# Artificial Intelligence

## Foundations of Computational Agents

### Third Edition

A comprehensive textbook for undergraduate and graduate AI courses, explaining modern artificial intelligence and its social impact, and integrating theory and practice. This extensively revised new edition now includes chapters on deep learning, including generative AI, the social impacts of AI, and causality.

Students and instructors will benefit from these features:

- The novel agent design space, which provides a coherent framework for teaching and learning, making both easier.
- Every concept or algorithm is illustrated with a motivating concrete example.
- Each chapter now has a social impact section, enabling students to understand the impact of the various techniques as they learn.
- Agent designs progress gradually from the simple to the complex.
- Every algorithm is presented in pseudocode and in open-source AIPython code, enabling students to experiment with and build on the implementations.
- Five larger case studies are developed throughout the book, and connect the design approaches to the applications.
- Appendices review the underlying mathematics, and provide the necessary mapping to open-source ML packages.

David L. Poole is Professor of Computer Science at the University of British Columbia. He is a former chair of the Association for Uncertainty in Artificial Intelligence, the winner of the Canadian AI Association (CAIAC) Lifetime Achievement Award, and a Fellow of AAAI and CAIAC.

Alan K. Mackworth is a Professor Emeritus of Computer Science at the University of British Columbia, where he co-founded the pioneering UBC Cognitive Systems Program. He served as President of CAIAC, IJCAII, and AAAI, and now acts as a consultant, writer, and lecturer. He is a Fellow of AAAI, CAIAC, CIFAR, AGE-WELL, and the Royal Society of Canada.

"This is an important textbook. Based on their broad experience, the authors harmonize some of the most exciting recent developments in the field, such as generative AI, with more traditional methods, within a unified agent framework. This will broaden the perspective of those relatively new to the field, for whom AI and deep learning appear almost synonymous."

*Yoav Shoham, Stanford University and AI21 Labs*

"This book is a tour de force. It provides a comprehensive introduction to so many topics in modern AI. The clarity of the exposition and the ability to capture the intuition underlying complex concepts make this book compelling and appealing to a broad audience."

*Pascal Van Hentenryck, Georgia Institute of Technology*

"This new edition offers an up-to-date account of AI, presenting the field in an accessible and unified manner. I particularly like the 'relations-late' approach, in which first-order logic and relational AI are covered later, after thoroughly covering more basic, feature-based methods. The hybrid data-driven/model-based approach to agent design that the authors propose will be essential to the development of reliable and trustworthy intelligent systems."

*Kevin Patrick Murphy, Google Brain, author of* Probabilistic Machine Learning

"Poole and Mackworth's now classic textbook has guided my senior undergraduate AI class since its first edition. Coupled with online resources, the book presents a comprehensive overview, with technical substance and many pointers for further study, in a coherent structure that fosters learning of key interrelated concepts. The third edition updates the content to cover the massive recent AI advances."

*Jesse Hoey, University of Waterloo*

"Machine learning has undergone spectacular advances over the last few years, but to harvest the new capabilities one needs an engineering framework to build computational agents. This book teaches students about the concepts and techniques that make that possible."

*Rodney Brooks, MIT and Robust AI*

"Wide-ranging, well-organized, up-to-date, and in-depth coverage of the AI world. The numerous figures, algorithms, and extensive references make this a valuable resource that readers will return to repeatedly. Instructors and students will benefit from the well-crafted end-of-chapter exercises. The thought-provoking social impact sections in each chapter and the social impact chapter admirably address the positive and harmful impacts on people. These complement the strong technical descriptions, wisely encouraging researchers and practitioners to limit the risks by highlighting human-centred AI. Poole and Mackworth are highly acclaimed experts who eagerly present their subject with enthusiasm and thoroughness."

*Ben Shneiderman, University of Maryland, author of* Human-Centered AI

"This revised and extended edition of *Artificial Intelligence: Foundations of Computational Agents* should become the standard text of AI education. Computer science students will find in this volume a broad and uniquely coherent perspective on many computational models of learning, reasoning, and decision-making. Students of causal inference, in particular, will rejoice at viewing the causal revolution reconnected to its roots in formal logic and probabilistic decision-making, strengthened and reinforced by concrete algorithms, challenging exercises, and open source AIPython codes. Highly recommended."

*Judea Pearl, UCLA, Turing Award winner and author of* Causality *and* The Book of Why

"This textbook is impressively comprehensive, covering all the major AI paradigms that have been introduced and studied over the years. At the same time, it is up to date with the latest technical advances and interdisciplinary perspectives on social impacts. I expect it to be a valuable resource for both teachers and students."

*Peter Stone, University of Texas at Austin*

"*Artificial Intelligence: Foundations of Computational Agents* is a great AI textbook written by prominent leaders in the field. It covers everything you want to know about AI in a very accessible style, accompanied by a wide range of thoughtful and challenging exercises. I find this book to be an extremely valuable resource, not only for teaching, but even more so for offering an updated reference to a wide spectrum of foundational subjects at the current frontier of AI."

*Rina Dechter, University of California, Irvine, author of* Constraint Programming

"Poole and Mackworth's book has been my go-to resource for students who need an introduction to Artificial Intelligence. While the previous versions have provided a complete overview of the field, the newer version organizes this information in a crystal clear manner. The division of the topics based on what the agent knows, what is in the world, and what the effects of its actions are allow for a logical flow of topics inside AI. As a comprehensive textbook for AI that includes slides, solutions, and code, this book is a must-have on the bookshelf for AI instructors, students, researchers, and practitioners."

*Sriram Natarajan, University of Texas at Dallas*

"This is a great foundational book on the science of AI, covering the main concepts and techniques using a simple structured approach. The extensive material on the social impact of AI provides much needed attention to the responsible design and use of AI. AI researchers can find here the indispensable foundational knowledge and the needed ethical attitude to create beneficial AI innovation."

*Francesca Rossi, IBM Fellow*

"The latest edition of Poole and Mackworth's book emphasizes the societal impacts of AI in every chapter, making it an essential read for anyone interested in AI, especially those who will shape its future to ensure these powerful technologies benefit society and minimize harms."

*Saleema Amershi, Microsoft Research*

"This textbook provides an amazing introduction to the field of AI. By bringing together learning, reasoning, and decision-making, it shows the rich interconnections across the various AI subfields. The writing is just at the right level to introduce students to the different facets of AI. The updated edition seamlessly integrates the exciting developments in deep learning into the broader AI context. The text also highlights the societal impact of AI, including AI ethics and computational sustainability."

*Carla Gomes, Cornell University*

"Poole and Mackworth – two pioneers of AI – present an admirably broad and complete introduction to the field, with a very useful focus on intelligent agents. From deep learning to causal reasoning, from Bayesian networks to knowledge graphs, from fundamental algorithms to effective heuristics, this book covers a wide range of important topics, each accompanied by a timely section on social impact. Highly recommended!"

*Holger Hoos, RWTH Aachen*

"Poole and Mackworth's *Artificial Intelligence: Foundations of Computational Agents 3e* is a tour de force. This is a comprehensive and clearly written text that takes the reader through core concepts in symbolic AI and machine learning, providing pathways for broad introductory undergraduate courses, or focused graduate courses. It's an outstanding resource for student and instructor alike. Whether you're a seasoned AI researcher or a student entering the field, you'll learn a great deal from reading this book."

*Sheila McIlraith, University of Toronto*

"An outstanding and lucid blast of fresh air, in a world that has lost contact with what AI should be about."

*Gary Marcus, NYU, author of* Rebooting AI

"*Artificial Intelligence: Foundations of Computational Agents* skillfully delivers a comprehensive exploration of AI ideas, demonstrating exceptional organization and clarity of presentation. Navigating the broad arc of important concepts and methods in AI, the book covers essential technical topics, historical context, and the growing importance of the societal influences of AI, making it an outstanding primary text for students and educators, and a valuable reference for professionals."

*Eric Horvitz, Technical Fellow and Chief Scientific Officer, Microsoft*

# Artificial Intelligence

## Foundations of Computational Agents

Third Edition

David L. Poole

*University of British Columbia, Vancouver*

Alan K. Mackworth

*University of British Columbia, Vancouver*

CAMBRIDGE
UNIVERSITY PRESS

CAMBRIDGE
UNIVERSITY PRESS

Shaftesbury Road, Cambridge CB2 8EA, United Kingdom

One Liberty Plaza, 20th Floor, New York, NY 10006, USA

477 Williamstown Road, Port Melbourne, VIC 3207, Australia

314–321, 3rd Floor, Plot 3, Splendor Forum, Jasola District Centre, New Delhi - 110025, India

103 Penang Road, #05–06/07, Visioncrest Commercial, Singapore 238467

Cambridge University Press is part of Cambridge University Press & Assessment, a department of the University of Cambridge.

We share the University's mission to contribute to society through the pursuit of education, learning and research at the highest international levels of excellence.

www.cambridge.org
Information on this title: www.cambridge.org/highereducation/isbn/9781009258197
DOI: 10.1017/9781009258227



First edition published 2010
Second edition published 2017
5th printing 2019
Third edition published 2023

*A catalogue record for this publication is available from the British Library.*

*A Cataloging-in-Publication data record for this book is available from the Library of Congress*

ISBN 978-1-009-25819-7 Hardback

Additional resources for this publication at www.cambridge.org/poole3e

To our families for their love, support, and patience

Jennifer, Alexandra, and Shannon

Marian, Bryn, Grant, and Tony

# Contents

# Preface

*Artificial Intelligence: Foundations of Computational Agents* is a book about the science of artificial intelligence (AI). AI is the study of intelligent computational agents. Our book is structured as a textbook but it is designed to be accessible to a wide audience.

We wrote this book because we are excited about the emergence of AI as an integrated science. As with any science being developed, AI has a coherent, formal theory and a rambunctious experimental wing. Here we balance theory and experiment and show how to link them together intimately. We develop the science of AI together with its engineering applications. We believe the adage, "There is nothing so practical as a good theory." The spirit of our approach is captured by the dictum, "Everything should be made as simple as possible, but not simpler." We must build the science on solid foundations; we present the foundations, but only sketch, and give some examples of, the complexity required to build useful intelligent systems. Although the resulting systems will be complex, the foundations and the building blocks should be simple.

## New to This Edition

This third edition results from extensive revision throughout the text. We have added three new chapters:

- Neural Networks and Deep Learning
- Causality
- The Social Impact of Artificial Intelligence

There is also a social impact section for each chapter, covering either beneficial applications or harmful impacts of AI, and often both. With the rise in the use of AI in society, it is imperative that all AI researchers and practitioners understand the possible social impact of their work.

We have restructured the material based on feedback from instructors who have used the book in classes. We have brought it up to date to reflect the current state of the art, made parts that were difficult for students more straightforward, added more intuitive explanations, and coordinated the pseudocode algorithms with open-source Python implementations at AIPython (aipython.org). We have resisted the temptation to cover every recent advance.

AI research is expanding so rapidly now that the volume of potential new text material is vast. However, research teaches us not only what works but also what does not work so well, allowing us to be highly selective. We have included more material on techniques that have proven successful. However, research also has trends and fashions. We have removed techniques that have been shown to be less promising, but we distinguish them from the techniques for problems that are merely out of fashion. We include some currently unfashionable material if the problems attacked still remain and the techniques have the potential to form the basis for future research and development. We have further developed the concept of a single design space for intelligent agents, showing how many bewilderingly diverse techniques can be seen in a simple, uniform framework. This allows us to emphasize the principles underlying the foundations of computational agents, making those ideas more accessible to students.

## Who This Book is For

The book can be used as an introductory text on artificial intelligence for advanced undergraduate or graduate students in computer science or related disciplines such as computer engineering, philosophy, cognitive science, or psychology. It will appeal more to the technically minded; parts are technically challenging, focusing on learning by doing: designing, building, and implementing systems. Any curious scientifically oriented reader will benefit from studying the book. Previous experience with computational systems is desirable, but prior study of the foundations upon which we build, including logic, probability, calculus, and control theory, is not necessary, because we develop the concepts as required.

The serious student will gain valuable skills at several levels ranging from expertise in the specification and design of intelligent agents to skills for implementing, testing, and improving real software systems for several challenging application domains. The thrill of participating in the emergence of a new science of intelligent agents is one of the attractions of this approach. The practical skills of dealing with a world of ubiquitous, intelligent, embedded agents are now in great demand in the marketplace.

## Our Approach

The focus is on an intelligent agent acting in an environment. We start with simple agents acting in simple, static environments and gradually increase the power of the agents to cope with more challenging worlds. We explore ten dimensions of complexity that allow us to introduce, gradually and with modularity, what makes building intelligent agents challenging. We have tried to structure the book so that the reader can understand each of the dimensions separately and we make this concrete by repeatedly illustrating the ideas with four different agent tasks: a delivery robot, a diagnostic assistant, a tutoring agent, and a trading agent.

The agent we want the student to envision is a hierarchically designed agent that acts intelligently in a stochastic environment that it can only partially observe – one that reasons online about individuals and relationships among them, has complex preferences, learns while acting, takes into account other agents, and acts appropriately given its own computational limitations. Of course, we cannot start with such an agent; it is still a research question to build such agents. So we introduce the simplest agents and then show how to add each of these complexities in a modular way.

We have made a number of design choices which distinguish this book from competing books, including our earlier book.

- We have tried to give a coherent framework in which to understand AI. We have chosen not to present disconnected topics that do not fit together. For example, we do not present disconnected logical and probabilistic views of AI, but we have presented a multidimensional design space in which students can understand the big picture, in which probabilistic and logical reasoning coexist.

- We decided that it is better to clearly explain the foundations upon which more sophisticated techniques can be built, rather than present all these more sophisticated techniques. This means that a larger gap may exist between what is covered in this book and the frontier of science. But it also means that the student will have a better foundation to understand current and future research.

- One of the more difficult decisions we made was how to linearize the design space. We have chosen a relations-late approach. This approach probably reflects better the research over the past few decades where there has been much progress in reasoning and learning for feature-based representations. The problems of relational learning and reasoning have not gone away, only become more urgent.

This should help students and instructors avoid being overwhelmed by the amount of technical details to be mastered before having a comprehensive view of AI.

## Online Resources

We provide open-source Python implementations of most of the algorithms at http://www.aipython.org. These are as close to pseudo-code as we can make them while they still run. We have chosen clarity over efficiency, with good asymptotic complexity. They are not a replacement for a well-engineered library, because they are sometimes a few orders of magnitude slower. However, by keeping everything as simple as possible, the student can see how the algorithms work. The code provides the basic algorithms, and variants can be used as exercises. One choice we have made that might not match every instructor's preference is to minimize the number of external Python libraries. We only use matplotlib, as we cannot get away without a plotting library if we want to present information.

## How to Use This Book in Your Course

We have chosen not to present an encyclopedic view of AI. Not every major idea that has been investigated is presented here. We have chosen some basic ideas upon which other, more sophisticated, techniques are based and have tried to explain the basic ideas in detail, sketching how these can be expanded. Once a student has understood the principles here they can go into more specialized topics such as vision, natural language understanding, or robotics.

Figure 1 (page xxv) shows the topics covered in the book. The solid lines depict prerequisites. Often the prerequisite structure does not include all subtopics. Given the medium of a book, we have had to linearize the topics. However, the book is designed so the topics are teachable in any order satisfying the prerequisite structure.

The references given at the end of each chapter are not meant to be comprehensive; we have referenced works that we have directly used and works that we think provide good overviews of the literature, by referencing both classic works and more recent surveys. We hope that no researchers feel slighted by their omission, and we are happy to have feedback where someone feels that an idea has been misattributed. Remember that this book is *not* a survey of AI research.

## Acknowledgments

Thanks to Saleema Amershi, Yoshua Bengio, Giuseppe Carenini, Jeff Clune, Mel Comisarow, Cristina Conati, Nando de Freitas, Rina Dechter, Bahare Fatemi, Randy Goebel, Robert Goldman, Jesse Hoey, Robert Holte, Christopher Mole, Kevin Murphy, Sriraam Natarajan, Alex Poole, Francesca Rossi, Justice Sefas, Ben Shneiderman, Peter van Beek, Geoffrey Woollard, and the anonymous reviewers for valuable feedback on this third edition.

Thanks to our editors, Lauren Cowles, Maggie Jeffers, Julie Lancashire, and Stefanie Seaton, our content manager, Rachel Norridge, and the staff at Cambridge University Press for all their support, encouragement, and help.

All remaining mistakes are ours.

We invite you to join us in an intellectual adventure: building a science of intelligent agents.

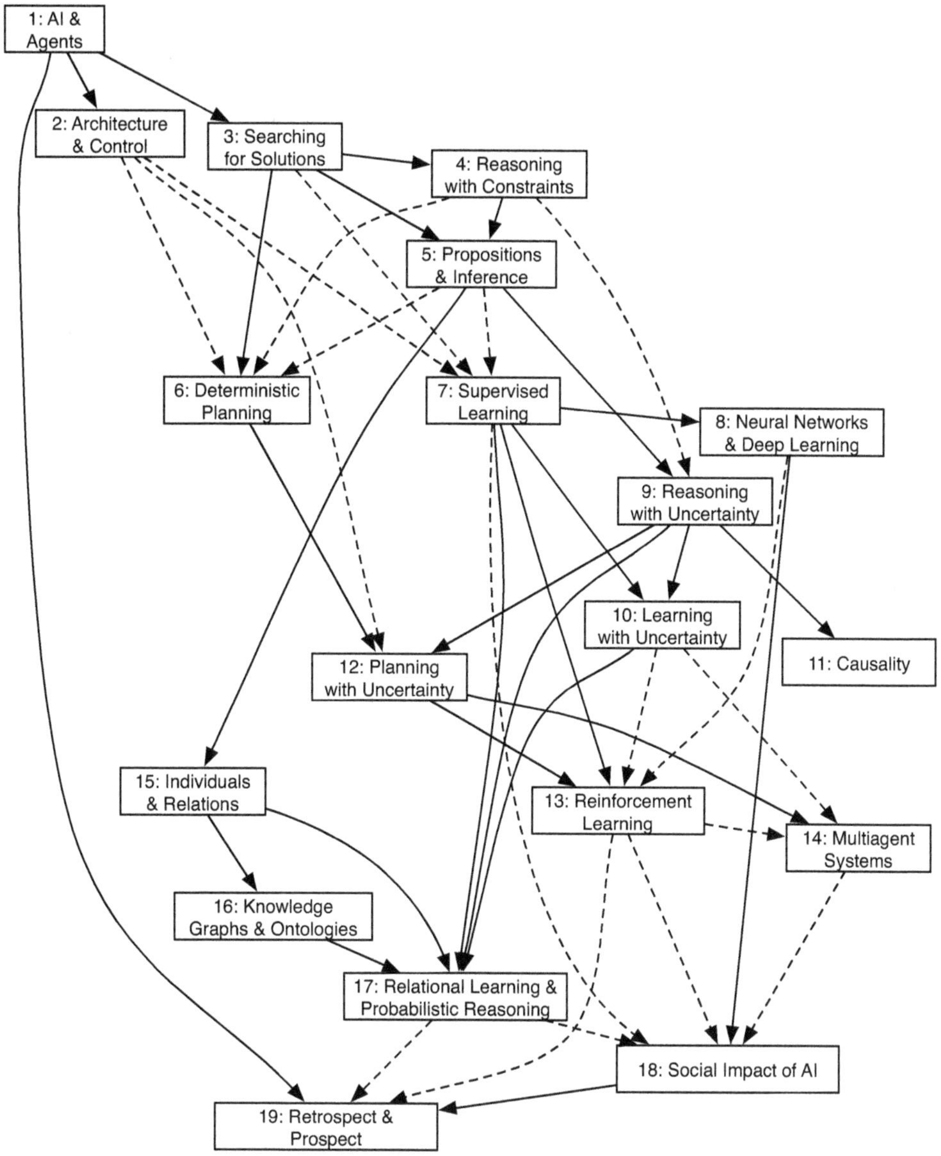


Figure 1: Overview of chapters and dependencies

# Part I

# Agents in the World

## What are Agents and How Can They be Built?

# Chapter 1

# Artificial Intelligence and Agents

*The history of AI is a history of fantasies, possibilities, demonstrations, and promise. Ever since Homer wrote of mechanical "tripods" waiting on the gods at dinner, imagined mechanical assistants have been a part of our culture. However, only in the last half century have we, the AI community, been able to build experimental machines that test hypotheses about the mechanisms of thought and intelligent behavior and thereby demonstrate mechanisms that formerly existed only as theoretical possibilities.*

– Bruce Buchanan [2005]

This book is about artificial intelligence (AI), a field built on centuries of thought, which has been a recognized discipline for over 60 years. As well as solving practical tasks, AI provides tools to test hypotheses about the nature of thought itself. Deep scientific and engineering problems have already been solved and many more are waiting to be solved. Many practical applications are currently deployed and the potential exists for an almost unlimited number of future applications. This book presents the principles that underlie intelligent computational agents.

## 1.1 What is Artificial Intelligence?

**Artificial intelligence**, or **AI**, is the field that studies *the synthesis and analysis of computational agents that act intelligently*. Consider each part of this definition.

An **agent** is something that acts in an environment; it does something. Agents include worms, dogs, thermostats, airplanes, robots, humans, companies, and countries.

An agent is judged solely by how it **acts**. Agents that have the same effect in the world are equally good.

**Intelligence** is a matter of degree. The aspects that go into an agent **acting intelligently** include

- what it does is appropriate for its circumstances, its goals, and its perceptual and computational limitations
- it takes into account the short-term and long-term consequences of its actions, including the effects on society and the environment
- it learns from experience
- it is flexible to changing environments and changing goals.

A **computational agent** is an agent whose decisions about its actions can be explained in terms of computation. That is, the decision can be broken down into primitive operations that can be implemented in a physical device. This computation can take many forms. In humans, this computation is carried out in "wetware"; in computers it is carried out in "hardware." Although there are some agents that are arguably not computational, such as the wind and rain eroding a landscape, it is an open question whether all intelligent agents are computational.

All agents are limited. No agent is omniscient (all knowing) or omnipotent (can do anything). Agents can only observe everything in very specialized and constrained domains. Agents have finite memory. Agents in the real world do not have unlimited time to act.

The central **scientific goal** of AI is to understand the principles that make intelligent behavior possible in natural or artificial systems. This is done by

- the **analysis** of natural and artificial agents
- formulating and testing hypotheses about what it takes to construct intelligent agents
- designing, building, and experimenting with computational systems that perform tasks commonly viewed as requiring intelligence.

As part of science, researchers build **empirical systems** to test hypotheses or to explore the space of possible designs. These are distinct from **applications** that are built to be useful for an application domain.

The definition is *not* for intelligent **thought**. The role of thought is to affect action and lead to more intelligent **behavior**.

The central **engineering goal** of AI is the **design** and **synthesis** of agents that act intelligently, which leads to useful artifacts.

Building general intelligence isn't the only goal of AI researchers. The aim of **intelligence augmentation** is to augment human intelligence and creativity. A diagnostic agent helps medical practitioners make better decisions, a search engine augments human memory, and natural language translation systems help people communicate. AI systems are often in **human-in-the-loop** mode, where humans and agents work together to solve problems. Sometimes the actions of artificial agents are to give advice to a human. Sometimes humans give advice or feedback to artificial agents, particularly for cases where decisions are made quickly or repeatedly.

### 1.1.1 Artificial and Natural Intelligence

Artificial intelligence (AI) is the established name for the field, but the term "artificial intelligence" is a source of much confusion because artificial intelligence may be interpreted as the opposite of real intelligence.

For any phenomenon, you can distinguish real versus fake, where the fake is non-real. You can also distinguish natural versus artificial. Natural means occurring in nature and artificial means made by people.

**Example 1.1** A tsunami is a large wave in an ocean. Natural tsunamis occur from time to time and are caused by earthquakes or landslides. You could imagine an artificial tsunami that was made by people, for example, by exploding a bomb in the ocean, yet which is still a real tsunami. One could also imagine fake tsunamis: either artificial, using computer graphics, or natural, such as a mirage that looks like a tsunami but is not one.

It is arguable that intelligence is different: you cannot have *fake* intelligence. If an agent behaves intelligently, it is intelligent. It is only the external behavior that defines intelligence; acting intelligently is being intelligent. Thus, artificial intelligence, if and when it is achieved, will be real intelligence created artificially.

This idea of intelligence being defined by external behavior was the motivation for a test for intelligence designed by Turing [1950], which has become known as the **Turing test**. The Turing test consists of an imitation game where an interrogator can ask a witness, via a text interface, any question. If the interrogator cannot distinguish the witness from a human, the witness must be intelligent. Figure 1.1 shows a possible dialog that Turing suggested. An agent that is not really intelligent could not fake intelligence for arbitrary topics.

**Interrogator:** In the first line of your sonnet which reads "Shall I compare thee to a summer's day," would not "a spring day" do as well or better?

**Witness:** It wouldn't scan.

**Interrogator:** How about "a winter's day," That would scan all right.

**Witness:** Yes, but nobody wants to be compared to a winter's day.

**Interrogator:** Would you say Mr. Pickwick reminded you of Christmas?

**Witness:** In a way.

**Interrogator:** Yet Christmas is a winter's day, and I do not think Mr. Pickwick would mind the comparison.

**Witness:** I don't think you're serious. By a winter's day one means a typical winter's day, rather than a special one like Christmas.

Figure 1.1: Part of Turing's possible dialog for the Turing test

There has been much debate about the usefulness of the Turing test. Unfortunately, although it may provide a test for how to recognize intelligence, it does not provide a way to realize intelligence.

Levesque [2014] suggested a new form of question, a **Winograd schema** after the following example of Winograd [1972]:

- The city councilmen refused the demonstrators a permit because they feared violence. Who feared violence?

- The city councilmen refused the demonstrators a permit because they advocated violence. Who advocated violence?

These two sentences only differ in one word – feared/advocated – but have the opposite answer.

Winograd schemas have the property that (a) humans can easily disambiguate them and (b) there is no simple grammatical or statistical test that could disambiguate them. For example, the sentences above would not qualify if the phrase "demonstrators feared violence" was much less or more likely than the phrase "councilmen feared violence" independently of the context, and similarly with advocating.

**Example 1.2** The following examples are due to Davis [2015]:

- Steve follows Fred's example in everything. He [admires/influences] him hugely. Who [admires/influences] whom?
- The table won't fit through the doorway because it is too [wide/narrow]. What is too [wide/narrow]?
- Grace was happy to trade me her sweater for my jacket. She thinks it looks [great/dowdy] on her. What looks [great/dowdy] on Grace?
- Bill thinks that calling attention to himself was rude [to/of] Bert. Who called attention to himself?

Each of these have their own reasons why one answer is preferred to the other. A computer that can reliably answer these questions needs to know about all of these reasons, and arguably requires the ability to do **commonsense reasoning**. Common sense should also allow it to reject sentences such as "The doorway won't fit through the chair because it is too narrow. What is too narrow?".

Figure 1.2 (page 7) shows some answers provided by **ChatGPT** [OpenAI, 2022], based on **GPT-3** [Brown et al., 2020], one of the most capable large language models in 2022. ChatGPT gives a different answer each time it is called. You can decide whether it solves this Winograd schema. The technology behind GPT-3 and related models is described in Section 8.5 (page 350).

Grosz [2012], arguing that language is inherently social and connected to human cooperation, suggested that a more appropriate test should involve purposeful natural language, not language just for the purpose of tricking a human. She suggested the question:

**Human**: The table won't fit through the doorway because it is too narrow. What is too narrow?

**ChatGPT**: If a table won't fit through a doorway because it is too narrow, it means that the width of the table is greater than the width of the doorway. In other words, the doorway is not wide enough to allow the table to pass through it. This can be a problem if you are trying to move the table from one room to another and the only way to do so is through the doorway. In order to solve this problem, you may need to remove the door or trim the table so that it fits through the doorway. Alternatively, you may need to find a different route to move the table, such as through a window or by taking it apart and reassembling it in the other room.

**Human**: The table won't fit through the doorway because it is too wide. What is too wide?

**ChatGPT**: If a table won't fit through a doorway because it is too wide, it means that the width of the doorway is smaller than the width of the table. In other words, the table is too big to fit through the doorway. This can be a problem if you are trying to move the table from one room to another and the only way to do so is through the doorway. In order to solve this problem, you may need to remove the door or trim the table so that it fits through the doorway. Alternatively, you may need to find a different route to move the table, such as through a window or by taking it apart and reassembling it in the other room.

**Human**: The doorway won't fit through the chair because it is too narrow. What is too narrow?

**ChatGPT**: "Too narrow" means that the doorway is not wide enough to fit through the chair. In this context, the doorway is the object that is being compared to the chair, and it is not wide enough to pass through the chair without encountering some difficulty or obstruction. This could be because the doorway is physically smaller in width than the chair, or because there is some other physical feature of the chair that is preventing the doorway from fitting through it. For example, the chair might have armrests or other protuberances that make it difficult for the doorway to pass through. In general, the phrase "too narrow" is used to describe something that is not wide enough to fit through or pass a particular opening or gap.

**Human**: The doorway won't fit through the chair because it is too narrow. What is too narrow?

**ChatGPT**: If a doorway is too narrow to fit through a chair, it means that the width of the doorway is smaller than the width of the chair. This can happen if the chair is too wide to fit through the doorway, or if the doorway is not wide enough to accommodate the chair. In either case, the chair will not be able to pass through the doorway because there is not enough space for it to fit.

Figure 1.2: ChatGPT answers to some Winograd schemas

> *Is it imaginable that a computer (agent) team member could behave, over the long term and in uncertain, dynamic environments, in such a way that people on the team will not notice it is not human?*
>
> – Barbara Grosz [2012]

An equal member of the team needs to be trusted enough to act in the world appropriately, know when to ask questions, and when to not act. This challenge also allows for incremental improvement; starting with simple group interactions before moving to complex ones.

Interacting in natural language is not the only aspect of intelligence. An agent acting in an environment needs **common sense**, "the ability to make effective use of ordinary, everyday, experiential knowledge in achieving ordinary, practical goals" [Brachman and Levesque, 2022b]. Here, **knowledge** is used in a general way to mean any non-transient information in an agent. Such knowledge is typically not stated in natural language; people do not state what everyone knows. Some knowledge, such as how to ride a bike or recognize a face, cannot be effectively conveyed by natural language. Formalizing common sense has a long history [McCarthy, 1958; Davis, 1990], including the development of representations and actual commonsense knowledge.

### 1.1.2 Natural Intelligence

The obvious naturally intelligent agent is the human being. Some people might say that worms, insects, or bacteria are intelligent, but more people would say that dogs, whales, or monkeys are intelligent (see Exercise 1.1 (page 48)). One class of intelligent agents that may be more intelligent than humans is the class of **organizations**. Ant colonies are a prototypical example of organizations. Each individual ant may not be very intelligent, but an ant colony can act more intelligently than any individual ant. The colony can discover food and exploit it very effectively, as well as adapt to changing circumstances. Corporations can be more intelligent than individual people. Companies develop, manufacture, and distribute products where the sum of the skills required is much more than any individual could master. Modern computers, from low-level hardware to high-level software, are more complicated than any single human can understand, yet they are manufactured daily by organizations of humans. Human **society** viewed as an agent is arguably the most intelligent agent known.

It is instructive to consider where human intelligence comes from. There are three main sources:

**Biology** Humans have evolved into adaptable animals that can survive in various habitats.

**Culture** Culture provides not only language, but also useful tools, useful concepts, and the wisdom that is passed from parents and teachers to children.

**Lifelong learning** Humans learn throughout their life and accumulate knowledge and skills.

These sources interact in complex ways. Biological evolution has provided stages of growth that allow for different learning at different stages of life. Biology and culture have evolved together; humans can be helpless at birth, presumably because of our culture of looking after infants. Culture interacts strongly with learning. A major part of lifelong learning is what people are taught by parents and teachers. Language, which is part of culture, provides distinctions in the world that are useful for learning.

When building an intelligent system, the designers have to decide which of these sources of intelligence need to be programmed in, and which can be learned. It is very unlikely that anyone will be able to build an agent that starts with a clean slate and learns everything, particularly for non-repetitive tasks. Similarly, most interesting and useful intelligent agents learn to improve their behavior.

## 1.2 A Brief History of Artificial Intelligence

Throughout human history, people have used technology to model themselves. There is evidence of this from ancient China, Egypt, and Greece, bearing witness to the universality of this activity. Each new technology has, in its turn, been exploited to build intelligent agents or models of mind. Clockwork, hydraulics, telephone switching systems, holograms, analog computers, and digital computers have all been proposed both as technological metaphors for intelligence and as mechanisms for modeling mind.

Hobbes (1588–1679), who has been described by Haugeland [1985, p. 85] as the "Grandfather of AI," espoused the position that thinking was symbolic reasoning, like talking out loud or working out an answer with pen and paper. The idea of symbolic reasoning was further developed by Descartes (1596–1650), Pascal (1623–1662), Spinoza (1632–1677), Leibniz (1646–1716), and others who were pioneers in the European philosophy of mind.

The idea of symbolic operations became more concrete with the development of computers. Babbage (1792–1871) designed the first general-purpose computer, the **Analytical Engine**. Leonardo Torres y Quevedo build a chess playing machine based on similar ideas in 1911 [Randell, 1982]. In the early part of the twentieth century, there was much work done on understanding computation. Several models of computation were proposed, including the **Turing machine** by Alan Turing (1912–1954), a theoretical machine that writes symbols on an infinitely long tape, and the **lambda calculus** of Church (1903–1995), which is a mathematical formalism for rewriting formulas. It can be shown that these very different formalisms are equivalent in that any function computable by one is computable by the others. This leads to the **Church–Turing thesis**:

> Any effectively computable function can be carried out on a Turing machine (and so also in the lambda calculus or any of the other equivalent formalisms).

**Effectively computable** means following well-defined operations. In Turing's day, "computers" were people who followed well-defined steps; computers as known today did not exist. This thesis says that all computation can be carried out on a Turing machine or one of the other equivalent computational machines. The Church–Turing thesis cannot be proved but it is a hypothesis that has stood the test of time. No one has built a machine that has carried out computation that cannot be computed by a Turing machine. There is no evidence that people can compute functions that are not Turing computable. This provides an argument that computation is more than just a metaphor for intelligence; reasoning *is* computation and computation can be carried out by a computer.

Some of the first applications of computers were AI programs. Samuel [1959] built a **checkers** program in 1952 and implemented a program that learns to play checkers in the late 1950s. His program beat the Connecticut state checkers champion in 1961. Wang [1960] implemented a program that proved every logic theorem (nearly 400) in *Principia Mathematica* [Whitehead and Russell, 1925, 1927]. Newell and Simon [1956] built a program, **Logic Theorist**, that discovers proofs in propositional logic.

In parallel, there was also much work on **neural networks** learning inspired by how **neurons** work. McCulloch and Pitts [1943] showed how a simple thresholding "formal neuron" could be the basis for a Turing-complete machine. Learning for artificial neural networks was first described by Minsky [1952]. One of the early significant works was the **perceptron** of Rosenblatt [1958]. The work on neural networks became less prominent for a number of years after the 1968 book by Minsky and Papert [1988], which argued that the representations learned were inadequate for intelligent action. Many technical foundations for neural networks were laid in the 1980s and 1990s [Rumelhart et al., 1986; Hochreiter and Schmidhuber, 1997; LeCun et al., 1998a]. Widespread adoption followed the success by Krizhevsky et al. [2012] for **ImageNet** [Deng et al., 2009], a dataset of over 3 million images labelled with over 5000 categories. Subsequent major advances include the introduction of **generative adversarial networks** (GANs) [Goodfellow et al., 2014] and **transformers** [Vaswani et al., 2017]. Neural networks in various forms are now the state of the art for predictive models for large perceptual datasets, including images, video, and speech, as well as some tasks for text. They are also used for **generative AI**, to generate images, text, code, molecules, and other structured output. See Chapter 8.

Neural networks are one of many **machine learning** tools used for making predictions from data in modern applications. Other methods have been developed though the years, including **decision trees** [Breiman et al., 1984; Quinlan, 1993] and **logistic regression**, introduced by Verhulst in 1832 [Cramer, 2002].

These have diverse applications in many areas of science. Combining these algorithms leads to the state-of-the-art **gradient-boosted trees** [Friedman, 2001; Chen and Guestrin, 2016], which demonstrates the close interconnections between **statistics** and machine learning.

While useful, making predictions is not sufficient to determine what an agent should do; an agent also needs to plan. **Planning** in AI was initially based on deterministic actions. Fikes and Nilsson [1971] used deterministic actions to control a mobile robot. Planning under uncertainty has a long history. **Markov decision processes (MDPs)**, the foundation for much of planning under uncertainty, and **dynamic programming**, a general way to solve them, were invented by Bellman [1957]. These were extended into **decision-theoretic planning** in the 1990's [Boutilier et al., 1999]. Decision-theoretic planning with learning is called **reinforcement learning**. The first reinforcement learning programs were due to Andreae [1963] and Michie [1963]. Major advances came with the inventions of **temporal-difference learning** [Sutton, 1988] and **Q-learning** [Watkins and Dayan, 1992]. Work in reinforcement learning has exploded, including superhuman performance in chess, Go and other games [Silver et al., 2017].

Planning requires representations. The need for representations was recognized early.

> *A computer program capable of acting intelligently in the world must have a general representation of the world in terms of which its inputs are interpreted. Designing such a program requires commitments about what knowledge is and how it is obtained. ... More specifically, we want a computer program that decides what to do by inferring in a formal language that a certain strategy will achieve its assigned goal. This requires formalizing concepts of causality, ability, and knowledge.*
>
> – McCarthy and Hayes [1969]

Many of the early representations were ad hoc, such as **frames** [Minsky, 1975], like the **schemas** of Kant [1787], Bartlett [1932], and Piaget [1953]. Later representations were based on **logic** [Kowalski, 1979], with knowledge being defined in logic and efficient inference. This resulted in languages such as **Prolog** [Kowalski, 1988; Colmerauer and Roussel, 1996].

Probabilities were eschewed in AI, because of the number of parameters required, until the breakthrough of **Bayesian networks** (**belief networks**) and **graphical models** [Pearl, 1988], which exploit conditional independence, and form a basis for modeling **causality**. Combining first-order logic and probability is the topic of **statistical relational AI** [De Raedt et al., 2016].

There has been a continual tension between how much knowledge is learned and how much is provided by human **experts** or is **innate** to an agent. It has long been recognized that learning is needed, and it is known that learning cannot be achieved with data alone (page 315). During the 1970s and 1980s,

**expert systems** came to prominence, where the aim was to capture the knowledge of an expert in some domain so that a computer could carry out expert tasks. **DENDRAL** [Buchanan and Feigenbaum, 1978], developed from 1965 to 1983 in the field of organic chemistry, proposed plausible structures for new organic compounds. **MYCIN** [Buchanan and Shortliffe, 1984], developed from 1972 to 1980, diagnosed infectious diseases of the blood, prescribed antimicrobial therapy, and explained its reasoning.

An alternative approach, de-emphasizing explicit knowledge representations, emphasized **situated embodied agents** [Brooks, 1990; Mackworth, 2009]. The hypothesis is that intelligence emerges, in evolution and individual development, through ongoing interaction and coupling with a real environment.

During the 1960s and 1970s, natural language understanding systems were developed for limited domains. For example, the **STUDENT** program of Bobrow [1967] could solve high-school algebra tasks expressed in natural language. Winograd's [1972] **SHRDLU** system could, using restricted natural language, discuss and carry out tasks in a simulated blocks world. CHAT-80 [Warren and Pereira, 1982] could answer geographical questions placed to it in natural language. Figure 1.3 (page 13) shows some questions that CHAT-80 answered based on a database of facts about countries, rivers, and so on. These systems could only reason in very limited domains using restricted vocabulary and sentence structure. Interestingly, IBM's **Watson**, which beat the world champion in the TV game show Jeopardy! in 2011, used a technique similar to **CHAT-80** [Lally et al., 2012] for understanding questions; see Section 15.7 (page 674).

In applications using language in the wild, such as speech recognition and translation in phones, many technologies are combined, including neural networks; see Chapter 8. Large language models (page 364), trained on huge datasets, can be used to predict the next word in a text, enabling predictive spelling and the creation of new text.

### 1.2.1 Relationship to Other Disciplines

AI is a very young discipline. Other disciplines as diverse as philosophy, neurobiology, evolutionary biology, psychology, economics, political science, sociology, anthropology, control engineering, statistics, and many more have been studying aspects of intelligence much longer.

The science of AI could be described as "synthetic psychology," "experimental philosophy," or "computational epistemology" – **epistemology** is the study of knowledge. AI can be seen as a way to study the nature of knowledge and intelligence, but with more powerful experimental tools than were previously available. Instead of being able to observe only the external behavior of intelligent systems, as philosophy, psychology, economics, and sociology have traditionally been able to do, AI researchers experiment with executable models of intelligent behavior. Most important, such models are open to inspection, redesign, and experimentation in a complete and rigorous way. Modern computers provide a way to construct the models about which philosophers have only been able to theorize. AI researchers can experiment with these models as opposed to just discussing their abstract properties. AI theories can be empirically grounded in implementations. Sometimes simple agents exhibit complex behavior, and sometimes sophisticated, theoretically motivated algorithms don't work in real-world domains, which would not be known without implementing the agents.

It is instructive to consider an analogy between the development of **flying machines** over the past few centuries and the development of thinking machines over the past few decades. There are several ways to understand flying. One is to dissect known flying animals and hypothesize their common structural features as necessary fundamental characteristics of any flying agent. With this method, an examination of birds, bats, and insects would suggest that flying involves the flapping of wings made of some structure covered with feathers or a membrane. Furthermore, the hypothesis could be tested by strapping feathers to one's arms, flapping, and jumping into the air, as Icarus did. An alternative methodology is to try to understand the principles of flying without restricting oneself to the natural occurrences of flying. This typically involves the construction of artifacts that embody the hypothesized principles,

---

Does Afghanistan border China?
What is the capital of Upper_Volta?
Which country's capital is London?
Which is the largest African country?
How large is the smallest American country?
What is the ocean that borders African countries and that borders Asian countries?
What are the capitals of the countries bordering the Baltic?
How many countries does the Danube flow through?
What is the total area of countries south of the Equator and not in Australasia?
What is the average area of the countries in each continent?
Is there more than one country in each continent?
What are the countries from which a river flows into the Black_Sea?
What are the continents no country in which contains more than two cities whose population exceeds 1 million?
Which country bordering the Mediterranean borders a country that is bordered by a country whose population exceeds the population of India?
Which countries with a population exceeding 10 million border the Atlantic?

Figure 1.3: Some questions CHAT-80 could answer

even if they do not behave like flying animals in any way except flying. This second method has provided both useful tools – airplanes – and a better understanding of the principles underlying flying, namely **aerodynamics**. Birds are still much better at flying though forests.

AI takes an approach analogous to that of aerodynamics. AI researchers are interested in testing general hypotheses about the nature of intelligence by building machines that are intelligent and that do not necessarily mimic humans or organizations. This also offers an approach to the question, "Can computers really think?" by considering the analogous question, "Can airplanes really fly?"

AI is intimately linked with the discipline of computer science because the study of computation is central to AI. It is essential to understand algorithms, data structures, and combinatorial complexity to build intelligent machines. It is also surprising how much of computer science started as a spinoff from AI, from timesharing to computer algebra systems.

Finally, AI can be seen as coming under the umbrella of **cognitive science**. Cognitive science links various disciplines that study cognition and reasoning, from psychology to linguistics to anthropology to neuroscience. AI distinguishes itself within cognitive science by providing tools to build intelligence rather than just studying the external behavior of intelligent agents or dissecting the inner workings of intelligent systems.

## 1.3 Agents Situated in Environments

AI is about practical reasoning: reasoning in order to do something. A coupling of perception, reasoning, and acting comprises an **agent**. An agent acts in an **environment**. An agent's environment often includes other agents. An agent together with its environment is called a **world**.

An agent could be, for example, a coupling of a computational engine with physical sensors and actuators, called a **robot**, where the environment is a physical setting. An **autonomous agent** is one that acts in the world without human intervention. A **semi-autonomous agent** acts with a **human-in-the-loop** who may provide perceptual information and carry out the task. An agent could be a program that acts in a purely computational environment, a **software agent**, often called a **bot**.

Figure 1.4 (page 15) shows a black-box view of an agent in terms of its inputs and outputs. At any time, what an agent does depends on:

- **prior knowledge** about the agent and the environment
- **stimuli** received from the environment, which can include **observations** about the environment (e.g., light, sound, keyboard commands, web requests) as well as actions that the environment imposes on the agent (e.g., bumping the agent)
- **past experiences**, including **history** of interaction with the environment (its previous actions and stimuli) and other data, from which it can learn

- **goals** that it must try to achieve or **preferences** over states of the world
- **abilities**, the primitive actions the agent is capable of carrying out.

Inside the black box, an agent has a **belief state** that can encode beliefs about its environment, what it has learned, what it is trying to do, and what it intends to do. An agent updates this internal state based on stimuli. It uses the belief state and stimuli to decide on its actions. Much of this book is about what is inside this black box.

**Purposive agents** have preferences or goals. They prefer some states of the world to other states, and they act to try to achieve the states they prefer most. The non-purposive agents are grouped together and called **nature**. Whether or not an agent is purposive is a modeling assumption that may, or may not, be appropriate. For example, for some applications it may be appropriate to model a dog as purposive, such as drug-sniffing dogs, and for others it may suffice to model a dog as non-purposive, such as when they are just part of the environment.

If an agent does not have preferences, by definition it does not care what world state it ends up in, and so it does not matter to it what it does. The reason to design an agent is to instill preferences in it – to make it prefer some world states and try to achieve them. An agent does not have to know its preferences explicitly. For example, a thermostat for a heater is an agent that senses the world and turns the heater either on or off. There are preferences embedded in the thermostat, such as to keep the room at a pleasant temperature, even though the thermostat arguably does not know these are its preferences. The preferences of an agent are often the preferences of the designer of the agent, but sometimes an agent can acquire goals and preferences at run time.

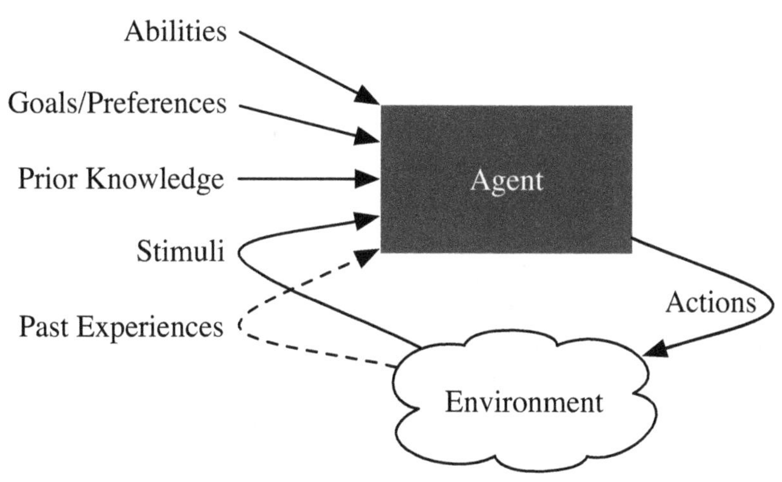


Figure 1.4: An agent interacting with an environment

This is an all-encompassing view of intelligent agents varying in complexity from a simple thermostat, to a diagnostic advising system whose perceptions and actions are mediated by human beings, to a team of mobile robots, to society itself. An agent does not have access to anything else; anything that does not affect one of these inputs cannot affect the agent's action.

## 1.4 Prototypical Applications

AI applications are widespread and diverse and include medical diagnosis, scheduling factory processes, robots for hazardous environments, game playing, autonomous cars, natural language translation systems, choosing advertisements, personal assistants, and tutoring agents. Rather than treating each application separately, we abstract the essential features of such applications to better understand the principles behind intelligent reasoning and action.

Five main application domains are developed in examples throughout the book. Although the particular examples presented are simple – otherwise they would not fit into the book – the application domains are representative of the range of domains in which AI techniques can be, and are being, used.

### 1.4.1 An Autonomous Delivery and Helping Robot

Imagine a robot with wheels and the ability to pick up, put down and manipulate objects. It has sensing capabilities allowing it to recognize objects and to avoid obstacles. It can be given orders in natural language and obey them, making reasonable choices about what to do when its goals conflict. Such a robot could deliver packages or coffee in an office environment, clean a home and put things in their appropriate place, or help caregivers in a hospital. Embedded in a wheelchair, it could help disabled people. It should be useful as well as safe.

In terms of the black-box characterization of an agent in Figure 1.4 (page 15), the autonomous delivery robot has as inputs:

- prior knowledge, provided by the agent designer, about the agent's capabilities, what objects it may encounter and have to differentiate, what requests mean, and perhaps about its environment, such as a map
- past experience obtained while acting, for instance, about the effects of its actions (and – hopefully limited – experiences of breaking objects), what objects are common in the world, and what requests to expect at different times of the day
- goals in terms of what it should deliver and when, as well as preferences specifying trade-offs, such as when it must forgo one goal to pursue another, or the trade-off between acting quickly and acting safely
- stimuli about its environment from observations from input devices such as cameras, sonar, touch, sound, laser range finders, or keyboards as well as stimuli such as the agent being forcibly moved or crashing.

The robot's outputs are motor controls specifying how its wheels should turn, where its limbs should move, and what it should do with its grippers. Other outputs may include speech and a video display.

**Example 1.3** Figure 1.5 depicts a typical laboratory environment for a delivery robot. This environment consists of four laboratories and many offices. In our examples, the robot can only push doors, and the directions of the doors in the diagram reflect the directions in which the robot can travel. Rooms require keys and those keys can be obtained from various sources. The robot must deliver parcels, beverages, and dishes from room to room. The environment also contains a stairway that is potentially hazardous to the robot.

### 1.4.2 A Diagnostic Assistant

A **diagnostic assistant** is intended to advise a human about some particular system such as a medical patient, the electrical system in a home, or an automobile. The diagnostic assistant should advise about potential underlying faults or diseases, what tests to carry out, and what treatment to prescribe. To give such advice, the assistant requires a model of the system, including knowledge of potential causes, available tests, available treatments, and observations of the system (which are often called **symptoms**).

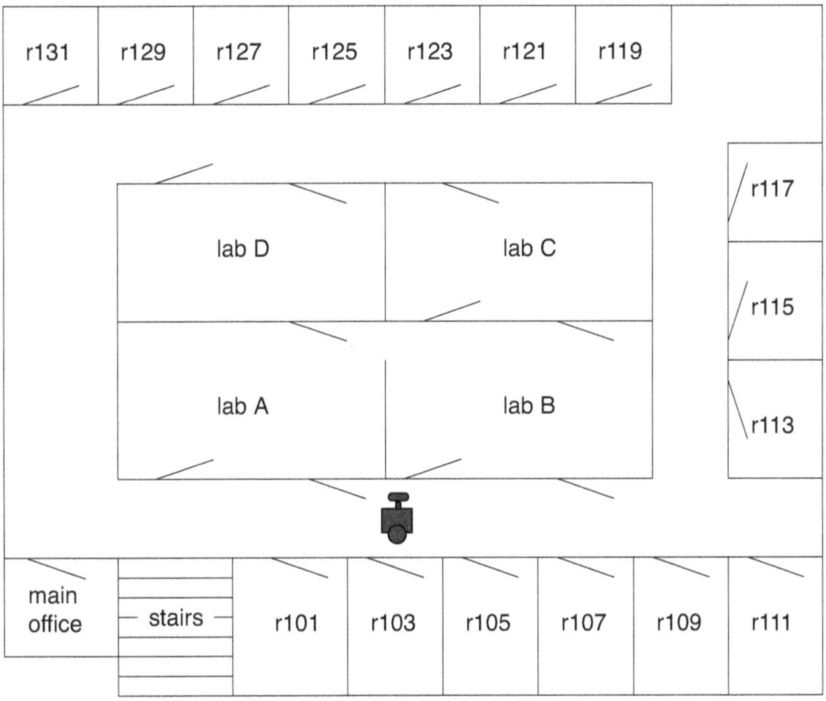


Figure 1.5: A typical laboratory environment for the delivery robot. This shows the locations of the doors and which way they open.

To be useful, the diagnostic assistant must provide added value, be easy for a human to use, and not be more trouble than it is worth. A diagnostic assistant connected to the Internet can draw on expertise from throughout the world, and its actions can be based on the most up-to-date research. However, it must be able to justify why the suggested diagnoses or actions are appropriate. Humans are, and should be, suspicious of computer systems that are opaque and impenetrable. When humans are responsible for what they do, even if their actions are based on a computer system's advice, the system needs to convince the human that the suggested actions are defensible.

**Example 1.4** Figure 1.6 shows an electrical distribution system in a home. In this home, power comes into the home through circuit breakers and then it goes to power outlets or to lights through light switches. For example, light $l_1$ is on if there is power coming into the home, if circuit breaker $cb_1$ is *on*, and if switches $s_1$ and $s_2$ are either both up or both down. This is the sort of model that someone may have of the electrical power in the home, which they could use to determine what is wrong given evidence about the position of the switches and which lights are on and which are off. The diagnostic assistant is there to help a resident or an electrician troubleshoot electrical problems.

In terms of the black-box definition of an agent in Figure 1.4 (page 15), the diagnostic assistant has as inputs:

- prior knowledge, such as how switches and lights normally work, how diseases or malfunctions manifest themselves, what information tests provide, the effects of repairs or treatments, and how to find out information

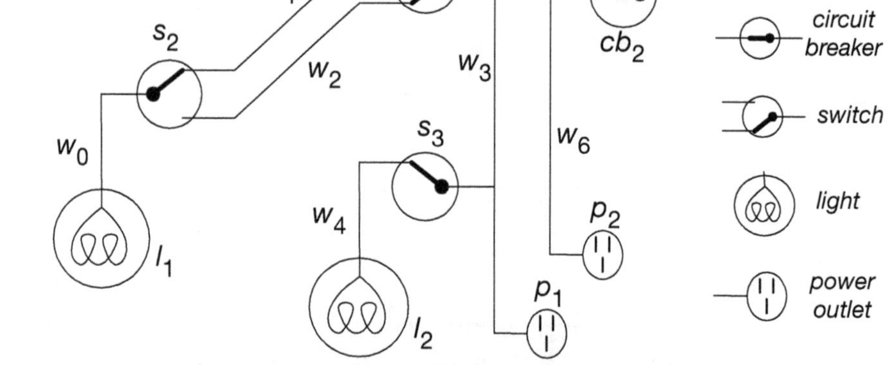


Figure 1.6: An electrical environment for the diagnostic assistant

- past experience, in terms of data of previous cases that include the effects of repairs or treatments, the prevalence of faults or diseases, the prevalence of symptoms for these faults or diseases, and the accuracy of tests
- goals of fixing the device or preferences between repairing or replacing components, or a patient's preferences between living longer or reducing pain
- stimuli that are observations of symptoms of a device or patient.

The output of the diagnostic assistant is in terms of recommendations of treatments and tests, along with a rationale for its recommendations.

### 1.4.3 A Tutoring Agent

A **tutoring agent** tutors students in some domain of study. The environment of the agent includes students who interact through a computer or tablet interface, and perhaps the students' parents and teachers.

**Example 1.5** Consider a tutoring agent to teach elementary physics, such as mechanics, that interacts with a student. In order to successfully tutor a student, the agent needs to be able to solve problems in the physics domain, determine the student's knowledge and misunderstanding based on interacting with them, and converse using natural language, mathematics, and diagrams.

In terms of the black-box definition of an agent in Figure 1.4 (page 15), a tutoring agent has the following as inputs:

- prior knowledge, provided by the agent designer, about the subject matter being taught, teaching strategies, possible student errors and misconceptions.
- past experience, which the tutoring agent has acquired by interacting with students, such as, what errors students make, how many examples and problems it takes various students to learn various topics, and what students forget; this can be information about students in general as well as about a particular student.
- preferences about the importance of each topic, the level of achievement of the student that is desired, and the importance given to student motivation and engagement; there are often complex trade-offs among these.
- stimuli include observations of a student's test results and observations of the student's interaction (or non-interaction) with the agent; students can also ask questions or request help on new examples and problems.

The actions of the tutoring agent include presenting the theory and worked-out examples, proposing suitable problems, providing help and feedback on a student's solution, asking the student questions, answering their questions, and producing reports for parents and teachers.

### 1.4.4 A Trading Agent

A **trading agent** is like a robot, but instead of interacting with a physical environment, it interacts with an information environment. Its task is to procure goods and services for a user. It must be able to be told the needs of a user, and it must interact with sellers (e.g., on the Web). The simplest trading agent involves proxy bidding for a user on an auction site, where the system will keep bidding until the user's price limit is reached. A more complicated trading agent will buy multiple complementary items, like booking a flight, a hotel, and a rental car that fit together, in addition to trading off competing preferences of the user. **Web services** provide tools on the Web designed to be combined by trading agents. Another example of a trading agent is one that monitors how much food and groceries are in a household, monitors the prices, and orders goods before they are needed, while trying to keep costs to a minimum.

In terms of the black-box definition of an agent in Figure 1.4 (page 15), the trading agent has as inputs:

- prior knowledge about types of goods and services, selling practices, and how auctions work
- past experience about where is the best place to look for specials, how prices vary with time in an auction, and when specials tend to turn up
- preferences in terms of what the user wants and how to trade off competing goals
- stimuli including observations about what items are available, their price, and, perhaps, how long they are available.

The output of the trading agent is either a recommendation the user can accept or reject, or an actual purchase.

Because of the personalized nature of the trading agent, it should be able to do better than a generic purchaser that, for example, only offers packaged tours.

### 1.4.5 Smart Home

A **smart home** is a home that looks after itself and its inhabitants. It can be seen as a mix of the other applications.

A smart home is an inside-out robot. It has physical sensors and actuators. It should be able to sense where people, pets, and objects are. It should be able to adjust lighting, sound, heat, etc., to suit the needs of its occupants, while reducing costs and minimizing environmental impacts. A smart home will not only have fixed sensors and actuators, but will be combined with mobile robots, and other actuators, such as arms on the kitchen walls to help with cooking, cleaning, and finding ingredients.

A purchaser of a smart home may expect it to be able to clean floors, dishes, and clothes and to put things where they are kept. It is easy to clean a floor with the assumption that everything small on the floor is garbage. It is much more difficult to know which of the small items are precious toys and which are junk that should be discarded, and this depends on the individual inhabitants and their age. Each person may have their own categorization of objects and where they are expected to be kept, which forces a smart home to adapt to the inhabitants.

A smart home also must act as a diagnostician. When something goes wrong, it should be able to determine what is the problem and fix it. It should also be able to observe the inhabitants and determine if there is something wrong, such as someone has been injured or there is a burglary.

Sometimes a smart home needs to act as a tutoring agent. It may have to teach the occupants how the appliances work, and how to interact with the home (e.g., what should an person expect to happen when they put their coffee cup on the vacuum cleaner). In order to do this, it has to take into account the knowledge and level of understanding of the person.

A smart home may also need to act as a purchasing agent. The home should notice when items, such as toilet paper, soap, or essential foodstuffs, are running low and order more of them. Given a decision about what food each inhabitant wants, it should make sure the ingredients are in stock. It might even need to decide when inessential items, such as junk food, should be kept in stock. It also might need to decide when to discard perishable items, without creating too much waste or putting people's health at risk.

A smart home would include energy management. For example, with solar energy providing power during daylight hours, it could determine whether to store the energy locally or buy and sell energy on the smart grid. It could manage appliances to minimize the cost of energy, such as washing clothes when water and electricity are cheaper.

## 1.5 Agent Design Space

Agents acting in environments range in complexity from thermostats to companies with multiple goals acting in competitive environments. The ten dimensions of complexity in the design of intelligent agents below are designed to help us understand work that has been done, as well as the potential and limits of AI. These dimensions may be considered separately but must be combined to build an intelligent agent. These dimensions define a **design space** for AI; different points in this space are obtained by varying the values on each dimension.

These dimensions give a coarse division of the design space for intelligent agents. There are many other design choices that must also be made to build an intelligent agent.

### 1.5.1 Modularity

The first dimension is the level of modularity.

**Modularity** is the extent to which a system can be decomposed into interacting modules that can be understood separately.

Modularity is important for reducing complexity. It is apparent in the structure of the brain, serves as a foundation of computer science, and is an important aspect of any large organization.

Modularity is typically expressed in terms of a hierarchical decomposition.

In the **modularity dimension**, an agent's structure is one of the following:

- **flat** – there is no organizational structure
- **modular** – the system is decomposed into interacting modules that can be understood on their own
- **hierarchical** – the system is modular, and the modules themselves are decomposed into simpler modules, each of which are hierarchical systems or simple components.

In a flat or modular structure the agent typically reasons at a single level of abstraction. In a hierarchical structure the agent reasons at multiple levels of abstraction. The lower levels of the hierarchy involve reasoning at a lower level of abstraction.

**Example 1.6** The delivery robot at the highest level has to plan its day, making sure it can deliver coffee on time, but still has time for longer trips and cleaning a room. At the lowest level, it needs to choose what motor controls to send to its wheels, and what movement its gripper should do. Even a task like picking up a glass involves many precise movements that need to be coordinated. Picking up a glass may be just one part of the larger task of cleaning part of a room. Cleaning the room might be one task that has to be scheduled into the robot's day.

In a flat representation, the agent chooses one level of abstraction and reasons at that level. A modular representation would divide the task into a number of subtasks that can be solved separately (e.g., pick up coffee, move from the corridor to lab B, put down coffee). In a hierarchical representation, the agent will solve these subtasks in a hierarchical way, until the task is reduced to simple tasks such a sending an http request or making a particular motor control.

**Example 1.7** A **tutoring** agent may have high-level teaching strategies, where it needs to decide which topics are taught and in what order. At a much lower level, it must design the details of concrete examples and specific questions for a test. At the lowest level it needs to combine words and lines in diagrams to express the examples and questions. Students can also be treated as learning in a hierarchical way, with detailed examples as well as higher-level concepts.

**Example 1.8** For the trading agent, consider the task of making all of the arrangements and purchases for a custom holiday for a traveler. The agent should be able to make bookings for flights that fit together. Only when it knows where the traveller is staying and when, can it make more detailed arrangements such as dinner and event reservations.

A hierarchical decomposition is important for reducing the complexity of building an intelligent agent that acts in a complex environment. Large organizations have a hierarchical organization so that the top-level decision makers are not overwhelmed by details and do not have to micromanage all activities of the organization. Procedural abstraction and object-oriented programming in computer science are designed to enable simplification of a system by exploiting modularity and abstraction. There is much evidence that biological systems are also hierarchical.

To explore the other dimensions, initially ignore the hierarchical structure and assume a flat representation. Ignoring hierarchical decomposition is often fine for small or moderately sized tasks, as it is for simple animals, small organizations, or small to moderately sized computer programs. When tasks or systems become complex, some hierarchical organization is required.

How to build hierarchically organized agents is discussed in Section 2.2 (page 58).

### 1.5.2 Planning Horizon

The planning horizon dimension is how far ahead in time the agent plans. For example, consider a dog as an agent. When a dog is called to come, it should turn around to start running in order to get a reward in the future. It does not act only to get an immediate reward. Plausibly, a dog does not act for goals arbitrarily far in the future (e.g., in a few months), whereas people do (e.g., working hard now to get a holiday next year).

How far the agent "looks into the future" when deciding what to do is called the **planning horizon**. For completeness, let's include the non-planning case where the agent is not reasoning in time. The time points considered by an agent when planning are called **stages**.

In the **planning horizon dimension**, an agent is one of the following:

- A **non-planning agent** is an agent that does not consider the future when it decides what to do or when time is not involved.
- A **finite horizon** planner is an agent that looks for a fixed finite number of stages. For example, a doctor may have to treat a patient but may have time for a test and so there may be two stages to plan for: a testing stage and a treatment stage. In the simplest case, a **greedy** or **myopic** agent only looks one time step ahead.
- An **indefinite horizon** planner is an agent that looks ahead some finite, but not predetermined, number of stages. For example, an agent that must get to some location may not know a priori how many steps it will

take to get there, but, when planning, it does not consider what it will do after it gets to the location.

- An **infinite horizon** planner is an agent that plans on going on forever. This is often called a **process**. For example, the stabilization module of a legged robot should go on forever; it cannot stop when it has achieved stability, because the robot has to keep from falling over.

The modules in a hierarchical decomposition may have different horizons, as in the following example.

**Example 1.9** For the delivery and helping agent, at the lowest level the module that keeps the robot stable, safe, and attentive to requests may be on an infinite horizon, assuming it is running forever. The task of delivering coffee to a particular person may be an indefinite horizon problem. Planning for a fixed number of hours may be a finite horizon problem.

**Example 1.10** In a **tutoring agent**, for some subtasks, a finite horizon may be appropriate, such as in a fixed teach, test, re-teach sequence. For other cases, there may be an indefinite horizon where the system may not know at design time how many steps it will take until the student has mastered some concept. It may also be possible to model teaching as an ongoing process of learning and testing with appropriate breaks, with no expectation of the system finishing.

### 1.5.3 Representation

The **representation dimension** concerns how the world is described.

The different ways the world could be are called **states**. A state of the world specifies the agent's internal state (its belief state) and the environment state.

At the simplest level, an agent can reason explicitly in terms of individually identified states.

**Example 1.11** A thermostat for a heater may have two belief states: *off* and *heating*. The environment may have three states: *cold*, *comfortable*, and *hot*. There are thus six states corresponding to the different combinations of belief and environment states. These states may not fully describe the world, but they are adequate to describe what a thermostat should do. The thermostat should move to, or stay in, *heating* if the environment is *cold* and move to, or stay in, *off* if the environment is *hot*. If the environment is *comfortable*, the thermostat should stay in its current state. The thermostat agent turns or keeps the heater on in the *heating* state and turns or keeps the heater off in the *off* state.

Instead of enumerating states, it is often easier to reason in terms of features of the state or propositions that are true or false of the state. A state may be described in terms of **features**, where a feature has a value in each state (see Section 4.1, page 127).

**Example 1.12** Consider designing an agent to diagnose electrical problems in the home of Figure 1.6 (page 18). It may have features for the position of each switch, the status of each switch (whether it is working okay, whether it is shorted, or whether it is broken), and whether each light works. The feature $position\_s_2$ may be a feature that has value *up* when switch $s_2$ is up and has value *down* when the switch is down. The state of the home's lighting may be described in terms of values for each of these features. These features depend on each other, but not in arbitrarily complex ways; for example, whether a light is on may just depend on whether it is okay, whether the switch is turned on, and whether there is electricity.

A **proposition** is a Boolean feature, which means that its value is either *true* or *false*. Thirty propositions can encode $2^{30} = 1,073,741,824$ states. It may be easier to specify and reason with the thirty propositions than with more than a billion states. Moreover, having a compact representation of the states indicates understanding, because it means that an agent has captured some regularities in the domain.

**Example 1.13** Consider an agent that has to recognize digits. Suppose the agent observes a binary image, a $28 \times 28$ grid of pixels, where each of the $28^2 =$ 784 grid points is either black or white. The action is to determine which of the digits $\{0,\ldots,9\}$ is shown in the image. There are $2^{784}$ different possible states of the image, and so $10^{2^{784}}$ different functions from the image state into the characters $\{a,\ldots,z\}$. You cannot represent such functions in terms of the state space. Instead, handwriting recognition systems define features of the image, such as line segments, and define the function from images to characters in terms of these features. Modern implementations learn the features that are useful; see Example 8.3 (page 336).

When describing a complex world, the features can depend on **relations** and **individuals**. An *individual* is also called a **thing**, an **object**, or an **entity**. A relation on a single individual is a **property**. There is a feature for each possible relationship among the individuals.

**Example 1.14** The agent that looks after a home in Example 1.12 could have the lights and switches as individuals, and relations *position* and *connected_to*. Instead of the feature $position\_s_2 = up$, it could use the relation $position(s_2, up)$. This relation enables the agent to reason about all switches or for an agent to have general knowledge about switches that can be used when the agent encounters a switch.

**Example 1.15** If an agent is enrolling students in courses, there could be a feature that gives the grade of a student in a course, for every student–course pair where the student took the course. There would be a *passed* feature for every student–course pair, which depends on the *grade* feature for that pair. It may be easier to reason in terms of individual students, courses, and grades, and the relations *grade* and *passed*. By defining how *passed* depends on *grade* once, the agent can apply the definition for each student and course. Moreover, this can be done before the agent knows which individuals exist, and so before it knows any of the features.

The two-argument relation *passed*, with 1000 students and 100 courses, can represent $1000 * 100 = 100,000$ propositions and so $2^{100,000}$ states.

By reasoning in terms of relations and individuals, an agent can reason about whole classes of individuals without ever enumerating the features or propositions, let alone the states. An agent may have to reason about infinite sets of individuals, such as the set of all numbers or the set of all sentences. To reason about an unbounded or infinite number of individuals, an agent cannot reason in terms of states or features; it must reason at the relational level.

In the **representation dimension**, the agent reasons in terms of

- states
- features, or
- individuals and relations (often called **relational representations**).

Some of the frameworks will be developed in terms of states, some in terms of features, and some in terms of individuals and relations.

Reasoning in terms of states is introduced in Chapter 3. Reasoning in terms of features is introduced in Chapter 4. Relational reasoning is considered starting from Chapter 15.

### 1.5.4 Computational Limits

Sometimes an agent can decide on its best action quickly enough for it to act. Often there are computational resource limits that prevent an agent from carrying out the best action. That is, the agent may not be able to find the best action quickly enough within its memory limitations to act while that action is still the best thing to do. For example, it may not be much use to take 10 minutes to derive what was the best thing to do 10 minutes ago, when the agent has to act *now*. Often, instead, an agent must trade off how long it takes to get a solution with how good the solution is; it may be better to find a reasonable solution quickly than to find a better solution later because the world will have changed during the computation.

The **computational limits dimension** determines whether an agent has

- **perfect rationality**, where an agent reasons about the best action without taking into account its limited computational resources, or
- **bounded rationality**, where an agent decides on the best action that it can find given its computational limitations.

Computational resource limits include computation time, memory, and numerical accuracy caused by computers not representing real numbers exactly.

An **anytime algorithm** is an algorithm where the solution quality improves with time. In particular, it is one that can produce its current best solution at any time, but given more time it could produce even better solutions. To ensure that the quality does not decrease, the agent can store the best solution found so far, and return that when asked for a solution. Although the solution quality may increase with time, waiting to act has a cost; it may be better for an agent to act before it has found what would be the best solution.

**Example 1.16** The delivery robot cannot think for a long time about how to avoid a person. There might be a best way to avoid the person and to achieve its other goals, however it might take time to determine that optimal path, and it might be better to act quickly and then recover from a non-optimal action. In the simplest case, a robot could just stop if it encounters a person, but even that is error prone as robots have momentum, so it cannot stop immediately and people behind may run into it if it stops suddenly.

**Example 1.17** Even a **tutoring agent** that can act at longer scales than a robot sometimes has to act quickly. When a student has completed a task and wants a new task, the agent needs to decide whether it should assign the student the best task it has found so far, or compute for longer, trying to find an even better task. As the student waits, they might become distracted, which might be worse than giving them a non-optimal task. The computer can be planning the next task when the student is working. Modern computers, as fast as they may be, cannot find optimal solutions to difficult problems quickly.

**Example 1.18** Figure 1.7 shows how the computation time of an anytime algorithm can affect the solution quality. The agent has to carry out an action but can do some computation to decide what to do. The absolute solution quality,

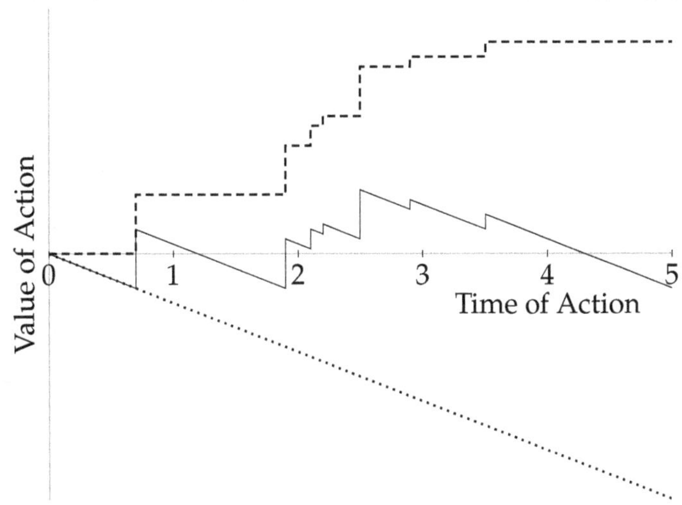


Figure 1.7: Solution quality as a function of time for an anytime algorithm. The meaning is described in Example 1.18

had the action been carried out at time zero, shown as the dashed line at the top, is improving as the agent takes time to reason. However, there is a penalty associated with taking time to act. In this figure, the penalty, shown as the dotted line at the bottom, is negative and proportional to the time taken before the agent acts. These two values can be added to get the discounted quality, the time-dependent value of computation; this is the solid line in the middle of the graph. For the example of Figure 1.7 (page 27), an agent should compute for about 2.5 time units, and then act, at which point the discounted quality achieves its maximum value. If the computation lasts for longer than 4.3 time units, the resulting discounted solution quality is worse than if the algorithm outputs the initial guess it can produce with virtually no computation. It is typical that the solution quality improves in jumps; when the current best solution changes, there is a jump in the quality. The penalty associated with waiting is rarely a straight line; it is typically a function of deadlines, which may not be known by the agent.

To take into account bounded rationality, an agent must decide whether it should act or reason for longer. This is challenging because an agent typically does not know how much better off it would be if it only spent a little bit more time reasoning. Moreover, the time spent thinking about whether it should reason may detract from actually reasoning about the domain.

### 1.5.5 Learning

In some cases, a designer of an agent may have a good model of the agent and its environment. But often a designer does not have a good model, and so an agent should use data from its past experiences and other sources to help it decide what to do.

The **learning dimension** determines whether

- **knowledge is given**, or
- **knowledge is learned** (from prior knowledge and data or past experience).

Learning typically means finding the best model that fits the data. Sometimes this is as simple as tuning a fixed set of parameters, but it can also mean choosing the best representation out of a class of representations. Learning is a huge field in itself but does not stand in isolation from the rest of AI. There are many issues beyond fitting data, including how to incorporate background knowledge, what data to collect, how to represent the data and the resulting representations, what learning biases are appropriate, and how the learned knowledge can be used to affect how the agent acts.

Learning is considered in Chapters 7, 8, 10, 13, and 17.

**Example 1.19** A robot has a great deal to learn, such as how slippery floors are as a function of their shininess, where each person hangs out at different parts of the day, when they will ask for coffee, and which actions result in the highest rewards.

Modern vision systems are trained to learn good features (such as lines and textures) on millions if not billions of images and videos. These features can be used to recognize objects and for other tasks, even if there have been few examples of the higher-level concepts. A robot might not have seen a baby crawling on a highway, or a particular mug, but should be able to deal with such situations.

**Example 1.20** Learning is fundamental to diagnosis. It is through learning and science that medical professionals understand the progression of diseases and how well treatments work or do not work. Diagnosis is a challenging domain for learning, because all patients are different, and each individual doctor's experience is only with a few patients with any particular set of symptoms. Doctors also see a biased sample of the population; those who come to see them usually have unusual or painful symptoms. Drugs are not given to people randomly. You cannot learn the effect of treatment by observation alone, but need a causal model of the causes and effects; see Chapter 11 for details on building causal models. To overcome the limitations of learning from observations alone, drug companies spend billions of dollars doing randomized controlled trials in order to learn the efficacy of drugs.

### 1.5.6 Uncertainty

An agent could assume there is no uncertainty, or it could take uncertainty in the domain into consideration. Uncertainty is divided into two dimensions: one for uncertainty from sensing and one for uncertainty about the effects of actions.

#### Sensing Uncertainty

In some cases, an agent can observe the state of the world directly. For example, in some board games or on a factory floor, an agent may know exactly the state of the world. In many other cases, it may have some noisy perception of the state and the best it can do is to have a probability distribution over the set of possible states based on what it perceives. For example, given a patient's symptoms, a medical doctor may not actually know which disease a patient has and may have only a probability distribution over the diseases the patient may have.

The **sensing uncertainty dimension** concerns whether the agent can determine the state from the stimuli:

- **Fully observable** means the agent knows the state of the world from the stimuli.

- **Partially observable** means the agent does not directly observe the state of the world. This occurs when many possible states can result in the same stimuli or when stimuli are misleading.

Assuming the world is fully observable is a common simplifying assumption to keep reasoning tractable.

**Example 1.21** The delivery robot does not know exactly where it is, or what else there is, based on its limited sensors. Looking down a corridor does not provide enough information to know where it is or who is behind the doors. Knowing where it was a second ago will help determine where it is now, but even robots can get lost. It may not know where the person who requested coffee is. When it is introduced into a new environment, it may have much more uncertainty.

**Example 1.22** The **tutoring agent** cannot directly observe the knowledge of the student. All it has is some sensing input, based on questions the student asks or does not ask, facial expressions, distractedness, and test results. Even test results are very noisy, as a mistake may be due to distraction or test anxiety instead of lack of knowledge, and a correct answer might be due to a lucky guess instead of real understanding. Sometimes students make mistakes in testing situations they wouldn't make at other times.

**Example 1.23** A trading agent does not know all available options and their availability, but must find out information that can become outdated quickly (e.g., if a hotel becomes booked up). A travel agent does not know whether a flight will be canceled or delayed, or whether the passenger's luggage will be lost. This uncertainty means that the agent must plan for the unanticipated.

### Effect Uncertainty

A model of the **dynamics** of the world is a model of how the world changes as a result of actions, including the case of how it changes if the action were to do nothing. In some cases an agent knows the effects of its action. That is, given a state and an action, the agent can accurately predict the state resulting from carrying out that action in that state. For example, a software agent interacting with the file system of a computer may be able to predict the effects of deleting a file given the state of the file system. However, in many cases, it is difficult to predict the effects of an action, and the best an agent can do is to have a probability distribution over the effects. For example, a teacher may not know the effects explaining a concept, even if the state of the students is known. At the other extreme, if the teacher has no inkling of the effect of its actions, there would be no reason to choose one action over another.

The dynamics in the **effect uncertainty dimension** can be

- **deterministic** when the state resulting from an action is determined by an action and the prior state, or

• **stochastic** when there is a probability distribution over the resulting states.

**Example 1.24** For the delivery robot, there can be uncertainty about the effects of an action, both at the low level, say due to slippage of the wheels, or at the high level because the agent might not know whether putting the coffee on a person's desk succeeded in delivering coffee to the person. This may depend on the individual preferences of users.

**Example 1.25** Even a trading agent does not know the effect of putting in a trade order, such as booking a flight or a hotel room. These can become unavailable at very short notice (consider two trading agents trying to book the same room at the same time), or the price can vary.

The effect dimension only makes sense when the world is fully observable. If the world is partially observable, a stochastic system can be modeled as a deterministic system where the effect of an action depends on unobserved features. It is a separate dimension because many of the frameworks developed are for the fully observable, stochastic action case.

Planning with deterministic actions is considered in Chapter 6. Planning with stochastic actions is considered in Chapter 12.

### 1.5.7 Preference

Agents normally act to have better outcomes. The only reason to choose one action over another is because the preferred action leads to more desirable outcomes.

An agent may have a simple goal, which is a proposition the agent wants to be true in a final state. For example, the goal of getting Sam coffee means the agent wants to reach a state where Sam has coffee. Other agents may have more complex preferences. For example, a medical doctor may be expected to take into account suffering, life expectancy, quality of life, monetary costs (for the patient, the doctor, and society), and the ability to justify decisions in case of a lawsuit. The doctor must trade these considerations off when they conflict, as they invariably do.

The **preference dimension** considers whether the agent has goals or richer preferences:

• A **goal** is either an **achievement goal**, which is a proposition to be true in some final state, or a **maintenance goal**, a proposition that must be true in all visited states. For example, the goals for a robot may be to deliver a cup of coffee and a banana to Sam, and not to make a mess or hurt anyone.
• **Complex preferences** involve trade-offs among the desirability of various outcomes, perhaps at different times. An **ordinal preference** is where only the ordering of the preferences is important. A **cardinal preference** is where the magnitude of the values matters. For example, an ordinal

preference may be that Sam prefers cappuccino over black coffee and prefers black coffee over tea. A cardinal preference may give a trade-off between the wait time and the type of beverage, and a mess versus taste trade-off, where Sam is prepared to put up with more mess in the preparation of the coffee if the taste of the coffee is exceptionally good.

**Example 1.26** The delivery robot could be given goals, such as "deliver coffee to Chris and make sure you always have power." A more complex goal may be to "clean up the lab, and put everything where it belongs", which can only be achieved to some degree. There can be complex preferences, such as "deliver mail when it arrives and service coffee requests as soon as possible, but it is more important to deliver messages marked as urgent, and Chris needs her coffee quickly when she asks for it."

**Example 1.27** For the diagnostic assistant, the goal may be as simple as "fix what is wrong," but often there are complex trade-offs involving costs, pain, life expectancy, and preferences related to the uncertainty that the diagnosis is correct and uncertainty as to efficacy and side-effects of the treatment. There is also a problem of whose preferences are to be taken into account; the patient, the doctor, the payer, and society may all have different preferences that must be reconciled.

**Example 1.28** Although it may be possible for the **tutoring agent** to have a simple goal such, as to teach some particular concept, it is more likely that complex preferences must be taken into account. One reason is that, with uncertainty, there may be no way to guarantee that the student knows the concept being taught; any method that tries to maximize the probability that the student knows a concept will be very annoying, because it will repeatedly teach and test if there is a slight chance that the student's errors are due to misunderstanding as opposed to fatigue or boredom. More complex preferences would enable a trade-off among fully teaching a concept, boring the student, the time taken, and the amount of retesting. The student may also have a preference for a teaching style that could be taken into account. The student, the teacher, the parents, and future employers may have different preferences. The student may have incompatible preferences, for example, to not work hard and to get a good mark. If the teacher is optimizing student evaluations, it might both allow the student to not work hard, and also give good marks. But that might undermine the goal of the student actually learning something.

**Example 1.29** For a trading agent, preferences of users are typically in terms of functionality, not components. For example, typical computer buyers have no idea of what hardware to buy, but they know what functionality they want and they also want the flexibility to be able to use new software features that might not even exist yet. Similarly, in a travel domain, what activities a user wants may depend on the location. Users also may want the ability to participate in a local custom at their destination, even though they may not know what those customs are. Even a simple path-finding algorithm, such as Google

Maps, which, at the time of writing, assumes all users' preferences are to minimize travel time, could take into account each individual user's preferences for diverse views or avoiding going too close to where some particular relative lives.

Goals are considered in Chapters 3 and 6. Complex preferences are considered in Chapter 12, and the following chapters.

### 1.5.8 Number of Agents

An agent reasoning about what it should do in an environment where it is the only agent is difficult enough. However, reasoning about what to do when there are other agents who are also reasoning is much more difficult. An agent in a multiagent setting may need to reason strategically about other agents; the other agents may act to trick or manipulate the agent or may be available to cooperate with the agent. With multiple agents, it is often optimal to act randomly because other agents can exploit deterministic strategies. Even when the agents are cooperating and have a common goal, the task of coordination and communication makes multiagent reasoning more challenging. However, many domains contain multiple agents and ignoring other agents' strategic reasoning is not always the best way for an agent to reason.

Taking the point of view of a single agent, the **number of agents dimension** considers whether the agent explicitly considers other agents:

- **Single agent** reasoning means the agent assumes that there are no other agents in the environment or that all other agents are part of **nature**, and so are non-purposive. This is a reasonable assumption if there are no other agents or if the other agents are not going to change what they do based on the agent's action.
- **Adversarial reasoning** considers another agent, where when one agent wins, the other loses. This is sometimes called a **two-player zero-sum game**, as the payoffs for the agents (e.g., $+1$ for a win and $-1$ for a loss) sum to zero. This is a simpler case than allowing for arbitrary agents as there is no need to cooperate or otherwise coordinate.
- **Multiple agent** reasoning (or **multiagent reasoning**) means the agent takes the reasoning of other agents into account. This occurs when there are other intelligent agents whose goals or preferences depend, in part, on what the agent does or if the agent must communicate with other agents. Agents may need to cooperate because coordinated actions can result in outcomes that are better for all agents than each agent considering the other agents as part of nature.

Reasoning in the presence of other agents is much more difficult if the agents can act simultaneously or if the environment is only partially observable. Multiagent systems are considered in Chapter 14. Note that the adversarial case is separate as there are some methods that only work for that case.

**Example 1.30** There can be multiple delivery robots, which can coordinate to deliver coffee and parcels more efficiently. They can compete for power outlets or for space to move. Only one might be able to go closest to the wall when turning a corner. There may also be children out to trick the robot, or pets that get in the way.

When automated vehicles have to go on a highway, it may be much more efficient and safer for them to travel in a coordinated manner, say one centimeter apart in a convoy, than to travel three vehicle lengths apart. It is more efficient because they can reduce wind drag, and many more vehicles can fit on a highway. It is safer because the difference in speeds is small; if one vehicle slams on its brakes or has engine problems, the car that might crash into the back is going approximately the same speed.

**Example 1.31** A trading agent has to reason about other agents. In commerce, prices are governed by supply and demand; this means that it is important to reason about the other competing agents. This happens particularly in a world where many items are sold by auction. Such reasoning becomes particularly difficult when there are items that must complement each other, such as flights and hotel bookings, and items that can substitute for each other, such as bus transport or taxis. You don't want to book the flights if there is no accommodation, or book accommodation if there are no flights.

### 1.5.9 Interactivity

In deciding what an agent will do, there are three aspects of computation that must be distinguished: (1) the **design-time computation** that goes into the design of the agent, carried out by the designer of the agent, not the agent itself; (2) the computation that the agent can do before it observes the world and needs to act; and (3) the computation that is done by the agent as it is acting.

The **interactivity dimension** considers whether the agent does

- only offline reasoning, where **offline reasoning** is the computation done by the agent before it has to act, and can include compilation, learning or finding solutions from every state the agent could find itself in; under this assumption, the agent can carry out simple fixed-cost computation while acting, sometimes even just looking up the action in a table
- significant online reasoning, where **online computation** is the computation done by the agent between observing the environment and acting.

An agent acting in the world usually does not have the luxury of having the world wait for it to consider the best option. However, offline reasoning, where the agent can reason about the best thing to do before having to act, is often a simplifying assumption. Online reasoning can include long-range strategic reasoning as well as determining how to react in a timely manner to the environment; see Chapter 2.

**Example 1.32** A delivery robot may be able to compute a plan for its day offline, but then it needs to be able to adapt to changes, for example, when someone wants coffee early or something urgent needs to be delivered. It cannot plan for who it will meet and need to avoid in the corridors. It either needs to be able to anticipate and plan for all possible eventualities, or it needs to reason online when it finds something unexpected.

**Example 1.33** A **tutoring agent** can determine the general outline of what should be taught offline. But then it needs to be able to react to unexpected behavior online when it occurs. It is difficult to be able to anticipate all eventualities, and might be easier to deal with them online when it encounters them.

### 1.5.10 Interaction of the Dimensions

Figure 1.8 summarizes the dimensions of complexity.

In terms of the dimensions of complexity, the simplest case for the robot is a flat system, represented in terms of states, with no uncertainty, with achievement goals, with no other agents, with given knowledge, and with perfect rationality. In this case, with an indefinite stage planning horizon, the problem of deciding what to do is reduced to the problem of finding a path in a graph of states. This is explored in Chapter 3.

In going beyond the simplest cases, these dimensions cannot be considered independently because they interact in complex ways. Consider the following examples of the interactions.

The representation dimension interacts with the modularity dimension in that some modules in a hierarchy may be simple enough to reason in terms of a finite set of states, whereas other levels of abstraction may require reasoning about individuals and relations. For example, in a delivery robot, a module

| Dimension | Values |
|---|---|
| Modularity | flat, modular, hierarchical |
| Planning horizon | non-planning, finite stage, indefinite stage, infinite stage |
| Representation | states, features, relations |
| Computational limits | perfect rationality, bounded rationality |
| Learning | knowledge is given, knowledge is learned |
| Sensing uncertainty | fully observable, partially observable |
| Effect uncertainty | deterministic, stochastic |
| Preference | goals, complex preferences |
| Number of agents | single agent, adversaries, multiple agents |
| Interactivity | offline, online |

Figure 1.8: Dimensions of complexity

that maintains balance may only have a few states. A module that must prioritize the delivery of multiple parcels to multiple people may have to reason about multiple individuals (e.g., people, packages, and rooms) and the relations between them. At a higher level, a module that reasons about the activity over the day may only require a few states to cover the different phases of the day (e.g., there might be three states of the robot: busy, available for requests, and recharging).

The planning horizon interacts with the modularity dimension. For example, at a high level, a dog may be getting an immediate reward when it comes and gets a treat. At the level of deciding where to place its paws, there may be a long time until it gets the reward, and so at this level it may have to plan for an indefinite stage.

Sensing uncertainty probably has the greatest impact on the complexity of reasoning. It is much easier for an agent to reason when it knows the state of the world than when it does not.

The uncertainty dimensions interact with the modularity dimension: at one level in a hierarchy, an action may be deterministic, whereas at another level, it may be stochastic. As an example, consider the result of flying to a particular overseas destination with a companion you are trying to impress. At one level you may know which country you are in. At a lower level, you may be quite lost and not know where you are on a map of the airport. At an even lower level responsible for maintaining balance, you may know where you are: you are standing on the ground. At the highest level, you may be very unsure whether you have impressed your companion.

Preference models interact with uncertainty because an agent needs to trade off between satisfying a very desirable goal with low probability or a less desirable goal with a higher probability. This issue is explored in Section 12.1 (page 518).

Multiple agents can also be used for modularity; one way to design a single agent is to build multiple interacting agents that share a common goal of making the higher-level agent act intelligently. Some researchers, such as Minsky [1986], argue that intelligence is an emergent feature from a "society" of unintelligent agents.

Learning is often cast in terms of learning with features – determining which feature values best predict the value of another feature. However, learning can also be carried out with individuals and relations. Learning with hierarchies, sometimes called **deep learning**, has enabled the learning of more complex concepts. Much work has been done on learning in partially observable domains, and learning with multiple agents. Each of these is challenging in its own right without considering interactions with multiple dimensions.

The interactivity dimension interacts with the planning horizon dimension in that when the agent is reasoning and acting online, it also needs to reason about the long-term horizon. The interactivity dimension also interacts with the computational limits; even if an agent is reasoning offline, it cannot take hundreds of years to compute an answer. However, when it has to reason about what to do in, say, 1/10 of a second, it needs to be concerned about the time taken to reason, and the trade-off between thinking and acting.

Two of these dimensions, modularity and bounded rationality, promise to make reasoning more efficient. Although they make the formalism more complicated, breaking the system into smaller components, and making the approximations needed to act in a timely fashion and within memory limitations, should help build more complex systems.

# 1.6 Designing Agents

Artificial agents are designed for particular tasks. Researchers have not yet got to the stage of designing an intelligent agent for the task of surviving and reproducing in a complex natural environment.

## 1.6.1 Simplifying Environments and Simplifying Agents

It is important to distinguish between the knowledge in the mind of an agent and the knowledge in the mind of the designer of the agent. Consider the extreme cases:

- At one extreme is a highly specialized agent that works well in the environment for which it was designed, but is helpless outside of this niche. The designer may have done considerable work in building the agent, but the agent can be extremely specialized to operate well. An example is a traditional thermostat. It may be difficult to design a thermostat so that it turns on and off at exactly the right temperatures, but the thermostat itself does not have to do much computation. Another example is a car-painting robot that always paints the same parts in an automobile factory. There may be much design time or offline computation to get it to work perfectly, but the painting robot can paint parts with little online computation; it senses that there is a part in position, but then it carries out its predefined actions. These very specialized agents do not adapt well to different environments or to changing goals. The painting robot would not notice if a different sort of part were present and, even if it did, it would not know what to do with it. It would have to be redesigned or reprogrammed to paint different parts or to change into a sanding machine or a dog-washing machine.
- At the other extreme is a very flexible agent that can survive in arbitrary environments and accept new tasks at run time. Simple biological agents such as insects can adapt to complex changing environments, but they cannot carry out arbitrary tasks. Designing an agent that can adapt to complex environments and changing goals is a major challenge. The agent will know much more about the particulars of a situation than the designer. Even biology has not produced many such agents. Humans

may be the only extant example, but even humans need time to adapt to new environments.

Even if the flexible agent is our ultimate dream, researchers have to reach this goal via more mundane goals. Rather than building a universal agent, which can adapt to any environment and solve any task, researchers have been restricted to particular agents for particular environmental niches. The designer can exploit the structure of the particular niche and the agent does not have to reason about other possibilities.

Two broad strategies have been pursued in building agents:

- The first is to simplify environments and build complex reasoning systems for these simple environments. For example, factory robots can do sophisticated tasks in the engineered environment of a factory, but they may be hopeless in a natural environment. Much of the complexity of the task can be reduced by simplifying the environment. This is also important for building practical systems because many environments can be engineered to make them simpler for agents.
- The second strategy is to build simple agents in natural environments. This is inspired by seeing how **insects** can survive in complex environments even though they have very limited reasoning abilities. Modern language systems can predict the probability of the next word in an arbitrary text, but this does not mean they can be used for decision making. Researchers then make the agents have more reasoning abilities as their tasks become more complicated.

One of the advantages of simplifying environments is that it may enable us to prove properties of agents or to optimize agents for particular situations. Proving properties or optimization typically requires a model of the agent and its environment. The agent may do a little or a lot of reasoning, but an observer or designer of the agent may be able to reason about the agent and the environment. For example, the designer may be able to prove whether the agent can achieve a goal, whether it can avoid getting into situations that may be bad for the agent (**safety**), whether it can avoid getting stuck somewhere (**liveness**), or whether it will eventually get around to each of the things it should do (**fairness**). Of course, the proof is only as good as the model.

The advantage of building agents for complex environments is that these are the types of environments in which humans live and where agents could be useful.

Even natural environments can be abstracted into simpler environments. For example, for an autonomous car driving on public roads the environment can be conceptually simplified so that everything is either a road, another car, or something to be avoided. Although autonomous cars have sophisticated sensors, they only have limited actions available, namely steering, accelerating, and braking.

Fortunately, research along both lines, and between these extremes, is being carried out. In the first case, researchers start with simple environments and make the environments more complex. In the second case, researchers increase the complexity of the behaviors that the agents can carry out.

### 1.6.2 Tasks

One way that AI representations differ from computer programs in traditional languages is that an AI representation typically specifies *what* needs to be computed, not *how* it is to be computed. You might specify that the agent should find the most likely disease a patient has, or specify that a robot should get coffee, but not give detailed instructions on how to do these things. Much AI reasoning involves searching through the space of possibilities to determine how to complete a task.

Typically, a task is only given informally, such as "deliver parcels promptly when they arrive" or "fix whatever is wrong with the electrical system of the home."

The general framework for solving tasks by computer is given in Figure 1.9. To solve a task, the designer of a system must:

- determine what constitutes a solution
- represent the task in a way a computer can reason about
- use the computer to compute an output; either answers presented to a user or actions to be carried out in the environment
- interpret the output as a solution to the task.

In AI, **knowledge** is long-term representation of a domain whereas **belief** is about the immediate environment, for example where the agent is and where other object are. In philosophy, knowledge is usually defined as *justified true belief*, but in AI the term is used more generally to be any relatively stable information, as opposed to belief, which is more transitory information. The reason for this terminology is that it is difficult for an agent to determine truth, and "justified" is subjective. Knowledge in AI can be represented in terms of logic,

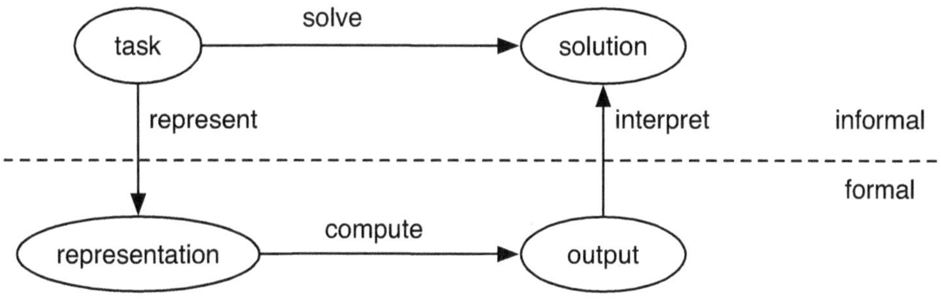


Figure 1.9: The role of representations in solving tasks

neural networks, or probabilistic models, but belief is typically represented as a distribution over the states.

A **representation** of some piece of knowledge is the particular data structures used to encode the knowledge so it can be reasoned with.

The form of representation – what is represented – is a compromise among many competing objectives. A representation should be:

- rich enough to express the knowledge needed to solve the task
- as close to a natural specification of the task as possible
- amenable to efficient computation
- able to be acquired from people, data, and past experiences.

Being as close to a natural specification of the task as possible means should be compact, natural, and maintainable. It should be easy to see the relationship between the representation and the domain being represented, so that it is easy to determine whether the knowledge represented is correct; a small change in the task should result in a small change in the representation of the task. There is an active debate about how much of the internal structure of reasoning should be explainable; the field of **explainable AI** is about how to make more aspects of the decision making amenable to being explained to a person.

Efficient computation enables the agent to act quickly enough to be effective. A **tractable** algorithm is one with reasonable **asymptotic complexity**, often meaning the computation time is polynomial in the input size (page 95), however often linear complexity is too slow. To ensure this, representations exploit features of the task for computational gain and trade off accuracy and computation time.

Many different representation languages have been designed. Many of these start with some of these objectives and are then expanded to include the other objectives. For example, some are designed for learning, perhaps inspired by neurons, and then expanded to allow richer task-solving and inference abilities. Some representation languages are designed with expressiveness in mind, and then inference and learning are added on. Some language designers focus on tractability and enhance richness, naturalness, and the ability to be acquired.

### 1.6.3 Defining a Solution

Given an informal description of a task, before even considering a computer, an agent designer should determine what would constitute a solution. This question arises not only in AI but in any software design. Much of **software engineering** involves refining the specification of the task.

Tasks are typically not well specified. Not only is there usually much left unspecified, but also the unspecified parts cannot be filled in arbitrarily. For example, if a user asks a trading agent to find out all the information about resorts that may have unsanitary food practices, they do not want the agent to return all the information about all resorts, even though all of the information requested is in the result. However, if the trading agent does not have complete knowledge about the resorts, returning all of the information may be the only way for it to guarantee that all of the requested information is there. Similarly, one does not want a delivery robot, when asked to take all of the trash to the garbage can, to take everything to the garbage can, even though this may be the only way to guarantee that all of the trash has been taken. Much work in AI is motivated by **commonsense reasoning**; the computer should be able to reach commonsense conclusions about the unstated assumptions.

Given a well-defined task, the next issue is whether it matters if the answer returned is incorrect or incomplete. For example, if the specification asks for all instances, does it matter if some are missing? Does it matter if there are some extra instances? Often a person does not want just any solution but the best solution according to some criteria. There are four common classes of solutions:

**Optimal solution** An **optimal solution** to a task is one that is the best solution according to some measure of solution quality. This measure is typically specified as an **ordinal**, where only the order matters. In some situations a **cardinal** measure, where the relative magnitudes also matter, is used. For example, a robot may need to take out as much trash as possible; the more trash it can take out, the better. In a more complex example, you may want the delivery robot to take as much of the trash as possible to the garbage can, minimizing the distance traveled, and explicitly specify a trade-off between the effort required and the proportion of the trash taken out. There are also costs associated with making mistakes and throwing out items that are not trash. It may be better to miss some trash than to waste too much time. One general measure of desirability that interacts with probability is **utility** (page 518).

**Satisficing solution** Often an agent does not need the best solution to a task but just needs some solution. A **satisficing solution** is one that is good enough according to some description of which solutions are adequate. For example, a person may tell a robot that it must take all of the trash out, or tell it to take out three items of trash.

**Approximately optimal solution** One of the advantages of a cardinal measure of success is that it allows for approximations. An **approximately optimal solution** is one whose measure of quality is close to the best that could theoretically be obtained. Typically, agents do not need optimal solutions to tasks; they only need to get close enough. For example, the robot may not need to travel the optimal distance to take out the trash but may only need to be within, say, 10% of the optimal distance. Some approximation algorithms guarantee that a solution is within some range of optimal, but for some algorithms no guarantees are available.

For some tasks, it is much easier computationally to get an approximately optimal solution than to get an optimal solution. However, for other tasks, it is just as difficult to find an approximately optimal solution that is guaranteed to be within some bounds of optimal as it is to find an optimal solution.

**Probable solution** A **probable solution** is one that, even though it may not actually be a solution to the task, is likely to be a solution. This is one way to approximate, in a precise manner, a satisficing solution. For example, in the case where the delivery robot could drop the trash or fail to pick it up when it attempts to, you may need the robot to be 80% sure that it has picked up three items of trash. Often you want to distinguish a **false-positive error** (positive answers that are not correct) from a **false-negative error** (negative answers that are correct). Some applications are much more tolerant of one of these types of errors than the other.

These categories are not exclusive. A form of learning known as **probably approximately correct (PAC)** learning considers probably learning an approximately correct concept.

### 1.6.4 Representations

Once you have some requirements on the nature of a solution, you must represent the task so a computer can solve it.

Computers and human minds are examples of **physical symbol systems**. A **symbol** is a meaningful pattern that can be manipulated. Examples of symbols are written words, sentences, gestures, marks on paper, or sequences of bits. A **symbol system** creates, copies, modifies, and destroys symbols. Essentially, a symbol is one of the patterns manipulated as a unit by a symbol system. The term "physical" is used, because symbols in a physical symbol system are physical objects that are part of the real world, even though they may be internal to computers and brains. They may also need to physically affect action or motor control.

The **physical symbol system hypothesis** of Newell and Simon [1976] is that:

> A physical symbol system has the necessary and sufficient means for general intelligent action.

This is a strong hypothesis. It means that any intelligent agent is necessarily a physical symbol system. It also means that a physical symbol system is all that is needed for intelligent action; there is no magic or as-yet-to-be-discovered quantum phenomenon required. It does not imply that a physical symbol system does not need a body to sense and act in the world.

One aspect of this hypothesis is particularly controversial, namely whether symbols are needed at all levels. For example, consider recognizing a "cat" in a picture. At the top level is the symbol for a cat. At the bottom level are pixels from a camera. There are many intermediate levels that, for example, combine pixels to form lines and textures. These intermediate features are learned from data, and are not learned with the constraint that they are interpretable. Although some people have tried to interpret them, it is reasonable to say that these are not symbols. However, at a high level, they are either trained to be symbols (e.g., by learning a mapping between pixels and symbols, such as *cat*) or can be interpreted as symbols.

An agent can use a physical symbol system to model the world. A **model** of a world is a representation of an agent's beliefs about what is true in the world or how the world changes. The world does not have to be modeled at the most detailed level to be useful. All models are **abstractions**; they represent only part of the world and leave out many of the details. An agent can have a very simplistic model of the world, or it can have a very detailed model of the world. The **level of abstraction** provides a partial ordering of abstraction. A lower-level abstraction includes more details than a higher-level abstraction. An agent can have multiple, even contradictory, models of the world. Models are judged not by whether they are correct, but by whether they are useful.

**Example 1.34** A delivery robot can model the environment at a high level of abstraction in terms of rooms, corridors, doors, and obstacles, ignoring distances, its size, the steering angles needed, the slippage of the wheels, the weight of parcels, the details of obstacles, the political situation in Canada, and virtually everything else. The robot could model the environment at lower levels of abstraction by taking some of these details into account. Some of these details may be irrelevant for the successful implementation of the robot, but some may be crucial for the robot to succeed. For example, in some situations the size of the robot and the steering angles may be crucial for not getting stuck around a particular corner. In other situations, if the robot stays close to the center of the corridor, it may not need to model its width or the steering angles.

Choosing an appropriate level of abstraction is difficult for the following reasons:

- A high-level description is easier for a human to specify and understand.
- A low-level description can be more accurate and more predictive. Often, high-level descriptions abstract away details that may be important for actually solving the task.
- The lower the level, the more difficult it is to reason with. This is because a solution at a lower level of detail involves more steps and many more possible courses of action exist from which to choose.
- An agent may not know the information needed for a low-level description. For example, the delivery robot may not know what obstacles it will encounter or how slippery the floor will be at the time that it must decide what to do.

It is often a good idea to model an environment at multiple levels of abstraction. This issue is discussed further in Section 2.2 (page 58).

Biological systems, and computers, can be described at multiple levels of abstraction. At successively lower levels of animals are the neuronal level, the biochemical level (what chemicals and what electrical potentials are being transmitted), the chemical level (what chemical reactions are being carried out), and the level of physics (in terms of forces on atoms and quantum phenomena). What levels above the neuronal level are needed to account for intelligence is still an open question. These levels of description are echoed in the hierarchical structure of science itself, where scientists are divided into physicists, chemists, biologists, psychologists, anthropologists, and so on. Although no level of description is more important than any other, it is plausible that you do not have to emulate every level of a human to build an AI agent but rather you can emulate the higher levels and build them on the foundation of modern computers. This conjecture is part of what AI studies.

The following are two levels that seem to be common to both biological and computational entities:

- The **knowledge level** is the level of abstraction that considers what an agent knows and believes and what its goals are. The knowledge level considers what an agent knows, but not how it reasons. For example, the delivery agent's behavior can be described in terms of whether it knows that a parcel has arrived or not and whether it knows where a particular person is or not. Both human and robotic agents are describable at the knowledge level. At this level, you do not specify how the solution will be computed or even which of the many possible strategies available to the agent will be used.
- The **symbol level** is a level of description of an agent in terms of the reasoning it does. To implement the knowledge level, an agent manipulates symbols to produce answers. Many cognitive science experiments are designed to determine what symbol manipulation occurs during reasoning. Whereas the knowledge level is about what the agent believes about the external world and what its goals are in terms of the outside world, the symbol level is about what goes on inside an agent to reason about the external world.

## 1.7 Social Impact

AI systems are now widely deployed in society. Individuals, corporations, governments, and other organizations are using AI for applications as varied as voice dictation, text synthesis, text-to-video generation, movie recommendations, personal finance, chatbots, credit scoring, screening employment applications, social media propagation and monitoring, face recognition, semi-autonomous cars, and warehouse automation. Many of these systems can be broadly beneficial. However, there are often adverse impacts on people in racialized populations and underserved communities, and on election results and vaccination campaigns.

There are significant ethical and social impacts of AI systems, leading to demands for human-centered AI that is explainable, transparent, and trustworthy. The inputs to an AI agent include the goals and preferences of the agent, but it is not clear whose preferences they are or should be.

Each chapter concludes with a social impact section discussing issues directly relevant to that chapter's topics. The social impact sections are of two types, sometimes containing both:

- broader impacts of AI, which includes intended or unintended downstream consequences of upstream decisions on the design of the AI system or on the choice of data

- use cases about user-facing applications of AI that have had an impact on society or science, either positive or negative.

Chapter 18 on the social impact of AI considers the effects of AI on the digital economy, work and automation, transportation and sustainability. It highlights the roles of human-centered AI, values, bias, ethics, certification, and regulation.

## 1.8 Overview of the Book

The rest of the book explores the design space defined by the dimensions of complexity. It considers each dimension separately, where this can be done sensibly.

Part I considers the big view of agents as a coherent vision of AI.

**Chapter 2** analyzes what is inside the black box of Figure 1.4 (page 15) and discusses the modular and hierarchical decomposition of intelligent agents.

Part II considers the case of no uncertainty, which is a useful abstraction of many domains.

**Chapter 3** considers the simplest case of determining what to do in the case of a single agent that reasons with explicit states, no uncertainty, and has goals to be achieved, but with an indefinite horizon. In this case, the task of solving the goal can be abstracted to searching for a path in a graph. It is shown how extra knowledge of the domain can help the search.

**Chapters 4 and 5** show how to exploit features. In particular, Chapter 4 considers how to find possible states given constraints on the assignments of values to features represented as variables. Chapter 5 presents reasoning with propositions in various forms.

**Chapter 6** considers the task of planning, in particular determining sequences of actions to solve a goal in deterministic domains.

Part III considers learning and reasoning with uncertainty. In particular, it considers sensing uncertainty and effect uncertainty.

**Chapter 7** shows how an agent can learn from past experiences and data. It covers the most common case of learning, namely supervised learning with features, where a function from input features into target features is learned from observational data. **Chapter 8** studies neural networks and deep learning and how features themselves can be learned from sensory observation.

**Chapter 9** shows how to reason with uncertainty, in particular with probability and graphical models of independence. **Chapter 10** introduces learning with uncertainty. **Chapter 11** shows how to model causality and learn the effects of interventions (which cannot be learned from observation alone).

Part IV considers planning and acting with uncertainty.

**Chapter 12** considers the task of planning with uncertainty. **Chapter 13** deals with reinforcement learning, where agents learn what to do. Chapter 14 expands planning to deal with issues arising from multiple agents.

Part V extends the state and feature-based representations to deal with relational representations, in terms of relations and individuals.

**Chapter 15** shows how to reason in terms of individuals and relations. **Chapter 16** discusses how to enable semantic interoperability using knowledge graphs and ontologies. **Chapter 17** shows how reasoning about individuals and relations can be combined with learning and probabilistic reasoning.

Part VI steps back from the details and gives the big picture.

In **Chapter 18** on the social impact of AI, further ethical and social concerns are addressed, by considering various questions, such as: What are the effects, benefits, costs, and risks of deployed AI systems for society? What are the ethical, equity, and regulatory considerations involved in building intelligent agents? How can you ensure that AI systems are fair, transparent, explainable, and trustworthy? How can AI systems be human-centered? What is the impact on sustainability?

Chapter 19 reviews the design space of AI and shows how the material presented can fit into that design space. It also considers some likely and possible future scenarios for the development of AI science and technology.

## 1.9 Review

The following are the main points you should have learned from this chapter:

- Artificial intelligence is the study of computational agents that act intelligently.
- An agent acts in an environment and only has access to its abilities, its prior knowledge, its history of stimuli, and its goals and preferences.
- A physical symbol system manipulates symbols to determine what to do.
- A designer of an intelligent agent should be concerned about modularity, how to describe the world, how far ahead to plan, uncertainty in both perception and the effects of actions, the structure of goals or preferences, other agents, how to learn from experience, how the agent can reason while interacting with the environment, and the fact that all real agents have limited computational resources.
- To solve a task by computer, the computer must have an effective representation with which to reason.

- To know when it has solved a task, an agent must have a definition of what constitutes an adequate solution, such as whether it has to be optimal, approximately optimal, or almost always optimal, or whether a satisficing solution is adequate.
- In choosing a representation, an agent designer should find a representation that is as close as possible to the task, so that it is easy to determine what is represented and so it can be checked for correctness and be able to be maintained. Often, users want an explanation of why they should believe the answer.
- The social impacts, both beneficial and harmful, of pervasive AI applications are significant, leading to calls for ethical and human-centered AI, certification and regulation.

## 1.10 References and Further Reading

The ideas in this chapter have been derived from many sources. Here, we try to acknowledge those that are explicitly attributable to particular authors. Most of the other ideas are part of AI folklore; trying to attribute them to anyone would be impossible.

Levesque [2012] provides an accessible account of how thinking can be seen in terms of computation. Haugeland [1997] contains a good collection of articles on the philosophy behind artificial intelligence, including that classic paper of Turing [1950] that proposes the Turing test. Grosz [2012] and Cohen [2005] discuss the Turing test from a more recent perspective. Winograd schemas are described by Levesque [2014]. Srivastava et al. [2022] provide a *Beyond the Imitation Game* benchmark (BIG-bench) consisting of 204 tasks designed to challenge modern learning systems. Grosz [2018] discusses research on what it takes to implement dialog, not just answering one-off questions. Zador et al. [2023] discuss an embodied Turing test, and the role of neuroscience in AI.

Nilsson [2010] and Buchanan [2005] provide accessible histories of AI. Chrisley and Begeer [2000] present many classic papers on AI. Jordan [2019] and the associated commentaries discuss intelligence augmentation.

For discussions on the foundations of AI and the breadth of research in AI, see Kirsh [1991a], Bobrow [1993], and the papers in the corresponding volumes, as well as Schank [1990] and Simon [1995]. The importance of knowledge in AI is discussed in Lenat and Feigenbaum [1991], Sowa [2000], Darwiche [2018], and Brachman and Levesque [2022b].

The physical symbol system hypothesis was posited by Newell and Simon [1976]. Simon [1996] discusses the role of symbol systems in a multidisciplinary context. The distinctions between real, synthetic, and artificial intelligence are discussed by Haugeland [1985], who also provides useful introductory material on interpreted, automatic formal symbol systems and the Church–Turing thesis. Brooks [1990] and Winograd [1990] critique the symbol system hypothesis. Nilsson [2007] evaluates the hypothesis in terms of such criticisms. Shoham [2016] and Marcus and Davis [2019] argue for the importance of symbolic knowledge representation in modern applications.

The use of anytime algorithms is due to Horvitz [1989] and Boddy and Dean [1994]. See Dean and Wellman [1991], Zilberstein [1996], and Russell [1997] for introductions to bounded rationality.

For overviews of cognitive science and the role that AI and other disciplines play in that field, see Gardner [1985], Posner [1989], and Stillings et al. [1987].

Conati et al. [2002] describe a tutoring agent for elementary physics. du Boulay et al. [2023] overview modern tutoring agents. Wellman [2011] overviews research in trading agents. Sandholm [2007] describes how AI can be used for procurement of multiple goods with complex preferences.

A number of AI texts are valuable as reference books complementary to this book, providing a different perspective on AI. In particular, Russell and Norvig [2020] give a more encyclopedic overview of AI. They provide an excellent complementary source for many of the topics covered in this book and also an outstanding review of the scientific literature, which we do not try to duplicate.

The Association for the Advancement of Artificial Intelligence (AAAI) provides introductory material and news at their *AI Topics* website (https://aitopics.org/). *AI Magazine*, published by AAAI, often has excellent overview articles and descriptions of particular applications. *IEEE Intelligent Systems* also provides accessible articles on AI research.

There are many journals that provide in-depth research contributions and conferences where the most up-to-date research is found. These include the journals *Artificial Intelligence*, the *Journal of Artificial Intelligence Research*, *IEEE Transactions on Pattern Analysis and Machine Intelligence*, and *Computational Intelligence*, as well as more specialized journals. Much of the cutting-edge research is published first in conferences. Those of most interest to a general audience are the International Joint Conference on Artificial Intelligence (IJCAI), the AAAI Annual Conference, the European Conference on AI (ECAI), the Pacific Rim International Conference on AI (PRICAI), various national conferences, and many specialized conferences, which are referred to in the relevant chapters.

## 1.11 Exercises

**Exercise 1.1** For each of the following, give five reasons why:

(a) A dog is more intelligent than a worm.
(b) A human is more intelligent than a dog.
(c) An organization is more intelligent than an individual human.

Based on these, give a definition of what "more intelligent" may mean.

**Exercise 1.2** Give as many disciplines as you can whose aim is to study intelligent behavior of some sort. For each discipline, find out what aspect of behavior is investigated and what tools are used to study it. Be as liberal as you can regarding what defines intelligent behavior.

**Exercise 1.3** Find out about two applications of AI (not classes of applications, but specific programs). For each application, write at most one typed page describing it. You should try to cover the following questions:

(a) What does the application actually do (e.g., control a spacecraft, diagnose a photocopier, provide intelligent help for computer users)?
(b) What AI technologies does it use (e.g., model-based diagnosis, belief networks, semantic networks, heuristic search, constraint satisfaction)?
(c) How well does it perform? (According to the authors or to an independent review? How does it compare to humans? How do the authors know how well it works?)
(d) Is it an experimental system or a fielded system? (How many users does it have? What expertise do these users require?)
(e) Why is it intelligent? What aspects of it make it an intelligent system?
(f) [optional] What programming language and environment was it written in? What sort of user interface does it have?
(g) References: Where did you get the information about the application? To what books, articles, or webpages should others who want to know about the application refer?

**Exercise 1.4** For each of the Winograd schemas in Example 1.2 (page 6), what knowledge is required to correctly answer the questions? Try to find a "cheap" method to find the answer, such as by comparing the number of results in a Google search for different cases. Try this for six other Winograd schemas of Davis [2015]. Try to construct an example of your own.

**Exercise 1.5** Choose four pairs of dimensions that were not compared in Section 1.5.10 (page 35). For each pair, give one commonsense example of where the dimensions interact.

# Chapter 2

# Agent Architectures and Hierarchical Control

*By a hierarchic system, or hierarchy, I mean a system that is composed of interrelated subsystems, each of the latter being in turn hierarchic in structure until we reach some lowest level of elementary subsystem. In most systems of nature it is somewhat arbitrary as to where we leave off the partitioning and what subsystems we take as elementary. Physics makes much use of the concept of "elementary particle," although the particles have a disconcerting tendency not to remain elementary very long ...*

*Empirically a large proportion of the complex systems we observe in nature exhibit hierarchic structure. On theoretical grounds we would expect complex systems to be hierarchies in a world in which complexity had to evolve from simplicity.*

– Herbert A. Simon [1996]

This chapter shows how an intelligent agent can perceive, reason, and act over time in an environment. In particular, it considers the internal structure of an agent. As Simon points out in the quote above, hierarchical decomposition is an important part of the design of complex systems such as intelligent agents. This chapter presents ways to design agents in terms of hierarchical decompositions and ways that agents can be built, taking into account the knowledge that an agent needs to act intelligently.

## 2.1 Agents and Environments

An **agent** (page 14) is something that acts in an environment. An agent can, for example, be a person, a robot, a dog, a worm, a lamp, a computer program that buys and sells, or a corporation.

Agents receive **stimuli** from their environment (Figure 1.4 (page 15)). Stimuli include light, sound, words typed on a keyboard, mouse movements, and physical bumps. The stimuli can also include information obtained from a webpage or from a database. Agents carry out **actions** that can affect the environment. Actions include steering, accelerating wheels, moving links of arms, speaking, displaying information, or sending a post command to a website.

An **agent** is made up of a **body** and a **controller**. Agents interact with the environment with a **body**. The controller receives **percepts** from the body and sends **commands** to the body. See Figure 2.1.

A body includes:

- **sensors** that convert stimuli into percepts
- **actuators**, also called **effectors**, that convert commands into the actions in the environment.

A body can also carry out actions that don't go through the controller, such as a stop button for a robot and reflexes of humans.

An **embodied agent** has a *physical* body. A **robot** is an artificial **purposive** (page 15) embodied agent. Sometimes agents that act only in an information space are called robots or **bots**.

Common sensors for robots include touch sensors, cameras, infrared sensors, sonar, microphones, keyboards, mice, and XML readers used to extract information from webpages. As a prototypical sensor, a camera senses light coming into its lens and converts it into a two-dimensional array of intensity values called **pixels**. Sometimes multiple pixel arrays represent different colors or multiple cameras. Such pixel arrays could be the percepts for our controller.

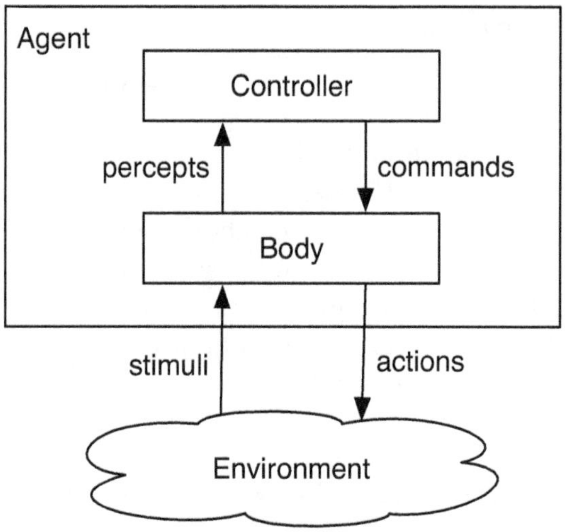


Figure 2.1: An agent system and its components

More often, percepts consist of higher-level features such as lines, edges, and depth information. Often the percepts are more specialized – for example, the positions of bright orange dots, the part of the display a student is looking at, or the hand signals given by a human. Sensors can be noisy, unreliable, or broken. Even when sensors are reliable there still may be ambiguity about the world given the sensor readings.

Commands include low-level commands such as to set the voltage of a motor to some particular value, and high-level specifications of the desired motion of a robot such as "stop" or "travel at 1 meter per second due east" or "go to room 103." Actuators, like sensors, are typically noisy and often slow and unreliable. For example, stopping takes time; a robot, governed by the laws of physics, has momentum, and messages take time to travel. The robot may end up going only approximately 1 meter per second, approximately east, and both speed and direction may fluctuate. Traveling to a particular room may fail for a number of reasons.

### 2.1.1 Controllers

Agents are situated in time; they receive sensory data in time and do actions in time.

Let $T$ be the set of **time** points. Assume that $T$ is totally ordered. $T$ is **discrete time** if there are only a finite number of time points between any two time points; for example, there is a time point every hundredth of a second, or every day, or there may be time points whenever interesting events occur. Discrete time has the property that, for all times, except perhaps a last time, there is always a next time. Initially, assume that time is discrete and goes on forever. Assume $t + 1$ as the next time after time $t$. The time points do not need to be equally spaced. Assume that $T$ has a starting point, which is defined to be 0.

Suppose $P$ is the set of all possible percepts. A **percept trace**, or **percept stream**, is a function from $T$ into $P$. It specifies which percept is received at each time.

Suppose $C$ is the set of all commands. A **command trace** is a function from $T$ into $C$. It specifies the command for each time point.

**Example 2.1** Consider a household trading agent that monitors the price of some commodity, such as toilet paper, by checking for deals online, as well as how much the household has in stock. It must decide whether to order more and how much to order. Assume the percepts are the price and the amount in stock. The command is the number of units the agent decides to order (which is zero if the agent does not order any). A percept trace specifies for each time point (e.g., each day) the price at that time and the amount in stock at that time. A percept trace is given in Figure 2.2 (page 54); at each time there is both a price and an amount in stock, here given as two graphs. A command trace specifies how much the agent decides to order at each time point. An example command trace is given in Figure 2.3 (page 54).

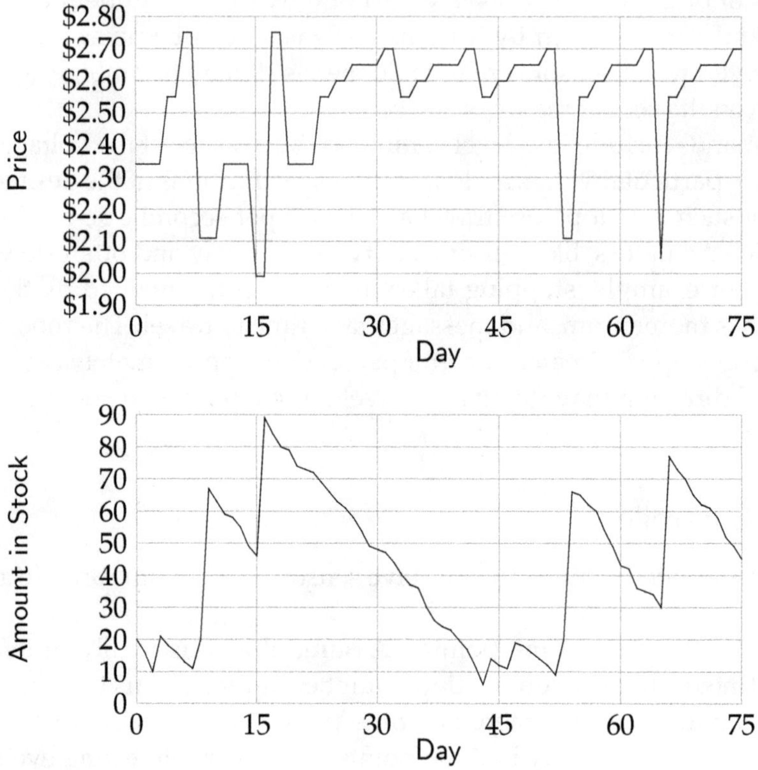


Figure 2.2: Percept traces for Example 2.1

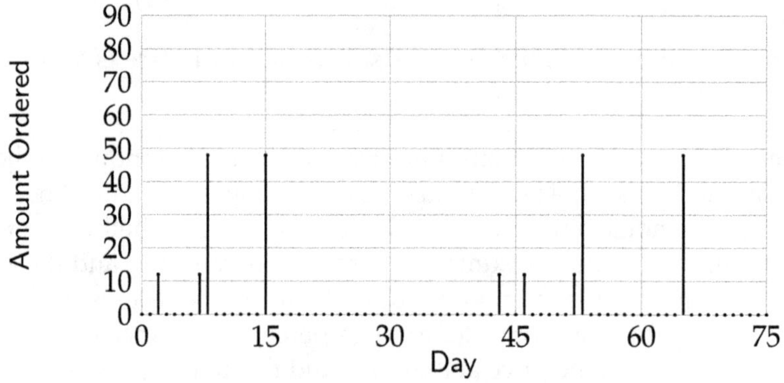


Figure 2.3: Command trace for Example 2.1 (page 53)

The action of actually buying depends on the command but may be different. For example, the agent could issue a command to buy 12 rolls of paper at \$2.10. This does not mean that the agent actually buys 12 rolls because there could be communication problems, the store could have run out of paper, or the price could change between deciding to buy and actually buying.

A percept trace for an agent is thus the sequence of all past, present, and future percepts received by the controller. A command trace is the sequence of all past, present, and future commands issued by the controller.

Because all agents are situated in time, an agent cannot actually observe full percept traces; at any time it has only experienced the part of the trace up to *now*. At time $t \in T$, an agent can only observe the value of the command and percept traces up to time $t$, and its commands cannot depend on percepts after time $t$.

The **history** of an agent at time $t$ is the agent's percept trace for all times before or at time $t$ and its command trace before time $t$.

A **transduction** is a function from the history of an agent at time $t$ to the command at time $t$.

Thus a transduction is a function from percept traces to command traces that is **causal** in that the command at time $t$ depends only on percepts up to and including time $t$.

A **controller** is an implementation of a transduction.

Note that this allows for the case where the agent can observe and act at the same time. This is useful when the time granularity is long enough. When time is measured finely enough, an agent may take time to react to percepts, in which case the action can be just a function of time before $t$.

**Example 2.2** Continuing Example 2.1 (page 53), a transduction specifies, for each time, how much of the commodity the agent should buy depending on the price history, the history of how much of the commodity is in stock (including the current price and amount in stock), and the past history of buying.

An example of a transduction is as follows: buy four dozen rolls if there are fewer than five dozen in stock and the price is less than 90% of the average price over the last 20 days; buy a dozen rolls if there are fewer than a dozen in stock; otherwise, do not buy any.

## 2.1.2 Belief States

Although a transduction is a function of an agent's history, it cannot be directly implemented because an agent does not have direct access to its entire history. It has access only to its current percepts and what it has remembered.

The **memory** or **belief state** of an agent at time $t$ is all the information the agent has remembered from the previous times. An agent has access only to the part of the history that it has encoded in its belief state. Thus, the belief state encapsulates all of the information about its history that the agent can use for current and future commands. At any time, an agent has access to its belief state and its current percepts.

The belief state can contain any information, subject to the agent's memory and processing limitations. This is a very general notion of belief.

Some instances of belief state include the following:

- The belief state for an agent that is following a fixed sequence of instructions may be a program counter that records its current position in the sequence, or a list of actions still to carry out.
- The belief state can contain specific facts that are useful – for example, where the delivery robot left a parcel when it went to find a key, or where it has already checked for the key. It may be useful for the agent to remember any information that it might need for the future that is reasonably stable and that cannot be immediately observed.
- The belief state could encode a model or a partial model of the state of the world. An agent could maintain its best guess about the current state of the world or could have a probability distribution over possible world states; see Section 9.6.2 (page 420).
- The belief state could contain an estimate of how good each action is for each world state. This belief state, called the *Q*-function, is used extensively in decison-theoretic planning (page 559) and reinforcement learning (page 583).
- The belief state could be a representation of the dynamics of the world – how the world changes – and some of its recent percepts. Given its percepts, the agent could reason about what is true in the world.
- The belief state could encode what the agent **desires**, the **goals** it still has to achieve, its **beliefs** about the state of the world, and its **intentions**, or the steps it intends to take to achieve its goals. These can be maintained as the agent acts and observes the world, for example, removing achieved goals and replacing intentions when more appropriate steps are found.

### 2.1.3 Agent Functions

A controller maintains the agent's belief state and determines what command to issue at each time. The information it has available when it must do this are its belief state and its current percepts. Figure 2.4 (page 57) shows how the agent function acts in time; the memories output at one time are the memories input at the next time.

A **belief state transition function** for discrete time is a function

$$remember : S \times P \rightarrow S$$

where $S$ is the set of belief states and $P$ is the set of possible percepts; $s_{t+1} = remember(s_t, p_t)$ means that $s_{t+1}$ is the belief state following belief state $s_t$ when $p_t$ is observed.

A **command function** is a function

$$command : S \times P \to C$$

where $S$ is the set of belief states, $P$ is the set of possible percepts, and $C$ is the set of possible commands; $c_t = command(s_t, p_t)$ means that the controller issues command $c_t$ when the belief state is $s_t$ and when $p_t$ is observed.

The belief-state transition function and the command function together specify a controller for the agent. Note that a transduction is a function of the agent's history, which the agent does not necessarily have access to, but a command function is a function of the agent's belief state and percepts, which it does have access to.

**Example 2.3** To implement the transduction of Example 2.2 (page 55), a controller can keep track of the rolling history of the prices for the previous 20 days and the average, using the variable *average*, updated using

$$average := average + \frac{new - old}{20}$$

where *new* is the new price and *old* is the oldest price remembered. It can then discard *old*. It must do something special for the first 20 days. See Section A.1 (page 797) for an analysis of rolling averages.

A simpler controller could, instead of remembering a rolling history in order to maintain the average, remember just a rolling estimate of the average and use that value as a surrogate for the oldest item. The belief state can then contain one real number (*ave*), with the state transition function

$$ave := ave + \frac{new - ave}{20}.$$

This controller is much easier to implement and is not as sensitive to what happened exactly 20 time units ago. It does not actually compute the average, as it

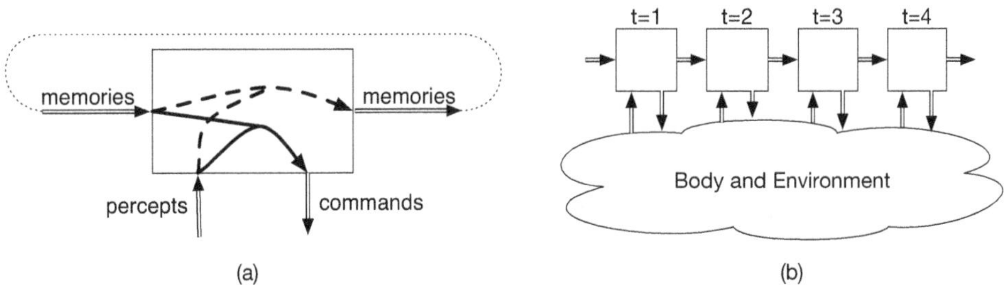


Figure 2.4: An agent function in time. In (a) the dashed line is the belief state transition function and the solid line is the command function (b) shows the controller in time. The controller treats the body and the environment together. The memory output of one time is the input for the next time

is biased towards recent data. This way of maintaining estimates of averages is the basis for temporal differences in reinforcement learning (page 588).

If there are a finite number of possible belief states, the controller is called a **finite state controller** or a **finite state machine**. A **factored representation** is one in which the belief states, percepts, or commands are defined by features (page 24). If there are a finite number of features, and each feature can only have a finite number of possible values, then the controller is a **factored finite state machine**. Richer controllers can be built using an unbounded number of values or an unbounded number of features. A controller that has an unbounded but countable number of states can compute anything that is computable by a Turing machine.

## 2.2 Hierarchical Control

One way that you could imagine building an agent depicted in Figure 2.1 (page 52) is to split the body into the sensors and actuators, with a complex perception system that feeds a description of the world into a reasoning engine implementing a controller that, in turn, outputs commands to the actuators. This turns out to be a bad architecture for intelligent systems. It is too slow and it is difficult to reconcile the slow reasoning about complex, high-level goals with the fast reaction that an agent needs for lower-level tasks such as avoiding obstacles. It also is not clear that there is a description of a world that is independent of what you do with it (see Exercise 2.1 (page 73)).

An alternative architecture is a hierarchy of controllers as depicted in Figure 2.5 (page 59). Each layer sees the layers below it as a **virtual body** from which it gets percepts and to which it sends commands.

The lower-level layers run much faster, react to those aspects of the world that need to be reacted to quickly, and deliver a simpler view of the world to the higher layers, hiding details that are not essential for the higher layers. The **planning horizon** (page 23) at lower levels is typically much shorter than the planning horizon at upper levels. People have to react to the world, at the lowest level, in fractions of a second, but plan at the highest level even for decades into the future. For example, the reason for doing some particular university course may be for the long-term career, but reading and answering a question in a university exam has to happen in minutes, if not seconds.

There is much evidence that people have multiple qualitatively different levels. Kahneman [2011] presents evidence for two distinct levels: **System 1**, the lower level, is fast, automatic, parallel, intuitive, instinctive, emotional, and not open to introspection; **System 2**, the higher level, is slow, deliberate, serial, open to introspection, and based on reasoning.

In a hierarchical controller there can be multiple channels – each representing a feature – between layers and between layers at different times.

There are three types of inputs to each layer at each time:

- features that come from the belief state, which are referred to as the remembered or previous values of these features
- features representing the percepts from the layer below in the hierarchy
- features representing the commands from the layer above in the hierarchy.

There are three types of outputs from each layer at each time:

- the higher-level percepts for the layer above
- the lower-level commands for the layer below
- the next values for the belief-state features.

An implementation of a layer specifies how the outputs of a layer are a function of its inputs. The definition of the **belief state transition function** (page 56), *remember*, and the **command function** (page 57), *command*, can be extended to include higher-level commands as inputs, and each layer also requires a **percept function**, represented as *tell* below. Thus a layer implements:

$$remember : S \times P_l \times C_h \rightarrow S$$

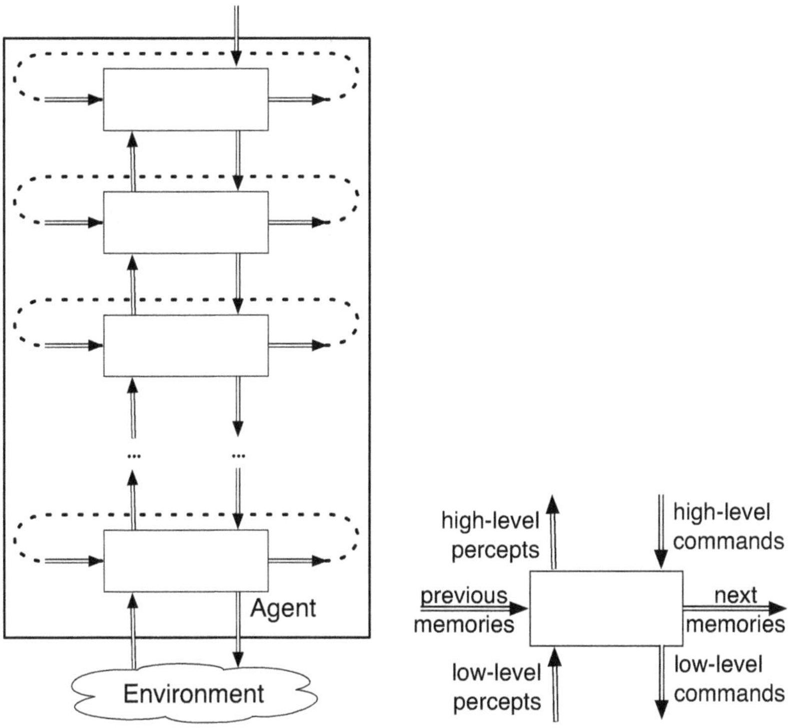


Figure 2.5: An idealized hierarchical agent system architecture. The unlabeled rectangles represent layers and the double lines represent information flow. The dashed lines show how the output at one time is the input for the next time

$$command : S \times P_l \times C_h \rightarrow C_l$$
$$tell : S \times P_l \times C_h \rightarrow P_h$$

where $S$ is the belief state, $C_h$ is the set of commands from the higher layer, $P_l$ is the set of percepts from the lower layer, $C_l$ is the set of commands for the lower layer, and $P_h$ is the set of percepts for the higher layer.

Computing these functions can involve arbitrary computation, but the goal is to keep each layer as simple as possible.

To implement a controller, each input to a layer must get its value from somewhere. Each percept or command input should be connected to an output of some other layer. Other inputs come from the remembered beliefs. The outputs of a layer do not have to be connected to anything, or they could be connected to multiple inputs.

**Example 2.4** Consider a delivery robot (page 17) able to carry out high-level

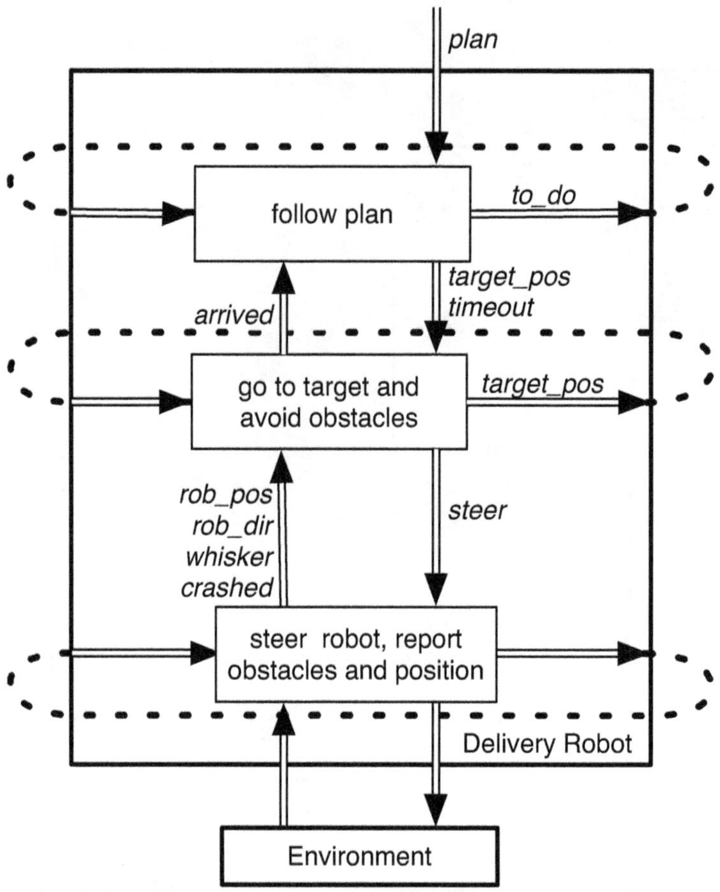


Figure 2.6: A hierarchical decomposition of the delivery robot

navigation tasks while avoiding obstacles. The delivery robot is required to visit a sequence of named locations in the environment of Figure 1.5 (page 17), avoiding obstacles it may encounter.

Assume the delivery robot has wheels, like a car, and at each time can either go straight, turn right, or turn left. It cannot stop. The velocity is constant and the only command is to set the steering angle to left, right, or straight. Assume turning the wheels is instantaneous, but turning to a certain direction takes time. Thus, the robot can only travel straight ahead or go around in circular arcs with a fixed radius.

The robot has a position sensor that gives its current coordinates and orientation. It has a single whisker sensor that sticks out in front and slightly to the right and detects when it has hit an obstacle. In the example below, the whisker points 30° to the right of the direction the robot is facing. The robot does not have a map, and the environment can change with obstacles moving.

A layered controller for the delivery robot is shown in Figure 2.6 (page 60). The robot is given a high-level plan consisting of a list of named locations to visit in sequence. The robot needs to sense the world and to move in the world in order to carry out the plan. The details of the lowest layer of the controller are not shown in this figure.

The top layer, called *follow plan*, is described in Example 2.6 (page 63). That layer takes in a plan to execute. The locations in the plan are selected in order. Each selected location becomes the current target. This layer determines the $x$–$y$ coordinates of the target. These coordinates are the target position for the middle layer. The top layer knows about the names of locations, but the lower layers only know about coordinates.

The top layer maintains a belief state consisting of a list of names of locations that the robot still needs to visit. It issues commands to the middle layer to go to the current target position but not to spend more than *timeout* steps. The percepts for the top layer indicate whether the robot has arrived at the target position or not. So the top layer abstracts the details of the robot and the environment.

The middle layer, which could be called *go to target and avoid obstacles*, tries to keep traveling towards the current target position, avoiding obstacles. The middle layer is described in Example 2.5 (page 62). The target position, *target_pos*, is received from the top layer. The middle layer needs to remember the current target position it is heading towards. When the middle layer has arrived at the target position or has reached the timeout, it signals to the top layer whether the robot has arrived at the target. When *arrived* becomes true, the top layer can change the target position to the coordinates of the next location on the plan.

The middle layer can access the robot's position, the robot's direction, and whether the robot's whisker sensor is on or off. It can use a simple strategy of trying to head towards the target unless it is blocked, in which case it turns left.

The middle layer is built on a lower layer that provides a simple view of the robot. This lower layer could be called *steer robot and report obstacles and position*. It takes in steering commands and reports the robot's position, orientation, and whether the whisker sensor is on or off.

Inside a layer are features that can be functions of other features and of the inputs to the layers. In the graphical representation of a controller, there is an arc into a feature from the features or inputs on which it is dependent. The features that make up the belief state can be written to and read from memory.

In the controller code in the following two examples, *lower.do*($C$) means that $C$ is the **do command** for the lower level to do.

**Example 2.5** The middle *go to location and avoid obstacles* layer steers the robot towards a target position while avoiding obstacles. The inputs and outputs of this layer are given in Figure 2.7.

The layer receives two high-level commands: a target position to head towards and a timeout, which is the number of steps it should take before giving up. It signals the higher layer when it has arrived or when the timeout is reached.

The robot has a single whisker sensor that detects obstacles touching the whisker. The one bit value that specifies whether the whisker sensor has hit an obstacle is provided by the lower layer. The lower layer also provides the robot position and orientation. All the robot can do is steer left by a fixed angle, steer right, or go straight. The aim of this layer is to make the robot head towards its current target position, avoiding obstacles in the process, and to report when it has arrived.

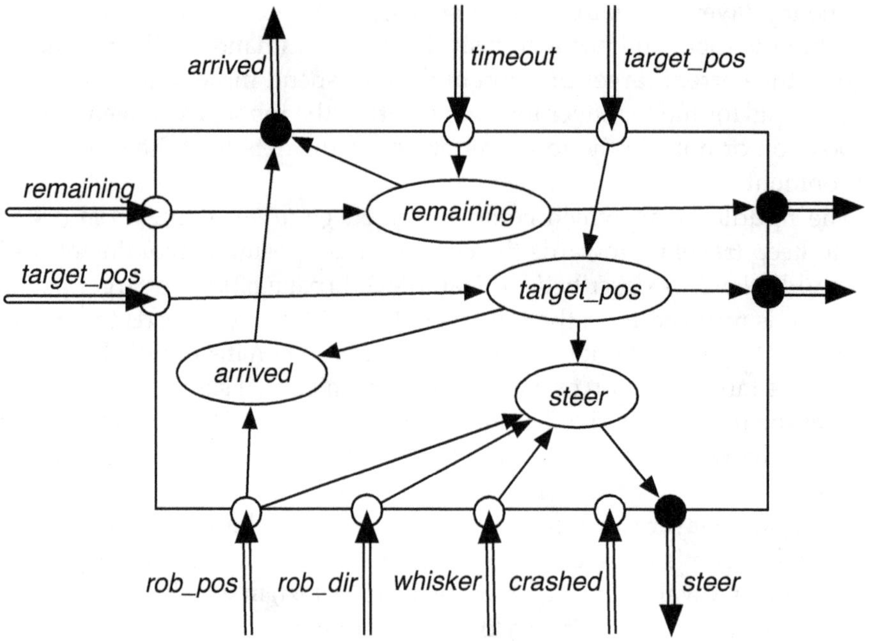


Figure 2.7: The middle layer of the delivery robot

This layer of the controller needs to remember the target position and the number of steps remaining. The command function specifies the robot's steering direction as a function of its inputs and whether the robot has arrived.

The robot has arrived if its current position is close to the target position. Thus, *arrived* is a function of the robot position and previous target position, and a threshold constant:

$$arrived() \equiv distance(target\_pos, rob\_pos) < threshold$$

where *distance* is the Euclidean distance and *threshold* is a distance in the appropriate units.

The robot steers left if the whisker sensor is on; otherwise it heads towards the target position. This can be achieved by assigning the appropriate value to the *steer* variable, given an integer *timeout* and *target_pos*:

```
remaining := timeout
while not arrived() and remaining ≠ 0
    if whisker_sensor = on
        then steer := left
    else if straight_ahead(rob_pos, robot_dir, target_pos)
        then steer := straight
    else if left_of(rob_pos, robot_dir, target_pos)
        then steer := left
    else steer := right
    lower.do(steer)
    remaining := remaining − 1
tell upper layer arrived()
```

where *straight_ahead*(*rob_pos*, *robot_dir*, *target_pos*) is true when the robot is at position *rob_pos*, facing the direction *robot_dir*, and when the current target position, *target_pos*, is straight ahead of the robot with some threshold (for later examples, this threshold is 11° of straight ahead). The function *left_of* tests if the target is to the left of the robot.

**Example 2.6** The top layer, *follow plan*, is given a plan – a list of named locations to visit in order. These are the kinds of targets that could be produced by a planner, such as those that are developed in Chapter 3. The top layer must output target coordinates to the middle layer and remember what it needs to carry out the plan. The layer is shown in Figure 2.8 (page 64).

This layer remembers the locations it still has to visit. The *to_do* feature has as its value a list of all pending locations to visit.

Once the middle layer has signaled that the robot has arrived at its previous target or it has reached the timeout, the top layer gets the next target position from the head of the *to_do* list. The plan given is in terms of named locations, so these must be translated into coordinates for the middle layer to use. The following code shows the top layer as a function of the plan:

```
to_do := plan
```

*timeout* := 200
while not *empty*(*to_do*)
    *target_pos* := *coordinates*(*first*(*to_do*))
    *middle.do*(*timeout*, *target_pos*)
    *to_do* := *rest*(*to_do*)

where *first*(*to_do*) is the first location in the *to_do* list and *rest*(*to_do*) is the rest of the *to_do* list. The function *coordinates*(*loc*) returns the coordinates of a named location *loc*. The controller tells the lower layer to go to the target coordinates, with a timeout here of 200 (which, of course, should be set appropriately). *empty*(*to_do*) is true when the *to_do* list is empty.

This layer determines the coordinates of the named locations. This could be done by simply having a database that specifies the coordinates of the locations. Using such a database is sensible if the locations do not move and are known a priori. If the locations can move, the lower layer must be able to tell the upper layer the current position of a location. See Exercise 2.7 (page 75).

A simulation of the plan [*goto*(*o*109), *goto*(*storage*), *goto*(*o*109), *goto*(*o*103)] with two obstacles is given in Figure 2.9 (page 65). The robot starts at position (0, 0) facing North, and the obstacles are shown with lines. The agent does not know about the obstacles before it starts.

Each layer is simple, and none model the full complexity of the problem. But, together they exhibit complex behavior. An implementation of the agent and environment is provided in AIPython (aipython.org).

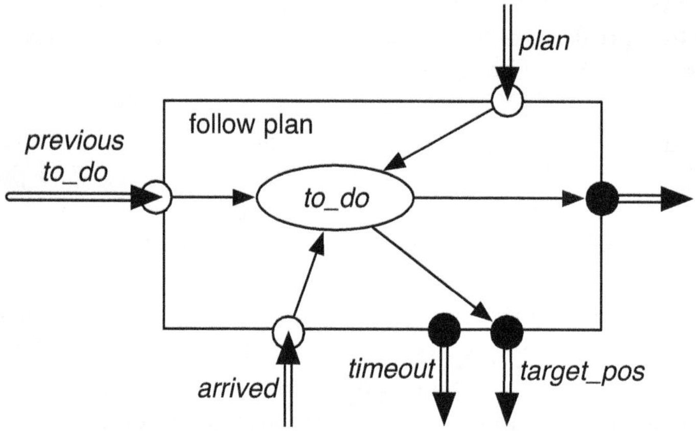


Figure 2.8: The top layer of the delivery robot controller. Notice how the lower level corresponds to the upper level of Figure 2.7 (page 62)

# 2.3 Designing Agents

## 2.3.1 Discrete, Continuous, and Hybrid

For **discrete time** (page 53) there are only a finite number of time steps between any two times; for example, there is a time point every hundredth of a second, or every day, or there may be time points whenever interesting events occur. An alternative is to assume **continuous** time that is measured by the real numbers.

Similarly, a feature can be **discrete**, with a finite or countable number of possible values, or the value can be any real number, in which case the feature is **continuous**. An example of a continuous value might be latitude, longitude, the distance to a wall, or the amount of fuel left. An example of a discrete value might be the room the robot is in, or whether it is carrying a particular item.

High-level reasoning, as carried out in the higher layers, is often discrete and qualitative, whereas low-level reasoning, as carried out in the lower layers, is often continuous and quantitative (see box on page 66). A controller that reasons in terms of both discrete and continuous values is called a **hybrid system**.

Discrete time means that there is a next time from any time, except perhaps a last time. For continuous time, there is no next time. Continuous time can be modeled by adding time and time intervals, for example adding 4:21 pm and

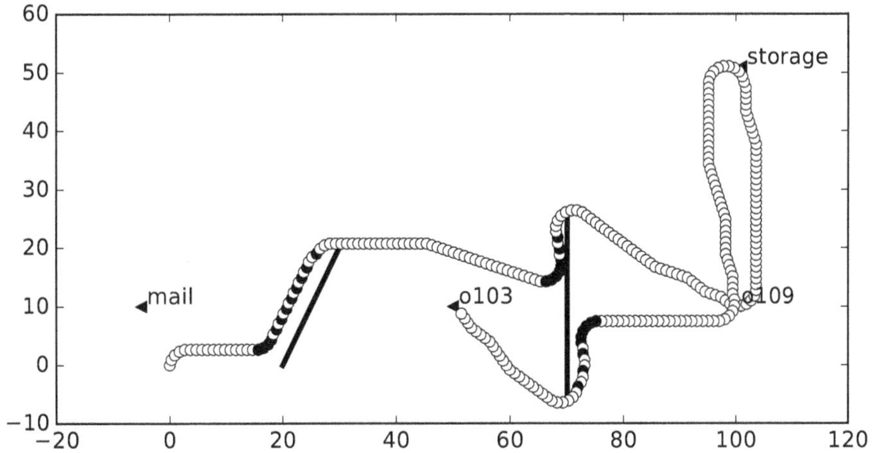


Figure 2.9: A simulation of the robot carrying out the plan of Example 2.6 (page 63). The black lines are obstacles. The robot starts at position (0,0) and follows the trajectory of the overlapping circles; the filled circles are when the whisker sensor is on. The robot goes to *o*109, *storage*, *o*109, and *o*103 in turn

### Qualitative versus Quantitative Representations

Much of science and engineering considers **quantitative reasoning** with numerical quantities, using differential and integral calculus as the main tools. **Qualitative reasoning** is reasoning, often using logic, about qualitative distinctions rather than numerical values for given parameters.

Qualitative reasoning is important for a number of reasons.

- An agent may not know what the exact values are. For example, for the delivery robot to pour coffee, it may not be able to compute the optimal angle that the coffee pot needs to be tilted, but a simple control rule may suffice to fill the cup to a suitable level.
- The reasoning may be applicable regardless of the quantitative values. For example, you may want a strategy for a robot that works regardless of what loads are placed on the robot, how slippery the floors are, or what the actual charge is of the batteries, as long as they are within some normal operating ranges.
- An agent needs to do qualitative reasoning to determine which quantitative laws are applicable. For example, if the delivery robot is filling a coffee cup, different quantitative formulas are appropriate to determine where the coffee goes when the coffee pot is not tilted enough for coffee to come out, when coffee comes out into a non-full cup, and when the coffee cup is full and the coffee is soaking into the carpet.

Qualitative reasoning uses discrete values, which can take a number of forms:

- **Landmarks** are values that make qualitative distinctions in the individual being modeled. In the coffee example, some important qualitative distinctions include whether the coffee cup is empty, partially full, or full. These landmark values are all that is needed to predict what happens if the cup is tipped upside down or if coffee is poured into the cup.
- **Orders-of-magnitude reasoning** involves approximate reasoning that ignores minor distinctions. For example, a partially full coffee cup may be full enough to deliver, half empty, or nearly empty. These **fuzzy terms** have ill-defined borders.
- **Qualitative derivatives** indicate whether some value is increasing, decreasing, or staying the same.

A flexible agent needs to do qualitative reasoning before it does quantitative reasoning. For simple agents, the qualitative reasoning is often done at design time, so the agent needs to only do quantitative reasoning online. Sometimes qualitative reasoning is all that is needed. An intelligent agent does not always need to do quantitative reasoning, but sometimes it needs to do both qualitative and quantitative reasoning.

0.003 seconds gives a new time.

Discrete features with continuous time provide an implicit discretization of time; there can be a next time whenever the state changes. A controller might model what is the next state and when it might occur.

When there is continuous state and continuous time, a controller needs to model how they vary together, which requires differential and integral calculus and is beyond the scope of this book.

### 2.3.2 Choosing Agent Functions

The definition of an agent function gives a great deal of latitude in the design of agents.

One extreme is for a purely **reactive system** that bases its actions only on the percepts; in this case, the agent function can have an empty or trivial belief state. The command function in this case is a function from percepts into actions. If sensors are very accurate, one might think that they can be relied on with no memory of the history. For example, a **global positioning system (GPS)** can locate a phone or robot within about 10 meters. However, it is much easier for a robot to locate itself if the GPS signal is combined with historical information about where it was a second ago, and even better if there is an estimate of the direction and speed of travel. A signal that suggests the robot jumped over a river might then be reconciled with the previous signals, and knowledge of how the robot moves.

At the other extreme, an agent could ignore the percepts and rely on a model of the environment and its memory. The agent can then determine what to do just by reasoning. This approach requires a model of the dynamics of the world and of the initial state. Given the state at one time and the dynamics, the state at the next time can be predicted. This process of maintaining the state by **forward prediction** is known as **dead reckoning**. For example, a robot could use a model to maintain its estimate of its position and update the estimate based on its actions. This may be appropriate when the world is fully observable (page 29) and deterministic (page 30). When there are unpredictable changes in the world or when there are noisy actuators (e.g., a wheel slips, the wheel is not of exactly the diameter specified in the model, or acceleration is not instantaneous), the noise accumulates, so that the estimates of position soon become very inaccurate. However, if the model is accurate at some level of detail, it may still be useful. For example, finding a route on a map, which can be seen as a high-level plan, is useful for an agent even if it doesn't specify all of the details and even if it is sometimes wrong.

A more promising approach is to combine the agent's prediction of the world state with sensing information. This can take a number of forms:

- If both the noise of forward prediction and sensor noise are modeled, the next belief state can be estimated using Bayes' rule (page 381). This is known as **filtering** (page 422).

- With more complicated sensors such as vision, a model can be used to predict where visual features can be found, and then vision can be used to look for these features close to the predicted location. This makes the vision task much simpler than the case where the agent has no idea where it is, and vision can greatly reduce the errors in position arising from forward prediction alone.

A control problem is **separable** if the best action can be obtained by first finding the best prediction of the state of the world and then using that prediction to determine the best action. Unfortunately, most control problems are not separable. This means that when the world is partially observable (page 30), the agent should consider multiple possible states to determine what to do. An agent could represent a probability distribution over the possible states (see Section 9.6, page 418), but this is often difficult to represent for complex domains, and often just a few representative hypotheses are chosen (see Section 9.7.6, page 445). Usually, there is no "best model" of the world that is independent of what the agent will do with the model.

### 2.3.3 Offline and Online Computation

Figure 2.10 shows a refinement of Figure 1.4 (page 15) showing the online and offline tasks. Offline, a learner creates a model that can be used online. The notion here of a learner is very general, and can include anything that takes data and background knowledge to make the online reasoner more accurate, have more ability, or carry out faster reasoning. The notion of a reasoner is also very general and can range from a simple function to decide actions, to an online learner, to a sophisticated reasoner that deals with all levels of complexity.

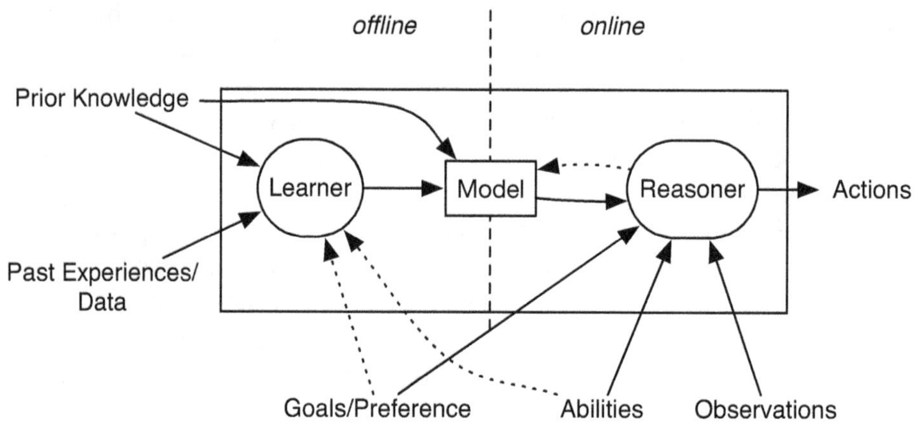


Figure 2.10: Offline and online decomposition of an agent

The goals and abilities are given offline, online, or both, depending on the agent. For example, a delivery robot could have general goals of keeping the lab clean and not damaging itself or other objects, but it could be given delivery goals at runtime. The online computation can be made simpler and so more efficient if the model is tuned for the particular goals and abilities. This is often not possible when the goals and abilities are only available at runtime.

**Offline**, before the agent has to act, the agent uses prior knowledge and past experiences (either its own past experiences or data it has been given) to **learn** (parts of) a model that is useful for acting online. Researchers have traditionally considered the case involving lots of data and very general, or even uninformative, prior knowledge in the field of statistics. The case of rich prior knowledge and little or no data from which to learn has been studied under the umbrella of **expert systems**. For most non-trivial domains, the agent needs whatever information is available, and so it requires both rich prior knowledge and observations from which to learn.

**Online** (page 34), when the agent is acting, the agent uses its model, its observations of the world, and its goals and abilities to choose what to do and update its belief state. Online, the information about the particular situation becomes available, and the agent has to act. The information includes the observations of the domain and often the preferences or goals. The agent can get observations from sensors, users, and other information sources, such as websites, although it typically does not have access to the domain experts or designers of the system.

An agent typically has much more time for offline computation than for online computation. During online computation it can take advantage of particular goals and particular observations.

For example, a medical diagnosis system offline can acquire knowledge about how diseases and symptoms interact and do some compilation to make inference faster. Online, it deals with a particular patient and needs to act in a timely manner. It can concentrate on the patient's symptoms and possible related symptoms, ignoring other symptoms, which helps it reason faster.

Online the following roles are involved:

- **Users** are people who have a need for expertise or have information about individual situations. For example, in a diagnostic system the users might include a patient or a receptionist in a doctor's office who enters the information. For a travel agent, the user might be a person looking for a holiday or someone providing accommodation or events. Users typically are not experts in the domain of the knowledge base. They often do not know what information is needed by the system. Thus, it is unreasonable to expect them to volunteer everything that is true about a particular situation. A simple and natural interface must be provided because users do not typically understand the internal structure of the system. Human users also only provide observations that are unusual; for example, a patient may specify that they have a bad cough, but not that they didn't get their arm damaged in an accident.

When users are using the output of the system, they must make informed decisions based on the recommendation of the system; thus, they require an explanation of why any recommendation is appropriate.

- **Sensors** provide information about the environment. For example, a thermometer is a sensor that can provide the current temperature at the location of the thermometer. Sensors may be more sophisticated, such as a vision sensor. At the lowest level, a vision sensor may simply provide an array of $1920 \times 1080$ pixels at 50 frames per second for each of red, green, and blue. At a higher level, a vision system may be able to provide information such as the location of particular features, where shoppers are in a store, or whether some particular individual is in the scene. A microphone can be used at a low level of abstraction to detect whether this is a sound and provide a trace of frequencies. At a higher level it may provide a sequence of spoken words.

  Sensors come in two main varieties. A **passive sensor** continuously feeds information to the agent. Passive sensors include thermometers, cameras, and microphones. The designer can typically choose where the sensors are or where they are pointing, but they just feed the agent information. In contrast, an **active sensor** is controlled or queried for information. Examples of an active sensor include a medical probe able to answer specific questions about a patient or a test given to a student in a tutoring agent. Often, sensors that are passive sensors at lower levels of abstraction can be seen as active sensors at higher levels of abstraction. For example, a camera could be asked whether a particular person is in the room. To do this, it may need to zoom in on the faces in the room, looking for distinguishing features of the person.

- An **external knowledge source**, such as a website or a database, might be asked questions and can provide the answer for a limited domain. An agent can ask a weather website for the temperature at a particular location or an airline website for the arrival time of a particular flight. The knowledge sources have various protocols and efficiency trade-offs. The interface between an agent and an external knowledge source is called a **wrapper**. A wrapper translates between the representation the agent uses and the queries the external knowledge source is prepared to handle. Often, wrappers are designed so that the agent is able to ask the same query of multiple knowledge sources. For example, an agent may want to know about airplane arrivals, but different airlines or airports may require very different protocols to access that information. When websites and databases adhere to a common vocabulary, as defined by an **ontology** (page 716), they can be used together because the same symbols have the same meaning. Having the same symbols mean the same thing is called **semantic interoperability**. When they use different ontologies, there must be mappings between the ontologies to allow them to interoperate.

## 2.4 Social Impact

> *...self-driving cars ...The technology is essentially here. We have machines that can make a bunch of quick decisions that could drastically reduce traffic fatalities, drastically improve the efficiency of our transportation grid, and help solve things like carbon emissions that are causing the warming of the planet. But ...what are the values that we're going to embed in the cars? There are gonna be a bunch of choices that you have to make, the classic problem being: If the car is driving, you can swerve to avoid hitting a pedestrian, but then you might hit a wall and kill yourself. It's a moral decision, and who's setting up those rules?*
>
> – Barack Obama, 2016 [Dadich, 2016]

Sometimes agents face decisions where there are no good choices. They just have to choose which of the bad choices to carry out. A designer has to either explicitly or implicitly decide what the agents should do in such circumstances. **Trolley problems** consider hypothetical scenarios where a trolley-car (tram, streetcar) has brake failure and has to decide which of two tracks to go down. Both tracks have bad outcomes; for example, one may kill three people who are not supposed to be there, and the other may kill a worker doing their job. As the scenarios vary, people are asked which they prefer. A number of philosophers, following Foot [1967], have used such problems to probe people's thinking about what to do when the interests of human beings conflict, including the difference between someone's responsibility for harms that they cause (more or less directly) and for harms that they merely allow to happen.

In a modern variant of the trolley problem, the **moral machines** experiment asked millions of people from 233 countries about what **autonomous vehicles** (**self-driving cars**) should do in various circumstances.

**Example 2.7** Suppose there is a self-driving car with sudden brake failure, and it has to choose:

- It can go straight ahead, which will result in the death of a man and a baby who are flouting the law by crossing on a red signal.
- It can swerve, which will result in the death of a pregnant woman who was abiding by the law.

What should it do?

The scenarios differed in the number of deaths, people versus animals, men versus women, young versus old, lawful versus unlawful, fit versus unfit. The global tendencies were to prefer sparing humans to animals, preference for sparing more lives, and preference for sparing young lives over old lives. Some preferences, such as the preference between genders and between social status (such as homeless person versus doctor), varied considerably between countries.

> *We can embrace the challenges of machine ethics as a unique opportunity to decide, as a community, what we believe to be right or wrong; and to make sure that machines, unlike humans, unerringly follow these moral preferences.*
>
> – Awad et al. [2018, p. 63]

This work showed that there are some principles that seem universal. There are some that are culturally specific. It also oversimplified in that it did not include any uncertainty; all of the outcomes were definitive. One interesting aspect is that, on average, people thought it was more important to save pedestrians than to save people in the vehicle; this means that it should not be up to the owners and drivers of the vehicles to choose their own policies, as people generally prefer to save their family than strangers.

## 2.5 Review

The main points you should have learned from this chapter are as follows:

- An agent system is composed of an agent and an environment.
- Agents have sensors and actuators to interact with the environment.
- An agent is composed of a body and interacting controllers.
- Agents are situated in time and must make decisions on what to do based on their history of interaction with the environment.
- An agent has direct access to what it has remembered (its belief state) and what it has just observed. At each point in time, an agent decides what to do and what to remember based on its belief state and its current observations.
- Complex agents are built modularly in terms of interacting hierarchical layers.
- An intelligent agent requires knowledge that is acquired at design time, offline or online.
- An agent's decisions implicitly convey the preferences of the agent. It is debatable whether it should be up to the owners or designers of agents (such as autonomous vehicles) to set the preferences, as they have different preferences than the rest of the population.

## 2.6 References and Further Reading

The model of agent systems is based on the constraint nets of Zhang and Mackworth [1995] and Rosenschein and Kaelbling [1995]. Walter [1950] presents a simple tortoise agent that has interesting behavior, and Walter [1951] describes a version that learns. Luenberger [1979] is a readable introduction to the classical theory of agents interacting with environments. *Turtle Geometry*, by Abelson and DiSessa [1981], investigates mathematics from the viewpoint of modeling simple reactive agents.

The hierarchical control is based on Albus [1981] and the subsumption architecture of Brooks [1986]. Simon [1996] argues for the importance of hierarchical control.

Kahneman [2011] provides compelling evidence for distinguishing two modes of human thought: fast, instinctive and, emotional versus slow, deliberate, and rational, which he calls **Systems 1 and 2** to avoid oversimplification.

For more detail on agent control, see Dean and Wellman [1991], Latombe [1991], and Agre [1995]. The methodology for building intelligent agents is discussed by Haugeland [1985], Brooks [1991], Kirsh [1991b], and Mackworth [1993].

Qualitative reasoning is described by Forbus and Hinrich [2017] and Forbus [2019].

The moral machines experiment is described by Awad et al. [2018, 2020] and Bonnefon [2021].

## 2.7 Exercises

**Exercise 2.1** The start of Section 2.2 (page 58) argued that it was impossible to build a representation of a world independently of what the agent will do with it. This exercise lets you evaluate this argument.

Choose a particular world, for example, the things on top of your desk right now.

(i) Get someone to list all of the individuals (things) that exist in this world (or try it yourself as a thought experiment).
(ii) Try to think of twenty individuals that they missed. Make these as different from each other as possible. For example, the ball at the tip of the rightmost ballpoint pen on the desk, the part of the stapler that makes the staples bend, or the third word on page 73 of a particular book on the desk.
(iii) Try to find an individual that cannot be described using your natural language (such as a particular component of the texture of the desk).
(iv) Choose a particular task, such as making the desk tidy, and try to write down all of the individuals in the world at a level of description relevant to this task.

Based on this exercise, discuss the following statements:

(a) What exists in a world is a property of the observer.
(b) We need ways to refer to individuals in ways other than expecting each individual to have a separate name.
(c) Which individuals exist is a property of the task as well as of the world.

(d) To describe the individuals in a domain, you need what is essentially a dictionary of a huge number of words and ways to combine them, and this should be able to be done independently of any particular domain.

**Exercise 2.2** Consider the top-level controller of Example 2.6 (page 63).

(a) If the lower level reached the timeout without getting to the target position, what does the agent do?
(b) The definition of the target position means that, when the plan ends, the top level stops. This is not reasonable for the robot that can only change direction and cannot stop. Change the definition so that the robot keeps going.

**Exercise 2.3** The obstacle avoidance implemented in Example 2.5 (page 62) can easily get stuck.

(a) Show an obstacle and a target for which the robot using the controller of Example 2.5 (page 62) would not be able to get around (and will crash or loop).
(b) Even without obstacles, the robot may never reach its destination. For example, if the robot is close to its target position, but not close enough to have arrived, it may keep circling forever without reaching its target. Design a controller that can detect this situation and find its way to the target.

**Exercise 2.4** Consider the "robot trap" in Figure 2.11.

(a) This question is to explore why it is so tricky for a robot to get to location $g$. Explain what the current robot does. Suppose one was to implement a robot that follows the wall using the "right-hand rule": the robot turns left when it hits an obstacle and keeps following a wall, with the wall always on its right. Is there a simple characterization of the situations in which the robot should keep following this rule or head towards the target?

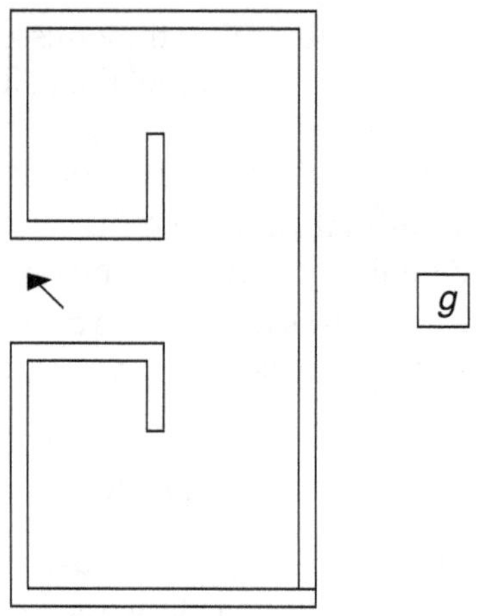


Figure 2.11: A robot trap

(b) An intuition of how to escape such a trap is that, when the robot hits a wall, it follows the wall until the number of right turns equals the number of left turns. Show how this can be implemented, explaining the belief state and the functions of the layer.

**Exercise 2.5** If the current target location were to be moved, the middle layer of Example 2.5 (page 62) travels to the original position of that target and does not try to go to the new position. Change the controller so that the robot can adapt to targets moving.

**Exercise 2.6** The current controller visits the locations in the *to_do* list sequentially.

(a) Change the controller so that it is opportunistic; when it selects the next location to visit, it selects the location that is closest to its current position. It should still visit all the locations.
(b) Give one example of an environment in which the new controller visits all the locations in fewer time steps than the original controller.
(c) Give one example of an environment in which the original controller visits all the locations in fewer time steps than the modified controller.
(d) Change the controller so that, at every step, the agent heads towards whichever target location is closest to its current position.
(e) Can the controller from part (d) get stuck and never reach a target in an example where the original controller will work? Either give an example in which it gets stuck and explain why it cannot find a solution, or explain why it gets to a goal whenever the original can.

**Exercise 2.7** Change the controller so that the robot senses the environment to determine the coordinates of a location. Assume that the body can provide the coordinates of a named location.

**Exercise 2.8** Suppose the robot has a battery that must be charged at a particular wall socket before it runs out. How should the robot controller be modified to allow for battery recharging?

**Exercise 2.9** Suppose you have a new job and must build a controller for an intelligent robot. You tell your bosses that you just have to implement a command function and a state transition function. They are very skeptical. Why these functions? Why only these? Explain why a controller requires a command function and a state transition function, but not other functions. Use proper English. Be concise.

**Exercise 2.10** Should the owners of autonomous cars be able to select the preferences for their vehicles? Give three reasons why, and three reasons why not. Which argument do you think is more persuasive? How should the preferences of autonomous cars be determined?

**Exercise 2.11** Consider the quote in Section 2.4 (page 71) from 2016: "self-driving cars ... The technology is essentially here." Looking back, was that an accurate assessment? Consider the subsequent development of self-driving cars and determine if that was accurate or overly optimistic. What is the current state of self-driving technology?

# Part II

# Reasoning and Planning with Certainty

How can an agent represent its knowledge, reason, and plan, under the assumption that it knows both what is true in the world and the effects of its actions?

# Chapter 3

# Searching for Solutions

*Have you ever watched a crab on the shore crawling backward in search of the Atlantic Ocean, and missing? That's the way the mind of man operates.*

– H. L. Mencken (1880–1956)

The previous chapter discussed how an agent perceives and acts, but not how its goals affect its actions. An agent could be programmed to act in the world to achieve a fixed goal or set of goals, but then it would not adapt to changing goals, and so would not be intelligent. An intelligent agent needs to reason about its abilities and goals to determine what to do. This chapter abstracts the problem of an agent deciding how to achieve a goal as the problem of searching for a path in a graph.

## 3.1 Problem Solving as Search

In the simplest case of an agent deciding what it should do, the agent has a perfect model of the world, with no uncertainty, and a goal to achieve. This is either a flat (non-hierarchical) representation or a single level of a hierarchy (page 58).

This problem can be abstracted to the mathematical problem of finding a path from the start node to a goal node in a directed graph. Many other problems can also be mapped to this abstraction, so it is worthwhile considering this level of abstraction. Most of this chapter explores various algorithms for finding such paths.

**Example 3.1** Computer maps provide path finding: showing how to go (drive, ride, walk, or take transit) from one location to another. Finding the best route from a current location to a destination is a search problem. The state includes mode of transportation (e.g., on foot or on a bus), the location of the traveler, and the direction of travel. A legal route will include the roads (going the correct way down one-way streets) and intersections the traveler will traverse.

The best route could mean

- the shortest (least distance) route
- the quickest route
- the route that uses the least energy
- the lowest-cost route, where the cost takes into account time, money (e.g., fuel and tolls), and the route's attractiveness.

Finding the shortest route is usually easiest to implement, because maps contain distances and they can be assumed to not change, ignoring detours due to roadworks or accidents. Estimating the time or the energy used is more difficult. The route planner might need to take into account regular traffic volumes, as well as local conditions, such as the weather or accidents. To estimate the time, machine learning algorithms can be used.

This example is discussed more in Section 3.9 (page 120) on social issues.

This notion of **search** is computation solely inside the agent. It is different from searching in the world, when an agent may have to act in the world; for example, a robot searching for keys, lifting up cushions, and so on. It is also different from searching the Web, which involves searching for information by indexing huge amounts of data and trying to find the best response for each search query. Searching in this chapter means finding a path to a goal node in a graph.

Search underlies much of AI. When an agent is given a problem, it is usually given only a description that lets it recognize a solution, not an algorithm to solve it. It has to search for a solution. The existence of NP-complete problems (page 89), with efficient means to recognize solutions but no efficient methods for finding them, indicates that searching is a necessary part of problem solving.

It is often believed that humans are able to use intuition to jump to solutions to difficult problems. However, humans cannot find optimal solutions to computationally difficult problems. Humans do not tend to solve general problems; instead, they solve specific instances about which they may know much more than the underlying search space. They often do not find optimal solutions, but find **satisficing**, or good enough, solutions. Problems with little structure, or ones in which the structure cannot be related to the physical world, are very difficult for humans to solve. The existence of public key encryption codes, where the search space is clear and the test for a solution is given – which humans nevertheless have no hope of solving and computers cannot solve in a realistic time frame – demonstrates the difficulty of search.

The difficulty of search and the fact that humans are able to solve some search problems efficiently suggests that computer agents should exploit knowledge about special cases to guide them to a solution. This extra knowledge beyond the search space is called **heuristic knowledge**. This chapter considers one kind of heuristic knowledge in the form of an estimate of the cost from a node to a goal.

## 3.2 State Spaces

One general formulation of intelligent action is in terms of a **state space**. A **state** contains all of the information necessary to predict the effects of an action and to determine whether a state satisfies the goal. State-space searching assumes:

- The agent has perfect knowledge of the state space.
- At any time, it knows what state it is in; the world is thus fully observable (page 29).
- The agent has a set of actions with known deterministic effects (page 30).
- The agent has a goal to achieve and can determine whether a state satisfies the goal.

A **solution** to a search problem is a sequence of actions that will get the agent from its current state to a state that satisfies the goal.

**Example 3.2** Consider the robot delivery domain of Figure 3.1, where there are offices around a central lab. The only way a robot can get through a doorway is to push the door open in the direction shown. The task is to find a path from one location to another. Assuming that the agent can use a lower-level controller to get from one location to a neighboring location, the actions for the search are traveling between neighboring locations. This can be modeled as a state-space search problem, where the states are locations. Some of the locations in Figure 3.1 are named and used as exemplars.

Consider an example problem where the robot starts at location $A$, and the goal is to get to location $G$. Thus, $G$ is the only state that satisfies the goal. A solution is a sequence of actions that moves the robot from $A$ to $G$.

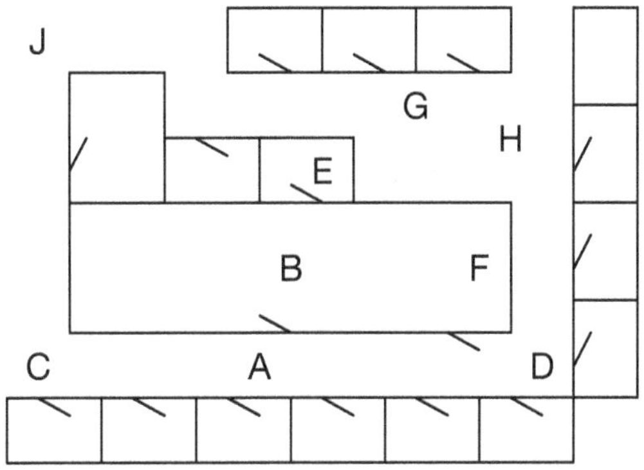


Figure 3.1: A delivery robot domain with interesting locations labeled

**Example 3.3** Consider a video game played on a grid, where an agent can move up, down, left, or right one step as long as the move is not blocked by a wall. The agent has to collect four coins, $C_1, \ldots, C_4$, where each coin starts at a known position. The agent uses one unit of fuel at each step, and cannot move if it has no fuel. It can get filled up (to 20 units of fuel) at the fuel station. In this case the state needs to take into account the position of the agent, the amount of fuel, and for each coin whether it has collected that coin. The state could be represented as the tuple

$$(x, y, fuel, c_1, c_2, c_3, c_4)$$

where $(x, y)$ is the position of the agent, *fuel* is the amount of fuel the agent has, and $c_i$ is true when the agent has collected coin $C_i$. True is written as $t$ and false as $f$ here. The goal might be for the agent to have collected all coins and be at position $(1, 1)$, which is the state

$$(1, 1, ?, t, t, t, t)$$

where ? means what the fuel is at the end does not matter. All states where the agent is at $(1, 1)$ and all $c_i$ are true are goal states.

Part of the environment is shown in Figure 3.2(a), where the agent cannot move into a blacked-out square. It could get filled up at position $(4, 9)$ and collect coin $C_3$ at position $(5, 7)$. The state where the agent, Rob, is at position $(5, 8)$ with 6 units of fuel, and has only collected coin $C_2$, is

$$(5, 8, 6, f, t, f, f).$$

Figure 3.2(b) shows part of the state space for this problem.

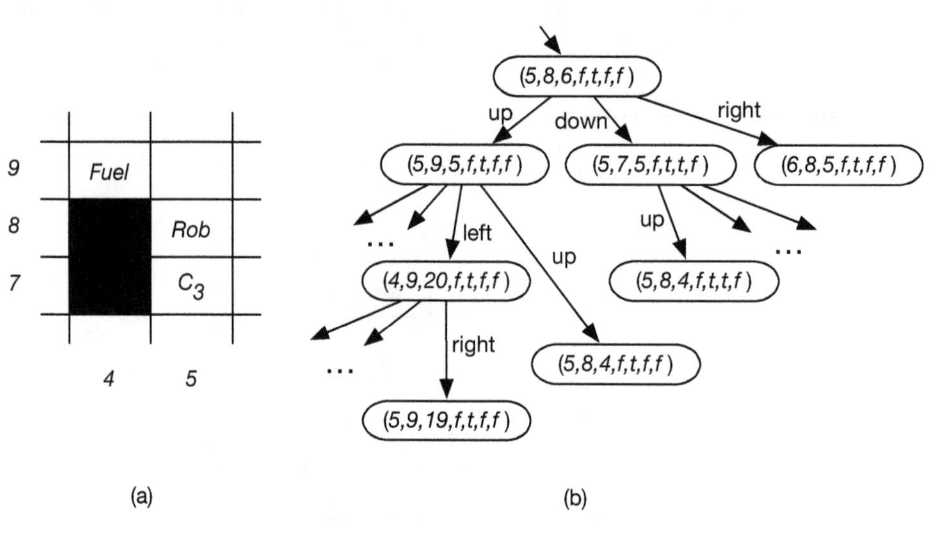


Figure 3.2: Part of the video game and state space of Example 3.3

**Example 3.4** The delivery robot may have a number of parcels to deliver to various locations, where each parcel has its own delivery destination. In this case, the state may consist of the location of the robot, which parcels the robot is carrying, and the locations of the other parcels. The possible actions may be for the robot to move, to pick up parcels that are at the same location as the robot, or to put down some or all of the parcels it is carrying. A goal state may be one in which some specified parcels are at their delivery destination. There may be many goal states because where the robot is or where some of the other parcels are in a goal state does not matter.

Notice that this representation has ignored many details, for example, how the robot is carrying the parcels (which may affect whether it can carry other parcels), the battery level of the robot, whether the parcels are fragile or damaged, and the color of the floor. Not having these details as part of the state space implies that they are not relevant to the problem at hand.

**Example 3.5** In a simplified **tutoring agent**, a state may consist of the set of topics that the student knows, and the topics they have been introduced to, but do not know yet. The action may be teaching a lesson on a particular topic, with preconditions that the student knows any prerequisite topic, and the result that the student knows the topic of the lesson. The aim is for a student to know a particular set of topics.

If the effect of teaching also depends on the aptitude of the student, this detail must be part of the state space as well. The state does not need to include the items the student is carrying if what they are carrying does not affect the result of actions or whether the goal is achieved.

A **state-space search problem** consists of:

- a set of states
- a distinguished state called the **start state**
- for each state, a set of actions available to the agent in that state
- an **action function** that, given a state and an action, returns a new state
- a **goal** specified as a Boolean function, $goal(s)$, that is true when state $s$ satisfies the goal, in which case $s$ is a **goal state**
- a criterion that specifies the quality of an acceptable solution; for example, any sequence of actions that gets the agent to the goal state may be acceptable, or there may be costs associated with actions and the agent may be required to find a sequence that has minimal total cost.

A solution that is best according to some criterion is called an **optimal solution**. An agent may be satisfied with any solution that is within, say, 10% of optimal.

This framework is extended in subsequent chapters to include cases where the states have structure that can be exploited, where the state is not fully observable (e.g., the robot does not know where the parcels are initially, or the teacher does not know the aptitude of the student), where the actions are stochastic (e.g., the robot may overshoot, or a student perhaps does not learn a topic that is taught), and with complex preferences in terms of rewards and punishments, not just a set of goal states.

## 3.3 Graph Searching

In this chapter, the problem of finding a sequence of actions to achieve a goal is abstracted as searching for paths in directed graphs. Searching in graphs provides an appropriate abstract model of problem solving independent of a particular domain.

A directed graph consists of a set of nodes and a set of directed arcs between nodes. The idea is to find a path along these arcs from the start node to a goal node.

The abstraction is necessary because there may be more than one way to represent a problem as a graph. The examples in this chapter are in terms of state-space searching, where nodes represent states and arcs represent actions. Future chapters consider other ways to use graphs for problem solving.

### 3.3.1 Formalizing Graph Searching

A **directed graph** consists of:

- a set $N$ of **nodes**
- a set $A$ of arcs, where an **arc** is an ordered pair of nodes.

In this definition, a node could be anything. There may be infinitely many nodes and arcs. A graph need not be represented explicitly; only a procedure to generate nodes and arcs as needed is required.

The arc $\langle n_1, n_2 \rangle$ is an **outgoing arc** from $n_1$ and an **incoming arc** to $n_2$.

A node $n_2$ is a **neighbor** of $n_1$ if there is an arc from $n_1$ to $n_2$; that is, if $\langle n_1, n_2 \rangle \in A$. Note that being a neighbor does not imply symmetry; just because $n_2$ is a neighbor of $n_1$ does not imply that $n_1$ is a neighbor of $n_2$. Arcs may be **labeled**, for example, with the action that will take the agent from a node to its neighbor or with the cost of an action or both.

A **path** from node $s$ to node $g$ is a sequence of nodes $\langle n_0, n_1, \ldots, n_k \rangle$ such that $s = n_0$, $g = n_k$, and $\langle n_{i-1}, n_i \rangle \in A$; that is, there is an arc from $n_{i-1}$ to $n_i$ for each $i$. Sometimes it is useful to view a path as the sequence of arcs, $\langle n_0, n_1 \rangle$, $\langle n_1, n_2 \rangle, \ldots, \langle n_{k-1}, n_k \rangle$, or a sequence of labels of these arcs. Path $\langle n_0, n_1, \ldots, n_i \rangle$ is an **initial part** of $\langle n_0, n_1, \ldots, n_k \rangle$, when $i \leq k$.

A **goal** is a Boolean function on nodes. Node $n$ is a **goal node** if $goal(n)$ is true.

To encode problems as graphs, one node is identified as the **start node**. A **solution** is a path from the start node to a goal node.

Sometimes there is a **cost** – a non-negative number – associated with arcs. The cost of arc $\langle n_i, n_j \rangle$ is written as $cost(\langle n_i, n_j \rangle)$.

The costs of arcs induce a cost of paths. Given a path $p = \langle n_0, n_1, \ldots, n_k \rangle$, the cost of path $p$ is the sum of the costs of the arcs in the path:

$$cost(p) = \sum_{i=1}^{k} cost(\langle n_{i-1}, n_i \rangle) = cost(\langle n_0, n_1 \rangle) + \cdots + cost(\langle n_{k-1}, n_k \rangle).$$

An **optimal solution** is one of the solutions that has the lowest cost. That is, an optimal solution is a path $p$ from the start node to a goal node such that there is no path $p'$ from the start node to a goal node where $cost(p') < cost(p)$.

A **state-space graph** is a special type of graph where the nodes are the states, and there is an arc $\langle n_i, n_j \rangle$ if there is an action that is possible to be carried out in $n_i$ and the effect of the action is to be in state $n_j$. Future chapters consider other ways to represent problems as graphs.

**Example 3.6** Consider the problem of the delivery robot finding a path from location $A$ to location $G$ in the domain shown in Figure 3.1 (page 81). The nodes are the labelled locations. Assume that the robot is only able to travel in one direction between the locations. Figure 3.3 shows the resulting graph where the nodes represent locations and the arcs represent possible single steps between locations. Each arc is shown with its associated cost, an estimate of the travel time of getting from one location to the next.

In this graph, the set of nodes is $\{A, B, C, D, E, F, G, H, J\}$ and the set of arcs is $\{\langle A, B\rangle, \langle A, C\rangle, \langle A, D\rangle, \langle B, E\rangle, \ldots\}$. Node $E$ has no neighbors. Node $B$ has two neighbors, namely $E$ and $F$. $A$ is not a neighbor of $B$ as there is no arc from $B$ to $A$.

There are three paths from $A$ to $G$:

$$\langle A, B, F, D, H, G\rangle$$
$$\langle A, D, H, G\rangle$$
$$\langle A, C, J, G\rangle$$

If $A$ were the start node and $G$ were the unique goal node, all three paths would be a solution to the graph-searching problem. The second, with cost $4 + 4 + 3 = 11$, is an optimal solution.

A **cycle** is a non-empty path where the end node is the same as the start node – that is, $\langle n_0, n_1, \ldots, n_k\rangle$ such that $n_0 = n_k$. A directed graph without any cycles is called a **directed acyclic graph (DAG)**. Note that this should be called an **acyclic directed graph**, because it is a directed graph that happens to

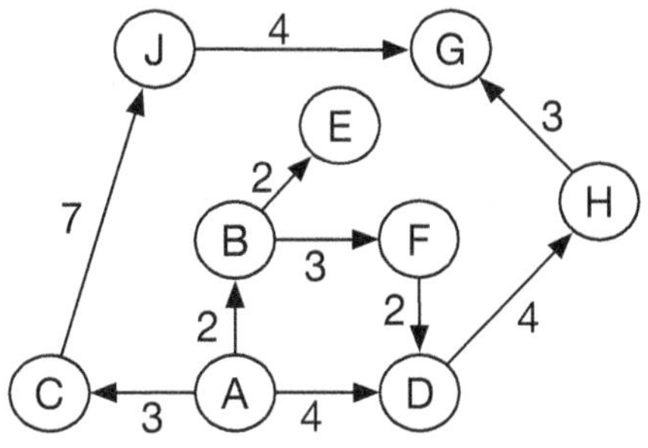


Figure 3.3: A graph with arc costs for the delivery domain of Figure 3.1

be acyclic, not an acyclic graph that happens to be directed, but DAG sounds better than ADG! The graph of Figure 3.3 (page 85) is a DAG.

A **tree** is a DAG where there is one node with no incoming arcs and every other node has exactly one incoming arc. The node with no incoming arcs is called the **root** of the tree. A node with no outgoing arcs is called a **leaf**. In a tree, an arc goes from a **parent** to a **child**; the family-tree metaphor, with grandparents, siblings, and so on, is often used.

In many problems the search graph is not given explicitly, but is dynamically constructed as needed. For the search algorithms, all that is required is a way to generate the neighbors of a node and to determine if a node is a goal node.

The **forward branching factor** of a node is the number of outgoing arcs from the node. The **backward branching factor** of a node is the number of incoming arcs to the node. These factors provide measures for the complexity of graph algorithms. In the time and space complexity discussed below, assume that the branching factors are bounded, meaning they are all less than some positive integer.

**Example 3.7** In the graph of Figure 3.3 (page 85), the forward branching factor of node $A$ is three because there are three outgoing arcs from node $A$. The backward branching factor of node $A$ is zero; there are no incoming arcs to node $A$. The forward branching factor of $E$ is zero and the backward branching factor of $E$ is one. The forward branching factor of node $B$ is two and the backward branching factor of $B$ is one.

The branching factor is an important key component in the size of the graph. If the forward branching factor for each node is $b$, and the graph is a tree, there are $b^n$ nodes that are $n$ arcs away from any node. (This is only possible if the tree is infinite.)

## 3.4 A Generic Searching Algorithm

This section describes a generic algorithm to search for a solution path in a graph. The algorithm calls procedures that can be coded to implement various search strategies.

The intuitive idea behind the generic search algorithm, given a graph, a start node, and a goal predicate, is to explore paths incrementally from the start node. This is done by maintaining a **frontier** (or **fringe**) of paths from the start node. The frontier contains all of the paths that could form initial segments of paths from the start node to a goal node. (See Figure 3.4 (page 87), where the frontier is the set of paths to the gray-shaded nodes.) Initially, the frontier contains the trivial path containing just the start node, and no arcs. As the search proceeds, the frontier expands into the unexplored nodes until a goal node is encountered. Different search strategies are obtained by providing an appropriate implementation of the frontier.

The **generic search algorithm** is shown in Figure 3.5 (page 88). The frontier is a set of paths. Initially, the frontier contains the path of zero cost consisting of just the start node. At each step, the algorithm removes a path $\langle n_0, \ldots, n_k \rangle$ from the frontier. If $goal(n_k)$ is true (i.e., $n_k$ is a goal node), it has **found a solution** and returns the path $\langle n_0, \ldots, n_k \rangle$. Otherwise, the path is extended by one more arc by finding the neighbors of $n_k$. For every neighbor $n$ of $n_k$, the path $\langle n_0, \ldots, n_k, n \rangle$ is added to the frontier. This step is known as **expanding** the path $\langle n_0, \ldots, n_k \rangle$.

This algorithm has a few features that should be noted:

- Which path is selected at line 13 defines the search strategy. The selection of a path can affect the efficiency; see the box on page 89 for more details on the use of "select".
- It is useful to think of the *return* at line 15 as a temporary return, where a caller can **retry** the search to get another answer by continuing the while loop. In languages that support object-oriented programming, such as Python, retry can be implemented by having a class that keeps the state of the search and a *search*() method that returns the next solution.

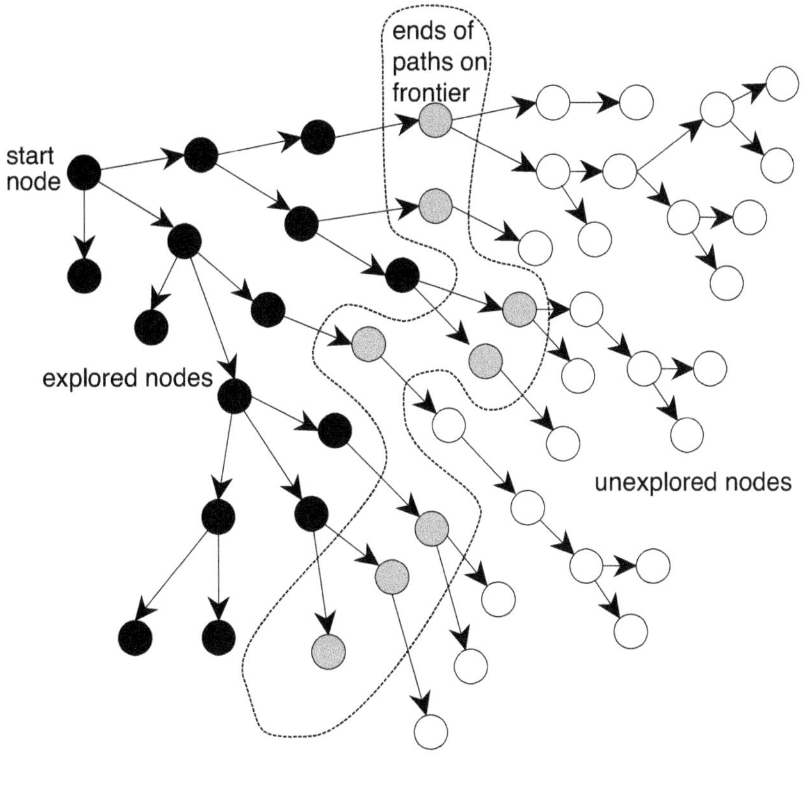


Figure 3.4: Problem solving by graph searching

- If the procedure returns $\bot$ ("**bottom**"), there are no solutions, or no remaining solutions if the search has been retried.
- The algorithm only tests if a path ends in a goal node *after* the path has been selected from the frontier, not when it is added to the frontier. There are two important reasons for this. There could be a costly arc from a node on the frontier to a goal node. The search should not always return the path with this arc, because a lower-cost solution may exist. This is crucial when the lowest-cost path is required. A second reason is that it may be expensive to determine whether a node is a goal node, and so this should be delayed in case the computation is not necessary.

## 3.5 Uninformed Search Strategies

A problem determines the graph, the start node, and the goal but not which path to select from the frontier. This is the job of a **search strategy**. A search strategy defines the order in which paths are selected from the frontier. It specifies which path is selected at line 13 of Figure 3.5. Different strategies are obtained by modifying how the selection of paths in the frontier is implemented.

This section presents four **uninformed search strategies** that do not take into account the location of the goal. Intuitively, these algorithms ignore where they are going until they find a goal and report success.

1: **procedure** *Search*$(G, S, goal)$<br>
2:     **Inputs**<br>
3:         $G$: graph with nodes $N$ and arcs $A$<br>
4:         $s$: start node<br>
5:         *goal*: Boolean function of nodes<br>
6:     **Output**<br>
7:         path from $s$ to a node for which *goal* is true<br>
8:         or $\bot$ if there are no solution paths<br>
9:     **Local**<br>
10:         *frontier*: set of paths<br>
11:     $frontier := \{\langle s \rangle\}$<br>
12:     **while** $frontier \neq \{\}$ **do**<br>
13:         **select** and **remove** $\langle n_0, \dots, n_k \rangle$ from *frontier*<br>
14:         **if** $goal(n_k)$ **then**<br>
15:             **return** $\langle n_0, \dots, n_k \rangle$<br>
16:         $frontier := frontier \cup \{\langle n_0, \dots, n_k, n \rangle : \langle n_k, n \rangle \in A\}$<br>
17:     **return** $\bot$

Figure 3.5: Search: generic graph-searching algorithm

### Non-deterministic Choice

In many AI programs, we want to separate the definition of a solution from how it is computed. Usually, the algorithms are **non-deterministic**, which means that there are choices in the program that are left unspecified. There are two forms of non-determinism:

- In **don't-care non-determinism**, if one selection does not lead to a solution, neither will other selections. Don't-care non-determinism is used in resource allocation, where a number of requests occur for a limited number of resources, and a scheduling algorithm has to select who gets which resource at each time. Correctness should not be affected by the selection, but efficiency and termination may be. When there is an infinite sequence of selections, a selection mechanism is **fair** if a request that is repeatedly available to be selected will eventually be selected. The problem of an element being repeatedly not selected is called **starvation**. In this context, a **heuristic** is a rule-of-thumb that can be used to select a value.
- In **don't-know non-determinism**, just because one choice did not lead to a solution does not mean that other choices will not. It is useful to think of an **oracle** that could specify, at each point, which choice will lead to a solution.

  Don't-know non-determinism plays a large role in computational complexity theory. A decision problem is a problem with a yes or no answer. The class $P$ consists of decision problems solvable in time complexity polynomial in the size of the problem. The class $NP$, of non-deterministic polynomial time problems, contains decision problems that could be solved in polynomial time with an **oracle** that chooses the correct value at each choice in constant time or, equivalently, if a solution is verifiable in polynomial time. It is widely conjectured that $P \neq NP$, which would mean that no such oracle can exist. One pivotal result of complexity theory is that the hardest problems in the $NP$ class are all equally complex; if one can be solved in polynomial time, they all can. These problems are **NP-complete**. A problem is **NP-hard** if it is at least as hard as an NP-complete problem.

  In a **non-deterministic procedure**, pretend that an oracle makes an appropriate choice at each time. A **choose** statement will result in a choice that will lead to success, or will **fail** if there are no such choices. A non-deterministic procedure may have multiple answers, where there are multiple choices that succeed, and will fail if there are no applicable choices. An explicit **fail** in the code indicates a choice that should not succeed. Because our agent does not have an oracle, it has to search through the space of alternate choices.

This book consistently uses the term **select** for don't-care non-determinism and **choose** for don't-know non-determinism.

### 3.5.1 Breadth-First Search

In **breadth-first search** the frontier is implemented as a **FIFO** (first-in, first-out) **queue**. Thus, the path that is selected from the frontier is the one that was added earliest. The paths from the start node are generated in order of the number of arcs in the path. One of the paths with the fewest arcs is selected at each iteration.

**Example 3.8** Consider the tree-shaped graph in Figure 3.6. Suppose the start node is the node at the top, and the children of a node are added in a left-to-right order. In breadth-first search, the order in which the paths are expanded does not depend on the location of the goal. The nodes at the end of the first 16 paths expanded are numbered in order of expansion in the figure. The shaded nodes are the nodes at the ends of the paths on the frontier after the first 16 iterations.

**Example 3.9** Consider breadth-first search from $A$ in the graph given in Figure 3.3 (page 85). The costs are ignored in breadth-first search, so it is searching in the space without weights, as shown in Figure 3.7 (page 91).

Initially, the frontier is $[\langle A\rangle]$. This is extended by $A$'s neighbors, making the frontier $[\langle A,B\rangle, \langle A,C\rangle, \langle A,D\rangle]$. These are the paths of length one starting at $A$. The next three paths expanded are $\langle A,B\rangle$, $\langle A,C\rangle$, and $\langle A,D\rangle$, after which the frontier is

$$[\langle A,B,E\rangle, \langle A,B,F\rangle, \langle A,C,J\rangle, \langle A,D,H\rangle].$$

These are the paths of length two starting at $A$. These are the next paths expanded, at which stage the frontier contains the paths of length three from $A$,

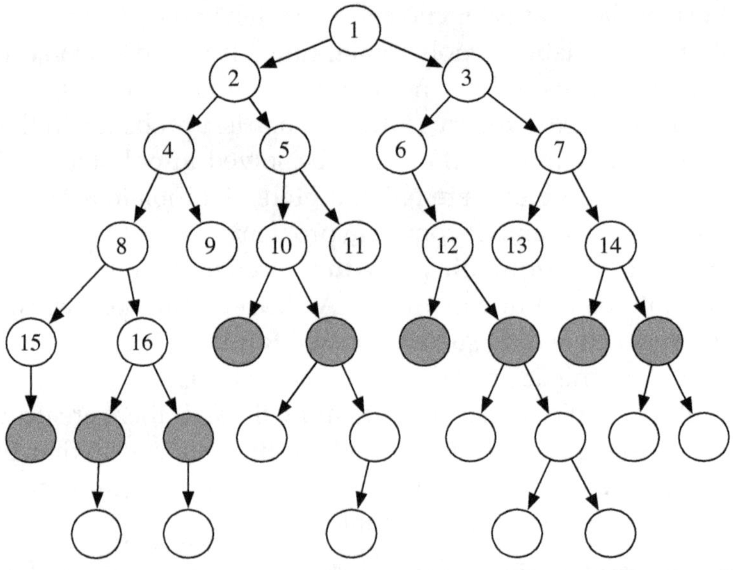


Figure 3.6: The order in which paths are expanded in breadth-first search

namely

$$[\langle A,B,F,D\rangle, \langle A,C,J,G\rangle, \langle A,D,H,G\rangle].$$

When $\langle A,C,J,G\rangle$ is selected, it is returned as a solution.

In breadth-first search, each path on the frontier has either the same number of arcs as, or one more arc than, the next path on the frontier that is expanded.

Suppose the branching factor of the search is $b$. If the next path to be selected on the frontier contains $n$ arcs, there are at least $b^{n-1}$ elements of the frontier. All of these paths contain $n$ or $n+1$ arcs. Thus, both space and time complexities to find a solution are exponential in the number of arcs of the path to a goal with the fewest arcs. This method is guaranteed to find a solution if one exists and will find a solution with the fewest arcs.

Breadth-first search is useful when

- the problem is small enough so that space is not a problem, such as when the graph is already stored, and
- a solution containing the fewest arcs is required.

It is a poor method when all solutions have many arcs or there is some heuristic knowledge available. It is not used very often for large problems where the graph is dynamically generated because of its exponential space complexity.

### 3.5.2 Depth-First Search

In **depth-first search**, the frontier acts like a **LIFO** (last-in, first-out) **stack** of paths. In a stack, elements are added and removed from the top of the stack. Using a stack means that the path selected and removed from the frontier at any time is the last path that was added.

**Example 3.10** Consider the tree-shaped graph in Figure 3.8 (page 92). Suppose the start node is the root of the tree (the node at the top). As depth-first search does not define the order of the neighbors, suppose for this graph that the children of each node are ordered from left to right, and are added to the

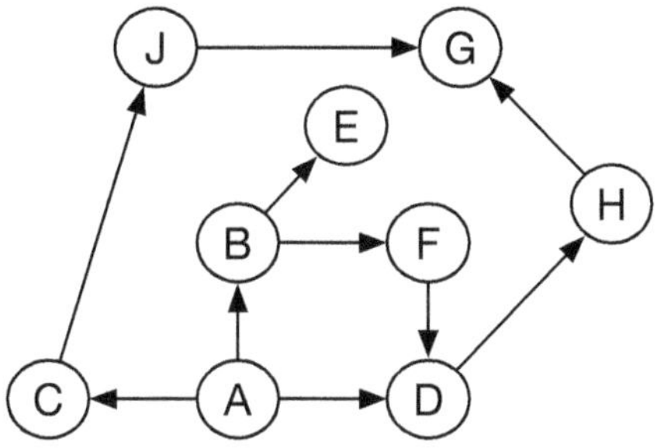


Figure 3.7: Delivery graph without arc costs

stack in reverse order so that the path to the leftmost neighbor is added to the stack last (and so removed first).

In depth-first search, like breadth-first search, the order in which the paths are expanded does not depend on the goal. The nodes at the end of the first 16 paths expanded are numbered in order of expansion in Figure 3.8. The shaded nodes are the nodes at the ends of the paths on the frontier after the first 16 steps, assuming none of the expanded paths end at a goal node.

The first six paths expanded, $\langle 1 \rangle$, $\langle 1,2 \rangle$, $\langle 1,2,3 \rangle$, $\langle 1,2,3,4 \rangle$, $\langle 1,2,3,4,5 \rangle$, and $\langle 1,2,3,4,5,6 \rangle$, are all initial parts of a single path. The node at the end of this path (node 6) has no neighbors. The seventh path expanded is $\langle 1,2,3,4,7 \rangle$. The next path expanded after path $p$ always contains an initial segment of path $p$ with one extra node.

Implementing the frontier as a stack results in paths being pursued in a depth-first manner – searching one path to its completion before trying an alternative path. This method is said to involve **backtracking**: the algorithm selects a first alternative at each node, and it *backtracks* to the next alternative when it has pursued all of the paths from the first selection. Some paths may be infinite when the graph has cycles or infinitely many nodes, in which case a depth-first search may never stop.

This algorithm does not specify the order in which the paths to the neighbors are added to the frontier. The efficiency of the algorithm can be sensitive to the order in which the neighbors are expanded.

Figure 3.9 (page 93) shows an alternative implementation of depth-first search that uses recursion to implement the stack. The call $DF\_search(G, \langle s \rangle, goal)$, if it halts, returns a path from node $s$ to a goal node, or $\perp$ if there is no path.

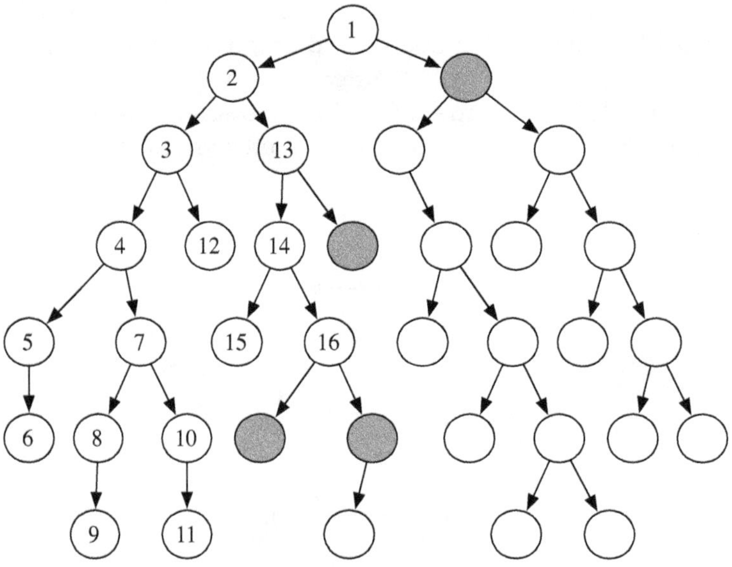


Figure 3.8: The order paths are expanded in depth-first search

Backtracking is achieved by the recursive call returning $\bot$ and the next neighbor being explored.

**Example 3.11** Consider depth-first search from $A$ to $G$ in the graph of Figure 3.3 (page 85). In this example, the frontier is shown as a list of paths with the top of the stack at the left of the list. The ordering of the neighbors matters; assume that the neighbors are ordered so they are expanded in alphabetic ordering.

Initially, the frontier is $\langle A \rangle$.

At the next stage, the frontier contains the paths

$$[\langle A,B \rangle, \langle A,C \rangle, \langle A,D \rangle].$$

Next, the path $\langle A,B \rangle$ is selected because it is at the top of the stack. It is expanded, giving the frontier

$$[\langle A,B,E \rangle, \langle A,B,F \rangle, \langle A,C \rangle, \langle A,D \rangle].$$

Next, the path $\langle A,B,E \rangle$ is removed. $E$ has no neighbors, and so no paths are added. The resulting frontier is

$$[\langle A,B,F \rangle, \langle A,C \rangle, \langle A,D \rangle].$$

At this stage, the path $\langle A,B,F \rangle$ is expanded, resulting in the frontier

$$[\langle A,B,F,D \rangle, \langle A,C \rangle, \langle A,D \rangle].$$

The next frontiers are

$$[\langle A,B,F,D,H \rangle, \langle A,C \rangle, \langle A,D \rangle],$$
$$[\langle A,B,F,D,H,G \rangle, \langle A,C \rangle, \langle A,D \rangle].$$

```
procedure DF_search(G, ⟨n0, ..., nk⟩, goal)
    Inputs
        G: graph with nodes N and arcs A
        ⟨n0, ..., nk⟩: path from node n0 to node nk
        goal: Boolean function on nodes
    Output
        path that extends ⟨n0, ..., nk⟩ to a goal node
        or ⊥ if there is no such path
    if goal(nk) then
        return ⟨n0, ..., nk⟩
    else
        for each arc ⟨nk, n⟩ ∈ A do
            res := DF_search(G, ⟨n0, ..., nk, n⟩, goal)
            if res ≠ ⊥ then
                return res
        return ⊥
```

Figure 3.9: Depth-first search using recursion

The path $\langle A, B, F, D, H, G\rangle$ is selected from the frontier and returned as the solution found.

Suppose $\langle n_0, \ldots, n_k\rangle$ is the path selected on line 13 of Figure 3.5 (page 88). In depth-first search, every other path on the frontier is of the form $\langle n_0, \ldots, n_i, m\rangle$, for some index $i < k$ and some node $m$ that is a neighbor of $n_i$; that is, it follows the selected path for a number of arcs and then has exactly one extra node. Thus, the frontier contains only the current path and paths to neighbors of the nodes on this path. If the branching factor is $b$ and the selected path, $p$, on the frontier has $k$ arcs, there can be at most $k * (b - 1)$ other paths on the frontier. These paths all follow an initial segment of path $p$, and have one extra node, a neighbor of a node in path $p$, and there are at most $(b - 1)$ neighbors from each node. Therefore, for depth-first search, the space used at any stage is linear in the number of arcs from the start to the current node.

If there is a solution on the first branch searched, the time complexity is linear in the number of arcs in the path. In the worst case, depth-first search can get trapped on infinite branches and never find a solution, even if one exists, for infinite graphs or for graphs with cycles. If the graph is a finite tree, with the forward branching factor less than or equal to $b$ and with all paths from the start having $k$ or fewer arcs, the worst-case time complexity is $O(b^k)$.

**Example 3.12** Consider the delivery graph presented in Figure 3.10 (page 96), in which the agent has more freedom in moving between locations, but can get into cycles. An infinite path leads from $A$ to $B$ to $F$ and back to $B$. Depth-first search may follow this path forever, never considering alternative paths. If the neighbors are selected in alphabetic ordering, the frontiers for the first few iterations of depth-first search from $A$ are

$$[\langle A\rangle]$$
$$[\langle A,B\rangle, \langle A,C\rangle, \langle A,D\rangle]$$
$$[\langle A,B,E\rangle, \langle A,B,F\rangle, \langle A,C\rangle, \langle A,D\rangle]$$
$$[\langle A,B,F\rangle, \langle A,C\rangle, \langle A,D\rangle]$$
$$[\langle A,B,F,B\rangle, \langle A,B,F,D\rangle, \langle A,C\rangle, \langle A,D\rangle]$$
$$[\langle A,B,F,B,E\rangle, \langle A,B,F,B,F\rangle, \langle A,B,F,D\rangle, \langle A,C\rangle, \langle A,D\rangle]$$
$$[\langle A,B,F,B,F\rangle, \langle A,B,F,D\rangle, \langle A,C\rangle, \langle A,D\rangle].$$

Depth-first search will never halt for this example. The last three paths are never explored.

Because depth-first search is sensitive to the order in which the neighbors are added to the frontier, care must be taken to do it sensibly. This ordering may be done statically (so that the order of the neighbors is fixed) or dynamically (where the ordering of the neighbors depends on the goal).

Depth-first search is appropriate when

- space is restricted

### Comparing Algorithms

Algorithms (including search algorithms) can be compared on

- the time taken
- the space used
- the quality or accuracy of the results.

The time taken, space used, and accuracy of an algorithm are a function of the inputs to the algorithm. Computer scientists talk about the **asymptotic complexity** of algorithms, which specifies how the time or space grows with the input size of the algorithm. An algorithm has time (or space) complexity $O(f(n))$ – read "big-oh of $f(n)$" – for input size $n$, where $f(n)$ is some function of $n$, if there exist constants $n_0$ and $k$ such that the time, or space, of the algorithm is less than $k * f(n)$ for all $n > n_0$. The most common types of functions are exponential functions such as $2^n$, $3^n$, or $1.015^n$; polynomial functions such as $n^5$, $n^2$, $n$, or $n^{1/2}$; and logarithmic functions, $\log n$. In general, exponential algorithms get worse more quickly than polynomial algorithms which, in turn, are worse than logarithmic algorithms.

An algorithm has time or space complexity $\Omega(f(n))$ for input size $n$ if there exist constants $n_0$ and $k$ such that the time or space of the algorithm is greater than $k * f(n)$ for all $n > n_0$. An algorithm has time or space complexity $\Theta(f(n))$ if it has complexity $O(f(n))$ and $\Omega(f(n))$. Typically, you cannot give a $\Theta(f(n))$ complexity on an algorithm, because most algorithms take different times for different inputs. Thus, when comparing algorithms, one has to specify the class of problems that will be considered.

Saying algorithm $A$ is better than $B$, using a measure of either time, space, or accuracy, could mean any one of:

- the worst case of $A$ is better than the worst case of $B$
- $A$ works better in practice, or the average case of $A$ is better than the average case of $B$, where you average over typical problems
- there is a subclass of problems for which $A$ is better than $B$, so which algorithm is better depends on the problem
- for every problem, $A$ is better than $B$.

The worst-case asymptotic complexity is often the easiest to show, but it is usually the least useful. Characterizing the subclass of problems for which one algorithm is better than another is usually the most useful, if it is easy to determine which subclass a given problem is in. Unfortunately, this characterization is usually very difficult to obtain.

Characterizing when one algorithm is better than the other can be done either theoretically using mathematics or empirically by building implementations. Theorems are only as valid as the assumptions on which they are based. Similarly, empirical investigations are only as good as the suite of test cases and the actual implementations of the algorithms. It is easy to disprove a conjecture that one algorithm is better than another for some class of problems by showing a counterexample, but it is usually much more difficult to prove such a conjecture.

- many solutions exist, perhaps with long paths, particularly for the case where nearly all paths lead to a solution, or
- the order in which the neighbors of a node are added to the stack can be tuned so that solutions are found on the first try.

It is a poor method when

- it is possible to get caught in infinite paths, which occurs when the graph is infinite or when there are cycles in the graph
- solutions exist at shallow depth, because in this case the search may explore many long paths before finding the short solutions, or
- there are multiple paths to a node, for example, on an $n \times n$ grid, where all arcs go right or down, there are exponentially many paths from the top-left node, but only $n^2$ nodes.

Depth-first search is the basis for a number of other algorithms, including iterative deepening, described next.

### 3.5.3 Iterative Deepening

Neither of the preceding methods is ideal. Breadth-first search, which guarantees that a path will be found, requires exponential space. Depth-first search may not halt on infinite graphs or graphs with cycles. One way to combine the space efficiency of depth-first search with the optimality of breadth-first search is to use **iterative deepening**. The idea is to recompute the elements of the breadth-first frontier rather than storing them. Each recomputation can be a depth-first search, which thus uses less space.

Iterative deepening repeatedly calls a **depth-bounded searcher**, a depth-first searcher that takes in an integer **depth bound** and never explores paths with more arcs than this depth bound. Iterative deepening first does a depth-first search to depth 1 by building paths of length 1 in a depth-first manner. If

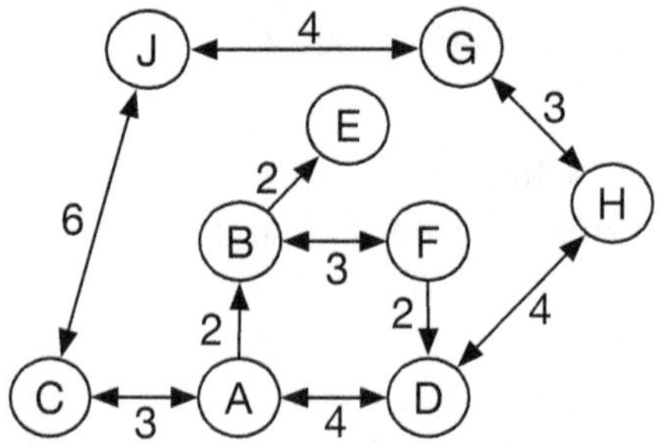


Figure 3.10: A graph, with cycles, for the delivery robot domain. Edges of the form $X \longleftrightarrow Y$ mean there is an arc from $X$ to $Y$ and an arc from $Y$ to $X$. That is, $\langle X,Y\rangle \in A$ and $\langle Y,X\rangle \in A$

that does not find a solution, it can build paths to depth 2, then depth 3, and so on until a solution is found. When a search with depth bound $n$ fails to find a solution, it can throw away all of the previous computation and start again with a bound of $n+1$. Eventually, it will find a solution if one exists, and, as it is enumerating paths in order of the number of arcs, a path with the fewest arcs will always be found first.

To ensure it halts for finite graphs, iterative deepening search needs to distinguish between

- failure because the depth bound was reached
- failure due to exhausting the search space.

In the first case, the search must be retried with a larger depth bound. In the second case, it is a waste of time to try again with a larger depth bound, because no path exists no matter what the depth, and so the whole search should fail.

Pseudocode for iterative deepening search, *ID_search*, is presented in Figure 3.11 (page 98). The local procedure *Depth_bounded_search* implements a depth-bounded depth-first search, using recursion to keep the stack, similar to Figure 3.9 (page 93), but with a limit on the length of the paths for which it is searching. It finds paths of length $k+b$, where $k$ is the path length of the given path from the start and $b$ is a non-negative integer.

The iterative deepening searcher calls *Depth_bounded_search* for increasing depth bounds. *Depth_bounded_search* only needs to check for a goal when $b = 0$, because it is only called when there are no solutions for lower bounds. *ID_search* explores the paths to goal nodes in the same order as breadth-first search, but regenerates the paths.

To ensure that iterative deepening search fails whenever breadth-first search would fail, it needs to keep track of when increasing the bound could help find an answer. A depth-bounded search **fails naturally** – it fails by exhausting the search space – if the search did not prune any paths due to the depth bound. In this case, the program can stop and report no paths. This is handled through the variable *hit_depth_bound*, which is false when *Depth_bounded_search* is called initially, and becomes true if the search is pruned due to the depth bound. If it is true at the end of a depth-bounded search, the search failed due to hitting the depth bound, and so the depth bound can be increased, and another depth-bounded search is carried out.

The obvious problem with iterative deepening is the wasted computation that occurs at each step. This, however, may not be as bad as one might think, particularly if the branching factor is high. Consider the running time of the algorithm. Assume a constant branching factor of $b > 1$. Consider the search where the bound is $k$. At depth $k$, there are $b^k$ nodes; each of these has been generated once. The nodes at depth $k-1$ have been generated twice, those at depth $k-2$ have been generated three times, and so on, and the nodes at depth 1 have been generated $k$ times. Thus, the total number of paths expanded is

$$b^k + 2b^{k-1} + 3b^{k-2} + \cdots + kb = b^k(1 + 2b^{-1} + 3b^{-2} + \cdots + kb^{1-k})$$

```
procedure ID_search(G, s, goal)
    Inputs
        G: graph with nodes N and arcs A
        s: start node
        goal: Boolean function on nodes
    Output
        path from s to a node for which goal is true
        or ⊥ if there is no such path
    Local
        hit_depth_bound: Boolean
        bound: integer
        procedure Depth_bounded_search(⟨n_0, ..., n_k⟩, b)
            Inputs
                ⟨n_0, ..., n_k⟩: path
                b: integer, b ≥ 0
            Output
                path to goal of length k + b if one exists
            if b > 0 then
                for each arc ⟨n_k, n⟩ ∈ A do
                    res := Depth_bounded_search(⟨n_0, ..., n_k, n⟩, b − 1)
                    if res ≠ ⊥ then
                        return res
            else if goal(n_k) then
                return ⟨n_0, ..., n_k⟩
            else if n_k has any neighbors then
                hit_depth_bound := true
            return ⊥
    bound := 0
    repeat
        hit_depth_bound := false
        res := Depth_bounded_search(⟨s⟩, bound)
        if res ≠ ⊥ then
            return res
        bound := bound + 1
    until not hit_depth_bound
    return ⊥
```

Figure 3.11: *ID_search*: iterative deepening search

$$< b^k \left( \sum_{i=1}^{\infty} i b^{(1-i)} \right)$$
$$= b^k \left( \frac{b}{b-1} \right)^2 .$$

Breadth-first search expands $\sum_{i=1}^{k} b^i = \left( \frac{b^{k+1}-1}{b-1} \right) = b^k \left( \frac{b}{b-1} \right) - \frac{1}{b-1}$ nodes. Thus, iterative deepening has an asymptotic overhead of $\frac{b}{(b-1)}$ times the cost of expanding the paths at depth $k$ using breadth-first search. Thus, when $b = 2$ there is an overhead factor of 2, and when $b = 3$ there is an overhead of 1.5. This algorithm is $O(b^k)$ and there cannot be an asymptotically better uninformed search strategy. Note that, if the branching factor is close to one, this analysis does not work because then the denominator would be close to zero; see Exercise 3.9 (page 125).

### 3.5.4 Lowest-Cost-First Search

For many domains, arcs have non-unit costs, and the aim is to find an **optimal solution**, a solution such that no other solution has a lower cost. For example, for a delivery robot, the cost of an arc may be resources (e.g., time, energy) required by the robot to carry out the action represented by the arc, and the aim is for the robot to solve a given goal using fewest resources. The cost for a tutoring agent (Example 3.5 (page 83)) may be the time and effort required by a student. In each of these cases, the searcher should try to minimize the cost of the path found to a goal.

The search algorithms considered thus far are not guaranteed to find the minimum-cost paths; they have not used the arc cost information at all. Breadth-first search finds a solution with the fewest arcs first, but the distribution of arc costs may be such that a path with the fewest arcs is not one of minimal cost.

The simplest search method that is guaranteed to find a minimum-cost path is **lowest-cost-first search** (also called **least-cost search** or **uniform-cost search**), which is similar to breadth-first search, but instead of expanding a path with the fewest number of arcs, it selects a path with the lowest cost. This is implemented by treating the frontier as a priority queue ordered by the *cost* function (page 84).

**Example 3.13** Consider lowest-cost-first search from $A$ to $F$ in the running example of the delivery graph given in Figure 3.3 (page 85). In this example, paths are shown with a subscript showing the cost of the path. The frontier is shown as a list of paths in order of cost.

Initially, the frontier is $[\langle A \rangle_0]$. At the next stage it is $[\langle A, B \rangle_2, \langle A, C \rangle_3, \langle A, D \rangle_4]$. The path $\langle A, B \rangle$ is expanded, with the resulting frontier

$$[\langle A, C \rangle_3, \langle A, B, E \rangle_4, \langle A, D \rangle_4 \, \langle A, B, F \rangle_5].$$

The path $\langle A, C \rangle$ is then expanded, resulting in the frontier

$$[\langle A, B, E \rangle_4, \langle A, D \rangle_4 \, \langle A, B, F \rangle_5, \langle A, C, J \rangle_{10}].$$

Next, the path $\langle A,B,E\rangle$ is expanded. $E$ has no neighbors, so the path is removed. Next, the path $\langle A,D\rangle$ is expanded, resulting in the frontier

$$[\langle A,B,F\rangle_5, \langle A,D,H\rangle_8, \langle A,C,J\rangle_{10}].$$

Then the path to $\langle A,B,F\rangle$ is expanded, resulting in the frontier

$$[\langle A,B,F,D\rangle_7, \langle A,D,H\rangle_8, \langle A,C,J\rangle_{10}].$$

Then the path $\langle A,B,F,D\rangle$ is expanded, and the resulting frontier is

$$[\langle A,D,H\rangle_8, \langle A,C,J\rangle_{10}, \langle A,B,F,D,H\rangle_{11}].$$

The path $\langle A,D,H\rangle$ is expanded, giving

$$[\langle A,C,J\rangle_{10}, \langle A,D,H,G\rangle_{11}, \langle A,C,F,D,H\rangle_{11}].$$

The path $\langle A,C,J\rangle_{10}$ is expanded, and then, depending on the order that ties are broken, the path $\langle A,D,H,G\rangle$ is selected and returned as the solution, either next or the step after.

If the costs of the arcs are all greater than a positive constant, known as **bounded arc costs**, and the branching factor is finite, the lowest-cost-first search is guaranteed to find an optimal solution – a solution with lowest path cost – if a solution exists. Moreover, the first path to a goal that is expanded is a path with lowest cost. Such a solution is optimal, because the algorithm expands paths from the start node in order of path cost, and the path costs never decrease as arc costs are positive. If a better path to a goal existed than the first solution found, it would have been expanded from the frontier earlier.

The bounded arc cost is used to guarantee the lowest-cost search will find a solution, when one exists, in graphs with finite branching factor. Without such a bound there can be infinite paths with a finite cost. For example, there could be nodes $n_0, n_1, n_2, \ldots$ with an arc $\langle n_{i-1}, n_i\rangle$ for each $i > 0$ with cost $1/2^i$. Infinitely many paths of the form $\langle n_0, n_1, n_2, \ldots, n_k\rangle$ all have a cost of less than 1. If there is an arc from $n_0$ to a goal node with a cost equal to 1, it will never be selected. This is the basis of **Zeno's paradox** that Aristotle wrote about more than 2300 years ago.

Suppose that all arc costs are greater than or equal to $\epsilon > 0$. Let $b$ be the maximum branching factor, $c$ the cost of a lowest-cost path to a goal, and $k = c/\epsilon$. $k$ is the maximum number of steps in a path that need to be considered in the search before finding a goal. In the worst case, the complexity for both space and time is $O(kb^k)$, as there may need to be $b^k$ paths explored where each path is of length $k$. It generates *all* paths from the start that have a cost less than the cost of a solution, and some of the paths that are of the cost of a solution, until it finds a path that is a solution.

## 3.6 Informed (Heuristic) Search

The search methods in the preceding section are **uninformed** in that they do not take the goal into account until they expand a path that leads to a goal node. Heuristic information about which nodes are most promising can guide the search by changing which node is selected in line 13 of the generic search algorithm in Figure 3.5 (page 88).

A **heuristic function** $h(n)$ takes a node $n$ and returns a non-negative real number that is an estimate of the cost of the least-cost path from node $n$ to a goal node. The function $h(n)$ is an **admissible heuristic** if $h(n)$ is always less than or equal to the actual cost of a lowest-cost path from node $n$ to a goal.

There is nothing magical about a heuristic function. It must use only information that can be readily obtained about a node. Typically there is a trade-off between the amount of work it takes to compute a heuristic value for a node and the accuracy of the heuristic value.

A standard way to derive a heuristic function is to solve a simpler problem and to use the cost to the goal in the simplified problem as the heuristic function of the original problem (see Section 3.6.3, page 108).

**Example 3.14** For the graph of Figure 3.3 (page 85), if the cost is the distance, the straight-line distance between the node and its closest goal can be used as the heuristic function.

The examples that follow assume the following heuristic function for the goal $G$:

$$\begin{aligned} h(A) &= 7 & h(B) &= 5 & h(C) &= 9 \\ h(D) &= 6 & h(E) &= 3 & h(F) &= 5 \\ h(G) &= 0 & h(H) &= 3 & h(J) &= 4. \end{aligned}$$

This $h$ function is an admissible heuristic because the $h$ value is less than or equal to the exact cost of a lowest-cost path from the node to a goal. It is the exact cost for node $H$. It is very much an underestimate of the cost to the goal for node $B$, which seems to be close, but there is only a long route to the goal. It is very misleading for $E$, which also seems close to the goal, but it has no path to the goal.

The $h$ function can be extended to be applicable to paths by making the heuristic value of a path equal to the heuristic value of the node at the end of the path. That is:

$$h(\langle n_o, \ldots, n_k \rangle) = h(n_k).$$

A simple use of a heuristic function in depth-first search is to order the neighbors that are added to the stack representing the frontier. The neighbors can be added to the frontier so that the best neighbor is selected first. This is known as **heuristic depth-first search**. This search selects the locally best path, but it explores all paths from the selected path before it selects another path.

Although it is often used, it suffers from the problems of depth-first search, is not guaranteed to find a solution, and may not find an optimal solution.

Another way to use a heuristic function is to always select a path on the frontier with the lowest heuristic value. This is called **greedy best-first search**. This method is not guaranteed to find a solution when there is one.

**Example 3.15** Consider the graph shown in Figure 3.12, where the heuristic value to $G$ is shown for each node. The arc costs are ignored and so are not shown. The aim is to find the shortest path from $A$ to $G$. A heuristic depth-first search and greedy best-first search will cycle forever in the nodes $B$, $E$, $F$ and will never terminate. Even if one could detect the cycles, it is possible to have a similar graph with infinitely many nodes connected, all with a heuristic value less that 6, which would still be problematic for heuristic depth-first search and greedy best-first search.

## 3.6.1 $A^*$ Search

$A^*$ **search** finds a least-cost path and can exploit heuristic information to improve the search. It uses both path cost, as in lowest-cost-first, and a heuristic function, as in greedy best-first search, in its selection of which path to expand. For each path $p$ on the frontier, $A^*$ uses an estimate of the total path cost from the start node to a goal node that follows $p$ then goes to a goal. It uses $cost(p)$, the cost of the path found, as well as the heuristic function $h(p)$, the estimated path cost from the end of $p$ to the goal.

For any path $p$ on the frontier, define $f(p) = cost(p) + h(p)$. This is an estimate of the total path cost to follow path $p$ then go to a goal node. If $n$ is the

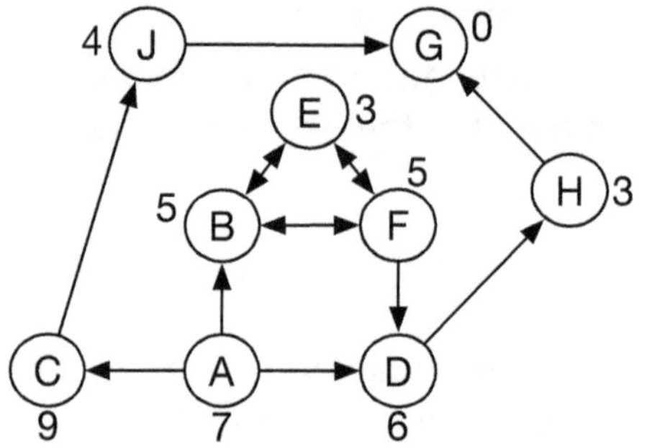


Figure 3.12: A graph with heuristic values that is bad for greedy best-first search

node at the end of path $p$, this can be depicted as

$$\underbrace{\underbrace{start \xrightarrow{\text{actual}} n}_{cost(p)} \underbrace{\xrightarrow{\text{estimate}} goal.}_{h(n)}}_{f(p)}$$

If $h(n)$ is an admissible heuristic (page 101) and so never overestimates the cost from node $n$ to a goal node, then $f(p)$ does not overestimate the path cost of going from the start node to a goal node via $p$.

$A^*$ is implemented using the generic search algorithm (page 88), treating the frontier as a priority queue ordered by $f(p)$.

**Example 3.16** Consider using $A^*$ search for the graph of Figure 3.3 (page 85) using the heuristic function of Example 3.14 (page 101), shown in Figure 3.13.

In this example, the paths on the frontier are shown using the final node of the path, subscripted with the $f$-value of the path. The frontier is initially $[\langle A\rangle_7]$, because $h(A) = 7$ and the cost of the path is zero. It is replaced by its neighbors, forming the frontier

$$[\langle A,B\rangle_7, \langle A,D\rangle_{10}, \langle A,C\rangle_{12}].$$

The first element of the frontier has $f(\langle A,B\rangle) = cost(\langle A,B\rangle) + h(B) = 2+5 = 7$. Because it has the lowest $f$-value, $\langle A,B\rangle$ is expanded, forming the frontier

$$[\langle A,B,E\rangle_7, \langle A,B,F\rangle_{10}, \langle A,D\rangle_{10}, \langle A,C\rangle_{12}].$$

The path to $E$ is selected, but $E$ has no neighbors, so the path is removed. Then there are two paths with the same $f$-value of 10. The algorithm does not specify which is selected. Suppose it expands the path to the node with the smallest heuristic value (see Exercise 3.6 (page 124)), which is the path to $F$. The resulting frontier is

$$[\langle A,D\rangle_{10}, \langle A,C\rangle_{12}, \langle A,B,F,D\rangle_{13}].$$

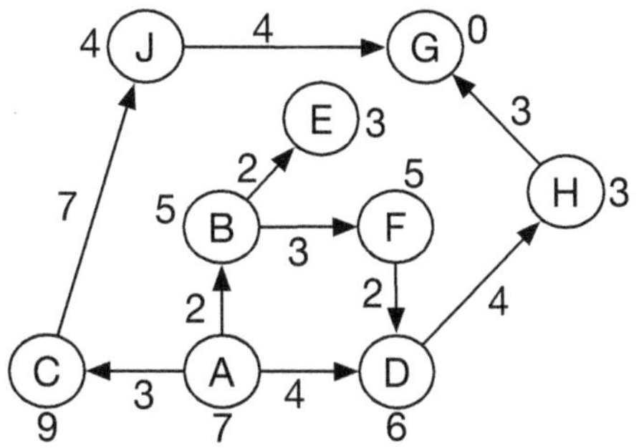


Figure 3.13: Delivery graph with arc costs and heuristic value of nodes

Then the path to $D$ is expanded, forming

$$[\langle A,D,H\rangle_{11}, \langle A,C\rangle_{12}, \langle A,B,F,D\rangle_{13}].$$

Next the path to $H$ is expanded, forming the frontier

$$[\langle A,D,H,G\rangle_{11}, \langle A,C\rangle_{12}, \langle A,B,F,D\rangle_{13}].$$

The path $\langle A,D,H,G\rangle$ is returned, as the shortest path to a goal with a cost of 11.

Notice how the path to $C$ was never selected. There could have been a huge network leading from $C$ which would never have been explored, as $A^*$ recognized that any such path could not be optimal.

**Example 3.17** Consider Figure 3.12 (page 102) with cycles. This was problematic for greedy best-first search that ignores path costs. Although $A^*$ initially searches through $E$, $B$, and $F$, eventually the cost of the path becomes so large that it selects the optimal path via $D$ and $H$.

A search algorithm is **admissible** if, whenever a solution exists, it returns an optimal solution. To guarantee admissibility, some conditions on the graph and the heuristic must hold. The following theorem gives sufficient conditions for $A^*$ to be admissible.

**Proposition 3.1.** *($A^*$ admissibility) If there is a solution, $A^*$ using heuristic function $h$ always returns an optimal solution if:*

- *the branching factor is bounded above by some number $b$ (each node has $b$ or fewer neighbors)*
- *all arc costs are greater than some $\epsilon > 0$*
- *$h$ is an* ***admissible heuristic*** *(page 101), which means that $h(n)$ is less than or equal to the actual cost of the lowest-cost path from node $n$ to a goal node.*

*Proof.* **Part A:** *A solution will be found.* If the arc costs are all greater than some $\epsilon > 0$, the costs are **bounded above zero**. If this holds and with a finite branching factor, eventually, for all paths $p$ in the frontier, $cost(p)$ will exceed any finite number and, thus, will exceed a solution cost if one exists (with each path having no greater than $c/\epsilon$ arcs, where $c$ is the cost of an optimal solution). Because the branching factor is finite, only a finite number of paths must be expanded before the search could get to this point, but the $A^*$ search would have found a solution by then. Bounding the arc costs above zero is a sufficient condition for $A^*$ to avoid suffering from Zeno's paradox (page 100), as described for lowest-cost-first search.

**Part B:** *The first path to a goal selected is an optimal path.* $h$ is admissible implies the $f$-value of a node on an optimal solution path is less than or equal to the cost of an optimal solution, which, by the definition of optimal, is less than the cost for any non-optimal solution. The $f$-value of a solution is equal to the cost of the solution if the heuristic is admissible. Because an element with minimum $f$-value is selected at each step, a non-optimal solution can never be selected while there is a path on the frontier that leads to an optimal solution. So, before it can select a non-optimal solution, $A^*$ will have to pick all of the nodes on an optimal path, including an optimal solution. □

It should be noted that the admissibility of $A^*$ does not ensure that every intermediate node selected from the frontier is on an optimal path from the start node to a goal node. Admissibility ensures that the first solution found will be optimal even in graphs with cycles. It does not ensure that the algorithm will not change its mind about which partial path is the best while it is searching.

To see how the heuristic function improves the efficiency of $A^*$, suppose $c$ is the cost of a least-cost path from the start node to a goal node. $A^*$, with an admissible heuristic, expands all paths from the start node in the set

$$\{p : cost(p) + h(p) < c\}$$

and some of the paths in the set

$$\{p : cost(p) + h(p) = c\}.$$

Increasing $h$ while keeping it admissible can help reduce the size of the first of these sets. Admissibility means that if a path $p$ is in the first set, then so are all of the initial parts of $p$, which means they will all be expanded. If the second set is large, there can be a great variability in the space and time of $A^*$. The space and time can be sensitive to the tie-breaking mechanism for selecting a path from those with the same $f$-value. It could, for example, select a path with minimal $h$-value or use a first-in, last-out protocol (the same as a depth-first search) for these paths; see Exercise 3.6 (page 124).

### 3.6.2 Branch and Bound

**Depth-first branch-and-bound search** is a way to combine the space saving of depth-first search with heuristic information for finding optimal paths. It is particularly applicable when there are many paths to a goal. As in $A^*$ search, the heuristic function $h(n)$ is non-negative and less than or equal to the cost of a lowest-cost path from $n$ to a goal node.

The idea of a branch-and-bound search is to maintain the lowest-cost path to a goal found so far, and its cost. Suppose this cost is *bound*. If the search encounters a path $p$ such that $cost(p) + h(p) \geq bound$, path $p$ can be pruned. If a non-pruned path to a goal is found, it must be better than the previous best path. This new solution is remembered and *bound* is reduced to the cost of this new solution. The searcher then proceeds to search for a better solution.

Once it has found one solution, branch-and-bound search generates a sequence of ever-improving solutions. The final solution found is the optimal solution.

Branch-and-bound search is typically used with depth-first search, where the space saving of the depth-first search can be achieved. It can be implemented similarly to depth-bounded search, but where the bound is in terms of path cost and reduces as shorter paths are found. The algorithm remembers the lowest-cost path found and returns this path when the search finishes.

The algorithm is shown in Figure 3.14. The internal procedure *cbsearch*, for cost-bounded search, uses the global variables to provide information to the main procedure.

Initially, *bound* can be set to infinity, but it is often useful to set it to an overestimate, $bound_0$, of the path cost of an optimal solution. This algorithm will return an optimal solution – a lowest-cost path from the start node to a goal node – if there is a solution with cost less than the initial bound $bound_0$.

If the initial bound is slightly above the cost of a lowest-cost path, this algorithm can find an optimal path expanding no more arcs than $A^*$ search. How-

```
procedure DF_branch_and_bound(G, s, goal, h, bound0)
    Inputs
        G: graph with nodes N and arcs A
        s: start node
        goal: Boolean function on nodes
        h: heuristic function on nodes
        bound0: initial depth bound (can be ∞ if not specified)
    Output
        a lowest-cost path from s to a goal node if there is a solution with cost less than bound0
        or ⊥ if there is no solution with cost less than bound0
    Local
        best_path: path or ⊥
        bound: non-negative real
        procedure cbsearch(⟨n0, ..., nk⟩)
            if cost(⟨n0, ..., nk⟩) + h(nk) < bound then
                if goal(nk) then
                    best_path := ⟨n0, ..., nk⟩
                    bound := cost(⟨n0, ..., nk⟩)
                else
                    for each arc ⟨nk, n⟩ ∈ A do
                        cbsearch(⟨n0, ..., nk, n⟩)
    best_path := ⊥
    bound := bound0
    cbsearch(⟨s⟩)
    return best_path
```

Figure 3.14: Depth-first branch-and-bound search

ever, it is rare to know the cost of a lowest-cost path. In general, once it has found an optimal path to the goal, it only explores paths whose $f$-value is lower than the optimal path. These are exactly the paths that $A^*$ explores to find one solution.

If it returns $\perp$ when $bound_0 = \infty$, there are no solutions. If it returns $\perp$ when $bound_0$ is some finite value, it means no solution exists with cost less than $bound_0$. This algorithm can be combined with iterative deepening to increase the bound until either a solution is found or it can show there is no solution, using a method similar to the use of *hit_depth_bound* in Figure 3.11 (page 98). See Exercise 3.11 (page 125).

**Example 3.18** Consider the tree-shaped graph in Figure 3.15. The goal nodes are shaded. Suppose that each arc has cost 1, and there is no heuristic information (i.e., $h(n) = 0$ for each node $n$). In the algorithm, suppose $bound_0 = \infty$ and the depth-first search always selects the leftmost child first. This figure shows the order in which the nodes are checked to determine if they are a goal node. The nodes that are not numbered are not checked for being a goal node.

The subtree under the node numbered "5" does not have a goal and is explored fully (or up to depth $bound_0$ if it had a finite value). The ninth node checked is a goal node. It has a path cost of 5, and so the bound is set to 5. From then on, only paths with a cost of less than 5 are checked for being a solution. The fifteenth node checked is also a goal. It has a path cost of 3, and so the bound is reduced to 3. There are no other goal nodes found, and so the path to the node labeled 15 is returned. It is an optimal path. Another optimal path is pruned; the algorithm never checks the children of the node labeled 18.

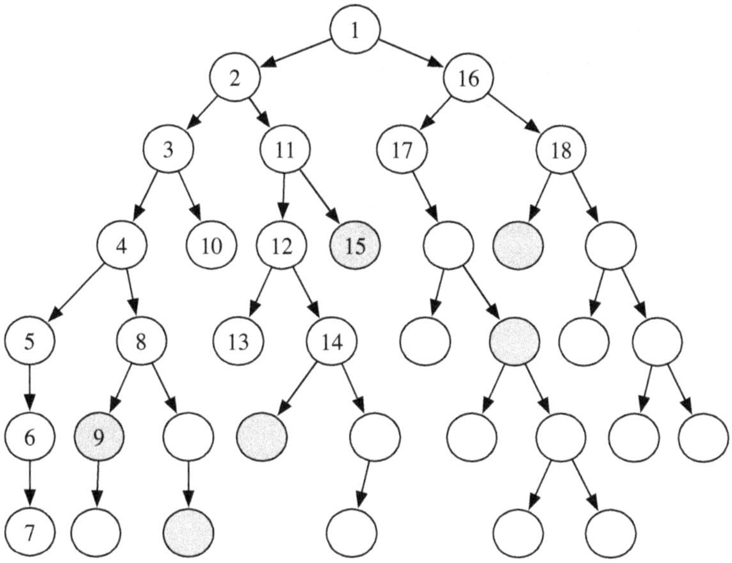


Figure 3.15: The paths expanded in depth-first branch-and-bound search. The shaded nodes are goal nodes

If there were heuristic information, it could also be used to prune parts of the search space, as in $A^*$ search.

### 3.6.3 Designing a Heuristic Function

An **admissible heuristic** (page 101) is a non-negative function $h$ of nodes, where $h(n)$ is never greater than the actual cost of the shortest path from node $n$ to a goal. The standard way to construct a heuristic function is to find a solution to a simpler problem, one with fewer states or fewer constraints. A problem with fewer constraints is often easier to solve (and sometimes trivial to solve). An optimal solution to the simpler problem cannot have a higher cost than an optimal solution to the full problem because any solution to the full problem is a solution to the simpler problem.

In many spatial problems where the cost is distance and the solution is constrained to go via predefined arcs (e.g., road segments), the straight-line Euclidean distance between two nodes is an admissible heuristic because it is the solution to the simpler problem where the agent is not constrained to go via the arcs.

For many problems one can design a better heuristic function, as in the following examples.

**Example 3.19** Consider the delivery robot of Example 3.4 (page 83), where the state space includes the parcels to be delivered. Suppose the cost function is the total distance traveled by the robot to deliver all the parcels. If the robot could carry multiple parcels, one possible heuristic function is the maximum of (a) and (b):

(a) the maximum delivery distance for any of the parcels that are not at their destination and not being carried, where the delivery distance of a parcel is the distance to that parcel's location plus the distance from that parcel's location to its destination

(b) the distance to the furthest destination for the parcels being carried.

This is not an overestimate because it is a solution to the simpler problem which is to ignore that it cannot travel though walls, and to ignore all but the most difficult parcel. Note that a maximum is appropriate here because the agent has to both deliver the parcels it is carrying and go to the parcels it is not carrying and deliver them to their destinations.

If the robot could only carry one parcel, one possible heuristic function is the sum of the distances that the parcels must be carried plus the distance to the closest parcel. Note that the reference to the closest parcel does not imply that the robot will deliver the closest parcel first, but is needed to guarantee that the heuristic is admissible.

**Example 3.20** In the route planning of Example 3.1 (page 79), when minimizing time, a heuristic could use the straight-line distance from the current location to the goal divided by the maximum speed – assuming the user could drive straight to the destination at top speed.

A more sophisticated heuristic may take into account the different maximum speeds on highways and local roads. One admissible heuristic is the minimum of (a) and (b):

(a) the estimated minimum time required to drive straight to the destination on slower local roads

(b) the minimum time required to drive to a highway on slow roads, then drive on highways to a location close to the destination, then drive on local roads to the destination.

The minimum is appropriate here because the agent can go via highways or local roads, whichever is quicker.

In the above examples, determining the heuristic did not involve search. Once the problem is simplified, it could be solved using search, which should be simpler than the original problem. The simpler search problem typically needs to be solved multiple times, even perhaps for all nodes. It is often useful to cache these results into a **pattern database** that maps the nodes of the simpler problem into the heuristic value. In the simpler abstract problem, there are often fewer nodes, with multiple original nodes mapped into a single node in the simplified graph, which can make storing the heuristic value for each of these nodes feasible.

# 3.7 Pruning the Search Space

The preceding algorithms can be improved by taking into account multiple paths to a node. The following presents two pruning strategies. The simplest strategy is to prune cycles; if the goal is to find a least-cost path, it is useless to consider paths with cycles. The other strategy is only ever to consider one path to a node and to prune other paths to that node.

## 3.7.1 Cycle Pruning

A graph representing a search space may include cycles. For example, in the robot delivery domain of Figure 3.10 (page 96), the robot can go back and forth between nodes $B$ and $F$. Some of the search methods presented so far can get trapped in cycles, continuously repeating the cycle and never finding an answer even in finite graphs. The other methods can loop through cycles, wasting time, but eventually still find a solution.

A simple method of pruning the search, while guaranteeing that a solution will be found in a finite graph, is to ensure that the algorithm does not consider neighbors that are already on the path from the start. **Cycle pruning**, or **loop pruning**, checks whether the last node on the path already appears earlier on the path from the start node to that node. A path $\langle n_0, \ldots, n_k, n\rangle$, where $n \in$

$\{n_0, \ldots, n_k\}$, is not added to the frontier at line 16 of Figure 3.5 (page 88) or is discarded when removed from the frontier.

The computational complexity of cycle pruning depends on which search method is used. For depth-first methods, the overhead can be as low as a constant factor, by storing the elements of the current path as a set (e.g., by maintaining a bit that is set when the node is in the path, or using a hash function). For the search strategies that maintain multiple paths – namely, all of those with exponential space in Figure 3.18 (page 114) – cycle pruning takes time linear in the length of the path being searched. These algorithms cannot do better than searching up the partial path being considered, checking to ensure they do not add a node that already appears in the path.

### 3.7.2 Multiple-Path Pruning

There is often more than one path to a node. If only one path is required, a search algorithm can prune from the frontier any path that leads to a node to which it has already found a path.

**Multiple-path pruning** is implemented by maintaining an **explored set** (traditionally called the **closed list**) of nodes that are at the end of paths that have been expanded. The explored set is initially empty. When a path $\langle n_0, \ldots, n_k \rangle$ is selected, if $n_k$ is already in the explored set, the path can be discarded. Otherwise, $n_k$ is added to the explored set, and the algorithm proceeds as before. See Figure 3.16 (page 111).

This approach does not necessarily guarantee that the least-cost path is not discarded. Something more sophisticated may have to be done to guarantee that an optimal solution is found. To ensure that the search algorithm can still find a lowest-cost path to a goal, one of the following can be done:

- Make sure that the first path found to any node is a lowest-cost path to that node, then prune all subsequent paths found to that node.
- If the search algorithm finds a lower-cost path to a node than one already found, it could remove all paths that used the higher-cost path to the node (because these cannot be on an optimal solution). That is, if there is a path $p$ on the frontier $\langle s, \ldots, n, \ldots, m \rangle$, and a path $p'$ to $n$ is found that has a lower cost than the portion of the path from $s$ to $n$ in $p$, then $p$ can be removed from the frontier.
- Whenever the search finds a lower-cost path to a node than a path to that node already found, it could incorporate a new initial section on the paths that have extended the initial path. Thus, if there is a path $p = \langle s, \ldots, n, \ldots, m \rangle$ on the frontier, and a path $p'$ to $n$ is found with a cost lower than the portion of $p$ from $s$ to $n$, then $p'$ can replace the initial part of $p$ to $n$.

The first of these alternatives allows the use of the explored set without losing the ability to find an optimal path. The others require more sophisticated algorithms.

In lowest-cost-first search, the first path found to a node (i.e., when the node is selected from the frontier) is the lowest-cost path to the node. Pruning subsequent paths to that node cannot remove a lower-cost path to that node, and thus pruning subsequent paths to each node still enables an optimal solution to be found.

$A^*$ (page 102) does not guarantee that when a path to a node is selected for the first time it is the lowest-cost path to that node. Note that the admissibility theorem guarantees this for every path to a *goal* node but not for every path to any node. Whether it holds for all nodes depends on properties of the heuristic function.

A **consistent heuristic** is a non-negative function $h(n)$ on nodes, such that $h(n) \leq cost(n, n') + h(n')$ for any two nodes $n'$ and $n$, where $cost(n, n')$ is the cost of the least-cost path from $n$ to $n'$. As $h(g) = 0$ for any goal $g$, a consistent heuristic is never an overestimate of the cost of going from a node $n$ to a goal.

Consistency can be guaranteed if the heuristic function satisfies the **monotone restriction**: $h(n) \leq cost(n, n') + h(n')$ for any arc $\langle n, n' \rangle$. It is easier to check the monotone restriction as it only depends on the arcs, whereas consistency depends on all pairs of nodes.

```
procedure SearchMPP(G, S, goal)
    Inputs
        G: graph with nodes N and arcs A
        s: start node
        goal: Boolean function of nodes
    Output
        path from s to a node for which goal is true
        or ⊥ if there are no solution paths
    Local
        frontier: set of paths
        explored: set of explored nodes
    frontier := {⟨s⟩}
    explored := {}
    while frontier ≠ {} do
        select and remove ⟨n0, ..., nk⟩ from frontier
        if nk ∉ explored then
            explored := explored ∪ {nk}
            if goal(nk) then
                return ⟨n0, ..., nk⟩
            frontier := frontier ∪ {⟨n0, ..., nk, n⟩ : ⟨nk, n⟩ ∈ A}
    return ⊥
```

Figure 3.16: SearchMPP: graph searching with multiple-path pruning

Consistency and the monotone restriction can be understood in terms of the **triangle inequality**, which specifies that the length of any side of a triangle cannot be greater than the sum of lengths of the other two sides. In consistency, the estimated cost of going from $n$ to a goal should not be more than the estimated cost of first going to $n'$ then to a goal (see Figure 3.17).

**Euclidean distance** – the straight-line distance in a multidimensional space – satisfies the triangle inequality. Therefore, when the cost function is the Euclidean distance, the heuristic function $h(n)$ that is the shortest distance between node $n$ and a goal satisfies the monotone restriction and so is consistent. A heuristic function that is a solution to a simplified problem that has shorter solutions also typically satisfies the monotone restriction and so is consistent.

With the monotone restriction, the $f$-values of the paths selected from the frontier are monotonically non-decreasing. That is, when the frontier is expanded, the $f$-values do not get smaller.

**Proposition 3.2.** *With a consistent heuristic, multiple-path pruning can never prevent $A^*$ search from finding an optimal solution.*

That is, under the conditions of Proposition 3.1 (page 104), which guarantee $A^*$ finds an optimal solution, if the heuristic function is consistent, $A^*$ with multiple-path pruning will always find an optimal solution.

*Proof.* The gist of the proof is to show that if the heuristic is consistent, when $A^*$ expands a path $p'$ to a node $n'$, no other path to $n'$ can have a lower cost than $p'$. Thus, the algorithm can prune subsequent paths to any node and will still find an optimal solution.

Let's use a proof by contradiction. Suppose the algorithm has selected a path $p'$ to node $n'$ for expansion, but there exists a lower-cost path to node $n'$, which it has not found yet. Then there must be a path $p$ on the frontier that is the initial part of the lower-cost path to $n'$. Suppose path $p$ ends at node $n$. It must be that $f(p') \leq f(p)$, because $p'$ was selected before $p$. This means that

$$cost(p') + h(p') \leq cost(p) + h(p).$$

If the path to $n'$ via $p$ has a lower cost than the path $p'$, then

$$cost(p) + cost(n, n') < cost(p')$$

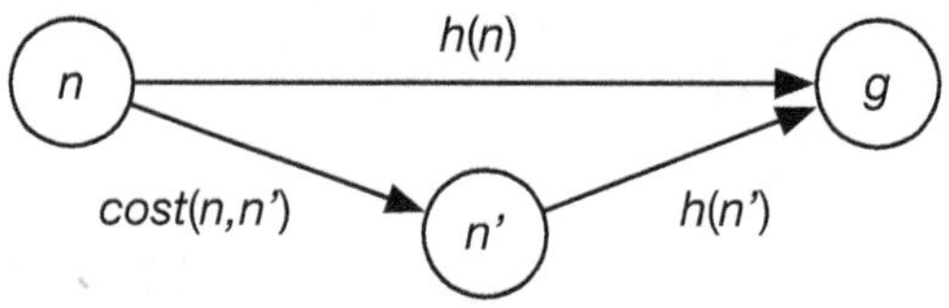


Figure 3.17: Triangle inequality: $h(n) \leq cost(n, n') + h(n')$

where $cost(n, n')$ is the actual cost of a lowest-cost path from node $n$ to $n'$. From these two equations, it follows that

$$cost(n, n') < cost(p') - cost(p) \leq h(p) - h(p') = h(n) - h(n')$$

where the last inequality follows because $h(p)$ is defined to be $h(n)$. This cannot happen if $h(n) - h(n') \leq cost(n, n')$, which is the consistency condition. □

$A^*$ **search** in practice includes multiple-path pruning; if $A^*$ is used without multiple-path pruning, the lack of pruning should be made explicit. It is up to the designer of a heuristic function to ensure that the heuristic is consistent, and so an optimal path will be found.

Multiple-path pruning subsumes cycle pruning, because a cycle is another path to a node and is therefore pruned. Multiple-path pruning can be done in constant time, by setting a bit on each node to which a path has been found if the graph is explicitly stored, or using a hash function. Multiple-path pruning is preferred over cycle pruning for breadth-first methods where virtually all of the nodes considered have to be stored anyway.

Depth-first search does not have to store all of the nodes at the end of paths already expanded; storing them in order to implement multiple-path pruning makes depth-first search exponential in space. For this reason, cycle pruning is preferred over multiple-path pruning for algorithms based on depth-first search, including depth-first branch and bound. It is possible to have a bounded size explored set, for example, by only keeping the newest elements, which enables some pruning without the space explosion.

### 3.7.3 Summary of Search Strategies

Figure 3.18 (page 114) summarizes the search strategies presented so far.

Lowest-cost-first, $A^*$, and depth-first branch-and-bound searches are guaranteed to find a lowest-cost solution, as long as the conditions of Proposition 3.1 (page 104) hold, even if the graph is infinite. Breadth-first search and iterative deepening will find a path with the fewest arcs as long as each node has a finite branching factor. Depth-first search and greedy best-first searches, when the graph is infinite or when there is no cycle pruning or multiple path pruning, sometimes do not halt, even if a solution exists.

A search algorithm is **complete** if it is guaranteed to find a solution if there is one. Those search strategies that are guaranteed to find a path with fewest arcs or the least cost are complete. They have worst-case time complexity which increases exponentially with the number of arcs on the paths explored. There can only be algorithms that are complete but better than exponential time complexity if $P = NP$ (page 89), which is not expected to be true. The algorithms that are not guaranteed to halt (depth-first and greedy best-first) have an infinite worst-case time complexity.

Depth-first search uses linear space with respect to the length of the longest path explored, but is not guaranteed to find a solution even if one exists. Breadth-first, lowest-cost-first, and $A^*$ may be exponential in both space and time, but are guaranteed to find a solution if one exists, even if the graph is infinite as long as there are finite branching factors and arc costs are bounded above zero. Iterative deepening reduces the space complexity at the cost of recomputing the elements on the frontier. Depth-first branch and bound (DF B&B) reduces the space complexity, but can search more of the space or fail to find a solution, depending on the initial bound.

## 3.8 Search Refinements

A number of refinements can be made to the preceding strategies. The direction of search – searching from the start to a goal or from a goal to the start – can make a difference in efficiency. Backward search can be used to find policies that give an optimal path from any position, and can be used to improve a heuristic function.

| Strategy | Selection from frontier | Path found | Space |
|---|---|---|---|
| Breadth-first | First node added | Fewest arcs | $O(b^d)$ |
| Depth-first | Last node added | ✘ | $O(bd)$ |
| Iterative deepening | N/A | Fewest arcs | $O(bd)$ |
| Greedy best-first | Minimal $h(p)$ | ✘ | $O(b^d)$ |
| Lowest-cost-first | Minimal $cost(p)$ | Least cost | $O(b^d)$ |
| $A^*$ | Minimal $cost(p) + h(p)$ | Least cost | $O(b^d)$ |
| DF B&B | N/A | Least cost | $O(bd)$ |

"Selection from frontier" refers to which element is selected in line 13 of the generic graph-searching algorithm of Figure 3.5 (page 88). Iterative deepening and depth-first branch and bound (DF B&B) are not instances of the generic search algorithm, and so the selection from the frontier is not applicable.

"Path found" refers to guarantees about the path found (for graphs with finite branching factor and arc costs bounded above zero). "✘" means the strategy is not guaranteed to find a path. Depth-first branch and bound (DF B&B) requires an initial finite bound that is greater than the cost of a least-cost solution.

"Space" refers to the worst-case space complexity; $d$, the depth, is the maximum number of arcs in a path expanded before a solution is found, and $b$ is a bound on the branching factor.

Figure 3.18: Summary of search strategies

### 3.8.1 Direction of Search

The size of the search space of the generic search algorithm, for a given pruning strategy, depends on the path length and the branching factor. Anything that can be done to reduce these can potentially give great savings. Sometimes it is possible to search backwards from a goal, which can be useful, particularly when it reduces the branching factor.

If the following conditions hold:

- the set of goal nodes, $\{n : goal(n)\}$, is finite and can be generated
- for any node $n$ the neighbors of $n$ in the **inverse graph**, namely $\{n' : \langle n', n \rangle \in A\}$, can be generated

then the graph-search algorithm can either begin with the start node and search forward for a goal node, or begin with a goal node and search backward for the start node. In many applications, the set of goal nodes, or the inverse graph, cannot easily be generated so backwards search may not be feasible; sometimes the purpose of the search is to just find a goal node and not the path to it.

In **backward search**, what was the start becomes the goal, and what was the goal becomes the start. If there is a single goal node, it can be used as the start node for backward search. If there can be multiple goal nodes, a new node, *goal*, is created, which becomes the start node of the backward search. The neighbors of *goal* in the backward graph are nodes $\{n : goal(n)\}$. The neighbors of the nodes, apart from *goal*, are given in the inverse graph. The goal of the backward search is the start node of the forward search.

**Forward search** searches from the start node to the goal nodes in the original graph.

For those cases where the goal nodes and the inverse graph can be generated, it may be more efficient to search in one direction than in the other. The size of the search space is typically exponential in the branching factor. It is often the case that forward and backward searches have different branching factors. A general principle is to search in the direction that has the smaller branching factor.

#### Bidirectional Search

The idea of **bidirectional search** is to search forwards from the start and backwards from the goal simultaneously. When the two search frontiers intersect, the algorithm needs to construct a single path that extends from the start node through the frontier intersection to a goal node. It is a challenge to guarantee that the path found is optimal.

A new problem arises during a bidirectional search, namely ensuring that the two search frontiers actually meet. For example, a depth-first search in both directions is not likely to work at all unless one is extremely lucky because its small search frontiers are likely to pass each other by. Breadth-first search in both directions would be guaranteed to meet.

A combination of depth-first search in one direction and breadth-first search in the other would guarantee the required intersection of the search frontiers, but the choice of which to apply in which direction may be difficult. The decision depends on the cost of saving the breadth-first frontier and searching it to check when the depth-first method will intersect one of its elements.

There are situations where a bidirectional search results in substantial savings. For example, if the forward and backward branching factors of the search space are both $b$, and the goal is at depth $k$, then breadth-first search will take time proportional to $b^k$, whereas a symmetric bidirectional search will take time proportional to $2b^{k/2}$, assuming the time overhead of determining intersection is negligible. This is an exponential saving in time, even though the time complexity is still exponential.

### Island-Driven Search

One of the ways that search may be made more efficient is to identify a limited number of places where the forward search and backward search could meet. For example, in searching for a path from two rooms on different floors, it may be appropriate to constrain the search to first go to the elevator on one level, go to the appropriate level, and then go from the elevator to the goal room. Intuitively, these designated positions are **islands** in the search graph, which are constrained to be on a solution path from the start node to a goal node.

When islands are specified, an agent can decompose the search problem into several search problems; for example, one from the initial room to the elevator, one from the elevator on one level to the elevator on the other level, and one from the elevator to the destination room. This reduces the search space by having three simpler problems to solve. Having smaller problems helps to reduce the combinatorial explosion of large searches and is an example of how extra knowledge about a problem is used to improve the efficiency of search.

To find a path between $s$ and $g$ using islands:

- identify a set of islands $i_0, \ldots, i_k$
- find paths from $s$ to $i_0$, from $i_{j-1}$ to $i_j$ for each $j$, and from $i_k$ to $g$.

Each of these search problems should be correspondingly simpler than the general problem and, therefore, easier to solve.

The identification of islands can be done by finding small **cut-sets** of arcs that, when removed, split the graph in two, or by using extra knowledge which may be beyond that which is in the graph. The use of inappropriate islands may make the problem more difficult (or even impossible to solve). It may also be possible to identify an alternate decomposition of the problem by choosing a different set of islands and searching through the space of possible islands. Whether this works in practice depends on the details of the problem. Island search sacrifices optimality unless one is able to guarantee that the islands are on an optimal path.

### Searching in a Hierarchy of Abstractions

The notion of islands can be used to define problem-solving strategies that work at multiple levels of detail or multiple levels of abstraction.

The idea of searching in a hierarchy of abstractions first involves abstracting the problem, leaving out as many details as possible. A solution to the abstract problem can be seen as a partial solution to the original problem. For example, the problem of getting from one room to another requires the use of many instances of turning, but an agent would like to reason about the problem at a level of abstraction where the steering details are omitted. It is expected that an appropriate abstraction solves the problem in broad strokes, leaving only minor problems to be solved.

One way this can be implemented is to generalize island-driven search to search over possible islands. Once a solution is found at the island level, this information provides a heuristic function for lower levels. Information that is found at a lower level can inform higher levels by changing the arc lengths. For example, the higher level may assume a particular distance between exit doors, but a lower-level search could find a better estimate of the actual distance.

The effectiveness of searching in a hierarchy of abstractions depends on how one decomposes and abstracts the problem to be solved. Once the problems are abstracted and decomposed, any of the search methods could be used to solve them. It is not easy, however, to recognize useful abstractions and problem decompositions.

## 3.8.2 Dynamic Programming

**Dynamic programming** is a general method for optimization that involves computing and storing partial solutions to problems. Solutions that have already been found can be retrieved rather than being recomputed. Dynamic programming algorithms are used throughout AI and computer science.

Dynamic programming can be used for finding paths in finite graphs by constructing a *cost_to_goal* function for nodes that gives the exact cost of a minimal-cost path from the node to a goal.

Let $cost\_to\_goal(n)$ be the actual cost of a lowest-cost path from node $n$ to a goal; $cost\_to\_goal(n)$ can be defined as

$$cost\_to\_goal(n) = \begin{cases} 0 & \text{if } goal(n) \\ \min_{\langle n,m\rangle \in A}(cost(\langle n,m\rangle) + cost\_to\_goal(m)) & \text{otherwise} \end{cases}$$

where $A$ is the set of arcs in the graph. The general idea is to build a table offline of the $cost\_to\_goal(n)$ value for each node. This is done by carrying out a lowest-cost-first search (page 99), with multiple-path pruning, from the goal nodes in the inverse graph (page 115), which is the graph with all arcs reversed. Rather than having a goal to search for, the dynamic programming algorithm records the *cost_to_goal* values for each node found. It uses the inverse graph to compute the costs from each node to the goal and not the costs from the goal to each node. In essence, dynamic programming works backwards from the goal, building the lowest-cost paths to the goal from each node in the graph.

**Example 3.21** For the graph given in Figure 3.3 (page 85), $G$ is a goal, so

$$cost\_to\_goal(G) = 0.$$

The next three steps of a lowest-cost-first search from G in the inverse graph give

$$cost\_to\_goal(H) = 3$$
$$cost\_to\_goal(J) = 4$$
$$cost\_to\_goal(D) = 7.$$

All of the *cost_to_goal* values are shown in Figure 3.19, where the numbers on the nodes are the cost to goal. $E$ has no path to G, so there is no value for $cost\_to\_goal(E)$.

A **policy** is a specification of which arc to take from each node. An **optimal policy** is a policy such that the cost of following that policy is not worse than the cost of following any other policy. Given a *cost_to_goal* function, which is computed offline, a policy can be computed as follows: From node $n$ it should go to a neighbor $m$ that minimizes $cost(\langle n, m\rangle) + cost\_to\_goal(m)$. This policy will take the agent from any node to a goal along a lowest-cost path.

Either this neighbor can be recorded for all nodes offline, and the mapping from node to node is provided to the agent for online action, or the *cost_to_goal* function is given to the agent and each neighbor can be computed online.

Dynamic programming takes time and space linear in the size of the graph to build the *cost_to_goal* table. Once the *cost_to_goal* function has been built, even if the policy has not been recorded, the time to determine which arc is optimal depends only on the number of neighbors for the node.

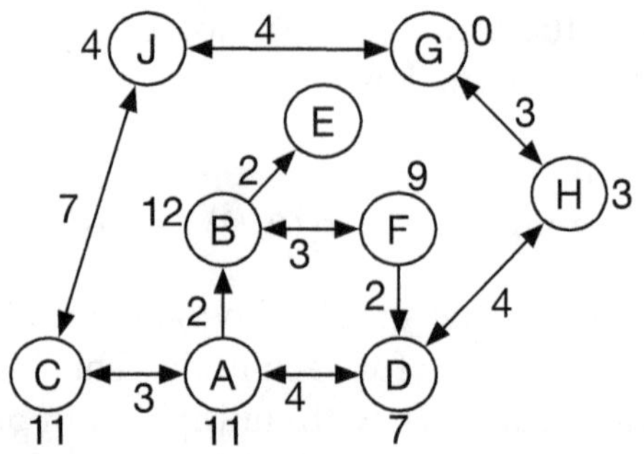


Figure 3.19: Cyclic delivery graph with node values computed by dynamic programming. Each node $n$ is shown with $cost\_to\_goal(n)$

**Example 3.22** Given the *cost_to_goal* of Figure 3.19 (page 118) for the goal of getting to $G$, if the agent is at $A$, it compares $2 + 12 = 14$ (the cost of going via $B$), $11 + 3 = 14$ (the cost of going via $C$), and $4 + 7 = 11$ (the cost of going straight to $D$). So it is shortest to go next to $D$.

## Partial Dynamic Programming as a Source of Heuristics

Dynamic programming does not have to be run to completion to be useful. Suppose $cost\_to\_goal(n)$ has a value for every node $n$ that has a path to a goal with cost less than $c$. Any node that does not have a *cost_to_goal* must have a cost of at least $c$. Suppose $h$ is an admissible heuristic function that satisfies the monotone restriction. Then the heuristic function

$$h'(n) = \begin{cases} cost\_to\_goal(n) & \text{if } cost\_to\_goal(n) \text{ is defined} \\ \max(c, h(n)) & \text{otherwise} \end{cases}$$

is an admissible heuristic function that satisfies the monotone restriction and, unless $h$ is already perfect for nodes within cost $c$ of a goal, improves $h$. It is perfect for all values less than $c$, but uses $h$ for values greater than $c$. This refined heuristic function can be dramatically more efficient than $h$.

Another way to build a heuristic function is to simplify the problem by leaving out some details. Dynamic programming can be used to find the cost of an optimal path to a goal in the simplified problem. This information forms a **pattern database** that can then be used as a heuristic for the original problem.

Dynamic programming is useful when

- the goal nodes are explicit (the methods based on the generic search algorithm only assumed a function that recognizes goal nodes)
- a lowest-cost path is needed
- the graph is finite and small enough to be able to store the *cost_to_goal* value for each node
- the goal does not change very often
- the policy is used a number of times for each goal, so that the cost of generating the *cost_to_goal* values can be amortized over many instances of the problem.

The main problems with dynamic programming are that

- it only works when the graph is finite and the table can be made small enough to fit into memory
- an agent must recompute a policy for each different goal
- the time and space required is linear in the size of the graph, where the graph size for finite graphs can be exponential in the path length.

## 3.9 Social Impact

The definition of a search problem assumes that you know what the goal and cost function are. Sometimes the goal or the cost provided by an application may not be what a user wants or there can be unintended side-effects. For example, consider route planning on maps, as in Example 3.1 (page 79). It is typical for the applications to ask for the start point and one or more destinations, and sometimes whether one wants to avoid highways or tolls (providing some modification of the graph), however they do not usually ask what cost a user might want to optimize. For example, a user may want to take a scenic route, one that avoids side streets as much as possible, or one that stays away from a relative's home. It is difficult to acquire these preferences and people may not even be able to articulate these preferences and trade-offs. But given the preferences, the problem reduces to one of searching, albeit with a complex cost function.

If a user wants to force a particular route in current apps, they can put them as intermediate destinations. However, it is difficult to determine what the user wants. If a user clicks on a town in a map, the system needs to decide whether they just want to go along the road that goes by the town, or they want to be directed to the exact location of the click. Misinterpreting the user's intentions can mean the user is not directed to where they want to go.

Route planning may have unintended side-effects. If the route planner is advising many people, and advises them all to take the same route, that route may become more congested because of the advice. It may be better for users to then deliberately avoid the advice. The system could avoid this by telling different users different routes. This may make users suspicious of this advice. It would be good for the system to guarantee that the user will not do better by ignoring the advice, which means that the system needs to do some load balancing so that all suggested routes have the same cost. What seemed like a simple search problem then becomes much more complicated.

It is impossible in general to avoid side streets, because the start or destination might be on a side street. If a main road or highway has congestion, it might be quicker for a driver to go via side streets. A system that advises drivers to go the quickest way will then send drivers on side streets until all side streets are also congested. In order to save a few drivers a few minutes, many more people become impacted. It might be better overall for the system to not optimize for the drivers. Instead, perhaps the system should optimize for some global preferences, but that is difficult to define clearly. Different people will have different preferences.

A challenge in path planning is that a driver might not actually take the route suggested, by design, perhaps visiting a place off the suggested route, by accident, such as taking a wrong turn, or where a road is closed. A challenge for the driver is over-relying on the directions, which has led to numerous incidents of what is colloquially known as **death by GPS** [Lin et al., 2017].

Collecting real-time location information for the purposes of congestion avoidance, also has privacy concerns if this information is used for other purposes or passed to third parties, such as advertisers or governments.

## 3.10 Review

The following are the main points you should have learned from this chapter:

- Many problems can be abstracted to the problem of searching to find paths in graphs.
- Breadth-first and depth-first searches can find paths in graphs without any extra knowledge beyond the graph.
- $A^*$ search can use a heuristic function that estimates the cost from a node to a goal. If a graph satisfies some reasonable condition (see Proposition 3.2 (page 112)) and the heuristic is admissible, $A^*$ is guaranteed to find a lowest-cost path to a goal if one exists.
- Multiple-path pruning and cycle pruning can be used to make search more efficient.
- Iterative deepening and depth-first branch-and-bound searches can be used to find lowest-cost paths with less memory than methods, such as $A^*$, which store multiple paths.
- When graphs are small enough to store all the nodes, dynamic programming records the actual cost of a lowest-cost path from each node to the goal, which can be used to find the next arc in an optimal path.
- When designing a search problem for the real world, you should ensure that there are no unintended social consequences, such as the ones of Section 3.9 (page 120).

## 3.11 References and Further Reading

There is a vast literature on search techniques in operations research, computer science, and AI. Search was seen early on as one of the foundations of AI. The AI literature emphasizes the use of heuristics in search.

Breadth-first search was invented by Moore [1959]. Lowest-cost-first search with multiple path pruning is one of the variants of **Dijkstra's algorithm** [Dijkstra, 1959], and is also equivalent to $A^*$ with a heuristic of zero. The $A^*$ algorithm was developed by Hart et al. [1968]. The optimality of $A^*$ is investigated by Dechter and Pearl [1985]. For a detailed analysis of heuristic search, see Pearl [1984].

Depth-first iterative deepening is described in Korf [1985]. Branch-and-bound search, developed in the operations research community, is described in Lawler and Wood [1966].

Dynamic programming is a general algorithm that will be used as a dual to search algorithms in other parts of this book. See Cormen et al. [2022] for more details on the general class of dynamic programming algorithms.

Bidirectional search was pioneered by Pohl [1971]. Chen et al. [2017] provide a bidirectional search algorithm with provable optimality.

The idea of using pattern databases as a source of heuristics for $A^*$ search was proposed by Culberson and Schaeffer [1998] and further developed by Felner et al. [2004]. Minsky [1961] discussed islands and problem reduction.

Dolgov et al. [2010] and Delling et al. [2015] describe real-world route planning for autonomous vehicles and Bing maps, respectively.

## 3.12 Exercises

**Exercise 3.1** Consider the graph of Figure 3.20, where the problem is to find a path from start $A$ to goal $G$. For each of the following algorithms, show the sequence of frontiers and give the path found.

(a) Depth-first search, where the neighbors are expanded in alphabetic ordering
(b) Breadth-first search
(c) Lowest-cost-first search ($A^*$ with $h(n) = 0$ for all nodes $n$)
(d) $A^*$ with $h(n) = |x(n) - x(G)| + |y(n) - y(G)|$ (the $x$-distance plus $y$-distance from $n$ to G), where $x(A) = 0$, $x(B) = 1$, $x(C) = 0$, $x(D) = 1$, $x(G) = 2$, $y(A) = 2$, $y(B) = 1$, $y(C) = 1$, $y(D) = 0$, and $y(G) = 0$.

**Exercise 3.2** Consider the problem of finding a path in the grid shown in Figure 3.21 (page 123) from the position $s$ to the position $g$. A piece can move on the grid horizontally or vertically, one square at a time. Each step has cost 1. No step may be made into a forbidden shaded area or outside the grid.

(a) For the grid shown in Figure 3.21 (page 123), number the nodes expanded (in order) for a depth-first search from $s$ to $g$, given that the order of the operators is up, down, left, right. Assume there is cycle pruning. What is the first path found?
(b) For the same grid, number the nodes expanded, in order, for a least-cost-first search with multiple-path pruning search from $s$ to $g$ (Dijkstra's algorithm). What is the first path found?

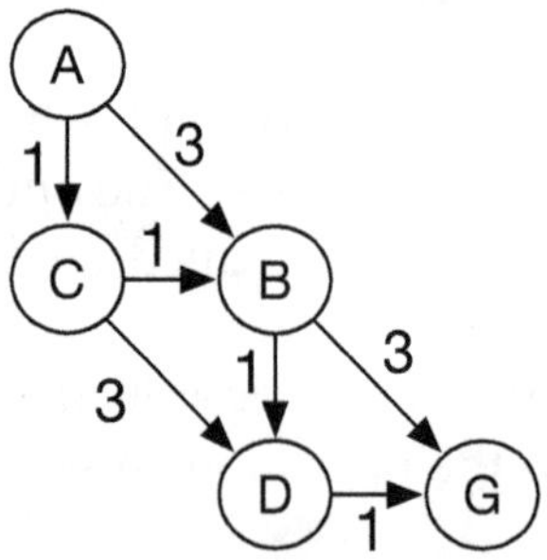


Figure 3.20: Graph for Exercise 3.1

(c) Number the nodes in order for an $A^*$ search, with multiple-path pruning, for the same grid, where the heuristic value for node $n$ is Manhattan distance from $n$ to the goal. The Manhattan distance between two points is the distance in the $x$-direction plus the distance in the $y$-direction. It corresponds to the distance traveled along city streets arranged in a grid. What is the path found?

(d) Show how to solve the same problem using dynamic programming. Give the *cost_to_goal* value for each node, and show which path is found.

(e) Based on this experience, discuss which algorithms are best suited for this problem.

(f) Suppose that the grid extended infinitely in all directions. That is, there is no boundary, but $s$, $g$, and the blocks are in the same positions relative to each other. Which methods would no longer find a path? Which would be the best method, and why?

**Exercise 3.3** This question investigates using graph searching to design video presentations. Consider a database of video segments, together with their length in seconds and the topics covered:

| Segment | Length | Topics Covered |
|---|---|---|
| seg0 | 10 | [welcome] |
| seg1 | 30 | [skiing, views] |
| seg2 | 50 | [welcome, artificial_intelligence, robots] |
| seg3 | 40 | [graphics, dragons] |
| seg4 | 50 | [skiing, robots] |

In the search graph, a node is a pair

$$\langle To\_Cover, Segs \rangle$$

where *Segs* is a list of segments that must be in the presentation, and *To_Cover* is a list of topics that also must be covered.

The neighbors of a node are obtained by first selecting a topic from *To_Cover*. There is a neighbor for each segment that covers the selected topic. The remaining

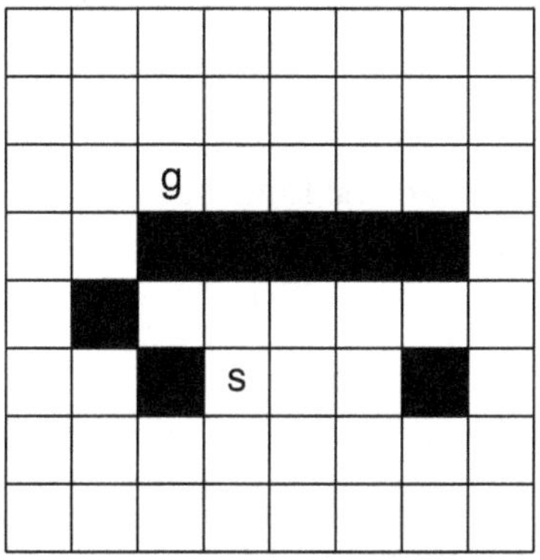


Figure 3.21: A grid-searching problem

topics are the topics not covered by the segment added. [Part of this exercise is to think about the exact structure of these neighbors.] Assume that the leftmost topic is selected at each step.

Given the above database, the neighbors of the node $\langle [welcome, robots], [] \rangle$, when *welcome* is selected, are $\langle [], [seg2] \rangle$ and $\langle [robots], [seg0] \rangle$.

Thus, each arc adds exactly one segment but can cover (and so remove) one or more topics. Suppose that the cost of the arc is equal to the time of the segment added.

The goal is to design a presentation that covers all of the topics in the list *MustCover*. The starting node is $\langle MustCover, [] \rangle$. The goal nodes are of the form $\langle [], Presentation \rangle$. The cost of the path from a start node to a goal node is the time of the presentation. Thus, an optimal presentation is a shortest presentation that covers all of the topics in *MustCover*.

(a) Suppose that the goal is to cover the topics $[welcome, skiing, robots]$ and the algorithm always selects the leftmost topic to find the neighbors for each node. Draw the search space expanded for a lowest-cost-first search until the first solution is found. This should show all nodes expanded, which node is a goal node, and the frontier when the goal was found.

(b) Give a non-trivial heuristic function $h$ that is admissible. [Note that $h(n) = 0$ for all $n$ is the trivial heuristic function.] Does it satisfy the monotone restriction for a heuristic function?

(c) Does the topic selected affect the result found? Why or why not?

**Exercise 3.4** Give two different admissible non-trivial heuristics for the video game of Example 3.3 (page 82) (depicted in Figure 3.2 (page 82)). Is one always less than or equal to the other? Explain why or why not.

**Exercise 3.5** Draw two different graphs, indicating start and goal nodes, for which forward search is better in one and backward search is better in the other.

**Exercise 3.6** The $A^*$ algorithm does not define what happens when multiple elements on the frontier have the same $f$-value. Compare the following tie-breaking conventions by first conjecturing which will work better, and then testing it on some examples. Try it on some examples where there are multiple optimal paths to a goal (such as finding a path from the bottom left of a rectangular grid to the top right of the grid, where the actions are step-up and step-right). Of the paths on the frontier with the same minimum $f$-value, select one:

(i) uniformly at random
(ii) that has been on the frontier the longest
(iii) that was most recently added to the frontier
(iv) with the smallest $h$-value
(v) with the least cost.

The last two may require other tie-breaking conventions when the cost and $h$ values are equal.

**Exercise 3.7** Consider what happens if the heuristic function is not admissible, but is still non-negative. What guarantees can be made when the path found by $A^*$ when the heuristic function:

(a) is less than $1 + \epsilon$ times the least-cost path (e.g., is less than 10% greater than the cost of the least-cost path)
(b) is less than $\delta$ more than the least-cost path (e.g., is always no more than 10 units greater than the cost of the optimal path)?

Develop a hypothesis about what would happen and show it empirically or prove your hypothesis. Does it change if multiple-path pruning is in effect or not?

Does loosening the heuristic in either of these ways improve efficiency? Try $A^*$ search where the heuristic is multiplied by a factor $1 + \epsilon$, or where a cost $\delta$ is added to the heuristic, for a number of graphs. Compare these on the time taken (or the number of nodes expanded) and the cost of the solution found for a number of values of $\epsilon$ or $\delta$.

**Exercise 3.8** How can depth-first branch and bound be modified to find a path with a cost that is not more than, say, 10% greater than the least-cost path. How does this algorithm compare to $A^*$ from the previous question?

**Exercise 3.9** The overhead for iterative deepening with $b - 1$ on the denominator (page 99) is not a good approximation when $b \approx 1$. Give a better estimate of the complexity of iterative deepening when $b \approx 1$. [Hint: Think about the case when $b = 1$.] How does this compare with $A^*$ for such graphs? Suggest a way that iterative deepening can have a lower overhead when the branching factor is close to 1.

**Exercise 3.10** Bidirectional search must be able to determine when the frontiers intersect. For each of the following pairs of searches, specify how to determine when the frontiers intersect:

(a) breadth-first search and depth-bounded depth-first search
(b) iterative deepening search and depth-bounded depth-first search
(c) $A^*$ and depth-bounded depth-first search
(d) $A^*$ and $A^*$.

**Exercise 3.11** The depth-first branch and bound of Figure 3.14 (page 106) is like a depth-bounded search in that it only finds a solution if there is a solution with cost less than *bound*. Show how this can be combined with an iterative deepening search to increase the depth bound if there is no solution for a particular depth bound. This algorithm must return $\perp$ in a finite graph if there is no solution. The algorithm should allow the bound to be incremented by an arbitrary amount and still return an optimal (least-cost) solution when there is a solution.

# Chapter 4

# Reasoning with Constraints

*Every task involves constraint,*
*Solve the thing without complaint;*
*There are magic links and chains*
*Forged to loose our rigid brains.*
*Structures, strictures, though they bind,*
*Strangely liberate the mind.*

– James Falen

Instead of reasoning explicitly in terms of states, it is typically better to describe states in terms of **features** and to reason in terms of these features, where a feature is a function on states. Features are described using **variables**. Often features are not independent and there are **hard constraints** that specify legal combinations of assignments of values to variables. As Falen's elegant poem emphasizes, the mind discovers and exploits constraints to solve tasks. Preferences over assignments are specified in terms of **soft constraints**. This chapter shows how to generate assignments that satisfy hard constraints and optimize soft constraints.

## 4.1 Variables and Constraints

### 4.1.1 Variables and Assignments

An **algebraic variable**, or **variable**, is used to name a feature. The **domain** of variable $X$, written $domain(X)$, is the set of values the variable can take.

A **discrete variable** is one whose domain is finite or countably infinite. A **binary variable** is a discrete variable with two values in its domain. One particular case of a binary variable is a **Boolean variable**, which is a variable with

## Symbols and Semantics

Algebraic variables are symbols.

Internal to a computer, a **symbol** is just a sequence of bits that is distinguished from other symbols. In a program we use constants to denote symbols. Some symbols have a fixed interpretation; for example, symbols that represent numbers and symbols that represent characters are predefined in most computer languages. Symbols with a user-defined meaning, but without a predefined meaning in the language, can be defined in many programming languages. Lisp refers to them as *atoms*. Python 3.4 introduced a symbol type called *enum*, but Python's strings are often used as symbols. Usually, symbols are implemented as indexes into a symbol table that gives the name to print out. The only operation performed on these symbols is equality, to determine whether two symbols are the same. This can be implemented by comparing the indexes in the symbol table.

To **users** of a computer, symbols can have meanings. A person who inputs constraints or interprets the output of a program associates meanings with the symbols making up the constraints or the outputs. They associate a symbol with some concept or object in the world. For example, the variable *SamsHeight*, to the computer, is just a sequence of bits. It has no relationship to *SamsWeight* or *AlsHeight*. To a person, this variable may mean the height, in particular units, of a particular person at a particular time.

The meaning associated with a variable–value pair must obey the **clarity principle**: an **omniscient agent** – a fictitious agent who knows the truth and the meanings associated with all of the symbols – should be able to determine the value of each variable. For example, the *height of Hagrid* only satisfies the clarity principle if the particular person being referred to and the particular time are specified as well as the units. For example, one may want to reason about the height, in centimeters, of Hagrid in a particular scene at the start of the second Harry Potter movie. This is different from the height, in inches, of Hagrid at the end of the third movie (although they are, of course, related). To refer to Hagrid's height at two different times, you need two variables.

You should have a consistent meaning for any symbols you use. When stating constraints, you must have the same meaning for the same variable and the same values, and you can use this meaning to interpret the output.

The bottom line is that symbols have meanings because you give them meanings. For this chapter, assume that the computer does not know what the symbols mean. A computer may know what a symbol means if it perceives and manipulates the environment.

domain $\{false, true\}$. We can also have variables that are not discrete; for example, a variable whose domain is the real numbers or a range of the real numbers is a **continuous variable**.

Given a set of variables, an **assignment** on the set of variables is a function from the variables into the domains of the variables. We write an assignment on $\{X_1, X_2, \ldots, X_k\}$ as $\{X_1 = v_1, X_2 = v_2, \ldots, X_k = v_k\}$, where $v_i$ is in $domain(X_i)$. This assignment specifies that, for each $i$, variable $X_i$ is assigned value $v_i$. A variable can only be assigned one value in an assignment.

A **total assignment** assigns a value to every variable.

**Example 4.1** The variable *Class_time* may denote the starting time for a particular class. The domain of *Class_time* may be the following set of possible times:

$$domain(Class\_time) = \{8, 9, 10, 11, 12, 1, 2, 3, 4, 5\}.$$

The variable *Height_joe* may refer to the height of a particular person, Joe, at a particular time and have as its domain the set of real numbers, in some range, that represent Joe's height in centimeters. *Raining* may be a random variable with domain $\{true, false\}$, which has value *true* if it is raining at a particular time.

The assignment $\{Class\_time = 11,\ Height\_joe = 165,\ Raining = false\}$ means the class starts at 11, Joe is 165 cm tall, and it is not raining.

**Example 4.2** In the electrical environment of Figure 1.6 (page 18), there may be a variable for the position of each switch that specifies whether the switch is up or down. There may be a variable for each light that specifies whether it is lit or not. There may be a variable for each component specifying whether it is working properly or if it is broken. Some variables that the following examples use include:

- $S_1\_pos$ is a binary variable denoting the position of switch $s_1$ with domain $\{up, down\}$, where $S_1\_pos = up$ means switch $s_1$ is up and $S_1\_pos = down$ means switch $s_1$ is down.
- $S_1\_st$ is a discrete variable denoting the status of switch $s_1$ with domain $\{ok, upside\_down, short, intermittent, broken\}$, where $S_1\_st = ok$ means switch $s_1$ is working normally, $S_1\_st = upside\_down$ means it is installed upside down, $S_1\_st = short$ means it is shorted and it allows electricity to flow whether it is up or down, $S_1\_st = intermittent$ means it is working intermittently, and $S_1\_st = broken$ means it is broken and does not allow electricity to flow.
- *Number_of_broken_switches* is an integer-valued variable denoting the number of switches that are broken.
- $Current\_w_1$ is a real-valued variable denoting the current, in amps, flowing through wire $w_1$. $Current\_w_1 = 1.3$ means there are 1.3 amps flowing through wire $w_1$. Inequalities between variables and constants form Boolean conditions; for example, $Current\_w_1 \geq 1.3$ is true when there are at least 1.3 amps flowing through wire $w_1$.

A total assignment specifies the position of every switch, the status of every device, and so on. For example, an assignment may be switch 1 is up, switch 2 is down, fuse 1 is okay, wire 3 is broken, etc.

**Example 4.3** Crossword puzzles, a popular form of recreation, involve filling in squares on a grid to make words that fit clues. There are two different representations of crossword puzzles in terms of variables:

- In one representation, the variables are the numbered squares with the direction of the word (down or across) and the domains are the set of possible words that can be used. For example, *one_across* could be a variable with domain {"ant", "big", "bus", "car", "has"}. A total assignment gives a word for each of the variables.
- In another representation of a crossword, the variables are the individual squares and the domain of each variable is the set of letters in the alphabet. For example, the top-left square could be a variable $p00$ with domain $\{a, \ldots, z\}$. A total assignment gives a letter to each square.

**Example 4.4** A trading agent, in planning a trip for a group of tourists, may be required to schedule a given set of activities. There could be two variables for each activity: one for the time, for which the domain is the set of possible times or days for the activity, and one for the location, for which the domain is the set of possible locations where it may occur. A total assignment gives a time and location for each activity.

An alternative representation may have the times as the variables (e.g., each hour for each day), with domains the set of possible activity–location pairs.

The number of total assignments is the product of the number of values in the domains of the variables.

**Example 4.5** If there are two variables, $A$ with domain $\{0, 1, 2\}$ and $B$ with domain $\{true, false\}$, there are six total assignments, which we name $w_0, \ldots, w_5$ as follows"

- $w_0 = \{A = 0, B = true\}$
- $w_1 = \{A = 0, B = false\}$
- $w_2 = \{A = 1, B = true\}$
- $w_3 = \{A = 1, B = false\}$
- $w_4 = \{A = 2, B = true\}$
- $w_5 = \{A = 2, B = false\}$

If there are $n$ variables, each with domain size $d$, there are $d^n$ total assignments.

One main advantage of reasoning in terms of variables is computational saving. Consider deciding whether to model in terms of states explicitly or to model the states in terms of binary variables. Many states can be described by a few variables:

- 10 binary variables can describe $2^{10} = 1024$ states

- 20 binary variables can describe $2^{20} = 1,048,576$ states
- 30 binary variables can describe $2^{30} = 1,073,741,824$ states
- 100 binary variables can describe $2^{100} = 1,267,650,600,228,229,401,496,703,205,376$ states.

Reasoning in terms of thirty variables may be easier than reasoning in terms of more than a billion states. One hundred variables is not that many, but reasoning in terms of more than $2^{100}$ states explicitly is not possible. Many real-world problems have thousands, if not millions, of variables.

### 4.1.2 Constraints

In many applications, not all possible assignments of values to variables are permissible. A **hard constraint**, or simply **constraint**, specifies legal combinations of assignments of values to some of the variables. The set of variables involved in the constraint is the **scope** of the constraint. A constraint specifies a **condition** on these variables that is true or false for each assignment to the variables in the scope.

A **unary constraint** is a constraint on a single variable (e.g., $B \leq 3$). A **binary constraint** is a constraint over a pair of variables (e.g., $A \leq B$). In general, a $k$-ary constraint has a scope of size $k$. For example, $A + B = C$ is a 3-ary (ternary) constraint.

A constraint can be evaluated in an assignment that assigns a superset of the variables in the scope. The extra variables are ignored. For example, $A \leq B$ is true of the assignment $\{A = 3, B = 7, C = 5\}$.

Assignment $A$ **satisfies** constraint $c$ if $A$ assigns the variables in the scope of $c$ and the condition of $c$ evaluates to true for $A$ restricted to the scope of $c$. Assignment $A$ **violates** constraint $c$ if $A$ assigns the variables in the scope of $c$ and the condition of $c$ evaluates to false for that assignment.

If an assignment $A$ satisfies a constraint, then any assignment that is a superset of $A$ also satisfies the constraint.

**Example 4.6** Suppose a robot needs to schedule a set of activities for a manufacturing process, involving casting, milling, drilling, and bolting. Each activity has a set of possible times at which it may start. The robot has to satisfy various constraints arising from prerequisite requirements and resource use limitations. For each activity there is a variable that represents the time that it starts. For example, it could use $D$ to represent the start time for the drilling, $B$ the start time of the bolting, and $C$ the start time for the casting. Drilling must start before bolting corresponds to the constraint $D < B$. Casting and drilling must not start at the same time corresponds to the constraint $C \neq D$. Bolting must start 3 time units after casting starts corresponds to the constraint $B = C + 3$.

Constraints are defined either by their **intension**, in terms of formulas, or by their **extension**, listing all the assignments that are true. Constraints defined extensionally can be seen as relations of legal assignments as in relational databases (page 800).

**Example 4.7** Consider a constraint on the possible dates for three activities. Let $A$, $B$, and $C$ be variables that represent the date of each activity. Suppose the domain of each variable is $\{1, 2, 3, 4\}$.

A constraint with scope $\{A, B, C\}$ could be described by its **intension**, using a logical formula to specify the legal assignments, such as

$$(A \le B) \land (B < 3) \land (B < C) \land \neg(A = B \land C \le 3)$$

where $\land$ means *and* and $\neg$ means *not*. This formula says that $A$ is on the same date or before $B$, and $B$ is before day 3, $B$ is before $C$, and it cannot be that $A$ and $B$ are on the same date when $C$ is on or before day 3.

The extensional definition of this constraint is defined using the following table specifying the legal assignments:

| A | B | C |
|---|---|---|
| 2 | 2 | 4 |
| 1 | 1 | 4 |
| 1 | 2 | 3 |
| 1 | 2 | 4 |

The first assignment is $\{A=2, B=2, C=4\}$, which assigns $A$ the value 2, $B$ the value 2, and $C$ the value 4. There are four legal assignments of the variables.

The assignment $\{A=1, B=2, C=3, D=3, E=1\}$ satisfies this constraint because when restricted to the scope of the relation, namely $\{A=1, B=2, C=3\}$, it is one of the legal assignments in the table.

**Example 4.8** Consider the constraints for the two representations of crossword puzzles of Example 4.3 (page 130):

- For the representation in which the domains are words, the constraint is that the letters where a pair of words intersect must be the same.
- For the representation in which the domains are letters, the constraint is that each contiguous sequence of letters must form a legal word.

### 4.1.3 Constraint Satisfaction Problems

A **constraint satisfaction problem** (CSP) consists of:

- a set of variables
- a domain for each variable
- a set of constraints.

A **solution** is a total assignment that satisfies all of the constraints.

**Example 4.9** Suppose the delivery robot must carry out a number of delivery activities, $a$, $b$, $c$, $d$, and $e$. Suppose that each activity happens at any of times 1, 2, 3, or 4. Let $A$ be the variable representing the time that activity $a$ will occur, and similarly for the other activities. The variable domains, which represent possible times for each of the deliveries, are

$$domain(A) = \{1,2,3,4\},\ domain(B) = \{1,2,3,4\},\ domain(C) = \{1,2,3,4\},$$
$$domain(D) = \{1,2,3,4\},\ domain(E) = \{1,2,3,4\}.$$

Suppose the following constraints must be satisfied:

$$\{(B \neq 3),\ (C \neq 2),\ (A \neq B),\ (B \neq C),\ (C < D),\ (A = D),$$
$$(E < A),\ (E < B),\ (E < C),\ (E < D),\ (B \neq D).\}$$

It is instructive for you to try to find a solution for this example; try to assign a value to each variable that satisfies these constraints.

Given a CSP, a number of tasks are useful:

- determine whether or not there is a solution
- find a solution when there is one
- count the number of solutions
- enumerate all of the solutions
- find a best solution, given a measure of how good solutions are
- determine whether some statement holds in all solutions.

The multidimensional aspect of CSPs, where each variable is a separate dimension, makes these tasks difficult to solve, but also provides structure that can be exploited.

CSPs are very common, so it is worth trying to find relatively efficient ways to solve them. Determining whether there is a solution for a CSP with finite domains is NP-complete (see box on page 89) and no known algorithms exist to solve such problems that do not use exponential time in the worst case. However, just because a problem is NP-complete does not mean that all instances are difficult to solve. Many instances have structure to exploit.

## 4.2 Solving CSPs by Searching

A finite CSP could be solved by exhaustively searching the total assignments.

The **generate-and-test** algorithm to find one solution is as follows: check each total assignment in turn; if an assignment is found that satisfies all of the constraints, return that assignment. A generate-and-test algorithm to find all solutions is the same except, instead of returning the first solution found, it enumerates the solutions.

**Example 4.10** In Example 4.9 (page 132), the assignment space is

$$S = \{\{A=1, B=1, C=1, D=1, E=1\},$$
$$\{A=1, B=1, C=1, D=1, E=2\}, \ldots,$$
$$\{A=4, B=4, C=4, D=4, E=4\}\}.$$

In this case there are $|S| = 4^5 = 1024$ different assignments to be tested. If there were fifteen variables instead of five, there would be $4^{15}$, which is about a billion, assignments to test. This method could not work for thirty variables.

If there are $n$ variables, each with domain size $d$, there are $d^n$ total assignments. If there are $e$ constraints, the total number of constraints tested is $O(ed^n)$. As $n$ becomes large, this becomes intractable very quickly.

The generate-and-test algorithm assigns values to all variables before checking the constraints. Because individual constraints only involve a subset of the variables, some constraints can be tested before all of the variables have been assigned values. If a partial assignment violates a constraint, any total assignment that extends the partial assignment will also violate the constraint. This can potentially prune a large part of the search space.

**Example 4.11** In the delivery scheduling problem of Example 4.9 (page 132), the assignment $\{A=1, B=1\}$ violates the constraint $A \neq B$ regardless of the values of the other variables. If the variables $A$ and $B$ are assigned values first, this violation can be discovered before any values are assigned to $C$, $D$, or $E$, thus saving a large amount of work.

Figure 4.1 gives a depth-first search-based algorithm to find all solutions for a CSP defined by variables *Vs* and constraints *Cs* that extend *context*, a partial or total assignment. *Vs* contains the variables not assigned in *context*, and *Cs* contains the constraints that involve at least one variable in *Vs*. It is called initially using

$$DFS\_solver(Vs, Cs, \{\})$$

```
procedure DFS_solver(Vs, Cs, context)
                    ▷ Returns the set of all solutions of constraints Cs that extend
    assignment context, where Vs are the variables not assigned in Cs
    Let ce = {c ∈ Cs | c can be evaluated in context}
    if context violates a constraint in ce then
        return {}
    else if Vs = {} then
        return {context}    ▷ all variables assigned and constraints satisfied
    else
        select variable var ∈ Vs
        sols := {}
        for val in domain(var) do
            sols := sols ∪ DFS_solver(Vs \ {var}, Cs \ ce, {var = val} ∪ context)
        return sols
```

Figure 4.1: Search-based algorithm to find all solutions to a CSP where $Vs$ is the set of all variables, and $Cs$ is the set of all constraints in a CSP, with *domain* implicit.

It first collects in *ce* the assignments that can be evaluated given the context. If the context violates a constraint that can be evaluated, there are no solutions that extend this context. If there are no variables in $Vs$, all variables have been assigned and so all constraints have been satisfied and it has found a solution. Otherwise, it selects a variable not assigned in the context and branches on all values of that variable.

This algorithm can be modified to implement generate and test by making it check the constraints only when all variables have been assigned.

The search-based algorithm carries out a depth-first search. It is possible to use any of the search strategies of the previous chapter to search the graph of assignments. However, as all of the solution paths are the same length – the length is the number of variables – there is not much point in doing so.

**Example 4.12** Consider a CSP with variables $A$, $B$, and $C$, each with domain $\{1,2,3,4\}$, and constraints $A < B$ and $B < C$. A possible search tree is shown in Figure 4.2. In this figure, a node corresponds to all of the assignments from the root to that node. The potential nodes that are pruned because they violate constraints are labeled ✘.

The leftmost ✘ corresponds to the assignment $\{A=1, B=1\}$. This violates the $A < B$ constraint, and so it is pruned.

This CSP has four solutions. The leftmost one is $\{A=1, B=2, C=3\}$. The size of the search tree, and thus the efficiency of the algorithm, depends on which variable is selected at each time. A static ordering, such as always splitting on $A$ then $B$ then $C$, is usually less efficient than the dynamic ordering used

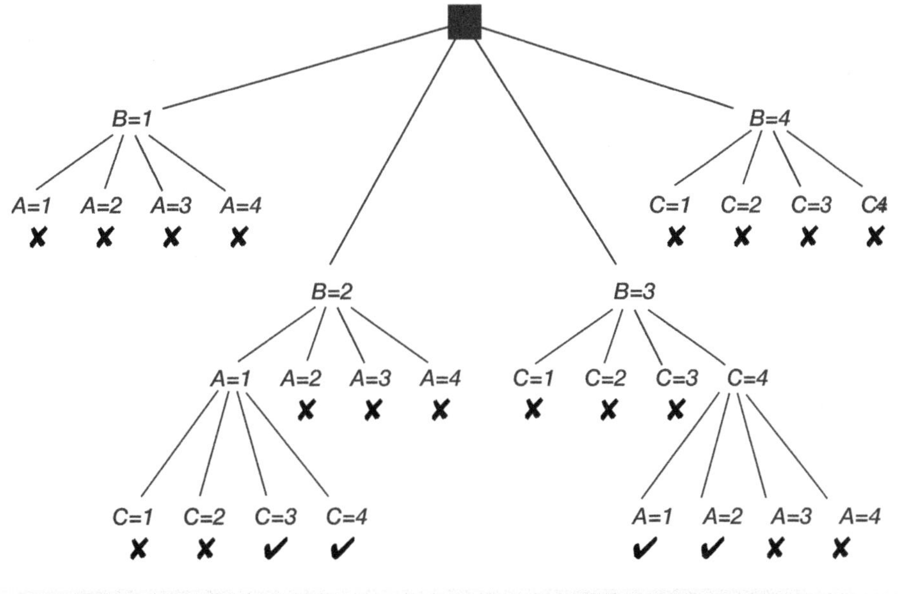


Figure 4.2: A possible search tree for the CSP of Example 4.12

here, but it might be more difficult to find the best dynamic ordering than to find the best static ordering. The set of answers is the same regardless of the variable ordering.

There would be $4^3 = 64$ total assignments tested in a generate-and-test algorithm. For the search method, there are 8 total assignments generated, and 16 other partial assignments that were tested as to whether they satisfy some of the constraints.

## 4.3 Consistency Algorithms

Although depth-first search over the search space of assignments is usually a substantial improvement over generate and test, it still has various inefficiencies that can be overcome.

**Example 4.13** In Example 4.12 (page 135), the variables $A$ and $B$ are related by the constraint $A < B$. The assignment $A = 4$ is inconsistent with each of the possible assignments to $B$ because $domain(B) = \{1, 2, 3, 4\}$. In the course of the backtrack search (see Figure 4.2), this fact is rediscovered for different assignments to $B$ and $C$. This inefficiency can be avoided by the simple expedient of deleting 4 from $domain(A)$, once and for all. This idea is the basis for the consistency algorithms.

The consistency algorithms are best thought of as operating over a **constraint network** defined as:

- There is a node (drawn as a circle or an oval) for each variable.
- There is a node (drawn as a rectangle) for each constraint.
- For every constraint $c$, and for every variable $X$ in the scope of $c$, there is an arc $\langle X, c\rangle$. The constraint network is thus a **bipartite graph**, with the two parts consisting of the variable nodes and the constraint nodes; each arc goes from a variable node to a constraint node.
- There is also a dictionary $dom$ with the variables as keys, where $dom[X]$ is a set of possible values for variable $X$. $dom[X]$ is initially the domain of $X$.

**Example 4.14** Consider Example 4.12 (page 135). There are three variables $A$, $B$, and $C$, each with domain $\{1, 2, 3, 4\}$. The constraints are $A < B$ and $B < C$. In the constraint network, shown in Figure 4.3, there are four arcs:

$$\langle A, A < B\rangle$$

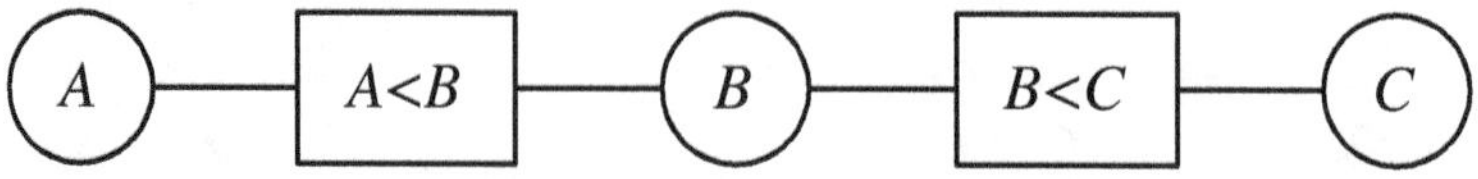


Figure 4.3: Constraint network for the CSP of Example 4.14

$$\langle B, A < B\rangle$$
$$\langle B, B < C\rangle$$
$$\langle C, B < C\rangle .$$

**Example 4.15** The constraint $X \neq 4$ has one arc:

$$\langle X, X \neq 4\rangle .$$

The constraint $X + Y = Z$ has three arcs:

$$\langle X, X + Y = Z\rangle$$
$$\langle Y, X + Y = Z\rangle$$
$$\langle Z, X + Y = Z\rangle .$$

In the simplest case, when a constraint has just one variable in its scope, the arc is **domain consistent** if every value of the variable satisfies the constraint.

**Example 4.16** The constraint $B \neq 3$ has scope $\{B\}$. With this constraint, and with $dom[B] = \{1, 2, 3, 4\}$, the arc $\langle B, B \neq 3\rangle$ is not domain consistent because $B = 3$ violates the constraint. If the value 3 were removed from the domain of $B$, then it would be domain consistent.

Suppose constraint $c$ has scope $\{X, Y_1, \ldots, Y_k\}$. Arc $\langle X, c\rangle$ is **arc consistent** if, for each value $x \in dom[X]$, there are values $y_1, \ldots, y_k$ where $y_i \in dom[Y_i]$, such that the assignment $\{X = x, Y_1 = y_1, \ldots, Y_k = y_k\}$ satisfies $c$. A network is arc consistent if all its arcs are arc consistent.

**Example 4.17** Consider the network of Example 4.14 (page 136) shown in Figure 4.3 (page 136). None of the arcs are arc consistent. The first arc, $\langle A, A < B\rangle$, is not arc consistent because for $A = 4$ there is no corresponding value for $B$ for which $A < B$. If 4 were removed from the domain of $A$, then it would be arc consistent. The second arc, $\langle B, A < B\rangle$, is not arc consistent because there is no corresponding value for $A$ when $B = 1$.

If an arc $\langle X, c\rangle$ is *not* arc consistent, there are some values of $X$ for which there are no values for $Y_1, \ldots, Y_k$ for which the constraint holds. In this case, all values of $X$ in $dom[X]$ for which there are no corresponding values for the other variables can be deleted from $dom[X]$ to make the arc $\langle X, c\rangle$ consistent. When a value is removed from a domain, this may make some other arcs that were previously consistent no longer consistent.

The **generalized arc consistency (GAC)** algorithm is given in Figure 4.4 (page 138). It takes in a CSP with variables *Vs*, constraints *Cs*, and (possibly reduced) domains specified by the dictionary *dom* and a set *to_do* of potentially inconsistent arcs. The set *to_do* initially consists of all arcs in the graph, $\{\langle X, c\rangle \mid c \in Cs \text{ and } X \in scope(c)\}$. It modifies *dom* to make the network arc consistent.

While *to_do* is not empty, an arc $\langle X, c\rangle$ is removed from the set and considered. If the arc is not arc consistent, it is made arc consistent by pruning the domain of variable $X$. All of the previously consistent arcs that could, as a result of pruning $X$, have become inconsistent are added to the set *to_do* if they are not already there. These are the arcs $\langle Z, c' \rangle$, where $c'$ is a constraint different from $c$ that involves $X$, and $Z$ is a variable involved in $c'$ other than $X$. When *to_do* is empty, the constraint graph is arc consistent.

**Example 4.18** Consider the *GAC* algorithm operating on the network from Example 4.14 (page 136), with constraints $A < B$, $B < C$. Initially, all of the arcs are in the *to_do* set. Here is one possible sequence of selections of arcs, showing what values are pruned and what is added to the set *to_do*.

| Arc | Domain reduced | Added to *to_do* |
|---|---|---|
| $\langle A, A < B \rangle$ | $dom[A] = \{1,2,3\}$ | – |
| $\langle B, A < B \rangle$ | $dom[B] = \{2,3,4\}$ | – |
| $\langle B, B < C \rangle$ | $dom[B] = \{2,3\}$ | $\langle A, A < B \rangle$ |
| $\langle A, A < B \rangle$ | $dom[A] = \{1,2\}$ | – |
| $\langle C, B < C \rangle$ | $dom[C] = \{3,4\}$ | – |

In the first step, the algorithm selects the arc $\langle A, A < B \rangle$. For $A = 4$, there is no value of $B$ that satisfies the constraint. Thus, 4 is pruned from the domain of $A$. Nothing is added to *to_do* because there is no arc involving $B$ not in *to_do*.

In the second step, 1 is removed from the domain of $B$. The arc $\langle A, A < B \rangle$ is not added back to *to_do* because it involves the same constraint as the arc visited.

In the third step, $\langle B, B < C \rangle$ is selected. The value 4 is removed from the domain of $B$. Because the domain of $B$ has been reduced, the arc $\langle A, A < B \rangle$ must be added back into the *to_do* set because the domain of $A$ could potentially be reduced further now that the domain of $B$ is smaller.

The algorithm then terminates with $dom[A] = \{1,2\}$, $dom[B] = \{2,3\}$, $dom[C] = \{3,4\}$. Although this has not fully solved the problem, it has greatly simplified it. For example, depth-first backtracking search (page 133) would now solve the problem more efficiently.

```
procedure GAC(Vs, dom, Cs, to_do)
        ▷ Returns arc-consistent domains for CSP ⟨Vs, dom, Cs⟩ given to_do
    while to_do ≠ {} do
        select and remove ⟨X, c⟩ from to_do
        let {Y1, ..., Yk} = scope(c) \ {X}
        ND := {x | x ∈ dom[X] and exists y1 ∈ dom[Y1] ... yk ∈ dom[Yk] such
that c(X=x, Y1=y1, ..., Yk=yk)}
        if ND ≠ dom[X] then
            to_do := to_do ∪ {⟨Z, c'⟩ | {X, Z} ⊆ scope(c'), c' ≠ c, Z ≠ X}
            dom[X] := ND
    return dom
```

Figure 4.4: Generalized arc consistency algorithm

**Example 4.19** Consider applying *GAC* to the scheduling problem of Example 4.9 (page 132). The network shown in Figure 4.5 has already been made domain consistent (the value 3 has been removed from the domain of $B$ and 2 has been removed from the domain of $C$). The following is a sequence of arcs processed for one sequence of selections from *to_do*, where the order of arcs is arbitrary:

| Arc | Domain Reduced | Added to *to_do* |
|---|---|---|
| $\langle B, B \neq C\rangle$ | – | – |
| $\langle D, C < D\rangle$ | $dom[D] = \{2,3,4\}$ | – |
| $\langle C, E < C\rangle$ | $dom[C] = \{3,4\}$ | $\langle D, C < D\rangle$, $\langle B, B \neq C\rangle$ |
| $\langle D, C < D\rangle$ | $dom[D] = \{4\}$ | – |
| $\langle B, B \neq C\rangle$ | – | – |
| $\langle C, C < D\rangle$ | $dom[C] = \{3\}$ | $\langle B, B \neq C\rangle$ |
| $\langle A, A = D\rangle$ | $dom[A] = \{4\}$ | – |
| $\langle B, B \neq D\rangle$ | $dom[B] = \{1,2\}$ | – |
| $\langle B, E < B\rangle$ | $dom[B] = \{2\}$ | $\langle B, B \neq D\rangle$ |
| $\langle E, E < B\rangle$ | $dom[E] = \{1\}$ | $\langle C, E < C\rangle$ |
| ... | – | – |

At the end, all the arcs are consistent, and so the algorithm terminates with the *to_do* set empty. The set of reduced variable domains is returned. In this case, the domains all have size 1 and there is a unique solution: $A = 4$, $B = 2$, $C = 3$, $D = 4$, $E = 1$.

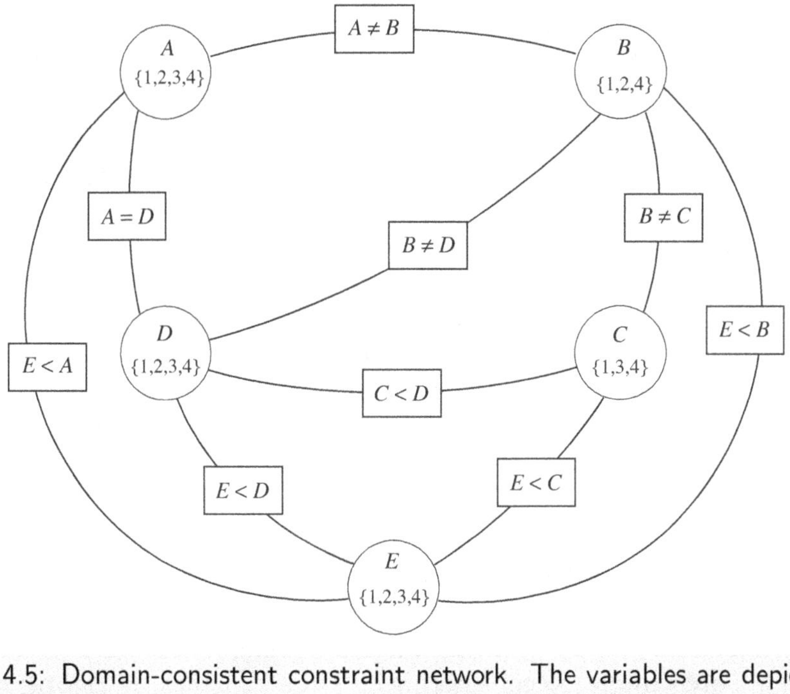


Figure 4.5: Domain-consistent constraint network. The variables are depicted as circles or ovals with their corresponding domain. The constraints are represented as rectangles. There is an arc between each variable and each constraint that involves that variable

Notice that at the third step, when $C$ is reduced, all processed constraints that involve $C$, but do not involve $E$, are added back to the set *to_do*.

Regardless of the order in which the arcs are considered, the algorithm will terminate with the same result, namely, an arc-consistent network and the same set of reduced domains. Three cases are possible, depending on the state of the network upon termination:

- In the first case, one domain becomes empty, indicating there is no solution for the CSP. Note that, as soon as any one domain becomes empty, all domains of connected nodes will become empty before the algorithm terminates.
- In the second case, each domain has a singleton value, indicating that there is a unique solution, as in Example 4.19 (page 139).
- In the third case, every domain is non-empty and at least one has multiple values. There may or may not be a solution. Methods to solve the problem in this case are explored in the following sections.

The following example shows that it is possible for a network to be arc consistent even though there is no solution.

**Example 4.20** Suppose there are variables, $A$, $B$, and $C$, each with the domain $\{1, 2, 3, 4\}$ and constraints $A = B$, $B = C$, and $A \neq C$. This is arc consistent: no domain can be pruned using any single constraint. However, there are no solutions; there is no assignment to the three variables that satisfies the constraints.

Consider the time complexity of the generalized arc-consistency algorithm for binary constraints. Suppose there are $c$ binary constraints, and the domain of each variable is of size $d$. There are $2c$ arcs. Checking an arc $\langle X, r(X, Y) \rangle$ involves, in the worst case, iterating through each value in the domain of $Y$ for each value in the domain of $X$, which takes $O(d^2)$ time. This arc may need to be checked once for every element in the domain of $Y$, thus *GAC* for binary variables can be done in time $O(cd^3)$, which is linear in $c$, the number of constraints. The space used is $O(nd)$, where $n$ is the number of variables and $d$ is the domain size. Exercise 4.5 (page 174) explores the complexity of more general constraints.

Various extensions to arc consistency are also possible. The domains need not be finite; they may be specified using intensions, such as $3 < X < 7$. Higher-order consistency techniques, such as **path consistency**, consider $k$-tuples of variables at a time, not just pairs of variables that are connected by a constraint. For example, by considering all three variables, an algorithm could recognize that there is no solution in Example 4.20. These higher-order methods are often less efficient for solving a problem than using arc consistency augmented with the methods described below.

## 4.4 Domain Splitting

To enable consistency methods to find all of the solutions, we need to incorporate search. While the search methods of Section 4.2 (page 133) can be adapted to allow for simplification of the domains, we can do better by **domain splitting**, a form of **case analysis** that interleaves search and arc consistency. The idea is to split a problem into a number of disjoint cases and solve each case separately. The set of all solutions to the initial problem is the union of the solutions to each case.

In the simplest case, suppose there is a binary variable $X$ with domain $\{t,f\}$. All of the solutions either have $X=t$ or $X=f$. One way to find all of the solutions is to set $X=t$, find all of the solutions with this assignment, and then assign $X=f$ and find all of the solutions with this assignment. Assigning a value to a variable gives a smaller *reduced* problem to solve. If we only want to find one solution, we can look for the solutions with $X=t$, and if we do not find any, we can look for the solutions with $X=f$.

If the domain of a variable has more than two elements, for example if the domain of $A$ is $\{1,2,3,4\}$, there are a number of ways to split it:

- Split the domain into a case for each value. For example, split $A$ into the four cases $A=1$, $A=2$, $A=3$, and $A=4$.
- Always split the domain into two disjoint non-empty subsets. For example, split $A$ into the two cases $A \in \{1,2\}$ and $A \in \{3,4\}$.

The first approach makes more progress with one split, but the second may allow for more pruning with fewer steps. For example, if the same values for $B$ can be pruned whether $A$ is 1 or 2, the second case allows this fact to be discovered once and not have to be rediscovered for each element of $A$. This saving depends on how the domains are split.

Recursively solving the cases using domain splitting, recognizing when there is no solution based on the assignments, is equivalent to the search algorithm of Section 4.2 (page 133). It can be more efficient to interleave arc consistency with the search.

One effective way to solve a CSP is to use arc consistency to simplify the network before each step of domain splitting. That is, to solve a problem:

- simplify the problem using arc consistency, and
- if the problem is not solved, select a variable whose domain has more than one element, split it, and recursively solve each case.

Arc consistency does not need to start from scratch after domain splitting. If the variable $X$ has its domain split, *to_do* can start with just the arcs that are possibly no longer arc consistent as a result of the split. These are all the arcs of the form $\langle Y, r\rangle$, where $X$ appears in $r$ and $Y$ is not $X$.

Figure 4.6 (page 142) shows how to solve a CSP with arc consistency and domain splitting. *Con_Solve*$(Vs, dom, Cs, to\_do)$ returns a solution to constraint satisfaction problem $Vs, dom, Cs$ if there is (at least) one, or *false* otherwise. Initially, *dom* contains the domain for each variable, and *to_do* is $\{\langle X, c\rangle \mid c \in Cs \text{ and } X \in scope(c)\}$. The "or" in line 14 is assumed to return the value of its first argument if it is not false, and otherwise returns the value of the second argument. *GAC* must not change *to_do*, otherwise the second *td* might have the wrong value.

It is possible to use essentially the same algorithm to find all solutions: line 5 should return the empty set, line 7 should return the set containing one element, and line 14 should return the union of the answers from each case.

**Example 4.21** In Example 4.18 (page 138), arc consistency simplified the network, but did not solve the problem. After arc consistency had completed, there were multiple elements in the domains. Suppose $B$ is split. There are two cases:

- $B=2$. In this case $A=2$ is pruned. Splitting on $C$ produces two of the answers.
- $B=3$. In this case $C=3$ is pruned. Splitting on $A$ produces the other two answers.

This search tree should be contrasted with the search tree of Figure 4.2 (page 135). The search space with arc consistency is much smaller.

Domain splitting forms a search space from which any of the methods of Chapter 3 can be used. However, as it is only the solution and not the path that is of interest, and because the search space is finite, depth-first search is often used for these problems.

One other enhancement can make domain splitting much more efficient when counting the number of solutions. If assigning values to the variables

1: **procedure** $Con\_Solve(Vs, dom, Cs, to\_do)$
2: ▷ Returns a solution to CSP $\langle Vs, dom, Cs\rangle$ or *false* otherwise
3: $dom_0 := GAC(Vs, dom, Cs, to\_do)$
4: **if** there is a variable $X$ such that $dom_0[X] = \{\}$ **then**
5: **return** *false*
6: **else if** for every variable $X$, $|dom_0[X]| = 1$ **then**
7: **return** solution with each variable $X$ having the value in $dom_0[X]$
8: **else**
9: select variable $X$ such that $|dom_0[X]| > 1$
10: partition $dom_0[X]$ into $D_1$ and $D_2$
11: $dom_1 :=$ a copy of $dom_0$ but with $dom_1[X] = D_1$
12: $dom_2 :=$ a copy of $dom_0$ but with $dom_2[X] = D_2$
13: $td := \{\langle Z, c'\rangle \mid \{X, Z\} \subseteq scope(c'), Z \neq X\}$
14: **return** $Con\_Solve(Vs, dom_1, Cs, td)$ **or** $Con\_Solve(Vs, dom_2, Cs, td)$

Figure 4.6: Finding a solution for a CSP using arc consistency and domain splitting disconnects the graph, each disconnected component can be solved separately. The solution to the complete problem is the product of the solutions to each component. For example, if one component has 100 solutions and the other component has 20 solutions, there are 2000 solutions. Treating them independently is more efficient than finding each of the 2000 solutions separately.

## 4.5 Variable Elimination

Arc consistency simplifies the network by removing values from the domains of variables. A complementary method is **variable elimination** (**VE**), which simplifies the network by removing variables.

The idea of VE is to remove the variables one by one. When removing a variable $X$, VE constructs a new constraint on some of the remaining variables reflecting the effects of $X$ on the other variables. This new constraint replaces all of the constraints that involve $X$, forming a reduced network that does not involve $X$. VE provides a way to construct a solution to the CSP that contains $X$ from a solution to the reduced CSP.

The following algorithm is described using the relational algebra operations of **join** and **project** (page 800).

When eliminating $X$, the influence of $X$ on the remaining variables is through the constraint relations that involve $X$. First, the algorithm collects all of the constraints that involve $X$. Let the join of all of these relations be the relation $r_X(X, \overline{Y})$, where $\overline{Y}$ is the set of other variables in the scope of $r_X$. Thus $\overline{Y}$ is the set of all variables that are neighbors of $X$ in the constraint graph. The algorithm then projects $r_X$ onto $\overline{Y}$; this relation replaces all of the relations that involve $X$. The algorithm thus creates a reduced CSP that involves one less variable, which it solves recursively. Once it has a solution for the reduced CSP, it extends that solution to a solution for the original CSP by joining the solution with $r_X$.

When only one variable is left, it returns the domain elements that are consistent with the constraints on this variable.

**Example 4.22** Consider a CSP that contains the variables $A$, $B$, and $C$, each with domain $\{1, 2, 3, 4\}$. Suppose the constraints that involve $B$ are $A < B$ and $B < C$. There may be many other variables, but if $B$ does not have any constraints in common with these variables, eliminating $B$ will not impose any new constraints on these other variables. To remove $B$, first join on the relations that involve $B$:

| $A$ | $B$ |
|---|---|
| 1 | 2 |
| 1 | 3 |
| 1 | 4 |
| 2 | 3 |
| 2 | 4 |
| 3 | 4 |

$\bowtie$

| $B$ | $C$ |
|---|---|
| 1 | 2 |
| 1 | 3 |
| 1 | 4 |
| 2 | 3 |
| 2 | 4 |
| 3 | 4 |

$=$

| $A$ | $B$ | $C$ |
|---|---|---|
| 1 | 2 | 3 |
| 1 | 2 | 4 |
| 1 | 3 | 4 |
| 2 | 3 | 4 |

To get the relation on $A$ and $C$ induced by $B$, project this join onto $A$ and $C$, which gives

| A | C |
|---|---|
| 1 | 3 |
| 1 | 4 |
| 2 | 4 |

This relation on $A$ and $C$ contains all of the information about the constraints on $B$ that affect the solutions of the rest of the network.

The original constraints on $B$ are replaced with the new constraint on $A$ and $C$. *VE* then solves the rest of the network, which is now simpler because it does not involve the variable $B$. To generate one or all solutions, the algorithm remembers the joined relation on $A, B, C$ to construct a solution that involves $B$ from a solution to the reduced network.

Figure 4.7 gives a recursive algorithm for variable elimination, *VE_CSP*, to find all solutions for a CSP.

The base case of the recursion occurs when only one variable is left. The constraints are on one variable, giving the set of allowable values for that variable. The values for that variable are the intersection of the sets for each constraint.

In the non-base case, a variable $X$ is selected for elimination (line 10). To eliminate variable $X$, the algorithm propagates the effect of $X$ onto those variables that $X$ is directly related to. This is achieved by joining all of the relations in which $X$ is involved (line 12) and then projecting $X$ out of the resulting relation (line 13). Thus, a simplified problem (with one less variable) has been

```
1:  procedure VE_CSP(Vs, Cs)
2:      Inputs
3:          Vs: a set of variables
4:          Cs: a set of constraints on Vs
5:      Output
6:          a relation containing all of the consistent variable assignments
7:      if Vs contains just one element then
8:          return the join of all relations in Cs
9:      else
10:         select variable X to eliminate
11:         CX := {C ∈ Cs : C involves X}
12:         R := join of all of the constraints in CX
13:         NR := R projected onto the variables other than X
14:         S := VE_CSP(Vs \ {X}, (Cs \ CX) ∪ {NR})
15:         return R ⋈ S
```

Figure 4.7: Variable elimination for finding all solutions to a CSP created that can be solved recursively. To get the possible values for $X$, the algorithm joins the solution of the simplified problem with the relation $R$ that defines the effect of $X$. If any value of $R$ in this algorithm contains no tuples, there are no solutions.

**Example 4.23** Consider the constraints of Example 4.9 (page 132), shown in Figure 4.5 (page 139). If the variables are selected in the elimination order $A$, $C$, $D$, $E$, the algorithm has the following sequence of constraints being joined ($CX$ in the algorithm) and new constraint created ($NR$ in the algorithm) where, for example, $c_1(B,D,E)$ is a new constraint on variables $\{B,D,E\}$:

| Variable Eliminated | Constraints Joined | New Constraint |
|---|---|---|
| $A$ | $A \neq B, A = D, E < A$ | $c_1(B,D,E)$ |
| $C$ | $B \neq C, C < D, E < C$ | $c_2(B,D,E)$ |
| $D$ | $E < D, B \neq D, c_1(B,D,E), c_2(B,D,E)$ | $c_3(B,E)$ |
| $E$ | $E < B, c_3(B,E)$ | $c_4(B)$ |

The legal assignment(s) for $B$ is given in $c_4(B)$.

The elimination order $B$, $C$, $A$, $E$ has the following constraints joined and new constraints:

| Variable Eliminated | Constraints Joined | New Constraint |
|---|---|---|
| $B$ | $A \neq B, B \neq D, B \neq C, E < B$ | $c_5(A,C,D,E)$ |
| $C$ | $C < D, E < C, c_5(A,C,D,E)$ | $c_6(A,D,E)$ |
| $A$ | $A = D, E < A, c_6(B,D,E)$ | $c_7(D,E)$ |
| $E$ | $E < D, c_7(D,E)$ | $c_8(D)$ |

These elimination orderings result in the same set of answers.

If you only wanted to find one solution, instead of returning $R \bowtie S$, the algorithm can return one element of the join. No matter which element it returns, that element is guaranteed to be part of a solution.

The order in which the variables are selected at line 10 is called the **elimination ordering**. The elimination ordering does not affect the correctness of the algorithm, but it may affect efficiency.

The intermediate structure – which variables the intermediate constraints are over – depends only on the graph structure of the constraint network and the elimination order. The maximum number of variables in the scope of an intermediate factor for a variable ordering is the **treewidth** of the graph for that variable ordering. The treewidth of a graph is the minimum treewidth for all orderings. The time complexity of variable elimination for finding one solution or counting the number of solutions is exponential in the treewidth and linear in the number of variables. The space is exponential in the treewidth. This can be compared to depth-first search (see Section 4.2, page 133), where the time is exponential in the number of variables, but the space is linear in the number of variables. The time complexity of the task for enumerating the solutions can be greater than this if there are many solutions.

Finding an elimination ordering that results in the smallest treewidth is NP-hard. However, some good heuristics exist. The two most common are:

- **Min-factor.** At each stage, select the variable that results in the smallest factors being created at that stage.
- **Minimum deficiency** or **minimum fill.** At each stage, select a variable that has the fewest pair variables in the new constraint that were not together in a constraint before the variable was eliminated. The **deficiency** of a variable $X$ is the number of pairs of variables that are in a constraint with $X$ that are not in another constraint with each other. The intuition is that it is okay to remove a variable that results in a large relation as long as it does not make the network more complicated.

The minimum deficiency has usually been found empirically to give a smaller treewidth than min-factor, but it is more difficult to compute.

*VE* can also be combined with *GAC* (page 137); whenever *VE* removes a variable, arc consistency can be used to further simplify the problem. This approach can result in smaller intermediate tables. For example, following eliminating one of the variables in Example 4.20 (page 140), arc consistency will result in empty domains (even if there were many other variables and constraints).

## 4.6 Local Search

The preceding algorithms systematically search the space of assignments of values to variables. If the space is finite, they will either find a solution or report that no solution exists. Unfortunately, many spaces are too big for systematic search and are possibly even infinite. In any reasonable time, systematic search will have failed to consider enough of the space to give any meaningful results. This section and the next consider methods intended to work in these very large spaces. The methods do not systematically search the whole search space but they are designed to find solutions quickly on average. They do not guarantee that a solution will be found even if one exists, and so they are not able to determine that no solution exists. They are often the method of choice for applications where solutions are known to exist or are very likely to exist.

Local search methods start with a total assignment of a value to each variable and try to improve this assignment iteratively by taking improving steps, by taking random steps, or by restarting with another total assignment. Many different local search techniques have been proposed. Understanding when these techniques work for different problems forms the focus of a number of research communities, in both operations research and AI.

A generic local search algorithm is given in Figure 4.8 (page 147). It maintains a total assignment in the dictionary $A$, which has the variables as the keys. Each iteration of the outer (repeat) loop is called a **try**. The first *for each* loop (line 11) assigns a random value to each variable. The first time it is executed is called a **random initialization**. At subsequent times it is a **random restart**. An alternative to random assignment is to use an informed guess, utilizing heuristic or prior knowledge, which is then iteratively improved.

The *while* loop (line 13 to line 15) does a **local search**, or a **walk**, through the assignment space. It considers a set of possible **successors** of the total assignment $A$, and selects one to be the next total assignment. In Figure 4.8, the possible successors of a total assignment are those assignments that differ in the assignment of a single variable.

This walk through assignments continues until either a satisfying assignment is found and returned or the *stop_walk*() condition is true, in which case the algorithm either does a random restart, starting again with a new assignment, or terminates with no solution found. A common case is that *stop_walk*() becomes true after a certain number of steps.

An algorithm is **complete** if it guarantees to find an answer whenever there is one. This algorithm can be complete or incomplete, depending on the selection of variable and value, and the *stop_walk* and *termination*() conditions.

One version of this algorithm is **random sampling**. In random sampling, the stopping criterion *stop_walk*() always returns *true* so that the *while* loop from line 13 is never executed. Random sampling keeps picking random assignments until it finds one that satisfies the constraints, and otherwise it does not halt. Random sampling is complete in the sense that, given enough time, it

```
1:  procedure Local_search(Vs, domain, Cs)
2:      Inputs
3:          Vs: a set of variables
4:          domain: a function such that domain(X) is the domain of variable X
5:          Cs: set of constraints to be satisfied
6:      Output
7:          total assignment that satisfies the constraints
8:      Local
9:          A a dictionary of values indexed by variables in Vs
10:     repeat
11:         for each variable X in Vs do
12:             A[X] := a (random or other) value in domain(X)
13:         while not stop_walk() & A is not a satisfying assignment do
14:             Select a variable Y and a value w ∈ domain(Y)
15:             A[Y] := w
16:         if A is a satisfying assignment then
17:             return A
18:     until termination()
```

Figure 4.8: Local search for finding a solution to a CSP

guarantees that a solution will be found if one exists, but there is no upper bound on the time it may take. It is typically very slow. The efficiency depends on the product of the domain sizes and how many solutions exist.

Another version is a **random walk** when *stop_walk*() is always false, and the variable and value are selected at random. Thus there are no random restarts, and the *while* loop is only exited when it has found a satisfying assignment. Random walk is also complete in the same sense as random sampling. Each step takes less time than resampling all variables, but it can take more steps than random sampling, depending on how the solutions are distributed. When the domain sizes of the variables differ, a random walk algorithm can either select a variable at random and then a value at random, or select a variable–value pair at random. The latter is more likely to select a variable when it has a larger domain.

### 4.6.1 Iterative Best Improvement

**Iterative best improvement** is a local search algorithm that selects a variable and value on line 14 of Figure 4.8 that most improves some **evaluation function**. If there are several possible successors that most improve the evaluation function, one is chosen at random. When the aim is to minimize a function, this algorithm is called **greedy descent**. When the aim is to maximize a function, this is called **hill climbing** or **greedy ascent**. We only consider minimization; to maximize a quantity, you can minimize its negation.

Iterative best improvement requires a way to evaluate each total assignment. For constraint satisfaction problems, a common evaluation function is the number of constraints that are violated. A violated constraint is called a **conflict**. With the evaluation function being the number of conflicts, a solution is a total assignment with an evaluation of zero. Sometimes this evaluation function is refined by weighting some constraints more than others.

A **local optimum** is an assignment such that no possible successor improves the evaluation function. This is also called a local minimum in greedy descent, or a local maximum in greedy ascent. A **global optimum** is an assignment that has the best value out of all assignments. All global optima are local optima, but there can be many local optima that are not a global optimum.

If the heuristic function is the number of conflicts, a satisfiable CSP has a global optimum with a heuristic value of 0, and an unsatisfiable CSP has a global optimum with a value above 0. If the search reaches a local minimum with a value above 0, you do not know if it is a global minimum (which implies the CSP is unsatisfiable) or not.

**Example 4.24** Consider the delivery scheduling in Example 4.9 (page 132). Suppose greedy descent starts with the assignment $A=2$, $B=2$, $C=3$, $D=2$, $E=1$. This assignment has an evaluation of 3, because it violates $A \neq B$, $B \neq D$, and $C < D$. One possible successor with the minimal evaluation has $B=4$ with an evaluation of 1 because only $C < D$ is unsatisfied. This assignment is selected. This is a local minimum. One possible successor with the fewest conflicts can be obtained by changing $D$ to 4, which has an evaluation of 2. It can then change $A$ to 4, with an evaluation of 2, and then change $B$ to 2, with an evaluation of 0, and a solution is found.

The following gives a trace of the assignments through the walk:

| $A$ | $B$ | $C$ | $D$ | $E$ | Evaluation |
|---|---|---|---|---|---|
| 2 | 2 | 3 | 2 | 1 | 3 |
| 2 | 4 | 3 | 2 | 1 | 1 |
| 2 | 4 | 3 | 4 | 1 | 2 |
| 4 | 4 | 3 | 4 | 1 | 2 |
| 4 | 2 | 3 | 4 | 1 | 0 |

Different initializations, or different choices when multiple assignments have the same evaluation, give different sequences of assignments to the variables and possibly different results.

Iterative best improvement considers the best successor assignment even if it is equal to or even worse than the current assignment. This means that if there are two or more assignments that are possible successors of each other and are all local, but not global, optima, it will keep moving between these assignments, and never reach a global optimum. Thus, this algorithm is not complete.

### 4.6.2 Randomized Algorithms

Iterative best improvement randomly picks one of the best possible successors of the current assignment, but it can get stuck in local minima that are not global minima.

Randomness can be used to escape local minima that are not global minima in two main ways:

- **random restart** (page 147), in which values for all variables are chosen at random; this lets the search start from a completely different part of the search space
- **random steps**, in which some random selections of variable and/or value are interleaved with the optimizing steps; with greedy descent, this process allows for upward steps that may enable random walk to escape a local minimum that is not a global minimum.

A random step is a cheap local operation only affecting a single variable, whereas a random restart is a global operation affecting all variables. For problems involving a large number of variables, a random restart can be quite expensive.

A mix of iterative best improvement with random steps is an instance of a class of algorithms known as **stochastic local search**.

Unfortunately, it is very difficult to visualize the search space to understand which algorithms work because there are often thousands or millions of dimensions (variables), each with a discrete, or even continuous, set of values. Some intuitions can be gleaned from lower-dimensional problems. Consider the two one-dimensional search spaces in Figure 4.9, where the objective is to find the minimum value. Suppose that a possible successor is obtained by a small step, either left or right of the current position. To find the global minimum in the search space (a), one would expect the greedy descent with random restart after a local optimum has been found to find the optimal value quickly. Once a random choice has found a point in the deepest valley, greedy descent quickly leads to the global minimum. One would not expect a random walk to work well in this example, because many random steps are required to exit one of the local, but not global, minima. However, for search space (b), a random restart quickly gets stuck on one of the jagged peaks and does not work very well. However, a random walk combined with greedy descent enables it to escape these local minima. A few random steps may be enough to escape a local minimum. Thus, one may expect that a random walk would work better in this search space.

Because it is difficult to determine which method would work best from examining the problem, practitioners evaluate many methods to see which one works well in practice for the particular problem. It is even possible that different parts of the search space have different characteristics. Some of the most efficient methods use **algorithm portfolios** – sets of algorithms, together with a learned function that, given a problem, chooses an appropriate algorithm from the portfolio.

### 4.6.3 Local Search Variants

There are many variants of iterative best improvement with randomness.

If the variables have small finite domains, a local search algorithm can consider all other values of the variable when considering the possible successors. If the domains are large, the cost of considering all the other values may be too high. An alternative is to consider only a few other values, often the close val-

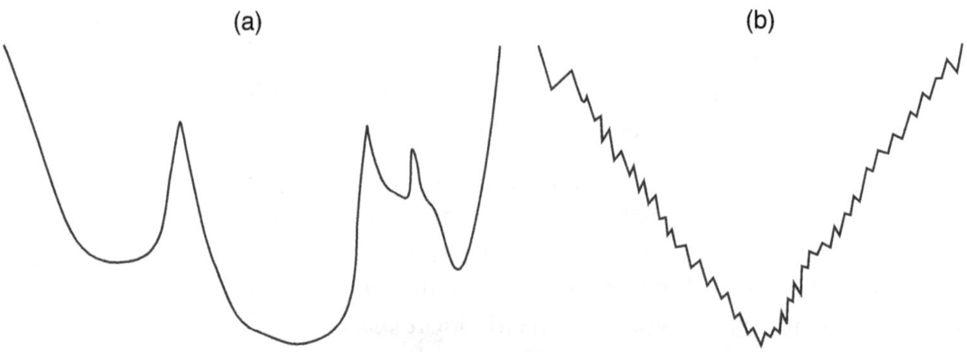


Figure 4.9: Two search spaces; find the minimum

ues, for one of the variables. Sometimes quite sophisticated methods are used to select an alternative value.

As presented, the local search has no memory. It does not remember anything about the search as it proceeds. A simple way to use memory to improve a local search is to use **tabu search**, which prevents recently changed variable assignments from being changed again. The idea is, when selecting a variable to change, not to select a variable that was changed in the last $t$ steps for some integer $t$, called the **tabu tenure**. If $t$ is small, tabu search can be implemented by having a list of the recently changed variables. If $t$ is larger, it can be implemented by including, for each variable, the step at which the variable got its current value. Tabu search prevents cycling among a few assignments. The tabu tenure is one of the parameters that can be optimized. A tabu list of size 1 is equivalent to not allowing the same assignment to be immediately revisited.

Algorithms differ in how much work they require to guarantee the best improvement step. At one extreme, an algorithm can guarantee to select one of the new assignments with the best improvement out of all possible successors. At the other extreme, an algorithm can select a new assignment at random and reject the assignment if it makes the situation worse. It is often better to make a quick choice than to spend a lot of time making the best choice. Which of these methods works best is, typically, an empirical question; it is difficult to determine theoretically whether large slow steps are better than small quick steps for a particular problem domain. There are many possible variants of which successor to select, some of which are explored in the next sections.

### Most Improving Step

The **most improving step** method always selects a variable–value pair that makes the best improvement. If there are many such pairs, one is chosen at random.

The naive way of implementing most improving step is, given the current total assignment, $A$, to linearly scan the variables, and for each variable $X$ and for each value $v$ in the domain of $X$ (other than the value of $X$ in $A$), evaluate the assignment $A$ but with $X=v$. Then select one of the variable–value pairs that results in the lowest evaluation. One step requires $O(ndr)$ evaluations of constraints, where $n$ is the number of variables, $d$ is the domain size, and $r$ is the number of constraints for each variable.

A more sophisticated alternative is to have a priority queue of variable–value pairs with associated weights. For each variable $X$, and each value $v$ in the domain of $X$ such that $X$ is not assigned to $v$ in $A$, the pair $\langle X,v \rangle$ is in the priority queue with weight the evaluation of $A$, but with $X=v$ minus the evaluation of $A$. This weight depends on values assigned to $X$ and the other variables in the constraints involving $X$ in the constraint, but does not depend on the values assigned to other variables. At each stage, the algorithm selects a variable–value pair with minimum weight, which gives a successor with the biggest improvement. Once a variable $X$ has been given a new value, the weights of all variable–value pairs that participate in a constraint that has been made satisfied or been made unsatisfied by the new assignment to $X$ must have their weights reassessed and, if changed, they need to be reinserted into the priority queue.

The size of the priority queue is $n(d-1)$, where $n$ is the number of variables and $d$ is the average domain size. To insert or remove an element takes time $O(\log nd)$. The algorithm removes one element from the priority queue, adds another, and updates the weights of at most $rk$ variables, where $r$ is the number of constraints per variable and $k$ is the number of variables per constraint. The complexity of one step of this algorithm is $O(rkd \log nd)$, where $n$ is the number of variables, $d$ is the average domain size, and $r$ is the number of constraints per variable. This algorithm spends much time maintaining the data structures to ensure that the most improving step is taken at each time.

### Two-Stage Choice

An alternative is to first select a variable and then select a value for that variable. The **two-stage choice** algorithm maintains a priority queue of variables, weighted by the number of conflicts (unsatisfied constraints) in which each variable participates. At each time, the algorithm selects a variable that participates in the maximum number of conflicts. Once a variable has been chosen, it can be assigned either a value that minimizes the number of conflicts or a value at random. For each constraint that becomes true or false as a result of this new assignment, the other variables participating in the constraint must have their weight re-evaluated.

The complexity of one step of this algorithm is $O(rk \log n)$, where $n$ is the number of variables and $r$ is the number of constraints per variable, and $k$ is the number of variables per constraint. Compared to selecting the best variable–value pair, this does less work for each step and so more steps are achievable for any given time period. However, the steps tend to give less improvement, giving a trade-off between the number of steps and the complexity per step.

### Any Conflict

Instead of choosing the best variable, an even simpler alternative is to select any variable participating in a conflict. A variable that is involved in a conflict is a **conflicting variable**. In the **any-conflict algorithm**, at each step, one of the conflicting variables is selected at random. The algorithm assigns to the chosen variable one of the values that minimizes the number of violated constraints or a value at random.

There are two variants of this algorithm, which differ in how the variable to be modified is selected:

- In the first variant, a conflict is chosen at random, and then a variable that is involved in the conflict is chosen at random.

- In the second variant, a variable that is involved in a conflict is chosen at random.

These differ in the probability that a variable in a conflict is chosen. In the first variant, the probability a variable is chosen depends on the number of conflicts it is involved in. In the second variant, all of the variables that are in conflicts are equally likely to be chosen.

Each of these algorithms requires maintaining data structures that enable a variable to be quickly selected at random. The data structure needs to be maintained as variables change their values. The first variant requires a set of conflicts from which a random element is selected, such as a binary search tree. The complexity of one step of this algorithm is thus $O(r \log c)$, where $r$ is the number of constraints per variable and $c$ is the number of constraints, because in the worst case $r$ constraints may need to be added or removed from the set of conflicts.

### Simulated Annealing

The last method maintains no data structure of conflicts; instead, it picks a variable and a new value for that variable at random and either rejects or accepts the new assignment.

**Annealing** is a metallurgical process where molten metals are slowly cooled to allow them to reach a low-energy state, making them stronger. Simulated annealing is an analogous method for optimization. It is typically described in terms of thermodynamics. The random movement corresponds to high temperature; at low temperature, there is little randomness. **Simulated annealing** is a stochastic local search algorithm where the temperature is reduced slowly, starting from approximately a random walk at high temperature, eventually becoming pure greedy descent as it approaches zero temperature. The randomness should allow the search to jump out of local minima and find regions that have a low heuristic value, whereas the greedy descent will lead to local minima. At high temperatures, worsening steps are more likely than at lower temperatures.

Like the other local search methods, simulated annealing maintains a current total assignment. At each step, it picks a variable at random, then picks a value for that variable at random. If assigning that value to the variable does not increase the number of conflicts, the algorithm accepts the assignment of that value to the variable, resulting in a new current assignment. Otherwise, it accepts the assignment with some probability, depending on the temperature and how much worse the new assignment is than the current assignment. If the change is not accepted, the current assignment is unchanged.

Suppose $A$ is the current total assignment and $h(A)$ is the evaluation of assignment $A$ to be minimized. For constraint solving, $h(A)$ is typically the number of conflicts of $A$. Simulated annealing selects a possible successor at random, which gives a new assignment $A'$. If $h(A') \leq h(A)$, it accepts the assignment and $A'$ becomes the new assignment. Otherwise, the new assignment is accepted randomly, using a **Gibbs distribution** or **Boltzmann distribution**, with probability

$$e^{-(h(A')-h(A))/T}$$

where $T$ is a positive real-valued temperature parameter. This is only used when $h(A') - h(A) > 0$, and so the exponent is always negative. If $h(A')$ is close to $h(A)$, the assignment is more likely to be accepted. If the temperature is high, the exponent will be close to zero, and so the probability will be close to one. As the temperature approaches zero, the exponent approaches $-\infty$, and the probability approaches zero.

Table 4.1 shows the probability of accepting worsening steps at different temperatures. In this figure, $k$-worse means that $h(A') - h(A) = k$. For example, if the temperature $T$ is 10, a change that is one worse (i.e., if $h(A') - h(A) = 1$) will be accepted with probability $e^{-0.1} \approx 0.9$; a change that is two worse will be accepted with probability $e^{-0.2} \approx 0.82$. If the temperature $T$ is 1, accepting a change that is one worse will happen with probability $e^{-1} \approx 0.37$. If the temperature is 0.1, a change that is one worse will be accepted with probability $e^{-10} \approx 0.00005$. At this temperature, it is essentially only performing steps that improve the value or leave it unchanged.

If the temperature is high, as in the $T = 10$ case, the algorithm tends to accept steps that only worsen a small amount; it does not tend to accept very large worsening steps. There is a slight preference for improving steps. As the temperature is reduced (e.g., when $T = 1$), worsening steps, although still possible, become much less likely. When the temperature is low (e.g., $T = 0.1$), it is very rare that it selects a worsening step.

Simulated annealing requires an **annealing schedule**, which specifies how the temperature is reduced as the search progresses. Geometric cooling is one of the most widely used schedules. An example of a geometric cooling schedule is to start with a temperature of 10 and multiply by 0.99 after each step; this will give a temperature of 0.07 after 500 steps. Finding a good annealing schedule is an art, and depends on the problem.

| Temperature | Probability of Acceptance | | |
|---|---|---|---|
| | 1-worse | 2-worse | 3-worse |
| 10 | 0.9 | 0.82 | 0.74 |
| 1 | 0.37 | 0.14 | 0.05 |
| 0.25 | 0.018 | 0.0003 | 0.000006 |
| 0.1 | 0.00005 | $2 * 10^{-9}$ | $9 * 10^{-14}$ |

Table 4.1: Probability of simulated annealing accepting worsening steps

### 4.6.4 Evaluating Randomized Algorithms

It is difficult to compare randomized algorithms when they give a different result and a different run time each time they are run, even for the same problem. It is especially difficult when the algorithms sometimes do not find an answer; they either run forever or must be stopped at an arbitrary point.

Unfortunately, summary statistics, such as the mean or median run time, are not very useful. For example, comparing algorithms on the mean run time requires deciding how to average in unsuccessful runs, where no solution was found. If unsuccessful runs are ignored in computing the average, an algorithm that picks a random assignment and then stops would be the best algorithm; it does not succeed very often, but when it does, it is very fast. Treating the non-terminating runs as having infinite time means all algorithms that do not find a solution will have infinite averages. A run that has not found a solution will need to be terminated. Using the time it was terminated in the average is more of a function of the stopping time than of the algorithm itself, although this does allow for a crude trade-off between finding some solutions fast versus finding more solutions.

If you were to compare algorithms using the median run time, you would prefer an algorithm that solves the problem 51% of the time but very slowly over one that solves the problem 49% of the time but very quickly, even though the latter is more useful. The problem is that the median (the 50th percentile) is just an arbitrary value; you could just as well consider the 47th percentile or the 87th percentile.

One way to visualize the run time of an algorithm for a particular problem is to use a **run-time distribution**, which shows the variability of the run time of a randomized algorithm on a single problem instance. The $x$-axis represents either the number of steps or the run time. The $y$-axis shows, for each value of $x$, the number of runs, or the proportion of the runs, solved within that run time or number of steps. Thus, it provides a cumulative distribution of how often the problem was solved within some number of steps or run time. For example, you can find the run time of the 30th percentile of the runs by finding the $x$-value that maps to 30% on the $y$-scale. The run-time distribution can be plotted (or approximated) by running the algorithm for a large number of times (say, 100 times for a rough approximation or 1000 times for a reasonably accurate plot) and then by sorting the runs by run time.

**Example 4.25** Five empirically generated run-time distributions for the CSP of Figure 4.5 (page 139) are shown in Figure 4.10 (page 156). On the $x$-axis is the number of steps, using a logarithmic scale. On the $y$-axis is the number of instances that were successfully solved out of 1000 runs. This shows five run-time distributions on the same problem instance.

The two dark lines (labeled $P(best) = 1$) use the same settings, and show an example of the variability of using 1000 runs. These solved the problem 20% of the time in 19 or fewer steps, but only solved the problem in around 55% of the cases.

The any-conflict case (labeled $P(best) = 0.00$, $P(ac) = 1.00$) took 32 steps to solve 20% of the runs, but managed to solve in all runs, taking up to 784 steps.

The other two cases, which chose the best node with probability 0.5 and otherwise chose a constraint in any conflict, solved all of the problems. Again these two cases used the same settings and show the variability of the experiment.

This only compares the number of steps; the time taken would be a better evaluation but is more difficult to measure for small problems and depends on the details of the implementation. The any-conflict algorithm takes less time than maintaining the data structures for finding a most-improving variable choice. The other algorithms that need to maintain the same data structures

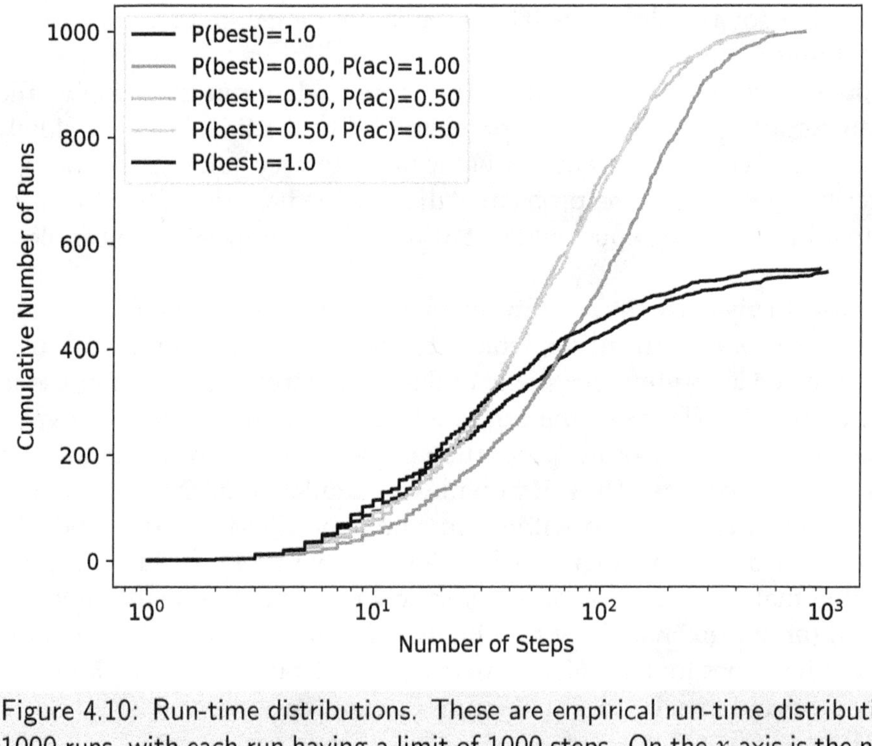


Figure 4.10: Run-time distributions. These are empirical run-time distributions of 1000 runs, with each run having a limit of 1000 steps. On the $x$-axis is the number of steps (using a logarithmic scale) and on the $y$-axis is the number of successes out of 1000 runs. This is generated using AIPython (aipython.org) for the network of Figure 4.5 (page 139). The dark lines (labeled $P(best) = 1$) are two separate runs for the two-stage greedy descent (picking a variable with the most conflicts). The line labeled $P(best) = 0.00$, $P(ac) = 1.00$ is any conflict, which picks a variable in a conflict at random. In the other two (labeled $P(best) = 0.50$, $P(ac) = 0.50$), with probability 0.5, a variable with the most conflicts is selected, otherwise a random variable in a random conflict is selected

take a similar time per step.

One algorithm strictly dominates another for this problem if its run-time distribution is completely to the left (and above) the run-time distribution of the second algorithm. Often two algorithms are incomparable under this measure. Which algorithm is better depends on how much time an agent has before it needs to use a solution or how important it is to actually find a solution.

**Example 4.26** In the run-time distributions of Figure 4.10 (page 156), the probabilistic mix $P(best) = 0.50$, $P(ac) = 0.50$ dominated $P(ac) = 1.0$. For any number of steps, it solved the problem in more runs.

This example was very small, and the empirical results here may not reflect performance on larger or different problems.

### 4.6.5 Random Restart

It may seem like a randomized algorithm that only succeeds, say, 20% of the time is not very useful if you need an algorithm to succeed, say, 99% of the time. However, a randomized algorithm that succeeds some of the time can be extended to an algorithm that succeeds more often by running it multiple times, using a random restart, and reporting any solution found.

Whereas a random walk, and its variants, are evaluated empirically by running experiments, the performance of random restart can also be predicted ahead of time, because the runs following a random restart are independent of each other.

A randomized algorithm for a problem that has a solution, and succeeds with probability $p$ independently each time, that is run $n$ times or until a solution is found, will find a solution with probability $1 - (1 - p)^n$. It fails to find a solution if it fails for each retry, and each retry is independent of the others.

For example, an algorithm that succeeds with probability $p = 0.5$ tried 5 times will find a solution around 96.9% of the time; tried 10 times it will find a solution 99.9% of the time. If each run succeeded with a probability $p = 0.1$, running it 10 times will succeed 65% of the time, and running it 44 times will give a 99% success rate. It is also possible to run these in parallel.

A run-time distribution allows us to predict how the algorithm will work with random restart after a certain number of steps. Intuitively, a random restart will repeat the lower left corner of the run-time distribution, suitably scaled down, at the stage where the restart occurs. A random restart after a certain number of greedy descent steps will make any algorithm that sometimes finds a solution into an algorithm that always finds a solution, given that one exists, if it is run for long enough.

**Example 4.27** In the distribution of Figure 4.10 (page 156), greedy search ($P(best) = 1.0$) solved more problems in the first 10 steps, after which it is not as effective as any-conflict search or a probabilistic mix. This may lead you to try to suggest using these settings with a random restart after 10 steps. This does, indeed, dominate the other algorithms for this problem instance, at least in terms of the number of steps (counting a restart as a single step). However, because the random restart is an expensive operation, this algorithm may not be the most efficient. This also does not necessarily predict how well the algorithm will work in other problem instances.

A random restart can be expensive if there are many variables. A **partial restart** randomly assigns just some not all of the variables, say 100 variables, or 10% of the variables, to move to another part of the search space. While this is often effective, the above theoretical analysis does not work because the partial restarts are not independent of each other.

## 4.7 Population-Based Methods

The preceding local search algorithms maintain a single total assignment. This section considers algorithms that maintain multiple total assignments. The first method, beam search, maintains the best $k$ assignments. The next algorithm, stochastic beam search, selects which assignments to maintain stochastically. In genetic algorithms, which are inspired by biological evolution, the $k$ assignments forming a population interact to produce the new population. In these algorithms, a total assignment of a value to each variable is called an **individual** and the set of current individuals is a **population**.

**Beam search** is a method similar to iterative best improvement, but it maintains up to $k$ assignments instead of just one. It reports success when it finds a satisfying assignment. At each stage of the algorithm, it selects $k$ best possible successors of the current individuals (or all of them if there are less than $k$) and picks randomly in the case of ties. It repeats with this new set of $k$ total assignments.

Beam search considers multiple assignments at the same time. Beam search is useful for memory-bounded cases, where $k$ can be selected depending on the memory available. The variants of stochastic local search presented earlier are also applicable to beam search; you can spend more time finding the best $k$, or spend less time and only approximate the best $k$.

**Stochastic beam search** is an alternative to beam search, which, instead of choosing the best $k$ individuals, selects $k$ of the individuals at random; the individuals with a better evaluation are more likely to be chosen. This is done by making the probability of being chosen a function of the evaluation function. A standard method is to use a **Gibbs distribution** or **Boltzmann distribution** (page 154) and select assignment $A$ with probability proportional to

$$e^{-h(A)/T}$$

where $h(A)$ is an evaluation function and $T$ is temperature.

Stochastic beam search tends to allow more diversity in the $k$ individuals than does plain beam search. As an analogy to evolution in biology, the evaluation function reflects the fitness of the individual; the fitter the individual, the more likely it is to pass its genetic material – here its variable assignment – on to the next generation. Stochastic beam search is like asexual reproduction; each individual gives slightly mutated children and then stochastic beam search proceeds with survival of the fittest. Note that under stochastic beam search it is possible for an individual to be selected multiple times at random.

**Genetic algorithms** further pursue the evolution analogy. Genetic algorithms are like stochastic beam searches, but each new element of the population is a combination of a pair of individuals – its parents. In particular, genetic algorithms use an operation known as **crossover** that selects pairs of individuals and then creates new offspring by taking some of the values for the offspring's variables from one of the parents and the rest of the values from the other parent, loosely analogous to how DNA is spliced in sexual reproduction.

A genetic algorithm is shown in Figure 4.11 (page 160). This maintains a population of $k$ individuals. At each step, a new generation of individuals is generated via the following steps until a solution is found:

- Randomly select pairs of individuals where the fitter individuals are more likely to be chosen. How much more likely a fit individual is to be chosen than a less fit individual depends on the difference in fitness levels and a temperature parameter. This is called **fitness proportional selection**.
- For each pair, perform a crossover (see below).
- Randomly mutate some (very few) values by choosing other values for some randomly chosen variables. This is a random walk step.

It proceeds in this way until it has created $k$ individuals, and then the operation proceeds to the next generation.

An alternative to fitness proportional selection is **tournament selection**, which involves selecting $t$ individuals, then choosing the fittest among them. The parameter $t$ determines how greedy the selection is.

The new operation in genetic algorithms is **crossover**. Uniform crossover takes two individuals (the parents) and creates two new individuals, called the **offspring**. The value for each variable in a child comes from one of the parents. A common method is **one-point crossover**, shown in the procedure *Crossover* in Figure 4.11 (page 160), which assumes a total ordering of the variables. An index $i$ is selected at random. One of the offspring is constructed by selecting the values for the variables up to $i$ from one of the parents, and the values for variables after $i$ from the other parent. The other child gets the other values. The effectiveness of the crossover depends on the total ordering of the variables. The ordering of the variables is part of the design of the genetic algorithm.

**Example 4.28** Consider Example 4.9 (page 132), where the evaluation function to be minimized is the number of unsatisfied constraints. The individual $A=2, B=2, C=3, D=1, E=1$ has an evaluation of 4. It has a low value mainly

**procedure** *Genetic_algorithm*$(Vs, Cs, S, k)$
**Inputs**
*Vs*: a set of variables
*Cs*: set of constraints to be satisfied
*S*: a cooling schedule for the temperature
*k*: population size
**Output**
total assignment that satisfies the constraints
**Local**
*Pop*: a set of total assignments
*T*: real
$Pop :=$ $k$ random total assignments
$T$ is assigned a value according to $S$
**repeat**
**if** some $A \in Pop$ satisfies all constraints in $Cs$ **then**
**return** $A$
$Npop := \{\}$
**repeat** $k/2$ **times**
$A_1 := Random\_selection(Pop, T)$
$A_1 := Random\_selection(Pop, T)$
$N_1, N_2 := Crossover(A_1, A_2)$
$Npop := Npop \cup \{mutate(N_1), mutate(N_2)\}$
$Pop := Npop$
$T$ is updated according to $S$
**until** *termination*()
**procedure** *Random_selection*$(Pop, T)$
select $A$ from $Pop$ with probability proportional to $e^{-h(A)/T}$
**return** $A$
**procedure** *Crossover*$(A_1, A_2)$
select integer $i$, $1 \leq i < |Vs|$ at random
Let $N_1 := \{(X_j = v_j) \in A_1 \text{ for } j \leq i\} \cup \{(X_j = v_j) \in A_2 \text{ for } j > i\}$
Let $N_2 := \{(X_j = v_j) \in A_2 \text{ for } j \leq i\} \cup \{(X_j = v_j) \in A_1 \text{ for } j > i\}$
**return** $N_1, N_2$

Figure 4.11: Genetic algorithm for finding a solution to a CSP because $E = 1$. Its offspring that preserve this property will tend to have a lower evaluation than those that do not and, thus, will be more likely to survive. Other individuals may have low values for different reasons; for example, the individual $A = 4$, $B = 2$, $C = 3$, $D = 4$, $E = 4$ also has an evaluation of 4. It is low mainly because of the assignment of values to the first four variables. Again, offspring that preserve this property will be fitter and more likely to survive than those that do not. If these two were to mate, some of the offspring would inherit the bad properties of both and would die off. Some, by chance, would inherit the good properties of both. These would then have a better chance of survival.

Efficiency is very sensitive to the variables used to describe the problem and the ordering of the variables. Getting this to work is an art. As with many other randomized algorithms, evolutionary algorithms have many degrees of freedom and, therefore, are difficult to configure or tune for good performance.

A large community of researchers are working on genetic algorithms to make them practical for real problems and there have been some impressive results. What we have described here is only one of the possible genetic algorithms.

## 4.8 Optimization

Instead of just having a total assignment satisfy constraints or not, we often have a **preference** relation over assignments, and we want a best total assignment according to the preference.

An **optimization problem** is given:

- a set of variables, each with an associated domain
- an **objective function** that maps total assignments to real numbers
- an **optimality criterion**, which is typically to find a total assignment that minimizes or maximizes the objective function.

The aim is to find a total assignment that is optimal according to the optimality criterion. For concreteness, we assume that the optimality criterion is to minimize the objective function. When minimizing, the function is often called the **cost function, loss function**, or **error function**.

A **constrained optimization problem** is an optimization problem that also has hard constraints. The set of assignments that does not violate a constraint is the set of **feasible** assignments. The aim is to find a feasible assignment that optimizes the objective function according to the optimality criterion.

**Example 4.29** The University of British Columbia (UBC) is one of the larger universities in Canada. It needs to schedule exams multiple times a year. Exam scheduling is a constrained optimization problem. In one term, there were 30,000 students taking exams, and 1700 course sections that needed to be scheduled into 52 time slots over 13 days, and 274 rooms. There any many courses that are divided into multiple sections, with lectures at different times, that must have exams at the same time, so there can be no simple mapping from lecture times to exam times. With the hard constraint that no student should have two exams at the same time – which seems reasonable – there are no possible exam schedules. Thus, soft constraints are needed. When an AI system started to be used for exam scheduling, the hard constraints were:

- There must be no more than 30 conflicts for a section, where a conflict is a student that has two exams at the same time.
- Each exam must fit into the allowable times and the allowable rooms for that exam (for the few cases where there are constraints on allowable times and rooms).
- There cannot be more students than the room capacity in a room.
- Each exam must go into a room that has the required room features.
- Unrelated exams cannot share a room.
- Cross-listed courses must have the same exam time.
- Evening courses must have evening exams.

The soft constraints that need to be minimized include:

- the number of conflicts
- the number of students with two or more exams on the same day
- the number of students with three or more exams in four consecutive time slots
- the number of students with back-to-back exams
- the number of students with less than eight time slots between exams
- the preferred times for each exam
- the preferred rooms for each exam
- first-year exams should not be on the last two days in the Fall (to allow time for large exams to be marked before the holidays)
- fourth-year exams should not be on the last two days in the Spring (so exams can be marked before graduation is determined).

These are not weighted equally.

One representation is that there is a *time* variable for each section with domain the set of possible time slots, and there is a *room* variable for each section, with domain the set of rooms.

This is simpler than many real-world scheduling problems as each exam only needs to be scheduled once and all of the time slots are the same length.

A huge literature exists on optimization. There are many techniques for particular forms of constrained optimization problems. For example, **linear programming** is the class of constrained optimization where the variables are real valued, the objective function is a linear function of the variables, and the hard constraints are linear inequalities. If the problem you are interested in solving falls into one of the classes for which there are more specific algorithms, or can be transformed into one, it is generally better to use those techniques than the more general algorithms presented here.

In a **factored optimization problem**, the objective function is factored into a set of soft constraints. A **soft constraint** has a **scope** that is a set of variables. The soft constraint is a function from the domains of the variables in its scope into a real number, a **cost**. A typical objective function is the sum of the costs of the soft constraints, and the optimality criterion is to minimize the objective function.

**Example 4.30** Suppose a number of delivery activities must be scheduled, similar to Example 4.9 (page 132), but, instead of hard constraints, there are preferences on times for the activities. The values of the variables are times. The soft constraints are costs associated with combinations of times associated with the variables. The aim is to find a schedule with the minimum total sum of the costs.

Suppose variables $A$, $C$, $D$, and $E$ have domain $\{1,2\}$, and variable $B$ has domain $\{1,2,3\}$. The soft constraints are $c_1$ with scope $\{A,B\}$, $c_2$ with scope $\{B,C\}$, and $c_3$ with scope $\{B,D\}$. Define their extension (page 131) as

$c_1$:

| $A$ | $B$ | Cost |
|---|---|---|
| 1 | 1 | 5 |
| 1 | 2 | 2 |
| 1 | 3 | 2 |
| 2 | 1 | 0 |
| 2 | 2 | 4 |
| 2 | 3 | 3 |

$c_2$:

| $B$ | $C$ | Cost |
|---|---|---|
| 1 | 1 | 5 |
| 1 | 2 | 2 |
| 2 | 1 | 0 |
| 2 | 2 | 4 |
| 3 | 1 | 2 |
| 3 | 2 | 0 |

$c_3$:

| $B$ | $D$ | Cost |
|---|---|---|
| 1 | 1 | 3 |
| 1 | 2 | 0 |
| 2 | 1 | 2 |
| 2 | 2 | 2 |
| 3 | 1 | 2 |
| 3 | 2 | 4 |

The constraint $c_4$, with scope $\{A,C\}$, has a cost of 3 if $A = C$, and 0 otherwise; $c_4$ provides a soft constraint that $A$ and $C$ should be different.

Soft constraints can be added point-wise. The sum of two soft constraints is a soft constraint with scope that is the union of their scopes. The cost of any assignment to variables in the scope is the sum of the costs of the constraints being added on that assignment.

**Example 4.31** Consider functions $c_1$ and $c_2$ in Example 4.30. $c_1 + c_2$ is a function with scope $\{A,B,C\}$, defined point-wise. For example, $c_1 + c_2$ evaluated in context $\{A=1, B=1, C=2\}$ is

$$\begin{aligned}(c_1 + c_2)(A=1, B=1, C=2) &= c_1(A=1, B=1) + c_2(B=1, C=2)\\ &= 5 + 2 = 7.\end{aligned}$$

Similarly, $c_1 + c_2 + c_3$ evaluated in context $\{A=1, B=1, C=2, D=2\}$ is

$$\begin{aligned}&(c_1 + c_2 + c_3)(A=1, B=1, C=2, D=1)\\ &\quad = c_1(A=1, B=1) + c_2(B=1, C=2) + c_3(B=1, D=1)\\ &\quad = 5 + 2 + 3 = 10.\end{aligned}$$

Hard constraints can be modeled as having a cost of infinity for violating a constraint. As long as the cost of an assignment is finite, it does not violate a hard constraint. An alternative is to use a large number – larger than the sum of the soft constraints could be – as the cost of violating a hard constraint. Then optimization can be used to find a solution with the fewest number of violated hard constraints and, among those, one with the lowest cost.

Optimization problems have one difficulty that goes beyond constraint satisfaction problems. It is difficult to know whether an assignment is optimal. Whereas, for a CSP, an algorithm can check whether an assignment is a solution by just considering the assignment and the constraints, in optimization problems an algorithm can only determine whether an assignment is optimal by comparing it to other assignments.

Many of the methods for solving hard constraints can be extended to optimization problems, as outlined in the following sections.

### 4.8.1 Systematic Methods for Discrete Optimization

When all of the variables have finite discrete domains, optimization is known as **discrete optimization**. In this case, it is possible to search through the space of assignments to find the least-cost assignment.

Any of the search algorithms of the previous chapter that minimize path cost can be used to search for the best solution. To do that, we need to define the optimization problem in terms of a search graph. The graph to search is defined as follows:

- The nodes are assignments of values to some subset of the variables.
- The neighbors of a node $n$ are obtained by selecting a variable *var* that is not assigned in node $n$ and by having a neighbor for each assignment of a value to *var*. The cost of the arc is the sum of the costs of the constraints that can be evaluated when *var* is assigned a value.

  Suppose node $n$ is the assignment $\{X_1 = v_1, \ldots, X_k = v_k\}$. To find the neighbors of $n$, select a variable $Y$ that is not in the set $\{X_1, \ldots, X_k\}$. For each value $y_i \in domain(Y)$, where $X_1 = v_1, \ldots, X_k = v_k, Y = y_i$ is consistent with each of the constraints, the node $\{X_1 = v_1, \ldots, X_k = v_k, Y = y_i\}$ is a neighbor of $n$. The cost of the arc is the sum of the constraints that involve only $\{X_1, \ldots, X_k, Y\}$ that were not previously evaluated in this branch.
- The start node is the empty assignment that does not assign a value to any variables.
- A goal node is a node that assigns a value to every variable. Note that this only exists if the assignment is consistent with all of the constraints.

By assigning costs as soon as a soft constraint is able to be evaluated, search algorithms such as $A^*$ or branch and bound can be used to find a minimal solution. These methods require each arc cost to be non-negative. To achieve this, the lowest cost in each soft constraint – even if it is negative – is subtracted from each of the costs in the soft constraint. This cost then needs to be added to the cost of a final solution.

**Example 4.32** Suppose $X$ and $Y$ are variables with domain $\{0,1\}$. The soft constraint

| $X$ | $Y$ | Cost |
|---|---|---|
| 0 | 0 | −4 |
| 0 | 1 | −1 |
| 1 | 0 | 6 |
| 1 | 1 | 5 |

is converted into non-negative form by subtracting −4 (i.e., adding 4) to each cost, so the costs range from 0 to 10, rather than from −4 to 6. The 4 is then subtracted from the cost of the solution.

Figure 4.12 (page 166) shows the **branch-and-bound search** of Figure 3.14 (page 106) for factored optimization. The heuristic function, $h(context, Cs)$, is an estimate of how much the soft constraints $Cs$ will cost, given *context*. It can be the sum of the minimum values for the constraints in $Cs$ given *context*. As long as $h$ is an underestimate, the algorithm will find the optimal solution. If all of the constraints are in non-negative form, $h$ always returning zero will be an underestimate, but we can typically do much better.

**Example 4.33** The soft constraint of Example 4.32 in non-negative form is

| $X$ | $Y$ | Cost |
|---|---|---|
| 0 | 0 | 0 |
| 0 | 1 | 3 |
| 1 | 0 | 10 |
| 1 | 1 | 9 |

In a context where $X = 1$, the heuristic value of this soft constraint is 9, the minimum cost for assignments with $X = 1$. In a context with $Y = 1$, the heuristic value is 3. The other contexts have value 0, because that is the minimum value for no assignments or for $X = 0$ or $Y = 0$.

This can be made more efficient by exploiting the structure of the constraint network. In particular, if the context disconnects the constraint graph (when the assigned variables are removed), the separate components can be solved independently. This can be recognized because $CCs$ can be partitioned into sets that have no variables in $CVs$ in common. Another way to exploit structure is to cache values that have already been computed. These two refinements are explored in more detail in an analogous algorithm for probabilistic reasoning (see Section 9.5.1, page 409).

**Arc consistency** (page 137) can be generalized to optimization problems by allowing pruning of dominated assignments. Suppose $c_1, \dots, c_k$ are the soft constraints that involve X. Let $c = c_1 + \cdots + c_k$. Suppose $Y_1, \ldots, Y_m$ are the variables, other than X, that are involved in c. A value v for variable X is **strictly dominated** if, for all values $y_1, \ldots, y_k$ of $Y_1, \ldots, Y_m$, some value $v'$ of X exists such that $c(X=v', Y_1=y_1, \ldots, Y_m=y_m) < c(X=v, Y_1=y_1, \ldots, Y_m=y_m)$. Pruning strictly dominated values does not remove a minimal solution. The pruning of domains can be done repeatedly, as in the *GAC* algorithm (page 138).

**Weakly dominated** has the same definition as strictly dominated, but with "less than" replaced by "less than or equal to." If only one solution is required, weakly dominated values can be pruned sequentially. Which weakly dominated values are removed may affect which optimal solution is found, but

```
procedure DF_branch_and_bound_const(Vs, domain, Cs, h, bound_0)
    Inputs
        (Vs, domain, Cs): CSP with variables (Vs), domain (dom), and constraints Cs
        h: heuristic function
        bound_0: initial depth bound (can be ∞ if not specified)
    Output
        a lowest-cost total assignment with cost less than bound_0
        or ⊥ if there is no solution with cost less than bound_0
    Local
        best_asst: total assignment or ⊥
        bound: non-negative real
        procedure cbsearch(CVs, CCs, context)
                ▷ context is an assignment, CVs is set of unassigned variables, CCs is set of unevaluated constraints
            can_eval := {c ∈ CCs | scope(c) ⊆ variables(context)}
            rem_Cs := CCs \ can_eval
            cost_context := Σ_{c∈can_eval} cost(c, context)
            if cost_context + h(context, rem_Cs) < bound then
                if CVs = {} then
                    best_asst := context
                    bound := cost_context
                else
                    select variable var ∈ CVs
                    for each val ∈ domain(var) do
                        cbsearch(CVs \ {var}, rem_Cs, {var = val} ∪ context)
    best_asst := ⊥
    bound := bound_0
    cbsearch(Vs, Cs, {})
    return best_asst
```

Figure 4.12: Depth-first branch-and-bound search for optimization removing a weakly dominated value does not remove all optimal solutions.

As with arc consistency for hard constraints, pruning (strictly or weakly) dominated values may greatly simplify the problem but does not, by itself, always solve the problem. Arc consistency can be combined with domain splitting (page 141) to build a search tree to find an optimal solution.

**Variable elimination** (page 143) can also be used for soft constraints. Instead of the join, sum the factors and select the value of the eliminated variable with the minimum cost.

### 4.8.2 Local Search for Optimization

Local search is directly applicable to optimization problems, where the local search is used to minimize the objective function, rather than find a solution. The algorithm runs for a certain amount of time (perhaps including random restarts to explore other parts of the search space), always keeping the best assignment found thus far, and returning this as its answer.

Local search for optimization has one extra complication that does not arise when there are only hard constraints. With only hard constraints, the algorithm has found a solution when there are no conflicts. For optimization, it is difficult to determine whether the best total assignment found is the best possible solution. A **local optimum** is a total assignment that is at least as good, according to the optimality criterion, as any of its possible successors. A **global optimum** is a total assignment that is at least as good as all of the other total assignments. Without systematically searching the other assignments, the algorithm may not know whether the best assignment found so far is a global optimum or whether a better solution exists in a different part of the search space.

When using local search to solve constrained optimization problems, with both hard and soft constraints, it is often useful to allow the algorithm to violate hard constraints on the way to a solution. This is done by making the cost of violating a hard constraint some large, but finite, value.

### 4.8.3 Gradient Descent for Continuous Functions

Local search for optimization with continuous domains requires a more refined definition of a successor of a total assignment.

Consider a function $f(x) = y$, where $x$ and $y$ are real numbers (e.g., $f(x) = exp(1.7 * x^2 + 0.3)$). $f$ is **continuous** if a small change in $x$ can only result in a small change in $y$. If $f$ is continuous, and $f(x) = y$, for each $x$ and $\epsilon$, there is an $\epsilon_y$ such that

$$f(x + \epsilon) = y + \epsilon_y.$$

Continuous means that if $\epsilon$ is small, then so is $\epsilon_y$. For example, the function $int(x)$ that returns the largest integer smaller than $x$ is not continuous.

$f$ is **smooth** if it doesn't have any abrupt angles. For example, $f(x) = max(x, 0)$ is continuous but not smooth. A continuous and smooth function can be approximated at a point by a linear function of $\epsilon$:

$$f(x+\epsilon) = f(x) + \epsilon * \delta.$$

This approximation gets better, the smaller that $\epsilon$ is. Solving for $\delta$ gives $\delta = (f(x+\epsilon) - f(x))/\epsilon$. For a continuous and smooth function, as $\epsilon$ gets closer to zero, this ratio gets closer to a value called the **derivative** of $f$ at $x$, written $(\frac{d}{dx}f)(x)$. Thus, $\frac{d}{dx}f$ is the function that returns the slope of $f$ at any point. You do not need to know how to derive the derivative; modern tools are good at automatically differentiating any function that is made up of addition, subtraction, exponentiation, and may other functions.

If $f$ is a function of one variable, the derivative is sometimes written $f'$. The function $f(v) + x * f'(v)$ is called the **tangent** of $f$ at $v$. The derivative of $f$ at a point gives the slope of the tangent at that point. The tangent of a function at $v$ approximates the function near $v$.

**Example 4.34** Consider the function $f(x) = 2 * (x - 1.3) * (x - 1.5) * (x - 2) * (x - 4.5) + 15$ plotted in Figure 4.13. The tangents of $f$ at 1 and 4.5 are shown. Notice how they form a good approximation to the function close to these points, even though they may be a poor approximation at further points.

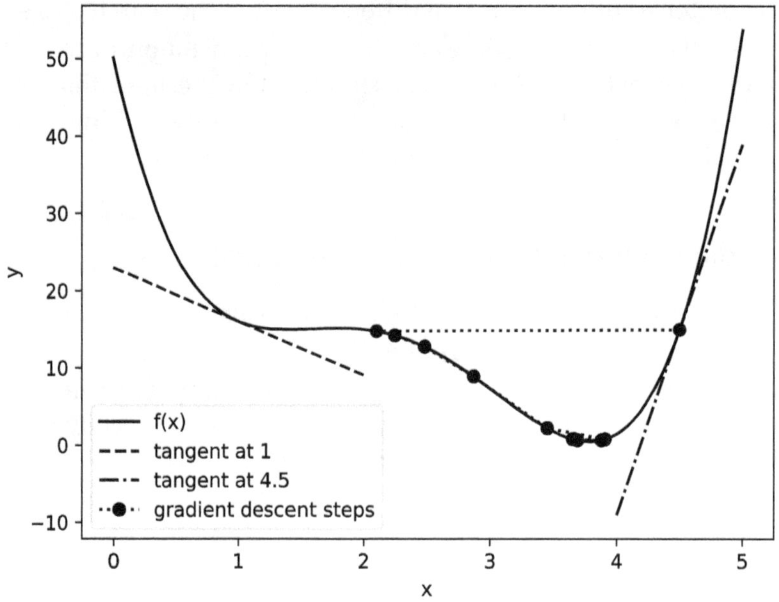


Figure 4.13: Derivatives and gradient decent

A (small) step in the direction of the derivative will increase the value unless the derivative is zero. A small step in the opposite direction will reduce the value. To find a minimum, **gradient descent** takes steps in the direction of the negative of the gradient. Gradient descent is like walking downhill and always taking a step in the direction that is locally downward. The successor of a total assignment is a step downhill, where the steps become bigger as the slope becomes steeper.

To minimize $f(x)$, where $x$ is a real-valued variable with current value of $v$, the next value

$$v - \eta * \left(\frac{df}{dx}\right)(v)$$

where $\eta$ is the **step size** determines how big a step to take. The algorithm is sensitive to the step size. If $\eta$ is too large, the algorithm can overshoot the minimum. If $\eta$ is too small, progress becomes very slow.

**Example 4.35** Consider finding the minimum value for a function $f(x)$ shown in Figure 4.13 (page 168). Suppose the step size is 0.05 and gradient descent starts at $x = 4.5$. The derivative is positive, so it steps to the left. Here it overshoots the minimum and the next position is $x = 2.1$, where the derivative is negative and has a smaller absolute value, so it takes a smaller step to the right. The steps are shown as the dotted trajectory in Figure 4.13 (page 168). It eventually finds a point close to the minimum. At that point the derivative is close to zero and so it makes very small steps.

If the step size was slightly larger, it could step into the shallow local minimum between 1.3 and 1.5, where the derivative is close to zero, and would be stuck there. If it took an even larger step, it might end up with $x$ close to zero or negative, in which case the derivative is larger in magnitude and will then step to a value greater than 4.5, and eventually diverges.

If the step size was much smaller, it might take a longer time to get to the local minimum. There is nothing special about 0.05. For example, if the $y$ values were 10 times as much, a step size of 0.005 would give the same behavior.

For multidimensional optimization, when there are many variables, the **partial derivative** of a function with respect to a variable is the derivative of the function with the other variables fixed. We write $\frac{\partial f}{\partial x}$ to be the derivative of $f$, with respect to variable $x$, with the other variables fixed.

Gradient descent takes a step in each direction proportional to the partial derivative of that direction. If $\langle x_1, \ldots, x_n \rangle$ are the variables that have to be assigned values, a total assignment corresponds to a tuple of values $\langle v_1, \ldots, v_n \rangle$. Assume that the evaluation function to be minimized, $h$, is continuous and smooth. The successor of the total assignment $\langle v_1, \ldots, v_n \rangle$ is obtained by moving in each direction in proportion to the slope of $h$ in that direction. The new value for $X_i$ is

$$v_i - \eta * \left(\frac{\partial h}{\partial x_i}\right)(v_1, \ldots, v_n)$$

where $\eta$ is the **step size**.

Gradient descent and variants are used for parameter learning (page 291); some large language models (page 364) have over $10^{12}$ parameters to be optimized. There are many variants of this algorithm. For example, instead of using a constant step size, the algorithm could do a binary search to determine a locally optimal step size. See Section 8.2 (page 336) for variants used in modern neural networks.

For smooth functions, where there is a minimum, if the step size is small enough, gradient descent will converge to a local minimum. If the step size is too big, it is possible that the algorithm will diverge. If the step size is too small, the algorithm will be very slow. If there is a unique local minimum which is the global minimum, gradient descent, with a small enough step size, will converge to that global minimum. When there are multiple local minima, not all of which are global minima, it may need to search to find a global minimum, for example by doing a random restart (page 147) or a random walk (page 149). These are not guaranteed to find a global minimum unless the whole search space is exhausted, but are often as good as we can get. The algorithms that power modern deep learning algorithms are described Section 8.2 (page 336); these adapt the step size for each dimension.

## 4.9 Social Impact

While it might seem that the main problem is how to optimize and how to solve a constraint problem, a perhaps more important problem is to decide on what to optimize. Consider the exam scheduling problem of Example 4.29 (page 161). A bad exam schedule can affect a student's performance, which could potentially affect whether they get into the career they want if they are on the borderline. The schedule found depends on the soft constraints, and their costs.

Students in a first-year class were asked their opinions on a perfect exam schedule, and they generally wanted one or two days off between each exam, no early morning exams, no evening exams, the first exam should be early in the exam period, and the last exam as early in the exam period as possible. Not all students can have such a schedule. Making a schedule better for some people may make it worse for others.

When the schedule was created by someone in an office (presumably by making adjustments to the previous schedule), it was not open to inspection. One of the hopes is that by making the preference function explicit, it can be criticized, and improved.

Constraint reasoning techniques are used to solve logistic problems of significant economic importance. Consider the routing problem of scheduling multiple vehicles to various customer locations where the items, of varying size, being transported must be picked up and delivered within given time windows. The task is to minimize the number of vehicles required by the schedule. Bent and Van Hentenryck [2004] show that a two-stage algorithm using simulated annealing followed by neighborhood search with branch and bound achieves excellent performance on standard benchmarks.

## 4.10 Review

The following are the main points you should have learned from this chapter:

- Instead of reasoning explicitly in terms of states, it is almost always much more efficient for an agent to reason in terms of variables or features.
- Constraint satisfaction problems are represented as a set of variables, domains for the variables, and a set of hard and/or soft constraints. A solution is an assignment of a value to each variable that satisfies a set of hard constraints or optimizes the sum of the soft constraints.
- Arc consistency and search can often be combined to find assignments that satisfy some constraints or to show that there is no assignment.
- Stochastic local search can be used to find satisfying assignments, but not to show there are no satisfying assignments. The efficiency depends on the trade-off between the time taken for each improvement and how much the value is improved at each step. Some method must be used to allow the search to escape local minima that are not solutions.
- Optimization can use systematic methods when the constraint graph is sparse. Local search can also be used, but the added problem arises of not knowing when the search is at a global optimum.
- In a scheduling task, it is important to consider the preferences and constraints of everyone involved in the task, and to consider any tradeoffs required.

## 4.11 References and Further Reading

Constraint satisfaction techniques are described by Mackworth [1977a], Dechter [2003], Freuder and Mackworth [2006], and Dechter [2019]. The *GAC* algorithm was invented by Mackworth [1977b].

Variable elimination for propositional satisfiability was proposed by Davis and Putnam [1960]. VE for optimization has been called **non-serial dynamic programming** and was invented by Bertelè and Brioschi [1972]. For a more recent overview see Dechter [2019], who calls variable elimination **bucket elimination** (the buckets contain the constraints to be joined).

Stochastic local search is described by Spall [2003] and Hoos and Stützle [2004]. The any-conflict algorithm is based on Minton et al. [1992]. Simulated annealing was invented by Kirkpatrick et al. [1983]. Xu et al. [2008] describe the use of **algorithm portfolios** to choose the best solver for each problem instance.

Genetic algorithms were pioneered by Holland [1975]. A huge literature exists on genetic algorithms; for overviews, see Mitchell [1996], Bäck [1996],

Goldberg [2002], Lehman et al. [2018], Stanley et al. [2019], and Katoch et al. [2021]

Gradient descent is due to Cauchy [1847].

Python implementations that emphasize readability over efficiency are available at AIPython (aipython.org).

## 4.12 Exercises

**Exercise 4.1** Consider the crossword puzzle shown in Figure 4.14.

You must find six three-letter words: three words read across (*1-across*, *4-across*, *5-across*) and three words read down (*1-down*, *2-down*, *3-down*). Each word must be chosen from the list of 18 possible words shown. Try to solve it yourself, first by intuition, then using domain consistency, and then arc consistency.

There are at least two ways to represent the crossword puzzle shown in Figure 4.14 as a constraint satisfaction problem.

The first is to represent the word positions (*1-across*, *4-across*, etc.) as variables, with the set of words as possible values. The constraints are that the letter is the same where the words intersect.

The second is to represent the nine squares as variables. The domain of each variable is the set of letters of the alphabet, $\{a, b, \ldots, z\}$. The constraints are that there is a word in the word list that contains the corresponding letters. For example, the top-left square and the center-top square cannot both have the value $a$, because there is no word starting with $aa$.

(a) Give an example of pruning due to domain consistency using the first representation (if one exists).

(b) Give an example of pruning due to arc consistency using the first representation (if one exists).

(c) Are domain consistency plus arc consistency adequate to solve this problem using the first representation? Explain.

(d) Give an example of pruning due to domain consistency using the second representation (if one exists).

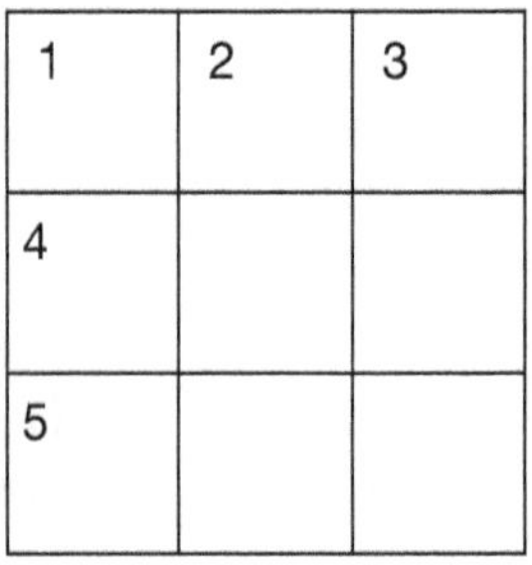


**Words:**
add, age, aid, aim, air, are, arm, art, bad, bat, bee, boa, dim, ear, eel, eft, lee, oaf

Figure 4.14: A crossword puzzle to be solved with six words

(e) Give an example of pruning due to arc consistency using the second representation (if one exists).
(f) Are domain consistency plus arc consistency adequate to solve this problem using the second representation?
(g) Which representation leads to a more efficient solution using consistency-based techniques? Give the evidence on which you are basing your answer.

**Exercise 4.2** Suppose you have a relation $v(N, W)$ that is true if there is a vowel (one o: a, e, i, o, u) as the $N$-th letter of word $W$. For example, $v(2, cat)$ is true because there is a vowel ("a") as the second letter of the word "cat"; $v(3, cat)$ is false because the third letter of "cat" is "t", which is not a vowel; and $v(5, cat)$ is also false because there is no fifth letter in "cat".

Suppose the domain of $N$ is $\{1, 3, 5\}$ and the domain of $W$ is $\{$*added, blue, fever, green, stare*$\}$.

(a) Is the arc $\langle N, v \rangle$ arc consistent? If so, explain why. If not, show what element(s) can be removed from a domain to make it arc consistent.
(b) Is the arc $\langle W, v \rangle$ arc consistent? If so, explain why. If not, show what element(s) can be removed from a domain to make it arc consistent.

**Exercise 4.3** Consider the crossword puzzles shown in Figure 4.15. The possible words for (a) are

> ant, big, bus, car, has, book, buys, hold, lane, year, ginger, search, symbol, syntax.

The available words for (b) are

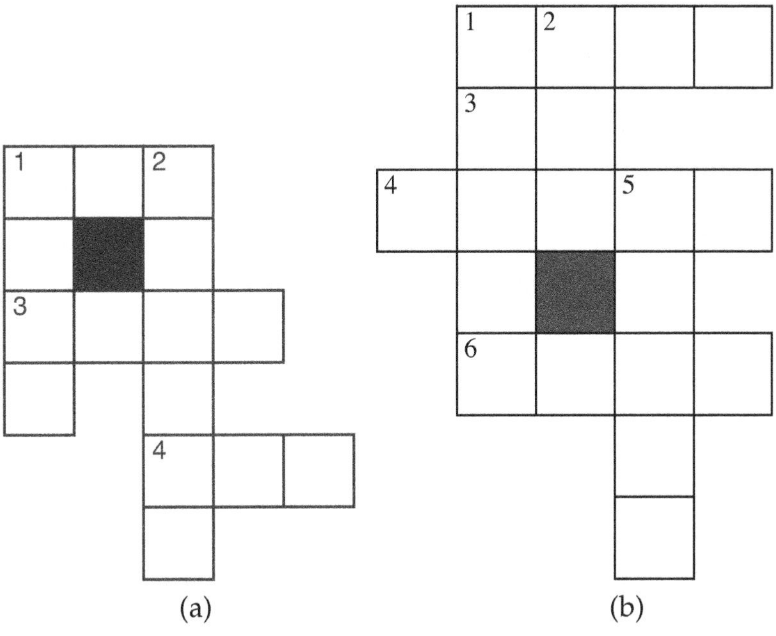


Figure 4.15: Two crossword puzzles

at, eta, be, hat, he, her, it, him, on, one, desk, dance, usage, easy, dove, first, else, loses, fuels, help, haste, given, kind, sense, soon, sound, this, think.

(a) Draw the constraint graph nodes for the positions (*1-across*, *2-down*, etc.) and words for the domains, after it has been made domain consistent.
(b) Give an example of pruning due to arc consistency.
(c) What are the domains after arc consistency has halted?
(d) Consider the dual representation in which the squares on the intersection of words are the variables. The domains of the variable contain the letters that could go in those positions. Give the domains after this network has been made arc consistent. Does the result after arc consistency in this representation correspond to the result in part (c)?
(e) Show how variable elimination solves the crossword problem. Start from the arc-consistent network from part (c).
(f) Does a different elimination ordering affect the efficiency? Explain.

**Exercise 4.4** Pose and solve the crypt-arithmetic problem $SEND + MORE = MONEY$ as a CSP. In a crypt-arithmetic problem, each letter represents a different digit, the leftmost digit cannot be zero (because then it would not be there), and the sum must be correct considering each sequence of letters as a base ten numeral. In this example, you know that $Y = (D + E) \bmod 10$ and that $E = (N + R + ((D + E) \div 10)) \bmod 10$, and so on.

**Exercise 4.5** Consider the complexity for generalized arc consistency beyond the binary case considered in the text (page 140). Suppose there are $n$ variables, $c$ constraints, where each constraint involves $k$ variables, and the domain of each variable is of size $d$. How many arcs are there? What is the worst-case cost of checking one arc as a function of $c$, $k$, and $d$? How many times must an arc be checked? Based on this, what is the time complexity of *GAC* as a function of $c$, $k$, and $d$? What is the space complexity?

**Exercise 4.6** For the constraints of Example 4.9 (page 132), shown in Figure 4.5 (page 139), show the variables eliminated, the constraints joined, and the new constraint (as in Example 4.23 (page 145)) for the variable ordering elimination ordering $A, B, C, D$.

**Exercise 4.7** Consider how stochastic local search can solve Exercise 4.3 (page 173). You can use the AIPython (aipython.org) code to answer this question. Start with the arc-consistent network.

(a) How well does random walking work?
(b) How well does iterative best improvement work?
(c) How well does the combination work?
(d) Which (range of) parameter settings works best? What evidence did you use to answer this question?

**Exercise 4.8** Consider a scheduling problem, where there are five activities to be scheduled in four time slots. Suppose we represent the activities by the variables $A$, $B$, $C$, $D$, and $E$, where the domain of each variable is $\{1, 2, 3, 4\}$ and the constraints are $A > D, D > E, C \neq A, C > E, C \neq D, B \geq A, B \neq C$, and $C \neq D + 1$. [Before you start this, try to find the legal schedule(s) using your own intuitions.]

(a) Show how backtracking solves this problem. To do this, you should draw the search tree generated to find all answers. Indicate clearly the valid schedule(s). Make sure you choose a reasonable variable ordering.

To indicate the search tree, write it in text form with each branch on one line. For example, suppose we had variables $X$, $Y$, and $Z$ with domains $t, f$ and constraints $X \neq Y$ and $Y \neq Z$. The corresponding search tree is written as

```
X=t Y=t failure
    Y=f Z=t solution
        Z=f failure
X=f Y=t Z=t failure
        Z=f solution
    Y=f failure
```

[Hint: It may be easier to write a program to generate such a tree for a particular problem than to do it by hand.]

(b) Show how arc consistency solves this problem. To do this you must

- draw the constraint graph
- show which arc is considered, the domain reduced, and the arcs added to the set *to_do* (similar to the table of Example 4.18 (page 138))
- show explicitly the constraint graph after arc consistency has stopped
- show how splitting a domain can be used to solve this problem.

**Exercise 4.9** Which of the following methods can

(a) determine that there is no model, if there is not one
(b) find a model if one exists
(c) find all models?

The methods to consider are

(i) arc consistency with domain splitting
(ii) variable elimination
(iii) stochastic local search
(iv) genetic algorithms.

**Exercise 4.10** Give the algorithm for variable elimination to return one of the models rather than all of them. How is finding one easier than finding all?

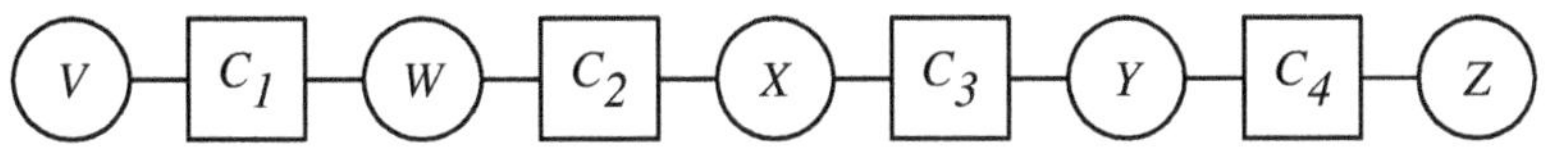


Figure 4.16: A chain constraint network

**Exercise 4.11** Consider the constraint network in Figure 4.16 (page 175). The form of the constraints are not given, but assume the network is arc consistent and there are multiple values for each variable. Suppose one of the search algorithms has split on variable $X$, so $X$ is assigned the value $a$.

(a) Suppose the aim is to count the number of solutions. Bao suggested that the subproblem with $X = a$ can be divided into two that can be solved separately. How can the solutions to each half be combined?

(b) Suppose the constraints are soft constraints (with costs for each assignment). Manpreet suggested that the problem with $X = a$ can be divided into two subproblems that can be solved separately, with the solution combined. What are the two independent subproblems? How can the optimal solution (the cost and the total assignment) be computed from a solution to each subproblem?

(c) How can the partitioning of constraints into non-empty sets such that the constraints in each set do not share a non-assigned variable (the sets that can be solved independently) be implemented?

**Exercise 4.12** Explain how arc consistency with domain splitting can be used to count the number of models. If domain splitting results in a disconnected graph, how can this be exploited by the algorithm?

**Exercise 4.13** Modify *VE_CSP* to count the number of models, without enumerating them all. [Hint: You do not need to save the join of all the constraints, but instead you can pass forward the number of solutions there would be.]

**Exercise 4.14** Consider the constraint graph of Figure 4.17 with named binary constraints. $r_1$ is a relation on $A$ and $B$, which we write as $r_1(A, B)$, and similarly for the other relations. Consider solving this network using variable elimination.

(a) Suppose you were to eliminate variable $A$. Which constraints are removed? A constraint is created on which variables? (You can call this $r_{11}$.)

(b) Suppose you were to subsequently eliminate $B$ (i.e., after eliminating $A$). Which relations are removed? A constraint is created on which variables?

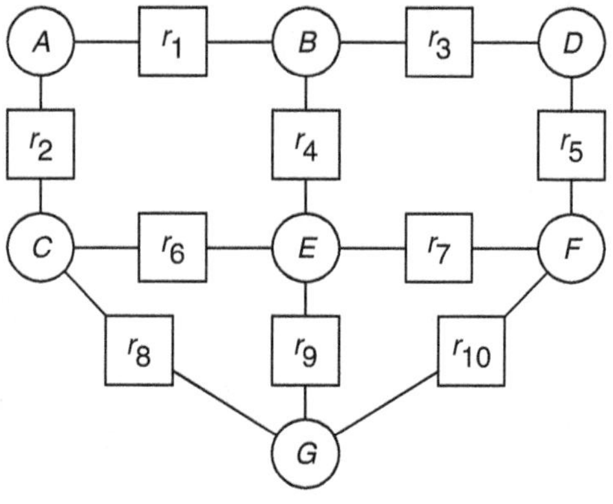


Figure 4.17: Abstract constraint network

# Chapter 5

# Propositions and Inference

*For when I am presented with a false theorem, I do not need to examine or even to know the demonstration, since I shall discover its falsity* a posteriori *by means of an easy experiment, that is, by a calculation, costing no more than paper and ink, which will show the error no matter how small it is ...*

*And if someone would doubt my results, I should say to him: "Let us calculate, Sir," and thus by taking to pen and ink, we should soon settle the question.*

– Gottfried Wilhelm Leibniz [1677]

This chapter considers simple forms of reasoning in terms of **propositions** – statements that can be true or false. Some reasoning includes model finding, finding logical consequences, and various forms of hypothetical reasoning. Semantics forms the foundations of specification of facts, reasoning, and debugging.

## 5.1 Propositions

### 5.1.1 Syntax of the Propositional Calculus

A **proposition** is a sentence, written in a language, that has a truth value (i.e., it is true or false) in a world. A proposition is built from atomic propositions and logical connectives.

An **atomic proposition**, or just an **atom**, is a symbol (page 128). Atoms are written as sequences of letters, digits, and the underscore (_) and start with a lower-case letter. For example, *a*, *ai_is_fun*, *lit_l*$_1$, *live_outside*, *mimsy*, and *sunny* are all atoms.

Propositions can be built from simpler propositions using logical connectives. A **proposition** or **logical formula** is either

- an atomic proposition or
- a **compound proposition** of the form

| | | |
|---|---|---|
| $\neg p$ | "not $p$" | **negation** of $p$ |
| $p \wedge q$ | "$p$ and $q$" | **conjunction** of $p$ and $q$ |
| $p \vee q$ | "$p$ or $q$" | **disjunction** of $p$ and $q$ |
| $p \rightarrow q$ | "$p$ implies $q$" | **implication** of $q$ from $p$ |
| $p \leftarrow q$ | "$p$ if $q$" | **implication** of $p$ from $q$ |
| $p \leftrightarrow q$ | "$p$ if and only if $q$" | **equivalence** of $p$ and $q$ |
| $p \oplus q$ | "$p$ XOR $q$" | **exclusive-or** of $p$ and $q$ |

where $p$ and $q$ are propositions.

The operators $\neg$, $\wedge$, $\vee$, $\rightarrow$, $\leftarrow$, $\leftrightarrow$, and $\oplus$ are **logical connectives.**

Parentheses can be used to make logical formulas unambiguous. When parentheses are omitted, the precedence of the operators is in the order they are given above. Thus, a compound proposition can be disambiguated by adding parentheses to the subexpressions in the order the operations are defined above. For example, $\neg a \vee b \wedge c \rightarrow d \wedge \neg e \vee f$ is an abbreviation for $((\neg a) \vee (b \wedge c)) \rightarrow ((d \wedge (\neg e)) \vee f)$.

### 5.1.2 Semantics of the Propositional Calculus

**Semantics** defines the meaning of the sentences of a language. The semantics of propositional calculus is defined below. Intuitively, propositions have meaning to someone who specifies propositions they claim are true, and then queries about what else must also be true. An interpretation is a way that the world could be. All that the system knows about the world is that the propositions specified are true, so the world must correspond to an interpretation in which those propositions hold.

An **interpretation** consists of a function $\pi$ that maps atoms to $\{true, false\}$. If $\pi(a) = true$, atom $a$ is **true** in the interpretation. If $\pi(a) = false$, atom $a$ is **false** in the interpretation. Sometimes it is useful to think of $\pi$ as the set of the atoms that map to *true*, and the rest of the atoms map to *false*.

Whether a compound proposition is true in an interpretation is inferred using the truth table of Figure 5.1 (page 179) from the truth values of the components of the proposition.

Truth values are only defined with respect to interpretations; propositions may have different truth values in different interpretations.

**Example 5.1** Suppose there are three atoms: *ai_is_fun*, *happy*, and *light_on*.

Suppose interpretation $I_1$ assigns *true* to *ai_is_fun*, *false* to *happy*, and *true* to *light_on*. That is, $I_1$ is defined by the function $\pi_1$:

$$\pi_1(ai\_is\_fun) = true, \quad \pi_1(happy) = false, \quad \pi_1(light\_on) = true.$$

Then

- *ai_is_fun* is true in $I_1$
- $\neg$*ai_is_fun* is false in $I_1$
- *happy* is false in $I_1$
- $\neg$*happy* is true in $I_1$
- *ai_is_fun* $\vee$ *happy* is true in $I_1$
- *ai_is_fun* $\leftarrow$ *happy* is true in $I_1$
- *happy* $\leftarrow$ *ai_is_fun* is false in $I_1$
- *ai_is_fun* $\leftarrow$ *happy* $\wedge$ *light_on* is true in $I_1$.

Suppose interpretation $I_2$ assigns *false* to *ai_is_fun*, *true* to *happy*, and *false* to *light_on*:

- *ai_is_fun* is false in $I_2$
- $\neg$*ai_is_fun* is true in $I_2$
- *happy* is true in $I_2$
- $\neg$*happy* is false in $I_2$
- *ai_is_fun* $\vee$ *happy* is true in $I_2$
- *ai_is_fun* $\leftarrow$ *happy* is false in $I_2$
- *ai_is_fun* $\leftarrow$ *light_on* is true in $I_2$
- *ai_is_fun* $\leftarrow$ *happy* $\wedge$ *light_on* is true in $I_2$.

A **knowledge base** is a set of propositions that are stated to be true. An element of the knowledge base is an **axiom**. The elements of a knowledge base are implicitly conjoined, so that a knowledge base is true when all of the axioms in it are true.

A **model** of knowledge base *KB* is an interpretation in which all the propositions in *KB* are true.

If *KB* is a knowledge base and $g$ is a proposition, $g$ is a **logical consequence** of *KB*, or $g$ **logically follows** from *KB*, or *KB* **entails** $g$, written

$$KB \models g$$

if $g$ is true in every model of *KB*. Thus, $g$ is not a logical consequence of *KB*, written $KB \not\models g$, when there is a model of *KB* in which $g$ is false.

| $p$ | $q$ | $\neg p$ | $p \wedge q$ | $p \vee q$ | $p \rightarrow q$ | $p \leftarrow q$ | $p \leftrightarrow q$ | $p \oplus q$ |
|---|---|---|---|---|---|---|---|---|
| *true* | *true* | *false* | *true* | *true* | *true* | *true* | *true* | *false* |
| *true* | *false* | *false* | *false* | *true* | *false* | *true* | *false* | *true* |
| *false* | *true* | *true* | *false* | *true* | *true* | *false* | *false* | *true* |
| *false* | *false* | *true* | *false* | *false* | *true* | *true* | *true* | *false* |

Figure 5.1: Truth table defining $\neg$, $\wedge$, $\vee$, $\leftarrow$, $\rightarrow$, $\leftrightarrow$, and $\oplus$

**Example 5.2** Suppose *KB* is the following knowledge base:

*sam_is_happy.*
*ai_is_fun.*
*worms_live_underground.*
*night_time.*
*bird_eats_apple.*
$apple\_is\_eaten \leftarrow bird\_eats\_apple.$
$switch\_1\_is\_up \leftarrow someone\_is\_in\_room \wedge night\_time.$

Given this knowledge base:

$KB \models bird\_eats\_apple.$
$KB \models apple\_is\_eaten.$

*KB* does not entail *switch_1_is_up* as there is a model of the knowledge base where *switch_1_is_up* is false. The atom *someone_is_in_room* must be false in that interpretation.

### The Human's View of Semantics

The description of semantics does not tell us why semantics is interesting or how it can be used as a basis to build intelligent systems. The basic idea behind the use of logic is that, when a **knowledge base designer** has a particular world to characterize, the designer can choose that world as an **intended interpretation**, choose meanings for the symbols with respect to that world, and write propositions about what is true in that world. When the system computes a logical consequence of a knowledge base, the designer can interpret this answer with respect to the intended interpretation.

The methodology used by a knowledge base designer to represent a world can be expressed as follows:

**Step 1** A knowledge base designer chooses a task domain or world to represent, which is the intended interpretation. This could be some aspect of the real world (for example, the structure of courses and students at a university, or a laboratory environment at a particular point in time), some imaginary world (such as the world of Alice in Wonderland, or the state of the electrical environment if a switch breaks), or an abstract world (for example, the world of numbers and sets).

**Step 2** The knowledge base designer selects atoms to represent propositions of interest. Each atom has a precise meaning to the designer with respect to the intended interpretation. This meaning of the symbols forms an **intended interpretation** or **conceptualization**.

**Step 3** The knowledge base designer **tells** the system propositions that are true in the intended interpretation. This is often called **axiomatizing the domain**, where the given propositions are the **axioms** of the domain.

**Step 4** A user can now **ask** questions about the intended interpretation. The system can answer these questions. A user who knows the intended interpretation is able to interpret the answers using the meaning assigned to the symbols.

Within this methodology, the designer does not actually tell the computer anything until step 3.

### The Computer's View of Semantics

A computer does not have access to the intended interpretation. All the computer knows about the intended interpretation is the knowledge base *KB*. If $KB \models g$, then $g$ must be true in the intended interpretation, because it is true in all models of the knowledge base. If $KB \not\models g$, meaning $g$ is not a logical consequence of *KB*, there is a model of *KB* in which $g$ is false. As far as the computer is concerned, the intended interpretation may be the model of *KB* in which $g$ is false, and so it does not know whether $g$ is true in the intended interpretation.

Given a knowledge base, the models of the knowledge base correspond to all of the ways that the world could be, given that the knowledge base is true.

**Example 5.3** Consider the knowledge base of Example 5.2 (page 180). The user could interpret these symbols as having some meaning. The computer does not know the meaning of the symbols, but it can still draw conclusions based on what it has been told. It can conclude that *apple_is_eaten* is true in the intended interpretation. It cannot conclude *switch_1_is_up* because it does not know if *someone_is_in_room* is true or false in the intended interpretation.

If the knowledge base designer tells lies – some axioms are false in the intended interpretation – the computer's answers are not guaranteed to be true in the intended interpretation.

## 5.2 Propositional Constraints

Chapter 4 shows how to reason with constraints. Logical formulas provide a concise form of constraints with structure that can be exploited.

There are a number of reasons for using propositions for specifying constraints and queries:

- It is often more concise and readable to give a logical statement about the relationship among some variables than to use an extensional representation.
- The form of the knowledge can be exploited to make reasoning more efficient.
- They are modular, so small changes to the problem result in small changes to the knowledge base. This also means that a knowledge base is easier to debug than other representations.

- The kind of queries may be richer than single assignments of values to variables.
- This language can be extended to reason about individuals (things, entities) and relations; see Chapter 15.

The class of **propositional satisfiability** or **SAT** problems have

- Boolean variable. A **Boolean variable** (page 127) is a variable with domain $\{true, false\}$. If $X$ is a Boolean variable, $X = true$ is written as its lower-case equivalent, $x$, and $X = false$ as $\neg x$.

  For example, the proposition *happy* means Boolean variable *Happy* is true ($Happy = true$), and $\neg happy$ means $Happy = false$.
- Clausal constraints. A **clause** is an expression of the form $l_1 \vee l_2 \vee \cdots \vee l_k$, where each $l_i$ is a literal. A **literal** is an atom or the negation of an atom; thus a literal is an assignment of a value to a Boolean variable. A clause is true in an interpretation if and only if at least one of the literals that make up the clause is true in that interpretation.

  If $\neg a$ appears in a clause, the atom $a$ is said to appear **negatively** in the clause. If $a$ appears unnegated in a clause, it is said to appear **positively** in a clause.

In terms of the propositional calculus, a set of clauses is a restricted form of logical formula. Any propositional formula can be converted into clausal form. A total assignment (page 129) corresponds to an interpretation (page 178).

In terms of constraints (page 131), a clause is a constraint on a set of Boolean variables that rules out one of the assignments of the literals in the clause. The clause $l_1 \vee l_2 \vee \cdots \vee l_k$ corresponds to the statement $\neg(\neg l_1 \wedge \neg l_2 \wedge \cdots \wedge \neg l_k)$, which says that not all of the $l_i$ are false.

**Example 5.4** The clause $happy \vee sad \vee \neg living$ is a constraint among the variables *Happy*, *Sad*, and *Living*, which is true if *Happy* has value *true*, *Sad* has value *true*, or *Living* has value *false*. The atoms *happy* and *sad* appear positively in the clause, and *living* appears negatively in the clause.

The assignment $\neg happy, \neg sad, living$ violates the constraint of clause $happy \vee sad \vee \neg living$. It is the only assignment of these three variables that violates this clause.

## 5.2.1 Clausal Form for CSPs

It is possible to convert any finite constraint satisfaction problem (CSP) (page 132) into a propositional satisfiable problem:

- A variable $Y$ with domain $\{v_1, \ldots, v_k\}$ can be converted into $k$ Boolean variables $\{Y_1, \ldots, Y_k\}$, where $Y_i$ is true when $Y$ has value $v_i$ and is false otherwise. Each $Y_i$ is called an **indicator variable**. Thus, $k$ atoms, $y_1, \ldots, y_k$, are used to represent the CSP variable.

- There are constraints that specify that $y_i$ and $y_j$ cannot both be true when $i \neq j$, namely the clause $\neg y_i \vee \neg y_j$ for $i < j$. There is also a constraint that one of the $y_i$ must be true, namely the clause $y_1 \vee \cdots \vee y_k$.
- To translate the constraints, notice that $\neg x_1 \vee \cdots \vee \neg x_k$ is equivalent to $\neg(x_1 \wedge \cdots \wedge x_k)$ for any atoms $x_1, \ldots, x_k$. One way to represent a constraint is to use a clause for each assignment of values that violates the constraint. Thus, for example, the clause $\neg x_5 \vee \neg y_7$ represents that $X = v_5$ and $Y = v_7$ is a combination that violates a constraint.

  Often we can use many fewer clauses than by applying this naively.

**Example 5.5** Consider two variables $A$ and $B$ each with domain $\{1,2,3,4\}$. For the variable $A$, construct four Boolean variables $a_1$, $a_2$, $a_3$, and $a_4$, where $a_1$ is true just when $A = 1$, $a_2$ is true just when $A = 2$, etc. Variables $a_1$, $a_2$, $a_3$, and $a_4$ are disjoint and covering which leads to the seven clauses

$$\neg a_1 \vee \neg a_2, \neg a_1 \vee \neg a_3, \neg a_1 \vee \neg a_4, \neg a_2 \vee \neg a_3, \neg a_2 \vee \neg a_4, \neg a_3 \vee \neg a_4,$$
$$a_1 \vee a_2 \vee a_3 \vee a_4.$$

Similarly for $B$.

The constraint $A < B$ implies that $a_4$ is false, $b_1$ is false, and the pairs that violate the constraint are also false, which gives the five clauses

$$\neg a_4, \neg b_1, \neg a_2 \vee \neg b_2, \neg a_3 \vee \neg b_3, \neg a_3 \vee \neg b_2.$$

Note that you don't need the clause $\neg a_1 \vee \neg b_1$ because this is implied by $\neg b_1$.

Consistency algorithms (page 136) can be made more efficient for propositional satisfiability problems than for general CSPs. When there are only two values, pruning a value from a domain is equivalent to assigning the opposite value. Thus, if $X$ has domain $\{true, false\}$, pruning *true* from the domain of $X$ is the same as assigning $X$ to have value *false*.

Arc consistency can be used to prune the set of values and the set of constraints. Assigning a value to a Boolean variable can simplify the set of constraints:

- If $X$ is assigned *true*, all of the clauses with $X = true$ become redundant; they are automatically satisfied. These clauses can be removed from consideration. Similarly, if $X$ is assigned *false*, clauses containing $X = false$ can be removed.
- If $X$ is assigned *true*, any clause with $X = false$ can be simplified by removing $X = false$ from the clause. Similarly, if $X$ is assigned *false*, then $X = true$ can be removed from any clause it appears in. This step is called **unit resolution**.

If, after pruning the clauses, there is a clause that contains just one assignment, $Y = v$, the other value can be removed from the domain of $Y$. This is a form of arc consistency. If all of the assignments are removed from a clause, the constraints are unsatisfiable.

**Example 5.6** Consider the clause $\neg x \vee y \vee \neg z$. If $X$ is assigned to *true*, the clause can be simplified to $y \vee \neg z$. If $Y$ is then assigned to *false*, the clause can be simplified to $\neg z$. Thus, *true* can be pruned from the domain of $Z$.

If, instead, $X$ is assigned to *false*, the clause can be removed.

If a variable has the same value in all remaining clauses, and the algorithm must only find one model, it can assign that value to that variable. For example, if variable $Y$ only appears as $Y = true$ (i.e., $\neg y$ is not in any clause), then $Y$ can be assigned the value *true*. That assignment does not remove all of the models; it only simplifies the problem because the set of clauses remaining after setting $Y = true$ is a subset of the clauses that would remain if $Y$ were assigned the value *false*. A variable that only has one value in all of the clauses is called a **pure literal**.

Pruning the domains and constraints, domain splitting, and assigning pure literals is the Davis–Putnam–Logemann–Loveland **(DPLL) algorithm**. It is a very efficient algorithm, as long as the data structures are indexed to carry out these tasks efficiently.

### 5.2.2 Exploiting Propositional Structure in Local Search

Stochastic local search (page 146) can be faster for CSPs in the form of propositional satisfiability problems (page 182) than for general CSPs, for the following reasons:

- Because only one alternative value exists for each assignment to a variable, the algorithm does not have to search through the alternative values.
- Changing any value in an unsatisfied clause makes the clause satisfied. As a result, it is easy to satisfy a clause, but this may make other clauses unsatisfied.
- If a variable is changed to be true, all of the clauses where it appears positively become satisfied, and only clauses where it appears negatively can become unsatisfied. Conversely, if a variable is changed to be false, all of the clauses where it appears negatively become satisfied, and only those clauses where it appears positively can become unsatisfied. This enables fast indexing of clauses.
- The search space is expanded. In particular, before a solution has been found, more than one of the indicator variables for a variable $Y$ could be true (which corresponds to $Y$ having multiple values) or all of the indicator variables could be false (which corresponds to $Y$ having no values). This can mean that some assignments that were local minima in the original problem may not be local minima in the new representation.
- Satisfiability has been studied much more extensively than most other types of CSPs and more efficient solvers exist because more of the space of potential algorithms has been explored by researchers.

Whether converting a particular CSP to a satisfiability problem makes search performance better is an empirical question, depending on the problem and the tools available.

## 5.3 Propositional Definite Clauses

The rest of this chapter considers some restricted languages and reasoning tasks that are useful and can be efficiently implemented.

The language of **propositional definite clauses** is a subset of propositional calculus that does not allow uncertainty or ambiguity. In this language, propositions have the same meaning as in propositional calculus, but not all compound propositions are allowed in a knowledge base.

The **syntax** of propositional definite clauses is defined as follows:

- An **atomic proposition** or **atom** is the same as in propositional calculus.
- A **definite clause** is of the form

  $$h \leftarrow a_1 \wedge \ldots \wedge a_m.$$

  where $h$ is an atom, the **head** of the clause, and each $a_i$ is an atom. It can be read "$h$ if $a_1$ and ... and $a_m$".

  If $m > 0$, the clause is called a **rule**, where $a_1 \wedge \ldots \wedge a_m$ is the **body** of the clause.

  If $m = 0$, the arrow can be omitted and the clause is called an **atomic clause** or **fact**. The clause has an **empty body**.
- A **knowledge base** is a set of definite clauses.

**Example 5.7** The elements of the knowledge base in Example 5.2 (page 180) are all definite clauses.

The following are *not* definite clauses:

$\neg apple\_is\_eaten.$

$apple\_is\_eaten \wedge bird\_eats\_apple.$

$sam\_is\_in\_room \wedge night\_time \leftarrow switch\_1\_is\_up.$

$Apple\_is\_eaten \leftarrow Bird\_eats\_apple.$

$happy \vee sad \vee \neg alive.$

The fourth statement is not a definite clause because an atom must start with a lower-case letter.

A definite clause $h \leftarrow a_1 \wedge \ldots \wedge a_m$ is false in interpretation $I$ (page 178) if $a_1, \ldots, a_m$ are all true in $I$ and $h$ is false in $I$; otherwise, the definite clause is true in $I$.

A definite clause is a restricted form of a clause (page 182). For example, the definite clause

$$a \leftarrow b \wedge c \wedge d$$

is equivalent to the clause

$$a \vee \neg b \vee \neg c \vee \neg d.$$

In general, a definite clause is equivalent to a clause with exactly one positive literal (non-negated atom). Propositional definite clauses cannot represent disjunctions of atoms (e.g., $a \vee b$) or disjunctions of negated atoms (e.g., $\neg c \vee \neg d$).

**Example 5.8** Consider how to axiomatize the electrical environment of Figure 5.2 following the methodology for the user's view of semantics (page 180). This axiomatization will allow us to simulate the electrical system. It will be expanded in later sections to let us diagnose faults based on observed symptoms.

The representation will be used to determine whether lights are on or off, based on switch positions and the status of circuit breakers.

The knowledge base designer must choose a level of abstraction. The aim is to represent the domain at the most general level that will enable the agent to solve the problems it must solve. We also want to represent the domain at a level that the agent will have information about. For example, we could represent the actual voltages and currents, but exactly the same reasoning would be done if this were a 12-volt DC system or a 120-volt AC system; the voltages and frequencies are irrelevant for questions about how switch positions (up or down) affect whether lights are on. Our agent is not concerned here with the color of the wires, the design of the switches, the length or weight of the wire, the date of manufacture of the lights and the wires, or any of the other myriad details one could imagine about the domain.

Let's represent this domain at a commonsense level that non-electricians may use to describe the domain, in terms of wires being live and currents flow-

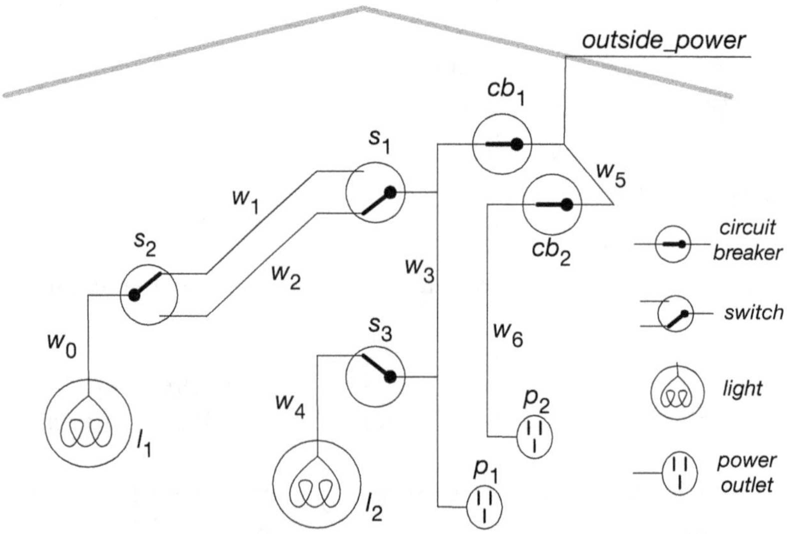


Figure 5.2: An electrical environment with components named

ing from the outside through wires to the lights, and that circuit breakers and light switches connect wires if they are turned on and working.

The designer must choose what to represent. Here we represent propositions about whether lights are lit, whether wires are live, whether switches are up or down, and whether components are working properly.

We then choose atoms with a specific meaning in the world. We can use descriptive names for these. For example, $up\_s_2$ is true when switch $s_2$ is up. $ok\_l_1$ is true when light $l_1$ is working properly (will be lit if it is has power coming into it). $live\_w_1$ is true when $w_1$ has power coming in. The computer does not know the meaning of these names and does not have access to the components of the atom's name.

At this stage, we have not told the computer anything. It does not know what the atoms are, let alone what they mean.

Once we have decided which symbols to use and what they mean, we tell the system, using definite clauses, background knowledge about what is true in the world. The simplest forms of definite clauses are those without bodies – the atomic clauses – such as

$light\_l_1.$ $light\_l_2.$ $ok\_l_1.$
$ok\_l_2.$ $ok\_cb_1.$ $ok\_cb_2.$
$live\_outside.$

The designer may look at part of the domain and know that light $l_1$ is live if wire $w_0$ is live, because they are connected together, but may not know whether $w_0$ is live. Such knowledge is expressible in terms of rules:

$live\_l_1 \leftarrow live\_w_0.$
$live\_w_0 \leftarrow live\_w_1 \land up\_s_2.$
$live\_w_0 \leftarrow live\_w_2 \land down\_s_2.$
$live\_w_1 \leftarrow live\_w_3 \land up\_s_1.$
$live\_w_2 \leftarrow live\_w_3 \land down\_s_1.$
$live\_l_2 \leftarrow live\_w_4.$
$live\_w_4 \leftarrow live\_w_3 \land up\_s_3.$
$live\_p_1 \leftarrow live\_w_3.$
$live\_w_3 \leftarrow live\_w_5 \land ok\_cb_1.$
$live\_p_2 \leftarrow live\_w_6.$
$live\_w_6 \leftarrow live\_w_5 \land ok\_cb_2.$
$live\_w_5 \leftarrow live\_outside.$
$lit\_l_1 \leftarrow light\_l_1 \land live\_l_1 \land ok\_l_1.$
$lit\_l_2 \leftarrow light\_l_2 \land live\_l_2 \land ok\_l_2.$

Online, the user is able to input the observations of the current switch positions, such as

$down\_s_1.$ $up\_s_2.$ $up\_s_3.$

The knowledge base consists of all the definite clauses, whether specified as background knowledge or as observations.

## 5.3.1 Queries and Answers

One reason to build a description of a real or imaginary world is to be able to determine what else must be true in that world. After the computer is given a knowledge base about a particular domain, a user might like to ask the computer questions about that domain. The computer can answer whether or not a proposition is a logical consequence of the knowledge base. A user that knows the meaning of the atoms, for example when is $up\_s_3$ true, can interpret the answer in terms of the domain.

A **query** is a way of asking whether a proposition is a logical consequence of a knowledge base. Once the system has been provided with a knowledge base, a query is used to ask whether a proposition is a logical consequence of the knowledge base. Queries have the form

ask $b$.

where $b$ is an atom or a conjunction of atoms (analogous to the body of a rule (page 185)).

A query is a question that has the **answer** *yes* if the body is a logical consequence of the knowledge base, or the answer *no* if the body is not a consequence of the knowledge base. The latter does not mean that *body* is false in the intended interpretation but rather that it is impossible to determine whether it is true or false based on the knowledge provided.

**Example 5.9** Once the computer has been told the knowledge base of Example 5.8 (page 186), it can answer queries such as

ask $light\_l_1$.

for which the answer is *yes*. The query

ask $light\_l_6$.

has answer *no*. The computer does not have enough information to know whether or not $l_6$ is a light. The query

ask $lit\_l_2$.

has answer *yes*. This atom is true in all models.

The user can interpret this answer with respect to the intended interpretation.

## 5.3.2 Proofs

So far, we have specified what an answer is, but not how it can be computed. The definition of $\models$ (page 179) specifies which propositions should be logical consequences of a knowledge base but not how to compute them. The problem of **deduction** is to determine if some proposition is a logical consequence of a knowledge base. Deduction is a specific form of **inference**.

A **proof** is a mechanically derivable demonstration that a proposition logically follows from a knowledge base. A **theorem** is a provable proposition. A **proof procedure** is a – possibly non-deterministic – algorithm for deriving consequences of a knowledge base. (See the box on page 89 for a description of non-deterministic choice.)

Given a proof procedure, $KB \vdash g$ means $g$ can be **proved** or **derived** from knowledge base $KB$.

A proof procedure's quality can be judged by whether it computes what it is meant to compute.

A proof procedure is **sound** with respect to the semantics if everything that can be derived from a knowledge base is a logical consequence of the knowledge base. That is, if $KB \vdash g$, then $KB \models g$.

A proof procedure is **complete** with respect to the semantics if there is a proof of each logical consequence of the knowledge base. That is, if $KB \models g$, then $KB \vdash g$.

We present two ways to construct proofs for propositional definite clauses: a bottom-up procedure and a top-down procedure.

## Bottom-Up Proof Procedure

A **bottom-up proof procedure** can be used to derive all logical consequences of a knowledge base. It is called bottom-up as an analogy to building a house, where each part of the house is built on the structure already completed. The bottom-up proof procedure builds on atoms that have already been established. It should be contrasted with a top-down approach (page 191), which starts from a query and tries to find definite clauses that can be used to prove the query. Sometimes we say that a bottom-up procedure is **forward chaining** on the definite clauses, in the sense of going forward from what is known rather than going backward from the query.

The general idea is based on one **rule of derivation**, a generalized form of the rule of inference called **modus ponens**:

> If "$h \leftarrow a_1 \wedge \ldots \wedge a_m$" is a definite clause in the knowledge base, and each $a_i$ has been derived, then $h$ can be derived.

An atomic clause (page 185) corresponds to the case of $m = 0$; modus ponens can always immediately derive any atomic clauses in the knowledge base.

Figure 5.3 (page 190) gives a procedure for computing the **consequence set** $C$ of a set $KB$ of definite clauses. Under this proof procedure, if $g$ is an atom, $KB \vdash g$ if $g \in C$ at the end of the *Prove_DC_BU* procedure. For a conjunction, $KB \vdash g_1 \wedge \cdots \wedge g_k$, if $\{g_1, \ldots, g_k\} \subseteq C$.

**Example 5.10** Given the knowledge base $KB$:

$$a \leftarrow b \wedge c. \qquad d.$$
$$b \leftarrow d \wedge e. \qquad e.$$
$$b \leftarrow g \wedge e. \qquad f \leftarrow a \wedge g.$$
$$c \leftarrow e.$$

one trace of the value assigned to $C$ in the bottom-up procedure is

$$\{\}$$
$$\{d\}$$
$$\{e, d\}$$

$\{c, e, d\}$
$\{b, c, e, d\}$
$\{a, b, c, e, d\}$.

The algorithm terminates with $C = \{a, b, c, e, d\}$. Thus, $KB \vdash a$, $KB \vdash b$, and so on.

The last rule in *KB* is never used. The bottom-up proof procedure cannot derive $f$ or $g$. This is as it should be because there is a model of the knowledge base in which $f$ and $g$ are both false.

The proof procedure of Figure 5.3 has a number of interesting properties:

**Soundness** The bottom-up proof procedure is sound. Every atom in $C$ is a logical consequence of *KB*. That is, if $KB \vdash g$ then $KB \models g$. To show this, assume that there is an atom in $C$ that is not a logical consequence of *KB*. If such an atom exists, let $h$ be the first atom added to $C$ that is not true in every model of *KB*. Suppose $I$ is a model of *KB* in which $h$ is false. Because $h$ has been generated, there must be some definite clause in *KB* of the form $h \leftarrow a_1 \wedge \ldots \wedge a_m$ such that $a_1, \ldots, a_m$ are all in $C$ (which includes the case where $h$ is an atomic clause and so $m = 0$). Because $h$ is the first atom added to $C$ that is not true in all models of *KB*, and the $a_i$ are generated before $h$, all of the $a_i$ are true in $I$. This clause's head is false in $I$, and its body is true in $I$. Therefore, by the definition of truth of clauses, this clause is false in $I$. This is a contradiction to the fact that $I$ is a model of *KB*. Thus, every element of $C$ is a logical consequence of *KB*.

**Complexity** The algorithm of Figure 5.3 halts, and the number of times the loop is repeated is bounded by the number of definite clauses in *KB*. This is easily seen because each definite clause is only used at most once. Thus, the time complexity of the bottom-up proof procedure is linear in the size

```
procedure Prove_DC_BU(KB)
    Inputs
        KB: a set of definite clauses
    Output
        Set of all atoms that are logical consequences of KB
    Local
        C is a set of atoms
    C := {}
    repeat
        select "h ← a1 ∧ ... ∧ am" in KB where ai ∈ C for all i, and h ∉ C
        C := C ∪ {h}
    until no more definite clauses can be selected
    return C
```

Figure 5.3: Bottom-up proof procedure for computing consequences of *KB* of the knowledge base if it indexes the definite clauses so that the inner loop is carried out in constant time.

**Fixed Point** The final $C$ generated in the algorithm of Figure 5.3 (page 190) is called a **fixed point** because any further application of the rule of derivation does not change $C$. $C$ is the **least fixed point** because there is no smaller fixed point.

Let $I$ be the interpretation in which every atom in the least fixed point is true and every atom not in the least fixed point is false. To show that $I$ must be a model of $KB$, suppose "$h \leftarrow a_1 \wedge \ldots \wedge a_m$" $\in KB$ is false in $I$. The only way this could occur is if $a_1, \ldots, a_m$ are in the fixed point, and $h$ is not in the fixed point. By construction, the rule of derivation can be used to add $h$ to the fixed point, a contradiction to it being the fixed point. Therefore, there can be no definite clause in $KB$ that is false in an interpretation defined by a fixed point. Thus, $I$ is a model of $KB$.

$I$ is the **minimal model** in the sense that it has the fewest true propositions. Every other model must also assign the atoms in $C$ to be true.

**Completeness** The bottom-up proof procedure is sound. Suppose $KB \models g$. Then $g$ is true in every model of $KB$, so it is true in the minimal model, and so it is in $C$, and so $KB \vdash g$.

### Top-Down Proof Procedure

An alternative proof method is to search *backwards* or *top-down* from a query to determine whether it is a logical consequence of the given definite clauses. This procedure is called **propositional definite clause resolution** or **SLD resolution**, where SL stands for Selecting an atom using a Linear strategy and D stands for Definite clauses. It is an instance of the more general **resolution** method.

The top-down proof procedure can be understood as refining an **answer clause** of the form

$$yes \leftarrow a_1 \wedge a_2 \wedge \ldots \wedge a_m$$

where *yes* is a special atom. Intuitively, *yes* is going to be true exactly when the answer to the query is "yes."

If the query is

$$\textsf{ask } q_1 \wedge \ldots \wedge q_m$$

then the initial answer clause is

$$yes \leftarrow q_1 \wedge \ldots \wedge q_m.$$

Given an answer clause $yes \leftarrow a_1 \wedge a_2 \wedge \ldots \wedge a_m$, the top-down algorithm selects an atom in the body of the answer clause. Suppose it selects the leftmost atom, $a_1$. The atom selected is called a **subgoal**. The algorithm proceeds by doing steps of **resolution**. In one step of resolution, it chooses a definite clause in *KB* with $a_1$ as the head. If there is no such clause, the algorithm fails.

Suppose the chosen clause is $a_1 \leftarrow b_1 \wedge \ldots \wedge b_p$.

The **resolvent** of the answer clause $yes \leftarrow a_1 \wedge a_2 \wedge \ldots \wedge a_m$ with the definite clause $a_1 \leftarrow b_1 \wedge \ldots \wedge b_p$ is the answer clause

$$yes \leftarrow b_1 \wedge \ldots \wedge b_p \wedge a_2 \wedge \ldots \wedge a_m.$$

That is, an atom is replaced by the body of a definite clause with that atom in the head.

An **answer** is an answer clause with an empty body ($m = 0$). That is, it is the answer clause $yes \leftarrow$ .

An **SLD derivation** of a query "ask $q_1 \wedge \ldots \wedge q_k$" from knowledge base *KB* is a sequence of answer clauses $\gamma_0, \gamma_1, \ldots, \gamma_n$ such that:

- $\gamma_0$ is the answer clause corresponding to the original query, namely the answer clause $yes \leftarrow q_1 \wedge \ldots \wedge q_k$
- $\gamma_i$ is the resolvent of $\gamma_{i-1}$ with a definite clause in *KB*
- $\gamma_n$ is an answer.

Another way to think about the algorithm is that the top-down algorithm maintains a collection (list or set) $G$ of atoms to prove. Each atom that must be proved is a **subgoal**. Initially, $G$ contains the atoms in the query. A clause $a \leftarrow b_1 \wedge \ldots \wedge b_p$ means $a$ can be replaced by $b_1, \ldots, b_p$. The query is proved when $G$ becomes empty.

Figure 5.4 specifies a non-deterministic procedure for solving a query. It follows the definition of a derivation. In this procedure, $G$ is the set of atoms in

```
non-deterministic procedure Prove_DC_TD(KB, Query)
    Inputs
        KB: a set of definite clauses
        Query: a set of atoms to prove
    Output
        yes if KB ⊨ Query and the procedure fails otherwise
    Local
        G is a set of atoms
    G := Query
    repeat
        select an atom a in G
        choose definite clause "a ← B" in KB with a as head
        G := B ∪ (G \ {a})
    until G = {}
    return yes
```

Figure 5.4: Top-down definite clause proof procedure

the body of the answer clause. The procedure is non-deterministic: at line 12 it has to *choose* a definite clause to resolve against. If there are choices that result in $G$ being the empty set, the algorithm returns *yes*; otherwise it fails, and the answer is *no*.

This algorithm treats the body of a clause as a set of atoms and $G$ is also a set of atoms. An alternative, used by the language **Prolog**, is to have $G$ as a list of atoms, in which case duplicates are not eliminated, as they would be if $G$ were a set. In Prolog, the order of the atoms is defined by the programmer. It does not have the overhead of checking for duplicates, which is needed for maintaining a set.

**Example 5.11** The system is given the knowledge base of Example 5.10:

$$\begin{array}{ll} a \leftarrow b \wedge c. & d. \\ b \leftarrow d \wedge e. & e. \\ b \leftarrow g \wedge e. & f \leftarrow a \wedge g. \\ c \leftarrow e. & \end{array}$$

It is asked the query

ask $a$.

The following shows a derivation that corresponds to a sequence of assignments to $G$ in the repeat loop of Figure 5.4 (page 192), where the leftmost atom in the body is selected:

| Answer Clause | Resolved with |
|---|---|
| $yes \leftarrow a$ | $a \leftarrow b \wedge c$ |
| $yes \leftarrow b \wedge c$ | $b \leftarrow d \wedge e$ |
| $yes \leftarrow d \wedge e \wedge c$ | $d$ |
| $yes \leftarrow e \wedge c$ | $e$ |
| $yes \leftarrow c$ | $c \leftarrow e$ |
| $yes \leftarrow e$ | $e$ |
| $yes \leftarrow$ | |

The following shows a sequence of choices, where the second definite clause for $b$ was chosen. This choice does not lead to a proof.

| Answer Clause | Resolved with |
|---|---|
| $yes \leftarrow a$ | $a \leftarrow b \wedge c$ |
| $yes \leftarrow b \wedge c$ | $b \leftarrow g \wedge e$ |
| $yes \leftarrow g \wedge e \wedge c$ | |

If $g$ is selected, there are no rules that can be chosen. This proof attempt is said to *fail*.

Note the use of **select** and **choose** (see box on page 89). Any atom in the body can be selected, and if one selection does not lead to a proof, other selections do not need to be tried. When choosing a clause, the algorithm may need to search for a choice that makes the proof succeed. Given a selection strategy, the algorithm induces a search graph. Each node in the search graph represents an answer clause. The neighbors of a node $yes \leftarrow a_1 \wedge \ldots \wedge a_m$, where $a_1$ is the selected atom, represent all of the possible answer clauses obtained by resolving on $a_1$. There is a neighbor for each definite clause whose head is $a_1$. The goal nodes of the search are of the form $yes \leftarrow$.

**Example 5.12** Given the knowledge base

| | | |
|---|---|---|
| $a \leftarrow b \wedge c.$ | $a \leftarrow g.$ | $a \leftarrow h.$ |
| $b \leftarrow j.$ | $b \leftarrow k.$ | $d \leftarrow m.$ |
| $d \leftarrow p.$ | $f \leftarrow m.$ | $f \leftarrow p.$ |
| $g \leftarrow m.$ | $g \leftarrow f.$ | $k \leftarrow m.$ |
| $h \leftarrow m.$ | $p.$ | |

and the query

ask $a \wedge d.$

the search graph for an SLD derivation, assuming the leftmost atom is selected in each answer clause, is shown in Figure 5.5.

The search graph is not defined statically, because this would require anticipating every possible query. Instead, the search graph is dynamically constructed as needed.

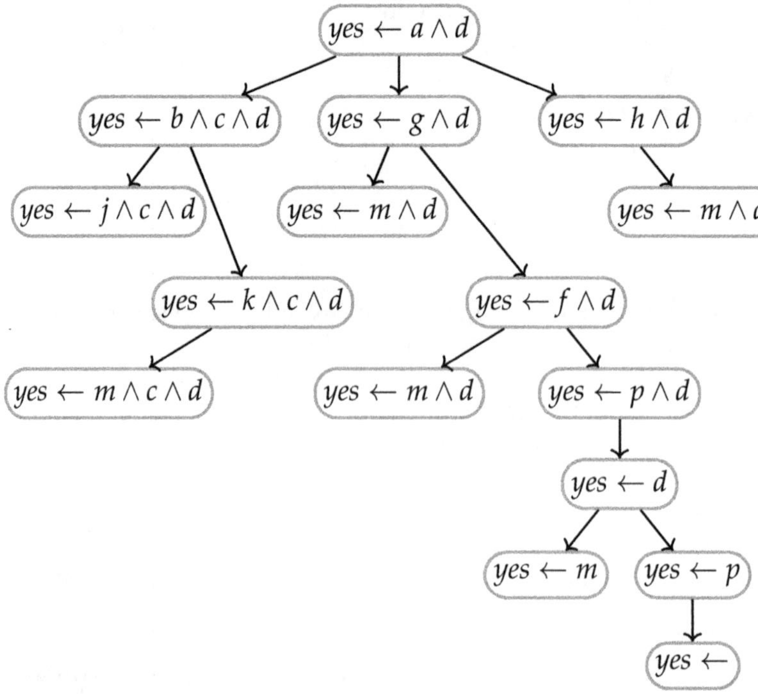


Figure 5.5: A search graph for a top-down derivation

Any of the search methods of Chapter 3 can be used to search the search space. The search space depends on the query and which atom is selected at each node. Whether the query is a logical consequence does not depend on the path found, so an optimal path is not necessary.

When the top-down procedure has derived the answer, the rules used in the derivation can be used in a bottom-up proof procedure to infer the query. Similarly, a bottom-up proof of an atom can be used to construct a corresponding top-down derivation. This equivalence can be used to show the soundness and completeness of the top-down proof procedure. As defined, the top-down proof procedure may spend extra time re-proving the same atom multiple times, whereas the bottom-up procedure proves each atom only once. However, the bottom-up procedure proves every atom, but the top-down procedure proves only atoms that are relevant to the query.

It is possible that the proof procedure can get into an infinite loop, as in the following example (without cycle pruning).

**Example 5.13** Consider the knowledge base

$$
\begin{array}{ll}
g \leftarrow a. & a \leftarrow b. \\
g \leftarrow c. & b \leftarrow a. \\
c. &
\end{array}
$$

Atoms $g$ and $c$ are the only atomic logical consequences of this knowledge base, and the bottom-up proof procedure will halt with fixed point $\{c, g\}$. However, the top-down proof procedure with a depth-first search, trying to prove $g$, will go on indefinitely, and not halt if the first clause for $g$ is chosen, and there is no cycle pruning.

The algorithm requires a selection strategy to decide which atom to select at each time. In the above examples the leftmost atom $a_1$ was selected, but any atom could be selected. Which atom is selected affects the efficiency and perhaps even whether the algorithm terminates if there is no cycle pruning. The best selection strategy is to select the atom that is most likely to fail. Ordering the atoms and selecting the leftmost atom is a common strategy, because this lets someone who is providing the rules provide heuristic knowledge about which atom to select.

## 5.4 Querying the User

An agent (page 15) receives some information as background knowledge and some as observations online. An **observation** (page 14) is information received online from users, sensors, or other knowledge sources. Assume an observation is a set of atomic propositions, which are implicitly conjoined.

A **user** (page 69) is a person who has need for expertise or has information about individual situations. Users cannot be expected to tell us everything that is true. First, they do not know what is relevant, and second, they do not know what vocabulary to use. An **ontology** (page 716) that specifies the meaning of the symbols, or a graphical user interface to allow the user to click on what is true, may help to solve the vocabulary problem. However, there can be too many possibly relevant truths to expect the user to specify everything that is true, even with a sophisticated user interface. We need to ensure that users are only asked to provide information that is potentially useful. Similarly, passive sensors (page 70) may be able to provide direct observations of conjunctions of atomic propositions, but **active sensors** (page 70) may have to be queried by the agent for the information that is necessary for a task.

A simple way to acquire information from a user or a sensor is to incorporate an **ask-the-user** mechanism, where an atom is **askable** if the user may know the truth value at run time, or it can be asked of an active sensor. The top-down proof procedure (page 191), when it has selected an atom to prove, either can use a clause in the knowledge base to prove it, or, if the atom is askable and hasn't already been asked, it can ask the user or an active sensor whether the atom is true. Users are thus only asked about atoms that are relevant for the query.

A bottom-up proof procedure can also be adapted to ask a user, but it should avoid asking about all askable atoms; see Exercise 5.5 (page 224).

**Example 5.14** In the electrical domain of Example 5.8 (page 186), one would not expect the designer of the model of the house wiring to know the switch positions (whether each switch is up or down). It is reasonable that all of the definite clauses of Example 5.8, except for the switch positions, should be given by the designer. The switch positions can then be made askable.

Here is a possible dialog, where the user asks a query and answers yes or no to the system's questions. The user interface here is minimal to show the basic idea; a real system would use a more sophisticated user-friendly interface.

ask $lit\_l_1$.
Is $down\_s_2$ true? no.
Is $up\_s_2$ true? yes.
Is $up\_s_1$ true? yes.
Answer: *True*.

The system only asks the user questions that the user is able to answer and that are relevant to the task at hand.

## 5.5 Knowledge-Level Debugging

The explicit use of semantics allows explanation and debugging at the **knowledge level** (page 44). To make a system usable by people, the system cannot just give an answer and expect the user to believe it. Consider the case of a system advising doctors who are legally responsible for the treatment that they carry out based on the diagnosis. The doctors must be convinced that the diagnosis is appropriate. The system must be able to justify that its answer is correct. The same mechanism can be used to explain how the system found a result and to debug the knowledge base; a good explanation should convince someone there are no bugs.

**Knowledge-level debugging** is the process of finding errors in knowledge bases with reference only to what the symbols mean and what is true in the world, not the reasoning steps.

Three types of non-syntactic errors arise in rule-based systems:

- An incorrect answer is produced; that is, some atom that is false in the intended interpretation was derived.
- An answer that was not produced; that is, the proof failed on a particular true atom when it should have succeeded.
- The program gets into an infinite loop. These can be handled for the top-down proof procedure in a similar way to cycle pruning (page 109), but where only the selected atoms need to be checked for cycles, and not the whole answer clause. The bottom-up proof procedure never gets into an infinite loop.

Ways to debug the first two of these types of error are examined below.

### 5.5.1 Incorrect Answers

An **incorrect answer**, or **false-positive error**, is an answer that has been proved yet is false in the intended interpretation. An incorrect answer is only produced by a sound proof procedure if a false clause was used in the proof. The aim is to find a false clause from an incorrect answer.

Suppose atom $g$ was proved yet is false in the intended interpretation. There must be a clause $g \leftarrow a_1 \wedge \ldots \wedge a_k$ in the knowledge base that was used to prove $g$. Either all of the $a_i$ are true, in which case the buggy clause has been found, or one of the $a_i$ is false. This $a_i$ can be debugged in the same way.

This leads to an algorithm, presented in Figure 5.6 (page 198) to **debug false positives**. It can find a false clause in a knowledge base when an atom that is false in the intended interpretation is derived. It only requires the person debugging the knowledge base to be able to answer true–false questions.

**Example 5.15** Consider Example 5.8 (page 186), involving the electrical domain, but assume there is a bug in the knowledge base. Suppose that the domain expert or user had inadvertently said that whether $w_1$ is connected to $w_3$ depends on the status of $s_3$ instead of $s_1$ (see Figure 5.2 (page 186)). Thus, the knowledge includes the following incorrect rule:

$$live\_w_1 \leftarrow live\_w_3 \wedge up\_s_3$$

instead of the rule with $up\_s_1$. All of the other axioms are the same as in Example 5.8. The atom $lit\_l_1$ can be derived, which is false in the intended interpretation.

The atom $lit\_l_1$ was derived using the following rule:

$$lit\_l_1 \leftarrow light\_l_1 \wedge live\_l_1 \wedge ok\_l_1.$$

The atoms $light\_l_1$ and $ok\_l_1$ are true in the intended interpretation, but $live\_l_1$ is false in the intended interpretation. The rule used to derive this atom is

$$live\_l_1 \leftarrow live\_w_0.$$

The atom $live\_w_0$ is false in the intended interpretation. It was proved using the clause

$$live\_w_0 \leftarrow up\_s_2 \wedge live\_w_1.$$

The atom $live\_w_1$ is false in the intended interpretation, and was proved using the clause

$$live\_w_1 \leftarrow up\_s_3 \wedge live\_w_3.$$

Both elements of the body are true in the intended interpretation, so this is a buggy rule.

## 5.5.2 Missing Answers

The second type of error occurs when an expected answer is not produced. This manifests itself by a failure when an answer is expected. An atom $g$ that is true in the domain, but is not a consequence of the knowledge base, is a **false-negative error**. The preceding algorithm does not work in this case; there is no proof.

An appropriate answer is not produced only if a definite clause or clauses are missing from the knowledge base. By knowing the intended interpretation of the symbols and by knowing what queries should succeed (i.e., what is true in the intended interpretation), a domain expert can debug a missing answer. Figure 5.7 (page 199) shows how to **debug** false negatives. Given $g$, a true atom for which there is no proof, it returns an atom for which there is a missing clause (or clauses).

**procedure** *Debug_false*$(g, KB)$
    **Inputs**
        $KB$ a knowledge base
        $g$ an atom: $KB \vdash g$ and $g$ is false in intended interpretation
    **Output**
        clause in $KB$ that is false
    Find the definite clause $g \leftarrow a_0 \wedge \ldots \wedge a_k \in KB$ used to prove $g$
    Present the rule to the user and ask if each $a_i$ is true
    **if** user specifies $a_i$ is false **then**
        **return** *Debug_false*$(a_i, KB)$
    **else if** user specifies all $a_i$ are true **then**
        **return** $g \leftarrow a_0 \wedge \ldots \wedge a_k$

Figure 5.6: An algorithm to debug false positive answers

It searches the space of plausible proofs until it finds an atom where there is no appropriate clause in the knowledge base.

**Example 5.16** Suppose that, for the axiomatization of the electrical domain in Example 5.8 (page 186), the world of Figure 5.2 (page 186) actually had $s_2$ down. Thus, it is missing the definite clause specifying that $s_2$ is down. The axiomatization of Example 5.8 fails to prove $lit\_l_1$ when it should succeed. Consider how to find the bug.

There is one clause with $lit\_l_1$ in the head:

$$lit\_l_1 \leftarrow light\_l_1 \wedge live\_l_1 \wedge ok\_l_1.$$

All of the elements of the body are true. The atoms $light\_l_1$ and $ok\_l_1$ can both be proved, but $live\_l_1$ fails, so the algorithm recursively debugs this atom. There is one rule with $live\_l_1$ in the head:

$$live\_l_1 \leftarrow live\_w_0.$$

The atom $live\_w_0$ is true in the intended interpretation and cannot be proved. The clauses for $live\_w_0$ are

$$live\_w_0 \leftarrow live\_w_1 \wedge up\_s_2.$$
$$live\_w_0 \leftarrow live\_w_2 \wedge down\_s_2.$$

The user can determine that the body of the second rule is true. There is a proof for $live\_w_2$. There are no clauses for $down\_s_2$, so this atom is returned. The correction is to add an appropriate clause, by stating it as a fact or providing a rule for it.

---

**procedure** $Debug\_missing(g, KB)$
    **Inputs**
        $KB$ a knowledge base
        $g$ an atom: $KB \nvdash g$ and $g$ is true in the intended interpretation
    **Output**
        atom for which there is a clause missing
    **if** there is a definite clause $g \leftarrow a_1 \wedge \ldots \wedge a_k \in KB$ such that all $a_i$ are true in the intended interpretation **then**
        **select** $a_i$ that cannot be proved
        **return** $Debug\_missing(a_i, KB)$
    **else**
        **return** $g$

Figure 5.7: An algorithm for debugging missing answers (false negatives)

## 5.6 Proving by Contradiction

Definite clauses can be used in a proof by contradiction by allowing rules that give contradictions. For example, in the electrical wiring domain (page 186), it is useful to be able to specify that some prediction, such as that light $l_2$ is on, is not true. This will enable diagnostic reasoning to deduce that some switches, lights, or circuit breakers are broken.

### 5.6.1 Horn Clauses

The definite-clause language does not allow a contradiction to be stated. However, a simple expansion of the language can allow proof by contradiction.

An **integrity constraint** is a clause of the form

$$false \leftarrow a_1 \land \ldots \land a_k.$$

where the $a_i$ are atoms and *false* is a special atom that is false in all interpretations.

A **Horn clause** is either a definite clause (page 185) or an integrity constraint. That is, a Horn clause has either *false* or a normal atom as its head.

Integrity constraints allow the system to prove that some conjunction of atoms is false in all models of a knowledge base. Recall (page 178) that $\neg p$ is the **negation** of $p$, which is true in an interpretation when $p$ is false in that interpretation, and $p \lor q$ is the **disjunction** of $p$ and $q$, which is true in an interpretation if $p$ is true or $q$ is true or both are true in the interpretation. The integrity constraint $false \leftarrow a_1 \land \ldots \land a_k$ is logically equivalent to $\neg a_1 \lor \ldots \lor \neg a_k$.

Unlike a definite-clause knowledge base, a Horn clause knowledge base can imply negations of atoms, as shown in Example 5.17.

**Example 5.17** Consider the knowledge base $KB_1$:

$$false \leftarrow a \land b.$$
$$a \leftarrow c.$$
$$b \leftarrow c.$$

The atom $c$ is false in all models of $KB_1$. To see this, suppose instead that $c$ is true in model $I$ of $KB_1$. Then $a$ and $b$ would both be true in $I$ (otherwise $I$ would not be a model of $KB_1$). Because *false* is false in $I$ and $a$ and $b$ are true in $I$, the first clause is false in $I$, a contradiction to $I$ being a model of $KB_1$. Thus, $\neg c$ is true in all models of $KB_1$, which can be written as

$$KB_1 \models \neg c.$$

Although the language of Horn clauses does not allow disjunctions and negations to be input, disjunctions of negations of atoms can be derived, as the following example shows.

**Example 5.18** Consider the knowledge base $KB_2$:

$$false \leftarrow a \wedge b.$$
$$a \leftarrow c.$$
$$b \leftarrow d.$$
$$b \leftarrow e.$$

Either $c$ is false or $d$ is false in every model of $KB_2$. If they were both true in some model $I$ of $KB_2$, both $a$ and $b$ would be true in $I$, so the first clause would be false in $I$, a contradiction to $I$ being a model of $KB_2$. Similarly, either $c$ is false or $e$ is false in every model of $KB_2$. Thus

$$KB_2 \models \neg c \vee \neg d$$
$$KB_2 \models \neg c \vee \neg e.$$

A set of clauses is **unsatisfiable** if it has no models. A set of clauses is provably **inconsistent** with respect to a proof procedure if *false* can be derived from the clauses using that proof procedure. If a proof procedure is sound and complete, a set of clauses is provably inconsistent if and only if it is unsatisfiable.

It is always possible to find a model for a set of definite clauses. The interpretation with all atoms true is a model of any set of definite clauses. Thus, a definite-clause knowledge base is always satisfiable. However, a set of Horn clauses can be unsatisfiable.

**Example 5.19** The set of clauses $\{a, false \leftarrow a\}$ is unsatisfiable. There is no interpretation that satisfies both clauses. Both $a$ and $false \leftarrow a$ cannot be true in any interpretation.

Both the top-down and the bottom-up proof procedures can be used to prove inconsistency, by using *false* as the query.

### 5.6.2 Assumables and Conflicts

Reasoning from contradictions is a very useful tool. For many activities it is useful to know that some combination of assumptions is incompatible. For example, it is useful in planning to know that some combination of actions an agent is contemplating is impossible. When designing a new artifact, it is useful to know that some combination of components cannot work together.

In a diagnostic application it is useful to be able to prove that some components working normally is inconsistent with the observations of the system. Consider a system that has a description of how it is supposed to work and some observations. If the system does not work according to its specification, a diagnostic agent should identify which components could be faulty.

To carry out these tasks it is useful to be able to make assumptions that can be proven to be false.

An **assumable** is an atom that can be assumed in a proof by contradiction. A proof by contradiction derives a disjunction of the negation of assumables.

With a Horn clause knowledge base and explicit assumables, if the system can prove a contradiction from some assumptions, it can extract those combinations of assumptions that cannot all be true. Instead of proving a query, the system tries to prove *false*, and collects the assumables that are used in a proof.

If *KB* is a set of Horn clauses, a **conflict** of *KB* is a set of assumables that, given *KB*, implies *false*. That is, $C = \{c_1, \ldots, c_r\}$ is a conflict of *KB* if

$$KB \cup \{c_1, \ldots, c_r\} \models false.$$

In this case, an **answer** is

$$KB \models \neg c_1 \vee \ldots \vee \neg c_r.$$

A **minimal conflict** is a conflict such that no strict subset is also a conflict.

**Example 5.20** In Example 5.18 (page 201), if $\{c, d, e, f, g, h\}$ is the set of assumables, then $\{c, d\}$ and $\{c, e\}$ are minimal conflicts of $KB_2$; $\{c, d, e, h\}$ is also a conflict, but not a minimal conflict.

In the examples that follow, assumables are specified using the assumable keyword followed by one or more assumable atoms separated by commas.

### 5.6.3 Consistency-Based Diagnosis

Making assumptions about what is working normally, and deriving what components could be abnormal, is the basis of **consistency-based diagnosis**. Suppose a **fault** is something that is wrong with a system. The aim of consistency-based diagnosis is to determine the possible faults based on a model of the system and observations of the system. By making the absence of faults assumable, conflicts can be used to prove what is wrong with the system.

**Example 5.21** Consider the house wiring example depicted in Figure 5.2 (page 186) and represented in Example 5.8 (page 186). Figure 5.8 (page 203) gives a background knowledge base suitable for consistency-based diagnosis. Normality assumptions, specifying that switches, circuit breakers, and lights must be ok to work as expected, are added to the clauses. There are no clauses for the *ok* atoms, but they are made assumable.

The user is able to observe the switch positions and whether a light is lit or dark.

A light cannot be both lit and dark. This knowledge is stated in the following integrity constraints:

$$false \leftarrow dark\_l_1 \wedge lit\_l_1.$$
$$false \leftarrow dark\_l_2 \wedge lit\_l_2.$$

Suppose the user observes that all three switches are up, and that $l_1$ and $l_2$ are both dark. This is represented by the atomic clauses

$$up\_s_1. \quad up\_s_2. \quad up\_s_3.$$
$$dark\_l_1. \quad dark\_l_2.$$

Given the knowledge of Figure 5.8 together with the observations, there are two minimal conflicts:

$$\{ok\_cb_1, ok\_s_1, ok\_s_2, ok\_l_1\}$$
$$\{ok\_cb_1, ok\_s_3, ok\_l_2\}.$$

Thus, it follows that

$$KB \models \neg ok\_cb_1 \vee \neg ok\_s_1 \vee \neg ok\_s_2 \vee \neg ok\_l_1$$
$$KB \models \neg ok\_cb_1 \vee \neg ok\_s_3 \vee \neg ok\_l_2$$

which means that at least one of the components $cb_1$, $s_1$, $s_2$, or $l_1$ must not be ok, and at least one of the components $cb_1$, $s_3$, or $l_2$ must not be ok.

Given the set of all conflicts, a user can determine what may be wrong with the system being diagnosed. However, sometimes it is more useful to give a disjunction of conjunctions of faults. This lets the user see whether all of the conflicts can be accounted for by a single fault or a pair of faults, or the system perhaps needs more faults.

Given a set of conflicts, a **consistency-based diagnosis** is a set of assumables that has at least one element in each conflict. A **minimal diagnosis** is a diagnosis such that no subset is also a diagnosis. For one of the diagnoses, all of its elements must be false in the world being modeled.

**Example 5.22** In Example 5.21 (page 202), the disjunction of the negation of the two conflicts is a logical consequence of the clauses. Thus, the conjunction

$$(\neg ok\_cb_1 \vee \neg ok\_s_1 \vee \neg ok\_s_2 \vee \neg ok\_l_1)$$
$$\wedge (\neg ok\_cb_1 \vee \neg ok\_s_3 \vee \neg ok\_l_2)$$

$light\_l_1.$ $\quad live\_w_0 \leftarrow live\_w_1 \wedge up\_s_2 \wedge ok\_s_2.$
$light\_l_2.$ $\quad live\_w_0 \leftarrow live\_w_2 \wedge down\_s_2 \wedge ok\_s_2.$
$live\_outside.$ $\quad live\_w_1 \leftarrow live\_w_3 \wedge up\_s_1 \wedge ok\_s_1.$
$live\_l_1 \leftarrow live\_w_0.$ $\quad live\_w_2 \leftarrow live\_w_3 \wedge down\_s_1 \wedge ok\_s_1.$
$live\_l_2 \leftarrow live\_w_4.$ $\quad live\_w_3 \leftarrow live\_w_5 \wedge ok\_cb_1.$
$live\_p_1 \leftarrow live\_w_3.$ $\quad live\_w_4 \leftarrow live\_w_3 \wedge up\_s_3 \wedge ok\_s_3.$
$live\_p_2 \leftarrow live\_w_6.$ $\quad live\_w_5 \leftarrow live\_outside.$
$lit\_l_1 \leftarrow light\_l_1 \wedge live\_l_1 \wedge ok\_l_1.$ $\quad live\_w_6 \leftarrow live\_w_5 \wedge ok\_cb_2.$
$lit\_l_2 \leftarrow light\_l_2 \wedge live\_l_2 \wedge ok\_l_2.$ $\quad false \leftarrow dark\_l_1 \wedge lit\_l_1.$
$false \leftarrow dark\_l_2 \wedge lit\_l_2.$
assumable $ok\_cb_1, ok\_cb_2, ok\_s_1, ok\_s_2, ok\_s_3, ok\_l_1, ok\_l_2.$

Figure 5.8: Knowledge for Example 5.21 (page 202)

follows from the knowledge base. This conjunction of disjunctions in **conjunctive normal form** (**CNF**) can be distributed into **disjunctive normal form** (**DNF**), a disjunction of conjunctions, here of negated atoms:

$$\neg ok\_cb_1 \vee$$
$$(\neg ok\_s_1 \wedge \neg ok\_s_3) \vee (\neg ok\_s_1 \wedge \neg ok\_l_2) \vee$$
$$(\neg ok\_s_2 \wedge \neg ok\_s_3) \vee (\neg ok\_s_2 \wedge \neg ok\_l_2) \vee$$
$$(\neg ok\_l_1 \wedge \neg ok\_s_3) \vee (\neg ok\_l_1 \wedge \neg ok\_l_2).$$

Thus, either $cb_1$ is broken or there is at least one of six double faults.

The propositions that are disjoined together correspond to the seven minimal diagnoses: $\{ok\_cb_1\}$, $\{ok\_s_1, ok\_s_3\}$, $\{ok\_s_1, ok\_l_2\}$, $\{ok\_s_2, ok\_s_3\}$, $\{ok\_s_2, ok\_l_2\}$, $\{ok\_l_1, ok\_s_3\}$, $\{ok\_l_1, ok\_l_2\}$. The system has proved that one of these combinations must be faulty.

### 5.6.4 Reasoning with Assumptions and Horn Clauses

This section presents a bottom-up implementation and a top-down implementation for finding conflicts in Horn clause knowledge bases.

#### Bottom-Up Implementation

The **bottom-up proof procedure** for assumables and Horn clauses is an augmented version of the bottom-up algorithm for definite clauses presented in Section 5.3.2 (page 189).

The modification to that algorithm is that the conclusions are pairs $\langle a, A\rangle$, where $a$ is an atom and $A$ is a set of assumables that imply $a$ in the context of the Horn clause knowledge base $KB$.

Initially, the conclusion set $C$ is $\{\langle a, \{a\}\rangle : a \text{ is assumable}\}$. Clauses can be used to derive new conclusions. If there is a clause $h \leftarrow b_1 \wedge \ldots \wedge b_m$ such that for each $b_i$ there is some $A_i$ such that $\langle b_i, A_i\rangle \in C$, then $\langle h, A_1 \cup \ldots \cup A_m\rangle$ can be added to $C$. This covers the case of atomic clauses, with $m = 0$, where $\langle h, \{\}\rangle$ is added to $C$.

Figure 5.9 (page 205) gives code for the algorithm. This algorithm is an **assumption-based truth maintenance system** (**ATMS**), and can be combined with the incremental addition of clauses and assumables.

When the pair $\langle false, A\rangle$ is generated, the assumptions $A$ form a conflict.

One refinement of this program is to prune supersets of assumptions. If $\langle a, A_1\rangle$ and $\langle a, A_2\rangle$ are in $C$, where $A_1 \subset A_2$, then $\langle a, A_2\rangle$ can be removed from $C$ or not added to $C$. There is no reason to use the extra assumptions to imply $a$. Similarly, if $\langle false, A_1\rangle$ and $\langle a, A_2\rangle$ are in $C$, where $A_1 \subseteq A_2$, then $\langle a, A_2\rangle$ can be removed from $C$ because $A_1$ and any superset – including $A_2$ – are inconsistent with the clauses given, and so nothing more can be learned from considering such sets of assumables.

**Example 5.23** Consider the axiomatization of Figure 5.8 (page 203), discussed in Example 5.21 (page 202).

Initially, in the algorithm of Figure 5.9, $C$ has the value

$$\{\langle ok\_l_1, \{ok\_l_1\}\rangle, \langle ok\_l_2, \{ok\_l_2\}\rangle, \langle ok\_s_1, \{ok\_s_1\}\rangle, \langle ok\_s_2, \{ok\_s_2\}\rangle,$$
$$\langle ok\_s_3, \{ok\_s_3\}\rangle, \langle ok\_cb_1, \{ok\_cb_1\}\rangle, \langle ok\_cb_2, \{ok\_cb_2\}\rangle\}.$$

The following shows a sequence of values added to $C$ under one sequence of selections:

$$\langle live\_outside, \{\}\rangle$$
$$\langle live\_w_5, \{\}\rangle$$
$$\langle live\_w_3, \{ok\_cb_1\}\rangle$$
$$\langle up\_s_3, \{\}\rangle$$
$$\langle live\_w_4, \{ok\_cb_1, ok\_s_3\}\rangle$$
$$\langle live\_l_2, \{ok\_cb_1, ok\_s_3\}\rangle$$
$$\langle light\_l_2, \{\}\rangle$$
$$\langle lit\_l_2, \{ok\_cb_1, ok\_s_3, ok\_l_2\}\rangle$$
$$\langle dark\_l_2, \{\}\rangle$$
$$\langle false, \{ok\_cb_1, ok\_s_3, ok\_l_2\}\rangle .$$

Thus, the knowledge base entails

$$\neg ok\_cb_1 \vee \neg ok\_s_3 \vee \neg ok\_l_2.$$

The other conflict can be found by continuing the algorithm.

```
procedure Prove_conflict_BU(KB, Assumables)
    Inputs
        KB: a set of Horn clauses
        Assumables: a set of atoms that can be assumed
    Output
        set of conflicts
    Local
        C is a set of pairs of an atom and a set of assumables
    C := {⟨a, {a}⟩ : a is assumable}
    repeat
        select clause "h ← b1 ∧ ... ∧ bm" in KB such that
            ⟨bi, Ai⟩ ∈ C for all i and
            ⟨h, A⟩ ∉ C where A = A1 ∪ ... ∪ Am
        C := C ∪ {⟨h, A⟩}
    until no more selections are possible
    return {A : ⟨false, A⟩ ∈ C}
```

Figure 5.9: Bottom-up proof procedure for computing conflicts

### Top-Down Implementation

The top-down implementation is similar to the top-down definite-clause interpreter described in Figure 5.4 (page 192), except the top-level query is to prove *false*, and the assumables encountered in a proof are not proved but collected.

The algorithm is shown in Figure 5.10. Different choices can lead to different conflicts being found. If no choices are available, the algorithm fails.

**Example 5.24** Consider the representation of the circuit in Example 5.21 (page 202). The following is a sequence of the values of $G$ for one sequence of selections and choices that leads to a conflict:

$$\{false\}$$
$$\{dark\_l_1, lit\_l_1\}$$
$$\{lit\_l_1\}$$
$$\{light\_l_1, live\_l_1, ok\_l_1\}$$
$$\{live\_l_1, ok\_l_1\}$$
$$\{live\_w_0, ok\_l_1\}$$
$$\{live\_w_1, up\_s_2, ok\_s_2, ok\_l_1\}$$
$$\{live\_w_3, up\_s_1, ok\_s_1, up\_s_2, ok\_s_2, ok\_l_1\}$$
$$\{live\_w_5, ok\_cb_1, up\_s_1, ok\_s_1, up\_s_2, ok\_s_2, ok\_l_1\}$$
$$\{live\_outside, ok\_cb_1, up\_s_1, ok\_s_1, up\_s_2, ok\_s_2, ok\_l_1\}$$
$$\{ok\_cb_1, up\_s_1, ok\_s_1, up\_s_2, ok\_s_2, ok\_l_1\}$$
$$\{ok\_cb_1, ok\_s_1, up\_s_2, ok\_s_2, ok\_l_1\}$$
$$\{ok\_cb_1, ok\_s_1, ok\_s_2, ok\_l_1\}.$$

**non-deterministic procedure** *Prove_conflict_TD*(*KB*, *Assumables*)
    **Inputs**
        *KB*: a set Horn clauses
        *Assumables*: a set of atoms that can be assumed
    **Output**
        A conflict
    **Local**
        $G$ is a set of atoms (that implies false)
    $G := \{false\}$
    **repeat**
        **select** an atom $a$ in $G$ such that $a \notin Assumables$
        **choose** clause "$a \leftarrow B$" in *KB* with $a$ as head
        $G := (G \setminus \{a\}) \cup B$
    **until** $G \subseteq Assumables$
    **return** $G$

Figure 5.10: Top-down Horn clause proof procedure to find conflicts

The set $\{ok\_cb_1, ok\_s_1, ok\_s_2, ok\_l_1\}$ is returned as a conflict. Different choices of the clause to use can lead to another answer.

## 5.7 Complete Knowledge Assumption

A database is often complete in the sense that anything not implied is false.

**Example 5.25** You may want the user to specify which switches are up and which circuit breakers are broken so that the system can conclude that any switch not mentioned as up is down and any circuit breaker not specified as broken is ok. Thus, down is the default value of switches and ok is the default value for circuit breakers. It is easier for users to communicate using defaults than it is to specify the seemingly redundant information about which switches are down and which circuit breakers are ok. To reason with such defaults, an agent must assume it has complete knowledge; a switch's position is not mentioned because it is down, not because the agent does not know whether it is up or down.

The given definite-clause logic does not allow the derivation of a conclusion from a lack of knowledge or a failure to prove. It does not assume that the knowledge is complete. In particular, the negation of an atom can never be a logical consequence of a definite-clause knowledge base.

The **complete knowledge assumption** assumes that, for every atom, the clauses with the atom as the head cover all the cases when the atom is true. In particular, an atom with no clauses is false. Under this assumption, an agent can conclude that an atom is false if it cannot derive that the atom is true. This is also called the **closed-world assumption**. It can be contrasted with the **open-world assumption**, which is that the agent does not know everything and so cannot make any conclusions from a lack of knowledge. The closed-world assumption requires that everything relevant about the world is known to the agent.

This assumption that there is a definition of each atom in terms of clauses is the basis of **logic programming**. Here we give the propositional version; richer variants are presented in Section 15.4 (page 655) and Section 15.6 (page 667).

Suppose the clauses for atom $a$ are

$$a \leftarrow b_1.$$
$$\vdots$$
$$a \leftarrow b_n.$$

where an atomic clause $a$ is treated as the rule $a \leftarrow true$. The complete knowledge assumption specifies that if $a$ is true in some interpretation then one of the $b_i$ must be true in that interpretation; that is,

$$a \rightarrow b_1 \vee \ldots \vee b_n.$$

Because the clauses defining $a$ are equivalent to

$$a \leftarrow b_1 \vee \ldots \vee b_n$$

the meaning of the clauses can be seen as the conjunction of these two propositions, namely, the equivalence

$$a \leftrightarrow b_1 \vee \ldots \vee b_n$$

where $\leftrightarrow$ is read as "if and only if" (see Figure 5.1 (page 179)). This equivalence is called **Clark's completion** of the clauses for $a$. Clark's completion of a knowledge base is the completion for each atom in the knowledge base.

Clark's completion means that if there are no rules for an atom $a$, then the completion of this atom is $a \leftrightarrow \mathit{false}$, which means that $a$ is false.

**Example 5.26** Consider the clauses from Example 5.8 (page 186):

$$\begin{aligned}
&\mathit{down_s_1}.\\
&\mathit{up_s_2}.\\
&\mathit{ok_cb_1}.\\
&\mathit{live_l_1} \leftarrow \mathit{live_w_0}.\\
&\mathit{live_w_0} \leftarrow \mathit{live_w_1} \wedge \mathit{up_s_2}.\\
&\mathit{live_w_0} \leftarrow \mathit{live_w_2} \wedge \mathit{down_s_2}.\\
&\mathit{live_w_1} \leftarrow \mathit{live_w_3} \wedge \mathit{up_s_1}.\\
&\mathit{live_w_2} \leftarrow \mathit{live_w_3} \wedge \mathit{down_s_1}.\\
&\mathit{live_w_3} \leftarrow \mathit{live_outside} \wedge \mathit{ok_cb_1}.\\
&\mathit{live_outside}.
\end{aligned}$$

Suppose that these are the only clauses for the atoms in the heads of these clauses, and there are no clauses for $\mathit{up\_s_1}$ or $\mathit{down\_s_2}$. The completion of these atoms is

$$\begin{aligned}
&\mathit{down_s_1} \leftrightarrow \mathit{true}.\\
&\mathit{up_s_1} \leftrightarrow \mathit{false}.\\
&\mathit{up_s_2} \leftrightarrow \mathit{true}.\\
&\mathit{down_s_2} \leftrightarrow \mathit{false}.\\
&\mathit{ok_cb_1} \leftrightarrow \mathit{true}.\\
&\mathit{live_l_1} \leftrightarrow \mathit{live_w_0}.\\
&\mathit{live_w_0} \leftrightarrow (\mathit{live_w_1} \wedge \mathit{up_s_2}) \vee (\mathit{live_w_2} \wedge \mathit{down_s_2}).\\
&\mathit{live_w_1} \leftrightarrow \mathit{live_w_3} \wedge \mathit{up_s_1}.\\
&\mathit{live_w_2} \leftrightarrow \mathit{live_w_3} \wedge \mathit{down_s_1}.\\
&\mathit{live_w_3} \leftrightarrow \mathit{live_outside} \wedge \mathit{ok_cb_1}.\\
&\mathit{live_outside} \leftrightarrow \mathit{true}.
\end{aligned}$$

This implies that $\mathit{up\_s_1}$ is false, $\mathit{live\_w_1}$ is false, and $\mathit{live\_w_2}$ is true.

With the completion, the system can derive negations, and so it is useful to extend the language to allow negations in the body of clauses. A **literal** is either an atom or the negation of an atom. The definition of a definite clause (page 185) can be extended to allow literals in the body rather than just atoms. We write the negation of atom $a$ under the complete knowledge assumption as $\sim a$ to distinguish it from classical negation that does not assume the completion. This negation is often called **negation as failure**.

Under negation as failure, body $g$ is a consequence of the knowledge base $KB$ if $KB' \models g$, where $KB'$ is Clark's completion of $KB$. A negation $\sim a$ in the body of a clause or the query becomes $\neg a$ in the completion. That is, a query follows from a knowledge base under the complete knowledge assumption means that the query is a logical consequence of the completion of the knowledge base.

**Example 5.27** Consider the axiomatization of Example 5.8 (page 186). Representing a domain can be made simpler by expecting the user to tell the system only what switches are up and by the system concluding that a switch is down if it has not been told the switch is up. This can be done by adding the following rules:

$$down\_s_1 \leftarrow \sim up\_s_1.$$
$$down\_s_2 \leftarrow \sim up\_s_2.$$
$$down\_s_3 \leftarrow \sim up\_s_3.$$

Similarly, the system may conclude that the circuit breakers are ok unless it has been told they are broken:

$$ok\_cb_1 \leftarrow \sim broken\_cb_1.$$
$$ok\_cb_2 \leftarrow \sim broken\_cb_2.$$

Although this may look more complicated than the previous representation, it means that it is easier for the user to specify what is occurring in a particular situation. The user has to specify only what is up and what is broken. This may save time if being down is normal for switches and being ok is normal for circuit breakers.

To represent the state of Figure 5.2 (page 186), the user specifies

$$up\_s_2.$$
$$up\_s_3.$$

The system can infer that $s_1$ must be down and both circuit breakers are ok.

The completion of the knowledge base consisting of the clauses above is

$$down\_s_1 \leftrightarrow \neg up\_s_1.$$
$$down\_s_2 \leftrightarrow \neg up\_s_2.$$
$$down\_s_3 \leftrightarrow \neg up\_s_3.$$
$$ok\_cb_1 \leftrightarrow \neg broken\_cb_1.$$
$$ok\_cb_2 \leftrightarrow \neg broken\_cb_2.$$
$$up\_s_1 \leftrightarrow false.$$

$up\_s_2 \leftrightarrow true.$

$up\_s_3 \leftrightarrow true.$

$broken\_cb_1 \leftrightarrow false.$

$broken\_cb_2 \leftrightarrow false.$

Notice that atoms that are in the bodies of clauses but are not in the head of any clauses are false in the completion.

Recall that a knowledge base is **acyclic** (page 85) if there is an assignment of natural numbers (non-negative integers) to the atoms so that the atoms in the body of a clause are assigned a lower number than the atom in the head. With negation as failure, non-acyclic knowledge bases become semantically problematic.

The following knowledge base is not acyclic:

$a \leftarrow \sim b.$

$b \leftarrow \sim a.$

Clark's completion of this knowledge base is equivalent to $a \leftrightarrow \neg b$, which just specifies that $a$ and $b$ have different truth values but not which one is true.

The following knowledge base is also not acyclic:

$a \leftarrow \sim a.$

Clark's completion of this knowledge base is $a \leftrightarrow \neg a$, which is logically inconsistent.

Clark's completion of an acyclic knowledge base is always consistent and always gives a unique truth value to each atom. For the rest of this chapter, we assume that the knowledge bases are acyclic.

### 5.7.1 Non-Monotonic Reasoning

A logic is **monotonic** if any proposition that can be derived from a knowledge base can also be derived when extra propositions are added to the knowledge base. That is, adding knowledge does not reduce the set of propositions that can be derived. The definite-clause logic is monotonic.

A logic is **non-monotonic** if some conclusions can be invalidated by adding more knowledge. The logic of definite clauses with negation as failure is non-monotonic. Non-monotonic reasoning is useful for representing defaults. A **default** is a rule that can be used unless it is overridden by an exception.

For example, to say that $b$ is normally true if $c$ is true, a knowledge base designer can write a rule of the form

$b \leftarrow c \wedge \sim ab\_a.$

where $ab\_a$ is an atom that means abnormal with respect to some aspect $a$. Given $c$, the agent can infer $b$ unless it is told $ab\_a$. Adding $ab\_a$ to the knowledge base can prevent the conclusion of $b$. Rules that imply $ab\_a$ can be used to prevent the default under the conditions of the body of the rule.

**Example 5.28** Suppose the purchasing agent is investigating purchasing holidays. A resort may be adjacent to a beach or away from a beach. This is not symmetric; if the resort were adjacent to a beach, the knowledge provider would specify this. Thus, it is reasonable to have the clause

$$away\_from\_beach \leftarrow \sim on\_beach.$$

This clause enables an agent to infer that a resort is away from the beach if the agent is not told it is on a beach.

A **cooperative system** tries to not mislead. If we are told the resort is on the beach, we would expect that resort users would have access to the beach. If they have access to a beach, we would expect them to be able to swim at the beach. Thus, we would expect the following defaults:

$$beach\_access \leftarrow on\_beach \wedge \sim ab\_beach\_access.$$
$$swim\_at\_beach \leftarrow beach\_access \wedge \sim ab\_swim\_at\_beach.$$

A cooperative system would tell us if a resort on the beach has no beach access or if there is no swimming. We could also specify that, if there is an enclosed bay and a big city, then there is no swimming, by default:

$$ab\_swim\_at\_beach \leftarrow enclosed\_bay \wedge big\_city \wedge \sim ab\_no\_swimming\_near\_city.$$

We could say that British Columbia (BC) is abnormal with respect to swimming near cities:

$$ab\_no\_swimming\_near\_city \leftarrow in\_BC \wedge \sim ab\_BC\_beaches.$$

Given only the preceding rules, an agent infers *away_from_beach*. If it is then told *on_beach*, it can no longer infer *away_from_beach*, but it can now infer *beach_access* and *swim_at_beach*. If it is also told *enclosed_bay* and *big_city*, it can no longer infer *swim_at_beach*. However, if it is then told *in_BC*, it can then infer *swim_at_beach*.

By having defaults of what is normal, a user can interact with the system by telling it what is abnormal, which allows for economy in communication. The user does not have to state the obvious.

One way to think about non-monotonic reasoning is in terms of **arguments**. The rules can be used as components of arguments, in which the negated abnormality gives a way to undermine arguments. Note that, in the language presented, only positive arguments exist, so these are the only ones that can be undermined. In more general theories, there can be positive and negative arguments that attack each other.

## 5.7.2 Proof Procedures for Negation as Failure

### Bottom-Up Procedure

The **bottom-up proof procedure** for negation as failure is a modification of the bottom-up procedure for definite clauses (page 189). The difference is that it can add literals of the form $\sim p$ to the set $C$ of consequences that have been derived; $\sim p$ is added to $C$ when it can determine that $p$ must fail.

Failure can be defined recursively: $p$ **fails** when every body of a clause with $p$ as the head fails. A body fails if one of the literals in the body fails. An atom $b_i$ in a body fails if $\sim b_i$ can be derived. A negation $\sim b_i$ in a body fails if $b_i$ can be derived.

Figure 5.11 gives a bottom-up negation-as-failure interpreter for computing consequents of a ground *KB*. Note that this includes the case of a clause with an empty body (in which case $m = 0$ and the atom at the head is added to C) and the case of an atom that does not appear in the head of any clause (in which case its negation is added to C).

**Example 5.29** Consider the following clauses:

$$p \leftarrow q \land \sim r.$$
$$p \leftarrow s.$$
$$q \leftarrow \sim s.$$
$$r \leftarrow \sim t.$$
$$t.$$
$$s \leftarrow w.$$

```
procedure Prove_NAF_BU(KB)
    Inputs
        KB: a set of clauses that can include negation as failure
    Output
        set of literals that follow from the completion of KB
    Local
        C is a set of literals
    C := {}
    repeat
        either
            select r ∈ KB such that
                r is "h ← b1 ∧ ... ∧ bm"
                bi ∈ C for all i, and
                h ∉ C;
            C := C ∪ {h}
        or
            select h such that ~h ∉ C and
                where for every clause "h ← b1 ∧ ... ∧ bm" ∈ KB
                    either for some bi, ~bi ∈ C
                    or some bi = ~g and g ∈ C
            C := C ∪ {~h}
    until no more selections are possible
```

Figure 5.11: Bottom-up negation as failure proof procedure

The following is a possible sequence of literals added to $C$:

$$t,\ \sim r,\ \sim w,\ \sim s,\ q,\ p$$

where $t$ is derived trivially because it is given as an atomic clause; $\sim r$ is derived because $t \in C$; $\sim w$ is derived as there are no clauses for $w$, and so the "for every clause" condition of line 18 of Figure 5.11 (page 212) trivially holds. Literal $\sim s$ is derived as $\sim w \in C$; and $q$ and $p$ are derived as the bodies are all proved.

## Top-Down Negation-as-Failure Procedure

The top-down procedure for the complete knowledge assumption proceeds by **negation as failure**. It is similar to the top-down definite-clause proof procedure of Figure 5.4 (page 192). This is a non-deterministic procedure (see the box on page 89) that can be implemented by searching over choices that succeed. When a negated atom $\sim a$ is selected, a new proof for atom $a$ is started. If the proof for $a$ fails, $\sim a$ succeeds. If the proof for $a$ succeeds, the algorithm fails and must make other choices. The algorithm is shown in Figure 5.12.

**Example 5.30** Consider the clauses from Example 5.29 (page 212). Suppose the query is ask $p$.

```
non-deterministic procedure Prove_NAF_TD(KB, Query)
    Inputs
        KB: a set of clauses that can include negation as failure
        Query: a set of literals to prove
    Output
        yes if completion of KB entails Query and fail otherwise
    Local
        G is a set of literals
    G := Query
    repeat
        select literal l ∈ G
        if l is of the form ~a then
            if Prove_NAF_TD(KB, a) fails then
                G := G \ {l}
            else
                fail
        else
            choose clause "l ← B" in KB with l as head
            G := G \ {l} ∪ B
    until G = {}
    return yes
```

Figure 5.12: Top-down negation as failure interpreter

Initially, $G = \{p\}$.

Using the first rule for $p$, $G$ becomes $\{q, \sim r\}$.

Selecting $q$, and replacing it with the body of the third rule, $G$ becomes $\{\sim s, \sim r\}$.

It then selects $\sim s$ and starts a proof for $s$. This proof for $s$ fails, and thus $G$ becomes $\{\sim r\}$.

It then selects $\sim r$ and tries to prove $r$. In the proof for $r$, there is the subgoal $\sim t$, and so it tries to prove $t$. This proof for $t$ succeeds. Thus, the proof for $\sim t$ fails and, because there are no more rules for $r$, the proof for $r$ fails. Therefore, the proof for $\sim r$ succeeds.

$G$ is empty and so it returns *yes* as the answer to the top-level query.

Note that this implements **finite failure**, because it makes no conclusion if the proof procedure does not halt. For example, suppose there is just the rule $p \leftarrow p$. The algorithm does not halt for the query ask $p$. The completion, $p \leftrightarrow p$, gives no information. Even though there may be a way to conclude that there will never be a proof for $p$, a sound proof procedure should not conclude $\sim p$, as it does not follow from the completion.

## 5.8 Abduction

**Abduction** is a form of reasoning where assumptions are made to explain observations. For example, if an agent were to observe that some light was not working, it hypothesizes what is happening in the world to explain why the light was not working. A **tutoring agent** could try to explain why a student gives some answer in terms of what the student understands and does not understand.

The term **abduction** was coined by Peirce (1839–1914) to differentiate this type of reasoning from **deduction**, which involves determining what logically follows from a set of axioms, and **induction**, which involves inferring general relationships from examples.

In abduction, an agent hypothesizes what may be true about an observed case. An agent determines what implies its observations – what could be true to make the observations true. Observations are trivially implied by contradictions (as a contradiction logically implies everything), so we want to exclude contradictions from our explanation of the observations.

To formalize abduction, we use the language of Horn clauses and assumables (page 201). The system is given:

- a knowledge base, *KB*, which is a set of of Horn clauses
- a set $A$ of atoms, called the **assumables**, which are the building blocks of hypotheses.

Instead of adding observations to the knowledge base, observations must be explained.

A **scenario** of $\langle KB, A \rangle$ is a subset $H$ of $A$ such that $KB \cup H$ is satisfiable. $KB \cup H$ is **satisfiable** if a model exists in which every element of $KB$ and every element $H$ is true. This happens if no subset of $H$ is a conflict of $KB$.

An **explanation** of proposition $g$ from $\langle KB, A \rangle$ is a scenario that, together with $KB$, implies $g$.

That is, an explanation of proposition $g$ is a set $H$, $H \subseteq A$ such that

$$KB \cup H \models g$$
$$KB \cup H \not\models \mathit{false}.$$

A **minimal explanation** of $g$ from $\langle KB, A \rangle$ is an explanation $H$ of $g$ from $\langle KB, A \rangle$ such that no strict subset of $H$ is also an explanation of $g$ from $\langle KB, A \rangle$.

**Example 5.31** Consider the following simplistic knowledge base and assumables for a diagnostic assistant:

$\mathit{bronchitis} \leftarrow \mathit{influenza}.$
$\mathit{bronchitis} \leftarrow \mathit{smokes}.$
$\mathit{coughing} \leftarrow \mathit{bronchitis}.$
$\mathit{wheezing} \leftarrow \mathit{bronchitis}.$
$\mathit{fever} \leftarrow \mathit{influenza}.$
$\mathit{fever} \leftarrow \mathit{infection}.$
$\mathit{sore\_throat} \leftarrow \mathit{influenza}.$
$\mathit{false} \leftarrow \mathit{smokes} \wedge \mathit{nonsmoker}.$
assumable $\mathit{smokes}, \mathit{nonsmoker}, \mathit{influenza}, \mathit{infection}.$

If the agent observes *wheezing*, there are two minimal explanations:

$\{\mathit{influenza}\}$ and $\{\mathit{smokes}\}$.

These explanations imply *bronchitis* and *coughing*.

If $\mathit{wheezing} \wedge \mathit{fever}$ is observed, the minimal explanations are

$\{\mathit{influenza}\}$ and $\{\mathit{smokes}, \mathit{infection}\}$.

If $\mathit{wheezing} \wedge \mathit{nonsmoker}$ was observed, there is one minimal explanation:

$\{\mathit{influenza}, \mathit{nonsmoker}\}$.

The other explanation of *wheezing* is inconsistent with being a non-smoker.

**Example 5.32** Consider the knowledge base

$\mathit{alarm} \leftarrow \mathit{tampering}.$
$\mathit{alarm} \leftarrow \mathit{fire}.$
$\mathit{smoke} \leftarrow \mathit{fire}.$

If *alarm* is observed, there are two minimal explanations:

$\{tampering\}$ and $\{fire\}$.

If $alarm \wedge smoke$ is observed, there is one minimal explanation:

$\{fire\}$.

Notice how, when *smoke* is observed, there is no need to hypothesize *tampering* to explain *alarm*; it has been **explained away** by *fire*.

Determining what is going on inside a system based on observations about the behavior is the problem of **diagnosis** or **recognition**. In **abductive diagnosis**, the agent hypothesizes diseases or malfunctions, as well as that some parts are working normally, to explain the observed symptoms.

This differs from consistency-based diagnosis (page 202) (CBD) in the following ways:

- In CBD, only normal behavior needs to be represented, and the hypotheses are assumptions of normal behavior. In abductive diagnosis, faulty behavior as well as normal behavior needs to be represented, and the assumables need to be for normal behavior and for each fault (or different behavior).
- In abductive diagnosis, observations need to be explained. In CBD, observations are added to the knowledge base, and *false* is proved.

Abductive diagnosis requires more detailed modeling and gives more detailed diagnoses, because the knowledge base has to be able to actually prove the observations from the knowledge base and the assumptions. Abductive diagnosis is also used to diagnose systems in which there is no normal behavior. For example, in a **tutoring agent**, by observing what a student does, the agent can hypothesize what the student understands and does not understand, which can guide the tutoring agent's actions.

Abduction can also be used for **design**, in which the query to be explained is a design goal and the assumables are the building blocks of the designs. The explanation is the design. Consistency means that the design is possible. The implication of the design goal means that the design provably achieved the design goal.

**Example 5.33** Consider the electrical domain of Figure 5.2 (page 186). Similar to the representation of the example for consistency-based diagnosis in Example 5.21 (page 202), we axiomatize what follows from the assumptions of what may be happening in the system. In abductive diagnosis, we must axiomatize what follows both from faults and from normality assumptions. For each atom that could be observed, we axiomatize how it could be produced.

A user could observe that $l_1$ is lit or is dark. We must write rules that axiomatize how the system must be to make these true. Light $l_1$ is lit if it is ok and there is power coming in. The light is dark if it is broken or there is no power. The system can assume $l_1$ is ok or broken, but not both:

$lit\_l_1 \leftarrow live\_w_0 \wedge ok\_l_1.$

$dark\_l_1 \leftarrow broken\_l_1.$

$dark\_l_1 \leftarrow dead\_w_0.$

assumable $ok\_l_1$.

assumable $broken\_l_1$.

$false \leftarrow ok\_l_1 \wedge broken\_l_1.$

You can then write rules on how $live\_w_0$ and $dead\_w_0$ depend on switch positions, the input to $w_0$, and assumptions of the status of the wire. Observing that some of the lights are lit gives explanations that can account for the observation.

Both the bottom-up and top-down implementations for assumption-based reasoning with Horn clauses can be used for abduction. The bottom-up algorithm of Figure 5.9 (page 205) computes the minimal explanations for each atom; at the end of the repeat loop, $C$ contains the minimal explanations of each atom (as well as potentially some non-minimal explanations). The refinement of pruning dominated explanations (page 204) can also be used. The top-down algorithm (page 206) can be used to find the explanations of any $g$ by first generating the conflicts and, using the same code and knowledge base, proving $g$ instead of *false*. The minimal explanations of $g$ are the minimal sets of assumables collected to prove $g$ such that no subset is a conflict.

## 5.9 Causal Models

A **primitive atom** is an atom that is defined using facts. A **derived atom** is an atom that is defined using rules. Typically, the designer writes axioms for the derived atoms and then expects a user to specify which primitive atoms are true. Thus, a derived atom will be inferred as necessary from the primitive atoms and other atoms that can be derived.

The designer of an agent must make many decisions when designing a knowledge base for a domain. For example, consider just two propositions, $a$ and $b$, both of which are true. There are multiple ways to write this. A designer could

- state both $a$ and $b$ as atomic clauses, treating both as primitive
- state the atomic clause $a$ and the rule $b \leftarrow a$, treating $a$ as primitive and $b$ as derived
- state the atomic clause $b$ and the rule $a \leftarrow b$, treating $b$ as primitive and $a$ as derived.

These representations are logically equivalent; they cannot be distinguished logically. However, they have different effects when the knowledge base is changed. Suppose $a$ was no longer true for some reason. In the first and third representations, $b$ would still be true, and in the second representation, $b$ would no longer true.

A **causal model**, or a model of **causality**, is a representation of a domain that predicts the results of interventions. An **intervention** is an action that forces a variable to have a particular value. That is, an intervention on a variable changes the value of the variable in some way other than as a side-effect of manipulating other variables in the model. Other variables may be affected by the change.

To predict the effect of interventions, a causal model represents how the cause implies its effect. When the cause is changed, its effect should be changed. An **evidential model** represents a domain in the other direction – from effect to cause. Note that there is no assumption that there is "the cause" of an effect; rather there are propositions, which together may cause the effect to become true.

A **structural causal model** defines a **causal mechanism** for each atom that is modeled. This causal mechanism specifies when the atom is true in terms of other atoms. If the model is manipulated to make an atom true or false, then the clauses for that atom are replaced by the appropriate assertion that the atom is true or false. The model is designed so that it gives appropriate answers for such interventions.

**Example 5.34** In the electrical domain depicted in Figure 5.2 (page 186), consider the relationship between switches $s_1$ and $s_2$ and light $l_1$. Assume all components are working properly. Light $l_1$ is lit whenever both switches are up or both switches are down. Thus,

$$lit\_l_1 \leftrightarrow (up\_s_1 \leftrightarrow up\_s_2) \tag{5.1}$$

which is logically equivalent to

$$up\_s_1 \leftrightarrow (lit\_l_1 \leftrightarrow up\_s_2).$$

This formula is symmetric between the three propositions; it is true if and only if an odd number of the propositions are true. However, in the world, the relationship between these propositions is not symmetric. Suppose both switches were up and the light was lit. Putting $s_1$ down does not make $s_2$ go down to preserve $lit\_l_1$. Instead, putting $s_1$ down makes $lit\_l_1$ false, and $up\_s_2$ remains true. Thus, to predict the result of interventions, formula (5.1) is not enough. A mechanism for each atom can make the relationship asymmetric, and account for interventions.

Assuming that nothing internal to the model causes the switches to be up or down, the state of Figure 5.2 (page 186) with $s_1$ up and $s_2$ down is represented as

$$lit\_l_1 \leftrightarrow (up\_s_1 \leftrightarrow up\_s_2)$$
$$up\_s_1$$

$$\neg up\_s_2$$

which can be written as a logic program using negation as failure as

$$lit\_l_1 \leftarrow up\_s_1 \wedge up\_s_2.$$
$$lit\_l_1 \leftarrow \sim up\_s_1 \wedge \sim up\_s_2.$$
$$up\_s_1.$$

The representation makes reasonable predictions when one of the values is changed. To intervene on the switch positions, assert or remove the propositions about the switch being up. This can change whether the light is lit. To intervene to make light $l_1$ unlit, replace the clauses defining $lit\_l_1$. This does not change the switch positions. Note that intervening to make the light off does not mean that the agent turns the light off by moving the corresponding switch, but rather by some other way, for example, removing the light bulb or breaking it.

An evidential model is

$$up\_s_1 \leftarrow lit\_l_1 \wedge up\_s_2.$$
$$up\_s_1 \leftarrow \sim lit\_l_1 \wedge \sim up\_s_2.$$

This can be used to answer questions about whether $s_1$ is up based on the position of $s_2$ and whether $l_1$ is lit. Its completion is also equivalent to formula (5.1). However, it does not accurately predict the effect of interventions.

For most purposes, it is preferable to use a causal model of the world as it is more transparent, stable, and modular than an evidential model. Causal models under uncertainty are explored in Chapter 11.

## 5.10 Social Impact

As society relies more and more on increasingly complex computational systems, the need for verifying the correctness of computer hardware and software, especially in safety-critical applications, has grown rapidly. Even in a computer chip that is not used in safety-critical applications, it is important to verify that its design is correct to avoid the enormous cost of withdrawing an incorrect design from the market and re-implementing it. In the early Intel Pentium processors, the so-called FDIV bug in the hardware of its floating point unit sometimes caused the processor to compute the wrong answer when dividing two floating point numbers. This bug caused Intel to recall the defective processors and take a US$475 million charge against earnings in 1994. Although simulating a design in software can catch some bugs, testing all possible inputs for faulty outputs creates a space of possible behaviors simply too large to search exhaustively, as shown by the FDIV bug. As a result, Intel and other hardware providers subsequently invested heavily in building groups that developed formal verification techniques that are useful to prove properties of hardware.

The development of solvers for the propositional satisfiability problem (SAT) has attracted very significant resources over the last few decades. Although SAT may be worst-case exponential, instances that occur in real applications, with millions of variables, can now be realistically solved. Some approaches to proving hardware and software correctness can exploit the progress in SAT solver performance. One method for doing that is to specify the range of desired behaviors of a system in terms of a logical formula constraining the system's inputs and outputs. Given a description of the design of the system, the problem then is to determine that the design always satisfies its formal specification. A technique known as bounded model checking (BMC) is widely used for hardware verification. BMC represents a bounded-length execution trace that would violate a required property. Each execution trace symbolically represents a large set of possible actual traces, thereby overcoming the difficulty of verifying the system by simulation on all possible inputs. The propositional formula that results is tested with a SAT solver. If the formula can be satisfied then the trace is feasible and the property has been violated. If not, then the bound is increased, repeating the process. BMC has also been applied to software verification, in a similar way, with some success. An alternative approach to the formal specification and verification of software and hardware systems is the TLA+ system, based on extensions to logic that include time (known as temporal logic).

SAT has many other significant industrial applications. One family of such applications is product configuration. A product line, such as a line of cars, is a family of similar products. Various features are available to be reused across the family. A product's configuration is the set of features it uses. A feature model characterizes the allowable configurations, specifying the constraints among the features that are used. A feature model, combined with user-supplied constraints, can be translated to a SAT formula to enumerate the set of acceptable legal configurations with a SAT solver. Formal methods were applied to the task of managing all possible configurations of the Mercedes lines of passenger cars and commercial vehicles. SAT solving was applied to the task of maintaining consistency in the database of thousands of logical constraints, and keeping it consistent as it constantly changes with the phasing in and out of models and parts.

Other important SAT applications include planning and scheduling for shift workers, sports tournaments, exams, and air traffic control.

## 5.11 Review

The following are the main points you should have learned from this chapter:

- Representing constraints in terms of propositions often enables constraint reasoning to be more efficient.
- A definite-clause knowledge base can be used to specify atomic clauses and rules about a domain when there is no uncertainty or ambiguity.

- Given a set of statements that are claimed to be true about a domain, the logical consequences characterize what else must be true.
- A sound and complete proof procedure can be used to determine the logical consequences of a knowledge base.
- Bottom-up and top-down proof procedures can be proven to be sound and complete.
- Proof by contradiction can be used to make inference from a Horn clause knowledge base.
- Negation as failure can be used to make conclusions assuming complete knowledge.
- Abduction can be used to explain observations.
- Consistency-based diagnosis and abductive diagnosis are alternative methods for troubleshooting systems.
- A causal model predicts the effect of interventions.
- SAT solvers play a critical role in many important applications.

## 5.12 References and Further Reading

Propositional logic has a long history; the semantics for propositional logic presented here is based on that of Tarski [1956].

The DPLL algorithm (page 184) is by Davis et al. [1962]. Levesque [1984] describes the tell–ask protocol for knowledge bases. Consistency-based diagnosis was formalized by de Kleer et al. [1992].

Much of the foundation of definite and Horn clause reasoning was developed in the context of a richer first-order logic that is presented in Chapter 15 and is studied under the umbrella of **logic programming**. Resolution was developed by Robinson [1965]. SLD resolution was pioneered by Kowalski [1974] and Colmerauer et al. [1973], building on previous work by Green [1969], Hayes [1973], and Hewitt [1969]. The fixed-point semantics was developed by van Emden and Kowalski [1976]. For more detail on the semantics and properties of logic programs, see Lloyd [1987].

The work on negation as failure (page 207) is based on the work of Clark [1978]. Apt and Bol [1994] provide a survey of different techniques and semantics for handling negation as failure. The bottom-up negation-as-failure proof procedure is based on the **truth maintenance system** (**TMS**) of Doyle [1979], who also considered incremental addition and removal of clauses; see Exercise 5.15 (page 229). The use of abnormality for default reasoning was advocated by McCarthy [1986].

The abduction framework presented here is based on the **assumption-based truth maintenance system** (**ATMS**) of de Kleer [1986] and on **Theorist** [Poole et al., 1987]. Kakas and Denecker [2002] review abductive reasoning. For an overview of the work of Peirce, who first characterized abduction, see Burch

[2022]. The bottom-up Horn implementation for the ATMS is more sophisticated in that it considers the problem of incremental addition of clauses and assumables also; see Exercise 5.16 (page 229).

Dung [1995] presents an abstract framework for arguments that provides a foundation for much of the work in this area. Chesnevar et al. [2000] and Besnard and Hunter [2008] survey work on arguments.

Causal models are discussed by Pearl [2009] and Spirtes et al. [2001]. See also Chapter 11.

The FDIV bug and the development of formal hardware verification at Intel is covered by Seger [2021]. Xu et al. [2008] and Biere et al. [2021] cover SAT, modern SAT solvers, and the applications for hardware and software verification. Sundermann et al. [2021] surveys product configuration using SAT. The application of formal methods to the Mercedes product lines is described by Sinz et al. [2003]. The TLA+ system is described by Lamport [2002] and Kuppe et al. [2019].

## 5.13 Exercises

Some of these exercises can use AIPython (aipython.org) or Prolog.

**Exercise 5.1** Suppose we want to be able to reason about an electric kettle plugged into one of the power outlets for the electrical domain of Figure 5.2 (page 186). Suppose a kettle must be plugged into a working power outlet, it must be turned on, and it must be filled with water, in order to heat. Write definite clauses that let the system determine whether kettles are heating.

You must

- give the intended interpretation of all symbols used
- write the clauses so they can be loaded into AIPython or Prolog
- show that the resulting knowledge base runs in AIPython or Prolog

**Exercise 5.2** Consider the domain of house plumbing shown in Figure 5.13.

In this diagram, $p_1$, $p_2$, and $p_3$ are cold water pipes; $t_1$, $t_2$, and $t_3$ are taps; $d_1$, $d_2$, and $d_3$ are drainage pipes.

Suppose you have the following atoms

- *pressurized_p*$_i$ is true if pipe $p_i$ has mains pressure in it
- *on_t*$_i$ is true if tap $t_i$ is on
- *off_t*$_i$ is true if tap $t_i$ is off
- *wet_b* is true if $b$ is wet ($b$ is either the sink, bath, or floor)
- *flow_p*$_i$ is true if water is flowing through $p_i$
- *plugged_sink* is true if the sink has the plug in
- *plugged_bath* is true if the bath has the plug in
- *unplugged_sink* is true if the sink does not have the plug in
- *unplugged_bath* is true if the bath does not have the plug in.

A definite-clause axiomatization for how water can flow down drain $d_1$ if taps $t_1$ and $t_2$ are on and the bath is unplugged is

$pressurized\_p_1.$

$pressurized\_p_2 \leftarrow on\_t_1 \land pressurized\_p_1.$

$flow\_shower \leftarrow on\_t_2 \land pressurized\_p_2.$

$wet\_bath \leftarrow flow\_shower.$

$flow\_d_2 \leftarrow wet\_bath \land unplugged\_bath.$

$flow\_d_1 \leftarrow flow\_d_2.$

$on\_t_1.$

$on\_t_2.$

$unplugged\_bath.$

(a) Finish the axiomatization for the sink in the same manner as the axiomatization for the bath. Test it in AIPython or Prolog.

(b) What information would you expect a resident of a house to be able to provide that the plumber who installed the system, who is not at the house, cannot? Change the axiomatization so that questions about this information are asked of the user.

(c) Axiomatize how the floor is wet if the sink overflows or the bath overflows. They overflow if the plug is in and water is flowing in. You may invent new atomic propositions as long as you give their intended interpretation. (Assume that the taps and plugs have been in the same positions for one hour; you do not have to axiomatize the dynamics of turning on the taps and inserting and removing plugs.) Test it in AIPython or Prolog.

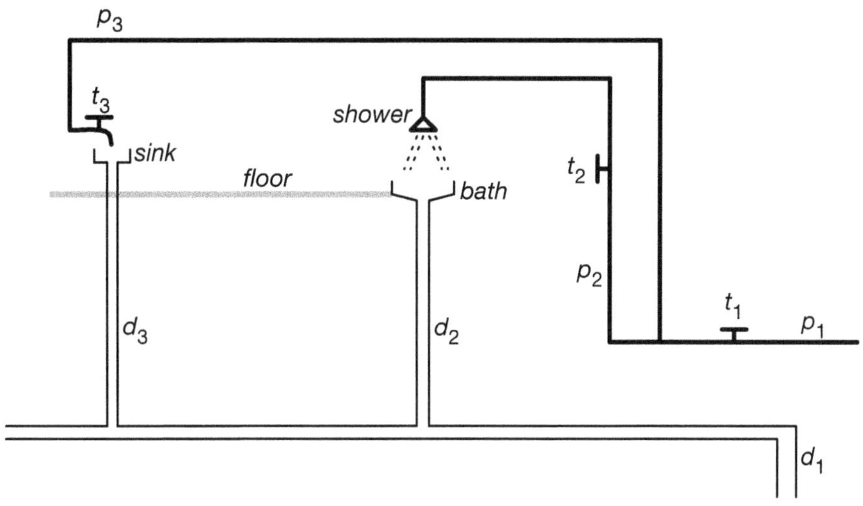


Figure 5.13: The plumbing domain

(d) Suppose a hot-water system is installed to the left of tap $t_1$. This has another tap in the pipe leading into it and supplies hot water to the shower and the sink (there are separate hot and cold water taps for each). Add this to your axiomatization. Give the denotation for all propositions you invent. Test it in AIPython or Prolog.

**Exercise 5.3** Consider the knowledge base

| | | |
|---|---|---|
| $a \leftarrow b \wedge c.$ | $b \leftarrow d.$ | $d \leftarrow h.$ |
| $a \leftarrow e \wedge f.$ | $b \leftarrow f \wedge h.$ | $f \leftarrow g.$ |
| $c \leftarrow e.$ | $e.$ | $g \leftarrow c.$ |

(a) Give a model of the knowledge base.

(b) Give an interpretation that is not a model of the knowledge base.

(c) Give two atoms that are logical consequences of the knowledge base.

(d) Give two atoms that are not logical consequences of the knowledge base.

**Exercise 5.4** Consider the knowledge base

| | | |
|---|---|---|
| $a \leftarrow b \wedge c.$ | $c.$ | $f \leftarrow g \wedge b.$ |
| $b \leftarrow d.$ | $d \leftarrow h.$ | $g \leftarrow c \wedge k.$ |
| $b \leftarrow e.$ | $e.$ | $j \leftarrow a \wedge b.$ |

(a) Show how the bottom-up proof procedure works for this example. Give all logical consequences of *KB*.

(b) $f$ is not a logical consequence of *KB*. Give a model of *KB* in which $f$ is false.

(c) $a$ is a logical consequence of *KB*. Give a top-down derivation for the query ask $a$.

**Exercise 5.5** A bottom-up proof procedure can incorporate an ask-the-user mechanism by asking the user about every askable atom. How can a bottom-up proof procedure still guarantee proof of all (non-askable) atoms that are a logical consequence of a definite-clause knowledge base without asking the user about every askable atom?

**Exercise 5.6** This question explores how having an explicit semantics can be used to debug programs. The file `elect_bug2` in the the book's website is an axiomatization of the electrical wiring domain of Figure 5.2 (page 186), but it contains a buggy clause (one that is false in the intended interpretation shown in the figure). The aim of this exercise is to to find the buggy clause, given the denotation of the symbols given in Example 5.8 (page 186). To find the buggy rule, you do not even need to look at the knowledge base! (You can look at the knowledge base to find the buggy clause if you like, but that will not help you in this exercise.) All you must know is the meaning of the symbols in the program and what is true in the intended interpretation.

The query *lit_l*$_1$ can be proved, but it is false in the intended interpretation. Use the *how* questions of AIPython to find a clause whose head is false in the intended interpretation and whose body is true. This is a buggy rule.

**Exercise 5.7** Consider the following knowledge base and assumables aimed to explain why people are acting suspiciously:

$goto\_forest \leftarrow walking.$

$get\_gun \leftarrow hunting.$

$goto\_forest \leftarrow hunting.$

$get\_gun \leftarrow robbing.$

$goto\_bank \leftarrow robbing.$

$goto\_bank \leftarrow banking.$

$fill\_withdrawal\_form \leftarrow banking.$

$false \leftarrow banking \wedge robbing.$

$false \leftarrow wearing\_good\_shoes \wedge goto\_forest.$

assumable $walking, hunting, robbing, banking.$

(a) Suppose $get\_gun$ is observed. What are all of the minimal explanations for this observation?
(b) Suppose $get\_gun \wedge goto\_bank$ is observed. What are all of the minimal explanations for this observation?
(c) Is there something that could be observed to remove one of these as a minimal explanation? What must be added to be able to explain this?
(d) What are the minimal explanations of $goto\_bank$?
(e) Give the minimal explanations of $goto\_bank \wedge get\_gun \wedge fill\_withdrawal\_form.$

**Exercise 5.8** Suppose there are four possible diseases a particular patient may have: $p$, $q$, $r$, and $s$. $p$ causes spots. $q$ causes spots. Fever could be caused by one (or more) of $q$, $r$, or $s$. The patient has spots and fever. Suppose you have decided to use abduction to diagnose this patient based on the symptoms.

(a) Show how to represent this knowledge using Horn clauses and assumables.
(b) Show how to diagnose this patient using abduction. Show clearly the query and the resulting answer(s).
(c) Suppose also that $p$ and $s$ cannot occur together. Show how that changes your knowledge base from part (a). Show how to diagnose the patient using abduction with the new knowledge base. Show clearly the query and the resulting answer(s).

**Exercise 5.9** Consider the following clauses and integrity constraints:

| | | |
|---|---|---|
| $false \leftarrow a \wedge b.$ | $a \leftarrow d.$ | $b \leftarrow d.$ |
| $false \leftarrow c.$ | $a \leftarrow g.$ | $b \leftarrow e.$ |
| $c \leftarrow h.$ | $a \leftarrow h.$ | |

Suppose the assumables are $\{d, e, f, g, h, i\}$. What are the minimal conflicts?

**Exercise 5.10** **Deep Space One** (http://nmp.jpl.nasa.gov/ds1/) was a spacecraft launched by NASA in October 1998 that used AI technology for its diagnosis and control. For more details, see Muscettola et al. [1998] or http://ti.arc.nasa.gov/tech/asr/planning-and-scheduling/remote-agent/ (although these references are not necessary to complete this question).

Figure 5.14 depicts a part of the actual DS1 engine design. To achieve thrust in an engine, fuel and oxidizer must be injected. The whole design is highly redundant to ensure its operation even in the presence of multiple failures (mainly stuck or inoperative valves). Note that whether the valves are black or white, and whether or not they have a bar, are irrelevant for this question.

Each valve can be ok (or not) and can be open (or not). The aim of this question is to axiomatize the domain so that we can do two tasks.

(a) Given an observation of the lack of thrust in an engine and given which valves are open, using consistency-based diagnosis, determine what could be wrong.
(b) Given the goal of having thrust and given the knowledge that some valves are ok, determine which valves should be opened.

For each of these tasks, you must think about what the clauses are in the knowledge base and what is assumable.

The atoms should be of the following forms:

- *open_V* is true if valve *V* is open. Thus the atoms should be $open\_v_1$, $open\_v_2$, and so on.
- *ok_V* is true if valve *V* is working properly.
- *pressurized_V* is true if the output of valve *V* is pressurized with gas. You should assume that $pressurized\_t_1$ and $pressurized\_t_2$ are true.
- *thrust_E* is true if engine *E* has thrust.
- *thrust* is true if no thrust exists in either engine.

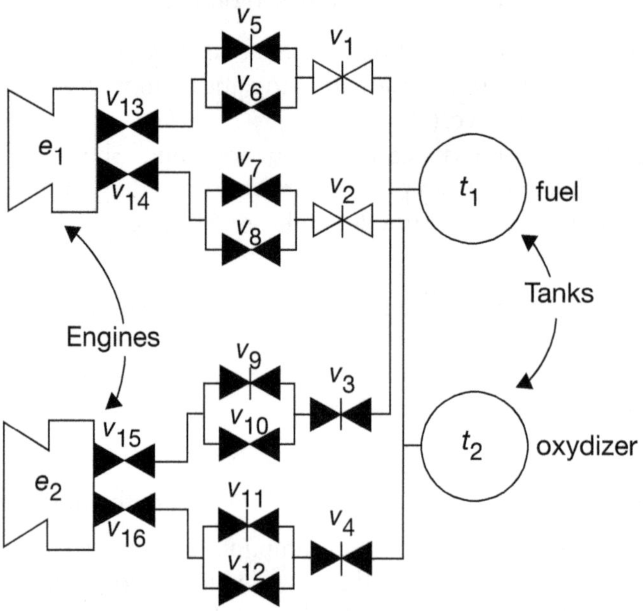


Figure 5.14: Deep Space One engine design

- *nothrust* is true if there is no thrust.

To make this manageable, only write rules for the input into engine $e_1$. Test your code using AIPython or Prolog on a number of examples.

**Exercise 5.11** Consider using abductive diagnosis on the problem in the previous question, with the following elaborations.

- Valves can be *open* or *closed*. Some valves may be specified as open or closed.
- A valve can be *ok*, in which case the gas will flow if the valve is open and not if it is closed; *broken*, in which case gas never flows; *stuck*, in which case gas flows independently of whether the valve is open or closed; or *leaking*, in which case gas flowing into the valve leaks out instead of flowing through.
- There are three gas sensors that can detect gas leaking (but not which gas); the first gas sensor detects gas from the rightmost valves ($v_1, \ldots, v_4$), the second gas sensor detects gas from the center valves ($v_5, \ldots, v_{12}$), and the third gas sensor detects gas from the leftmost valves ($v_{13}, \ldots, v_{16}$).

(a) Axiomatize the domain so the system can explain thrust or no thrust in engine $e_1$ and the presence of gas in one of the sensors. For example, it should be able to explain why $e_1$ is thrusting. It should be able to explain why $e_1$ is not thrusting and there is a gas detected by the third sensor.

(b) Test your axiomatization on some non-trivial examples.

(c) Some of the queries have many explanations. Suggest how the number of explanations could be reduced or managed so that the abductive diagnoses are more useful.

**Exercise 5.12** You are tasked with axiomatizing the plumbing in your home and you have an axiomatization similar to that of Exercise 5.2 (page 222). A new tenant is going to sublet your home and may want to use your system to determine what may be going wrong with the plumbing (before calling you or the plumber).

There are some atoms that you will know the rules for, some that the tenant will know, and some that neither will know. Divide the atomic propositions into these three categories, and suggest which should be made askable and which should be assumable. Show what the resulting interaction will look like under your division.

**Exercise 5.13** This question explores how integrity constraints and consistency-based diagnosis can be used in a purchasing agent that interacts with various information sources on the web. The purchasing agent will ask a number of the information sources for facts. However, information sources are sometimes wrong. It is useful to be able to automatically determine which information sources may be wrong when a user gets conflicting information.

This question uses meaningless symbols such as $a, b, c, \ldots$, but in a real domain there will be meaning associated with the symbols, such as $a$ meaning "there is skiing in Hawaii" and $z$ meaning "there is no skiing in Hawaii" or $a$ meaning "butterflies do not eat anything" and $z$ meaning "butterflies eat nectar". We will use meaningless symbols in this question because the computer does not have access to the meanings and must simply treat them as meaningless symbols.

Suppose the following information sources and associated information are provided.

- Source $s_1$ claims the following clauses are true:

  $a \leftarrow h. \quad d \leftarrow c.$

- Source $s_2$ claims the following clauses are true:

  $e \leftarrow d. \quad f \leftarrow k.$
  $z \leftarrow g. \quad j.$

- Source $s_3$ claims the following clause is true:

  $h \leftarrow d.$

- Source $s_4$ claims the following clauses are true:

  $a \leftarrow b \wedge e. \quad b \leftarrow c.$

- Source $s_5$ claims the following clause is true:

  $g \leftarrow f \wedge j.$

- You know that the following clauses are true:

  $\mathit{false} \leftarrow a \wedge z. \quad c. \quad k.$

Not every source can be believed, because together they produce a contradiction.

(a) Code the knowledge provided by the users into AIPython using assumables. To use a clause provided by one of the sources, you must assume that the source is reliable.
(b) Use the program to find the conflicts about what sources are reliable. (To find conflicts you can just ask *false*.)
(c) Suppose you would like to assume that as few sources as possible are unreliable. Which single source, if it was unreliable, could account for a contradiction (assuming all other sources were reliable)?
(d) Which pairs of sources could account for a contradiction (assuming all other sources are reliable) such that no single one of them could account for the contradiction?

**Exercise 5.14** Suppose you have a job at a company that is building online teaching tools. Because you have taken an AI course, your boss wants to know your opinion on various options under consideration.

They are planning on building a tutoring system for teaching elementary physics (e.g., mechanics and electromagnetism). One of the things that the system must do is to diagnose errors that a student may be making.

For each of the following, answer the explicit questions and use proper English. Answering parts not asked or giving more than one answer when only one is asked for will annoy the boss. The boss also does not like jargon, so please use straightforward English.

The boss has heard of consistency-based diagnosis and abductive diagnosis but wants to know what they involve *in the context of building a tutoring system for teaching elementary physics.*

(a) Explain what knowledge (about physics and about students) is required for consistency-based diagnosis.
(b) Explain what knowledge (about physics and about students) is required for abductive diagnosis.
(c) What is the main advantage of using abductive diagnosis over consistency-based diagnosis in this domain?
(d) What is the main advantage of consistency-based diagnosis over abductive diagnosis in this domain?

**Exercise 5.15** Consider the bottom-up negation-as-failure proof procedure of Figure 5.11 (page 212). Suppose we want to allow for incremental addition and deletion of clauses. How does $C$ change as a clause is added? How does $C$ change if a clause is removed?

**Exercise 5.16** Suppose you are implementing a bottom-up Horn clause explanation reasoner and you want to incrementally add clauses or assumables. When a clause is added, how are the minimal explanations affected? When an assumable is added, how are the minimal explanations affected?

**Exercise 5.17** Figure 5.15 (page 230) shows a simplified redundant communication network between an unmanned spacecraft (*sc*) and a ground control center (*gc*). There are two indirect high-bandwidth (high-gain) links that are relayed through satellites ($s_1$, $s_2$) to different ground antennae ($a_1$, $a_2$). Furthermore, there is a direct, low-bandwidth (low-gain) link between the ground control center's antenna ($a_3$) and the spacecraft. The low-gain link is affected by atmospheric disturbances – it works if there are no disturbances (*no_dist*) – and the spacecraft's low-gain transmitter (*sc_lg*) and antenna 3 are ok. The high-gain links always work if the spacecraft's high-gain transmitter (*sc_hg*), the satellites' antennae ($s_1$*_ant*, $s_2$*_ant*), the satellites' transmitters ($s_1$*_trans*, $s_2$*_trans*), and the ground antennae ($a_1$, $a_2$) are ok.

To keep matters simple, consider only messages from the spacecraft going through these channels to the ground control center.

The following knowledge base formalizes the part of the communication network we are interested in:

$$send\_signal\_lg\_sc \leftarrow ok\_sc\_lg \wedge alive\_sc.$$
$$send\_signal\_hg\_sc \leftarrow ok\_sc\_hg \wedge alive\_sc.$$
$$get\_signal\_s_1 \leftarrow send\_signal\_hg\_sc \wedge ok\_s_1\_ant.$$
$$get\_signal\_s_2 \leftarrow send\_signal\_hg\_sc \wedge ok\_s_2\_ant.$$
$$send\_signal\_s_1 \leftarrow get\_signal\_s_1 \wedge ok\_s_1\_trans.$$
$$send\_signal\_s_2 \leftarrow get\_signal\_s_2 \wedge ok\_s_2\_trans.$$
$$get\_signal\_gc \leftarrow send\_signal\_s_1 \wedge ok\_a_1.$$
$$get\_signal\_gc \leftarrow send\_signal\_s_2 \wedge ok\_a_2.$$
$$get\_signal\_gc \leftarrow send\_signal\_lg\_sc \wedge ok\_a_3 \wedge no\_dist.$$

Ground control is worried, because it has not received a signal from the spacecraft (*no_signal_gc*). It knows for sure that all ground antennae are ok (i.e., $ok\_a_1$, $ok\_a_2$, and $ok\_a_3$) and satellite $s_1$'s transmitter is ok ($ok\_s_1\_trans$). It is not sure about the state of the spacecraft, its transmitters, the satellites' antennae, $s_2$'s transmitter, and atmospheric disturbances.

(a) Specify a set of assumables and an integrity constraint that model the situation.
(b) Using the assumables and the integrity constraints from part (a), what is the set of minimal conflicts?
(c) What is the consistency-based diagnosis for the given situation? In other words, what are the possible combinations of violated assumptions that could account for why the control center cannot receive a signal from the spacecraft?

**Exercise 5.18**

(a) Explain why NASA may want to use abduction rather than consistency-based diagnosis for the domain of Exercise 5.17 (page 229).
(b) Suppose that an atmospheric disturbance *dist* could produce static or no signal in the low-bandwidth signal. To receive the static, antenna $a_3$ and the spacecraft's low-bandwidth transmitter *sc_lg* must be working. If $a_3$ or *sc_lg* are not working or *sc* is dead, there is no signal. What rules and assumables must be added to the knowledge base of Exercise 5.17 so that we can explain the possible observations *no_signal_gc*, *get_signal_gc*, or *static_gc*? You may ignore the high-bandwidth links. You may invent any symbols you need.

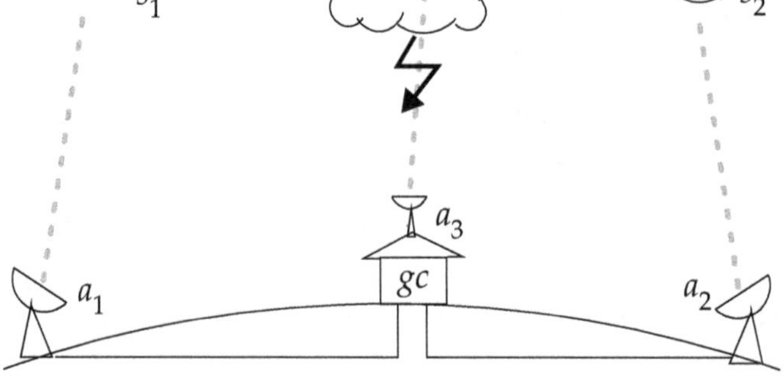


Figure 5.15: A space communication network

## Chapter 6

# Deterministic Planning

*...our Homo sapiens ancestors: their newly acquired causal imagination enabled them to do many things more efficiently through a tricky process we call "planning." Imagine a tribe preparing for a mammoth hunt. What would it take for them to succeed? My mammoth-hunting skills are rusty, I must admit, but as a student of thinking machines, I have learned one thing: a thinking entity (computer, caveman, or professor) can only accomplish a task of such magnitude by planning in advance – by deciding how many hunters to recruit; by gauging, given wind conditions, the direction from which to approach the mammoth; in short, by imagining and comparing the consequences of several hunting strategies. To do this, the thinking entity must possess, consult, and manipulate a mental model of its reality.*

– Pearl and Mackenzie [2018, p. 25]

**Deterministic planning** is the process of finding a sequence of actions to achieve a goal. Because an agent does not usually achieve its goals in one step, what it should do at any time depends on what it will do in the future. What it will do in the future depends on the state it is in, which, in turn, depends on what it has done in the past. This chapter presents representations of actions and their effects, and some offline algorithms for an agent to find a plan to achieve its goals from a given state.

This chapter makes the following simplifying assumptions:

- There is a single agent.
- The agent's actions are deterministic and the agent can predict the consequences of its actions.
- There are no exogenous events beyond the control of the agent that change the state of the environment.

- The environment is fully observable; thus, the agent can observe the current state of the environment.
- Time progresses discretely from one state to the next.
- Goals are predicates of states that must be achieved.

Some of these assumptions are relaxed in the following chapters.

## 6.1 Representing States, Actions, and Goals

To reason about what to do, assume an agent has goals, a model of the environment, and a model of its actions.

A deterministic **action** is a partial function from states to states. It is partial because not every action is able to be carried out in every state. For example, a robot cannot pick up a particular object if it is nowhere near the object. The **precondition** of an action specifies when the action can be carried out. The **effect** of an action specifies the resulting state.

**Example 6.1** Consider a delivery robot (page 16) with mail and coffee to deliver. Assume a simplified problem domain with four locations as shown in Figure 6.1. The robot, called Rob, can buy coffee at the coffee shop, pick up mail in the mail room, move, and deliver coffee and/or mail. Delivering the coffee to Sam's office will stop Sam from wanting coffee. There could be mail

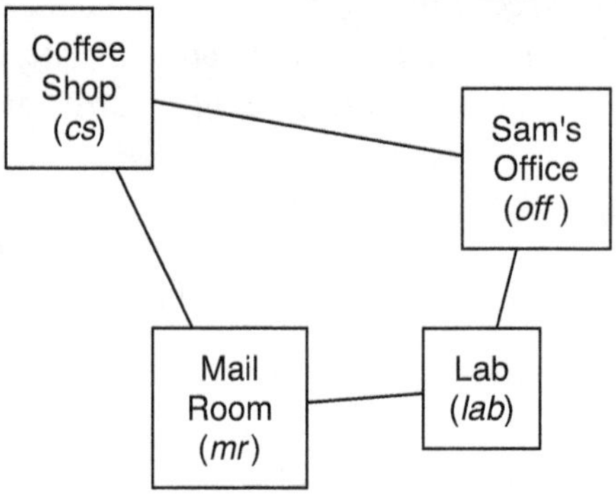


| **Features to describe states** | | **Actions** | |
|---|---|---|---|
| *RLoc* | – Rob's location | *mc* | – move clockwise |
| *RHC* | – Rob has coffee | *mcc* | – move counterclockwise |
| *SWC* | – Sam wants coffee | *puc* | – pick up coffee |
| *MW* | – Mail is waiting | *dc* | – deliver coffee |
| *RHM* | – Rob has mail | *pum* | – pick up mail |
| | | *dm* | – deliver mail |

Figure 6.1: The delivery robot domain

waiting at the mail room to be delivered to Sam's office. This domain is quite simple, yet it is rich enough to demonstrate many of the issues in representing actions and in planning.

The state is described in terms of the following features:

- *RLoc*, the robot's location, which is one of the coffee shop (*cs*), Sam's office (*off*), the mail room (*mr*), or the laboratory (*lab*).
- *RHC*, whether the robot has coffee. The atom *rhc* means Rob has coffee (i.e., $RHC = true$) and $\neg rhc$ means Rob does not have coffee (i.e., $RHC = false$).
- *SWC*, whether Sam wants coffee. The atom *swc* means Sam wants coffee and $\neg swc$ means Sam does not want coffee.
- *MW*, whether mail is waiting at the mail room. The atom *mw* means there is mail waiting and $\neg mw$ means there is no mail waiting.
- *RHM*, whether the robot is carrying the mail. The atom *rhm* means Rob has mail, and $\neg rhm$ means Rob does not have mail.

Rob has six actions:

- Rob can move clockwise (*mc*).
- Rob can move counterclockwise (*mcc*).
- Rob can pick up coffee if Rob is at the coffee shop. Let *puc* mean that Rob picks up coffee. The precondition of *puc* is $\neg rhc \wedge RLoc = cs$; that is, Rob can pick up coffee in any state where its location is *cs*, and it is not already holding coffee. The effect of this action is to make *RHC* true. It does not affect the other features.
- Rob can deliver coffee if Rob is carrying coffee and is at Sam's office. Let *dc* mean that Rob delivers coffee. The precondition of *dc* is $rhc \wedge RLoc = off$. The effect of this action is to make *RHC* false and make *SWC* false. Rob can deliver coffee whether or not Sam wants it.
- Rob can pick up mail if Rob is at the mail room and there is mail waiting there. Let *pum* mean Rob picks up the mail.
- Rob can deliver mail if Rob is carrying mail and at Sam's office. Let *dm* mean Rob delivers mail.

Assume that it is only possible for Rob to do one action at a time. We assume that a lower-level controller is able to implement these actions, as described in Chapter 2.

### 6.1.1 Explicit State-Space Representation

One possible representation of the effect and precondition of actions is to explicitly enumerate the states and, for each state, specify the actions that are possible in that state and, for each state–action pair, specify the state that results from carrying out the action in that state. This would require a table such as the following:

| State | Action | Resulting State |
|---|---|---|
| $s_7$ | $act_{47}$ | $s_{94}$ |
| $s_7$ | $act_{14}$ | $s_{83}$ |
| $s_{94}$ | $act_5$ | $s_{33}$ |
| ... | ... | ... |

The first tuple in this relation specifies that it is possible to carry out action $act_{47}$ in state $s_7$ and, if it were to be carried out in state $s_7$, the resulting state would be $s_{94}$.

Thus, this is the explicit representation of a graph, where the nodes are states and the acts are actions. This is a **state-space graph** (page 85). This is the sort of graph that was used in Chapter 3. Any of the algorithms of Chapter 3 can be used to search the space.

**Example 6.2** In Example 6.1 (page 232), the states are the quintuples specifying the robot's location, whether the robot has coffee, whether Sam wants coffee, whether mail is waiting, and whether the robot is carrying the mail. For example, the tuple

$$\langle lab, \neg rhc, swc, \neg mw, rhm \rangle$$

represents the state where Rob is at the lab, Rob does not have coffee, Sam wants coffee, there is no mail waiting, and Sam has mail. The tuple

$$\langle lab, rhc, swc, mw, \neg rhm \rangle$$

represents the state where Rob is at the lab carrying coffee, Sam wants coffee, there is mail waiting, and Rob is not holding any mail.

In this example, there are $4 \times 2 \times 2 \times 2 \times 2 = 64$ states. Intuitively, all of them are possible, even if one would not expect that some of them would be reached by an intelligent robot.

There are six actions, not all of which are applicable in each state.

The actions are defined in terms of the state transitions:

| State | Action | Resulting State |
|---|---|---|
| $\langle lab, \neg rhc, swc, \neg mw, rhm \rangle$ | $mc$ | $\langle mr, \neg rhc, swc, \neg mw, rhm \rangle$ |
| $\langle lab, \neg rhc, swc, \neg mw, rhm \rangle$ | $mcc$ | $\langle off, \neg rhc, swc, \neg mw, rhm \rangle$ |
| $\langle off, \neg rhc, swc, \neg mw, rhm \rangle$ | $dm$ | $\langle off, \neg rhc, swc, \neg mw, \neg rhm \rangle$ |
| $\langle off, \neg rhc, swc, \neg mw, rhm \rangle$ | $mcc$ | $\langle cs, \neg rhc, swc, \neg mw, rhm \rangle$ |
| $\langle off, \neg rhc, swc, \neg mw, rhm \rangle$ | $mc$ | $\langle lab, \neg rhc, swc, \neg mw, rhm \rangle$ |
| ... | ... | ... |

This table shows the transitions for two of the states. The complete representation includes the transitions for the other 62 states.

This is not a good representation for three main reasons:

- There are usually too many states to represent, to acquire, and to reason with.

- Small changes to the model mean a large change to the representation. Adding another feature means changing the whole representation. For example, to model the level of power in the robot, so that it can recharge itself in the lab, every state has to change.
- It does not represent the structure of states; there is much structure and regularity in the effects of actions that is not reflected in the state transitions. For example, most actions do not affect whether Sam wants coffee, but this cannot be specified directly.

An alternative is to model how the actions affect the features.

### 6.1.2 The STRIPS Representation

The **STRIPS representation** is an action-centric representation which, for each action, specifies when the action can occur and the effects of the action. STRIPS, which stands for "STanford Research Institute Problem Solver," was the planner used in Shakey, one of the first robots built using AI technology.

To represent a planning problem in STRIPS, first divide the features that describe the state of the world into **primitive** and **derived** features. The STRIPS representation is used to specify the values of primitive features in a state based on the previous state and the action taken by the agent. Definite clauses are used to determine the value of derived features from the values of the primitive features in any given state.

The **STRIPS representation** for an action consists of:

- the **precondition**, a set of assignments of values to features that must hold for the action to occur
- the **effect**, a set of assignments of values to primitive features that specifies the features that change, and the values they change to, as the result of the action.

The **precondition** of an action is a proposition – the conjunction of the elements of the set – that must be true before the action is able to be carried out. In terms of constraints, the robot is constrained so it can only choose an action for which the precondition holds.

**Example 6.3** In Example 6.1 (page 232), the action of Rob to pick up coffee (*puc*) has precondition $\{cs, \neg rhc\}$. That is, Rob must be at the coffee shop (*cs*), not carrying coffee ($\neg rhc$), to carry out the *puc* action. As a constraint, this means that *puc* is not available for any other location or when *rhc* is true.

The action to move clockwise is always possible. Its precondition is the empty set, $\{\}$, which represents the proposition *true*.

The STRIPS representation is based on the idea that most things are not affected by a single action. The semantics relies on the **STRIPS assumption**: the values of all of the primitive features not mentioned in the effects of the action are unchanged by the action.

Primitive feature $X$ has value $v$ after action *act* if action *act* is possible (its preconditions hold) and either

- $X = v$ is in the effect of *act* or
- $X$ is not mentioned in the effect of *act* and $X$ has value $v$ immediately before *act*.

The values of non-primitive features can be derived from the values of the primitive features for each time.

**Example 6.4** In Example 6.1 (page 232), the action of Rob to pick up coffee (*puc*) has the following STRIPS representation:

**precondition** $\{cs, \neg rhc\}$
**effect** $\{rhc\}$

That is, in order to be able to pick up coffee, the robot must be at the coffee shop and not have coffee. After the action, *rhc* holds (i.e., $RHC = true$). All other feature values are unaffected by this action.

**Example 6.5** The action of delivering coffee (*dc*) can be defined by

**precondition** $\{off, rhc\}$
**effect** $\{\neg rhc, \neg swc\}$

The robot can deliver coffee when it is in the office and has coffee. The robot does not have coffee after the action, and Sam does not want coffee after the action. Thus, the effects are to make $RHC = false$ and $SWC = false$. According to this model, the robot can deliver coffee whether or not Sam wants coffee. In either case, Sam does not want coffee immediately after the action.

STRIPS cannot directly define **conditional effects**, where the effect of an action depends on what is true initially. However, conditional effects can be modeled by introducing new actions, as shown in the following example.

**Example 6.6** Consider representing the action *mc* to move clockwise. The effect of *mc*, where the robot ends up, depends on the robot's location before *mc* was carried out.

To represent this in the STRIPS representation, we can construct multiple actions that differ in what is true initially. For example, the action *mc_cs* (move clockwise from coffee shop) has a precondition $\{RLoc = cs\}$ and effect $\{RLoc = off\}$. The action *mc_off* (move clockwise from office) has a precondition $\{RLoc = off\}$ and effect $\{RLoc = lab\}$. STRIPS thus requires four move clockwise actions (one for each location) and four move counterclockwise actions.

### 6.1.3 Feature-Based Representation of Actions

Whereas STRIPS is an action-centric representation, a feature-centric representation is more flexible, as it allows for conditional effects, and non-local effects.

A **feature-based representation of actions** models:

- the precondition of each action
- for each feature, the feature values in the next state as a function of the feature values of the previous state and the action.

The feature-based representation of actions uses definite clauses to specify the value of each variable in the state resulting from an action. The bodies of these rules can include propositions about the action carried out and propositions about values of features in the previous state. We assume these propositions can be equalities and inequalities between features and values.

The rules have two forms:

- A **causal rule** specifies when a feature gets a new value.
- A **frame rule** specifies when a feature keeps its value.

It is useful to think of these as two separate cases: what makes the feature change its value, and what makes it keep its value.

**Example 6.7** In Example 6.1 (page 232), Rob's location depends on its previous location and where it moved. Let $RLoc'$ be the variable that specifies the location in the resulting state. The following rules specify the conditions under which Rob is at the coffee shop:

$$RLoc' = cs \leftarrow RLoc = off \land Act = mcc.$$
$$RLoc' = cs \leftarrow RLoc = mr \land Act = mc.$$
$$RLoc' = cs \leftarrow RLoc = cs \land Act \neq mcc \land Act \neq mc.$$

The first two rules are causal rules and the last rule is a frame rule.

Whether the robot has coffee in the resulting state depends on whether it has coffee in the previous state and its action. A causal rule specifies that picking up the coffee causes the robot to have coffee in the next time step:

$$rhc' \leftarrow Act = puc.$$

A frame rule specifies that the robot having coffee persists unless the robot delivers the coffee:

$$rhc' \leftarrow rhc \land Act \neq dc.$$

The rule implicitly implies that the robot cannot drop the coffee, drink it or lose it, and the coffee cannot be stolen.

The feature-based representation is more powerful than the STRIPS representation; it can represent anything representable in STRIPS, but can also represent conditional effects. It may be more verbose because it requires explicit frame axioms, which are implicit in the STRIPS representation.

The mapping from STRIPS to the feature-based representation for Boolean features is as follows. If the effect of an action *act* is $\{e_1, \ldots, e_k\}$, then the STRIPS representation is equivalent to the causal rules

$$e_i' \leftarrow act.$$

for each $e_i$ that is made true by the action and the frame rules

$$c' \leftarrow c \land act.$$

for each condition $c$ that does not involve a variable on the effects list. Thus each $e_i$ that assigns a feature to be false does not result in a rule. The precondition of each action is the same in both representations. Non-Boolean features may require multiple rules for the different values of the feature.

A **conditional effect** of an action depends on the value of other features. The feature-based representation is able to specify conditional effects, whereas STRIPS cannot represent these directly. Example 6.6 (page 236) shows how to represent in STRIPS the action moving clockwise, where the effect depends on the previous state, by inventing new actions. Example 6.7 (page 237) shows how the feature-based representation can represent actions without needing to invent those new actions by adding conditions to the rules. The feature-based representation also allows for non-local effects, as in the following example.

**Example 6.8** Suppose that all of the actions make the robot dirty, except for the *wash* action that makes the robot clean. In STRIPS this would entail having dirty as an effect of every action. In the feature-based representation, we could add a rule that the robot is dirty after every action that is not *wash*:

$$robot\_dirty' \leftarrow Act \neq wash.$$

## 6.1.4 Initial States and Goals

In a typical planning problem, where the world is fully observable and deterministic, the initial state is defined by specifying the value for each feature for the initial state.

There are several different kinds of **goals**:

- An **achievement goal** is a proposition that must be true in the final state.
- A **maintenance goal** is a proposition that must be true in every state through which the agent passes. These are often **safety goals** – the goal of staying away from bad states.
- A **transient goal** is a proposition that must be achieved somewhere in the plan.
- A **resource goal** is the goal of minimizing some resource in the plan. For example, the goal may be to minimize fuel consumption or the time required to execute the plan.

In the rest of this chapter, we concentrate on achievement goals, where the goal is a set of assigned values to features, all of which must hold in the final state.

## 6.2 Forward Planning

A deterministic **plan** is a sequence of actions to achieve a **goal** from a given starting state. A deterministic **planner** produces a plan given an initial world description, a specification of the actions available to the agent, and a goal description.

A forward planner treats the planning problem as a path planning problem in the **state-space graph** (page 85), which can be explored. In a state-space graph, nodes are states and arcs correspond to actions from one state to another. The arcs coming out of state $s$ correspond to all of the legal actions that can be carried out in that state. That is, for each state, there is an arc for each action $a$ whose precondition holds in state $s$. A plan is a path from the initial state to a state that satisfies the achievement goal.

A **forward planner** searches the state-space graph from the initial state looking for a state that satisfies a goal description. It can use any of the search strategies described in Chapter 3.

The search graph is defined as follows:

- The nodes are states of the world, where a state is a total assignment of a value to each feature.
- The arcs correspond to actions. In particular, an arc from node $s$ to $s'$, labeled with action *act*, means *act* is possible in $s$ and carrying out *act* in state $s$ results in state $s'$.
- The start node is the initial state.
- The goal condition for the search, $goal(s)$, is true if state $s$ satisfies the achievement goal.
- A path corresponds to a plan that achieves the goal.

**Example 6.9** For the running example, a state can be represented as a quintuple

$$\langle Loc, RHC, SWC, MW, RHM\rangle$$

of values for the respective variables.

Figure 6.2 (page 240) shows part of the search space (without showing the loops) starting from the state where Rob is at the coffee shop, Rob does not have coffee, Sam wants coffee, there is mail waiting, and Rob does not have mail. The search space is the same irrespective of the goal state.

Using a forward planner is not the same as making an explicit state-based representation of the actions (page 233), because the relevant parts of the graph are created dynamically from the representations of the actions.

A complete search strategy, such as $A^*$ with multiple-path pruning or depth-first branch and bound, is guaranteed to find a solution. The complexity of the search space is defined by the forward branching factor (page 84) of the graph. The branching factor is the set of all possible actions at any state, which may be quite large. For the simple robot delivery domain, the branching factor is three for the initial situation and is up to four for other situations. This complexity may be reduced by finding good heuristics, so that not all of the space is searched if there is a solution.

For a forward planner, a heuristic function for a state is an estimate of the cost of solving the goal from the state.

**Example 6.10** For the delivery robot plan, if all actions have a cost of 1, a possible admissible heuristic function (page 101) given a particular goal, is the maximum of:

- the distance from the robot location in the state $s$ to the goal location, if there is one
- the distance from the robot's location in state $s$ to the coffee shop plus three (because the robot has to, at least, get to the coffee shop, pick up the coffee and get to the office to deliver the coffee) if the goal includes $SWC = false$ and state $s$ has $SWC = true$ and $RHC = false$.

A state can be represented as either

(a) *a complete world description*, in terms of an assignment of a value to each primitive proposition, or

(b) *a path from an initial state*; that is, by the sequence of actions that were used to reach that state from the initial state. In this case, what holds in a state is computed from the axioms that specify the effects of actions.

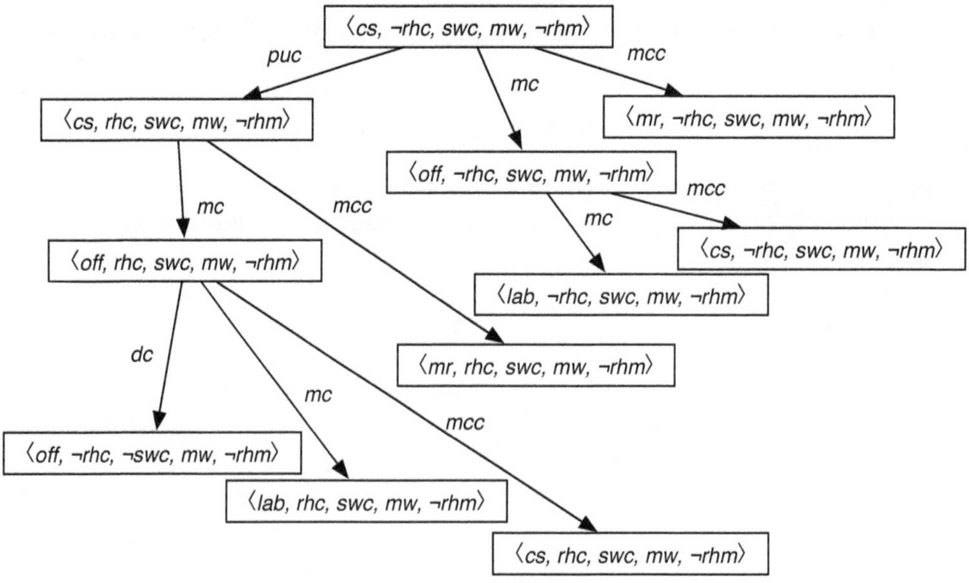


Figure 6.2: Part of the search space for a state-space planner

Choice (a) involves computing a whole new world description for each world created, whereas (b) involves computing what holds in a state as needed. Alternative (b) may save on space (particularly if there is a complex world description) and may allow faster creation of a new node, however it is slower to determine what actually holds in any given world. Each representation requires a way to determine whether two states are the same if cycle pruning or multiple-path pruning are used.

State-space searching has been presented as a forward search method, but it is also possible to search backward (page 115) from the set of states that satisfy the goal. Typically, the goal does not fully specify a state, so there may be many goal states that satisfy the goal. If there are multiple states, create a node, *goal*, that has, as neighbors, all of the goal states, and use this as the start node for backward search. Once *goal* is expanded, the frontier has as many elements as there are goal states, which can be very large, making backward search in the state space impractical for non-trivial domains.

## 6.3 Regression Planning

Regression planning involves searching backwards from a goal, asking the question: what does the agent need to do to achieve this goal, and what needs to hold to enable this action to solve the goal? What needs to hold before the action becomes a **subgoal**, which either holds initially or becomes a new goal to solve.

**Example 6.11** If the goal is for the robot to hold coffee, and the robot isn't already holding coffee, then the action that achieves this is to pick up coffee. This action requires the robot to be in the coffee shop, which becomes a new subgoal.

If the goal, instead, is for the robot to be holding coffee in the office, then the actions to achieve that involve moving to the office from a neighboring location, while holding coffee. This results in the subgoal of being in a neighboring location holding coffee. Picking up coffee cannot achieve the goal of holding coffee in the office, because picking up coffee can only be done in the coffee shop, and so the result of picking up coffee is that the robot is in the coffee shop, not the office.

**Regression planning** is searching in the graph defined by the following:

- The nodes are subgoals, where a **subgoal** is an assignment to some of the features.
- The arcs correspond to actions. In particular, an arc from node $g$ to $g'$, labeled with action *act*, means
  - *act* is the last action that is carried out before subgoal $g$ is achieved
  - node $g'$ is a subgoal that must be true immediately before *act* so that $g$ is true immediately after *act*.

- The start node is the planning goal to be achieved.
- The goal condition for the search, *goal*($g$), is true if $g$ is true of the initial state.

Given a node that represents subgoal $g$, a neighbor of $g$ exists for every action *act* such that:

- *act* is **possible**, it is possible for *act* to be carried out and for $g$ to be true immediately after *act*
- *act* is **useful**, *act* achieves part of $g$.

Consider the subgoal $g = \{X_1 = v_1, \ldots, X_n = v_n\}$. In terms of the STRIPS representation, *act* is useful for solving $g$ if, for some $i$, $X_i = v_i$ is an effect of action *act*. Immediately before *act*, the preconditions of *act*, as well as any $X_k = v_k$ not achieved by *act*, must hold. Thus, the neighbor of subgoal $g$ on the arc labeled *act* is the subgoal $precondition(act) \cup (g \setminus effects(act))$, as long as *act* is possible. Action *act* is possible if:

- for each $X_j = v_j$ in $g$, there is no effect $X_j = v_j$ of *act* where $v'_j \neq v_j$
- $precondition(act) \cup (g \setminus effects(act))$ does not include two different assignments to any feature.

**Example 6.12** Suppose the goal is to ensure that Sam does not want coffee, which is $\neg swc$. Therefore, the start node is $\{\neg swc\}$. If this is true in the initial state, the planner stops. If not, it chooses an action that achieves $\neg swc$. In this case, there is only one such action: *dc* (deliver coffee). The precondition of *dc* is $\{off, rhc\}$. Thus, there is one arc:

$$\langle \{\neg swc\}, \{off, rhc\} \rangle \text{ labeled with } dc.$$

Consider the node $\{off, rhc\}$. There are two actions that can achieve *off*, namely *mc* from *cs* and *mcc* from *lab*. There is one action that can achieve *rhc*, namely *puc*. However, *puc* has as precondition $\{cs, \neg rhc\}$, but *cs* and *off* are inconsistent (because they involve different assignments to the variable *RLoc*). Therefore, *puc* is not a possible last action; it is not possible that, immediately after *puc*, the condition $\{off, rhc\}$ holds.

Figure 6.3 (page 243) shows the first three levels of the search space (without cycle pruning or multiple-path pruning). Note that the search space is the same no matter what the initial state is. The starting state has two roles: to serve as a stopping criterion and as a source of heuristics.

If a subgoal contains a number of assignments, regression can often determine which of the assignments to achieve last, as in the following example.

**Example 6.13** Suppose the goal is for Sam to not want coffee and for the robot to have coffee: $\{\neg swc, rhc\}$. The last action cannot be *dc* to achieve $\neg swc$, because this achieves $\neg rhc$. The only last action must be *puc* to achieve *rhc*. Thus, the resulting subgoal is $\{\neg swc, cs\}$. Again, the last action before this subgoal cannot be to achieve $\neg swc$ because this has as a precondition *off*, which is inconsistent with *cs*. Therefore, the second-to-last action must be a move action to achieve *cs*.

In terms of the feature-based representation of actions, an action *act* is useful if there is a causal rule that achieves $X_i = v_i$ for some $i$, using action *act*. The neighbor of this node along the arc labeled with action *act* is the proposition

$$precondition(act) \land body(X_1 = v_1, act) \land \cdots \land body(X_n = v_n, act)$$

where $body(X_i = v_i, act)$ is the set of assignments of variables in the body of a rule that specifies when $X_i = v_i$ is true immediately after *act*. There is no such neighbor if there is no corresponding rule for some $i$, or if the proposition is inconsistent (i.e., assigns different values to a variable). Note that, if multiple rules are applicable for the same action, there will be multiple neighbors.

Search algorithms such as $A^*$ and branch and bound can make use of heuristic knowledge. For a regression planner, the heuristic value of a node is an estimate of the cost to achieve the subgoal represented by the node from the initial state. This form of heuristic as an estimate of the cost of achieving a subgoal from a state is the same as used in a forward planner. So, for example, the heuristic of Example 6.10 (page 240) could also be used for a regression planner. However, an effective heuristic for a regression planner may not be very useful for a forward planner, and vice versa (see Exercise 6.4 (page 255)).

One problem that arises in regression planning is that a subgoal may not be achievable. Deciding whether a subgoal is achievable is often difficult to infer from the definitions of the actions. For example, consider the restriction that an object cannot be at two different places at the same time; sometimes this is not explicitly represented and is only implicit in the effects of an action, and the fact that the object is only in one position initially. It is possible to have domain knowledge to prune nodes that can be shown to be inconsistent.

Cycle pruning and multiple-path pruning may be incorporated into a regression planner. The regression planner does not have to visit exactly the

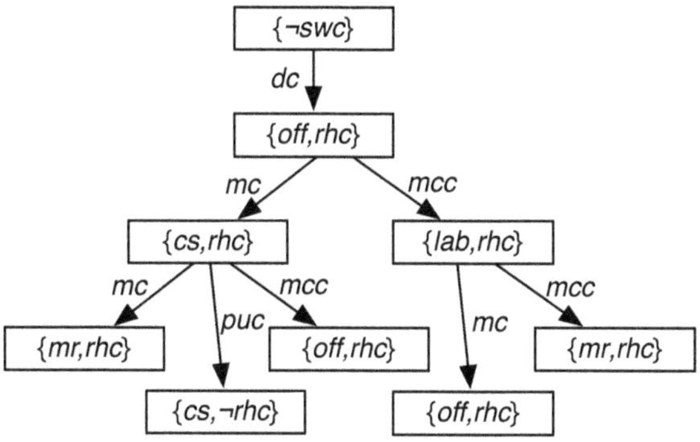


Figure 6.3: Part of the search space for a regression planner

same node to prune the search. If the subgoal represented by a node $n$ is a superset of a subgoal on the path to $n$, node $n$ can be pruned. Similarly for multiple-path pruning, see Exercise 6.9 (page 256).

## 6.4 Planning as a CSP

In forward planning, the search is constrained by the initial state and only uses the goal as a stopping criterion and as a source for heuristics. In regression planning, the search is constrained by the goal and only uses the start state as a stopping criterion and as a source for heuristics. By converting the problem to a constraint satisfaction problem (CSP), the initial state can be used to prune what is not reachable and the goal to prune what is not useful. The CSP will be defined for a finite number of steps; the number of steps can be adjusted to find the shortest plan. Any of the CSP methods from Chapter 4 can then be used to solve the CSP and thus find a plan.

To construct a CSP from a planning problem, first choose a fixed planning **horizon**, which is the number of time steps over which to plan. Suppose the horizon is $k$. The CSP has the following variables:

- A **state variable** for each feature and each time from 0 to $k$. If there are $n$ features for a horizon of $k$, there are $n * (k + 1)$ state variables. The domain of the state variable is the domain of the corresponding feature.
- An **action variable**, $Action_t$, for each time $t$ in the range 0 to $k - 1$. The domain of $Action_t$ is the set of all possible actions. The value of $Action_t$ represents the action that takes the agent from the state at time $t$ to the state at time $t + 1$.

There are several types of constraints:

- A **precondition constraint** between a state variable at time $t$ and the variable $Action_t$ constrains what actions are legal at time $t$.
- An **effect constraint** between $Action_t$ and a state variable at time $t + 1$ constrains the values of a state variable that is a direct effect of the action.
- A **frame constraint** among a state variable at time $t$, the variable $Action_t$, and the corresponding state variable at time $t + 1$ specifies when the variable that does not change as a result of an action has the same value before and after the action.
- An **initial-state constraint** constrains a variable on the initial state (at time 0). The initial state is represented as a set of domain constraints on the state variables at time 0.
- A **goal constraint** constrains the final state to be a state that satisfies the achievement goal. These are domain constraints on the variables that appear in the goal.
- A **state constraint** is a constraint among variables at the same time step. These can include physical constraints on the state or can ensure that states that violate maintenance goals (page 238) are forbidden. This is

extra knowledge beyond the power of the feature-based or STRIPS representations of the action.

The STRIPS representation gives precondition, effect, and frame constraints for each time $t$ as follows:

- For each $Var = v$ in the precondition of action $A$, there is a precondition constraint

$$Var_t = v \leftarrow Action_t = A$$

that specifies that if the action is to be $A$, $Var_t$ must have value $v$ immediately before. This constraint is violated when $Action_t = A$ and $Var_t \neq v$, and thus is equivalent to $\neg(Var_t \neq v \wedge Action_t = A)$.
- For each $Var = v$ in the effect of action $A$, there is an effect constraint

$$Var_{t+1} = v \leftarrow Action_t = A$$

which is violated when $Var_{t+1} \neq v \wedge Action_t = A$, and thus is equivalent to $\neg(Var_{t+1} \neq v \wedge Action_t = A)$.
- For each $Var$, there is a frame constraint, where $As$ is the set of actions that include $Var$ in the effect of the action:

$$Var_{t+1} = Var_t \leftarrow Action_t \notin As$$

which specifies that the feature $Var$ has the same value before and after any action that does not affect $Var$.

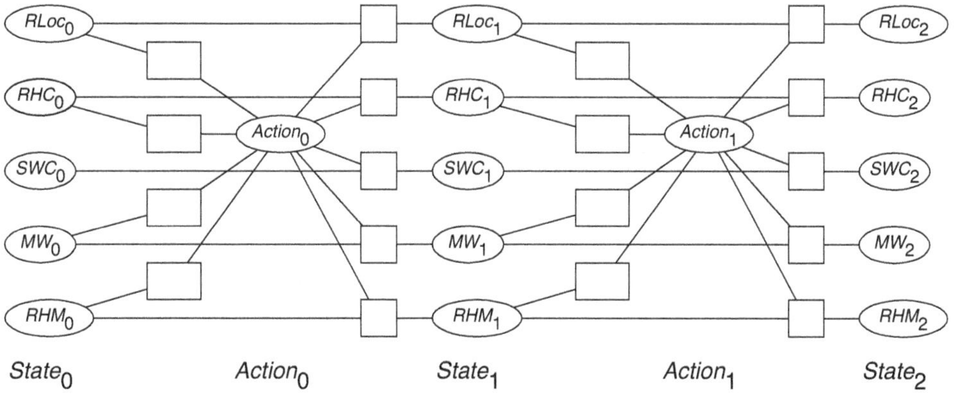


$RLoc_i$ – Rob's location
$RHC_i$ – Rob has coffee
$SWC_i$ – Sam wants coffee
$MW_i$ – Mail is waiting
$RHM_i$ – Rob has mail
$Action_i$ – Rob's action

Figure 6.4: The delivery robot CSP planner for a planning horizon of $k = 2$

**Example 6.14** Figure 6.4 (page 245) shows a CSP representation of the delivery robot example, with a planning horizon of $k = 2$. There are three copies of the state variables: one at time 0, the initial state; one at time 1; and one at time 2, the final state. There are action variables for times 0 and 1.

**Precondition constraints:** The constraints to the left of the action variable for each time are the precondition constraints. There is a separate constraint for each element of the precondition of the action.

The precondition for the action deliver coffee, *dc*, is $\{RLoc = off, rhc\}$; the robot has to be in the office and it must have coffee. Thus there are two precondition constraints for delivers coffee:

$$RLoc_t = office \leftarrow Action_t = dc$$
$$RHC_t = true \leftarrow Action_t = dc.$$

**Effect constraints:** The effect of delivering coffee (*dc*) is $\{\neg rhc, \neg swc\}$. Therefore there are two effect constraints:

$$RHC_{t+1} = false \leftarrow Action_t = dc$$
$$SWC_{t+1} = false \leftarrow Action_t = dc.$$

**Frame constraints:** Rob has mail (*rhm*) is not one of the effects of delivering coffee (*dc*). Thus there is a frame constraint:

$$RHM_{t+1} = RHM_t \leftarrow Act_t = dc$$

which is violated when $RHM_{t+1} \neq RHM_t \wedge Act_t = dc$.

**Example 6.15** Consider finding a plan to get Sam coffee, where initially, Sam wants coffee but the robot does not have coffee. This can be represented as initial-state constraints: $SWC_0 = true$ and $RHC_0 = false$.

With a planning horizon of 2, the goal is represented as the domain constraint $SWC_2 = false$, and there is no solution.

With a planning horizon of 3, the goal is represented as the domain constraint $SWC_3 = false$. This has many solutions, all with $RLoc_0 = cs$ (the robot has to start in the coffee shop), $Action_0 = puc$ (the robot has to pick up coffee initially), $Action_1 = mc$ (the robot has to move to the office), and $Action_2 = dc$ (the robot has to deliver coffee at time 2).

The CSP representation assumes a fixed planning horizon (i.e., a fixed number of steps). To find a plan over any number of steps, the algorithm can be run for a horizon of $k = 0, 1, 2, \ldots$ until a solution is found. For the stochastic local search algorithm, it is possible to search multiple horizons at once, searching for all horizons, $k$ from 0 to $n$, and allowing $n$ to vary slowly. When solving the CSP using arc consistency and domain splitting, it is sometimes possible to determine that trying a longer plan will not help. That is, by analyzing why no solution exists for a horizon of $n$ steps, it may be possible to show that there can be no plan for any length greater than $n$. This will enable the planner to halt when there is no plan. See Exercise 6.10 (page 257).

### 6.4.1 Action Features

So far we have assumed that actions are atomic and that an agent can only do one action at any time. For the CSP representation, it can be useful to describe the actions in terms of features – to have a factored representation of actions as well as a factored representation of states. The features representing actions are called **action features** and the features representing states are called **state features**. The action features can be considered as actions in themselves that are carried out in the same time step.

In this case, there can be an extra set of constraints called **action constraints** to specify which action features cannot co-occur. These are sometimes called mutual exclusion or **mutex constraints**.

**Example 6.16** Another way to model the actions of Example 6.1 (page 232) is that, at each step, Rob gets to choose

- whether it will pick up coffee – let *PUC* be a Boolean variable that is true when Rob picks up coffee
- whether it will deliver coffee – let *DelC* be a Boolean variable that is true when Rob delivers coffee
- whether it will pick up mail – let *PUM* be a Boolean variable that is true when Rob picks up mail
- whether it will deliver mail – let *DelM* be a Boolean variable that is true when Rob delivers mail
- whether it moves. Let *Move* be a variable with domain $\{mc, mcc, nm\}$ that specifies whether Rob moves clockwise, moves counterclockwise, or does not move (*nm* means "not move").

Thus the agent can be seen as doing more than one action in a single stage. For some of the actions at the same stage, the robot can do them in any order, such as delivering coffee and delivering mail. Some of the actions at the same stage need to be carried out in a particular order, for example, the agent must move after the other actions.

**Example 6.17** Consider finding a plan to get Sam coffee, where initially, Sam wants coffee but the robot does not have coffee. The initial state can be represented as two domain constraints: $SWC_0 = true$ and $RHC_0 = false$. The goal is that Sam no longer wants coffee, $SWC_k = false$.

With a planning horizon of 2, the CSP is shown in Figure 6.5 (page 248). The goal is represented as the domain constraint $SWC_2 = false$, there is a solution $RLoc_0 = cs$ (the robot has to start in the coffee shop), $PUC_0 = true$ (the robot has to pick up coffee initially), $Move_0 = mc$ (the robot has to move to the office), and $DC_1 = true$ (the robot has to deliver coffee at time 1).

Note that in the representation without factored actions, the problem cannot be solved with a horizon of 2; it requires a horizon of 3, as there are no concurrent actions.

## 6.5 Partial-Order Planning

The forward and regression planners enforce a total ordering on actions at all stages of the planning process. The CSP planner commits to the particular time that the action will be carried out. This means that those planners have to commit to an ordering of actions when adding them to a partial plan, even if there is no particular reason to put one action before another.

A **partial-order planner** maintains a partial ordering between actions and only commits to an ordering between actions when forced. This is sometimes also called a **nonlinear planner**, which is a misnomer because such planners often produce a linear plan.

Because the same action may be used a number of times in the same plan, for example, the robot may need to move clockwise a number of times, the partial ordering will be between **action instances**, where an action instance is just a pair of an action and an integer, which we will write as *act#i*. By the preconditions and effects of the action instance, we mean the precondition and

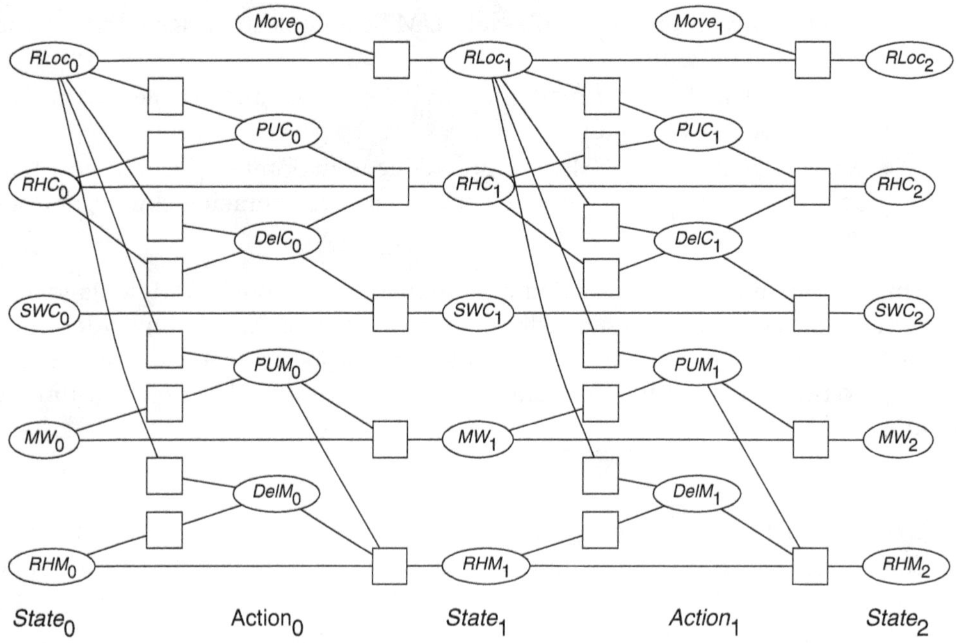


| | | | |
|---|---|---|---|
| $RLoc_i$ | – Rob's location | $Move_i$ | – Rob's move action |
| $RHC_i$ | – Rob has coffee | $PUC_i$ | – Rob picks up coffee |
| $SWC_i$ | – Sam wants coffee | $DelC$ | – Rob delivers coffee |
| $MW_i$ | – Mail is waiting | $PUM_i$ | – Rob picks up mail |
| $RHM_i$ | – Rob has mail | $DelM_i$ | – Rob delivers mail |

Figure 6.5: The delivery robot CSP planner with factored actions

the effects of the action.

A partial ordering is a binary relation that is transitive and asymmetric. A **partial-order plan** is a set of action instances together with a partial ordering between them, representing a "before" relation on action instances. Write $act_0 < act_1$ if action instance $act_0$ is before action instance $act_1$ in the partial order. This means that the action of $act_0$ must occur before the action of $act_1$. The aim of the planner is to produce a partial ordering of the action instances so that any total ordering that is consistent with the partial ordering will solve the goal from the initial state.

There are two special action instances, *start*, that achieves the relations that are true in the initial state, and *finish*, whose precondition is the goal to be solved. Every other action instance is after *start* and before *finish* in the partial ordering. The use of these as action instances means that the algorithm does not require special cases for the initial situation and for the goals. When the preconditions of *finish* are achieved, the goal is solved.

Any action instance, other than *start* or *finish*, will be in a partial-order plan to achieve a precondition of an action instance in the plan. Each precondition $P$ of an action instance $act_1$ in the plan is either true in the initial state, and so achieved by *start*, or there will be an action instance $act_0$ in the plan that achieves $P$. The action instance $act_0$ that achieves $P$ must be before $act_1$; that is, $act_0 < act_1$. To be correct, the algorithm must also ensure that nothing makes $P$ false in between $act_0$ and $act_1$.

A **causal link** is a triple $\langle act_0, P, act_1 \rangle$, where $act_0$ and $act_1$ are action instances and $P$ is a $Var = val$ assignment that is in the precondition of $act_1$, and in the effect of $act_0$. This means that $act_0$ makes $P$ hold for $act_1$. With this causal link, any other action instance that makes $P$ false must either be before $act_0$ or after $act_1$.

Informally, a partial-order planner works as follows. Begin with the action instances *start* and *finish* and the partial order $start < finish$. The planner maintains an agenda that is a set of $\langle P, A \rangle$ pairs, where $A$ is an action instance in the plan and $P$ is a variable-value assignment that is a precondition of $A$ that remains to be achieved. Initially, the agenda contains pairs $\langle G, finish \rangle$, where $G$ is an assignment that must be true in the goal state.

At each stage in the planning process, a pair $\langle G, act_1 \rangle$ is chosen from the agenda, where $P$ is in the precondition for action instance $act_1$. Then an action instance, $act_0$, is chosen to achieve $P$. That action instance is either already in the plan – it could be the *start* action, for example – or it is a new action instance that is added to the plan. Action instance $act_0$ must happen before $act_1$ in the partial order. The planner adds a causal link that records that $act_0$ achieves $P$ for action $act_1$. Any action in the plan that makes $P$ false must happen either before $act_0$ or after $act_1$. If $act_0$ is a new action, its preconditions are added to the agenda, and the process continues until the agenda is empty.

The algorithm *Partial_order_planner* is given in Figure 6.6 (page 251). This is a non-deterministic procedure. The "choose" and the "either ... or ..." form choices that must be searched over. There are two choices that require search:

- which action is chosen to achieve $P$
- whether an action instance that deletes $P$ happens before $act_0$ or after $act_1$.

The function $add\_const(A_0 < A_1, Constraints)$ returns the constraints formed by adding the constraint $A_0 < A_1$ to *Constraints*, and it fails if $A_0 < A_1$ is incompatible with *Constraints*. There are many ways this function can be implemented. See Exercise 6.11.

The function $protect(\langle A_0, G, A_1 \rangle, A)$ checks whether $A \neq A_0$, $A \neq A_1$, and the effect of $A$ is inconsistent with $G$. If so, either $A < A_0$ is added to the set of constraints or $A_1 < A$ is added to the set of constraints. This is a non-deterministic choice that is searched over.

**Example 6.18** Consider the goal of Sam not wanting coffee and no mail waiting (i.e., $\neg swc \wedge \neg mw$), where in the initial state Rob is in the lab, Sam wants coffee, Rob does not have coffee, there is mail waiting, and Rob does not have mail, i.e., $RLoc = lab, swc, \neg rhc, mw, \neg rhm$.

In the following, instances of action *Act* are written as *Act#n*, where $n$ is a unique integer.

Initially, the agenda is

$$\{\langle \neg swc, finish \rangle, \langle \neg mw, finish \rangle\}.$$

Suppose $\langle \neg swc, finish \rangle$ is chosen and removed from the agenda. One action can achieve $\neg swc$, namely deliver coffee, *dc*, with preconditions *off* and *rhc*. So it inserts an instance, say *dc#6*, into the plan. After the first time through the **repeat** loop, *Agenda* contains

$$\{\langle off, dc\#6 \rangle, \langle rhc, dc\#6 \rangle, \langle \neg mw, finish \rangle\}.$$

At this stage, the value of *Constraints* is $\{start < finish, start < dc\#6, dc\#6 < finish\}$. There is one causal link, $\langle dc\#6, \neg swc, finish \rangle$. This causal link means that no action that undoes $\neg swc$ is allowed to happen between *dc#6* and *finish*.

Suppose $\langle \neg mw, finish \rangle$ is chosen from the agenda. One action can achieve this, *pum*, with precondition $\{mw, RLoc = mr\}$. The algorithm constructs a new action instance, say *pum#7*. The causal link $\langle pum\#7, \neg mw, finish \rangle$ is added to the set of causal links; $\langle mw, pum\#7 \rangle$ and $\langle mr, pum\#7 \rangle$ are added to the agenda.

Suppose $\langle mw, pum\#7 \rangle$ is chosen from the agenda. The action *start* achieves *mw*, because *mw* is true initially. The causal link $\langle start, mw, pum\#7 \rangle$ is added to the set of causal links. Nothing is added to the agenda.

At this stage, there is no ordering imposed between *dc#6* and *pum#7*.

Suppose $\langle off, dc\#6 \rangle$ is removed from the agenda. There are two actions that can achieve *off*: *mc_cs* with preconditions *cs*, and *mcc_lab* with preconditions *lab*. The algorithm searches over these choices. Suppose it chooses the action instance *mc_cs#9*. The causal link $\langle mc\_cs\#9, off, dc\#6 \rangle$ is added.

The first violation of a causal link occurs when a move action is used to achieve $\langle mr, pum\#7 \rangle$. This action violates the causal link $\langle mc\_cs\#9, off, dc\#6 \rangle$, and so must happen after *dc#6* (the robot goes to the mail room after delivering coffee) or before *mc_cs#9*.

```
non-deterministic procedure Partial_order_planner(As, Gs)
    Inputs
        As: possible actions
        Gs: goal, a set of variable-value assignments to achieve
    Output
        linear plan to achieve Gs
    Local
        Agenda: set of ⟨P, A⟩ pairs where P is an atom and A an action instance
        Actions: set of action instances in the current plan
        Constraints: set of temporal constraints on action instances
        CausalLinks: set of ⟨act0, P, act1⟩ triples
    Agenda := {⟨G, finish⟩ : G ∈ Gs}
    Actions := {start, finish}
    Constraints := {start < finish}
    CausalLinks := {}
    repeat
        select and remove ⟨G, act1#i⟩ from Agenda
        either
            choose act0#j ∈ Actions such that act0 achieves G
        Or
            choose act0 ∈ As such that act0 achieves G
            select unique integer j
            Actions := Actions ∪ {act0#j}
            Constraints := add_const(start < act0#j, Constraints)
            for each CL ∈ CausalLinks do
                Constraints := protect(CL, act0#j, Constraints)
            Agenda := Agenda ∪ {⟨P, act0#j⟩ : P is a precondition of act0}
        Constraints := add_const(act0#j < act1#i, Constraints)
        new_cl := ⟨act0#j, G, act1#i⟩
        CausalLinks := CausalLinks ∪ {new_cl}
        for each A ∈ Actions do
            Constraints := protect(new_cl, A, Constraints)
    until Agenda = {}
    return total ordering of Actions consistent with Constraints
```

Figure 6.6: Partial-order planner

Eventually, it finds a plan of action instances, such as

$$start; mc\_lab\#15; pum\#7; mc\_mr\#40; puc\#11; mc\_cs\#9; dc\#6; finish.$$

This is the only total ordering consistent with the partial ordering.

A partial-order planner works particularly well when no ordering of actions can achieve a goal, as it does not need to search over all permutations of the actions. It also works well when many orderings can solve the goal, in which case it can find a flexible plan for the robot.

## 6.6 Social Impact

The spectacular growth of the video game sector has major economic, technological, social, and psychological impacts. The commercial video game industry generates more revenue than the movie industry and the music industry combined. In 2022, the revenue from video games was estimated to be about $200 billion. In commercial video games, the non-player characters (NPCs) have to generate and execute a wide variety of believable behaviors responding to other agents' behaviors and changes in the environment. The simplest form of planning is path planning in a spatial environment. $A^*$ (page 102) for path planning was widely adopted in video games. Autonomous NPCs have used a variety of representations of the set of possible behaviors. Early video games typically used finite state machines (page 58) with explicitly programmed belief-state transition functions and command functions. Behavior trees specify complex behaviors as tree structures of tasks with interior nodes represent the agent's higher-level tasks and leaf nodes corresponding to primitive actions, implementing a form of hierarchical control (page 58). Behavior trees allow for more expressive representations but they require pre-specifying all possible behavior explicitly.

Planners are now increasingly being used in video games instead of finite state machines or behavior trees. The advantage of planners is that they allow the agent to look further ahead in time, and they also allow much richer behavioral repertoires. *F.E.A.R.*, published in 2005, was one of the first games to use planning successfully. Its planner used a simplified STRIPS approach, known as goal-oriented action planning, GOAP. The successful use of GOAP in *F.E.A.R.* inspired the use of STRIPS-like planners in many other games, such as *Tomb Raider* (2013) and *Middle-Earth: Shadow of Mordor* (2014).

Another successful AI planning approach is the hierarchical task network (HTN). The HTN model is a generalization of the STRIPS approach. An HTN provides a set of tasks, made up of primitive tasks (similar to the actions of STRIPS), compound tasks composed of simpler tasks, and goal tasks (generalizations of STRIPS goals). *Killzone 2*, published in 2009, was the first commercial video game built using the HTN approach to planning. Other games built subsequently using HTN include *Transformers: Fall of Cybertron* (2012, 2016) and *Dying Light* (2015).

The planners described here assume deterministic actions and complete knowledge of the world. Relaxing those restrictions requires the approaches to planning and acting with uncertainty described in Chapters 12, 13, and 14. Many of those techniques are used in modern video games.

## 6.7 Review

The following are the main points you should have learned from this chapter:

- Planning is the process of choosing a sequence of actions to achieve a goal.
- An action is a partial function from a state to a state. Two representations for actions that exploit structure in states are the STRIPS representation, which is an action-centric representation, and the feature-based representation of actions, which is a feature-centric representation.
- Planning algorithms can be used to convert a planning problem into a search problem.
- A forward planner searches in the state space from the initial state to a goal state.
- A regression planner searches backwards from the goal, where each node in the search space is a subgoal to be achieved.
- A planning problem for a fixed horizon can be represented as a CSP, and any of the CSP algorithms can be used to solve it. The planner may need to search over horizons to find a plan.
- A partial-order planner does not enforce an ordering between actions unless there is a reason to make such an ordering.
- The video game industry has successfully exploited AI planning techniques.

## 6.8 References and Further Reading

There is much ongoing research into how to plan sequences of actions. Geffner and Bonet [2013] and Yang [1997] present overviews of automated planning.

The STRIPS representation was developed by Fikes and Nilsson [1971]. The Planning Domain Definition Language (PDDL) [Haslum et al., 2019] is a language that extends STRIPS in various ways, including conditional effects (when the effect only occurs when some condition holds), constraints on intermediate states, and explicit time durations. PDDL and its extensions have been used for international planning competitions.

Forward planning with good heuristics [Bacchus and Kabanza, 1996] is the basis for the most efficient algorithms [Geffner and Bonet, 2013]. (See Exercise 6.4 (page 255).)

Regression planning was pioneered by Waldinger [1977]. The use of weakest preconditions is based on the work of Dijkstra [1976], where it was used to define the semantics of imperative programming languages. This should not be too surprising because the commands of an imperative language are actions that change the state of the computer.

Planning as CSP is based on Graphplan [Blum and Furst, 1997] and Satplan [Kautz and Selman, 1996] and is also investigated by Lopez and Bacchus [2003] and van Beek and Chen [1999]. Bryce and Kambhampati [2007] survey the field.

Partial-order planning was introduced in Sacerdoti's [1975] NOAH and followed up in Tate's [1977] NONLIN system, Chapman's [1987] TWEAK algorithm, and McAllester and Rosenblitt's [1991] systematic nonlinear planning (SNLP) algorithm. See Weld [1994] for an overview of partial-order planning and Kambhampati et al. [1995] for a comparison of the algorithms. The version presented here is based on SNLP.

Wilkins [1988] discusses practical issues in planning. Weld [1999], McDermott and Hendler [1995], and Nau [2007] and associated papers provide overviews.

Neufeld et al. [2019] provide a comprehensive survey of the use of planners in video games. Orkin [2006] describes the GOAP model and its use in *F.E.A.R.* The HTN approach is described by Ghallab et al. [2004]. Yannakakis and Togelius [2018] provide an overview of the roles of AI in game development, including planning. Colledanchise and Ögren [2018] describe behavior trees and their relationship to the subsumption architecture developed by Brooks [1986].

Planning research is published at general AI journals and conferences and specialized conferences, most notably the International Conference on Planning and Scheduling (ICAPS); https://www.icaps-conference.org.

## 6.9 Exercises

**Exercise 6.1** Consider the planning domain in Figure 6.1 (page 232).

(a) Give the STRIPS representations for the pick up mail (*pum*) and deliver mail (*dm*) actions.
(b) Give the feature-based representation of the *MW* and *RHM* features.

**Exercise 6.2** Change the representation of the delivery robot world of Example 6.1 (page 232) so that the robot cannot carry both *mail* and *coffee* at the same time. Test it on an example that gives a different solution than the original representation.

**Exercise 6.3** Suppose the robot cannot carry both *mail* and *coffee* at the same time, but the robot can carry a box in which it can place objects (so it can carry the box and the box can hold the mail and the coffee). Suppose boxes can be picked up and dropped off at any location. Give the STRIPS representation for the resulting problem and test it on the problem of starting from the lab with mail waiting; the robot must deliver coffee and the mail to Sam's office.

**Exercise 6.4** This exercise involves designing a heuristic function that is better than the heuristic of Example 6.10 (page 240).

(a) For each of the forward and regression planners, test how effective each of the individual parts of the heuristic for Example 6.10 is, as well as the maximum. Explain why the results you observed occurred.
(b) Give an admissible heuristic function for the forward planner that expands fewer nodes than the forward planner does with that heuristic.
(c) Give an admissible heuristic function for the regression planner that expands fewer nodes than the regression planner does with that heuristic.

AIPython (aipython.org) has an an implementation of the heuristic that can be modified.

**Exercise 6.5** Suppose you must solve planning problems for cleaning a house. Various rooms can be dusted (making the room dust-free) or swept (making the room have a clean floor), but the robot can only sweep or dust a room if it is in that room. Sweeping causes a room to become dusty (i.e., not dust-free). The robot can only dust a room if the dustcloth is clean; but dusting rooms that are extra-dusty, like the garage, cause the dustcloth to become dirty. The robot can move directly from any room to any other room.

Assume there are only two rooms, the garage – which, if it is dusty, is extra-dusty – and the living room – which is not extra-dusty. Assume the following features:

- *Lr_dusty* is true when the living room is dusty.
- *Gar_dusty* is true when the garage is dusty.
- *Lr_dirty_floor* is true when the living room floor is dirty.
- *Gar_dirty_floor* is true when the garage floor is dirty.
- *Dustcloth_clean* is true when the dust cloth is clean.
- *Rob_loc* is the location of the robot, with values $\{garage, lr\}$.

Suppose the robot can do one of the following actions at any time:

- *move*: move to the other room
- *dust*: dust the room the robot is in, as long as the room is dusty and the dustcloth is clean
- *sweep*: sweep the floor the robot is in.

(a) Give the STRIPS representation for *dust*. [Hint: Because STRIPS cannot represent conditional effects, you may need to use two separate actions that depend on the robot's location.]
(b) Give the feature-based representation for *lr_dusty*.
(c) Suppose that the initial state is that the robot is in the garage, both rooms are dusty but have clean floors and the goal is to have both rooms not dusty. Draw the first two levels (with two actions, so the root has children and grandchildren) of a forward planner with multiple-path pruning, showing the actions (but do not give the state descriptions). Show explicitly what nodes are pruned through multiple-path pruning.
(d) Pick two of the states at the second level (after two actions) and show what is true in those states.

(e) Suppose that the initial state is that the robot is in the garage, both rooms are dusty but have clean floors, and the goal is to have both rooms not dusty. Draw the first two levels (with two actions, so the root has children and grandchildren) of a regression planner, showing the actions but do not show what the nodes represent.

(f) Pick two of the nodes at the second level (after two actions) and show what the subgoal is at those nodes.

(g) Draw the CSP for a planning horizon of two. Describe each constraint in English by specifying which values are (in)consistent.

(h) In designing the actions, the above description made one choice of what to include as preconditions of the actions. Consider the choices of whether to have the room is dusty as a precondition for cleaning the room, and whether to have the floor is dirty as a precondition for sweeping. Do these choices make a difference to (i) the shortest plan, (ii) the size of the search space for a forward planner, or (iii) the size of the search space for a regression planner?

**Exercise 6.6** Given a STRIPS representation for actions $a_1$ and $a_2$, define the STRIPS representation for the composite action $a_1; a_2$, which means that the agent does $a_1$ then does $a_2$.

(a) What are the effects for this composite action?

(b) When is the composite action impossible? (That is, when is it impossible for $a_2$ to be immediately after $a_1$?)

(c) Assuming the action is not impossible, what are the preconditions for this composite action?

(d) Using the delivery robot domain of Example 6.1 (page 232), give the STRIPS representation for the composite action *puc*; *mc*.

(e) Give the STRIPS representation for the composite action *puc*; *mc*; *dc* made up of three primitive actions.

(f) Give the STRIPS representation for the composite action *mcc*; *puc*; *mc*; *dc* made up of four primitive actions.

**Exercise 6.7** In a forward planner, a state can be represented in terms of the sequence of actions that lead to that state.

(a) Explain how to check whether the precondition of an action is satisfied, given such a representation.

(b) Explain how to do cycle pruning (page 109) in such a representation. You can assume that all of the states are legal. (Some other program has ensured that the preconditions hold.)

[Hint: Consider the composite action (Exercise 6.6) consisting of the first $k$ or the last $k$ actions at any stage.]

**Exercise 6.8** For the delivery robot domain, give a non-trivial admissible heuristic function for the regression planner. A non-trivial heuristic function is non-zero for some nodes, and always non-negative. Does it satisfy the monotone restriction?

**Exercise 6.9** Explain how multiple-path pruning can be incorporated into a regression planner. When can a node be pruned? See the discussion, page 244.

**Exercise 6.10** Give a condition for the CSP planner that, when arc consistency with search fails at some horizon, implies there can be no solutions for any longer horizon. [Hint: Think about a very long horizon where the forward search and the backward search do not influence each other.] Implement it.

**Exercise 6.11** To implement the function $add\_constraint(A_0 < A_1, Constraints)$ used in the partial-order planner, you have to choose a representation for a partial ordering. Implement the following as different representations for a partial ordering:

(a) Represent a partial ordering as a set of less-than relations that entail the ordering – for example, as the list $[1 < 2, 2 < 4, 1 < 3, 3 < 4, 4 < 5]$.

(b) Represent a partial ordering as the set of all the less-than relations entailed by the ordering – for example, as the list $[1 < 2, 2 < 4, 1 < 4, 1 < 3, 3 < 4, 1 < 5, 2 < 5, 3 < 5, 4 < 5]$.

(c) Represent a partial ordering as a set of pairs $\langle E, L \rangle$, where $E$ is an element in the partial ordering and $L$ is the list of all elements that are after $E$ in the partial ordering. For every $E$, there exists a unique term of the form $\langle E, L \rangle$. An example of such a representation is $[\langle 1, [2,3,4,5] \rangle, \langle 2, [4,5] \rangle, \langle 3, [4,5] \rangle, \langle 4, [5] \rangle, \langle 5, [\,] \rangle]$.

For each of these representations, how big can the partial ordering be? How easy is it to check for consistency of a new ordering? How easy is it to add a new less-than ordering constraint? Which do you think would be the most efficient representation? Can you think of a better representation?

# Part III

# Learning and Reasoning with Uncertainty

**How can an agent learn and reason, relaxing the assumption that it knows what is in the world?**

# Chapter 7

# Supervised Machine Learning

*Who so neglects learning in his youth, loses the past and is dead for the future.*

– Euripides (484 BCE – 406 BCE), Phrixus, Frag. 927

*From 2016 to 2020, the entire machine learning and data science industry has been dominated by two approaches: deep learning and gradient boosted trees. Specifically, gradient boosted trees is used for problems where structured data is available, whereas deep learning is used for perceptual problems such as image classification. ...These are the two techniques you should be most familiar with in order to be successful in applied machine learning today.*

– Chollet [2021, pp. 19,20]

**Learning** is the ability of an agent to improve its behavior based on experience. This could mean the following:

- The range of behaviors is expanded; the agent can do more.
- The accuracy on tasks is improved; the agent can do things better.
- The speed is improved; the agent can do things faster.

The most common goal of machine learning is for an agent to understand the world using **data**. The aim is *not* to model the data, but to model the world that generates the data. Having better models of the world allows the agent to make better decisions and to carry out better actions.

Learning is an important aspect of acting intelligently (page 4). As Euripides pointed out, learning involves an agent remembering its past in a way that is useful for its future. Learning is one of the fundamental skills of an intelligent agent; however, it is usually not an end in itself. For example, a bank may learn from who has defaulted on a loan, in order to make decisions about who to give a loan to, but the bank may not want future decisions to be based purely on the inequities of the past. A self-driving car may learn to recognize people and faces in order to drive safely and recognize its owners, but the cost of being wrong – running over a person or opening for the wrong person – can be very high. For a smart watch predicting the activity, location, or health of a person, if it is just suggesting measuring activity or tracking a run, a good guess might be adequate; however, if it is calling an ambulance, it needs to be accurate and reliable.

This chapter considers general issues of learning and the problem of making a prediction as supervised learning: given a collection of training **examples** made up of input–output pairs, predict the **output** of a new example where only the inputs are given. What we call examples are sometimes called **samples**. The output – what is being predicted – is often called the **target**. Two predominant base algorithms from which other more sophisticated algorithms are built are presented. Section 7.5 presents more sophisticated models based on these, including one of the dominant approaches in Chollet's quote above. The other dominant approach is presented in the next chapter. Future chapters include other learning paradigms, as well as how to reason and make decisions with learned models.

## 7.1 Learning Issues

The following components are part of any learning problem:

**Task** The behavior or task that is being improved.

**Data** The experiences that are used to improve performance in the task, either as a bag of examples or as a temporal sequence of examples. A **bag** is a set that allows for repeated elements, also known as a **multiset**. A bag is used when the order of the examples conveys no information.

**Measure of improvement** How the improvement is measured – for example, new skills that were not present initially, increasing accuracy in prediction, or improved speed.

Consider the agent internals of Figure 2.10 (page 68). The problem of **learning** is to take in prior knowledge and data (including the experiences of the agent) and to create an internal representation (a **model**) that is used by the agent as it acts.

Learning techniques face the following issues:

**Task** Virtually any task for which an agent can get data or experiences might be learned. The most commonly studied learning task is **supervised learning**: given some input features, some target output features, and a set of **training examples** where values of the input features and target features are specified, predict the value of each target feature for new examples given their values on the input features. This is called **classification** when the target features are discrete and **regression** when the target features are continuous. Other variants include **structured prediction** where the target is a more complex data structure, such as the constituents and shape of a molecule.

Other learning tasks include learning when the examples do not have targets defined (unsupervised learning), learning what to do based on rewards and punishments (reinforcement learning), and learning richer representations such as graphs (graph learning) or programs (inductive programming). These are considered in later chapters.

**Feedback** Learning tasks can be characterized by the feedback given to the learner. In **supervised learning**, the value of what should be learned is specified for each training example. **Unsupervised learning** occurs when no targets are given and the learner must discover clusters and regularities in the data. Feedback often falls between these extremes, such as in **reinforcement learning**, where the feedback in terms of rewards and punishments can occur after a sequence of actions.

**Measuring success** Learning is defined in terms of improving performance based on some measure. To know whether an agent has learned, you need a measure of success. The measure is usually not how well the agent performs on the training data, but how well the agent performs for new data.

In classification, being able to correctly classify all training examples is not the goal. For example, consider predicting a Boolean (true/false) feature based on a set of examples. Suppose that there were two agents $P$ and $N$. Agent $P$ claims that all of the negative examples seen are the only negative examples and that every other instance is positive. Agent $N$ claims that the positive examples in the training set are the only positive examples and that every other instance is negative. Both agents correctly classify every example in the training set but disagree on every other example. Success in learning should not be judged on correctly classifying the training set but on being able to correctly classify unseen examples. Thus, the learner must **generalize**: go beyond the specific given examples to classify unseen examples.

To measure a prediction, a **loss** (or **error**) function specifies how close the prediction is to the correct answer; **utility** (page 518) provides a measure of preferences, often in terms of **rewards** (page 552), when there is no correct answer.

A standard way to **evaluate** a learning method is to divide the given examples into **training examples** and **test examples**. A predictive model is built using the training examples, and the predictions of the model are measured on the test examples. To evaluate the method properly, the test cases should not be used in any way for the training. Using a test set is only an approximation of what is wanted; the real measure is its performance on future tasks. In **deployment** of a model in an application –

using a prediction to make decisions – an explicit test set is not usually required. A learned model is applied to new examples, and when the ground truth of these is eventually determined, the model can be evaluated using those examples in an ongoing manner. It is typical to relearn on all of the data, including the old data and the new data. In some applications, it is appropriate to remove old data, particularly when the world is changing or the quality of data is improving.

**Bias** The tendency to prefer one hypothesis over another is called a **bias**. Consider the agents $N$ and $P$ introduced earlier. Saying that a hypothesis is better than the hypotheses of $N$ or $P$ is not something that is obtained from the data – both $N$ and $P$ accurately predict all of the data given – but is something external to the data. Without a bias, an agent cannot make any predictions on unseen examples (see Section 7.6, page 315).

The set of all assumptions that enable generalization to unseen examples is called the **inductive bias**. What constitutes a good bias is an empirical question about which biases work best in practice; we do not imagine that either $P$'s or $N$'s biases work well in practice.

**Representation** For an agent to use its experiences, the experiences must affect the agent's internal representation. This internal representation could be the raw experiences themselves, but it is typically a **model**, a compact representation that generalizes the data. The choice of the possible representations for models provides a **representation bias** – only models that can be represented are considered. The preference for one model over another is called a **preference bias**.

There are two principles that are at odds in choosing a representation:

- *The richer the representation, the more useful it is for subsequent problem solving*. For an agent to learn a way to solve a task, the representation must be rich enough to express a way to solve the task.
- *The richer the representation, the more difficult it is to learn.* A very rich representation is difficult to learn because it requires a great deal of data, and often many different hypotheses are consistent with the data.

The representations required for intelligence are a compromise among many desiderata. The ability to learn the representation is one of them, but it is not the only one.

Much of machine learning is studied in the context of particular representations such as decision trees, linear models, or neural networks.

**Learning as search** Given a class of representations and a bias, the problem of learning can be reduced to one of search. Learning becomes a search through the space of possible models, trying to find a model or models that best fit the data given the bias. The search spaces are typically prohibitively large for systematic search, except for the simplest of cases. Nearly all of the search techniques used in machine learning can be seen as forms of local search (page 146) through a space of representations.

The definition of the learning algorithm then becomes one of defining the search space, the evaluation function, and the search method. A **search bias** occurs when the search only returns one of the many possible models that could be found.

**Imperfect data** In most real-world situations, data are not perfect. There can be **noise** where the observed features are not adequate to predict the classification or when the process generating the data is inherently noisy, **missing data** where the observations of some of the features for some or all of the examples are missing, and **errors** where some of the features have been assigned wrong values. One of the important properties of a learning algorithm is its ability to handle imperfect data in all of its forms.

**Interpolation and extrapolation** For domains with a natural interpretation of "between," such as where the features are about time or space, **interpolation** involves making a prediction between cases for which there are examples. **Extrapolation** involves making a prediction that goes beyond the seen examples. Extrapolation is usually less accurate than interpolation. For example, in ancient astronomy, the Ptolemaic system developed about 150 CE made detailed models of the movement of the solar system in terms of epicycles (cycles within cycles). The parameters for the models could be made to fit the data very well and they were very good at interpolation; however, the models were very poor at extrapolation. As another example, it is often easy to predict a stock price on a certain day given data about the prices on the days before and the days after that day. It is very difficult to predict the price that a stock will be tomorrow given historical data, although it would be very profitable to do so. An agent must be careful if its test cases mostly involve interpolating between data points, but the learned model is used for extrapolation.

**Curse of dimensionality** When examples are described in terms of features, each feature can be seen as a dimension. As the dimensionality increases, the number of possible examples grows exponentially, and even large datasets can be very sparse in large dimensions. For example, a single frame in a 4k video has about 8 million pixels, where each pixel value can be considered a dimension. The space is so large that it is extremely unlikely that any example is between the other examples in all dimensions of the multidimensional space. Any one of the dimensions is often not important; for example, changing just one of the pixels in an image does not change what the image is. In predicting diseases based on electronic health records, with images, text, laboratory results, and other information, the number of dimensions varies for different patients and can be enormous.

**Online and offline** In **offline learning**, all of the training examples are available to an agent before it needs to act. In **online learning**, training examples arrive as the agent is acting. An agent that learns online requires some representation of its previously seen examples before it has seen all of its examples. As new examples are observed, the agent must update its representation. Typically, an agent never sees all of the examples it could possibly see, and often cannot store all of the examples seen. **Active learning** is a form of online learning in which the agent acts to acquire new useful examples from which to learn. In active learning, the agent reasons about which examples would be most useful to learn from and acts to collect those examples.

## 7.2 Supervised Learning Foundations

A common learning task is **supervised learning**, where there is a set of examples, described by features, which are partitioned into input features and target features. The aim is to predict the values of the target features from the values of the input features for each possible example.

A **feature** is a function from examples into a value. If $e$ is an example, and $F$ is a feature, $F(e)$ is the value of feature $F$ for example $e$. The **domain** of a feature is the set of values it can return. Note that this is the *range* of the function defining the feature, but becomes the *domain* of a function that takes features and makes predictions. A **Boolean feature** is one with domain $\{false, true\}$.

A feature has exactly one value for each example. Suppose an example is a news article. The topic of an article can be a feature, with domain the set of possible topics (perhaps including "none" if it is possible there is no topic), if each article has a unique topic. If each article can have multiple topics, *topic* would not be a feature. Instead, there could be a Boolean feature for each possible topic. Alternatively, there could be a feature that maps each news article to the set of topics it covers.

In a supervised learning task, the learner is given

- a set of **input features**, $X_1, \dots, X_m$
- a set of **target features**, $Y_1, \dots, Y_k$
- a **bag** (page 262) of **training examples**, where each example $e$ is a pair $(x_e, y_e)$, where $x_e = (X_1(e), \dots, X_m(e))$ is a tuple of a value for each input feature and $y_e = (Y_1(e), \dots, Y_k(e))$ is a tuple of a value for each target feature.

The output is a **predictor**, a function that predicts $Y$s from $X$s. The aim is to predict the values of the target features for examples that the learner has not seen. For this book, consider only a single target feature, except where explicitly noted.

Supervised learning is called **regression** when the domain of the target is (a subset of) the real numbers. It is called **classification** when the domain of the target is a fixed finite set, for example, the domain could be Boolean $\{false, true\}$, clothing sizes {XS, S, M, L, XL, ...}, or countries of birth (countries, or *None* for those people who were born outside of any country). Other forms of supervised learning include **relational learning**, such as predicting a person's birth mother when test examples might be from a different population of people from training examples, and **structured prediction**, such as predicting the shape of a molecule.

Some examples of applications of supervised learning are

- a smart watch predicting the activity of the wearer (e.g., sleeping, sitting, walking, running, driving) from their heart rate and movement
- predicting how likely a location will be to flood in the next decade or century, based on the local topography, climate, geology, and land use, which might be used for insurance or for a decision about whether to build in the location
- predicting the words that someone may have hand-written in a phone or tablet based on their writing, perhaps taking the order of the strokes into account
- in a machine translation system, predicting Indonesian text that corresponds to some Swahili text (where the training examples might include text in other languages).

Before tackling sophisticated applications such as these, you need to understand the basics.

**Example 7.1** Figure 7.1 (page 268) shows training examples typical of a classification task. The aim is to predict whether a person reads an article posted to a threaded discussion website given properties of the article. The input features are *Author*, *Thread*, *Length*, and *Where_read*. There is one target feature, *User_action*. The domain of *Author* is $\{known, unknown\}$, the domain of *Thread* is $\{new, followup\}$, and so on.

There are eighteen training examples, each of which has a value for all of the features. In this dataset, $Author(e_{11}) = unknown$, $Thread(e_{11}) = followup$, and $User\_action(e_{11}) = skips$.

There are two new cases, $e_{19}$ and $e_{20}$, for which the model needs to predict the user action.

**Example 7.2** Figure 7.2 (page 268) shows some data for a regression task, where the aim is to predict the value of feature $Y$ on examples for which the value of feature $X$ is provided. This is a regression task because $Y$ is a real-valued feature. Predicting a value of $Y$ for example $e_8$ is an interpolation problem, as its value for the input feature is between two of the values of the training examples. Predicting a value of $Y$ for example $e_9$ is an extrapolation problem, because its $X$ value is outside the range of the training examples.

| *Example* | *Author* | *Thread* | *Length* | *Where_read* | *User_action* |
|---|---|---|---|---|---|
| $e_1$ | *known* | *new* | *long* | *home* | *skips* |
| $e_2$ | *unknown* | *new* | *short* | *work* | *reads* |
| $e_3$ | *unknown* | *followup* | *long* | *work* | *skips* |
| $e_4$ | *known* | *followup* | *long* | *home* | *skips* |
| $e_5$ | *known* | *new* | *short* | *home* | *reads* |
| $e_6$ | *known* | *followup* | *long* | *work* | *skips* |
| $e_7$ | *unknown* | *followup* | *short* | *work* | *skips* |
| $e_8$ | *unknown* | *new* | *short* | *work* | *reads* |
| $e_9$ | *known* | *followup* | *long* | *home* | *skips* |
| $e_{10}$ | *known* | *new* | *long* | *work* | *skips* |
| $e_{11}$ | *unknown* | *followup* | *short* | *home* | *skips* |
| $e_{12}$ | *known* | *new* | *long* | *work* | *skips* |
| $e_{13}$ | *known* | *followup* | *short* | *home* | *reads* |
| $e_{14}$ | *known* | *new* | *short* | *work* | *reads* |
| $e_{15}$ | *known* | *new* | *short* | *home* | *reads* |
| $e_{16}$ | *known* | *followup* | *short* | *work* | *reads* |
| $e_{17}$ | *known* | *new* | *short* | *home* | *reads* |
| $e_{18}$ | *unknown* | *new* | *short* | *work* | *reads* |
| $e_{19}$ | *unknown* | *new* | *long* | *work* | ? |
| $e_{20}$ | *unknown* | *followup* | *short* | *home* | ? |

Figure 7.1: Example data of a user's behavior. These are fictitious examples obtained from observing a user deciding whether to read articles posted to a threaded discussion website depending on whether the author is known or not, whether the article started a new thread or was a follow-up, the length of the article, and whether it is read at home or at work. $e_1, \ldots, e_{18}$ are the training examples. The aim is to make a prediction for the user action on $e_{19}$, $e_{20}$, and other, currently unseen, examples

| Example | $X$ | $Y$ |
|---|---|---|
| $e_1$ | 0.7 | 1.7 |
| $e_2$ | 1.1 | 2.4 |
| $e_3$ | 1.3 | 2.5 |
| $e_4$ | 1.9 | 1.7 |
| $e_5$ | 2.6 | 2.1 |
| $e_6$ | 3.1 | 2.3 |
| $e_7$ | 3.9 | 7 |
| $e_8$ | 2.9 | ? |
| $e_9$ | 5.0 | ? |

Figure 7.2: Examples for a toy regression task

### 7.2.1 Evaluating Predictions

Suppose *Es* is a bag of examples and $Y$ is a target feature. Given example $e \in Es$, the actual value of $Y$ for $e$, the **ground truth**, is $Y(e)$. $|Es|$ is the number of examples in *Es*.

A **predictor** for target feature $Y$ is a function from the domains of the input features into the domain of $Y$. A predictor for $Y$ is written as $\widehat{Y}$, so $\widehat{Y}(e)$ is the predicted value for target feature $Y$ on example $e$. $\widehat{Y}$ can only use the input features of an example for its prediction. $\widehat{Y}$ is built using examples in *Es*, but should be applicable for all possible examples.

A **point estimate** for target feature $Y$ on example $e$ is a prediction of $\widehat{Y}(e)$ that is a number if $Y$ is real or Boolean, or can be a vector if $Y$ has a finite set of possible values or is vector-valued. For example, if $Y$ is Boolean, or has domain $\{0, 1\}$, a point prediction could be 1 or 0.7 or even 1.3 (although 1.3 would never be a good prediction). An example of a prediction that is *not* a point estimate is the prediction that the value of real-valued variable $Y$ lies between 1.7 and 1.8. If $Y$ is discrete with values red, yellow, and green, the prediction can be a vector containing a number for each of the three values.

The **loss** for example $e$ on feature $Y$ is a measure of how close the prediction $\widehat{Y}(e)$ is to the actual value $Y(e)$. The measures below define a nonnegative real-valued function $loss(p, a)$ that gives the loss for prediction $p$ on an example when the actual value is $a$.

A common error function on a dataset is the **mean loss**, which for predictor $\widehat{Y}$ on a dataset *Es* is

$$\frac{1}{|Es|} \sum_{e \in Es} loss(\widehat{Y}(e), Y(e))$$

where $|Es|$ is the number of examples in *Es*. An alternative error is the **sum of losses** (without $1/|Es|$). When finding a predictor to minimize the error, either the mean or sum can be used, because they are a minimum for the same predictors. When implementing an algorithm, it is important to check whether the mean or the sum is used, particularly when this value is added to another one. The mean loss is typically reported as the error for a dataset because it can be interpreted without knowing the number of examples.

#### Real-valued Target Features

Real-valued features are used when the values are totally ordered, and the differences are meaningful. This covers cases where the values are all integers as well as cases where the values can be arbitrary reals. For example, height in centimeters, student marks, and number of children could all be real-valued features. Clothing sizes, when mapped to numbers, could also be considered real-valued.

For regression, when the target feature $Y$ is real-valued, when both the actual and the prediction are numbers, the following losses are common:

- The **0–1 loss**, or ***L*0 loss**, has

$$loss(p,a) = \begin{cases} 1 & \text{if } p \neq a \\ 0 & \text{if } p = a \end{cases}$$

This is sometimes written as $\mathbf{1}(p \neq a)$, where $\mathbf{1}$ is a function from Booleans into $\{0,1\}$, defined by $\mathbf{1}(true) = 1$ and $\mathbf{1}(false) = 0$.

The mean 0–1 loss of a dataset is the average number of predictions that are wrong. It does not take into account how wrong the predictions are, just whether they are correct or not. The **accuracy** of a predictor on a dataset is one minus the mean 0–1 loss, which is the number of correct predictions divided by the number of examples. Accuracy is maximized when 0–1 loss is minimized.

Testing equality for real or floating-point numbers is unreliable. This means that 0–1 loss may not be appropriate for the prediction of the mean, but is still applicable for predicting the mode or the median.

- The **absolute loss**, or ***L*1 loss**, is

$$loss(p,a) = |p - a|$$

the absolute difference between the predicted and actual value. This is always nonnegative. The mean absolute loss of a dataset is only zero when the predictions exactly fit the observed values. Unlike for the 0–1 loss, close predictions are better than far-away predictions.

- The **squared loss**, or ***L*2 loss**, is

$$loss(p,a) = (p - a)^2.$$

This measure treats large losses as much worse than small losses. For example, a loss of 2 on an example is as bad as 4 losses of 1, and a loss of 10 on one example is as bad as 100 losses of 1. Minimizing mean squared loss is equivalent to minimizing the **root-mean-square (RMS) error**, the square root of the mean squared loss, because the square root function is a monotonically increasing function on nonnegative values.

Sometimes you might see squared loss as $\frac{1}{2}(p - a)^2$. The $\frac{1}{2}$ does not affect the minimization, but makes some calculations simpler (in particular, when taking derivatives).

- The **worst-case loss**, or ***L*∞ loss**, on examples *Es* is the maximum absolute difference

$$\max_{e \in Es} \left| \widehat{Y}(e) - Y(e) \right| .$$

In this case, the learner is evaluated by its worst prediction. This is the only error covered that is not a mean or sum.

**Example 7.3** Consider the data of Figure 7.2 (page 268). Figure 7.3 shows a plot of the training data (filled circles) and three lines, $L1$, $L2$, and $L\infty$, that predict the $Y$-value for all $X$ points. $L1$ minimizes the mean absolute loss, $L2$ minimizes the mean squared loss, and $L\infty$ minimizes the mean worst-case loss of the training examples.

As no three points are collinear, any line through any pair of the points minimizes the 0–1, $L0$, loss.

Lines $L1$ and $L2$ give similar predictions for $X = 1.1$; namely, $L1$ predicts 1.805 and $L2$ predicts 1.709, whereas the data contain a data point $(1.1, 2.4)$. $L\infty$ predicts 0.7. They give predictions within 1.5 of each other when interpolating in the range $[1, 3]$. Their predictions diverge when extrapolating from the data. $L1$ and $L\infty$ give very different predictions for $X = 5$.

An **outlier** is an example that does not follow the pattern of the other examples. The difference between the lines that minimize the various error measures is most pronounced in how they handle outliers. The point $(3.9, 7)$ can be seen as an outlier as the other points are approximately in a line.

The prediction with the lowest worse-case loss for this example, $L\infty$, only depends on three data points, $(1.1, 2.4)$, $(3.1, 2.3)$, and $(3.9, 7)$, each of which has the same worst-case loss for prediction $L\infty$. The other data points could be at different locations, as long as they are not farther away from $L\infty$ than these three points.

A prediction that minimizes the absolute loss, $L1$, does not change as a function of the actual $Y$-value of the training examples, as long as the points above the line stay above the line, and those below the line stay below. For example, the prediction that minimizes the absolute loss would be the same, even if the last data point was $(3.9, 107)$ instead of $(3.9, 7)$.

Prediction $L2$ is sensitive to all of the data points; if the $Y$-value for any point changes, the line that minimizes the squared loss will change. Changes

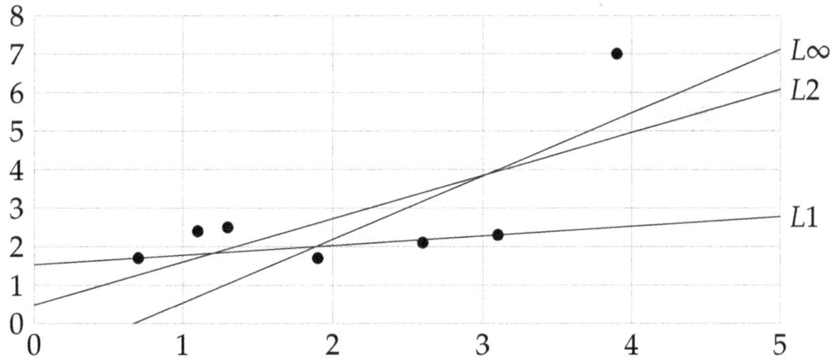


Figure 7.3: Linear regression predictions for a simple prediction example. Filled circles are the training examples. $L1$ is the prediction that minimizes the mean absolute loss of the training examples. $L2$ is the prediction that minimizes the mean squared loss of the training examples. $L\infty$ is the prediction that minimizes the worst-case loss of the training examples. See Example 7.3

to outliers will have more effect on the line than changes to points close to the line.

### Categorical Features

A **categorical feature** is one where the domain is a fixed finite set. Examples include the main topic of a news article (when each news article only has one main topic), the species of an animal, the country of birth of a person (perhaps with the extra value for those who were not born in a country), or the letter of the alphabet for a hand-written letter.

Suppose target variable $Y$ is categorical with domain $D = \{v_1, \ldots, v_k\}$. A **point estimate** is one of the following two forms:

- A **definitive prediction** where the prediction is one of $v_1, \ldots, v_k$.

- A **probabilistic prediction** $p$, a function or dictionary that maps the domain into nonnegative real numbers such that $\sum_{v \in D} p[v] = 1$, where $p[v]$ is the value that prediction $p$ makes for value $v$. Thus a probabilistic prediction makes a nonnegative prediction for each value in the domain, and the sum of the predictions is 1.

A definitive prediction of $v_j$ is equivalent to the probabilistic prediction with $p[v_j] = 1$ and the other numbers in the probabilistic prediction are all 0.

Whether a variable is real-valued or categorical is often a matter of data design – how the data is represented.

**Example 7.4** A trading agent wants to learn a person's preference for the length of holidays. The holiday can be for 1, 2, 3, 4, 5, or 6 days. See Figure 7.4 for example data. Note that there are no input features, and one output feature in this example.

One representation is to treat the target as a real-valued variable $Y$ that is the number of days in the holiday. A prediction for a new example $e$ can be any real number, such as $\widehat{Y}(e) = 3.2$.

| Example | $Y$ |
|---|---|
| $e_1$ | 1 |
| $e_2$ | 6 |
| $e_3$ | 6 |
| $e_4$ | 2 |
| $e_5$ | 1 |

Figure 7.4: Fictitious data of the number of days of a holiday

The target could also be treated as categorical with domain $\{1,2,3,4,5,6\}$. A definitive prediction for example $e$ might be the prediction $\widehat{Y}(e) = 1$. A probabilistic prediction for example $e$ might be the prediction $\widehat{Y}(e)$ represented by the dictionary $p$ with

$$p[1] = 0.25 \quad p[2] = 0.2 \quad p[3] = 0.1$$
$$p[4] = 0.1 \quad p[5] = 0.1 \quad p[6] = 0.25$$

which means that it is predicting the holiday is of length 1 with probability 0.25, length 2 with probability 0.2, and so on.

The losses used for real-valued target features can be applied to categorical features by using $loss(p[a], 1)$ for an actual $a$. For example, if the actual is $a$, the squared loss of probabilistic prediction is $(1 - p[a])^2$.

It is common to report mean accuracy. **Accuracy** for a definitive prediction is 1 if the prediction is correct, and 0 otherwise. For probabilistic predictions, the accuracy is 1 when there is a unique mode (the $v$ with the highest corresponding $p[v]$) that corresponds to the actual value. Accuracy is a crude measure of how accurate probabilistic predictions are, as it only depends on the mode.

A probabilistic prediction $p$ is typically optimized with **categorical log loss** or **categorical cross entropy**, often just known as **log loss**, where the loss for prediction $p$ for actual $a$ is

$$logloss(p, a) = -\log p[a].$$

That is, when the actual is $a$, log loss selects the corresponding prediction, $p[a]$, and returns its negative logarithm.

The log loss is always greater than or equal to 0. It is only 0 when $p[a] = 1$ and all other probabilities are 0.

For categorical $Y$ and dataset $Es$, predictor $\widehat{Y}$ has **mean log loss**

$$-\frac{1}{|Es|} \sum_e \log \widehat{Y}(e)[Y(e)]$$

where $\widehat{Y}(e)[Y(e)]$ is the value of the prediction $\widehat{Y}(e)$ evaluated for the actual $Y(e)$ for example $e$.

**Example 7.5** The probabilistic prediction from Example 7.4 (page 272) for the dataset of Figure 7.4 (page 272), with four data points ($e_1$, $e_2$, $e_3$, and $e_5$) having the prediction 0.25, and one ($e_4$) having the prediction 0.2 has mean log loss (where the logarithm is base 2):

$$-\frac{4 * \log_2 0.25 + \log_2 0.2}{5} \approx 2.064.$$

The log loss of the prediction with $p[1] = p[6] = 0.4$ and $p[2] = 0.2$, with the others 0, has mean log loss (base 2)

$$-\frac{4 * \log_2 0.4 + \log_2 0.2}{5} \approx 1.522.$$

Thus, the second prediction, which is using the proportion of the data for each value, is better than the other prediction.

There are two main justifications for log loss; one is in terms of probability, and one in terms of decision making.

- You might want the model that best predicts the data; this is the model where the data is most likely given the model. The **likelihood** of the examples $Es$ given model $\widehat{Y}$, assuming that the examples are independent, is the product of the prediction for each example:

  $$\prod_{e \in Es} \widehat{Y}(e)[Y(e)].$$

  Taking the logarithm gives the **log-likelihood**

  $$\sum_{e \in Es} \log \widehat{Y}(e)[Y(e)].$$

  The mean log loss is negative of the log-likelihood divided by the number of examples. Thus, log loss is minimized when the log likelihood – and so also the likelihood – is maximized.

- Mean log loss is appropriate when the prediction is used as a probability for gambling and other reasoning under uncertainty (see Chapter 9). For example, under squared loss, $10^{-7}$ and $10^{-6}$ are very close; a prediction of $10^{-7}$ will have a very similar error to a prediction of $10^{-6}$. However, as probabilities they are very different. An insurance company making its decisions based on a probability of $10^{-7}$ will lose a lot of money if the correct probability is $10^{-6}$; the event will occur 10 times as much as expected. This difference is reflected in the log loss, but not in the losses that only use the differences between the actual and predicted.

The logarithm of 0 is undefined. As $\epsilon > 0$ gets closer to 0, $-\log \epsilon$ gets larger. For this reason, log loss of the prediction of 0 is usually treated as infinity. Averaging infinity with any finite set of numbers is infinity. Log loss discourages any probabilistic prediction of 0 for a value that is possible.

Log loss is closely related to the notion of **entropy** (page 275). The log loss (when the base of the logarithm is 2) can be seen as the mean number of bits it will take to encode the data given a code that is based on $\widehat{Y}$ treated as a probability. The base of the logarithm provides a constant difference, which doesn't matter when the goal is to minimize the loss. However, when reporting results it is important to specify the base of the logarithm, where both 2 and $e$ (the base of the natural logarithm) are common.

**Information Theory**

A **bit** is a binary digit. Because a bit has two possible values (0 and 1), it can be used to distinguish two items. Two bits can distinguish four items, each associated with either 00, 01, 10, or 11. In general, $n$ bits can distinguish $2^n$ items. Thus, $n$ items can be distinguished with $\log_2 n$ bits (or the smallest integer greater than or equal to this value). It may be surprising, but you can do better than this using probabilities.

Consider this code to distinguish the elements of the set $\{a, b, c, d\}$, with $P(a) = \frac{1}{2}, P(b) = \frac{1}{4}, P(c) = \frac{1}{8}$, and $P(d) = \frac{1}{8}$:

| | | | |
|---|---|---|---|
| $a$ | 0 | $c$ | 110 |
| $b$ | 10 | $d$ | 111 |

This code sometimes uses one bit, sometimes two bits and sometimes three bits. On average, it uses

$$P(a) * 1 + P(b) * 2 + P(c) * 3 + P(d) * 3 = \frac{1}{2} + \frac{2}{4} + \frac{3}{8} + \frac{3}{8} = 1\frac{3}{4} \text{ bits.}$$

For example, the string *aacabbda* with 8 characters has code 00110010101110, which uses 14 bits.

With this code, $-\log_2 P(a) = 1$ bit is required to distinguish $a$ from the other symbols. Distinguishing $b$ uses $-\log_2 P(b) = 2$ bits. Distinguishing $c$ or $d$ requires $-\log_2 P(c) = 3$ bits.

It is possible to build a code that, to identify $x$, requires $-\log_2 P(x)$ bits (or the smallest integer greater than this). Suppose there is a sequence of symbols you want to transmit or store and you know the probability distribution over the symbols. A symbol $x$ with probability $P(x)$ can use $-\log_2 P(x)$ bits. To transmit a sequence, each symbol requires, on average,

$$\sum_x -P(x) * \log_2 P(x)$$

bits to send, where the sum is over each value $x$ in a domain. This is called the **information content** or **entropy** of the distribution.

Suppose $P$ and $Q$ are both probability distributions. The expected number of bits to describe $Q$ using a code optimized for $P$ is

$$\sum_x -Q(x) * \log_2 P(x).$$

This is the **cross entropy** of distribution $P$ relative to $Q$. For a fixed $Q$, cross entropy is minimized when $P = Q$. In machine learning, $P$ is typically the learned model and $Q$ the distribution of the data. Log loss (page 273) allows for a separate prediction for each example.

### Boolean and Other Binary Features

When the domain of $Y$ is binary, one value can be associated with 0, the other value with 1. For Boolean features, with domain $\{false, true\}$, it is traditional to associate 0 with *false* and 1 with *true*. Boolean variables are very common; for example, predicting the topics of a news article that can have multiple topics can be modeled using a Boolean variable for each topic.

A Boolean target variable can be treated either as a real-valued prediction or as a categorical prediction. The real-valued prediction $p$ for variable $Y$ is equivalent to the categorical prediction where the prediction for 1 is $p$ and the prediction for 0 is $1 - p$.

The **binary log loss**, or **binary cross-entropy loss**, for prediction $p$ and actual value $a$ is defined by

$$logloss(p, a) = -a \log p - (1 - a) \log(1 - p)$$

and by convention, $logloss(1, 1) = logloss(0, 0) = 0$, even though $\log 0$ is undefined (or infinity). Log loss is $\log p$ when $a = 1$ and $\log(1 - p)$ when $a = 0$, and so is the same as categorical log loss where the prediction for value 1 is $p$ and the prediction for value 0 is $1 - p$. The term *log loss* includes both categorical log loss and binary log loss; which is meant should be clear from the context.

A binary point prediction could be any real number or could be restricted to be 0 or 1. Here we assume that the prediction can be any real number, except where explicitly noted.

## 7.2.2 Point Estimates with No Input Features

The simplest case for learning is when there is a single target feature and the input features are ignored (or there are no input features). In this case, a learning algorithm predicts a single value for the target feature for all of the examples. This forms a **naive baseline** that any more sophisticated algorithm should be able to beat. It is also the base case for some of the learning algorithms.

Suppose $Es$ is a bag of $n$ examples, $Y$ is a numeric feature, and the learner makes a point estimate, $p$, for all examples.

The optimal prediction depends on the optimality criterion. Figure 7.5 (page 277) gives the optimal prediction for various optimality criteria for the case with no input features and a single real-valued feature $Y$, where the training set consisting of $n$ examples, namely the numbers $Y(e_1), \ldots, Y(e_m)$. The **mode** is the value that occurs most often. The **median** is the middle value after sorting the values; if there are two middle values, either of them, or any value between them, will minimize the absolute error. The **mean** is the sum of the values divided by the number of values. The best worst-case error is the mean of the minimum value and the maximum value. Exercise 7.1 (page 320) asks about the proofs.

When the target feature has domain $\{0, 1\}$, the $n$ training examples can be summarized in two numbers: $n_1$, the number of examples with value 1 and $n_0$, the number of examples with value 0 ($n_0 = n - n_1$). The mean is the **empirical frequency**: the proportion of 1s in the training data, namely $n_1/n$. This is also the **maximum likelihood estimate**, and the prediction with the minimum log loss. The 0–1 error and the absolute error are minimized by predicting which of 0 or 1 occurs more often.

When the target feature is categorical with domain $\{v_1, \ldots, v_k\}$, a dataset can be summarized by $k$ numbers $n_1, \ldots, n_k$, where $n_i$ is the number of occurrences of $v_i$ in the dataset. In this case, the prediction that minimizes log loss on the training set is the empirical frequency. The prediction that minimizes 0–1 error and maximizes accuracy is to predict the mode; a value that appears most often.

**Example 7.6** Consider the length of holiday data of Example 7.4 (page 272). Suppose only the target is given, and there are no input features, so all of the examples get the same prediction.

In the first representation, the prediction of 1 and the prediction of 6 both minimize 0–1 error and so maximize accuracy on the training data. The prediction that minimizes the absolute loss is 2, with an total absolute loss of 10, and a mean absolute loss of 2. The prediction that minimizes the squared error on the training data is 3.2. The prediction the minimizes the worst-case error is 3.5.

Treating the feature as categorical, the prediction that minimizes log loss in training error is $(0.4, 0.2, 0, 0, 0.4)$, which is the empirical distribution of the training data.

Thus, which prediction is preferred depends on how the prediction is represented and how it will be evaluated.

| Loss | Error for prediction $p$ for training data | Optimal prediction for training data |
|---|---|---|
| mean 0–1 loss | $\frac{1}{n}\sum_e \mathbf{1}(Y(e) \neq p)$ | *mode* |
| mean absolute loss | $\frac{1}{n}\sum_e \lvert Y(e) - p\rvert$ | *median* |
| mean squared loss | $\frac{1}{n}\sum_e (Y(e) - p)^2$ | *mean* |
| worst case | $\max_e \lvert Y(e) - p\rvert$ | $(min + max)/2$ |

Special case for domain of $Y$ is $\{0, 1\}$, $n_1 = \sum_e (Y(e))$, $n_0 = n - n_1$.

| | | |
|---|---|---|
| mean log loss | $-\frac{n_1}{n} * \log p - \frac{n_0}{n} * \log(1-p)$ | $\frac{n_1}{n}$ |

For categorical $Y$ with domain $\{v_1, \ldots, v_k\}$, value $v_i$ occurs $n_i$ times in training data, and prediction $p$ has $p[v_i] = p_i$.

| | | |
|---|---|---|
| mean log loss | $-\sum_i \frac{n_i}{n} * \log p_i$ | $p[v_i] = \frac{n_i}{n}$ |

Figure 7.5: Optimal predictions on training data with no input features. The training data consist of $n$ examples $e_1, \ldots, e_n$ with single real-valued feature $Y$

This analysis does not specify the optimal prediction for unseen examples. You should *not* expect the empirical frequency of the training data to be the optimal prediction for new examples when maximizing the likelihood or minimizing the log loss. If one $n_i = 0$, the corresponding $v_i$ does not appear in the training data. However, if just one test example has value $v_i$, the likelihood would be 0 (its lowest possible value) and the log loss would be infinite (or undefined). This is an example of overfitting (page 297). See Exercise 7.1 (page 320).

Figure 7.6 provides mean losses that any method for binary target domains should beat, as a function of the optimality criterion. The naive prediction is a prediction that can be made before seeing any data. These losses act as a quick check for determining if a method is not working. For example, if the mean squared loss of a predictor for 0/1 variable is greater than 0.25, the method is not working.

Given a dataset, for the optimality criterion used, you should compute the average loss for the optimal prediction on the training set – ignoring the input features – as a baseline to beat. Often you will find such a baseline is difficult to beat by a lot.

### 7.2.3 Types of Errors

Not all errors are equal; the consequences of some errors may be much worse than others. For example, it may be much worse to predict a patient does not have a disease that they actually have, so that the patient does not get appropriate treatment, than it is to predict that a patient has a disease they do not actually have, which will force the patient to undergo further tests, but may result in more anxiety.

Consider a simple case where the domain of the target feature is Boolean (which you can consider as "positive" and "negative") and the predictions are restricted to be Boolean. One way to evaluate a prediction independently of the decision is to consider the four cases between the predicted value and the actual value:

| Optimality Criterion | Naive Prediction | Mean Loss |
|---|---|---|
| mean 0–1 loss | 1 | $\leq 1$ |
| mean absolute loss | 0.5 | 0.5 |
| mean squared loss | 0.5 | 0.25 |
| worst case error | 0.5 | 0.5 |
| mean log loss (base 2) | 0.5 | 1 |
| mean log loss (base $e$) | 0.5 | 0.693... |

Figure 7.6: Baseline errors any method should beat, for target domain $\{0, 1\}$

| | actual positive (*ap*) | actual negative (*an*) |
|---|---|---|
| predict positive (*pp*) | true positive (*tp*) | false positive (*fp*) |
| predict negative (*pn*) | false negative (*fn*) | true negative (*tn*) |

A **false-positive error** or **type I error** is a positive prediction that is wrong (i.e., the predicted value is positive and the actual value is negative). A **false-negative error** or **type II error** is a negative prediction that is wrong (i.e., the predicted value is negative and the actual value is positive). For a given predictor for a given set of examples, suppose *tp* is the number of true positives, *fp* is the number of false positives, *fn* is the number of false negatives, and *tn* is the number of true negatives.

Different choices of learning algorithm or parameters can affect the number of false positives and false negatives. Suppose false positives are $c$ times as bad as false negatives. $c < 1$ means false negatives are worse than false positives, $c = 1$ means they are equally as bad, and $c > 1$ means false positives are worse than false negatives. Assuming the costs of errors can be added, the **cost** of a prediction is proportional to

$$c * fp + fn.$$

One would then select the predictor with the lowest cost.

Sometimes you want to evaluate a predictor without knowing anything about the relative costs of different types of errors.

The following measures are often used:

- The **recall** or **true-positive rate** is $\frac{tp}{tp+fn}$, the proportion of actual positives that are predicted to be positive.
- The **false-positive rate** is $\frac{fp}{fp+tn}$, the proportion of actual negatives predicted to be positive.

An agent should try to maximize the true-positive rate and minimize the false-positive rate; however, these goals are incompatible. An agent can maximize the true-positive rate by making positive predictions about all cases it is sure about (assuming it is correct about these). However, this choice maximizes the false-positive rate because more of the positives will be wrong.

Predictor $A$ **dominates** $B$ if $A$ has a higher true-positive rate and a lower false-positive rate than $B$. If $A$ dominates $B$ then $A$ has a lower cost (and so is better) than $B$ for *all* cost functions that depend only on the number of false positives and false negatives (assuming the costs to be minimized are additive and nonnegative). See Exercise 7.3 (page 321).

For a given set of examples where both the prediction and the actual are given, a **receiver operating characteristic space**, or an **ROC space**, plots the false-positive rate against the true-positive rate for various predictors. Each predictor becomes a point in the space.

**Example 7.7** Consider a case where there are 100 examples that are actually positive ($ap$) and 1000 examples that are actually negative ($an$). Figure 7.7 shows the performance of six possible predictors for these 1100 examples. Predictor (a) predicts 70 of the positive examples correctly and 850 of the negative examples correctly. Predictor (e) predicts every example as positive, and (f) predicts all examples as negative.

In the ROC space, any predictor lower and to the right of another predictor is dominated by the other predictor. For example, (d) is dominated by (c); there would be no reason to choose (d) if (c) were available as a predictor.

Consider predictions (a) and (c) in Figure 7.7. The true-positive rate of (a) is 0.7 and the false-positive rate is 0.15. Predictor (c) has a true-positive rate of 0.98 and a false-positive rate of 0.2. If false positives were much more important than false negatives, then (a) would be better than (c), as it has fewer false positives. If false negatives were much more important (much worse) than false positives, then (c) would be better than (a), as it has fewer false negatives. Neither dominates the other in the ROC space.

Any predictor that is below the upper envelope of predictors (shown with line segments in Figure 7.7) is dominated by the other predictors. For example, although (a) is not dominated by (b) or by (c), it is dominated by the randomized predictor: with probability 0.5 use the prediction of (b), else use the prediction of (c). This randomized predictor would expect to have 26 false negatives and 112.5 false positives. The line between (b) and (c) reflects all probabilistic

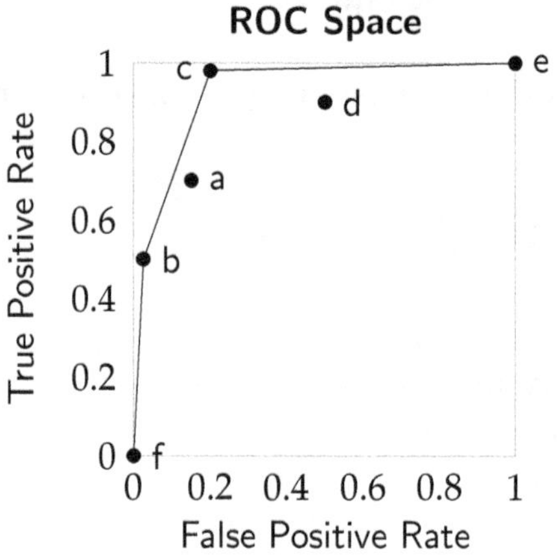


| (a) | $ap$ | $an$ |
|---|---|---|
| $pp$ | 70 | 150 |
| $pn$ | 30 | 850 |

| (b) | $ap$ | $an$ |
|---|---|---|
| $pp$ | 50 | 25 |
| $pn$ | 50 | 975 |

| (c) | $ap$ | $an$ |
|---|---|---|
| $pp$ | 98 | 200 |
| $pn$ | 2 | 800 |

| (d) | $ap$ | $an$ |
|---|---|---|
| $pp$ | 90 | 500 |
| $pn$ | 10 | 500 |

| (e) | $ap$ | $an$ |
|---|---|---|
| $pp$ | 100 | 1000 |
| $pn$ | 0 | 0 |

| (f) | $ap$ | $an$ |
|---|---|---|
| $pp$ | 0 | 0 |
| $pn$ | 100 | 1000 |

Figure 7.7: Six predictors in the ROC space

mixes of (b) and (c).

For some algorithms, there is a parameter which, when varied, results in predictors with different false-positive and true-positive rates. For example, a model that returns a real value can predict true if the output value is greater than a threshold, and false if the output value is less than the threshold. As the threshold varies, so do the predictions. In such cases, a single algorithm can provide a curve in the ROC space. One algorithm is better than another algorithm if its curve is above and to the left of the other. Often two algorithms have different parts of the curve where they dominate, in which case the preferred algorithm depends on the relative costs of the two types of errors. The **area under the ROC curve** (**AUROC**) is a single number that can be used to compare algorithms across the whole parameter space. One predictor having a larger AUROC than another means it is better for some cost functions, but does not imply it is better for all cost functions.

Another common measure is **precision**, which is $\frac{tp}{tp+fp}$, the proportion of positive predictions that are actual positives. Some have suggested comparing algorithms just using precision and recall. However, it is possible that one algorithm might have a better (higher) recall and a better (higher) precision than another but be a worse algorithm for some cost functions. See Exercise 7.3 (page 321).

## 7.3 Basic Models for Supervised Learning

Supervised learning methods take the input features, the target features, and the training data and return **predictors**, functions on input features that predict values for the target features. Learning methods are often characterized by how the predictors are represented. This section considers some basic methods from which other methods are built. Initially assume a single target feature and the learner returns a predictor on this target.

### 7.3.1 Learning Decision Trees

A decision tree is a simple representation for classifying examples. Decision tree learning is one of the simplest useful techniques for supervised classification learning.

A **decision tree** is a tree in which

- each internal (non-leaf) node is labeled with a condition, a Boolean function of examples
- each internal node has two branches, one labeled *true* and the other *false*
- each leaf of the tree is labeled with a **point estimate** (page 269).

Decision trees are also called **classification trees** when the target (leaf) is a classification, and **regression trees** when the target is real-valued.

To classify an example, filter it down the tree, as follows. Each condition encountered in the tree is evaluated and the arc corresponding to the result is followed. When a leaf is reached, the classification corresponding to that leaf is returned. A decision tree corresponds to a nested if–then–else structure in a programming language.

**Example 7.8** Figure 7.8 shows two possible decision trees for the examples of Figure 7.1 (page 268). Each decision tree can be used to classify examples according to the user's action. To classify a new example using the tree on the left, first determine the length. If it is long, predict *skips*. Otherwise, check the thread. If the thread is new, predict *reads*. Otherwise, check the author and predict *reads* only if the author is known. This decision tree can correctly classify all examples in Figure 7.1 (page 268).

The left tree corresponds to the program defining $\widehat{UserAction}(e)$:

**define** $\widehat{UserAction}(e)$:
  if $long(e)$: return *skips*
  else if $new(e)$: return *reads*
  else if $unknown(e)$: return *skips*
  else: return *reads*

The tree on the right returns a numerical prediction for *reads*:

**define** $\widehat{UserAction}(e)$:
  if $long(e)$: return 0
  else $new(e)$: return 0.82

To use decision trees as a target representation, there are a number of questions that arise.

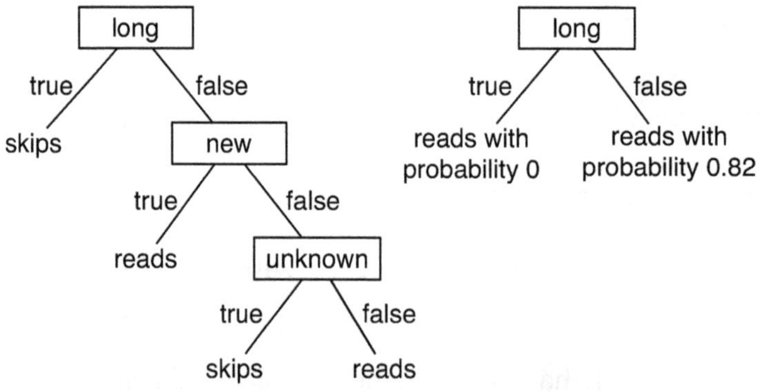


Figure 7.8: Two decision trees

- Given some training examples, what decision tree should be generated? Because a decision tree can represent any function of discrete input features, the bias that is necessary is incorporated into the preference of one decision tree over another. One proposal is to prefer the smallest tree that is consistent with the data, which could mean the tree with the least depth or the tree with the fewest nodes. Which decision trees are the best predictors of unseen data is an empirical question.
- How should an agent go about building a decision tree? One way is to search the space of decision trees for the smallest decision tree that fits the data. Unfortunately, the space of decision trees is enormous (see Exercise 7.7 (page 323)). A practical solution is to carry out a greedy search on the space of decision trees, with the goal of minimizing the error. This is the idea behind the algorithm described below.

### Searching for a Good Decision Tree

A decision tree can be seen as a branching program, that takes an example and returns a prediction for that example. The program is either

- a function that ignores its argument and returns a point prediction for all of the examples that reach this point (which corresponds to a leaf), or
- of the form "if $c(e)$ then $t_1(e)$ else $t_0(e)$" where $c$ is a Boolean condition, and $t_1$ and $t_0$ are decision trees; $t_1$ is the tree that is used when the condition $c$ is true of example $e$, and $t_0$ is the tree used when $c(e)$ is false.

The algorithm *Decision_tree_learner* of Figure 7.9 (page 284) mirrors the recursive decomposition of a tree. It builds a decision tree from the top down as follows. The input to the algorithm is a set of input conditions (Boolean functions of examples that use only input features), the target feature, a set of training examples, and a real-valued parameter, $\gamma$, discussed below. If the input features are Boolean, they can be used directly as the conditions.

A **greedy optimal split** is a condition that results in the lowest error if the learner were allowed only one split and it splits on that condition. $sum\_loss(Es)$ gives the sum of losses of training examples $Es$ for the loss function assumed, given that the optimal prediction is used for that loss function, as given in Figure 7.5 (page 277). The procedure *select_split* returns a greedy optimal split if the sum of losses after the split improves the sum of losses before the split by at least the threshold $\gamma$. If there is no such condition, *select_split* returns *None*.

Adding a split increases the size of the tree by 1. The threshold $\gamma$ can be seen as a penalty for increasing the size of the tree by 1. If positive, $\gamma$ is also useful to prevent $val < best\_val$ holding solely due to rounding error.

If *select_split* returns *None*, the decision tree learning algorithm creates a leaf. The function $leaf\_value(Es)$ returns the value that is used as a prediction of the target for examples $Es$ that reach this node. It ignores the input features for these examples and returns a point estimate (page 269), which is the case considered in Section 7.2.2 (page 276). The decision tree algorithm returns a function that takes an example and returns that point estimate.

If *select_split* returns condition $c$, the learner splits on condition $c$ by partitioning the training examples into those examples $e$ with $c(e)$ true and those examples with $c(e)$ false. It recursively builds a subtree for each of these bags of examples. It returns a function that, given an example, tests whether $c$ is true of the example, and then uses the prediction from the appropriate subtree.

**Example 7.9** Consider applying *Decision_tree_learner* to the classification data of Figure 7.1 (page 268), with $\gamma = 0$. The initial call is

$$decisionTreeLearner(\{known, new, long, home\}, User\_action, \{e_1, e_2, \ldots, e_{18}\}, 0)$$

```
procedure Decision_tree_learner(Cs, Y, Es, γ)
    Inputs
        Cs: set of possible conditions
        Y: target feature
        Es: set of training examples
        γ: minimum improvement needed to expand a node (γ ≥ 0)
    Output
        function to predict a value of Y for an example
    c := select_split(Es, Cs, γ)
    if c = None then                                    ▷ stopping criterion is true
        v := leaf_value(Es)
        define T(e) = v
        return T
    else
        true_examples := {e ∈ Es : c(e)}
        t1 := Decision_tree_learner(Cs \ {c}, Y, true_examples, γ)
        false_examples := {e ∈ Es : ¬c(e)}
        t0 := Decision_tree_learner(Cs \ {c}, Y, false_examples, γ)
        define T(e) = if c(e) then t1(e) else t0(e)
        return T
    procedure select_split(Es, Cs, γ)
        best_val := sum_loss(Es) − γ
        best_split := None
        for c ∈ Cs do
            val := sum_loss({e ∈ Es | c(e)}) + sum_loss({e ∈ Es | ¬c(e)})
            if val < best_val then
                best_val := val
                best_split := c
        return best_split   ▷ best_split = None means stopping criterion is true
```

Figure 7.9: Decision tree learner; returns a predicting function where *known* is true when $Author = known$, and similarly for the other conditions.

Suppose the stopping criterion is not true and the algorithm selects the condition *long* to split on. It then calls

$$decisionTreeLearner(\{known, new, home\}, User\_action,$$
$$\{e_1, e_3, e_4, e_6, e_9, e_{10}, e_{12}\}, 0)$$

where $\{e_1, e_3, e_4, e_6, e_9, e_{10}, e_{12}\}$ is the set of training examples with $Length = long$.

All of these examples agree on the user action; therefore, the algorithm returns the prediction *skips*. The second step of the recursive call is

$$decisionTreeLearner(\{known, new, home\}, User\_action,$$
$$\{e_2, e_5, e_7, e_8, e_{11}, e_{13}, e_{14}, e_{15}, e_{16}, e_{17}, e_{18}\}, 0).$$

Not all of the examples agree on the user action, so assuming the stopping criterion is false, the algorithm selects a condition to split on. Suppose it selects *new*. Eventually, this recursive call returns the function on example *e* in the case when *Length* is *short*:

if $new(e)$ then *reads*
else if $unknown(e)$ then *skips* else *reads*.

The final result is the first predictor of Example 7.8 (page 282).

When the loss is log loss (page 276) with base 2, the mean of the losses, $sum\_losses(Es)/|Es|$, is the **entropy** (page 275) of the empirical distribution of $|Es|$. The number of bits to describe *Es* after testing the condition *c* is *val*, defined on line 25 of Figure 7.9 (page 284). The entropy of the distribution created by the split is $val/|Es|$. The difference of these two is the **information gain** of the split. Sometimes information gain is used even when the optimality criterion is some other error measure, for example, when maximizing accuracy it is possible to select a split to optimize log loss, but return the mode as the leaf value. See Exercise 7.6 (page 323).

The following example shows details of the split choice for the case where the split is chosen using log loss, and the empirical distribution is used as the leaf value.

**Example 7.10** In the running example of learning the user action from the data of Figure 7.1 (page 268), suppose the aim is to minimize the log loss. The algorithm greedily chooses a split that minimizes the log loss. Suppose $\gamma$ is 0.

Without any splits, the optimal prediction on the training set is the empirical frequency (page 277). There are nine examples with $User\_action = reads$ and nine examples with $User\_action = skips$, and so *known* is predicted with probability 0.5. The mean log loss is equal to $(-18 * \log_2 0.5)/18 = 1$.

Consider splitting on *Author*. This partitions the examples into $[e_1, e_4, e_5, e_6, e_9, e_{10}, e_{12}, e_{13}, e_{14}, e_{15}, e_{16}, e_{17}]$ with $Author = known$ and $[e_2, e_3, e_7, e_8, e_{11}, e_{18}]$ with $Author = unknown$, each of which is evenly split between the different user actions. The optimal prediction for each partition is again 0.5, and so the log loss after the split is again 1. In this case, finding out whether the author is known, by itself, provides no information about what the user action will be.

Splitting on *Thread* partitions the examples into $[e_1, e_2, e_5, e_8, e_{10}, e_{12}, e_{14}, e_{15}, e_{17}, e_{18}]$ with *Thread* = *new* and $[e_3, e_4, e_6, e_7, e_9, e_{11}, e_{13}, e_{16}]$ with *Thread* = *followup*. The examples with *Thread* = *new* contains three examples with *User_action* = *skips* and seven examples with *User_action* = *reads*, thus the optimal prediction for these is to predict reads with probability 7/10. The examples with *Thread* = *followup* have two *reads* and six *skips*. Thus, the best prediction for these is to predict *reads* with probability 2/8. The mean log loss after the split is

$$
\begin{aligned}
&-(3 * \log_2(3/10) + 7 * \log_2(7/10) + 2 * \log_2(2/8) + 6 * \log_2(6/8))/18 \\
&\approx 15.3/18 \approx 0.85.
\end{aligned}
$$

Splitting on *Length* divides the examples into $[e_1, e_3, e_4, e_6, e_9, e_{10}, e_{12}]$ and $[e_2, e_5, e_7, e_8, e_{11}, e_{13}, e_{14}, e_{15}, e_{16}, e_{17}, e_{18}]$. The former all agree on the value of *User_action* and predict with probability 1. The user action divides the second set 9 : 2, and so the mean log loss is

$$
-(7 * \log_2 1 + 9 * \log_2 9/11 + 2 * \log_2 2/11)/18 \approx 7.5/18 \approx 0.417.
$$

Therefore, splitting on *Length* is better than splitting on *Thread* or *Author*, when greedily optimizing the log loss.

## Constructing Conditions

In the decision tree learning algorithm (Figure 7.9), Boolean input features can be used directly as the conditions. Non-Boolean input features are handled in a number of ways.

- Suppose input variable $X$ is categorical, with domain $\{v_1, \ldots, v_k\}$. A binary **indicator variable** (page 182), $X_i$, can be associated with each value $v_i$, where $X_i(e) = 1$ if $X(e) = v_i$ and $X_i(e) = 0$ otherwise. For each example $e$, exactly one of $X_1(e), \ldots, X_k(e)$ is 1 and the others are 0.
- When the domain of a feature is totally ordered, the feature is called an **ordinal feature**. This includes real-valued features as a special case, but might also include other features such as clothing sizes (S, M, L, XL, etc.), and highest level of education (none, primary, secondary, bachelor, etc.).

  For an ordinal input feature $X$ and for a given value $v$, a Boolean feature can be constructed as a **cut**: a new feature that has value 1 when $X > v$ and 0 otherwise. Combining cuts allows for features that are true for intervals; for example, a branch might include the conditions $X > 9$ is true and $X > 17$ is false, which corresponds to the interval $9 < X \leq 17$.

  Suppose the domain of input variable $X$ is totally ordered. To select the optimal value for the cut value $v$, sort the examples on the value of $X$ and sweep through the examples to consider each split value and select the best. See Exercise 7.8 (page 323).

- For ordinal features (including real-valued features), **binning** involves choosing a set of thresholds, creating a feature for each interval between the thresholds. The thresholds $\alpha_1 < \alpha_2 < \cdots < \alpha_k$, make $k + 1$ Boolean features, one that is true for $X$ when $X \le \alpha_1$, one for $\alpha_k < X$, and one for $\alpha_i < X \le \alpha_{i+1}$ for each $i \le i < k$. A bin of the form $\alpha_i < X \le \alpha_{i+1}$ would require two splits to represent using cuts. The $\alpha_i$ can be chosen upfront, for example, using percentiles of the training data, or chosen depending on the target.
- For categorical feature $X$, there might be a better split of the form $X \in S$ where $S$ is a set of values, rather than only splitting on a single value, as is done with indicator variables. When the target $Y$ is Boolean, to find an appropriate set $S$, sort the values of $X$ by the proportion of $Y$ that are true; a greedy optimal split will be between values in this sorted list.
- It is possible to expand the algorithm to allow multiway splits. To split on a multivalued variable, there would be a child for each value in the domain of the variable. This means that the representation of the decision tree becomes more complicated than the simple if–then–else form used for binary features. There are two main problems with this approach. The first is what to do with values of a feature for which there are no training examples. The second is that for most greedy splitting heuristics, including information gain, it is generally better to split on a variable with a larger domain because it produces more children and so can fit the data better than splitting on a feature with a smaller domain. However, splitting on a feature with a smaller domain keeps the representation more compact. A four-way split, for example, is equivalent to three binary splits; they both result in four leaves.

### Alternative Design Choices

The algorithm does not split when *select_split* returns *None*. This occurs when there are no examples, when there are no conditions remaining, when all examples have the same value on each condition, when all of the examples have the same target value, and when the improvement of the evaluation is less than the parameter $\gamma$. A number of other criteria have been suggested for stopping earlier.

- Minimum child size: do not split more if one of the children will have fewer examples than a threshold.
- Maximum depth: do not split more if the depth reaches a maximum.

It is possible that one condition may only work well in conjunction with other conditions, and the greedy method may not work when this occurs. One particularly tricky case is a parity function of $k$ Boolean variables that is true if an odd (or even) number of variables are true; knowing the values of fewer than $k$ of the variables gives no information about the value of the parity function. The simplest parity functions (for $k = 2$) are exclusive-or and equivalence. Parity functions have complicated decision trees.

In some cases, greedy splitting does not find a simplest decision tree and it is often useful to simplify the tree resulting from the top-down algorithm, as shown in the following example.

**Example 7.11** Consider a dataset with inputs $x$, $y$, and $z$ and target $t$. The target is true if $x$ is true and $y$ is true, or $x$ is false and $z$ is true. Figure 7.10 (a) shows a tree representation of this function. This tree can generate the data in the center (b). Although the simplest tree first splits on $x$, splitting on $x$ provides no information; there is the same proportion of $t$ true when $x$ is true as when $x$ is false. Instead, the algorithm can split on $y$. When $y$ is true, there is a larger proportion of $t$ true than when $y$ is false. For the case where $y$ is true, splitting on $x$ perfectly predicts the target when $x$ is true. The resulting tree is given in Figure 7.10(c). Following the paths to $t=1$, this tree corresponds to $t$ being true when $(x \wedge y) \vee (y \wedge \neg x \wedge z) \vee (\neg y \wedge \neg x \wedge z)$, which can be simplified to $(x \wedge y) \vee (\neg x \wedge z)$. This is essentially the original tree.

## 7.3.2 Linear Regression and Classification

Linear functions provide a basis for many learning algorithms. This section first covers regression, then considers classification.

**Linear regression** is the problem of fitting a linear function to a set of training examples, in which the input and target features are real numbers.

Suppose the input features, $X_1, \ldots, X_m$, are all real numbers (which includes the $\{0, 1\}$ case) and there is a single target feature $Y$. A **linear function** of the

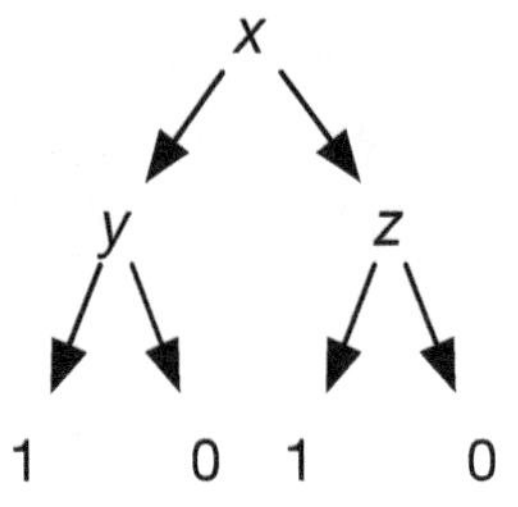


| $x$ | $y$ | $z$ | $t$ |
|---|---|---|---|
| 0 | 0 | 0 | 0 |
| 0 | 0 | 1 | 1 |
| 0 | 1 | 0 | 0 |
| 0 | 1 | 1 | 1 |
| 1 | 0 | 0 | 0 |
| 1 | 0 | 1 | 0 |
| 1 | 1 | 0 | 1 |
| 1 | 1 | 1 | 1 |

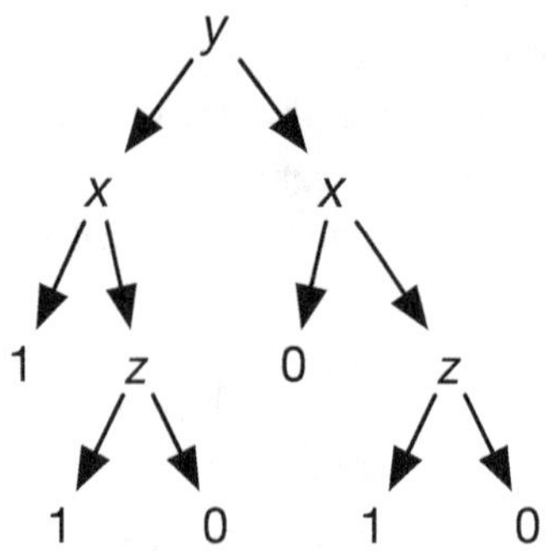


(a) (b) (c)

Figure 7.10: Generator, training data, and learned tree for "if $x$ then $t=y$ else $t=z$". In the decision trees, the left branches correspond to "true" and the right branches to "false". The prediction for $t$ is at the leaves input features is a function of the form

$$\begin{aligned}\widehat{Y}^{\overline{w}}(e) &= w_0 + w_1 * X_1(e) + \cdots + w_m * X_m(e)\\ &= \sum_{i=0}^{m} w_i * X_i(e)\end{aligned}$$

where $\overline{w} = \langle w_0, w_1, \ldots, w_n \rangle$ is a vector (tuple) of **weights**, and $X_0$ is a special feature whose value is always 1.

Suppose $Es$ is a set of examples. The mean squared loss (page 270) on examples $Es$ for target $Y$ is the error

$$\begin{aligned}error(Es, \overline{w}) &= \frac{1}{|Es|} \sum_{e \in Es} (\widehat{Y}^{\overline{w}}(e) - Y(e))^2\\ &= \frac{1}{|Es|} \sum_{e \in Es} \left( \sum_{i=0}^{m} w_i * X_i(e) - Y(e) \right)^2 . \qquad (7.1)\end{aligned}$$

Consider minimizing the mean squared loss. There is a unique minimum, which occurs when the partial derivatives with respect to the weights are all zero. The partial derivative of the error in Equation (7.1) with respect to weight $w_i$ is

$$\frac{\partial}{\partial w_i} error(Es, \overline{w}) = \frac{1}{|Es|} \sum_{e \in Es} 2 * \delta(e) * X_i(e) \qquad (7.2)$$

where $\delta(e) = \widehat{Y}^{\overline{w}}(e) - Y(e)$, a linear function of the weights. The weights that minimize the error can be computed analytically by setting the partial derivatives to zero and solving the resulting linear equations in the weights (see Exercise 7.11 (page 324)).

### Squashed Linear Functions

Consider binary classification, where the domain of the target variable is $\{0, 1\}$.

A linear function does not work well for such classification tasks; a learner should never make a prediction greater than 1 or less than 0. However, a linear function could make a prediction of, say, 3 for one example just to fit other examples better.

A **squashed linear function** is of the form

$$\begin{aligned}\widehat{Y}^{\overline{w}}(e) &= \phi(w_0 + w_1 * X_1(e) + \cdots + w_m * X_m(e))\\ &= \phi(\sum_{i} w_i * X_i(e))\end{aligned}$$

where $\phi$, an **activation function**, is a function from the real line $[-\infty, \infty]$ into some subset of the real line, such as $[0, 1]$.

A prediction based on a squashed linear function is a **linear classifier**.

One differentiable activation function is the **sigmoid** or **logistic function**:

$$sigmoid(x) = \frac{1}{1 + exp(-x)}$$

where $exp(v) = e^v$, where $e$ is Euler's number (approximately 2.718). The sigmoid function, depicted in Figure 7.11, squashes the real line into the interval $(0, 1)$, which is appropriate for classification because you would never want to make a prediction of greater than 1 or less than 0. The sigmoid function can be justified in terms of probabilities (page 400). It is also differentiable, with derivative

$$\frac{d}{dx} sigmoid(x) = sigmoid(x) * (1 - sigmoid(x)).$$

The problem of determining weights for the sigmoid of a linear function that minimize an error on a set of examples is called **logistic regression**.

The mean **log loss** (page 276) for logistic regression is

$$LL(E, \overline{w}) = -\frac{1}{|Es|} * \sum_{e \in Es} \left( Y(e) * \log \widehat{Y}(e) + (1 - Y(e)) * \log(1 - \widehat{Y}(e)) \right)$$

where $\widehat{Y}(e) = sigmoid \left( \sum_{i=0}^{m} w_i * X_i(e) \right)$. To minimize this, consider weight $w_i$. The partial derivative with respect to weight $w_i$ is

$$\frac{\partial}{\partial w_i} LL(E, \overline{w}) = \frac{1}{|Es|} \sum_{e \in E} \delta(e) * X_i(e) \tag{7.3}$$

where $\delta(e) = \widehat{Y^{\overline{w}}}(e) - Y(e)$. This is very similar to Equation (7.2) (page 289), the main difference is the definition of the predicted value. Unlike Equation (7.2) (page 289), this is not a linear function of the parameters (because $\widehat{Y^{\overline{w}}}(e)$ is not linear in the parameters) and is difficult to solve analytically.

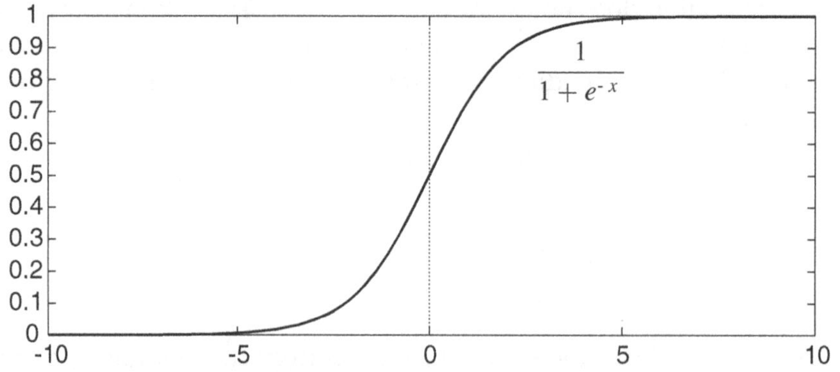


Figure 7.11: The sigmoid or logistic function

### Stochastic Gradient Descent

The problem of finding a set of parameters to minimize errors is an optimization problem; see Section 4.8 (page 161).

**Gradient descent** (page 169) is an iterative method to find a local minimum of a function. To find a set of weights to minimize an error, it starts with an initial set of weights. In each step, it decreases each weight in proportion to its partial derivative:

$$w_i := w_i - \eta * \frac{\partial}{\partial w_i} error(Es, \overline{w})$$

where $\eta$, the gradient descent step size, is called the **learning rate**. The learning rate, as well as the features and the data, is given as input to the learning algorithm. The partial derivative specifies how much a small change in the weight would change the error.

For linear regression with squared error and logistic regression with log loss, the derivatives, given in Equation (7.2) (page 289) and Equation (7.3) (page 290). For each of these (ignoring the constant factor of 2), gradient descent has the update

$$w_i := w_i - \eta * \frac{1}{|Es|} * \sum_{e \in Es} \delta(e) * X_i(e) \tag{7.4}$$

where $\delta(e) = \widehat{Y}^{\overline{w}}(e) - Y(e)$.

A direct implementation of gradient descent does not update any weights until all examples have been considered. This can be very wasteful for large datasets. It is possible to make progress with a subset of the data. This gradient descent step takes a mean value. Often you can compute means approximately by using a random sample of examples. For example, you can get a good estimate of the mean height of a large population of people by selecting 100 or 1000 people at random and using their mean height.

Instead of using all of the data for an update, **stochastic gradient descent** uses a random sample of examples to update the weights. It is called stochastic because of the random sampling. Random sampling is explored more in Section 9.7 (page 436). The set of $b$ examples used in each update is called a **minibatch** or a **batch**.

The stochastic gradient descent algorithm for logistic regression is shown in Figure 7.12 (page 292). This returns a function, *pred*, that can be used for predictions on new examples. The algorithm collects the update for each weight $w_i$ for a batch in a corresponding $d_i$, and updates the weights after each batch. The learning rate $\eta$ is assumed to be per example, and so the update needs to be divided by the batch size.

An **epoch** is $\lceil |Es|/b \rceil$ batches, which corresponds to one pass through all of the data, on average. Epochs are useful when reporting results, particularly with different batch sizes.

**Example 7.12** Consider learning a squashed linear function for classifying the data of Figure 7.1 (page 268). One function that correctly classifies the examples is

$$\widehat{Reads}(e) = sigmoid(-8 + 7 * Short(e) + 3 * New(e) + 3 * Known(e)),$$

where $f$ is the sigmoid function. A function similar to this can be found with about 3000 iterations of stochastic gradient descent with a learning rate $\eta = 0.05$. According to this function, $\widehat{Reads}(e)$ is true (the predicted value for example $e$ is closer to 1 than 0) if and only if $Short(e)$ is true and either $New(e)$ or $Known(e)$ is true. Thus, in this case, the linear classifier learns the same function as the decision tree learner.

Smaller batch sizes tend to learn faster as fewer examples are required for

```
procedure Linear_learner(Xs, Y, Es, η, m)
    Inputs
        Xs: set of input features, Xs = {X_1, ..., X_m}. Assume X_0 = 1
        Y: target feature
        Es: set of training examples
        η: learning rate
        b: batch size
    Output
        function to make prediction on examples
    Local
        w_0, ..., w_m: real numbers
        d_0, ..., d_m: real numbers
    initialize w_0, ..., w_m randomly
    define pred(e) = φ(Σ_i w_i * X_i(e))
    repeat
        for each i ∈ [0, n] do
            d_i := 0
        select batch B ⊆ Es of size b
        for each example e in B do
            error := pred(e) − Y(e)
            for each i ∈ [0, n] do
                d_i := d_i + error * X_i(e)
        for each i ∈ [0, n] do
            w_i := w_i − η * d_i / b
    until termination
    return pred
```

Figure 7.12: Stochastic gradient descent for linear and logistic regression. For linear regression, $\phi$ is the identity function. For logistic regression, $\phi$ is *sigmoid* an update. However, smaller batches may not converge to a local optimum solution, whereas more data, up to all of the data, will. To see this, consider being at an optimum. A batch containing all of the examples would end up with all of the $d_i$ being zero. However, for smaller batches, the weights will vary and later batches will be using non-optimal parameter settings and so use incorrect derivatives. It is common to start with small batch size and increase the batch size until convergence, or good enough performance has been obtained.

**Incremental gradient descent**, or **online gradient descent**, is a special case of stochastic gradient descent using minibatches of size 1. In this case, there is no need to store the intermediate values in $d_i$, but the weights can be directly updated. This is sometimes used for streaming data where each example is used once and then discarded. If the examples are not selected at random, it can suffer from **catastrophic forgetting**, where it fits the later data and forgets about earlier examples.

### Linear Separability

Each input feature can be seen as a dimension; $m$ features results in an $m$-dimensional space. A **hyperplane** in an $m$-dimensional space is a set of points that all satisfy a constraint that some linear function of the variables is zero. The hyperplane forms an $(m-1)$-dimensional space. For example, in a (two-dimensional) plane, a hyperplane is a line, and in a three-dimensional space, a hyperplane is a plane. A Boolean classification is **linearly separable** if there exists a hyperplane where the classification is true on one side of the hyperplane and false on the other side.

The *Logistic_regression_learner* algorithm can learn any linearly separable binary classification. The error can be made arbitrarily small for arbitrary sets of examples if, and only if, the target classification is linearly separable. The hyperplane is the set of points where $\sum_i w_i * X_i = 0$ for the learned weights $\overline{w}$. On one side of this hyperplane, the prediction is greater than 0.5; on the other side, the prediction is less than 0.5.

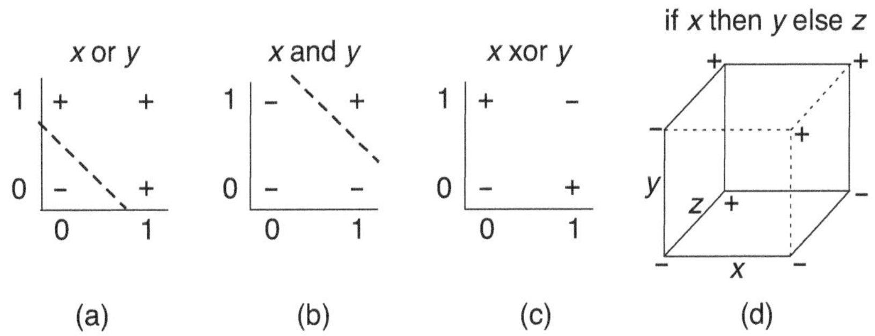


Figure 7.13: Linear separators for Boolean functions

**Example 7.13** Figure 7.13 (page 293) shows linear separators for "or" (a) and "and" (b). The dashed line separates the positive (true) cases from the negative (false) cases. One simple function that is not linearly separable is the **exclusive-or** (xor) function (c). There is no straight line that separates the positive examples from the negative examples. As a result, a linear classifier cannot represent, and therefore cannot learn, the exclusive-or function.

Suppose there are three input features $x$, $y$, and $z$, each with domain $\{0,1\}$, and the ground truth is the function "if $x$ then $y$ else $z$" (represented by $t$ in Figure 7.10 (page 288)). This function is depicted by the cube in Figure 7.13(d) with the origin ($x$, $y$, $z$ all zero) at the bottom left and the ground truth for $t$ labelled with $+$ and $-$. This function is not linearly separable.

The following example shows what happens in gradient descent for logistic regression when the data is not linearly separable.

**Example 7.14** Consider target $t$ from the previous example that is true if $x$ is true and $y$ is true, or $x$ is false and $z$ is true. The prediction of $t$ is not linearly separable, as shown in Figure 7.13(d) – there is no hyperplane that separates the positive and negative cases of $t$.

After 1000 epochs of gradient descent with a learning rate of 0.05, one run found the following weights (to two decimal points):

$$\begin{aligned} lin(e) &= -0.12 * x(e) + 4.06 * y(e) + 4.06 * z(e) - 3.98 \\ \widehat{t}(e) &= sigmoid(lin(e)) \,. \end{aligned}$$

The linear function $lin$ and the prediction for each example are shown in Figure 7.14(b). Four examples are predicted reasonably well, and the other four are predicted with a value of approximately 0.5. This function is quite stable with different initializations. Increasing the number of iterations makes the predictions approach 0, 1, or 0.5.

| $x$ | $y$ | $z$ | $t$ |
|---|---|---|---|
| 0 | 0 | 0 | 0 |
| 0 | 0 | 1 | 1 |
| 0 | 1 | 0 | 0 |
| 0 | 1 | 1 | 1 |
| 1 | 0 | 0 | 0 |
| 1 | 0 | 1 | 0 |
| 1 | 1 | 0 | 1 |
| 1 | 1 | 1 | 1 |

(a)

| $lin$ | $\widehat{t}$ |
|---|---|
| −3.98 | 0.02 |
| 0.08 | 0.52 |
| 0.08 | 0.52 |
| 4.14 | 0.98 |
| −4.10 | 0.02 |
| −0.04 | 0.49 |
| −0.04 | 0.49 |
| 4.14 | 0.98 |

(b)

Figure 7.14: Logistic regression for conditional; target $t$ is "if $x$ then $t=y$ else $t=z$" (a) training data (b) prediction

### Categorical Target Features

When the domain of the target variable is categorical with more than two values, indicator variables (page 286) can be used to convert the classification to binary variables. These binary variables could be learned separately. Because exactly one of the values must be true for each example, the predicted probabilities should add to 1. One way to handle this is to learn for all-but-one value, and predict the remaining value as 1 minus the sum of the other values. This is effectively how the binary case works. However, this introduces an asymmetry in the values by treating one value differently from the other values. This is problematic because the errors for the other values accumulate, making for a poor prediction on the value treated specially; it's even possible that the prediction for the remaining value is negative if the others sum to more than 1.

The standard alternative is to learn a linear function for each value of the target variable, exponentiate, and normalize. This has more parameters than necessary to represent the function (it is said to be **over-parametrized**) but treats all of the values in the same way. Suppose the target $Y$ is categorical with domain represented by the tuple of values $(v_1, \ldots, v_k)$. The **softmax** function takes a vector (tuple) of real numbers, $(\alpha_1, \ldots, \alpha_k)$, and returns a vector of the same size, where the $i$th component of the result is

$$softmax((\alpha_1, \ldots, \alpha_k))_i = \frac{exp(\alpha_i)}{\sum_{j=1}^{k} exp(\alpha_j)}.$$

This ensures that the resulting values are all positive and sum to 1, and so can be considered as a probability distribution.

Sigmoid and softmax are closely related:

$$\begin{aligned} sigmoid(x) &= \frac{1}{exp(-x)+1} \\ &= \frac{exp(x)}{exp(0)+exp(x)} \\ &= softmax((0,x))_2 \end{aligned}$$

where $(0, x)$ corresponds to the values $(false, true)$ and $softmax((0, x))_2$ is the second component of the pair that results from the softmax. The second equality follows from multiplying the numerator and the denominator by $exp(x)$, and noticing that $exp(x) * exp(-x) = exp(0) = 1$. Thus, *sigmoid* is equivalent to *softmax* where the false component is fixed to be 0.

A softmax, like a sigmoid, cannot represent zero probabilities.

The generalization of logistic regression to predicting a categorical feature is called **softmax regression**, **multinomial logistic regression**, or **multinomial logit**. It involves a linear equation for each value in the domain of the target variable, $Y$. Suppose $Y$ has domain $(v_i, \ldots, v_k)$. The prediction for example $e$ is a tuple of $k$ values, $softmax((u_1(e), \ldots, u_k(e)))$, where the $j$th component is the prediction for $Y = v_j$ and

$$u_j(e) = w_{0,j} + X_1(e) * w_{1,j} * + \cdots + X_m(e) * w_{m,j}.$$

This is typically optimized with categorical log loss (page 273).

Consider weight $w_{ij}$ that is used for input $X_i$ for output value $v_j$, and example $e$ that has $Y(e) = v_q$:

$$\begin{aligned}
&\frac{\partial}{\partial w_{ij}} logloss(softmax((u_1(e), \ldots, u_k(e))), v_q) \\
&= \frac{\partial}{\partial w_{ij}} - \log\left(\frac{exp(u_q(e))}{\sum_j exp(u_j(e))}\right) \\
&= \frac{\partial}{\partial w_{ij}} (\log(\sum_j exp(u_j(e))) - u_q(e)) \\
&= ((\widehat{Y}(e))_j - \mathbf{1}(j = q)) * X_i
\end{aligned}$$

where $\mathbf{1}(j = q)$ is 1 if $j$ is the index of the observed value, $v_q$, and $(\widehat{Y}(e))_j$ is the $j$th component of the prediction. This is the predicted value minus the actual value.

To implement this effectively, you need to consider how computers represent numbers. Taking the exponential of a large number can result in a number larger than the largest number able to be represented on the computer, resulting in **overflow**. For example, $exp(800)$ will overflow for most modern CPUs. Taking exponentials of a large negative number can result in a number that is represented as zero, resulting in **underflow**. For example, $exp(-800)$ results in zero on many CPUs. Adding a constant to each $\alpha_i$ in a softmax does not change the value of the softmax. To prevent overflow and prevent all values from underflowing, the maximum value can be subtracted from each value, so there is always a zero, and the rest are negative. On GPUs and similar parallel hardware, often lower precision is used to represent weights, and so it becomes more important to correct for underflow and overflow.

When there is a large number of possible values, the computation of the denominator can be expensive, as it requires summing over all values. For example, in natural language, we may want to predict the next word in a text, in which case the number of values could be up to a million or more (particularly when phrases and names such as "Mahatma Gandhi" are included). In this case, it is possible to represent the prediction in terms of a binary tree of the values, forming **hierarchical softmax**. This implements the same function as softmax, just more efficiently for large domains.

### Creating Input Features

The definitions of linear and logistic regression assume that the input features are numerical.

Categorical features can be converted into features with domain $\{0, 1\}$ by using **indicator variables**, as was done for decision tree learning (page 286). This is known as a **one-hot encoding**.

A real-valued feature can be used directly as long as the target is a linear function of that input feature, when the other input features are fixed. If the target is not a linear function, often some transformation of the feature is used to create new features.

For **ordinal features**, including real-valued features, **cuts** (page 286) can be used to define a Boolean feature from a real feature. For input feature $x$, choose a value $v$ and use a feature that is true if $x > v$, or equivalently $x - v > 0$. It is also common to use **binning** (page 287). Binning involves choosing a set of thresholds, $\alpha_1 < \alpha_2 < \cdots < \alpha_k$, and using a feature with domain $\{0, 1\}$ for each interval between $\alpha_i$ and $\alpha_{i+1}$. Binning allows for a piecewise constant function. Constructing a feature using $max(x - v, 0)$ allows for a connected piecewise linear approximation; this is the basis of the **rectified linear unit (ReLU)**, further investigated in the next chapter (page 330).

Designing appropriate features is called **feature engineering**. It is often difficult to design good features. Gradient-boosted trees (page 311) use conjunctions of input features. Learning features is part of **representation learning**; see Chapter 8.

## 7.4 Overfitting

**Overfitting** occurs when the learner makes predictions based on regularities that appear in the training examples but do not appear in the test examples or in the world from which the data is taken. It typically happens when the model tries to find signal in randomness – spurious correlations in the training data that are not reflected in the problem domain as a whole – or when the learner becomes overconfident in its model. This section outlines methods to detect and avoid overfitting.

The following example shows a practical example of overfitting.

**Example 7.15** Consider a website where people submit ratings for restaurants from 1 to 5 stars. Suppose the website designers would like to display the best restaurants, which are those restaurants that future patrons would like the most. It is tempting to return the restaurants with the highest mean rating, but that does not work.

It is extremely unlikely that a restaurant that has many ratings, no matter how outstanding it is, will have a mean of 5 stars, because that would require all of the ratings to be 5 stars. However, given that 5-star ratings are not that uncommon, it would be quite likely that a restaurant with just one rating will have 5 stars. If the designers used the mean rating, the top-rated restaurants will be ones with very few ratings, and these are unlikely to be the best restaurants. Similarly, restaurants with few ratings but all low are unlikely to be as bad as the ratings indicate.

The phenomenon that extreme predictions will not perform as well on test cases is analogous to **regression to the mean**. Regression to the mean was discovered by Galton [1886], who called it *regression to mediocrity*, after discovering that the offspring of plants with larger than average seeds are more like average seeds than their parents are. In both the restaurant and the seed cases, this occurs because ratings, or the size, will be a mix of quality and luck (e.g., who gave the rating or what genes the seeds had). Restaurants that have a very high rating will have to be high in quality and be lucky (and be very lucky if the quality is not very high). More data averages out the luck; it is very unlikely that someone's luck does not run out. Similarly, the seed offspring do not inherit the part of the size of the seed that was due to random fluctuations.

Overfitting can also be caused by **model complexity**: a more complex model, with more parameters, can almost always fit data better than a simple model.

**Example 7.16** A polynomial of degree $k$ is of the form

$$y = w_0 + w_1 * x + w_2 * x^2 + \cdots + w_k * x^k.$$

Linear regression can be used unchanged to learn the weights of the polynomial that minimize the squared error, simply by using $1, x, x^2, \ldots, x^k$ as the input features to predict $y$.

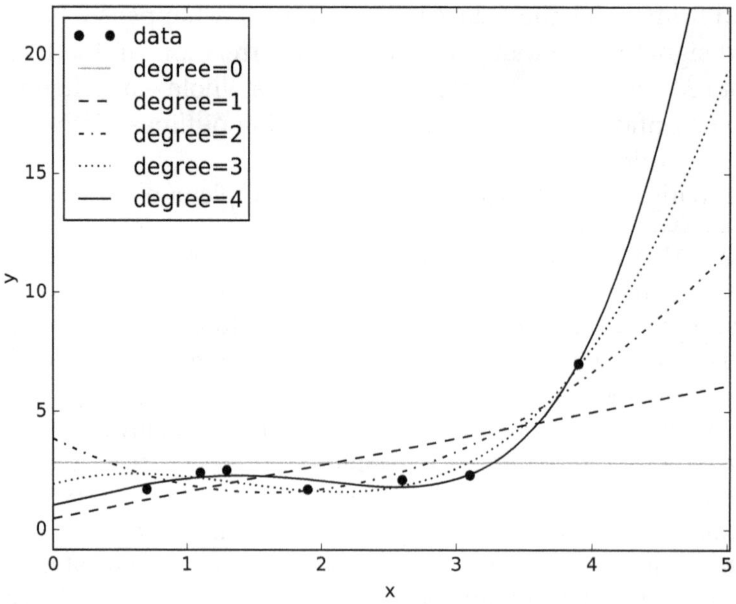


Figure 7.15: Fitting polynomials to the data of Figure 7.2 (page 268)

Figure 7.15 (page 298) shows polynomials up to degree 4 for the data of Figure 7.2 (page 268). Higher-order polynomials can fit the data better than lower-order polynomials, but that does not make them better on the test set.

Notice how the higher-order polynomials get more extreme in extrapolation. All of the polynomials, except the degree 0 polynomials, go to plus or minus infinity as $x$ gets bigger or smaller, which is almost never what you want. Moreover, if the maximum value of $k$ for which $w_k \neq 0$ is even, then as $x$ approaches plus or minus infinity, the predictions will have the same sign, going to either plus infinity or minus infinity. The degree-4 polynomial in the figure approaches $\infty$ as $x$ approaches $-\infty$, which does not seem reasonable given the data. If the maximum value of $k$ for which $w_k \neq 0$ is odd, then as $x$ approaches plus or minus infinity, the predictions will have opposite signs.

Example 7.15 (page 297) shows how more data can allow for better predictions. Example 7.16 (page 298) shows how complex models can lead to overfitting the data. Given a fixed dataset, the problem arises as to how to make predictions that make good predictions on test sets.

The test set error is caused by bias, variance, and/or noise:

- **Bias**, the error due to the algorithm finding an imperfect model. The bias is low when the model learned is close to the **ground truth**, the process in the world that generated the data. The bias can be divided into **representation bias** caused by the representation not containing a hypothesis close to the ground truth, and a **search bias** caused by the algorithm not searching enough of the space of hypotheses to find the best hypothesis. For example, with discrete features, a decision tree can represent any function, and so has a low representation bias. With a large number of features, there are too many decision trees to search systematically, and decision tree learning can have a large search bias. Linear regression, if solved directly using the analytic solution, has a large representation bias and zero search bias. There would also be a search bias if the gradient descent algorithm was used.

- **Variance**, the error due to a lack of data. A more complicated model, with more parameters to tune, will require more data. Thus, with a fixed amount of data, there is a **bias–variance trade-off**; you can have a complicated model which could be accurate, but you do not have enough data to estimate it appropriately (with low bias and high variance), or a simpler model that cannot be accurate, but you can estimate the parameters reasonably well given the data (with high bias and low variance).

- **Noise**, the inherent error due to the data depending on features not modeled or because the process generating the data is inherently stochastic.

Overfitting results in **overconfidence**, where the learner is more confident in its prediction than the data warrants. For example, in the predictions in Figure 7.14 (page 294), trained on eight examples, the probabilities are much more extreme than could be justified by eight examples. The first prediction, that there is approximately 2% chance of $t$ being true when $x$, $y$, and $z$ are false, does not seem to be reasonable given only one example of this case. As the search proceeds, it becomes even more confident. This overconfidence is reflected in test error, as in the following example.

**Example 7.17** Figure 7.16 shows a typical plot of how the training and test errors change with the number of iterations of gradient descent. The error on the training set decreases as the number of iterations increases. For the test set, the error reaches a minimum and then increases as the number of iterations increases. As it overfits to the training examples, errors in the test set become bigger because it becomes more confident in its imperfect model.

The following sections discuss three ways to avoid overfitting. The first, pseudocounts, explicitly allows for regression to the mean, and can be used for cases where the representations are simple. The second, regularization, pro-

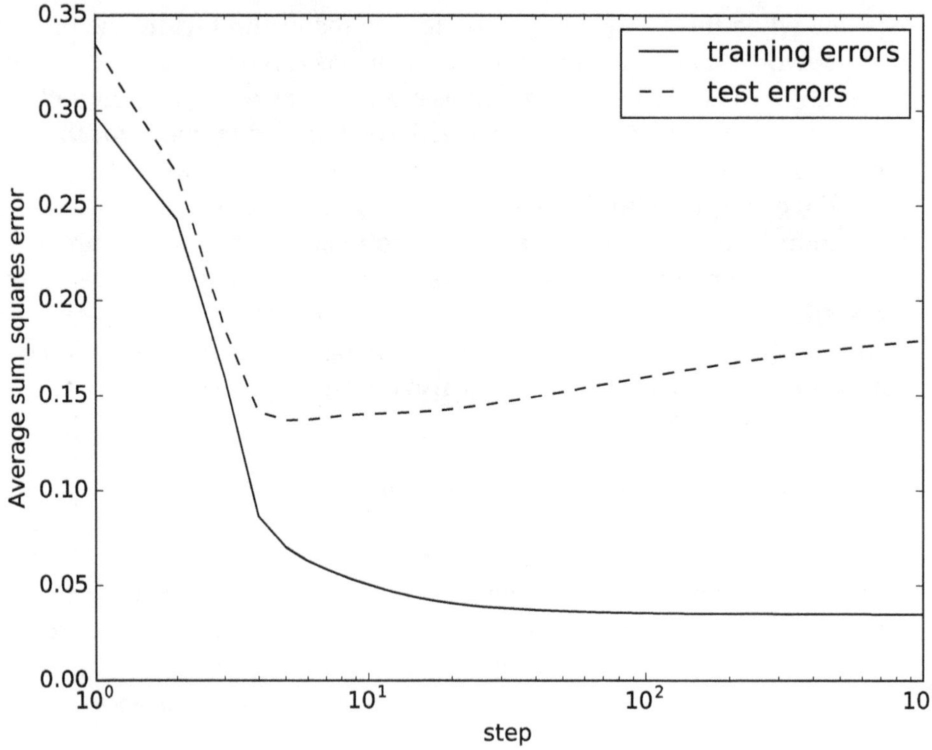


Figure 7.16: Training and test set error as a function of number of steps. On the $x$-axis is the step count of a run of a learner using gradient descent. On the $y$-axis is the mean squared error (the squared error divided by the number of examples) for the training set (solid line) and the test set (dashed line)

vides an explicit trade-off between model complexity and fitting the data. The third, cross validation, is to use some of the training data to detect overfitting.

### 7.4.1 Pseudocounts

For many of the prediction measures, the optimal prediction on the training data is the mean. In the case of Boolean data (assuming true is represented as 1, and false as 0), the mean can be interpreted as a probability. However, the empirical mean, the mean of the training set, is typically not a good estimate of the probability of new cases, as was shown in Example 7.15 (page 297).

A simple way both to solve the zero-probability problem and to take prior knowledge into account is to use **pseudo-examples**, which are added to the given examples. The number of pseudo-examples used is a nonnegative **pseudocount** or **prior count**, which is not necessarily an integer.

Suppose the examples are values $v_1, \ldots, v_n$ and you want to make a prediction for the next $v$, written as $\widehat{v}$. When $n = 0$, assume you use prediction $a_0$ (which you cannot get from data as there are no data for this case). For the other cases, use

$$\widehat{v} = \frac{c * a_0 + \sum_i v_i}{c + n}$$

where $c$ is a nonnegative real-value constant, which is the number of assumed fictional data points. This is assuming there are $c$ pseudo-examples, each with a value of $a_0$. The count $c$ does not have to be an integer, but can be any nonnegative real value. If $c = 0$, the prediction is the mean value, but that prediction cannot be used when there is no data (when $n = 0$). The value of $c$ controls the relative importance of the initial hypothesis (the **prior**) and the data.

**Example 7.18** Consider how to better estimate the ratings of restaurants in Example 7.15 (page 297). The aim is to predict the mean rating over the test data, not the mean rating of the seen ratings.

You can use the existing data about other restaurants to make estimates about the new cases, assuming that the new cases are like the old. Before seeing anything, it may be reasonable to use the mean rating of the restaurants as the value for $a_0$. This would be like assuming that a new restaurant is like an average restaurant (which may or may not be a good assumption). Suppose you are most interested in being accurate for top-rated restaurants. To estimate $c$, consider a restaurant with a single 5-star rating. You could expect this rating to be like other 5-star ratings. Let $a'$ be the mean rating of the restaurants with 5-star ratings (where the mean is weighted by the number of 5-star ratings each restaurant has). This is an estimate of the restaurant quality for a random 5-star rating by a user, and so may be reasonable for the restaurant with a single 5-star rating. In the equation above, with $n = 1$ and $\sum_i v_i = 5$, this gives $a' = (c * a_0 + 5)/(c + 1)$. Solving for $c$ gives $c = (5 - a')/(a' - a_0)$.

Suppose the mean rating for all restaurants ($a_0$) is 3, and the mean rating for the restaurants with a 5-star rating $a'$ is 4.5. Then $c = 1/3$. If the mean for restaurants with 5-star ratings was instead 3.5, then $c$ would be 3. See Exercise 7.13 (page 324).

Section 17.2.1 (page 734) shows how to do better than this by taking into account the other ratings of the person giving the rating.

Consider the following thought experiment (or, better yet, implement it):

- Select a number $p$ at random uniformly from the range $[0, 1]$. Suppose this is the ground truth for the probability that $Y = 1$ for a variable $Y$ with domain $\{0, 1\}$.

- Generate $n$ training examples with $P(Y=1) = p$. To do this, for each example, generate by a random number uniformly in range $[0, 1)$, and record $Y=1$ if the random number is less than $p$, and $Y=0$ otherwise. Let $n_1$ be the number of examples with $Y=1$ and so there are $n_0 = n - n_1$ samples with $Y=0$.

- Generate some (e.g., 10) test cases with the same $p$.

The learning problem for this scenario is: from $n_0$ and $n_1$ create the estimator $\widehat{p}$ with the smallest error on the test cases. If you try this for a number of values of $n$, such as $1, 2, 3, 4, 5, 10, 20, 100, 1000$ and repeat this 1000 times, you will get a good idea of what is going on.

With squared error or log loss, you will find that the empirical mean $\widehat{p} = n_1/(n_0 + n_1)$, which has the smallest error on the training set, works poorly on the test set, with the log loss typically being infinity. The log loss is infinity when one of 0 or 1 does not appear in the training set (so the corresponding $n_i$ is zero) but appears in the test set.

**Laplace smoothing**, defined by $\widehat{p} = (n_1 + 1)/(n_0 + n_1 + 2)$, has the smallest log loss and squared error of all estimators on the test set. This is equivalent to two pseudo-examples: one of 0 and one of 1. A theoretical justification for Laplace smoothing is presented in Section 10.2 (page 460). If $p$ were selected from some distribution other than the uniform distribution, Laplace smoothing may not result in the best predictor.

### 7.4.2 Regularization

**Ockham's razor** specifies that you should prefer simpler hypotheses over more complex ones. William of Ockham was an English philosopher who was born in about 1285 and died, apparently of the plague, in 1349. (Note that "Occam" is the French spelling of the English town "Ockham" and is often used.) He argued for economy of explanation: "What can be done with fewer [assumptions] is done in vain with more."

An alternative to optimizing fit-to-data is to optimize fit-to-data plus a term that rewards model simplicity and penalizes complexity. The penalty term is a **regularizer**.

The typical form for a regularizer is to find a predictor $\widehat{Y}$ to minimize

$$\left(\sum_e loss(\widehat{Y}(e), Y(e))\right) + \lambda * regularizer(\widehat{Y}) \tag{7.5}$$

where $loss(\widehat{Y}(e), Y(e))$ is the loss of example $e$ for predictor $\widehat{Y}$, which specifies how well $\widehat{Y}$ fits example $e$, and $regularizer(\widehat{Y})$ is a penalty term that penalizes complexity. The **regularization parameter**, $\lambda$, trades off fit-to-data and model simplicity. As the number of examples increases, the leftmost sum tends to dominate and the regularizer has little effect. The regularizer has most effect when there are few examples. The regularization parameter is needed because the error and complexity terms are typically in different units.

A **hyperparameter** is a parameter used to define what is being optimized, or how it is optimized. It can be chosen by prior knowledge, past experience with similar problems, or **hyperparameter tuning** to choose the best values using cross validation (page 304).

The regularization parameter, $\lambda$ above, is a hyperparameter. In learning a decision tree one complexity measure is the number of leaves in a decision tree (which is one more than the number of splits for a binary decision tree). When building a decision tree, you could optimize the sum of a loss plus a function of the size of the decision tree, minimizing

$$\left(\sum_{e \in Es} loss(\widehat{Y}(e), Y(e))\right) + \gamma * |tree|$$

where $|tree|$ is the number of leaves in a tree representation of $\widehat{Y}$. This uses $\gamma$ instead of $\lambda$, following the convention in gradient-boosted trees (see below). A single split on a leaf increases the number of leaves by 1. When splitting, a single split is worthwhile if it reduces the sum of losses by $\gamma$. This regularization is implemented in the decision tree learner (Figure 7.9 (page 284)).

For models where there are real-valued parameters, an ***L2* regularizer** penalizes the sum of squares of the parameters. To optimize the squared error for linear regression (page 288) with an *L2* regularizer, minimize

$$\left(\sum_{e \in Es} \left(Y(e) - \sum_{i=0}^{m} w_i * X_i(e)\right)^2\right) + \lambda \left(\sum_{i=0}^{m} w_i^2\right)$$

which is known as **ridge regression**. Note that this is equivalent to $\lambda$ pseudo-examples with a value of 0 for the target, and a value of 1 for each input feature.

It is possible to use multiple regularizers, for example including both $\gamma$ for tree size and $\lambda$ for *L2* regularization.

To optimize the log loss (page 276) error for logistic regression (page 290) with an *L2* regularizer, minimize

$$-\left(\sum_{e \in Es} \left(Y(e) \log \widehat{Y}(e) + (1 - Y(e)) \log(1 - \widehat{Y}(e))\right)\right) + \lambda \left(\sum_{i=0}^{m} w_i^2\right)$$

where $\widehat{Y}(e) = sigmoid\,(\sum_{i=0}^{m} w_i * X_i(e))$.

An $L2$ regularization is implemented for stochastic gradient descent by adding

$$w_i := w_i - \eta * \lambda * m/|Es| * w_i$$

after line 24 of Figure 7.12 (page 292) (in the scope of "for each"). The $m/|Es|$ is because the regularization is $\lambda$ for the whole dataset, but the update occurs for each batch. Note that $\eta * \lambda * m/|Es|$ changes rarely, if ever, and so can be stored until one of its constituents change.

An ***L*1 regularizer** adds a penalty for the sum of the absolute values of the parameters.

To optimize the squared error for linear regression (page 288) with an $L1$ regularizer, minimize

$$\left(\sum_{e \in Es}\left(Y(e) - \sum_{i=0}^{m} w_i * X_i(e)\right)^2\right) + \lambda\left(\sum_{i=0}^{m}|w_i|\right)$$

which is called **lasso** (least absolute shrinkage and selection operator).

Adding an $L1$ regularizer to the log loss entails minimizing

$$-\left(\sum_{e \in Es}\left(Y(e)\log\widehat{Y}(e) + (1 - Y(e))\log(1 - \widehat{Y}(e))\right)\right) + \lambda\left(\sum_{i=0}^{m}|w_i|\right).$$

The partial derivative of the sum of absolute values with respect to $w_i$ is the sign of $w_i$, either 1 or $-1$ (defined as $sign(w_i) = w_i/|w_i|$), at every point except at 0. You do not need to make a step at 0, because the value is already a minimum. To implement an $L1$ regularizer, each parameter is moved towards zero by a constant, except if that constant would change the sign of the parameter, in which case the parameter becomes zero. An $L1$ regularizer can be incorporated into the gradient descent algorithm of Figure 7.12 (page 292) by adding after line 24 (in the scope of "for each"):

$$w_i := sign(w_i) * max(0, |w_i| - \eta * \lambda * m/|Es|).$$

This is called **iterative soft-thresholding** and is a special case of the *proximal-gradient method*.

$L1$ regularization with many features tends to make many weights zero, which means the corresponding feature is ignored. This is a way to implement **feature selection**. An $L2$ regularizer tends to make all of the parameters smaller, but not zero.

### 7.4.3 Cross Validation

The problem with the previous methods is that they require a notion of simplicity to be known before the agent has seen any data. It would seem that an agent should be able to determine, from the training data, how complicated a model needs to be. Such a method could be used when the learning agent has no prior information about the world.

Figure 7.17 shows a general pattern for learning and evaluating learning algorithms. Recall (page 263) that you need to remove some of the examples as the test set and only ever use these for the final evaluation. The aim is to predict examples that the agent has not seen, and the test set acts as a surrogate for these unseen examples, and so cannot be used in any part of training.

The idea of **cross validation** is to use part of the non-test data as a surrogate for test data. In the simplest case, split the non-test data into two: a set of examples to train with, and a **validation set**, also called the **dev (development) set** or **holdout**. The agent uses the remaining examples as the training set to build models. The validation set can act as a surrogate for the test set in evaluating the predictions from the training set.

The evaluation of the validation set is used to choose **hyperparameters** of the learner. The **hyperparameters** are any choices that need to be made for the learner, including the choice of the learning algorithm, the values of regularization parameters, and other choices that affect the model learned.

Once the hyperparameters have been set, the whole non-test dataset can be used to build a predictor, which is evaluated on the test set.

To see how the validation error could be used, consider a graph such as

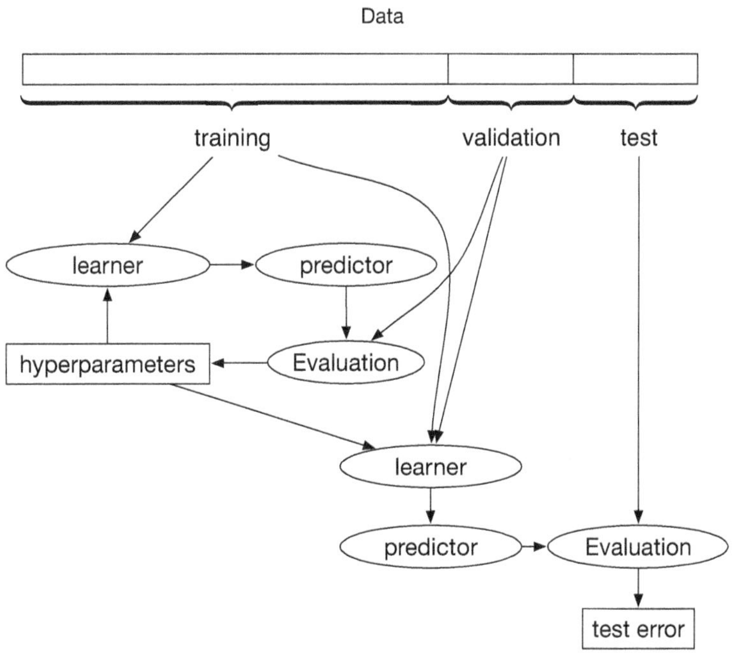


Figure 7.17: Using a validation set in learning

the one in Figure 7.16 (page 300), but where the test errors instead come from the validation set. The error on the training set gets smaller as the size of the tree grows. However, on the validation set (and the test set), the error typically improves for a while and then starts to get worse. The idea of cross validation is to choose a parameter setting or a representation in which the error of the validation set is a minimum. The hyperparameter here is how many steps to train for before returning a predictor. This is known as **early stopping**. The hypothesis is that the parameter setting where the validation set is a minimum is also where the error on the test set is a minimum.

Typically, you want to train on as many examples as possible, because then you get better models. However, a larger training set results in a smaller validation set, and a small validation set may or may not fit well just by luck.

To overcome this problem for small datasets, ***k*-fold cross validation** allows examples to be used for both training and validation, but still use all of the data for the final predictor. It has the following steps:

- Partition the non-test examples randomly into $k$ sets, of approximately equal size, called **folds**.
- To evaluate a parameter setting, train $k$ times for that parameter setting, each time using one of the folds as the validation set and the remaining folds for training. Thus each fold is used as a validation set exactly once. The accuracy is evaluated using the validation set. For example, if $k = 10$, then 90% of the training examples are used for training and 10% of the examples for validation. It does this 10 times, so each example is used once in a validation set.
- Optimize parameter settings based on the error on each example when it is used in the validation set.
- Return the model with the selected parameter settings, trained on all of the data.

**Example 7.19** One of the possible hyperparameters for the decision tree learner is the minimum number of examples that needs to be in a child, so the stopping criterion for the decision tree learner of Figure 7.9 (page 284) will be true if the number of examples in a child is less than *min_child_size*. If this threshold is too small, the decision tree learner will tend to overfit, and if it is too large, it will tend not to generalize. Figure 7.18 (page 307) shows the validation error for 5-fold cross validation as a function of the hyperparameter *min_child_size*. For each point on the $x$-axis, the decision tree was run five times, and the mean log loss was computed for the validation set. The error is at a minimum at 39, and so this is selected as the best value for this parameter. This plot also shows the error on the test set for trees with various settings for the minimum number of examples, and 39 is a reasonable parameter setting based on the test set. A learner does not get to see the error on the test set when selecting a predictor.

At one extreme, when $k$ is the number of training examples, $k$-fold cross validation becomes **leave-one-out cross validation**. With $m$ examples in the training set, it learns $m$ times; for each example $e$, it uses the other examples as training set, and evaluates on $e$. This is not practical if each training is done independently, because it increases the complexity by the number of training examples. However, if the model from one run can be adjusted quickly when one example is removed and another added, this can be very effective.

One special case is when the data is temporal and the aim is to extrapolate; to predict the future from the past. To work as a surrogate for predicting the future, the test set should be the latest examples. The validation set can then be the examples immediately before these. The analogy to leave-one-out cross validation is to learn each example using only examples before it.

The final predictor to be evaluated on the test can use all of the non-test examples in its predictions. This might mean adjusting some of the hyperparameters to account for the different size of the final training set.

## 7.5 Composite Models

Decision trees and (squashed) linear functions provide the basis for many other supervised learning techniques. Although decision trees can represent any discrete function, many simple functions have very complicated decision trees.

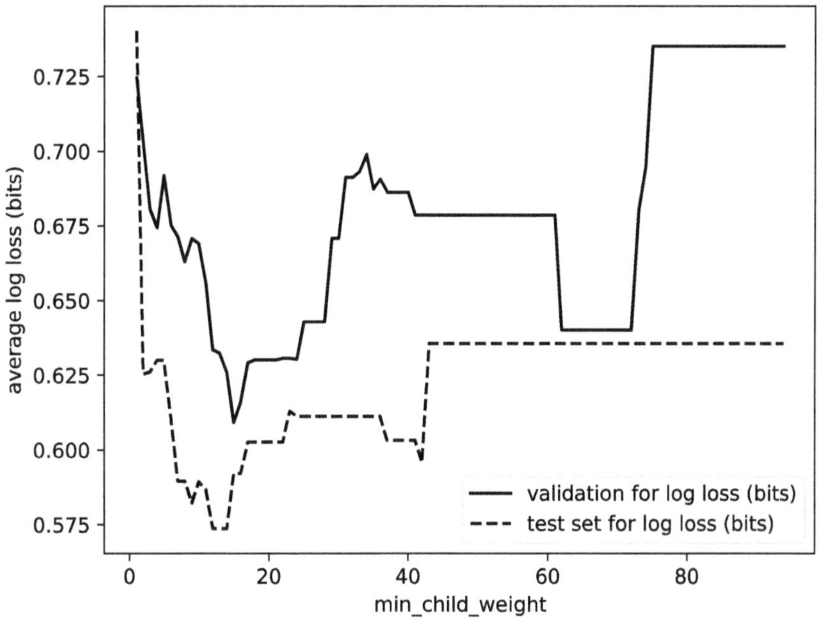


Figure 7.18: Validation error and test set error for determining the minimum number of examples in a child needed to split in a decision tree learner

Linear functions and linear classifiers (without inventing new features) are very restricted in what they can represent.

One way to make the linear function more powerful is to have the inputs to the linear function be some nonlinear function of the original inputs. Adding these new features can increase the dimensionality, making some functions that were not linear (or linearly separable) in the lower-dimensional space linear in the higher-dimensional space.

**Example 7.20** The exclusive-or function, $x_1$ xor $x_2$, is linearly separable in the space where the dimensions are $x_1$, $x_2$, and $x_1x_2$, where $x_1x_2$ is a feature that is true when both $x_1$ and $x_2$ are true. To visualize this, consider Figure 7.13(c); with the product as the third dimension, the top-right point will be lifted out of the page, allowing for a linear separator (in this case a plane) to go underneath.

A **kernel function** is a function that is applied to the input features to create new features. For example, a product of features could either replace or augment the existing features. Adding such features can allow for linear separators where there was none before. Another example is, for a feature $x$, adding $x^2$ and $x^3$ to the features allows a linear learner to find the best degree-3 polynomial fit. Note that when the feature space is augmented, overfitting can become more of a problem. The use of the term *kernel function* is often restricted to cases where learning in the augmented space can be implemented very efficiently, but that is beyond the scope of this book.

Neural networks (Chapter 8) allow the inputs to the (squashed) linear function to be a squashed linear function with weights to be tuned. Having multiple layers of squashed linear functions as inputs to (squashed) linear functions allows more complex functions to be represented.

Another nonlinear representation is a **regression tree**, which is a decision tree with a constant function at each leaf, which represents a **piecewise constant function**. A decision tree for regression with a linear function at each leaf represents a **piecewise linear function**. It is even possible to have neural networks or other classifiers at the leaves of the decision tree. To classify a new example, the example is filtered down the tree, and the classifier at the leaves is then used to classify the example.

Another possibility is to use a number of classifiers that have each been trained on the data and to combine their outputs using mode, median, or mean, depending on the loss function (see Figure 7.5 (page 277)). In **ensemble learning**, an agent takes a number of learners and combines their predictions to make a prediction for the ensemble. The algorithms being combined are called **base-level algorithms**.

One simple yet effective composite model is to have an ensemble of decision trees, known as a **random forest**. The idea is to have a number of decision trees, each of which can make a prediction on each example. Once the trees have been trained, the predictions on the trees are combined, using a method appropriate for the optimality criterion, such as the mode of the tree predictions for maximizing accuracy or the mean of the tree predictions for minimizing squared error or log loss.

In order to make this work effectively, the trees that make up the forest need to make diverse predictions. There are a number of ways that you can ensure diversity, including:

- Each tree could use a different subset of the examples to train on. If there are many examples, each tree could use just a random subset of them. In **bagging**, a random subset (with replacement) of $|Es|$ examples – the same size as the dataset – is selected for each tree to train on. In each of these sets, some examples are not chosen and some are duplicated. On average, each set contains about 63% of the original examples.

- A subset of the conditions could be used for each tree (or each split). Rather than considering all of the conditions when selecting a split, a random subset of them (e.g., a third of them) could be made available to split on.

### 7.5.1 Boosting

In **boosting**, there is a sequence of learners in which each one learns from the errors of the previous ones. The features of a boosting algorithm are:

- There is a sequence of **base learners** (that may be different from each other or the same as each other), such as small decision trees or (squashed) linear functions.

- Each learner is trained to fit the examples that the previous learners did not fit well.

- The final prediction uses a mix (e.g., sum, weighted mean, or mode) of the predictions of each learner.

The base learners can be **weak learners**, in that they do not need to be very good; they just need to be better than random. These weak learners are then boosted to be components in the ensemble that performs better than any of them.

A simple boosting algorithm is **functional gradient boosting**, which can be used for regression as follows. The algorithm is given the hyperparameter $K$, which is the number of rounds of boosting, corresponding to the number of base learners in the ensemble. The final prediction, as a function of the inputs, is the sum

$$p_0 + d_1(X) + \cdots + d_K(X)$$

where $p_0$ is an initial prediction, say the mean, and each $d_i$ is the difference from the previous prediction. The $i$th prediction is

$$p_i(X) = p_0 + d_1(X) + \cdots + d_i(X).$$

Then $p_i(X) = p_{i-1}(X) + d_i(X)$. Each $d_i$ is constructed so that the error of $p_i$ is minimal, given that $p_{i-1}$ is fixed. At each stage, the base learner learns $\widehat{d_i}$ to minimize

$$\sum_e loss(p_{i-1}(e) + \widehat{d_i}(e), Y(e)) = \sum_e loss(\widehat{d_i}(e), Y(e) - p_{i-1}(e)).$$

for any loss based on the difference between the actual and predicated value. This includes the losses considered for real-valued target features (page 269), but does not include log loss, which is not of this form.

The $i$th learner learns $d_i(e)$ to fit $Y_i(e) - p_{i-1}(e)$. This is equivalent to learning from a modified dataset, where the previous prediction is subtracted from the actual value of the training set. In this way, each learner is made to correct the errors of the previous prediction.

The algorithm is shown in Figure 7.19. Each $p_i$ is a function that, given an example, returns a prediction for that example. $E_i$ is a new set of examples, where for each $e \in Es$, the latest prediction, $p_{i-1}(e)$, is subtracted from the value of the target feature $Y(e)$. The new learner is therefore learning from the errors of the old learner. The function $d_i$ is computed by applying the base learner to the examples $E_i$.

$E_i$ could either be stored or the new targets for the examples can be generated as needed.

**Example 7.21** Figure 7.20 (page 311) shows a plot of the squared error of the validation set as the number of trees increases for functional gradient boosting

**procedure** *Boosting_learner*($Xs, Y, Es, L, K$)
  **Inputs**
    $Xs$: set of input features
    $Y$: target feature
    $Es$: set of examples from which to learn
    $L$: base learner
    $K$: number of components in the ensemble
  **Output**
    function to make prediction on examples
  $mean := \sum_{e \in Es} Y(e)/|Es|$
  define $p_0(e) = mean$
  **for each** $i$ from 1 to $K$ **do**
    let $E_i = \{\langle Xs(e), Y(e) - p_{i-1}(e)\rangle$ for $e \in Es\}$
    let $d_i = L(E_i)$
    define $p_i(e) = p_{i-1}(e) + d_i(e)$
  **return** $p_k$

Figure 7.19: Functional gradient-boosting regression learner of decision trees. The different lines are for different values of the parameter $\gamma$ in the decision tree learner. This is for the case where the minimum child size is 20 (no nodes have fewer than 20 examples). The point for zero trees is the error for predicting the mean. When $\gamma = 10$, the trees are degenerate and it always predicts the mean. The other values of $\gamma$ have similar errors for a single tree. When $\gamma = 1$, the subsequent trees do not extract useful information. For both the other values of $\gamma$, boosting helped improve the prediction. The code is available as part of AIPython (aipython.org).

## 7.5.2 Gradient-Boosted Trees

Gradient-boosted trees are a mix of some of the techniques presented previously. They are a linear model (page 288) where the features are decision trees (page 281) with binary splits, learned using boosting (page 309).

Let $K$ be the number of boosting rounds, which corresponds to the number of decision trees in the linear model.

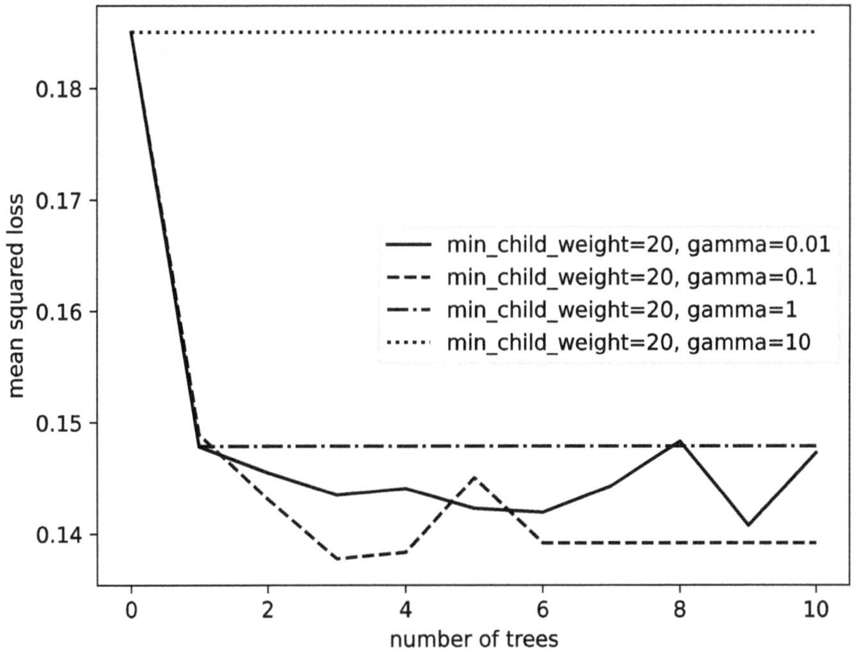


Figure 7.20: Validation error of functional gradient boosting as a function of $\gamma$ and number of trees

For regression, the prediction for example $(x_e, y_e)$ is

$$\widehat{y_e} = \sum_{k=1}^{K} f_k(x_e)$$

where each $f_k$ is a decision tree. Each decision tree is represented by a vector of weights, $w$, one weight for each leaf, and a function $q$ that maps the input features into the corresponding leaf. $q$ is an implementation of the if–then–else structure of the tree. $w_j$ is the $j$th component of $w$. The value of the decision tree applied to an example with input feature values $x$ is $w_{q(x)}$, the weight for the leaf numbered $q(x)$. $|w|$ is the number of leaves in the tree, which is one more than the number of splits in the tree.

For regression, the loss function is the regularized squared error

$$\left(\sum_{e}(\widehat{y_e} - y_e)^2\right) + \sum_{k=1}^{K} \Omega(f_k).$$

The regularization term $\Omega(f) = \gamma * |w| + \frac{1}{2}\lambda * \sum_j w_j^2$, where $w$ is the vector of weights for $f$; $\gamma$ and $\lambda$ are nonnegative numbers. This allows for regularizing on both the size of the tree and the values of the parameters.

For classification, the prediction is the sigmoid (or softmax) of the sum of trees

$$\widehat{y_e} = sigmoid(\sum_{k=1}^{K} f_k(x_e))$$

and the error to be optimized is the sum of log loss with the same regularization term used for regression:

$$\left(\sum_{e} logloss(\widehat{y_e}, y_e)\right) + \sum_{k=1}^{K} \Omega(f_k).$$

## Choosing Leaf Values

The model is learned using boosting (page 309), so the trees are learned one at a time. Consider building the $t$th tree, where the previous trees are fixed. Assume for now that the tree structure ($q$) for the $t$th tree is fixed. Consider a single weight $w_j$ that is used for the examples that map to the $j$th leaf of the tree. Let $I_j = \{e \mid q(x_e) = j\}$, the set of training examples that map to the $j$th leaf.

When choosing the value of $w_j$ to minimize loss, $\gamma * |w|$ does not depend on the value of $w_j$ and so can be ignored in the minimization.

The $t$th tree is learned with the previous ones fixed. For regression, the loss for the $t$th tree is

$$\mathcal{L}^{(t)} = \frac{1}{2}\lambda * \sum_{j} w_j^2 + \sum_{e}(y_e - \sum_{k=1}^{t} f_k(x_e))^2 + constant$$

where *constant* is the regularization values for the previous trees and the size, which can be ignored when learning the parameters for the $t$th tree.

Ignoring the constant, this is the same as the squared error of the dataset of differences between the observed values and the previous trees, for those examples that map to this leaf, with $\lambda$ extra pseudo-examples of value 0. Thus,

$$w_j = \frac{\sum_{e \in I_j} (y_e - \widehat{y_e}^{(t-1)})}{|I_j| + \lambda}$$

where $\widehat{y_e}^{(t-1)} = \sum_{k=1}^{t-1} f_k(x_e)$ is the previous prediction for example $e$.

For classification, the prediction is the sigmoid (or softmax) of the sum of trees, and the error to be optimized for the $t$th tree is log loss with $L2$ regularization:

$$\widehat{y_e}^{(t)} = sigmoid(\sum_{k=1}^{t} f_k(x_e))$$

$$\mathcal{L}^{(t)} = \frac{1}{2}\lambda * \sum_j w_j^2 + \sum_e logloss(\widehat{y_e}^{(t)}, y_e) + constant$$

where the constant again can be ignored in the minimization.

Taking the derivative of the loss with respect to $w_j$:

$$\frac{\partial}{\partial w_j} \mathcal{L}^{(t)} = \lambda * w_j + \sum_{e \in I_j} (\widehat{y_e} - y_e)$$

where the sum is over examples in $I_j$ because the predicted value is constant with respect to $w_j$ outside of this set. Finding the weights where the derivative is zero, which would be a minimum, is difficult to solve analytically.

For classification, starting with each $w_j$ in the new tree as zero, a single step in the opposite direction of the gradient gives the weights for a new tree. A second-order approximation (based on the Newton–Raphson method, which we do not cover) provides a step size for the weight:

$$w_j = \frac{\sum_{e \in I_j} (y_e - \widehat{y_e}^{(t-1)})}{\sum_{e \in I_j} \widehat{y_e}^{(t-1)} * (1 - \widehat{y_e}^{(t-1)}) + \lambda}$$

where $\widehat{y_e}^{(t-1)}$ is the previous prediction for example $e$.

### Choosing Splits

What remains is to choose the tree structure: choosing the splits of the tree. This is done in a greedy fashion (as in the decision-tree learner of Figure 7.9). Initially, the tree has a single leaf. The algorithm searches for a best leaf to expand. For each leaf, it chooses a feature to split by searching through the choices to make the split that most decreases the loss. For small datasets, the best split can be found by sorting the values on the feature and testing every split. For larger datasets, suggested splits can be made by subsampling the data or using pre-computed percentiles.

The regularization term $\gamma$ gives a direct penalty for larger trees; splitting stops when the optimal split does not decrease the loss by at least $\gamma$. Note that the *L*2 regularization parameter, $\lambda$, when positive, also penalizes larger trees: consider a split that provides no information; with the split, $\lambda$ applied to each child provides more regularization because each child has fewer examples, and so will fit the training data worse.

The implementation of gradient-tree boosting for classification shown in

```
procedure Gradient_boosted_tree_learner(Cs, Y, Es, K, λ, γ, η, css, ss)
    Inputs
        Cs: set of possible conditions
        Y: target feature
        Es: set of training examples
        K: number of boosting rounds
        λ: L2 regularization
        γ: penalty for increasing tree size
        η: weight shrinkage
        css: proportion of features (columns) subsampled for each tree
        ss: proportion of data subsampled for each tree
    Output
        function to predict a value of Y for an example
    Ts := []
    repeat K times
        append Decision_tree_learner(sample(Cs, css), Y, sample(Es, ss), γ) to Ts
    procedure leaf_value(Es)                    ▷ called by Decision_tree_learner
                       ▷ Es is the set of training examples that reach this leaf
        numerator := 0
        denominator := λ
        for e ∈ Es do
            pred := sigmoid(∑_{t∈Ts} t(e))
            numerator := numerator + Y(e) − pred
            denominator := denominator + pred ∗ (1 − pred)
        return η ∗ numerator / denominator
    procedure sum_loss(Es)
        new_val := leaf_value(Es)   ▷ value of leaf that would be constructed
        return ∑_{e∈Es} logloss(sigmoid(new_val + ∑_{t∈Ts} t(e)), Y(e))
```

Figure 7.21: Gradient-boosted trees classification learner. *Decision_tree_learner* is defined in Figure 7.9 (page 284)

Figure 7.21 calls the decision-tree learner of Figure 7.9 (page 284) iteratively, once for each decision tree in the ensemble. The gradient-boosted-tree learner overrides the *leaf_value* function called by *Decision_tree_learner*. The leaf value is no longer the prediction for each example that reaches the leaf, but is a component that goes into predicting the target value of examples that reach the leaf. The function $sample(S, p)$ returns a bag containing each member of $S$ chosen with probability $p$, without replacement. This allows for regularization by subsampling the data or the features.

There are a number of hyperparameters that are used in Figure 7.21 to reduce overfitting:

- $K$, the number of boosting rounds, which is the number of trees in the resulting ensemble.
- $\lambda$, the $L2$ regularization term.
- $\gamma$, the penalty for increasing the number of leaves by 1.
- $\eta$, the amount the weights for a tree are shrunk to make the algorithm more conservative.
- *css*, the proportions of columns (features) that are used .
- *ss*, the proportion of the data used for each tree; e.g., if $ss = 0.8$, then 80% of the data is selected for each tree.

The corresponding parameter names and default values for the open-source packages **XGBoost** and **LightGBM** are given in Appendix B.1.

Other common hyperparameters include:

- The maximum depth of a tree.
- The minimum number of training examples that map to a child for a split to be considered.
- The maximum number of leaves in a tree. Note that this value is a property of the whole tree and is not a property of a single node. If used as a criterion to stop when the number of leaves has been reached, the result depends on how the leaves are selected. Rather than the depth-first algorithm of Figure 7.9 (page 284), it is common to enumerate the leaves in a best-first manner (choosing the best split based on all of the leaves).

## 7.6 Limitations

> *Even after the observation of the frequent or constant conjunction of objects, we have no reason to draw any inference concerning any object beyond those of which we have had experience.*
>
> – Hume [1739–40], Book I, Part 3, Section 12

One might think that one can learn just based on the data, without any need to appeal to biases or any extra information. This is not possible. There are a number of results that show why preferences over hypotheses are needed.

The **no-free-lunch theorem** for machine learning specifies that no matter what the training set, for any two definitive predictors $A$ and $B$, there are as many functions from the input features to the target features that are consistent with the evidence for which $A$ is better than $B$ on the off-training set (the examples not in the training set) as when $B$ is better than $A$ on the off-training set. This includes when $B$ is chosen randomly or even is the worst predictor on the training set. Thus, if the functions are all equally likely to be the ground truth, no predictor is better than any other predictor.

As a simple illustration of this, consider the case with $m$-Boolean input features, and the aim is a Boolean classification. There are $2^m$ assignments of the input features, and so $2^{2^m}$ functions from assignments into $\{0,1\}$. With no probability to exploit (or assuming a uniform distribution over functions), the best one can do is to use $2^m$ bits to represent a function – one bit for each assignment, which is effectively just memorizing the training data. A training set of size $n$ will set $n$ of these bits, but the remaining bits – those that are used for off-training examples – are free to be assigned in any way.

This result does not mean learning is impossible. Rather, learning is possible because not all functions are equally likely. Or put another way, learning would be impossible if the world was random, however, because we can learn, the world cannot be random. It does mean that you cannot learn just from data without any extra information; you need a **bias** (page 264).

The most common bias is to choose the simplest hypothesis that fits the data by appealing to **Ockham's razor** (page 302). The simplest hypothesis depends on the language used to represent hypotheses and how data is represented, as shown in the following example.

**Example 7.22** Consider defining propositions using three Boolean variables, $x$, $y$, and $z$, as in Example 7.11 (page 288). The set of assignments is shown in Figure 7.22(a). Suppose, instead, that the space of assignments was represented using variables $a$, $b$, and $c$, where $a \equiv x \oplus y \oplus z$, $b \equiv (x \oplus y)$, and $c \equiv (y \oplus z)$, where $\oplus$ is exclusive-or (Figure 5.1 (page 179)). The exclusive-or of propositions is true whenever an odd number of them are true. Figure 7.22(b) shows the truth values for $a$, $b$, and $c$ given the values of $x$, $y$, and $z$.

As can be verified from the figure, the same space can be described using features $a$, $b$, and $c$ as using $x$, $y$, and $z$. What is simple in one representation may be complicated in the other. For example, $x \oplus y \oplus z$ is complicated to represent using $x$, $y$, $z$ – it requires a big decision tree and is not linearly separable – but is trivial in the other; it is just $a$. Similarly $a \oplus b \oplus c$ is complicated to represent using $a$, $b$, and $c$, but is trivial in the other; it is just $y$. The representation for $t$ – see Figure 7.22(c) – is more complicated in terms of one representation than the other.

One might think that $x$, $y$, and $z$ is simpler because the other has a complex description in terms of $x$, $y$, and $z$. However, $x$, $y$, and $z$ also has a complex description in terms of $a$, $b$, and $c$; see Exercise 7.15 (page 325).

It might appear problematic that simplicity depends on the language and the vocabulary. However, language has evolved to be useful, so this should not necessarily make one suspicious. Data is often represented to make learning useful, and to make biases towards simplicity appropriate. For example, there are many ways to represent an image; representing an image as a grid of pixel values enables some learning algorithms to work well. However, a representation that allows the image to be incrementally improved as it is delivered over time may cause the same algorithms to fail to learn.

## 7.7 Social Impact

> *Preventing discrimination requires that we have means of detecting it, and this can be enormously difficult when human beings are making the underlying decisions. As applied today, algorithms can increase the risk of discrimination. But . . . algorithms by their nature require a far greater level of specificity than is usually possible with human decision making, and this specificity makes it possible to probe aspects of the decision in additional ways. With the right changes to legal and regulatory systems, algorithms can thus potentially make it easier to detect – and hence to help prevent – discrimination.*
>
> – Kleinberg et al. [2020]

Machine learning algorithms make predictions based on the selection of input features, the target, the data, and the evaluation criteria. Numerous machine learning models have been shown to incorporate systematic biases based on race, gender, and level of poverty. These can depend crucially on the input features and target. Obermeyer et al. [2019] report on a learned model for determining which patients will require more intensive care. Using historical data, the model predicted the costs of medical treatments, with the higher predicted

| $x$ | $y$ | $z$ | $a$ | $b$ | $c$ | $t$ |
|---|---|---|---|---|---|---|
| 0 | 0 | 0 | 0 | 0 | 0 | 0 |
| 0 | 0 | 1 | 1 | 0 | 1 | 1 |
| 0 | 1 | 0 | 1 | 1 | 1 | 0 |
| 0 | 1 | 1 | 0 | 1 | 0 | 1 |
| 1 | 0 | 0 | 1 | 1 | 0 | 0 |
| 1 | 0 | 1 | 0 | 1 | 1 | 0 |
| 1 | 1 | 0 | 0 | 0 | 1 | 1 |
| 1 | 1 | 1 | 1 | 0 | 0 | 1 |

(a) (b) (c)

Figure 7.22: Alternative representations of a Boolean space

costs getting more proactive treatment. They found that for the same symptoms, black people were systematically recommended to require less proactive treatment. This occurred because blacks have historically had less money spent on their healthcare. Even though the race was not an input feature, it was correlated with other features that were used in the prediction. While the amount on money spent may be an easy to measure proxy for health for those jurisdictions that track money, it does not correspond to the health, which is much harder to measure. Obermeyer et al. [2019] argued that the predictive model was flawed because the data was biased. In their case, they worked with the model designers to make the target more appropriate for the actual decision, and developed models that were much fairer.

Understanding the reasons behind predictions and actions is the subject of **explainable AI**. It might seem obvious that it is better if a system can explain its conclusion. Having a system that can explain an incorrect conclusion, particularly if the explanation is approximate, might do more harm than good.

There have been similar cases of biases in training data in many other domains, including models that predict crime as used in **predictive policing** [Lum and Isaac, 2016], and models of who to hire [Ajunwa, 2020]. The algorithms might have worked as intended, predicting patterns in the data to train them, but the data was biased. Datasets for **facial recognition** lead to models that are more prone to false positives for some populations than others [Buolamwini and Gebru, 2018], and mugshot datasets exacerbate over-surveillance of marginalized populations, perpetuating systemic racism.

People might legitimately disagree on the appropriate label for training data, such as toxicity and misinformation of social media posts. Different groups of people may have irreconcilable disagreements about the ground truth. Predicting the mode or average label can mean that minorities, who are often most at risk, are ignored [Gordon et al., 2021].

A model that performs well on held-out (validation) data might not work well in an application [Liao et al., 2021], due to internal or external validity. **Internal validity** refers to issues that arise in the learning problem in isolation, such as overfitting to standard validation sets – choosing the solutions that are best on validation or test sets – and using them for new problems. **External validity** refers to problems that arise on using the model for some task for which it might seem appropriate, such as due to differences in the dataset or the appropriate evaluation.

Data is invariably based on the past, but you might not want the future to be like the past. As Agrawal et al. [2022] argue, prediction is not an end in itself. Knowing predictions based on the past is useful, but does not directly specify what you should do. What an agent should do (page 14) also depends on the values and preferences as well as what actions are available. How to make decisions based on predictions is the basis for much of the rest of the book.

## 7.8 Review

The following are the main points you should have learned from this chapter:

- Learning is the ability of an agent to improve its behavior based on experience.
- Supervised learning is the problem of predicting the target of a new input, given a set of input–target pairs.
- Given some training examples, an agent builds a representation that can be used for new predictions.
- Linear models and decision trees are representations which are the basis for more sophisticated models.
- Overfitting occurs when a prediction fits the training set well but does not fit the test set or future predictions.
- Gradient-boosted trees are an efficient and effective representation for many learning problems.
- Data is invariably about the past. If data is used for acting in the future, the predictor may no longer work as well, and we might want the future to be different from the past.

## 7.9 References and Further Reading

For overviews of machine learning, see Mitchell [1997], Duda et al. [2001], Bishop [2008], Hastie et al. [2009], and [Murphy, 2022]. Halevy et al. [2009] discuss the unreasonable effectiveness of big data.

The UCI machine learning repository [Dua and Graff, 2017] is a collection of classic machine learning datasets. **Kaggle** (https://www.kaggle.com) runs machine learning competitions and has many datasets available for testing algorithms.

The collection of papers by Shavlik and Dietterich [1990] contains many classic learning papers. Michie et al. [1994] give empirical evaluation of many early learning algorithms on multiple problems. Davis and Goadrich [2006] discuss precision, recall, and ROC curves. Settles [2012] overviews active learning.

The approach to combining expert knowledge and data was proposed by Spiegelhalter et al. [1990].

Logistic regression dates back to 1832 by Verhulst [see Cramer, 2002], and has a long history in many areas, including the economics Nobel prize to McFadden [2000]. Decision tree learning is discussed by Breiman et al. [1984] and Quinlan [1993]. Gelman et al. [2020] provide theory and practice for linear and logistic regression, with many practical examples. Ng [2004] compares $L1$ and $L2$ regularization for logistic regression. Hierarchical softmax is due to Morin and Bengio [2005].

Feurer and Hutter [2019] overview automatic hyperparameter optimization, or **hyperparameter tuning**, part of **autoML** [Hutter et al., 2019], which involves search to choose algorithms and hyperparameters for machine learning. Shahriari et al. [2016] review Bayesian optimization, one of the most useful tools for hyperparameter optimization. Stanley et al. [2019] and Real et al. [2020] show how genetic algorithms (page 159) can be successfully used for autoML.

Random forests were introduced by Breiman [2001], and are compared by Dietterich [2000a] and Denil et al. [2014]. For reviews of ensemble learning, see Dietterich [2002]. Boosting is described in Schapire [2002] and Meir and Rätsch [2003]. Gradient tree boosting is by Friedman [2001]. The notation used in that section follows Chen and Guestrin [2016], who develop the algorithm in much more generality, and discuss many efficiency refinements. **XGBoost** [Chen and Guestrin, 2016] and **LightGBM** [Ke et al., 2017] are modern implementations (see Appendix B).

The no-free-lunch theorem for machine learning is due to Wolpert [1996].

Rudin et al. [2022] review interpretable machine learning, which involves building models that can be understood.

For research results on machine learning, see the journals *Journal of Machine Learning Research (JMLR)*, *Machine Learning*, the annual *International Conference on Machine Learning (ICML)*, the *Proceedings of the Neural Information Processing Society (NeurIPS)*, or general AI journals such as *Artificial Intelligence* and the *Journal of Artificial Intelligence Research*, and many specialized conferences and journals.

## 7.10 Exercises

**Exercise 7.1** The aim of this exercise is to prove and extend the table of Figure 7.5 (page 277).

(a) Prove the optimal predictions for training data of Figure 7.5. To do this, find the minimum value of the absolute error, the squared error, the log loss, and the value that gives the maximum likelihood. The maximum or minimum value is either at an end point or where the derivative is zero. [Hints: For squared error and log loss, take the derivative and set to zero. For the absolute error, consider how the error changes when moving from one data point to the next (in order). It might help to consider first the case where the data points are at consecutive integers, and then generalize.]

(b) To determine the best prediction for the test data, assume that the data cases are generated stochastically according to some true parameter $p$. [See the thought experiment (page 302).] Try the following for a number of different values for $p$ selected uniformly in the range $[0, 1]$. Generate $n$ training examples (try various values for $n$, some small, say 2, 3, or 5, and some large, say 1000) by sampling with probability $p_0$ from these training examples. Let $n_0$ be the number of false examples and $n_1$ be the number of true examples in the training set (so $n_0 + n_1 = n$). Generate a test set of size, say, 20, that contains many test cases using the same parameter $p$. Repeat this for 1000 times to get a reasonable average. Which of the following gives a lower error on the test set for each of the optimality criteria: (I) absolute error; (II) squared error; and (III) log loss.

(i) The mode.
(ii) $n_1/n$.
(iii) If $n_1 = 0$, use 0.001, if $n_0 = 0$, use 0.999, else use $n_1/n$. Try this for different numbers when the counts are zero.
(iv) $(n_1 + 1)/(n + 2)$
(v) $(n_1 + \alpha)/(n + 2\alpha)$ for different values of $\alpha > 0$.
(vi) Another predictor that is a function of $n_0$ and $n_1$.

(For the mathematically sophisticated, try to prove what the optimal predictor is for each criterion.)

**Exercise 7.2** In the context of a point estimate of a feature with domain $\{0, 1\}$ with no inputs, it is possible for an agent to make a stochastic prediction with a parameter $p \in [0, 1]$ such that the agent predicts 1 with probability $p$ and predicts 0 otherwise. For each of the following error measures, give the expected error on a training set with $n_0$ occurrences of 0 and $n_1$ occurrences of 1 (as a function of $p$). What is the value of $p$ that minimizes the error? Is this worse or better than the prediction of Figure 7.5 (page 277)?

(a) Mean absolute loss.
(b) Mean squared loss.
(c) Worst-case error.

**Exercise 7.3**

(a) Prove that for any two predictors $A$ and $B$ on the same dataset, if $A$ dominates $B$ (page 279), that is, $A$ has a higher true-positive rate and lower false-positive rate than $B$, then $A$ has a lower cost (and so is better) than $B$ for *all* cost functions that depend only on the number of false positives and false negatives (assuming the costs to be minimized are non-negative). [Hint: Prove that the conditions of the statement imply the number of false negatives and the number of false positives is less (or, perhaps, equal), which in turn implies the conclusion.]
(b) Consider the predictors (a) and (c) in Figure 7.7 (page 280).
   (i) Which of (a) and (c) has a better recall (true-positive rate)? (See Example 7.7.)
   (ii) What is the precision of (a)? (Give both a ratio and the decimal value to 3 decimal points.)
   (iii) What is the precision of (c)?
   (iv) Which of (a) and (c) is better in terms of precision?
   (v) Suppose false positives were 1000 times worse than false negatives, which of (a) and (c) would have a lower cost? (Consider the cost of a false negative to be 1 and a false positive to be 1000.)
   (vi) Suppose false negatives were 1000 times worse than false positives, which of (a) and (c) would have a lower cost?

**Exercise 7.4** Suppose you need to define a system that, given data about a person's TV-watching likes, recommends other TV shows the person may like. Each show has features specifying whether it is a comedy, whether it features doctors, whether it features lawyers, and whether it has guns. You are given the fictitious examples of Figure 7.23 about whether the person likes various TV shows. We want to use this dataset to learn the value of *Likes* (i.e., to predict which TV shows the person would like based on the attributes of the TV show).

This is designed to be small enough to do it manually, however you may find the AIPython (aipython.org) code or useful to check your answers.

(a) Suppose the error is the sum of absolute errors. Give the optimal decision tree with only one node (i.e., with no splits). What is the error of this tree?
(b) Do the same as in part (a), but with the squared error.
(c) Suppose the error is the sum of absolute errors. Give the optimal decision tree of depth 2 (i.e., the root node is the only node with children). For each leaf in the tree, give the examples that are filtered to that node. What is the error of this tree?
(d) Do the same as in part (c) but with the squared error.
(e) What is the smallest tree that correctly classifies all training examples? Does a top-down decision tree that optimizes the information gain at each step represent the same function?
(f) Give two instances not appearing in the examples of Figure 7.23 and show how they are classified using the smallest decision tree. Use this to explain the bias inherent in the tree. (How does the bias give you these particular predictions?)
(g) Is this dataset linearly separable? Explain why or why not.

**Exercise 7.5** Consider the decision tree learning algorithm of Figure 7.9 (page 284) and the data of Figure 7.1 (page 268). Suppose, for this question, the stopping criterion is that all of the examples have the same classification. The tree of Figure

| Example | *Comedy* | *Doctors* | *Lawyers* | *Guns* | *Likes* |
|---|---|---|---|---|---|
| $e_1$ | *false* | *true* | *false* | *false* | *false* |
| $e_2$ | *true* | *false* | *true* | *false* | *true* |
| $e_3$ | *false* | *false* | *true* | *true* | *true* |
| $e_4$ | *false* | *false* | *true* | *false* | *false* |
| $e_5$ | *false* | *false* | *false* | *true* | *false* |
| $e_6$ | *true* | *false* | *false* | *true* | *false* |
| $e_7$ | *true* | *false* | *false* | *false* | *true* |
| $e_8$ | *false* | *true* | *true* | *true* | *true* |
| $e_9$ | *false* | *true* | *true* | *false* | *false* |
| $e_{10}$ | *true* | *true* | *true* | *false* | *true* |
| $e_{11}$ | *true* | *true* | *false* | *true* | *false* |
| $e_{12}$ | *false* | *false* | *false* | *false* | *false* |

Figure 7.23: Training examples for Exercise 7.4

7.8 (page 282) was built by selecting a feature that gives the maximum information gain. This question considers what happens when a different feature is selected.

(a) Suppose you change the algorithm to always select the first element of the list of features. What tree is found when the features are in the order [*Author*, *Thread*, *Length*, *WhereRead*]? Does this tree represent a different function than that found with the maximum information gain split? Explain.
(b) What tree is found when the features are in the order [*WhereRead*, *Thread*, *Length*, *Author*]? Does this tree represent a different function than that found with the maximum information gain split or the one given for the preceding part? Explain.
(c) Is there a tree that correctly classifies the training examples but represents a different function than those found by the preceding algorithms? If so, give it. If not, explain why.

**Exercise 7.6** In the decision tree learner of Figure 7.9 (page 284), it is possible to mix the leaf predictions (what is returned by *leaf_value*) and which loss is used in *sum_loss*. For each loss in the set {*0–1 loss*, *absolute loss*, *squared loss*, *log loss*}, and for each leaf choice in {*empirical distribution*, *mode*, *median*}, build a tree to greedily optimize the loss when choosing the split, and use the leaf choice. For each tree, give the number of leaves and the evaluation of a test set for each loss. Try this for at least two datasets.

(a) Which split choice gives the smallest tree?
(b) Is there a loss that is consistently improved by optimizing a different loss when greedily choosing a split?
(c) Try to find a different leaf choice that would be better for some optimization criterion.
(d) For each optimization criterion, which combination of split choice and leaf choice has the best performance on the test set?

**Exercise 7.7** The aim of this exercise is to determine the size of the space of decision trees. Suppose there are $n$ binary features in a learning problem. How many different decision trees are there? How many different functions are represented by these decision trees? Is it possible that two different decision trees give rise to the same function?

**Exercise 7.8** Implement a decision tree learner that handles input features with ordered domains. You can assume that any numerical feature is ordered. The condition should be a cut on a single variable, such as $X \leq v$, which partitions the training examples according to the value $v$. A cut-value can be chosen for a feature $X$ by sorting the examples on the value of $X$, and sweeping through the examples in order. While sweeping through the examples, the evaluation of each partition should be computed from the evaluation of the previous partition. Does this work better than, for example, selecting the cuts arbitrarily?

**Exercise 7.9** Give the weights for a logistic regression model that can approximate the following logical operations. Assume true is represented as 1, and false as 0. Assume that $sigmoid(5)$ is a close enough approximation to 1, $sigmoid(-5)$ is close enough to 0.

(a) and: $x_1 \land x_2$
(b) or: $x_1 \lor x_2$
(c) negation: $\neg x_1$
(d) nand: $\neg(x_1 \land x_2)$. Note that nand (not and) is of interest because all Boolean functions can be built using nand.

Use $w_0$ for the bias term (the weight multiplied by 1) and $w_i$ is the weight for $x_i$.

**Exercise 7.10** Show how gradient descent can be used for learning a linear function that minimizes the absolute error. [Hint: Do a case analysis of the error; for each example the absolute value is either the positive or the negative of the value. What is appropriate when the value is zero?]

**Exercise 7.11** Consider minimizing Equation (7.1) (page 289), which gives the error of a linear prediction. This can be solved by finding the zero(s) of its derivative. The general case involves solving linear equations, for which there are many techniques, but it is instructive to do a simple case by hand.

(a) Give a formula for the weights that minimize the error for the case where $n = 2$ (i.e., when there are only two input features). [Hint: For each weight, differentiate with respect to that weight and set to zero. Solve the resulting equations.]
(b) Write pseudocode to implement this.
(c) Why is it hard to minimize the error analytically when using a sigmoid function as an activation function, for $n = 2$? (Why doesn't the same method as in part (a) work?)

**Exercise 7.12** Suppose you want to optimize the mean squared loss (page 270) for the sigmoid of a linear function.

(a) Modify the algorithm of Figure 7.12 (page 292) so that the update is proportional to the gradient of the squared error. Note that this question assumes you know differential calculus, in particular, the chain rule for differentiation.
(b) Does this work better than the algorithm that minimizes log loss when evaluated according to the squared error?

**Exercise 7.13** Consider how to estimate the quality of a restaurant from the ratings of 1 to 5 stars as in Example 7.18 (page 301).

(a) What would this predict for a restaurant that has two 5-star ratings? How would you test from the data whether this is a reasonable prediction?
(b) Suppose you wanted not to optimize just for the 5-star restaurants, but for all restaurants. How can this be done?
(c) Can $c$, as computed in Example 7.18, be negative? Give a scenario where this might occur.
(d) Why might we choose not to use the average rating for $a_0$? What else might you use? [Hints: A new restaurant may be quite different from a well-established restaurant. Picking a restaurant at random, and then a rating at random, will have a different average than picking a rating at random.]

It might be useful to try this on some real data. For example, Movielens makes a dataset of movie ratings available, which can be used to test such hypotheses (albeit on movies, not restaurants).

**Exercise 7.14** It is possible to define a regularizer to minimize $\sum_e (loss(\widehat{Y}(e), Y(e)) + \lambda * regularizer(\widehat{Y}))$ rather than formula (7.5) (page 303). How is this different than the existing regularizer? [Hint: Think about how this affects multiple datasets or for cross validation.]

Suppose $\lambda$ is set by $k$-fold cross validation, and then the model is learned for the whole dataset. How would the algorithm be different for the original way(s) of defining a regularizer and this alternative way? [Hint: There is a different number of examples used for the regularization than there is the full dataset; does this matter?] Which works better in practice?

**Exercise 7.15** Given the parameterizations of Example 7.22 (page 316):

(a) When the features are $a$, $b$, and $c$, what decision tree will the decision-tree learning algorithm find to represent $t$ (assuming it maximizes information gain and only stops when all examples at a leaf agree)?

(b) When the features are $a$, $b$, and $c$, what is a smallest decision tree that can represent $t$? How does this compare to using $x$, $y$, and $z$.

(c) How can $x$, $y$, and $z$ be defined in terms of $a$, $b$, and $c$?

Chapter 8

# Neural Networks and Deep Learning

*Deep learning allows computational models that are composed of multiple processing layers to learn representations of data with multiple levels of abstraction. These methods have dramatically improved the state-of-the-art in speech recognition, visual object recognition, object detection and many other domains such as drug discovery and genomics. Deep learning discovers intricate structure in large data sets by using the backpropagation algorithm to indicate how a machine should change its internal parameters that are used to compute the representation in each layer from the representation in the previous layer. Deep convolutional nets have brought about breakthroughs in processing images, video, speech and audio, whereas recurrent nets have shone light on sequential data such as text and speech.*

– Y. LeCun, Y. Bengio, and G. Hinton [2015]

The previous chapter assumed that the input were features; you might wonder where the features come from. The inputs to real-world agents are diverse, including pixels from cameras, sound waves from microphones, or character sequences from web requests. Using these directly as inputs to the methods from the previous chapter often does not work well; useful features need to be created from the raw inputs. This could be done by designing features from the raw inputs using **feature engineering**. Learned features, however, are now state-of-the-art for many applications, and can beat engineered features for cases that have abundant data.

This chapter is about how to learn features. The methods here learn features that are useful for the tasks trained on, even though they may not have an interpretation that can be easily explained. Often features learned for some tasks are useful for other tasks.

Learning the features that are useful for prediction is called **representation learning**. The most common form of representation reasoning is in terms of multilayer **neural networks**. These networks are inspired by the **neurons** in the brain but do not actually simulate neurons. Artificial neurons are called **units**. Each unit has many real-valued parameters. Large artificial neural networks (in 2022) contain on the order of one hundred billion ($10^{11}$) trained parameters, which is approximately the number of neurons in the human brain. Neurons are much more complicated than the units in artificial neural networks. For example, the roundworm *Caenorhabditis elegans*, which is about 1 mm long, has 302 neurons and exhibits complex behavior, which simple models of neurons cannot account for.

As pointed out by LeCun et al., above, artificial neural networks (ANNs) have had considerable success in unstructured and perception tasks for which there is abundant training data, such as for image interpretation, speech recognition, machine translation, and game playing. The models used in state-of-the-art applications are trained on huge datasets, including more cats than any one person has ever seen, more sentences than any one person has ever read, and more games than any one person has played. They can take advantage of the data because they are very flexible, with the capability of inventing low-level features that are useful for the higher-level task.

Artificial neural networks are interesting to study for a number of reasons:

- As part of neuroscience, to understand real neural systems, researchers are simulating the neural systems of simple animals such as worms, which promises to lead to an understanding of which aspects of neural systems are necessary to explain the behavior of these animals.
- Some researchers seek to automate not only the functionality of intelligence (which is what the field of artificial intelligence is about) but also the mechanism of the brain, suitably abstracted. One hypothesis is that the best way to build the functionality of the brain is to use the mechanism of the brain. This hypothesis can be tested by attempting to build intelligence using the mechanism of the brain, as well as attempting it without using the mechanism of the brain.
- The brain inspires a new way to think about computation that contrasts with traditional computers. Unlike conventional computers, which have a few processors and a large but essentially inert memory, the brain consists of a huge number of asynchronous distributed processes, all running concurrently with no master controller. Conventional computers are not the only architecture available for computation. Current neural network systems are often implemented on parallel architectures, including GPUs and specialized tensor processing units.
- As far as learning is concerned, neural networks provide a different measure of simplicity as a learning bias than, for example, boosted deci-

sion trees. Multilayer neural networks, like decision trees, can represent any function of a set of discrete features. However, the bias is different; functions that correspond to simple neural networks do not necessarily correspond to simple ensembles of decision trees. In neural networks, low-level features that are useful for multiple higher-level features are learned.

## 8.1 Feedforward Neural Networks

There are many different types of neural networks. A **feedforward neural network** implements a prediction function given inputs $x$ as

$$f(x) = f_n(f_{n-1}(\dots f_2(f_1(x)))). \tag{8.1}$$

Each function $f_i$ maps a **vector** (array or list) of values into a vector of values. The function $f_i$ is the $i$th **layer**. The number of functions composed, $n$, is the **depth** of the neural network. The last layer, $f_n$, is the **output layer**. The other layers are called **hidden layers**. Sometimes the input, $x$, is called the **input layer**. Each component of the output vector of a layer is called a **unit**. The "**deep**" in deep learning refers to the depth of the network.

In a feedforward network, each layer $f_i$ is a linear function (page 288) with learnable parameters of each output given the input, similar to linear or logistic regression, followed by a nonlinear **activation function**, $\phi$ (page 289). The

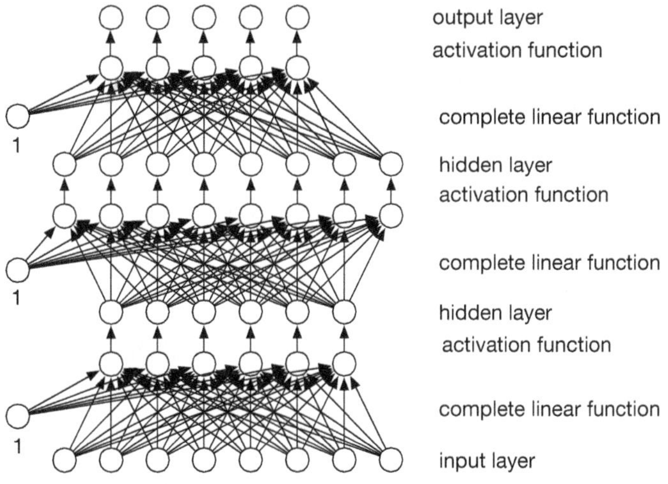


Figure 8.1: A feedforward neural network of depth three. On the bottom is the input layer which is fed the input features. On the top is the output layer that makes predictions for the target features. In each dense linear function, the left-most input is clamped at 1, and there is a parameter for each arc. The activation function is applied to each value

linear function takes a vector *in* of values for the inputs to the layer (and, as in linear regression (page 288), an extra constant input that has value "1"), and returns a vector *out* of output values, so that

$$out[j] = \phi(\sum_k in[k] * w[k,j])$$

for a two-dimensional array $w$ of weights. The weight associated with the extra 1 input is the **bias**. There is a weight $w[i,j]$ for each input–output pair of the layer, plus a bias for each output. The outputs of one layer are the inputs to the next. See Figure 8.1 (page 329).

The activation function $\phi$ for the hidden layers is a **nonlinear function**. If it is a linear function (or the identity), the layer is redundant as a linear function of a linear function is another linear function. An activation function should be (almost everywhere) differentiable so that methods based on gradient descent work.

A common activation function for hidden layers is the **rectified linear unit (ReLU)**: defined by $\phi(x) = max(0,x)$. That is

$$\phi(x) = \begin{cases} 0 & \text{if } x < 0 \\ x & \text{if } x \geq 0. \end{cases}$$

$\phi$ has derivative 0 for $x < 0$ and 1 for $x > 0$. Although it does not have a derivative for $x = 0$, assume the derivative is 0. If all the hidden layers use ReLU activation, the network implements a piecewise linear function.

The activation function for the output layer depends on the type of the output $y$ and the error function (loss) that is being optimized.

- If $y$ is real and the average **squared loss** (page 270) is optimized, the activation function is typically the identity function: $\phi(x) = x$.

- If $y$ is Boolean with **binary log loss** (page 276) optimized, the activation function is typically the **sigmoid** (page 290): $\phi(x) = sigmoid(x) = 1/(1+\exp(-x))$. Sigmoid has a theoretical justification in terms of probability (page 400).

- If $y$ is categorical, but not binary, and **categorical log loss** (page 273) is optimized, the activation function is typically **softmax** (page 295). The output layer has one unit for each value in the domain of $y$.

In each of these choices, the activation function and the loss **complement** each other to have a simple derivative. For each of these, the derivative of the error is proportional to $\widehat{Y}(e) - Y(e)$.

**Example 8.1** Consider the function with three Boolean inputs $x$, $y$, and $z$ and where the Boolean target has the value of $y$ if $x$ is true, and has the value of $z$ if $x$ is false (see Figure 7.10 (page 288)). This function is not linearly separable (see

Example 7.13 (page 294)) and logistic regression fails for a dataset that follows this structure (Example 7.11 (page 288)).

This function can be approximated using a neural network with one hidden layer containing two units. As the target is Boolean, a sigmoid is used for the output.

The function is equivalent to the logical formula $(x \land y) \lor (\neg x \land z)$. Each of these operations can be represented in terms of rectified linear units or approximated by sigmoids. The first layer can be represented as the function with two outputs, $h_1$ and $h_2$, defined as

$$h_1 = relu(x + y - 1)$$
$$h_2 = relu(-x + z).$$

Then $h_1$ is 1 when $(x \land y)$ is true and $h_2$ is 1 when $(\neg x \land z)$ is true, and they are 0 otherwise. The output is $sigmoid(-5 + 10 * h_1 + 10 * h_2)$, which approximates the function $h_1 \lor h_2$ with approximately a 0.7% error. The resulting two-layer neural network is shown in Figure 8.2.

Neural networks can have multiple real-valued inputs. Non-binary categorical features can be transformed into indicator variables (page 286), which results in a **one-hot encoding**.

The **width** of a layer is the number of elements in the vector output of the layer. The **width** of a neural network is the maximum width over all layers. The architectural design of a network includes the depth of the network (number of layers) and the width of each hidden layer. The size of the output and input are usually specified as part of the problem definition. A network with one hidden layer – as long as it is wide enough – can approximate any continuous function on an interval of the reals, or any function of discrete inputs

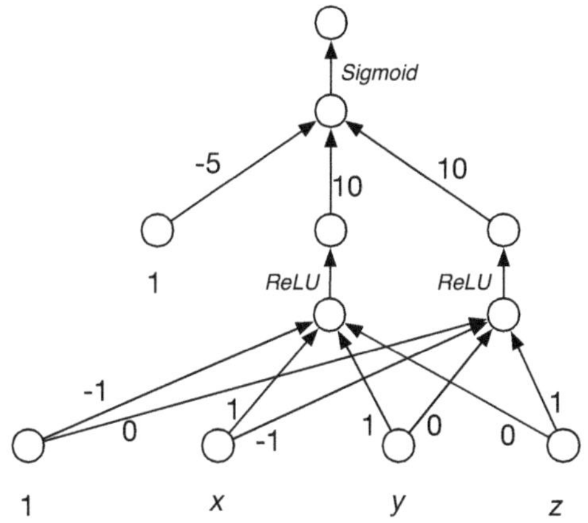


Figure 8.2: A neural network with one hidden layer for "if $x$ then $y$ else $z$" with ReLU hidden activation and sigmoid output activation functions

to discrete outputs. The width required may be prohibitively wide, and it is typically better for a network to be deep than be very wide. Lower-level layers can provide useful features to make the upper layers simpler.

### 8.1.1 Parameter Learning

**Backpropagation** implements (stochastic) gradient descent for all weights. Recall that **stochastic gradient descent** (page 291) involves updating each weight $w$ proportionally to $-\frac{\partial}{\partial w}error(e)$, for each example $e$ in a batch.

There are two properties of differentiation used in backpropagation.

- **Linear rule**: the derivative of a linear function, $aw + b$, is given by

$$\frac{\partial}{\partial w}(aw + b) = a$$

so the derivative is the number that is multiplied by $w$ in the linear function.

- **Chain rule**: if $g$ is a function of $w$ and function $f$, which does not depend on $w$, is applied to $g(w)$, then

$$\frac{\partial}{\partial w}f(g(w)) = f'(g(w)) * \frac{\partial}{\partial w}g(w)$$

where $f'$ is the derivative of $f$.

Let $f(e) = f_n(f_{n-1}(\ldots f_2(f_1(x_e))))$, the output of the prediction function (Equation (8.1)) for example $e$, with input features $x_e$. The $f_i$ are parametrized by weights. Suppose $v_i = f_i(f_{i-1}(\ldots f_2(f_1(x_e))))$, which means $v_i = f_i(v_{i-1})$ and $v_0 = x_e$. The values for $v_i$ for $1 \le i \le n$ can be computed with one pass through the nested functions.

Consider a single weight $w$ that is used in the definition of $f_j$. The $f_i$ for $i \neq j$ do not depend on $w$. The derivative of $error(f(e))$ with respect to weight $w$:

$$\begin{aligned}
\frac{\partial}{\partial w}error(f(e)) &= error'(v_n) * \frac{\partial}{\partial w}f_n(v_{n-1}) \\
&= error'(v_n) * \frac{\partial}{\partial w}f_n(f_{n-1}(v_{n-2})) \\
&= error'(v_n) * f_n'(v_{n-1}) * \frac{\partial}{\partial w}(f_{n-1}(v_{n-2})) \\
&= error'(v_n) * f_n'(v_{n-1}) * f_{n-1}'(v_{n-2}) * \frac{\partial}{\partial w}(f_{n-2}(v_{n-3})) \\
&= error'(v_n) * f_n'(v_{n-1}) * f_{n-1}'(v_{n-2}) * \cdots * \frac{\partial}{\partial w}(f_j(v_{j-1}))
\end{aligned}$$

where $f_i'$ is the derivative of $f_i$ with respect to its inputs. The expansion can stop at $f_j$. The last partial derivative is not an instance of the chain rule because $v_{j-1}$

is not a function of $w$. Instead, the linear rule is used, where $w$ is multiplied by the appropriate component of $v_{j-1}$.

**Backpropagation** determines the update for every weight with two passes through the network for each example.

- Prediction: given the values on the inputs for each layer, compute a value for the outputs of the layer. That is, the $v_i$ are computed. In the algorithm below, each $v_i$ is stored in a *values* array associated with the layer.

- Back propagate: go backwards through the layers to determine the update of all of the weights of the network (the weights in the linear layers). Going backwards, the $error'(v_n) * \prod_{i=0}^{k} f'_{n-i}(v_{n-i-1})$ for $k$ starting from 0 are computed and passed to the lower layers. This input is the error term for a layer, which is combined with the values computed in the prediction pass, to update all of the weights for the layer, and compute the error term for the lower layer.

Storing the intermediate results makes backpropagation a **dynamic programming** form of (stochastic) gradient descent.

A layer is represented by a linear function (page 288) and an activation function in the algorithm below. Each function is implemented modularly as a class (in the sense of object-oriented programming) that implements forward prediction and backpropagation for each example, and the updates for the weights after a batch.

The class *Dense* implements a **dense linear function**, where each output unit is connected to all input units. The array $w$ stores the weights, so the weight for input unit $i$ connected to output unit $j$ is $w[i,j]$, and the bias (the weight associated with the implicit input that is always 1) for output $j$ is in $w[n_i, j]$. The methods *output* and *Backprop* are called for each example. *Backprop* accumulates the gradients for each $w[i,j]$ in $d[i,j]$, and returns an error term for the lower levels. The *update* method updates the parameters given the gradients of the batch, and resets $d$. The method *output* remembers any information necessary for *Backprop* for each example.

Figure 8.3 (page 334) shows a modular version of backpropagation. The variable *functions* is the sequence of possibly parameterized functions that defines the neural network (typically a linear function and an activation function for each layer). Each function is implemented as a class that can carry out the forward and backward passes and remembers any information it needs to.

The first function for the lowest layer has as many inputs as there are input features. For each subsequent function, the number of inputs is the same as the number of outputs of the previous function. The number of outputs of the final function is the number of target features, or the number of values for a (non-binary) categorical output feature.

The pseudocode of Figure 8.3 assumes the type of the output activation function is made to complement the error (loss) function, so that the derivative is proportional to the predicted value minus the actual value. This is true

The class for each function implements the methods:

- *output*(*in*) returns the output values for the input values of vector *in*
- *Backprop*(*error*) returns vector of input errors, and updates gradients
- *update*() updates the weights for a batch

Each class stores *in* and *out* if needed for *Backprop*

```
class Dense(n_i, n_o)                          ▷ n_i is # inputs, n_o is #outputs
    for each 0 ≤ i ≤ n_i and each 0 ≤ j < n_o do
        d[i,j] := 0; w[i,j] := a random value
    method output(in)                          ▷ in is array with length n_i
        for each j do out[j] := w[n_i,j] + Σ_i in[i] * w[i,j]
        return out
    method Backprop(error)                     ▷ error is array with length n_o
        for each i,j do d[i,j] := d[i,j] + in[i] * error[j]
        for each i do ierror[i] := Σ_j w[i,j] * error[j]
        return ierror
    method update()                ▷ update all weights. This implements SGD.
        for each i,j do
            w[i,j] := w[i,j] − η/batch_size * d[i,j]        ▷ η is learning rate
            d[i,j] := 0
procedure Neural_network_learner(Xs, Ys, Es, functions, η, batch_size)
    Inputs
        Xs: input features, Xs = (X_1, ..., X_n)
        Ys: target features
        Es: set of training examples
        functions: the sequence of functions that defines the network
        batch_size: number of examples in each batch
        η: learning rate (gradient descent step size)
    repeat
        batch := random sample of batch_size examples
        for each example e in batch do
            for each input unit i do values[i] := X_i(e)
            for each fun in functions from lowest to highest do
                values := fun.output(values)
            for each output unit j do error[j] := φ_o(values[j]) − Ys[j]
            for each fun in functions from highest to lowest do
                error := fun.Backprop(error)
        for each fun in functions that contains weights do
            fun.update()
    until termination
```

Figure 8.3: Backpropagation with stochastic gradient descent of the identity activation for squared error (Equation (7.1) (page 289)), the sigmoid activation for binary log loss (Equation (7.3) (page 290)), and softmax for categorical log loss (page 295). The final activation function, $\phi_o$, is used in *Neural_network_learner*, but is not implemented as a class. Other combinations of error functions and loss might have a different form; modern tools automate taking derivatives so you do not need to program it directly.

Figure 8.4 shows the pseudocode for two common activation functions. ReLU is typically used for hidden layers in modern deep networks. Sigmoid was common in classical neural networks, and is still used in models such as the long short-term memory network (LSTM) (page 357).

Mappings to the parameters of **Keras** and **PyTorch**, two common deep learning libraries, are presented in Appendix B.2.

**Example 8.2** Consider training the parameters of the network of Figure 8.2 (page 331) using the "if $x$ then $y$ else $z$" data of Figure 7.10(b) (page 288).

This network is represented by the call to *Neural_network_learner* with

$$functions = [Dense(3,2), ReLU(), Dense(2,1)].$$

In one run with 10,000 epochs, learning rate of 0.01, and batch size 8 (including all examples in a batch), the weights learned gave the network represented by the following equations (to three significant digits), where $h_1$ and $h_2$ are the hidden units:

$$h_1 = relu(2.47 * x + 0.0000236 * y - 2.74 * z + 2.74)$$
$$h_2 = relu(3.62 * x + 4.01 * y + 0.228 * z - 3.84)$$

```
class ReLU()
    method output(in)                                  ▷ in is a vector with length n_i
        for each i : 0 ≤ i < n_i do out[i] := max(0, in[i])
        return out                                     ▷ out is a vector with length n_i
    method Backprop(error)                             ▷ error is a vector with length n_i
        for each i : 0 ≤ i < n_i do
            ierror[i] := error[i] if (in[i] > 0) else 0
        return ierror
class sigmoid()
    method output(in)                                  ▷ in is a vector with length n_i
        for each i : 0 ≤ i < n_i do out[i] := 1/(1 + exp(−in[i]))
        return out                                     ▷ out is a vector with length n_i
    method Backprop(error)                             ▷ error is a vector with length n_i
        for each i : 0 ≤ i < n_i do ierror[i] := out[i] * (1 − out[i]) * error[i]
        return ierror
```

Figure 8.4: Backpropagation for some activation functions

$$output = sigmoid(-4.42 * h_1 + 6.64 * h_2 + 4.95).$$

This has learned to approximate the function to 1% error in the worst case. The prediction with the largest log loss is the prediction of 0.99 for the example with $\neg x \wedge \neg y \wedge z$, which should be 1.

Different runs can give quite different weights. For small examples like this, you could try to interpret the target. In this case (very approximately) $h_1$ is positive unless $x = 0, z = 1$ and $h_2$ is only large when $x = 1, y = 1$. Notice that, even for a simple example like this, it is difficult to explain (or understand) why it works. Easy-to-explain weights, like Example 8.1 (page 330), do not arise in practice. Realistic problems have too many parameters to even try to interpret them.

**Example 8.3** **MNIST** (Modified National Institute of Standards and Technology database) is a dataset of grayscale images of hand-written digits. Each image consists of a $28 \times 28$ grid of pixels, where each pixel is an integer in the range $[0, 255]$ specifying its intensity. Some examples are shown in Figure 8.5 (page 337). There are 60,000 training images and 10,000 test images. MNIST has been used for many perceptual learning case studies.

This was trained with a network with 784 input units (one for each pixel), and one hidden layer containing 512 units with ReLU activation. There are 10 output units, one for each digit, combined with a softmax. It was optimized for categorical cross entropy, and trained for five epochs (each example was used five times, on average, in the training), with a batch size of 128.

After training, the model has a training log loss (base $e$) of 0.21, with an accuracy of 98.4% (the mode is the correct label). On the test set the log loss is 0.68, with an accuracy of 97.0%. If trained for more epochs, the fit to the training data gets better, but on the test set, the log loss becomes much worse and accuracy improves to test 97.7% after 15 more epochs. This is run with the default parameters of **Keras**; different runs might have different errors, and different extreme examples.

Often, insights can be obtained by looking at the incorrect predictions. Figure 8.5 (page 337) shows some of the predictions for the images in the training set and the test set. The first two sets of examples are the incorrect predictions that are closest to 0.5; one for the training set and one for the test set. The other two sets of examples are the most extreme incorrect classifications. They have more extreme probabilities than would be justified by the examples.

## 8.2 Improved Optimization

Stochastic gradient descent (page 291) is the workhorse for parameter learning in neural networks. However, setting the step size is challenging. The structure of the multidimensional search space – the error as a function of the parameter settings – is complex. For a model with, say, a million parameters, the search space has a million dimensions, and the local structure can vary across the dimensions.

The most uncertain (closest to 0.5) incorrect predictions for the training set

| | | | | | |
|---|---|---|---|---|---|
| Actual=4 | Actual=7 | Actual=6 | Actual=1 | Actual=9 | Actual=5 |
| P(4)=0.4735 | P(7)=0.4762 | P(6)=0.4765 | P(1)=0.4767 | P(9)=0.4916 | P(5)=0.4970 |
| P(8)=0.5265 | P(9)=0.5238 | P(4)=0.5235 | P(7)=0.5233 | P(7)=0.5084 | P(3)=0.5030 |

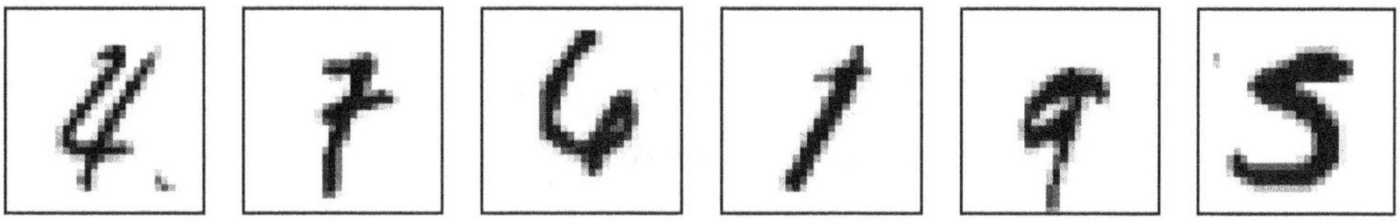

and for the test set:

| | | | | | |
|---|---|---|---|---|---|
| Actual=8 | Actual=3 | Actual=9 | Actual=9 | Actual=8 | Actual=4 |
| P(8)=0.4529 | P(3)=0.4772 | P(9)=0.4788 | P(9)=0.4895 | P(8)=0.4921 | P(4)=0.4984 |
| P(7)=0.5471 | P(8)=0.5228 | P(5)=0.5212 | P(3)=0.5105 | P(3)=0.5079 | P(9)=0.5016 |

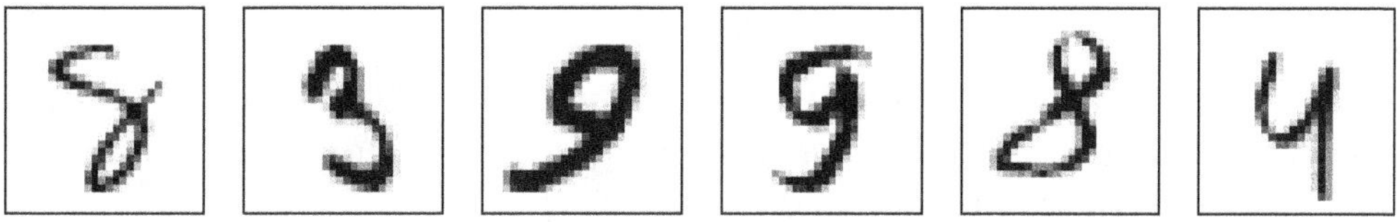

The predictions with highest log loss for the training set are as follows (where $0.0e+00$ indicates the number is less than machine precision for a GPU ($\approx 10^{-38}$), and because most of the mode predictions are 1.0 to machine precision, they are written as $1-\epsilon$, for the given $\epsilon$):

| | | | | | |
|---|---|---|---|---|---|
| Actual=1 | Actual=4 | Actual=1 | Actual=7 | Actual=4 | Actual=0 |
| P(1)=0.0e+00 | P(4)=2.0e-31 | P(1)=4.9e-29 | P(7)=8.0e-29 | P(4)=1.5e-28 | P(0)=2.3e-28 |
| P(2)=1-2.4e-35 | P(7)=1-7.2e-21 | P(8)=1-1.9e-22 | P(2)=1-3.3e-23 | P(0)=1-4.7e-04 | P(8)=1-5.6e-13 |

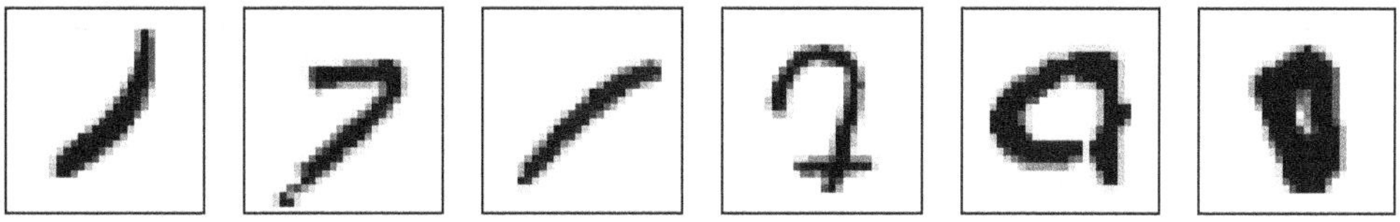

and for the test set:

| | | | | | |
|---|---|---|---|---|---|
| Actual=4 | Actual=6 | Actual=2 | Actual=6 | Actual=9 | Actual=6 |
| P(4)=0.0e+00 | P(6)=0.0e+00 | P(2)=0.0e+00 | P(6)=0.0e+00 | P(9)=0.0e+00 | P(6)=0.0e+00 |
| P(2)=1-1.1e-21 | P(0)=1-0.0e+00 | P(0)=1-0.0e+00 | P(1)=1-1.6e-30 | P(7)=1-5.9e-29 | P(4)=1-1.4e-25 |

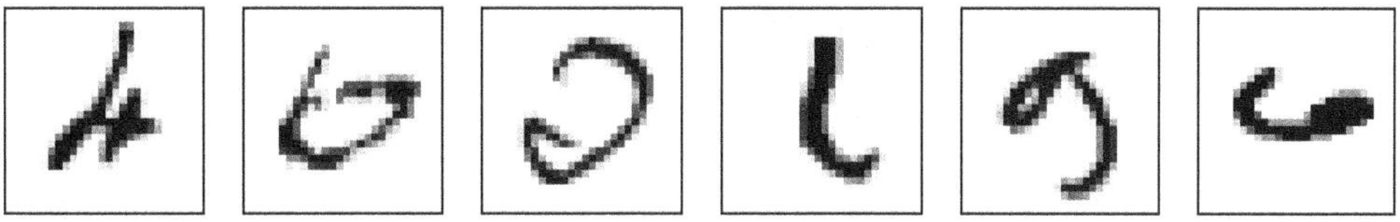

Figure 8.5: Predictions of MNIST digits for the architecture of Example 8.3 (page 336) for one run with five epochs. The actual label, the prediction of the actual label, and the prediction for the label with the greatest predicted probability (the mode) are given

One particular challenge is a **canyon**, where there is a U-shaped error function in one dimension and another dimension has a downhill slope. Another is a **saddle point**, where a minimum in one dimension meets a maximum of another. Close to a saddle point, moving along the dimension that is at a maximum, there is a canyon, so a way to handle canyons should also help with saddle points.

**Example 8.4** Figure 8.6 depicts a canyon with two parameters. The error is plotted as a function of parameters $x$ and $y$. In the $x$-direction the error has a steep valley, but in the $y$-direction there is a gentle slope. A large step size would keep jumping from side-to-side of the valley, perhaps diverging. A small step size is needed for the $x$-value to decrease. However, a small step size in the $y$-direction means very slow convergence. Ideally, you would like small steps in the $x$-direction and large steps in the $y$-direction.

There are two main approaches to adapting step size to handle canyons and related problems. Both have a separate step size for each parameter. They can be combined. The intuition behind each is:

- If the sign of the gradient doesn't change, the step size can be larger; if the sign keeps changing, the step size should be smaller.
- Each weight update should follow the direction of the gradient, and the magnitude should depend on whether the gradient is more or less than its historic value.

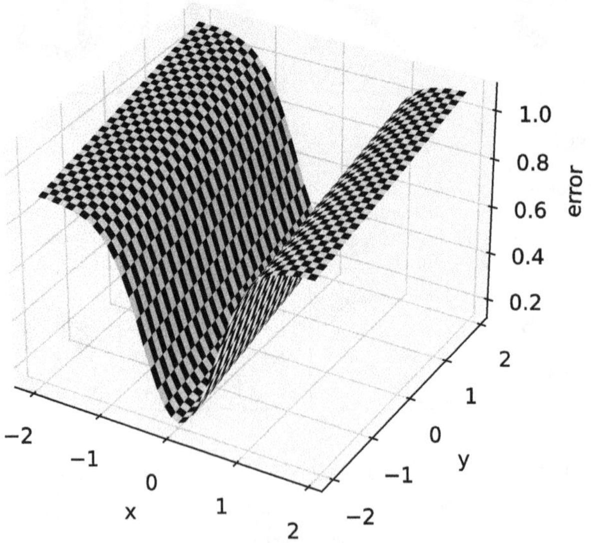


Figure 8.6: A canyon with two parameters

## 8.2.1 Momentum

The **momentum** for each parameter acts like a velocity of the update for each parameter, with the standard stochastic gradient descent update acting like an acceleration. The momentum acts as the step size for the parameter. It is increased if the acceleration is the same sign as the momentum and is decreased if the acceleration is the opposite sign.

To implement momentum, a velocity $v[i,j]$ is stored for each weight $w[i,j]$. Hyperparameter $\alpha$, with $0 \leq \alpha < 1$, specifies how much of the momentum should be used for each batch. The *update* method for *Dense* in Figure 8.3 (page 334) becomes

```
method update()                                  ▷ update all weights
    for each i, j do
        v[i,j] := α * v[i,j] − η/batch_size * d[i,j]
        w[i,j] := w[i,j] + v[i,j]
        d[i,j] := 0.
```

The change in weight is not necessarily in the direction of the gradient of the error, because the momentum might be too great.

The value of $\alpha$ affects how much the step size can increase. Common values for $\alpha$ are 0.5, 0.9, and 0.99. If the gradients have the same value, the step size will approach $\sum_{i=0}^{\infty} \alpha^i = 1/(1-\alpha)$ times the step size without momentum. If $\alpha$ is 0.5, the step size could double. If $\alpha$ is 0.9, the step size could increase up to 10 times, and $\alpha = 0.99$ allows the step size to increase by up to 100 times.

**Example 8.5** Consider the error surface of Figure 8.6 (page 338), described in Example 8.4 (page 338). In the $y$-direction, the gradients are consistent, and so momentum will increase the step size, up to $1/(1-\alpha)$ times. In the $x$-direction, as the valley is crossed, the sign of the gradient changes, and the momentum, and so the steps, get smaller. This means that it eventually makes large steps in the $y$-direction, but small steps in the $x$-direction, enabling it to move down the canyon.

As well as handling canyons, momentum can average out noise due to the batches not including all the examples.

## 8.2.2 RMS-Prop

**RMS-Prop** (root mean squared propagation) is the default optimizer for the **Keras** deep learning library. The idea is that the magnitude of the change in each weight depends on how (the square of) the gradient for that weight compares to its historic value, rather than depending on the absolute value of the gradient. For each weight, a rolling average (page 797) of the square of the gradient is maintained. This is used to determine how much the weight should change. A correction to avoid numeric instability of dividing by approximately zero is also used.

The hyperparameters for RMS-Prop are the learning rate $\eta$ (with a default of 0.001 in Keras), $\rho$ (with a default of 0.9 in Keras) that controls the time horizon of the rolling average, and $\epsilon$ (defaults to $10^{-7}$ in Keras) to ensure numerical stability. The algorithm below maintains a rolling average of the square of the gradient for $w[i,j]$ in $r[i,j]$. The *update* method for *Dense* in Figure 8.3 becomes

```
method update()                                      ▷ update weights
    for each i, j do
        g := d[i,j] / batch_size
        r[i,j] := ρ * r[i,j] + (1 − ρ) * g^2
        w[i,j] := w[i,j] − (η * g) / sqrt(r[i,j] + ε)
        d[i,j] := 0 .
```

To understand the algorithm, assume the value of $r[i,j]$ is initially much bigger than $\epsilon$, so that $r[i,j] + \epsilon \approx r[i,j]$.

- When $r[i,j] \approx g^2$, the ratio $g/\sqrt{r[i,j]+\epsilon}$ is approximately 1 or $-1$, depending on the sign of $g$, so the magnitude of the change in weight is approximately $\eta$.
- When $g^2$ is bigger than $r[i,j]$, the error has a larger magnitude than its historical value, $r[i,j]$ is increased, and the step size increases.
- When $g^2$ is smaller than $r[i,j]$, the value $r[i,j]$ is decreased, and the step size decreases. When a local minimum is approached, the values of $g^2$ and $r[i,j]$ become smaller than the magnitude of $\epsilon$, so the updates are dominated by $\epsilon$, and the step is small.

RMS-Prop only affects the magnitude of the step; the direction of change of $w[i,j]$ is always opposite to $d[i,j]$.

**Example 8.6** Consider the error surface of Figure 8.6 (page 338), described in Example 8.4 (page 338). In the $y$-direction, the gradients are consistent, and so $g$ will be approximately the same as the square root of $r[i,j]$, the average squared value of $g$, and so, assuming $r[i,j]$ is much greater than $\epsilon$, the change in $w[i,j]$ will have magnitude approximately $\eta$.

In the $x$-direction, it might start with a large gradient, but when it encounters a flatter region, $g^2$ becomes less than the rolling average $r[i,j]$, so the step size is reduced. As $g$ for that parameter becomes very small, the steps get very small because they are less than their historical value, eventually becoming dominated by $\epsilon$.

### 8.2.3 Adam

**Adam**, for "adaptive moments", is an optimizer that uses both momentum and the square of the gradient, similar to RMS-Prop. It also uses corrections for the parameters to account for the fact that they are initialized at 0, which is not a good estimate to average with. Other mixes of RMS-Prop and momentum are also common.

It takes as hyperparameters: learning-rate ($\eta$), with a default of 0.001; $\beta_1$, with a default of 0.9; $\beta_2$, with a default of 0.999; and $\epsilon$, with a default of $10^{-7}$. (Names and defaults are consistent with **Keras**.)

Adam takes the gradient, $d[i,j]/bath\_size$, for the weight $w[i,j]$ and maintains a rolling average of the gradient in $s[i,j]$, a rolling average of the square of the gradient in $r[i,j]$, and the step number, $t$. These are all initialized to zero. To implement Adam, the *update* method for *Dense* in Figure 8.3 becomes:

1: **method** *update*() ▷ update weights
2: $\quad t := t + 1$
3: $\quad$ **for each** $i, j$ **do**
4: $\quad\quad g := d[i,j]/batch\_size$
5: $\quad\quad s[i,j] := \beta_1 * s[i,j] + (1 - \beta_1) * g$
6: $\quad\quad r[i,j] := \beta_2 * r[i,j] + (1 - \beta_2) * g^2$
7: $\quad\quad w[i,j] := w[i,j] - \dfrac{\eta * s[i,j]/(1 - \beta_1^t)}{\sqrt{r[i,j]/(1 - \beta_2^t)} + \epsilon}$
8: $\quad\quad d[i,j] := 0.$

The weight update step (line 7) is like RMS-Prop but uses $s[i,j]$ instead of the gradient in the numerator, and corrects it by dividing by $1 - \beta_1^t$. Note that $\beta_1$ and $\beta_2$ are the names of the parameters, but the superscript is the power. In the first update, when $t = 1$, $s[i,j]/(1 - \beta_1^t)$ is equal to $g$; it corrects subsequent updates similarly. It also corrects $r[i,j]$ by dividing by $1 - \beta_2^t$. Note that $\epsilon$ is inside the square root in RMS-Prop, but is outside in Adam.

### 8.2.4 Initialization

For convergence, it helps to normalize the input parameters, and sensibly initialize the weights.

For example, consider a dataset of people with features including height (in cm), the number of steps walked in a day, and a Boolean which specifies whether they have passed high school. These use very different units, and might have very different utility in predictions. To make it learn independently of the units, it is typical to **normalize** each real-valued feature, by subtracting the mean, so the result has a mean of 0, and dividing by the standard deviation, so the result has a standard deviation and variance of 1. Each feature is scaled independently.

Categorical inputs are usually represented as **indicator variables** (page 182), so that categorical variable $X$ with domain $\{v_1, \ldots, v_k\}$ is represented as $k$ inputs, $X_1, \ldots, X_k$. An input example with $X = v_j$ is represented with $X_j = 1$ and every other $X_{j'} = 0$. This is also called a **one-hot encoding**.

The weights for the linear functions in hidden layers cannot all be assigned the same value, otherwise they will converge in lock-step, never learning different features. If the $w[i,j]$ parameters are initialized to the same value, all of the units at one layer will implement the same function. Thus they need to be initialized to random values. In **Keras**, the default initializer is the **Glorot uniform initializer**, which chooses values uniformly in the interval between $\pm\sqrt{6/(n_i+n_O)}$, where $n_i$ is the number of inputs and $n_o$ is the number of outputs for the linear function. This has a theoretical basis and tends to work well in practice for many cases. The biases (the weights multiplied by input unit 1) are typically initialized to 0.

For the output units, the bias can be initialized to the value that would predict best when all of the other inputs are zero. This is the mean for regression, or the inverse-sigmoid of the empirical probability for binary classification. The other output weights can be set to 0. This allows the gradient descent to learn the signal from the inputs, and not the background average.

## 8.3 Improving Generalization

When building a new model, it is often useful to ensure initially that the model can fit the training data, and then tackle overfitting.

First make sure it is learning something. The error on the training set should be able to beat the naive baseline corresponding to the loss being evaluated (page 276); for example, it should do better than the mean of the training data targets for squared loss or log loss. If it does not, the algorithm is not learning, and the algorithm, architecture, optimization algorithm, step size, or initialization might need to be changed. You should try one of the algorithms from the previous chapter, as well as a neural network.

If it beats the naive baseline, but does not perform as well as you might expect on the training set, try changing the model. You know it won't do as well on the test set and on new examples as it does on the training set, so if it is poor on the training set, it will be poor on new cases. Poor performance on the training set is an indication of under fitting; the model is too simple to represent the data. One example of under fitting is using logistic regression for a function that is not linearly separable (see Example 7.11 (page 288)). Try increasing the capacity (e.g., the width and/or depth), but also check other algorithms and parameter settings. It also might be the case that the input features do not contain enough information to predict the target features, in which case the naive baseline might be the best you can do.

Once you know the algorithm can at least fit the training set, test the error on validation set (page 305). If the validation error does not improve as the algorithm proceeds, it means the learning is not generalizing, and it is fitting to noise. In this case, it is probably overfitting and the model should be simplified. When there is little data, models with more than one or two hidden layers tend to severely overfit. In general, small amounts of data require small models.

At this stage it is useful to carry out **hyperparameter tuning** (page 305) using **cross validation** (page 304). Automating hyperparameter tuning, a process known as **autoML**, is often the best way to select the hyperparameters.

When there is little data available, $k$**-fold cross validation** (page 306) works well, but might not be needed if there is a lot of data.

Some of the hyperparameters that can be tuned include:

- the algorithm (a decision tree or gradient-boosted trees (page 311) may be more appropriate than a neural network)
- number of layers
- width (page 331) of each layer
- number of epochs, to allow for early stopping (page 306)
- learning rate
- batch size
- regularization parameters (page 302); $L1$ and $L2$ regularization are often useful when there is little data.

One effective mechanism for deep networks is **dropout**, which involves randomly dropping some units during training. Ignoring a unit is equivalent to temporarily setting its output to zero. Dropout is controlled by a parameter *rate*, which specifies the proportion of values that are zeroed. It is common that *rate* is 0.5 for hidden units, and 0.2 for input units. These probabilities are applied to each unit independently for each example in a batch.

This can be implemented by treating dropout as a layer consisting of a single function, as in Figure 8.7. This function is used when learning, but not when making a prediction for a new example.

If $rate = 0.5$, half of the values are used, and so the sum would be half, on average, of what it would be without dropout. To make the learner with dropout comparable to the one without, the output should be doubled. In general, the output needs to be scaled by $1/(1 - rate)$, which is the value of *scaling* in Figure 8.7.

Improving the algorithm is not the only way to improve the prediction. Other methods that are useful to building a better model include the following.

```
class Dropout(rate)                      ▷ rate is probability of an input being zeroed
    method output(in)                                  ▷ in is array with length n_i
        scaling := 1/(1 − rate)
        for each i ∈ [0, n_i) do
            mask[i] := 0 with probability rate else 1
            out[i] := in[i] ∗ mask[i] ∗ scaling
        return out
    method Backprop(error)                          ▷ error is array with length n_i
        for each i ∈ [0, n_i) do
            ierror[i] := error[i] ∗ mask[i]
        return ierror
```

Figure 8.7: Pseudocode for dropout

- Collecting more data is sometimes the most cost-effective way to improve a model.

- Sometimes more data can be obtained by **data augmentation**: using the existing data, for example in recognizing objects from images by translating, scaling, or rotating the image (but be careful it doesn't change the class, e.g., a rotation of a "6" might become a "9"), adding noise or changing the context (e.g., once you have a picture of a cat, put it in different contexts).

- Feature engineering is still useful when the data is limited or there are limited resources for trainings. For example, there are many representations for the positions of a hand on a clock, and some are much easier to learn with than others; it is much easier to learn the time from the angles of the hands than from an image of the clock.

- It is sometimes easier to learn a model for a task for which there is limited data, by sharing the lower-level features among multiple tasks. The lower-level features then have many more examples to learn from than they would with any single task. This is known as **multi-task learning**. In a neural network, it can be achieved by sharing the lower layers (those closest to the inputs), with the different tasks having their own higher layers. When learning a task, all of the weights for the units used for the task (including the shared lower-level units) are updated. An alternative, which is used when one task has already been learned, is for a new task with limited data to use the lower-level features of the original task and only learn higher-level features for the new task. This is explored more in Section 8.5.5 (page 364).

## 8.4 Convolutional Neural Networks

Imagine using a neural network for recognizing objects in large images using a dense network, as in Example 8.3 (page 336). There are two aspects that might seem strange. First, it does not take into account any spatial locality, if the pixels were shuffled consistently in all of the images, the neural network would act the same. Humans would not be able to recognize objects any more, because humans take the spatial proximity into account. Second, it would have to learn to recognize cats, for example, separately when they appear in the bottom-left of an image and when they appear in the bottom-right and in the top-middle of an image. Convolutional neural networks tackle these problems by using filters that act on small patches of an image, and by sharing the parameters so they learn useful features no matter where in an image they occur.

In a **convolutional neural network (CNN)**, a **kernel** (sometimes called a **convolution mask**, or **filter**) is a learned linear operator that is applied to local patches. The following first covers one-dimensional kernels, used for sequences such as sound or text, then two-dimensional kernels, as used in images. Higher-dimensional kernels are also used, for example in video.

In one dimension, suppose the input is a sequence (list) $[x_0, \ldots, x_{m-1}]$ and there is structure so that $x_i$ is close to $x_{i+1}$ in some sense. For example, $x_i$ could be the $i$th value of a speech signal in time, and $x_{i+1}$ is the next one in time. In a spectrum, $x_i$ could be the value of one frequency, and $x_{i+1}$ the value for the next frequency measured.

A **one-dimensional kernel** is a vector $[w_0, \ldots, w_{k-1}]$, where $k$ is the **kernel size**, which when applied to the sequence $x = [x_0, \ldots, x_{m-1}]$ produces a sequence $y = [y_0, \ldots, y_{m-k}]$ where

$$y[i] = \sum_{j=0}^{k-1} x[i+j] * w[j].$$

**Example 8.7** Suppose a signal consists of the values

$$[0, 1, 2, 3, 7, 5, 8, 10, 12, 9, 6, 3, 0, 2, 4, 6, 8]$$

in order. Thus, $x_0 = 0$, $x_6 = 7$, $x_7 = 5$, etc. This is shown in Figure 8.8(a).

Consider the kernel $[0.5, 0.5]$. Applying this to the signal gives the sequence

$$[0.5, 1.5, 2.5, 5.0, 6.0, 6.5, 9.0, 11.0, 10.5, 7.5, 4.5, 1.5, 1.0, 3.0, 5.0, 7.0]$$

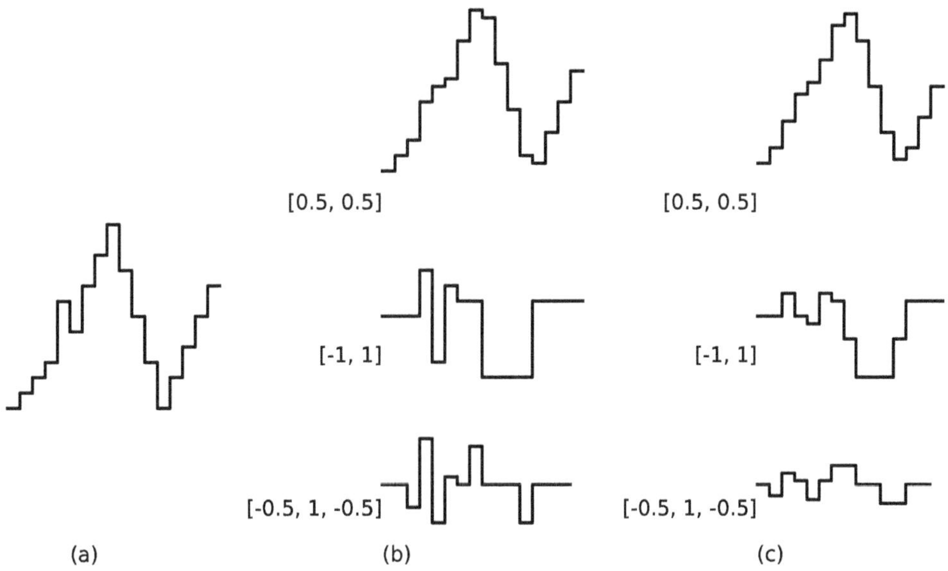


Figure 8.8: Result of simple one-dimensional kernels: (a) is the original signal; (b) shows the kernels $[0.5, 0.5]$, $[-1, 1]$, and $[-0.5, 1, -0.5]$ applied to the signal (a); (c) shows the same kernels applied to the top signal in (b)

shown in Figure 8.8(b), top. Each value is the mean of two adjoining values in the original signal. This kernel smooths a sequence.

Applying the kernel $[-1,1]$ to the original sequence results in the sequence

$$[1,1,1,4,-2,3,2,2,-3,-3,-3,-3,2,2,2,2]$$

which is the slope; it is positive when the value is increasing and negative when the value is decreasing. See Figure 8.8(b), middle.

The kernel $[-0.5,1,-0.5]$ finds peaks and troughs. It is positive when the value is locally higher than its neighbors, and negative when the value is lower than its neighbors. The magnitude reflects how much it is greater or less. See Figure 8.8(b), bottom.

Figure 8.8(c) shows the same kernels applied to the smoothed signal (Figure 8.8(b), top).

A **two-dimensional kernel** is a $k \times k$ array $w[i,j]$, where $k$ is the kernel size, which when applied to the two-dimensional array *in* produces a two-dimensional array *out* where

$$out[x,y] := \sum_{i=0}^{k-1}\sum_{j=0}^{k-1} in[x+i,y+j] * w[i,j].$$

The kernel size, $k$, is usually much smaller than the size of either dimension of *in*. Two-dimensional kernels are used for images, where they are applied to patches of adjacent pixels.

**Example 8.8** Consider the following kernels that could be applied to a black-and-white image where the value of $in[x,y]$ is the brightness of the pixel at position $(x,y)$:

(a)

| | |
|---|---|
| 0 | 1 |
| −1 | 0 |

(b)

| | |
|---|---|
| 1 | 0 |
| 0 | −1 |

(c)

| | | |
|---|---|---|
| −1 | 0 | 1 |
| −2 | 0 | 2 |
| −1 | 0 | 1 |

(d)

| | | |
|---|---|---|
| 1 | 2 | 1 |
| 0 | 0 | 0 |
| −1 | −2 | −1 |

Kernels (a) and (b) were invented by Roberts [1965]. The result of (a) is positive when the top-right pixel in a $2 \times 2$ block is greater than the pixel one down and to the left. This can be used to detect the direction of a change in shading. Kernels (a) and (b) together can recognize various directions of the change in shading; when (a) and (b) are both positive, the brightness increases going up. When (a) is positive and (b) is negative, the brightness increases going right. When (a) is positive and (b) close to zero, the brightness increases going up-right.

Kernels (c) and (d) are the **Sobel-Feldman operators** for edge detection, where (c) finds edges in the $x$-direction and (d) finds edges in the $y$-direction; together they can find edges in other directions.

Before machine learning dominated image interpretation, kernels were hand designed to have particular characteristics. Now kernels are mostly learned.

**Convolutional neural networks** learn the weights for the kernels from data. Two main aspects distinguish convolutional neural networks from ordinary neural networks.

- **Locality**: the values are a function of neighboring positions, rather than being based on all units as they are in a fully-connected layer. For example, a $5 \times 5$ kernel for vision uses two pixels in each direction of a point to give a value for the point for the next layer. Multiple applications of kernels can increase the size of influence. For example, in image interpretation, when two consecutive convolutional layers use $5 \times 5$ kernels, the values of the second one depend on four pixels in each direction in the original image.

- **Parameter sharing** or **weight tying** means that, for a single kernel, the same parameters are used at all locations in the image.

---

**class** *Conv2D*($k$)
    Create $w[i,j]$ for each $0 \leq i,j < k$, initialize randomly
    Create $d[i,j]$ for each $0 \leq i,j < k$, initialize to 0
    **method** *output*(*input*) ▷ *input* is $xd \times yd$ array
        Create $out[x,y]$ for each $0 \leq x \leq xd-k,\ 0 \leq y \leq yd-k$
        **for each** $x : 0 \leq x \leq xd-k$ **do**
            **for each** $y : 0 \leq y \leq yd-k$ **do**
$$out[x,y] := \sum_{i=0}^{k-1}\sum_{j=0}^{k-1} in[x+i,y+j] * w[i,j]$$
        **return** *out*
    **method** *Backprop*(*error*) ▷ *error* is $xd-k+1 \times yd-k+1$ array
        Create $ierror[x,y]$ for each $0 \leq x < xd,\ 0 \leq j < yd$ initialized to 0
        **for each** $x : 0 \leq x \leq xd-k$ **do**
            **for each** $y : 0 \leq y \leq yd-k$ **do**
                **for each** $i : 0 \leq i < k$ **do**
                    **for each** $j : 0 \leq j < k$ **do**
                        $d[i,j] := d[i,j] + in[x+i,y+j] * error[x,y]$
                        $ierror[x+i,y+j] := ierror[x+i,y+j] + error[x,y] * w[i,j]$
        **return** *ierror*
    **method** *update*() ▷ update all weights
        Same as for *Dense* (Figure 8.3 (page 334))

Figure 8.9: Two-dimensional convolution pseudocode

---

Figure 8.9 shows the algorithm for a two-dimensional convolutional layer, where only one kernel is applied to the input array. The kernel is a $k \times k$ square. The input is an $xd \times yd$ rectangle. The output is smaller than the input, removing $k-1$ values from each dimension. In backpropagation, the input error (*ierror*) and $d$ are updated once for each time the corresponding input or weight is used to compute an output. Unlike in the dense linear function (Figure 8.3 (page 334)), parameter sharing means that during backpropagation each $d[i,j]$ is updated multiple times for a single example.

Real convolutional neural networks are more sophisticated than this, including the following features:

- The kernel does not need to be square, but can be any rectangular size. This affects the size of $d$ and $w$.

- Because the algorithm above requires each array index to be in range, it removes elements from the edges. This is problematic for deep networks, as the model eventually shrinks to zero as the number of layers increases. It is common to add **zero padding**: expand the input (or the output) by zeros symmetrically – with the same number of zeros on each side – so that the output is the same size as the input. The use of padding means it is reasonable for the kernel indexes to start from 0, whereas it was traditional to have them be symmetric about 0, such as in the range $[-2,2]$.

- Multiple kernels are applied concurrently. This means that the output consists of multiple two-dimensional arrays, one for each kernel used. These multiple arrays are called **channels**. To stack these into layers, the input also needs to be able to handle multiple channels. A color image typically has three channels corresponding to the colors red, green, and blue. (Cameras for scientific purposes can contain many more channels.)

  To represent multiple channels for the input and the output, the weight array, $w$, becomes four-dimensional; one for $x$, one for $y$, one for the input channel, and one for the output channel. The pseudocode needs to be expanded, as follows. If the input is $in[x,y,ic]$ for input channel $ic$ and the output is $out[x,y,oc]$ for output channel $oc$, there is a weight for each $x,y,ic,oc$. In the method *output*, there is an extra loop over $oc$, and the output assignment becomes

  $$out[x,y,oc] := \sum_{ic}\sum_{i}\sum_{j} in[x+i,y+j,ic] * w[i,j,ic,oc].$$

  *Backprop* needs also to loop over the input channels and the output channels, updating each parameter.

  Instead of all input channels being connected to all output channels, sometimes they are grouped so that only the input and output channels in the same group are connected.

- The above algorithm does not include a **bias** term – the weight multiplied by 1. Whether to use a bias is a parameter in most implementations, with a default of using a bias.

- This produces an output of the same size as the input, perhaps with a fixed number of pixels removed at the sides. It is also possible to **down-sample**, selecting every second (which would halve the size of each dimension) or every third value (which would divide the size of each dimension by three), for example. While this could be done with an extra layer to down-sample, it is more efficient to not compute the values to be thrown away, thus down-sampling is usually incorporated into the convolutional layer.

  A **stride** for a dimension is a positive integer $s$ such that each $s$th value is used in the output. For two dimensions, a stride of 2 for each dimension will halve the size of each dimension, and so the output will be a quarter the size of the input. For example, a $256 \times 265$ image with a stride of 2 for each dimension will output a $128 \times 128$ array, which in later layers can use another stride of 2 in each dimension to give a $64 \times 64$ array. A stride of 1 selects all output values, and so is like not having a stride. There can be a separate stride for each dimension.

- In a **pooling** layer, instead of a learnable linear kernel, a fixed function of the outputs of the units is applied in a kernel. A common pooling layer is **max-pooling**, which is like a convolution, but where the maximum is used instead of a linear function. Pooling is typically combined with a stride greater than 1 to down-sample as well. It is typical to use a convolution layer, followed by a nonlinear function, such as ReLU, followed by a pooling layer, the output of which is then input to a convolution layer and so on.

- When used for classification of the whole image (e.g., detecting whether there is a cat or a baby in the image), a convolutional neural network typically ends with fully-connected layers. Note that to use standard fully-connected layers, the array needs to be **flattened** into a vector; this is done by concatenating the rows or the columns. A **fully convolutional neural network** has a number of convolution layers, but no fully-connected layer. This is used to classify each point in an image (e.g., whether each pixel is part of a cat or part of the background).

- A **shortcut connection** or a **skip connection** in a deep network is a connection that skips some layers. In particular, some of the input channels of a layer come from the previous layer and some from lower-level layers. In a **residual network**, the values from one layer are added to the values from a lower layer. In this case, the intermediate layers – those between the two layers being added – become trained to predict the error, in a similar way to boosting (page 309). The first residual network

[He et al., 2015] won many competitions for classification from images. One of their models had a depth of 152 layers with over a million parameters, and was trained on an ImageNet dataset with 1000 classes and 1.28 million training examples.

## 8.5 Neural Models for Sequences

Fully-connected networks, perhaps including convolutional layers, can handle fixed-size images and sequences. It is also useful to consider **sequential data** consisting of variable-length sequences. Sequences arise in natural language processing, biology, and any domain involving time, such as the controllers of Chapter 2. Here, natural language is used as the canonical example of sequences. We first give some background for **neural language models** that will be expanded for language as a sequence of frequencies, phonemes, characters, or words.

A **corpus** is the text used for training. The corpus could be, for example, a novel, a set of news articles, all of Wikipedia, or a subset of the text on the web. A **token** is a sequence of characters that are grouped together, such as all of the characters between blanks or punctuation. The process of splitting a corpus into tokens is called **tokenization**. Along with the corpus is a **vocabulary**, the set of **words** that will be considered, such as all of the tokens that appear in the corpus, the words in a fixed dictionary, or all of the tokens that appear more than, say, 10 times in the corpus. The vocabulary typically includes not only the words in common dictionaries, but also often names, common phrases (such as "artificial intelligence" and "hot dog"), slang (such as "zzz", which is used to indicate snoring), punctuation, and a markers for the beginning and end of sentences, written as "⟨*start*⟩" and "⟨*stop*⟩". While *word* can be synonymous with *token*, sometimes there is more processing to group words into tokens, or to split words into tokens (such as the word "eating" becoming the tokens "eat" and "ing"). In a character-level model, the vocabulary could be the set of Unicode characters that appear in the corpus.

### 8.5.1 Word Embeddings

The first model, shown in Figure 8.10 (page 351), takes a single word and makes a prediction about what word appears near it. It might take a word and predict the next word in a text, or the word that was two words before. Each word is mapped to a **word embedding**, a vector representing some mix of syntax and semantics that is useful for predicting words that appear with the word.

The input layer uses **indicator variables** (page 286), forming a **one-hot encoding** for words. That is, there is an input unit for each word in a dictionary. For a given word, the corresponding unit has value 1, and the rest of the units have value 0. This input layer can feed into a hidden layer using a dense linear function, as at the bottom of Figure 8.10. This dense linear layer is called an

**encoder**, as it encodes each word into a vector. Suppose $u$ defines the weights for the encoder, so $u[i,j]$ is the weight for the $i$th word for the $j$th unit in the hidden layer. The bias term for the linear function can be used for unknown words – words in a text that were not in the dictionary, so all of the input units are 0 – but let's ignore them for now and set the bias to 0.

The one-hot encoding has an interesting interaction with a dense linear layer that may follow it. The one-hot encoding essentially selects one weight for each hidden unit. The vector of values in the hidden layer for the input word $i$ is $[u[i,0], u[i,1], u[i,2], \dots]$, which is called a **word embedding** for that word.

To predict another word from this embedding, another dense linear function can be used to map the embedding into predictions for the words, with one unit per word, as shown in Figure 8.10. This function from the embeddings to words is a **decoder**. Suppose $v$ defines the weights for the decoder, so $v[j,k]$ is the weight for the $k$th word for the $j$th unit in the hidden layer.

Notice that, ignoring the softmax output, the relationship between the $i$th input word and the $k$th output word is $\sum_j u[i,j] * v[j,k]$. This combination of linear functions is **matrix multiplication**, where a matrix is a two-dimensional array of weights (see box on page 352).

Suppose you want to predict a word in a text given the previous words, and training on a corpus consisting of the sequence of words $w_0, w_1, w_2, \dots$. The models can be trained using input–output pairs of the form $(w_{i-1}, w_i)$ for each $i > 0$. The sequence $w_{i-k}, \dots, w_{i-1}$ is the **context** for $w_i$. As you are predicting

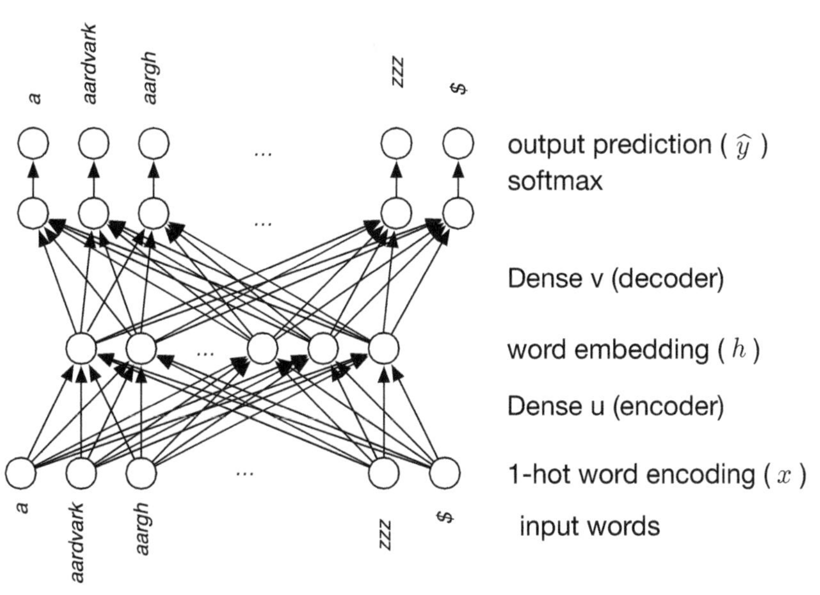


Figure 8.10: A shallow neural network for word embeddings

### Vectors, Matrices, Tensors, and Arrays

A **vector** is a fixed-length array of numbers. A **matrix** is a two-dimensional rectangular array of numbers with a fixed size of each dimension. A **tensor** generalizes these to allow multiple dimensions. A vector is thus a one-dimensional tensor, a matrix is a two-dimensional tensor, a number is a zero-dimensional tensor. Four-dimensional tensors are used for video, with dimensions for the frame number, $x$ and $y$ positions, and the color channel. A collection of fixed-size video clips can be represented as a five-dimensional tensor, with the extra dimension representing the clip.

For a matrix $M$, the $i,j$th element is $M_{ij}$ in mathematical notation, $M[i,j]$ in standard programming language notation, or $M[i][j]$ in Python. Python natively only has one-dimensional arrays, which are very flexible, where the elements of the arrays can be of heterogenous types (e.g., integers or other arrays). A tensor has a fixed dimensionality and fixed sizes of each dimension, which makes them more inflexible than Python arrays. The inflexibility can result in greater efficiency because the looping can be determined at compile time, as is exploited in the **NumPy** package and in **graphics processing units (GPUs)**.

A vector can represent an assignment of values to a set of variables (given a total ordering of the variables). A linear function (page 288) from one set of variables to another can be represented by a matrix. What also distinguishes matrices and vectors from arbitrary arrays is that they have particular operations defined on them. Matrix–vector multiplication represents the application of a linear function, represented by matrix $A$, to a vector $v$ representing an assignment of values to the variables. The result is $Av$, a vector defined by

$$(Av)[i] = \sum_j A[i,j] * v[j].$$

Linear function composition is defined by **matrix multiplication**; if $A$ and $B$ are matrices, $AB$ represents the linear function that is the composition of these two functions, defined by

$$(AB)[i,k] = \sum_j A[i,j] * B[j,k].$$

Later chapters define various generalizations of matrix multiplication. Section 17.2.2 (page 740) defines a form of tensor multiplication that multiplies three matrices to get a three-dimensional tensor. The factors of Section 9.5.2 (page 413) allow multiple arrays to be multiplied before summing out a variable.

a single next word, softmax (page 295), implemented as hierarchical softmax (page 296) when the vocabulary is large, is appropriate.

**Example 8.9** Suppose the text starts with "The history of AI is a history of fantasies, possibilities, demonstrations, and promise". Let's ignore punctuation, and use ⟨*start*⟩ as the start of a sentence. The training data might be:

| Input | Target |
|---|---|
| ⟨*start*⟩ | the |
| the | history |
| history | of |
| of | ai |
| ai | is |
| is | a |
| a | history |
| history | of |
| of | fantasies |

As you may imagine, learning a model that generalizes well requires a large corpus. Some of the original models were trained on corpuses of billions of words with a vocabulary of around a million words.

It usually works better to make predictions based on multiple surrounding words, rather than just one. In the following two methods, the $k$ surrounding words form the **context**. For example, if $k$ were 3, to predict a word, the three words before and the three words after in the training corpus would form the context. In these two methods, the order or position of the context words is ignored. These two models form **Word2vec**.

- In the **continuous bag of words (CBOW)** model, all words in the context contribute $n/(2*k)$ in the one-hot encoding of Figure 8.10 (page 351), where $n$ is the number of times the word appears in the context. This gives a weighted average of the embeddings of the word used.
- In the **Skip-gram model**, the model of Figure 8.10 (page 351) is used for each $(w_{i+j}, w_i)$, for $j \in \{-k, \ldots, -1, 1, \ldots, k\}$, and the prediction of $w_i$ is proportional to the product of each of the predictions. Thus, this assumes that each context word gives an independent prediction of word $w_i$.

**Example 8.10** Consider the sentence "the history of AI is a history of fantasies possibilities demonstrations and promise" from Example 8.9. Suppose the context is the three words to the left and right, and case is ignored. In the prediction for the fourth word ("ai"), the bag of context words is {a, history, history, is, of, the}. For the following word ("is"), the bag of context words is {a, ai, history, history, of, of}.

In the CBOW model, the positive training example for the fourth word ("ai"), has inputs "the", "of", "is", and "a" with weight 1/6 in the one-hot encoding, "history" with weight 2/6, and the other words with weight 0 and the target is "ai".

In the Skip-gram model, for the fourth word, there are six positive training examples, namely (a,ai), (history,ai), (history,ai), (is,ai), (of,ai), (the ai). At test time, there is a prediction for each of [a, history, history, is, of, the] being the input. The prediction for a target word is the product of the predictions for these.

The embeddings resulting from these models can be added or subtracted point-wise, for example $Paris - France + Japan \approx Tokyo$. The idea is that $Paris - France$ represents the "capital of" relationship, which when added to the embedding of *Japan* gives *Tokyo*. Mikolov et al. [2013], the originators of these methods, trained them on a corpus of 1.6 billion words, with up to 600 hidden units. Some other relationships found using the Skip-gram model were the following, where the value after "$\approx$" is the mode of the resulting prediction:

$$\begin{aligned}
&scientist - Einstein + Messi \approx midfielder\\
&scientist - Einstein + Mozart \approx violinist\\
&scientist - Einstein + Picasso \approx painter\\
&sushi - Japan + Germany \approx bratwurst\\
&sushi - Japan + USA \approx pizza\\
&sushi - Japan + France \approx tapas.
\end{aligned}$$

There was about 60% accuracy picking the mode compared to what the authors considered to be the correct answer.

It has been found that Skip-gram is better for small datasets and CBOW is faster and better for more frequent words. How important it is to represent rare words usually dictates which method to use.

### 8.5.2 Recurrent Neural Networks

The previous methods ignored the order of the words in the context. A **recurrent neural network (RNN)** explicitly models sequences by augmenting the model of Figure 8.10 (page 351) with a hidden state. The following description assumes sequences are ordered in time, as the actions of an agent or speech would be.

Figure 8.11 (page 355) shows a recurrent neural network that takes a sequence of values

$$x^{(0)}, x^{(1)}, x^{(2)}, x^{(3)} \ldots$$

and outputs a sequence of values

$$y^{(0)}, y^{(1)}, y^{(2)}, y^{(3)} \ldots$$

where $y^{(i)}$ only depends on $x^{(j)}$ for $j \le i$. This is a **matched RNN** because there is an output for each input. For example, the input could be a sequence of words and the output the same sequence of words shifted right by 1 (so $x^{(0)}$ is the $\langle start \rangle$ token and $y^{(i)} = x^{(i+1)}$), so the model is predicting the next word in the sequence. There is also a $\langle stop \rangle$ token to mean the end of the text output.

Between the inputs and the outputs for each time is a **memory** or **belief state** (page 55), $h^{(t)}$, which represents the information remembered from the previous times. A recurrent neural network represents a **belief state transition function** (page 56), which specifies how the belief state, $h^{(t)}$, depends on the percept, $x^{(t)}$, and the previous belief state, $h^{(t-1)}$, and a **command function** (page 57), which specifies how the output $y^{(t)}$ depends on the input and the belief state $h^{(t)}$ and the input $x^{(t)}$. For a basic recurrent neural network, both of these are represented using a linear function followed by an activation function. More sophisticated models use other differentiable functions, such as deep networks, to represent these functions.

The vector $h^{(t)}$ has as the $i$th component

$$h^{(t)}[i] = \phi\left(b[i] + \sum_j w[i,j] * h^{(t-1)}[j] + \sum_k u[i,k] * x^{(t)}[k]\right) \tag{8.2}$$

for a nonlinear activation function $\phi$, bias weight vector $b$, weight matrices $w$ and $u$, which do not depend on time, $t$. Thus, a recurrent neural network uses **parameter sharing** (page 347) for the weights because the same weights are used every time. The prediction to time $t$ is the vector $\widehat{y}^{(t)}$, where

$$\widehat{y}^{(t)}[m] = sigmoid(b'[m] + \sum_i v[m,i] * h^{(t)}[i])$$

where $b'$ is a vector and $v$ is a weight matrix similar to Figure 8.10 (page 351).

Figure 8.12 (page 356) shows a recurrent neural network with a single output at time $T$. This has a similar parametrization to that of Figure 8.11. It could be used for determining the sentiment of some text, such as whether an online review of a product is positive or negative. It could be used to generate an im-

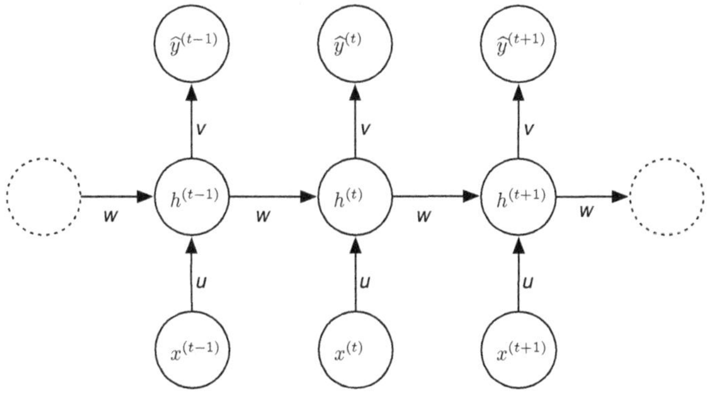


Figure 8.11: A recurrent neural network with matched input–output

age from a text. In this case, the hidden state accumulates the evidence needed to make the final prediction.

Figure 8.13 shows an **encoder–decoder recurrent neural network** which does **sequence-to-sequence mapping** where the inputs and the outputs are not matched. The input is a sequence $x^{(0)}, x^{(1)}, \ldots, x^{(n_x)}$ and the output is a sequence $y^{(0)}, y^{(1)}, \ldots, y^{(n_y)}$. These sequences could be of very different lengths. There are two extra tokens, $\langle start \rangle$ and $\langle stop \rangle$; one for the beginning of a sequence and one for the end. Encoder–decoder networks are used for speech-to-text and for machine translation. In a speech recognition system, the input could be a sequence of sounds, and the output a sequence of words.

The **encoder**, shown on the left of Figure 8.13, is the same as the matched RNN, but without the output. The hidden layer at the end of the encoder, $c$, becomes the context for the decoder. This context contains all of the information about the input sequence that can be used to generate the output sequence.

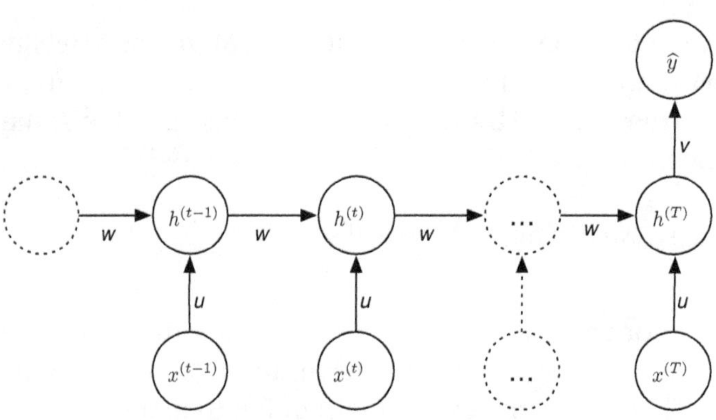


Figure 8.12: A recurrent neural network with a single output

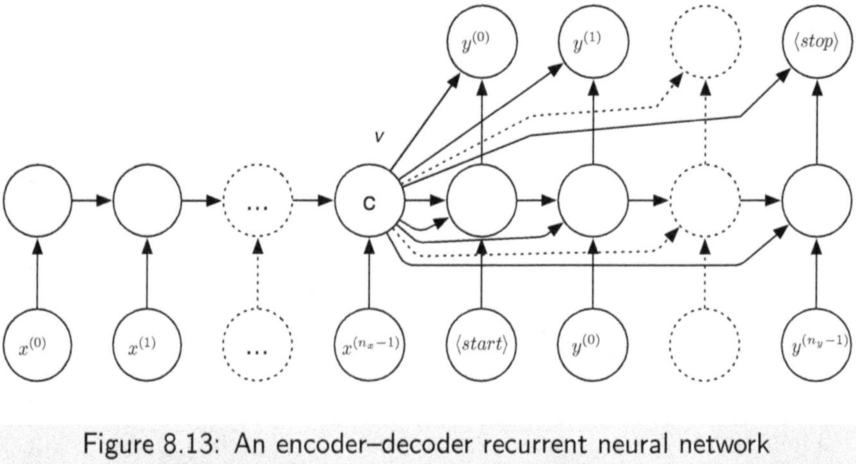


Figure 8.13: An encoder–decoder recurrent neural network

(The start and stop tokens are ignored here.)

The **decoder**, shown on the right of Figure 8.13 (page 356), is a **generative language model** that takes the context and emits an output sequence. It is like the matched RNN (page 354), but also includes the hidden vector, $c$, as an input for each hidden value and each output value. The output sequence is produced one element at a time. The input to the first hidden layer of the decoder is the $\langle start \rangle$ token and the context (twice). The hidden layer and the context are used to predict $y^{(0)}$. For each subsequent prediction of $y^{(i)}$, the hidden layer takes as input the previous output, $y^{(i-1)}$, the context, $c$, and the value of the previous hidden layer. Then $y^{(i)}$ is predicted from the hidden layer and the context. This is repeated until the $\langle stop \rangle$ token is produced.

During training, all of the $y^{(i)}$ can be predicted at once based on the output shifted by 1. Note that $y^{(i)}$ can only use the $x^{(j)}$ and the previous $y^{(j)}$; it cannot use $y^{(i)}$ as an input. When generating text for the prediction for $y^{(i)}$, a value for $y^{(i-1)}$ is input. If the most likely value of $\widehat{y}^{(i-1)}$ is used, it is called **greedy decoding**. It is usually better to search through the predicted values, using one of the methods of Chapter 3, where the log-probability or log loss (page 273) is the cost. Beam search (page 158) is a common method.

For a given input size, recurrent neural networks are feedforward networks with shared parameters. Stochastic gradient descent and related methods work, with the proviso that during backpropagation, the (shared) weights are updated whenever they were used in the prediction. Recurrent neural networks are challenging to train because for a parameter that is reduced in each backpropagation step, its influence, and so its gradient vanishes, dropping exponentially. A parameter that is increased at each step has its gradient increasing exponentially and thus exploding.

### 8.5.3 Long Short-Term Memory

Consider the sentence "I grew up in Indonesia, where I had a wonderful childhood, speaking the local dialect of Indonesian." Predicting the last word requires information that is much earlier in the sentence (or even in previous sentences). The problem of vanishing gradients means that it is difficult to learn long dependencies such as the one in this sentence.

One way to think about recurrent neural networks is that the hidden layer at any time represents the agent's short-term memory at that time. At the next time, the memory is replaced by a combination of the old memory and new information, using the formula of Equation (8.2) (page 355). While parameter values can be designed to remember information from long ago, the vanishing and exploding gradients mean that the long-term dependencies are difficult to learn.

A **long short-term memory (LSTM)** network is a special kind of recurrent neural network designed so that the memory is maintained unless replaced by new information. This allows it to better capture long-term dependencies than is done in a traditional RNN. Intuitively, instead of learning the function from $h^{(t-1)}$ to $h^{(t)}$, it learns the change in $h$, which we write $\Delta h^{(t)}$, so that $h^{(t)} = h^{(t-1)} + \Delta h^{(t)}$. Then the value of $h^{(t)}$ is $h^{(0)} + \sum_{i \le t} \Delta h^{(i)}$. This means that the error in $h^{(t)}$ is passed to all predecessors, and is not vanishing exponentially as it does in a traditional RNN.

In an LSTM, a hidden unit at time $t$ takes in the previous hidden state ($h^{(t-1)}$), the previous output ($o^{(t-1)}$), and the new input ($x^{(t)}$). It needs to produce the next state and the next output.

A construct that is used in the steps of an LSTM is that if $v_1$ and $v_2$ are vectors of the same length, a vector with element $i$ being $v_1[i] * sigmoid(v_2[i])$ will select elements of $v_1$ where $v_2[i] \gg 0$, and will zero-out the elements where $v_2[i] \ll 0$. This allows a model to learn which elements to keep, and which to discard.

An LSTM consists of four dense linear functions (page 333), as implemented in *Dense* in Figure 8.3. Each takes as input the vectors $o^{(t-1)}$ and $x^{(t)}$ appended together, of length $n_h + n_i$, and the output is the same size as $h^{(t)}$, namely $n_h$. Thus an LSTM has $4 * (1 + n_h + n_i) * n_h$ parameters, where $n_i$ is the number of input units at each time and $n_h$ is the number of hidden units for each time, which is also the size of the output for each time. The "1" is for the bias of each linear function.

The state transition function and the command function are defined by the following steps, where all of the linear functions use learnable parameters that do not depend on time.

- Forgetting: the model decides what to forget. It uses a dense linear function, $f(x)$, where $x$ is of length $n_h + n_i$, that outputs a vector of length $n_h$. The function $f$ is used to determine which components of the hidden state to forget, by point-wise multiplying the sigmoid of $f(x)$ to the hidden state. The bias of the dense linear function should be initialized to a large value, such as 1 or 2, or an extra bias of 1 should be added, so that the default behavior is to remember each value.

- Remembering: the model decides what to add, using two dense linear functions, $r(x)$ and $w(x)$, where $x$ is a vector of length $n_h + n_i$, and each output a vector of length $n_h$. The function $w$ specifies what to remember and traditionally uses the **hyperbolic tangent, tanh**, activation function, where $tanh(x) = 2 * sigmoid(2 * x) - 1$, which squashes the real line into the interval $[-1, 1]$. The *tanh* function is used because it is symmetric about 0, which makes subsequent learning easier. The function $r$ determines whether each hidden value should be remembered and so has a sigmoid activation function.

- The resulting hidden state is a combination of what is forgotten and what is remembered:

$$h^{(t)}[i] = sigmoid(f(v^{(t)})[i]) * h^{(t-1)}[i] + sigmoid(r(v^{(t)})[i]) * \phi(w(v^{(t)})[i])$$

for each component $i$, where $v^{(t)}$ is the concatenation of $o^{(t-1)}$ and $x^{(t)}$, and $\phi$ is an activation function (typically *tanh*).

- It then needs to decide what to output. It outputs components of a function of the hidden state, selected by another linear function, $s$, of $y^{(t-1)}$ and $x^{(t)}$, similar to $f$ and $r$. The output is a vector where the $i$th component is

$$y^{(t)}[i] = sigmoid(s(v^{(t)})[i]) * \phi(h^{(t)}[i]).$$

Figure 8.14 shows the data flow of an LSTM for one of the belief states of the HMM of Figure 8.11 (page 355). In an LSTM, the belief state consists of both $h^{(t)}$ and $o^{(t)}$.

Jozefowicz et al. [2015] evaluated over 10,000 different RNN architectures, with 220 hyperparameter settings, on average, for each one, and concluded "the fact a reasonable search procedure failed to dramatically improve over the LSTM suggests that, at the very least, if there are architectures that are much better than the LSTM, then they are not trivial to find."

**Example 8.11** Karpathy [2015] describes an experiment using a character-to-character LSTM. (This example is based on his blog, and is reproduced with permission of the author.)

The input to the model is a sequence of characters; $x^{(t)}$ is a one-hot encoding of the $t$th character. The prediction $y^{(t)}$ is the next character. It is trained so that there is a training example for every character in the text; it predicts that character from the previous text. At test time, it predicts a distribution over the next character, selects the mode of that distribution, and uses that character as

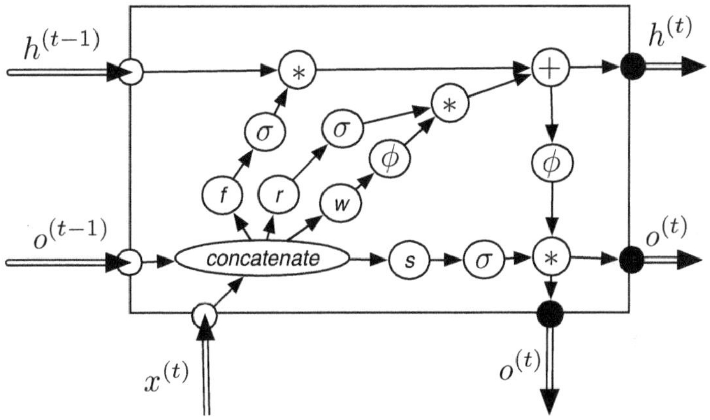


Each of $f$, $r$, $w$, and $s$ is a dense linear function with parameters shared across time. $\sigma$ is sigmoid, $\phi$ is *tanh*. Each arithmetic function acts point-wise.

Figure 8.14: An LSTM showing the data flow for each time

the next input. It thus uses a greedy decoding (page 357) of a matched RNN. In this way it can produce a sequence of characters from the learned model.

Karpathy uses examples of training from Shakespeare, Wikipedia, a book on algebraic geometry, the linux source code, and baby names. In each case, a new text is created based on a model learned from the original corpus.

In one experiment, Karpathy trained an LSTM on Leo Tolstoy's *War and Peace* and then generated samples every 100 iterations of training. The LSTM had 512 hidden nodes, about 3.5 million parameters, dropout of 0.5 after each layer, and a batch size of 100 examples. At iteration 100 the model output

```
tyntd-iafhatawiaoihrdemot lytdws e ,tfti, astai f ogoh
eoase rrranbyne 'nhthnee e plia tklrgd t o idoe ns,smtt
h ne etie h,hregtrs nigtike,aoaenns lng
```

which seems like gibberish. At iteration 500 the model had learned simple words and produced

```
we counter. He stutn co des. His stanted out one ofler
that concossions and was to gearang reay Jotrets and with
fre colt otf paitt thin wall. Which das stimn
```

At iteration 500 the model had learned about quotation marks and other punctuation, and hard learned more words:

```
"Kite vouch!" he repeated by her door. "But I would be
done and quarts, feeling, then, son is people...."
```

By about iteration 2000 it produced

```
"Why do what that day," replied Natasha, and wishing to
himself the fact the princess, Princess Mary was easier,
fed in had oftened him. Pierre aking his soul came to the
packs and drove up his father-in-law women.
```

This is a very simple model, with a few million parameters, trained at the character level on a single book. While it does not produce great literature, it is producing something that resembles English.

### 8.5.4 Attention and Transformers

A way to improve sequential models is to allow the model to pay attention to specific parts of the input. **Attention** uses a probability distribution over the words in a text or regions of an image to compute an expected embedding for each word or region. Consider a word like "bank" that has different meanings depending on the context. Attention uses the probability that other words in a window – a sentence or a fixed-size sequence of adjacent words – are related to a particular instance of "bank" to infer a word embedding for the instance of "bank" that takes the whole window into account. Attention in an image might use the probability that a pixel is part of the head of one of the people in an image. For concreteness, the following description uses text – sequences of words – as the canonical example.

There can be multiple instances of the same word in a sentence, as in the sentence "The bank is on the river bank." There is a dictionary that gives a learnable embedding for each word. The whole sentence (or words in a window) can be used to give an embedding for each instance of each word in the sentence.

**Self-attention** for text in a window inputs three embeddings for each word instance in the window and outputs an embedding for each word that takes the whole window into account. For each word $w$, it infers a probability distribution over all the words, and uses this distribution to output an embedding for $w$. For example, consider an instance of the word "bank" that appears with "river". Both words might have a high probability in the attention distribution for the instance of "bank". The attention would output an embedding for that instance of "bank" that is a mix of the input embeddings for the words "bank" and "river". If "bank" appears with "money", the output embedding for "bank" might be a mix of the embedding for "money" and "bank". In this way, instances of the same word can use different embeddings depending on the context.

An attention mechanism uses three sequences, called **query**, **keys**, and **values**. In self-attention, these are all the same sequence. For translation from a source to a target, the keys and values can be the source text, and the query the target text.

The input to attention is three matrices, each representing an embedding for each element of the corresponding sequence:

- $q$, where $q[i,j]$ is the $j$th value of the **query embedding** for the $i$th word in *query*
- $k$, where $k[i,j]$ is the $j$th value of the **key embedding** for the $i$th word in *keys*
- $v$, where $v[i,j]$ is the $j$th value of the **value embedding** for the $i$th word in *values*.

It returns a new embedding for the elements of *values*. This new embedding takes the embeddings of the other elements in *values* into account, where the mix is determined by *query* and *keys*.

It first determines the similarity between each query word $i$ and each key word $j$:

$$r[i,j] = \sum_{l} q[i,l] * k[j,l].$$

It uses this to compute a probability distribution over the key words for each word in query:

$$a[i,j] = \frac{exp(r[i,j])}{\sum_l exp(r[i,l])}$$

which is the softmax (page 295) of the $j$s for each $i$.

This probability distribution is then used to create a new embedding for the values defined by

$$c[i,l] = \sum_j a[i,j] * v[j,l]$$

where $i$ is the $i$th word in the values sequence, and $l$ is the position in the embedding. The array $c$ is the output of the attention mechanism.

Note that $r$, $a$, and $c$ have no learnable parameters. The query, key, and value embeddings are typically the outputs of dense linear layers, which have learnable parameters.

**Example 8.12** Consider the text "the bank is on the river bank" which makes up one window. The inputs for self-attention ($q$, $k$, and $v$) are of the following form, where each row, labelled with a word–position pair, represents the embedding of the word at that position, and the columns represent the embedding positions:

| | | | | | | | |
|---|---|---|---|---|---|---|---|
| the-0 | | | | | | | |
| bank-1 | | | | | | | |
| is-2 | | | | | | | |
| on-3 | | | | | | | |
| the-4 | | | | | | | |
| river-5 | | | | | | | |
| bank-6 | | | | | | | |

(8.3)

The intermediate matrices $r$ and $v$ are of the same form, with $v$ represented as a probability distribution for each word, such as the following (to one significant digit):

| | the-0 | bank-1 | is-2 | on-3 | the-4 | river-5 | bank-6 |
|---|---|---|---|---|---|---|---|
| the-0 | 0.4 | 0.6 | 0 | 0 | 0 | 0 | 0 |
| bank-1 | 0.2 | 0.4 | 0.1 | 0.3 | 0 | 0 | 0 |
| is-2 | 0 | 0.4 | 0.2 | 0.4 | 0 | 0 | 0 |
| on-3 | 0 | 0 | 0 | 0.4 | 0 | 0 | 0.6 |
| the-4 | 0 | 0 | 0 | 0 | 0.4 | 0 | 0.6 |
| river-5 | 0 | 0 | 0 | 0 | 0 | 0.5 | 0.5 |
| bank-6 | 0 | 0 | 0 | 0 | 0.2 | 0.4 | 0.4 |

The output of self-attention, $c$, is of the same form as (8.3), with an embedding for each word in the window. The embedding for the first occurrence of "bank" is a mix of the value embeddings of "the-0", "bank-1", "is-2", and "on-6". The output embedding for the second occurrence of "bank" is a mix of the value embeddings of "the-4", "river-5", and "bank-6".

**Transformers** are based on attention, interleaved with dense linear layers and activation functions, with the following features:

- There can be multiple attention mechanisms, called **heads**, applied in parallel. The heads are each preceded by separate dense linear functions so that they compute different values. The output of the **multi-head attention** is the concatenation of the output of these attention layers.
- There can be multiple layers of attention, each with a shortcut connection, as in a residual network (page 349), so that the information from the attention is added to the input.
- The input to the lowest level is the array of the word embeddings, with a **positional encoding** of the position at which the word appears, which is added to the embedding of the word. The positional encoding can be learned, or given a priori.

**Example 8.13** Consider the text "the bank is on the river bank", as in Example 8.12 (page 362). A transformer learns the parameters of the dense layers, and an embedding for each word in the dictionary. At the lowest level, the embedding for "bank" is combined with the positional encoding for 1 (counting the elements from 0), giving the embedding for the first occurrence of "bank" (labelled "bank-1" in (8.3)). The embedding for "bank" is combined with the positional encoding for 6 to give the embedding for the second occurrence of "bank" (labelled "bank-6"). This forms a matrix representation of the window of the form of (8.3), which can be input into dense linear layers and attention mechanisms.

The output of an attention module can be input into a dense linear layer and other attention layers. Different heads can implement different functions by being preceded by separate dense linear functions. This enables them to have different properties, perhaps one where verbs attend to their subject and one where verbs attend to their object.

Sequence-to-sequence mapping, such as translation between languages, can be implemented using an encoder–decoder architecture (similar to Figure 8.13 (page 356)) to build a representation of one sequence, which is decoded to construct the resulting sequence. This can be implemented as layers of self-attention in both the encoder and the decoder, followed by a layer where the query is from the target and the keys and values are from the input sequence. This is then followed by layers of self-attention in the target. One complication is that, while the encoder has access to the whole input sequence, the decoder should only have access to the input before the current one, so it can learn to predict the next word as a function of the input sequence, and the words previously generated.

Caswell and Liang [2020] report that a transformer for the encoder and an LSTM for the decoder works better than transformers for both the encoder and decoder, and so that architecture was used in **Google translate**.

Transformers have been used for other sequence modeling tasks, including **protein folding**, a fundamental problem in **biology**. Proteins are made of long chains of amino acid residues, and the aim of protein folding is to determine the three-dimensional structure of these residues. In the transformer, the residues form the role of words in the above description. The attention mechanism uses all pairs of residues in a protein. Proteins can contain thousands of residues.

### 8.5.5 Large Language Models

With a large corpus and a large number of parameters, transformer-based language models have been shown to keep improving on the metrics they are trained on, whereas other methods such as $n$-gram models (page 433) for small $n$ and LSTMs (page 357) tend to hit a plateau of performance. Transformer-based models used for language generation can be seen as $n$-gram models with a large $n$ (the window size); 2048 is used in GPT-3, for example.

It is very expensive to train a large language model on a large corpus, and so only a few organizations can afford to do so. Similarly, to train a large image model on an Internet-scale number of images requires huge resources.

Recently, there has been a number of large language models trained on huge corpora of text or huge collections of images. The texts include all of (English or Chinese) Wikipedia (about 4 billion words), documents linked from Reddit, collections of books, and text collected from the Internet.

Figure 8.15 shows some large language models, with the number of parameters (trainable weights) and the sizes of the training dataset size. This infor-

| Year | Model | # Parameters | Dataset Size |
|---|---|---|---|
| 2018 | ELMo | $9.36 * 10^7$ | $\approx$ 6 GB * |
| 2019 | BERT | $3.4 * 10^8$ | 16 GB |
| 2019 | Megatron-LM | $8.3 * 10^9$ | 174 GB |
| 2020 | **GPT-3** | $1.75 * 10^{11}$ | 570 GB |
| 2020 | GShard | $6.00 * 10^{11}$ | † |
| 2021 | Switch-C | $1.57 * 10^{12}$ | 745 GB |
| 2021 | Gopher | $2.8 * 10^{11}$ | $\approx$ 1800 GB ‡ |
| 2022 | PaLM | $5.4 * 10^{11}$ | $\approx$ 4680 GB $ |

Those that did not report dataset size in GB are approximated with 6 bytes per word (5 characters in a word plus a space):

* * 1 billion words
* † 25 billion training examples (100 languages)
* ‡ 300 billion tokens
* $ 780 billion tokens.

ELMo uses character-based LSTMs; the others use transformers or variants.

Source: Parts extracted from Bender et al. [2021].

Figure 8.15: Some pre-trained large language models

mation is confidential for some more recent models, such as GPT-4 [OpenAI, 2023].

To put the sizes of the datasets in perspective, someone who reads a 400-page book each week takes about 30 years to read 180 million words, which is approximately 1 GB of text. Someone who reads a 400-page book each day for 30 years will only read 1% of the data used to train Switch-C. This model is trained on more text than any one person and all of their ancestors put together has read.

Some models are trained just to predict the next word, which lets them continue stories and answer questions, but others are trained on multiple tasks. The aim is to have representations that are useful for as many tasks as possible.

For a particular application, these models can be fine-tuned on specialized corpora. However, adjusting all the weights is expensive. An alternative is to train a new task on the high-level features of the model, with the lower layers fixed.

Large language models are controversial because of the claims that are made. In particular, there is a lot to be impressed with if you set out to be impressed, however there is a lot to be critical of if you set out to be critical. There are many examples of answering questions well, and giving sensible answers, but the failures are interesting. Hofstadter [2022] gives the following examples of interactions with **GPT-3** [Brown et al., 2020]:

> *Person: When was the Golden Gate Bridge transported for the second time across Egypt?*
> *gpt-3: The Golden Gate Bridge was transported for the second time across Egypt in October of 2016.*
> *Person: How many pieces of sound are there in a typical cumulonimbus cloud?*
> *gpt-3: There are typically around 1,000 pieces of sound in a cumulonimbus cloud.*
> *Person: How many parts will the Andromeda galaxy break into if a grain of salt is dropped on it?*
> *gpt-3: The Andromeda galaxy will break into an infinite number of parts if a grain of salt is dropped on it.*

It is not clear that the problem is with the large models, but with the nature of language itself. People tend to only write what is unusual and notable. Even when people are lying or trying to spread disinformation, they write a tiny proportion of what is not true; there are too many statements that are false. The models, however, are not able to distinguish fact from fiction or disinformation; they take all of the corpus as input and try to predict the next word (or phrase), with no way to determine whether its output is true or not (see Section 8.7). While some have argued that such models show true intelligence, even consciousness, others argue that examples like this "reveal a mind-boggling hollowness hidden just beneath its flashy surface" [Hofstadter, 2022].

## 8.6 Other Neural Network Models

### 8.6.1 Autoencoders

An encoder takes an input and maps it into a vector that can be used for prediction. The **dimension** of a vector is the number of values in the vector. Figure 8.10 (page 351) shows a network that embeds words in a smaller embedding than the one-hot embedding on the input. Figure 8.13 (page 356) shows an encoder for sequences. An encoder is a way to carry out **dimensionality reduction** when the encoding has a smaller dimension than the input.

An **autoencoder** is an encoder where the inputs and the outputs are the same. For images, an autoencoder can take an image, map it to a vector, and then map that vector back into the same image. The vector forms a **representation** of the image, or an **encoding** of the image. The network learns both to **compress** (the part of the network between the input and the representation) and to decompress (the part of the network between the representation and the output) images.

An autoencoder can be used as a **generative image model**, to generate random images or images from text. Consider an autoencoder for images, where the vector representation is small enough so there is little redundant information. An image is mapped to an encoding, which is mapped back to the same image. As the dimensionality of the encoding increases, more detail can be represented. If a random bit vector is used as the embedding, the decoder can be used to produce images, similar to how a decoder produced text in Example 8.11. When the network producing them is a deep network, the generated images are **deep fakes**. This method by itself does not produce very good images; see Section 8.6.2 below.

An autoencoder can also be used to generate images from text. Given an autoencoder for images, you can train a network to predict the embedding of an image from its caption; the embedding is treated as the target for the language model. Then, given a caption, the language model can produce a vector representation of an image and the decoder part of the autoencoder can be used to produce an image. The autoencoder is useful in this case because it allows for a form of **semi-supervised learning**, where not all of the images have captions; it uses all the images to train the autoencoder, and the images with captions to train the caption to embedding mapping. It is easier to get images without captions than images with captions.

### 8.6.2 Adversarial Networks

An **adversarial network**, such as a **generative adversarial network** (**GAN**), is trained both to be able to predict some output, and also not to be able to predict some other output.

One example is in **adversarial debiasing** for recruitment, where you want to predict whether someone is suitable for a job, but to be blind to race or gender. It is not enough to just remove race and gender from the inputs, because other inputs are correlated with race and gender (e.g., postcodes, poverty, current occupation). One way to make the network blind to race and gender is to create a layer from which race or gender cannot be predicted. The idea is to train the network to predict suitability, but have an adversary that adjusts the embedding of an intermediate layer so that race and gender cannot be predicted from it.

As another example, suppose there is a **deep fake** model able to generate images from vector representations, as in the decoder of the last section, for which the images are not very realistic. They can be made much more realistic by also training a network $N$ that, given an image, predicts whether the image is real or fake. The image generator can then be trained so that $N$ cannot determine if its output is real or fake. This might produce details that make the output look realistic, even though the details might be just fiction.

### 8.6.3 Diffusion Models

**Diffusion models** are effective methods for **generative AI**, particularly for image generation. The idea is to build a sequence of more noisy images, starting with the data and repeatedly add noise until the result is just noise, and then learn the inverse of this process.

Suppose an input image is $x_0$, and $x_t$ is produced from $x_{t-1}$ by adding noise, until $x_T$, for some $T$ (say 1000), is indistinguishable from noise. $T$ neural networks are trained, when network $N_t$ is trained with input $x_t$ and output $x_{t-1}$. Thus each network is learning to **denoise** – reduce the amount of noise in – an image. An image can be generated by starting with random noise, $y_T$, and running it through the networks $N_T$ to $N_1$ to produce an image $y_0$. Different noise inputs produce different images.

The details of diffusion models are beyond the scope of this book, with a theory and practice more sophisticated than the characterization here.

## 8.7 Social Impact

ELIZA, written in 1964–66, was one of the first programs that conversed in English. A version, called DOCTOR, analyzed language and used a script for the role of a psychotherapist. The author, Joseph Weizenbaum [1976], was shocked by the reaction to the program:

> *A number of practicing psychiatrists seriously believed the DOCTOR computer program could grow into a nearly completely automatic form of psychotherapy. ...*
>
> *I was startled to see how quickly and how very deeply people conversing with DOCTOR became emotionally involved with the computer and how unequivocally they anthropomorphized it. ...*

> *Another widespread, and to me surprising, reaction to the ELIZA program was the spread of a belief that it demonstrated a general solution to the problem of computer understanding of natural language.*
>
> – J. Weizenbaum [1976]

Over 50 years after ELIZA, natural language systems are much more sophisticated and much more widespread. The issues that Weizenbaum outlined have become more pressing, and new issues have arisen.

Bender et al. [2021] outline many problems with modern systems based on learning from huge corpora. These include the following:

- Data: biases in large uncurated data include stereotypical and derogatory language along gender, race, ethnicity, and disability status. Most content on the Internet is created by the privileged; those who have the time and the access to create content, whereas the marginalized experience harassment which discourages participation in open fora. Increasing the size does not guarantee diversity, because while the number of diverse views might increase, their proportion tends not to. Datasets curated for other reasons, such as Wikipedia, have biases about who is included ("notable" people), and how much information is included about each person. Blodgett et al. [2020] provide a review of biases in natural language processing. Bender et al. [2021] recommend significant resources allocated to dataset curation and documentation practices in order to mitigate the biases.

- Learning: once you have the data, training the models is very energy intensive. Generating the energy creates greenhouse gases, or diverts energy from other sources that create greenhouse gases. Only rich corporations and governments can afford to train them, and accrue the benefits, but it is poor countries that disproportionately accrue the risks. The expense of training only increases inequality.

- Use of models: once the models have been trained, they can be used in various ways. Used as a **generative language model**, they are particularly useful for those who want to spread misinformation; they can generate seemingly plausible text which may or may not correspond with the truth. For example, consider saying you want fiction and asking for a completion for "the atrocities committed by <target> included", and spreading this as factual information, in order to recruit people to a cause against <target>. AI systems are trained to optimize some score, which may not correspond to what the user wants to optimize. McGuffie and Newhouse [2020] discuss the risk of large language models for radicalization and weaponization by extremists.

- Large language models are trained on text only, but language understanding also involves meaning; there is typically a world that text is about, and understanding meaning involves not just the text but the interaction of the text, the world, and the intent of the author [Bender and Koller, 2020; Bisk et al., 2020]. People will assume that the output is the truth; but, when the data used to train isn't necessarily the truth, and the inference is opaque, there is no reason to have confidence in the outputs. The preoccupation with improving scores on well-defined, but artificial, tasks – those the AI systems are trained to optimize – has diverted resources away from other research.

*Feeding AI systems on the world's beauty, ugliness and cruelty and expecting it to reflect only the beauty is a fantasy.*

– Prabhu and Birhane [2020]

Deep learning has had success in science fields where large datasets can be created. For example, the problem of **protein folding** – determining the three-dimensional structure of proteins – is one of the successes of transformer-based models. The predictions of these programs have changed how chemists work:

*Today, thanks to programs like AlphaFold2 and RoseTTAFold, researchers like me can determine the three-dimensional structure of proteins from the sequence of amino acids that make up the protein – at no cost – in an hour or two. Before AlphaFold2 we had to crystallize the proteins and solve the structures using X-ray crystallography, a process that took months and cost tens of thousands of dollars per structure.*

– M. Zimmer [2022]

Better predictions promise to enable improved medicine, drug design, and understanding of biochemistry, which can have enormous social impacts. Ma et al. [2022] used deep learning to identify many new candidates for potential antimicrobials drugs, which may be important as drug-resistant bacteria kill millions of people each year. These programs make predictions that still need to be verified in the real world before being accepted.

## 8.8 Review

- Artificial neural networks are parametrized models for predictions, typically made of multiple layers of parameterized linear functions and nonlinear activation functions.

- The output is typically a linear function for a real-valued prediction, with a sigmoid for a Boolean prediction, or with a softmax for a categorical prediction. Other outputs, such as sequences or structured predictions, use specialized methods.

- Neural networks that use ReLU for all hidden units define piecewise linear functions if they have a linear output, or piecewise linear separators if they have a sigmoid output.
- Backpropagation can be used for training parameters of differentiable (almost everywhere) functions.
- Gradient descent is used to train by making steps proportional to the negation of the gradient; many variants improve the basic algorithm by adjusting the step size and adding momentum.
- Convolutional neural networks apply learnable filters to multiple positions on a grid.
- Recurrent neural networks can be used for sequences. An LSTM is a type of RNN that solves the vanishing gradients problem.
- Attention for text is used to compute the expected embedding of words based on their relationship with other words. Attention is also used for speech, vision, and other tasks.
- Transformers, using layers of linear transformation and attention, are the workhorse for modern language processing, computer vision, and biology.
- Neural networks are used for **generative AI**, for the generation of images, text, code, molecules, and other structured output.
- Neural networks are very successful for applications where there are large training sets, or where training data can be generated from a model.
- It can be dangerous to make decisions based on data of dubious quality; large quantity and high quality are difficult to achieve together.

## 8.9 References and Further Reading

Goodfellow et al. [2016] provide an overview of neural networks and deep learning. Schmidhuber [2015] provides a comprehensive history and extensive references to the literature. Chollet [2021] provides a readable intuitive overview of deep learning with code (using Python and the **Keras** library).

McCulloch and Pitts [1943] define a formal neuron. Minsky [1952] showed how such representations can be learned from data. Rosenblatt [1958] introduced the perceptron. Minsky and Papert [1988] is a classic work that analyzed the limitations of the neural networks of the time.

Backpropagation is introduced in Rumelhart et al. [1986]. LeCun et al. [1998b] describe how to effectively implement backpropagation. Ng [2018] provides practical advice on how to build deep learning applications.

LeCun et al. [2015] review how multilayer neural networks have been used for deep learning in many applications. Hinton et al. [2012a] review neural networks for speech recognition, Goldberg [2016] for natural language processing, and Lakshmanan et al. [2021] for vision.

Different activation functions, including ReLU, are investigated in Jarrett et al. [2009] and Glorot et al. [2011]. Ruder [2016] gives an overview of many variants of gradient descent. Nocedal and Wright [2006] provide practical advice on gradient descent and related methods. Karimi et al. [2016] analyze how many iterations of stochastic gradient descent are needed. The Glorot uniform initializer is by Glorot and Bengio [2010]. Dropout is described by Hinton et al. [2012b].

Convolutional neural networks and the MNIST dataset are by LeCun et al. [1998a]. Krizhevsky et al. [2012] describe AlexNet, which used convolutional neural networks to significantly beat the state-of-the-art on ImageNet [Russakovsky et al., 2014], a dataset to predict which of 1000 categories is in an image. Residual networks are described by He et al. [2015].

Jurafsky and Martin [2023] provide a textbook introduction to speech and language processing, which includes more detail on some of the language models presented here. LSTMs were invented by Hochreiter and Schmidhuber [1997]. Gers et al. [2000] introduced the forget gate to LSTMs. Word embeddings were pioneered by Bengio et al. [2003]. The CBOW and Skip-gram models, collectively known as **Word2vec**, are by Mikolov et al. [2013]. Olah [2015] presents a tutorial introduction to LSTMs.

Attention for machine translation was pioneered by Bahdanau et al. [2015]. Transformers are due to Vaswani et al. [2017]. Alammar [2018] provides a tutorial introduction, and Phuong and Hutter [2022] provide a self-contained introduction, with pseudocode, to transformers. Tay et al. [2022] survey the time and memory complexity of transformer variants. AlphaFold [Senior et al., 2020; Jumper et al., 2021] and RoseTTAFold [Baek et al., 2021] used transformers and other deep learning techniques for protein folding.

Large pre-trained language models are surveyed by Qiu et al. [2020] and Minaee et al. [2021]. Bommasani et al. [2021], calling them **foundation models**, outlined a research program for large pre-trained models of language, vision, science, and other domains. The language models in Figure 8.15 (page 364) are ELMo [Peters et al., 2018], BERT [Devlin et al., 2019], Magetron-ML [Shoeybi et al., 2019], GPT-3 [Brown et al., 2020], GShard [Lepikhin et al., 2021], Switch-C [Fedus et al., 2021], Gopher [Rae et al., 2021], and PaLM [Chowdhery et al., 2022]. Shanahan [2022] and Zhang et al. [2022b] discuss what large language models actually learn and what they do not learn.

Srivastava et al. [2022] provide challenge benchmarks of 204 diverse tasks that are more precisely specified than the Turing test (page 5) and are beyond the capabilities of current language models. Lertvittayakumjorn and Toni [2021] and Qian et al. [2021] survey explainability in natural language systems.

Generative adversarial networks were invented by Goodfellow et al. [2014]. Adversarial debiasing is based on Zhang et al. [2018]. Sohl-Dickstein et al.

[2015] and Ho et al. [2020] present diffusion probabilistic models.

Bender et al. [2021] and Weidinger et al. [2021] discuss issues with large pre-trained models, and include a diverse collection of references.

## 8.10 Exercises

**Exercise 8.1** Give the weights and structure of a neural network with a sigmoid output activation and one hidden layer with an ReLU activation, that can represent the exclusive-or function ($\oplus$) of two Booleans, which is true when the inputs have different truth values; see Figure 7.13 (page 293). Assume true is represented as 1, and false as 0. [Hint: Write exclusive-or in terms of other logical operators. See Exercise 7.9 (page 323) and Example 8.1 (page 330). You need to think about how many units need to be in the hidden layer.]

**Exercise 8.2** Run the AIPython (aipython.org) neural network code or an other learner on the "Mail reading" data of Figure 7.1 (page 268) with a single hidden layer with two hidden units.

(a) Suppose that you decide to use any predicted value from the neural network greater than 0.5 as true, and any value less than 0.5 as false. How many examples are misclassified initially? How many examples are misclassified after 40 iterations? How many examples are misclassified after 80 iterations?
(b) Try the same example and the same initial values, with different step sizes for the gradient descent. Try at least $\eta = 0.1$, $\eta = 1.0$, and $\eta = 5.0$. Comment on the relationship between step size and convergence.
(c) Given the final parameter values you found, give a logical formula for what each of the units is computing. [Hint: As a brute-force method, for each of the units, build the truth tables for the input values and determine the output for each combination, then simplify the resulting formula.] Is it always possible to find such a formula?
(d) All of the parameters were set to different initial values. What happens if the parameter values are all set to the same (random) value? Test it out for this example, and hypothesize what occurs in general.
(e) For the neural network algorithm, comment on the following stopping criteria.

    (i) Learn for a limited number of iterations, where the limit is set initially.
    (ii) Stop when the squared error is less than some threshold close to zero.
    (iii) Stop when the derivatives all become within some $\epsilon$ of zero.
    (iv) Split the data into training data and validation data, train on the training data and stop when the error on the validation data increases.

    Which would you expect to better handle overfitting? Which criteria guarantee the gradient descent will stop? Which criteria would guarantee that, if it stops, the network can be used to predict the test data accurately?

**Exercise 8.3** Adam (page 340) was described as a combination of momentum and RMS-Prop. Using AIPython (aipython.org), Keras, or PyTorch (see Appendix B.2), find two datasets and compare the following:

(a) How does Adam with $\beta_1 = \beta_2 = 0$, differ from plain stochastic gradient descent without momentum? [Hint: How does setting $\beta_1 = \beta_2 = 0$ simplify Adam, considering first the case where $\epsilon \ll g$?] Which works better on the datasets selected?

(b) How does Adam with $\beta_2 = 0$ differ from stochastic gradient descent, when the $\alpha$ momentum parameter is equal to $\beta_1$ in Adam? [Hint: How does setting $\beta_2 = 0$ simplify Adam, considering first the case where $\epsilon \ll g$?] Which works better on the datasets selected?

(c) How does Adam with $\beta_1 = 0$ differ from RMS-Prop, where the $\rho$ parameter in RMS-Prop is equal to $\beta_2$ in Adam? Which works better on the datasets selected?

**Exercise 8.4** The Conv2D code of Figure 8.9 does not include a stride (page 349). Show how a stride can be incorporated into the pseudocode, where the stride is a pair of numbers, one for each dimension. Implement it in AIPython (aipython.org).

**Exercise 8.5** Give the pseudocode for Conv1D, for one-dimensional convolutions (the one-dimensional version of Figure 8.9). What hyperparameters are required? This pseudocode does not include all of the hyperparameters of Keras or PyTorch. For two of the hyperparameters of one of these, show how the pseudocode can be extended to include this.

**Exercise 8.6** In Exercise 8.11 (page 359), the LSTM was character-based, and there were about 3.5 million parameters.

(a) How many parameters would there be in an LSTM if it was word-based with a vocabulary of 1000 words and a hidden state of size 1000?

(b) How many parameters would there be if the vocabulary had 10,000 words and the hidden state was of size 10,000?

(c) Consider a simple character-based transformer with a single attention mechanism that performs self-attention to predict the next character in a text. Suppose the window size is 100, an embedding size is 1000, and there are 64 characters. Suppose as part of the transformer there are dense functions for $q$, $k$, and $v$ as inputs to the attention mechanism, and the output of the attention goes directly into a softmax. How many parameters are there?

(d) Suppose instead of the character-based transformer in (c), the transformer was word-based, with a vocabulary of 10,000 words. How many parameters are there?

**Exercise 8.7** Take the text of some classic work, such as can be found on gutenberg.org. Repeat the experiment of Example 8.11 (page 359) with that text. Increase the number of hidden nodes from 512 to 2048 and double the number of epochs. Is the performance better? What evidence can you provide to show it is better?

# Chapter 9

# Reasoning with Uncertainty

*It is remarkable that a science which began with the consideration of games of chance should become the most important object of human knowledge ... The most important questions of life are, for the most part, really only problems of probability ...*

*The theory of probabilities is at bottom nothing but common sense reduced to calculus.*

– Pierre Simon de Laplace [1812]

Agents in real environments are inevitably forced to make decisions based on incomplete information. Even when an agent senses the world to find out more information, it rarely finds out the exact state of the world. For example, a doctor does not know exactly what is going on inside a patient, a teacher does not know exactly what a student understands, and a robot does not know what is in a room it left a few minutes ago. When an intelligent agent must act, it has to use whatever information it has. The previous chapters considered learning probabilities, which is useful by itself when many similar cases have been observed, however novel situations require **reasoning**, not just learning. This chapter considers **reasoning with uncertainty** that is required whenever an intelligent agent is not omniscient, and cannot just rely on having seen similar situations many times.

## 9.1 Probability

To make a good decision, an agent cannot simply assume what the world is like and act according to that assumption. It must consider multiple hypotheses when making a decision, and not just act on the most likely prediction. Consider the following example.

**Example 9.1** Many people consider it sensible to wear a seat belt when traveling in a car because, in an accident, wearing a seat belt reduces the risk of serious injury. However, consider an agent that commits to assumptions and bases its decision on these assumptions. If the agent assumes it will not have an accident, it will not bother with the inconvenience of wearing a seat belt. If it assumes it will have an accident, it will not go out. In neither case would it wear a seat belt! A more intelligent agent may wear a seat belt because the inconvenience of wearing a seat belt is far outweighed by the increased risk of injury or death if it has an accident. It does not stay at home too worried about an accident to go out; the benefits of being mobile, even with the risk of an accident, outweigh the benefits of the extremely cautious approach of never going out. The decisions of whether to go out and whether to wear a seat belt depend on the likelihood of having an accident, how much a seat belt helps in an accident, the inconvenience of wearing a seat belt, and how important it is to go out. The various trade-offs may be different for different agents. Some people do not wear seat belts, and some people do not go in cars because of the risk of accident.

Reasoning with uncertainty has been studied in the fields of probability theory and decision theory. Probability is the calculus needed for **gambling**. When an agent makes decisions and is uncertain about the outcomes of its actions, it is gambling on the outcomes. However, unlike a gambler at the casino, an agent that has to survive in the real world cannot opt out and decide not to gamble; whatever it does – including doing nothing – involves uncertainty and risk. If it does not take the probabilities of possible outcomes into account, it will eventually lose at gambling to an agent that does. This does not mean, however, that making the best decision guarantees a win.

**Probability** is the calculus of belief; probability theory tells us how to update beliefs based on new information. When an agent doesn't have any information about the particular situation; it will still have beliefs. The belief of an agent before it observes anything is its **prior probability**. As it discovers information – typically by observing the environment – it updates its beliefs, giving a **posterior probability**.

The view of probability as a measure of belief is known as **Bayesian probability** or **subjective probability**. The term *subjective* here means "belonging to the subject" (as opposed to *subjective* meaning *arbitrary*). Different agents may have different information, and so different beliefs.

Assume that the uncertainty is **epistemological** – pertaining to an agent's beliefs about the world – rather than **ontological** – how the world is. For example, if you are told that someone is very tall, you know they have some height but you only have vague knowledge about the actual value of their height.

Belief in some proposition, $\alpha$, is measured in terms of a number between 0 and 1. The probability of $\alpha$ is 0 means that $\alpha$ is believed to be definitely false (no new evidence will shift that belief), and the probability of $\alpha$ is 1 means that $\alpha$ is believed to be definitely true. Using 0 and 1 is purely a convention; you could just as well use 0 and 100. If an agent's probability of $\alpha$ is greater than zero and less than one, this does not mean that $\alpha$ is true to some degree but rather that the agent is ignorant of whether $\alpha$ is true or false. The probability reflects the agent's ignorance.

### 9.1.1 Semantics of Probability

The semantics is defined in terms of **possible worlds**, each of which is one way the world could be. An omniscient agent knows which world is the true world, but real agents are not omniscient.

A **random variable** (or just **variable**) is a function on worlds. Given a world, it returns a value. The set of values a random variable could return is the **domain** of the variable.

For example, a variable *Coughs* with domain $\{true, false\}$ might be true in worlds where the patient under consideration coughs and false in worlds where the patient doesn't cough. The variable *Distance_to_wall* might be a random variable whose value might be the distance (in centimeters) of the agent from the wall closest to it.

Variables are written starting with an uppercase letter. A **discrete variable** has a domain that is a finite or countable set. A **binary variable** is a variable where the domain has two values. A **Boolean variable** is a binary variable with domain $\{true, false\}$. The assignment of *true* to a Boolean variable is written as the lower-case variant of the variable (e.g., $Happy = true$ is written as *happy* and $Fire = true$ is *fire*).

A **primitive proposition** (page 177) is an assignment of a value to a variable, or an inequality between a variable and a value, or between variables (e.g., $A = true$, $X < 7$, or $Y > Z$). A primitive proposition is true in a possible world whenever that condition holds in the world. Propositions are built from primitive propositions using logical connectives (page 178). A proposition is either true or false in a world.

A **probability measure** is a function $\mu$ from sets of worlds into the nonnegative real numbers that satisfies two constraints:

- if $\Omega_1$ and $\Omega_2$ are disjoint sets of worlds (they have no elements in common), then $\mu(\Omega_1 \cup \Omega_2) = \mu(\Omega_1) + \mu(\Omega_2)$
- $\mu(\Omega) = 1$ where $\Omega$ is the set of all possible worlds.

These should not be controversial. For example, the number of people in two groups of people is the sum of the number in each group if the groups don't have any members in common. The second constraint is just by convention; we could have chosen any other value.

The **probability** of proposition $\alpha$, written $P(\alpha)$, is the measure of the set of possible worlds in which $\alpha$ is true. That is,

$$P(\alpha) = \mu(\{\omega : \alpha \text{ is true in } \omega\}).$$

**Example 9.2** Consider the ten possible worlds of Figure 9.1, with Boolean variable *Filled* and with variable *Shape* with domain $\{circle, triangle, star\}$. Each world is defined by its shape, whether it's filled, and its position. Suppose the measure of each singleton set of worlds is 0.1. Then $P(Shape = circle) = 0.5$, as there are five circles and $P(Filled = false) = 0.4$, as there are four unfilled shapes. $P(Shape = circle \wedge Filled = false) = 0.1$ (where "$\wedge$" means "and"), as there is only one unfilled circle.

If $X$ is a random variable, a **probability distribution**, $P(X)$, over $X$ is a function from the domain of $X$ into the real numbers such that, given a value $x \in domain(X)$, $P(x)$ is the probability of the proposition $X = x$. A probability distribution over a set of variables is a function from the values of those variables into a probability. For example, $P(X, Y)$ is a probability distribution over $X$ and $Y$ such that $P(X = x, Y = y)$, where $x \in domain(X)$ and $y \in domain(Y)$, has the value $P(X = x \wedge Y = y)$, where $X = x \wedge Y = y$ is the proposition representing the conjunction (and) of the assignments to the variables, and $P$ is the function on propositions defined above. Whether $P$ refers to a function on propositions or a probability distribution should be clear from the context.

If $X_1, \ldots, X_n$ are all of the random variables, an assignment to those random variables corresponds to a world, and the probability of the proposition defining a world is equal to the probability of the world. The distribution over all worlds, $P(X_1, \ldots, X_n)$, is called the **joint probability distribution**.

### 9.1.2 Conditional Probability

Probability is a measure of belief. Beliefs need to be updated when new evidence is observed.

The measure of belief in proposition $h$ given proposition $e$ is called the **conditional probability** of $h$ **given** $e$, written $P(h \mid e)$.

A proposition $e$ representing the conjunction of *all* of the agent's **observations** of the world is called **evidence**. Given evidence $e$, the conditional probability $P(h \mid e)$ is the agent's **posterior probability** of $h$. The probability $P(h)$

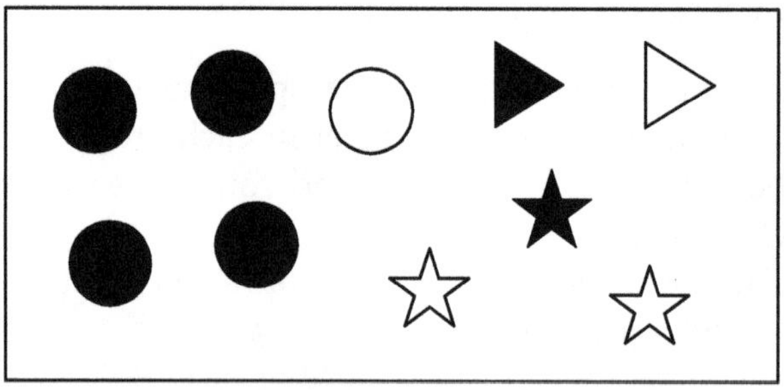

Figure 9.1: Ten possible worlds described by variables *Filled* and *Shape*

## Beyond Finitely Many Worlds

The definition of probability is straightforward when there are only finitely many worlds. When there are infinitely many worlds, there are some technical issues that need to be confronted.

There are infinitely many worlds when

- the domain of a variable is infinite, for example, the domain of a variable *height* might be the set of nonnegative real numbers or
- there are infinitely many variables, for example, there might be a variable for the location of a robot for every millisecond from now infinitely far into the future.

When there are infinitely many worlds there are uncountably many sets of worlds, which is more than can be described with a language with finite sentences. We do not need to define the measure for *all* sets of worlds, just those that can be defined by logical formulas. This is the basis for the definition of a $\sigma$-algebra used in many probability texts.

For variables with continuous domains, the probability of $X = v$ can be zero for all $v$, even though the probability of $v_0 < X < v_i$ is positive for $v_0 < v_1$. For variables with real-valued domains, a **probability density function**, written as $p$, is a function from reals into nonnegative reals that integrates to 1. The probability that a real-valued variable $X$ has value between $a$ and $b$ is

$$P(a \leq X \leq b) = \int_a^b p(X)\, dX.$$

A **parametric distribution** is one where the probability or density function is described by a formula with free parameters. Not all distributions can be described by formulas, or any finite representation. Sometimes statisticians use the term **parametric** to mean a distribution described using a fixed, finite number of parameters. A **nonparametric distribution** is one where the number of parameters is not fixed, such as in a decision tree. (Oddly, nonparametric typically means "many parameters".)

An alternative is to consider **discretization** of continuous variables. For example, only consider height to the nearest centimeter or micron, and only consider heights up to some finite number (e.g., a kilometer). Or only consider the location of the robot for a millennium. With finitely many variables, there are only finitely many worlds if the variables are discretized. A challenge is to define representations that work for any (fine enough) discretization.

It is common to work with a parametric distribution when the solutions can be computed analytically and where there is theoretical justification for some particular distribution or the parametric distribution is close enough.

is the **prior probability** of $h$ and is the same as $P(h \mid true)$ because it is the probability before the agent has observed anything.

The evidence used for the posterior probability is *everything* the agent observes about a particular situation. Everything observed, and not just a few select observations, must be conditioned on to obtain the correct posterior probability.

**Example 9.3** For the diagnostic agent, the prior probability distribution over possible diseases is used before the diagnostic agent finds out about the particular patient. Evidence is obtained through discussions with the patient, observing symptoms, and the results of lab tests. Essentially, any information that the diagnostic agent finds out about the patient is evidence. The agent updates its probability to reflect the new evidence in order to make informed decisions.

**Example 9.4** The information that the delivery robot receives from its sensors is its evidence. When sensors are noisy, the evidence is what is known, such as the particular pattern received by the sensor, not that there is a person in front of the robot. The robot could be mistaken about what is in the world but it knows what information it received.

### Semantics of Conditional Probability

Evidence $e$, where $e$ is a proposition, will rule out all possible worlds that are incompatible with $e$. Like the definition of logical consequence, the given proposition $e$ selects the possible worlds in which $e$ is true.

Evidence $e$ induces a new measure, $\mu_e$, over sets of worlds. Any set of worlds which all have $e$ false has measure 0 in $\mu_e$. The measure of a set of worlds for which $e$ is true in all of them is its measure in $\mu$ multiplied by a constant:

$$\mu_e(S) = \begin{cases} c * \mu(S) & \text{if } e \text{ is true in } \omega \text{ for all } \omega \in S \\ 0 & \text{if } e \text{ is false in } \omega \text{ for all } \omega \in S \end{cases}$$

where $c$ is a constant (that depends on $e$) to ensure that $\mu_e$ is a proper measure.

For $\mu_e$ to be a probability measure over worlds for each $e$:

$$\begin{aligned} 1 &= \mu_e(\Omega) \\ &= \mu_e(\{w : e \text{ is true in } w\}) + \mu_e(\{w : e \text{ is false in } w\}) \\ &= c * \mu(\{w : e \text{ is true in } w\}) + 0 \\ &= c * P(e). \end{aligned}$$

Therefore, $c = 1/P(e)$. Thus, the conditional probability is only defined if $P(e) > 0$. This is reasonable, as if $P(e) = 0$, $e$ is impossible.

The conditional probability of proposition $h$ given evidence $e$ is the sum of the conditional probabilities of the possible worlds in which $h$ is true. That is:

$$P(h \mid e) = \mu_e(\{\omega : h \text{ is true in } \omega\})$$

$$= \mu_e(\{\omega : h \wedge e \text{ is true in } \omega\}) + \mu_e(\{\omega : h \wedge \neg e \text{ is true in } \omega\})$$
$$= \frac{1}{P(e)} * \mu(\{\omega : h \wedge e \text{ is true in } \omega\}) + 0$$
$$= \frac{P(h \wedge e)}{P(e)}.$$

The last form above is typically given as the definition of conditional probability. Here we have derived it as a consequence of a more basic definition. This more basic definition is used when designing algorithms; set the assignments inconsistent with the observations to have probability zero, and normalize at the end.

**Example 9.5** As in Example 9.2, consider the worlds of Figure 9.1 (page 378), with each singleton set having a measure of 0.1. Given the evidence $Filled = false$, only four worlds have a nonzero measure, with

$$P(Shape = circle \mid Filled = false) = 0.25$$
$$P(Shape = star \mid Filled = false) = 0.5.$$

A **conditional probability distribution**, written $P(X \mid Y)$ where $X$ and $Y$ are variables or sets of variables, is a function of the variables: given a value $x \in domain(X)$ for $X$ and a value $y \in domain(Y)$ for $Y$, it gives the value $P(X = x \mid Y = y)$, where the latter is the conditional probability of the propositions.

The definition of conditional probability allows the decomposition of a conjunction into a product of conditional probabilities. The definition of conditional probability gives $P(e \wedge h) = P(h \mid e) * P(e)$. Repeated application of this product can be used to derive the **chain rule**:

$$\begin{aligned} &P(\alpha_1 \wedge \alpha_2 \wedge \ldots \wedge \alpha_n) \\ &\quad = P(\alpha_n \mid \alpha_1 \wedge \cdots \wedge \alpha_{n-1}) * P(\alpha_1 \wedge \cdots \wedge \alpha_{n-1}) \\ &\quad = P(\alpha_n \mid \alpha_1 \wedge \cdots \wedge \alpha_{n-1}) * \cdots * P(\alpha_2 \mid \alpha_1) * P(\alpha_1) \\ &\quad = \prod_{i=1}^{n} P(\alpha_i \mid \alpha_1 \wedge \cdots \wedge \alpha_{i-1}) \end{aligned}$$

where the base case is $P(\alpha_1 \mid true) = P(\alpha_1)$, the empty conjunction being *true*.

## Bayes' Rule

An agent using probability updates its belief when it observes new evidence. A new piece of evidence is conjoined to the old evidence to form the complete set of evidence. Bayes' rule specifies how an agent should update its belief in a proposition based on a new piece of evidence.

Suppose an agent has a current belief in proposition $h$ based on evidence $k$ already observed, given by $P(h \mid k)$, and subsequently observes $e$. Its new belief in $h$ is $P(h \mid e \wedge k)$. Bayes' rule tells us how to update the agent's belief in hypothesis $h$ as new evidence arrives.

**Proposition 9.1.** *(Bayes' rule) As long as* $P(e \mid k) \neq 0$*:*

$$P(h \mid e \wedge k) = \frac{P(e \mid h \wedge k) * P(h \mid k)}{P(e \mid k)}.$$

This is often written with the background knowledge $k$ implicit. In this case, if $P(e) \neq 0$, then

$$P(h \mid e) = \frac{P(e \mid h) * P(h)}{P(e)}.$$

$P(e \mid h)$ is the **likelihood** and $P(h)$ is the **prior probability** of the hypothesis $h$. Bayes' rule states that the **posterior probability** is proportional to the likelihood times the prior.

*Proof.* The commutativity of conjunction means that $h \wedge e$ is equivalent to $e \wedge h$, and so they have the same probability given $k$. Using the rule for multiplication in two different ways:

$$\begin{aligned} & P(h \wedge e \mid k) = P(h \mid e \wedge k) * P(e \mid k) \\ = & P(e \wedge h \mid k) = P(e \mid h \wedge k) * P(h \mid k). \end{aligned}$$

The theorem follows from dividing the right-hand sides by $P(e \mid k)$, which is not 0 by assumption. □

Generally, one of $P(e \mid h \wedge k)$ or $P(h \mid e \wedge k)$ is much easier to estimate than the other. Bayes' rule is used to compute one from the other.

**Example 9.6** In medical diagnosis, the doctor observes a patient's symptoms, and would like to know the likely diseases. Thus the doctor would like $P(\mathit{Disease} \mid \mathit{Symptoms})$. This is difficult to assess as it depends on the context (e.g., some diseases are more prevalent in hospitals). It is typically easier to assess $P(\mathit{Symptoms} \mid \mathit{Disease})$ because how the disease gives rise to the symptoms is typically less context dependent. These two are related by Bayes' rule, where the prior probability of the disease, $P(\mathit{Disease})$, reflects the context.

**Example 9.7** The diagnostic assistant may need to know whether the light switch $s_1$ of Figure 1.6 (page 18) is broken or not. You would expect that the electrician who installed the light switch in the past would not know if it is broken now, but would be able to specify how the output of a switch is a function of whether there is power coming into the switch, the switch position, and the status of the switch (whether it is working, shorted, installed upside-down, etc.). The prior probability for the switch being broken depends on the maker of the switch and how old it is. Bayes' rule lets an agent infer the status of the switch given the prior and the evidence.

### 9.1.3 Expected Values

The expected value of a numerical random variable (one whose domain is the real numbers or a subset of the reals) is the variable's weighted average value, where sets of worlds with higher probability have higher weight.

Let $X$ be a numerical random variable. The **expected value** of $X$, written $\mathbb{E}_P(X)$, with respect to probability $P$ is

$$\mathbb{E}_P(X) = \sum_{v \in domain(X)} v * P(X{=}v)$$

when the domain is $X$ is finite or countable. When the domain is continuous, the sum becomes an integral.

One special case is if $\alpha$ is a proposition, treating *true* as 1 and *false* as 0, where $\mathbb{E}_P(\alpha) = P(\alpha)$.

**Example 9.8** In an electrical domain, if *number_of_broken_switches* is the number of switches broken:

$$\mathbb{E}_P(number\_of\_broken\_switches)$$

would give the expected number of broken switches given by probability distribution $P$. If the world acted according to the probability distribution $P$, this would give the long-run average number of broken switches. If there were three switches, each with a probability of 0.7 of being broken independently of the others, the expected number of broken switches is

$$0 * 0.3^3 + 1 * 3 * 0.7 * 0.3^2 + 2 * 3 * 0.7^2 * 0.3 + 3 * 0.7^3 = 2.01$$

where $0.3^3$ is the probability that no switches are broken, $0.7 * 0.3^2$ is the probability that one switch is broken, which is multiplied by 3 as there are three ways that one switch can be broken.

In a manner analogous to the semantic definition of conditional probability (page 380), the **conditional expected value** of $X$ conditioned on evidence $e$, written $\mathbb{E}(X \mid e)$, is

$$\mathbb{E}(X \mid e) = \sum_{v \in domain(X)} v * P(X{=}v \mid e).$$

**Example 9.9** The expected number of broken switches given that light $l_1$ is not lit is given by

$$\mathbb{E}(number\_of\_broken\_switches \mid \neg lit(l_1)).$$

This is obtained by averaging the number of broken switches over all of the worlds in which light $l_1$ is not lit.

If a variable is Boolean, with *true* represented as 1 and *false* as 0, the expected value is the probability of the variable. Thus any algorithms for expected values can also be used to compute probabilities, and any theorems about expected values are also directly applicable to probabilities.

## 9.2 Independence

The axioms of probability are very weak and provide few constraints on allowable conditional probabilities. For example, if there are $n$ **binary variables**, there are $2^n - 1$ **free parameters**, which means there are $2^n - 1$ numbers to be assigned to give an arbitrary probability distribution.

A useful way to limit the amount of information required is to assume that each variable only directly depends on a few other variables. This uses assumptions of conditional independence. Not only does it reduce how many numbers are required to specify a model, but also the independence structure may be exploited for efficient reasoning.

As long as the value of $P(h \mid e)$ is not 0 or 1, the value of $P(h \mid e)$ does not constrain the value of $P(h \mid f \wedge e)$. This latter probability could have any value in the range $[0, 1]$. It is 1 when $f$ implies $h$, and it is 0 if $f$ implies $\neg h$. A common kind of qualitative knowledge is of the form $P(h \mid e) = P(h \mid f \wedge e)$, which specifies $f$ is irrelevant to the probability of $h$ given that $e$ is observed. This idea applies to random variables, as in the following definition.

Random variable $X$ is **conditionally independent** of random variable $Y$ **given** a set of random variables $Zs$ if

$$P(X \mid Y, Zs) = P(X \mid Zs)$$

whenever the probabilities are well defined. That is, given a value of each variable in $Zs$, knowing $Y$'s value does not affect the belief in the value of $X$.

**Example 9.10** Consider a probabilistic model of students and exams. It is reasonable to assume that the random variable *Intelligence* is independent of *Works_hard*, given no observations. If you find that a student works hard, it does not tell you anything about their intelligence.

The answers to the exam (the variable *Answers*) would depend on whether the student is intelligent and works hard. Thus, given *Answers*, *Intelligent* would be dependent on *Works_hard*; if you found someone had insightful answers, and did not work hard, your belief that they are intelligent would go up.

The grade on the exam (variable *Grade*) should depend on the student's answers, not on the intelligence or whether the student worked hard. Thus, *Grade* would be independent of *Intelligence* given *Answers*. However, if the answers were not observed, *Intelligence* will affect *Grade* (because highly intelligent students would be expected to have different answers than not so intelligent students); thus, *Grade* is dependent on *Intelligence* given no observations.

**Proposition 9.2.** *The following four statements are equivalent, as long as the conditional probabilities are well defined:*

1. *$X$ is conditionally independent of $Y$ given $Z$.*
2. *$Y$ is conditionally independent of $X$ given $Z$.*
3. *$P(X{=}x \mid Y{=}y \wedge Z{=}z) = P(X{=}x \mid Y{=}y' \wedge Z{=}z)$ for all values $x$, $y$, $y'$, and $z$. That is, in the context that you are given a value for $Z$, changing the value of $Y$ does not affect the belief in $X$.*

4. $P(X, Y \mid Z) = P(X \mid Z)P(Y \mid Z)$.

The proof is left as an exercise. See Exercise 9.1 (page 451).

Variables $X$ and $Y$ are **unconditionally independent** if $P(X, Y) = P(X)P(Y)$, that is, if they are conditionally independent given no observations. Note that $X$ and $Y$ being unconditionally independent does not imply they are conditionally independent given some other information $Z$.

Conditional independence is a useful assumption that is often natural to assess and can be exploited in inference. It is rare to have a table of probabilities of worlds and assess independence numerically.

Another useful concept is **context-specific independence**. Variables $X$ and $Y$ are independent with respect to context $Zs = vs$ if

$$P(X \mid Y, Zs = vs) = P(X \mid Zs = zs)$$

whenever the probabilities are well defined. That is, for all $x \in domain(X)$ and for all $y \in domain(Y)$, if $P(Y = y \wedge Zs = zs) > 0$:

$$P(X = x \mid Y = y \wedge Zs = zs) = P(X = x \mid Zs = zs).$$

This is like conditional independence, but is only for one of the values of $Zs$. This is discussed in more detail when representing conditional probabilities in terms of decision trees (page 396).

## 9.3 Belief Networks

The notion of conditional independence is used to give a concise representation of many domains. The idea is that, given a random variable $X$, there may be a few variables that directly affect the $X$'s value, in the sense that $X$ is conditionally independent of other variables given these variables. The set of locally affecting variables is called the **Markov blanket**. This locality is exploited in a belief network.

A **belief network** is a directed acyclic graph representing conditional dependence among a set of random variables. The random variables are the nodes. The arcs represent direct dependence. The conditional independence implied by a belief network is determined by an ordering of the variables; each variable is independent of its predecessors in the total ordering given a subset of the predecessors called its parents. Independence in the graph is indicated by missing arcs.

To define a belief network on a set of random variables, $\{X_1, \ldots, X_n\}$, first select a total ordering of the variables, say, $X_1, \ldots, X_n$. The chain rule (Proposition 9.1.2 (page 381)) shows how to decompose a conjunction into conditional probabilities:

$$P(X_1 = v_1 \wedge X_2 = v_2 \wedge \cdots \wedge X_n = v_n)$$

$$= \prod_{i=1}^{n} P(X_i = v_i \mid X_1 = v_1 \wedge \cdots \wedge X_{i-1} = v_{i-1}).$$

Or, in terms of random variables:

$$P(X_1, X_2, \ldots, X_n) = \prod_{i=1}^{n} P(X_i \mid X_1, \ldots, X_{i-1}). \tag{9.1}$$

Define the **parents** of random variable $X_i$, written *parents*$(X_i)$, to be a minimal set of predecessors of $X_i$ in the total ordering such that the other predecessors of $X_i$ are conditionally independent of $X_i$ given *parents*$(X_i)$. Thus $X_i$ **probabilistically depends on** each of its parents, but is independent of its other predecessors. That is, $parents(X_i) \subseteq \{X_1, \ldots, X_{i-1}\}$ such that

$$P(X_i \mid X_1, \ldots, X_{i-1}) = P(X_i \mid parents(X_i)).$$

This conditional independence characterizes a belief network.

When there are multiple minimal sets of predecessors satisfying this condition, any minimal set may be chosen to be the parents. There can be more than one minimal set only when some of the predecessors are deterministic functions of others.

Putting the chain rule and the definition of parents together gives

$$P(X_1, X_2, \ldots, X_n) = \prod_{i=1}^{n} P(X_i \mid parents(X_i)).$$

The probability over all of the variables, $P(X_1, X_2, \ldots, X_n)$, is called the **joint probability distribution**. A belief network defines a **factorization** of the joint probability distribution into a product of conditional probabilities.

A **belief network**, also called a **Bayesian network**, is an acyclic directed graph (DAG), where the nodes are random variables. There is an arc from each element of *parents*$(X_i)$ into $X_i$. Associated with the belief network is a set of conditional probability distributions that specify the conditional probability of each variable given its parents (which includes the prior probabilities of those variables with no parents).

Thus, a belief network consists of

- a DAG, where each node is labeled by a random variable
- a domain for each random variable, and
- a set of conditional probability distributions giving $P(X \mid parents(X))$ for each variable $X$.

A belief network is acyclic by construction. How the chain rule decomposes a conjunction depends on the ordering of the variables. Different orderings can result in different belief networks. In particular, which variables are eligible to be parents depends on the ordering, as only predecessors in the ordering can be parents. Some of the orderings may result in networks with fewer arcs than other orderings.

**Example 9.11** Consider the four variables of Example 9.10 (page 384), with the ordering: *Intelligent*, *Works_hard*, *Answers*, *Grade*. Consider the variables in order. *Intelligent* does not have any predecessors in the ordering, so it has no parents, thus $parents(Intelligent) = \{\}$. *Works_hard* is independent of *Intelligent*, and so it too has no parents. *Answers* depends on both *Intelligent* and *Works_hard*, so

$$parents(Answers) = \{Intelligent, Works\_hard\}.$$

*Grade* is independent of *Intelligent* and *Works_hard* given *Answers* and so

$$parents(Grade) = \{Answers\}.$$

The corresponding belief network is given in Figure 9.2.

This graph defines the decomposition of the joint distribution:

$$\begin{aligned} &P(Intelligent, Works\_hard, Answers, Grade) \\ &\quad = P(Intelligent) * P(Works\_hard) * P(Answers \mid Intelligent, Works\_hard) \\ &\qquad * P(Grade \mid Answers). \end{aligned}$$

In the examples below, the domains of the variables are simple, for example the domain of *Answers* may be $\{insightful, clear, superficial, vacuous\}$ or it could be the actual text answers.

The independence of a belief network, according to the definition of parents, is that each variable is independent of all of the variables that are not descendants of the variable (its non-descendants) given the variable's parents.

### 9.3.1 Observations and Queries

A belief network specifies a joint probability distribution from which arbitrary conditional probabilities can be derived. The most common probabilistic inference task – the task required for decision making – is to compute the **posterior distribution** of a **query variable**, or variables, given some evidence, where the evidence is a conjunction of assignment of values to some of the variables.

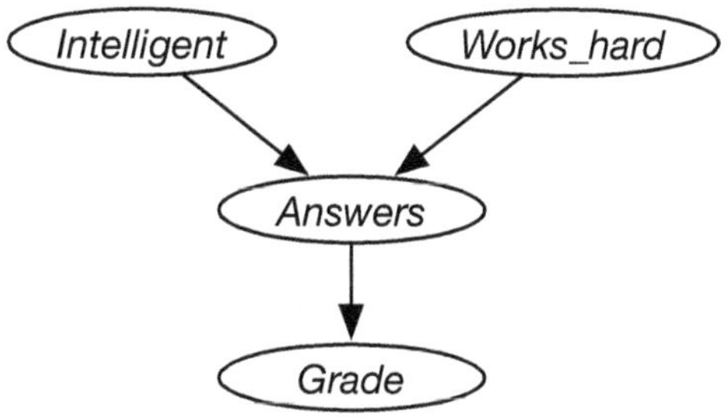


Figure 9.2: Belief network for exam answering of Example 9.11

**Example 9.12** Before there are any observations, the distribution over intelligence is $P(Intelligent)$, which is provided as part of the network. To determine the distribution over grades, $P(Grade)$, requires inference.

If a grade of $A$ is observed, the posterior distribution of *Intelligent* is given by

$$P(Intelligent \mid Grade = A).$$

If it was also observed that *Works_hard* is false, the posterior distribution of *Intelligent* is

$$P(Intelligent \mid Grade = A \land Works\_hard = false).$$

Although *Intelligent* and *Works_hard* are independent given no observations, they are dependent given the grade. This might explain why some people claim they did not work hard to get a good grade; it increases the probability they are intelligent.

## 9.3.2 Constructing Belief Networks

To represent a domain in a belief network, the designer of a network must consider the following questions.

- What are the relevant variables? In particular, the designer must consider:
  - What the agent may observe in the domain. Each feature that may be observed should be a variable, because the agent must be able to condition on all of its observations.
  - What information the agent is interested in knowing the posterior probability of. Each of these features should be made into a variable that can be queried.
  - Other **hidden variables** or **latent variables** that will not be observed or queried but make the model simpler. These variables either account for dependencies, reduce the size of the specification of the conditional probabilities, or better model how the world is assumed to work.
- What values should these variables take? This involves considering the level of detail at which the agent should reason to answer the sorts of queries that will be encountered.

  For each variable, the designer should specify what it means to take each value in its domain. What must be true in the world for a (non-hidden) variable to have a particular value should satisfy the **clarity principle** (page 128): an omniscient agent should be able to know the value of a variable. It is a good idea to explicitly document the meaning of all variables and their possible values. The only time the designer may not want to do this is for hidden variables whose values the agent will want to learn from data (see Section 10.4.1, page 482).

- What is the relationship between the variables? This should be expressed by adding arcs in the graph to define the parent relation.
- How does the distribution of a variable depend on its parents? This is expressed in terms of the conditional probability distributions.

**Example 9.13** Suppose you want to use the diagnostic assistant to diagnose whether there is a fire in a building and whether there has been some tampering with equipment based on noisy sensor information and possibly conflicting explanations of what could be going on. The agent receives a report from Sam about whether everyone is leaving the building. Suppose Sam's report is noisy: Sam sometimes reports leaving when there is no exodus (a false positive), and sometimes does not report when everyone is leaving (a false negative). Suppose that leaving only depends on the fire alarm going off. Either tampering or fire could affect the alarm. Whether there is smoke only depends on whether there is fire.

Suppose you use the following variables in the following order:

- *Tampering* is true when there is tampering with the alarm.
- *Fire* is true when there is a fire.
- *Alarm* is true when the alarm sounds.
- *Smoke* is true when there is smoke.
- *Leaving* is true if there are many people leaving the building at once.
- *Report* is true if Sam reports people leaving. *Report* is false if there is no report of leaving.

Assume the following conditional independencies:

- *Fire* is conditionally independent of *Tampering* (given no other information).
- *Alarm* depends on both *Fire* and *Tampering*. This is making no independence assumptions about how *Alarm* depends on its predecessors given this variable ordering.
- *Smoke* depends only on *Fire* and is conditionally independent of *Tampering* and *Alarm* given whether there is *Fire*.
- *Leaving* only depends on *Alarm* and not directly on *Fire* or *Tampering* or *Smoke*. That is, *Leaving* is conditionally independent of the other variables given *Alarm*.
- *Report* only directly depends on *Leaving*.

The belief network of Figure 9.3 (page 390) expresses these dependencies. This network represents the factorization

$$\begin{aligned} &P(Tampering, Fire, Alarm, Smoke, Leaving, Report) \\ &\quad = P(Tampering) * P(Fire) * P(Alarm \mid Tampering, Fire) \end{aligned}$$

$$* P(Smoke \mid Fire) * P(Leaving \mid Alarm) * P(Report \mid Leaving).$$

Note that the alarm is *not* a smoke alarm, which would be affected by the smoke, and not directly by the fire, but rather it is a heat alarm that is directly affected by the fire. This is made explicit in the model in that *Alarm* is independent of *Smoke* given *Fire*.

You also must define the domain of each variable. Assume that the variables are Boolean; that is, they have domain $\{true, false\}$. We use the lower-case variant of the variable to represent the true value and use negation for the false value. Thus, for example, $Tampering = true$ is written as *tampering*, and $Tampering = false$ is written as $\neg tampering$.

The examples that follow assume the following conditional probabilities:

$$P(tampering) = 0.02$$
$$P(fire) = 0.01$$
$$P(alarm \mid fire \wedge tampering) = 0.5$$
$$P(alarm \mid fire \wedge \neg tampering) = 0.99$$
$$P(alarm \mid \neg fire \wedge tampering) = 0.85$$
$$P(alarm \mid \neg fire \wedge \neg tampering) = 0.0001$$
$$P(smoke \mid fire) = 0.9$$
$$P(smoke \mid \neg fire) = 0.01$$
$$P(leaving \mid alarm) = 0.88$$
$$P(leaving \mid \neg alarm) = 0.001$$
$$P(report \mid leaving) = 0.75$$
$$P(report \mid \neg leaving) = 0.01.$$

Before any evidence arrives, the probability is given by the priors. The following probabilities follow from the model (all of the numbers here are to about three decimal places):

$$P(tampering) = 0.02$$
$$P(fire) = 0.01$$
$$P(report) = 0.028$$
$$P(smoke) = 0.0189.$$

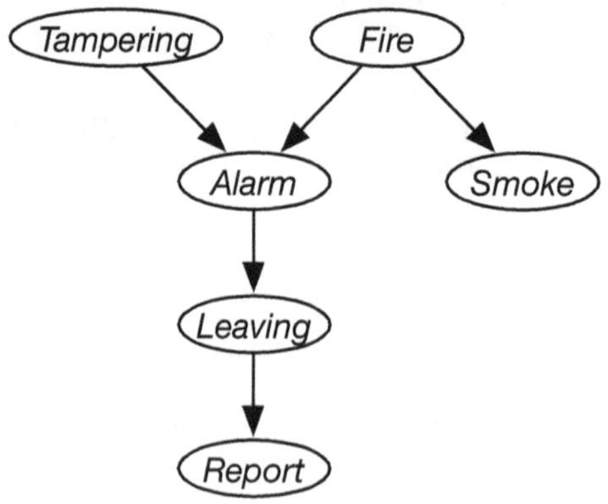


Figure 9.3: Belief network for report of leaving of Example 9.13

Observing a report gives the following:

$$P(\mathit{tampering} \mid \mathit{report}) = 0.399$$
$$P(\mathit{fire} \mid \mathit{report}) = 0.2305$$
$$P(\mathit{smoke} \mid \mathit{report}) = 0.215.$$

As expected, the probabilities of both *tampering* and *fire* are increased by the report. Because the probability of *fire* is increased, so is the probability of *smoke*.

Suppose instead that *smoke* alone was observed:

$$P(\mathit{tampering} \mid \mathit{smoke}) = 0.02$$
$$P(\mathit{fire} \mid \mathit{smoke}) = 0.476$$
$$P(\mathit{report} \mid \mathit{smoke}) = 0.320.$$

Note that the probability of *tampering* is not affected by observing *smoke*; however, the probabilities of *report* and *fire* are increased.

Suppose that both *report* and *smoke* were observed:

$$P(\mathit{tampering} \mid \mathit{report} \wedge \mathit{smoke}) = 0.0284$$
$$P(\mathit{fire} \mid \mathit{report} \wedge \mathit{smoke}) = 0.964.$$

Observing both makes *fire* even more likely. However, in the context of *report*, the presence of *smoke* makes *tampering* less likely. This is because *report* is **explained away** by *fire*, which is now more likely.

Suppose instead that *report*, but not *smoke*, was observed:

$$P(\mathit{tampering} \mid \mathit{report} \wedge \neg \mathit{smoke}) = 0.501$$
$$P(\mathit{fire} \mid \mathit{report} \wedge \neg \mathit{smoke}) = 0.0294.$$

In the context of *report*, *fire* becomes much less likely and so the probability of *tampering* increases to explain *report*.

This example illustrates how the belief net independence assumption gives commonsense conclusions and also demonstrates how explaining away is a consequence of the independence assumption of a belief network.

**Example 9.14** Consider the problem of diagnosing why someone is sneezing and perhaps has a fever. Sneezing could be because of influenza or because of hay fever. They are not independent, but are correlated due to the season. Suppose hay fever depends on the season because it depends on the amount of pollen, which in turn depends on the season. The agent does not get to observe sneezing directly, but rather observed just the "Achoo" sound. Suppose fever depends directly on influenza. These dependency considerations lead to the belief network of Figure 9.4 (page 392).

**Example 9.15** Consider the wiring example of Figure 1.6 (page 18). Let's have variables for whether lights are lit, for the switch positions, for whether lights and switches are faulty or not, and for whether there is power in the wires. The variables are defined in Figure 9.5 (page 393).

Let's try to order the variables so that each variable has few parents. In this case there seems to be a natural causal order where, for example, the variable for whether a light is lit comes after variables for whether the light is working and whether there is power coming into the light.

Whether light $l_1$ is lit depends only on whether there is power in wire $w_0$ and whether light $l_1$ is working properly. Other variables, such as the position of switch $s_1$, whether light $l_2$ is lit, or who is the Queen of Canada, are irrelevant. Thus, the parents of $L_1\_lit$ are whether there is power in wire $w_0$ (variable $W_0$), and the status of light $l_1$ (variable $L_1\_st$); see Figure 9.5 for the meaning of the variables.

Consider variable $W_0$, which represents whether there is power in wire $w_0$. If you knew whether there was power in wires $w_1$ and $w_2$, and knew the position of switch $s_2$ and whether the switch was working properly, the value of the other variables (other than $L_1\_lit$) would not affect the belief in whether there is power in wire $w_0$. Thus, the parents of $W_0$ should be $S_2\_Pos$, $S_2\_st$, $W_1$, and $W_2$.

Figure 9.5 (page 393) shows the resulting belief network after the independence of each variable has been considered. The belief network also contains the domains of the variables and conditional probabilities of each variable given its parents.

Note the independence assumption embedded in this model. The DAG specifies that the lights, switches, and circuit breakers break independently. To model dependencies among how the switches break, you could add more arcs and perhaps more variables. For example, if some lights do not break independently because they come from the same batch, you could add an extra node modeling the batch, and whether it is a good batch or a bad batch, which is made a parent of the $L_i\_st$ variables for each light $L_i$ from that batch. When you have evidence that one light is broken, the probability that the batch is bad may increase and thus make it more likely that other lights from that batch are broken. If you are not sure whether the lights are indeed from the same batch, you could add variables representing this, too. The important point is that the

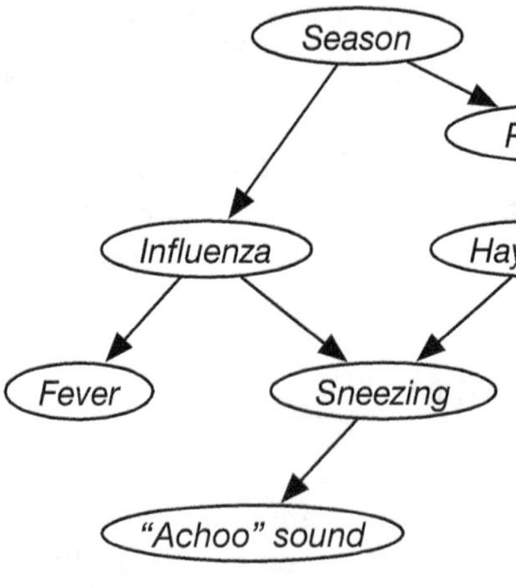


Figure 9.4: Belief network for Example 9.14

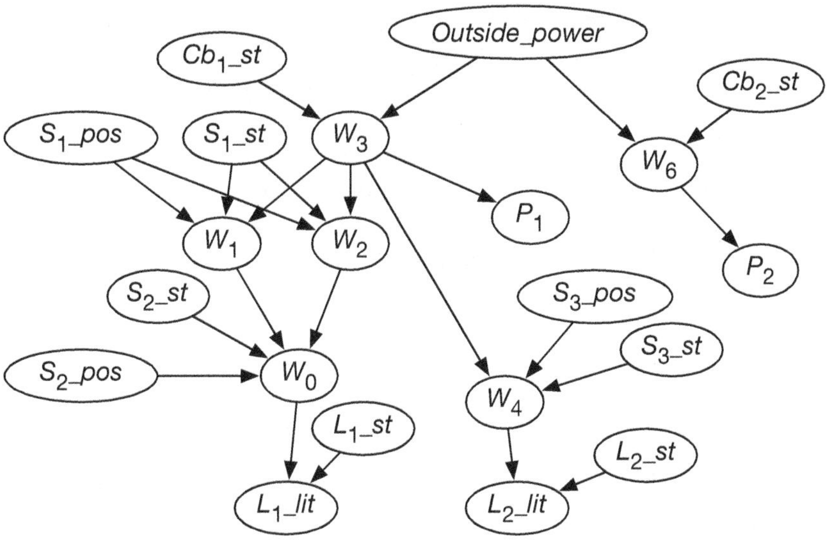


- For each wire $w_i$, there is a random variable, $W_i$, with domain $\{live, dead\}$, which denotes whether there is power in wire $w_i$. $W_i = live$ means wire $w_i$ has power. $W_i = dead$ means there is no power in wire $w_i$.
- *Outside_power* with domain $\{live, dead\}$ denotes whether there is power coming into the building.
- For each switch $s_i$, variable $S_i\_pos$ denotes the position of $s_i$. It has domain $\{up, down\}$.
- For each switch $s_i$, variable $S_i\_st$ denotes the state of switch $s_i$. It has domain $\{ok, upside\_down, short, intermittent, broken\}$. $S_i\_st = ok$ means switch $s_i$ is working normally. $S_i\_st = upside\_down$ means switch $s_i$ is installed upside-down. $S_i\_st = short$ means switch $s_i$ is shorted and acting as a wire. $S_i\_st = broken$ means switch $s_i$ is broken and does not allow electricity to flow.
- For each circuit breaker $cb_i$, variable $Cb_i\_st$ has domain $\{on, off\}$. $Cb_i\_st = on$ means power could flow through $cb_i$ and $Cb_i\_st = off$ means power could not flow through $cb_i$.
- For each light $l_i$, variable $L_i\_st$ with domain $\{ok, intermittent, broken\}$ denotes the state of the light. $L_i\_st = ok$ means light $l_i$ will light if powered, $L_i\_st = intermittent$ means light $l_i$ intermittently lights if powered, and $L_i\_st = broken$ means light $l_i$ does not work.

Figure 9.5: Belief network for the electrical domain of Figure 1.6

belief network provides a specification of independence that lets us model dependencies in a natural and direct manner.

The model implies that there is no possibility of shorts in the wires or that the house is wired differently from the diagram. For example, it implies that $w_0$ cannot be shorted to $w_4$ so that wire $w_0$ gets power from wire $w_4$. You could add extra dependencies that let each possible short be modeled. An alternative is to add an extra node that indicates that the model is appropriate. Arcs from this node would lead to each variable representing power in a wire and to each light. When the model is appropriate, you could use the probabilities of Example 9.15 (page 391). When the model is inappropriate, you could, for example, specify that each wire and light works at random. When there are weird observations that do not fit in with the original model – they are impossible or extremely unlikely given the model – the probability that the model is inappropriate will increase.

### 9.3.3 Representing Conditional Probabilities and Factors

A **factor** is a function of a set of variables; the variables on which it depends are the **scope** of the factor. Given an assignment of a value to each variable in the scope, the factor evaluates to a number.

A conditional probability is a factor representing $P(Y \mid X_1, \ldots, X_k)$, which is a function from the variables $Y, X_1, \ldots, X_k$ into nonnegative numbers. It must satisfy the constraints that for each assignment of values to all of $X_1, \ldots, X_k$, the values for $Y$ sum to 1. That is, given values for all of the variables, the function returns a number that satisfies the constraint

$$\forall x_1 \ldots \forall x_k \sum_{y \in domain(Y)} P(Y = y \mid X_1 = x_1, \ldots, X_k = x_k) = 1. \tag{9.2}$$

The following gives a number of ways of representing conditional probabilities, and other factors.

#### Conditional Probability Tables

A representation for a conditional probability that explicitly stores a value for each assignment to the variables is called a **conditional probability table** or **CPT**. This can be done whenever there is a finite set of variables with finite domains. The space used is exponential in the number of variables; the size of the table is the product of the sizes of the domains of the variables in the scope.

One such representation is to use a multidimensional table, storing $P(Y = y \mid X_1 = v_1, \ldots, x_k = v_k)$ in $p\_y[v_1] \ldots [v_k][y]$ (using Python's notation for arrays, and exploiting its ambiguity of arrays and dictionaries).

**Example 9.16** Figure 9.6 shows the conditional probabilities for $P(alarm \mid Fire, Tampering)$. The probability for *Alarm* being false can be computed from the given probabilities, for example:

$$P(Alarm = false \mid Fire = false, Tampering = true) = 1 - 0.85 = 0.15$$

Given a total ordering of the variables, $[Fire, Tampering, Alarm]$, the values mapped to the nonnegative integers; *false* to 0 and *true* to 1.

$P(Alarm \mid Fire, Tampering)$ of Figure 9.6 can be represented as the Python array

$$cpt = [[[0.9999, 0.0001], [0.15, 0.85]], [[0.01, 0.99], [0.5, 0.5]]].$$

Given particular values of $Fire = f, Tampering = t, Alarm = a$, where $f$, $t$, and $a$ are each 0 or 1, the value can be found at $cpt[f][t][a]$. If the domain of a variable is not of the form $\{0, \ldots, n-1\}$, a dictionary can be used. Other languages have different syntaxes.

There are a number of refinements, which use different space-time trade-offs, including the following.

- Tables can be implemented as one-dimensional arrays. Given an ordering of the variables (e.g., alphabetical) and an ordering for the values, and using a mapping from the values into nonnegative integers, there is a unique representation using the lexical ordering of each factor as a one-dimensional array that is indexed by natural numbers. This is a space-efficient way to store a table.

- If the child variable is treated the same as the parent variables, the information is redundant; more numbers are specified than is required. One way to handle this is to store the probability for all-but-one of the values of the child, $Y$. The probability of the other value can be computed as 1 minus the sum of other values for a set of parents. In particular, if $Y$ is Boolean, you only need to represent the probability for one value, say $Y = true$ given the parents; the probability for $Y = false$ can be computed from this.

- It is also possible to store **unnormalized probabilities**, which are nonnegative numbers that are proportional to the probability. The probability is computed by dividing each value by the sum of the values. This is common when the unnormalized probabilities are counts (see Section 10.2.1, page 461).

| *Fire* | *Tampering* | $P(alarm \mid Fire, Tampering)$ |
|---|---|---|
| *false* | *false* | 0.0001 |
| *false* | *true* | 0.85 |
| *true* | *false* | 0.99 |
| *true* | *true* | 0.5 |

Figure 9.6: Conditional probability of $Alarm = true$ given *Fire* and *Tampering*

## Decision Trees

The tabular representation of conditional probabilities can be enormous when there are many parents. There is often insufficient evidence – either from data or from experts – to provide all the numbers required. Fortunately, there is often structure in conditional probabilities which can be exploited.

One such structure exploits **context-specific independence** (page 385), where one variable is conditionally independent of another, given particular values for some other variables.

**Example 9.17** Suppose a robot can go outside or get coffee, so *Action* has domain $\{go\_out, get\_coffee\}$. Whether it gets wet (variable *Wet*) depends on whether there is rain (variable *Rain*) in the context that it went out or on whether the cup was full (variable *Full*) if it got coffee. Thus *Wet* is independent of *Rain* given context $Action = get\_coffee$, but is dependent on *Rain* given contexts $Action = go\_out$. Also, *Wet* is independent of *Full* given $Action = go\_out$, but is dependent on *Full* given $Action = get\_coffee$.

A conditional probability table that represents such independencies is shown in Figure 9.7.

Context-specific independence may be exploited in a representation by not requiring numbers that are not needed. A simple representation for conditional probabilities that models context-specific independence is a **decision tree** (page 281), where the parents in a belief network correspond to the input features that form the splits, and the child corresponds to the target feature. Each leaf of the decision tree contains a probability distribution over the child variable.

**Example 9.18** The conditional probability $P(Wet \mid Action, Rain, Full)$ of Figure 9.7 could be represented as a decision tree, where the number at the leaf is the probability for $Wet = true$:

| *Action* | *Rain* | *Full* | $P(Wet = true \mid Action, Rain, Full)$ |
|---|---|---|---|
| *go_out* | *false* | *false* | 0.1 |
| *go_out* | *false* | *true* | 0.1 |
| *go_out* | *true* | *false* | 0.8 |
| *go_out* | *true* | *true* | 0.8 |
| *get_coffee* | *false* | *false* | 0.3 |
| *get_coffee* | *false* | *true* | 0.6 |
| *get_coffee* | *true* | *false* | 0.3 |
| *get_coffee* | *true* | *true* | 0.6 |

Figure 9.7: A conditional probability that a robot will get wet

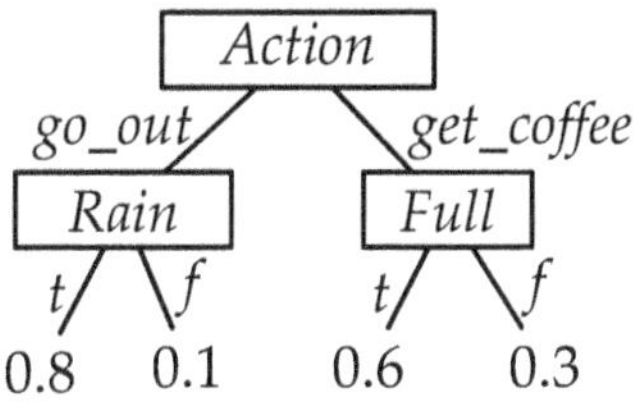


How to learn a decision tree from data was explored in Section 7.3.1 (page 281). Context-specific inference can be exploited in probabilistic inference because a factor represented by a decision tree can be evaluated in an assignment when the values down a path in the tree hold; you don't need to know the value of all parent variables.

### Deterministic System with Noisy Inputs

An alternative representation of conditional distributions is in terms of a deterministic system, with probabilistic inputs. The deterministic system can range from a logical formula to a program. The inputs to the system are the parent variables and stochastic inputs. The **stochastic inputs** – often called **noise variables** or **exogenous variables** – can be considered as random variables that are unconditionally independent (page 385) of each other. There is a deterministic system that defines the non-leaf variables of the belief network, the **endogenous variables**, as a deterministic function of the exogenous variables and the parents.

When the deterministic system is Clark's completion of a logic program (page 208), it is known as **probabilistic logic programming** and when the deterministic system is a program, it is known as **probabilistic programming**. When the deterministic system is specified by a logical formula, the probabilistic inference is known as **weighted model counting**.

**Example 9.19** The decision tree of Example 9.7 (page 396) for the conditional distribution of Figure 9.6 (page 395) can be represented as the logical formula (page 178)

$$\begin{aligned} wet \leftrightarrow\ & ((go\_out \wedge rain \wedge n_0) \\ & \vee (go\_out \wedge \neg rain \wedge n_1) \\ & \vee (\neg go\_out \wedge full \wedge n_2) \\ & \vee (\neg go\_out \wedge \neg full \wedge n_3)) \end{aligned}$$

where the $n_i$ are independent noise variables, with

$$P(n_0) = 0.8,\ P(n_1) = 0.1,\ P(n_2) = 0.6,\ P(n_3) = 0.3.$$

So if, for example, *go_out* is true and *rain* is false, then *wet* is true whenever $n_1$ is true, which occurs with probability 0.1.

This conditional distribution can be represented as a program:

```
if go_out:
   if rain:
      wet := flip(0.8)
   else:
      wet := flip(0.1)
else:
   if full:
      wet := flip(0.6)
   else:
      wet := flip(0.3)
```

```
flip(x) = (random() < x)
```

where `random()` returns a random number uniformly in the range [0,1), so `flip(x)` makes a new independent random variable that is true with probability x. The logical formula gave these random variables names.

Logical formulas allow for much more complicated expressions than presented here. Probabilistic programming allows for the full expressivity of the underlying programming language to express probabilistic models. Typically a single program is used to represent the distribution of all variables, rather than having a separate program for each conditional probability.

### Noisy-or

There are many cases where something is true if there is something that makes it true. For example, someone has a symptom if there is a disease that causes that symptom; each of the causes can be probabilistic. In natural language understanding, topics may have words probabilistically associated with them; a word is used if there is a topic that makes that word appear. Each of these examples follows the same pattern, called a noisy-or.

In a **noisy-or** model of a conditional probability, the child is true if one of the parents is activated and each parent has a probability of activation. So the child is an "or" of the activations of the parents.

If $Y$ has Boolean parents $X_1, \ldots, X_k$, the **noisy-or** model of probability is defined by $k+1$ parameters $w_0, \ldots, w_k$. $Y$ is defined in terms of a deterministic system with noisy inputs, where

$$Y \equiv n_0 \vee (n_1 \wedge x_1) \vee \cdots \vee (n_k \wedge x_k).$$

The $n_i$ are unconditionally independent **noise variables** (page 397), with $P(n_i) = w_i$, and $x_i$ means $X_i = true$.

The same distribution for $P(Y \mid X_1, X_2, \ldots, X_k)$ can be defined using $k+1$ Boolean variables $A_0, A_1, \ldots, A_k$, where for each $i > 0$, $A_i$ has $X_i$ as its only parent. See Figure 9.8 (page 399). $P(A_i = true \mid X_i = true) = w_i$ and $P(A_i = true \mid X_i = false) = 0$. The variable $A_0$ has $P(A_0 = true) = w_0$. The variables $A_0, \ldots, A_k$ are the parents of $Y$. The conditional probability for $Y$, $P(Y \mid A_0, A_1, \ldots, A_k)$, is

1 if any of the $A_i$ are true and 0 if all of the $A_i$ are false. Thus, $w_0$ is the probability of $Y$ when all of $X_i$ are false; the probability of $Y$ increases as more of the $X_i$ become true.

**Example 9.20** Suppose the robot could get wet from rain or coffee. There is a probability that it gets wet from rain if it rains, and a probability that it gets wet from coffee if it has coffee, and a probability that it gets wet for other reasons. The robot gets wet if it gets wet from one of the reasons, giving the "or". You could have $P(wet\_from\_rain \mid rain) = 0.3$, $P(wet\_from\_coffee \mid coffee) = 0.2$, and, for the bias term, $P(wet\_for\_other\_reasons) = 0.1$. The robot is wet if it is wet from rain, wet from coffee, or wet for other reasons.

### Log-linear Models and Logistic Regression

In a **log-linear model** unnormalized probabilities are specified using a product of terms, and probabilities are inferred by normalization. When the terms being multiplied are all positive, a product can be represented as the exponential of a sum. A sum of terms is often a convenient term to work with.

The simplest case is for a Boolean variable. To represent conditional probabilities of a Boolean variable $h$:

$$\begin{aligned}
P(h \mid e) &= \frac{P(h \wedge e)}{P(e)} \\
&= \frac{P(h \wedge e)}{P(h \wedge e) + P(\neg h \wedge e)} \\
&= \frac{1}{1 + P(\neg h \wedge e)/P(h \wedge e)} \\
&= \frac{1}{1 + \exp(-(\log P(h \wedge e)/P(\neg h \wedge e)))} \\
&= sigmoid(\log odds(h \mid e)).
\end{aligned}$$

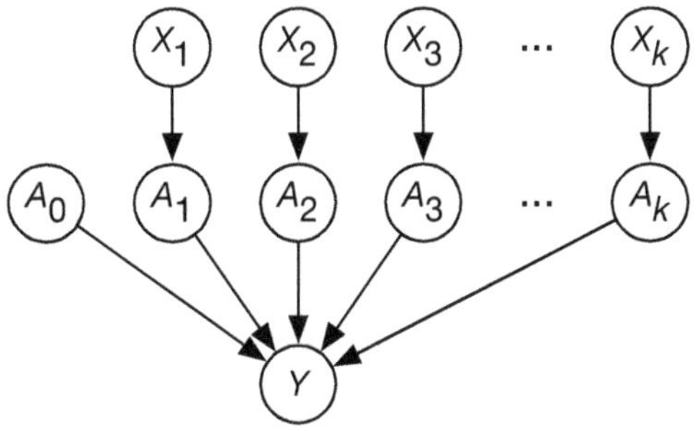


Figure 9.8: Noisy-or $P(Y \mid X_1, X_2, \ldots, X_k)$ as a belief network

- The **sigmoid function**, $sigmoid(x) = 1/(1 + \exp(-x))$, plotted in Figure 7.11 (page 290), has been used previously in this book for logistic regression (page 290) and neural networks (page 330).

- The **conditional odds** (as often used by bookmakers in gambling)

$$\begin{aligned} odds(h \mid e) &= \frac{P(h \wedge e)}{P(\neg h \wedge e)} \\ &= \frac{P(h \mid e)}{P(\neg h \mid e)} \\ &= \frac{P(h \mid e)}{1 - P(h \mid e)}. \end{aligned}$$

  Decomposing $P(h \wedge e)$ into $P(e \mid h) * P(h)$, and analogously for the numerator, gives

$$odds(h \mid e) = \frac{P(e \mid h)}{P(e \mid \neg h)} * \frac{P(h)}{P(\neg h)}$$

  where $\frac{P(h)}{P(\neg h)} = \frac{P(h)}{1-P(h)}$ is the **prior odds** and $\frac{P(e|h)}{P(e|\neg h)}$ is the **likelihood ratio**. When $P(e \mid h)/P(e \mid \neg h)$ is a product of terms, the log is a sum of terms.

The **logistic regression** (page 290) model of a conditional probability $P(Y \mid X_1, \dots, X_k)$ is of the form

$$P(Y = true \mid X_1, \dots, X_k) = sigmoid\left(\sum_i w_i * X_i\right). \tag{9.3}$$

Assume a dummy input $X_0$ which is always 1; $w_0$ is the bias. This corresponds to a decomposition of the conditional probability, where the likelihood ratio is a product of terms, one for each $X_i$.

Note that $P(Y \mid X_1 = 0, \dots, X_k = 0) = sigmoid(w_0)$. Thus, $w_0$ determines the probability when all of the parents are zero. Each $w_i$ specifies a value that should be added as $X_i$ changes. $P(Y \mid X_1 = 0, \dots, X_i = 1, \dots, X_k = 0) = sigmoid(w_0 + w_i)$. The logistic regression model makes the independence assumption that the influence of each parent on the child does not depend on the other parents. In particular, it assumes that the odds can be decomposed into a product of terms that each only depend on a single variable. When learning logistic regression models (Section 7.3.2 (page 288)), the training data does not need to obey that independence, but rather the algorithm tries to find a logistic regression model that best predicts the training data (in the sense of having the lowest squared error or log loss).

**Example 9.21** Suppose the probability of *wet* given whether there is rain, coffee, kids, or whether the robot has a coat, $P(wet \mid Rain, Coffee, Kids, Coat)$, is

$$sigmoid(-1.0 + 2.0 * Rain + 1.0 * Coffee + 0.5 * Kids - 1.5 * Coat).$$

This implies the following conditional probabilities:

$$P(wet \mid \neg rain \wedge \neg coffee \wedge \neg kids \wedge \neg coat) = sigmoid(-1.0) = 0.27$$
$$P(wet \mid rain \wedge \neg coffee \wedge \neg kids \wedge \neg coat) = sigmoid(1.0) = 0.73$$
$$P(wet \mid rain \wedge \neg coffee \wedge \neg kids \wedge coat) = sigmoid(-0.5) = 0.38.$$

This requires fewer parameters than the $2^4 = 16$ parameters required for a tabular representation, but makes more independence assumptions.

Noisy-or and logistic regression models are similar, but different. Noisy-or is typically used when the causal assumption that a variable is true if it is caused to be true by one of the parents, is appropriate. Logistic regression is used when the various parents add up to influence the child. See the box on page 402.

One way to extend logistic regression to be able to represent more conditional probabilities is to allow weights for conjunctions of Boolean properties. For example, if Boolean $Y$ has Booleans $X_1$ and $X_2$ as parents, four weights can be used to define the conditional distribution:

$$P(Y \mid X_1, X_2) = w_0 + w_1 * X_1 + w_2 * X_2 + w_3 * X_1 * X_2$$

where $X_1 * X_2$ is 1 only when both $X_1$ and $X_2$ are true – the product of variables with domain $\{0,1\}$ corresponds to conjunction. Then $w_0 = P(Y \mid X_1=0, X_2=0)$, $w_1 = P(Y \mid X_1=1, X_2=0) - w_0$, $w_2 = P(Y \mid X_1=0, X_2=1) - w_0$ and $w_3 = P(Y \mid X_1=1, X_2=1) - w_0 - w_1 - w_2$. In general, for $P(Y \mid X_1, \dots, X_k)$ there are $2^k$ parameters, one for each subset of $\{X_1, \dots, X_k\}$ being conjoined (or multiplied). This is known as the **canonical representation** for Boolean conditional probabilities. This has the same number of parameters as a conditional probability table, but can be made simpler by not representing the zero weights. Logistic regression is the extreme form where all of the interaction (product) weights are zero. It is common to start with the logistic regression form and add as few interaction terms as needed.

A logistic regression model for Boolean variables can be represented using weighted logical formulas, where a **weighted logical formula** is a pair of a formula and a weight, such that $P(Y = true \mid X_1, \dots, X_k)$ is proportional to the exponential of the sum of the weights for the formulas for which $Y$ is true, and the $X_i$ have their given value. The model of Equation (9.3) (page 400) can be specified by $(y, w_0)$ and $(y \wedge x_i, w_i)$ for each $i$, where $x_i$ means $X_i = true$. For the canonical representation, more complicated formulas can be used; for example, the case in the previous paragraph is represented by adding the weighted formula $(y \wedge x_1 \wedge x_2, w_3)$ to the logistic regression weighted formulas.

The extension of logistic regression to non-binary discrete variables is softmax regression (page 295); the softmax of linear functions.

**Noisy-or Compared to Logistic Regression**

Noisy-or and logistic regression when used for Boolean parents are similar in many ways. They both take a parameter for each parent plus another parameter that is used when all parents are false. Logistic regression cannot represent zero probabilities. Noisy-or cannot represent cases where a parent being true makes the child less probable (although the negation can be a parent).

They can both represent the probability exactly when zero or one parent is true (as long as there are no zero probabilities for logistic regression). They are quite different in how they handle cases when multiple parents are true.

To see the difference, consider representing $P(Y \mid X_1, X_2, X_3, X_4)$, using parameters $w_0, \ldots, w_4$. Assume the following probabilities when zero or one parent is true:

| $X_1$ | $X_2$ | $X_3$ | $X_4$ | *Prob* |
|---|---|---|---|---|
| *False* | *False* | *False* | *False* | $p_0 = 0.01$ |
| *True* | *False* | *False* | *False* | $p_1 = 0.05$ |
| *False* | *True* | *False* | *False* | $p_2 = 0.1$ |
| *False* | *False* | *True* | *False* | $p_3 = 0.2$ |
| *False* | *False* | *False* | *True* | $p_4 = 0.2$ |

For noisy-or, $w_0 = p_0$. $1 - (1 - w_0)(1 - w_i) = p_i$. Solving for $w_i$ gives $w_i = 1 - (1 - p_i)/(1 - w_0)$.

For logistic regression, $sigmoid(w_0) = p_0$ and $sigmoid(w_0 + w_i) = p_i$.

The predictions for $Y = true$ for the other assignments to Xs are:

| $X_1$ | $X_2$ | $X_3$ | $X_4$ | Noisy-or | Logistic Regression |
|---|---|---|---|---|---|
| *False* | *False* | *True* | *True* | 0.353535 | 0.860870 |
| *False* | *True* | *False* | *True* | 0.272727 | 0.733333 |
| *False* | *True* | *True* | *False* | 0.272727 | 0.733333 |
| *False* | *True* | *True* | *True* | 0.412305 | 0.985520 |
| *True* | *False* | *False* | *True* | 0.232323 | 0.565714 |
| *True* | *False* | *True* | *False* | 0.232323 | 0.565714 |
| *True* | *False* | *True* | *True* | 0.379655 | 0.969916 |
| *True* | *True* | *False* | *False* | 0.136364 | 0.366667 |
| *True* | *True* | *False* | *True* | 0.302112 | 0.934764 |
| *True* | *True* | *True* | *False* | 0.302112 | 0.934764 |
| *True* | *True* | *True* | *True* | 0.436050 | 0.997188 |

Logistic regression is much more extreme than noisy-or when multiple $X_i$ are true. With noisy-or, each $X_i = true$ probabilistically forces $Y$ to be true. With logistic regression, each $X_i = true$ provides independent evidence for $Y$.

If the probability $p_0$ is increased, to say, 0.05, with $p_1, \ldots, p_4$ fixed, the probability of $Y = true$ given assignments with multiple $X_i$ true for noisy-or goes up (as there are more ways $Y$ could be true) and for logistic regression goes down (as each $X_i$ true provides less evidence of exceptionality).

**Directed and Undirected Graphical Models**

A belief network is a directed model; all of the arcs are directed. The model is defined in terms of conditional probabilities.

An alternative is an **undirected model**. A **factor graph** consists of a set of variables and a set of nonnegative factors (page 394), each with scope a subset of the variables. There is an arc between each variable and the factors it is in the scope of, similar to a constraint network (page 136). It is sometimes written as a **Markov random field** or **Markov network** where the factors are implicit: the nodes are the variables, with an edge between any pair of nodes if there is a factor containing both.

The joint probability is defined by

$$P(X_1 = v_1 \land X_2 = v_2 \land \cdots \land X_n = v_n) \propto \prod_F F(X_F = v_f)$$

where $X_F$ is the tuple of variables in factor $F$ and $v_F$ is the tuple of corresponding values.

The constant of proportionality,

$$\sum_{X_1,\ldots,X_n} \prod_F F(X_F)$$

is called the **partition function**. The exact algorithms of Section 9.5 (page 405) can be used to compute the partition function; those algorithms just assume a set of factors.

Sometimes the factors are defined in terms of weights, so that $F(X_{F_1}, \ldots, X_{F_k}) = \exp(w_F(X_{F_1}, \ldots, X_{F_k}))$. This changes the product above to

$$P(X_1 = v_1 \land X_2 = v_2 \land \cdots \land X_n = v_n) \propto \exp(\sum_F w_F(X_F = v_f))$$

giving a **log-linear model**, which is useful for learning as the derivative is simpler and the nonnegative constraint happens automatically, although zero probabilities cannot be represented.

Note that a belief network can also be seen as a factor graph, where the factors are defined in terms of conditional probabilities. The directed and undirected models are collectively called **graphical models**.

A **canonical representation** is a representation that has a unique form. One problem with undirected models is that there is no canonical representation for a probability distribution. For example, modifying a factor on $X_i$ by multiplying $X_i = v_i$ by a constant and modifying another factor on $X_i$ by dividing by the same constant gives the same model. This means that the model cannot be learned modularly; each factor depends on the others. A belief network forces a particular factorization that gives a canonical representation for a distribution.

## 9.4 Probabilistic Inference

The most common and useful **probabilistic inference** task is to compute the **posterior distribution** of a query variable or variables given some evidence. Unfortunately, even the problem of estimating the posterior probability in a belief network within an absolute error (of less than 0.5), or within a constant multiplicative factor, is NP-hard (page 89), so general efficient implementations will not be available. Computing the posterior probability of a variable is in a complexity class called *#NP* (pronounced "sharp-NP"). *NP* is the complexity of determining whether there is a solution to a decision problem where solutions can be verified in polynomial time. *#NP* is the complexity of counting the number of solutions. These are for the worst case, however, there is often structure that can be exploited, such as conditional independence.

The main approaches for probabilistic inference in belief networks are:

**Exact inference** where the probabilities are computed exactly. A naive way is to enumerate the worlds that are consistent with the evidence, but this algorithm takes time exponential in the number of variables. It is possible to do much better than this by exploiting the structure of the network. The recursive conditioning and variable elimination algorithms (below) are exact algorithms that exploit conditional independence so that they can be much more efficient for networks that are not highly interconnected.

**Approximate inference** where probabilities are approximated. Such methods are characterized by the guarantees they provide:

- They could produce **guaranteed bounds** on the probabilities. That is, they return a range $[l, u]$ where the exact probability $p$ is guaranteed to have $l \leq p \leq u$. An **anytime algorithm** (page 26) may guarantee that $l$ and $u$ get closer to each other as computation time (and perhaps space) increases.
- They could produce **probabilistic bounds** on the error. Such algorithms might guarantee that the error, for example, is within 0.1 of the correct answer 95% of the time. They might also have guarantees that, as time increases, probability estimates will converge to the exact probability. Some even have guarantees of the rates of convergence. Stochastic simulation (page 436) is a class of algorithms, many of which have such guarantees.
- They could make a best effort to produce an approximation that may be good enough, even though there may be cases where they do not work very well. One such class of techniques is called **variational inference**, where the idea is to find an approximation to the problem that is easy to compute. First choose a class of representations that are easy to compute. This class could be as simple as the set of disconnected belief networks (with no arcs). Next try to find a member

of the class that is closest to the original problem. That is, find an easy-to-compute distribution that is as close as possible to the posterior distribution to be computed. Thus, the problem reduces to an optimization problem of minimizing the error, followed by a simple inference problem.

This book presents some exact methods and some stochastic simulation methods.

## 9.5 Exact Probabilistic Inference

The task of **probabilistic inference** is to compute the probability of a query variable $Q$ given evidence $e$, where $e$ is a conjunction of assignments of values to some of the variables; that is, to compute $P(Q \mid e)$. This is the task that is needed for decision making.

Given evidence $e$, and query variable or variables $Q$, the problem of computing the posterior distribution on $Q$ can be reduced to the problem of computing the probability of conjunctions, using the definition of conditioning:

$$\begin{aligned} P(Q \mid e) &= \frac{P(Q \wedge e)}{P(e)} \\ &= \frac{P(Q \wedge e)}{\sum_{Q} P(Q \wedge e)} \end{aligned} \tag{9.4}$$

where $\sum_{Q}$ means summing over all of the values of $Q$, which is called **marginalizing** $Q$ and $\sum_{Q} P(Q \wedge e)$ is an abbreviation for $\sum_{v \in domain(Q)} P(Q = v \wedge e)$, where $Q = v$ is the proposition that is true when $Q$ has value $v$.

To compute the probability of a product, first introduce all of the other variables. With all of the variables, the definition of a belief network is used to decompose the resulting joint probability into a product of factors.

Suppose $\{X_1, \ldots, X_n\}$ is the set of all variables in the belief network and the evidence $e$ is $Y_1 = v_1, \ldots, Y_j = v_j$, where $\{Y_1, \ldots, Y_j\} \subseteq \{X_1, \ldots, X_n\}$.

Suppose $Z_1, \ldots, Z_k$ is a total ordering of the variables in the belief network other than the observed variables, $Y_1, \ldots, Y_j$, and the query variable, $Q$. That is:

$$\{Z_1, \ldots, Z_k\} = \{X_1, \ldots, X_n\} \setminus \{Q, Y_1, \ldots, Y_j\}.$$

The probability of $Q$ conjoined with the evidence is

$$p(Q, e) = \sum_{Z_1} \cdots \sum_{Z_k} P(X_1, \ldots, X_n)_e$$

where the subscript $e$ means that the observed variables are set to their observed values.

Once all of the variables are modeled, the definition of a belief network, Equation (9.1) (page 386), shows how to decompose the joint probability:

$$P(X_1, \ldots, X_n) = \prod_{i=1}^{n} P(X_i \mid parents(X_i))$$

where $parents(X_i)$ is the set of parents of variable $X_i$.

So

$$p(Q,e) = \sum_{Z_1} \cdots \sum_{Z_k} \prod_{i=1}^{n} P(X_i \mid parents(X_i))_e. \qquad (9.5)$$

The belief-network inference problem is thus reduced to a problem of summing out a set of variables from a product of factors.

### Naive Search-Based Algorithm

The naive search-based algorithm shown in Figure 9.9 computes Equation (9.5) from the outside-in. The algorithm is similar to the search-based algorithm for constraint satisfaction problems (see Figure 4.1 (page 134)).

The algorithm takes in a context, *Con*, an assignment of values to some of the variables, and a set, *Fs*, of factors. The aim is to compute the value of the product of the factors, evaluated with the assignment *Con*, after all of the

```
procedure prob_dfs(Con, Fs)
    Inputs
        Con: context
        Fs: set of factors
    Output
        Σ_{v1,...,vk} Π_{f∈Fs} f_Con where {v1, ..., vk} = vars(Fs) \ vars(Con)
    if Fs = {} then
        return 1
    else if there is f ∈ Fs that can be evaluated in Con then
        return eval(f, Con) * prob_dfs(Con, Fs \ {f})
    else
        select variable var in vars(Fs) \ vars(Con)
        sum := 0
        for val in domain(var) do
            sum := sum + prob_dfs(Con ∪ {var = val}, Fs)
        return sum
```

Figure 9.9: Naive search-based inference algorithm

variables not in the context are summed out. Initially the context is usually the observations and an assignment of a value to the query variable, and the factors are the conditional probabilities of a belief network.

In this algorithm, the function *vars* returns the set of variables in a context or set of factors, so *vars*(*context*) is the set of variables assigned in *context* and *vars*(*factors*) is the set of all variables that appear in any factor in *factors*. Thus, *vars*(*factors*) $\setminus$ *vars*(*context*) is the set of variables that appear in factors that are not assigned in the context. The algorithm returns the value of the product of the factors with all of these variables summed out. This is the probability of the context, given the model specified by the factors.

If there are no factors, the probability is 1. Factors are evaluated as soon as they can be. A factor on a set of variables can be evaluated when all of the variables in the factor are assigned in the context. Some representations of factors, such as decision trees, may be able to be evaluated before all of the variables are assigned. The function *eval*($f$, *context*) returns the value of factor $f$ in *context*; it is only called when it can return a value.

If neither of the previous conditions arise, the algorithm selects a variable and branches on it, summing the values. This is **marginalizing** the selected variable. Which variable is selected does not affect the correctness of the algorithm, but may affect the efficiency.

### Exploiting Independence in Inference

The naive search-based algorithm evaluates the sum of Equation (9.5) (page 406) directly. However, it is possible to do much better.

The **distribution law** specifies that a sum of products, such as $xy + xz$, can be simplified by distributing out the common factors (here $x$), which results in $x(y + z)$. The resulting form is more efficient to compute, because it has only one addition and one multiplication. Distributing out common factors is the essence of the efficient exact algorithms. The elements multiplied together are called "factors" because of the use of the term in algebra.

**Example 9.22** Consider the simple chain belief network of Figure 9.10. Suppose you want to compute $P(D)$, the probability of $D$ with no observations; the denominator of Equation (9.4) (page 405) is 1, so let's ignore that. The variable order $A, B, C$, results in the factorization

$$P(D) = \sum_A \sum_B \sum_C P(A, B, C, D)$$

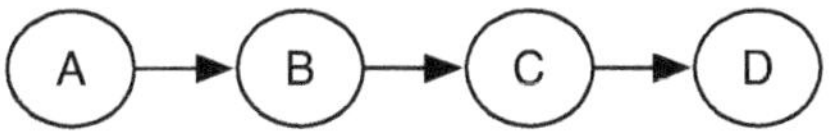


Figure 9.10: A simple chain belief network

$$= \sum_A \sum_B \sum_C P(A)P(B \mid A)P(C \mid B)P(D \mid C).$$

Consider the rightmost sum ($\sum_C$). The left two terms do not include $C$ and can be distributed out of that sum, giving

$$P(D) = \sum_A \sum_B P(A)P(B \mid A) \sum_C P(C \mid B)P(D \mid C).$$

Similarly, $P(A)$ can be distributed out of $\sum_B$, giving

$$P(D) = \sum_A P(A) \sum_B P(B \mid A) \sum_C P(C \mid B)P(D \mid C).$$

The search-based algorithms, described below, start at the leftmost sum and sum the values. Variable elimination (see Section 9.5.2, page 413) is the dynamic programming variant that creates factors from the inside-out; in this case creating an explicit representation for $\sum_C P(C \mid B)P(D \mid C)$, which is multiplied by $P(B \mid A)$, and then $B$ is summed out, and so on.

You could choose a different ordering of the variables, which can result in a different factorization. For example, the variable order $C, B, A$ gives

$$\begin{aligned} P(D) &= \sum_C \sum_B \sum_A P(A,B,C,D) \\ &= \sum_C \sum_B \sum_A P(A)P(B \mid A)P(C \mid B)P(D \mid C) \\ &= \sum_C P(D \mid C) \sum_B P(C \mid B) \sum_A P(A)P(B \mid A). \end{aligned}$$

**Example 9.23** Consider the query $P(B \mid D{=}true)$ in the simple chain belief network of Figure 9.10 (page 407). Let's write $D{=}true$ as $d$. Equation (9.4) (page 405) gives

$$P(B \mid d) = \frac{P(B,d)}{\sum_D P(B,d)}.$$

Computing $P(B,d)$ with the variable order $A, C$ gives

$$\begin{aligned} P(B,d) &= \sum_A \sum_C P(A,B,C,d) \\ &= \sum_A \sum_C P(A)P(B \mid A)P(C \mid B)P(d \mid C). \end{aligned}$$

Distributing the factors out of the sums gives

$$P(B,d) = \left(\sum_A P(A)P(B \mid A)\right)\left(\sum_C P(C \mid B)P(d \mid C)\right).$$

This gives two independent problems that can be solved separately. Note that, in this case, the variable order $C, A$ gives the same factorization.

### 9.5.1 Recursive Conditioning

Recursive conditioning is one of the most efficient exact algorithms. It adds two features to the naive search-based inference algorithm of Figure 9.9 (page 406), namely caching and recognizing subproblems that can be solved independently. The motivation for this can be seen in the following two examples.

**Example 9.24** Consider the chain belief network of Figure 9.10 (page 407) with the last factorization of Example 9.22 (page 407). First splitting on $D$, then $C$, $B$, $A$, results in the tree of Figure 9.11(a). In general, you need to split on the values of the query variable to compute the normalizing constant; while it is not necessary here (because there is no evidence, it must be 1), we show it anyway.

The left branch is for the variable having value *false*, and the right branch for the variable having value *true*.

Part (b) of the figure shows the stage where each factor can be evaluated. $P(D \mid C)$ can be evaluated when $D$ and $C$ are assigned values. $P(C \mid B)$ can be evaluated when $D$, $C$, and $B$ have been assigned values. For this variable ordering, all variables need to be split before $P(A)$ and $P(B \mid A)$ can be evaluated.

Consider the first recursive call after $D$ and $C$ have been assigned *false*, and $P(D \mid C)$ has been evaluated:

$$prob\_dfs(\{D = false, C = false\}, \{P(C \mid B), P(B \mid A), P(A)\}).$$

Notice that the factors do not involve $D$, and so this call will have the same value as when the context is $\{D = true, C = false\}$.

Recursive conditioning "forgets" $D$, and stores the computed value for

$$prob\_dfs(\{C = false\}, \{P(C \mid B), P(B \mid A), P(A)\})$$

in a cache (a dictionary), and then retrieves that value for the $D = true$ case.

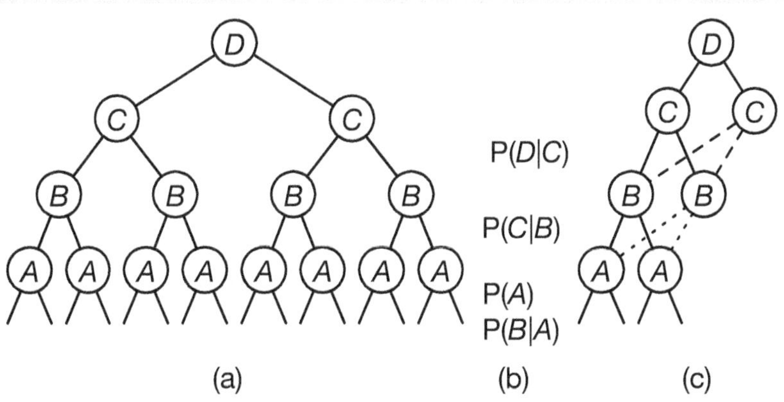


Figure 9.11: Search space of (a) naive search and (c) recursive conditioning, with (b) the factors that can be evaluated

Similarly, after $D, C$, and $B$ have been assigned a value, the factors are $\{P(B \mid A), P(A)\}$, which will give the same values for $C = true$ as for $C = false$. Again, recursive conditioning saves the result of $prob\_dfs(\{B = false\}, \{P(B \mid A), P(A)\})$ in a cache and retrieves that value for the other value of $C$.

This results in the search space of Figure 9.11(c), where the dashed lines indicate a cache lookup.

**Example 9.25** Consider the query $P(B \mid d)$ for the belief network in Example 9.23 (page 408). The assigned value, $D = true$, is given as the initial context. After $B$ is assigned a value (which is needed for the denominator of Equation (9.4) (page 405)), the naive search algorithm has the recursive call

$$prob\_dfs(\{B = false, D = true\}, \{P(D \mid C), P(C \mid B), P(B \mid A), P(A)\}).$$

This can be decomposed into two independent problems, one using the factors $P(D \mid C), P(C \mid B)$, which has the same value independently of the assignment to $A$, and the other for the factors $P(B \mid A), P(A)$, which has the same value independently of the assignment to $C$. These factors only have $B$ in common, which has been assigned a value in the context.

Thus, this call can be decomposed into the product:

$$\begin{aligned} &prob\_dfs(\{B = false, D = true\}, \{P(D \mid C), P(C \mid B)\}) \\ &\quad * prob\_dfs(\{B = false, D = true\}, \{P(B \mid A), P(A)\}). \end{aligned}$$

The recursive conditioning algorithm is shown in Figure 9.12 (page 411).

The function *vars* returns the set of variables, as described previously for the naive algorithm.

The cache is a global dictionary that can be reused through recursive calls. It remembers what has already been computed. The keys are $(Con, Fs)$ pairs. In order to cover the base case, the cache is initialized to have value 1 for the key $(\{\}, \{\})$.

The first condition (line 7) is to check whether the answer has already been computed and stored in the cache. If it has, the stored value is returned. Note that because of the initialization of the cache, this can replace the base case for the naive search.

The second condition (line 9) checks whether there are variables in the context that are not in any factors, and "forgets" them. This is needed so that the caching works properly, as in Example 9.24 (page 409).

The third condition (line 11) checks whether some factors can be evaluated in the given context. If so, these factors are evaluated and removed from the factors of the recursive call.

The fourth condition (line 13) checks whether the problem can be split into independent parts that can be solved separately and multiplied. Here $\uplus$ is the **disjoint union**, where $Fs = Fs_1 \uplus Fs_2$ means that non-empty sets $Fs_1$ and $Fs_2$ have no element in common and together contain all of the elements of $Fs$. Thus, $Fs_1$ and $Fs_2$ are a partition of $Fs$. If all of the variables in common are assigned in the context, the problem can be decomposed into two independent problems. The algorithm could, alternatively, split into multiple nonempty sets of factors that have no unassigned variables in any pair. They would then be the connected components, where the two factors are connected if they both contain a variable that is not assigned in the context. If there are more than two connected components, the algorithm of Figure 9.12 would find the connected components in recursive calls. Note that the subsequent recursive calls typically result in forgetting the variables that are only in the other partition, so it does not need to be done explicitly here.

If none of the other conditions hold (line 15), the algorithm branches. It selects a variable, and sums over all of the values of this variable. Which variable is selected does not affect the result, but can affect the efficiency. Finding the optimal variable to select is an NP-hard problem. Often the algorithm is given a split-order of variables in the order they should be branched on. The algorithm saves the computed result in the cache.

Examples of the application of recursive conditioning are given in Example 9.24 (page 409) and Example 9.25 (page 410).

---

1: **procedure** $prob\_RC(Con, Fs)$
2:     **Inputs**
3:         $Con$: context
4:         $Fs$: set of factors
5:     **Output**
6:         $\sum_{v_1,\dots,v_k} \prod_{f \in Fs} f_{Con}$ where $\{v_1, \dots, v_k\} = vars(Fs) \setminus vars(Con)$
7:     **if** $(Con, Fs)$ in *cache* with value $v$ **then**
8:         **return** $v$
9:     **else if** there is $X = v$ in $Con$ such that $X \notin vars(Fs)$ **then**
10:         **return** $prob\_RC(\{X = v \in Con : X \in vars(Fs)\}, Fs)$
11:     **else if** $fs = \{f \in Fs : f$ can be evaluated in $Con\}$ is not empty **then**
12:         **return** $\left(\prod_{f \in fs} eval(f, Con)\right) * prob\_RC(Con, Fs \setminus fs)$
13:     **else if** $Fs = Fs_1 \uplus Fs_2$ where $vars(Fs_1) \cap vars(Fs_2)$ are all assigned in Con **then**
14:         **return** $prob\_RC(Con, Fs_1) * prob\_RC(Con, Fs_2)$
15:     **else**
16:         select variable $var$ in $vars(Fs) \setminus vars(Con)$
17:         $sum := 0$
18:         **for** $val$ in $domain(var)$ **do**
19:             $sum := sum + prob\_RC(Con \cup \{var = val\}, Fs)$
20:         add $(Con, Fs)$ to cache with value $sum$
21:         **return** $sum$

Figure 9.12: Recursive conditioning algorithm

---

**Example 9.26** Consider Example 9.13 (page 389) with the query

$$P(Tampering \mid Smoke = true \wedge Report = true).$$

The initial call (using abbreviated names, and lower-case letters for true value) for the $Ta = false$ case is

$$prob\_RC(\{sm, re, \neg ta\}, \{P(Ta), P(Fi), P(Al \mid Ta, Fi), P(Sm \mid Fi), P(Le \mid Al), P(Re \mid Le)\}).$$

$P(Ta)$ can be evaluated. If it then splits on *Le*, the call is

$$prob\_RC(\{sm, re, \neg ta, \neg le\}, \{P(Fi), P(Al \mid Ta, Fi), P(Sm \mid Fi), P(Le \mid Al), P(Re \mid Le)\}).$$

At this stage $P(Re \mid Le)$ can be evaluated, and then *Re* is not in the remaining factors, so *re* can be forgotten in the context. If it then splits on *Al*, the call is

$$prob\_RC(\{sm, \neg ta, \neg le, \neg al\}, \{P(Fi), P(Al \mid Ta, Fi), P(Sm \mid Fi), P(Le \mid Al)\}).$$

Then $P(Le \mid Al)$ can be evaluated, and $\neg le$ forgotten. Splitting on *Fi* results in the call

$$prob\_RC(\{sm, \neg ta, \neg al, \neg fi\}, \{P(Fi), P(Al \mid Ta, Fi), P(Sm \mid Fi)\}).$$

All of the factors can be evaluated, and so this call returns the value $P(\neg fi) * P(\neg al \mid \neg ta, \neg fi) * P(sm \mid \neg fi)$.

The search continues; where the variables are forgotten, the cache is used to look up values rather than computing them. This can be summarized as

| Variable Split on | Factors Evaluated | Forgotten |
|---|---|---|
| *Ta* | $P(Ta)$ | |
| *Le* | $P(Re \mid Le)$ | *Re* |
| *Al* | $P(Le \mid Al)$ | *Le* |
| *Fi* | $P(Fi), P(Al \mid Ta, Fi), P(Sm \mid Fi)$ | |

Different variable orderings can result in quite different evaluations, for example, for the same query $P(Ta \mid sm, re)$, for the splitting order *Ta*, *Fi*, *Al*, *Le*:

| Variable Split on | Factors Evaluated | Forgotten |
|---|---|---|
| *Ta* | $P(Ta)$ | |
| *Fi* | $P(Fi), P(Sm \mid Fi)$ | *Sm* |
| *Al* | $P(Al \mid Ta, Fi)$ | *Fi*, *Ta* |
| *Le* | $P(Le \mid Al), P(Re \mid Le)$ | |

If *Al* was split before *Fi* and *Le*, there are two independent subproblems that can be solved separately; subproblem 1 involving *Fi* and subproblem 2 involving *Le*:

| Variable Split on | Factors Evaluated | Forgotten |
|---|---|---|
| *Ta* | $P(Ta)$ | |
| *Al* | | |
| subproblem 1: | | |
| *Fi* | $P(Fi), P(Sm \mid Fi), P(Al \mid Ta, Fi)$ | *Sm*, *Fi* |
| subproblem 2: | | |
| *Le* | $P(Le \mid Al), P(Re \mid Le)$ | *Le*, *Re* |

The solutions to the subproblems are multiplied.

Some of the conditions checked in Figure 9.12 (page 411) only depend on the variables in the context, and not on the values of the variables. The results of these conditions can be precomputed and looked up during the search, saving a lot of time.

Some representations of factors (e.g., tables or logistic regression) require all variables to be assigned before they can be evaluated, whereas other representations (e.g., decision trees or weighted logical formula) can often be evaluated before all variables involved have been assigned values. To exploit this short-circuiting effectively, there needs to be good indexing to determine which factors can be evaluated.

## 9.5.2 Variable Elimination for Belief Networks

**Variable elimination** (VE) is the **dynamic programming** variant of recursive conditioning. Consider the decomposition of probability of the query $Q$ and the evidence $e$ (Equation (9.5) (page 406), reproduced here):

$$p(Q,e) = \sum_{Z_1} \cdots \sum_{Z_k} \prod_{i=1}^{n} P(X_i \mid parents(X_i))_e.$$

VE carries out the rightmost sum, here $\sum_{Z_k}$ first, eliminating $Z_k$, producing an explicit representation of the resulting factor. The resulting factorization then contains one fewer variables. This can be repeated until there is an explicit representation of $P(Q,e)$. The resulting factor is a function just of $Q$; given a value for $Q$, it evaluates to a number that is the probability of the evidence conjoined with the value for $Q$. The conditional probability can be obtained by normalization (dividing each value by the sum of the values).

To compute the posterior distribution of a query variable given observations:

1. Construct a factor for each conditional probability distribution.
2. Eliminate each of the non-query variables:

   - if the variable is observed, its value is set to the observed value in each of the factors in which the variable appears
   - otherwise, the variable is summed out.

     To sum out a variable $Z$ from a product $f_1, \ldots, f_k$ of factors, first partition the factors into those not containing $Z$, say $f_1, \ldots, f_i$, and those containing $Z$, $f_{i+1}, \ldots, f_k$; then distribute the common factors out of the sum:

$$\sum_Z f_1 * \cdots * f_k = f_1 * \cdots * f_i * \left( \sum_Z f_{i+1} * \cdots * f_k \right).$$

Variable elimination explicitly constructs a representation (in terms of a multidimensional array, a tree, or a set of rules) of the rightmost factor. We have then simplified the problem to have one fewer variable.

3. Multiply the remaining factors and normalize.

Figure 9.13 gives pseudocode for the VE algorithm. The elimination ordering could be given a priori or computed on the fly. This algorithm assigns the values to the observations as part of the elimination. It is worthwhile to select observed variables first in the elimination ordering, because eliminating these simplifies the problem.

This algorithm assumes that the query variable is not observed. If it is observed to have a particular value, its posterior probability is just 1 for the observed value and 0 for the other values.

**Example 9.27** Consider Example 9.13 (page 389) with the query

$$P(Tampering \mid Smoke = true \wedge Report = true).$$

Suppose it first eliminates the observed variables, *Smoke* and *Report*. This created a factor for $P(Smoke = yes \mid Fire)$ which is just a function of *Fire*; call it

```
procedure VE_BN(Vs, Ps, e, Q)
    Inputs
        Vs: set of variables
        Ps: set of factors representing the conditional probabilities
        e: the evidence, a variable-value assignment to some of the variables
        Q: a query variable
    Output
        posterior distribution on Q
    Fs := Ps                                   ▷ Fs is the current set of factors
    for each X ∈ Vs − {Q} using some elimination ordering do
        if X is observed then
            for each F ∈ Fs that involves X do
                assign X in F to its observed value in e
        else
            Rs := {F ∈ Fs : F involves X}
            let T be the product of the factors in Rs
            construct an explicit representation for N = Σ_X T
            Fs := Fs \ Rs ∪ {N}
    let T be the product of the factors in Fs
    N := Σ_Q T
    return T/N
```

Figure 9.13: Variable elimination for belief networks

$f_0(Fire)$. Given a value for *Fire*, this evaluates to a number. $P(Report = yes \mid Leaving)$ becomes a factor $f_1(Leaving)$.

Suppose *Fire* is next in the elimination ordering. To eliminate *Fire*, collect all of the factors containing *Fire*, namely $P(Fire)$, $P(Alarm \mid Tampering, Fire)$, and $f_0(Fire)$, and replace them with an explicit representation of the resulting factor. This factor is on *Tampering* and *Alarm* as these are the other variables in the factors being multiplied. Call it $f_2(Tampering, Alarm)$:

$$f_2(Tampering, Alarm) = \sum_{Fire} P(Fire) * (Alarm \mid Tampering, Fire) * f_0(Fire).$$

We explicitly store a number for each value for *Tampering* and *Alarm*. For example, $f_2(Tampering = t, Alarm = f)$ has value

$$\sum_{v \in domain(Fire)} P(Fire = v) * P(Alarm = f \mid Tampering = t, Fire = v) * f_0(Fire = v).$$

At this stage, *Fs* contains the factors

$$P(Tampering), P(Leaving \mid Alarm), f_1(Leaving), f_2(Tampering, Alarm).$$

Suppose *Alarm* is eliminated next. VE multiplies the factors containing *Alarm* and sums out *Alarm* from the product, giving a factor, call it $f_7$:

$$f_3(Tampering, Leaving) = \sum_{Alarm} P(Leaving \mid Alarm) * f_2(Tampering, Alarm).$$

*Fs* then contains the factors

$$P(Tampering), f_1(Leaving), f_3(Tampering, Leaving).$$

Eliminating *Leaving* results in the factor

$$f_4(Tampering) = \sum_{Leaving} f_1(Leaving) * f_3(Tampering, Leaving).$$

The posterior distribution over *Tampering* is given by

$$\frac{P(Tampering) * f_4(Tampering)}{\sum_{Tampering} P(Tampering) * f_4(Tampering)}.$$

Note that the denominator is the prior probability of the evidence, namely $P(Smoke = true \wedge Report = true)$.

**Example 9.28** Consider the same network as in the previous example but with the query

$$P(Alarm \mid Fire = true).$$

When *Fire* is eliminated, the factor $P(Fire)$ becomes a factor of no variables; it is just a number, $P(Fire = true)$.

Suppose *Report* is eliminated next. It is in one factor, which represents $P(Report \mid Leaving)$. Summing over all of the values of *Report* gives a factor on *Leaving*, all of whose values are 1. This is because $P(Report = true \mid Leaving = v) + P(Report = false \mid Leaving = v) = 1$ for any value $v$ of *Leaving*.

If *Leaving* is eliminated next, a factor that is all 1 is multiplied by a factor representing $P(Leaving \mid Alarm)$ and *Leaving* is summed out. This, again, results in a factor all of whose values are 1.

Similarly, eliminating *Smoke* results in a factor of no variables, whose value is 1. Note that even if smoke had also been observed, eliminating *Smoke* would result in a factor of no variables, which would not affect the posterior distribution on *Alarm*.

Eventually, there is only the factor on *Alarm* that represents its posterior probability and a constant factor that will cancel in the normalization.

### 9.5.3 Exploiting Structure and Compilation

When the ordering of the splits in recursive conditioning is the *reverse* of the elimination ordering of variable elimination, the two algorithms carry out the same multiplications and additions, and the values stored in the factors of variable elimination are the same numbers as stored in the cache of recursive conditioning. The main differences are:

- Recursive conditioning just evaluates the input factors, whereas variable elimination requires an explicit representation of intermediate factors. This means that recursive conditioning can be used where the conditional probabilities can be treated as black boxes that output a value when enough of their variables are instantiated. Thus, recursive conditioning allows for diverse representations of conditional probabilities, such as presented in Section 9.3.3 (page 394). This also enables it to exploit structure when all of the variables need not be assigned. For example, in a decision tree representation of a conditional probability, it is possible to evaluate a factor before all values are assigned.

- A straightforward implementation of variable elimination can use a more space-efficient tabular representation of the intermediate factors than a straightforward implementation of the cache in recursive conditioning.

- When there are zeros in a product, there is no need to compute the rest of the product. Zeros arise from constraints where some combination of values to variables is impossible. This is called **determinism**. Determinism can be incorporated into recursive conditioning in a straightforward way.

- Recursive conditioning can act as an **any-space algorithm**, which can use any amount of space by just not storing some values in the cache, but instead recomputing them, trading off space for time.

To speed up the inference, variables that are irrelevant to a conditional probability query can be **pruned**. In particular, any node that has no observed or queried descendants and is itself not observed or queried may be pruned. This may result in a smaller network with fewer factors and variables. For example, to compute $P(Alarm \mid Fire = true)$, in the running example, the variables *Report*, *Leaving*, and *Smoke* may be pruned.

The complexity of the algorithms depends on a measure of complexity of the network. The size of a tabular representation of a factor is exponential in the number of variables in the factor. The **treewidth** (page 145) of a network for an elimination ordering is the maximum number of variables in a factor created by variable elimination summing out the variables in the elimination ordering. The **treewidth** of a belief network is the minimum treewidth over all elimination orderings. The treewidth depends only on the graph structure and is a measure of the sparseness of the graph. The complexity of recursive conditioning and variable elimination is exponential in the treewidth and linear in the number of variables. Finding the elimination ordering with minimum treewidth is NP-hard, but there are some good elimination ordering heuristics, as discussed for CSP VE (page 146).

**Example 9.29** Consider the belief network of Figure 9.4 (page 392). To compute the probability of *Sneezing*, the variables *Fever* and *"Achoo" sound* may be pruned, as they have no children and are not observed or queried. Summing out *Season* involves multiplying the factors

$$P(Season), P(Pollen \mid Season), P(Influenza \mid Season)$$

and results in a factor on *Influenza* and *Pollen*. The treewidth of this belief network is 2; there is an ordering of the variables that only constructs factors of size 1 or 2, and there is no ordering of the variables that has a smaller treewidth.

Many modern exact algorithms **compile** the network into a secondary structure, by essentially carrying out variable elimination or recursive conditioning symbolically, summing out all of the variables, to produce a **probabilistic circuit** that just contains the symbolic variables combined by sum and product. The circuit is like Figure 9.11 (page 409), where the branches in (c) form the sums and the conditional probabilities in (b) are multiplied at the appropriate place, as in the factorization of Example 9.22 (page 407). The circuit is an arithmetic expression with shared structure. When all variables are summed out, the circuit provides an expensive way to compute the value 1. When some variables are observed, the circuit uses the observed values instead of summing out these variables; the output is the probability of the evidence. When a query variable is then set to a value, the circuit outputs the probability of the evidence and the query variable, from which a conditional probability can be computed. It is possible to compute the posterior probability of all variables with two passes through the circuit, but that is beyond the scope of this book.

Compilation is appropriate when the same belief network is used for many multiple queries, or where observations are added incrementally. Unfortunately, extensive preprocessing, allowing arbitrary sequences of observations and deriving the posterior on each variable, precludes pruning the network. So for each application you need to choose whether you will save more by pruning irrelevant variables for each query or by preprocessing before there are any observations or queries.

## 9.6 Sequential Probability Models

Special types of belief networks with repeated structure are used for reasoning about time and other sequences, such as sequences of words in a sentence. Such probabilistic models may have an unbounded number of random variables. Reasoning with time is essential for agents in the world. Reasoning about text with unbounded size is important for understanding language.

### 9.6.1 Markov Chains

A **Markov chain** is a belief network with random variables in a sequence, where each variable only directly depends on its predecessor in the sequence. Markov chains are used to represent sequences of values, such as the sequence of states in a dynamic system or language model (page 357). Each point in the sequence is called a **stage**.

Figure 9.14 shows a generic Markov chain as a belief network. The network has five stages, but does not have to stop at stage 4; it can extend indefinitely. The belief network conveys the independence assumption

$$P(S_{i+1} \mid S_0, \ldots, S_i) = P(S_{i+1} \mid S_i)$$

which is called the **Markov assumption**.

Often the sequences are in time, and $S_t$ represents the **state** at time $t$. The state conveys all of the information about the history that could affect the future. The independence assumption of the Markov chain can be seen as "the future is conditionally independent of the past given the state."

A Markov chain is a **stationary model** or **time-homogenous model** if the variables all have the same domain, and the transition probabilities are the

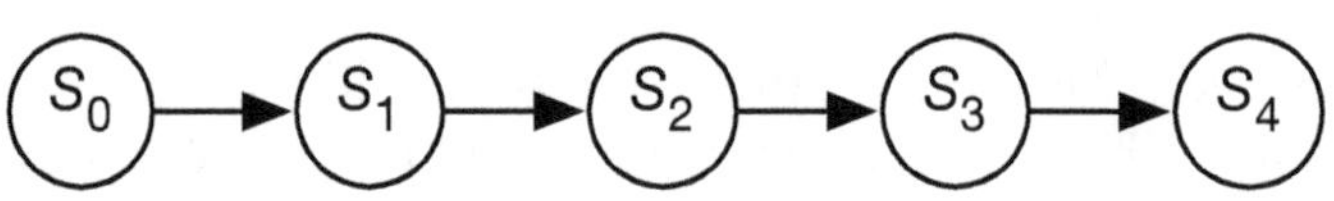


Figure 9.14: A Markov chain as a belief network

same for each stage:

$$\text{for all } i \geq 0,\ P(S_{i+1} \mid S_i) = P(S_1 \mid S_0).$$

To specify a stationary Markov chain, two conditional probabilities are provided:

- $P(S_0)$ specifies the initial conditions
- $P(S_{i+1} \mid S_i)$ specifies the **dynamics**, which is the same for each $i \geq 0$.

The sharing of the parameters for the conditional probability is known as **parameter sharing** or **weight tying**, as used in **convolutional neural networks** (page 347).

Stationary Markov chains are of interest for the following reasons:

- They provide a simple model that is easy to specify.
- The assumption of stationarity is often the natural model, because the dynamics of the world typically does not change in time. If the dynamics does change in time, it is usually because of some other feature that could also be modeled as part of the state.
- The network extends indefinitely. Specifying a small number of parameters gives an infinite network. You can ask queries or make observations about any arbitrary points in the future or the past.

To determine the probability distribution of state $S_i$, variable elimination can be used to sum out the preceding variables. The variables after $S_i$ are irrelevant to the probability of $S_i$ and need not be considered. To compute $P(S_i \mid S_k)$, where $i > k$, only the variables between $S_i$ and $S_k$ need to be considered, and if $i < k$, only the variables less than $k$ need to be considered.

A **stationary distribution** of a Markov chain is a distribution of the states such that if it holds at one time, it holds at the next time. Thus, $P$ is a stationary distribution if for each state $s$, $P(S_{i+1}=s) = P(S_i=s)$. Thus

$$P(S_i=s) = \sum_{s'} P(S_{i+1}=s \mid S_i=s') * P(S_i=s').$$

Every Markov chain with a finite number of states has at least one stationary distribution. The distribution over states encountered in one infinite run (or the limit as the number of steps approaches infinity) is a stationary distribution. Intuitively, if an agent is lost at time $i$, and doesn't observe anything, it is still lost at time $i+1$. Different runs might result in different parts of the state space being reached, and so result in different stationary distributions. There are some general conditions that result in unique stationary distributions, which are presented below.

A Markov chain is **ergodic** if, for any two states $s_1$ and $s_2$, there is a nonzero probability of eventually reaching $s_2$ from $s_1$.

A Markov chain is **periodic** with period $p$ if the difference between the times when it visits the same state is always divisible by $p$. For example, consider a Markov chain where the step is per day, so $S_{i+1}$ is the state on the day after $S_i$, and where the day of the week is part of the state. A state where the day is Monday is followed by a state where the day is Tuesday, etc. The period will be (a multiple of) 7; a state where the day is Monday can only be a multiple of 7 days from a state where the day is also Monday. If the only period of a Markov chain is a period of 1, then the Markov chain is **aperiodic**.

If a Markov chain is ergodic and aperiodic, then there is a unique stationary distribution, and this is the **equilibrium distribution** that will be approached from any starting state. Thus, for any distribution over $S_0$, the distribution over $S_i$ will get closer and closer to the equilibrium distribution, as $i$ gets larger.

The box on page 421 gives an application of Markov chains that formed the basis of Google's initial search engine.

### 9.6.2 Hidden Markov Models

A **hidden Markov model (HMM)** is an augmentation of a Markov chain to include observations. A hidden Markov model includes the state transition of the Markov chain, and adds to it observations at each time that depend on the state at the time. These observations can be **partial** in that different states map to the same observation and **noisy** in that the same state can map to different observations at different times.

The assumptions behind an HMM are:

- The state at time $t+1$ only directly depends on the state at time $t$ for $t \geq 0$, as in the Markov chain.
- The observation at time $t$ only directly depends on the state at time $t$.

The observations are modeled using the variable $O_t$ for each time $t$ whose domain is the set of possible observations. The belief-network representation of an HMM is depicted in Figure 9.15 (page 422). Although the belief network is shown for five stages, it extends indefinitely.

A stationary HMM includes the following probability distributions:

- $P(S_0)$ specifies initial conditions
- $P(S_{t+1} \mid S_t)$ specifies the **dynamics** or the **belief state transition function**
- $P(O_t \mid S_t)$ specifies the sensor model.

**Example 9.30** Suppose you want to keep track of an animal in a triangular enclosure using sound. You have three microphones that provide unreliable (noisy) binary information at each time step. The animal is either near one of the three vertices of the triangle or close to the middle of the triangle. The state has domain $\{m, c_1, c_2, c_3\}$, where $m$ means the animal is in the middle and $c_i$ means the animal is in corner $i$.

The dynamics of the world is a model of how the state at one time depends on the previous time. If the animal is in a corner, it stays in the same corner with probability 0.8, goes to the middle with probability 0.1, or goes to one of the other corners with probability 0.05 each. If it is in the middle, it stays in the

PageRank

**Google**'s initial search engine [Brin and Page, 1998] was based on **PageRank** [Page et al., 1999], a probability measure over web pages where the most influential web pages have the highest probability. It is based on a Markov chain of a web surfer who starts on a random page, and with some probability $d$ picks one of the pages at random that is linked from the current page, and otherwise (if the current page has no outgoing links or with probability $1 - d$) picks a page at random. The Markov chain is defined as follows:

- The domain of $S_i$ is the set of all web pages.
- $P(S_0)$ is the uniform distribution of web pages: $P(S_0 = p_j) = 1/N$ for each web page $p_j$, where $N$ is the number of web pages.
- The transition is defined as follows:

$$P(S_{i+1} = p_j \mid S_i = p_k)$$
$$= (1-d)/N + d * \begin{cases} 1/n_k & \text{if } p_k \text{ links to } p_j \\ 1/N & \text{if } p_k \text{ has no links} \\ 0 & \text{otherwise} \end{cases}$$

  where there are $N$ web pages and $n_k$ links on page $p_k$. The way to think about this is that $p_k$ is the current web page, and $p_j$ is the next web page. If $p_k$ has no outgoing links, then $p_j$ is a page at random, which is the effect of the middle case. If $p_k$ has outgoing links, with probability $d$ the surfer picks a random page linked from $p_k$, and otherwise picks a page at random.
- $d \approx 0.85$ is the probability someone picks a link on the current page.

This Markov chain converges to a stationary distribution over web pages. Page et al. [1999] reported the search engine had converged to "a reasonable tolerance" for $i = 52$ with 322 million links.

PageRank provides a measure of influence. To get a high PageRank, a web page should be linked from other pages with a high PageRank. It is difficult, yet not impossible, to manipulate PageRank for selfish reasons. One could try to artificially boost PageRank for a specific page, by creating many pages that point to that page, but it is difficult for those referring pages to also have a high PageRank.

In the initial reported version, Brin and Page [1998] used 24 million web pages and 76 million links. The web is more complex now, with many pages being dynamically generated, and search engines use much more sophisticated algorithms.

middle with probability 0.7, otherwise it moves to one of the corners, each with probability 0.1.

The sensor model specifies the probability of detection by each microphone given the state. If the animal is in a corner, it will be detected by the microphone at that corner with probability 0.6, and will be independently detected by each of the other microphones with probability 0.1. If the animal is in the middle, it will be detected by each microphone with probability 0.4.

Initially the animal is in one of the four states, with equal probability.

There are a number of tasks that are common for HMMs.

The problem of **filtering** or belief-state **monitoring** is to determine the current state based on the current and previous observations, namely to determine

$$P(S_i \mid O_0, \ldots, O_i).$$

All state and observation variables after $S_i$ are irrelevant because they are not observed and can be ignored when this conditional distribution is computed.

**Example 9.31** Consider filtering for Example 9.30 (page 420).

The following table gives the observations for each time, and the resulting state distribution.

| | Observation | | | Posterior State Distribution | | | |
|---|---|---|---|---|---|---|---|
| Time | Mic#1 | Mic#2 | Mic#3 | $P(m)$ | $P(c_1)$ | $P(c_2)$ | $P(c_3)$ |
| initially | – | – | – | 0.25 | 0.25 | 0.25 | 0.25 |
| 0 | 0 | 1 | 1 | 0.46 | 0.019 | 0.26 | 0.26 |
| 1 | 1 | 0 | 1 | 0.64 | 0.084 | 0.019 | 0.26 |

Thus, even with only two time steps of noisy observations from initial ignorance, it is very sure that the animal is not at corner 1 or corner 2. It is most likely that the animal is in the middle.

Note that the posterior distribution at any time only depended on the observations up to that time. Filtering does not take into account future observations that provide more information about the initial state.

The problem of **smoothing** is to determine a state based on past and future observations. Suppose an agent has observed up to time $k$ and wants to

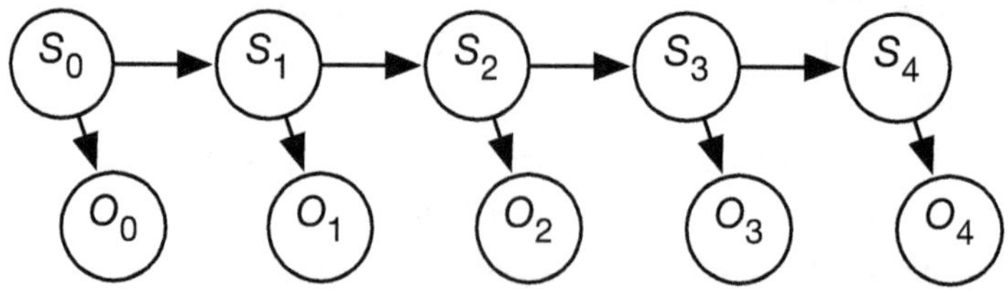


Figure 9.15: A hidden Markov model as a belief network

determine the state at time $i$ for $i < k$; the smoothing problem is to determine

$$P(S_i \mid O_0, \ldots, O_k).$$

All of the variables $S_i$ and $V_i$ for $i > k$ can be ignored.

### Localization

Suppose a robot wants to determine its location based on its history of actions and its sensor readings. This is the problem of **localization**. Figure 9.16 shows a belief-network representation of the localization problem. There is a variable $Loc_i$ for each time $i$, which represents the robot's location at time $i$. There is a variable $Obs_i$ for each time $i$, which represents the robot's observation made at time $i$. For each time $i$, there is a variable $Act_i$ that represents the robot's action at time $i$. In this section, assume that the robot's actions are observed. (The case in which the robot chooses its actions is discussed in Chapter 12.)

This model assumes the following dynamics: at time $i$, the robot is at location $Loc_i$, it observes $Obs_i$, then it acts, it observes its action $Act_i$, and time progresses to time $i+1$, where it is at location $Loc_{i+1}$. Its observation at time $t$ only depends on the state at time $t$. The robot's location at time $t+1$ depends on its location at time $t$ and its action at time $t$. Its location at time $t+1$ is conditionally independent of previous locations, previous observations, and previous actions, given its location at time $t$ and its action at time $t$.

The localization problem is to determine the robot's location as a function of its observation history:

$$P(Loc_t \mid Obs_0, Act_0, Obs_1, Act_1, \ldots, Act_{t-1}, Obs_t).$$

**Example 9.32** Consider the domain depicted in Figure 9.17 (page 424). There is a circular corridor, with 16 locations numbered 0 to 15. The robot is at one of these locations at each time. This is modeled with, for every time $i$, a variable $Loc_i$ with domain $\{0, 1, \ldots, 15\}$.

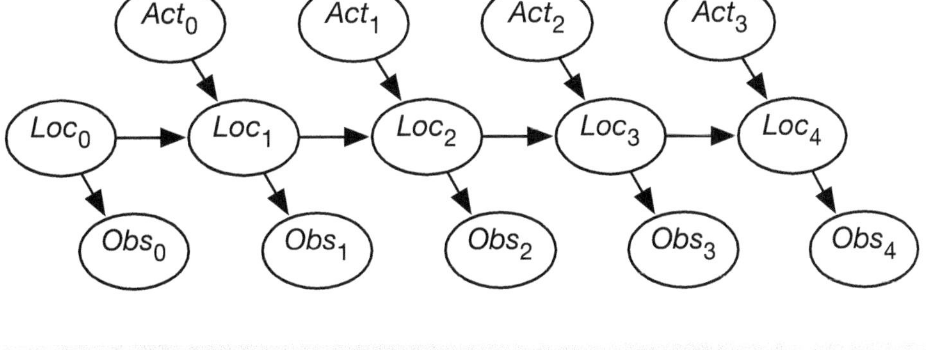


Figure 9.16: A belief network for localization

- There are doors at positions 2, 4, 7, and 11 and no doors at other locations.
- The robot has a sensor that noisily senses whether or not it is in front of a door. This is modeled with a variable $Obs_i$ for each time $i$, with domain $\{door, nodoor\}$. Assume the following conditional probabilities:

$$P(Obs_t = door \mid atDoor_t) = 0.8$$
$$P(Obs_t = door \mid \neg AtDoor_t) = 0.1$$

where $atDoor_t$ is true when the robot is at states 2, 4, 7, or 11 at time $t$.

Thus, the observation is partial in that many states give the same observation and it is noisy in the following way: in 20% of the cases in which the robot is at a door, the sensor gives a negative reading (a false negative). In 10% of the cases where the robot is not at a door, the sensor records that there is a door (a false positive).

- The robot can, at each time, move left, move right, or stay still. Assume that the *stay still* action is deterministic, but the dynamics of the moving actions are stochastic. Just because the robot carries out the *goRight* action does not mean that it actually goes one step to the right – it is possible that it stays still, goes two steps right, or even ends up at some arbitrary location (e.g., if someone picks up the robot and moves it). Assume the following dynamics, for each location $L$:

$$P(Loc_{t+1} = L \mid Act_t = goRight \wedge Loc_t = L) = 0.1$$
$$P(Loc_{t+1} = L+1 \mid Act_t = goRight \wedge Loc_t = L) = 0.8$$
$$P(Loc_{t+1} = L+2 \mid Act_t = goRight \wedge Loc_t = L) = 0.074$$
$$P(Loc_{t+1} = L' \mid Act_t = goRight \wedge Loc_t = L) = 0.002 \text{ for } L' \neq L.$$

All location arithmetic is modulo 16. The action *goLeft* works the same way but to the left.

The robot starts at an unknown location and must determine its location.

It may seem as though the domain is too ambiguous, the sensors are too noisy, and the dynamics is too stochastic to do anything. However, it is possible to compute the probability of the robot's current location given its history of actions and observations.

Figure 9.18 (page 425) gives the robot's probability distribution over its locations, assuming it starts with no knowledge of where it is and experiences the following observations: observe door, go right, observe no door, go right, and then observe door. Location 4 is the most likely current location, with posterior probability of 0.42. That is, in terms of the network of Figure 9.16 (page 423):

$$P(Loc_2 = 4 \mid Obs_0 = door, Act_0 = goRight, Obs_1 = nodoor,$$

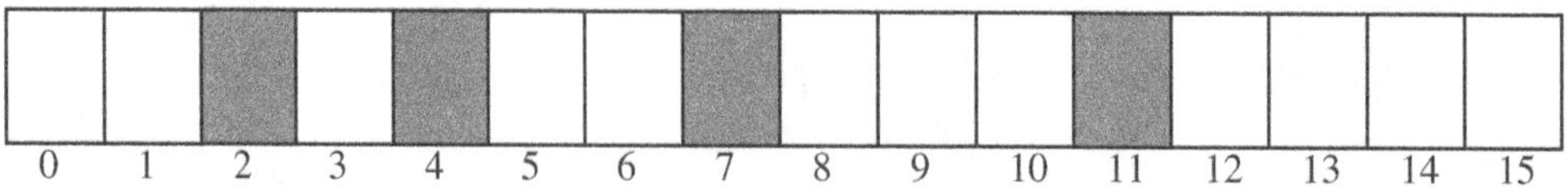


Figure 9.17: Localization domain

$$Act_1 = goRight, Obs_2 = door) = 0.42.$$

Location 7 is the second most likely current location, with posterior probability of 0.141. Locations 0, 1, 3, 8, 12, and 15 are the least likely current locations, with posterior probability 0.011.

You can see how well this works for other sequences of observations using the AIPython (aipython.org) code.

**Example 9.33** Let us augment Example 9.32 (page 423) with another sensor. Suppose that, in addition to a door sensor, there is also a light sensor. The light sensor and the door sensor are conditionally independent given the state. Suppose the light sensor is not very informative; it only gives yes-or-no information about whether it detects any light, and this is very noisy, and depends on the location.

This is modeled in Figure 9.19 (page 426) using the following variables:

- $Loc_t$ is the robot's location at time $t$
- $Act_t$ is the robot's action at time $t$
- $D_t$ is the door sensor value at time $t$
- $L_t$ is the light sensor value at time $t$.

Conditioning on both $L_i$ and $D_i$ lets it combine information from the light sensor and the door sensor. This is an instance of **sensor fusion**. It is not necessary to define any new mechanisms for sensor fusion given the belief-network

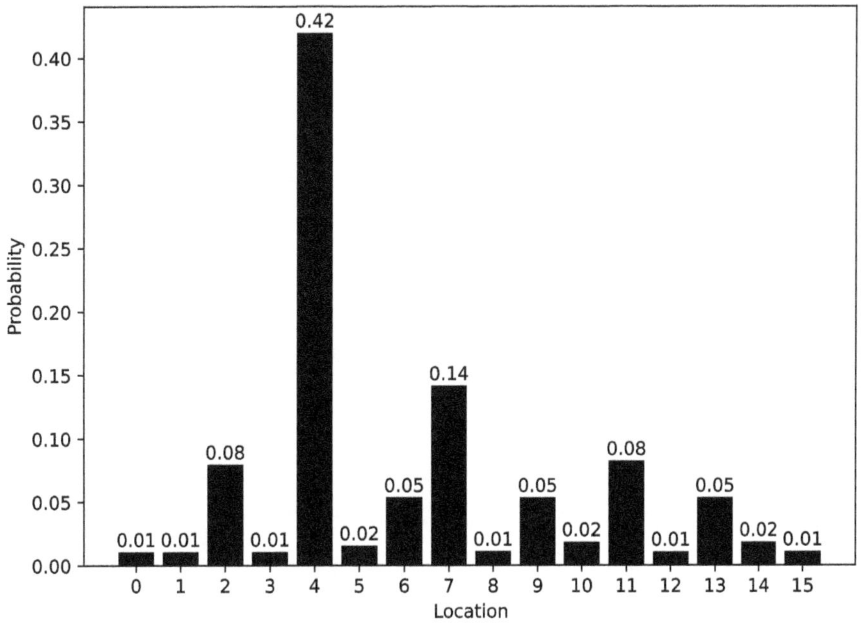


Figure 9.18: Posterior distribution over locations after the sequence of observations: observe door, move right, observe no door, move right, observe door. See Example 9.32 (page 423). The probability is given to two decimal places.

model; standard probabilistic inference combines the information from both sensors. In this case, the sensors provide independent information, but a (different) belief network could model dependent information.

### 9.6.3 Algorithms for Monitoring and Smoothing

Standard belief-network algorithms, such as recursive conditioning or variable elimination, can be used to carry out monitoring or smoothing. However, it is possible to take advantage of the fact that time moves forward and that the agent is getting observations in time and is interested in its state at the current time.

In **belief monitoring** or **filtering**, an agent computes the probability of the current state given the history of observations. The history can be forgotten. In terms of the HMM of Figure 9.15 (page 422), for each time $i$, the agent computes $P(S_i \mid o_0, \dots, o_i)$, the distribution over the state at time $i$ given the observation of $o_0, \dots, o_i$. As in exact inference (page 407), a variable is introduced and summed out to enable the use of known probabilities:

$$\begin{aligned}
P(S_i \mid o_0, \dots, o_i) &\propto P(S_i, o_0, \dots, o_i)\\
&= P(o_i \mid S_i) P(S_i, o_0, \dots, o_{i-1})\\
&= P(o_i \mid S_i) \sum_{S_{i-1}} P(S_i, S_{i-1}, o_0, \dots, o_{i-1})\\
&= P(o_i \mid S_i) \sum_{S_{i-1}} P(S_i \mid S_{i-1}) P(S_{i-1}, o_0, \dots, o_{i-1})\\
&\propto P(o_i \mid S_i) \sum_{S_{i-1}} P(S_i \mid S_{i-1}) P(S_{i-1} \mid o_0, \dots, o_{i-1}). \qquad (9.6)
\end{aligned}$$

Suppose the agent has computed the previous belief based on the observations received up until time $i - 1$. That is, it has a factor representing $P(S_{i-1} \mid$

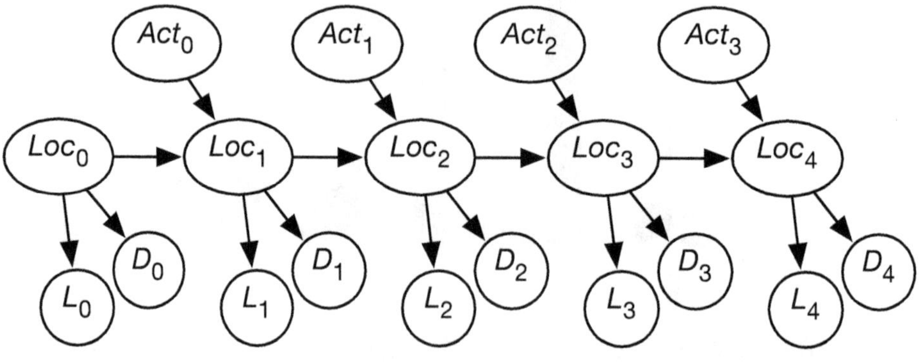


Figure 9.19: Localization with multiple sensors

$o_0, \ldots, o_{i-1})$. This is just a factor on $S_{i-1}$. To compute the next belief, it multiplies this by $P(S_i \mid S_{i-1})$, sums out $S_{i-1}$, multiplies this by the factor $P(o_i \mid S_i)$, and normalizes.

Multiplying a factor on $S_{i-1}$ by the factor $P(S_i \mid S_{i-1})$ and summing out $S_{i-1}$ is an instance of **matrix multiplication** (page 352). Multiplying the result by $P(o_i \mid S_i)$ is the **dot product** (page 352).

**Example 9.34** Consider the domain of Example 9.32 (page 423). An observation of a door involves multiplying the probability of each location $L$ by $P(door \mid Loc = L)$ and renormalizing. A move right involves, for each state, doing a forward simulation of the move-right action in that state weighted by the probability of being in that state.

**Smoothing** (page 422) is the problem of computing the probability distribution of a state variable in an HMM given past and future observations. The use of future observations can make for more accurate predictions. Given a new observation, it is possible to update all previous state estimates with one sweep through the states using variable elimination; see Exercise 9.14 (page 456).

**Recurrent neural networks (RNNs)** (page 354) can be seen as neural network representations of reasoning in a hidden Markov model. An RNN models how $S_i$ depends on $o_i$ and $S_{i-1}$ using a differentiable function. They need to be trained on data for the task being performed, typically smoothing. An HMM is designed to be more modular (page 22); learning transition functions and sensor models separately allows for different forms of reasoning, such as smoothing, and the ability to modularly add sensors or modify the dynamics.

### 9.6.4 Dynamic Belief Networks

The state at a particular time need not be represented as a single variable. It is often more natural to represent the state in terms of features.

A **dynamic belief network (DBN)** is a **discrete time** (page 53) belief network with regular repeated structure. It is like a (hidden) Markov model, but the states and the observations are represented in terms of features. If $F$ is a feature, we write $F_t$ as the random variable that represented the value of variable $F$ at time $t$. A dynamic belief network makes the following assumptions:

- The set of features is the same at each time.
- For any time $t > 0$, the parents of variable $F_t$ are variables at time $t$ or time $t - 1$, such that the graph for any time is acyclic. The structure does not depend on the value of $t$ (except $t = 0$ is a special case).
- The conditional probability distribution of how each variable depends on its parents is the same for every time $t > 0$. This is called a **stationary model**.

Thus, a dynamic belief network specifies a belief network for time $t = 0$, and for each variable $F_t$ specifies $P(F_t \mid parents(F_t))$, where the parents of $F_t$ are in the same or previous time steps. As in a belief network, directed cycles are not allowed.

The model for a dynamic belief network is represented as a **two-step belief network**, which represents the variables at the first two times (times 0 and 1). That is, for each feature $F$ there are two variables, $F_0$ and $F_1$. The set of parents of $F_0$, namely $parents(F_0)$, can only include variables for time 0. The resulting graph must be acyclic. Associated with the network are the probabilities $P(F_0 \mid parents(F_0))$ and $P(F_1 \mid parents(F_1))$.

The two-step belief network is **unfolded** into a belief network by replicating the structure for subsequent times. In the unfolded network, $P(F_i \mid parents(F_i))$, for $i > 1$, has exactly the same structure and the same conditional probability values as $P(F_1 \mid parents(F_1))$.

**Example 9.35** Suppose a trading agent (page 20) wants to model the dynamics of the price of a commodity such as paper. To represent this domain, the designer models variables affecting the price and the other variables. Suppose the cost of pulp and the transportation costs directly affect the price of paper. The transportation costs are affected by the weather. The pulp cost is affected by the prevalence of tree pests, which in turn depend on the weather. Suppose that each variable depends on its value at the previous time step. A two-stage dynamic belief network representing these dependencies is shown in Figure 9.20 (page 429).

According to this figure, the variables are independent at time 0.

This two-stage dynamic belief network can be expanded into a regular dynamic belief network by replicating the nodes for each time step, and the parents for future steps are a copy of the parents for the time 1 variables. An expanded belief network for a horizon of 3 is shown in Figure 9.21 (page 429). The subscripts represent the time that the variable is referring to.

## 9.6.5 Time Granularity

One of the problems with the definition of an HMM or a dynamic belief network is that the model depends on the time granularity. The **time granularity** specifies how often a dynamic system transitions from one state to the next. The time granularity could either be fixed, for example each day or each thirtieth of a second, or it could be event based, where a time step occurs when something interesting occurs. If the time granularity were to change, for example from daily to hourly, the conditional probabilities would also change.

One way to model the dynamics independently of the time granularity is to model **continuous time**, where for each variable and each value for the variable, the following are specified:

- a distribution of how long the variable is expected to keep that value (e.g., an exponential decay) and
- what value it will transition to when its value changes.

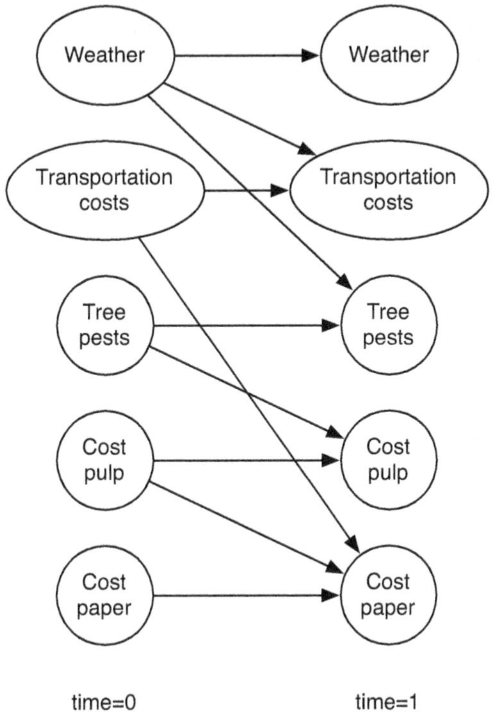


Figure 9.20: Two-stage dynamic belief network for paper pricing

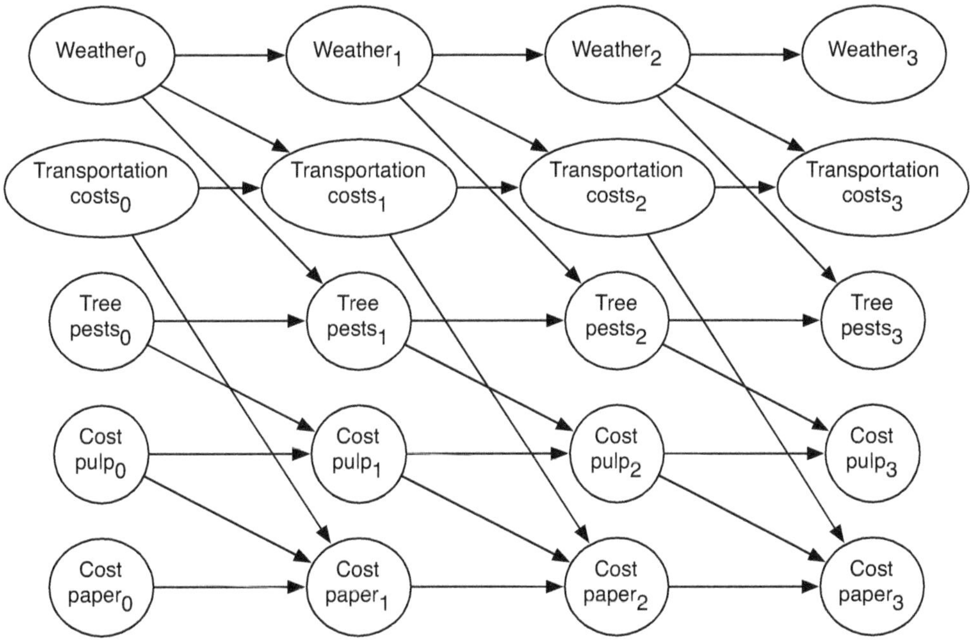


Figure 9.21: Expanded dynamic belief network for paper pricing

Given a **discretization** of time, where time moves from one state to the next in discrete steps, a dynamic belief network can be constructed from this information. If the discretization of time is fine enough, ignoring multiple value transitions in each time step will result only in small errors.

### 9.6.6 Probabilistic Language Models

Markov chains are the basis of simple language models, which have proved to be very useful in various **natural language processing** tasks in daily use.

Assume that a **document** is a sequence of sentences, where a **sentence** is a sequence of **words**. Consider the sorts of sentences that people may speak to a system or ask as a query to a help system. They may not be grammatical, and often contain words such as "thx" or "zzz", which may not be typically thought of as words.

In the **set-of-words model**, a sentence (or a document) is treated as the set of words that appear in the sentence, ignoring the order of the words or whether the words are repeated. For example, the sentence "how can I phone my phone" would be treated as the set {"can", "how", "I", "my", "phone"}.

To represent the set-of-words model as a belief network, as in Figure 9.22, there is a Boolean random variable for each word. In this figure, the words are independent of each other (but they do not have to be). This belief network requires the probability of each word appearing in a sentence: $P(\text{"}a\text{"})$, $P(\text{"}aardvark\text{"})$, ..., $P(\text{"}zzz\text{"})$. To condition on the sentence "how can I phone my phone", all of the words in the sentence are assigned true, and all of the other words are assigned false. Words that are not defined in the model are either ignored, or are given a default (small) probability. The probability of sentence $S$ is $(\prod_{w \in S} P(w)) * (\prod_{w \notin S} (1 - P(w)))$.

A set-of-words model is not very useful by itself, but is often used as part of a larger model, as in the following example.

**Example 9.36** Suppose you want to develop a **help system** to determine which help page users are interested in based on the keywords they give in a query to a help system.

The system will observe the words that the user gives. Instead of modeling the sentence structure, assume that the set of words used in a query will be sufficient to determine the help page.

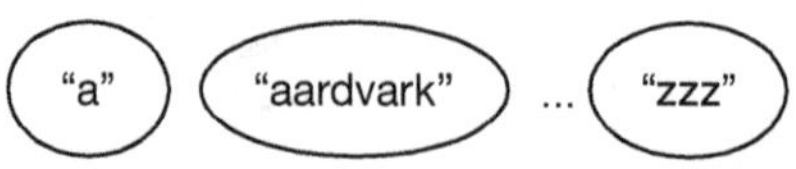


$$domain(\text{"}a\text{"}) = domain(\text{"}aardvark) = \cdots = domain(\text{"}zzz\text{"}) = \{true, false\}$$

Figure 9.22: Set-of-words language model

The aim is to determine which help page the user wants. Suppose that the user is interested in one and only one help page. Thus, it seems reasonable to have a node $H$ with domain the set of all help pages, $\{h_1, \dots, h_k\}$.

One way this could be represented is as a **naive Bayes classifier**. A naive Bayes classifier is a belief network that has a single node – the class – that directly influences the other variables, and the other variables are independent of each other given the class. Figure 9.23 shows a naive Bayes classifier for the help system. The value of the class is the help page the user is interested in. The other nodes represent the words used in a query. This network embodies the independence assumption: the words used in a query depend on the help page the user is interested in, and the words are conditionally independent of each other given the help page.

This network requires $P(h_i)$ for each help page $h_i$, which specifies how likely it is that a user would want this help page given no information. This network assumes the user is interested in exactly one help page, and so $\sum_i P(h_i) = 1$.

The network also requires, for each word $w_j$ and for each help page $h_i$, the probability $P(w_j \mid h_i)$. These may seem more difficult to acquire but there are a few heuristics available. The sum of these values should be the average number of words in a query. We would expect words that appear in the help page to be more likely to be used when asking for that help page than words not in the help page. There may also be keywords associated with the page that may be more likely to be used. There may also be some words that are just used more, independently of the help page the user is interested in. Example 10.5 (page 469) shows how to learn the probabilities of this network from experience.

To condition on the set of words in a query, the words that appear in the query are observed to be true and the words that are not in the query are observed to be false. For example, if the help text was "the zoom is absent", the words "the", "zoom", "is", and "absent" would be observed to be true, and the other words would be observed to be false. Once the posterior for $H$ has been computed, the most likely few help topics can be shown to the user.

Some words, such as "the" and "is", may not be useful in that they have the same conditional probability for each help topic and so, perhaps, would

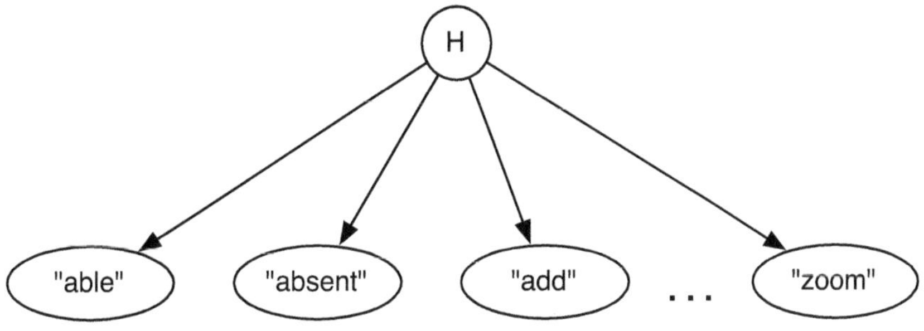


Figure 9.23: Naive belief network with a set-of-words model for a help system

be omitted from the model. Some words that may not be expected in a query could also be omitted from the model.

Note that the conditioning included the words that were not in the query. For example, if page $h_{73}$ was about printing problems, you might expect that people who wanted page $h_{73}$ would use the word "print". The non-existence of the word "print" in a query is strong evidence that the user did not want page $h_{73}$.

The independence of the words given the help page is a strong assumption. It probably does not apply to words like "not", where which word "not" is associated with is very important. There may even be words that are complementary, in which case you would expect users to use one and not the other (e.g., "type" and "write") and words you would expect to be used together (e.g., "go" and "to"); both of these cases violate the independence assumption. It is an empirical question as to how much violating the assumptions hurts the usefulness of the system.

In a **bag-of-words** or **unigram** model, a sentence is treated as a bag (multiset) of words, representing the number of times a word is used in a sentence, but not the order of the words. Figure 9.24 shows how to represent a unigram as a belief network. For the sequence of words, there is a variable $W_i$ for each position $i$, with domain of each variable the set of all words, such as $\{"a", "aardvark", \dots, "zzz"\}$. The domain is often augmented with a symbol, "$\bot$", representing the end of the sentence, and with a symbol "?" representing a word that is not in the model.

To condition on the sentence "how can I phone my phone", the word $W_1$ is observed to be "how", the variable $W_2$ is observed to be "can", etc. Word $W_7$ is assigned $\bot$. Both $W_4$ and $W_6$ are assigned the value "phone". There are no variables $W_8$ onwards.

The unigram model assumes a stationary distribution, where the prior distribution of $W_i$ is the same for each $i$. The value of $P(W_i = w)$ is the probability that a randomly chosen word is $w$. More common words have a higher probability than less common words.

In a **bigram model**, the probability of each word depends on the previous word in the sentence. It is called a bigram model because it depends on pairs of words. Figure 9.25 (page 433) shows the belief-network representation of a bigram model. This needs a specification of $P(W_i \mid W_{i-1})$.

$$domain(W_i) = \{"a", "aarvark", \dots, "zzz", "\bot", "?"\}$$

Figure 9.24: Bag-of-words or unigram language model

To make $W_1$ not be a special case, introduce a new word $\perp$; intuitively $\perp$ is the "word" between sentences. For example, $P(\textit{"cat"} \mid \perp)$ is the probability that the word "cat" is the first word in a sentence. $P(\perp \mid \textit{"cat"})$ is the probability that the sentence ends after the word "cat".

In a **trigram** model, each triple of words is modeled. This is represented as a belief network in Figure 9.26. This requires $P(W_i \mid W_{i-2}, W_{i-1})$; the probability of each word given the previous two words.

In general, in an ***n*-gram** model, the probability of each word given the previous $n-1$ words is modeled. This requires considering each sequence of $n$ words, and so the complexity of representing this as a table grows with $w^n$, where $w$ is the number of words. Figure 9.27 shows some common unigram, bigram, and trigram probabilities.

The conditional probabilities are typically not represented as tables, because the tables would be too large, and because it is difficult to assess the probability of a previously unknown word, or the probability of the next word given a previously unknown word or given an uncommon phrase. Instead, one could use context-specific independence (page 385), such as, for trigram models, represent the probability of the next word conditioned on some of the pairs of words, and if none of these hold, use $P(W_i \mid W_{i-1})$, as in a bigram model. For example, the phrase "frightfully green" is not common, and so to compute the probability of the next word, $P(W \mid \textit{"frightfully"}, \textit{"green"})$, it is typical to use $P(W \mid \textit{"green"})$, which is easier to assess and learn.

**Transformers** (page 360), when used in **generative language models**, are $n$-gram models, where $n$ – the window size of the transformer – is very large (in GPT-3, $n$ is 2048). A neural network, using attention, gives the probability of the next word given the previous words in the window. Note that a trans-

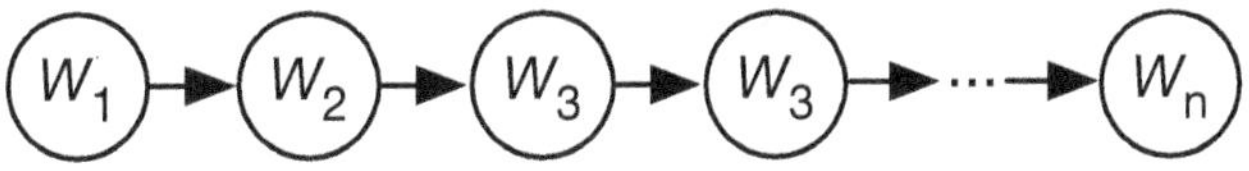


$$domain(W_i) = \{\textit{"a"}, \textit{"aarvark"}, \ldots, \textit{"zzz"}, \textit{"}\perp\textit{"}, \textit{"?"}\}$$

Figure 9.25: Bigram language model

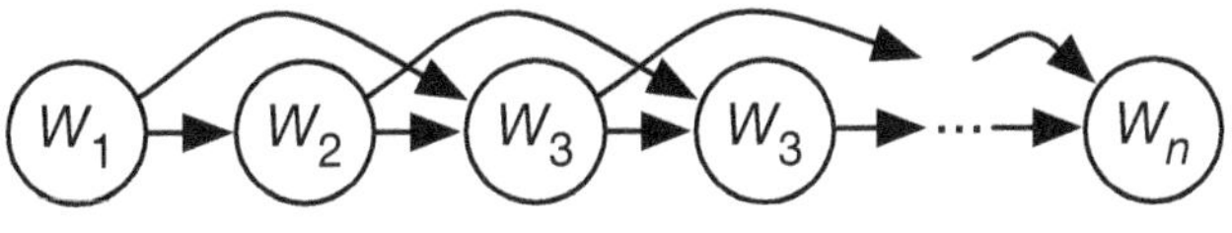


$$domain(W_i) = \{\textit{"a"}, \textit{"aarvark"}, \ldots, \textit{"zzz"}, \textit{"}\perp\textit{"}, \textit{"?"}\}$$

Figure 9.26: Trigram language model

former model used in an encoder to find a representation for a text uses the words after, as well as the words before, each word.

Any of these models could be used in the help system of Example 9.36 (page 430), instead of the set-of-words model used there. These models may be combined to give more sophisticated models, as in the following example.

**Example 9.37** Consider the problem of spelling correction as users type into a phone's onscreen keyboard to create sentences. Figure 9.28 gives a predictive typing model that does this (and more).

| *Word* | $P_1$ | *Word* | $P_2$ | *Word* | $P_3$ |
|---|---|---|---|---|---|
| the | 0.0464 | same | 0.01023 | time | 0.15236 |
| of | 0.0294 | first | 0.00733 | as | 0.04638 |
| and | 0.0228 | other | 0.00594 | way | 0.04258 |
| to | 0.0197 | most | 0.00558 | thing | 0.02057 |
| in | 0.0156 | world | 0.00428 | year | 0.00989 |
| a | 0.0152 | time | 0.00392 | manner | 0.00793 |
| is | 0.00851 | two | 0.00273 | in | 0.00739 |
| that | 0.00806 | whole | 0.00197 | day | 0.00705 |
| for | 0.00658 | people | 0.00175 | kind | 0.00656 |
| was | 0.00508 | great | 0.00102 | with | 0.00327 |

Unigram, bigram, and trigram probabilities derived from the Google books Ngram viewer (https://books.google.com/ngrams/) for the year 2000. $P_1$ is $P(Word)$ for the top 10 words, which are found by using the query "*" in the viewer. $P_2$ is part of a bigram model that represents $P(Word \mid "the")$ for the top 10 words. This is derived from the query "the *" in the viewer. $P_3$ is part of a trigram model; the probabilities given represent $P(Word \mid "the", "same")$, which is derived from the query "the same *" in the viewer.

Figure 9.27: Some of the most-likely *n*-grams

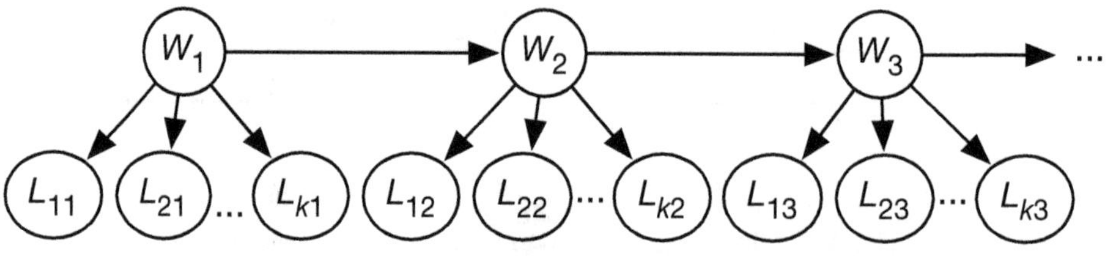


$$domain(W_i) = \{"a", "aarvark", \ldots, "zzz", "\perp", "?"\}$$
$$domain(L_{ji}) = \{"a", "b", "c", \ldots, "z"\}$$

Figure 9.28: Predictive typing model

The variable $W_i$ is the $i$th word in the sentence. The domain of each $W_i$ is the set of all words. This uses a bigram model for words, and assumes $P(W_i \mid W_{i-1})$ is provided as the language model. A stationary model is typically appropriate.

The $L_{ji}$ variable represents the $j$th letter in word $i$. The domain of each $L_{ji}$ is the set of characters that could be typed. This uses a unigram model for each letter given the word, but it would not be a stationary model, as for example the probability distribution of the first letter given the word "print" is different from the probability distribution of the second letter given the word "print". We would expect $P(L_{ji} = c \mid W_i = w)$ to be close to 1 if the $j$th letter of word $w$ is $c$. The conditional probability could incorporate common misspellings and common typing errors (e.g., switching letters, or if someone tends to type slightly higher on the phone's screen).

For example, $P(L_{1j} = "p" \mid W_j = "print")$ would be close to 1, but not equal to 1, as the user could have mistyped. Similarly, $P(L_{2j} = "r" \mid W_j = "print")$ would be high. The distribution for the second letter in the word, $P(L_{2j} \mid W_j = "print")$, could take into account mistyping adjacent letters ("e" and "t" are adjacent to "r" on the standard keyboard) and missing letters (maybe "i" is more likely because it is the third letter in "print"). In practice, these probabilities are typically extracted from data of people typing known sentences, without needing to model why the errors occurred.

The word model allows the system to predict the next word even if no letters have been typed. Then, as letters are typed, it predicts the word, based on the previous words and the typed letters, even if some of the letters are mistyped. For example, if the user types "I cannot pint", it might be more likely that the last word is "print" than "pint" because of the way the model combines all of the evidence.

A **topic model** predicts the topics of a document from the sentences typed. Knowing the topic of a document helps people find the document or similar documents even if they do not know what words are in the document.

**Example 9.38** Figure 9.29 shows a simple topic model based on a set-of-words language model. There is a set of topics (four are given) which are a priori

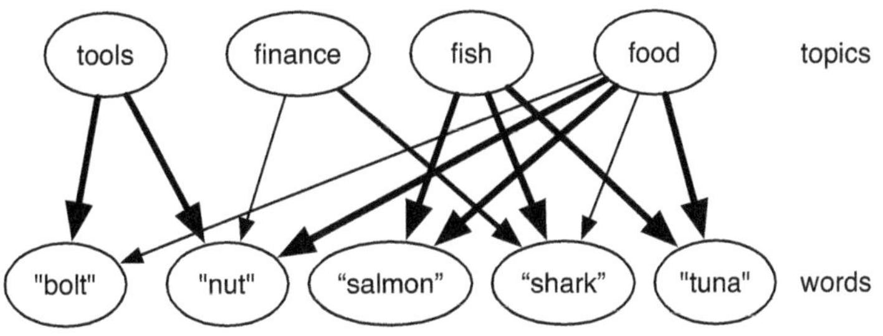


Figure 9.29: Simple topic model with a set-of-words. The thickness of the lines indicates the strength of the connection. See Example 9.38

independent of each other. In this model, the words are independent of each other given the topic. A noisy-or (page 398) is used to model how each word depends on the topics.

The **noisy-or** model can be represented by having a variable for each topic–word pair where the word is relevant for the topic. For example, the *tools_bolt* variable represents the probability that the word *bolt* is in the document because the topic is *tools*. This variable has probability zero if the topic is not *tools* and has the probability that the word would appear when the topic is *tools* (and there are no other relevant topics). The word *bolt* would appear, with probability 1 if *tools_bolt* is true or if an analogous variable, *food_bolt*, is true, and with a small probability otherwise (the probability that it appears without one of the topics). Thus, each topic–word pair where the word is relevant to the topic is modeled by a single weight. In Figure 9.29 (page 435), the higher weights are shown by thicker lines.

Given the words, the topic model is used to infer the distribution over topics. Once a number of words that are relevant to a topic are given, the topic becomes more likely, and so other words related to that topic also become more likely. Indexing documents by the topic lets us find relevant documents even if different words are used to look for a document.

This model is based on **Google**'s **Rephil**, which has 12,000,000 words (where common phrases are treated as words), a million topics and 350 million topic–word pairs with nonzero probability. In Rephil, the topics are structured hierarchically into a tree.

It is possible to mix these patterns, for example by using the current topics to predict the word in a predictive typing model with a topic model.

Models based on $n$-grams cannot represent all of the subtleties of natural language, as exemplified by the following example.

**Example 9.39** Consider the sentence

A tall person with a big hairy cat drank the cold milk.

In English, this is unambiguous; the person drank the milk. Consider how an $n$-gram might fare with such a sentence. The problem is that the subject ("person") is far away from the verb ("drank"). It is also plausible that the cat drank the milk. It is easy to think of variants of this sentence where the word "person" is arbitrarily far away from the object of the sentence ("the cold milk") and so would not be captured by any $n$-gram, unless $n$ was very large. Such sentences can be handled using a hidden state as in a long short-term memory (LSTM) (page 357) or by explicitly building a parse tree, as described in Section 15.7 (page 674).

## 9.7 Stochastic Simulation

Many problems are too big for exact inference, so one must resort to **approximate inference** (page 404). Some of the most effective methods are based on generating random samples from the (posterior) distribution that the network specifies.

**Stochastic simulation** is a class of algorithms based on the idea that a set of samples can be mapped to and from probabilities. For example, the probability $P(a) = 0.14$ means that out of 1000 samples, about 140 will have $a$ true. Inference can be carried out by going from probabilities into samples and from samples into probabilities.

The following sections consider three problems:

- how to generate samples
- how to infer probabilities from samples
- how to incorporate observations.

These form the basis for methods that use sampling to compute the posterior distribution of a variable in a belief network, including rejection sampling, importance sampling, particle filtering, and Markov chain Monte Carlo.

## 9.7.1 Sampling from a Single Variable

The simplest case is to generate the probability distribution of a single variable. This is the base case the other methods build on.

### From Probabilities to Samples

To generate samples from a single discrete or real-valued variable, $X$, first totally order the values in the domain of $X$. For discrete variables, if there is no natural order, just create an arbitrary ordering. Given this ordering, the **cumulative probability distribution** is a function of $x$, defined by $f(x) = P(X \leq x)$.

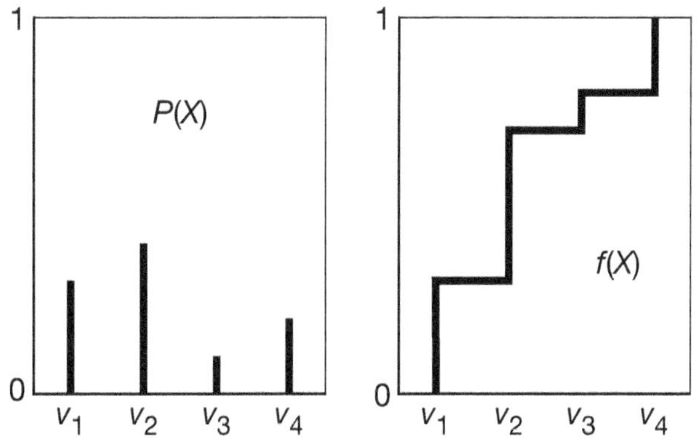


Figure 9.30: A cumulative probability distribution

To generate a random sample for X, select a random number $y$ in the domain $[0,1]$. We select $y$ from a uniform distribution to ensure that each number between 0 and 1 has the same chance of being chosen. Let $v$ be the value of X that maps to $y$ in the cumulative probability distribution. That is, $v$ is the element of *domain*(X) such that $f(v) = y$ or, equivalently, $v = f^{-1}(y)$. Then, $X = v$ is a random sample of X, chosen according to the distribution of X.

**Example 9.40** Consider a random variable $X$ with domain $\{v_1, v_2, v_3, v_4\}$. Suppose $P(X=v_1) = 0.3$, $P(X=v_2) = 0.4$, $P(X=v_3) = 0.1$, and $P(X=v_4) = 0.2$. First, totally order the values, say $v_1 < v_2 < v_3 < v_4$. Figure 9.30 (page 437) shows $P(X)$, the distribution for X, and $f(X)$, the cumulative distribution for X. Consider value $v_1$; 0.3 of the domain of $f$ maps back to $v_1$. Thus, if a sample is uniformly selected from the Y-axis, $v_1$ has a 0.3 chance of being selected, $v_2$ has a 0.4 chance of being selected, and so forth.

## From Samples to Probabilities

Probabilities can be estimated from a set of samples using the sample average. The **sample average** of a proposition $\alpha$ is the number of samples where $\alpha$ is true divided by the total number of samples. The sample average approaches the true probability as the number of samples approaches infinity by the **law of large numbers**.

**Hoeffding's inequality** provides an estimate of the error of the sample average, $s$, given $n$ independent samples compared to the true probability, $p$. $|s - p| > \epsilon$ means that the error is larger than $\epsilon$, for $0 < \epsilon < 1$.

**Proposition 9.3** (Hoeffding). *Suppose p is the true probability, and s is the sample average from n independent samples; then*

$$P(|s-p| > \epsilon) \leq 2\exp(-2n\epsilon^2).$$

This theorem can be used to determine how many samples are required to guarantee a **probably approximately correct (PAC)** estimate of the probability. To guarantee that the error is *always* less than some $\epsilon < 0.5$, infinitely many samples are required. However, if you are willing to have an error greater than $\epsilon$ in $\delta$ of the cases, solve $2\exp(-2n\epsilon^2) < \delta$ for $n$, which gives

$$n > \frac{-\ln\frac{\delta}{2}}{2\epsilon^2}.$$

For example, suppose you want an error less than 0.1, 19 times out of 20; that is, you are only willing to tolerate an error bigger than 0.1 in less than 5% of the cases. You can use Hoeffding's bound by setting $\epsilon$ to 0.1 and $\delta$ to 0.05, which gives $n > 184$. The following table gives some required number $n$ of examples for various combinations of values for $\epsilon$ and $\delta$:

| $\epsilon$ | $\delta$ | $n$ |
|---|---|---|
| 0.1 | 0.05 | 185 |
| 0.01 | 0.05 | 18445 |
| 0.1 | 0.01 | 265 |
| 0.01 | 0.01 | 26492 |

Notice that many more examples are required to get accurate probabilities (small $\epsilon$) than are required to get good approximations (small $\delta$).

### 9.7.2 Forward Sampling

Using the cumulative distribution (page 437) to generate samples only works for a single dimension, because all of the values must be put in a total order. Sampling from a distribution defined by multiple variables is difficult in general, but is straightforward when the distribution is defined using a belief network.

**Forward sampling** is a way to generate a sample of every variable in a belief network so that each sample is generated in proportion to its probability. This enables us to estimate the prior probability of any variable.

Suppose $X_1, \dots, X_n$ is a total ordering of the variables so that the parents of each variable come before the variable in the total order. Forward sampling draws a sample of all of the variables by drawing a sample of each variable $X_1, \dots, X_n$ in order. First, it samples $X_1$ using the cumulative distribution, as described above. For each of the other variables, due to the total ordering of variables, when it comes time to sample $X_i$, it already has values for all of the parents of $X_i$. It now samples a value for $X_i$ from the distribution of $X_i$ given the values already assigned to the parents of $X_i$. Repeating this for every variable generates a sample containing values for all of the variables. The probability distribution of a query variable is estimated by considering the proportion of the samples that have assigned each value of the variable.

**Example 9.41** To create a set of samples for the belief network of Figure 9.3 (page 390), suppose the variables are ordered: *Tampering, Fire, Alarm, Smoke, Leaving, Report*.

First the algorithm samples *Tampering*, using the cumulative distribution (page 437). Suppose it selects $Tampering = false$. Then it samples *Fire* using the same method. Suppose it selects $Fire = true$. Then it samples a value for *Alarm*, using the distribution $P(Alarm \mid Tampering = false, Fire = true)$. Suppose it selects $Alarm = true$. Next, it samples a value for *Smoke* using $P(Smoke \mid Fire = true)$. And so on for the other variables. It has thus selected a value for each variable and created the first sample of Figure 9.31 (page 440). Notice that it has selected a very unlikely combination of values. This does not happen very often; it happens in proportion to how likely the sample is. It repeats this until it has enough samples. In Figure 9.31 (page 440), it generated 1000 samples.

The probability that *Report* = *true* is estimated from the proportion of the samples where the variable *Report* has value *true*.

Forward sampling is used in **(large) language models** (page 364), to generate text. A neural network, such as an LSTM (page 357) or transformer (page 360), is used to represent the probability of the next word given the previous words. Forward sampling then generates a sample of text. Different runs produce different text, with a very low probability of repeating the same text. Forward sampling is also used in game playing, where it can be used to predict the distribution of outcomes of a game from a game position, given a probability distribution of the actions from a position, in what is called **Monte Carlo tree search**; see Section 14.7.3 (page 636).

## 9.7.3 Rejection Sampling

Given some evidence *e*, rejection sampling estimates $P(h \mid e)$ using the formula

$$P(h \mid e) = \frac{P(h \wedge e)}{P(e)}.$$

This is computed by considering only the samples where *e* is true and by determining the proportion of these in which *h* is true. The idea of **rejection sampling** is that samples are generated as before, but any sample where *e* is false is rejected. The proportion of the remaining, non-rejected, samples where *h* is true is an estimate of $P(h \mid e)$. If the evidence is a conjunction of assignments of values to variables, a sample is rejected when any variable is assigned a value different from its observed value.

**Example 9.42** Figure 9.32 (page 441) shows how rejection sampling is used to estimate $P(tampering \mid smoke \wedge \neg report)$. Any sample with *Smoke* = *false* is rejected. The sample is rejected without considering any more variables. Any

| Sample | Tampering | Fire | Alarm | Smoke | Leaving | Report |
|---|---|---|---|---|---|---|
| $s_1$ | *false* | *true* | *true* | *true* | *false* | *false* |
| $s_2$ | *false* | *false* | *false* | *false* | *false* | *false* |
| $s_3$ | *false* | *true* | *true* | *true* | *true* | *true* |
| $s_4$ | *false* | *false* | *false* | *false* | *false* | *true* |
| $s_5$ | *false* | *false* | *false* | *false* | *false* | *false* |
| $s_6$ | *false* | *false* | *false* | *false* | *false* | *false* |
| $s_7$ | *true* | *false* | *false* | *true* | *true* | *true* |
| $s_8$ | *true* | *false* | *false* | *false* | *false* | *true* |
| ... | | | | | | |
| $s_{1000}$ | *true* | *false* | *true* | *true* | *false* | *false* |

Figure 9.31: Sampling for a belief network

sample with *Report* = *true* is rejected. The sample average from the remaining samples (those marked with ✔) is used to estimate the posterior probability of *tampering*.

Because $P(smoke \wedge \neg report) = 0.0128$, we would expect about 13 samples out of the 1000 to have $smoke \wedge \neg report$ true; the other 987 samples would have $smoke \wedge \neg report$ false, and so would be rejected. Thus, 13 is used as $n$ in Hoeffding's inequality, which, for example, guarantees an error for any probability computed from these samples of less than 0.25 in about 86% of the cases, which is not very accurate.

The error in the probability of $h$ depends on the number of samples that are not rejected, which is proportional to $P(e)$. Hoeffding's inequality can be used to estimate the error of rejection sampling, where $n$ is the number of non-rejected samples. Therefore, the error depends on $P(e)$.

Rejection sampling does not work well when the evidence is unlikely. This may not seem like that much of a problem because, by definition, unlikely evidence is unlikely to occur. But, although this may be true for simple models, for complicated models with complex observations, every possible observation may be unlikely. Also, for many applications, such as in diagnosis, the user is interested in determining the probabilities because unusual observations are involved.

### 9.7.4 Likelihood Weighting

Instead of creating a sample and then rejecting it, it is possible to mix sampling with inference to reason about the probability that a sample would be rejected. In **importance sampling** methods, each sample has a weight, and the sample average uses the weighted average. **Likelihood weighting** is a simple form where the variables are sampled in the order defined by a belief network, and evidence is used to update the weights. The weights reflect the probability that

| Sample | *Tampering* | *Fire* | *Alarm* | *Smoke* | *Leaving* | *Report* | |
|---|---|---|---|---|---|---|---|
| $s_1$ | *false* | *false* | *true* | *false* | ✘ | | |
| $s_2$ | *false* | *true* | *false* | *true* | *false* | *false* | ✔ |
| $s_3$ | *false* | *true* | *true* | *false* | ✘ | | |
| $s_4$ | *false* | *true* | *false* | *true* | *false* | *false* | ✔ |
| $s_5$ | *false* | *true* | *true* | *true* | *true* | *true* | ✘ |
| $s_6$ | *false* | *false* | *false* | *true* | *false* | *false* | ✔ |
| $s_7$ | *true* | *false* | *false* | *false* | ✘ | | |
| $s_8$ | *true* | *true* | *true* | *true* | *true* | *true* | ✘ |
| ... | | | | | | | |
| $s_{1000}$ | *true* | *false* | *true* | *false* | ✘ | | |

Figure 9.32: Rejection sampling for $P(tampering \mid smoke \wedge \neg report)$

a sample would not be rejected. More general forms of importance sampling are explored in Section 9.7.5 (page 443).

**Example 9.43** Consider the belief network of Figure 9.3 (page 390). In this $P(fire) = 0.01$, $P(smoke \mid fire) = 0.9$, and $P(smoke \mid \neg fire) = 0.01$. Suppose $Smoke = true$ is observed, and another descendant of *Fire* is queried.

Starting with 1000 samples, approximately 10 will have $Fire = true$, and the other 990 samples will have $Fire = false$. In rejection sampling, of the 990 with $Fire = false$, 1%, which is approximately 10, will have $Smoke = true$ and so will not be rejected. The remaining 980 samples will be rejected. Of the 10 with $Fire = true$, about 9 will not be rejected. Thus, about 98% of the samples are rejected.

In likelihood weighing, instead of sampling *Smoke* and rejecting most samples, the samples with $Fire = true$ are weighted by 0.9 and the samples with $Fire = false$ are weighted with 0.01. This potentially give a much better estimate of any of the probabilities that use these samples.

```
procedure Likelihood_weighting(B, e, Q, n):
    Inputs
        B: belief network
        e: the evidence; a variable-value assignment to some of the variables
        Q: query variable
        n: number of samples to generate
    Output
        posterior distribution on Q
    Local
        array sample[var], where sample[var] ∈ domain(var)
        real array counts[k] for k ∈ domain(Q), initialized to 0
    repeat n times
        sample := {}
        weight := 1
        for each variable X in B, in order do
            if X = v is in e then
                sample[X] := v
                weight := weight * P(X = v | parents(X))
            else
                sample[X] := a random sample from P(X | parents(X))
        v := sample[Q]
        counts[v] := counts[v] + weight
    return counts / Σ_v counts[v]
```

Figure 9.33: Likelihood weighting for belief-network inference

Figure 9.33 (page 442) shows the details of the likelihood weighting for computing $P(Q \mid e)$ for query variable $Q$ and evidence $e$. The *for* loop (from line 15) creates a sample containing a value for all of the variables. Each observed variable changes the weight of the sample by multiplying by the probability of the observed value given the assignment of the parents in the sample. The variables not observed are sampled according to the probability of the variable given its parents in the sample. Note that the variables are sampled in an order to ensure that the parents of a variable have been assigned in the sample before the variable is selected.

To extract the distribution of the query variable $Q$, the algorithm maintains an array *counts*, such that *counts*$[v]$ is the sum of the weights of the samples where $Q = v$. This algorithm can also be adapted to the case where the query is some complicated condition on the values by counting the cases where the condition is true and those where the condition is false.

**Example 9.44** Consider using likelihood weighting to compute $P(Tampering \mid smoke \wedge \neg report)$.

The following table gives a few samples. In this table, $s$ is the sample; $e$ is $\neg smoke \wedge report$. The weight is $P(e \mid s)$, which is equal to $P(smoke \mid Fire) * P(\neg report \mid Leaving)$, where the values for *Fire* and *Leaving* are from the sample.

| *Tampering* | *Fire* | *Alarm* | *Smoke* | *Leaving* | *Report* | Weight |
|---|---|---|---|---|---|---|
| *false* | *true* | *false* | *true* | *true* | *false* | $0.9 * 0.25 = 0.225$ |
| *true* | *true* | *true* | *true* | *false* | *false* | $0.9 * 0.99 = 0.891$ |
| *false* | *false* | *false* | *true* | *true* | *false* | $0.01 * 0.25 = 0.0025$ |
| *false* | *true* | *false* | *true* | *false* | *false* | $0.9 * 0.99 = 0.891$ |

$P(tampering \mid \neg smoke \wedge report)$ is estimated from the weighted proportion of the samples that have *Tampering* true.

## 9.7.5 Importance Sampling

Likelihood weighting is an instance of importance sampling. **Importance samplingin** general has:

- Samples are weighted.
- The samples do not need to come from the actual distribution, but can be from (almost) any distribution, with the weights adjusted to reflect the difference between the distributions.
- Some variables can be summed out and some sampled.

This freedom to sample from a different distribution allows the algorithm to choose better sampling distributions to give better estimates.

Stochastic simulation can be used to compute the expected value (page 383) of real-valued variable $f$ under probability distribution $P$ using

$$\mathbb{E}_P(f) = \sum_w f(w) * P(w)$$

$$\approx \frac{1}{n}\sum_{s} f(s)$$

where $s$ is a sample that is sampled with probability $P$, and $n$ is the number of samples. The estimate gets more accurate as the number of samples grows.

Suppose it is difficult to sample with the distribution $P$, but it is easy to sample from a distribution $Q$. We adapt the previous equation to estimate the expected value from $P$, by sampling from $Q$ using

$$\begin{aligned}\mathbb{E}_P(f) &= \sum_{w} f(w) * P(w) \\ &= \sum_{w} f(w) * (P(w)/Q(w)) * Q(w) \\ &\approx \frac{1}{n}\sum_{s} f(s) * P(s)/Q(s)\end{aligned}$$

where the last sum is over $n$ samples selected according to the distribution $Q$. The distribution $Q$ is called a **proposal distribution**. The only restriction on $Q$ is that it should not be zero for any cases where $P$ is not zero (i.e., if $Q(c) = 0$ then $P(c) = 0$).

Recall (page 383) that for Boolean variables, with *true* represented as 1 and *false* as 0, the expected value is the probability. So the methods here can be used to compute probabilities.

The algorithm of Figure 9.33 (page 442) can be adapted to use a proposal distribution as follows: in line 20, it should sample from $Q(X \mid parents(X))$, and in a new line after that, it updates the value of *weight* by multiplying it by $P(X \mid parents(X))/Q(X \mid parents(X))$.

**Example 9.45** In the running alarm example, $P(smoke) = 0.0189$. As explained in Example 9.43 (page 442), if the algorithm samples according to the prior probability, $Smoke = true$ would only be true in about 19 samples out of 1000. Likelihood weighting ended up with a few samples with high weights and many samples with low weights, even though the samples represented similar numbers of cases.

Suppose, instead of sampling according to the probability, the proposal distribution with $Q(fire) = 0.5$ is used. Then $Fire = true$ is sampled 50% of the time. According to the model $P(fire) = 0.01$, thus each sample with $Fire = true$ is weighted by $0.01/0.5 = 0.02$ and each sample with $Fire = false$ is weighted by $0.99/0.5 = 1.98$.

With importance sampling with $Q$ as the proposal distribution, half of the samples will have $Fire = true$, and the model specifies $P(smoke \mid fire) = 0.9$. Given the evidence $e$, these will be weighted by $0.9 * 0.02 = 0.018$. The other half of the samples will have $A = false$, and the model specifies $P(smoke \mid \neg fire) = 0.01$. These samples will have a weighting of $0.01 * 1.98 = 0.0198$. Notice how all of the samples have weights of the same order of magnitude. This means that the estimates from these are much more accurate.

Importance sampling can also be combined with exact inference. Not all variables need to be sampled. The variables not sampled can be summed out by variable elimination.

The best proposal distribution is one where the samples have approximately equal weight. This occurs when sampling from the posterior distribution. In **adaptive importance sampling**, the proposal distribution is modified to approximate the posterior probability of the variable being sampled.

### 9.7.6 Particle Filtering

Importance sampling enumerates the samples one at a time and, for each sample, assigns a value to each variable. It is also possible to start with all of the samples and, for each variable, generate a value for that variable for each sample. For example, for the data of Figure 9.31 (page 440), the same data could be generated by generating all of the samples for *Tampering* before generating the samples for *Fire*. The **particle filtering** algorithm or **sequential Monte Carlo (SMC)** generates all the samples for one variable before moving to the next variable. It does one sweep through the variables, and for each variable it does a sweep through all of the samples. This algorithm is advantageous when variables are generated dynamically and when there are unboundedly many variables, as in the sequential models (page 418). It also allows for a new operation of resampling.

In particle filtering, the samples are called particles. A **particle** is a *variable-value* dictionary, where a **dictionary** is a representation of a partial function from keys into values; here the key is a variable and the particle maps to its value. A particle has an associated weight. A set of particles is a **population**.

The algorithm starts with a population of $n$ empty dictionaries. The algorithm repeatedly selects a variable according to an ordering where a variable is selected after its parents. If the variable is not observed, for each particle, a value for the variable for that particle is sampled from the distribution of the variable given the assignment of the particle. If the variable is observed, each particle's weight is updated by multiplying by the probability of the observation given the assignment of the particle.

Given a population of $n$ particles, **resampling** generates a new population of $n$ particles, each with the same weight. Each particle is selected with probability proportional to its weight. Resampling can be implemented in the same way that random samples for a single random variable are generated (page 437), but particles, rather than values, are selected. Some particles may be selected multiple times and others might not be selected at all.

The particle filtering algorithm is shown in Figure 9.34 (page 446). Line 16 assigns $X$ its observed value. Line 17, which is used when $X$ is observed, updates the weights of the particles according to the probability of the observation on $X$. Line 22 assigns $X$ a value sampled from the distribution of $X$ given the values of its parents in the particle.

This algorithm resamples after each observation. It is also possible to resample less often, for example, after a number of variables are observed.

Importance sampling is equivalent to particle filtering without resampling. The principal difference is the order in which the particles are generated. In particle filtering, each variable is sampled for all particles, whereas, in importance sampling, each particle (sample) is sampled for all variables before the next particle is considered.

Particle filtering has two main advantages over importance sampling. First, it can be used for an unbounded number of variables, as in hidden Markov models (page 420) and dynamic belief networks (page 427). Second, resampling enables the particles to better cover the distribution over the variables. Whereas importance sampling will result in some particles that have very low probability, with only a few of the particles covering most of the probability mass, resampling lets many particles more uniformly cover the probability

```
procedure Particle_filtering(B, e, Q, n):
    Inputs
        B: belief network
        e: the evidence; a variable-value assignment to some of the variables
        Q: query variable
        n: number of samples to generate
    Output
        posterior distribution on Q
    Local
        particles is a set of particles
        array counts[k] where k in domain(Q)
    particles := list of n empty particles
    for each variable X in B, in order do
        if X = v is observed in e then
            for each part in particles do
                part[X] := v
                weight[part] := weight * P(X = v | part[parents(X)])
            particles := n particles selected from particles according to weight
        else
            for each part in particles do
                sample v from distribution P(X | part[parents(X)])
                part[X] := v
    for each v in domain(Q) do
        counts[v] := (number of part in particles s.th. part[Q] = v)/n
    return counts
```

Figure 9.34: Particle filtering for belief-network inference mass.

**Example 9.46** Consider using particle filtering to compute $P(tampering \mid smoke \wedge report)$ for the belief network of Figure 9.3 (page 390). First generate the particles $s_1, \ldots, s_{1000}$. Suppose it first samples *Fire*. Out of the 1000 particles, about 10 will have $Fire = true$ and about 990 will have $Fire = false$ (as $P(fire) = 0.01$). It then absorbs the evidence $Smoke = true$. Those particles with $Fire = true$ will be weighted by 0.9 as $P(smoke \mid fire) = 0.9$ and those particles with $Fire = false$ will be weighted by 0.01 as $P(smoke \mid \neg fire) = 0.01$. It then resamples; each particle is chosen in proportion to its weight. The particles with $Fire = true$ will be chosen in the ratio $990 * 0.01 : 10 * 0.9$. Thus, about 524 particles will be chosen with $Fire = true$, and the remainder with $Fire = false$. The other variables are sampled, in turn, until *Report* is observed, and the particles are resampled. At this stage, the probability of $Tampering = true$ will be the proportion of the samples with tampering being true.

Note that in particle filtering the particles are not independent, so Hoeffding's inequality (page 438) is not directly applicable.

### 9.7.7 Markov Chain Monte Carlo

The previously described methods went forward through the network (parents were sampled before children), and were not good at passing information back through the network. The method described in this section can sample variables in any order.

A **stationary distribution** (page 419) of a Markov chain (page 418) is a distribution of its variables that is not changed by the transition function of the Markov chain. If the Markov chain mixes enough, there is a unique stationary distribution, which can be approached by running the Markov chain long enough. The idea behind **Markov chain Monte Carlo (MCMC)** methods to generate samples from a distribution (e.g., the posterior distribution given a belief network) is to construct a Markov chain with the desired distribution as its (unique) stationary distribution and then sample from the Markov chain; these samples will be distributed according to the desired distribution. The first few samples are typically discarded in a **burn-in** period, as these samples may be far from the stationary distribution.

One way to create a Markov chain from a belief network with observations, is to use **Gibbs sampling**. The idea is to clamp observed variables to the values they were observed to have, and sample the other variables. Each variable is sampled from the distribution of the variable given the current values of the other variables. Note that each variable only depends on the values of the variables in its Markov blanket (page 385). The **Markov blanket** of a variable $X$ in a belief network contains $X$'s parents, $X$'s children, and the other parents of $X$'s children; these are all of the variables that appear in factors with $X$.

Figure 9.35 (page 448) gives pseudocode for Gibbs sampling. The only part not defined is how to randomly sample from $P(X \mid markov\_blanket(X))$. This can be computed by noticing that for each value of $X$, the probability $P(X \mid markov\_blanket(X))$ is proportional to the product of the values of the factors in which $X$ appears projected onto the current value of all of the other variables.

**Example 9.47** Consider using particle filtering to compute $P(Tampering \mid smoke \wedge \neg report)$ for the belief network of Figure 9.3 (page 390). Figure 9.36 (page 449) shows a sequence of samples, where the underlined value is selected at each step. *Smoke* and *Report* are clamped at *true* and *false*, respectively.

Sample $s_1$ is generated at random and the variable *Tampering* is selected. *Fire* and *Alarm* form the Markov blanket for *Tampering*, so a random sample for $P(Tampering \mid fire \wedge \neg alarm)$ is drawn; suppose it is *true*. This gives sample $s_2$.

Given $s_2$, a random value from $P(Fire \mid tampering \wedge \neg alarm \wedge smoke)$ is drawn. Suppose it is *true*. This gives sample $s_3$. Next a random value from $P(Alarm \mid tampering \wedge fire \wedge \neg leaving)$ is drawn; suppose it is *true*.

At the end, the estimate of probability of *tampering* is the proportion of *true* cases in the samples after the burn-in period.

Gibbs sampling will approach the correct probabilities as long as there are no zero probabilities. How quickly it approaches the distribution depends on

```
procedure Gibbs_sampling(B, e, Q, n, burn_in):
    Inputs
        B: belief network
        e: the evidence; a variable-value assignment to some of the variables
        Q: query variable
        n: number of samples to generate
        burn_in: number of samples to discard initially
    Output
        posterior distribution on Q
    Local
        array sample[var], where sample[var] ∈ domain(var)
        real array counts[k] for k ∈ domain(Q), initialized to 0
    initialize sample[X] = e[X] if X observed, otherwise assign randomly
    repeat burn_in times
        for each non-observed variable X, in any order do
            sample[X] := a random sample from P(X | markov_blanket(X))
    repeat n times
        for each non-observed variable X, in any order do
            sample[X] := a random sample from P(X | markov_blanket(X))
        v := sample[Q]
        counts[v] := counts[v] + 1
    return counts / Σ_v counts[v]
```

Figure 9.35: Gibbs sampling for belief-network inference

how quickly the probabilities mix (how much of the probability space is explored), which depends on how extreme the probabilities are. Gibbs sampling works well when the probabilities are not extreme (very close to 0 or 1).

**Example 9.48** As a problematic case for Gibbs sampling, consider a simple example with three Boolean variables $A$, $B$, and $C$, with $A$ as the parent of $B$, and $B$ as the parent of $C$. Suppose $P(a) = 0.5$, $P(b \mid a) = 0.99$, $P(b \mid \neg a) = 0.01$, $P(c \mid b) = 0.99$, and $P(c \mid \neg b) = 0.01$. There are no observations and the query variable is $C$. The two assignments with all variables having the same value are equally likely and are much more likely than the other assignments. Gibbs sampling will quickly get to one of these assignments, and will take a long time to transition to the other assignments (as it requires some very unlikely choices). If 0.99 and 0.01 were replaced by numbers closer to 1 and 0, it would take even longer to converge.

## 9.8 Social Impact

The **global positioning system (GPS)** as used on modern smartphones has a mean accuracy of about 5 meters radius under an open sky [van Diggelen and Enge, 2015; U.S. Government, 2022]. GPS becomes less accurate in cities, where buildings cause occlusion and reflection of GPS signals. Smartphones and self-driving cars use probabilistic localization (page 423), which improves accuracy by keeping track of the distribution over immediately preceding locations. Using hidden Markov models (page 420), current sensing information, with error estimates, is combined with the distribution of the previous position to give a distribution of the current position. You can tell if your phone does not combine previous estimates with sensing; it re-estimates your position at each time and the location estimation tends to jump around. For example, suppose you are walking along the side of a river, as you walk under a bridge the GPS reading becomes inaccurate, and can predict that you jump across the river. Keeping track of the distribution of where you just were and taking into account

| Sample | *Tampering* | *Fire* | *Alarm* | *Smoke* | *Leaving* | *Report* |
|---|---|---|---|---|---|---|
| $s_1$ | *true* | *true* | *false* | *true* | *false* | *false* |
| $s_2$ | *true* | *true* | *false* | *true* | *false* | *false* |
| $s_3$ | *true* | *true* | *false* | *true* | *false* | *false* |
| $s_4$ | *true* | *true* | *true* | *true* | *false* | *false* |
| $s_5$ | *true* | *true* | *true* | *true* | *true* | *false* |
| $s_5$ | *false* | *true* | *true* | *true* | *true* | *false* |
| ... | | | | | | |
| $s_{10000}$ | *false* | *true* | *true* | *true* | *true* | *false* |

Figure 9.36: Gibbs sampling for $P(tampering \mid smoke \wedge \neg report)$

the accuracy of the signal can be used to give a much more accurate estimate of location. It is unlikely you jumped across the river. A similar methodology is used to guess activity in a smart watch, combining GPS, heart rate, and movement; the different activities each make predictions, which can be used as sensing information for a distribution of the activity of the wearer at each time.

For self-driving cars, accurate positioning is important as a single error can take the vehicle on the wrong route. The most reliable way to do this is to only travel on well-mapped routes. A mapping vehicle can pre-drive the routes with all of the sensors (e.g., GPS, lidar, radar, sonar, vision), so the self-driving car knows what sensor values to expect. The sensing needs to work under all weather conditions. It also needs to recognize events for which action is required, such as roadworks or someone running across the road. For a vehicle to travel on unmapped routes (e.g., on a detour because of an accident ahead), it needs to rely on more general capabilities. Techniques for positioning can also work indoors, using vision without GPS, as shown by Viswanathan et al. [2011] for an intelligent wheelchair.

Robots in a novel environment can simultaneously estimate location and construct a map (known as **simultaneous localization and mapping (SLAM)**). This is filtering (page 422) with a richer representation of a state. The state now includes the map as well as the location, which makes the state space enormous. Thrun et al. [2005] overview the use of probability in robotics.

## 9.9 Review

The following are the main points you should have learned from this chapter:

- Probability is a measure of belief in a proposition.
- The posterior probability is used to update an agent's beliefs based on evidence.
- A Bayesian belief network is a representation of conditional independence of random variables.
- Exact inference can be carried out efficiently for sparse graphs (with low treewidth) using recursive conditioning or variable elimination.
- A hidden Markov model or a dynamic belief network can be used for probabilistic reasoning about sequences, such as changes over time or words in sentences, with applications such as robot localization and extracting information from language.
- Stochastic simulation is used for approximate inference.

## 9.10 References and Further Reading

Introductions to probability from an AI perspective, and belief (Bayesian) networks, are by Pearl [1988], Koller and Friedman [2009], Darwiche [2009], and

[Murphy, 2023]. Halpern [2003] overviews foundations of probability. van de Meent et al. [2018] overview probabilistic programming (page 397).

Recursive conditioning is due to Darwiche [2001]. **Variable elimination** for belief networks, also called **bucket elimination**, is presented in Zhang and Poole [1994] and Dechter [1996]. Darwiche [2009] and Dechter [2019] compare these and other methods. Bodlaender [1993] discusses treewidth. Choi et al. [2020] overview probabilistic circuits.

For comprehensive reviews of information theory, see Cover and Thomas [2006], MacKay [2003], and Grünwald [2007].

Brémaud [1999] describes theory and applications of Markov chains. HMMs are described by Rabiner [1989]. Dynamic Bayesian networks were introduced by Dean and Kanazawa [1989]. Markov localization and other issues on the relationship of probability and robotics are described by Thrun et al. [2005]. The use of particle filtering for localization is due to Dellaert et al. [1999].

Shannon and Weaver [1949] pioneered probabilistic models of natural language and forecast many future developments. Manning and Schütze [1999] and Jurafsky and Martin [2023] present probabilistic and statistical methods for natural language. The topic model of Example 9.38 is based on Google's Rephil, described in the supplementary material of Murphy [2023].

For introductions to stochastic simulation, see Rubinstein [1981] and Andrieu et al. [2003]. Likelihood weighting in belief networks is based on Henrion [1988]. Importance sampling in belief networks is based on Cheng and Druzdzel [2000], who also consider how to learn the proposal distribution. There is a collection of articles on particle filtering in Doucet et al. [2001].

The annual Conference on Uncertainty in Artificial Intelligence, and the general AI conferences, provide up-to-date research results.

## 9.11 Exercises

**Exercise 9.1** Using only the axioms of probability and the definition of conditional independence, prove Proposition 9.2 (page 384).

**Exercise 9.2** Consider the belief network of Figure 9.37. This is the "Simple

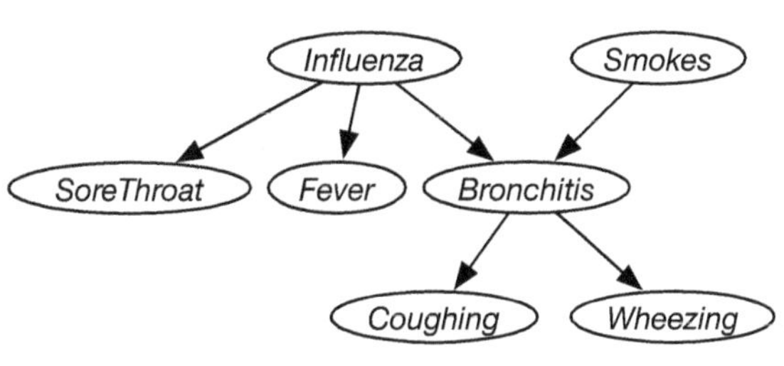


Figure 9.37: A simple diagnostic belief network

diagnostic example" in AIPython (aipython.org). For each of the following, first predict the answer based on your intuition, then run the belief network to check it. Explain the result you found by carrying out the inference.

(a) The posterior probabilities of which variables change when *Smokes* is observed to be true? That is, for which $X$ is $P(X \mid Smoke = true) \neq P(X)$.
(b) Starting from the original network, the posterior probabilities of which variables change when *Fever* is observed to be true? That is, specify the $X$ where $P(X \mid Fever = true) \neq P(X)$.
(c) Does the probability of *Fever* change when *Wheezing* is observed to be true? That is, is $P(Fever \mid Wheezing = true) \neq P(Fever)$? Explain why (in terms of the domain, in language that could be understood by someone who did not know about belief networks).
(d) Suppose *Wheezing* is observed to be true. Does the observing *Fever* change the probability of *Smokes*? That is, is $P(Smokes \mid Wheezing) \neq P(Smokes \mid Wheezing, Fever)$? Explain why (in terms that could be understood by someone who did not know about belief networks).
(e) What could be observed so that subsequently observing *Wheezing* does not change the probability of *SoreThroat*. That is, specify a variable or variables $X$ such that $P(SoreThroat \mid X) = P(SoreThroat \mid X, Wheezing)$, or state that there are none. Explain why.
(f) Suppose *Allergies* could be another explanation of *Sore Throat*. Change the network so that *Allergies* also affects *Sore Throat* but is independent of the other variables in the network. Give reasonable probabilities.
(g) What could be observed so that observing *Wheezing* changes the probability of *Allergies*? Explain why.
(h) What could be observed so that observing *Smokes* changes the probability of *Allergies*? Explain why.

Note that parts (a), (b), and (c) only involve observing a single variable.

**Exercise 9.3** Consider the belief network of Figure 9.38 (page 453), which extends the electrical domain to include an overhead projector. Answer the following questions about how knowledge of the values of some variables would affect the probability of another variable.

(a) Can knowledge of the value of *Projector_plugged_in* affect the belief in the value of *Sam_reading_book*? Explain.
(b) Can knowledge of *Screen_lit_up* affect the belief in *Sam_reading_book*? Explain.
(c) Can knowledge of *Projector_plugged_in* affect your belief in *Sam_reading_book* given that you have observed a value for *Screen_lit_up*? Explain.
(d) Which variables could have their probabilities changed if just *Lamp_works* was observed?
(e) If just *Power_in_projector* was observed, which variables could have their probabilities changed?

**Exercise 9.4** Kahneman [2011, p. 166] gives the following example.

A cab was involved in a hit-and-run accident at night. Two cab companies, Green and Blue, operate in the city. You are given the following data:

- 85% of the cabs in the city are Green and 15% are Blue.
- A witness identified the cab as Blue. The court tested the reliability of the witness in the circumstances that existed on the night of the accident and concluded that the witness correctly identifies each one of the two colors 80% of the time and fails 20% of the time.

What is the probability that the cab involved in the accident was Blue?

(a) Represent this story as a belief network. Explain all variables and conditional probabilities. What is observed, what is the answer?

(b) Suppose there were three independent witnesses, two of whom claimed the cab was Blue and one of whom claimed the cab was Green. Show the corresponding belief network. What is the probability the cab was Blue? What if all three claimed the cab was Blue?

(c) Suppose it was found that the two witnesses who claimed the cab was Blue were not independent, but there was a 60% chance they colluded. (What might this mean?) Show the corresponding belief network, and the relevant probabilities. What is the probability that the cab is Blue (both for the case where all three witnesses claim that the cab was Blue and the case where the other witness claimed the cab was Green)?

(d) In a variant of this scenario, Kahneman [2011, p. 167] replaced the first condition with: "The two companies operate the same number of cabs, but Green cabs are involved in 85% of the accidents." How can this new scenario be represented as a belief network? Your belief network should allow observations about whether there is an accident as well as the color of the cab. Show examples of inferences in your network. Make reasonable choices for anything that is not fully specified. Be explicit about any assumptions you make.

**Exercise 9.5** Represent the same scenario as in Exercise 5.8 (page 225) using a belief network. Show the network structure. Give all of the initial factors, making

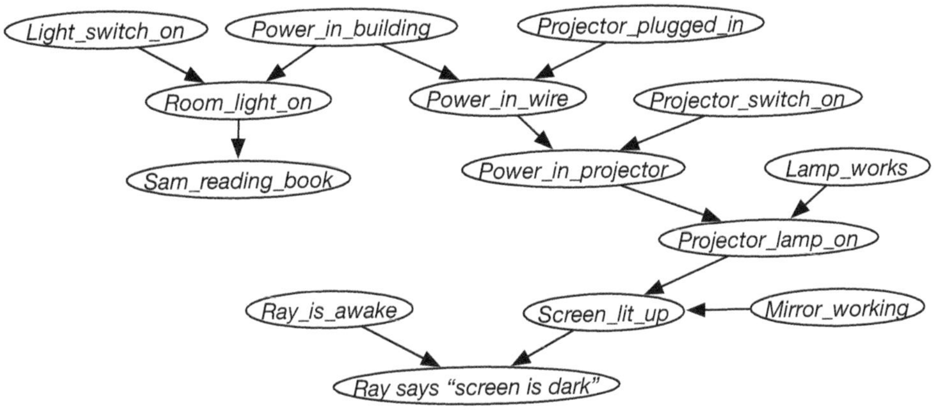


Figure 9.38: Belief network for an overhead projector

reasonable assumptions about the conditional probabilities (they should follow the story given in that exercise, but allow some noise). Give a qualitative explanation of why the patient has spots and fever.

**Exercise 9.6** In this question, you will build a belief-network representation of the Deep Space 1 (DS1) spacecraft considered in Exercise 5.10 (page 225). Figure 5.14 (page 226) depicts a part of the actual DS1 engine design.

Consider the following scenario:

- Valves are *open* or *closed*.
- A value can be *ok*, in which case the gas will flow if the valve is open and not if it is closed; *broken*, in which case gas never flows; *stuck*, in which case gas flows independently of whether the valve is open or closed; or *leaking*, in which case gas flowing into the valve leaks out instead of flowing through.
- There are three gas sensors that can detect whether some gas is leaking (but not which gas); the first gas sensor detects gas from the rightmost valves ($v_1, \dots, v_4$), the second sensor detects gas from the center valves ($v_5, \dots, v_{12}$), and the third sensor detects gas from the leftmost valves ($v_{13}, \dots, v_{16}$).

(a) Build a belief-network representation of the valves that feed into engine $e_1$. Make sure there are appropriate probabilities.

(b) Test your model on some non-trivial examples.

**Exercise 9.7** Consider the following belief network:

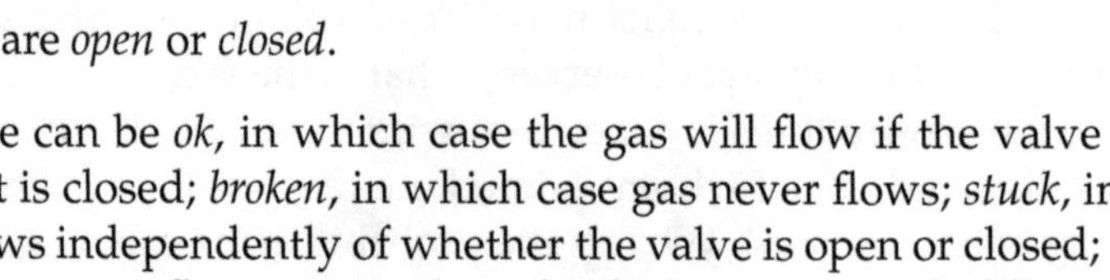


with Boolean variables ($A = true$ is written as $a$ and $A = false$ as $\neg a$, and similarly for the other variable) and the following conditional probabilities:

| | |
|---|---|
| $P(a) = 0.9$ | $P(d \mid b) = 0.1$ |
| $P(b) = 0.2$ | $P(d \mid \neg b) = 0.8$ |
| $P(c \mid a, b) = 0.1$ | $P(e \mid c) = 0.7$ |
| $P(c \mid a, \neg b) = 0.8$ | $P(e \mid \neg c) = 0.2$ |
| $P(c \mid \neg a, b) = 0.7$ | $P(f \mid c) = 0.2$ |
| $P(c \mid \neg a, \neg b) = 0.4$ | $P(f \mid \neg c) = 0.9.$ |

(a) Compute $P(e)$ using variable elimination (VE). You should first prune irrelevant variables. Show the factors that are created for a given elimination ordering.

(b) Suppose you want to compute $P(e \mid \neg f)$ using VE. How much of the previous computation is reusable? Show the factors that are different from those in part (a).

**Exercise 9.8** Sam suggested that the recursive conditioning algorithm only needs to cache answers resulting from forgetting, rather than all answers. Is Sam's suggestion better (in terms of space or search space reduced) than the given code for a single query? What about for multiple queries that share a cache? Give evidence (either theoretical or empirical) for your results.

**Exercise 9.9** Explain how to extend VE to allow for more general observations and queries. In particular, answer the following:

(a) How can the VE algorithm be extended to allow observations that are disjunctions of values for a variable (e.g., of the form $X = a \vee X = b$)?
(b) How can the VE algorithm be extended to allow observations that are disjunctions of values for different variables (e.g., of the form $X = a \vee Y = b$)?
(c) How can the VE algorithm be extended to allow for the probability on a set of variables (e.g., asking for the $P(X, Y \mid e)$)?

**Exercise 9.10** In a nuclear research submarine, a sensor measures the temperature of the reactor core. An alarm is triggered ($A = true$) if the sensor reading is abnormally high ($S = true$), indicating an overheating of the core ($C = true$). The alarm and/or the sensor could be defective ($S\_ok = false$, $A\_ok = false$), which causes them to malfunction. The alarm system is modeled by the belief network of Figure 9.39.

(a) What are the initial factors for this network? For each factor, state what it represents and what variables it is a function of.
(b) Show how VE can be used to compute the probability that the core is overheating, given that the alarm does not go off; that is, $P(c \mid \neg a)$. For each variable eliminated, show which variable is eliminated, which factor(s) are removed, and which factor(s) are created, including what variables each factor is a function of. Explain how the answer is derived from the final factor.
(c) Suppose we add a second, identical sensor to the system and trigger the alarm when either of the sensors reads a high temperature. The two sensors break and fail independently. Give the corresponding extended belief network.

**Exercise 9.11** This exercise continues Exercise 5.14 (page 228).

(a) Explain what knowledge (about physics and about students) a belief-network model requires.

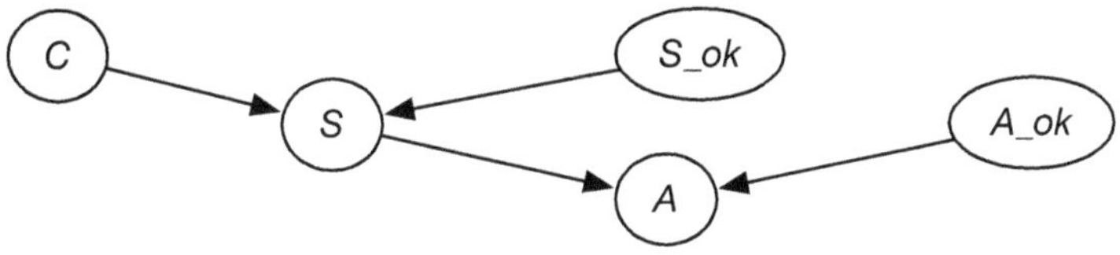


Figure 9.39: Belief network for a nuclear submarine

(b) What is the main advantage of using belief networks over using abductive diagnosis or consistency-based diagnosis in this domain?
(c) What is the main advantage of using abductive diagnosis or consistency-based diagnosis over using belief networks in this domain?

**Exercise 9.12** Extend Example 9.30 (page 420) so that it includes the state of the animal, which is either sleeping, foraging, or agitated.

If the animal is sleeping at any time, it does not make a noise, does not move, and at the next time point it is sleeping with probability 0.8 or foraging or agitated with probability 0.1 each.

If the animal is foraging or agitated, it tends to remain in the same state of composure (with probability 0.8), move to the other state of composure with probability 0.1, or go to sleep with probability 0.1.

If the animal is foraging in a corner, it will be detected by the microphone at that corner with probability 0.5, and if the animal is agitated in a corner, it will be detected by the microphone at that corner with probability 0.9. If the animal is foraging in the middle, it will be detected by each of the microphones with probability 0.2. If it is agitated in the middle, it will be detected by each of the microphones with probability 0.6. Otherwise, the microphones have a false positive rate of 0.05.

(a) Represent this as a two-stage dynamic belief network. Draw the network, give the domains of the variables and the conditional probabilities.
(b) What independence assumptions are embedded in the network?
(c) Implement either variable elimination or particle filtering for this problem.
(d) Does being able to hypothesize the internal state of the agent (whether it is sleeping, foraging, or agitated) help localization? Explain why.

**Exercise 9.13** Suppose Sam built a robot with five sensors and wanted to keep track of the location of the robot, and built a hidden Markov model (HMM) with the following structure (which repeats to the right):

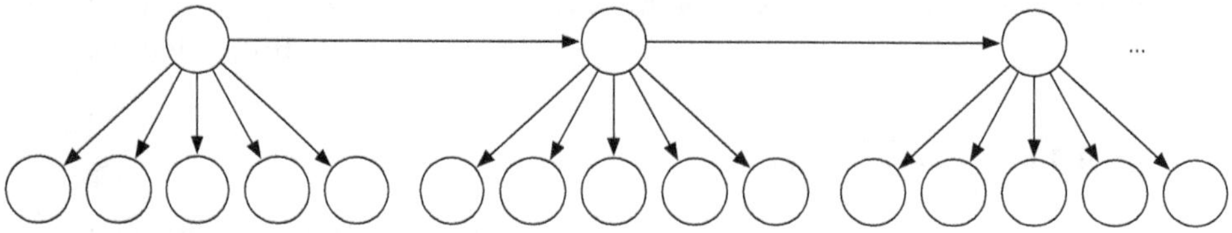

(a) What probabilities does Sam need to provide? You should label a copy of the diagram, if that helps explain your answer.
(b) What independence assumptions are made in this model?
(c) Sam discovered that the HMM with five sensors did not work as well as a version that only used two sensors. Explain why this may have occurred.

**Exercise 9.14** Consider the problem of filtering in HMMs (page 426).

(a) Give a formula for the probability of some variable $X_j$ given future and past observations. You can base this on Equation (9.6) (page 426). This should involve obtaining a factor from the previous state and a factor from the next state and combining them to determine the posterior probability of $X_k$.

[Hint: Consider how VE, eliminating from the leftmost variable and eliminating from the rightmost variable, can be used to compute the posterior distribution for $X_j$.]

(b) Computing the probability of all of the variables can be done in time linear in the number of variables by not recomputing values that were already computed for other variables. Give an algorithm for this.

(c) Suppose you have computed the probability distribution for each state $S_1$, ..., $S_k$, and then you get an observation for time $k+1$. How can the posterior probability of each variable be updated in time linear in $k$? [Hint: You may need to store more than just the distribution over each $S_i$.]

**Exercise 9.15** Which of the following algorithms suffers from underflow (real numbers that are too small to be represented using double precision floats): rejection sampling, importance sampling, particle filtering? Explain why. How could underflow be avoided?

**Exercise 9.16**

(a) What are the independence assumptions made in the naive Bayes classifier for the help system of Example 9.36 (page 430).

(b) Are these independence assumptions reasonable? Explain why or why not.

(c) Suppose we have a topic-model network like the one of Figure 9.29 (page 435), but where all of the topics are parents of all of the words. What are all of the independencies of this model?

(d) Give an example where the topics would not be independent.

**Exercise 9.17** How well does particle filtering work for Example 9.48 (page 449)? Try to construct an example where Gibbs sampling works much better than particle filtering. [Hint: Consider unlikely observations after a sequence of variable assignments.]

# Chapter 10

# Learning with Uncertainty

*Learning without thought is labor lost; thought without learning is perilous.*

– Confucius [500 BCE]

*It can scarcely be denied that the supreme goal of all theory is to make the irreducible basic elements as simple and as few as possible without having to surrender the adequate representation of a single datum of experience.*

– Albert Einstein [1934]

In Chapters 7 and 8, learning was divorced from reasoning. An alternative is to explicitly use probabilistic reasoning, as in Chapter 9, with **data** providing **evidence** that can be conditioned on. This provides a theoretical basis for much of machine learning, including regularization and measures of simplicity. This chapter uses probability for supervised and unsupervised learning, as well as learning of belief networks.

## 10.1 Probabilistic Learning

Training examples provide evidence that can be conditioned on. **Bayes' rule** (page 381) specifies how to determine the probability of model $m$ given examples $Es$:

$$P(m \mid Es) = \frac{P(Es \mid m) * P(m)}{P(Es)} . \tag{10.1}$$

The **likelihood**, $P(Es \mid m)$, is the probability that this model would have produced this dataset. It is high when the model is a good fit to the data. The **prior probability**, $P(m)$, encodes a **learning bias** and specifies which models are a priori more likely, and can be used to bias the learning toward simpler models. The denominator, $P(Es)$, is the **partition function**, a normalizing constant to make sure that the probabilities sum to 1.

In Chapter 7, the aim was to fit the data as well as possible, using the **maximum likelihood model** – the model that maximizes $P(Es \mid m)$ – but then we had to use seemingly ad hoc regularization (page 302) to avoid **overfitting** and better fit to test data. One problem with choosing the maximum likelihood model is that, if the space of models is rich enough, a model exists that specifies that this particular dataset will be produced, which has $P(Es \mid m) = 1$. For example, a decision tree (page 281) can represent any discrete function, but can overfit training data.

The model that maximizes $P(m \mid Es)$ is called the **maximum a posteriori probability model**, or **MAP model**. Because the denominator of Equation (10.1) (page 459) is independent of the model, it may be ignored when choosing the most likely model. Thus, the MAP model is the model that maximizes

$$P(Es \mid m) * P(m)\,. \tag{10.2}$$

It takes into account both the likelihood (fit to the data) and the prior, which can be used as a learning bias, such as a preference for simpler models.

## 10.2 Bayesian Learning

Instead of just choosing the most likely hypothesis, it is typically more useful to use the posterior probability distribution of hypotheses, in what is called **Bayesian learning.**

Suppose $Es$ is the set of training examples and a test example has inputs $X = x$ (written as $x$) and target $Y$. The aim is to compute $P(Y \mid x \wedge Es)$. This is the probability distribution of the target variable given the particular inputs and the examples. The role of a model is to be the assumed generator of the examples. If $M$ is a set of disjoint and covering models:

$$\begin{aligned} P(Y \mid x \wedge Es) &= \sum_{m \in M} P(Y \wedge m \mid x \wedge Es) \\ &= \sum_{m \in M} P(Y \mid m \wedge x \wedge Es) * P(m \mid x \wedge Es) \\ &= \sum_{m \in M} P(Y \mid m \wedge x) * P(m \mid Es)\,. \end{aligned} \tag{10.3}$$

The first two equalities follow from the definition of (conditional) probability (page 378). The last equality relies on two assumptions: the model includes all the information about the examples that is necessary for a particular prediction,

$P(Y \mid m \wedge x \wedge Es) = P(Y \mid m \wedge x)$, and the model does not change depending on the inputs of the new example, $P(m \mid x \wedge Es) = P(m \mid Es)$. Instead of choosing the best model, Bayesian learning relies on **model averaging**, averaging over the predictions of all the models, where each model is weighted by its posterior probability given the training examples, as in Equation (10.3) (page 460).

$P(m \mid Es)$ can be computed using Bayes' rule (Equation (10.1)), in terms of the prior $P(Es)$, the likelihood $P(Es \mid m)$, and a normalization term.

A common assumption is that examples $Es = \{e_1, \ldots, e_k\}$ are **independent and identically distributed (i.i.d.)** given model $m$, which means examples $e_i$ and $e_j$, for $i \neq j$, are independent given $m$:

$$P(Es \mid m) = \prod_{i=1}^{k} P(e_i \mid m) .$$

The i.i.d. assumption can be represented as the belief network of Figure 10.1. A standard reasoning technique in such a network is to condition on the observed $e_i$ and to either query an unobserved $e_j$ variable, which provides a probabilistic prediction for unseen examples, or query $m$, which provides a distribution over models.

The inference methods of the previous chapter could be used to compute the posterior probabilities. However, the exact methods presented are only applicable when $m$ is finite, because they involve enumerating the domains of the variables. However, $m$ is usually more complicated (often including real-valued components) than these exact techniques can handle, and approximation methods are required. For some cases, the inference can be exact using special-case algorithms.

The simplest case (Section 10.2.1) is to learn probabilities of a single discrete variable. Bayesian learning can also be used for learning decision trees (Section 10.2.3 (page 471)), learning the structure and probabilities of belief networks (Section 10.4 (page 481)), and more complicated cases.

## 10.2.1 Learning Probabilities

The simplest learning task is to learn a single Boolean random variable, $Y$, with no input features, as in Section 7.2.2 (page 276). The aim is to learn the posterior

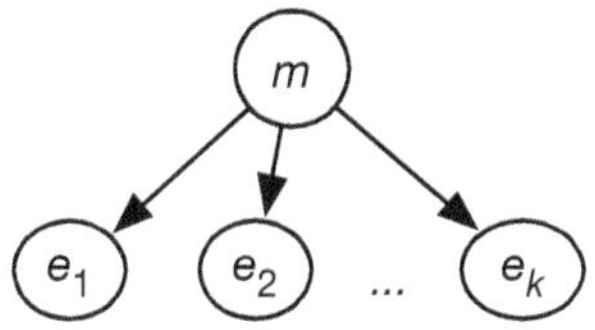


Figure 10.1: The i.i.d. assumption as a belief network

distribution of $Y$ conditioned on the training examples.

**Example 10.1** Consider the problem of predicting the next toss of a thumbtack (drawing pin), where the outcomes *Tails* and *Heads* are as follows:

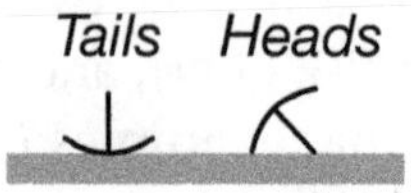


Suppose you tossed a thumbtack a number of times and observed *Es*, a particular sequence of $n_0$ instances of *Tails* and $n_1$ instances of *Heads*. Assume the tosses are independent, and that *Heads* occurs with probability $\phi$. The likelihood is

$$P(Es \mid \phi) = \phi^{n_1} * (1-\phi)^{n_0}.$$

This is a maximum when the log-likelihood (page 274)

$$\log P(Es \mid \phi) = n_1 * \log \phi + n_0 * \log(1-\phi)$$

is a maximum, and the negation of the average log-likelihood, the categorical log loss (page 273), is a minimum, which occur when $\phi = \frac{n_1}{n_0+n_1}$.

Note that if $n_1 = 0$, then $\phi$ is zero, which would indicate that *Heads* is impossible; similarly, $n_1 = 0$ would predict that *Tails* is impossible, which is an instance of **overfitting** (page 297). A MAP model would also take into account a prior.

Reverend Thomas Bayes [1763] had the insight to treat a probability as a real-valued random variable. For a Boolean variable, $Y$, a real-valued variable, $\phi$, on the interval $[0,1]$ represents the probability of $Y$. Thus, by definition of $\phi$, $P(Y=true \mid \phi) = \phi$ and $P(Y=false \mid \phi) = 1-\phi$.

Suppose, initially, an agent considers all values in the interval $[0,1]$ equally likely to be the value of $\phi$. This can be modeled with the variable $\phi$ having a uniform distribution over the interval $[0,1]$. This is the probability density function labeled $n_0=0, n_1=0$ in Figure 10.2 (page 463).

The probability distribution of $\phi$ is updated by conditioning on observed examples. Let the examples *Es* be the particular sequence of observations that resulted in $n_1$ occurrences of $Y=true$ and $n_0$ occurrences of $Y=false$. Bayes' rule and the i.i.d. assumption gives

$$\begin{aligned} P(\phi \mid Es) &= \frac{P(Es \mid \phi) * P(\phi)}{P(Es)} \\ &\propto \phi^{n_1} * (1-\phi)^{n_0} * P(\phi). \end{aligned}$$

The denominator is a normalizing constant to ensure the area under the curve is 1.

**Example 10.2** Consider the thumbtack of Example 10.1 (page 462) with a uniform prior.

With a uniform prior and no observations, shown as the $n_0 = 1, n_1 = 2$ line of Figure 10.2, the MAP estimate is undefined – every point is a maximum – and the expected value (page 383) is 0.5.

When a single heads and no tails is observed, the distribution is a straight line from point $(0,0)$ to point $(1,2)$. The most likely prediction – the MAP estimate – is $\phi = 1$. The expected value of the resulting distribution is $\phi = 2/3$.

When two heads and one tails are observed, the resulting distribution is the $n_0 = 1, n_1 = 2$ line of Figure 10.2. The mode is at $2/3$ and the expected value is $3/5$.

Figure 10.2 gives some posterior distributions of the variable $\phi$ based on different sample sizes, given a uniform prior. The cases are $(n_0 = 1, n_1 = 2)$, $(n_0 = 2, n_1 = 4)$, and $(n_0 = 4, n_1 = 8)$. Each of these peak at the same place, namely at $\frac{2}{3}$. More training examples make the curve sharper.

When eight heads and four tails are observed, the mode is at $2/3$ and the expected value is $5/14$. Notice how the expected value for this case is closer to the empirical proportion of heads in the training data than when $n_0 = 1, n_1 = 2$, even though the modes are the same empirical proportion.

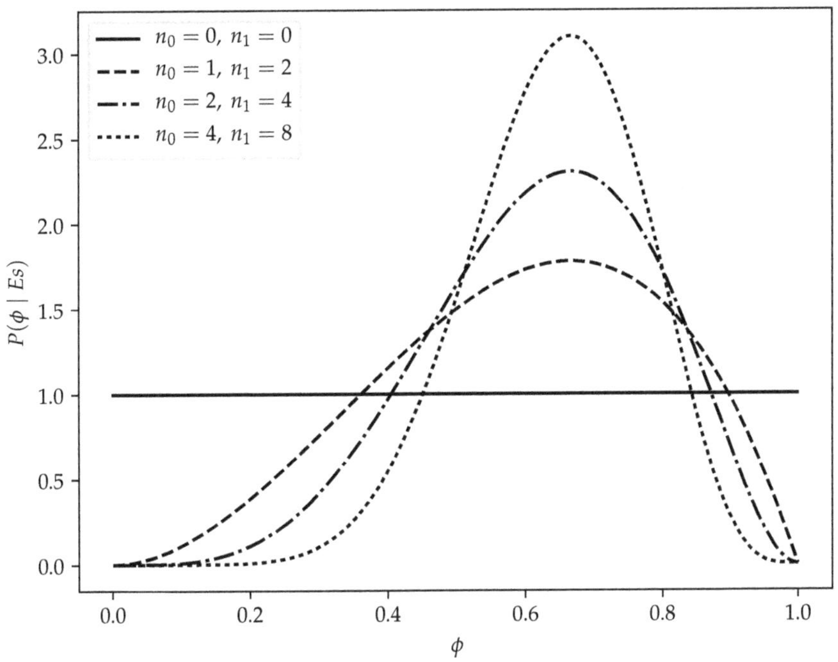


Figure 10.2: Beta distribution based on different samples

The distribution of this example is known as the **beta distribution**; it is parameterized by two counts, $\alpha_0$ and $\alpha_1$, and a probability $\phi$. Traditionally, the $\alpha_i$ parameters for the beta distribution are one more than the counts; thus, $\alpha_i = n_i + 1$. The beta distribution is

$$Beta^{\alpha_0,\alpha_1}(\phi) = \frac{\phi^{\alpha_1-1} * (1-\phi)^{\alpha_0-1}}{Z}$$

where $Z$ is a normalizing constant that ensures the integral over all values is 1. Thus, the uniform distribution on $[0,1]$ is the beta distribution $Beta^{1,1}$.

The **mode** – the value with the maximum probability – of the beta distribution $Beta^{\alpha_0,\alpha_1}$ is $\phi = \frac{\alpha_0-1}{\alpha_0+\alpha_0-2}$.

The expected value of the beta distribution $Beta^{\alpha_0,\alpha_1}$ is $\phi = \frac{\alpha_0}{\alpha_0+\alpha_0}$

Thus, the expectation of the beta distribution with a uniform prior gives **Laplace smoothing** (page 302). This shows that Laplace smoothing is optimal for the thought experiment (page 302) where a probability was selected uniformly in [0,1], training and test data were generated using that probability, and evaluated on test data.

The prior does not need to be the uniform distribution. A common prior is to use a beta distribution for the prior of $\phi$, such as

$$P(\phi) = \phi^{c_1-1} * (1-\phi)^{c_0-1}$$

corresponding to $c_1$ pseudo-examples (page 301) with outcome *true*, and $c_0$ *false* pseudo-examples. In this case, the posterior probability given examples *Es* that consists of a particular sequence of $n_0$ *false* and $n_1$ *true* examples is

$$P(\phi \mid Es) \propto \phi^{c_1+n_1-1} * (1-\phi)^{c_0+n_0-1}.$$

In this case, the MAP estimate for $\phi$, the probability of *true*, is

$$p = \frac{c_1+n_1-1}{c_0+n_0+c_1+n_1-2}$$

and the expected value is

$$p = \frac{c_1+n_1}{c_0+n_0+c_1+n_1}.$$

This prior has the same form as the posterior; both are described in terms of a ration of counts. A prior that has the same form as a posterior is called a **conjugate prior**.

Note that *Es* is the particular sequence of observations made. If the observation was just that there were a total of $n_0$ occurrences of $Y = false$ and $n_1$ occurrences of $Y = true$, you would get a different answer, because you would have to take into account all the possible sequences that could have given this count. This is known as the **binomial distribution**.

In addition to using the posterior distribution of $\phi$ to derive the expected value, it can be used to answer other questions such as: What is the probability that the posterior probability, $\phi$, is in the range $[a, b]$? In other words, derive $P((\phi \geq a \wedge \phi \leq b) \mid Es)$. This is the problem that Bayes [1763] solved in his posthumously published paper. The solution published – although in much more cumbersome notation because calculus had not been invented when it was written – was

$$\frac{\int_a^b p^n * (1-p)^{m-n}}{\int_0^1 p^n * (1-p)^{m-n}}.$$

This kind of knowledge is used in poll surveys when it may be reported that a survey is correct with an error of at most 5%, 19 times out of 20, and in a **probably approximately correct (PAC)** (page 438) estimate. It guarantees an error at most $\epsilon$ at least $1-\delta$ of the time as follows:

- If an agent predicts $\frac{a+b}{2}$, the midpoint of the range $[a, b]$, it will have error less than or equal to $\epsilon = \frac{b-a}{2}$, exactly when the hypothesis is in $[a, b]$.
- Let $\delta = 1 - P(\phi \geq a \wedge \phi \leq b \mid Es)$. Then $1-\delta$ is $P(\phi \geq a \wedge \phi \leq b \mid Es)$, so
- choosing the midpoint will result in an error at most $\epsilon$ in $1-\delta$ of the time.

**Hoeffding's inequality** (page 438) gives worst-case results, whereas the Bayesian estimate gives the expected number. The worst case provides looser bounds than the expected case.

### Categorical Variables

Suppose $Y$ is a **categorical variable** (page 272) with $k$ possible values. A distribution over a categorical variable is called a **multinomial distribution**. The Dirichlet distribution is the generalization of the beta distribution to cover categorical variables. The **Dirichlet distribution** with two sorts of parameters, the "counts" $\alpha_1, \ldots, \alpha_k$, and the probability parameters $p_1, \ldots, p_k$, is

$$Dirichlet^{\alpha_1,\ldots,\alpha_k}(p_1, \ldots, p_k) = \frac{\prod_{j=1}^k p_j^{\alpha_j - 1}}{Z}$$

where $p_i$ is the probability of the $i$th outcome (and so $0 \leq p_i \leq 1$) and $\alpha_i$ is a positive real number and $Z$ is a normalizing constant that ensures the integral over all the probability values is 1. You can think of $a_i$ as one more than the count of the $i$th outcome, $\alpha_i = n_i + 1$. The Dirichlet distribution looks like Figure 10.2 (page 463) along each dimension (i.e., as each $p_j$ varies between 0 and 1).

For the Dirichlet distribution, the expected value outcome $i$ (averaging over all $p_j$) is

$$\frac{\alpha_i}{\sum_j \alpha_j}.$$

The reason that the $\alpha_i$ parameters are one more than the counts in the definitions of the beta and Dirichlet distributions is to make this formula simple.

Suppose an agent must predict a value for $Y$ with domain $\{y_1, \ldots, y_k\}$, and there are no inputs. The agent starts with a positive pseudocount $c_i$ for each $y_i$. These counts are chosen before the agent has seen any of the data. Suppose the agent observes training examples with $n_i$ data points having $Y = y_i$. The probability of $Y$ is estimated using the expected value

$$P(Y = y_i) = \frac{c_i + n_i}{\sum_{i'} c_{i'} + n_{i'}}.$$

When the dataset is empty (all $n_i = 0$), the $c_i$ are used to estimate probabilities. An agent does not have to start with a uniform prior; it could start with any prior distribution. If the agent starts with a prior that is a Dirichlet distribution, its posterior will be a Dirichlet distribution.

Thus, the beta and Dirichlet distributions provide a justification for using **pseudocounts** (page 301) for estimating probabilities. A pseudocount of 1 corresponds to **Laplace smoothing** (page 302).

### Probabilities from Experts

The use of pseudocounts also gives us a way to combine **expert knowledge** and data. Often a single agent does not have good data but may have access to multiple experts who have varying levels of expertise and who give different probabilities.

There are a number of problems with obtaining probabilities from experts:

- experts' reluctance to give an exact probability value that cannot be refined
- representing the uncertainty of a probability estimate
- combining the estimates from multiple experts
- combining expert opinion with actual data.

Rather than expecting experts to give probabilities, the experts can provide counts. Instead of giving a real number for the probability of $A$, an expert gives a pair of numbers as $\langle n, m \rangle$ that is interpreted as though the expert had observed $n$ occurrences of $A$ out of $m$ trials. Essentially, the experts provide not only a probability, but also an estimate of the size of the dataset on which their estimate is based.

The counts from different experts can be combined together by adding the components to give the pseudocounts for the system. You should not necessarily believe an expert's sample size, as people are often overconfident in their abilities. Instead, the size can be estimated taking into account the experiences of the experts. Whereas the ratio between the counts reflects the probability, different levels of confidence are reflected in the absolute values. Consider different ways to represent the probability 2/3. The pair $\langle 2, 3 \rangle$, with two positive examples out of three examples, reflects extremely low confidence that would quickly be dominated by data or other experts' estimates. The pair $\langle 20, 30\rangle$ reflects more confidence – a few examples would not change it much, but tens of examples would. Even hundreds of examples would have little effect on the prior counts of the pair $\langle 2000, 3000\rangle$. However, with millions of data points, even these prior counts would have little impact on the resulting probability estimate.

### 10.2.2 Probabilistic Classifiers

A **Bayes classifier** is a probabilistic model that is used for supervised learning. A Bayes classifier is based on the idea that the role of a **class** is to predict the values of features for members of that class. Examples are grouped in classes because they have common values for some of the features. The learning agent learns how the features depend on the class and uses that model to predict the classification of a new example.

The simplest case is the **naive Bayes classifier**, which makes the independence assumption that the input features are conditionally independent of each other given the classification. The independence of the naive Bayes classifier is embodied in a belief network where the features are the nodes, the target feature (the classification) has no parents, and the target feature is the only parent of each input feature. This belief network requires the probability distributions $P(Y)$ for the target feature, or class, $Y$ and $P(X_i \mid Y)$ for each input feature $X_i$. For each example, the prediction is computed by conditioning on observed values for the input features and querying the classification. Multiple target variables can be modeled and learned separately.

**Example 10.3** Suppose an agent wants to predict the user action given the data of Figure 7.1 (page 268). For this example, the user action is the classification. The naive Bayes classifier for this example corresponds to the belief network of Figure 10.3. The input features form variables that are children of the classification.

The model of Figure 10.3 corresponds to $m$ in Figure 10.1.

Given an example with inputs $X_1 = v_1, \ldots, X_k = v_k$, Bayes' rule (page 381) is used to compute the posterior probability distribution of the example's classi-

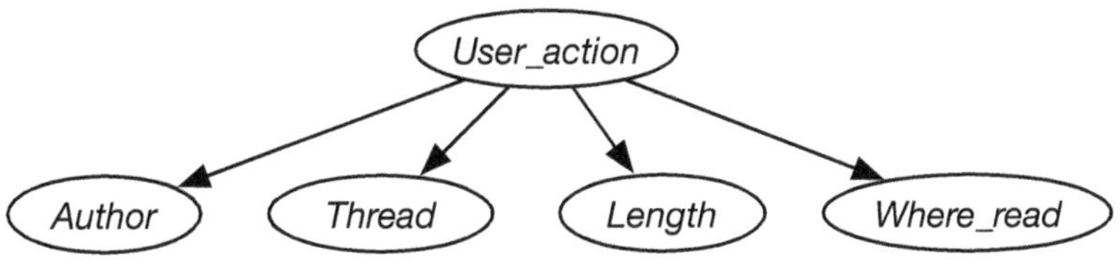


Figure 10.3: Belief network corresponding to a naive Bayes classifier

fication, $Y$:

$$P(Y \mid X_1 = v_1, \dots, X_k = v_k) = \frac{P(X_1 = v_1, \dots, X_k = v_k \mid Y) * P(Y)}{P(X_1 = v_1, \dots, X_k = v_k)} = \frac{P(Y) * \prod_{i=1}^{k} P(X_i = v_i \mid Y)}{\sum_Y P(Y) * \prod_{i=1}^{k} P(X_i = v_i \mid Y)}$$

where the denominator is a normalizing constant to ensure the probabilities sum to 1.

Unlike many other models of supervised learning, the naive Bayes classifier can handle **missing data** where not all features are observed; the agent conditions on the features that are observed, which assumes the data is missing at random (page 498). Naive Bayes is optimal – it makes no independence assumptions beyond missing at random – if only a single $X_i$ is observed. As more of the $X_i$ are observed, the accuracy depends on how independent the $X_i$ are given $Y$.

If $Y$ is Boolean and every $X_i$ is observed, naive Bayes is isomorphic to a **logistic regression** (page 290) model; see page 400 for a derivation. They have identical predictions when the logistic regression weight for $X_i$ is the logarithm of the likelihood ratio, $\log P(X_i \mid h)/P(X_i \mid \neg h)$. They are typically learned differently – but don't need to be – with logistic regression trained to minimize log loss and naive Bayes trained for the conditional probabilities to be the MAP model or the expected value, given a prior.

To learn a classifier, the distributions of $P(Y)$ and $P(X_i \mid Y)$ for each input feature can be learned from the data. Each conditional probability distribution $P(X_i \mid Y)$ may be treated as a separate learning problem for each value of $Y$, for example using beta or Dirichlet distributions (page 461).

**Example 10.4** Suppose an agent wants to predict the user action given the data of Figure 7.1 (page 268). For this example, the user action is the classification. The naive Bayes classifier for this example corresponds to the belief network of Figure 10.3 (page 467). The training examples are used to determine the probabilities required for the belief network.

Suppose the agent uses the empirical frequencies as the probabilities for this example. (Thus, it is not using any pseudocounts.) The maximum likelihood probabilities that can be derived from these data are

$$P(User\_action = reads) = 9/18 = 0.5$$
$$P(Author = known \mid User\_action = reads) = 2/3$$
$$P(Author = known \mid User\_action = skips) = 2/3$$
$$P(Thread = new \mid User\_action = reads) = 7/9$$
$$P(Thread = new \mid User\_action = skips) = 1/3$$
$$P(Length = long \mid User\_action = reads) = 0$$

$$P(Length = long \mid User\_action = skips) = 7/9$$
$$P(Where\_read = home \mid User\_action = reads) = 4/9$$
$$P(Where\_read = home \mid User\_action = skips) = 4/9\,.$$

Based on these probabilities, the features *Author* and *Where_read* have no predictive power because knowing either does not change the probability that the user will read the article.

If the maximum likelihood probabilities are used, some conditional probabilities may be zero. This means that some features become predictive: knowing just one feature value can rule out a category. It is possible that some combinations of observations are impossible, and the classifier will have a divide-by-zero error if these are observed. See Exercise 10.1 (page 487). This is a problem not necessarily with using a Bayes classifier, but rather with using empirical frequencies as probabilities.

The alternative to using the empirical frequencies is to incorporate **pseudocounts** (page 301). Pseudocounts can be engineered to have desirable behavior, before any data is observed and as more data is acquired.

**Example 10.5** Consider how to learn the probabilities for the **help system** of Example 9.36 (page 430), where a helping agent infers what help page a user is interested in based on the words in the user's query to the help system. Let's treat the query as a set of words (page 430).

The learner must learn $P(H)$. It could start with a pseudocount (page 301) for each $h_i$. Pages that are a priori more likely should have a higher pseudocount.

Similarly, the learner needs the probability $P(w_j \mid h_i)$, the probability that word $w_j$ will be used given the help page is $h_i$. Because you may want the system to work even before it has received any data, the prior for these probabilities should be carefully designed, taking into account the frequency of words in the language, the words in the help page itself, and other information obtained by experience with other (help) systems.

Assume the following positive counts, which are observed counts plus suitable pseudocounts:

- $c_i$ the number of times $h_i$ was the correct help page
- $s = \sum_i c_i$ the total count
- $u_{ij}$ the number of times $h_i$ was the correct help page and word $w_j$ was used in the query.

From these counts an agent can estimate the required probabilities

$$P(h_i) = c_i/s$$
$$P(w_j \mid h_i) = u_{ij}/c_i$$

from which $P(H \mid q)$, the posterior distribution of help pages conditioned on the set of words $q$ in a user's query, can be computed; see Example 10.3 (page 488). It is necessary to use the words not in the query as well as the words in the query. For example, if a help page is about printing, the work "print" may be very likely to be used. The fact that "print" is not in a query is strong evidence that this is not the appropriate help page.

The system could present the help page(s) with the highest probability given the query.

When a user claims to have found the appropriate help page, the counts for that page and the words in the query are updated. Thus, if the user indicates that $h_i$ is the correct page, the counts $s$ and $c_i$ are incremented, and for each word $w_j$ used in the query, $u_{ij}$ is incremented. This model does not use information about the wrong page. If the user claims that a page is not the correct page, this information is not used.

The biggest challenge in building such a help system is not in the learning but in acquiring useful data. In particular, users may not know whether they have found the page they were looking for. Thus, users may not know when to stop and provide the feedback from which the system learns. Some users may never be satisfied with a page. Indeed, there may not exist a page they are satisfied with, but that information never gets fed back to the learner. Alternatively, some users may indicate they have found the page they were looking for, even though there may be another page that was more appropriate. In the latter case, the correct page may end up with its counts so low, it is never discovered. See Exercise 10.2 (page 487).

Although there are some cases where the naive Bayes classifier does not produce good results, it is extremely simple, easy to implement, and often works very well. It is a good method to try for a new problem.

In general, the naive Bayes classifier works well when the independence assumption is appropriate, that is, when the class is a good predictor of the other features and the other features are independent given the class. This may be appropriate for **natural kinds**, where the classes have evolved because they are useful in distinguishing the objects that humans want to distinguish. Natural kinds are often associated with nouns, such as the class of dogs or the class of chairs.

The naive Bayes classifier can be expanded in a number of ways:

- Some input features could be parents of the classification and some be children. The probability of the classification given its parents could be represented as a decision tree or a squashed linear function or a neural network.

- The children of the classification do not have to be modeled as independent. In a **tree-augmented naive Bayes (TAN) network**, the children of the class variable are allowed to have zero or one other parents as long as the resulting graph is acyclic. This allows for a simple model that accounts for interdependencies among the children, while retaining efficient inference, as the tree structured in the children has a small treewidth (page 417).

- Structure can be incorporated into the class variable. A **latent tree model** decomposes the class variable into a number of latent variables that are connected together in a tree structure. Each observed variable is a child of one of the latent variables. The latent variables allow a model of the dependence between the observed variables.

### 10.2.3 Probabilistic Learning of Decision Trees

The previous examples did not need the prior on the structure of models, as all the models were equally complex. However, learning decision trees (page 281) requires a bias, typically in favor of smaller decision trees. The prior probability provides this bias.

If there are no examples with the same values for the input features but different values for the target feature, there are always multiple decision trees that fit the data perfectly. For every assignment of values that did not appear in the training set, there are decision trees that perfectly fit the training set, and make opposite predictions on the unseen examples. See the no-free-lunch theorem (page 315). If there is a possibility of noise, none of the trees that perfectly fit the training set may be the best model.

**Example 10.6** Consider the data of Figure 7.1 (page 268), where the learner is required to predict the user's actions.

One possible decision tree is the one given on the left of Figure 7.8 (page 282). Call this decision tree $d_2$; the subscript being the depth. The likelihood of the data is $P(Es \mid d_2) = 1$. That is, $d_2$ accurately fits the data.

Another possible decision tree is the one with no internal nodes, and a single leaf that predicts *reads* with probability $\frac{1}{2}$. This is the most likely tree with no internal nodes, given the data. Call this decision tree $d_0$. The likelihood of the data given this model is

$$P(Es \mid d_0) = \left(\frac{1}{2}\right)^9 * \left(\frac{1}{2}\right)^9 \approx 1.5 * 10^{-6}.$$

Another possible decision tree is one on the right of Figure 7.8 (page 282), with one split on *Length* and with probabilities on the leaves given by $P(reads \mid Length = long) = 0$ and $P(reads \mid Length = short) = \frac{9}{11}$. Note that $\frac{9}{11}$ is the empirical frequency of *reads* among the training set with $Length = short$. Call this decision tree $d_{1a}$. The likelihood of the data given this model is

$$P(Es \mid d_{1a}) = 1^7 * \left(\frac{9}{11}\right)^9 * \left(\frac{2}{11}\right)^2 \approx 0.0543.$$

These are just three of the possible decision trees. Which is best depends on the prior on trees. The likelihood of the data is multiplied by the prior probability of the decision trees to determine the posterior probability of the decision tree.

### 10.2.4 Description Length

To find a most likely model $m$ given examples $Es$ – a model that maximizes $P(m \mid Es)$ – you can apply Bayes' rule, ignore the denominator (which doesn't depend on $m$), and so maximize $P(Es \mid m) * P(m)$; see formula (10.2) (page 460). Taking the negative of the logarithm (base 2), means you can minimize

$$-\log_2 P(Es \mid m) - \log_2 P(m).$$

This can be interpreted in terms of **information theory** (page 275). The term $-\log_2 P(Es \mid m)$ is the number of **bits** it takes to describe the data given the model $m$. The term $-\log_2 P(m)$ is the number of bits it takes to describe the model. A model that minimizes this sum is a **minimum description length (MDL)** model. The **MDL principle** is to choose the model that minimizes the number of bits it takes to describe both the model and the data given the model.

One way to think about the MDL principle is that the aim is to communicate the data as succinctly as possible. To communicate the data, first communicate the model, then communicate the data in terms of the model. The number of bits it takes to communicate the data using a model is the number of bits it takes to communicate the model plus the number of bits it takes to communicate the data in terms of the model.

As the logarithm function is monotonically increasing, the MAP model is the same as the MDL model. Choosing a model with the highest posterior probability is the same as choosing a model with a minimum description length.

The description length provides common units for probabilities and model complexity; they can both be described in terms of bits.

**Example 10.7** In Example 10.6 (page 471), the definition of the priors on decision trees was left unspecified. The notion of a description length provides a basis for assigning priors to decision trees.

One code for a tree for a Boolean output with Boolean input features might be as follows. A decision tree is either 0 followed by a fixed-length probability, or 1 followed by a bit string representing a condition (an input feature) followed by the tree when the condition is false followed by the tree for when the condition is true. The condition might take $\lceil \log_2 m \rceil$, where $m$ is the number of input features. The probability could either be a fixed-length bit string, or depend on the data (see below). See Exercise 10.8 (page 489).

It is often useful to approximate the description length of the model. One way to approximate the description length is to consider just representing the probabilistic parameters of the model. Let $|t|$ be the number of probabilistic parameters of the model $t$. For a decision tree with probabilities at the leaves, $|t|$ is the number of leaves. For a linear function or a neural network, $|t|$ is the number of numerical parameters.

Suppose $|Es|$ is the number of training examples. There are at most $|Es| + 1$ different probabilities the model needs to distinguish, because that probability is derived from the counts, and there can be from 0 to $|Es|$ examples with a particular value true in the dataset. It takes $\log_2(|Es| + 1) \approx \log_2(|Es|)$ bits to distinguish these probabilities. Thus, the problem of finding the MDL model can be approximated by minimizing

$$-\log_2 P(Es \mid t) + |t| * \log_2(|Es|).$$

This value is the **Bayesian information criteria (BIC)** score.

## 10.3 Unsupervised Learning

This chapter has so far considered supervised learning, where target features are observed in the training data. In **unsupervised learning**, the target features are not given in the training examples.

One general method for unsupervised learning is **clustering**, which partitions the examples into **clusters**. Each cluster predicts feature values for the examples in the cluster. The best clustering is the one that minimizes the prediction error, such as squared error or log loss.

Often the term *class* is used as a semantically meaningful term, but while you might want the clusters to be semantically meaningful, they are not always.

**Example 10.8** A diagnostic assistant may want to group treatments into groups that predict the desirable and undesirable effects of the treatment. The assistant may not want to give a patient a drug because similar drugs may have had disastrous effects on similar patients.

A tutoring agent may want to cluster students' learning behavior so that strategies that work for one member of a cluster may work for other members.

In **hard clustering**, each example is placed definitively in a cluster. The cluster is then used to predict the feature values of the example. The alternative to hard clustering is **soft clustering**, in which each example has a probability distribution over clusters. The prediction of the values for the features of an example is the weighted average of the predictions of the clusters the example is in, weighted by the probability of the example being in the cluster. Soft clustering is described in Section 10.3.2 (page 478).

### 10.3.1 *k*-Means

The ***k*-means algorithm** is used for hard clustering. The training examples, *Es*, and the number of clusters, *k*, are given as input. It requires the value of each feature to be a (real) number, so that differences in values make sense.

The algorithm constructs *k* clusters, a prediction of a value for each feature for each cluster, and an assignment of examples to clusters.

Suppose the input features, $X_1, \dots, X_n$, are observed for each example. Let $X_j(e)$ be the value of input feature $X_j$ for example $e$. Associate a cluster with each integer $c \in \{1, \dots, k\}$.

The $k$-means algorithm constructs

- a function $cluster : Es \rightarrow \{1, \dots, k\}$ that maps each example to a cluster (if $cluster(e) = c$, example $e$ is said to be in cluster $c$)
- a function $prediction(j, c)$ that returns the predicted value of each element of cluster $c$ on feature $X_j$.

Example $e$ is thus predicted to have value $prediction(j, cluster(e))$ for feature $X_j$.

The aim is to find the functions *cluster* and *prediction* that minimize the sum of **squared loss** (page 270):

$$\sum_{e \in Es} \sum_{j=1}^{n} \left(prediction(j, cluster(e)) - X_j(e)\right)^2 .$$

To minimize the squared loss, the prediction of a cluster should be the mean of the prediction of the examples in the cluster; see Figure 7.5 (page 277). Finding an optimal clustering is NP-hard. When there are only a few examples, it is possible to enumerate the assignments of examples to clusters. For more than a few examples, there are too many partitions of the examples into $k$ clusters for exhaustive search to be feasible.

The $k$-means algorithm iteratively improves the squared loss. Initially, it randomly assigns the examples to clusters. Then it carries out the following two steps:

- For each cluster $c$ and feature $X_j$, make $prediction(j, c)$ be the mean value of $X_j(e)$ for each example $e$ in cluster $c$:

$$\frac{\sum_{e:cluster(e)=c} X_j(e)}{|\{e : cluster(e) = c\}|}$$

  where the denominator is the number of examples in cluster $c$.

- Reassign each example to a cluster: assign each example $e$ to a cluster $c$ that minimizes

$$\sum_{j=1}^{n} \left(prediction(j, c) - X_j(e)\right)^2 .$$

These two steps are repeated until the second step does not change the assignment of any example.

An algorithm that implements $k$-means is shown in Figure 10.4 (page 475). It constructs **sufficient statistics** to compute the mean of each cluster for each feature, namely

- $cc[c]$ is the number of examples in cluster $c$
- $fs[j,c]$ is the sum of the value for $X_j(e)$ for examples in cluster $c$.

These are sufficient statistics because they contain all of the information from the data necessary to compute $cluster(e)$ and $prediction(j,c)$. The current values of $fs$ and $cc$ are used to determine the next values (in $fs\_new$ and $cc\_new$).

The random initialization could be assigning each example to a cluster at random, selecting $k$ points at random to be representative of the clusters, or assigning some, but not all, of the examples to construct the initial sufficient statistics. The latter two methods may be more useful if the dataset is large, as they avoid a pass through the whole dataset for initialization.

An assignment of examples to clusters is **stable** if an iteration of $k$-means does not change the assignment. Stability requires that *arg min* in the definition

```
procedure k-means(Xs, Es, k)
    Inputs
        Xs set of features, X = {X_1, ..., X_n}
        Es set of training examples
        k number of clusters
    Output
        cluster: function from examples to clusters
        predicion: function from feature and cluster to a value for that feature
    Local
        integer cc[c], cc_new[c]        ▷ old and new cluster count for cluster c
        real fs[j,c], fs_new[j,c]       ▷ sum of feature X_j for cluster c
        Boolean stable
    Initialize fs and cc randomly based on data
    define prediction(j,c) = fs[j,c]/cc[c]        ▷ estimate of X̂_j(c)
    define cluster(e) = arg min_c Σ_{j=1}^{n} (prediction(j,c) − X_j(e))^2
    repeat
        fs_new and cc_new initialized to be all zero
        for each example e ∈ Es do
            c := cluster(e)
            cc_new[c] += 1
            for each feature X_j ∈ Xs do
                fs_new[j,c] += X_j(e)
        stable := (fs_new = fs) and (cc_new = cc)
        fs := fs_new
        cc := cc_new
    until stable
    return cluster, prediction
```

Figure 10.4: $k$-Means for unsupervised learning

of *cluster* gives a consistent value for each example in cases where more than one cluster is minimal. This algorithm has reached a stable assignment when each example is assigned to the same cluster in one iteration as in the previous iteration. When this happens, *fs* and *cluster_count* do not change, and so the Boolean variable *stable* becomes *true*.

This algorithm will eventually converge to a stable local minimum. This is easy to see because the sum-of-squares error keeps reducing and there are only a finite number of reassignments. This algorithm often converges in a few iterations.

**Example 10.9** Suppose an agent has observed the $\langle X, Y\rangle$ pairs

$$\langle 0.7, 5.1\rangle,\ \langle 1.5, 6.1\rangle,\ \langle 2.1, 4.5\rangle,\ \langle 2.4, 5.5\rangle,\ \langle 3.1, 4.4\rangle,\ \langle 3.5, 5.1\rangle,\ \langle 4.5, 1.5\rangle,$$
$$\langle 5.2, 0.7\rangle,\ \langle 5.3, 1.8\rangle,\ \langle 6.2, 1.7\rangle,\ \langle 6.7, 2.5\rangle,\ \langle 8.5, 9.2\rangle,\ \langle 9.1, 9.7\rangle,\ \langle 9.5, 8.5\rangle.$$

These data points are plotted in Figure 10.5(a). The agent wants to cluster the data points into two clusters ($k = 2$).

In Figure 10.5(b), the points are randomly assigned into the clusters; one cluster is depicted as $+$ and the other as $*$. The mean of the points marked with $+$ is $\langle 4.6, 3.65\rangle$, shown with $\oplus$. The mean of the points marked with $*$ is $\langle 5.2, 6.15\rangle$, shown with $\circledast$.

In Figure 10.5(c), the points are reassigned according to the closer of the two means. After this reassignment, the mean of the points marked with $+$ is then $\langle 3.96, 3.27\rangle$. The mean of the points marked with $*$ is $\langle 7.15, 8.34\rangle$.

In Figure 10.5(d), the points are reassigned to the closest mean. This assignment is stable in that no further reassignment will change the assignment of the examples.

A different initial assignment to the points can give different clustering. One clustering that arises in this dataset is for the lower points (those with a $Y$-value less than 3) to be in one cluster, and for the other points to be in another cluster.

Running the algorithm with three clusters ($k = 3$) typically separates the data into the top-right cluster, the left-center cluster, and the lower cluster. However, there are other possible stable assignments that could be reached, such as having the top three points in two different clusters, and the other points in another cluster.

Some stable assignments may be better, in terms of sum-of-squares error, than other stable assignments. To find the best assignment, it is often useful to try multiple starting configurations, using a **random restart** (page 147) and selecting a stable assignment with the lowest sum-of-squares error. Note that any permutation of the labels of a stable assignment is also a stable assignment, so there are invariably multiple local and global minima.

One problem with the $k$-means algorithm is that it is sensitive to the relative scale of the dimensions. For example, if one feature is *height* in centimeters, another feature is *age*, and another is a binary ($\{0, 1\}$) feature, the different values need to be scaled so that they can be compared. How they are scaled relative to each other affects the clusters found. It is common to scale the dimensions to between 0 and 1 or with a mean of 0 and a variance of 1, but this assumes that all dimensions are relevant and independent of each other.

Finding an appropriate number of clusters is a classic problem in trading off model complexity and fit to data. One solution is to use the **Bayesian information criteria (BIC)** score (page 473), similar to its use in decision trees where the number of clusters is used instead of the number of leaves. While it is possible to construct $k+1$ clusters from $k$ clusters, the optimal division into three clusters, for example, may be quite different from the optimal division into two clusters.

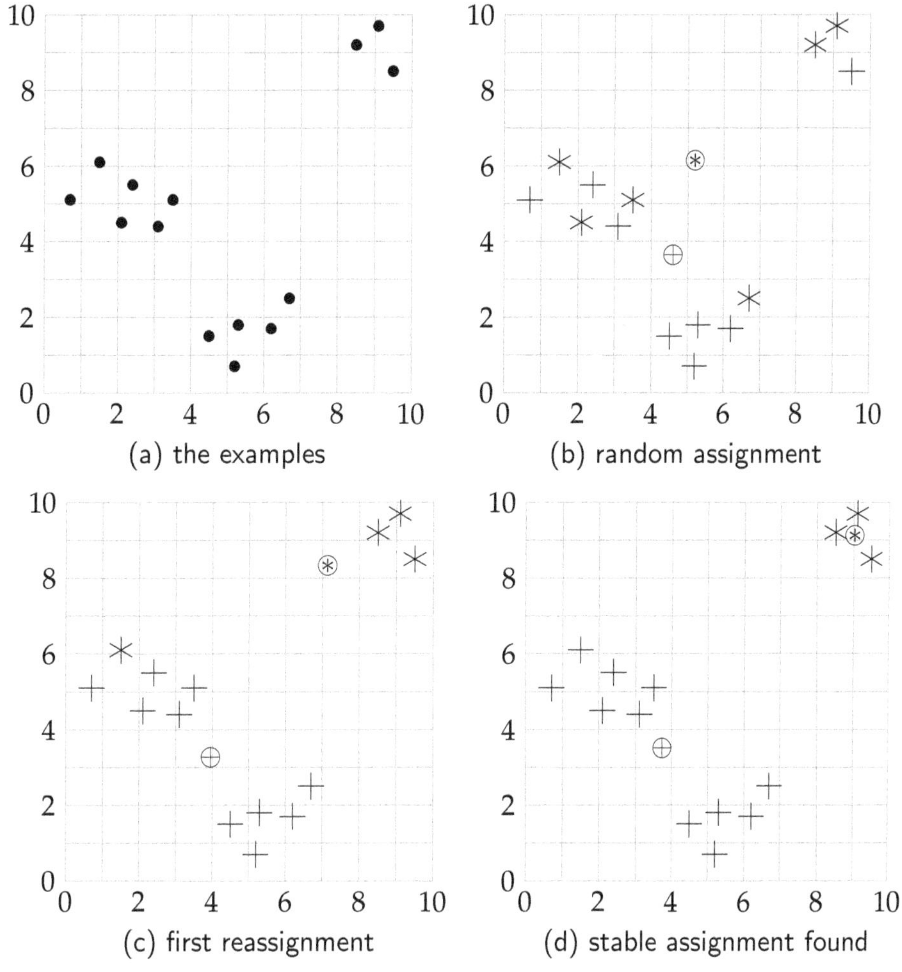


Figure 10.5: A trace of the $k$-means algorithm for $k = 2$ for Example 10.9

### 10.3.2 Expectation Maximization for Soft Clustering

A **hidden variable** or **latent variable** is a probabilistic variable that is not observed in a dataset. A Bayes classifier can be the basis for **unsupervised learning** by making the class a hidden variable.

The **expectation maximization (EM)** algorithm can be used to learn probabilistic models with hidden variables. Combined with a **naive Bayes classifier** (page 467), it does soft clustering, similar to the $k$-means algorithm, but where examples are probabilistically in clusters.

As in the $k$-means algorithm, the training examples and the number of clusters, $k$, are given as input.

Given the data, a naive Bayes model is constructed where there is a variable for each feature in the data and a hidden variable for the class. The class variable is the only parent of the other features. This is shown in Figure 10.6. The class variable has domain $\{1, 2, \ldots, k\}$, where $k$ is the number of classes. The probabilities needed for this model are the probability of the class $C$ and the probability of each feature given $C$. The aim of the EM algorithm is to learn probabilities that best fit the data.

The EM algorithm conceptually augments the data with a class feature, $C$, and a count column. Each original example gets mapped into $k$ augmented examples, one for each class. The counts for these examples are assigned so that they sum to 1.

For four features and three classes, the example $\langle X_1 = t, X_2 = f, X_3 = t, X_4 = t \rangle$ is mapped into the three tuples, shown in the table on the left of Figure 10.7 (page 479). EM works by iteratively determining the count from the model, and the model from the count.

The EM algorithm repeats the following two steps:

- **E step**. Update the augmented counts based on the probability distribution. For each example $\langle X_1 = v_1, \ldots, X_n = v_n \rangle$ in the original data, the count associated with $\langle X_1 = v_1, \ldots, X_n = v_n, C = c \rangle$ in the augmented data is updated to

$$P(C = c \mid X_1 = v_1, \ldots, X_n = v_n).$$

**Data**

| $X_1$ | $X_2$ | $X_3$ | $X_4$ |
|---|---|---|---|
| $t$ | $f$ | $t$ | $t$ |
| $f$ | $t$ | $t$ | $f$ |
| $f$ | $f$ | $t$ | $t$ |
| | ... | | |

**Model**

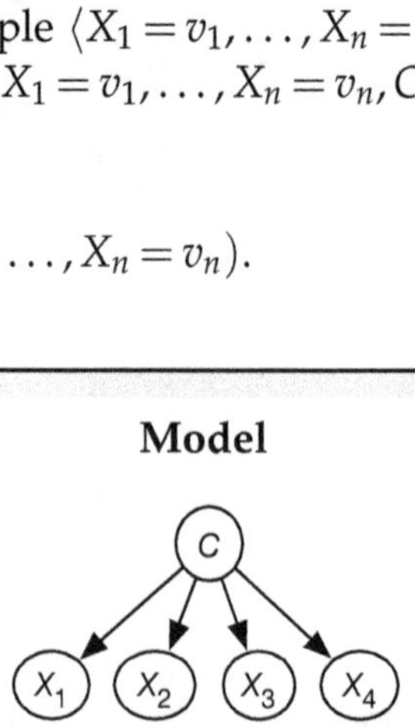


⇨ **Probabilities**

$P(C)$
$P(X_1 \mid C)$
$P(X_2 \mid C)$
$P(X_3 \mid C)$
$P(X_4 \mid C)$

Figure 10.6: EM algorithm: Bayes classifier with hidden class

This step involves probabilistic inference. If multiple examples have the same values for the input features, they can be treated together, with the probabilities multiplied by the number of examples. This is an **expectation** step because it computes the expected values.

- **M step**. Infer the probabilities for the model from the augmented data. Because the augmented data has values associated with all the variables, this is the same problem as learning probabilities from data in a naive Bayes classifier (page 467). This is a **maximization** step because it computes the maximum likelihood estimate or the maximum a posteriori probability (MAP) (page 460) estimate of the probability.

The EM algorithm starts with random probabilities or random counts. EM will converge to a local maximum of the likelihood of the data.

This algorithm returns a probabilistic model, which is used to classify an existing or new example. An example is classified using

$$P(C=c \mid X_1=v_1,\ldots,X_n=v_n) = \frac{P(C=c) * \prod_{i=1}^{n} P(X_i=v_i \mid C=c)}{\sum_{c'} P(C=c') * \prod_{i=1}^{n} P(X_i=v_i \mid C=c')}.$$

The algorithm does not need to store the augmented data, but can maintain a set of **sufficient statistics**, which is enough information to compute the required probabilities. Assuming categorical features, sufficient statistics for this algorithm are

- $cc$, the class count, a $k$-valued array such that $cc[c]$ is the sum of the counts of the examples in the augmented data with $class = c$
- $fc$, the feature count, a three-dimensional array; for $i$ from 1 to $n$, for each value $v$ in $domain(X_i)$, and for each class $c$, $fc[i, v, c]$ is the sum of the counts of the augmented examples $t$ with $X_i(t) = v$ and $class(t) = c$.

In each iteration, it sweeps through the data once to compute the sufficient statistics. The sufficient statistics from the previous iteration are used to infer the new sufficient statistics for the next iteration.

| $X_1$ | $X_2$ | $X_3$ | $X_4$ | $C$ | *Count* |
|---|---|---|---|---|---|
| ⋮ | ⋮ | ⋮ | ⋮ | ⋮ | ⋮ |
| *t* | *f* | *t* | *t* | 1 | 0.4 |
| *t* | *f* | *t* | *t* | 2 | 0.1 |
| *t* | *f* | *t* | *t* | 3 | 0.5 |
| ⋮ | ⋮ | ⋮ | ⋮ | ⋮ | ⋮ |

E-step ⟵

M-step ⟶

$P(C)$
$P(X_1 \mid C)$
$P(X_2 \mid C)$
$P(X_3 \mid C)$
$P(X_4 \mid C)$

Figure 10.7: EM algorithm for unsupervised learning

The probabilities required of the model can be computed from *cc* and *fc*:

$$P(C=c) = \frac{cc[c]}{|Es|}$$

where $|Es|$ is the number of examples in the original dataset (which is the same as the sum of the counts in the augmented dataset).

$$P(X_i=v \mid C=c) = \frac{fc[i,v,c]}{cc[c]}.$$

The algorithm of Figure 10.8 computes the sufficient statistics. Evaluating $P(C=c \mid X_1=v_1,\ldots,X_n=v_n)$ in line 17 relies on the counts in *cc* and *fc*. This algorithm has glossed over how to initialize the counts. One way is for $P(C \mid X_1=v_1,\ldots,X_n=v_n)$ to return a random distribution for the first iteration, so the counts come from the data. Alternatively, the counts can be assigned randomly before seeing any data. See Exercise 10.7 (page 488).

```
1: procedure EM(Xs, Es, k)
2:     Inputs
3:         Xs set of features, Xs = {X_1, ..., X_n}
4:         Es set of training examples
5:         k number of classes
6:     Output
7:         sufficient statistics for probabilistic model on X
8:     Local
9:         real cc[c], cc_new[c]                # old and new class count
10:        real fc[i,v,c], fc_new[i,v,c]        # old and new feature count
11:        real dc         # class probability for current example and class
12:        Boolean stable
13:    repeat
14:        cc_new[c] and fc_new[i,v,c] initialized to be all zero
15:        for each example ⟨v_1, ..., v_n⟩ ∈ Es do
16:            for each c ∈ [1,k] do
17:                dc := P(C=c | X_1=v_1, ..., X_n=v_n)
18:                cc_new[c] := cc_new[c] + dc
19:                for each i ∈ [1,n] do
20:                    fc_new[i,v_i,c] := fc_new[i,v_i,c] + dc
21:        stable := (cc ≈ cc_new) and (fc ≈ fc_new)
22:        cc := cc_new
23:        fc := fc_new
24:    until stable
25:    return cc,fc
```

Figure 10.8: EM for unsupervised learning

The algorithm will eventually converge when *cc* and *fc* do not change significantly in an iteration. The threshold for the approximately equal in line 21 can be tuned to trade off learning time and accuracy. An alternative is to run the algorithms for a fixed number of iterations.

**Example 10.10** Consider Figure 10.7 (page 479).

When example $\langle x_1, \neg x_2, x_3, x_4 \rangle$ is encountered in the dataset, the algorithm computes

$$\begin{aligned}
&P(C=c \mid x_1 \wedge \neg x_2 \wedge x_3 \wedge x_4) \\
&\quad \propto P(X_1=1 \mid C=c) * P(X_2=0 \mid C=c) * P(X_3=1 \mid C=c) \\
&\qquad * P(X_4=1 \mid C=c) * P(C=c) \\
&\quad = \frac{fc[1,1,c]}{cc[c]} * \frac{fc[2,0,c]}{cc[c]} * \frac{fc[3,1,c]}{cc[c]} * \frac{fc[4,1,c]}{cc[c]} * \frac{cc[c]}{|Es|} \\
&\quad \propto \frac{fc[1,1,c] * fc[2,0,c] * fc[3,1,c] * fc[4,1,c]}{cc[c]^3}
\end{aligned}$$

for each class $c$ and normalizes the results. Suppose the value computed for class 1 is 0.4, class 2 is 0.1, and class 3 is 0.5 (as in the augmented data in Figure 10.7). Then $cc\_new[1]$ is incremented by 0.4, $cc\_new[2]$ is incremented by 0.1, etc. Values $fc\_new[1,1,1], fc\_new[2,0,1]$, etc. are each incremented by 0.4. Next, $fc\_new[1,1,2], fc\_new[2,0,2]$ are each incremented by 0.1, etc.

Notice the similarity with the $k$-means algorithm. The E step (probabilistically) assigns examples to classes, and the M step determines what the classes predict.

As long as $k > 1$, EM, like $k$-means, virtually always has multiple local and global maxima. In particular, any permutation of the class labels will give the same probabilities. To try to find a global maximum, multiple restarts can be tried, and a model with the lowest log-likelihood returned.

## 10.4 Learning Belief Networks

A **belief network** (page 385) gives a probability distribution over a set of random variables. We cannot always expect an expert to be able to provide an accurate model; often we want to learn a network from data.

Learning a belief network from data has many variants, depending on how much prior information is known and how complete the dataset is. The complexity of learning depends on whether all of the variables are known (or need to be invented), whether the structure is given, and whether all variables are observed, which can vary by example.

The simplest case occurs when a learning agent is given the structure of the model and all variables have been observed. The agent must learn the conditional probabilities, $P(X_i \mid parents(X_i))$, for each variable $X_i$. Learning the conditional probabilities is an instance of **supervised learning** (page 262), where $X_i$ is the target feature and the parents of $X_i$ are the input features. Any of the methods of Chapter 7, Chapter 8, or Section 10.1 (page 459) can be used to learn the conditional probabilities.

### 10.4.1 Hidden Variables

The next simplest case is where the model is given, but not all variables are observed. A **hidden variable** or a **latent variable** is a variable in a belief network whose value is not observed for any of the examples. That is, there is no column in the data corresponding to that variable.

**Example 10.11** Figure 10.9 shows a typical case. Assume that all the variables are binary with domain $\{f, t\}$. The model contains a hidden variable $E$ that is in the model but not the dataset. The aim is to learn the parameters of the model that includes the hidden variable $E$. There are 10 parameters to learn.

Note that, if $E$ was not part of the model, the algorithm would have to learn $P(A)$, $P(B)$, $P(C \mid AB)$, $P(D \mid ABC)$, which has 14 parameters. The reason for introducing hidden variables is, paradoxically, to make the model simpler and, therefore, less prone to overfitting.

The **expectation maximization (EM)** algorithm for learning belief networks with hidden variables is essentially the same as the EM algorithm for clustering (page 478). The E step, depicted in Figure 10.10 (page 483), involves probabilistic inference for each example to infer the probability distribution of the hidden variable(s) given the observed variables for that example. The M step of inferring the probabilities of the model from the augmented data is the same as in the fully observable case discussed in the previous section, but, in the augmented data, the counts are not necessarily integers.

### 10.4.2 Missing Data

Data can be incomplete in ways other than having an unobserved variable. A dataset could simply be missing the values of some variables for some of the examples. When some of the values of the variables are missing, one must be

**Model**

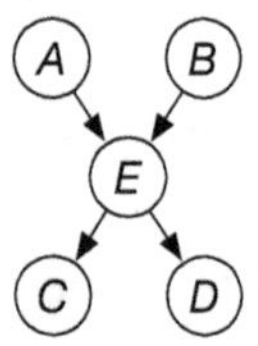


**Data**

| $A$ | $B$ | $C$ | $D$ |
|---|---|---|---|
| $t$ | $f$ | $t$ | $t$ |
| $f$ | $t$ | $t$ | $t$ |
| $t$ | $t$ | $f$ | $t$ |
| | ... | | |

➪ **Probabilities**

$P(A)$
$P(B)$
$P(E \mid A, B)$
$P(C \mid E)$
$P(D \mid E)$

Figure 10.9: Deriving probabilities with a hidden variable

very careful in using the dataset because the missing data may be correlated with the phenomenon of interest.

A simple case is when only categorical variables with no parents that are not themselves queried have missing values. A probability distribution from which other variables can be queried can be modeled by adding an extra value "missing" to the domain of the variables with missing values. This can also be modeled by having a 0/1 indicator variable (page 286) for each value in the domain of the variable, where all of the indicator variables are 0 if the value is missing.

**Example 10.12** Consider a case where someone volunteers information about themself. If someone has a sibling, they are likely to volunteer that; if they do not have a sibling, it is unusual for them to state that. Similarly, if someone doesn't have anxiety, they are unlikely to mention anxiety, but might mention that they are not anxious. There are too many ailments and other conditions that humans have for them to mention the ones they don't have. Suppose there is a model of when someone fears isolation ($f$) that depends on whether they have a sibling ($S$) and whether they have anxiety ($A$). A logistic regression model could be

$$P(f) = sigmoid(w_0 + w_1 * (S = true) + w_2 * (S = false) \\ + w_3 * (A = true) + w_4 * (A = false))$$

where $S = true$ has value 1 when $S$ is reported to be true, and $S = false$ has value 1 when $S$ is reported to be false, and both have value 0 when the value is missing. The learned bias, $w_0$, is the value used when both $S$ and $A$ are missing.

In general, missing data cannot be ignored, as in the following example.

**Example 10.13** Suppose there is a drug that is a (claimed) treatment for a disease that does not actually affect the disease or its symptoms. All it does is make sick people sicker. Suppose patients were randomly assigned to the

| $A$ | $B$ | $C$ | $D$ | $E$ | Count |
|---|---|---|---|---|---|
| ⋮ | ⋮ | ⋮ | ⋮ | ⋮ | ⋮ |
| $t$ | $f$ | $t$ | $t$ | $t$ | 0.71 |
| $t$ | $f$ | $t$ | $t$ | $f$ | 0.29 |
| $f$ | $f$ | $t$ | $t$ | $f$ | 4.2 |
| ⋮ | ⋮ | ⋮ | ⋮ | ⋮ | ⋮ |
| $f$ | $t$ | $t$ | $t$ | $f$ | 2.3 |

E-step $\longleftarrow$

M-step $\longrightarrow$

$P(A)$
$P(B)$
$P(E \mid A, B)$
$P(C \mid E)$
$P(D \mid E)$

Figure 10.10: EM algorithm for belief networks with hidden variables; $E$ is a hidden variable. The E-step computes $P(E \mid A, B, C, D)$ for each example, and the M-step learns probabilities from complete data treatment, but the sickest people dropped out of the study, because they became too sick to participate. The sick people who took the treatment were sicker and so would drop out at a faster rate than the sick people who did not take the treatment. Thus, if the patients with missing data are ignored, it looks like the treatment works; there are fewer sick people among the people who took the treatment and remained in the study!

Handling missing data requires more than a probabilistic model that models correlation. It requires a causal model of how the data is missing; see Section 11.2 (page 497).

### 10.4.3 Structure Learning

Suppose a learning agent has complete data and no hidden variables, but is not given the structure of the belief network. This is the setting for **structure learning** of belief networks.

There are two main approaches to structure learning:

- The first is to use the definition of a belief network in terms of conditional independence (page 385). Given a total ordering of variables, the parents of a variable $X$ are defined to be a subset of the predecessors of $X$ in the total ordering that render the other predecessors independent of $X$. Using the definition directly has two main challenges: the first is to determine the best total ordering; the second is to find a way to measure independence. It is difficult to determine conditional independence when there is limited data.
- The second method is to have a score for networks, for example, using the MAP model (page 460), which takes into account fit to the data and model complexity. Given such a measure, it is feasible to search for the structure that minimizes this error.

This section presents the second method, often called a **search and score** method.

Assume that the data is a set $Es$ of examples, where each example has a value for each variable. The aim of the search and score method is to choose a model $m$ that maximizes

$$P(m \mid Es) \propto P(Es \mid m) * P(m).$$

The likelihood, $P(Es \mid m)$, is the product of the probability of each example. Using the product decomposition, the product of each example given the model is the product of the probability of each variable given its parents in the model. Thus

$$\begin{aligned} P(Es \mid m) * P(m) &= \left( \prod_{e \in Es} P(e \mid m) \right) * P(m) \\ &= \left( \prod_{e \in Es} \prod_{X_i} P^e_m(X_i \mid par(X_i, m)) \right) * P(m) \end{aligned}$$

where $par(X_i, m)$ denotes the parents of $X_i$ in the model $m$, and $P^e_m(\cdot)$ denotes the probability of example $e$ as specified in the model $m$.

This is maximized when its logarithm is maximized. When taking logarithms, products become sums:

$$\log P(Es \mid m) + \log P(m) = \left( \sum_{e \in Es} \sum_{X_i} \log P^e_m(X_i \mid par(X_i, m)) \right) + \log P(m).$$

To make this approach feasible, assume that the prior probability of the model decomposes into components for each variable. That is, we assume the probability of the model decomposes into a product of probabilities of local models for each variable. Let $m(X_i)$ be the local model for variable $X_i$.

Thus, we want to maximize

$$\begin{aligned} &\left( \sum_{e \in Es} \sum_{X_i} \log P^e_m(X_i \mid par(X_i, m)) \right) + \sum_{X_i} \log P(m(X_i)) \\ &\quad = \sum_{X_i} \left( \sum_{e \in Es} \log P^e_m(X_i \mid par(X_i, m)) \right) + \sum_{X_i} \log P(m(X_i)) \\ &\quad = \sum_{X_i} \left( \sum_{e \in Es} \log P^e_m(X_i \mid par(X_i, m)) + \log P(m(X_i)) \right). \end{aligned}$$

Each variable could be optimized separately, except for the requirement that a belief network is acyclic. However, if you had a total ordering of the variables, there is an independent supervised learning problem to predict the probability of each variable given the predecessors in the total ordering. To approximate $\log P(m(X_i))$, the BIC score (page 473) can be used. To find a good total ordering of the variables, a learning agent could search over total orderings, using search techniques such as local search (page 146) or branch-and-bound search (page 105).

### 10.4.4 General Case of Belief Network Learning

The general case has unknown structure, hidden variables, and missing data; we may not even know which variables should be part of the model. Two main problems arise. The first is the problem of missing data discussed earlier. The second is computational; although there may be a well-defined search space, it is prohibitively large to try all combinations of variable ordering and hidden variables. If one only considers hidden variables that simplify the model (as is reasonable), the search space is finite, but enormous.

One can either select the best model (e.g., the model with the highest posterior probability) or average over all models. Averaging over all models gives better predictions, but it is difficult to explain to a person who may have to understand or justify the model.

## 10.5 Social Impact

Most modern mail systems use **spam filters** to filter out unwanted email. A common form of spam filtering analyzes the content of the message and the subject to determine the probability that the email should be classified as junk. What is junk to one person might not be junk to another; determining what is junk requires feedback from the user. A user can only give a limited amount of feedback, so data-hungry approaches, like deep learning, trained on the user's feedback are not appropriate.

A standard way to implement content-based spam filtering is to use a naive Bayes classifier (page 467), where the classification is Boolean (spam or not spam). The features can include words, phrases, capitalization, and punctuation. Because the unnormalized probability is a product and taking logs gives a sum, the decision can be seen as a sum of weights for each feature that has a different prediction for spam and non-spam.

The advantage of thinking about this in terms of probability is that it enables learning from user feedback. In particular, having an informed prior, and using, for example, beta (page 464) or Dirichlet (page 465) distributions, allows the model to work initially with no feedback, using the priors, and then to learn from personalized feedback. How quickly the model adapts to new data is controlled by the prior counts, the sum of which is an **expected sample size**. The expected sample size controls how much new experience is weighted compared to the prior model, and can be tuned for good user experience. One way to think about this is that it can use data from everyone (in the prior) but weight personalized data for each user much more.

There is no perfect way to control spam when there is an adversary trying to thwart the spam filter. The issue of acting with adversaries (and other agents) is explored more in Chapter 14.

## 10.6 Review

The main points you should have learned from this chapter are:

- Bayes' rule provides a way to incorporate prior knowledge into learning and a way to trade off fit-to-data and model complexity.
- Bayesian learning replaces making a prediction from the best model with finding a prediction by averaging over all of the models conditioned on the data.
- EM and $k$-means are iterative methods for unsupervised learning that learn the parameters of models with hidden variables (including the case in which the classification is hidden).
- The probabilities and the structure of belief networks can be learned from complete data. The probabilities can be derived from counts. The structure can be learned by searching for the best model given the data.

- Missing values cannot just be ignored. Why values are missing is important to be modeled and often needs to be determined from extra information.
- Bayesian techniques can help solve the practical problem of eliminating spam email.

## 10.7 References and Further Reading

Bayesian learning is overviewed by Jaynes [2003], MacKay [2003], Howson and Urbach [2006], and Ghahramani [2015]. See also books on Bayesian statistics such as Gelman et al. [2020], [McElreath, 2020], or, for more rigor, Gelman et al. [2013]. Murphy [2022, 2023] provides a comprehensive coverage of the topics of this chapter.

Bayes classifiers are discussed by Duda et al. [2001] and Langley et al. [1992]. TAN networks are described by Friedman et al. [1997], who also discuss how the naive Bayes classifier can be generalized to allow for more appropriate independence assumptions. Latent tree models are described by Zhang [2004]. Bayesian learning of decision trees is described in Buntine [1992]. Grünwald [2007] discusses the MDL principle.

The $k$-means algorithm was invented by 1957 by Lloyd [1982]. Schubert [2022] discusses how to choose the number of clusters. EM is due to Dempster et al. [1977]. Unsupervised learning is discussed by Cheeseman et al. [1988].

For an overview of learning belief networks, see Heckerman [1999], Darwiche [2009], and Koller and Friedman [2009]. The Bayesian information criteria is due to Schwarz [1978]. Our definition (page 473) is slightly different; the definition of Schwarz is justified by a more complex Bayesian argument.

## 10.8 Exercises

**Exercise 10.1** Try to construct an artificial example where a naive Bayes classifier can give divide-by-zero error in test cases when using empirical frequencies as probabilities. Specify the network and the (non-empty) training examples. [Hint: You can do it with two features, say $A$ and $B$, and a binary classification, say $C$, that has domain $\{0, 1\}$. Construct a dataset where the empirical probabilities give $P(a|C = 0) = 0$ and $P(b|C = 1) = 0$.] What observation is inconsistent with the model?

**Exercise 10.2** Consider designing a help system based on Example 10.5 (page 469). Discuss how your implementation can handle the following issues, and if it cannot, whether it is a major problem.

(a) What should be the initial $u_{ij}$ counts? Where might this information be obtained?

(b) What if the most likely page is not the correct page?

(c) What if users cannot find the correct page?

(d) What if users mistakenly think they have the correct page?
(e) Can some pages never be found?
(f) What should it do with common words that are independent of the help page?
(g) What about words that affect the meaning, such as "not"?
(h) How should it handle words it has never seen before?
(i) How can new help pages be incorporated?

**Exercise 10.3** Consider the help system of Example 10.5 (page 469).

(a) Using the $c_1$ and $w_{ij}$ counts in that example, give the probability of $P(H \mid q)$, the distribution over help pages given $q$, the set of words in a user query. Note that this probability needs to also depend on the words not in $q$.
(b) How can this be computed in time proportional to the number of words in $q$, rather than the size of the vocabulary. [Hint: Consider the probability of $H$ given no words were in the query – which is *not* the prior of $H$ – and then adjust for the words in the query.]

**Exercise 10.4** Suppose you have designed a help system based on Example 10.5 (page 469) and much of the underlying system which the help pages are about has changed. You are now very unsure about which help pages will be requested, but you may have a good model of which words will be used given the help page. How can the help system be changed to take this into account? [Hint: You may need different counts for $P(h_i)$ and $P(w_j \mid h_i)$.]

**Exercise 10.5** Consider the unsupervised data of Figure 10.5 (page 477).

(a) How many different stable assignments of examples to classes does the $k$-means algorithm find when $k = 2$? [Hint: Try running the algorithm on the data with a number of different starting points, but also think about what assignments of examples to classes are stable.] Do not count permutations of the labels as different assignments.
(b) Estimate how many different stable assignments there are when $k = 3$.
(c) Estimate many different stable assignments there are when $k = 4$.
(d) Why might someone suggest that three is the natural number of classes in this example? Give a definition for "natural" number of classes, and use this data to justify the definition.

**Exercise 10.6** Suppose the $k$-means algorithm is run for an increasing sequence of values for $k$, and that it is run for a number of times for each $k$ to find the assignment with a global minimum error. Is it possible that a number of values of $k$ exist for which the error plateaus and then has a large improvement (e.g., when the errors for $k = 3$, $k = 4$, and $k = 5$ are about the same, but the error for $k = 6$ is much lower)? If so, give an example. If not, explain why.

**Exercise 10.7** To initialize the EM algorithm in Figure 10.8 (page 480) consider two alternatives:

(a) allow $P$ to return a random distribution the first time through the loop
(b) initialize $cc$ and $fc$ to random values.

By running the algorithm on some datasets, determine which, if any, of these alternatives is better in terms of log loss (page 276) of the training data, as a function of the number of loops through the dataset. Does it matter if *cc* and *fc* are not consistent with the semantics (counts that should be equal are not)?

**Exercise 10.8** Consider the code for decision trees in Example 10.7 (page 472), and the Bayesian information criteria (BIC) (page 473) for decision trees. Consider the three cases: the BIC, the decision tree code with a 32-bit representation for probabilities, and the decision tree code that uses $\log_2(|Es|)$ bits to represent a probability.

(a) For each case, how many extra bits does introducing a split incur?
(b) Which method has the biggest preference for smaller trees?
(c) For each of the three methods, is there a value of $\gamma$ in the decision tree learner (Figure 7.9 (page 284)) that corresponds to that method? If so, give it, if not, why not?

# Chapter 11

# Causality

> *The word* cause *is not in the vocabulary of standard probability theory. It is an embarrassing yet inescapable fact that probability theory, the official mathematical language of many empirical sciences, does not permit us to express sentences such as "Mud does not cause rain"; all we can say are that the two events are mutually correlated, or dependent – meaning that if we find one, we can expect to encounter the other. Scientists seeking causal explanations for complex phenomenon or rationales for policy decisions must therefore supplement the language of probability with a vocabulary for causality, one in which the symbolic representation for "Mud does not cause rain" is distinct from the symbolic representation for "Mud is independent of rain". Oddly, such distinctions have yet to be incorporated into standard scientific analysis.*
>
> – Judea Pearl [2009]

In the example from Pearl (above), mud and rain are correlated, but the relationship between mud and rain is not symmetric. Creating mud (e.g., by pouring water on dirt) does not make rain. However, if you were to cause rain (e.g., by seeding clouds), mud will result. There is a causal relationship between mud and rain: rain causes mud, and mud does not cause rain. This causal relationship holds even when you ignore the other necessary conditions, such as the existence of dirt, and the absence of a cover on the dirt to prevent it getting wet. It also depends on the level of abstraction: arguably, rain causes dirt to get wet, which in turn makes mud.

It is known that ice-cream consumption and drowning deaths are positively correlated. But that doesn't mean that if one wanted to reduce drowning deaths one should ban ice-cream.

As another example, taking marijuana and taking hard drugs are positively correlated. This has led to the theory that marijuana is a gateway drug; taking marijuana leads to harder drugs. But the correlation doesn't tell us what happens when you intervene to force taking marijuana false or true. It is indeed possible that the use of hard drugs will decrease if you give people marijuana. You can get indirect evidence from places where marijuana has been legalized, but you can't determine the causal relationship just from passive observation, without making assumptions that go beyond the data.

A **causal model** (page 218) is a model that predicts the effects of interventions, where an **intervention** on a variable is the action of setting the variable to a particular value, in some way other than manipulating other variables in the model. For example, when a light is connected to a switch, as in Example 5.34 (page 218), intervening to make the light off might involve unscrewing the bulb or breaking it, if these are not modeled, but would not include flipping the switch, if the switch position is part of the model.

A causal model is obtained from observational data, interventional data, and modeling assumptions. Observational data alone is not sufficient to determine causality; knowing a probability distribution is not enough information to determine the consequences of actions. Drug manufacturers, for example, spend billions of dollars on controlled randomized trials in order to determine causality; namely, the effects of giving someone a drug.

This is *not* referring to "the (unique) cause" of an effect, but all of the factors that together lead to the effect. An effect typically has multiple causes. For example, to cause mud, you need water, dirt, and for them to actually mix. None by itself is *the* cause. The variables in a causal model need not be observable; most of the challenges arise because some variables cannot be observed.

## 11.1 Probabilistic Causal Models

A **direct cause** of variable $Y$ is a variable $X$ such that intervening on $X$, holding all other variables constant, can affect $Y$. For example, if making rain would affect whether there is mud, with all other variables fixed, then rain is a direct cause of mud. If making mud does not affect rain, then mud is not a direct cause of rain.

Assume that there are no causal cycles. Examples of apparent causal cycles, such as poverty causes sickness and sickness causes poverty, are handled by considering time – each variable is about an event at some time; sickness at one time causes poverty at a future time, and poverty at one time causes sickness at future times.

Suppose you knew the direct causes of a variable and have not made any observations. The only way to affect the variable is to intervene on that variable or affect one of its direct causes. A variable is not independent of the variables it eventually causes, but is independent of the other variables given its direct causes. This is exactly the independence assumption of a belief network (page 385) when the causes of each variable are before it in the total ordering of variables; thus, a belief network is an appropriate representation for a causal model. All of the reasoning in a belief network followed from that independence, and so is applicable to causal models.

A **structural causal model** defines a **causal mechanism** for each modeled variable. A causal mechanism defines a conditional probability for a variable given its parents, where the probability of the variable when the parents are set to some values by intervention is the same as it is when the parents are observed to have those values. For example, $P(light\_on \mid switch\_up)$ is a causal mechanism if the probability that the light is on is the same when intervening to make the light switch up as it is when observing it is up. $P(switch\_up \mid light\_off)$ would not be a causal mechanism if observing the light off results in a different belief about the switch than intervening to make the light off. Any of the representations for conditional probability (page 394) can be used to represent causal mechanisms. A structural causal model defines a **causal network**, a belief network where the probability of each variable given its parents is the same when the parents are observed as when they are intervened on.

The following example is based on Pearl [2009, p. 15]:

**Example 11.1** Suppose some grass can be wet because of rain or a sprinkler. Whether it rains depends on the season. Whether the sprinkler was on also depends on the season. Wet grass causes it to be shiny and causes my shoes to get wet. A belief network for this story is given in Figure 11.1(a). Observing the sprinkler is on (or off) tells us something about the season (e.g., the sprinkler is more likely to be on during the dry season than the wet season), which in turn affects our belief in rain.

However, turning the sprinkler on or off does not affect (our belief in) the season. To model this intervention, replace the mechanism for the sprinkler,

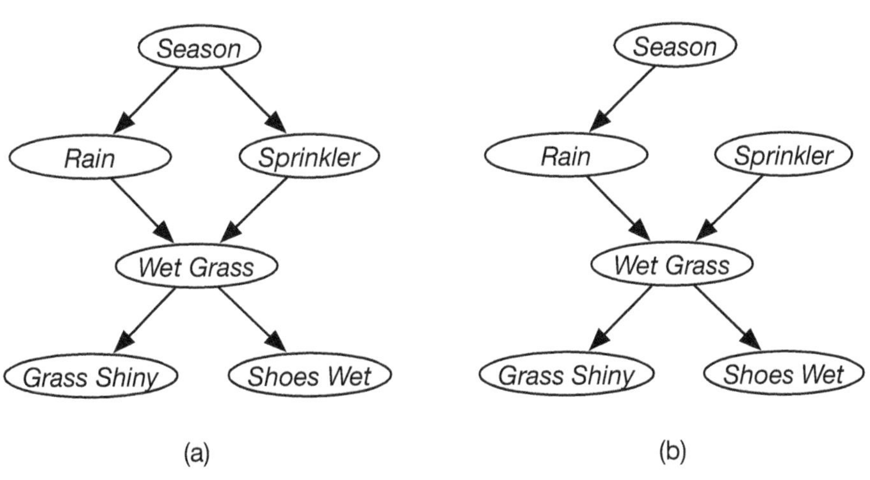


Figure 11.1: Causal network causes of wet grass (a) and intervening by turning on the sprinkler (b)

namely $P(Sprinkler \mid Season)$, with $P(Sprinkler)$, a deterministic conditional probability distribution (with probability 1 that the sprinkler is in the position selected), resulting in the network of Figure 11.1(b). This has the same probabilities for the season and rain as in (a) with no observations, but different probabilities for the remaining variables, as the probability the sprinkler is on has changed.

**Example 11.2** As discussed at the start of this chapter, taking marijuana and taking hard drugs are positively correlated. One possible causal relationship is given in Figure 11.2. A parametrization for this that fits the story below is given at AIPython (aipython.org). The side-effects may be ill effects or satisfying curiosity, both of which (for the point of this example) may decrease the appetite for hard drugs. Observing taking marijuana increases the probability of being drug prone and having side-effects, which in turn can increase the probability that the person takes hard drugs. This means that taking marijuana and taking hard drugs would be positively correlated. However, intervening to give someone marijuana would only increase the probability of side-effects (providing no information about whether they are drug prone), which in turn may decrease the probability that they take hard drugs. Similarly, depriving someone of marijuana (which would be an intervention making taking marijuana false) would increase the probability that they take hard drugs. You could debate whether this is a reasonable model, but with only observational data about the correlation between taking marijuana and taking hard drugs, it is impossible to infer the effect of intervening on taking marijuana.

### 11.1.1 Do-notation

The **do-notation** adds interventions to the language of probability:

$$P(x \mid do(z), y)$$

where $x$, $y$, and $z$ are propositions (possibly using complex formulas including conjunction) is the probability that $x$ is true after doing $z$ and then observing $y$.

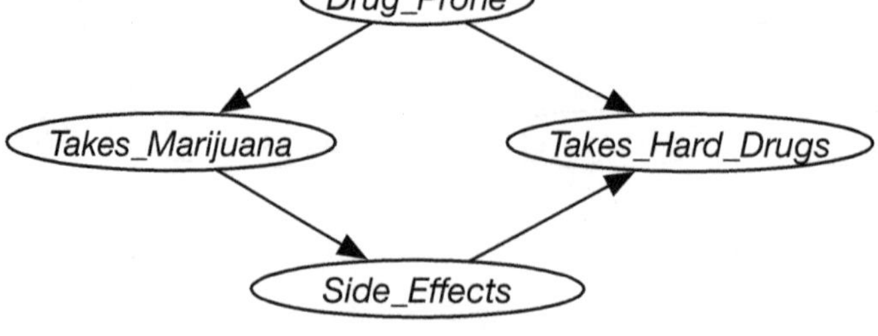


Figure 11.2: Possible causal graph for marijuana as a gateway drug

(Intervening after observing is counterfactual reasoning (page 508) because the intervention could make the observation no longer true.)

**Example 11.3** Consider Example 11.1 (page 493), with the belief network of Figure 11.1(a) (page 493). The probability that the shoes are wet given the sprinkler is (observed to be) on is

$$P(\mathit{shoes\_wet} \mid \mathit{sprinkler})$$

which can be answered with standard probabilistic inference, as covered in Chapter 9. Observing the sprinkler is on can provide information about the season; *Sprinkler* and *Season* have an arc between them in Figure 11.1(a).

The probability that shoes are wet given you turned the sprinkler on

$$P(\mathit{shoes\_wet} \mid do(\mathit{sprinkler}))$$

can be answered using probabilistic inference in the network of Figure 11.1(b) conditioned on $\mathit{Sprinkler} = \mathit{true}$. Intervening on *Sprinkler* has no effect on *Season*, because they are independent in this network.

The probability that the shoes are wet given that you turned the sprinkler on and then observed the grass was not shiny is given by

$$P(\mathit{shoes\_wet} \mid do(\mathit{sprinkler}),\ \neg \mathit{grass\_shiny})$$

which can be answered by conditioning on *sprinkler* and $\neg$*grass_shiny*, and querying *Shoes_wet* in the graph of Figure 11.1(b).

The use of the do-notation allows you to ask questions about the manipulated graphs in terms of the original graph.

### 11.1.2 D-separation

The definition of a belief network – each variable is independent of the variables that are not its descendants given its parents – implies independencies among the variables. The graphical criterion used to determine independence is called **d-separation**.

In a belief network, there are three ways two arcs can meet at a node, as shown in Figure 11.3 (page 496), where an arc involving $A$ and $B$ meets an arc involving $B$ and $C$. Assuming that all arrows represent true dependency (the conditional probabilities do not imply more independencies than the graph):

(a) In a chain ($A \rightarrow B \rightarrow C$), $A$ and $C$ are dependent if $B$ is not observed, and are independent given $B$. This is the same independence as the chain in the opposite direction ($A \leftarrow B \leftarrow C$).

(b) In a fork ($A \leftarrow B \rightarrow C$), $A$ and $C$ are dependent if $B$ is not observed, and are independent given $B$. This is the same independence structure as the chain; the chain and fork cannot be distinguished by observational data.

(c) In a collider ($A \rightarrow B \leftarrow C$), $A$ and $C$ are dependent given $B$ or one of its descendants. $A$ and $C$ are independent if $B$ and none of its descendants are observed.

Consider a path $p$ between two nodes in a directed acyclic graph, where the path can follow arcs in either direction. Recall that a path (page 84) is a sequence of nodes where adjacent nodes in the sequence are connected by an arc. A set of nodes $Z$ **blocks** path $p$ if and only if

- $p$ contains a chain ($A \rightarrow B \rightarrow C$ or $A \leftarrow B \leftarrow C$) or a fork ($A \leftarrow B \rightarrow C$) such that $B$ is in $Z$, or
- $p$ contains a collider ($A \rightarrow B \leftarrow C$) such that $B$ is *not* in $Z$ and no descendant of $B$ is in $Z$.

Nodes $X$ and $Y$ are **d-separated** by nodes $Z$ if $Z$ blocks every path from $X$ to $Y$.

**Example 11.4** Consider the belief network of Figure 11.4. There are two paths between $X$ and $Y$, both of which must be blocked for $X$ and $Y$ to be d-separated.

- $X$ and $Y$ are not d-separated by $\{\}$ because the top path is not blocked.
- $X$ and $Y$ are d-separated by $\{K\}$ because both paths are blocked

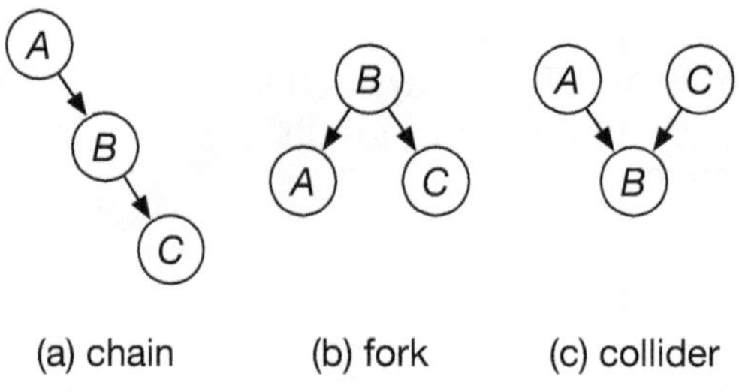


Figure 11.3: Three types of meetings between arcs

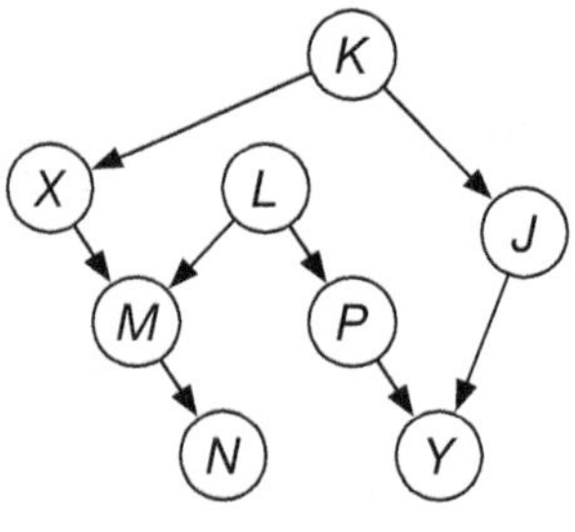


Figure 11.4: A belief network to demonstrate d-separation

- $X$ and $Y$ are not d-separated by $\{K, N\}$ because the bottom path is not blocked because $N$ is observed.
- $X$ and $Y$ are d-separated by $\{K, N, P\}$ because both paths are blocked.

These independencies can be determined just from the graphical structure without considering the conditional distributions.

It can be proved that in a belief network, $X$ and $Y$ are independent given $Z$ for all conditional probability distributions if and only if $X$ and $Y$ are d-separated by $Z$.

There can be independencies that hold even when d-separation doesn't hold, due to the actual numbers in the conditional distributions. However, these are unstable in that changing the distribution slightly makes the variables dependent.

## 11.2 Missing Data

When data is missing some values for some features, the missing data cannot be ignored. Example 10.13 (page 483) gives an example where ignoring missing data leads to wrong conclusions. Making inference from missing data is a causality problem, as it cannot be solved by observation, but requires a causal model.

A **missingness graph**, or ***m*-graph** for short, is used to model data where some values might be missing. Start with a belief network model of the domain. In the *m*-graph, all variables in the original graph exist with the same parents. For each variable $V$ that could be observed with some values missing, the *m*-graph contains two extra variables:

- $M\_V$, a Boolean variable that is true when $V$'s value is missing. The parents of this node can be whatever variables the missingness is assumed to depend on.
- A variable $V^*$, with domain $dom(V) \cup \{missing\}$, where *missing* is a new value (not in the domain of $V$). The only parents of $V^*$ are $V$ and $M\_V$. The conditional probability table contains only 0 and 1, with the 1s being

$$P(V^* = missing \mid M\_V = true) = 1$$
$$P(V^* = v \mid M\_V = false \land V = v) = 1.$$

If the value of $V$ is observed to be $v$, then $V^* = v$ is conditioned on. If the value for $V$ is missing, $V^* = missing$ is conditioned on. Note that $V^*$ is *always* observed and conditioned on, and $V$ is never conditioned on, in this augmented model. When modeling a domain, the parents of $M\_V$ specify what the missingness depends on.

**Example 11.5** Example 10.13 (page 483) gives a problematic case of a drug that just makes people sicker and so drop out, giving missing data. A graphical model for it is shown in Figure 11.5. Assume *Take_drug* is Boolean and the domains of *Sick_before* and *Sick_after* are $\{well, sick, very\_sick\}$. Then the domain of *Sick_after** is $\{well, sick, very\_sick, missing\}$. The variable *M_Sick_after* is Boolean.

Suppose there is a dataset from which to learn, with *Sick_before* and *Take_drug* observed for each example, and some examples have *Sick_after* observed and some have it missing. To condition the *m*-graph on an example, all of the variables except *Sick_after* are conditioned on. *Sick_after** has the value of *Sick_after* when it is observed, and has value *missing* otherwise.

You might think that you can learn the missing data using expectation maximization (EM) (page 482), with *Sick_after* as a hidden variable. There are, however, many probability distributions that are consistent with the data. All of the missing cases could have value *well* for *Sick_after*, or they all could be *very_sick*; you can't tell from the data. EM can converge to any one of these distributions that are consistent with the data. Thus, although EM may converge, it does not converge to something that makes predictions that can be trusted.

To determine appropriate model parameters, one should find some data about the relationship between *Sick_after* and *M_Sick_after*. When doing a human study, the designers of the study need to try to find out why people dropped out of the study. These cases cannot just be ignored.

A distribution is **recoverable** or **identifiable** from missing data if the distribution can be accurately measured from the data, even with parts of the data missing. Whether a distribution is recoverable is a property of the underlying graph. A distribution that is not recoverable cannot be reconstructed from observational data, no matter how large the dataset. The distribution in Example 11.5 is not recoverable.

Data is **missing completely at random (MCAR)** if $V$ and $M\_V$ are independent. If the data is missing completely at random, the examples with missing values can be ignored. This is a strong assumption that rarely occurs in practice, but is often implicitly assumed when missingness is ignored.

A weaker assumption is that a variable $Y$ is **missing at random (MAR)**, which occurs when $Y$ is independent of $M\_Y$ given the observed variables $V_o$. That is, when $P(Y \mid V_o, M\_Y) = P(Y \mid V_o)$. This occurs when the reason the

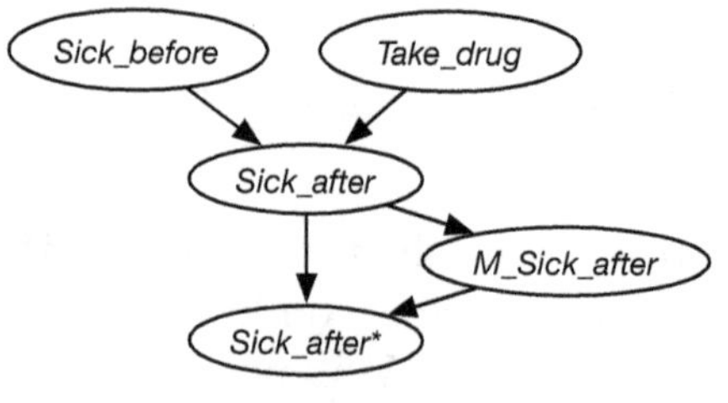


Figure 11.5: Missingness graph for Example 11.5

data is missing can be observed. The distribution over $Y$ and the observed variables is recoverable by $P(Y, V_o) = P(Y \mid V_o, M\_Y = \mathit{false}) P(V_o)$. Thus, the non-missing data is used to estimate $P(Y \mid V_o)$ and all of the data is used to estimate $P(V_o)$.

**Example 11.6** Suppose you have a dataset of education and income, where the income values are often missing, and have modeled that income depends on education. You want to learn the joint probability of *Income* and *Education*.

If income is missing completely at random, shown in Figure 11.6(a), the missing data can be ignored when learning the probabilities:

$$P(Income, Education) = P(Income^*, Education \mid M\_Income = false)$$

since *M_Income* is independent of *Income* and *Education*.

If income is missing at random, shown in Figure 11.6(b), the missing data cannot be ignored when learning the probabilities, however

$$\begin{aligned} &P(Income, Education) \\ &\quad = P(Income \mid Education) * P(Education) \\ &\quad = P(Income \mid Education \wedge M\_Income = false) * P(Education) \\ &\quad = P(Income^* \mid Education \wedge M\_Income = false) * P(Education). \end{aligned}$$

Both of these can be estimated from the data. The first probability can ignore the examples with *Income* missing, and the second cannot.

If *Income* is missing not at random, as shown in Figure 11.6(c), which is similar to Figure 11.5 (page 498), the probability $P(Income, Education)$ cannot be learned from data, because there is no way to determine whether those who don't report income are those with very high income or very low income. While algorithms like EM converge, what they learn is fiction, converging to one of the many possible hypotheses about how the data could be missing.

The main points to remember are:

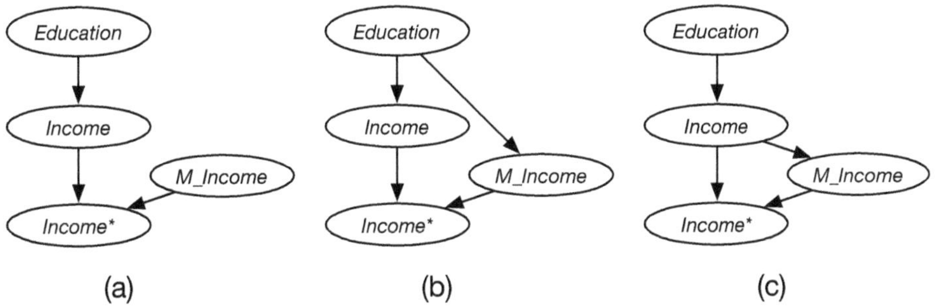


Figure 11.6: Missing data. *Education* is observed but *Income* might have missing values: (a) completely at random, (b) missing at random, (c) missing not at random

- You cannot learn from missing data without making modeling assumptions.
- Some distributions are not recoverable from missing data, and some are. It depends on the independence structure of the underlying graph.
- If the distribution is not recoverable, a learning algorithm still may be able to learn parameters, but the resulting distributions should not be trusted.

## 11.3 Inferring Causality

You cannot determine the effect of intervention from observational data. However, you can infer causality if you are prepared to make assumptions. A problem with inferring causality is that there can be **confounders**, other variables correlated with the variables of interest. A confounder between $X$ and $Y$ is a variable $Z$ such that $P(Y \mid X, do(Z)) \neq P(Y \mid X)$ and $P(X \mid do(Z)) \neq P(X)$. A confounder can account for the correlation between $X$ and $Y$ by being a common cause of both.

**Example 11.7** Consider the effect of a drug on a disease. The effect of the drug cannot be determined by considering the correlation between taking the drug and the outcome. The reason is that the drug and the outcome can be correlated for other reasons than just the effect of the drug. For example, the severity of a disease and the gender of the patient may be correlated with both, and so potential confounders. If the drug is only given to the sickest people, the drug may be positively correlated with a poor outcome, even though the drug might work very well – it makes each patient less sick than they would have been if they were not given the drug.

The story of how the variables interact could be represented by the network of Figure 11.7. In this figure, the variable *Drug* could represent whether the patient was given the drug or not. Whether a patient is given a drug depends on the severity of the disease (variable *Severity*) and the gender of the person (variable *Gender*). You might not be sure whether *Gender* is a confounder, but because there is a possibility, it can be included to be safe.

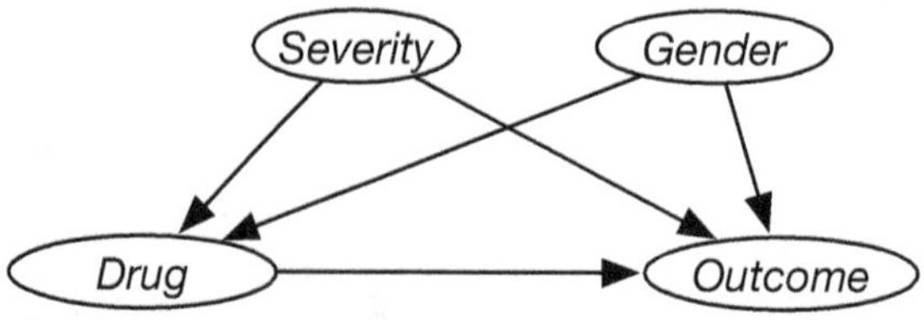


Figure 11.7: Measuring the effectiveness of a drug

From observational data, $P(outcome \mid drug)$ can be determined, but to determine whether a drug is useful requires $P(outcome \mid do(drug))$, which is potentially different because of the confounders. The important part of the network of Figure 11.7 (page 500) are the missing nodes and arcs; this assumes that there are no other confounders.

In a **randomized controlled trial** one variable (e.g., a drug) is given to patients at random, selected using a random number generator, independently of its parents (e.g., independently of how severe the disease is). In a causal network, this is modeled by removing the arcs into that variable, as it is assumed that the random number generator is not correlated with other variables. This then allows us to determine the effect of making the variable true with all confounders removed.

## 11.3.1 Backdoor Criterion

If one is prepared to commit to a model, in particular to identify all possible confounders, it is possible to determine causal knowledge from observational data. This is appropriate when you identify all confounders and enough of them are observable.

**Example 11.8** In Example 11.7 (page 500), there are three reasons why the drug and outcome are correlated. One is the direct effect of the drug on the outcome. The others are due to the confounders of the severity of the disease and the gender of the patient. The aim to measure the direct effect. If the severity and gender are the only confounders, you can adjust for them by considering the effect of the drug on the outcome for each severity and gender separately, and weighting the outcome appropriately:

$$\begin{aligned} &P(Outcome \mid do(Drug)) \\ &\quad = \sum_{Severity} \sum_{Gender} P(Severity) * P(Gender) \\ &\qquad\qquad * P(Outcome \mid do(Drug), Severity, Gender) \\ &\quad = \sum_{Severity} \sum_{Gender} P(Severity) * P(Gender) \\ &\qquad\qquad * P(Outcome \mid Drug, Severity, Gender). \end{aligned}$$

The last step follows because *Drug*, *Severity*, *Gender* are all the parents of *Outcome*, for which, because of the assumption of a causal network, observing and doing have the same effect. These can all be judged without acting.

This analysis relies on the assumptions that severity and gender are the only confounders and both are observable.

The previous example is a specific instance of the backdoor criterion. A set of variables $Z$ satisfies the **backdoor criterion** for $X$ and $Y$ with respect to directed acyclic graph $G$ if

- $Z$ can be observed
- no node in $Z$ is a descendant of $X$, and
- $Z$ blocks (page 496) every path between $X$ and $Y$ that contains an arrow into $X$.

If $Z$ satisfies the backdoor criterion, then

$$P(Y \mid do(X)) = \sum_Z P(Y \mid X, Z) * P(Z).$$

The aim is to find an observable set of variables $Z$ which blocks all spurious paths from $X$ to $Y$, leaves all directed paths from $X$ to $Y$, and doesn't create any new spurious paths. If $Z$ is observable, the above formula can be estimated from observational data.

It is often challenging, or even impossible, to find a $Z$ that is observable. For example, even though "drug prone" in Example 11.2 (page 494) blocks all paths in Figure 11.2, because it cannot be measured, it is not useful.

### 11.3.2 Do-calculus

The **do-calculus** tells us how probability expressions involving the do-operator can be simplified. It is defined in terms of the following three rules:

- If $Z$ blocks (page 496) all of the paths from $W$ to $Y$ in the graph obtained after removing all of the arcs into $X$:

  $$P(Y \mid do(X), Z, W) = P(Y \mid do(X), Z).$$

  This rule lets us remove observations from a conditional probability. This is effectively d-separation in the manipulated graph.

- If $Z$ satisfies the backdoor criterion, for $X$ and $Y$:

  $$P(Y \mid do(X), Z) = P(Y \mid X, Z).$$

  This rule lets us convert an intervention into an observation.

- If there are no directed paths from $X$ to $Y$, or from $Y$ to $X$:

  $$P(Y \mid do(X)) = P(Y).$$

  This only can be used when there are no observations, and tells us that the only effects of an intervention are on the descendants of the intervened variable.

These three rules are complete in the sense that all cases where interventions can be reduced to observations follow from applications of these rules.

### 11.3.3 Front-Door Criterion

Sometimes the backdoor criterion is not applicable because the confounding variables are not observable. One case where it is still possible to derive the effect of an action is when there is an intermediate, **mediating variable** or variables between the intervention variable and the effect, and where the mediating variable is not affected by the confounding variables, given the intervention variable. This case is covered in the **front-door criterion**.

Consider the generic network of Figure 11.8, where the aim is to predict $P(E \mid do(C))$, where the confounders $U$ are unobserved and the intermediate **mediating variable** $M$ is independent of $U$ given $C$. This pattern can be created by collecting all confounders into $U$, and all mediating variables into $M$, and marginalizing other variables to fit the pattern.

The backdoor criterion is not applicable here, because $U$ is not observed. When $M$ is observed and is independent of $U$ given $C$, the do-calculus can be used to infer the effect on $E$ of intervening on $C$.

Let's first introduce $M$ and marginalize it out, as in belief network inference:

$$
\begin{aligned}
P(E \mid do(C)) &= \sum_M P(E \mid do(C), M) * P(M \mid do(C)) \\
&= \sum_M P(E \mid do(C), do(M)) * P(M \mid do(C)) && (11.1)\\
&= \sum_M P(E \mid do(C), do(M)) * P(M \mid C) && (11.2)\\
&= \sum_M P(E \mid do(M)) * P(M \mid C). && (11.3)
\end{aligned}
$$

Step (11.1) follows using the second rule of the do-calculus because $C$ blocks the backdoor between $M$ and $E$. Step (11.2) uses the second rule of the do-calculus as $\{\}$ satisfies the backdoor criterion between $C$ and $M$; there are no backdoors between $C$ and $M$, given nothing is observed. Step (11.3) uses the third rule of the do-calculus as there are no causal paths from $C$ to $E$ in the graph obtained by removing the arcs into $M$ (which is the effect of $do(M)$).

The intervention on $C$ does not affect $P(E \mid do(M))$. This conditional probability can be computed by introducing $C$ and marginalizing it from the network

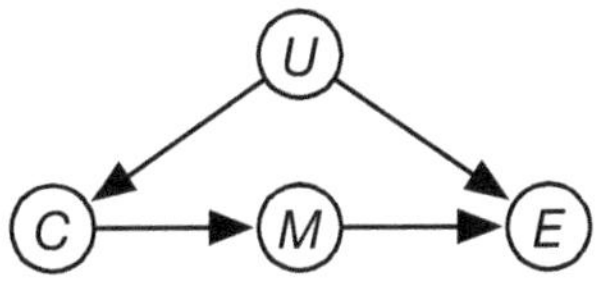


Figure 11.8: A generic network showing the front-door criterion

of Figure 11.8. The $C$ is not intervened on, so let's give it a new name, $C'$:

$$P(E \mid do(M)) = \sum_{C'} P(E \mid do(M), C') * P(C' \mid do(M)).$$

As $C'$ closes the backdoor between $M$ and $E$, by the second rule, and there are no backdoors between $M$ and $C$:

$$\begin{aligned} P(E \mid do(M)) &= \sum_{C'} P(E \mid M, C') * P(C' \mid do(M)) \\ &= \sum_{C'} P(E \mid M, C') * P(C'). \end{aligned}$$

Thus, $P(E \mid do(C))$ reduces to observable quantities only:

$$P(E \mid do(C)) = \sum_{M} P(M \mid C) * \sum_{C'} P(E \mid M, C') * P(C').$$

Thus the intervention on $M$ can be inferred from observable data only as long as $C$ is observable and the mediating variable $M$ is observable and independent of all confounders given $C$.

One of the lessons from this is that it is possible to make causal conclusions from observational data and assumptions on causal mechanisms. Indeed, it is not possible to make causal conclusions without assumptions on causal mechanisms. Even randomized trials require the assumption that the randomizing mechanism is independent of the effects.

### 11.3.4 Simpson's Paradox

**Simpson's paradox** occurs when considering subpopulations gives different conclusions than considering the population as a whole. This is a case where different conclusions are drawn from the same data, depending on an underlying causal model.

**Example 11.9** Consider the following (fictional) dataset of 1000 students, 500 of whom were using a particular method for learning a concept (the treatment variable $T$), and whether they were judged to have understood the concept (evaluation $E$) for two subpopulations (one with $C = true$ and one with $C = false$):

| $C$ | $T$ | $E = true$ | $E = false$ | Rate |
|---|---|---|---|---|
| *true* | *true* | 90 | 10 | $90/(90+10) = 90\%$ |
| *true* | *false* | 290 | 110 | $290/(290+110) = 72.5\%$ |
| *false* | *true* | 110 | 290 | $110/(110+290) = 27.5\%$ |
| *false* | *false* | 10 | 90 | $10/(10+90) = 10\%$ |

where the integers are counts, and the rate is the proportion that understood ($E = true$). For example, there were 90 students with $C = true$, $T = true$, and $E = true$, and 10 students with $C = true$, $T = true$, and $E = false$, and so 90% of the students with $C = true$, $T = true$ have $E = true$.

For both subpopulations, the understanding rate for those who used the method is better than for those who didn't use the method. So it looks like the method works.

Combining the subpopulations gives

| $T$ | $E = true$ | $E = false$ | Rate |
|---|---|---|---|
| *true* | 200 | 300 | $200/(200 + 300) = 40\%$ |
| *false* | 300 | 200 | $300/(300 + 200) = 60\%$ |

where the understanding was better for the students who didn't use the method.

For making decisions for a student, it isn't clear whether it is better to determine whether the condition is true of the student, in which case it is better to use the method, or to ignore the condition, in which case it is better not to use the method. The data doesn't tell us which is the correct answer.

In the previous example, the data does not specify what to do. You need to go beyond the data by building a causal model.

**Example 11.10** In Example 11.9, to make a decision on whether to use the method, consider whether $C$ is a cause for $T$ or $T$ is a cause of $C$. Note that these are not the only two cases; more complicated cases are beyond the scope of this book.

In Figure 11.9(a), $C$ is used to select which treatment was chosen (e.g., $C$ might be the student's prior knowledge). In this case, the data for each condition is appropriate, so based on the data of Example 11.9, it is better to use the method.

In Figure 11.9(b), $C$ is a consequence of the treatment, such as whether the students learned a particular technique. In this case, the aggregated data is appropriate, so based on the data of Example 11.9, it is better not to use the method.

The best treatment is not only a function of the data, but also of the assumed causality.

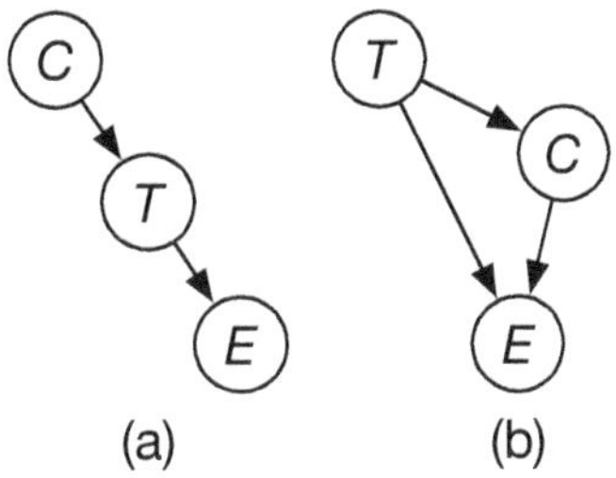


Figure 11.9: Two of the possible causal models for Simpson's paradox

## 11.4 Instrumental Variables

Sometimes it is difficult to manipulate a variable; for example, someone carrying out a medical trial can't force someone to take a drug, all they can do is try to convince them, for example by paying them. An **instrumental variable** is a variable that can be used as a surrogate for a variable that is difficult to manipulate. Observable or controllable variable $Z$ is an instrumental variable for variable $X$ in predicting $Y$ if:

- $Z$ is independent of the possible confounders (page 500) between $X$ and $Y$. One way to ensure independence is to randomize $Z$.
- $Y$ is independent of $Z$ given $X$. The only way for $Z$ to affect $Y$ is to affect $X$.
- There is a strong association between $Z$ and $X$.

The variable $Z$ can be used to manipulate $X$, thus giving an artificial experiment. There is no causation between $X$ and $Y$ that holds for all conditional probabilities in this setup, so the do-calculus cannot be used to infer causation. However, based on the actual probabilities, some bounds can be inferred, as in the following example.

**Example 11.11** Suppose you wanted to know the effect of a drug on a disease, that is, you want to compute $P(\mathit{Disease} \mid do(\mathit{Drug}))$, how likely is the disease if someone takes the drug versus not taking the drug. You create a randomized experiment where some people are assigned the drug and some are assigned a placebo. However, some people might not take the pill prescribed for them.

Figure 11.10 shows a model of the relationship between being assigned a drug and taking a drug, and the effect on a disease. You don't know what the possible confounders are, and so can't measure them. The participants were assigned the drug randomly and so that is independent of the confounders. The participants did not know whether they were assigned the drug or a placebo, so it is reasonable to assume that assignment is also independent of the outcome given the drug.

The do-calculus does not help here; the propensity to not take the drug might be highly correlated with the outcome. The people who would not take

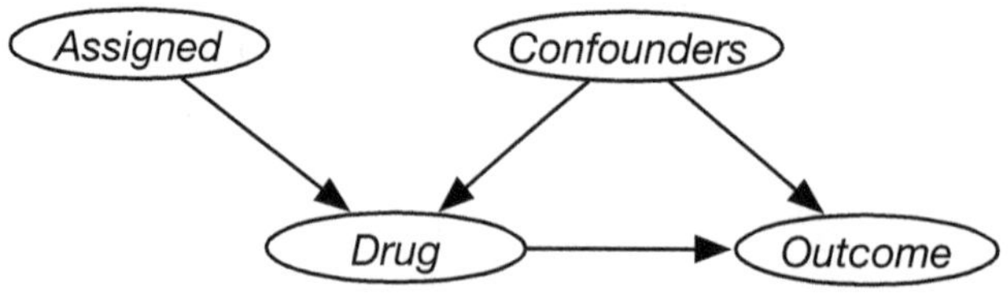


Figure 11.10: *Assigned* is an instrumental variable for *Drug*: an experiment provides $P(\mathit{Outcome} \mid do(\mathit{Assigned}))$; the aim is to estimate $P(\mathit{Outcome} \mid do(\mathit{Drug}))$

the drug might be those who would have a good (or bad) outcome. There is no method that can produce an answer based only on the graphical model.

Consider the following fictional data:

| *Assigned* | *Drug* | *Outcome* | Count |
|---|---|---|---|
| true | true | good | 300 |
| true | true | bad | 50 |
| true | false | good | 25 |
| true | false | bad | 125 |
| false | true | good | 0 |
| false | true | bad | 0 |
| false | false | good | 100 |
| false | false | bad | 400 |

No one who was not assigned the drug, actually took it, which is reasonable for a clinical trial for a new drug.

While you may not be able to determine $P(Outcome = good \mid do(Drug = true))$, it is possible to bound the effect by considering what would have happened to the non-compliers (those assigned the drug who did not take it). The following analysis ignores regularization, and so is expected to overfit.

At one extreme, none of the non-compliers would have had a good outcome if they had been forced to take the drug. In this case, 300 of the patients would have a good outcome. Thus, intervening on the drug would have resulted in 300/500 having a good outcome.

At the other extreme, all of the non-compliers would have had a good outcome if they had been forced to take the drug. In this case, 450 of the patients would have a good outcome. Thus, intervening on the drug would result in 450/500 having a good outcome.

Putting the two extremes together gives

$$0.6 \leq P(Outcome = good \mid do(Drug = true)) \leq 0.9.$$

Because there was full compliance of those not assigned the drug:

$$P(Outcome = good \mid do(Drug = false)) = 0.2.$$

In this analysis, the outcome of those that were assigned the drug and didn't take it was ignored, but the non-compliance cannot be ignored. Just removing non-compliant people from the sample, resulting in the conclusion that the outcome was good with probability 3/4 when the drug was taken, would be equivalent to assuming there are no confounders, which may not be a reasonable assumption.

It is often useful to consider the effect of the drug as the difference between (or ratio of) the outcome when the drug was taken and the outcome when the drug was not taken.

It is also possible to make other assumptions to allow for inference from instrumental variables. A common assumption for real-valued variables is that each variable is a linear function of its parents. Solving for the coefficients can give a unique solution.

## 11.5 Counterfactual Reasoning

The preceding analysis was for intervening before observing. The other case is observing then intervening. When the intervention is different from what actually happened, this is **counterfactual reasoning**, which is asking "what if something else were true?" Here we use a more general notion of counterfactual, where you can ask "what if $x$ were true?" without knowing whether $x$ were true.

Pearl [2009] created the following example.

**Example 11.12** Consider a case of a firing squad, where a captain can give an order to a number of shooters who can each shoot to kill. One reason for using a firing squad is that each shooter can think "I wasn't responsible for killing the prisoner, because the prisoner would be dead even if I didn't shoot."

Suppose the captain has some probability of giving the order. The shooters each probabilistically obey the order to shoot or the order to not shoot. Assume they deviate from orders with low probabilities. The prisoner is dead if any of the shooters shoot.

One counterfactual is "if the second shooter shot, what would have happened if the second shooter had not shot?" The fact that the second shooter shot means that the order probably was given, and so the first shooter probably also shot, so the prisoner would probably be dead. The following analysis shows how to construct the probability distribution for the variables in the resulting situation.

Another counterfactual query is "if the prisoner died, what would have happened if the second shooter had not shot?" In a narrow reading, this might not be a counterfactual, as the second shooter might not have actually shot. However, this case is also covered below.

Counterfactual reasoning is useful when you need to assign blame. For example, in a self-driving car that has an accident, it might be useful to ask what would have happened if it had turned left instead of braking or if it had used its horn, when it sensed something on the road. If there is nothing it could have done, perhaps the accident was not its fault. Assigning blame is used in the law to provide penalties for those who make bad choices (e.g., would a death have occurred if they did not do some action), in the hope that they and others will make better decisions in the future.

Suppose you have a causal network (page 493). To model observing $O$, and asking "what if $a$" consists of three steps:

1. Determining what must be true for $O$ to be observed. This is an instance of abduction (page 214).

2. Intervening to make $a$ true.

3. Querying the resulting model, using the posterior probabilities from the first step.

This can be implemented by constructing an appropriate belief network, from which queries from the counterfactual situation can be made. The construction of the belief network for the counterfactual "what if $a$", where $a$ is one of the values for variable $A$, is as follows:

- Represent the problem using a causal network, where conditional probabilities are in terms of a deterministic system with stochastic inputs (page 397), such as a **probabilistic logic program** (page 397) or a **probabilistic program** (page 397).
- Create a node $A'$ with the same domain as $A$ but with no parents ($A'$ is called a primed variable below).
- For each descendant $D$ of $A$ in the original model, create a node $D'$ sharing the same parents and conditional probability as $D$, apart from any descendant of $A$, for which the primed version is used.
- Condition on $A' = a$ and condition on the observations of the initial situation using unprimed variables.

The primed variables are the variables for the counterfactual scenario. The non-primed variables are for the original scenario. Variables that are not a descendant of $A$ have no primed version and are the same in the original and the counterfactual scenario. This includes all probabilistic variables, because of the representation for conditional probabilities.

Any of the original variables can be conditioned on to give the initial situation, and any primed variables can be queried to answer queries about the counterfactual situation. Any belief network inference algorithm (page 404) can be used to compute the posterior probabilities.

**Example 11.13** Figure 11.11(a) shows a model of a firing squad as in Example 11.12 (page 508). The captain can give an order to two shooters who can shoot to kill; when one of them shoots, the prisoner dies. *Order* is true when the

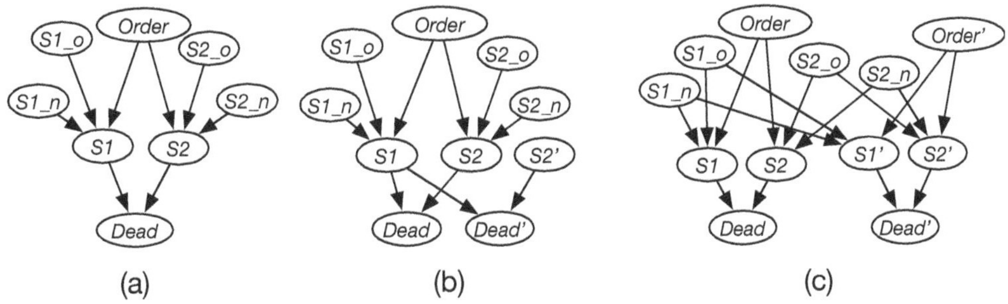


Figure 11.11: Causal network for firing squad example: (a) original; (b) what if shooter 2 shot (or didn't shoot); (c) what if the order was given (or not given)

order is given to shoot. $S1$ is true when shooter 1 shoots to kill. $S1\_o$ is true when shooter 1 would follow the order to shoot and $S1\_n$ is true when shooter 1 would shoot when the order is not to shoot. Thus, shooter 1 shoots when the order is given and $S1\_o$ is true or when the order is not given and $S1\_n$ is true:

$$s1 \leftrightarrow order \wedge s1\_o \vee \neg order \wedge s1\_n$$

where *order* means $Order = true$, and similarly for other variables. The model for the second shooter is similar.

Figure 11.11(b) shows the network used when considering the alternative "what if shooter 2 did shoot?" or "what if shooter 2 did not shoot?" In this case there is a new variable $S2'$ that is true when shooter 2 shot in the alternative scenario. Everything in the alternative scenario is the same as in the initial scenario, except that the consequences of shooter 2 shooting might be different. In this case, the variable $Dead'$ represents the proposition that the prisoner is dead in the second scenario.

The counterfactual "the second shooter shot; what is the probability that the prisoner would be dead if the second shooter did not shoot?" can be computed by querying

$$P(dead' \mid s2 \wedge \neg s2')$$

in the network of Figure 11.11(b).

The counterfactual "the prisoner is dead; what is the probability that the prisoner would be dead if the second shooter did not shoot?" can be computed by querying

$$P(dead' \mid dead \wedge \neg s2')$$

in the network of Figure 11.11(b).

Figure 11.11(c) shows the counterfactual network for "what if the order was not given". The counterfactual "shooter 1 didn't shoot and the prisoner was dead; what is the probability the prisoner is dead if the order was not given?" can be answered with the query

$$P(dead' \mid \neg s1 \wedge dead \wedge \neg order')$$

in the network of Figure 11.11(c).

## 11.6 Social Impact

**Randomized clinical trials** are conducted for each new drug or medical device to demonstrate safety and efficacy for the European Medicines Agency (EMA) and the U.S. Food and Drug Administration (USFDA), for example, to approve it. Moore et al. [2020] estimated the median cost of clinical trials for 101 therapeutic drugs approved by USFDA in 2015–17 was US$48 million per approved drug. The aim of a clinical trial for a drug is to assess the effects of intervening to give someone the drug. The effects include both the beneficial and harmful effects, where the benefits have to outweigh the harms.

The main assumption behind a randomized clinical trial is that the random assignment of the drug means that there are no confounders. Missing data (page 497) – when some patients drop out of the trial – makes the naive analysis of such data problematic. The conductors of the trial need to find out why the patients dropped out, or to consider the worst case (similar to the analysis of instrumental variables, page 506).

Randomized controlled trials are a standard mechanism in much of science, including the social sciences, however they may not be appropriate or possible in all situations. For example, a randomized trial to gauge the impact of an intervention in schools might be unethical because, although the study might provide information that can help future students, some of the students in the trial are not being provided with the best education available. It is also difficult to only vary a single condition in a study on students. The tools of causal analysis and making causal assumptions explicit should enable more cases where the effect of interventions can be inferred. Explicit assumptions are open to scrutiny and debate.

One of the promising ways to **explain** a prediction of an otherwise inscrutable method, such as a **neural network**, is a **counterfactual explanation**. Given a prediction, a minimal counterfactual explanation is a minimal change to the inputs that would result in a different conclusion. For example, if someone was denied a loan, it is reasonable to ask for the smallest changes that would have resulted in the loan being approved. There are generally many minimal changes that could have resulted in a different conclusion.

## 11.7 Review

- The do-notation extends the language of conditional probability to include intervention on some variables and observing other variables.

- A **causal network** is a belief network where $P(X \mid parents(X)) = P(X \mid do(parents(X)))$ for each variable $X$ – intervening on the parents of a variable has the same effect as observing them.

- D-separation characterizes which conditional independencies follow from the independencies of a directed graphical model (belief network). The do-calculus extends d-separation to include interventions.

- The do-calculus can be used to show cases where the effect of interventions can be computed from observational data, including the backdoor and front-door criteria.

- There are cases, such as in Simpson's paradox, where the probabilistic inferences depend on the causal model and not just the data.

- Counterfactual reasoning can be used to answer "what-if" queries.
- Causal assumptions can be used to go beyond randomized clinical trials, if the assumptions are accepted.

## 11.8 References and Further Reading

Pearl and Mackenzie [2018] provide a readable overview of causality and its historical context. For a more technical description, see Pearl [2009], Spirtes et al. [2001] and Veitch and D'Amour [2023]. Geffner et al. [2022] overview the work of Judea Pearl, one of the pioneers of causality in AI, and include many papers on causality.

Huang and Valtorta [2006] and Shpitser and Pearl [2008] independently showed that the do-calculus is complete; it completely characterizes when interventions impact probabilities given only the causal structure.

Modeling missing data is discussed by Rubin [1976], Little and Rubin [1987], Marlin et al. [2011], and Mohan et al. [2013]. Mohan [2022] provides an overview.

## 11.9 Exercises

**Exercise 11.1** Suppose Kim has a camper van (a mobile home) and likes to keep it at a comfortable temperature and noticed that the energy use depended on the elevation. Kim knows that the elevation affects the outside temperature. Kim likes the camper warmer at higher elevation. Note that not all of the variables directly affect electrical usage.

(a) Show how this can be represented as a causal network, using the variables *Elevation, Electrical Usage, Outside Temperature*, and *Thermostat Setting*.
(b) Give an example where intervening has an effect different from conditioning for this network.

**Exercise 11.2** Exercise 9.2 (page 451) asked to intuitively explore independence in Figure 9.37. For parts (c), (d), and (e) of Exercise 9.2, express the question in terms of conditional independence, and use d-separation (page 495) to infer the answer. Show your working.

**Exercise 11.3** Consider the causal network of Figure 11.12 (page 513). For each part, explain why the independence holds or doesn't hold, using the definition of d-separation. The independence asked needs to hold for all probability distributions (which is what d-separation tells us).

(a) Is $J$ independent of $A$ given $\{\}$ (i.e., given no observations)?
(b) Is $J$ independent of $A$ given $\{G\}$ (i.e., given only $G$ is observed)?
(c) Is $J$ independent of $A$ given $\{F\}$?
(d) Is $J$ independent of $A$ given $\{G, F\}$ (i.e., given only $G$ and $F$ are observed)?
(e) Is $G$ independent of $J$ given $\{\}$?
(f) Is $G$ independent of $J$ given $\{I\}$?

(g) Is $G$ independent of $J$ given $\{B\}$?
(h) Is $G$ independent of $J$ given $\{B, I\}$?
(i) What needs to be observed, and what needs to be not observed for $G$ to be independent of $J$? Give a complete characterization.

**Exercise 11.4** Consider the causal network of Figure 11.12. The following can be answered intuitively or using the do-calculus. Explain your reasoning:

(a) Does $P(I \mid B) = P(I \mid do(B))$?
(b) Does $P(I \mid G) = P(J \mid do(G))$?
(c) Does $P(I \mid G, B) = P(J \mid do(G), B)$?
(d) Does $P(B \mid I) = P(B \mid do(I))$?

**Exercise 11.5** Bickel et al. [1975] report on gender biases for graduate admissions at UC Berkeley. This example is based on that case, but the numbers are fictional.

There are two departments, which we will call *dept#1* and *dept#2* (so *Dept* is a random variable with values *dept#1* and *dept#2*), which students can apply to. Assume students apply to one, but not both. Students have a gender (male or female), and are either admitted or not. Consider the table of the percent of students in each category of Figure 11.13.

In the semantics of possible worlds, we will treat the students as possible worlds, with the measure of a set of worlds corresponding to the number of students in the set.

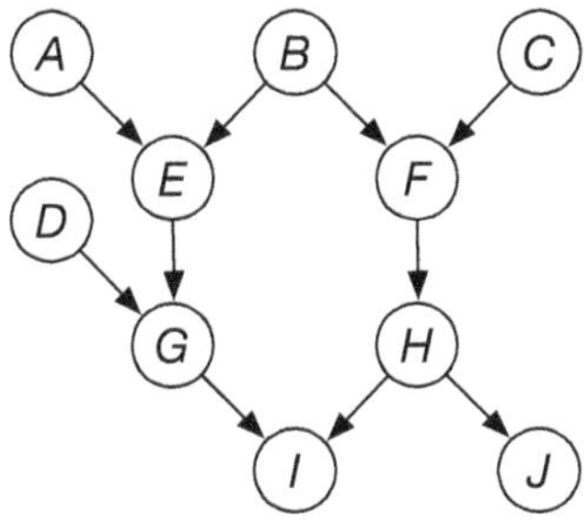


Figure 11.12: An example causal network

| *Dept* | *Gender* | *Admitted* | Percent |
|---|---|---|---|
| *dept#1* | *male* | *true* | 32 |
| *dept#1* | *male* | *false* | 18 |
| *dept#1* | *female* | *true* | 7 |
| *dept#1* | *female* | *false* | 3 |
| *dept#2* | *male* | *true* | 5 |
| *dept#2* | *male* | *false* | 14 |
| *dept#2* | *female* | *true* | 7 |
| *dept#2* | *female* | *false* | 14 |

Figure 11.13: Fictional counts for students in departments

(a) What is $P(Admitted = true \mid Gender = male)$?
What is $P(Admitted = true \mid Gender = female)$?
Which gender is more likely to be admitted?

(b) What is $P(Admitted = true \mid Gender = male, Dept = dept\#1)$?
What is $P(Admitted = true \mid Gender = female, Dept = dept\#1)$?
Which gender is more likely to be admitted to *dept#1*?

(c) What is $P(Admitted = true \mid Gender = male, Dept = dept\#2)$?
What is $P(Admitted = true \mid Gender = female, Dept = dept\#2)$?
Which gender is more likely to be admitted to *dept#2*?

(d) This is an instance of Simpson's paradox. Why is it a paradox? Explain why it happened in this case.

(e) Does this provide evidence that the university has a bias against women? See Section 11.3.4 (page 504).

(f) Give another scenario where Simpson's paradox occurs.

**Exercise 11.6** Suppose someone provided the source code for a recursive conditioning (page 409) program that computes conditional probabilities in belief networks. Your job is to use it to build a program that also works for interventions, that is for queries of the form $P(Y \mid do(a_1, \ldots, a_k), b_1, \ldots, b_m)$. Explain how you would proceed.

**Exercise 11.7** Consider a two-variable causal network with Boolean variables $A$ and $B$, where $A$ is a parent of $B$, and the following conditional probabilities:

$$P(a) = 0.2$$
$$P(b \mid a) = 0.9$$
$$P(b \mid \neg a) = 0.3.$$

Consider the counterfactual: "$B$ is observed to be true; what is the probability of $B$ if $A$ was false?"

Draw the belief network that can be used to answer this question. Give all (conditional) probabilities. What needs to be conditioned on and what is queried to answer this counterfactual question? What is the resulting answer? (This can be done by hand or using any belief network implementation.)

# Part IV

# Planning and Acting with Uncertainty

**How can an agent plan and act, relaxing the assumption that it knows the effects of its actions and the current state of the world?**

# Chapter 12

# Planning with Uncertainty

> *In retrospect... it is interesting to note that the original problem that started my research is still outstanding – namely the problem of planning or scheduling dynamically over time, particularly planning dynamically under uncertainty. If such a problem could be successfully solved it could eventually through better planning contribute to the well-being and stability of the world.*
>
> – George B. Dantzig (1991)

An agent that is not omniscient cannot just plan a fixed sequence of steps, as was assumed in Chapter 6. Planning must take into account the fact that an agent in the real world does not know what will actually happen when it acts, nor what it will observe in the future. An agent should plan to react to its environment.

What an agent should do at any time depends on what it will do in the future. For example, in a medical situation, sometimes tests hurt patients, but they are useful because they enable future actions. When an agent cannot precisely predict the effects of its actions, what it will do in the future depends on what it does now and what it will observe before it acts.

With uncertainty, an agent typically cannot guarantee to satisfy its goals, and even trying to maximize the probability of achieving a goal may not be sensible. For example, an agent whose goal is to minimize the probability of injury in a car accident would not get into a car or walk down a sidewalk or even go to the ground floor of a building, each of which increases the probability of being injured in a car accident, however slightly. An agent that does not guarantee to satisfy a goal can fail in many ways, some of which may be much worse than others.

This chapter is about how to take planning, reacting, observing, succeeding, and failing into account simultaneously. As George Dantzig, the inventor of linear programming, points out in the quote above, planning under uncertainty is essential for an intelligent agent.

An agent's decision on what to do at any time (see Figure 2.10 (page 68)) depends on:

- *The agent's ability.* The agent has to select from the actions available to it.
- *What the agent believes and observes.* An agent might like to condition its action on what is true in the world, but it only has access to the world via its sensors. When an agent has to decide what to do, it only has access to what it has remembered and what it observes (page 55). Sensing the world updates an agent's beliefs. Beliefs and observations are the only information about the world available to an agent at any time.
- *The agent's preferences.* When an agent must reason with uncertainty, it has to consider not only what is most likely to happen but also what may happen. Some possible outcomes may have much worse consequences than others. The simple notion of a *goal*, considered in Chapter 6, is not adequate when reasoning under uncertainty because the designer of an agent has to trade off between different outcomes that may occur. For example, if an action results in a good outcome most of the time, but sometimes results in a disastrous outcome, it must be compared with performing an alternative action that results in the good outcome less often and the disastrous outcome less often and some mediocre outcome most of the time. Decision theory specifies how to trade off the desirability of outcomes with the probabilities of those outcomes.

## 12.1 Preferences and Utility

What an agent decides to do should depend on its preferences. This section specifies some intuitive properties of preferences and gives some consequences of those properties. The properties are **axioms of rationality**. You should consider whether each axiom is reasonable for a **rational agent** to follow; if you accept them all as reasonable, you should accept their consequences. If you do not accept the consequences, you need to give up one or more of the axioms.

### 12.1.1 Axioms for Rationality

An agent chooses actions based on their **outcomes**. Outcomes are whatever the agent has **preferences** over. If an agent does not prefer any outcome to any other outcome, it does not matter what the agent does. Initially, let's consider outcomes without considering the associated actions. Assume there are only a finite number of outcomes.

Let's define a **preference relation** over outcomes. Suppose $o_1$ and $o_2$ are outcomes. Outcome $o_1$ is **weakly preferred** to outcome $o_2$, written $o_1 \succeq o_2$, if outcome $o_1$ is at least as desirable as outcome $o_2$.

We write $o_1 \not\succeq o_2$ to mean the negation of $o_1 \succeq o_2$, that is, $o_1$ is not weakly preferred to outcome $o_2$.

Define $o_1 \sim o_2$ to mean $o_1 \succeq o_2$ and $o_2 \succeq o_1$. That is, $o_1 \sim o_2$ means outcomes $o_1$ and $o_2$ are equally preferred. In this case, we say that the agent is **indifferent** between $o_1$ and $o_2$.

Define $o_1 \succ o_2$ to mean $o_1 \succeq o_2$ and $o_2 \not\succeq o_1$. That is, the agent weakly prefers outcome $o_1$ to outcome $o_2$, but does not weakly prefer $o_2$ to $o_1$, and is not indifferent between them. In this case, we say that outcome $o_1$ is **strictly preferred** to outcome $o_2$.

Typically, an agent does not know the outcome of its actions. A **lottery** is defined to be a finite distribution over outcomes, written

$$[p_1 : o_1, p_2 : o_2, \ldots, p_k : o_k]$$

where each $o_i$ is an outcome and each $p_i$ is a non-negative real number such that $\sum_i p_i = 1$. The lottery specifies that outcome $o_i$ occurs with probability $p_i$. In all that follows, assume that outcomes may include lotteries. This includes lotteries where the outcomes are also lotteries (called lotteries over lotteries).

**Axiom 12.1.** *(Completeness) An agent has preferences between all pairs of outcomes:*

$$o_1 \succeq o_2 \text{ or } o_2 \succeq o_1.$$

The rationale for this axiom is that an agent must act; if the actions available to it have outcomes $o_1$ and $o_2$ then, by acting, it is explicitly or implicitly preferring one outcome over the other.

**Axiom 12.2.** *(Transitivity) Preferences are transitive:*

$$\text{if } o_1 \succeq o_2 \text{ and } o_2 \succ o_3 \text{ then } o_1 \succ o_3.$$

To see why this is reasonable, suppose it is false, in which case $o_1 \succeq o_2$ and $o_2 \succ o_3$ and $o_3 \succeq o_1$. Because $o_2$ is strictly preferred to $o_3$, the agent should be prepared to pay some amount to get from $o_3$ to $o_2$. Suppose the agent has outcome $o_2$; then $o_1$ is at least as good so the agent would just as soon have $o_1$. $o_3$ is at least as good as $o_1$, so the agent would just as soon have $o_3$ as $o_1$. Once the agent has $o_3$, it is again prepared to pay to get to $o_2$. It has gone through a cycle of preferences and paid money to end up where it is. This cycle that involves paying money to go through it is known as a **money pump** because, by going through the loop enough times, the amount of money that an agent must pay can exceed any finite amount. It seems reasonable to claim that being prepared to pay money to cycle through a set of outcomes is irrational; hence, a rational agent should have transitive preferences.

It follows from the transitivity and completeness axioms that transitivity holds for mixes of $\succ$ and $\succeq$, so that if $o_1 \succeq o_2$ and $o_2 \succeq o_3$, then $o_1 \succeq o_3$ and if one or both of the preferences in the premise of the transitivity axiom is strict, then the conclusion is strict. Thus, if $o_1 \succ o_2$ and $o_2 \succeq o_3$, then $o_1 \succ o_3$. See Exercise 12.1 (page 573).

**Axiom 12.3.** *(Monotonicity) An agent prefers a larger chance of getting a better outcome than a smaller chance of getting the better outcome, other things being equal. That is, if $o_1 \succ o_2$ and $p > q$, then*

$$[p : o_1, (1-p) : o_2] \succ [q : o_1, (1-q) : o_2].$$

Note that, in this axiom, $\succ$ between outcomes represents the agent's preference, whereas $>$ between $p$ and $q$ represents the familiar comparison between numbers.

The following axiom specifies that lotteries over lotteries only depend on the outcomes and probabilities.

**Axiom 12.4.** *(Decomposability) ("no fun in gambling") An agent is indifferent between lotteries that have the same probabilities over the same outcomes, even if one or both is a lottery over lotteries. For example:*

$$[p : o_1, (1-p) : [q : o_2, (1-q) : o_3]] \\ \sim [p : o_1, (1-p) * q : o_2, (1-p) * (1-q) : o_3].$$

*Also $o_1 \sim [1 : o_1, 0 : o_2]$ for any outcomes $o_1$ and $o_2$.*

This axiom specifies that it is only the outcomes and their probabilities that define a lottery. If an agent had a preference for gambling, that would be part of the outcome space.

These four axioms imply some structure on the preference between outcomes and lotteries. Suppose that $o_1 \succ o_2$ and $o_2 \succ o_3$. Consider whether the agent would prefer

- $o_2$ or
- the lottery $[p : o_1, (1-p) : o_3]$

for different values of $p \in [0, 1]$. When $p = 1$, the agent prefers the lottery (because, by decomposability, the lottery is equivalent to $o_1$ and $o_1 \succ o_2$). When $p = 0$, the agent prefers $o_2$ (because the lottery is equivalent to $o_3$ and $o_2 \succ o_3$). At some stage, as $p$ is varied, the agent's preferences flip between preferring $o_2$ and preferring the lottery. Figure 12.1 (page 521) shows how the preferences must flip as $p$ is varied. On the $X$-axis is $p$ and the $Y$-axis shows which of $o_2$ or the lottery is preferred. The following proposition formalizes this intuition.

**Proposition 12.1.** *If an agent's preferences are complete, transitive, and follow the monotonicity axiom, and if $o_1 \succ o_2$ and $o_2 \succ o_3$, there exists a number $p_2$ such that $0 \leq p_2 \leq 1$ and*

- *for all $p < p_2$, the agent prefers $o_2$ to the lottery (i.e., $o_2 \succ [p : o_1, (1-p) : o_3]$) and*
- *for all $p > p_2$, the agent prefers the lottery (i.e., $[p : o_1, (1-p) : o_3] \succ o_2$).*

*Proof.* By monotonicity and transitivity, if $o_2 \succeq [p : o_1, (1-p) : o_3]$ for any $p$, then, for all $p' < p$, $o_2 \succ [p' : o_1, (1-p') : o_3]$. Similarly, if $[p : o_1, (1-p) : o_3] \succeq o_2$ for any $p$, then, for all $p' > p$, $[p' : o_1, (1-p') : o_3] \succ o_2$.

By completeness, for each value of $p$, either $o_2 \succ [p : o_1, (1-p) : o_3]$, $o_2 \sim [p : o_1, (1-p) : o_3]$, or $[p : o_1, (1-p) : o_3] \succ o_2$. If there is some $p$ such that $o_2 \sim [p : o_1, (1-p) : o_3]$, then the theorem holds. Otherwise, a preference for either $o_2$ or the lottery with parameter $p$ implies preferences for either all values greater than $p$ or for all values less than $p$. By repeatedly subdividing the region that we do not know the preferences for, we will approach, in the limit, a value filling the criteria for $p_2$. □

The preceding proposition does not specify what the preference of the agent is at the point $p_2$. The following axiom specifies that the agent is indifferent at this point.

**Axiom 12.5.** *(Continuity) Suppose $o_1 \succ o_2$ and $o_2 \succ o_3$, then there exists a $p_2 \in [0,1]$ such that*

$$o_2 \sim [p_2 : o_1, (1-p_2) : o_3].$$

The next axiom specifies that replacing an outcome in a lottery with an outcome that is not worse, cannot make the lottery worse.

**Axiom 12.6.** *(Substitutability) If $o_1 \succeq o_2$ then the agent weakly prefers lotteries that contain $o_1$ instead of $o_2$, everything else being equal. That is, for any number $p$ and outcome $o_3$:*

$$[p : o_1, (1-p) : o_3] \succeq [p : o_2, (1-p) : o_3].$$

A direct corollary of this is that outcomes to which the agent is indifferent can be substituted for one another, without changing the preferences.

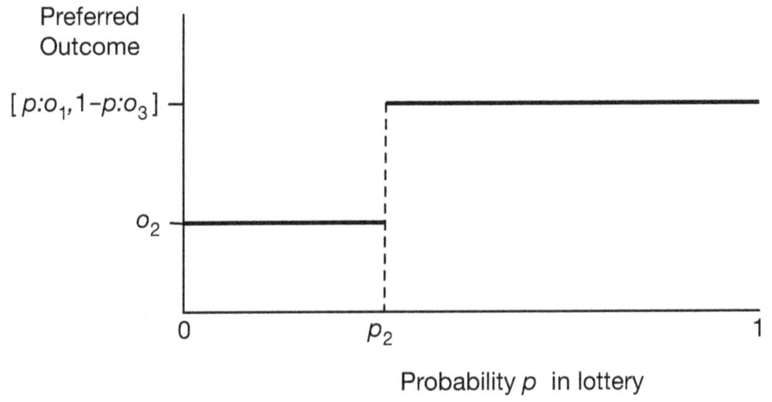


Figure 12.1: The preference between $o_2$ and the lottery, as a function of $p$

**Proposition 12.2.** *If an agent obeys the substitutability axiom and $o_1 \sim o_2$, then the agent is indifferent between lotteries that only differ by $o_1$ and $o_2$. That is, for any number $p$ and outcome $o_3$, the following indifference relation holds:*

$$[p : o_1, (1-p) : o_3] \sim [p : o_2, (1-p) : o_3].$$

This follows because $o_1 \sim o_2$ is equivalent to $o_1 \succeq o_2$ and $o_2 \succeq o_1$, and we can use substitutability for both cases.

An agent is defined to be **rational** if it obeys the completeness, transitivity, monotonicity, decomposability, continuity, and substitutability axioms.

It is up to you to determine if this technical definition of rationality matches your intuitive notion of rationality. In the rest of this section, we show more consequences of this definition.

Although preferences may seem to be complicated, the following theorem shows that a rational agent's value for an outcome can be measured by a real number. Those value measurements can be combined with probabilities so that preferences with uncertainty can be compared using expectation. This is surprising for two reasons:

- It may seem that preferences are too multifaceted to be modeled by a single number. For example, although one may try to measure preferences in terms of dollars, not everything is for sale or easily converted into dollars and cents.
- One might not expect that values could be combined with probabilities. An agent that is indifferent between the money $\$(px + (1-p)y)$ and the lottery $[p : \$x,\ (1-p)\$y]$ for all monetary values $x$ and $y$ and for all $p \in [0,1]$ is known as an **expected monetary value** (EMV) agent. Most people are not EMV agents, because they have, for example, a strict preference between \$1,000,000 and the lottery $[0.5 : \$0,\ 0.5 : \$2,000,000]$. (Think about whether you would prefer a million dollars or a coin toss where you would get nothing if the coin lands heads or two million if the coin lands tails.) Money cannot be simply combined with probabilities, so it may be surprising that there is a value that can be.

**Proposition 12.3.** *If an agent is rational, then for every outcome $o_i$ there is a real number $u(o_i)$, called the **utility** of $o_i$, such that*

- *$o_i \succ o_j$ if and only if $u(o_i) > u(o_j)$ and*
- *utilities are linear with probabilities*

$$u([p_1 : o_1, p_2 : o_2, \ldots, p_k : o_k]) = p_1 u(o_1) + p_2 u(o_2) + \cdots + p_k u(o_k).$$

*Proof.* If the agent has no strict preferences (i.e., the agent is indifferent between all outcomes), then define $u(o) = 0$ for all outcomes $o$.

Otherwise, choose the best outcome, $o_{best}$, and the worst outcome, $o_{worst}$, and define, for any outcome $o$, the utility of $o$ to be the value $p$ such that

$$o \sim [p : o_{best}, (1-p) : o_{worst}].$$

The first part of the proposition follows from substitutability and monotonicity.

To prove the second part, any lottery can be reduced to a single lottery between $o_{best}$ and $o_{worst}$ by replacing each $o_i$ by its equivalent lottery between $o_{best}$ and $o_{worst}$, and using decomposability to put it in the form $[p : o_{best}, (1-p) : o_{worst}]$, with $p$ equal to $p_1 u(o_1) + p_2 u(o_2) + \cdots + p_k u(o_k)$. The details are left as an exercise. □

Thus, an **ordinal preference** that follows the axioms is a **cardinal preference** (page 31) where utility defines the values to be compared.

In this proof the utilities are all in the range $[0, 1]$, but any linear scaling gives the same result. Sometimes $[0, 100]$ is a good scale to distinguish it from probabilities, and sometimes negative numbers are useful to use when the outcomes have costs. In general, a program should accept any scale that is intuitive to the user.

A linear relationship does not usually exist between money and utility, even when the outcomes have a monetary value. People often are **risk averse** when it comes to money: they would rather have \$$n$ in their hand than some randomized setup where they expect to receive \$$n$ but could possibly receive more or less.

**Example 12.1** Figure 12.2 shows a possible money–utility relationship for three agents. The topmost line represents an agent that is risk averse, with a concave utility function. The agent with a straight-line plot is risk neutral. The lowest line represents an agent with a convex utility function that is risk seeking.

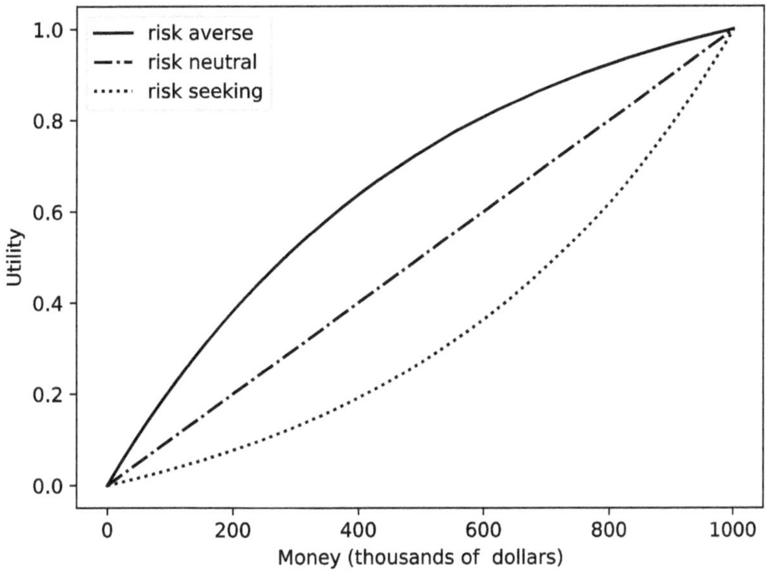


Figure 12.2: Money–utility relationships for agents with different risk profiles

The risk-averse agent in Figure 12.2 would rather have \$300,000 than a 50% chance of getting either nothing or \$1,000,000, but would prefer the gamble on the million dollars to \$275,000. This can be seen by checking the value for $utility = 0.5$. They would also require more than a 73% chance of winning a million dollars to prefer this gamble to half a million dollars.

For the risk-averse agent, $u(\$999,000) \approx 0.9997$. Thus, given this utility function, the risk-averse agent would be willing to pay \$1000 to eliminate a 0.03% chance of losing all of their money. This is why **insurance** companies exist. By paying the insurance company, say, \$600, the risk-averse agent can change the lottery that is worth \$999,000 to them into one worth \$1,000,000 and the insurance companies expect to pay out, on average, about \$300, and so expect to make \$300. The insurance company can get its expected value by insuring enough houses. It is good for both parties.

Rationality does not impose any conditions on what the utility function looks like.

**Example 12.2** Figure 12.3 shows a possible money–utility relationship for Chris who really wants a toy worth \$30, but would also like one worth \$20, and would like both even better. Apart from these, money does not matter much to Chris. Chris is prepared to take risks. For example, if Chris had \$29, Chris would be very happy to bet \$9 against a single dollar of another agent on a fair bet, such as a coin toss. This is reasonable because that \$9 is not much use to Chris, but the extra dollar would enable Chris to buy the \$30 toy. Chris does not want more than \$60, because then Chris will worry about it being lost or stolen.

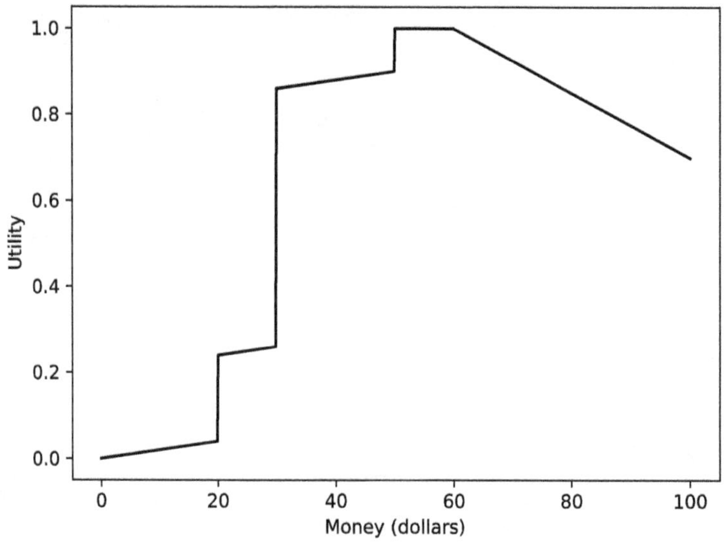


Figure 12.3: Possible money–utility relationship from Example 12.2

**Challenges to Expected Utility**

There have been a number of challenges to the theory of expected utility. The **Allais Paradox**, presented in 1953 [Allais and Hagen, 1979], is as follows. Which would you prefer of the following two alternatives?

A: \$1m – one million dollars
B: lottery [0.10 : \$2.5m, 0.89 : \$1m, 0.01 : \$0].

Similarly, what would you choose between the following two alternatives?

C: lottery [0.11 : \$1m, 0.89 : \$0]
D: lottery [0.10 : \$2.5m, 0.9 : \$0].

It turns out that many people prefer *A* to *B*, and prefer *D* to *C*. This choice is inconsistent with the axioms of rationality. To see why, both choices can be put in the same form:

A,C: lottery [0.11 : \$1m, 0.89 : *X*]
B,D: lottery [0.10 : \$2.5m, 0.01 : \$0, 0.89 : *X*].

In *A* and *B*, *X* is a million dollars. In *C* and *D*, *X* is zero dollars. Concentrating just on the parts of the alternatives that are different seems intuitive, but people seem to have a preference for certainty.

Tversky and Kahneman [1974], in a series of human experiments, showed how people systematically deviate from utility theory. One such deviation is the **framing effect** of a problem's presentation. Consider the following.

- A disease is expected to kill 600 people. Two alternative programs have been proposed:

  Program A: 200 people will be saved
  Program B: with probability 1/3, 600 people will be saved, and with probability 2/3, no one will be saved.

  Which program would you favor?
- A disease is expected to kill 600 people. Two alternative programs have been proposed:

  Program C: 400 people will die
  Program D: with probability 1/3, no one will die, and with probability 2/3, 600 will die.

  Which program would you favor?

Tversky and Kahneman showed that 72% of people in their experiments chose program A over program B, and 22% chose program C over program D. However, these are exactly the same choice, just described in a different way.

**Prospect theory** (page 528), developed by Kahneman and Tversky, is an alternative to expected utility that better fits human behavior.

### 12.1.2 Factored Utility

Utility for an agent is a function of outcomes or states. Representing utilities in terms of features or variables typically results in more compact representations that are easier to reason with and more natural to acquire.

Suppose each outcome can be described in terms of features $X_1, \ldots, X_n$. An **additive utility** is one that can be decomposed into a sum of terms:

$$u(X_1, \ldots, X_n) = f_1(X_1) + \cdots + f_n(X_n).$$

Such a decomposition is making the assumption of **additive independence**.

When this can be done, it greatly simplifies **preference elicitation** – the problem of acquiring preferences from the user. This decomposition is not unique, because adding a constant to one of the terms and subtracting it from another gives the same utility. A **canonical representation** for additive utility has a unique decomposition. Canonical forms are easier to acquire as each number can be acquired without considering the other numbers. To put additive utility into canonical form, for each feature $X_i$, define a local utility function $u_i(X_i)$ that has a value of 0 for the value of $X_i$ in the worst outcome and 1 for the value of $X_i$ in the best outcome, and a non-negative real weight, $w_i$. The $w_i$ weights should sum to 1. The utility as a function of the variables is

$$u(X_1, \ldots, X_n) = w_1 * u_1(X_1) + \cdots + w_n * u_n(X_n).$$

To elicit such a utility function requires eliciting each local utility function and assessing the weights. Each feature, if it is relevant, must have a best value for an agent and a worst value for the agent. Assessing the local functions and weights can be done as follows. Consider just $X_1$; the other features then can be treated analogously. For feature $X_1$, values $x_1$ and $x_1'$ for $X_1$, and fixed values $x_2, \ldots, x_n$ for $X_2, \ldots, X_n$:

$$u(x_1, x_2, \ldots, x_n) - u(x_1', x_2, \ldots, x_n) = w_1 * (u_1(x_1) - u_1(x_1')). \quad (12.1)$$

The weight $w_1$ can be derived when $x_1$ is the best outcome and $x_1'$ is the worst outcome (because then $u_1(x_1) - u_1(x_1') = 1$). The values of $u_1$ for the other values in the domain of $X_1$ can be computed using Equation (12.1), making $x_1'$ the worst outcome (as then $u_1(x_1') = 0$).

Assuming additive independence entails making a strong independence assumption. In particular, in Equation (12.1), the difference in utilities must be the same for all values $x_2, \ldots, x_n$ for $X_2, \ldots, X_n$.

Additive independence is often not a good assumption. Consider binary features $X$ and $Y$, with domains $\{x_0, x_1\}$ and $\{y_0, y_1\}$.

- Two values of $X$ and $Y$ are **complements** if having both is better than the sum of having the two separately. More formally, values $x_1$ and $y_1$ are complements if getting one when the agent has the other is more valuable than when the agent does not have the other:

$$u(x_1, y_1) - u(x_0, y_1) > u(x_1, y_0) - u(x_0, y_0).$$

- Two values are **substitutes** if having both is not worth as much as the sum of having each one. More formally, values $x_1$ and $y_1$ are substitutes if getting one when the agent has the other is less valuable than getting one when the agent does not have the other:

$$u(x_1, y_0) - u(x_0, y_0) > u(x_1, y_1) - u(x_0, y_1).$$

**Example 12.3** For a purchasing agent in the travel domain, consider the utility function for having a plane booking for a particular day and a hotel booking for the same day:

| *Plane* | *Hotel* | Utility |
|---|---|---|
| *true* | *true* | 100 |
| *true* | *false* | 0 |
| *false* | *true* | 10 |
| *false* | *false* | 20 |

Thus

$$u(plane, hotel) - u(\neg plane, hotel) = 90$$
$$> u(plane, \neg hotel) - u(\neg plane, \neg hotel) = -20.$$

Thus, a plane booking and a hotel booking are complements: one without the other does not give a good outcome.

If the person taking the holiday would enjoy one outing, but not two, on the same day, the two outings on the same day would be substitutes.

Additive utility assumes there are no substitutes or complements. When there is interaction, we require a more sophisticated model, such as a **generalized additive independence** model, which represents utility as a sum of terms, where each term can be a factor over multiple variables. Elicitation of the generalized additive independence model is much more involved than eliciting an additive model, because a variable can appear in many factors.

For Boolean features, it is possible to represent arbitrary utility using the analogy to the **canonical representation** (page 401) for probability. This extends the additive utility to allow weights for the conjunctions of atoms (which corresponds to the product when *true* is 1 and *false* is 0), including a bias term. Complements have a positive weight for the conjunction, and substitutes have a negative weight for the conjunction.

**Example 12.4** Consider Example 12.3. The utility for a plane and a hotel for the same day, as shown in the table, can be represented using

$$utility(Plane, Hotel) = w_0 + w_1 * Plane + w_2 * Hotel + w_3 * Plane * Hotel$$

where $w_0 = 20$, $w_1 = -20$, $w_2 = -10$, $w_3 = 110$.

For the two trips in Example 12.3, where the person does not want both, the weight for the product term would be negative.

It is common to start with representing just the simpler interactions, such as only representing the weights of single atoms and some pairwise products, and only introducing products of more atoms when necessary. If all conjunctions were included, there would be $2^n$ weights for $n$ propositions, which is the same as a table of all combinations of truth values. The canonical representation is useful when many of the weights are zero, and so don't need to be represented at all.

### 12.1.3 Prospect Theory

Utility theory is a **normative theory** of rational agents that is justified by a set of axioms. **Prospect theory** is a **descriptive theory** of people that seeks to describe how humans make decisions. A descriptive theory is evaluated by making observations of human behavior and by carrying out controlled psychology experiments.

Rather than having preferences over outcomes, prospect theory considers the context of the preferences. The idea that humans do not perceive absolute values, but values in context, is well established in psychology. Consider the Müller-Lyer illusion shown in Figure 12.4. The horizontal lines are of equal length, but in the context of the other lines, they appear to be different. As another example, if you have one hand in cold water and one in hot water, and then put both into warm water, the warm water will feel very different to each hand. People's preferences also depend on context. Prospect theory is based on the observation that it is not the outcomes that people have preferences over; what matters is how much the choice differs from the current situation.

The relationship between money and value that is predicted by prospect theory is shown in Figure 12.5 (page 529). Rather than having the absolute wealth on the $x$-axis, this graph shows the difference from the current wealth. The origin of the $x$-axis is the current state of the person's wealth. This position is called the **reference point**. Prospect theory predicts:

- For gains, people are risk averse. This can be seen as the curve above the current wealth is concave.

- For losses, people are risk seeking. This can be seen as the curve below the current wealth is convex.

Figure 12.4: Human perception of length depends on the context

- Losses are approximately twice as bad as gains. The slope for losses is steeper than that for gains.

It is not just money that has such a relationship, but anything that has value. Prospect theory makes different predictions about how humans will act than does utility theory, as in the following examples from Kahneman [2011, pp. 275, 291].

**Example 12.5** Consider Anthony and Betty:

- Anthony's current wealth is $1 million.
- Betty's current wealth is $4 million.

They are both offered the choice between a gamble and a sure thing.

- Gamble: equal chance to end up owning $1 million or $4 million.
- Sure thing: own $2 million.

Utility theory predicts that, assuming they have the same utility curve, Anthony and Betty will make the same choice, as the outcomes are identical. Utility theory does not take into account the current wealth. Prospect theory makes different predictions for Anthony and Betty. Anthony is making a gain and so will be risk averse, and so will probably go with the sure thing. Betty is making a loss, and so will be risk seeking and go with the gamble. Anthony will be happy with the $2 million, and does not want to risk being unhappy. Betty will be unhappy with the $2 million, and has a chance to be happy if she takes the gamble.

**Example 12.6** Twins Andy and Bobbie, have identical tastes and identical starting jobs. There are two jobs that are identical, except that

- job A gives a raise of $10,000
- job B gives an extra day of vacation per month.

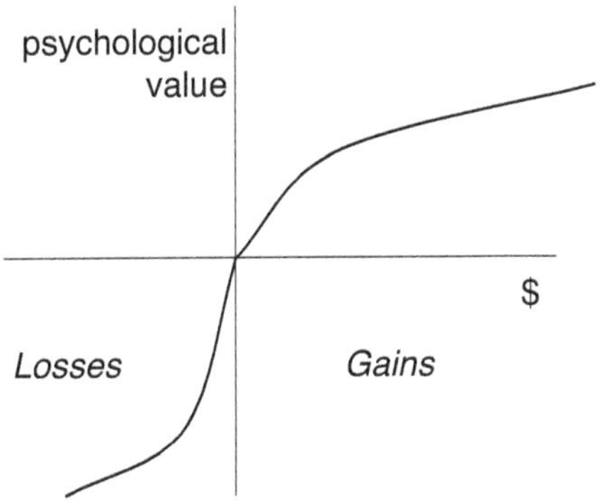


Figure 12.5: Money–value relationship for prospect theory

They are each indifferent to the outcomes and toss a coin. Andy takes job A, and Bobbie takes job B.

Now the company suggests they swap jobs with a $500 bonus.

Utility theory predicts that they will swap. They were indifferent and now can be $500 better off by swapping.

Prospect theory predicts they will not swap jobs. Given they have taken their jobs, they now have different reference points. Andy thinks about losing $10,000. Bobbie thinks about losing 12 days of holiday. The loss is much worse than the gain of the $500 plus the vacation or salary. They each prefer their own job.

Empirical evidence supports the hypothesis that prospect theory is better than utility theory in predicting human decisions. However, just because it better matches a human's choices does not mean it is the best for an artificial agent. An artificial agent that must interact with humans should, however, take into account how humans reason. For the rest of this chapter we assume utility theory as the basis for an artificial agent's decision making and planning.

## 12.2 One-Off Decisions

Basic decision theory applied to intelligent agents relies on the following assumptions:

- Agents know what actions they can carry out.
- The effect of each action can be described as a probability distribution over outcomes.
- An agent's preferences are expressed by utilities of outcomes.

It is a consequence of Proposition 12.3 (page 522) that, if agents only act for one step, a rational agent should choose an action with the highest expected utility.

**Example 12.7** Consider the problem of the delivery robot in which there is uncertainty in the outcome of its actions. In particular, consider the problem of going from position *o*109 in Figure 3.1 (page 81) to the *mail* position, where there is a chance that the robot will slip off course and fall down the stairs. Suppose the robot can get pads that will not change the probability of an accident but will make an accident less severe. Unfortunately, the pads add extra weight. The robot could also go the long way around, which would reduce the probability of an accident but make the trip much slower.

Thus, the robot has to decide whether to wear the pads and which way to go (the long way or the short way). What is not under its direct control is whether there is an accident, although this probability can be reduced by going the long way around. For each combination of the agent's choices and whether there is an accident, there is an outcome ranging from severe damage to arriving quickly without the extra weight of the pads.

Whose Values?

Any computer program or person who acts or gives advice is using some value system to judge what is important and what is not.

> *Alice ... went on "Would you please tell me, please, which way I ought to go from here?"*
>
> *"That depends a good deal on where you want to get to," said the Cat.*
>
> *"I don't much care where –" said Alice.*
>
> *"Then it doesn't matter which way you go," said the Cat.*
>
> – Lewis Carroll (1832–1898)
> *Alice's Adventures in Wonderland*, 1865

We all, of course, want computers to work on *our* value system, but they cannot act according to everyone's value system. When you build programs to work in a laboratory, this is not usually a problem. The program acts according to the goals and values of the program's designer, who is also the program's user. When there are multiple users of a system, you must be aware of whose value system is incorporated into a program. If a company sells a medical diagnostic program to a doctor, does the advice the program gives reflect the values of society, the company, the doctor, the patient, or whoever is paying (all of whom may have very different value systems)? Does it determine the doctor's or the patient's values?

For autonomous cars, do the actions reflect the utility of the owner or the utility of society? Consider the choice between injuring $n$ people walking across the road or injuring $m$ family members by swerving to miss the pedestrians. How do the values of the lives trade off for different values of $n$ and $m$, and different chances of being injured or killed? Drivers who most want to protect their family would have different trade-offs than the pedestrians. This situation has been studied using **trolley problems**, where the trade-offs are made explicit and people give their moral opinions. See Section 2.4 (page 71).

If you want to build a system that gives advice to someone, you should find out what is true as well as what their values are. For example, in a medical diagnostic system, the appropriate procedure depends not only on patients' symptoms but also on their priorities. Are they prepared to put up with some pain in order to be more aware of their surroundings? Are they willing to put up with a lot of discomfort to live longer? What risks are they prepared to take? Always be suspicious of a program or person that tells you what to do if it does not ask you what you want to do! As builders of programs that do things or give advice, you should be aware of whose value systems are incorporated into the actions or advice. If people are affected, their preferences should be taken into account, or at least they should be aware of whose preferences are being used as a basis for decisions.

In one-off decision making, a **decision variable** is used to model an agent's choice. A decision variable is like a random variable, but it does not have an associated probability distribution. Instead, an agent gets to choose a value for a decision variable. A **possible world** specifies values for both random and decision variables. Each possible world has an associated utility. For each combination of values to decision variables, there is a probability distribution over the random variables. That is, for each assignment of a value to each decision variable, the measures of the worlds that satisfy that assignment sum to 1.

Figure 12.6 shows a **decision tree** that depicts the different choices available to the agent and the outcomes of those choices. To read the decision tree, start at the root (on the left in this figure). For the decision nodes, shown as squares, the agent gets to choose which branch to take. For each random node, shown as a circle, the agent does not get to choose which branch will be taken; rather, there is a probability distribution over the branches from that node. Each leaf corresponds to a world, which is the **outcome** if the path to that leaf is followed.

**Example 12.8** In Example 12.7 (page 530) there are two decision variables, one corresponding to the decision of whether the robot wears pads and one to the decision of which way to go. There is one random variable, whether there is an accident or not. Eight possible worlds correspond to the eight paths in the decision tree of Figure 12.6.

What the agent should do depends on how important it is to arrive quickly, how much the pads' weight matters, how much it is worth to reduce the damage from severe to moderate, and the likelihood of an accident.

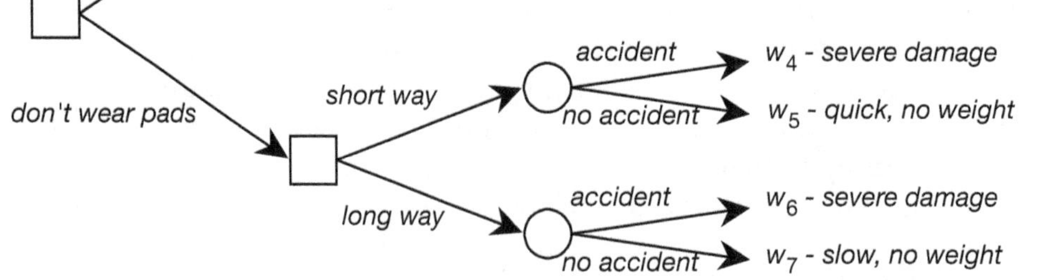


Figure 12.6: A decision tree for the delivery robot. Square boxes represent decisions that the robot can make. Circles represent random variables that the robot cannot observe before making its decision

The proof of Proposition 12.3 (page 522) specifies how to measure the desirability of the outcomes. Suppose we decide to have utilities in the range [0,100]. First, choose the best outcome, which would be $w_5$, and give it a utility of 100. The worst outcome is $w_6$, so assign it a utility of 0. For each of the other worlds, consider the lottery between $w_6$ and $w_5$. For example, $w_0$ may have a utility of 35, meaning the agent is indifferent between $w_0$ and $[0.35 : w_5, 0.65 : w_6]$, which is slightly better than $w_2$, which may have a utility of 30. $w_1$ may have a utility of 95, because it is only slightly worse than $w_5$.

**Example 12.9** In medical **diagnosis**, decision variables correspond to various treatments and tests. The utility may depend on the costs of tests and treatment and whether the patient gets better, stays sick, or dies, and whether they have short-term or chronic pain. The outcomes for the patient depend on the treatment the patient receives, the patient's physiology, and the details of the disease, which may not be known with certainty.

The same approach holds for diagnosis of artifacts such as airplanes; engineers test components and fix them. In airplanes, you may hope that the utility function is to minimize accidents (maximize safety), but the utility incorporated into such decision making is often to maximize profit for a company and accidents are simply costs taken into account.

In a one-off decision, the agent chooses a value for each decision variable simultaneously. This can be modeled by treating all the decision variables as a single composite decision variable, $D$. The domain of this decision variable is the cross product of the domains of the individual decision variables.

Each world $\omega$ specifies an assignment of a value to the decision variable $D$ and an assignment of a value to each random variable. Each world has a utility, given by the variable $u$.

A **single decision** is an assignment of a value to the decision variable. The **expected utility** of single decision $D = d_i$ is $\mathbb{E}(u \mid D = d_i)$, the expected value (page 383) of the utility conditioned on the value of the decision. This is the average utility of the worlds, where the worlds are weighted according to their probability:

$$\mathbb{E}(u \mid D = d_i) = \sum_{\omega : D(\omega) = d_i} u(\omega) * P(\omega)$$

where $D(\omega)$ is the value of variable $D$ in world $\omega$, $u(\omega)$ is the value of utility in $\omega$, and $P(\omega)$ is the probability of world $\omega$.

An **optimal single decision** is the decision whose expected utility is maximal. That is, $D = d_{max}$ is an optimal decision if

$$\mathbb{E}(u \mid D = d_{max}) = \max_{d_i \in domain(D)} \mathbb{E}(u \mid D = d_i)$$

where $domain(D)$ is the domain of decision variable $D$. Thus

$$d_{max} = \arg \max_{d_i \in domain(D)} \mathbb{E}(u \mid D = d_i).$$

**Example 12.10** The delivery robot problem of Example 12.7 (page 530) is a single decision problem where the robot has to decide on the values for the variables *Wear_pads* and *Which_way*. The single decision is the complex decision variable $\langle Wear\_pads, Which\_way \rangle$. Each assignment of a value to each decision variable has an expected value. For example, the expected utility of $Wear\_pads = true \land Which\_way = short$ is given by

$$\begin{aligned}&\mathbb{E}(u \mid wear\_pads \land Which\_way = short)\\&\quad = P(accident \mid wear\_pads \land Which\_way = short) * u(w_0)\\&\quad + (1 - P(accident \mid wear\_pads \land Which\_way = short)) * u(w_1)\end{aligned}$$

where $u(w_i)$ is the value of the utility in worlds $w_i$, the worlds $w_0$ and $w_1$ are as in Figure 12.6 (page 532), and *wear_pads* means $Wear\_pads = true$.

## 12.2.1 Single-Stage Decision Networks

A decision tree is a state-based representation where each path from a root to a leaf corresponds to a state. It is, however, often more natural and more efficient to represent and reason directly in terms of features, represented as variables.

A **single-stage decision network** is an extension of a belief network with three kinds of nodes:

- **Decision nodes**, drawn as rectangles, represent decision variables. The agent gets to choose a value for each decision variable. Where there are multiple decision variables, we assume there is a total ordering of the decision nodes, and the decision nodes before a decision node $D$ in the total ordering are the parents of $D$.
- **Chance nodes**, drawn as ovals, represent random variables. These are the same as the nodes in a belief network. Each chance node has an associated domain and a conditional probability of the variable, given its parents. As in a belief network, the parents of a chance node represent conditional dependence: a variable is independent of its non-descendants, given its parents. In a decision network, both chance nodes and decision nodes can be parents of a chance node.
- A single **utility node**, drawn as a diamond, represents the utility. The parents of the utility node are the variables on which the utility depends. Both chance nodes and decision nodes can be parents of the utility node.

Each chance variable and each decision variable has a domain. There is no domain for the utility node. Whereas the chance nodes represent random variables and the decision nodes represent decision variables, there is no utility variable.

Associated with a decision network is a conditional probability for each chance node given its parents (as in a belief network) and a utility as a function of the utility node's parents. In the specification of the network, there are no functions associated with a decision (although the algorithm will construct a function).

**Example 12.11** Figure 12.7 gives a decision network representation of Example 12.7 (page 530). There are two decisions to be made: which way to go and whether to wear padding. Whether the agent has an accident only depends on which way they go. The utility depends on all three variables.

This network requires two factors: a factor representing the conditional probability, $P(Accident \mid Which\_way)$, and a factor representing the utility as a function of *Which_way*, *Accident*, and *Wear_pads*. Tables for these factors are shown in Figure 12.7.

A **policy** for a single-stage decision network is an assignment of a value to each decision variable. Each policy has an expected utility. An **optimal policy** is a policy whose expected utility is maximal. That is, it is a policy such that no other policy has a higher expected utility. The **value** of a decision network is the expected utility of an optimal policy for the network.

Figure 12.8 (page 536) shows how **variable elimination** (page 413) is used to find an optimal policy in a single-stage decision network. After pruning irrelevant nodes and summing out all random variables, there will be a single factor that represents the expected utility for each combination of decision variables. This factor does not have to be a factor on *all* of the decision variables;

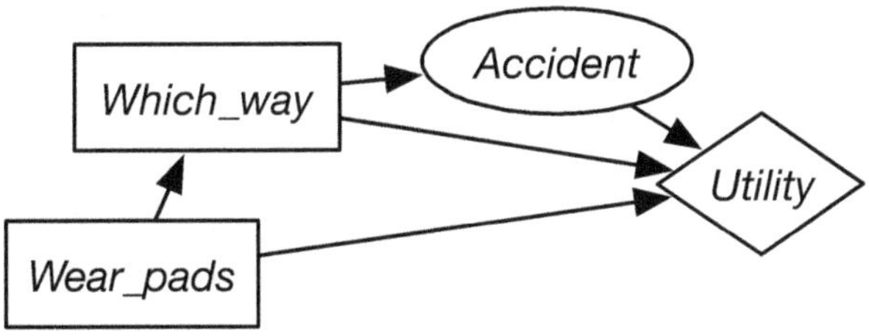


| *Which_way* | *Accident* | Value |
|---|---|---|
| *short* | *true* | 0.2 |
| *short* | *false* | 0.8 |
| *long* | *true* | 0.01 |
| *long* | *false* | 0.99 |

| *Wear_pads* | *Which_way* | *Accident* | Utility |
|---|---|---|---|
| *true* | *short* | *true* | 35 |
| *true* | *short* | *false* | 95 |
| *true* | *long* | *true* | 30 |
| *true* | *long* | *false* | 75 |
| *false* | *short* | *true* | 3 |
| *false* | *short* | *false* | 100 |
| *false* | *long* | *true* | 0 |
| *false* | *long* | *false* | 80 |

Figure 12.7: Single-stage decision network for the delivery robot

however, those decision variables that are not included are not relevant to the decision.

**Example 12.12** Consider running *VE_SSDN* on the decision network of Figure 12.7 (page 535). No nodes are able to be pruned, so it sums out the only random variable, *Accident*. To do this, it multiplies both factors because they both contain *Accident*, and sums out *Accident*, giving the following factor:

| *Wear_pads* | *Which_way* | Value |
|---|---|---|
| *true* | *short* | $0.2 * 35 + 0.8 * 95 = 83$ |
| *true* | *long* | $0.01 * 30 + 0.99 * 75 = 74.55$ |
| *false* | *short* | $0.2 * 3 + 0.8 * 100 = 80.6$ |
| *false* | *long* | $0.01 * 0 + 0.99 * 80 = 79.2$ |

Thus, the policy with the maximum value – the optimal policy – is to take the short way and wear pads, with an expected utility of 83.

## 12.3 Sequential Decisions

Generally, agents do not make decisions in the dark without observing something about the world, nor do they make just a single decision. A more typical scenario is that the agent makes an observation, decides on an action, carries out that action, makes observations in the resulting world, then makes another decision conditioned on the observations, and so on. Subsequent actions can depend on what is observed, and what is observed can depend on previous actions. In this scenario, it is often the case that the sole reason for carrying out an action is to provide information for future actions. Actions that are carried out just to acquire information are called **information-seeking actions**. Such actions are only ever needed in partially observable environments. The formalism does not need to distinguish information-seeking actions from other

**procedure** *VE_SSDN*(*DN*)
  **Inputs**
    *DN* a single-stage decision network
  **Output**
    An optimal policy and the expected utility of that policy.
  Prune all nodes that are not ancestors of the utility node.
  Sum out all chance nodes.
  – at this stage there is a single factor *F* that was derived from utility
  Let $v$ be the maximum value in *F*
  Let *d* be an assignment that gives the maximum value
  return *d*, $v$

Figure 12.8: Variable elimination for a single-stage decision network actions. Typically actions will have both information outcomes as well as effects on the world.

A **sequential decision problem** models

- what actions are available to the agent at each stage
- what information is, or will be, available to the agent when it has to act
- the effects of the actions, and
- the desirability of these effects.

**Example 12.13** Consider a simple case of diagnosis where a doctor first chooses some tests and then treats a patient, taking into account the outcome of the tests. The reason the doctor may decide to do a test is so that some information (the test results) will be available at the next stage when treatment may be performed. The test results will be information that is available when the treatment is decided, but not when the test is decided. It is often a good idea to test, even if testing itself may harm the patient.

The actions available are the possible tests and the possible treatments. When the test decision is made, the information available will be the symptoms exhibited by the patient. When the treatment decision is made, the information available will be the patient's symptoms, what tests were performed, and the test results. The effect of the test is the test result, which depends on what test was performed and what is wrong with the patient. The effect of the treatment is some function of the treatment and what is wrong with the patient. The utility may include, for example, costs of tests and treatments, the pain and inconvenience to the patient in the short term, and the long-term prognosis.

### 12.3.1 Decision Networks

A **decision network** (also called an **influence diagram**) is a graphical representation of a finite sequential decision problem. Decision networks extend belief networks to include decision variables and utility. A decision network extends the single-stage decision network (page 534) to allow for sequential decisions, and allows both chance nodes and decision nodes to be parents of decision nodes.

In particular, a **decision network** is a directed acyclic graph (DAG) with chance nodes (drawn as ovals), decision nodes (drawn as rectangles), and a utility node (drawn as a diamond). The meaning of the arcs is as follows.

- Arcs coming into decision nodes represent the information that will be available when the decision is made.

- Arcs coming into chance nodes represent probabilistic dependence.

- Arcs coming into the utility node represent what the utility depends on.

**Example 12.14** Figure 12.9 shows a simple decision network for a decision of whether the agent should take an umbrella when it goes out. The agent's utility depends on the weather and whether it takes an umbrella. The agent does not get to observe the weather; it only observes the forecast. The forecast probabilistically depends on the weather.

As part of this network, the designer must specify the domain for each random variable and the domain for each decision variable. Suppose the random variable *Weather* has domain $\{norain, rain\}$, the random variable *Forecast* has domain $\{sunny, rainy, cloudy\}$, and the decision variable *Umbrella* has domain $\{take\_it, leave\_it\}$. There is no domain associated with the utility node. The designer also must specify the probability of the random variables given their parents. Suppose $P(Weather)$ is defined by

$$P(Weather = rain) = 0.3.$$

$P(Forecast \mid Weather)$ is given by

| *Weather* | *Forecast* | Probability |
|---|---|---|
| *norain* | *sunny* | 0.7 |
| *norain* | *cloudy* | 0.2 |
| *norain* | *rainy* | 0.1 |
| *rain* | *sunny* | 0.15 |
| *rain* | *cloudy* | 0.25 |
| *rain* | *rainy* | 0.6 |

Suppose the utility function, $u(Weather, Umbrella)$, is

| *Weather* | *Umbrella* | *Utility* |
|---|---|---|
| *norain* | *take_it* | 20 |
| *norain* | *leave_it* | 100 |
| *rain* | *take_it* | 70 |
| *rain* | *leave_it* | 0 |

There is no table specified for the *Umbrella* decision variable. It is the task of the planner to determine which value of *Umbrella* to select, as a function of the forecast.

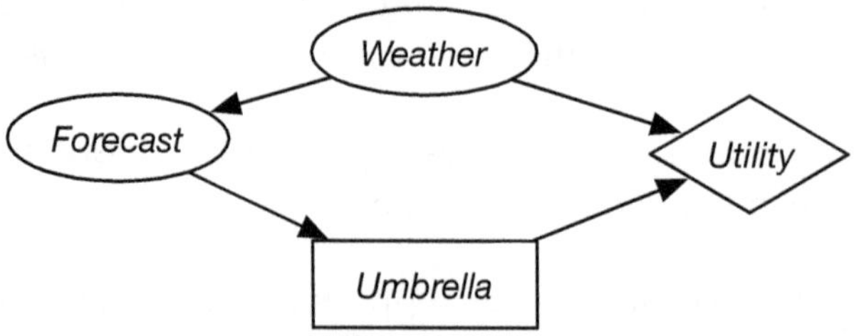


Figure 12.9: Decision network for decision of whether to take an umbrella

**Example 12.15** Figure 12.10 shows a decision network that represents the idealized diagnosis scenario of Example 12.13 (page 537). The symptoms depend on the disease. What test to perform is decided based on the symptoms. The test result depends on the disease and the test performed. The treatment decision is based on the symptoms, the test performed, and the test result. The outcome depends on the disease and the treatment. The utility depends on the costs of the test and on the outcome.

The outcome does not depend on the test, but only on the disease and the treatment, so the test presumably does not have side-effects. The treatment does not directly affect the utility; any cost of the treatment can be incorporated into the outcome. The utility needs to depend on the test unless all tests cost the same amount.

The diagnostic assistant that is deciding on the tests and the treatments never actually finds out what disease the patient has, unless the test result is definitive, which it, typically, is not.

**Example 12.16** Figure 12.11 (page 540) gives a decision network that is an extension of the belief network of Figure 9.3 (page 390). The agent can receive a report of people leaving a building and has to decide whether or not to call the fire department. Before calling, the agent can check for smoke, but this has some cost associated with it. The utility depends on whether it calls, whether there is a fire, and the cost associated with checking for smoke.

In this sequential decision problem, there are two decisions to be made. First, the agent must decide whether to check for smoke. The information that will be available when it makes this decision is whether there is a report of people leaving the building. Second, the agent must decide whether or not to call the fire department. When making this decision, the agent will know whether there was a report, whether it checked for smoke, and whether it can see smoke. Assume that all of the variables are binary.

The information necessary for the decision network includes the conditional probabilities of the belief network and

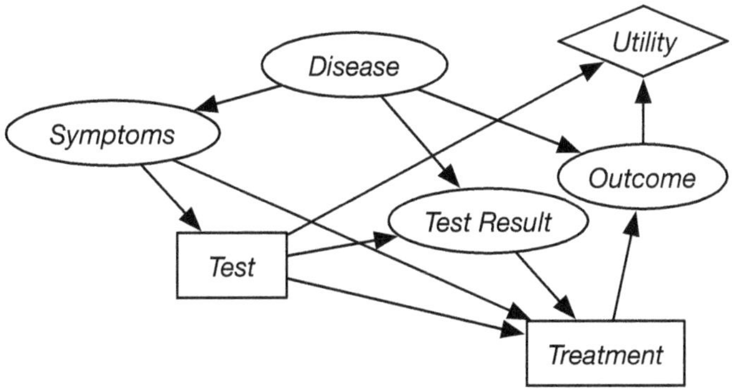


Figure 12.10: Decision network for idealized test–treat diagnosis scenario

- $P(See\_smoke \mid Smoke, Check\_smoke)$ – how seeing smoke depends on whether the agent looks for smoke and whether there is smoke. Assume that the agent has a perfect sensor for smoke. It will see smoke if and only if it looks for smoke and there is smoke. See Exercise 12.9 (page 578).
- $u(Check\_smoke, Fire, Call)$ – how the utility depends on whether the agent checks for smoke, whether there is a fire, and whether the fire department is called. Figure 12.12 provides this utility information. This utility function expresses the cost structure that calling has a cost of 200, checking has a cost of 20, but not calling when there is a fire has a cost of 5000. The utility is the negative of the cost.

A **no-forgetting agent** is an agent whose decisions are totally ordered in time, and the agent remembers its previous decisions and any information that was available to a previous decision.

A **no-forgetting decision network** is a decision network in which the decision nodes are totally ordered and, if decision node $D_i$ is before $D_j$ in the total

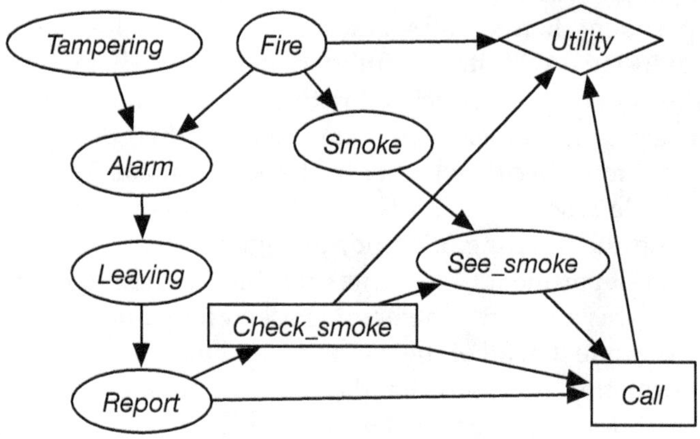


Figure 12.11: Decision network for the fire alarm decision problem

| *Check_smoke* | *Fire* | *Call* | *Utility* |
|---|---|---|---|
| *yes* | *true* | *yes* | −220 |
| *yes* | *true* | *no* | −5020 |
| *yes* | *false* | *yes* | −220 |
| *yes* | *false* | *no* | −20 |
| *no* | *true* | *yes* | −200 |
| *no* | *true* | *no* | −5000 |
| *no* | *false* | *yes* | −200 |
| *no* | *false* | *no* | 0 |

Figure 12.12: Utility for fire alarm decision network

ordering, then $D_i$ is a parent of $D_j$, and any parent of $D_i$ is also a parent of $D_j$.

Thus, any information available to $D_i$ is available to any subsequent decision, and the action chosen for decision $D_i$ is part of the information available for subsequent decisions. The no-forgetting condition is sufficient to make sure that the following definitions make sense and that the following algorithms work.

## 12.3.2 Policies

A **policy** specifies what the agent should do under all contingencies. A policy consists of a decision function for each decision variable. A **decision function** for a decision variable is a function that specifies a value for the decision variable for each assignment of values to its parents. Thus, a policy specifies, for each decision variable, what the agent will do for each of the possible observations.

**Example 12.17** In Example 12.14 (page 538), some of the policies are:

- Always bring the umbrella.
- Bring the umbrella only if the forecast is "rainy."
- Bring the umbrella only if the forecast is "sunny."

There are eight different policies, because there are three possible forecasts and there are two choices for each forecast.

**Example 12.18** In Example 12.16 (page 539), a policy specifies a decision function for *Check_smoke* and a decision function for *Call*. Some of the policies are:

- Never check for smoke, and call only if there is a report.
- Always check for smoke, and call only if it sees smoke.
- Check for smoke if there is a report, and call only if there is a report and it sees smoke.
- Check for smoke if there is no report, and call when it does not see smoke.
- Always check for smoke and never call.

There are four decision functions for *Check_smoke*. There are $2^8$ decision functions for *Call*; for each of the eight assignments of values to the parents of *Call*, the agent can choose to call or not. Thus there are $4 * 2^8 = 1024$ different policies.

### Expected Utility of a Policy

Each policy has an expected utility for an agent that follows the policy. A rational agent should adopt the policy that maximizes its expected utility.

A **possible world** specifies a value for each random variable and each decision variable. A possible world $\omega$ **satisfies** policy $\pi$ if for every decision variable $D$, $D(\omega)$ has the value specified by the policy given the values of the parents of $D$ in the possible world.

A possible world corresponds to a complete history and specifies the values of all random and decision variables, including all observed variables. Possible world $\omega$ satisfies policy $\pi$ if $\omega$ is one possible unfolding of history given that the agent follows policy $\pi$.

The **expected utility** of policy $\pi$ is

$$\mathbb{E}(u \mid \pi) = \sum_{\omega \text{ satisfies } \pi} u(\omega) * P(\omega)$$

where $P(\omega)$, the probability of world $\omega$, is the product of the probabilities of the values of the chance nodes given their parents' values in $\omega$, and $u(\omega)$ is the value of the utility $u$ in world $\omega$.

**Example 12.19** Consider Example 12.14 (page 538), let $\pi_1$ be the policy to take the umbrella if the forecast is cloudy and to leave it at home otherwise. The worlds that satisfy this policy are:

| *Weather* | *Forecast* | *Umbrella* |
|---|---|---|
| *norain* | *sunny* | *leave_it* |
| *norain* | *cloudy* | *take_it* |
| *norain* | *rainy* | *leave_it* |
| *rain* | *sunny* | *leave_it* |
| *rain* | *cloudy* | *take_it* |
| *rain* | *rainy* | *leave_it* |

Notice how the value for the decision variable is the one chosen by the policy. It only depends on the forecast.

The expected utility of this policy is obtained by averaging the utility over the worlds that satisfy this policy:

$$\begin{aligned}\mathbb{E}(u \mid \pi_1) = {} & P(norain) * P(sunny \mid norain) * u(norain, leave\_it) \\ & + P(norain) * P(cloudy \mid norain) * u(norain, take\_it) \\ & + P(norain) * P(rainy \mid norain) * u(norain, leave\_it) \\ & + P(rain) * P(sunny \mid rain) * u(rain, leave\_it) \\ & + P(rain) * P(cloudy \mid rain) * u(rain, take\_it) \\ & + P(rain) * P(rainy \mid rain) * u(rain, leave\_it)\end{aligned}$$

where *norain* means *Weather* $=$ *norain*, *sunny* means *Forecast* $=$ *sunny*, and similarly for the other values.

An **optimal policy** is a policy $\pi^*$ such that $\mathbb{E}(u \mid \pi^*) \geq \mathbb{E}(u \mid \pi)$ for all policies $\pi$. That is, an optimal policy is a policy whose expected utility is maximal over all policies.

Suppose a binary decision node has $n$ binary parents. There are $2^n$ different assignments of values to the parents and, consequently, there are $2^{2^n}$ different possible decision functions for this decision node. The number of policies is the product of the number of decision functions for each of the decision variables. Even small examples can have a huge number of policies. An algorithm that simply enumerates the policies looking for the best one will be very inefficient.

### 12.3.3 Optimizing Decision Networks using Search

The recursive conditioning algorithm for belief networks (page 409) can be extended to decision networks as follows:

- It takes a context, a set of factors for the conditional distributions of the random variables and the utility, and a set of decision variables.
- It returns a value for the optimal policy given the context and optimal decision functions for the decision variables for that context. The decision functions are represented as a set of $\langle context, d = v\rangle$ pairs, which means the optimal decision has decision variable $d$ taking value $v$ in *context*.
- The splitting order has the parents of each decision node come before the node, and these are the only nodes before the decision node. In particular, it cannot select a variable to split on that is not a parent of all remaining decision nodes. Thus, it is only applicable to no-forgetting decision networks (page 540). If it were to split on a variable $X$ that is not a parent of a decision variable $d$, it can make a different choice of a value for $d$ depending on the value of $X$, which cannot be implemented by an agent that does not know the value of $X$ when it has to do $d$.
- The utility node does not need to be treated differently from the factors defining probabilities; the utility just provides a number that is multiplied by the probabilities.
- To split on a decision node, the algorithm chooses a value that maximizes the values returned for each assignment of a value for that node.

Figure 12.13 (page 544) extends the naive search algorithm of Figure 9.9 (page 406) to solve decision networks. It is easiest to think of this algorithm as computing a sum over products, choosing the maximum value when there is a choice. The value returned by the recursive call is a mix of the probability and utility.

**Example 12.20** Consider Example 12.16 (page 539). The algorithm first splits on *Report* as it is a parent of all decision nodes. Consider the *false* branch. It then calls *DN_dfs* with context $\{Report = false\}$, and the decision variable *Check_smoke* is split. The recursive call will determine whether it is better to check when the report is false. It then splits on *See_smoke* and then *Call*. The other factors can be eliminated in any order.

The call to *DN_dfs* with context $\{Report = false\}$ returns the pair

$$\langle P(Report = false) * utility(\pi), \pi \rangle$$

where $\pi$ is the optimal policy when $Report = false$.

Table 12.1 (page 545) shows what factors can be evaluated for one variable ordering. It is difficult to interpret the numbers being returned by the recursive calls. Some are just products of probability (recursive calls after the *Utility* factor is evaluated), and some are a mix of probability and utility. The easiest way to think about this is that the algorithm is computing the sum of a product of numbers, maximizing for a choice at the decision nodes.

The algorithm of Figure 12.13 does not exploit the independence of graphical structure, but all of the enhancements of recursive conditioning (page 409), namely recognizing disconnected components and judicious caching can be incorporated unchanged.

### 12.3.4 Variable Elimination for Decision Networks

Variable elimination (page 413) can be adapted to find an optimal policy. The

```
procedure DN_dfs(Con, Fs, Ds)
            # Con:contest, Fs: set of factors, Ds: set of decision variables
            # Returns a value, and set of ⟨context, d = v⟩ pairs
    if Fs = {} then
        return (1, {})
    else if f ∈ Fs can be evaluated in Con then
        (v, p) := DN_dfs(Con, Fs \ {f}, Ds)
        return (eval(f, Con) * v, p)
    else if Con assigns all parents of decision node d ∈ Ds then
        max_value := −∞;  opt_decn := ⊥
        for val in domain(d) do
            (v, p) := DN_dfs(Con ∪ {d = val}, Fs, Ds \ {d})
            if v > max_value then
                max_value := v;  opt_decn := {⟨Con, d = val⟩} ∪ p
        return (max_value, opt_decn)
    else
        select variable var in vars(Fs) \ vars(Con) that is a parent of all d ∈ Ds
        sum := 0; policy = {}
        for val in domain(var) do
            (v, p) := DN_dfs(Con ∪ {var = val}, Fs, Ds)
            sum := sum + v; policy := policy ∪ p
        return (sum, policy)
```

Figure 12.13: Search-based optimization algorithm for decision networks idea is first to consider the *last* decision, find an optimal decision for each value of its parents, and produce a factor of these maximum values. This results in a new decision network, with one less decision, that can be solved recursively.

Figure 12.14 (page 546) shows how to use **variable elimination** for decision networks. Essentially, it computes the expected utility of an optimal decision. It eliminates the random variables that are not parents of a decision node by summing them out according to some elimination ordering. The ordering of the random variables being eliminated does not affect correctness and so it can be chosen for efficiency.

After eliminating all of the random variables that are not parents of a decision node, in a no-forgetting decision network, there must be one decision variable $D$ that is in a factor $F$ where all of the variables, other than $D$, in $F$ are parents of $D$. This decision $D$ is the *last* decision in the ordering of decisions.

To eliminate that decision node, *VE_DN* chooses the values for the decision that result in the maximum utility. This maximization creates a new factor on the remaining variables and a decision function for the decision variable being eliminated. This decision function created by maximizing is one of the decision functions in an optimal policy.

**Example 12.21** In Example 12.14 (page 538), there are three initial factors representing $P(Weather)$, $P(Forecast \mid Weather)$, and $u(Weather, Umbrella)$. First, it eliminates *Weather* by multiplying all three factors and summing out *Weather*, giving a factor on *Forecast* and *Umbrella*, shown on left of Table 12.2 (page 546). To maximize over *Umbrella*, for each value of *Forecast*, *VE_DN* selects the value of *Umbrella* that maximizes the value of the factor. For example, when the forecast is *sunny*, the agent should leave the umbrella at home for a value of 49.0. The resulting decision function is shown in Table 12.2 (page 546) (center), and the resulting factor is shown in Table 12.2 (page 546) (right).

It now sums out *Forecast* from this factor, which gives the value 77.0. This is the expected value of the optimal policy.

| Variable | Factor(s) Evaluated |
|---|---|
| *Report* | – |
| *Check_smoke* | – |
| *See_Smoke* | – |
| *Call* | – |
| *Tampering* | $P(Tampering)$ |
| *Fire* | $P(Fire), Utility(Fire, See\_smoke, Call)$ |
| *Smoke* | $P(Fire \mid Smoke), P(See\_smoke \mid Smoke)$ |
| *Alarm* | $P(Alarm \mid Tampering, Fire)$ |
| *Leaving* | $P(Leaving \mid Alarm), P(Report \mid Leaving)$ |

Table 12.1: Variables split on and factors evaluated for Example 12.20 (page 543)

**Example 12.22** Consider Example 12.16 (page 539). The initial factors are shown in Table 12.3 (page 547). The expected utility is the product of the probability and the utility, as long as the appropriate actions are chosen.

Table 12.3 (page 547) (bottom) shows the factors that are removed and created for one elimination ordering. The random variables that are not parents of a decision node are summed out first.

The factor $f_{16}$ is a number that is the expected utility of the optimal policy.

The following gives more detail of one of the factors. After summing out *Tampering*, *Fire*, *Alarm*, *Smoke*, and *Leaving*, there is a single factor, $f_{12}$, part of which (to two decimal places) is

```
procedure VE_DN(DN):
    Inputs
        DN a decision network
    Output
        An optimal policy and its expected utility
    Local
        DFs: a set of decision functions, initially empty
        Fs: a set of factors
    Remove all variables that are not ancestors of the utility node
    Create a factor in Fs for each conditional probability
    Create a factor in Fs for the utility
    while there are decision nodes remaining do
        Sum out each random variable that is not a parent of a decision node
        Let D be the last decision remaining
                # D is only in a factor F(D, V1, ..., Vk) where V1, ..., Vk are parents of D
        Add max_D F to Fs.
        Add arg max_D F to DFs.
    Sum out all remaining random variables
    Return DFs and the product of remaining factors
```

Figure 12.14: Variable elimination for decision networks

| *Forecast* | *Umbrella* | Value |
|---|---|---|
| *sunny* | *take_it* | 12.95 |
| *sunny* | *leave_it* | 49.0 |
| *cloudy* | *take_it* | 8.05 |
| *cloudy* | *leave_it* | 14.0 |
| *rainy* | *take_it* | 14.0 |
| *rainy* | *leave_it* | 7.0 |

| *Forecast* | *Umbrella* |
|---|---|
| *sunny* | *leave_it* |
| *cloudy* | *leave_it* |
| *rainy* | *take_it* |

| *Forecast* | *Value* |
|---|---|
| *sunny* | 49.0 |
| *cloudy* | 14.0 |
| *rainy* | 14.0 |

Table 12.2: Factors and decision functions created in Example 12.21 (page 545)

| *Report* | *See_smoke* | *Check_smoke* | *Call* | Value |
|---|---|---|---|---|
| *true* | *true* | *yes* | *yes* | −1.33 |
| *true* | *true* | *yes* | *no* | −29.30 |
| *true* | *true* | *no* | *yes* | 0 |
| *true* | *true* | *no* | *no* | 0 |
| *true* | *false* | *yes* | *yes* | −4.86 |
| *true* | *false* | *yes* | *no* | −3.68 |
| ... | ... | ... | ... | ... |

From this factor, an optimal decision function can be created for *Call* by selecting a value for *Call* that maximizes *Value* for each assignment to *Report*, *See_smoke*, and *Check_smoke*.

Consider the case when *Report* = *true*, *See_smoke* = *true*, and *Check_smoke* = *yes*. The maximum of −1.33 and −29.3 is −1.33, so for this case, the optimal action is *Call* = *yes* with value −1.33. This maximization is repeated for the other values of *Report*, *See_smoke*, and *Check_smoke*.

An optimal decision function for *Call* is

---

Initial factors:

| *Meaning* | *Factor* |
|---|---|
| $P(Tampering)$ | $f_0(Tampering)$ |
| $P(Fire)$ | $f_1(Fire)$ |
| $P(Alarm \mid Tampering, Fire)$ | $f_2(Tampering, Fire, Alarm)$ |
| $P(Smoke \mid Fire)$ | $f_3(Fire, Smoke)$ |
| $P(Leaving \mid Alarm)$ | $f_4(Alarm, Leaving)$ |
| $P(Report \mid Leaving)$ | $f_5(Leaving, Report)$ |
| $P(See\_smoke \mid Check\_smoke, Smoke)$ | $f_6(Smoke, See\_smoke, Check\_smoke)$ |
| $u(Fire, Check\_smoke, Call)$ | $f_7(Fire, Check\_smoke, Call)$ |

The factors that are removed and created for one elimination ordering:

| Variable | How | Removed | Factor Created |
|---|---|---|---|
| *Tampering* | sum | $f_0, f_2$ | $f_8(Fire, Alarm)$ |
| *Fire* | sum | $f_1, f_8, f_3, f_7$ | $f_9(Alarm, Smoke, Check\_Smoke, Call)$ |
| *Alarm* | sum | $f_4, f_9$ | $f_{10}(Smoke, Check\_Smoke, Call, Leaving)$ |
| *Smoke* | sum | $f_{10}, f_6$ | $f_{11}(Check\_Smoke, Leaving, See\_Smoke, Call)$ |
| *Leaving* | sum | $f_5, f_{11}$ | $f_{12}(Report, See\_Smoke, Check\_Smoke, Call)$ |
| *Call* | max | $f_{12}$ | $f_{13}(Check\_Smoke, See\_Smoke, Report)$ |
| *See_smoke* | sum | $f_{13}$ | $f_{14}(Check\_Smoke, Report)$ |
| *Check_smoke* | max | $f_{14}$ | $f_{15}(Report)$ |
| *Report* | sum | $f_{15}$ | $f_{16}$ |

Table 12.3: Initial and created factors in Example 12.22 (page 546)

---

| *Report* | *See_smoke* | *Check_smoke* | *Call* |
|---|---|---|---|
| *true* | *true* | *yes* | *yes* |
| *true* | *true* | *no* | *yes* |
| *true* | *false* | *yes* | *no* |
| ... | ... | ... | ... |

The value for *Call* when *Report* = *true*, *See_smoke* = *true*, and *Check_smoke* = *no* is arbitrary. It does not matter what the agent plans to do in this situation, because the situation never arises. The algorithm does not need to treat this as a special case.

The factor resulting from maximizing *Call* contains the maximum values for each combination of *Report*, *See_smoke*, and *Check_smoke*:

| *Report* | *See_smoke* | *Check_smoke* | Value |
|---|---|---|---|
| *true* | *true* | *yes* | −1.33 |
| *true* | *true* | *no* | 0 |
| *true* | *false* | *yes* | −3.68 |
| ... | ... | ... | ... |

Summing out *See_smoke* gives the factor

| *Report* | *Check_smoke* | Value |
|---|---|---|
| *true* | *yes* | −5.01 |
| *true* | *no* | −5.65 |
| *false* | *yes* | −23.77 |
| *false* | *no* | −17.58 |

Maximizing *Check_smoke* for each value of *Report* gives the decision function

| *Report* | *Check_smoke* |
|---|---|
| *true* | *yes* |
| *false* | *no* |

and the factor

| *Report* | Value |
|---|---|
| *true* | −5.01 |
| *false* | −17.58 |

Summing out *Report* gives the expected utility of −22.60 (taking into account rounding errors).

Thus, the policy returned can be seen as the rules

*check_smoke* ← *report*.

*call* ← *see_smoke*.

*call* ← *report* ∧ ¬*check_smoke* ∧ ¬*see_smoke*.

The last of these rules is never used because the agent following the optimal policy does check for smoke if there is a report. It remains in the policy because *VE_DN* has not determined an optimal policy for *Check_smoke* when it is optimizing *Call*.

Note also that, in this case, even though checking for smoke has an immediate negative reward, checking for smoke is worthwhile because the information obtained is valuable.

The following example shows how the factor containing a decision variable can contain a subset of its parents when the VE algorithm optimizes the decision.

**Example 12.23** Consider Example 12.14 (page 538), but with an extra arc from *Weather* to *Umbrella*. That is, the agent gets to observe both the weather and the forecast. In this case, there are no random variables to sum out, and the factor that contains the decision node and a subset of its parents is the original utility factor. It can then maximize *Umbrella*, giving the decision function and the factor:

| *Weather* | *Umbrella* |
|---|---|
| *norain* | *leave_it* |
| *rain* | *take_it* |

| *Weather* | *Value* |
|---|---|
| *norain* | 100 |
| *rain* | 70 |

Note that the forecast is irrelevant to the decision. Knowing the forecast does not give the agent any useful information. Summing out *Forecast* gives a factor where all of the values are 1.

Summing out *Weather*, where $P(Weather = norain) = 0.7$, gives the expected utility $0.7 * 100 + 0.3 * 70 = 91$.

Variable elimination for decision networks of Figure 12.14 (page 546) has similar complexity to the combination of depth-first search of Figure 12.13 (page 544) with recursive conditioning (page 409). They are carrying out the same computations on a different order. In particular, the values stored in the cache of recursive conditioning are the same as the values in the factors of variable elimination. Recursive conditioning allows for the exploitation of various representations of conditional probability, but storing the values in a cache is less efficient than storing the values using a tabular representation. When the networks are infinite, as below, the more sophisticated algorithms are usually based on one or the other.

## 12.4 The Value of Information and Control

Information can be valuable to agents if it helps them make better decisions.

**Example 12.24** In Example 12.22 (page 546), the action *Check_smoke* provides information about fire. Checking for smoke costs 20 units and does not provide any direct reward; however, in an optimal policy, it is worthwhile to check for smoke when there is a report because the agent can condition its further actions on the information obtained. Thus, the information about smoke is valuable to the agent, even though smoke only provides imperfect information about whether there is fire.

One of the important lessons from this example is that an information-seeking action, such as *Check_smoke*, can be treated in the same way as any other action, such as *Call*. An optimal policy often includes actions whose only purpose is to find information, as long as subsequent actions can condition on some effect of the action. Most actions do not just provide information; they also have a more direct effect on the world.

If $X$ is a random variable and $D$ is a decision variable, the **value of information** about $X$ for decision $D$ is how much extra utility can be obtained by knowing the value for $X$ when decision $D$ is made. This depends on what is controlled and what else is observed for each decision, which is the information provided in a decision network.

The value of information about $X$ for decision $D$ in a no-forgetting decision network $N$ is

- the value of decision network $N$ with an arc added from $X$ to $D$, and with arcs added from $X$ to the decisions after $D$ to ensure that the network remains a no-forgetting decision network (page 540)
- minus the value of the decision network $N$ where $D$ does not have information about $X$, and the no-forgetting arcs are not added.

This is only defined when $X$ is not a successor of $D$, because that would cause a cycle. (Something more sophisticated must be done when adding the arc from $X$ to $D$ causes a cycle.)

**Example 12.25** In Example 12.14 (page 538), consider how much it could be worth to get a better forecast. The value of getting perfect information about the weather for the decision about whether to take an umbrella is the difference between the value of the network with an arc from *Weather* to *Umbrella* which, as calculated in Example 12.23 (page 549), is 91 and the original network, which, as computed in Example 12.14 (page 538), is 77. Thus, the value of information about *Weather* for the *Umbrella* decision is $91 - 77 = 14$.

The value of information has some interesting properties:

- The value of information is never negative. The worst that can happen is that the agent can ignore the information.
- If an optimal decision is to do the same thing no matter which value of $X$ is observed, the value of information $X$ is zero. If the value of information $X$ is zero, there is an optimal policy that does not depend on the value of $X$ (i.e., the same action can be chosen no matter which value of $X$ is observed).

The value of information is a bound on the amount the agent should be willing to pay (in terms of loss of utility) for information $X$ for decision $D$. It is an upper bound on the amount that **imperfect information** about the value of $X$ at decision $D$ would be worth. Imperfect information is the information available from a noisy sensor of $X$. It is not worth paying more for a sensor of $X$ than the value of information about $X$ for the earliest decision that could use the information of $X$.

**Example 12.26** In the fire alarm problem of Example 12.22 (page 546), the agent may be interested in knowing whether it is worthwhile to try to detect tampering. To determine how much a tampering sensor could be worth, consider the value of information about tampering.

The following are the values (the expected utility of the optimal policy, to one decimal point) for some variants of the network. Let $N_0$ be the original network.

- The network $N_0$ has a value of −22.6.
- Let $N_1$ be the same as $N_0$ but with an arc added from *Tampering* to *Call*. $N_1$ has a value of −21.3.
- Let $N_2$ be the same as $N_1$ except that it also has an arc from *Tampering* to *Check_smoke*. $N_2$ has a value of −20.9.
- Let $N_3$ be the same as $N_2$ but without the arc from *Report* to *Check_smoke*. $N_3$ has the same value as $N_2$.

The difference in the values of the optimal policies for the first two decision networks, namely 1.3, is the value of information about *Tampering* for the decision *Call* in network $N_0$. The value of information about *Tampering* for the decision *Check_smoke* in network $N_0$ is 1.7. Therefore, installing a tampering sensor could at most give an increase of 1.7 in expected utility.

In the context $N_3$, the value of information about *Tampering* for *Check_smoke* is 0. In the optimal policy for the network with both arcs, the information about *Alarm* is ignored in the optimal decision function for *Check_smoke*; the agent never checks for smoke when deciding whether to call in the optimal policy when *Alarm* is a parent of *Call*.

The **value of control** specifies how much it is worth to control a variable. In its simplest form, it is the change in value of a decision network where a random variable is replaced by a decision variable, and arcs are added to make it a no-forgetting network. If this is done, the change in utility is non-negative; the resulting network always has an equal or higher expected utility than the original network.

**Example 12.27** In the fire alarm decision network of Figure 12.11 (page 540), you may be interested in the value of controlling *Tampering*. This could, for example, be used to estimate how much it is worth to add security guards to prevent tampering. To compute this, compare the value of the decision network of Figure 12.11 (page 540) to the decision network where *Tampering* is a decision node and a parent of the other two decision nodes.

To determine the value of control, turn the *Tampering* node into a decision node and make it a parent of the other two decisions. The value of the resulting network is −20.7. This can be compared to the value of $N_3$ in Example 12.26 (which has the same arcs, and differs in whether *Tampering* is a decision or random node), which was −20.9. Notice that control is more valuable than information.

The previous description assumed the parents of the random variable that is being controlled become parents of the decision variable. In this case, the value of control is never negative. However, if the parents of the decision node do not include all of the parents of the random variable, it is possible that control is less valuable than information. In general, one must be explicit about what information will be available when controlling a variable.

**Example 12.28** Consider controlling the variable *Smoke* in the network of Figure 12.11. If *Fire* is a parent of the decision variable *Smoke*, it has to be a parent of *Call* to make it a no-forgetting network. The expected utility of the resulting network with *Smoke* coming before *Check_smoke* is −2.0. The value of controlling *Smoke* in this situation is due to observing *Fire*. The resulting optimal decision is to call if there is a fire and not call otherwise.

Suppose the agent were to control *Smoke* without observing *Fire*. That is, the agent can decide to make smoke or prevent smoke, and *Fire* is not a parent of any decision. This situation can be modeled by making *Smoke* a decision variable with no parents. In this case, the expected utility is −23.20, which is worse than the initial decision network, because blindly controlling *Smoke* loses its ability to act as a sensor for *Fire*.

## 12.5 Decision Processes

Recall that the **planning horizon** (page 23) is how far ahead an agent considers when planning. The decision networks of Section 12.3.1 (page 537) were for finite-stage, partially observable domains. This section considers indefinite-horizon and infinite-horizon problems.

Often an agent must reason about an ongoing process or it does not know how many actions it will be required to do. These are called **infinite-horizon** problems when the process may go on forever or **indefinite-horizon** problems when the agent will eventually stop, but it does not know when it will stop.

For ongoing processes, it may not make sense to consider only the utility at the end, because the agent may never get to the end. Instead, an agent can receive a sequence of rewards. **Rewards** provide a way to factor utility (page 522) through time, by having a reward for each time, and accumulating (page 555) the rewards to determine utility. Rewards can incorporate action costs in addition to any prizes or penalties that may be awarded. Negative rewards are called **punishments**. Indefinite-horizon problems can be modeled using a stopping state. A **stopping state** or **absorbing state** is a state in which all actions have no effect; that is, when the agent is in that state, all actions immediately return to that state with a zero reward. Goal achievement can be modeled by having a reward for entering such a stopping state.

A Markov decision process can be seen as a Markov chain (page 418) augmented with actions and rewards or as a decision network extended in time. At each stage, the agent decides which action to perform; the reward and the resulting state depend on both the previous state and the action performed.

Unless noted, assume a **stationary model** (page 418), where the state transitions and the rewards do not depend on the time.

A **Markov decision process**, or **MDP**, consists of

- $S$, a set of states of the world
- $A$, a set of actions
- $P : S \times S \times A \rightarrow [0,1]$, which specifies the **dynamics**. This is written as $P(s' \mid s,a)$, the probability of the agent transitioning into state $s'$ given that the agent is in state $s$ and does action $a$. Thus

$$\forall s \in S\ \forall a \in A\ \sum_{s' \in S} P(s' \mid s,a) = 1.$$

- $R : S \times A \times S \rightarrow \Re$, where $R(s,a,s')$, the **reward function**, gives the expected immediate reward from doing action $a$ and transitioning to state $s'$ from state $s$. Sometimes it is convenient to use $R(s,a)$, the expected value of doing $a$ in state $s$, which is $R(s,a) = \sum_{s'} R(s,a,s') * P(s' \mid s,a)$.

A finite part of a Markov decision process can be depicted using a decision network as in Figure 12.15.

**Example 12.29** Suppose Sam wanted to make an informed decision about whether to party or relax over the weekend. Sam prefers to party, but is worried about getting sick. Such a problem can be modeled as an MDP with two states, *healthy* and *sick*, and two actions, *relax* and *party*. Thus

$$S = \{healthy, sick\}$$
$$A = \{relax, party\}.$$

Based on experience, Sam estimates that the dynamics $P(s' \mid s,a)$ is given by

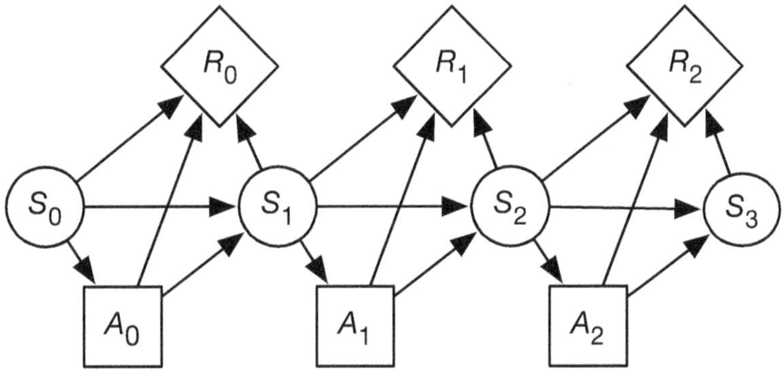


Figure 12.15: Decision network representing a finite part of an MDP

| $S$ | $A$ | Probability of $s' = healthy$ |
|---|---|---|
| *healthy* | *relax* | 0.95 |
| *healthy* | *party* | 0.7 |
| *sick* | *relax* | 0.5 |
| *sick* | *party* | 0.1 |

So, if Sam is healthy and parties, there is a 30% chance of becoming sick. If Sam is healthy and relaxes, Sam will more likely remain healthy. If Sam is sick and relaxes, there is a 50% chance of getting better. If Sam is sick and parties, there is only a 10% chance of becoming healthy.

Sam estimates the rewards to be the following, irrespective of the resulting state:

| $S$ | $A$ | Reward |
|---|---|---|
| *healthy* | *relax* | 7 |
| *healthy* | *party* | 10 |
| *sick* | *relax* | 0 |
| *sick* | *party* | 2 |

Thus, Sam always enjoys partying more than relaxing. However, Sam feels much better overall when healthy, and partying results in being sick more than relaxing does.

The problem is to determine what Sam should do each weekend.

**Example 12.30** A grid world is an idealization of a robot in an environment. At each time, the robot is at some location and can move to neighboring locations, collecting rewards and punishments. Suppose that the actions are stochastic, so that there is a probability distribution over the resulting states given the action and the state.

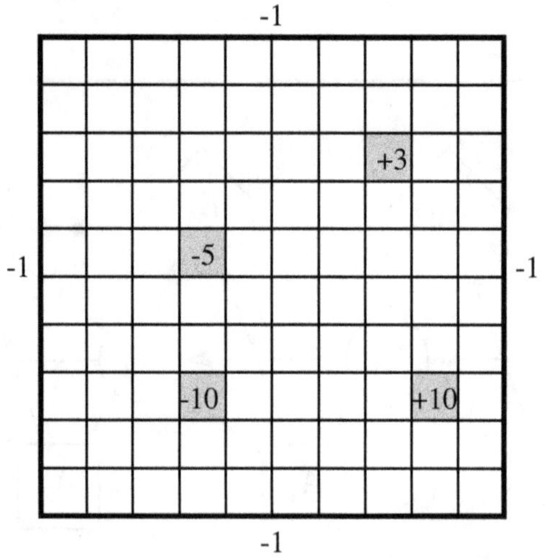


Figure 12.16: The grid world of Example 12.30

Figure 12.16 (page 554) shows a $10 \times 10$ grid world, where the robot can choose one of four actions: up, down, left, or right. If the agent carries out one of these actions, it has a 0.7 chance of going one step in the desired direction and a 0.1 chance of going one step in any of the other three directions. If it bumps into the outside wall (i.e., the location computed is outside the grid), there is a penalty of 1 (i.e., a reward of $-1$) and the agent does not actually move. There are four rewarding states (apart from the walls), one worth $+10$ (at position $(9,8)$; 9 across and 8 down), one worth $+3$ (at position $(8,3)$), one worth $-5$ (at position $(4,5)$), and one worth $-10$ (at position $(4,8)$). In each of these states, the agent gets the reward after it carries out an action in that state, not when it enters the state. When the agent reaches one of the states with positive reward (either $+3$ or $+10$), no matter what action it performs, at the next step it is flung, at random, to one of the four corners of the grid world.

Note that the reward in this example depends on both the initial state and the final state. The agent bumped into the wall, and so received a reward of $-1$, if and only if the agent remains in the same state. Knowing just the initial state and the action, or just the final state and the action, does not provide enough information to infer the reward.

As with decision networks (page 537), the designer also has to consider what information is available to the agent when it decides what to do. There are two variations:

- In a **fully observable Markov decision process (MDP)**, the agent gets to observe the current state when deciding what to do.
- A **partially observable Markov decision process (POMDP)** is a combination of an MDP and a **hidden Markov model (HMM)** (page 420). At each time, the agent gets to make some (ambiguous and possibly noisy) observations that depend on the state. The agent only has access to the history of rewards, observations, and previous actions when making a decision. It cannot directly observe the current state.

## Rewards

To decide what to do, the agent compares different sequences of rewards. The most common way to do this is to convert a sequence of rewards into a number called the **return**, the **cumulative reward**, or the **value**. This is a number that specifies the utility to an agent of the current and future rewards. To compute the return, the agent combines the current reward with other rewards in the future. Suppose the agent receives the sequence of rewards

$$r_1, r_2, r_3, r_4, \ldots.$$

Three common reward criteria are used to combine rewards into a value $V$:

**Total reward** $V = \sum_{i=1}^{\infty} r_i$. In this case, the value is the sum of all of the rewards. This works when you can guarantee that the sum is finite; but if the sum is infinite, it does not give any opportunity to compare which sequence of rewards is preferable. For example, a sequence of 1 rewards has the same total as a sequence of 100 rewards (both are infinite). One case where the total reward is finite is when there are stopping states (page 552) and the agent always has a non-zero probability of eventually entering a stopping state.

**Average reward** $V = \lim_{n \to \infty}(r_1 + \cdots + r_n)/n$. In this case, the agent's value is the average of its rewards, averaged over for each time period. As long as the rewards are finite, this value will also be finite. However, whenever the total reward is finite, the average reward is zero, and so the average reward will fail to allow the agent to choose among different actions that each have a zero average reward. Under this criterion, the only thing that matters is where the agent ends up. Any finite sequence of bad actions does not affect the limit. For example, receiving 1,000,000 followed by rewards of 1 has the same average reward as receiving 0 followed by rewards of 1 (they both have an average reward of 1).

**Discounted reward** $V = r_1 + \gamma r_2 + \gamma^2 r_3 + \cdots + \gamma^{i-1} r_i + \cdots$, where $\gamma$, the **discount factor**, is a number in the range $0 \leq \gamma < 1$. Under this criterion, future rewards are worth less than the current reward. If $\gamma$ was 1, this would be the same as the total reward. When $\gamma = 0$, the agent ignores all future rewards. Having $0 \leq \gamma < 1$ guarantees that, whenever the rewards are finite, the total value will also be finite.

The discounted reward can be rewritten as

$$\begin{aligned} V &= \sum_{i=1}^{\infty} \gamma^{i-1} r_i \\ &= r_1 + \gamma r_2 + \gamma^2 r_3 + \cdots + \gamma^{i-1} r_i + \cdots \\ &= r_1 + \gamma(r_2 + \gamma(r_3 + \cdots)). \end{aligned}$$

Suppose $V_k$ is the reward accumulated from time $k$:

$$\begin{aligned} V_k &= r_k + \gamma(r_{k+1} + \gamma(r_{k+2} + \cdots)) \\ &= r_k + \gamma V_{k+1}. \end{aligned}$$

To understand the properties of $V_k$, suppose $S = 1 + \gamma + \gamma^2 + \gamma^3 + \cdots$, then $S = 1 + \gamma S$. Solving for $S$ gives $S = 1/(1-\gamma)$. Thus, with the discounted reward, the value of all of the future is at most $1/(1-\gamma)$ times as much as the maximum reward and at least $1/(1-\gamma)$ times as much as the minimum reward. Therefore, the eternity of time from now only has a finite value compared with the immediate reward, unlike the average reward, in which the immediate reward is dominated by the cumulative reward for the eternity of time.

In economics, $\gamma$ is related to the interest rate: getting \$1 now is equivalent to getting \$$(1+i)$ in one year, where $i$ is the interest rate. You could also see the discount rate as the probability that the agent survives; $\gamma$ can be seen as the probability that the agent keeps going.

The rest of this chapter considers discounted rewards, referred to as the **return** or **value**.

### 12.5.1 Policies

In a fully-observable Markov decision process, the agent gets to observe its current state before deciding which action to carry out. For now, assume that the Markov decision process is fully observable. A **policy** for an MDP specifies what the agent should do as a function of the state it is in. A **stationary policy** is a function $\pi : S \to A$. In a non-stationary policy the action is a function of the state and the time; we assume policies are stationary.

Given a reward criterion, a policy has an **expected return**, often referred to as the **expected value**, for every state. Let $V^{\pi}(s)$ be the expected value of following $\pi$ in state $s$. This is the utility an agent that is in state $s$ and following policy $\pi$ receives, on average. Policy $\pi$ is an **optimal policy** if for every policy $\pi'$ and state $s$, $V^{\pi}(s) \geq V^{\pi'}(s)$. That is, an optimal policy is at least as good as any other policy for every state.

**Example 12.31** For Example 12.29 (page 553), with two states and two actions, there are $2^2 = 4$ policies:

- Always relax.
- Always party.
- Relax if healthy and party if sick.
- Party if healthy and relax if sick.

The total reward for all of these is infinite because the agent never stops, and can never continually get a reward of 0. To determine the average reward is left as an exercise (Exercise 12.15 (page 580)). How to compute the discounted reward is discussed in the next section.

**Example 12.32** In the grid-world MDP of Example 12.30 (page 554), there are 100 states and 4 actions, therefore there are $4^{100} \approx 10^{60}$ stationary policies. Each policy specifies an action for each state.

For infinite-horizon problems, a stationary MDP always has an optimal stationary policy. However, for finite-stage problems, a non-stationary policy might be better than all stationary policies. For example, if the agent had to stop at time $n$, for the last decision in some state, the agent would act to get the largest immediate reward without considering the future actions, but for earlier decisions it may decide to get a lower reward immediately to obtain a larger reward later.

### Foundations of Discounting

You might wonder whether there is something special about discounted rewards, or they are just an arbitrary way to define utility over time. Utility follows from the axioms of Section 12.1.1 (page 518). **Discounting** can be proved to follow from a set of assumptions, as follows.

With an infinite sequence of outcomes $\langle o_1, o_2, o_3, \dots \rangle$ the following assumptions hold

- the first time period matters, so there exist $o_1, o_2, o_3, \dots$ and $o_1'$ such that

$$\langle o_1, o_2, o_3, \dots \rangle \succ \langle o_1', o_2, o_3, \dots \rangle$$

- a form of additive independence (page 526), where preferences for the first two time periods do not depend on the future:

$$\langle x_1, x_2, o_3, o_4 \dots \rangle \succ \langle y_1, y_2, o_3, o_4 \dots \rangle$$
if and only if
$$\langle x_1, x_2, o_3', o_4' \dots \rangle \succ \langle y_1, y_2, o_3', o_4' \dots \rangle$$

- time stationarity, where if the first outcome is the same, preference depends on the remainder:

$$\langle o_1, o_2, o_3, \dots \rangle \succ \langle o_1, o_2', o_3', \dots \rangle$$
if and only if
$$\langle o_2, o_3, \dots \rangle \succ \langle o_2', o_3', \dots \rangle$$

- some extra technical conditions specifying that the agent is only concerned about finite subspaces of infinite time

if and only if there exists a discount factor $\gamma$ and function $r$ such that

$$utility(\langle o_1, o_2, o_3, \dots \rangle) = \sum_i \gamma^{i-1} r(o_i)$$

where $r$ does not depend on the time, only the outcome. These are quite strong assumptions, for example, disallowing complements and substitutes (page 526). It is standard to engineer the rewards to make them true.

### Value of a Policy

Consider how to compute the expected value, using the discounted reward of a policy, given a discount factor of $\gamma$. The value is defined in terms of two interrelated functions:

- $V^\pi(s)$ is the expected value for an agent that is in state $s$ and following policy $\pi$.
- $Q^\pi(s,a)$ is the expected value for an agent that is starting in state $s$, then doing action $a$, then following policy $\pi$. This is called the **Q-value** of policy $\pi$.

$Q^\pi$ and $V^\pi$ are defined recursively in terms of each other. If the agent is in state $s$, performs action $a$, and arrives in state $s'$, it gets the immediate reward of $R(s,a,s')$ plus the discounted future return, $\gamma V^\pi(s')$. When the agent is planning it does not know the actual resulting state, so it uses the expected value, averaged over the possible resulting states:

$$\begin{aligned} Q^\pi(s,a) &= \sum_{s'} P(s' \mid s,a)(R(s,a,s') + \gamma V^\pi(s')) \\ &= R(s,a) + \gamma \sum_{s'} P(s' \mid s,a) V^\pi(s') \end{aligned} \tag{12.2}$$

where $R(s,a) = \sum_{s'} P(s' \mid s,a) R(s,a,s')$.

$V^\pi(s)$ is obtained by doing the action specified by $\pi$ and then following $\pi$:

$$V^\pi(s) = Q^\pi(s, \pi(s)).$$

### Value of an Optimal Policy

Let $Q^*(s,a)$, where $s$ is a state and $a$ is an action, be the expected value of doing $a$ in state $s$ and then following the optimal policy. Let $V^*(s)$, where $s$ is a state, be the expected value of following an optimal policy from state $s$.

$Q^*$ can be defined analogously to $Q^\pi$:

$$\begin{aligned} Q^*(s,a) &= \sum_{s'} P(s' \mid s,a)(R(s,a,s') + \gamma V^*(s')) \\ &= R(s,a) + \gamma \sum_{s'} P(s' \mid s,a) \gamma V^*(s'). \end{aligned}$$

$V^*(s)$ is obtained by performing the action that gives the best value in each state:

$$V^*(s) = \max_a Q^*(s,a).$$

An optimal policy $\pi^*$ is one of the policies that gives the best value for each state:

$$\pi^*(s) = \arg\max_a Q^*(s,a)$$

where $\arg\max_a Q^*(s,a)$ is a function of state $s$, and its value is an action $a$ that results in the maximum value of $Q^*(s,a)$.

### 12.5.2 Value Iteration

Value iteration is a method of computing an optimal policy for an MDP and its value.

Value iteration starts at the "end" and then works backward, refining an estimate of either $Q^*$ or $V^*$. There is really no end, so it uses an arbitrary end point. Let $V_k$ be the value function assuming there are $k$ stages to go, and let $Q_k$ be the Q-function assuming there are $k$ stages to go. These can be defined recursively. Value iteration starts with an arbitrary function $V_0$. For subsequent stages, it uses the following equations to get the functions for $k+1$ stages to go from the functions for $k$ stages to go:

$$Q_{k+1}(s,a) = R(s,a) + \gamma * \sum_{s'} P(s' \mid s,a) * V_k(s')$$

$$V_k(s) = \max_a Q_k(s,a).$$

Value iteration can either save a $V[S]$ array or a $Q[S,A]$ array. Saving the $V$ array results in less storage, but it is more difficult to determine an optimal action, and one more iteration is needed to determine which action results in the greatest value.

Figure 12.17 (page 561) shows the value iteration algorithm when the $V$ array is stored. This procedure converges no matter what the initial value function $V_0$ is. An initial value function that approximates $V^*$ converges quicker than one that does not. The basis for many abstraction techniques for MDPs is to use some heuristic method to approximate $V^*$ and to use this as an initial seed for value iteration.

**Example 12.33** Consider the two-state MDP of Example 12.29 (page 553) with discount $\gamma = 0.8$. We write the value function as $[healthy\_value, sick\_value]$ and the Q-function as $[[healthy\_relax, healthy\_party], [sick\_relax, sick\_party]]$. Suppose initially the value function is $[0,0]$. The next Q-value is $[[7,10],[0,2]]$, so the next value function is $[10,2]$ (obtained by Sam partying). The next Q-value is then

| *State* | *Action* | Value | | |
|---|---|---|---|---|
| *healthy* | *relax* | $7 + 0.8 * (0.95 * 10 + 0.05 * 2)$ | = | 14.68 |
| *healthy* | *party* | $10 + 0.8 * (0.7 * 10 + 0.3 * 2)$ | = | 16.08 |
| *sick* | *relax* | $0 + 0.8 * (0.5 * 10 + 0.5 * 2)$ | = | 4.8 |
| *sick* | *party* | $2 + 0.8 * (0.1 * 10 + 0.9 * 2)$ | = | 4.24 |

So the next value function is $[16.08, 4.8]$. After 1000 iterations, the value function is $[35.71, 23.81]$. So the Q-function is $[[35.10, 35.71], [23.81, 22.0]]$. Therefore, the optimal policy is to party when healthy and relax when sick.

**Example 12.34** Consider the nine squares around the +10 reward of Example 12.30 (page 554). The discount is $\gamma = 0.9$. Suppose the algorithm starts with $V_0[s] = 0$ for all states $s$.

The values of $V_1$, $V_2$, and $V_3$ (to one decimal point) for these nine cells are

| | | |
|---|---|---|
| 0 | 0 | −0.1 |
| 0 | 10 | −0.1 |
| 0 | 0 | −0.1 |

$V_1$

| | | |
|---|---|---|
| 0 | 6.3 | −0.1 |
| 6.3 | 9.8 | 6.2 |
| 0 | 6.3 | −0.1 |

$V_2$

| | | |
|---|---|---|
| 4.5 | 6.2 | 4.4 |
| 6.2 | 9.7 | 6.6 |
| 4.5 | 6.1 | 4.4 |

$V_3$

After the first step of value iteration (in $V_1$), the nodes get their immediate expected reward. The center node in this figure is the +10 reward state. The right nodes have a value of −0.1, with the optimal actions being up, left, and down; each of these has a 0.1 chance of crashing into the wall for an immediate expected reward of −1.

$V_2$ are the values after the second step of value iteration. Consider the node that is immediately to the left of the +10 reward state. Its optimal value is to go to the right; it has a 0.7 chance of getting a reward of 10 in the following state, so that is worth 9 (10 times the discount of 0.9) to it now. The expected reward for the other possible resulting states is 0. Thus, the value of this state is $0.7 * 9 = 6.3$.

Consider the node immediately to the right of the +10 reward state after the second step of value iteration. The agent's optimal action in this state is to

**procedure** *Value_iteration*$(S, A, P, R)$
    **Inputs**
        $S$ is the set of all states
        $A$ is the set of all actions
        $P$ is the state transition function specifying $P(s' \mid s, a)$
        $R$ is a reward function $R(s, a)$
    **Output**
        $\pi[S]$ approximately optimal policy
        $V[S]$ value function
    **Local**
        real array $V_k[S]$ is a sequence of value functions
        action array $\pi[S]$
    assign $V_0[S]$ arbitrarily
    $k := 0$
    **repeat**
        $k := k + 1$
        **for each** state $s$ **do**
            $V_k[s] = \max_a R(s, a) + \gamma * \sum_{s'} P(s' \mid s, a) * V_{k-1}[s']$
    **until** termination
    **for each** state $s$ **do**
        $\pi[s] = \arg\max_a R(s, a) + \gamma * \sum_{s'} P(s' \mid s, a) * V_k[s']$
    **return** $\pi, V_k$

Figure 12.17: Value iteration for MDPs, storing $V$

go left. The value of this state is

| | Prob | Reward | | Future Value | |
|---|---|---|---|---|---|
| | $0.7 * ($ | $0$ | $+$ | $0.9 * 10)$ | *Agent goes left* |
| $+$ | $0.1 * ($ | $0$ | $+$ | $0.9 * -0.1)$ | *Agent goes up* |
| $+$ | $0.1 * ($ | $-1$ | $+$ | $0.9 * -0.1)$ | *Agent goes right* |
| $+$ | $0.1 * ($ | $0$ | $+$ | $0.9 * -0.1)$ | *Agent goes down* |

which evaluates to 6.173, which is approximated to 6.2 in $V_2$ above.

The +10 reward state has a value less than 10 in $V_2$ because the agent gets flung to one of the corners and these corners look bad at this stage.

After the next step of value iteration, shown on the right-hand side of the figure, the effect of the +10 reward has progressed one more step. In particular, the corners shown get values that indicate a reward in three steps.

The value iteration algorithm of Figure 12.17 (page 561) has an array for each stage, but it really only needs to store the current and previous arrays. It can update one array based on values from the other.

A common refinement of this algorithm is **asynchronous value iteration**. Rather than sweeping through the states to create a new value function, asynchronous value iteration updates the states one at a time, in any order, and stores the values in a single array. Asynchronous value iteration can store either the $Q[s,a]$ array or the $V[s]$ array. Figure 12.18 (page 563) shows asynchronous value iteration when the $Q$-array is stored. It converges faster than value iteration and is the basis of some of the algorithms for reinforcement learning (page 583). Termination can be difficult to determine if the agent must guarantee a particular error, unless it is careful about how the actions and states are selected. Often, this procedure is run indefinitely as an **anytime algorithm** (page 26), where it is always prepared to give its best estimate of the optimal action in a state when asked.

Asynchronous value iteration could also be implemented by storing just the $V[s]$ array. In that case, the algorithm selects a state $s$ and carries out the update

$$V[s] := \max_a R(s,a) + \gamma * \sum_{s'} P(s' \mid s,a) * V[s'].$$

Although this variant stores less information, it is more difficult to extract the policy. It requires one extra backup to determine which action $a$ results in the maximum value. This can be done using

$$\pi[s] := \arg\max_a R(s,a) + \gamma * \sum_{s'} P(s' \mid s,a) * V[s'].$$

**Example 12.35** In Example 12.34 (page 560), the state one step up and one step to the left of the +10 reward state only had its value updated after three value iterations, in which each iteration involved a sweep through all of the states.

In asynchronous value iteration, the +10 reward state can be chosen first. Next, the node to its left can be chosen, and its value will be $0.7 * 0.9 * 10 = 6.3$. Next, the node above that node could be chosen, and its value would become $0.7 * 0.9 * 6.3 = 3.969$. Note that it has a value that reflects that it is close to a +10 reward after considering three states, not 300 states, as does value iteration.

### 12.5.3 Policy Iteration

**Policy iteration** starts with a policy and iteratively improves it. It starts with an arbitrary policy $\pi_0$ (an approximation to the optimal policy works best) and carries out the following steps, starting from $i = 0$.

- Policy evaluation: determine $V^{\pi_i}(S)$. The definition of $V^{\pi}$ is a set of $|S|$ linear equations in $|S|$ unknowns. The unknowns are the values of $V^{\pi_i}(S)$. There is an equation for each state. These equations can be solved by a linear equation solution method (such as Gaussian elimination) or they can be solved iteratively.
- Policy improvement: choose $\pi_{i+1}(s) = \arg\max_a Q^{\pi_i}(s, a)$, where the Q-value can be obtained from $V$ using Equation (12.2) (page 559). To detect

```
procedure Asynchronous_value_iteration(S, A, P, R)
    Inputs
        S is the set of all states
        A is the set of all actions
        P is the state transition function specifying P(s' | s, a)
        R is a reward function R(s, a)
    Output
        π[s] policy
        Q[S, A] value function
    Local
        real array Q[S, A]
        action array π[S]
    assign Q[S, A] arbitrarily
    repeat
        select a state s
        select an action a
        Q[s, a] = R(s, a) + γ * Σ_s' P(s' | s, a) * max_a' Q[s', a']
    until termination
    for each state s do
        π[s] = arg max_a Q[s, a]
    return π, Q
```

Figure 12.18: Asynchronous value iteration for MDPs

when the algorithm has converged, it should only change the policy if the new action for some state improves the expected value; that is, it should set $\pi_{i+1}(s)$ to be $\pi_i(s)$ if $\pi_i(s)$ is one of the actions that maximizes $Q^{\pi_i}(s,a)$.

- Stop if there is no change in the policy, if $\pi_{i+1} = \pi_i$, otherwise increment $i$ and repeat.

The algorithm is shown in Figure 12.19. Note that it only keeps the latest policy and notices if it has changed. This algorithm always halts, usually in a small number of iterations. Unfortunately, solving the set of linear equations is often time consuming.

A variant of policy iteration, called **modified policy iteration**, is obtained by noticing that the agent is not required to evaluate the policy to improve it; it can just carry out a number of backup steps using Equation (12.2) (page 559)

```
procedure Policy_iteration(S, A, P, R)
    Inputs
        S is the set of all states
        A is the set of all actions
        P is the state transition function specifying P(s' | s, a)
        R is a reward function R(s, a)
    Output
        optimal policy π
    Local
        action array π[S]
        Boolean variable noChange
        real array V[S]
    set π arbitrarily
    repeat
        noChange := true
        Solve V[s] = R(s, a) + γ * Σ_{s'∈S} P(s' | s, π[s]) * V[s']
        for each s ∈ S do
            QBest := V[s]
            for each a ∈ A do
                Qsa := R(s, a) + γ * Σ_{s'∈S} P(s' | s, a) * V[s']
                if Qsa > QBest then
                    π[s] := a
                    QBest := Qsa
                    noChange := false
    until noChange
    return π
```

Figure 12.19: Policy iteration for MDPs

and then do an improvement.

Policy iteration is useful for systems that are too big to be represented explicitly as MDPs. One case is when there is a large action space, and the agent does not want to enumerate all actions at each time. The algorithm also works as long as an improving action is found, and it only needs to find an improving action probabilistically, for example, by testing some promising actions, rather than all.

Suppose a controller has some parameters that can be varied. An estimate of the derivative of the cumulative discounted reward of a parameter $a$ in some context $s$, which corresponds to the derivative of $Q(a, s)$, can be used to improve the parameter. Such an iteratively improving controller can get into a local maximum that is not a global maximum. Policy iteration for state-based MDPs does not result in non-optimal local maxima, because it is possible to improve an action for a state without affecting other states, whereas updating parameters can affect many states at once.

### 12.5.4 Dynamic Decision Networks

A Markov decision process is a state-based representation. Just as in classical planning (page 231), where reasoning in terms of features can allow for more straightforward representations and more efficient algorithms, planning under uncertainty can also take advantage of reasoning in term of features. This forms the basis for **decision-theoretic planning**.

A **dynamic decision network** (DDN) can be seen in a number of different ways:

- a factored representation of MDPs, where the states are described in terms of features
- an extension of decision networks to allow repeated structure for indefinite or infinite-horizon problems
- an extension of dynamic belief networks (page 427) to include actions and rewards
- an extension of the feature-based representation of actions (page 237) or the CSP representation of planning (page 244) to allow for rewards and for uncertainty in the effect of actions.

A **dynamic decision network** consists of

- a set of state features
- a set of possible actions
- a two-stage decision network with chance nodes $F_0$ and $F_1$ for each feature $F$ (for the features at time 0 and time 1, respectively) and decision node $A_0$, such that
    - the domain of $A_0$ is the set of all actions
    - the parents of $A_0$ are the set of time 0 features (these arcs are often not shown explicitly)

- the parents of time 0 features do not include $A_0$ or time 1 features, but can include other time 0 features as long as the resulting network is acyclic
- the parents of time 1 features can contain $A_0$ and other time 0 or time 1 features as long as the graph is acyclic
- there are probability distributions for $P(F_0 \mid parents(F_0))$ and $P(F_1 \mid parents(F_1))$ for each feature $F$
- the reward function depends on any subset of the action and the features at times 0 or 1.

As in a dynamic belief network, a dynamic decision network can be **unfolded** into a decision network by replicating the features and the action for each subsequent time. For a time horizon of $n$, there is a variable $F_i$ for each feature $F$ and for each time $i$ for $0 \leq i \leq n$. For a time horizon of $n$, there is a variable $A_i$ for each time $i$ for $0 \leq i < n$. The horizon, $n$, can be unbounded, which allows us to model processes that do not halt.

Thus, if there are $k$ features for a time horizon of $n$, there are $k * (n + 1)$ chance nodes (each representing a random variable) and $k$ decision nodes in the unfolded network.

The parents of $A_i$ are random variables $F_i$ (so that the agent can observe the state). Each $F_{i+1}$ depends on the action $A_i$ and the features at time $i$ and $i + 1$ in the same way, with the same conditional probabilities, as $F_1$ depends on the action $A_0$ and the features at time 0 and 1. The $F_0$ variables are modeled directly in the two-stage decision network.

**Example 12.36** Example 6.1 (page 232) models a robot that can deliver coffee and mail in a simple environment with four locations. Consider representing a stochastic version of Example 6.1 as a dynamic decision network. We use the same features as in that example.

Feature *RLoc* models the robot's location. The parents of variables $RLoc_1$ are $Rloc_0$ and $A$.

Feature *RHC* is true when the robot has coffee. The parents of $RHC_1$ are $RHC_0$, $A_0$, and $RLoc_0$; whether the robot has coffee depends on whether it had coffee before, what action it performed, and its location. The probabilities can encode the possibilities that the robot does not succeed in picking up or delivering the coffee, that it drops the coffee, or that someone gives it coffee in some other state (which we may not want to say is impossible).

Variable *SWC* is true when Sam wants coffee. The parents of $SWC_1$ include $SWC_0$, $RHC_0$, $A_0$, and $RLoc_0$. You would not expect $RHC_1$ and $SWC_1$ to be independent because they both depend on whether or not the coffee was successfully delivered. This could be modeled by having one be a parent of the other.

The two-stage belief network representing how the state variables at time 1 depend on the action and the other state variables is shown in Figure 12.20 (page 567). This figure also shows the reward as a function of the action, whether Sam stopped wanting coffee, and whether there is mail waiting.

Figure 12.21 (page 568) shows the unfolded decision network for a horizon of 3.

**Example 12.37** An alternate way to model the dependence between $RHC_1$ and $SWC_1$ is to introduce a new variable, $CSD_1$, which represents whether coffee was successfully delivered at time 1. This variable is a parent of both $RHC_1$ and $SWC_1$. Whether Sam wants coffee is a function of whether Sam wanted coffee before and whether coffee was successfully delivered. Whether the robot has coffee depends on the action and the location, to model the robot picking up coffee. Similarly, the dependence between $MW_1$ and $RHM_1$ can be modeled by introducing a variable $MPU_1$, which represents whether the mail was successfully picked up. The resulting DDN unfolded to a horizon of 2, but omitting the reward, is shown in Figure 12.22 (page 568).

If the reward comes only at the end, variable elimination for decision networks, shown in Figure 12.14 (page 546), can be applied directly. Variable elimination for decision networks corresponds to value iteration. Note that in fully observable decision networks, variable elimination does not require the no-forgetting condition. Once the agent knows the state, all previous decisions are irrelevant. If rewards are accrued at each time step, the algorithm must be augmented to allow for the addition (and discounting) of rewards. See Exercise 12.19 (page 582).

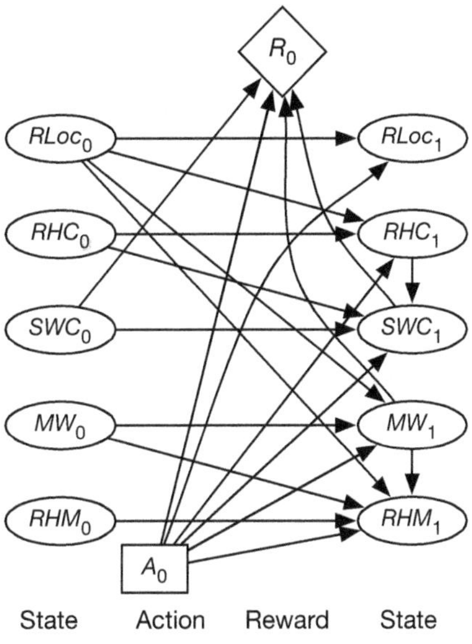


Figure 12.20: Two-stage dynamic decision network

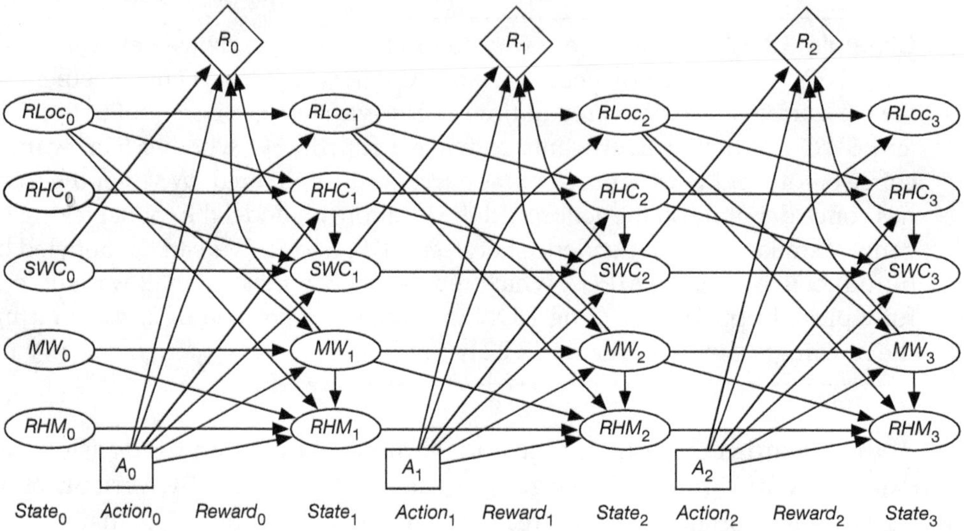


Figure 12.21: Dynamic decision network unfolded for a horizon of 3

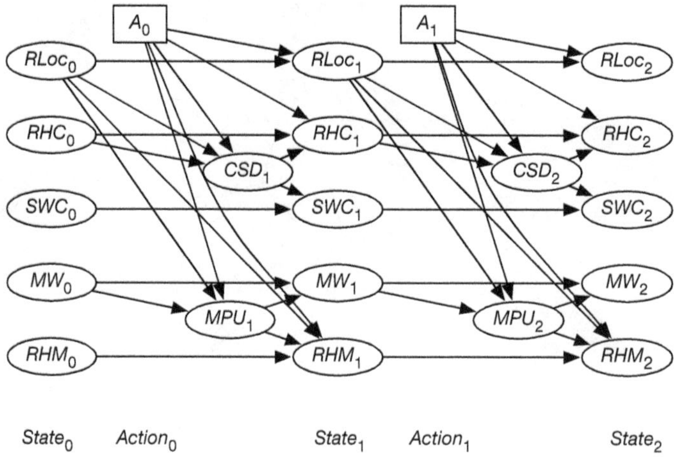


Figure 12.22: Dynamic decision network with intermediate variables for a horizon of 2, omitting the reward nodes

### 12.5.5 Partially Observable Decision Processes

A **partially observable Markov decision process (POMDP)** is a combination of an MDP (page 553) and a hidden Markov model (HMM) (page 420). Whereas the state in an MPD is assumed to be fully observable, the environment state in a POMDP is **partially observable** (page 30), which means the agent receives partial and/or noisy observations of the environment before it has to act.

A POMDP can be expressed as the infinite extension of the decision network of Figure 12.23, which explicitly shows the **belief state** (page 55) of the agent. The network extends indefinitely to the right.

A POMDP consists of the following variables and factors defining the external behavior of the agent:

- $S$, a set of states of the world
- $A$, a set of actions
- $O$, a set of possible observations
- $P(S_0)$, the probability distribution of the starting state
- $P(S' \mid S, A)$, the **dynamics** of the environment, is the probability of getting to state $S'$ by doing action $A$ from state $S$
- $R(S, A)$, the expected **reward** of starting in state $S$, doing action $A$
- $P(O \mid S, A, R)$, the probability of observing $O$ given the state is $S$, the previous action is $A$, and the reward is $R$.

$P(S' \mid S, A)$ and $R(S, A)$ are the same as in an MDP (page 553). The arc from $S_i$ to $O_i$ means that what the agent observes can depend on the state. The arc from $A_{i-1}$ to $O_i$ allows the agent to have actions that don't affect the environment, but affect its observations, such as paying **attention** to some part of the

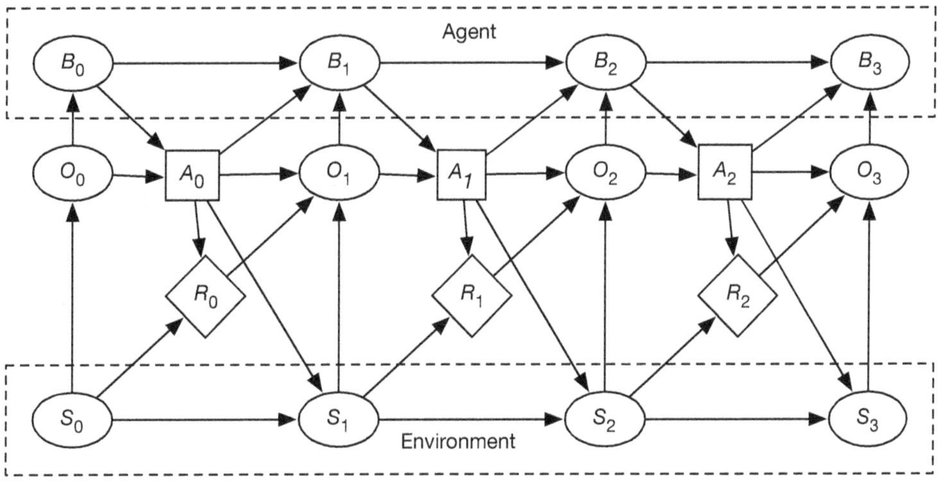


Figure 12.23: A POMDP with explicit belief states

environment. The arc from $R_{i-1}$ to $O_i$ indicates that the agent's observation can depend on the reward received; the agent is not assumed to observe the reward directly, as sometimes the rewards are only seen in retrospect. Observing the reward can often provide hints about the state that the agent might not actually be able to observe.

Internally, an agent has

- $B$, the set of possible belief states
- $T(B, A, O)$, a **belief state transition function** (page 56), which specifies the agent's new belief state given the previous belief state $B$, the action the agent did, $A$, and the observation, $O$; the belief state at stage $i$ is $B_i = T(B_{i-1}, A_{i-1}, O_i)$.
- $\pi(A_i \mid B_i, O_i)$, a **command function** (page 57) or **policy**, which specifies a **conditional plan** defining what the agent will do as a function of the belief state and the observation.

A policy might be stochastic to allow for exploration (page 591) or to confound other agents (page 623). The belief-state transition function is typically deterministic, representing probability distributions, that are updated based on the action and new observations.

Planning in a POMDP involves creating both a belief state transition function and a command function. The $B_i$ variables are special in that the world does not specify the domain or structure of these variables; an agent or its designer gets to choose the structure of a belief state, and how the agent acts based on its belief state, previous action, and latest observations. The belief state encodes all that the agent has remembered about its history.

There are a number of ways to represent a belief state and to find the optimal policy:

- The decision network of Figure 12.23 (page 569) can be solved using variable elimination for decision networks, shown in Figure 12.14 (page 546), extended to include discounted rewards. Adding the no-forgetting arcs (page 540) is equivalent to a belief state being the sequence of observations and actions; $B_i$ is $A_{i-1}$ and $O_i$ appended to the sequence $B_{i-1}$. The problem with this approach is that the history is unbounded, and the size of a policy is exponential in the length of the history. This is only practical when the history is short or is deliberately cut short.
- The belief state can be a probability distribution over the states of the environment. Maintaining the belief state is then the problem of filtering (page 422) in the associated hidden Markov model. The problem with this approach is that, with $n$ world states, the set of belief states is an $(n-1)$-dimensional real space. The agent then needs to find the optimal function from this multidimensional real space into the actions. The value of a sequence of actions only depends on the world states; as the belief state is a probability distribution over world states, the expected value of a belief state is a linear function of the values of the world states.

Not all points in $\Re^{n-1}$ are possible belief states, only those resulting from sequences of observations are possible. Policies can be represented as a **decision tree** with conditions being (functions of) the observations. The observations dictate which path in the tree the agent will follow. The value function for an agent choosing the best policy for any finite look-ahead is piecewise linear and convex. Although this is simpler than a general $\Re^{n-1}$ function, the number of conditional policies grows like $O^t$, where $O$ is the set of possible observations, and $t$ is the stage.

- In general, the belief state can be anything. A belief state can include probability distributions over some of the variables, and remembered observations and actions. The agent can search over the space of controllers for the best controller (page 55). Thus, the agent searches over what to remember (the belief state) and what to do based on its belief state. Note that the first two proposals are instances of this approach: the agent's belief state is all of its history, or the agent's belief state is a probability distribution over world states, both of which are intractable. Because the general case is unconstrained over what to remember, the search space is enormous.

## 12.6 Social Impact

Open and accountable decision making requires making utilities explicit, where they are open to scrutiny and people can argue why they are appropriate or not; see the box on page 531. When a decision is proposed, sensitivity analysis – exploring how the decision changes as utilities change – can determine just how much the utility matters. Making utilities explicit and open is particularly important for decisions in the public sphere that affect many people, however these are often controversial because people do not have a common utility function.

Designing utilities and rewards so that the policies have desirable properties is called **utility engineering** or **reward engineering**. This is particularly difficult for unobservable constructs such as socioeconomic status, teacher effectiveness, and risk of recidivism for decisions on poverty reduction, education, or crime. These cannot be measured directly, but need to be inferred from a **measurement model** of observable properties, such as death rate, student ratings, or rearrests. However, an agent optimizing for the measurement model might not actually optimize for what is desired. Jacobs and Wallach [2021] analyze the interaction of measurement models and **fairness**.

One case where explicit utilities have been used is for resource allocation in health care, particularly for jurisdictions where the allocation is based on need, not ability to pay. A measure used in a number of countries is the **quality-adjusted life year (QALY)**, a utility-based measure for evaluating medical interventions, such as (expensive) drugs or surgeries. For each possible intervention, it uses a utility of 1 for a healthy life for a year and 0 for death. The utility can be negative for outcomes that are considered worse than death. Outcomes are assessed as a lottery between the maximum and minimum utilities. The utility of the intervention is the sum of this value over each expected year of life. If the intervention is ongoing and constant in the future, the utility is the life expectancy times the yearly value. The QALY provides a measure that incorporates the quantity and quality of life. When there are limited resources, the cost/QALY ratio is used as a cost-effectiveness measure for decision making in many countries.

Society must make decisions that affect everyone. Finding a utility that works for everyone is controversial. For example, for most sighted people, going blind would have a low utility; they consider going blind to be very bad as they would need to relearn the way they interact with the world. So the utility for blindness for a year would be low. However, this implies that blind people are less valued than sighted people, an **ableist** assumption. There have been suggestions for incorporating individual reference points, as in prospect theory (page 528).

Sometimes society needs to make life-and-death decisions. For example, consider how much to spend on earthquake-proofing public schools. A severe earthquake when pupils are in school might cause multiple deaths. It is possible to compute the probability of an earthquake in a location and the probability that a particular structure will collapse when students are present. Money can be spent to reduce the chance of a collapse. Deciding whether to spend the money is a classic example of decision making under uncertainty, which requires trading off money with children's lives. Many decision makers are reluctant to explicitly trade off money and the lives of children. However, when they don't make an explicit trade-off they tend to undervalue children's lives.

As AI tools become more common, and more decisions are automated, society will need to come to terms with the uncomfortable conversations of assigning utilities. Not having these conversations will mean that someone else's utilities are embedded in AI tools.

## 12.7 Review

- Utility is a measure of preference that combines with probability.
- A decision network can represent a finite-stage, partially observable sequential decision problem in terms of features.
- An MDP can represent an infinite-stage or indefinite-stage sequential decision problem in terms of states.
- A fully observable MDP can be solved with value iteration or policy iteration.
- A dynamic decision network allows for the representation of an MDP in terms of features.

- Utility-based decision making in the public realm can be made more transparent and accountable if the utility measures are made explicit.

## 12.8 References and Further Reading

Utility theory, as presented here, was developed by Neumann and Morgenstern [1953] and further developed by Savage [1972]. Keeney and Raiffa [1976] discuss utility theory, concentrating on multi-attribute (feature-based) utility functions. The axioms for discounting are by Koopmans [1972]; Bleichrodt et al. [2008] provide a debugged version and a proof. For work on graphical models of utility and preferences, see Bacchus and Grove [1995] and Boutilier et al. [2004]. Walsh [2007] and Rossi et al. [2011] overview the use of preferences in AI.

Kahneman [2011] discusses the psychology behind how people make decisions under uncertainty and motivates prospect theory. Wakker [2010] provides a textbook overview of utility and prospect theories.

Decision networks or influence diagrams were invented by Howard and Matheson [1984]. A method using dynamic programming for solving influence diagrams can be found in Shachter and Peot [1992]. The value of information and control is discussed by Matheson [1990].

MDPs were invented by Bellman [1957] and are discussed by Puterman [1994] and Bertsekas [2017]. Mausam and Kolobov [2012] overview MDPs in AI. Boutilier et al. [1999] review lifting MDPs to features, known as decision-theoretic planning.

Kochenderfer et al. [2022] provide an introduction to planning under uncertainty. Kochenderfer [2015] provides many real-world case studies. Lehman et al. [2018] provide examples of the effect of misspecification of reward functions.

The quality-adjusted life year (QALY) is due to Torrance [1970]; Fanshel and Bush [1970]. Spencer et al. [2022] overviews the history of QALY, with many references.

## 12.9 Exercises

**Exercise 12.1** Prove that the completeness and/or transitivity axioms (page 519), imply the following statements. What axiom(s) do your proofs rely on?

(a) $o_2 \not\succeq o_1$ is equivalent to $o_1 \succ o_2$
(b) if $o_1 \succ o_2$ and $o_2 \succ o_3$ then $o_1 \succ o_3$
(c) if $o_1 \succ o_2$ and $o_2 \succeq o_3$ then $o_1 \succ o_3$
(d) if $o_1 \succeq o_2$ and $o_2 \succeq o_3$ then $o_1 \succeq o_3$.

**Exercise 12.2** Consider the following two alternatives:

(i) In addition to what you currently own, you have been given \$1000. You are now asked to choose one of these options:
50% chance to win \$1000 or get \$500 for sure.

(ii) In addition to what you currently own, you have been given \$2000. You are now asked to choose one of these options:
50% chance to lose \$1000 or lose \$500 for sure.

Explain how the predictions of utility theory and prospect theory differ for these alternatives.

**Exercise 12.3** One of the decisions we must make in real life is whether to accept an invitation even though we are not sure we can or want to go to an event. Figure 12.24 gives a decision network for such a problem. Suppose that all of the decision and random variables are Boolean (i.e., have domain {*true*, *false*}). You can accept the invitation, but when the time comes, you still must decide whether or not to go. You might get sick in between accepting the invitation and having to decide to go. Even if you decide to go, if you have not accepted the invitation you may not be able to go. If you get sick, you have a good excuse not to go. Your utility depends on whether you accept, whether you have a good excuse, and whether you actually go.

(a) Give a table representing a possible utility function. Assume the unique best outcome is that you accept the invitation, you do not have a good excuse, but you do go. The unique worst outcome is that you accept the invitation, you do not have a good excuse, and you do not go. Make your other utility values reasonable.

(b) Suppose that you get to observe whether you are sick before accepting the invitation. Note that this is a different variable than if you are sick after accepting the invitation. Add to the network so that this situation can be modeled. You must not change the utility function, but the new observation must have a positive value of information. The resulting network must be no-forgetting.

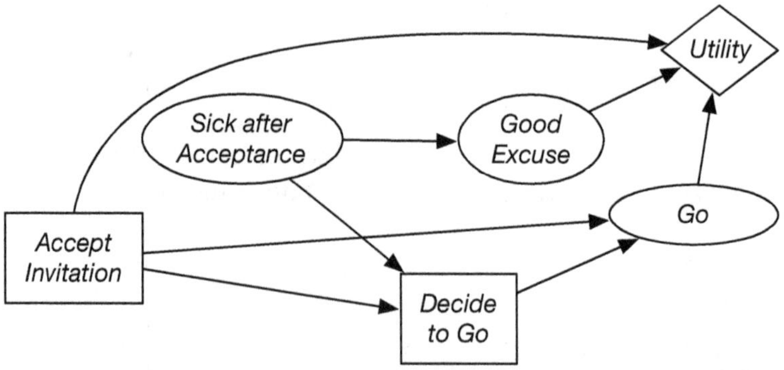


Figure 12.24: A decision network for an invitation decision

(c) Suppose that, after you have decided whether to accept the original invitation and before you decide to go, you can find out if you get a better invitation (to an event that clashes with the original event, so you cannot go to both). Suppose you would prefer the later invitation than the original event you were invited to. (The difficult decision is whether to accept the first invitation or wait until you get a better invitation, which you may not get.) Unfortunately, having another invitation does not provide a good excuse. On the network, add the node "better invitation" and all relevant arcs to model this situation. [You do not have to include the node and arcs from part (b).]

(d) If you have an arc between "better invitation" and "accept invitation" in part (c), explain why (i.e., what must the world be like to make this arc appropriate). If you did not have such an arc, which way could it go to still fit the preceding story; explain what must happen in the world to make this arc appropriate.

(e) If there was not an arc between "better invitation" and "accept invitation" (whether or not you drew such an arc), what must be true in the world to make this lack of arc appropriate?

**Exercise 12.4** Students have to make decisions about how much to study for each course. The aim of this question is to investigate how to use decision networks to help them make such decisions.

Suppose students first have to decide how much to study for the midterm. They can study a lot, study a little, or not study at all. Whether they pass the midterm depends on how much they study and on the difficulty of the course. As a rough approximation, they pass if they study hard or if the course is easy and they study a bit. After receiving their midterm grade, they have to decide how much to study for the final exam. The final exam result depends on how much they study and on the difficulty of the course. Their final grade (A, B, C, or F) depends on which exams they pass; generally they get an A if they pass both exams, a B if they only pass the final, a C if they only pass the midterm, or an F if they fail both. Of course, there is a great deal of noise in these general estimates.

Suppose that their utility depends on their subjective total effort and their final grade. Suppose their subjective total effort (a lot or a little) depends on their effort in studying for the midterm and the final.

(a) Draw a decision network for a student decision based on the preceding story.

(b) What is the domain of each variable?

(c) Give appropriate conditional probability tables.

(d) What is the best outcome (give this a utility of 100) and what is the worst outcome (give this a utility of 0)?

(e) Give an appropriate utility function for a student who is lazy and just wants to pass (not get an F). The total effort here measures whether they (thought they) worked a lot or a little overall. Explain the best outcome and the worst outcome. Fill in a copy of the table of Table 12.4 (page 576); use 100 for the best outcome and 0 for the worst outcome.

(f) Given your utility function for the previous part, give values for the missing terms for one example that reflects the utility function you gave above:

Comparing outcome ____________________
and lottery [$p$ : ____________________, $1 - p$ : ____________________]
when $p$ = ____________ the outcome is preferred to the lottery
when $p$ = ____________ the lottery is preferred to the outcome.

(g) Give an appropriate utility function for a student who does not mind working hard and really wants to get an A, and would be very disappointed with a B or lower. Explain the best outcome and the worst outcome. Fill in a copy of the table of Table 12.4; use 100 for the best outcome and 0 for the worst outcome.

**Exercise 12.5** Some students choose to cheat on exams, and instructors want to make sure that cheating does not pay. A rational model would specify that the decision of whether to cheat depends on the costs and the benefits. Here we will develop and critique such a model.

Consider the decision network of Figure 12.25. This diagram models a student's decisions about whether to cheat at two different times. If students cheat

| Grade | Total Effort | Utility |
|---|---|---|
| A | lot | |
| A | little | |
| B | lot | |
| B | little | |
| C | lot | |
| C | little | |
| F | lot | |
| F | little | |

Table 12.4: Utility function for the study decision

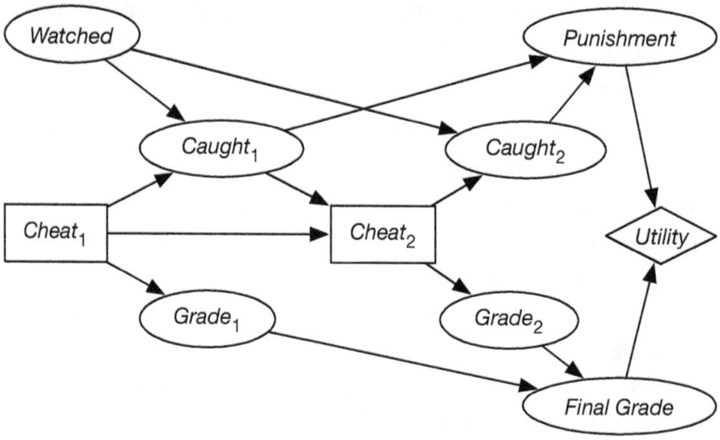


Figure 12.25: Decision about whether to cheat

they may be caught cheating, but they could also get higher grades. The punishment (either suspension, cheating recorded on the transcript, or none) depends on whether they get caught at either or both opportunities. Whether they get caught depends on whether they are being watched and whether they cheat. The utility depends on their final grades and their punishment.

The cheating decision network in AIPython (aipython.org) provides probabilities to use for the following questions.

(a) What is an optimal policy? Give a description in English of an optimal policy. (The description should not use any jargon of AI or decision theory.) What is the value of an optimal policy?

(b) What happens to the optimal policy when the probability of being watched goes up? [Modify the probability of "Watched".] Try a number of values. Explain what happens and why.

(c) What is an optimal policy when the rewards for cheating are reduced? Try a number of different parameterizations.

(d) Change the model so that once students have been caught cheating, they will be watched more carefully. [Hint: Whether they are watched at the first opportunity needs to be a different variable than whether they are watched at the second opportunity.] Show the resulting model (both the structure and any new parameters), and give the policies and expected utilities for various settings of the parameters.

(e) What does the current model imply about how cheating affects future grades? Change the model so that cheating affects subsequent grades. Explain how the new model achieves this.

(f) How could this model be changed to be more realistic (but still be simple)? [For example: Are the probabilities reasonable? Are the utilities reasonable? Is the structure reasonable?]

(g) Suppose the university decided to set up an honor system so that instructors do not actively check for cheating, but there is severe punishment for first offenses if cheating is discovered. How could this be modeled? Specify a model for this and explain what decision is optimal (for a few different parameter settings).

(h) Should students and instructors be encouraged to think of the cheating problem as a rational decision in a game? Explain why or why not in a single paragraph.

**Exercise 12.6** Suppose that, in a decision network, the decision variable *Run* has parents *Look* and *See*. Suppose you are using VE to find an optimal policy and, after eliminating all of the other variables, you are left with a single factor:

| *Look* | *See* | *Run* | *Value* |
|---|---|---|---|
| *true* | *true* | *yes* | 23 |
| *true* | *true* | *no* | 8 |
| *true* | *false* | *yes* | 37 |
| *true* | *false* | *no* | 56 |
| *false* | *true* | *yes* | 28 |
| *false* | *true* | *no* | 12 |
| *false* | *false* | *yes* | 18 |
| *false* | *false* | *no* | 22 |

(a) What is the resulting factor after eliminating *Run*? [Hint: You do not sum out *Run* because it is a decision variable.]
(b) What is the optimal decision function for *Run*?
(c) What is the value of information about *Look* for the decision *Run* for the decision network where *See* is a parent of *Run*? That is, if the agent has the information about *See*, how much more is the information about *Look* worth?

**Exercise 12.7** Suppose that, in a decision network, there were arcs from random variables "contaminated specimen" and "positive test" to the decision variable "discard sample." You solved the decision network and discovered that there was a unique optimal policy:

| Contaminated Specimen | Positive Test | Discard Sample |
|---|---|---|
| *true* | *true* | *yes* |
| *true* | *false* | *no* |
| *false* | *true* | *yes* |
| *false* | *false* | *no* |

What can you say about the value of information in this case?

**Exercise 12.8** How sensitive are the answers from the decision network of Example 12.16 (page 539) to the probabilities? Test the program with different conditional probabilities and see what effect this has on the answers produced. Discuss the sensitivity both to the optimal policy and to the expected value of the optimal policy.

**Exercise 12.9** In Example 12.16 (page 539), suppose that the fire sensor was noisy in that it had a 20% false positive rate

$$P(see\_smoke|report \wedge \neg smoke) = 0.2$$

and a 15% false negative rate

$$P(see\_smoke|report \wedge smoke) = 0.85.$$

Is it still worthwhile to check for smoke?

**Exercise 12.10** This exercise is to compare variable elimination and conditioning for the decision network of Example 12.16 (page 539).

(a) For the *inverse* of the variable ordering for search used in Example 12.20 (page 543) (i.e., from *Leaving* to *Report*) show the sequence of factors removed and created for variable elimination, in a table similar to Example 12.22 (page 546) (only the variable ordering changes).

(b) For the splitting order that is the inverse of the variable ordering of Example 12.22, specify what variables can be evaluated for each split (similar to Example 12.20, but with a different variable ordering. Also show what variables can be forgotten, as in Example 9.26 (page 412).

(c) How does the evaluation of the factors in recursive conditioning relate to the factors created for variable elimination, when the variable orderings are the inverse of each other? Be as specific as you can.

**Exercise 12.11** Consider the belief network of Exercise 9.10 (page 455). When an alarm is observed, a decision is made whether or not to shut down the reactor. Shutting down the reactor has a cost $c_s$ associated with it (independent of whether the core was overheating), whereas not shutting down an overheated core incurs a cost $c_m$ that is much higher than $c_s$.

(a) Draw the decision network to model this decision problem for the original system (i.e., with only one sensor).

(b) Specify the tables for all new factors that must be defined (you should use the parameters $c_s$ and $c_m$ where appropriate in the tables). Assume that *utility* is the negative of *cost*.

(c) Show how variable elimination can be used to find the optimal decision. For each variable eliminated, show which variable is eliminated, how it is eliminated (through summing or maximization), which factors are removed, what factor is created, and what variables this factor is over (similar to Example 12.22 (page 546)). You are not required to give the tables.

**Exercise 12.12** Consider the following decision network:

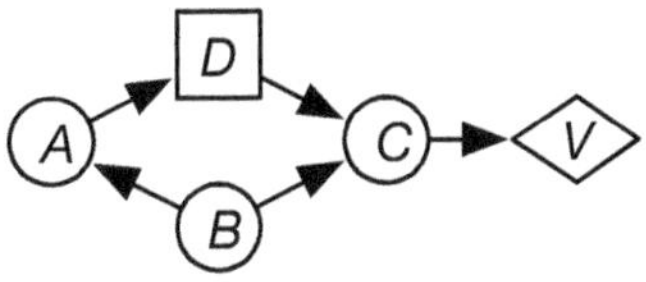


(a) What are the initial factors? (Give the variables in the scope of each factor, and specify any associated meaning of each factor.)

(b) Give a legal splitting order, and the order that variables can be evaluated (similar to Example 12.20 (page 543)).

(c) Show what factors are created in variable elimination when optimizing the decision function and computing the expected value, for one of the legal elimination orderings. At each step explain which variable is being eliminated, whether it is being summed out or maximized, what factors are being combined, and what factors are created (give the variables they depend on, not the tables).

(d) If the value of information of $A$ at decision $D$ is zero, what does an optimal policy look like? (Give the most specific statement you can make about any optimal policy.)

**Exercise 12.13** What is the main difference between asynchronous value iteration and standard value iteration? Why does asynchronous value iteration often work better than standard value iteration?

**Exercise 12.14** Explain why we often use discounting of future rewards in MDPs. How would an agent act differently if the discount factor was 0.6 as opposed to 0.9?

**Exercise 12.15** Consider the MDP of Example 12.31 (page 557).

(a) As the discount varies between 0 and 1, how does the optimal policy change? Give an example of a discount that produces each different policy that can be obtained by varying the discount.
(b) How can the MDP and/or discount be changed so that the optimal policy is to relax when healthy and to party when sick? Give an MDP that changes as few of the probabilities, rewards, or discount as possible to have this as the optimal policy.
(c) The optimal policy computed in Example 12.33 (page 560) was to party when healthy and relax when sick. What is the distribution of states that the agent following this policy will visit? [Hint: The policy induces a Markov chain (page 418), which has a stationary distribution.] What is the average reward of this policy? [Hint: The average reward can be obtained by computing the expected value of the immediate rewards with respect the stationary distribution.]

**Exercise 12.16** Consider a game world

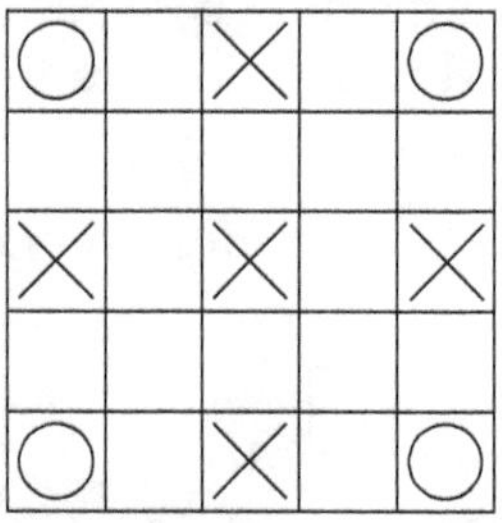

The robot can be at any one of the 25 locations on the grid. There can be a treasure on one of the circles at the corners. When the robot reaches the corner where the treasure is, it collects a reward of 10, and the treasure disappears. When there is no treasure, at each time step, there is a probability $P_1 = 0.2$ that a treasure appears, and it appears with equal probability at each corner. The robot knows its position and the location of the treasure.

There are monsters at the squares marked with an $\times$. Each monster randomly and independently, at each time step, checks whether the robot is on its square. If the robot is on the square when the monster checks, it has a reward of $-10$ (i.e., it loses 10 points). At the center point, the monster checks at each time step with probability $p_2 = 0.4$; at the other four squares marked with an $\times$, the monsters check at each time step with probability $p_3 = 0.2$.

Assume that the rewards are immediate upon entering a state: that is, if the robot enters a state with a monster, it gets the (negative) reward on entering the state, and if the robot enters the state with a treasure, it gets the reward upon entering the state, even if the treasure arrives at the same time.

The robot has eight actions corresponding to the eight neighboring squares. The diagonal moves are noisy; there is a $p_4 = 0.6$ probability of going in the direction chosen and an equal chance of going to each of the four neighboring squares closest to the desired direction. The vertical and horizontal moves are also noisy; there is a $p_5 = 0.8$ chance of going in the requested direction and an equal chance of going to one of the adjacent diagonal squares. For example, the actions up-left and up have the following results:

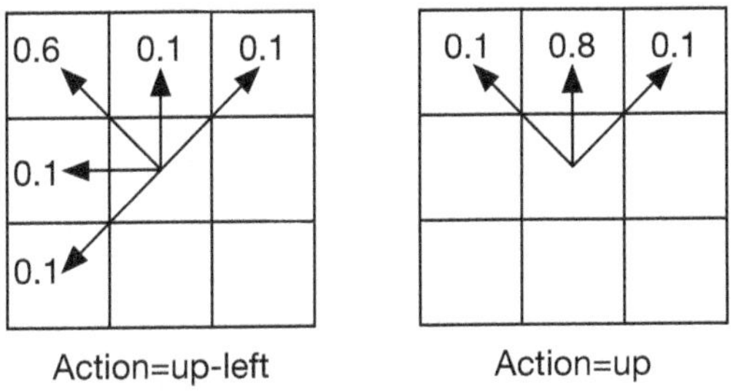


If the action results in crashing into a wall, the robot has a reward of −2 (i.e., loses 2) and does not move.

There is a discount factor of $p_6 = 0.9$.

(a) How many states are there? (Or how few states can you get away with?) What do they represent?

(b) What is an optimal policy?

(c) Suppose the game designer wants to design different instances of the game that have non-obvious optimal policies for a game player. Give three assignments to the parameters $p_1$ to $p_6$ with different optimal policies. If there are not that many different optimal policies, give as many as there are and explain why there are no more than that.

**Exercise 12.17** Consider a $5 \times 5$ grid game similar to the game of the previous question. The agent can be at one of the 25 locations, and there can be a treasure at one of the corners or no treasure.

Assume the "up" action has same dynamics as in the previous question. That is, the agent goes up with probability 0.8 and goes up-left with probability 0.1 and up-right with probability 0.1.

If there is no treasure, a treasure can appear with probability 0.2. When it appears, it appears randomly at one of the corners, and each corner has an equal probability of treasure appearing. The treasure stays where it is until the agent lands on the square where the treasure is. When this occurs the agent gets an immediate reward of +10 and the treasure disappears in the next state transition. The agent and the treasure move simultaneously so that if the agent arrives at a square at the same time the treasure appears, it gets the reward.

Suppose we are doing asynchronous value iteration and have the value for each state as in the following grids. The number in a square represent the value of that state and empty squares have a value of zero. It is irrelevant to this question how these values got there.

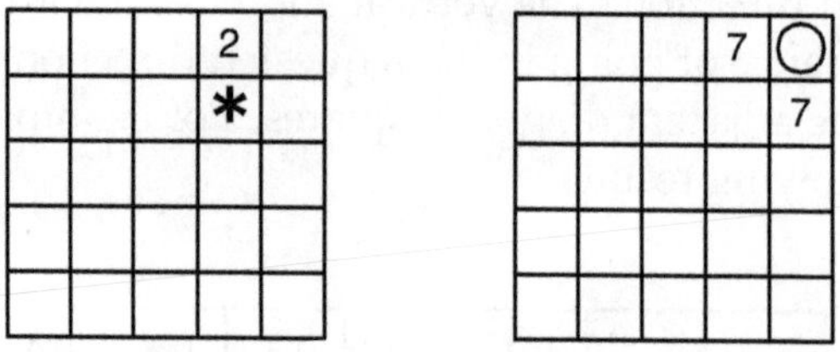


The left grid shows the values for the states where there is no treasure and the right grid shows the values of the states when there is a treasure at the top-right corner. There are also states for the treasures at the other three corners, but assume that the current values for these states are all zero.

Consider the next step of asynchronous value iteration. For state $s_{13}$, which is marked by $*$ in the figure, and the action $a_2$, which is "up," what value is assigned to $Q[s_{13}, a_2]$ on the next value iteration? You must show all your work but do not have to do any arithmetic (i.e., leave it as an expression). Explain each term in your expression.

**Exercise 12.18** In a decision network, suppose that there are multiple utility nodes, where the values must be added. This lets us represent a generalized additive utility function. How can the VE for decision networks algorithm, shown in Figure 12.14 (page 546), be altered to include such utilities?

**Exercise 12.19** How can variable elimination for decision networks, shown in Figure 12.14 (page 546), be modified to include additive discounted rewards? That is, there can be multiple utility (reward) nodes, to be added and discounted. Assume that the variables to be eliminated are eliminated from the latest time step forward.

# Chapter 13

# Reinforcement Learning

> *[W]e hypothesise that intelligence, and its associated abilities, can be understood as subserving the maximisation of reward. Accordingly, reward is enough to drive behaviour that exhibits abilities studied in natural and artificial intelligence, including knowledge, learning, perception, social intelligence, language, generalisation and imitation.*
>
> – Silver et al. [2021]

A **reinforcement learning** (**RL**) agent acts in an environment, observing its state and receiving rewards. From its experience of a stream of acting then observing the resulting state and reward, it must determine what to do given its goal of maximizing accumulated reward. This chapter considers fully observable (page 29), single-agent reinforcement learning. Section 14.7.2 (page 633) describes multiagent reinforcement learning. This is an extension of decision-theoretic planning (page 552) to the case where the transition and reward models are not specified.

We have already seen results showing the universality of utility (page 522). Silver et al. [2021] argue that decomposing utility into rewards can be a basis of intelligent action.

## 13.1 Reinforcement Learning Problem

A reinforcement learning agent is characterized as follows:

- The learning agent is given the possible states of the world and the set of actions it can carry out.

- At each time the agent observes the state of the world (the environment and the agent) and the reward received.
- After observing the state and reward, the agent carries out an action.
- The goal of the agent is to maximize its discounted reward (page 556), for some discount factor $\gamma$.

Reinforcement learning can be formalized in terms of **Markov decision processes** (MDPs) (page 552), in which the agent initially only knows the set of possible states and the set of possible actions. The dynamics, $P(s' \mid a, s)$, and the reward function, $R(s, a)$, are not given to the agent. As in an MDP, after each action, the agent observes the state it is in and receives a reward.

**Example 13.1** Consider the domain shown in Figure 13.1. There are six states the agent could be in, labeled $s_0, \ldots, s_5$. The agent has four actions: *upR*, *upC*, *left*, *right*. That is all the agent knows before it starts. It does not know how the states are configured, what the actions do, or how rewards are earned.

Figure 13.1 shows the configuration of the six states. Suppose the actions work as follows:

**right** The agent moves to the right in states $s_0$ ,$s_2$, and $s_4$, with a reward of 0 and stays still in the other states, with a reward of $-1$.

**left** The agent moves one state to the left in states $s_1$, $s_3$, and $s_5$, with a reward of 0. In state $s_0$, it stays in state $s_0$ and has a reward of $-1$. In state $s_2$, it has a reward of $-100$ and stays in state $s_2$. In state $s_4$, it receives a reward of 10 and moves to state $s_0$.

**upC** (for "up carefully") The agent goes up, except in states $s_4$ and $s_5$, where the agent crashes and stays still. It receives a reward of $-1$, except when it crashes, in which case there is a reward of $-2$.

**upR** (for "up risky") With a probability of 0.8 it acts like *upC*, except the reward is $-1$ when it crashes, and 0 otherwise. With probability 0.1 it acts as a *left*, and with probability 0.1 it acts as a *right*.

There is a discounted reward (page 556) with a discount of $\gamma = 0.9$. This can be translated as having a 0.1 chance of the agent leaving the game at any step,

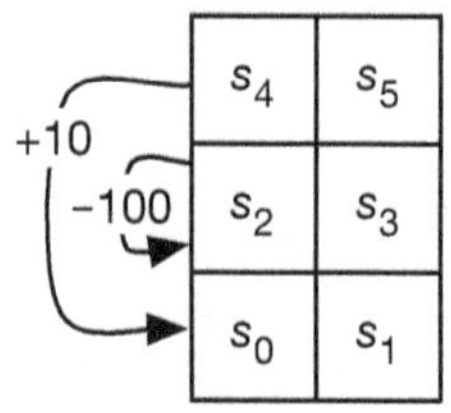


Figure 13.1: The environment of a tiny reinforcement learning problem

or as a way to encode that the agent prefers immediate rewards over future rewards.

The agent should try to go left from $s_4$ as often as possible, to collect the reward of +10. Getting from $s_0$ to $s_4$, it can go past a dangerous cliff at $s_2$ where there is a risk of falling off the cliff and getting a large negative reward, or going the longer and safer way around. Initially, it does not know this, but this is what it needs to learn.

**Example 13.2** Figure 13.2 shows the domain of a more complex game. There are 25 grid locations the agent could be in. A prize could be on one of the corners, or there could be no prize. When the agent lands on a prize, it receives a reward of 10 and the prize disappears. When there is no prize, for each time step there is a probability that a prize appears on any one of the corners. Monsters can appear at any time on one of the locations marked $M$. The agent gets damaged if a monster appears on the square the agent is on. If the agent is already damaged, it receives a reward of $-10$. The agent can get repaired (so it is no longer damaged) by visiting the repair station marked $R$.

In this example, the state consists of four components: $\langle X, Y, D, P \rangle$, where $X$ is the $X$-coordinate of the agent, $Y$ is the $Y$-coordinate of the agent, $D$ is Boolean and is true when the agent is damaged, and $P$ is the position of the prize ($P = 0$ if there is no prize, $P = i$ if there is a prize at position $P_i$). Because the monsters are transient – knowing whether a monster appeared at a time does not provide any information about the future – it is not necessary to include them as part of the state. There are therefore $5 * 5 * 2 * 5 = 250$ states. The environment is fully observable, so the agent knows what state it is in. The agent does not know the meaning of the states; it doesn't know about the four components and it has no idea initially about being damaged or what a prize is.

The agent has four actions: *up*, *down*, *left*, and *right*. These move the agent one step – usually one step in the direction indicated by the name, but sometimes in one of the other directions. If the agent crashes into an outside wall or

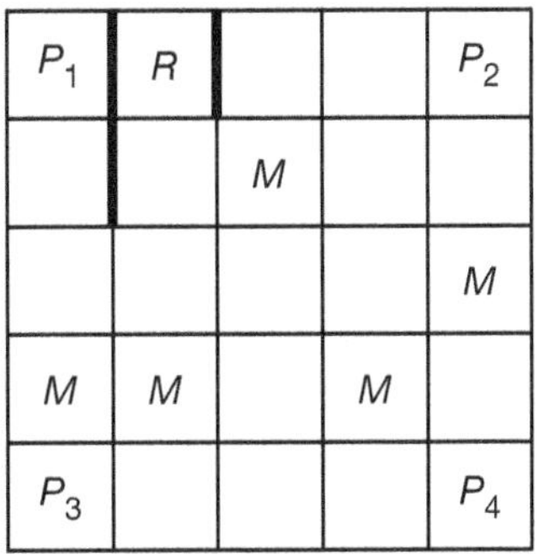


Figure 13.2: The environment of a monster game

one of the interior walls (the thick lines near the location $R$), it remains where is was and receives a reward of $-1$.

The agent does not know any of the story given here. It just knows there are 250 states and four actions, which state it is in at each time, and what reward was received at each time.

This game is simple, but it is surprisingly difficult to write a good controller for it. There are implementations available on the book's website that you can play with and modify. Try to write a controller by hand for it; it is possible to write a controller that accumulates a reward of about 500 for each 1000 steps. This game is also difficult to learn, because visiting $R$ is seemingly useless until the agent eventually learns that being damaged is bad, and that visiting $R$ makes it not damaged. It must stumble on this while trying to collect the prizes. The states where there is no prize available do not last very long. Moreover, it has to learn this without being given the concept of *damaged*; all it knows, initially, is that there are 250 states and four actions.

Reinforcement learning is difficult for a number of reasons:

- The **credit assignment problem**, or **blame attribution problem**, is the problem of determining which action was responsible for a reward or punishment. The action responsible may have occurred a long time before the reward was received. Moreover, not just a single action but rather a combination of actions carried out in the appropriate circumstances may be responsible for a reward. For example, you could teach an agent to play a game by rewarding it when it wins or loses; it must determine the brilliant moves, which usually occur long before the end, that were needed to win. As another example, you may try to train a dog by saying "bad dog" when you come home and find a mess. The dog has to determine, out of all of the actions it did, which of them were the actions that were responsible for the reprimand.
- Even if the dynamics of the world does not change, the effect of an action of the agent depends on what the agent will do in the future. What may initially seem like a bad thing for the agent to do may end up being the best action because of what the agent does in the future. This is common among planning problems, but it is complicated in the reinforcement learning context because the agent does not know, a priori, the effects of its actions.
- The **explore–exploit dilemma**: if an agent has worked out a good course of actions, should it continue to follow these actions (exploiting what it has determined) or should it explore to find better actions? An agent that never explores may act forever in a way that could have been much better if it had explored earlier. An agent that always explores will never use what it has learned. Exploration may lead to irreversible damage. This dilemma is discussed further in Section 13.5 (page 591).

## 13.2 Evolutionary Algorithms

One way to solve reinforcement algorithms is to treat this as an optimization problem (page 161), with the aim of selecting a policy that maximizes the expected discounted reward. This can be done with a **policy search** through the space of policies to find the best policy. A policy is a controller (page 55) that can be evaluated by running it in the agent acting in the environment.

Policy search is often solved as a stochastic local search algorithm (page 149) by searching in the space of policies. A policy can be evaluated by running it in the environment a number of times.

A diverse set of initial policies can be repeatedly evaluated in the environment and iteratively improved. This process is called an **evolutionary algorithm** because each policy, considered as an agent, is evaluated on how well it survives. This is often combined with genetic algorithms (page 159), which allows the combination of components of the policies with the aim of having a diverse collection of controllers. Often these controllers are represented as neural networks, which is the foundation of **neuroevolution**.

These algorithms have the advantage of being able to explore a diverse set of controllers.

Algorithms based on evaluating policies as a whole have a number of issues. The first is the size of the state space. If there are $n$ states and $m$ actions, there are $m^n$ policies. For example, for the game described in Example 13.1 (page 584), there are $4^6 = 4096$ different policies. For the game of Example 13.2 (page 585), there are 250 states, and so $4^{250} \approx 10^{150}$ policies. This is a very small game, but it has more policies than there are particles in the universe.

Second, evolutionary algorithms use experiences very wastefully. If an agent was in state $s_2$ of Example 13.1 (page 584) and it moved left, you would like it to learn that it is bad to go left from state $s_2$. But evolutionary algorithms, as presented, wait until the agent has finished and judge the policy as a whole. Stochastic local search will randomly try doing something else in state $s_2$ and so may eventually determine that that action was not good, but it is very indirect. Genetic algorithms are slightly better in that the policies that have the agent going left in state $s_2$ will die off, but again this is very indirect.

Third, the performance of evolutionary algorithms can be very sensitive to the representation of the policy. The representation for a genetic algorithm should be such that crossover preserves the good parts of the policy. The representations are often tuned for the particular domain.

An alternative pursued in the rest of this chapter is to learn after every action. The components of the policy are learned, rather than the policy as a whole. By learning what to do in each state, learning can have linear or polynomial time and space complexity in the number of states, rather than exponential in the number of states. However, evolutionary algorithms can sometimes find creative solutions to problems that elude other methods; see Section 13.9.2 (page 603).

## 13.3 Temporal Differences

To understand how reinforcement learning works, consider how to average values that arrive to an agent sequentially. Section A.1 (page 797) discusses how to maintain rolling averages, which is the basis of temporal differences.

Suppose there is a sequence of numerical values, $v_1, v_2, v_3, \ldots$, and the aim is to predict the next. A rolling average $A_k$ is maintained, and updated using the **temporal difference equation**, derived in Section A.1:

$$\begin{aligned} A_k &= (1 - \alpha_k) * A_{k-1} + \alpha_k * v_k \\ &= A_{k-1} + \alpha_k * (v_k - A_{k-1}) \end{aligned} \tag{13.1}$$

where $\alpha_k = \frac{1}{k}$. The difference, $v_k - A_{k-1}$, is called the **temporal difference error** or **TD error**; it specifies how different the new value, $v_k$, is from the old prediction, $A_{k-1}$. The old estimate, $A_{k-1}$, is updated by $\alpha_k$ times the TD error to get the new estimate, $A_k$.

A qualitative interpretation of the temporal difference equation is that if the new value is higher than the old prediction, increase the predicted value; if the new value is less than the old prediction, decrease the predicted value. The change is proportional to the difference between the new value and the old prediction. Note that this equation is still valid for the first value, $k = 1$, in which case $A_1 = v_1$.

In reinforcement learning, the values are often estimates of the effects of actions; more recent values are more accurate than earlier values because the agent is learning, and so they should be weighted more. One way to weight later examples more is to use Equation (13.1), but with $\alpha$ as a constant ($0 < \alpha \leq 1$) that does not depend on $k$. This does not converge to the average value when there is variability in the values of the sequence, but it can track changes when the underlying process generating the values changes. See Section A.1.

One way to give more weight to more recent experiences, but also converge to the average, is to set $\alpha_k = (r+1)/(r+k)$ for some $r > 0$. For the first experience $\alpha_1 = 1$, so it ignores the prior $A_0$. If $r = 9$, after 11 experiences, $\alpha_{11} = 0.5$ so it weights that experience as equal to all of its prior experiences. The parameter $r$ should be set to be appropriate for the domain.

Guaranteeing convergence to the average is not compatible with being able to adapt to make better predictions when the underlying process generating the values changes, for non-stationary (page 418) dynamics or rewards.

## 13.4 Learning from Experiences

In reinforcement learning, an agent tries to learn the optimal policy from its history of interaction with the environment. A **history** of an agent is a sequence of state–action–rewards:

$$\langle s_0, a_0, r_1, s_1, a_1, r_2, s_2, a_2, r_3, s_3, a_3, r_4, s_4 \ldots \rangle$$

which means that the agent was in state $s_0$ and did action $a_0$, which resulted in it receiving reward $r_1$ and being in state $s_1$; then it did action $a_1$, received reward $r_2$, and ended up in state $s_2$; then it did action $a_2$, received reward $r_3$, and ended up in state $s_3$; and so on.

We treat this history of interaction as a sequence of experiences, where an **experience** is a tuple

$$\langle s, a, r, s' \rangle$$

which means that the agent was in state $s$, it did action $a$, it received reward $r$, and it went into state $s'$. These experiences will be the data from which the agent can learn what to do. As in decision-theoretic planning, the aim is for the agent to maximize its value, which is usually the discounted reward (page 556).

### 13.4.1 Q-learning

Recall (page 559) that $Q^*(s, a)$, where $a$ is an action and $s$ is a state, is the expected value (cumulative discounted reward) of doing $a$ in state $s$ and then following the optimal policy.

**Q-learning** uses temporal differences to estimate the value of $Q^*(s, a)$. In Q-learning, the agent maintains a table of $Q[S, A]$, where $S$ is the set of states and $A$ is the set of actions. $Q[s, a]$ represents its current estimate of $Q^*(s, a)$.

An experience $\langle s, a, r, s' \rangle$ provides one data point for the value of $Q(s, a)$. The data point is that the agent received the future value of $r + \gamma V(s')$, where $V(s') = \max_{a'} Q(s', a')$; this is the actual current reward plus the discounted estimated future value. This new data point is called a **return**. The agent can use the temporal difference equation (13.1) to update its estimate for $Q(s, a)$:

$$Q[s, a] := Q[s, a] + \alpha * \left( r + \gamma \max_{a'} Q[s', a'] - Q[s, a] \right)$$

or, equivalently:

$$Q[s, a] := (1 - \alpha) * Q[s, a] + \alpha * \left( r + \gamma \max_{a'} Q[s', a'] \right).$$

Figure 13.3 (page 590) shows a Q-learning controller, where the agent is acting and learning at the same time. The **do command**, $do(a)$, on line 17 specifies that the action $a$ is the **command** (page 52) the controller sends to the body. The reward and the resulting state are the **percepts** (page 52) the controller receives from the body.

The algorithm of Figure 13.3 also maintains an array $N[s, a]$, which counts the number of times action $a$ was performed in state $s$. The function $alpha\_fun$ computes $\alpha$ from the count. $alpha\_fun(c) = 10/(9 + c)$ often works well; see Exercise 13.6 (page 607). When $\alpha$ is fixed, the $N$ array does not need to be maintained (but it is also used for some exploration strategies; see below).

The Q-learner learns (an approximation of) the optimal Q-function as long as the agent explores enough, and there is no bound on the number of times it tries an action in any state (i.e., it does not always do the same subset of actions in a state).

**Example 13.3** Consider the two-state MDP of Example 12.29 (page 553). The agent knows there are two states $\{healthy, sick\}$ and two actions $\{relax, party\}$. It does not know the model and it learns from the $s, a, r, s'$ experiences. With a discount, $\gamma = 0.8$, $\alpha = 0.3$, and $Q$ initially 0, the following is a possible trace (to a few significant digits and with the states and actions abbreviated):

| $s$ | $a$ | $r$ | $s'$ | $Update = (1-\alpha) * Q[s,a] + \alpha(r + \gamma max_{a'} Q[s',a'])$ |
|---|---|---|---|---|
| $he$ | $re$ | 7 | $he$ | $Q[he, re] = 0.7 * 0 + 0.3 * (7 + 0.8 * 0) = 2.1$ |
| $he$ | $re$ | 7 | $he$ | $Q[he, re] = 0.7 * 2.1 + 0.3 * (7 + 0.8 * 2.1) = 4.07$ |
| $he$ | $pa$ | 10 | $he$ | $Q[he, pa] = 0.7 * 0 + 0.3 * (10 + 0.8 * 4.07) = 3.98$ |
| $he$ | $pa$ | 10 | $si$ | $Q[he, pa] = 0.7 * 3.98 + 0.3 * (10 + 0.8 * 0) = 5.79$ |
| $si$ | $pa$ | 2 | $si$ | $Q[si, pa] = 0.7 * 0 + 0.3 * (2 + 0.8 * 0) = 0.06$ |
| $si$ | $re$ | 0 | $si$ | $Q[si, re] = 0.7 * 0 + 0.3 * (0 + 0.8 * 0.06) = 0.014$ |
| $si$ | $re$ | 0 | $he$ | $Q[si, re] = 0.7 * 0.014 + 0.3 * (0 + 0.8 * 5.79) = 1.40$ |

```
controller Q-learning(S, A, γ, alpha_fun)
    Inputs
        S is a set of states
        A is a set of actions
        γ the discount
        alpha_fun is a function to compute step size from counts
    Local
        real array Q[S, A]
        integer array N[S, A]
        states s, s'
        action a
    initialize Q[S, A] arbitrarily
    initialize N[S, A] to 0
    observe current state s
    repeat
        select an action a
        do(a)
        N[s, a] := N[s, a] + 1
        α := alpha_fun(N[s, a])
        observe reward r and state s'
        Q[s, a] := Q[s, a] + α * (r + γ * max_a' Q[s', a'] − Q[s, a])
        s := s'
    until termination()
```

Figure 13.3: Q-learning controller

With $\alpha$ fixed, the $Q$-values will approximate, but not converge to, the values obtained with value iteration in Example 12.33 (page 560). The smaller $\alpha$ is, the closer it will converge to the actual $Q$-values, but the slower it will converge.

## 13.5 Exploration and Exploitation

An estimate of a $Q$-function is not enough to determine what the agent should actually do (which action is selected in line 16 of Figure 13.3 (page 590)). There are two competing goals for what an agent should do:

- It could **exploit** the knowledge that it has found to get higher rewards by, in state $s$, doing one of the actions $a$ that maximizes $Q[s, a]$.
- It could **explore** to build a better estimate of the $Q$-function, by, for example, selecting an action at random at each time.

An agent only gets a good estimate of the $Q$-values for states and actions it has tried many times. If an agent exploits all of the time, it will keep trying the same action in a state, and not explore enough to find an action with lower current $Q$-value that could be better than the action with the current highest $Q$-value.

Random exploration will not allow the agent to exploit what it has found until after it has finished learning, which might never occur. Note that $Q$-learning will converge eventually to the optimal $Q$-function even with random exploration. Random exploration can take an inordinate amount of time to find interesting parts of the state space – the parts of the state space the agent will try to be in – and so even if the aim is to learn then exploit, it might be better to have more purposeful exploration.

There are a number of ways to combine exploitation and exploration:

- In **optimism in the face of uncertainty**, the $Q$-values are initialized to values that encourage exploration. If the $Q$-values are initialized to high values, the unexplored areas will look good, so that pure exploitation will tend to explore. This does encourage exploration; however, the agent can hallucinate that some state–action pairs are good for a long time, even though there is no real evidence for them being good. A state only gets to look bad when all its actions look bad; but when all of these actions lead to states that look good, it takes a long time to get a realistic view of the actual values. This is a case where old estimates of the $Q$-values can be quite bad estimates of the actual $Q$-value, and these can remain bad estimates for a long time. To get fast convergence, the initial values should be as close as possible to the final values; trying to make them an overestimate will make convergence slower. In noisy environments, where the effect of an action has some randomness, optimism in the face of uncertainty with no other mechanism for exploration can mean that a good action never gets explored more because, by random chance, it gets a low $Q$-value from which it cannot recover. Optimism in the face of uncertainty can be used in conjunction with other methods.

- In an **$\epsilon$-greedy exploration strategy**, where $0 \leq \epsilon \leq 1$, the agent selects a random action $\epsilon$ of the time, and otherwise an action that maximizes $Q[s, a]$. It is possible to change $\epsilon$ through time. Intuitively, early in the life of the agent, it should act more randomly to encourage initial exploration and, as time progresses, it should act more greedily (reducing $\epsilon$).
- One problem with an $\epsilon$-greedy strategy is that it treats all of the actions, apart from the best action, equivalently. If there are a few seemingly good actions and other actions that look much less promising, it may be more sensible to select among the good actions: putting more effort towards determining which of the promising actions is best, and less effort towards exploring the actions that look worse. One way to do that is to select action $a$ with a probability depending on the value of $Q[s, a]$. This is known as a **softmax** action selection. A common method is to use a **Gibbs** or **Boltzmann distribution**, where the probability of selecting action $a$ in state $s$ is proportional to $e^{Q[s,a]/\tau}$. Thus, in state $s$, the agent selects action $a$ with probability

$$\frac{e^{Q[s,a]/\tau}}{\sum_a e^{Q[s,a]/\tau}}$$

  where $\tau > 0$ is the **temperature** specifying how randomly values should be chosen. How the difference in temperatures affects the probability of being selected is given in Figure 4.1 (page 154); for example, at a temperature of 1, if action $a_1$ has a utility two less than action $a_2$, it will be chosen approximately 14% of the time that $a_1$ is chosen. When $\tau$ is high, the actions are chosen in almost equal amounts. As the temperature is reduced, the higher-valued actions are more likely to be chosen and, in the limit as $\tau \to 0$, the best action is always chosen. Often the temperature can be reduced as the search progresses.
- A problem with the previous methods is that they do not distinguish the actions that the agent has tried many times, for which there is a good estimate of the actual $Q$-value, from those actions that have not been tried much, for which the estimate is very poor. Another group of methods models a distribution of the uncertainty of the estimate of the expected values, not just the current expected value. As the agent gets more information, the uncertainty about the expected value reduces, and it can become more sure of the expected value. The **upper confidence bound** is an upper estimate of the expected value; the aim is to pick a value such that it will be very unlikely that the actual value is greater than this. The upper confidence bound is the sum of two terms, the $Q$ estimate and a confidence bound that depends on the number of times the action has been chosen. Suppose $N[s, a]$ is the number of times action $a$ has been selected for state $s$, and $N(s) = \sum_a N[s, a]$ is the number of times state $s$

has been visited. $N(s)$ can be stored or computed on demand. The upper confidence bound **UCB1** (where the name is from Auer et al. [2002], who analyze a number of algorithms) is

$$UCB1(s,a) = Q[s,a] + C * \sqrt{\frac{\log N(s)}{N[s,a]}}$$

where $C$ is a constant that depends on the magnitude of the $Q$-values; if the values are all in range $[0,1]$ and the samples are independent, then $C = \sqrt{2}$ has good theoretical properties. In reinforcement learning the samples are rarely independent. In a state $s$, the agent can balance exploration and exploitation by choosing action $a$ that has the highest $UCB1(s,a)$ value.

- The successive values of $Q(s,a)$ computed provide more and more refined estimates its the mean value. Those estimates can be used to create a distribution over the mean. An alternative to choosing the upper confidence bound is to sample from this distribution. In **Thompson sampling**, given a state, for each action, $a$, a value $v_a$ is selected from the distribution of the mean (page 437); the action with the highest $v_a$ is chosen to be carried out.

  If the values are all 0 or 1 (for example, if the reward is just a win or loss at the end), the beta distribution (page 464), represented by counts of the number of 0s and the number of 1s, is appropriate.

  If the return is a real number it is common to assume it is a Gaussian, which is parameterized by the mean and the variance. For each state, choose the action $a$ that maximizes

$$Q[s,a] + C * \frac{randn()}{\sqrt{N[s,a]}}$$

  where $randn()$ returns a random number using the standard normal distribution (mean 0, variance 1). $C$ is chosen to reflect the scale of the $Q$-values.

  Sometimes neither the beta nor normal distributions are appropriate, in which case there is a large literature of other methods that are available.

Much of the theoretical work in the exploration–exploitation tradeoff has been for the single-state case, called the **multi-armed bandit** problem; a "**bandit**" is the slang for a slot machine that gives rewards randomly and independently each time. The explore–exploit trade-off in reinforcement learning is more complicated than in the bandit setting, because rewards may be delayed and so the initial estimates of a $Q$-value may be not a random sample, and because the estimates are not independent. This means that we typically have to resort to testing what works in practice; see, for example, Exercise 13.4 (page 606).

## 13.6 Evaluating RL Algorithms

We can judge a reinforcement learning algorithm either by how good a policy it finds or by how much reward it receives while acting and learning. Which is more important depends on how the agent will be deployed. If there is sufficient time for the agent to learn safely before it is deployed, the final policy may be the most important. If the agent has to learn while being deployed, it may never get to the stage where it no longer needs to explore, and the agent needs to maximize the reward it receives while learning.

One way to show the performance of a reinforcement learning algorithm is to plot the cumulative reward (the sum of all rewards received so far) as a function of the number of steps. One algorithm dominates another if its plot is consistently above the other.

**Example 13.4** Figure 13.4 compares four runs of the $Q$-learner on the game of Example 13.2 (page 585).

The plots are for different runs that varied according to whether $\alpha$ was fixed, according to the initial values of the $Q$-function, and according to the randomness in the action selection. They all used greedy exploit of 80% (i.e., $\epsilon = 0.2$) for the first 100,000 steps, and 100% (i.e., $\epsilon = 0.0$) for the next 100,000 steps. The top plot dominated the others.

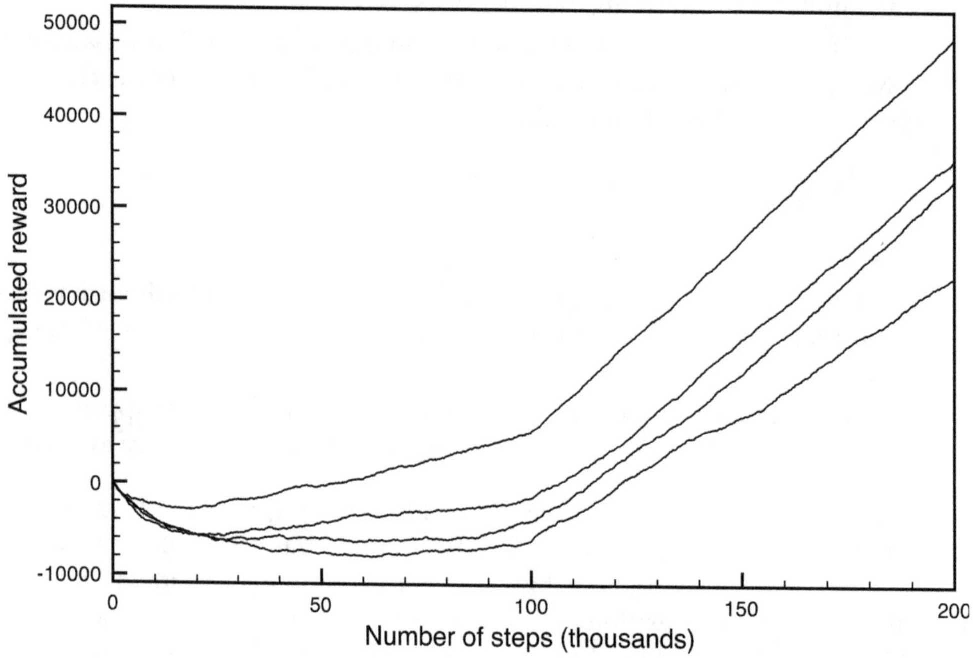


Figure 13.4: Cumulative reward as a function of the number of steps

There can be a great deal of variability of each algorithm on different runs, so to actually compare these algorithms, the same algorithm must be run multiple times.

There are three statistics of this plot that are important:

- The asymptotic slope shows how good the policy is after the algorithm has stabilized.
- The minimum of the curve shows how much reward must be sacrificed before it starts to improve.
- The zero crossing shows how long it takes until the algorithm has recouped its cost of learning.

The last two statistics are applicable when both positive and negative rewards are available and having these balanced is reasonable behavior. For other cases, the cumulative reward should be compared with reasonable behavior that is appropriate for the domain; see Exercise 13.3 (page 606).

It is also possible to plot the average reward (the accumulated reward per time step). This more clearly shows the value of policy eventually learned and whether the algorithm has stopped learning (when it is flat), but often has large variations for early times.

One thing that should be noted about the cumulative reward plot is that it measures total reward, yet the algorithms optimize discounted reward at each step. In general, you should optimize for, and evaluate your algorithm using, the optimality criterion that is most appropriate for the domain.

## 13.7 On-Policy Learning

$Q$-learning is an off-policy learner. An **off-policy learner** learns the value of an optimal policy independently of the agent's actions, as long as it explores enough. An off-policy learner can learn the optimal policy even if it is acting randomly. An off-policy learner that is exploring does not learn the value of the policy it is following, because it includes exploration steps.

There may be cases, such as where there are large negative rewards, where ignoring what the agent actually does is dangerous. An alternative is to learn the value of the policy the agent is actually carrying out, which includes exploration steps, so that that policy can be iteratively improved. The learner can thus take into account the costs associated with exploration. An **on-policy learner** learns the value of the policy being carried out by the agent, including the exploration steps.

**SARSA** (so called because it uses state–action–reward–state–action experiences to update the $Q$-values) is an *on-policy* reinforcement learning algorithm that estimates the value of the policy being followed. An experience in SARSA is of the form $\langle s, a, r, s', a' \rangle$, which means that the agent was in state $s$, did action

$a$, received reward $r$, and ended up in state $s'$, from which it decided to do action $a'$. This provides a new experience to update $Q(s,a)$. The new value that this experience provides is $r + \gamma Q(s',a')$.

Figure 13.5 gives the SARSA algorithm. The $Q$-values that SARSA computes depend on the current exploration policy which, for example, may be greedy with random steps. It can find a different policy than $Q$-learning in situations where exploring may incur large penalties. For example, when a robot goes near the top of a flight of stairs, even if this is an optimal policy, it may be dangerous for exploration steps. SARSA will discover this and adopt a policy that keeps the robot away from the stairs. It will find a policy that is optimal, taking into account the exploration inherent in the policy.

**Example 13.5** In Example 13.1 (page 584), the optimal policy is to go up from state $s_0$ in Figure 13.1 (page 584). However, if the agent is exploring, this action may be bad because exploring from state $s_2$ is very dangerous.

If the agent is carrying out the policy that includes exploration, "when in state $s$, 80% of the time select the action $a$ that maximizes $Q[s,a]$, and 20% of the time select an action at random," going up from $s_0$ is not optimal. An on-policy learner will try to optimize the policy the agent is following, not the optimal policy that does not include exploration.

```
controller SARSA(S, A, γ, α)
    Inputs
        S is a set of states
        A is a set of actions
        γ the discount
        α is the step size
    Local
        real array Q[S, A]
        state s, s'
        action a, a'
    initialize Q[S, A] arbitrarily
    observe current state s
    select an action a using a policy based on Q[s, a]
    repeat
        do(a)
        observe reward r and state s'
        select an action a' using a policy based on Q[s', a']
        Q[s, a] := Q[s, a] + α * (r + γ * Q[s', a'] − Q[s, a])
        s := s'
        a := a'
    until termination()
```

Figure 13.5: SARSA: on-policy reinforcement learning

The $Q$-values of the optimal policy are less in SARSA than in $Q$-learning. The values for $Q$-learning and for SARSA (the exploration rate in parentheses) for the domain of Example 13.1, for a few state–action pairs, are

| Algorithm | $Q[s_0, right]$ | $Q[s_0, up]$ | $Q[s_2, upC]$ | $Q[s_2, up]$ | $Q[s_4, left]$ |
|---|---|---|---|---|---|
| $Q$-learning | 19.48 | 23.28 | 26.86 | 16.9 | 30.95 |
| SARSA (20%) | 9.27 | 7.9 | 14.8 | 4.43 | 18.09 |
| SARSA (10%) | 13.04 | 13.95 | 18.9 | 8.93 | 22.47 |

The optimal policy using SARSA with 20% exploration is to go right in state $s_0$, but with 10% exploration the optimal policy is to go up in state $s_0$. With 20% exploration, this is the optimal policy because exploration is dangerous. With 10% exploration, going into state $s_2$ is less dangerous. Thus, if the rate of exploration is reduced, the optimal policy changes. However, with less exploration, it would take longer to find an optimal policy. The value $Q$-learning converges to does not depend on the exploration rate.

SARSA is useful when deploying an agent that is exploring in the world. If you want to do offline learning, and then use that policy in an agent that does not explore, $Q$-learning may be more appropriate.

## 13.8 Model-Based RL

In many applications of reinforcement learning, plenty of time is available for computation between each action. For example, a physical robot may have many seconds between each action. $Q$-learning, which only does one backup per action, will not make full use of the available computation time.

An alternative to doing one $Q$-value update after each action is to use the experiences to learn a model. An agent can explicitly learn $P(s' \mid s, a)$ and $R(s, a)$. For each action that the agent carries out in the environment, the agent can do a number of steps of asynchronous value iteration (page 562) to give a better estimate of the $Q$-function.

Figure 13.6 (page 598) shows a generic model-based reinforcement learner. As with other reinforcement learning programs, it keeps track of $Q[S, A]$, but it also maintains a model of the dynamics, represented here as $T$, where $T[s, a, s']$ is the count of the number of times that the agent has done $a$ in state $s$ and ended up in state $s'$. This also maintains $C[s, a]$, which is the count of the number of times action $a$ was carried out in state $s$. Note that $C[s, a] = \sum_{s'} T[s, a, s']$, and so we could save space but increase runtime by not storing $C$, but computing it when needed. The $R[s, a]$ array maintains the average reward obtained when doing action $a$ in state $s$.

After each action, the agent observes the reward $r$ and the resulting state $s'$. It then updates the transition-count matrices $T$ and $C$, as well as the average reward $R$. It then does a number of steps of asynchronous value iteration, using the updated probability model derived from $T$ and the updated reward model.

There are three main undefined parts to this algorithm:

- Which $Q$-values should be updated? It seems reasonable that the algorithm should at least update $Q[s,a]$, because more data have been received on the transition probability and reward. From there it can either do random updates or determine which $Q$-values would change the most. The elements that potentially have their values changed the most are the $Q[s_1,a_1]$ with the highest probability of ending up at a $Q$-value that has changed the most (i.e., where $Q[s_2,a_2]$ has changed the most). This can be implemented by keeping a priority queue of $Q$-values to con-

**controller** *RL_Model_learner*$(S, A, \gamma)$
    **Inputs**
        $S$ is a set of states
        $A$ is a set of actions
        $\gamma$ the discount
    **Local**
        real array $Q[S,A]$
        real array $R[S,A]$
        integer array $T[S,A,S]$
        integer array $C[S,A]$
    initialize $Q[S,A]$ arbitrarily
    initialize $R[S,A]$ arbitrarily
    initialize $T[S,A,S]$ to zero
    initialize $C[S,A]$ to zero
    observe current state $s$
    select action $a$
    $do(a)$
    **repeat**
        observe reward $r$ and state $s'$
        $T[s,a,s'] := T[s,a,s'] + 1$
        $C[s,a] := C[s,a] + 1$
        $R[s,a] := R[s,a] + \frac{r - R[s,a]}{C[s,a]}$
        $s := s'$
        select action $a$
        $do(a)$
        **repeat**
            select state $s_1$, action $a_1$ such that $C[s_1,a_1] \neq 0$
            $Q[s_1,a_1] := R[s_1,a_1] + \gamma * \sum_{s_2} \frac{T[s_1,a_1,s_2]}{C[s_1,a_1]} * \max_{a_2} Q[s_2,a_2]$
        **until** an observation arrives
    **until** *termination*()

Figure 13.6: Model-based reinforcement learner

sider. To ensure there is no divide-by-zero error, it should only choose $s_1, a_1$ state–action pairs for which $C[s_1, a_1] \neq 0$, or include pseudocounts (page 301) for the transitions.

- How many steps of asynchronous value iteration should be done between actions? An agent could continue doing $Q$-updates until it has to act or until it gets new information. Figure 13.6 (page 598) assumes that the agent acts and then does $Q$-updates until an observation arrives. When an observation arrives, the agent acts as soon as possible. There are may variants, including doing a fixed number of updates, which may be appropriate in games where it can act at any time. It is also possible to run the update in parallel with observing and acting.
- What should be the initial values for $Q[S, A]$? It requires some value for the transitions it has never experienced when updating $Q$. If it is using the exploration strategy of optimism in the face of uncertainty (page 591), it can use *Rmax*, the maximum reward possible, as the initial value for $R$, to encourage exploration. However, as in value iteration (page 560), the algorithm converges faster if it initializes $Q$ to be as close as possible to the final $Q$-value.

This algorithm assumes that the rewards depend on the initial state and the action. If there are separate action costs and rewards for being in a state, and the agent can separately observe the costs and rewards, the reward function can be decomposed into $C[A]$ and $R[S]$, leading to more efficient learning.

It is difficult to directly compare the model-based and model-free reinforcement learners. Typically, model-based learners are much more efficient in terms of experience; many fewer experiences are needed to learn well. However, the model-free methods use less memory and often use less computation time. If experience was cheap, such as in a computer game, a different comparison would be needed than if experience was expensive, such as for a robot.

## 13.9 RL with Generalization

Usually, there are too many states to reason about explicitly. The alternative to reasoning explicitly in terms of states is to reason in terms of features, which can either be provided explicitly or learned.

Figure 13.7 (page 600) shows a generic reinforcement on-policy learner that incorporates a supervised learner. This assumes the learner can carry out the operations

- $add(x, y)$ which adds a new example to the dataset, with input $x$ and target value $y$
- $predict(x)$ which gives a point prediction for the target for an example with input $x$.

In *SARSA_with_Generalization*, the input $x$ for the learner is a state–action pair, and the target for pair $(s, a)$ is an estimate of $Q^*(s, a)$.

The only difference from the learners considered in Chapters 7 and 8 is that the learner must be able to incrementally add examples, and make predictions based on the examples it currently has. Newer examples are often better approximations than old examples, and the algorithms might need to take this into account.

Selecting the next action $a'$ on line 10 with pure exploitation means selecting an $a'$ that maximizes $Learner.predict((s', a'))$; exploration can be carried out using one of the exploration techniques of Section 13.5 (page 591).

Generalization in this algorithm occurs by the learner generalizing. The learner could be, for example, a linear function (see next section), a decision tree learner, or a neural network. SARSA is an instance of this algorithm where the learner memorizes, but does not generalize.

In **deep reinforcement learning**, a deep neural network (page 327) is used as the learner. In particular, a neural network can be used to represent the $Q$-function, the value function, and/or the policy. Deep learning requires a large amount of data, and many iterations to learn, and can be sensitive to the architecture provided. While it has been very successful in games such as Go or Chess (see Section 14.7.3 (page 636)), it is notoriously difficult to make it work, and it is very computationally intensive. A linear function is usually better for smaller problems.

```
1: controller SARSA_with_Generalization(Learner, γ)
2:     Inputs
3:         Learner with operations Learner.add(x, y) and Learner.predict(x).
4:         γ ∈ [0, 1]: discount factor
5:     observe current state s
6:     select action a
7:     repeat
8:         do(a)
9:         observe reward r and state s'
10:        select action a' based on Learner.predict((s', a'))
11:        Learner.add((s, a), r + γ * Learner.predict((s', a')))
12:        s := s'
13:        a := a'
14:    until termination()
```

Figure 13.7: SARSA with generalization

### 13.9.1 SARSA with Linear Function Approximation

Consider an instance of SARSA with generalization (Figure 13.7) that is a linear function of features of the state and the action. While there are more complicated alternatives, such as using a decision tree or neural network, the linear function often works well, but requires **feature engineering**.

The feature-based learners require more information about the domain than the reinforcement-learning methods considered so far. Whereas the previous reinforcement learners were provided only with the states and the possible actions, the feature-based learners require extra domain knowledge in terms of features. This approach requires careful selection of the features; the designer should find features adequate to represent the $Q$-function.

The algorithm **SARSA with linear function approximation**, *SARSA_LFA*, uses a linear function of features to approximate the $Q$-function. It is based on incremental gradient descent (page 293), a variant of stochastic gradient descent that updates the parameters after every example. Suppose $F_1, \dots, F_n$ are numerical features of the state and the action. $F_i(s, a)$ provides the value for the $i$th feature for state $s$ and action $a$. These features will be used to represent the linear $Q$-function

$$Q_{\overline{w}}(s, a) = w_0 + w_1 * F_1(s, a) + \cdots + w_n * F_n(s, a)$$

for some tuple of weights $\overline{w} = \langle w_0, w_1, \dots, w_n \rangle$ that have to be learned. Assume that there is an extra feature $F_0(s, a)$ whose value is always 1, so that $w_0$ is not a special case.

An experience in SARSA of the form $\langle s, a, r, s', a' \rangle$ (the agent was in state $s$, did action $a$, received reward $r$, and ended up in state $s'$, in which it decided to do action $a'$) provides the new estimate $r + \gamma * Q_{\overline{w}}(s', a')$ to update $Q_{\overline{w}}(s, a)$. This experience can be used as a data point for **linear regression** (page 288). Let $\delta = Q_{\overline{w}}(s, a) - (r + \gamma * Q_{\overline{w}}(s', a'))$. Using Equation (7.4) (page 291), weight $w_i$ is updated by

$$w_i := w_i - \eta * \delta * F_i(s, a).$$

This update can then be incorporated into SARSA, giving the algorithm shown in Figure 13.8 (page 602).

Although this program is simple to implement, **feature engineering** – choosing what features to include – is non-trivial. The linear function must not only convey the best action to carry out, it must also convey the information about what future states are useful.

**Example 13.6** Consider the monster game of Example 13.2 (page 585). From understanding the domain, and not just treating it as a black box, some possible features that can be computed and might be useful are

- $F_1(s, a)$ has value 1 if action $a$ would most likely take the agent from state $s$ into a location where a monster could appear and has value 0 otherwise.

- $F_2(s, a)$ has value 1 if action $a$ would most likely take the agent into a wall and has value 0 otherwise.
- $F_3(s, a)$ has value 1 if step $a$ would most likely take the agent toward a prize.
- $F_4(s, a)$ has value 1 if the agent is damaged in state $s$ and action $a$ takes it toward the repair station.
- $F_5(s, a)$ has value 1 if the agent is damaged and action $a$ would most likely take the agent into a location where a monster could appear and has value 0 otherwise. That is, it is the same as $F_1(s, a)$ but is only applicable when the agent is damaged.
- $F_6(s, a)$ has value 1 if the agent is damaged in state $s$ and has value 0 otherwise.
- $F_7(s, a)$ has value 1 if the agent is not damaged in state $s$ and has value 0 otherwise.
- $F_8(s, a)$ has value 1 if the agent is damaged and there is a prize ahead in direction $a$.
- $F_9(s, a)$ has value 1 if the agent is not damaged and there is a prize ahead in direction $a$.
- $F_{10}(s, a)$ has the value of the $x$-value in state $s$ if there is a prize at location $P_0$ in state $s$. That is, it is the distance from the left wall if there is a prize at location $P_0$.

---

**controller** *SARSA_LFA*($\overline{F}, \gamma, \eta$)
**Inputs**
$\overline{F} = \langle F_1, \ldots, F_n \rangle$: a set of features. Define $F_0(s, a) = 1$.
$\gamma \in [0, 1]$: discount factor
$\eta > 0$: step size for gradient descent
**Local**
weights $\overline{w} = \langle w_0, \ldots, w_n \rangle$, initialized arbitrarily
observe current state $s$
select action $a$
**repeat**
*do*($a$)
observe reward $r$ and state $s'$
select action $a'$ (using a policy based on $Q_{\overline{w}}$)
$\delta := Q_{\overline{w}}(s, a) - (r + \gamma * Q_{\overline{w}}(s', a'))$
**for** $i = 0$ to $n$ **do**
$w_i := w_i - \eta * \delta * F_i(s, a)$
$s := s'$
$a := a'$
**until** *termination*()

Figure 13.8: SARSA_LFA: SARSA with linear function approximation

- $F_{11}(s,a)$ has the value $4 - x$, where $x$ is the horizontal position in state $s$ if there is a prize at location $P_0$ in state $s$. That is, it is the distance from the right wall if there is a prize at location $P_0$.
- $F_{12}(s,a)$ to $F_{29}(s,a)$ are like $F_{10}$ and $F_{11}$ for different combinations of the prize location and the distance from each of the four walls. For the case where the prize is at location $P_0$, the $y$-distance could take into account the wall.

An example linear function is

$$Q(s,a) = 2.0 - 1.0 * F_1(s,a) - 0.4 * F_2(s,a) - 1.3 * F_3(s,a) - \\ 0.5 * F_4(s,a) - 1.2 * F_5(s,a) - 1.6 * F_6(s,a) + 3.5 * F_7(s,a) + \\ 0.6 * F_8(s,a) + 0.6 * F_9(s,a) - 0.0 * F_{10}(s,a) + 1.0 * F_{11}(s,a) + \cdots .$$

These are the learned values (to one decimal place) for one run of the *SARSA_LFA* algorithm in Figure 13.8 (page 602).

AIPython (aipython.org) has an open-source Python implementation of this algorithm for this monster game. Experiment with stepping through the algorithm for individual steps, trying to understand how each step updates each parameter. Now run it for a number of steps. Consider the performance using the evaluation measures of Section 13.6 (page 594). Try to make sense of the values of the parameters learned.

This algorithm tends to overfit to current experiences, and to forget about old experiences, so that when it returns to a part of the state space it has not visited recently, it will have to relearn all over again. This is known as **catastrophic forgetting**. One modification is to remember old experiences ($\langle s,a,r,s'\rangle$ tuples) and to carry out some steps of **action replay**, by doing some weight updates based on random previous experiences. Updating the weights requires the use of the next action $a'$, which should be chosen according to the current policy, not the policy that was under effect when the experience occurred. When memory size becomes an issue, some of the old experiences can be discarded.

### 13.9.2 Escaping Local Optima

State-based MDPs and state-based reinforcement learning algorithms such as Q-learning (page 589), SARSA (page 595), and the model-based reinforcement learner (page 597) have no local maxima that are not global maxima. This is because each state can be optimized separately; improving a policy for one state cannot negatively impact another state.

However, when there is generalization, improving on one state can make other states worse. This means that the algorithms can converge to local optima (page 148) with a value that is not the best possible. They can work better when there is some way to escape local optima. A standard way to escape local maxima is to use randomized algorithms (page 149), for example using population-based methods (page 158), similar to particle filtering (page 445), where multiple initial initializations are run in parallel, and the best policy chosen. There has been some notable – arguably creative – solutions that have been found using **evolutionary algorithms** (page 587), where the individual runs are combined using a genetic algorithm (page 160).

## 13.10 Social Impact

One of the main problems with the real-world deployment of reinforcement learning is that of **accidents**: unintended or harmful behavior, which may be the result of poor design.

Amodei et al. [2016] gives five challenges to real-world deployment of reinforcement learning agents.

- Avoiding negative **side-effects**. A side-effect is something unintended that happens as a consequence of an agent's action. For example, a delivery robot should not spill coffee on the carpet or run over cats, but it may be unavoidable to run over ants if delivering outside. If you specify to be as quick as possible, the optimal course of action – based on its specified rewards – may be to have some of these side-effects. There are too many possible ways the robot could go wrong to specify them all for each task.

- Avoiding **reward hacking**. Reward hacking occurs when an agent optimizes a reward by doing something that was not the intention of whoever specified the reward. The delivery robot could put all of the mail in the garbage in order to have no undelivered mail, or if its goal is to have no unfulfilled tasks it could hide so that it cannot be given new tasks. A cleaning robot that is rewarded for cleaning messes might be able to get most reward by creating messes it can clean.

- **Scalable oversight** occurs when a human is giving rewards to ensure an agent is doing the right thing, but a human cannot give unlimited feedback. When the agent does something unintended, as in the examples above, it needs to be corrected. However, such oversight cannot be continual; a human does not want to continually evaluate a deployed robot.

- **Safe exploration**. Even though the optimal way to deliver coffee might be safe, while exploring it might try actions that are dangerous, such as hitting people or throwing coffee, only to be given a negative reward. The actions of the agent even when exploring need to be safe; it should be able to explore but only within a safety-constrained environment.

- Robustness to **distributional shift**. The environment during deployment will undoubtedly be different from the environment the agent is trained on. Environments change in time, and agents should be able to take changes in stride. The probability distribution of different outcomes can shift, and an agent should be robust to these changes or be able to quickly adapt to them.

Amodei et al. [2016] provide references to other researchers who have considered these issues.

## 13.11 Review

The following are the main points you should have learned from this chapter:

- A Markov decision process is an appropriate formalism for reinforcement learning. A common method is to learn an estimate of the value of doing each action in a state, as represented by the $Q(S, A)$ function.
- In reinforcement learning, an agent should trade off exploiting its knowledge and exploring to improve its knowledge.
- Off-policy learning, such as $Q$-learning, learns the value of the optimal policy. On-policy learning, such as SARSA, learns the value of the policy the agent is actually carrying out (which includes the exploration).
- Model-based reinforcement learning separates learning the dynamics and reward models from the decision-theoretic planning of what to do given the models.
- For large state or action spaces, reinforcement learning algorithms can be designed to use generalizing learners such as neural networks) to represent the value function, the $Q$-function and/or the policy.

## 13.12 References and Further Reading

For an introduction to reinforcement learning, see Sutton and Barto [2018], Szepesvári [2010], Kochenderfer et al. [2022], and Powell [2022]. Silver et al. [2021] argue that many problems can be formulated in terms of reward maximization and reinforcement learning.

Langton [1997], De Jong [2006], Salimans et al. [2017], and Such et al. [2017] overview evolutionary computation, including how it is used in reinforcement learning. Stanley et al. [2019] review **neuroevolution**. Such et al. [2017] show how genetic algorithms can be competitive for hard reinforcement learning algorithms. Lehman et al. [2018] provide many examples of the creativity of evolutionary algorithms.

Temporal-difference learning is by Sutton [1988]. $Q$-learning is by Watkins and Dayan [1992].

The use of the upper confidence bound for bandit problems was analyzed by Auer et al. [2002]. Russo et al. [2018] provide a tutorial on Thompson [1933] sampling. Kearns et al. [2002] analyze tree search, and Kocsis and Szepesvári [2006] combine tree search with smart exploration.

Schmidhuber [1990] shows how neural networks can simultaneously learn a model and a policy. Mnih et al. [2015] describe how reinforcement learning combined with neural networks was used to solve classic Atari computer games. Silver et al. [2016] show how learning can be used for the game of Go, and Silver et al. [2017] describe AlphaZero that also has superhuman performance in the games of chess and shogi. François-Lavet et al. [2018] and Li [2018] survey deep reinforcement learning.

The social impact section is based on Amodei et al. [2016].

## 13.13 Exercises

**Exercise 13.1** Explain how Q-learning fits in with the agent architecture of Section 2.1.1 (page 53). Suppose that the Q-learning agent has discount factor $\gamma$, a step size of $\alpha$, and is carrying out an $\epsilon$-greedy exploration strategy.

(a) What are the components of the belief state of the Q-learning agent?
(b) What are the percepts?
(c) What is the command function of the Q-learning agent?
(d) What is the belief-state transition function of the Q-learning agent?

**Exercise 13.2** Suppose a Q-learning agent, with fixed $\alpha$ and discount $\gamma$, was in state 34, did action 7, received reward 3, and ended up in state 65. What value(s) get updated? Give an expression for the new value. (Be as specific as possible.)

**Exercise 13.3** For the plot of the total reward as a function of time as in Figure 13.4 (page 594), the minimum and zero crossing are only meaningful statistics when balancing positive and negative rewards is reasonable behavior. Suggest what should replace these statistics when zero reward is not an appropriate definition of reasonable behavior. [Hint: Think about the cases that have only positive reward or only negative reward.]

**Exercise 13.4** Compare the different parameter settings for Q-learning for the game of Example 13.2 (page 585) (the "monster game" in AIPython (aipython.org)) In particular, compare the following situations:

(i) $step\_size(c) = 1/c$ and the Q-values are initialized to 0.0.
(ii) $step\_size(c) = 10/(9 + c)$ varies, and the Q-values are initialized to 0.0.
(iii) $\alpha$ varies (using whichever of (i) and (ii) is better) and the Q-values are initialized to 5.0.
(iv) $\alpha$ is fixed to 0.1 and the Q-values are initialized to 0.0.
(v) $\alpha$ is fixed to 0.1 and the Q-values are initialized to 5.0.
(vi) Some other parameter settings.

For each of these, carry out multiple runs and compare

(a) the distributions of minimum values
(b) the zero crossing
(c) the asymptotic slope for the policy that includes exploration
(d) the asymptotic slope for the policy that does not include exploration (to test this, after the algorithm has explored, set the exploitation parameter to 100% and run additional steps).

Which of these settings would you recommend? Why?

**Exercise 13.5** For the following reinforcement learning algorithms:

(i) $Q$-learning with fixed $\alpha$ and 80% exploitation.
(ii) $Q$-learning with fixed $\alpha_k = 1/k$ and 80% exploitation.
(iii) $Q$-learning with $\alpha_k = 1/k$ and 100% exploitation.
(iv) SARSA learning with $\alpha_k = 1/k$ and 80% exploitation.
(v) SARSA learning with $\alpha_k = 1/k$ and 100% exploitation.
(vi) Feature-based SARSA learning with softmax action selection.
(vii) A model-based reinforcement learner with 50% exploitation.

(a) Which of the reinforcement learning algorithms will find the optimal policy, given enough time?
(b) Which ones will actually follow the optimal policy?

**Exercise 13.6** Consider four different ways to derive the value of $\alpha_k$ from $k$ in $Q$-learning (note that for $Q$-learning with varying $\alpha_k$, there must be a different count $k$ for each state–action pair).

(i) Let $\alpha_k = 1/k$.
(ii) Let $\alpha_k = 10/(9+k)$.
(iii) Let $\alpha_k = 0.1$.
(iv) Let $\alpha_k = 0.1$ for the first 10,000 steps, $\alpha_k = 0.01$ for the next 10,000 steps, $\alpha_k = 0.001$ for the next 10,000 steps, $\alpha_k = 0.0001$ for the next 10,000 steps, and so on.

(a) Which of these will converge to the true $Q$-value in theory?
(b) Which converges to the true $Q$-value in practice (i.e., in a reasonable number of steps)? Try it for more than one domain.
(c) Which are able to adapt if the environment changes slowly?

**Exercise 13.7** The model-based reinforcement learner allows for a different form of optimism in the face of uncertainty. The algorithm can be started with each state having a transition to a "nirvana" state, which has very high $Q$-value (but which will never be reached in practice, and so the probability will shrink to zero).

(a) Does this perform differently than initializing all $Q$-values to a high value? Does it work better, worse, or the same?
(b) How high does the $Q$-value for the nirvana state need to be to work most effectively? Suggest a reason why one value might be good, and test it.
(c) Could this method be used for the other RL algorithms? Explain how or why not.

**Exercise 13.8** The grid game of Example 13.6 (page 601) included features for the $x$-distance to the current treasure and are the $y$-distance to the current treasure. Chris thought that these were not useful as they do not depend on the action. Do these features make a difference? Explain why they might or might not. Do they make a difference in practice?

**Exercise 13.9** In SARSA with linear function approximation, using linear regression to minimize $r + \gamma Q_{\overline{w}}(s', a') - Q_{\overline{w}}(s, a)$ gives a different algorithm than Figure 13.8 (page 602). Explain what you get and why what is described in the text may be preferable (or not). [Hint: what should the weights be adjusted to better estimate?]

**Exercise 13.10** In Example 13.6 (page 601), some of the features are perfectly correlated (e.g., $F_6$ and $F_7$). Does having such correlated features affect what functions are able to be represented? Does it help or hurt the speed at which learning occurs? Test this empirically on some examples.

# Chapter 14

# Multiagent Systems

*Imagine a personal software agent engaging in electronic commerce on your behalf. Say the task of this agent is to track goods available for sale in various online venues over time, and to purchase some of them on your behalf for an attractive price. In order to be successful, your agent will need to embody your preferences for products, your budget, and in general your knowledge about the environment in which it will operate. Moreover, the agent will need to embody your knowledge of other similar agents with which it will interact (e.g., agents who might compete with it in an auction, or agents representing store owners) – including their own preferences and knowledge. A collection of such agents forms a multiagent system.*

– Yoav Shoham and Kevin Leyton-Brown [2008]

What should an agent do when there are other agents, with their own goals and preferences, who are also reasoning about what to do? An intelligent agent should not ignore other agents or treat them as noise in the environment. This chapter considers the problems of determining what an agent should do in an environment that includes other agents who have their own utilities.

## 14.1 Multiagent Framework

This chapter considers environments that contain multiple agents, with the following assumptions:

- The agents can act autonomously, each with its own information about the world and the other agents.
- The outcome can depend on the actions of all the agents.

- Each agent has its own utility that depends on the outcome. Agents act to maximize their own utility.

A **mechanism** specifies what actions are available to each agent and how the actions of the agents lead to outcomes. An agent acts **strategically** when it decides what to do based on its goals or utilities.

Sometimes **nature** is treated as an agent. Nature is defined as being a special agent that does not have preferences and does not act strategically. It just acts, perhaps stochastically. In terms of the agent architecture shown in Figure 1.4 (page 15), nature and the other agents form the environment for an agent. Agents that are not acting strategically are treated as part of nature. A strategic agent should not treat other strategic agents as part of nature, but rather should be open to coordination, cooperation, and perhaps negotiation with other strategic agents.

There are two extremes in the study of multiagent systems:

- fully **cooperative**, where the agents share the same utility function
- fully **competitive**, when one agent can only win when another loses; in **zero-sum games**, for every outcome, the sum of the utilities for the agents is zero.

Most interactions are between these two extremes, where the agents' utilities are synergistic in some aspects, competing in some, and other aspects are independent. For example, two commercial agents with stores next door to each other may both share the goal of having the street area clean and inviting; they may compete for customers, but may have no preferences about the details of the other agent's store. Sometimes their actions do not interfere with each other, and sometimes they do. Often agents are better off if they coordinate their actions through cooperation and negotiation.

Multiagent interactions have mostly been studied using the terminology of games, following the seminal work of Neumann and Morgenstern [1953]. Many issues of interaction among agents can be studied in terms of games. Even quite small games highlight deep issues. However, the study of games is meant to be about general multiagent interactions, not just artificial games.

Multiagent systems are ubiquitous in AI robot soccer, to interactive video games (page 252), to agents acting in complex economic systems, games are integral to AI. Games were one of the first applications of AI. The first operating checkers program dates back to 1952. A program by Samuel [1959] beat the Connecticut state checker champion in 1961. There was great fanfare when Deep Blue [Campbell et al., 2002] beat the world chess champion in 1997 and when AlphaGo [Silver et al., 2016] beat one of the world's top Go players in 2016. Although large, these games are conceptually simple because the agents observe the state of the world perfectly (they are fully observable). In most real-world interactions, the state of the world is only partially observable. There is now much interest in partially observable games like poker, where the environment is predictable (as the proportion of cards is known, even if the particular cards dealt are unknown), and robot soccer, where the environment is much less predictable. But all of these games are much simpler than the multiagent interactions people perform in their daily lives, let alone the strategizing needed for bartering in marketplaces or on the Internet, where the rules are less well defined and the utilities are much more multifaceted.

## 14.2 Representations of Games

A mechanism represents the actions available to each agent and the (distribution over) outcomes for their joint actions. There are many representations for mechanisms in games, and multiagent interactions in general, that have been proposed in economics and AI. In AI, these representations typically allow the designer to model aspects of games that can be exploited for computational gain.

Three representations are presented; two of these are classic representations from economics. The first abstracts away all structure of the policies of the agents. The second models the sequential structure of games and is the foundation for much work on representing board games. The third representation moves away from the state-based representation to allow the representation of games in terms of features.

### 14.2.1 Normal-Form Games

The most basic representation of games is the **normal-form game**, also known as the **strategic-form game**. A normal-form game consists of

- a finite set $I$ of agents, typically identified with the integers $I = \{1, \dots, n\}$
- a set of actions $A_i$ for each agent $i \in I$
- a utility function $u_i$ for each agent $i \in I$ that, given an assignment of action to every agent, returns the expected utility for agent $i$; each agent is trying to maximize its own utility.

An **action profile** is a tuple $\langle a_1, \dots, a_n \rangle$, which specifies that agent $i \in I$ carries out action $a_i$, where $a_i \in A_i$. An action profile produced an **outcome**. Each agent has a utility over each outcome. The utility for an agent is meant to encompass everything that the agent is interested in, including fairness, altruism, and societal well-being.

**Example 14.1** The game rock–paper–scissors is a common game played by children, and there is even a world championship. Suppose there are two agents (players), Alice and Bob. There are three actions for each agent, so that

$$A_{Alice} = A_{Bob} = \{rock, paper, scissors\}.$$

For each combination of an action for Alice and an action for Bob, there is a utility for Alice and a utility for Bob. This is often drawn in a table as in Figure 14.1 (page 612). This is called a **payoff matrix**. Alice chooses a row and

Bob chooses a column, simultaneously. This gives a pair of numbers: the first number is the payoff to the row player (Alice) and the second gives the payoff to the column player (Bob). Note that the utility for each of them depends on what both players do. An example of an action profile is $\langle scissors_{Alice}, rock_{Bob} \rangle$, where Alice chooses scissors and Bob chooses rock. In this action profile, Alice receives the utility of $-1$ and Bob receives the utility of 1. This game is a zero-sum game because one person wins only when the other loses.

This representation of a game may seem very restricted, because it only gives a one-off payoff for each agent based on single actions, chosen simultaneously, for each agent. However, the interpretation of an action in the definition is very general.

Typically, an "action" is not just a simple choice, but a **strategy**: a specification of what the agent will do under the various contingencies. The normal form, essentially, is a specification of the utilities given the possible strategies of the agents. This is why it is called the strategic form of a game.

More generally, the "action" in the definition of a normal-form game can be a **controller** (page 55) for the agent. Thus, each agent chooses a controller and the utility gives the expected outcome of the controllers run for each agent in an environment. Although the examples that follow are for simple actions, the general case has an enormous number of possible actions (possible controllers) for each agent.

### 14.2.2 Extensive Form of a Game

Whereas the normal form of a game represents controllers as single units, it is often more natural to specify the unfolding of a game through time. The extensive form of a game is an extension of a single-agent **decision tree** (page 532). Let's first give a definition that assumes the game is fully observable (called *perfect information* in game theory).

A **perfect-information game** in **extensive form**, or a **game tree**, is a finite tree where the nodes are states and the arcs correspond to actions by the agents. In particular:

- Each internal node is labeled with an agent (or with *nature*). The agent is said to control the node.

| | | Bob | | |
|---|---|---|---|---|
| | | *rock* | *paper* | *scissors* |
| | *rock* | 0,0 | −1,1 | 1,−1 |
| Alice | *paper* | 1,−1 | 0,0 | −1,1 |
| | *scissors* | −1,1 | 1,−1 | 0,0 |

Figure 14.1: Normal form for the rock–paper–scissors game

- Each arc out of a node labeled with agent $i$ corresponds to an action for agent $i$.
- Each internal node labeled with *nature* has a probability distribution over its children.
- The leaves represent final outcomes and are labeled with a utility for each agent.

The extensive form of a game specifies a particular unfolding of the game. Each path to a leaf, called a **run**, specifies one particular way that the game could proceed, depending on the choices of the agents and nature.

A **strategy** for agent $i$ is a function from nodes controlled by agent $i$ into actions. That is, a strategy selects a child for each node that agent $i$ controls. A **strategy profile** consists of a strategy for each agent.

**Example 14.2** Consider a sharing game where there are two agents, Andy and Barb, and there are two identical items to be divided between them. Andy first selects how they will be divided: Andy keeps both items, they share and each person gets one item, or he gives both items to Barb. Then Barb gets to either reject the allocation and they both get nothing, or accept the allocation and they both get the allocated amount.

The extensive form of the sharing game is shown in Figure 14.2. Andy has 3 strategies. Barb has $2^3 = 8$ strategies; one for each combination of assignments to the nodes she controls. As a result, there are 24 strategy profiles.

Given a strategy profile, each node has a utility for each agent. The utility for an agent at a node is defined recursively from the bottom up:

- The utility for each agent at a leaf is given as part of the leaf.
- The utility for an agent at a node controlled by that agent is the utility for the agent of the child node that is selected by the agent's strategy.
- The utility for agent $j$ at a node controlled by another agent $i$ is the utility for agent $j$ of the child node that is selected by agent $i$'s strategy.

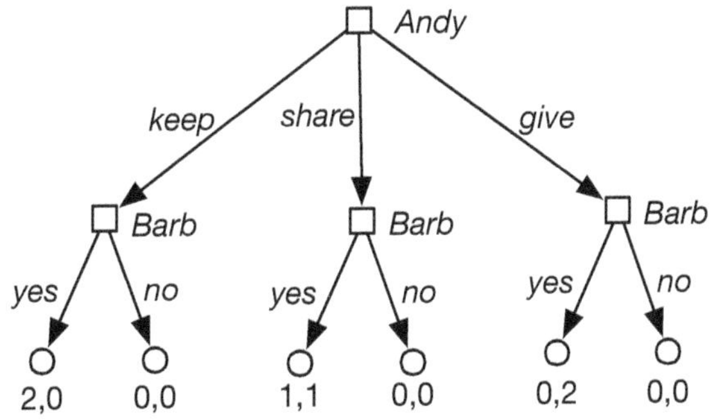


Figure 14.2: Extensive form of the sharing game

- The utility for agent $i$ for a node controlled by nature is the expected value of the utility for agent $i$ of the children. That is, $u_i(n) = \sum_c P(c)u_i(c)$, where the sum is over the children $c$ of node $n$, and $P(c)$ is the probability that nature will choose child $c$.

**Example 14.3** In the sharing game, consider the following strategy profile: Andy, not knowing what Barb will do, chooses *keep*. Barb chooses *no*, *yes*, *yes* for each of the nodes she gets to choose for. Under this strategy profile, the utility for Andy at the leftmost internal node is 0, the utility for Andy at the center internal node is 1, and the utility for Andy at the rightmost internal node is 0. For this strategy profile, the utility for Andy at the root is 0.

The preceding definition of the extensive form of a game assumes that the agents can observe the state of the world (i.e., at each stage they know which node they are at). This means that the state of the game must be fully observable. In a **partially observable game** or an **imperfect-information game**, the agents do not necessarily know the state of the world when they have to decide what to do. This includes **simultaneous-action games**, where more than one agent needs to decide what to do at the same time. In such cases, the agents do not know which node they are at in the game tree. To model these games, the extensive form of a game is extended to include information sets. An **information set** is a set of nodes, all controlled by the same agent and all with the same set of available actions. The idea is that the agent cannot distinguish the elements of the information set. The agent only knows the game state is at one of the nodes in the information set, not which of those nodes. In a strategy, the agent chooses one action for each information set; the same action is carried out at each node in the information set. Thus, in the extensive form, a strategy specifies a function from information sets to actions.

**Example 14.4** Figure 14.3 gives the extensive form for the rock–paper–scissors game of Example 14.1 (page 611). The elements of the information set are in a

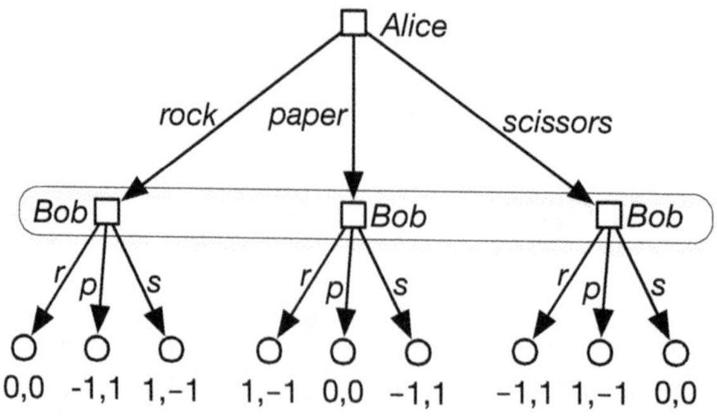


Figure 14.3: Extensive form of the rock–paper–scissors game

rounded rectangle. In a strategy, Bob must treat each node in the information set the same. When Bob gets to choose his action, he does not know which action Alice has chosen.

### 14.2.3 Multiagent Decision Networks

The extensive form of a game is a state-based representation of the game. It is often more concise to describe states in terms of features. A **multiagent decision network** is a factored representation of a multiagent decision problem. It is like a **decision network** (page 537), except that each decision node is labeled with an agent that gets to choose a value for the node. There is a utility node for each agent specifying the utility for that agent. The parents of a decision node specify the information that will be available to the agent when it has to act.

**Example 14.5** Figure 14.4 gives a multiagent decision network for a fire alarm example. In this scenario, there are two agents, Agent 1 and Agent 2. Each has its own noisy sensor of whether there is a fire. However, if they both call, it is possible that their calls will interfere with each other and neither call will work. Agent 1 gets to choose a value for decision variable $Call_1$ and only observes the value for the variable $Alarm_1$. Agent 2 gets to choose a value for decision variable $Call_2$ and only observes the value for the variable $Alarm_2$. Whether the call works depends on the values of $Call_1$ and $Call_2$. Whether the fire department comes depends on whether the call works. Agent 1's utility depends on whether there was a fire, whether the fire department comes, and whether they called – similarly for Agent 2.

A multiagent decision network can be converted into a normal-form game; however, the number of strategies may be enormous. If a decision variable

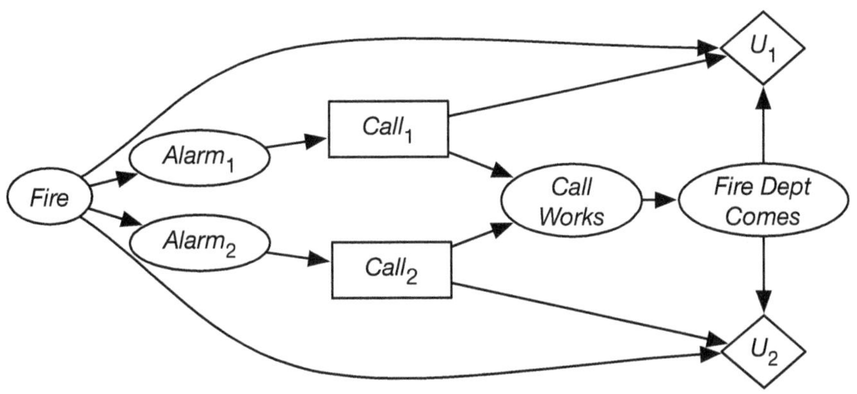


Figure 14.4: Multiagent decision network for Example 14.5

has $d$ states and $n$ binary parents, there are $2^n$ assignments of values to parents and so $d^{2^n}$ strategies. That is just for a single decision node; more complicated networks are even bigger when converted to normal form. Thus, algorithms that depend on enumerating strategies are impractical for anything but the smallest multiagent decision networks.

Other representations exploit other structures in multiagent settings. For example, the utility of an agent may depend on the number of other agents who do some action, but not on their identities. An agent's utility may depend on what a few other agents do, not directly on the actions of all other agents. An agent's utility may only depend on what the agents at neighboring locations do, and not on the identity of these agents or on what other agents do.

## 14.3 Solving Perfect Information Games

**Fully observable** (page 29) with multiple agents is typically called **perfect information**. In perfect-information games, agents act sequentially and, when an agent has to act, it gets to observe the state of the world before deciding what to do. Each agent acts to maximize its own utility.

A perfect-information game can be represented as an extensive-form game where the information sets all contain a single node. They can also be represented as a multiagent decision network where the decision nodes are totally ordered and, for each decision node, the parents of that decision node include the preceding decision node and all of their parents (so they are a multiagent counterpart of no-forgetting decision networks (page 540)).

Perfect-information games are solvable in a manner similar to fully observable single-agent systems. They can be solved backward, from the last decisions to the first, using dynamic programming, or forward using search. The multiagent algorithm maintains a utility for each agent and, for each move, it selects an action that maximizes the utility of the agent making the move. The dynamic programming variant, called **backward induction**, starts from the end of the game, computing and caching the values and the plan of each node for each agent.

Figure 14.5 (page 617) gives a top-down, depth-first search algorithm for evaluating a game tree for a perfect information game. It enumerates the whole tree. At each internal node, the agent that controls the node selects a child that is best for it. This arbitrarily chooses the first child that maximizes the agent's score (the $>$ on line 12), but as the following example shows, which one is selected can affect the utility.

**Example 14.6** Consider the sharing game of Figure 14.2 (page 613). In the recursive calls, Barb gets to choose the value that maximizes her utility. Thus, she will choose "yes" for the right two nodes she controls, and would choose either for the leftmost node she controls. Suppose she chooses "no" for this node, then Andy gets to choose one of his actions: *keep* has utility 0 for him, *share* has utility 1, and *give* has utility 0, so he chooses to share. If Barb had chosen "yes" for the leftmost node, Andy would keep, and so Andy would get both items.

### 14.3.1 Adversarial Games

The case where two agents are competing, so that a positive reward for one is a negative reward for the other, is a two-agent **zero-sum game**. An agent that plays such a game well requires **adversarial reasoning** (page 33). The value of such a game can be characterized by a single number that one agent is trying to maximize and the other agent is trying to minimize, which leads to a **minimax** search space. Each node is either a MAX node, if it is controlled by the agent trying to maximize, or a MIN node, if it is controlled by the agent trying to minimize.

Figure 14.5 implements a minimax algorithm for zero-sum perfect information games, by the MAX agent choosing an action with the maximum value, and the MIN agent choosing an action with the maximum of the *negation* of the value.

The game-tree search of Figure 14.5 traverses the whole game tree. It is possible to prune part of the search tree for minimax games by showing that some part of the tree will never be part of an optimal play.

**Example 14.7** Consider searching in the game tree of Figure 14.6 (page 618). In this figure, the square MAX nodes are controlled by the maximizing agent, and the round MIN nodes are controlled by the minimizing agent.

```
procedure GameTreeSearch(n)
    Inputs
        n a node in a game tree
    Output
        A pair of a value for each agent for node n, path that gives this value
    if n is a leaf node then
        return {i : evaluate(i, n)}, None
    else if n is controlled by agent i then
        max_score_for_i := −∞
        for each child c of n do
            score, path := Minimax(c)
            if score[i] > max_score_for_i then
                max_score_for_i := score[i]
                best := c : path
        return score, best
```

Figure 14.5: Evaluating a perfect-information game tree (without nature)

Suppose the values of the leaf nodes are given or are computed given the definition of the game. The numbers at the bottom show some of these values. The other values are irrelevant, as shown here. Suppose you are doing a left-first, depth-first traversal of this tree. The value of node $h$ is 7, because it is the minimum of 7 and 9. Just by considering the leftmost child of $i$ with a value of 6, you know that the value of $i$ is less than or equal to 6. Therefore, at node $d$, the maximizing agent will go left. You do not have to evaluate the other child of $i$. Similarly, the value of $j$ is 11, so the value of $e$ is at least 11, and so the minimizing agent at node $b$ will choose to go left.

The value of $l$ is less than or equal to 5, and the value of $m$ is less than or equal to 4; thus, the value of $f$ is less than or equal to 5, so the value of $c$ will be less than or equal to 5. So, at $a$, the maximizing agent will choose to go left. Notice that this argument did not depend on the values of the unnumbered leaves. Moreover, it did not depend on the size of the subtrees that were not explored.

The previous example analyzed what can be pruned. Minimax with **alpha–beta ($\alpha$–$\beta$) pruning** is a depth-first **search** algorithm that prunes by passing pruning information down in terms of parameters $\alpha$ and $\beta$. In this depth-first search, a node has a score, which has been obtained from (some of) its descendants.

The parameter $\alpha$ is used to prune MIN nodes. Initially, it is the highest current value for all MAX ancestors of the current node. Any MIN node whose current value is less than or equal to its $\alpha$ value does not have to be explored further. This cutoff was used to prune the other descendants of nodes $l$, $m$, and $c$ in the previous example.

The $\beta$ parameter is used to prune MAX nodes in an analogous way.

The minimax algorithm with $\alpha$–$\beta$ pruning is given in Figure 14.7 (page 619). It is called, initially, with $MinimaxAlphaBeta(R, -\infty, \infty)$, where $R$ is the root

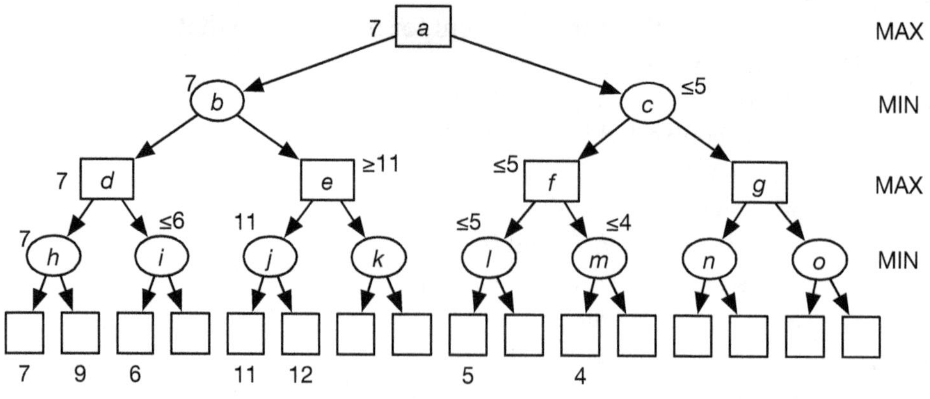


Figure 14.6: A zero-sum game tree showing which nodes can be pruned

node. It returns a pair of the value for the node $n$ and a path of choices that lead to this value. (Note that this path does not include $n$.) Line 13 performs $\beta$ pruning; at this stage the algorithm knows that the current path will never be chosen, and so returns a current score. Similarly, line 22 performs $\alpha$-pruning. Line 17 and line 26 concatenate $c$ to the path, as it has found a best path for the agent. In this algorithm, the path "*None*" is sometimes returned for non-leaf nodes; this only occurs when the algorithm has determined this path will not be used.

**Example 14.8** Consider running *MinimaxAlphaBeta* on the tree of Figure 14.6 (page 618). Consider the recursive calls (and the values returned, but not the paths). Initially, it calls

$$MinimaxAlphaBeta(a, -\infty, \infty)$$

```
1: procedure Minimax_alpha_beta(n, α, β)
2:     Inputs
3:         n a node in a game tree
4:         α, β real numbers
5:     Output
6:         A pair of a value for node n, path that gives this value
7:     best := None
8:     if n is a leaf node then
9:         return evaluate(n), None
10:    else if n is a MAX node then
11:        for each child c of n do
12:            score, path := MinimaxAlphaBeta(c, α, β)
13:            if score ≥ β then
14:                return score, None
15:            else if score > α then
16:                α := score
17:                best := c : path
18:        return α, best
19:    else
20:        for each child c of n do
21:            score, path := MinimaxAlphaBeta(c, α, β)
22:            if score ≤ α then
23:                return score, None
24:            else if score < β then
25:                β := score
26:                best := c : path
27:        return β, best
```

Figure 14.7: Minimax with $\alpha$–$\beta$ pruning

which then calls, in turn:

$$MinimaxAlphaBeta(b, -\infty, \infty)$$

$$MinimaxAlphaBeta(d, -\infty, \infty)$$

$$MinimaxAlphaBeta(h, -\infty, \infty).$$

This last call finds the minimum of both of its children and returns 7. Next the procedure calls

$$MinimaxAlphaBeta(i, 7, \infty)$$

which then gets the value for the first of $i$'s children, which has value 6. Because $\alpha \geq \beta$, it returns 6. The call to $d$ then returns 7, and it calls

$$MinimaxAlphaBeta(e, -\infty, 7).$$

Node $e$'s first child returns 11 and, because $\alpha \geq \beta$, it returns 11. Then $b$ returns 7, and the call to $a$ calls

$$MinimaxAlphaBeta(c, 7, \infty)$$

which in turn calls

$$MinimaxAlphaBeta(f, 7, \infty)$$

which eventually returns 5, and so the call to $c$ returns 5, and the whole procedure returns 7.

By keeping track of the values, the maximizing agent knows to go left at $a$, then the minimizing agent will go left at $b$, and so on.

The amount of pruning provided by this algorithm depends on the ordering of the children of each node. It works best if a highest-valued child of a MAX node is selected first and if a lowest-valued child of a MIN node is returned first. In implementations of real games, much of the effort is made to try to ensure this ordering.

Most real games are too big to carry out minimax search, even with $\alpha$–$\beta$ pruning. For these games, instead of only stopping at leaf nodes, it is possible to stop at any node. The value returned at the node where the algorithm stops is an estimate of the value for this node. The function used to estimate the value is an **evaluation function**. Much work goes into finding good evaluation functions. There is a trade-off between the amount of computation required to compute the evaluation function and the size of the search space that can be explored in any given time. It is an empirical question as to the best compromise between a complex evaluation function and a large search space.

## 14.4 Reasoning with Imperfect Information

In an **imperfect-information game**, or a **partially observable game**, an agent does not fully know the state of the world or the agents act simultaneously.

Partial observability for the multiagent case is more complicated than the fully observable multiagent case or the partially observable single-agent case. The following simple examples show some important issues that arise even in the case of two agents, each with a few choices.

**Example 14.9** Consider the case of a penalty kick in soccer as depicted in Figure 14.8. If the kicker kicks to their right and the goalkeeper jumps to their right, the probability of a goal is 0.9, and similarly for the other combinations of actions, as given in the figure.

What should the kicker do, given that they want to maximize the probability of a goal and the goalkeeper wants to minimize the probability of a goal? The kicker could think that it is better kicking to their right, because the pair of numbers for their right kick is higher than the pair for the left. The goalkeeper could then think that if the kicker will kick right, they should jump left. However, if the kicker thinks that the goalkeeper will jump left, they should then kick left. But then, the goalkeeper should jump right. Then the kicker should kick right...

Each agent is potentially faced with an infinite regression of reasoning about what the other agent will do. At each stage in their reasoning, the agents reverse their decision. One could imagine cutting this off at some depth; however, the actions then are purely a function of the arbitrary depth. Even worse, if the goalkeeper knew the depth limit of reasoning for the kicker, they could exploit this knowledge to determine what the kicker will do and choose their action appropriately.

An alternative is for the agents to choose actions stochastically. Imagine that the kicker and the goalkeeper each secretly toss a coin to decide what to do. Consider whether the coins should be biased. Suppose that the kicker decides to kick to their right with probability $p_k$ and that the goalkeeper decides to jump

| | | Goalkeeper left | Goalkeeper right |
|---|---|---|---|
| Kicker | left | 0.6 | 0.2 |
| | right | 0.3 | 0.9 |

Probability of a goal

Figure 14.8: Soccer penalty kick. The kicker can kick to their left or right. The goalkeeper can jump to their left or right to their right with probability $p_g$. The probability of a goal is then

$$P(goal) = 0.9p_kp_g + 0.3p_k(1-p_g) + 0.2(1-p_k)p_g + 0.6(1-p_k)(1-p_g)$$

where the numbers (0.9, 0.3, etc.) come from Figure 14.8 (page 621).

Figure 14.9 shows the probability of a goal as a function of $p_k$. The different lines correspond to different values of $p_g$.

There is something special about the value $p_k = 0.4$. At this value, the probability of a goal is 0.48, independent of the value of $p_g$. That is, no matter what the goalkeeper does, the kicker expects to get a goal with probability 0.48. If the kicker deviates from $p_k = 0.4$, they could do better or could do worse, depending on what the goalkeeper does.

The plot for $p_g$ is similar, with all of the lines meeting at $p_g = 0.3$. Again, when $p_g = 0.3$, the probability of a goal is 0.48.

The strategy with $p_k = 0.4$ and $p_g = 0.3$ is special in the sense that neither agent can do better by unilaterally deviating from the strategy. However, this does not mean that they cannot do better; if one of the agents deviates from this equilibrium, the other agent could do better by also deviating from the equilibrium. However, this equilibrium is safe for an agent in the sense that, even if the other agent knew the agent's strategy, the other agent cannot force a worse outcome for the agent. Playing this strategy means that an agent does not have to worry about double-guessing the other agent. In this game, each agent will get the best payoff it could guarantee to obtain.

So let us now extend the definition of a strategy to include randomized strategies.

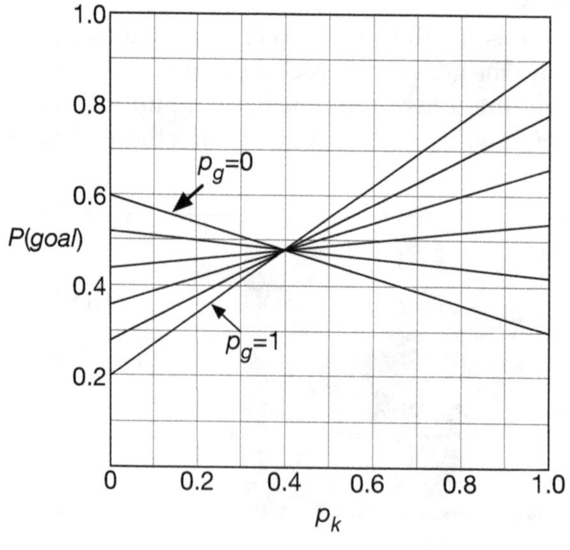


Figure 14.9: Probability of a goal as a function of action probabilities

Consider the normal form of a game where each agent chooses an action simultaneously. Each agent chooses an action without knowing what the other agents choose.

A **strategy** for an agent is a probability distribution over the actions for this agent. In a **pure strategy**, one of the probabilities will be 1 and the rest will be 0. Thus, an agent following a pure strategy is acting deterministically. The alternative to a pure strategy is a **stochastic strategy**, where none of the probabilities are 1, and so more than one action has a non-zero probability. The set of actions with a non-zero probability in a strategy is the **support set** of the strategy.

A **strategy profile** is an assignment of a strategy to each agent. If $\sigma$ is a strategy profile, let $\sigma_i$ be the strategy of agent $i$ in $\sigma$, and let $\sigma_{-i}$ be the strategies of the other agents. Then $\sigma$ is $\sigma_i\sigma_{-i}$. If the strategy profile is made up of pure strategies, it is often called an **action profile** (page 611), because each agent is playing a particular action.

A strategy profile $\sigma$ has an expected utility for each agent. Let $utility(\sigma, i)$ be the expected utility of strategy profile $\sigma$ for agent $i$. The utility of a stochastic strategy profile can be computed by averaging the utilities of the basic actions that make up the profile given the probabilities of the actions.

A **best response** for an agent $i$ to the strategies $\sigma_{-i}$ of the other agents is a strategy that has maximal utility for that agent. That is, $\sigma_i$ is a best response to $\sigma_{-i}$ if, for all other strategies $\sigma'_i$ for agent $i$:

$$utility(\sigma_i\sigma_{-i}, i) \geq utility(\sigma'_i\sigma_{-i}, i).$$

A strategy profile $\sigma$ is a **Nash equilibrium** if, for each agent $i$, strategy $\sigma_i$ is a best response to $\sigma_{-i}$. That is, a Nash equilibrium is a strategy profile such that no agent can do better by unilaterally deviating from that profile.

One of the great results of game theory, proved by Nash [1950], is that every finite game has at least one Nash equilibrium.

**Example 14.10** In Example 14.9 (page 621), there is a unique Nash equilibrium where $p_k = 0.4$ and $p_g = 0.3$. This has the property that, if the kicker is playing $p_k = 0.4$, it does not matter what the goalkeeper does; the goalkeeper will have the same payoff, and so $p_g = 0.3$ is a best response (as is any other strategy). Similarly, if the goalkeeper is playing $p_g = 0.3$, it does not matter what the kicker does; and so every strategy, including $p_k = 0.4$, is a best response.

The only reason an agent would consider randomizing between two actions is if the actions have the same expected utility. All probabilistic mixtures of the two actions have the same utility. The reason to choose a particular value for the probability of the mixture is to prevent the other agent from exploiting a deviation.

Games can have multiple Nash equilibria. Consider the following two-agent, two-action game.

**Example 14.11** Suppose there is a resource that two agents may want to fight over. Each agent chooses to act as a hawk or as a dove. Suppose the resource is worth $R$ units, where $R > 0$. If both agents act as doves, they share the resource. If one agent acts as a hawk and the other as a dove, the hawk agent gets the resource and the dove agent gets nothing. If they both act like hawks, there is destruction of the resource and the reward to both is $-D$, where $D > 0$. This is depicted by the following payoff matrix:

| | | Agent 2 | |
|---|---|---|---|
| | | dove | hawk |
| Agent 1 | dove | $R/2, R/2$ | $0, R$ |
| | hawk | $R, 0$ | $-D, -D$ |

In this matrix, Agent 1 gets to choose the row, Agent 2 gets to choose the column, and the payoff in the cell is a pair consisting of the reward to Agent 1 and the reward to Agent 2. Each agent is trying to maximize its own reward.

In this game there are three Nash equilibria:

- In one equilibrium, Agent 1 acts as a hawk and Agent 2 as a dove. Agent 1 does not want to deviate because then they have to share the resource. Agent 2 does not want to deviate because then there is destruction.
- In the second equilibrium, Agent 1 acts as a dove and Agent 2 as a hawk.
- In the third equilibrium, both agents act stochastically. In this equilibrium, there is some chance of destruction. The probability of acting like a hawk goes up with the value $R$ of the resource and goes down as the value $D$ of destruction increases. See Exercise 14.3 (page 640).

In this example, you could imagine each agent doing some posturing to try to indicate what it will do to try to force an equilibrium that is advantageous to it.

Having multiple Nash equilibria does not come from being adversaries, as the following example shows.

**Example 14.12** Suppose there are two people who want to be together. Agent 1 prefers they both go to the football game and Agent 2 prefers they both go shopping. They both would be unhappy if they are not together. Suppose they both have to choose simultaneously what activity to do. This is depicted by the following payoff matrix:

| | | Agent 2 | |
|---|---|---|---|
| | | football | shopping |
| Agent 1 | football | 2,1 | 0,0 |
| | shopping | 0,0 | 1,2 |

In this matrix, Agent 1 chooses the row, and Agent 2 chooses the column.

In this game, there are three Nash equilibria. One equilibrium is where they both go shopping, one is where they both go to the football game, and one is a randomized strategy.

This is a **coordination** problem. Knowing the set of equilibria does not actually tell either agent what to do, because what an agent should do depends on what the other agent will do. In this example, you could imagine conversations to determine which equilibrium they would choose.

Even when there is a unique Nash equilibrium, that Nash equilibrium does not guarantee the maximum payoff to each agent. The following example is a variant of what is known as the **prisoner's dilemma**.

**Example 14.13** Imagine you are on a game show with a stranger who you will never see again. You each have the choice of

- taking \$100 for yourself, or
- giving \$1000 to the other person.

This is depicted as the following payoff matrix:

| | | Player 2 | |
|---|---|---|---|
| | | take | give |
| Player 1 | take | 100, 100 | 1100, 0 |
| | give | 0, 1100 | 1000, 1000 |

No matter what the other agent does, each agent is better off if it takes rather than gives. However, both agents are better off if they both give rather than if they both take.

Thus, there is a unique Nash equilibrium, where both agents take. This strategy profile results in each player receiving \$100. The strategy profile where both players give results in each player receiving \$1000. However, in this strategy profile, each agent is rewarded for deviating.

There is a large body of research on the prisoner's dilemma, because it does not seem to be so rational to be greedy, where each agent tries to do the best for itself, resulting in everyone being worse off. One case where giving becomes preferred is when the game is played a number of times. This is known as the **sequential prisoner's dilemma**. One strategy for the sequential prisoner's dilemma is **tit-for-tat**: each player gives initially, then does the other agent's previous action at each step. This strategy is a Nash equilibrium as long as there is no last action that both players know about. See Exercise 14.8 (page 641).

Having multiple Nash equilibria arises not just from partial observability. It is possible to have multiple equilibria with a perfect-information game, and it is even possible to have infinitely many Nash equilibria, as the following example shows.

**Example 14.14** Consider the sharing game of Example 14.2 (page 613). In this game there are infinitely many Nash equilibria. There is a set of equilibria where Andy shares, and Barb says *yes* to sharing for the center choice and can randomize between the other choices, as long as the probability of saying *yes* in the left-hand choice is less than or equal to 0.5. In these Nash equilibria, they both get 1. There is another set of Nash equilibria where Andy keeps, and Barb randomizes among her choices, so that the probability of saying *yes* in the left branch is greater than or equal to 0.5. In these equilibria, Barb gets 0 and Andy gets some value in the range [1, 2] depending on Barb's probability. There is a third set of Nash equilibria where Barb has a 0.5 probability of selecting *yes* at the leftmost node, selects *yes* at the center node, and Andy randomizes between *keep* and *share* with any probability.

Suppose the sharing game were modified slightly so that Andy offered a small bribe for Barb to say *yes*. This could be done by changing the 2, 0 payoff to be 1.9, 0.1. Andy may think, "Given the choice between getting 0.1 or 0, Barb will choose to get 0.1, so then I should *keep*." But Barb could think, "I should say *no* to 0.1, so that Andy shares and I get 1." In this example (even ignoring the rightmost branch), there are multiple pure Nash equilibria. One is where Andy keeps and Barb says *yes* at the leftmost branch. In this equilibrium, Andy gets 1.9 and Barb gets 0.1. There is another Nash equilibrium where Barb says *no* at the leftmost choice node and *yes* at the center branch and Andy chooses *share*. In this equilibrium, they both get 1. It would seem that this is the one preferred by Barb. However, Andy could think that Barb is making an empty **threat**. If he actually decided to *keep*, Barb, acting to maximize her utility, would not actually say *no*.

The backward-induction algorithm only finds one of the equilibria in the modified sharing game of the previous example. It computes a **subgame-perfect equilibrium**, where it is assumed that the agents choose the action with greatest utility for them at every node where they get to choose. It assumes that agents do not carry out threats that it is not in their interest to carry out at the time. In the modified sharing game of the previous example, it assumes that Barb will say *yes* to the small bribe. However, when dealing with real opponents, you should be aware that they may follow through with threats that you may not think rational. Indeed, it might be better for an agent not to (appear to) be rational!

## 14.4.1 Computing Nash Equilibria

To compute a Nash equilibrium for a game in normal form, there are three steps:

1. Eliminate dominated strategies.
2. Determine the **support set**, the set of actions which have non-zero probabilities.
3. Determine the probability for the actions in the support set.

It turns out that the second of these is the most difficult.

### Eliminating Dominated Strategies

A strategy $s_1$ for agent $A$ is **dominated** by strategy $s_2$ for $A$ if, for every action of the other agents, the utility of $s_1$ for agent $A$ is lower than the utility of $s_2$ for agent $A$. This is formalized below. Any pure strategy dominated by another strategy can be eliminated from consideration. The dominating strategy could be a randomized strategy. Removing dominated strategies can be done repeatedly.

**Example 14.15** Consider the following payoff matrix, where the first agent chooses the row and the second agent chooses the column. In each cell is a pair of payoffs: the payoff for Agent 1 and the payoff for Agent 2. Agent 1 has actions $\{a_1, b_1, c_1\}$. Agent 2 has actions $\{d_2, e_2, f_2\}$.

| | | Agent 2 | | |
|---|---|---|---|---|
| | | $d_2$ | $e_2$ | $f_2$ |
| | $a_1$ | 3,5 | 5,1 | 1,2 |
| Agent 1 | $b_1$ | 1,1 | 2,9 | 6,4 |
| | $c_1$ | 2,6 | 4,7 | 0,8 |

(Before looking at the solution, try to work out what each agent should do.)

Action $c_1$ can be removed because it is dominated by action $a_1$: Agent 1 will never do $c_1$ if action $a_1$ is available to it. Notice how the payoff for Agent 1 is greater doing $a_1$ than doing $c_1$, no matter what the other agent does.

Once action $c_1$ is eliminated, action $f_2$ can be eliminated because it is dominated for Agent 2 by the randomized strategy $0.5 * d_2 + 0.5 * e_2$.

Once $c_1$ and $f_2$ have been eliminated, $b_1$ is dominated by $a_1$, and so Agent 1 will do action $a_1$. Given that Agent 1 will do $a_1$, Agent 2 will do $d_2$. Thus the unique Nash equilibrium has Agent 1 doing $a_1$ and Agent 2 doing $d_2$, with a payoff of 3 for Agent 1 and 5 for Agent 2.

Strategy $s_1$ **strictly dominates** strategy $s_2$ for Agent $i$ if, for all action profiles $\sigma_{-i}$ of the other agents:

$$utility(s_1\sigma_{-i}, i) > utility(s_2\sigma_{-i}, i)$$

in which case $s_2$ is **strictly dominated** by $s_1$. If $s_2$ is a pure strategy that is strictly dominated by some strategy $s_1$, then $s_2$ can never be in the support set of any Nash equilibrium. This holds even if $s_1$ is a stochastic strategy. Repeated elimination of strictly dominated strategies gives the same result, regardless of the order in which the strictly dominated strategies are removed.

There are also weaker notions of domination, where the greater than symbol in the preceding formula is replaced by greater than or equal. If the weaker notion of domination is used, there is always a Nash equilibrium with support of the non-dominated strategies. However, some Nash equilibria may be lost. Which equilibria are lost can depend on the order in which the dominated strategies are removed.

## Computing Randomized Strategies

An agent will only randomize among actions if the actions all have the same utility to the agent, given the strategies of the other agents. This idea leads to a set of constraints that can be solved to compute a Nash equilibrium. If these constraints can be solved with numbers in the range $(0, 1)$, and the mixed strategies computed for each agent are not dominated by another strategy for the agent, then this strategy profile is a Nash equilibrium.

Recall that a support set (page 623) is a set of pure strategies that each have non-zero probability in a Nash equilibrium.

Once dominated strategies have been eliminated, an agent can search over support sets to determine whether the support sets form a Nash equilibrium. Note that, if there are $n$ actions available to an agent, there are $2^n - 1$ non-empty subsets, and we have to search over combinations of support sets for the various agents. This is not feasible unless there are only a few non-dominated actions or there are Nash equilibria with small support sets. To find simple (in terms of the number of actions in the support set) equilibria, an agent can search from smaller support sets to larger sets.

Suppose agent $i$ is randomizing actions $a_i^1, \ldots, a_i^{k_i}$ in a Nash equilibrium, each with a non-zero probability. Let $p_i^j$ be the probability that agent $i$ does action $a_i^j$. Let $\sigma_{-i}$ be the strategies for the other agents, which is a function of their probabilities. The fact that this is a Nash equilibrium gives the following constraints: $p_i^j > 0$, $\sum_{j=1}^{k_i} p_i^j = 1$, and, for all $j, j'$

$$utility(a_i^j \sigma_{-i}, i) = utility(a_i^{j'} \sigma_{-i}, i).$$

You also require that the utility of doing $a_i^j$ is not less than the utility of doing an action outside of the support set. Thus, for all $a' \notin \{a_i^1, \ldots, a_i^{k_i}\}$:

$$utility(a_i^j \sigma_{-i}, i) \geq utility(a' \sigma_{-i}, i).$$

**Example 14.16** In Example 14.9 (page 621), suppose the goalkeeper jumps right with probability $p_g$ and the kicker kicks right with probability $p_k$.

If the goalkeeper jumps right, the probability of a goal is

$$0.9p_k + 0.2(1 - p_k).$$

If the goalkeeper jumps left, the probability of a goal is

$$0.3p_k + 0.6(1 - p_k).$$

The only time the goalkeeper would randomize is if these are equal; that is, if

$$0.9p_k + 0.2(1 - p_k) = 0.3p_k + 0.6(1 - p_k).$$

Solving for $p_k$ gives $p_k = 0.4$.

Similarly, for the kicker to randomize, the probability of a goal must be the same whether the kicker kicks left or right:

$$0.2p_g + 0.6(1 - p_g) = 0.9p_g + 0.3(1 - p_g).$$

Solving for $p_g$ gives $p_g = 0.3$.

Thus, the only Nash equilibrium has $p_k = 0.4$ and $p_g = 0.3$.

## 14.5 Group Decision Making

Often, groups of people have to make decisions about what the group will do. It may seem that voting is a good way to determine what a group wants, and when there is a clear most-preferred choice, it is. However, there are major problems with voting when there is not a clear preferred choice, as shown in the following example.

**Example 14.17** Consider a purchasing agent that has to decide on a holiday destination for a group of people, based on their preference. Suppose there are three people, Alice, Bob, and Cory, and three destinations, $X$, $Y$, and $Z$. Suppose the agents have the following preferences, where $\succ$ means strictly prefers (page 519):

- Alice: $X \succ Y \succ Z$
- Bob: $Y \succ Z \succ X$
- Cory: $Z \succ X \succ Y$.

Given these preferences, in a pairwise vote, $X \succ Y$ because two out of the three prefer $X$ to $Y$. Similarly, in the voting, $Y \succ Z$ and $Z \succ X$. Thus, the preferences obtained by voting are not transitive (page 519). This example is known as the **Condorcet paradox**. Indeed, it is not clear what a group outcome should be in this case, because it is symmetric among the outcomes.

A **social preference function** gives a preference relation for a group. We would like a social preference function to depend on the preferences of the individuals in the group. It may seem that the Condorcet paradox is a problem unique to pairwise voting; however, the following result due to Arrow [1963] shows that such paradoxes occur with any social preference function.

**Proposition 14.1** (Arrow's impossibility theorem). *If there are three or more outcomes, the following properties cannot simultaneously hold for any social preference function:*

- *The social preference function is complete and transitive (page 519).*
- *Every individual preference that is complete and transitive is allowed.*
- *If every individual prefers outcome $o_1$ to $o_2$, the group prefers $o_1$ to $o_2$.*
- *The group preference between outcomes $o_1$ and $o_2$ depends only on the individual preferences on $o_1$ and $o_2$ and not on the individual preferences on other outcomes.*
- *No individual gets to unilaterally decide the outcome (non-dictatorship).*

When building an agent that takes the individual preferences and gives a social preference, you should be aware that you cannot have all of these intuitive and desirable properties. Rather than giving a group preference that has undesirable properties, it may be better to point out to the individuals how their preferences cannot be reconciled.

## 14.6 Mechanism Design

The earlier discussion on agents choosing their actions assumed that each agent gets to play in a predefined game. The problem of **mechanism design** is to design a game with desirable properties for various agents to play.

A **mechanism** specifies the actions available to each agent and the outcomes of each action profile. We assume that agents have utilities over outcomes.

There are two common properties that are desirable for a mechanism:

- A mechanism should be easy for agents to use. Given an agent's utility, it should be easy for the agent to determine what to do. A **dominant strategy** is a strategy for an agent that is best for the agent, no matter what the other agents do. If an agent has a dominant strategy, it can do its best action without the complicated strategic reasoning described in the previous sections. A mechanism is dominant-strategy **truthful** if it has a dominant strategy for each agent and, in the dominant strategy, an agent's best strategy is to declare its true preferences. In a mechanism that is dominant-strategy truthful, an agent simply declares its true preferences; the agent cannot do better by trying to manipulate the mechanism for its own gain.
- A mechanism should give the best outcome aggregated over all of the agents. A mechanism is **economically efficient** if the outcome chosen is one that maximizes the sum of the utilities of the agents.

**Example 14.18** Suppose you want to design a meeting scheduler, where users input the times they are available and the scheduler chooses a time for the meeting. One mechanism is for the users to specify when they are available or not, and for the scheduler to select the time that has the most people available. A second mechanism is for the users to specify their utility for the various times, and the scheduler chooses the time that maximizes the sum of the utilities. Neither of these mechanisms is dominant-strategy truthful.

For the first mechanism, users may declare that they are unavailable at some time to force a time they prefer. It is not clear that being available at a certain time is well defined; at some stage, users must decide whether it is easier to reschedule what they would have otherwise done at some particular time, rather than say they are unavailable at this time. Different people may have different thresholds as to what other activities can be moved.

For the second mechanism, suppose there are three people, Alice, Bob, and Cory, and they have to decide whether to meet on Monday, Tuesday, or Wednesday. Suppose they have the following utilities for the meeting days:

| | Monday | Tuesday | Wednesday |
|---|---|---|---|
| Alice | 0 | 8 | 10 |
| Bob | 3 | 4 | 0 |
| Cory | 11 | 7 | 6 |

The economically efficient outcome is to meet on Tuesday. However, if Alice were to change her evaluation of Tuesday to be 2, the mechanism would choose

Wednesday. Thus, Alice has an incentive to misrepresent her values. It is not in Alice's interest to be honest.

Note that, if there is a mechanism that has dominant strategies, there is a mechanism that is dominant-strategy truthful. This is known as the **revelation principle**. To implement a dominant-strategy truthful mechanism, we could, in principle, write a program that accepts from an agent its actual preferences and provides to the original mechanism the optimal input for that agent. This program would optimally lie for the agent.

It turns out that it is essentially impossible to design a reasonable mechanism that is dominant-strategy truthful. Gibbard [1973] and Satterthwaite [1975] proved that, as long as there are three or more outcomes that are possible to be chosen, the only mechanisms with dominant strategies have a **dictator**: there is one agent whose preferences determine the outcome. This is known as the **Gibbard–Satterthwaite theorem**.

One way to obtain dominant-strategy truthful mechanisms is to introduce money. Assume that money can be added to utility so that, for any two outcomes $o_1$ and $o_2$, for each agent there is some (possibly negative) amount $d$ such that the agent is indifferent between the outcomes $o_1$ and $o_2 + d$. By allowing agents to be paid to accept an outcome they would not otherwise prefer, or to pay for an outcome they want, we can ensure an agent does not gain by lying.

In a **VCG (Vickrey–Clarke–Groves) mechanism**, the agents declare their values for each of the outcomes. The outcome that maximizes the sum of the declared values is chosen. Agents pay according to how much their participation affects the outcome. Agent $i$ pays the sum of the value for the *other* agents if $i$ had not participated minus the sum of the values for the other agents if $i$ had participated. Thus the agent needs to pay the amount that its participation cost the others.

**Example 14.19** Consider the values of Example 14.18 (page 630). Suppose the values given can be interpreted as equivalent to dollars; for example, Alice is indifferent between meeting on Monday or meeting on Tuesday and paying \$8.00 (she is prepared to pay \$7.99 to move the meeting from Monday to Tuesday, but not \$8.01). Given these declared values, Tuesday is chosen as the meeting day. If Alice had not participated, Monday would have been chosen, and so the other agents have a net loss of 3, so Alice has to pay \$3.00. The net value to her is then 5; the utility of 8 for the Tuesday minus the payment of 3. The declarations, payments, and net values are given in the following table:

| | Monday | Tuesday | Wednesday | Payment | Net Value |
|---|---|---|---|---|---|
| Alice | 0 | 8 | 10 | 3 | 5 |
| Bob | 3 | 4 | 0 | 1 | 3 |
| Cory | 11 | 7 | 6 | 0 | 7 |
| Total | 14 | 19 | 16 | | |

Consider what would happen if Alice had changed her evaluation of Tuesday to 2. In this case, Wednesday would be the chosen day, but Alice would have had to pay \$8.00, with a net value of 2, and so would be worse off. Alice cannot gain an advantage by lying to the mechanism. One way to think about the payment is that Alice needs to bribe the mechanism to go along with her favorite choice.

The VCG mechanism is both economically efficient and dominant-strategy truthful, assuming that agents only care about their utility and not about other agents' utilities or other agents' payments.

One common mechanism for selling an item, or a set of items, is an **auction**. A common auction type for selling a single item is an ascending auction, where there is a current offering price for the item that increases by a predetermined increment when the previous offering price has been met. Offering to buy the item at the current price is called a bid. Only one person may put in a bid for a particular price. The item goes to the person who put in the highest bid, and the person pays the amount of that bid.

Consider a VCG mechanism for selling a single item. Suppose there are a number of people who each put in a bid for how much they value an item. The outcome that maximizes the payoffs is to give the item to the person who had the highest bid. If they had not participated, the item would have gone to the second-highest bidder. Therefore, according to the VCG mechanism, the top bidder should get the item and pay the value of the second-highest bid. This is known as a **second-price auction**. The second-price auction is equivalent (up to bidding increments) to having an ascending auction, where people specify how much they want to pay as a proxy bid, and there is an agent to convert the proxy bids into real bids. Bidding in a second-price auction is straightforward because the agents do not have to do complex strategic reasoning. It is also easy to determine a winner and the appropriate payment.

## 14.7 Multiagent Reinforcement Learning

### 14.7.1 Perfect-Information Games

For a **perfect-information game** (page 612), where agents take turns and observe the state of the world before acting, and each agent acts to maximize its own utility, the single-agent reinforcement learning algorithms of Chapter 13 can work unchanged. Each agent can assume that the other agents are part of the environment. This works whether the opponent is playing its optimal strategy or is also learning. The reason this works is that there is a unique Nash equilibrium which is the value for the agent of the current node in the game tree (page 612). This strategy is the best response to the other agents.

If the opponent is not playing its optimal strategy or converging to an optimal strategy, a learning agent could converge to a non-optimal strategy. It is possible for an opponent to train a learning agent to carry out a non-optimal strategy by playing badly, and then for the opponent to change to another strategy in order to exploit the agent's sub-optimal strategy. However, the learning agent could then learn from the (now) better opponent.

It is possible to use reinforcement learning to simulate both players in a game, and to learn for both. For two-player, zero-sum, perfect-information games, as in **minimax** (page 617), the game can be characterized by a single value that one agent is trying to minimize and the other is trying to maximize. In that case, an agent could learn $Q(s, a)$, an estimate of this value for being in state $s$ and carrying out action $a$. The algorithms can remain essentially the same, but need to know which player's turn it is, and the $Q$-value would then be updated by maximizing or minimizing depending on which player's turn it is.

### 14.7.2 Reinforcement Learning with Stochastic Policies

For multiple agents with imperfect information (page 621), including simultaneous action games, it is possible that there are multiple Nash equilibria, and that no deterministic strategy is optimal. Due to the existence of multiple equilibria, in many cases it is not clear what an agent should actually do, even if it knows all of the outcomes for the game and the utilities of the agents. However, most real strategic encounters are much more difficult, because the agents do not know the outcomes or the utilities of the other agents.

For games where the only Nash equilibria consist of randomized strategies, such as in the soccer penalty kick (Figure 14.8 (page 621)), learning any deterministic policy is not a good idea because any deterministic strategy can be exploited by the other agent. For other games with multiple Nash equilibria, such as those explored in Section 14.4 (page 621), agents may need to play multiple games to coordinate on a strategy profile where neither wants to deviate.

Reinforcement learning can be extended to such situations by explicitly representing **stochastic policies**, which are policies that specify a probability distribution over actions. This automatically allows for a form of exploration, because any action with a non-zero probability will be tried repeatedly.

This section presents a variant of SARSA (page 595), where each player represents a stochastic policy using counts for each action, as in a Dirichlet distribution (page 465). The agent updates the counts of its actions based on the rewards received.

The **stochastic policy iteration** controller of Figure 14.10 (page 634) is similar to the SARSA algorithm (page 596) but learns a **stochastic policy**, a probability distribution over actions for each state. The policy is represented in $\pi$ as counts, as in a Dirichlet distribution (page 465), over which action has highest $Q$ value (plus pseudo counts). The stochastic policy is obtained by normalizing the $\pi$ array, so that the probability of doing action $a$ in state $s$ is $\pi[s, a] / \sum_{a'} \pi[s, a']$

The algorithm is the same as SARSA (page 595), except that it updates $\pi$ by adding one to the value for an action with highest estimated $Q$-value.

To trade off exploration and exploitation, $P$ is initialized with counts that are not close to zero (e.g., 5 is used in the examples below) so that one policy does not become dominant quickly and/or by initializing $Q$ with a high value to encourage explorations. An open-source implementation of this learning controller is available from AIPython (aipython.org).

If there is a unique Nash equilibrium in pure strategies, and all of the agents use this algorithm, they will converge to this equilibrium. Dominated strategies will have their probability converge to zero. In Example 14.15 (page 627), it will find the Nash equilibrium. Similarly for the prisoner's dilemma in Example 14.13 (page 625), it will converge to the unique equilibrium where both agents take. Thus, this algorithm does *not* learn to **cooperate**, where cooperating agents will both *give* in the prisoner's dilemma to maximize their payoffs.

If there are multiple pure equilibria, this algorithm will converge to one of them. The agents thus learn to **coordinate**. For example, in the football–shopping game of Example 14.12 (page 624), it will converge to one of the equilibria of both shopping or both going to the football game.

---

**controller** *Stochastic_policy_iteration*$(S, A, \gamma, \alpha, q\_init, pi\_init)$
    **Inputs**
        $S$ set of states
        $A$ set of actions
        $\gamma$ discount factor
        $\alpha$ step size
        *q_init* initial $Q$ value
        *pi_init* initial $\pi$ value (must be greater than 0)
    **Local**
        $\pi[S, A]$ unnormalized probability of doing $A$ in state $S$
        $Q[S, A]$ an estimate of the value of doing $A$ in state $S$
    $\pi[s, a] := p\_init$ for all $s \in S, a \in A$
    $Q[s, a] := q\_init$ for each $s \in S, a \in A$
    observe state $s$, choose action $a$ at random
    **repeat**
        $do(a)$
        **observe** reward $r$, state $s'$
        **select** action $a'$ based on $\pi[s', a'] / \sum_{a''} \pi[s', a'']$
        $Q[s, a] := Q[s, a] + \alpha * (r + \gamma * Q[s', a'] - Q[s, a])$
        $a\_best := \arg\max_a(Q[s, a])$
        $\pi[s, a\_best] = \pi[s, a\_best] + 1$
        $s := s'; a := a'$
    **until** *termination*()

Figure 14.10: Reinforcement learning with stochastic policies

---

**Example 14.20** Consider the penalty kick game of Example 14.9 (page 621). Figure 14.11 shows a plot of two players using the learning algorithm for Example 14.9. This figure plots the probabilities for the goalkeeper jumping right and the kicker kicking right for one run of the learning algorithm. That is, it shows the *right* value for the normalized $P$ function. In this run, $Q$ is initialized to 1, and the counts in $P$ are initialized to 5. At equilibrium, the kicker kicks right with probability 0.4 and the goalkeeper jumps right with probability 0.3.

Consider a two-agent competitive game where there is only a randomized Nash equilibrium. If agents $A$ and $B$ are competing and agent $B$ is playing a Nash equilibrium, it does not matter which action in its support set is performed by agent $A$; they all have the same value to $A$. This algorithm tends to find a Nash equilibrium, and then one agent diverges from the equilibrium because there is no penalty for doing so when the other agent is playing an equilibrium strategy. After the agent deviates, the other can change its strategy

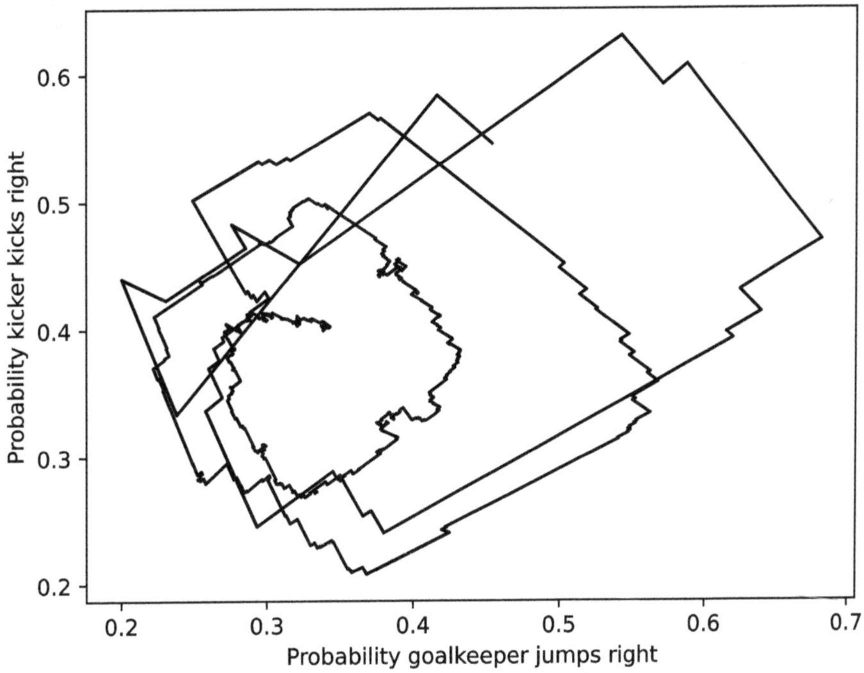


A plot of the policy of two players using the stochastic reinforcement learning algorithm of Figure 14.10 (page 634) (with $S$ having a single element, $\gamma = 0$, $\alpha = 0.1$, $q\_init = 1$, $pi\_init = 5$) for the soccer penalty kick of Example 14.9 (page 621).

After the first action, the policy is the position (0.455, 0.545) and follows the line, ending up at the point (0.338, 0.399). The Nash equilibrium is the point (0.3, 0.4), as derived in Example 14.16 (page 628).

Figure 14.11: Learning for the soccer penalty kick example

to exploit the deviation. This is one explanation for the cycling behavior.

There are many variants of this algorithm, including weighting more recent experiences more than older ones, adjusting the probabilities by a constant (being careful to ensure the probabilities are between 0 and 1 and sum to 1). See Exercise 14.9 (page 642).

An agent using this algorithm does not need to know the game or the payoffs. When an agent knows the game, another simple strategy is **fictitious play**, where the agent collects the statistics of the other player and, assuming those statistics reflect the stochastic policy of the other agent, plays a best response. Both players using fictitious play converges to a Nash equilibrium for many types of games (including two-player zero-sum games).

Note that there is no perfect learning strategy. If an opposing agent knew the exact strategy (whether learning or not) agent $A$ was using, and could predict what agent $A$ would do, it could exploit that knowledge.

**Example 14.21** Suppose two agents are playing the penalty kick game (Example 14.9 (page 621)) and one agent (Agent 1) is using fictitious play. Agent 1 has a deterministic strategy (except for a few cases). The opposing player, Agent 2, if they know Agent 1 is using fictitious play, could predict what Agent 1 is going to do, and carry out the best response. They will almost always be able to beat Agent 1.

The only time Agent 2 is not guaranteed to beat Agent 1 is when Agent 2's history corresponds to a Nash equilibrium, in which case Agent 1 could be stochastic. In that case, at the next step, Agent 2 will have a different ratio, and so will not be playing an equilibrium strategy, and then can beat Agent 1.

This property is not a feature of fictitious play. Indeed, if Agent 1 can convince Agent 2 that Agent 1 is using fictitious play, then Agent 1 could predict what Agent 2 will do, and play to beat that. Agent 2, if they consider the hypothesis that Agent 1 is not actually using fictitious play, should be able to determine that Agent 1 is not using fictitious play, and change their strategy.

### 14.7.3 State-of-the-Art Game Players

In 2016 the computer program AlphaGo beat Lee Sedol, one of the top Go players in the world, in a five-game Go match. **AlphaZero**, the follow-on program with zero programmed prior knowledge of the games – beyond a simulator of the games – plays world-class chess, shogi, and Go. The main features of AlphaZero are:

- It implements modified policy iteration (page 564), using a deep neural network with the board position as the input and the output is both the value function (the expected value with $+1$ for a win, 0 for a draw, and $-1$ for a loss) and a stochastic policy (a probability distribution using softmax over the possible moves, incorporating the upper confidence bound (page 592)). The parameters of the neural network are optimized with respect to the sum of the squared loss of the value function, the log loss of the distribution representing the stochastic policy, and an L2 regularization term.

- At each step, it carries out a stochastic simulation – forward sampling (page 439), as there are no observations – of the rest of the game, following the stochastic policy. This stochastic simulation is used to estimate the expected value of each action. This is known as **Monte Carlo tree search (MCTS)**. Note that MCTS relies on a model; it has to be able to restart the search from any point.

- It was trained on self-play, playing itself for tens of millions of games, using first and second-generation tensor processing units as the hardware.

## 14.8 Social Impact

The multiagent version of the prisoner's dilemma is the **tragedy of the commons**, named because common resources (such as the air we breathe) do not become a priority for anyone acting to maximize their utility, making everyone worse off, as in the following numerical example.

**Example 14.22** Suppose there are 100 people and there is an action that each person can choose (such as driving an internal combustion engine car) that gives them 10 units of utility but costs the environment 100, which, shared among everyone, corresponds to $-1$ for everyone; otherwise each agent can do an action with utility 1 for them and 0 for the environment (such as walking). When each person considers driving, they have a reward of 10 minus their share of the environment, which is $-1$, so driving has a utility for them of 9, so they are better off driving. This is independent of what anyone else does. So then everyone drives, with a driving reward of 1000 minus 10,000, which is the utility for the environment, giving a total utility of $-9000$, which is $-90$ for each person. Everyone would be much better off if no one drove, even though individually each person has a great utility by driving.

One way to solve that is to implement a VCG mechanism (page 631), where each person pays a tax. In this case, the mechanism would specify that each person would have to pay a tax of 99, which corresponds to the cost of their action on the others. Then each person would be rational to not drive.

One problem with the scenario in the last example is to convince people to implement the tax. After all, the only reason they are not driving is because of the tax, and they want to drive. One major problem is to compute the cost of changing the environment, where the cost may occur a long time into the future, so depends on how future values are discounted (page 556), and where the impact may be in other locations, and so depends on how others' suffering and loss of habitable land should be measured. This is a key problem for efforts to restrict greenhouse gas emissions to mitigate climate change. It occurs at the individual level as well as at the country level, with countries not reducing their carbon emissions because it is better for them not to.

AI can potentially help in a number of ways. It can make better predictions of the future costs, however, it cannot determine how these future values are discounted, as this depends on society's values (and each person might value the future differently). It might be able to help by promoting posts on social media that are known to be true, not promoting posts known to be false, and only promoting posts that have appropriate caveats, rather that maximizing engagement, which is known to lead to promoting extreme views [Acemoglu et al., 2021]. However, actually determining whether a post is true or false is very difficult.

Perrault et al. [2020] describe a research agenda about multiagent systems to address complex societal problems. They present many successful deployed systems in three application areas: public safety and security, wildlife conservation, and public health in low-resource communities. Much of their work is framed in the context of **Stackelberg security games**. A two-player Stackelberg security game is played between a defender and an attacker. Using limited intervention resources, the defender moves first to protect a number of targets from the attacker. Perrault et al. [2020] show how AI can play an important role in fighting social injustice and improving society.

## 14.9 Review

This chapter has touched on some of the issues that arise with multiple agents. The following are the main points to remember:

- A multiagent system consists of multiple agents who act autonomously and have their own utility over outcomes. The outcomes depend on the actions of all the agents. Agents can compete, cooperate, coordinate, communicate, and negotiate.
- The strategic form or normal form of a game specifies the expected outcome given controllers for each agent.
- The extensive form of a game models agents' actions and information through time in terms of game trees.
- A multiagent decision network models probabilistic dependency and information availability.
- Perfect-information games can be solved by backing up values in game trees or searching the game tree using minimax with $\alpha$–$\beta$ pruning.
- In partially observable domains, sometimes it is optimal to act stochastically.
- A Nash equilibrium is a strategy profile for each agent such that no agent can increase its utility by unilaterally deviating from the strategy profile.
- By introducing payments, it is possible to design a mechanism that is dominant-strategy truthful and economically efficient.

- Game-theoretic AI can be used to model and promote prosocial environmental behavior.

## 14.10 References and Further Reading

For overviews of multiagent systems, see Leyton-Brown and Shoham [2008], Shoham and Leyton-Brown [2008], Wooldridge [2009], Vlassis [2007], Stone and Veloso [2000], and Jackson [2011]. See also Kochenderfer et al. [2022].

Multiagent decision networks are based on the MAIDs of Koller and Milch [2003]. Genesereth and Thielscher [2014] describe **general game playing**, which uses logical representations for games.

Minimax with $\alpha$–$\beta$ pruning was first published by Hart and Edwards [1961]. Knuth and Moore [1975] and Pearl [1984] analyze $\alpha$–$\beta$ pruning and other methods for searching game trees. Ballard [1983] discusses how minimax can be combined with chance nodes.

The **Deep Blue** chess computer, which beat Garry Kasparov, the world **chess** champion, in May 1997 is described by Campbell et al. [2002]. Silver et al. [2016] describe **AlphaGo**, the program that beat a top-ranked **Go** player in 2016. **AlphaZero** is by Silver et al. [2017]. **Pluribus** [Brown and Sandholm, 2019] beat top human professionals in six-player no-limit Texas hold'em **poker**, a popular form of poker; this is the only one of these superhuman players that was not playing a two-player zero-sum game. **Cicero** [Bakhtin et al., 2022], playing in an anonymous online blitz league for the game **Diplomacy**, achieved more than double the average score of human players and ranked in the top 10% of participants. Only one human player suspected it was a computer program.

Robot soccer was proposed, and implemented, as an embodied AI challenge by Mackworth [1993]. Busoniu et al. [2008] survey multiagent reinforcement learning.

Mechanism design is described by Shoham and Leyton-Brown [2008] and Nisan [2007]. Ordeshook [1986] describes group decision making and game theory.

Hardin [1968] introduced the concept of the **tragedy of the commons**. Ostrom [1990], on the other hand, showed that the commons can be, and is, governable.

Gal and Grosz [2022] describe technical and ethical challenges. Perrault et al. [2020] describe how multiagent systems are having a social impact in public safety and security, wildlife conservation and public health.

This chapter has only covered **non-cooperative games**, where agents make decisions in isolation, without coordinating their actions. It has not covered **cooperative games**, where agents can communicate, negotiate, and perhaps participate in payments and enforceable conflicts. Many of the above references cover cooperative games. Kramár et al. [2022] describe an AI system that learns to play the game **Diplomacy**, which requires negotiation to play well.

The state space is enormous, as it includes the actions involved in negotiation. Siu et al. [2021] evaluated how well AI systems can cooperate with humans to play the cooperative card game **Hanabi**, and concluded "We find that humans have a clear preference toward a rule-based AI teammate (SmartBot) over a state-of-the-art learning-based AI teammate (Other-Play) across nearly all subjective metrics, and generally view the learning-based agent negatively, despite no statistical difference in the game score."

## 14.11 Exercises

**Exercise 14.1** Modify Figure 14.5 (page 617) to include nature moves. Test it on a (simple) perfect information game that includes randomized moves (e.g., coin toss or roll of a dice). Recall (page 612) that in an extensive form of a game, each internal node labeled with *nature* has a probability distribution over its children.

**Exercise 14.2** Consider the game of Tic-Tac-Toe (also called *noughts and crosses*), which is played by two players, an "X" player and an "O" player who alternate putting their symbol in a blank space on a $3 \times 3$ game board. A player's goal is to win by placing three symbols in a row, column, or diagonal; the game ends when a player wins or the board is filled. In the game shown below, player O has just made its third turn. It is X's turn to make its fourth move. The playing agent needs to decide intelligently which of the available three moves X should choose next: X1, X2, or X3. We have started the search tree, with three branches for the three possible moves for X:

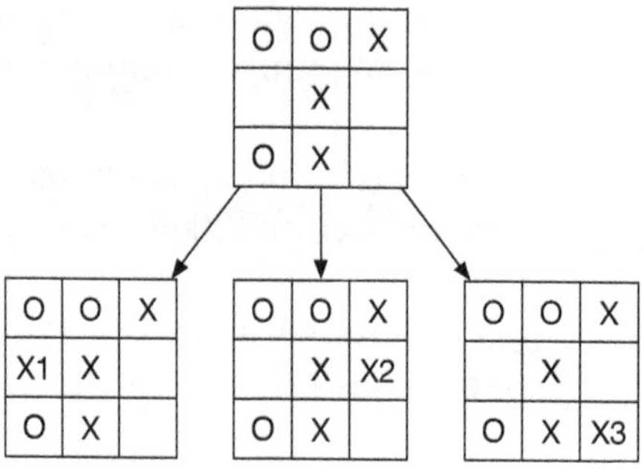


Draw the rest of the game tree. Assume the value of the tree is $+1$ for an X win, $-1$ for an O win, and 0 for a draw. Show how the values are backed up to give a value for each of the nodes. What should X do? Is it likely to win, lose, or draw?

Could $\alpha$–$\beta$ pruning prune any of the tree?

**Exercise 14.3** For the hawk–dove game of Example 14.11 (page 624), where $D > 0$ and $R > 0$, each agent is trying to maximize its utility. Is there a Nash equilibrium with a randomized strategy? What are the probabilities? What is the expected payoff to each agent? (These should be expressed as functions of $R$ and $D$.) Show your calculations.

**Exercise 14.4** Which of the following games in normal form have a Nash equilibrium made up of pure strategies? For those that do, specify the pure strategy Nash equilibria. For those that do not, explain how you know there is no pure strategy Nash equilibrium.

(a)

| | | Player 2 | |
|---|---|---|---|
| | | a2 | b2 |
| Player 1 | a1 | 10, 10 | 110, 0 |
| | b1 | 0, 110 | 100, 100 |

(b)

| | | Player 2 | |
|---|---|---|---|
| | | a2 | b2 |
| Player 1 | a1 | 10, 10 | 11, 20 |
| | b1 | 0, 11 | 20, 1 |

(c)

| | | Player 2 | |
|---|---|---|---|
| | | a2 | b2 |
| Player 1 | a1 | 10, 20 | 5, 10 |
| | b1 | 7, 11 | 20, 12 |

**Exercise 14.5** In Example 14.12 (page 624), what is the Nash equilibrium with randomized strategies? What is the expected value for each agent in this equilibrium?

**Exercise 14.6** Consider the following normal-form game where the row player can choose action $A$, $B$, or $C$ and the column player could choose action $D$, $E$, or $F$:

| | $D$ | $E$ | $F$ |
|---|---|---|---|
| $A$ | 40, 40 | 120, 10 | 60, 30 |
| B | 30, 60 | 110, 60 | 90, 90 |
| C | 30, 110 | 100, 100 | 70, 120 |

where the pairs give the value of the outcome for the row player followed by the value for the column player.

(a) When eliminating dominated strategies, what strategies (if any) can be eliminated? Explain what is eliminated, and what cannot be eliminated.

(b) Specify a Nash equilibrium for this game. (For a randomized strategy, give just the actions that are randomized; you do not need to give the probabilities). Explain why it is a Nash equilibrium.

(c) Is there more than one Nash equilibrium? If so, give another one. If not explain why there is no other one.

(d) If the agents could coordinate, could they get a better outcome than in a Nash equilibrium? Explain why or why not.

**Exercise 14.7** Answer the same questions as in the previous exercise for the following games:

(i)

| | $D$ | $E$ | $F$ |
|---|---|---|---|
| $A$ | 2, 11 | 10, 10 | 3, 12 |
| B | 5, 7 | 12, 1 | 6, 5 |
| C | 6, 5 | 13, 2 | 4, 6 |

(ii)

| | $D$ | E | $F$ |
|---|---|---|---|
| $A$ | 80, 130 | 20, 10 | 130, 80 |
| B | 130, 80 | 30, 20 | 80, 130 |
| C | 20, 10 | 100, 100 | 30, 20 |

**Exercise 14.8** Consider the sequential prisoner's dilemma (page 625).

(a) Suppose the agents play for a fixed number of times (say three times). Give two equilibria if there are two or more, otherwise, give the unique equilibrium and explain why there is only one. [Hint: Consider the last time first.]
(b) Suppose there is a discount factor (page 556) of $\gamma$, which means there is a probability $\gamma$ of stopping at each stage. Is tit-for-tat a Nash equilibrium for all values of $\gamma$? If so, prove it. If not, for which values of $\gamma$ is it a Nash equilibrium?

**Exercise 14.9** Consider the following alternative ways to update the probability $P$ in the stochastic policy iteration algorithm of Figure 14.10 (page 634).

(i) Make more recent experiences have more weight by multiplying the counts in $P$ by $(1 - \beta)$, for small $\beta$ (such as 0.01), before adding 1 to the best action.
(ii) Add some small value, $\epsilon$ (such as 0.01 or 0.001), to the probability of the best action and subtract values from the other actions to make sure the probabilities are non-negative and sum to 1.

(a) Which of the original, (i), or (ii) has the best payoffs for the game of Example 14.15 (page 627), where there is a unique Nash equilibrium but another strategy profile has a better payoff for both agents?
(b) Which one has the best payoffs in the penalty kick game of Example 14.9 (page 621) when played against the others?
(c) Which of the original and the alternatives, if any, converge to a Nash equilibrium in the strategies played (averaging over all of the actions played)? (Do this experimentally, creating hypotheses from your observations, and then try to prove your hypotheses.)

**Exercise 14.10** The stochastic policy iteration algorithm of Figure 14.10 (page 634) is based on SARSA (page 596)). How could it be modified to be off-policy as in Q-learning (page 590)? [Hint: Q-learning updates using the best action, SARSA updates by the one using the policy and stochastic policy iteration updates using the expected value.] Does this work better for the example domains?

# Part V

# Representing Individuals and Relations

**How can an agent reason, learn, and act in more complex environments where there are individuals (things, entities, objects) with complex relations among them?**

# Chapter 15

# Individuals and Relations

*There is a real world with real structure. The program of mind has been trained on vast interaction with this world and so contains code that reflects the structure of the world and knows how to exploit it. This code contains representations of real objects in the world and represents the interactions of real objects. The code is mostly modular..., with modules for dealing with different kinds of objects and modules generalizing across many kinds of objects.... The modules interact in ways that mirror the real world and make accurate predictions of how the world evolves....*

*You exploit the structure of the world to make decisions and take actions. Where you draw the line on categories, what constitutes a single object or a single class of objects for you, is determined by the program of your mind, which does the classification. This classification is not random but reflects a compact description of the world, and in particular a description useful for exploiting the structure of the world.*

– Eric B. Baum [2004, pp. 169–170]

This chapter is about how to represent individuals (things, entities, objects) and relationships among them. As Baum suggests in the quote above, the real world contains objects and compact representations of those objects and relationships can make reasoning about them tractable. Such representations can be much more compact than representations in terms of features alone. This chapter considers logical representations and gives detailed examples of how to use such representations for natural language interfaces to databases. Later chapters address knowledge graphs, ontologies and communicating meaning, and integrating relations into learning and reasoning under uncertainty.

## 15.1 Exploiting Relational Structure

One of the main lessons of AI is that successful agents exploit the structure of the world. Previous chapters showed how states can be represented, learned, and reasoned with, in terms of features. Representing domains using features can be much more compact than representing states explicitly, and algorithms that exploit this compactness can be much more efficient. There is, however, usually much more structure that can be exploited beyond features for representation and inference. In particular, this chapter considers reasoning in terms of individuals and relations:

- **Individuals** are things in the world, whether they are concrete individuals such as people and buildings, imaginary individuals such as unicorns and programs that can reliably pass the Turing test, processes such as reading a book or going on a holiday, or abstract concepts such as money, a course (such as the course MCS-224 at a particular university), an offering of a course (such as the 2026 Spring offering of MCS-224) and times. Individuals are also called **entities**, **objects**, or **things**.
- **Relations** specify what is true about these individuals. This is meant to be as general as possible and includes **unary relations** that are true or false of single individuals, **propositions** (page 177), which are true or false independently of any individuals, as well as relationships among multiple individuals.

**Example 15.1** In the representation of the electrical domain in Example 5.8 (page 186), the propositions $up\_s_2$, $up\_s_3$, and $ok\_s_2$ have no internal structure. There is no notion that the propositions $up\_s_2$ and $up\_s_3$ are about the same relation, but with different individuals, or that $up\_s_2$ and $ok\_s_2$ are about the same switch. There is no notion of individuals and relations.

An alternative is to represent explicitly the individual switches $s_1$, $s_2$, $s_3$, and the properties *up* and *ok*. Using this representation, "switch $s_2$ is up" is represented as $up(s_2)$. By knowing what *up* and $s_1$ represent, you do not require a separate definition of $up(s_1)$. A binary relation, like *connected_to*, can be used to relate two individuals, such as $connected\_to(w_1, s_1)$.

Modeling in terms of individuals and relations has a number of advantages over just using features:

- It is often the natural representation. Often features are properties of individuals, and this internal structure is lost in converting to features.
- An agent may have to model a domain without knowing what the individuals are, or how many there will be, and, thus, without knowing what the features are. When interacting with the environment, the agent can construct the features when it finds out which individuals are in the particular environment.

- An agent can do some reasoning without caring about the particular individuals. For example, it may be able to derive that something holds for all individuals without identifying any individuals. An agent may be able to derive that some individual exists that has some properties, without caring about other individuals. There may be some queries an agent can answer for which it does not have to distinguish the individuals. For example, a cleaning robot might be able to infer that someone or something created a mess, without knowing which entity did.
- The existence of individuals could depend on actions or could be uncertain. For example, in planning in a manufacturing context, whether there is a working component may depend on many other subcomponents working and being put together correctly; some of these may depend on the agent's actions, and some may not be under the agent's control. Thus, an agent may have to act without knowing what features there are or what features there will be.
- Often there are infinitely many individuals an agent is reasoning about, and so infinitely many features. For example, if the individuals are sentences, the agent may only have to reason about a very limited set of sentences (e.g., those that could be meant by a person speaking, or those that may be sensible to generate), even though there may be infinitely many possible sentences, and so infinitely many features.

## 15.2 Symbols and Semantics

The basic idea behind the use of logic (see Chapter 5) is that, when knowledge base designers have a particular world they want to characterize, they can select that world as an **intended interpretation**, select meanings for the symbols with respect to that interpretation, and write, as axioms, what is true in that world. When a system computes a logical consequence of a knowledge base, a user that knows the meanings of the symbols can interpret this answer with respect to the intended interpretation. Because the intended interpretation is a model, and a logical consequence is true in all models, a logical consequence must be true in the intended interpretation. This chapter expands the propositional logic (page 177) to allow reasoning about individuals and relations. Atomic propositions now have internal structure in terms of relations and individuals.

**Example 15.2** Figure 15.1 (page 648) illustrates the general idea of semantics with individuals and relations. The person who is designing the knowledge base has a meaning for the symbols. The person knows what the symbols *kim*, *r*123, and *in* refer to in the domain and supplies a knowledge base of sentences in the representation language to the computer. The knowledge includes specific facts "*kim* is in *r*123" and "*r*123 is part of *cs_building*", and the general rule that says "if any $Z$ is part of $Y$ and any $X$ is in $Z$ then $X$ is in $Y$", where $X$, $Y$, and $Z$ are logical variables. These sentences have meaning to that person. They can ask queries using these symbols and with the particular meaning she has for them. The computer takes these sentences and queries, and it computes answers. The computer does not know what the symbols mean. However, the person who supplied the information can use the meaning associated with the symbols to interpret the answer with respect to the world.

The mapping between the symbols in the mind and the individuals and relations denoted by these symbols is called a **conceptualization**. This chapter assumes that the conceptualization is in the user's head, or written informally, in comments. Making conceptualizations explicit is the role of a formal ontology (page 714).

What is the correct answer is defined independently of how it is computed. The correctness of a knowledge base is defined by the semantics, not by a particular algorithm for proving queries. As long as an inference algorithm is faithful to the semantics, it can be optimized for efficiency. This separation of meaning from computation lets an agent optimize performance while maintaining correctness.

## 15.3 Predicate Calculus

**Predicate calculus**, often just known as **predicate logic**, extends propositional calculus (page 177) in two ways:

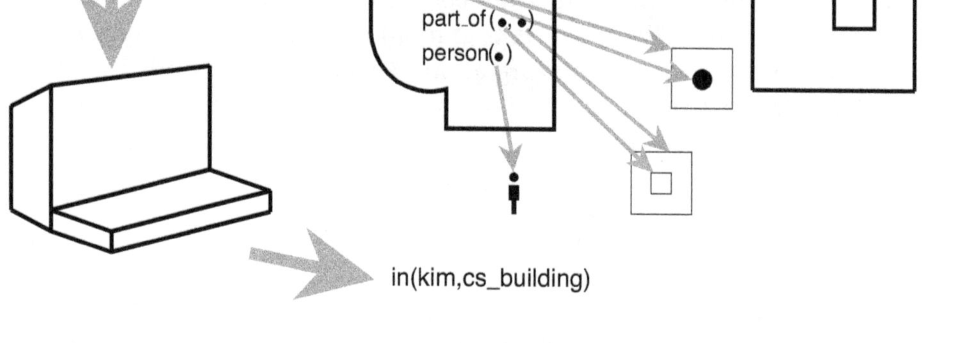


Figure 15.1: The role of semantics. The meanings of the symbols are in the user's head. The computer takes in symbols and outputs symbols. The output can be interpreted by the user according to the meaning the user places on the symbols

- atoms have structure and can include logical variables
- quantification of logical variables.

This book follows the syntactic conventions of **Prolog**, where variables start with an upper-case letter. In mathematics, variables typically are $x$, $y$, and $z$. In Prolog, as in other programming languages, longer names are typically used to make code more readable. The upper case is used to make variables stand out.

The **syntax** of the predicate calculus extends the syntax of the propositional calculus (page 177) as follows, where a **symbol** is a sequence of letters, digits, or an underscore ("_"):

- A **logical variable** is a symbol starting with an upper-case letter or with "_". For example, *X*, *Room*, *_B4*, *Raths*, and *The_big_guy* are all variables.
- A **constant** is a symbol that starts with a lower-case letter, or is a number constant or a string.
- A **predicate symbol** is a symbol that starts with a lower-case letter. Constants and predicate symbols are distinguishable by their context in a knowledge base.

  For example, *kim*, *r123*, *f*, *grandfather*, and *borogroves* can be constants or predicate symbols, depending on the context; 725 is a constant.
- A **term** is either a variable or a constant.

  For example, *X*, *kim*, *cs422*, *mome*, or *Raths* can be terms.
- An **atomic symbol**, or simply an **atom**, is of the form $p$ or $p(t_1, \dots, t_n)$, where $p$ is a predicate symbol and each $t_i$ is a term. Each $t_i$ is called an **argument** to the predicate.

  For example, $teaches(sue, cs422)$, $in(kim, r123)$, $father(bill, Y)$, $happy(C)$, $outgrabe(mome, Raths)$, and $sunny$ can all be atoms. From context in the atom $outgrabe(mome, Raths)$, the symbol *outgrabe* is a predicate symbol and *mome* is a constant.

A **logical formula** is built from the atoms using the connectives of the propositional calculus (page 177), and the quantifiers. The following are also logical formula:

- $\forall X\ p$, where $X$ is a variable, and $p$ is a logical formula (typically containing $X$), is read "**for all** $X$, $p$". Variable $X$ is said to be **universally quantified**.
- $\exists X\ p$, where $X$ is a variable, and $p$ is a logical formula, is read "**there exists** an $X$ **such that** $p$". Variable $X$ is said to be **existentially quantified**.

**Example 15.3** The following are logical formulas:

$$\forall G\ (grandfather(sam, G) \leftarrow \exists P\ (father(sam, P) \land parent(P, G))).$$

$$in(X, Y) \leftarrow part\_of(Z, Y) \land in(X, Z).$$

$$slithy(toves) \leftarrow \forall Raths\ (mimsy \land borogroves \land outgrabe(mome, Raths)).$$

From context, *sam*, *toves*, and *mome* are constants; *grandfather*, *father*, *parent*, *in*, *part_of*, *slithy*, *mimsy*, *borogroves*, and *outgrabe* are predicate symbols; and $G$, $P$, $X$, $Y$, $Z$, and *Raths* are variables.

The first two formulas may make some intuitive sense, even without an explicitly provided formal specification for the meaning of formulas. However, regardless of the mnemonic names' suggestiveness, as far as the computer is concerned, the first two formulas have no more meaning than the third. Meaning is provided only by virtue of a semantics.

An expression is **ground** if it does not contain any variables. For example, *teaches*(*chris*, *cs*322) is ground, but *teaches*(*Prof*, *Course*) is not ground.

The next sections define the semantics. First consider ground expressions and then extend the semantics to include variables.

### 15.3.1 Semantics of Ground Logical Formulas

The first step in giving the semantics of predicate calculus is to give the semantics for the ground (variable-free) case.

An **interpretation** is a triple $I = \langle D, \phi, \pi \rangle$:

- $D$ is a non-empty set called the **domain**. Elements of $D$ are **individuals**.
- $\phi$ is a mapping that assigns to each constant an element of $D$.
- $\pi$ is a mapping that assigns to each $n$-ary predicate symbol a function from $D^n$ into $\{true, false\}$.

$\phi$ is a function from names into individuals in the world. The constant $c$ is said to **denote** the individual $\phi(c)$. Here $c$ is a symbol but $\phi(c)$ can be anything: a real physical individual such as a person or a virus, an abstract concept such as a course, love, the number 2, or a symbol.

$\pi(p)$ specifies whether the relation denoted by the $n$-ary predicate symbol $p$ is true or false for each $n$-tuple of individuals. If predicate symbol $p$ has no arguments, then $\pi(p)$ is either *true* or *false*. Thus, for predicate symbols with no arguments, this semantics reduces to the semantics of the propositional calculus (page 178).

**Example 15.4** Consider the world consisting of three individuals on a table:

| ✂ ✈ ✎ |
|---|

These are drawn in this way because they are things in the world, not symbols. ✂ is a pair of scissors, ✈ is a model airplane, and ✎ is a pencil.

Suppose the constants in our language are *plane*, *pencil*, and *model*, and predicate symbols are *noisy* and *left_of*. Assume *noisy* is a unary predicate (it takes a single argument) and that *left_of* is a binary predicate (it takes two arguments).

An example interpretation that represents the individuals on the table is

- $D = \{$✂, ✈, ✎$\}$.

- $\phi(plane) =$ ✈, $\phi(pencil) =$ ✎, $\phi(model) =$ ✈.
- $\pi(noisy)$:

| | | | | | |
|---|---|---|---|---|---|
| ⟨✂⟩ | *false* | ⟨✈⟩ | *true* | ⟨✎⟩ | *false* |

$\pi(left\_of)$:

| | | | | | |
|---|---|---|---|---|---|
| ⟨✂,✂⟩ | *false* | ⟨✂,✈⟩ | *true* | ⟨✂,✎⟩ | *true* |
| ⟨✈,✂⟩ | *false* | ⟨✈,✈⟩ | *false* | ⟨✈,✎⟩ | *true* |
| ⟨✎,✂⟩ | *false* | ⟨✎,✈⟩ | *false* | ⟨✎,✎⟩ | *false* |

Because *noisy* is unary, it takes a singleton individual and has a truth value for each individual.

Because *left_of* is a binary predicate, it takes a pair of individuals and is true when the first element of the pair is left of the second element. Thus, for example, $\pi(left\_of)(\langle$✂,✈$\rangle) = true$, because the scissors are to the left of the model; $\pi(left\_of)(\langle$✎,✎$\rangle) = false$, because the pencil is not to the left of itself.

Note how the $D$ is a set of things in the world. The relations are among the individuals in the world, not among the names. As $\phi$ specifies that *plane* and *model* refer to the same individual, exactly the same statements are true about them in this interpretation.

**Example 15.5** Consider the interpretation of Figure 15.1 (page 648).

$D$ is the set with four elements: the person Kim, room 123, room 023, and the CS building. This is not a set of four symbols, but it is the set containing the actual person, the actual rooms, and the actual building. It is difficult to write down this set and, fortunately, you never really have to. To remember the meaning and to convey the meaning to another person, knowledge base designers typically describe $D$, $\phi$, and $\pi$ by pointing to the physical individuals, or a depiction of them (as is done in Figure 15.1), or describe the meaning in natural language.

The constants are *kim*, *r*123, *r*023, and *cs_building*. The mapping $\phi$ is defined by the gray arcs from each of these constants to an individual in the world in Figure 15.1.

The predicate symbols are *person*, *in*, and *part_of*. The meanings of these are meant to be conveyed in the figure by the arcs from the predicate symbols.

Thus, the person called Kim is in room *r*123 and is also in the CS building, and these are the only instances of the *in* relation that are true. Similarly, room *r*123 and room *r*023 are part of the CS building, and there are no other *part_of* relationships that are true in this interpretation.

Each ground term denotes an individual in an interpretation. A constant $c$ denotes in $I$ the individual $\phi(c)$.

A ground atom is either true or false in an interpretation. Atom $p(t_1, \ldots, t_n)$ is **true** in $I$ if $\pi(p)(\langle t'_1, \ldots, t'_n \rangle) = true$, where $t'_i$ is the individual denoted by term $t_i$, and is **false** in $I$ otherwise.

**Example 15.6** The atom $in(kim, r123)$ is true in the interpretation of Example 15.5, because the person denoted by *kim* is indeed in the room denoted by *r*123. Similarly, $person(kim)$ is true, as is $part\_of(r123, cs\_building)$. The atoms $in(cs\_building, r123)$ and $person(r123)$ are false in this interpretation.

Logical connectives have the same meaning as in the propositional calculus (page 178); see Figure 5.1 (page 179) for the truth tables for the logical connectives.

### 15.3.2 Interpreting Variables

To define the semantics of logical formulas with variables, a **variable assignment**, $\rho$, is a function from the variables into the domain $D$. Thus, a variable assignment assigns an element of the domain to each variable. Given interpretation $\langle D, \phi, \pi \rangle$ and variable assignment $\rho$, each term denotes an individual in the domain. If the term is a constant, the individual is given by $\phi$. If the term is a variable, the individual is given by $\rho$. Given an interpretation and a variable assignment for all variables, each atom is either true or false, using the same definition as earlier.

The semantics of quantification is as follows:

- **Universally quantified formula** $\forall X\ p$ is true in an interpretation if $p$ is true for all variable assignments of $X$ to an individual. Thus, a formula is false in an interpretation whenever there is a variable assignment to $X$ under which the formula is false. The formula $p$ is the **scope** of $X$.

- **Existentially quantified formula** $\exists X\ p$ is true in an interpretation if $p$ is true for some variable assignment of $X$ to an individual. The individual that exists can depend on universally quantified variables that $\exists X\ p$ is in the scope of. For example, in $\forall Y\ (\exists X\ p)$, the $X$ can depend on $Y$; for every number $Y$ there is an $X$ such that $X = Y + 1$. In $\exists X\ (\forall Y\ p)$, the $X$ cannot depend on $Y$ because $X$ is not in the scope of $Y$; there does not exist an $X$ such that for every number $Y$, $X = Y + 1$.

A formula that contains a variable that does not have an enclosing qualification is said to be **open**, and does not have a truth value, because not all variables have a variable assignment.

**Example 15.7** The formula

$$\forall X\ \forall Y\ \mathit{part\_of}(X, Y) \leftarrow \mathit{in}(X, Y).$$

is false in the interpretation of Example 15.5 (page 651), because under the variable assignment with $X$ denoting Kim and $Y$ denoting Room 123, $\mathit{in}(X, Y)$ is true and $\mathit{part\_of}(X, Y)$ is false.

The formula

$$\forall X\ \forall Y\ \forall Z\ \mathit{in}(X, Y) \leftarrow \mathit{part\_of}(Z, Y) \wedge \mathit{in}(X, Z).$$

is true in that interpretation, because $\mathit{in}(X, Y)$ is true in all variable assignments where $\mathit{part\_of}(Z, Y) \wedge \mathit{in}(X, Z)$ is true.

Logical consequence is defined in the same way as it was for propositional calculus in Section 5.1.2 (page 179): $g$ is a **logical consequence** of $KB$, written $KB \models g$, if $g$ is true in every model of $KB$.

**Example 15.8** Suppose the knowledge base $KB$ is the conjunction of the formulas

$$in(kim, r123).$$
$$part\_of(r123, cs\_building).$$
$$\forall X\, \forall Y \forall Z \;\; in(X,Y) \leftarrow part\_of(Z,Y) \wedge in(X,Z).$$

The interpretation defined in Example 15.5 (page 651) is a model of $KB$, because each formula is true in that interpretation.

$KB \models in(kim, r123)$, because this is stated explicitly in the knowledge base. If every formula in $KB$ is true in an interpretation, then $in(kim, r123)$ must be true in that interpretation.

$KB \not\models in(kim, r023)$. The interpretation defined in Example 15.5 is a model of $KB$, in which $in(kim, r023)$ is false.

$KB \not\models part\_of(r023, cs\_building)$. Although $part\_of(r023, cs\_building)$ is true in the interpretation of Example 15.5, there is another model of $KB$ in which $part\_of(r023, cs\_building)$ is false. In particular, the interpretation which is like the interpretation of Example 15.5, but where

$$\pi(part\_of)(\langle \phi(r023), \phi(cs\_building) \rangle) = false$$

is a model of $KB$ in which $part\_of(r023, cs\_building)$ is false.

$KB \models in(kim, cs\_building)$. If the formula in $KB$ are true in interpretation $I$, it must be the case that $in(kim, cs\_building)$ is true in $I$, otherwise, there is an instance of the third formula of $KB$ that is false in $I$ – a contradiction to $I$ being a model of $KB$.

### The Human's View of Semantics

The formal description of semantics does not tell us why semantics is interesting or how it can be used as a basis to build intelligent systems. The methodology for using semantics for propositional logic programs (page 180) can be extended to predicate logic:

**Step 1** Select the task domain or world to represent. This could be some aspect of the real world, for example, the structure of courses and students at a university or a laboratory environment at a particular point in time, some imaginary world, such as the world of Alice in Wonderland, or the state of the electrical environment if a switch breaks, or an abstract world, for example, the world of money, numbers, and sets. Within this world, let the domain $D$ be the set of all individuals or things that you want to be able to refer to and reason about. Also, select which relations to represent.

**Step 2** Associate constants in the language with individuals in the world that you want to name. For each element of $D$ you want to refer to by name, assign a constant in the language. For example, you may select the name "*kim*" to denote a particular professor and the name "*cs*322" for a particular introductory AI course. Each of these names **denotes** the corresponding individual in the world.

**Step 3** For each relation that you may want to represent, associate a predicate symbol in the language. Each $n$-ary predicate symbol denotes a function from $D^n$ into $\{true, false\}$, which specifies the subset of $D^n$ for which the relation is true. For example, the predicate symbol "*teaches*" of two arguments (a teacher and a course) may correspond to the binary relation that is true when the individual denoted by the first argument teaches the course denoted by the second argument.

The association of symbols with their meanings forms an **intended interpretation**. This specifies what the symbols are intended to mean.

**Step 4** Write formulas that are true in the intended interpretation. This is often called **axiomatizing the domain**, where the given formulas are the **axioms** of the domain, or the **knowledge base**. For example, if the person denoted by the symbol *kim* teaches the course denoted by the symbol *cs*322, you can assert the formula $teaches(kim, cs322)$ as being true in the intended interpretation. Not everything that is true needs to be written down; there is no need to state what is implied by other axioms.

**Step 5** Ask queries about the intended interpretation. The system gives answers that you can interpret using the meaning assigned to the symbols.

Following this methodology, the knowledge base designer does not actually tell the computer anything until step 4. The first three steps are carried out in the head of the designer. Of course, the designer should document the denotations to make their knowledge base understandable to other people, so that they remember each symbol's denotation, and so that they can check the truth of the formulas.

The world itself does not prescribe what the individuals are.

**Example 15.9** In one conceptualization of a domain, *pink* may be a predicate symbol of one argument that is true when the individual denoted by that argument is pink. In another conceptualization, *pink* may be an individual that is the color pink, and it may be used as the second argument to a binary predicate *color*, which says that the individual denoted by the first argument has the color denoted by the second argument. Alternatively, someone may want to describe the world at a level of detail where various shades of *red* are not distinguished, and so the color *pink* would not be included. Someone else may describe the world in more detail, and decide that *pink* is too general a term, and use the terms *coral* and *salmon*.

When the individuals in the domain are real physical things, it is usually difficult to give the denotation without physically pointing at the individual. When the individual is an abstract individual – for example, a university course or the concept of love – it is virtually impossible to write the denotation. However, this does not prevent the system from representing and reasoning about such concepts.

## 15.4 Datalog: A Relational Rule Language

**Datalog** expands the language of propositional definite clauses (page 185) to include individuals and relations. It can be seen as a restricted form of the predicate logic where

- The only formulas allowed are **definite clauses**, of the form $h \leftarrow a_1 \wedge \ldots \wedge a_m$, where $h$ is the head and $a_1 \wedge \ldots \wedge a_m$ is the body. If $m > 0$, the clause is called a **rule**. If $m = 0$, the "$\leftarrow$" is ignored and the clause is called a **fact**.

- There is no explicit quantification; all variables are assumed to be universally quantified at the outside of the clause.

  The clause $h(X) \leftarrow b(X,Y)$ thus means $\forall X\ \forall Y\ (h(X) \leftarrow b(X,Y))$, which is equivalent to $\forall X\ (h(X) \leftarrow \exists Y\ b(X,Y))$.

Datalog is of interest because it is a database language for defining and querying relations.

**Example 15.10** A relation is often written as a table:

| Course | Section | Time | Room |
|---|---|---|---|
| cs111 | 7 | 830 | dp101 |
| cs422 | 2 | 1030 | cc208 |
| cs502 | 1 | 1230 | dp202 |

This can be represented using a relation *scheduled*(*Course*, *Section*, *Time*, *Room*), with the knowledge base containing the facts

*scheduled*(*cs*111, 7, 830, *dp*101).
*scheduled*(*cs*422, 2, 1030, *cc*208).
*scheduled*(*cs*502, 1, 1230, *dp*202).

Suppose the relation *enrolled*(*StudentNum*, *Course*, *Section*) is also defined by facts. The relation *busy*(*StudentNum*, *Time*), which is the join of these relations, projected into student number and time, can be represented using the rule

*busy*(*StudentNum*, *Time*) $\leftarrow$
  *enrolled*(*StudentNum*, *Course*, *Section*) $\wedge$
  *scheduled*(*Course*, *Section*, *Time*, *Room*).

A student is busy at a time if they are enrolled in a section of a course that is scheduled at that time.

**Example 15.11** Example 5.8 (page 186) represented the electrical environment of Figure 5.2 (page 186) using propositions. Using individuals and relations can make the representation more intuitive, because the general knowledge about how switches work can be clearly separated from the knowledge about a specific house.

To represent this domain, the first step is to decide what individuals exist in the domain. In what follows, assume that each switch, each light, and each power outlet is an individual. Each wire between two switches and between a switch and a light is also an individual. Someone may claim that, in fact, there are pairs of wires joined by connectors and that the electricity flow must obey Kirchhoff's laws. Someone else may decide that even that level of abstraction is inappropriate because the flow of electrons should be modeled. However, an appropriate level of abstraction is one that is useful for the task at hand. A resident of the house may not know the whereabouts of the connections between the individual strands of wire or even the voltage. Therefore, let's assume a flow model of electricity, where power flows from the outside of the house through wires to lights. This model is appropriate for the task of determining whether a light should be lit or not, but it may not be appropriate for other tasks.

Next, give names to each individual to which you want to refer. This is done in Figure 5.2 (page 186) by writing the name next to the component. For example, the individual $w_0$ is the wire between light $l_1$ and switch $s_2$.

Next, choose which relationships to represent. Assume the following predicates with their associated intended interpretations:

- $light(L)$ is true if the individual denoted by $L$ is a light.
- $lit(L)$ is true if the light $L$ is lit and emitting light.
- $live(W)$ is true if there is power coming into $W$; that is, $W$ is live.
- $up(S)$ is true if switch $S$ is up.
- $down(S)$ is true if switch $S$ is down.
- $ok(E)$ is true if $E$ is not faulty; $E$ can be either a circuit breaker or a light.
- $connected\_to(X, Y)$ is true if component $X$ is connected to $Y$ such that current would flow from $Y$ to $X$.

At this stage, the computer has not been told anything. It does not know what the predicates are, let alone what they mean. It does not know which individuals exist or their names.

Before anything about the particular house is known, the system can be told general rules such as

$$lit(L) \leftarrow light(L) \land live(L) \land ok(L).$$

This means that a light is lit if it has electricity coming in and is not broken.

Recursive rules let you state what is live from what is connected to what:

$$live(X) \leftarrow connected\_to(X, Y) \land live(Y).$$
$$live(outside).$$

This specifies that there is electricity coming into the building, and if there is electricity coming into $Y$ and $X$ is connected to $Y$, then there will be electricity coming into X. Note that the order of clauses and the order of the elements of the body has no effect on the semantics.

For the particular house and configuration of components and their connections, the following facts about the world can be told to the computer:

$$
\begin{array}{l}
light(l_1).\quad light(l_2).\quad down(s_1).\\
up(s_2).\quad ok(cb_1).\\
connected\_to(w_0, w_1) \leftarrow up(s_2).\\
connected\_to(w_0, w_2) \leftarrow down(s_2).\\
connected\_to(w_1, w_3) \leftarrow up(s_1).\\
connected\_to(w_3, outside) \leftarrow ok(cb_1).
\end{array}
$$

These rules and atomic clauses are all that the computer is told. It does not know the meaning of these symbols. However, it can now answer queries about this particular house.

## 15.4.1 Queries with Variables

Queries are used to ask whether some statement is a logical consequence of a knowledge base. With propositional queries (page 187), a user can only ask yes-or-no queries. **Queries** with variables allow users to ask for the individuals that make the query true.

An **instance** of a query is obtained by substituting terms for the variables in the query. Each occurrence of a distinct variable in a query must be replaced by the same term; if variable X appears in a formula, each occurrence of X must be replaced by the same term.

Given a query with free variables, an **answer** is either an instance of the query that is a logical consequence of the knowledge base, or "*no*", meaning that no instances of the query logically follow from the knowledge base. Instances of the query are specified by providing values for the variables in the query. Determining which instances of a query follow from a knowledge base is known as **answer extraction**.

An answer of "no" does *not* mean that the query is false in the intended interpretation; it simply means that there is no instance of the query that is a logical consequence.

**Example 15.12** Consider the facts about some of the counties in South America in Figure 15.2 (page 658). The computer knows nothing about geography or South America. All it knows are the clauses it is given, however it can compute logical consequences. Note that the constants denoting the countries and languages start with a lower-case letter, as that is the convention of the language used; English has the opposite convention, where proper nouns start with an upper-case letter.

The user can ask the following query:

$$language(chile, spanish).$$

```
% country(C) is true if C is a country

country(argentina).
    country(brazil).
    country(chile).
    country(paraguay).
    country(peru).

% area(C,A) is true if C is a country and A is its area in square kilometers

area(argentina, 2780400).
    area(brazil, 8515767).
    area(chile, 756102).
    area(paraguay, 406756).
    area(peru, 1285216).

% language(C,L) is true if L is the principal language of country C

language(argentina, spanish).
    language(brazil, portuguese).
    language(chile, spanish).
    language(paraguay, spanish).
    language(peru, spanish).

% borders0(C1,C2) is true if countries C1 and C2 border each other and C1 is
% alphabetically before C2

borders0(chile,peru).
    borders0(argentina,chile).
    borders0(brazil,peru).
    borders0(brazil,argentina).
    borders0(brazil,paraguay).
    borders0(argentina,paraguay).

% borders(C1,C2) is true if country C1 borders country C2

borders(X,Y) ← borders0(X,Y).
    borders(X,Y) ← borders0(Y,X).
```

Figure 15.2: Some facts about South America

and the answer is *yes*. The user can ask the query

$language(venezuela, spanish).$

and the answer is *no*. This means it is not a logical consequence, not that it is false. There is not enough information in the database to determine the principal language of *venezuela*.

The query

$language(C, spanish).$

has four answers. The answer with $X = chile$ means $language(chile, spanish)$ is a logical consequence of the clauses.

The *borders* relation is true of two countries when they share a border. This relation is symmetric; $borders(X, Y)$ if and only if $borders(Y, X)$. To represent this, Figure 15.2 represents one of the pairs (arbitrarily, with the alphabetically first one as the first argument) using *borders0*, and then *borders* is derived from this. This uses half as many facts as would be if *borders* were represented directly, with the extra cost of two rules.

The query

ask $borders0(paraguay, X).$

has no answers. The query

ask $borders(paraguay, X).$

has two answers: $X = argentina$ and $X = brazil$.

The query

ask $borders(X, Y).$

has 12 answers.

To ask for a country that borders Chile with an area greater than two million square kilometers, one could give the query

ask $borders(chile, Y) \wedge area(Y, A) \wedge A > 2000000.$

where $>$ is a predicate that is true if its arguments are numbers and its left argument is greater than its right argument. As is traditional in mathematics, this predicate is written using infix notation.

**Example 15.13** Figure 15.3 (page 660) gives more facts about some South American countries and their capitals. Note how it distinguishes the name of the country from the country itself. The constant *chile* denotes the county, and the constant *"Chile"* denotes the string that is the name of the country. These are very different, for example *"Chile"* is five characters long, whereas *chile* is 4270 kilometers long (from North to South).

To ask for the name of the capital city of Chile, one would ask

ask $capital(chile, C) \wedge name(C, N).$

## 15.5 Proofs and Substitutions

Both the bottom-up and top-down propositional proof procedures of Section 5.3.2 (page 188) can be extended to Datalog. A proof procedure extended for variables must account for the fact that a free variable in a clause means that all instances of the clause are true. A proof may have to use different instances of the same clause in a single proof.

### 15.5.1 Instances and Substitutions

An **instance** of a clause is obtained by uniformly substituting terms for variables in the clause. All occurrences of a particular variable are replaced by the same term.

The specification of which value is assigned to each variable is called a substitution. A **substitution** is a set of the form $\{V_1/t_1, \ldots, V_n/t_n\}$, where each $V_i$ is a distinct variable and each $t_i$ is a term. The element $V_i/t_i$ is a **binding** for variable $V_i$. A substitution is in **normal form** if no $V_i$ appears in any $t_j$.

**Example 15.14** For example, $\{X/Y, Z/chile\}$ is a substitution in normal form that binds $X$ to $Y$ and binds $Z$ to *chile*. The substitution$\{X/Y, Z/X\}$ is not in normal form, because the variable $X$ occurs both on the left and on the right of a binding.

% *capital*$(A, B)$ is true if $B$ is the capital city of $A$

*capital(argentina, beunos_aires).*
*capital(chile, santiago).*
*capital(peru, lima).*
*capital(brazil, brasilia).*
*capital(paraguay, asuncion).*

% *name*$(E, N)$ is true if string $N$ is the name of individual $E$

*name(beunos_aires, "Buenos Aires").*
*name(santiago, "Santiago").*
*name(lima, "Lima").*
*name(brasilia, "Brasilia").*
*name(asuncion, "Asunción").*
*name(argentina, "Argentina").*
*name(chile, "Chile").*
*name(peru, "Peru").*
*name(brazil, "Brazil").*
*name(paraguay, "Paraguay").*

Figure 15.3: Some facts about South American capitals

The **application** of a substitution $\sigma = \{V_1/t_1, \ldots, V_n/t_n\}$ to expression $e$, written $e\sigma$, is an expression that is the same as the original expression $e$ except that each occurrence of $V_i$ in $e$ is replaced by the corresponding $t_i$. The expression $e\sigma$ is called an **instance** of $e$. If $e\sigma$ does not contain any variables, it is called a **ground instance** of $e$.

**Example 15.15** Some applications of substitutions are

$$borders(peru, X)\{X/chile\} = borders(peru, chile).$$
$$borders(Y, chile)\{Y/peru\} = borders(peru, chile).$$
$$borders(peru, X)\{Y/peru, Z/X\} = borders(peru, X).$$
$$p(X, X, Y, Y, Z)\{X/Z, Y/brazil\} = p(Z, Z, brazil, brazil, Z).$$

Substitutions can apply to clauses, atoms, and terms. For example, the result of applying the substitution $\{X/Y, Z/peru\}$ to the clause

$$p(X, Y) \leftarrow q(peru, Z, X, Y, Z)$$

is the clause

$$p(Y, Y) \leftarrow q(peru, peru, Y, Y, peru).$$

A substitution $\sigma$ is a **unifier** of expressions $e_1$ and $e_2$ if $e_1\sigma$ is identical to $e_2\sigma$; expressions $e_1$ and $e_2$ are said to **unify**. That is, a unifier of two expressions is a substitution that when applied to each expression results in the same expression.

**Example 15.16** Substitution $\{X/chile, Y/peru\}$ is a unifier of $borders(peru, X)$ and $borders(Y, chile)$. Applying this substitution to either gives $borders(peru, chile)$.

$\{X/a, Y/b\}$ is a unifier of $t(a, Y, c)$ and $t(X, b, c)$ as

$$t(a, Y, c)\{X/a, Y/b\} = t(X, b, c)\{X/a, Y/b\} = t(a, b, c).$$

Expressions can have many unifiers.

**Example 15.17** Atoms $p(X, Y)$ and $p(Z, Z)$ have many unifiers, including $\{X/b, Y/b, Z/b\}$, $\{X/c, Y/c, Z/c\}$, $\{X/Z, Y/Z\}$, and $\{Y/X, Z/X\}$. The last two unifiers are more general than the first two, because the first two both have $X$ the same as $Z$ and $Y$ the same as $Z$ but make more commitments to what these values are.

Substitution $\sigma$ is a **most general unifier** (**MGU**) of expressions $e_1$ and $e_2$ if

- $\sigma$ is a unifier of the two expressions, and
- if substitution $\sigma'$ is also a unifier of $e_1$ and $e_2$, then $e\sigma'$ must be an instance of $e\sigma$ for all expressions $e$.

**Example 15.18** $\{X/Z, Y/Z\}$ and $\{Z/X, Y/X\}$ are both most general unifiers of $p(X,Y)$ and $p(Z,Z)$. $\{X/a, Y/a, Z/a\}$ is a unifier, but not a most general unifier, of these. The resulting applications are

$$p(X,Y)\{X/Z,Y/Z\} = p(Z,Z)\{X/Z,Y/Z\} = p(Z,Z)$$
$$p(X,Y)\{Z/X,Y/X\} = p(Z,Z)\{Z/X,Y/X\} = p(X,X)$$
$$p(X,Y)\{X/a,Y/a,Z/a\} = p(Z,Z)\{X/a,Y/a,Z/a\} = p(a,a).$$

Note that $p(a,a)$ is an instance of $p(Z,Z)$ and an instance of $p(X,X)$, but these are not instances of $p(a,a)$. $p(Z,Z)$ and $p(X,X)$ are instances of each other.

The definition of MGU refers to "all expressions $e$" to preclude a substitution such as $\{X/Z, Y/Z, W/a\}$ being a most general unifier of $p(X,Y)$ and $p(Z,Z)$, because it affects other expressions such as $r(W)$.

Expression $e_1$ is a **renaming** of $e_2$ if they differ only in the names of variables. In this case, they are both instances of each other.

If two expressions have a unifier, they have at least one MGU. The expressions resulting from applying the MGUs to the expressions are all renamings of each other. That is, if $\sigma$ and $\sigma'$ are both MGUs of expressions $e_1$ and $e_2$, then $e_1\sigma$ is a renaming of $e_1\sigma'$.

## 15.5.2 Bottom-Up Procedure for Datalog

The propositional bottom-up proof procedure (page 189) can be extended to Datalog by using ground instances of the clauses. A **ground instance** of a clause is obtained by uniformly substituting constants for the variables in the clause. The constants required are those appearing in the knowledge base or in the query. If there are no constants in the knowledge base or the query, one must be invented.

**Example 15.19** Suppose the knowledge base is

| | | |
|---|---|---|
| $q(a)$. | $q(b)$. | $r(a)$. |
| $s(W) \leftarrow r(W)$. | $p(X,Y) \leftarrow q(X) \wedge s(Y)$. | |

The set of all ground instances is

| | | |
|---|---|---|
| $q(a)$. | $q(b)$. | $r(a)$. |
| $s(a) \leftarrow r(a)$. | $s(b) \leftarrow r(b)$. | $p(a,a) \leftarrow q(a) \wedge s(a)$. |
| $p(a,b) \leftarrow q(a) \wedge s(b)$. | $p(b,a) \leftarrow q(b) \wedge s(a)$. | $p(b,b) \leftarrow q(b) \wedge s(b)$. |

The propositional bottom-up proof procedure of Section 5.3.2 (page 189) can be applied to the grounding to derive $q(a), q(b), r(a), s(a), p(a,a)$, and $p(b,a)$ as the ground instances that are logical consequences.

**Example 15.20** Suppose the knowledge base is

$p(X,Y)$.

$g \leftarrow p(W,W)$.

The bottom-up proof procedure for query "ask $g$" must invent a new constant symbol, say $c$. The set of all ground instances is then

$$p(c,c).$$
$$g \leftarrow p(c,c).$$

The propositional bottom-up proof procedure will derive $p(c,c)$ and $g$.

If the query were "ask $p(b,d)$" the set of ground instances would change to reflect the constants $b$ and $d$.

The bottom-up proof procedure applied to the grounding of the knowledge base is sound, because each instance of each rule is true in every model. This procedure is essentially the same as the variable-free case, but it uses the set of ground instances of the clauses, all of which are true because the variables in a clause are universally quantified.

This bottom-up procedure will eventually halt for Datalog because there are only finitely many grounded atoms, and one ground atom is added to the consequence set each time through the loop.

This procedure is also complete for ground atoms. That is, if a ground atom is a consequence of the knowledge base, it will be derived. To prove this, as in the propositional case (page 191), construct a particular generic model. Recall that a model specifies the domain, what the constants denote, and what is true. A **Herbrand interpretation** is an interpretation where the domain is symbolic and consists of all constants of the language. A constant is invented if there are no constants in the knowledge base or the query. In a Herbrand interpretation, each constant denotes itself. Thus, in the definition of an interpretation (page 650), $D$ and $\phi$ are fixed for a given program, and all that needs to be specified is $\pi$, which defines the predicate symbols.

Consider the Herbrand interpretation where the true atoms are the ground instances of the relations that are eventually derived by the bottom-up procedure. It is easy to see that this Herbrand interpretation is a model of the rules given. As in the variable-free case (page 189), it is a **minimal model** in that it has the fewest true atoms of any model. If $KB \models g$ for ground atom $g$, then $g$ is true in the minimal model and, thus, is eventually derived.

### 15.5.3 Unification

A computer does not need to reason at the propositional level by grounding. Instead, it can reason in terms of variables instead of multiple ground instances. Sometimes, it needs to replace variables by other variables or by constants.

The problem of **unification** is the following: given two atoms or terms, determine whether they unify, and, if they do, return a unifier of them. The unification algorithm finds a **most general unifier** (MGU) of two atoms or returns $\perp$ if they do not unify.

The unification algorithm is given in Figure 15.4. $E$ is a set of equality statements implying and implied by the unification of $t_1$ and $t_2$. $S$ is a substitution in normal form; if $\alpha/\beta$ is in the substitution $S$, then, by construction, $\alpha$ is a variable that does not appear elsewhere in $S$ or in $E$. In line 20, $\alpha$ and $\beta$ must have the same predicate and the same number of arguments; otherwise the unification fails.

**Example 15.21** Consider the call $Unify(p(X,Y,Y), p(a,Z,b))$. Initially $E$ is $\{p(X,Y,Y) = p(a,Z,b)\}$. The first time through the while loop, $E$ becomes $\{X = a, Y = Z, Y = b\}$. Suppose $X = a$ is selected next. Then $S$ becomes $\{X/a\}$ and $E$ becomes $\{Y = Z, Y = b\}$. Suppose $Y = Z$ is selected. Then $Y$ is replaced by $Z$ in $S$ and $E$. $S$ becomes $\{X/a, Y/Z\}$ and $E$ becomes $\{Z = b\}$. Finally $Z = b$ is selected, $Z$ is replaced by $b$, $S$ becomes $\{X/a, Y/b, Z/b\}$, and $E$ becomes empty. The substitution $\{X/a, Y/b, Z/b\}$ is returned as an MGU.

Consider unifying $p(a,Y,Y)$ with $p(Z,Z,b)$. $E$ starts off as $\{p(a,Y,Y) = p(Z,Z,b)\}$. In the next step, $E$ becomes $\{a = Z, Y = Z, Y = b\}$. Then $Z$ is replaced by $a$ in $E$, and $E$ becomes $\{Y = a, Y = b\}$. Then $Y$ is replaced by $a$ in

```
1: procedure Unify(t1, t2)
2:     Inputs
3:         t1, t2: atoms or terms
4:     Output
5:         most general unifier of t1 and t2 if it exists or ⊥ otherwise
6:     Local
7:         E: a set of equality statements
8:         S: substitution
9:     E ← {t1 = t2}
10:    S = {}
11:    while E ≠ {} do
12:        select and remove α = β from E
13:        if β is not identical to α then
14:            if α is a variable then
15:                replace α with β everywhere in E and S
16:                S ← {α/β} ∪ S
17:            else if β is a variable then
18:                replace β with α everywhere in E and S
19:                S ← {β/α} ∪ S
20:            else if α is p(α1, ..., αn) and β is p(β1, ..., βn) then
21:                E ← E ∪ {α1 = β1, ..., αn = βn}
22:            else
23:                return ⊥
24:    return S
```

Figure 15.4: Unification algorithm for Datalog

$E$, and $E$ becomes $\{a = b\}$, and then $\perp$ is returned indicating that there is no unifier.

### 15.5.4 Definite Resolution with Variables

The **top-down proof procedure** for propositional definite clauses (page 191) can be extended to handle variables by allowing instances of rules to be used in the derivation.

A **generalized answer clause** is of the form

$$yes(t_1, \ldots, t_k) \leftarrow a_1 \wedge a_2 \wedge \ldots \wedge a_m$$

where $t_1, \ldots, t_k$ are terms and $a_1, \ldots, a_m$ are atoms. The use of *yes* enables **answer extraction**: determining which instances of the query variables are a logical consequence of the knowledge base.

Initially, the generalized answer clause for query $q$ is

$$yes(V_1, \ldots, V_k) \leftarrow q$$

where $V_1, \ldots, V_k$ are the variables that appear in the query $q$. Intuitively this means that an instance of $yes(V_1, \ldots, V_k)$ is true if the corresponding instance of the query is true.

The proof procedure maintains a current generalized answer clause.

At each stage, the algorithm selects an atom in the body of the generalized answer clause. It then chooses a clause in the knowledge base whose head unifies with the atom.

The **SLD resolution** where SLD stands for *selection linear definite*, of the generalized answer clause

$$yes(t_1, \ldots, t_k) \leftarrow a_1 \wedge a_2 \wedge \ldots \wedge a_m$$

on $a_1$ with the chosen clause

$$a \leftarrow b_1 \wedge \ldots \wedge b_p$$

where $a_1$ and $a$ have most general unifier $\sigma$, is the answer clause

$$(yes(t_1, \ldots, t_k) \leftarrow b_1 \wedge \ldots \wedge b_p \wedge a_2 \wedge \ldots \wedge a_m)\sigma$$

where the body of the chosen clause has replaced $a_1$ in the answer clause, and the MGU $\sigma$ is applied to the whole answer clause.

An **SLD derivation** is a sequence of generalized answer clauses $\gamma_0$, $\gamma_1$, ..., $\gamma_n$ such that

- $\gamma_0$ is the answer clause corresponding to the original query. If the query is $q$, with free variables $V_1, \ldots, V_k$, the initial generalized answer clause $\gamma_0$ is

$$yes(V_1, \ldots, V_k) \leftarrow q.$$

- $\gamma_i$ is obtained by selecting an atom $a_1$ in the body of $\gamma_{i-1}$; choosing a *copy* of a clause $a \leftarrow b_1 \wedge \ldots \wedge b_p$ in the knowledge base whose head, $a$, unifies with $a_i$; replacing $a_1$ with the body, $b_1 \wedge \ldots \wedge b_p$; and applying the unifier to the whole resulting answer clause.

  The main difference between this and the propositional top-down proof procedure (page 191) is that, for clauses with variables, the proof procedure must take *copies* of clauses from the knowledge base. The copying renames the variables in the clause with new names. This is both to remove name clashes between variables and because a single proof may use different instances of a clause.
- $\gamma_n$ is an answer. That is, it is of the form

  $$yes(t_1, \ldots, t_k) \leftarrow .$$

  When this occurs, the algorithm returns the answer

  $$V_1 = t_1, \ldots, V_k = t_k.$$

Notice how the answer is extracted; the arguments to *yes* keep track of the instances of the variables in the initial query that lead to a successful proof.

Figure 15.5 gives a non-deterministic algorithm that answers queries by searching for SLD derivations. This is non-deterministic (page 89) in the sense that all derivations can be found by making appropriate choices that do not fail. If all choices fail, the algorithm fails, and there are no derivations. The "choose"

**non-deterministic procedure** *Prove_datalog_TD*$(KB, q)$
    **Inputs**
        *KB*: a set of definite clauses
        Query $q$: a set of atoms to prove, with variables $V_1, \ldots, V_k$
    **Output**
        substitution $\theta$ if $KB \models q\theta$ and fail otherwise
    **Local**
        $G$ is a generalized answer clause
    Set $G$ to generalized answer clause $yes(V_1, \ldots, V_k) \leftarrow q$
    **while** $G$ is not an answer **do**
        Suppose $G$ is $yes(t_1, \ldots, t_k) \leftarrow a_1 \wedge a_2 \wedge \ldots \wedge a_m$
        **select** atom $a_1$ in the body of $G$
        **choose** clause $a \leftarrow b_1 \wedge \ldots \wedge b_p$ in *KB*
        Rename all variables in $a \leftarrow b_1 \wedge \ldots \wedge b_p$ to have new names
        Let $\sigma$ be *Unify*$(a_1, a)$. Fail if *Unify* returns $\bot$.
        $G := (yes(t_1, \ldots, t_k) \leftarrow b_1 \wedge \ldots \wedge b_p \wedge a_2 \wedge \ldots \wedge a_m)\sigma$
    **return** $\{V_1 = t_1, \ldots, V_k = t_k\}$ where $G$ is $yes(t_1, \ldots, t_k) \leftarrow$

Figure 15.5: Top-down definite-clause proof procedure for Datalog on line 13 is implemented using search, as in Example 5.12 (page 194). Recall that $Unify(a_i, a)$ returns an MGU of $a_i$ and $a$, if there is one, and $\perp$ if they do not unify. The algorithm for *Unify* is given in Figure 15.4 (page 664).

**Example 15.22** The singer Shakira was born in Barranquilla, the capital of Atlántico Department in Colombia. It follows that she was born in Colombia and so also in South America. Consider the following propositions (as part of a larger knowledge base):

$$born\_in(shakira, barranquilla).$$
$$born\_in(P, L) \leftarrow part\_of(S, L) \wedge born\_in(P, S).$$
$$part\_of(barranquilla, atlantico).$$
$$part\_of(atlantico, colombia).$$
$$part\_of(colombia, south\_america).$$

A query to ask who is born in Colombia is

ask $born\_in(P, colombia)$.

Figure 15.6 (page 668) shows a successful derivation with answer $P = shakira$.
Note that this derivation used two instances of the rule

$$born\_in(P, L) \leftarrow part\_of(S, L) \wedge born\_in(P, S).$$

One instance eventually substituted *colombia* for $S$, and one instance substituted *atlantico* for $S$.

## 15.6 Function Symbols and Data Structures

Datalog requires a name, using a constant, for every individual about which the system reasons. Often it is simpler to identify an individual in terms of its components, rather than requiring a separate constant for each individual.

**Example 15.23** In many domains, you want to be able to refer to a time as an individual. You may want to say that some course is held at 11:30 a.m. You do not want a separate constant for each possible time, although this is possible. It is better to define times in terms of, say, the number of hours past midnight and the number of minutes past the hour. Similarly, you may want to reason with facts about particular dates. You cannot give a constant for each date arbitrarily far in the future, as there are infinitely many possible dates. It is easier to define a date in terms of the year, the month, and the day.

Using a constant to name each individual means that the knowledge base can only represent a finite number of individuals, and the number of individuals is fixed when the knowledge base is built. However, you may want to reason about a potentially infinite set of individuals.

**Example 15.24** Suppose you want to build a system that takes questions in English and answers them by consulting an online database. In this case, each sentence is an individual. You do not want to have to give each sentence its own name, because there are too many English sentences to name them all. It may be better to name the words and then to specify a sentence in terms of the sequence of words in the sentence. This approach may be more practical because there are far fewer words to name than sentences, and each word has its own natural name. You may also want to specify the words in terms of the letters in the word or in terms of their constituent parts.

Function symbols allow you to describe individuals indirectly. Rather than using a constant to describe an individual, an individual is described in terms of other individuals. Function symbols enable the language to represent rich **data structures**; a function symbol gives a structured collection of other entities.

Syntactically a **function symbol** is a word starting with a lower-case letter. The definition of a term (page 649) is extended so that a **term** is either a variable, a constant, or of the form $f(t_1, \ldots, t_n)$, where $f$ is a function symbol and each $t_i$

$yes(P) \leftarrow born\_in(P, colombia)$

  resolve with: $born\_in(P_1, L_1) \leftarrow part\_of(S_1, L_1) \land born\_in(P_1, S_1)$

  substitution: $\{P_1/P, L_1/colombia\}$

$yes(P) \leftarrow part\_of(S_1, colombia) \land born\_in(P, S_1)$

  select leftmost conjunct

  resolve with: $part\_of(atlantico, colombia)$

  substitution: $\{S_1/atlantico\}$

$yes(P) \leftarrow born\_in(P, atlantico)$

  resolve with: $born\_in(P_2, L_2) \leftarrow part\_of(S_2, L_2) \land born\_in(P_2, S_2)$

  substitution: $\{P_2/P, L_2/atlantico\}$

$yes(P) \leftarrow part\_of(S_2, atlantico) \land born\_in(P, S_2)$

  resolve with: $part\_of(barranquilla, atlantico)$

  substitution: $\{S_2/barranquilla\}$

$yes(P) \leftarrow born\_in(P, barranquilla)$

  resolve with: $born_in(shakira, barranquilla)$

  substitution: $\{P/shakira\}$

$yes(shakira) \leftarrow$

Figure 15.6: A derivation for query $born\_in(P, colombia)$

is a term. Apart from extending the definition of terms, the language stays the same.

Terms only appear within predicate symbols. You do not write clauses that imply terms. You may, however, write clauses that include atoms that use function symbols.

The semantics of Datalog (page 650) must be expanded to reflect the new syntax. The definition of $\phi$ (page 650) is extended so that $\phi$ also assigns to each $n$-ary function symbol a function from $D^n$ into $D$. A constant can be seen as a 0-ary function symbol (i.e., one with no arguments). Thus, $\phi$ specifies which individual is denoted by each ground term.

**Example 15.25** Suppose you want to define dates, such as 20 July 1969, which is the date the first time a human was on the moon. You can use the function symbol *ce* (common era), so that $ce(Y, M, D)$ denotes a date with year $Y$, month $M$, and day $D$. For example, $ce(1969, jul, 20)$ may denote 20 July 1969. Similarly, you can define the symbol *bce* to denote a date before the common era.

The only way to use the function symbol is to write clauses that define relations using the function symbol. There is no notion of *defining* the *ce* function; dates are not in a computer any more than people are.

To use function symbols, you can write clauses that are quantified over the arguments of the function symbol. For example, Figure 15.7 defines the $before(D_1, D_2)$ relation that is true if date $D_1$ is before date $D_2$ in a day.

This assumes the predicate "<" represents the relation "less than" between integers. This could be represented in terms of clauses, but is often predefined,

% $before(D_1, D_2)$ is true if date $D_1$ is before date $D_2$

$$before(ce(Y1, M1, D1), ce(Y2, M2, D2)) \leftarrow$$
$$Y1 < Y2.$$
$$before(ce(Y, M1, D1), ce(Y, M2, D2)) \leftarrow$$
$$month(M1, N1) \land$$
$$month(M2, N2) \land$$
$$N1 < N2.$$
$$before(ce(Y, M, D1), ce(Y, M, D2)) \leftarrow$$
$$D1 < D2.$$

% $month(M, N)$ is true if month $M$ is the $N$th month of the year

| | | |
|---|---|---|
| $month(jan, 1).$ | $month(feb, 2).$ | $month(mar, 3).$ |
| $month(apr, 4).$ | $month(may, 5).$ | $month(jun, 6).$ |
| $month(jul, 7).$ | $month(aug, 8).$ | $month(sep, 9).$ |
| $month(oct, 10).$ | $month(nov, 11).$ | $month(dec, 12).$ |

Figure 15.7: Axiomatizing a "before" relation for dates in the common era

as it is in Prolog. The months are represented by constants that consist of the first three letters of the month.

A knowledge base consisting of clauses with function symbols can compute any computable function. Thus, a knowledge base can be interpreted as a program, called a **logic program**. Logic programs are Turing complete; they can compute any function computable on a digital computer.

This expansion of the language has a major impact. With just one function symbol and one constant, the language contains infinitely many ground terms and infinitely many ground atoms. The infinite number of terms can be used to describe an infinite number of individuals.

Function symbols are used to build data structures, as in the following example.

**Example 15.26** A tree is a useful data structure. You could use a tree to build a syntactic representation of a sentence for a natural language processing system. You could decide that a labeled tree is either of the form $node(N, LT, RT)$ or of the form $leaf(L)$. Thus, *node* is a function from a name, a left tree, and a right tree into a tree. The function symbol *leaf* denotes a function from the label of a leaf node into a tree.

The relation $at\_leaf(L, T)$ is true if label $L$ is the label of a leaf in tree $T$. It can be defined by

$$at\_leaf(L, leaf(L)).$$
$$at\_leaf(L, node(N, LT, RT)) \leftarrow$$
$$\quad at\_leaf(L, LT).$$
$$at\_leaf(L, node(N, LT, RT)) \leftarrow$$
$$\quad at\_leaf(L, RT).$$

This is an example of a structural recursive program. The rules cover all of the cases for each of the structures representing trees.

The relation $in\_tree(L, T)$, which is true if label $L$ is the label of an interior node of tree $T$, can be defined by

$$in\_tree(L, node(L, LT, RT)).$$
$$in\_tree(L, node(N, LT, RT)) \leftarrow$$
$$\quad in\_tree(L, LT).$$
$$in\_tree(L, node(N, LT, RT)) \leftarrow$$
$$\quad in\_tree(L, RT).$$

**Example 15.27** A **list** is an ordered sequence of elements. You can reason about lists using just function symbols and constants, without the notion of a list being predefined in the language. A list is either the empty list or an element followed by a list. You can invent a constant to denote the empty list. Suppose you use the constant *nil* to denote the empty list. You can choose a function symbol, say $cons(Hd, Tl)$, with the intended interpretation that it denotes a list with first element *Hd* and rest of the list *Tl*. The list containing the elements *a*, *b*, *c* would then be represented as

$$cons(a, cons(b, cons(c, nil))).$$

To use lists, one must write predicates that do something with them. For example, the relation $append(X, Y, Z)$ that is true when $X$, $Y$, and $Z$ are lists, such that $Z$ contains the elements of $X$ followed by the elements of $Z$, can be defined recursively by

$append(nil, L, L).$
$append(cons(Hd, X), Y, cons(Hd, Z)) \leftarrow$
$\quad append(X, Y, Z).$

There is nothing special about *cons* or *nil*; you could have just as well used *foo* and *bar*.

## 15.6.1 Proof Procedures with Function Symbols

The proof procedures with variables carry over for the case with function symbols. The main difference is that the class of terms is expanded to include function symbols.

The use of function symbols involves infinitely many terms. To be complete, forward chaining on the clauses has to ensure that the selection criterion for selecting clauses is fair (page 89).

**Example 15.28** To see why fairness is important, consider the following clauses:

$num(0).$
$num(s(N)) \leftarrow num(N).$
$a \leftarrow b.$
$b.$

An unfair strategy could initially select the first clause to forward chain on and, for every subsequent selection, select the second clause. The second clause can always be used to derive a new consequence. This strategy never selects either of the last two clauses and thus never derives *a* or *b*.

This problem of ignoring some clauses forever is known as **starvation**. A **fair** selection criterion is one such that any clause available to be selected will eventually be selected. The bottom-up proof procedure can generate an infinite sequence of consequences and if the selection is fair, each consequence will eventually be generated and so the proof procedure is complete.

The top-down proof procedure is the same as for Datalog (see Figure 15.5 (page 666)). Unification becomes more complicated, because it must recursively descend into the structure of terms. There is one change to the unification algorithm (page 664): a variable $X$ does not unify with a term $t$ in which $X$

**First-Order and Second-Order Logic**

**First-order predicate calculus** is a logic that extends propositional calculus (page 177) to include atoms with function symbols and logical variables. All logical variables must have explicit quantification in terms of "for all" ($\forall$) and "there exists" ($\exists$) (page 649). The semantics of first-order predicate calculus is like the semantics of logic programs presented in this chapter, but with a richer set of operators.

The language of logic programs forms a pragmatic subset of first-order predicate calculus, which has been developed because it is useful for many tasks. First-order predicate calculus can be seen as a language that adds disjunction and explicit quantification to logic programs.

First-order logic is *first order* because it allows quantification over individuals in the domain. First-order logic allows neither predicates as variables nor quantification over predicates.

**Second-order logic** allows for quantification over first-order relations, and allows for predicates whose arguments are first-order relations. These are second-order relations. For example, the second-order logic formula

$$\forall R\ symmetric(R) \leftrightarrow (\forall X \forall Y\ R(X,Y) \rightarrow R(Y,X))$$

defines the second-order relation *symmetric*, which is true if its argument is a symmetric relation.

Second-order logic seems necessary for many applications because transitive closure is not first-order definable. For example, suppose you want *before* to be the transitive closure of *next*, where $next(X, s(X))$ is true. Think of *next* meaning the "next millisecond" and *before* denoting "before." The natural first-order definition would be the definition

$$\forall X \forall Y\ before(X,Y) \leftrightarrow (Y = s(X) \vee before(s(X),Y)) . \tag{15.1}$$

This expression does not accurately capture the definition, because, for example:

$$\forall X \forall Y\ before(X,Y) \rightarrow \exists W\ Y = s(W)$$

does not logically follow from formula (15.1), because there are nonstandard models of formula (15.1) with $Y$ denoting *infinity*. To capture the transitive closure, you require a formula stating that *before* is the minimal predicate that satisfies the definition. This can be stated using second-order logic.

First-order logic is **semi-decidable**, which means that a sound and complete proof procedure exists in which every true statement can be proved, but it may not halt. Second-order logic is undecidable; no sound and complete proof procedure can be implemented on a Turing machine.

occurs and is not $X$ itself. The algorithm should return $\perp$ if $X/t$ is to be added to $S$ where variable $X$ occurs in term $t$. Checking for this condition is known as the **occurs check**. The occurs check is sometimes omitted (e.g., in Prolog), because removing it makes the proof procedure more efficient, even though removing it makes the proof procedure unsound, as shown in the following example.

**Example 15.29** Consider the knowledge base with only one clause:

$$lt(X, s(X)).$$

Suppose the intended interpretation is the domain of integers in which $lt$ means "less than" and $s(X)$ denotes the integer after $X$. The query ask $lt(Y, Y)$ should fail because it is false in the intended interpretation; there is no number less than itself. However, if $X$ and $s(X)$ could unify, this query would succeed. In this case, the proof procedure would be unsound because something could be derived that is false in a model of the axioms.

The following example shows the details of SLD resolution with function symbols.

**Example 15.30** Consider the clauses

$$append(c(A, X), Y, c(A, Z)) \leftarrow$$
$$\quad append(X, Y, Z).$$
$$append(nil, Z, Z).$$

For now, ignore what this may mean. Like the computer, treat this as a problem of symbol manipulation. Consider the following query:

ask $append(F, c(L, nil), c(l, c(i, c(s, c(t, nil))))).$

The following is a derivation:

$yes(F, L) \leftarrow append(F, c(L, nil), c(l, c(i, c(s, c(t, nil)))))$
  resolve with $append(c(A_1, X_1), Y_1, c(A_1, Z_1)) \leftarrow append(X_1, Y_1, Z_1)$
  substitution: $\{F/c(l, X_1), Y_1/c(L, nil), A_1/l, Z_1/c(i, c(s, c(t, nil)))\}$
$yes(c(l, X_1), L) \leftarrow append(X_1, c(L, nil), c(i, c(s, c(t, nil))))$
  resolve with $append(c(A_2, X_2), Y_2, c(A_2, Z_2)) \leftarrow append(X_2, Y_2, Z_2)$
  substitution: $\{X_1/c(i, X_2), Y_2/c(L, nil), A_2/i, Z_2/c(s, c(t, nil))\}$
$yes(c(l, c(i, X_2)), L) \leftarrow append(X_2, c(L, nil), c(s, c(t, nil)))$
  resolve with $append(c(A_3, X_3), Y_3, c(A_3, Z_3)) \leftarrow append(X_3, Y_3, Z_3)$
  substitution: $\{X_2/c(s, X_3), Y_3/c(L, nil), A_3/s, Z_3/c(t, nil)\}$
$yes(c(l, c(i, c(s, X_3))), L) \leftarrow append(X_3, c(L, nil), c(t, nil))$

At this stage both clauses are applicable. Choosing the first clause gives

  resolve with $append(c(A_4, X_4), Y_4, c(A_4, Z_4)) \leftarrow append(X_4, Y_4, Z_4)$

substitution: $\{X_3/c(t,X_4), Y_4/c(L,nil), A_4/t, Z_4/nil\}$

$yes(c(l,c(i,c(s,X_3))),L) \leftarrow append(X_4,c(L,nil),nil).$

At this point, there are no clauses whose head unifies with the atom in the generalized answer clause's body. The proof fails.

Choosing the second clause instead of the first gives

resolve with $append(nil,Z_5,Z_5)$

substitution: $\{Z_5/c(t,nil), X_3/nil, L/t\}$

$yes(c(l,c(i,c(s,nil))),t) \leftarrow .$

At this point, the proof succeeds, with answer $F = c(l,c(i,c(s,nil))), L = t$.

For the rest of this chapter, the "syntactic sugar" notation of Prolog for representing lists is used. The empty list, *nil*, is written as $[\,]$. The list with first element $E$ and the rest of the list $R$, which is $cons(E,R)$ in Example 15.27 (page 670), is written as $[E \mid R]$. There is one other notational simplification: $[X \mid [Y]]$ is written as $[X,Y]$, where $Y$ can be a sequence of values. For example, $[a \mid [\,]]$ is written as $[a]$, and $[b \mid [a \mid [\,]]]$ is written as $[b,a]$. The term $[a \mid [b \mid C]]$ is written as $[a,b \mid C]$.

**Example 15.31** Using the list notation, *append* from the previous example can be written as

$append([A \mid X],Y,[A \mid Z]) \leftarrow$
$\quad append(X,Y,Z).$
$append([\,],Z,Z).$

The query

ask $append(F,[L],[l,i,s,t])$

has an answer $F = [l,i,s], L = t$. The proof is exactly as in the previous example. As far as the proof procedure is concerned, nothing has changed; there is just a renamed function symbol and constant.

## 15.7 Applications in Natural Language

Natural language processing is an interesting and difficult domain in which to develop and evaluate representation and reasoning theories. Many of the problems of AI arise in this domain; solving "the natural language problem" is almost as difficult as solving "the AI problem" because any domain can be expressed in natural language. The field of **computational linguistics** has a wealth of techniques and knowledge. This book only gives an overview.

There are at least three reasons for studying natural language processing:

- Users want to communicate on their own terms and many prefer natural language to some artificial language or a graphical user interface. This is particularly important for casual users and those users, such as managers and children, who have neither the time nor the inclination to learn new interaction skills.
- There is a vast store of information recorded in natural language that could be accessible using computers. Information is constantly generated in the form of tweets, blogs, books, news, business and government reports, and scientific papers, many of which are available online. A system requiring a great deal of information must be able to process natural language to retrieve much of the information available on computers.
- Many of the problems of AI arise in a very clear and explicit form in natural language processing and, thus, it is a good domain in which to experiment with general theories.

### Two Traditions for Natural Language Processing

Natural language processing systems in AI have generally followed two traditions:

- Systems with broad coverage, trying to understand language in the wild, but being content with some errors.

- Systems in a constrained domain where the users can be expected to use controlled natural language, and the results can be unambiguous.

Systems of the first type are used for predictive typing in smartphones and for broad-coverage language translation. Systems of the second type are used when the same people interact with the system on an ongoing basis, such as database queries for supermarket inventories, games, or when the language is stylized – such as parsing the question in the game of Jeopardy! (as was done by the Watson system; see references).

One difference is how to treat ungrammatical sentences or questions, or unfamiliar words. In the first type, these are treated like grammatical ones. However, systems of the second type may ask for clarification or rephrasing, or even fail for such sentences.

Translation using the systems for broad coverage are good for casual use with low cost for being wrong or when the person you are communicating with can ask a question and interact to find the appropriate meaning. However, you might not want to use such a system when there is a large cost for errors or misunderstanding, such as for legal contracts.

The state of the art for systems with broad coverage is to learn them from data, for example using neural networks and deep learning (page 327).

This chapter considers systems of the second type, where the techniques presented here are still used.

There are at least three major aspects of natural language:

**Syntax** The syntax describes the form of the language. Natural language is much more complicated than the formal languages used for logics and computer programs. Syntax is usually specified by a grammar. Some natural language models are represented using neural networks that predict each word from its context (see Section 8.5, page 350), without explicitly building a parse tree.

**Semantics** The semantics provides the meaning of utterances or sentences of the language. Although general semantic theories exist, when natural language processing systems are built for a particular application, it is typical to use the simplest representation available. For example, in the development that follows, there is a fixed mapping between words and concepts in the knowledge base, which is inappropriate for many domains but simplifies development. There can be different senses for the same word (such as a bank of a river and a bank to keep money). Neural models typically represent words using fixed-length vectors called embeddings (page 350), which represent enough semantics to predict each word in context or other tasks they are trained on.

**Pragmatics** The pragmatic component explains how the utterances relate to the world. To understand language, an agent should consider more than the sentence; it has to take into account the context of the sentence, the state of the world, the goals of the speaker and the listener, special conventions, and the like.

To understand the difference among these aspects, consider the following sentences, which might appear at the start of an AI textbook:

- *This book is about artificial intelligence.*
- *The green frogs sleep soundly.*
- *Colorless green ideas sleep furiously.*
- *Furiously sleep ideas green colorless.*

The first sentence would be quite appropriate at the start of such a book; it is syntactically, semantically, and pragmatically well formed. The second sentence is syntactically and semantically well formed, but it would appear very strange at the start of an AI book; it is not pragmatically well formed for that context. The last two sentences are by the linguist Noam Chomsky [1957]. The third sentence is syntactically well formed, but it is semantically nonsensical. The fourth sentence is syntactically ill formed; it does not make any sense – syntactically, semantically, or pragmatically.

The next section shows how to write a natural language query answering system that is applicable to very narrow domains using stylized natural language that users have to adhere to. This approach may be adequate for domains in which little, if any, ambiguity exists. At the other extreme are shallow but broad systems, such as the help system presented in Example 9.36 (page 430) and Example 10.5 (page 469).

### 15.7.1 Using Definite Clauses for Context-Free Grammars

This section shows how to use definite clauses to represent aspects of the syntax and semantics of natural language.

**Languages** are defined by their legal sentences. A **sentence** is a sequence of **tokens**, which typically represent **words** in the language, common phrases (such as "artificial intelligence"), and often include punctuation. Some models represent words in terms of their parts, for example, splitting off the ending such as "ing" and "er" as separate tokens or using sequences of characters (as in Example 8.11 (page 359)). Sentences are represented here using lists, and tokens as strings written in double quotes.

The legal sentences are specified by a grammar. A **context-free grammar** is defined by a set of **rewrite rules**, with **non-terminal** symbols transforming into a sequence of terminal and non-terminal symbols. A sentence of the language is a sequence of **terminal symbols** generated by such rewriting rules. For example, the grammar rule

$$sentence \longmapsto noun\_phrase, verb\_phrase$$

means that a non-terminal symbol *sentence* can be a *noun_phrase* followed by a *verb_phrase*. The symbol "$\longmapsto$" means "can be rewritten as."

A context-free grammar provides a first approximation of the grammar of some natural languages. For natural languages, the terminal symbols are the tokens of the language. If a sentence of natural language is represented as a list of tokens, the following definite clause means that a list of words is a sentence if it is a noun phrase followed by a verb phrase:

$$sentence(S) \leftarrow noun\_phrase(N) \land verb\_phrase(V) \land append(N, V, S).$$

To say that the word "country" is a noun, you could write

$$noun(["country"]).$$

An alternative, simpler, representation of grammar rules, known as a **definite-clause grammar (DCG)**, uses definite clauses without requiring an explicit *append*. To represent a context-free grammar, each non-terminal symbol $s$ becomes a predicate with two arguments, $s(L_1, L_2)$, which is true when list $L_2$ is an ending of list $L_1$ such that all of the words in $L_1$ before $L_2$ form a sequence of words of the category $s$. Lists $L_1$ and $L_2$ together form a **difference list** of words that make the class given by the non-terminal symbol, because it is the difference of these that forms the syntactic category.

**Example 15.32** Under this representation, $noun\_phrase(L_1, L_2)$ is true if list $L_2$ is an ending of list $L_1$ such that all of the words in $L_1$ before $L_2$ form a noun phrase. $L_2$ is the part of $L_1$ after the noun phrase.

$$noun\_phrase(["large", "country", "bordering", "Paraguay", "borders", "Chile"],$$
$$["bordering", "Paraguay", "borders", "Chile"])$$

is true in the intended interpretation because "large country" forms a noun phrase.

$$noun\_phrase(["large","country","bordering","Paraguay","borders","Chile"],\\ ["borders","Chile"])$$

is also true because "large country bordering Paraguay" forms a noun phrase.

The grammar rule

$$sentence \longmapsto noun\_phrase, verb\_phrase$$

means that there is a sentence between some $L_0$ and $L_2$ if there exists a noun phrase between $L_0$ and $L_1$ and a verb phrase between $L_1$ and $L_2$:

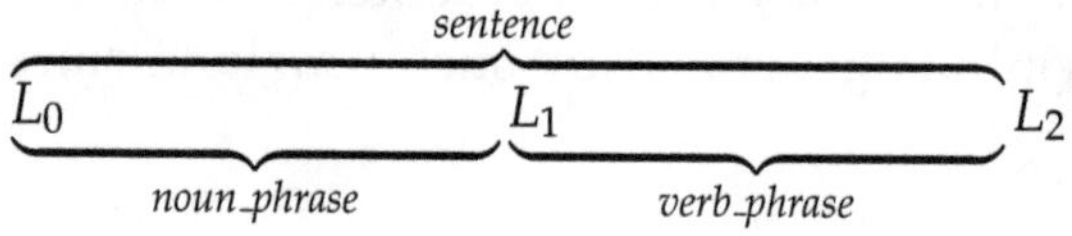


This grammar rule can be specified as the clause

$$\begin{aligned} &sentence(L_0, L_2) \leftarrow \\ &\quad noun\_phrase(L_0, L_1) \wedge \\ &\quad verb\_phrase(L_1, L_2). \end{aligned}$$

In general, the rule

$$h \longmapsto b_1, b_2, \ldots, b_n$$

says that $h$ is composed of a $b_1$ followed by a $b_2$, ..., followed by a $b_n$, and is written as the definite clause

$$\begin{aligned} &h(L_0, L_n) \leftarrow \\ &\quad b_1(L_0, L_1) \wedge \\ &\quad b_2(L_1, L_2) \wedge \\ &\quad \vdots \\ &\quad b_n(L_{n-1}, L_n). \end{aligned}$$

using the interpretation

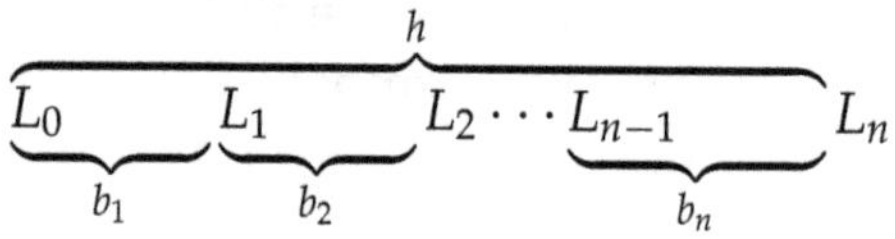


where the $L_i$ are unique variables.

To say that non-terminal $h$ gets mapped to the terminal symbols, $t_1, \ldots, t_n$, one would write

$$h([t_1, \ldots, t_n \mid T], T)$$

using the interpretation

$$\overbrace{t_1, \ldots, t_n}^{h} T$$

Thus, $h(L_1, L_2)$ is true if $L_1 = [t_1, \ldots, t_n \mid L_2]$.

**Example 15.33** The rule that specifies that the non-terminal $h$ can be rewritten to the non-terminal $a$ followed by the non-terminal $b$ followed by the terminal symbols $c$ and $d$, followed by the non-terminal symbol $e$ followed by the terminal symbol $f$ and the non-terminal symbol $g$, can be written as

$$h \longmapsto a, b, [c, d], e, [f], g$$

and can be represented as

$$\begin{aligned} & h(L_0, L_6) \leftarrow \\ & \quad a(L_0, L_1) \land \\ & \quad b(L_1, [c, d \mid L_3]) \land \\ & \quad e(L_3, [f \mid L_5]) \land \\ & \quad g(L_5, L_6). \end{aligned}$$

Note that the translations $L_2 = [c, d \mid L_3]$ and $L_4 = [f \mid L_5]$ were done manually.

Figure 15.8 (page 680) shows a simple grammar of English questions. Note that % indicates that the rest of the line is a comment. Figure 15.9 (page 681) gives a simple dictionary of words and their parts of speech, which can be used with this grammar. The first rule for *question* allows for questions such as "What country borders Chile?" or "What large county bordering Paraguay borders Chile?" while the second rules allows for "What is bordering Chile?"

**Example 15.34** Consider the question "What large county bordering Paraguay borders Chile?" This is represented as a list of strings, one for each word.

For the grammar of Figure 15.8 (page 680), the dictionary of Figure 15.9 (page 681), and the definition of *name* of Figure 15.3 (page 660), the query

ask *noun_phrase(["large","country","bordering",*
*"Paraguay","borders","Chile"], R).*

has an answer

$$R = [\text{"bordering"}, \text{"Paraguay"}, \text{"borders"}, \text{"Chile"}]$$

meaning "large country" is a noun phrase.

Another answer is

$$R = [\text{"borders"}, \text{"Chile"}]$$

meaning "large country bordering Paraguay" is a noun phrase.

% A noun phrase is a determiner (or article, such as "the" or "a") followed by
% adjectives followed by a noun followed by an optional modifying phrase

$$
\begin{aligned}
&noun\_phrase(L_0, L_4) \leftarrow \\
&\quad det(L_0, L_1) \wedge \\
&\quad adjectives(L_1, L_2) \wedge \\
&\quad noun(L_2, L_3) \wedge \\
&\quad omp(L_3, L_4).
\end{aligned}
$$

% Adjectives consist of a (possibly empty) sequence of adjectives

$$
\begin{aligned}
&adjectives(L, L). \\
&adjectives(L_0, L_2) \leftarrow \\
&\quad adj(L_0, L_1) \wedge \\
&\quad adjectives(L_1, L_2).
\end{aligned}
$$

% A modifying phrase is a relation (verb or preposition) followed by a noun phrase

$$
\begin{aligned}
&mp(L_0, L_2) \leftarrow \\
&\quad reln(L_0, L_1) \wedge \\
&\quad noun\_phrase(L_1, L_2).
\end{aligned}
$$

% An optional modifying phrase is a modifying phrase or nothing

$$
\begin{aligned}
&omp(L, L). \\
&omp(L_0, L_1) \leftarrow mp(L_0, L_1).
\end{aligned}
$$

% Some simple questions are "What" and "What is" questions

$$
\begin{aligned}
&question(["What"|L_0], L_2) \leftarrow \\
&\quad noun\_phrase(L_0, L_1) \wedge \\
&\quad mp(L_1, L_2). \leftarrow \\
&question(["What", "is"|L_0], L_1) \leftarrow \\
&\quad mp(L_0, L_1).
\end{aligned}
$$

Figure 15.8: A context-free grammar for simple English questions

## 15.7.2 Augmenting the Grammar

A context-free grammar does not adequately express the complexity of the grammar of natural languages, such as English. Two mechanisms can be added to this grammar to make it more expressive:

- extra arguments to the non-terminal symbols
- arbitrary constraints on the rules.

The extra arguments enable us to do several things, including constructing a parse tree and representing a query to a database. The use of arbitrary arguments and conditions means that a definite-clause grammar can represent much more than a context-free grammar; it can represent anything computable by a Turing machine (see Exercise 15.13 (page 700)).

## 15.7.3 Building a Natural Language Interface to a Database

The preceding grammar can be augmented to implement a simple natural language interface to a database. Instead of transforming sub-phrases into parse trees, you can transform them directly into the entity the part of speech is about. To do this, let's make the following simplifying assumptions, which are not always true, but form a useful first approximation:

- Proper nouns (such as "Chile") correspond to individuals.
- **Nouns** (e.g., "country") and **adjectives** (e.g., "large") correspond to properties.
- **Verbs** (e.g., "borders") and **prepositions** (e.g., "next to") correspond to a binary relation between two individuals, the **subject** and the **object**.

In this case, a noun phrase represents an individual with a set of properties defining it. To answer a question, the system can find an individual that has

---

*det*(*L*, *L*).
*det*([*a* | *L*], *L*).
*det*([*the* | *L*], *L*).
*noun*(["*country*"|*L*], *L*).
*noun*(["*city*"|*L*], *L*).
*noun*([*N*|*L*], *L*) : −*name*(*E*,*N*).
*adj*(["*large*" | *L*], *L*).
*reln*(["*bordering*" | *L*], *L*).
*reln*(["*borders*" | *L*], *L*).
*reln*(["*next*", "*to*" | *L*], *L*).
*reln*(["*the*", "*name*", "*of*" | *L*], *L*).

Figure 15.9: A simple dictionary

these properties. A modifying phrase (such as a propositional phrase or relative clause) describes an individual in terms of a relation with another individual. The following assumes only the linguistic structure required to implement database queries from limited natural language.

**Example 15.35** In the sentence "What large country borders Chile?" the phrase "large country" is the subject of the verb 'borders" and "Chile" is the object. Assume the geographic database of Figure 15.2 (page 658). For the individual $S$ that is the subject, $large(S)$ and $country(S)$ are true. The object is the individual *chile* and the verb specifies $borders(S, chile)$. Thus, the question "'What large country borders Chile?" can be converted into the query

$$\text{ask } large(S) \wedge country(S) \wedge borders(S, chile)$$

where *large* is a predicate that might be true of countries larger than two million square kilometers.

The question "What is the name of the capital of a Spanish-speaking country that borders Argentina?" could be translated into asking for a value of $S$ for the query

$$\begin{aligned}\text{ask } & name(C, S) \wedge capital(X, C) \wedge language(X, spanish) \\ & \wedge borders(X, argentina).\end{aligned}$$

Figure 15.10 (page 683) shows a simple grammar that parses an English question and answers it at the same time. This ignores most of the grammar of English, such as the differences between prepositions and verbs or between determiners and adjectives, and makes a guess at the meaning, even if the question is not grammatical. Adjectives, nouns, and noun phrases refer to an individual. The extra argument to the predicates is an individual which satisfies the adjectives and nouns. Here an *mp* is a modifying phrase, which could be a prepositional phrase or a relative clause. A *reln*, either a verb or a preposition, is a relation between two individuals, the subject and the object, so these are extra arguments to the *reln* predicate.

**Example 15.36** Suppose $question(Q, A)$ means $A$ is an answer to question $Q$, where a question is a list of words. The following provides some ways questions can be asked from the clauses of Figure 15.10 (page 683), even given the very limited vocabulary used there. The following ignores punctuation.

The following rule is used to answer questions such as "What is next to Chile?"

$$\begin{aligned}& question(["What", "is" \mid L_0], Ind) \leftarrow \\ & \quad mp(L_0, [\,], Ind).\end{aligned}$$

Note that [] means that in the question there is nothing after the modifying phrase.

The following rule is used to answer questions such as "What is a large Spanish-speaking country next to Chile?"

$$question(["What", "is" \mid L], Ind) \leftarrow$$

% A noun phrase is a determiner followed by adjectives followed by a noun
% followed by an optional modifying phrase, all about the same individual

$noun\_phrase(L_1, L_4, Ind) \leftarrow$
$\quad adjectives(L_1, L_2, Ind) \wedge$
$\quad noun(L_2, L_3, Ind) \wedge$
$\quad omp(L_3, L_4, Ind).$

% Adjectives consist of a sequence of adjectives about the same individual

$adjectives(L_0, L_2, Ind) \leftarrow$
$\quad adj(L_0, L_1, Ind) \wedge$
$\quad adjectives(L_1, L_2, Ind).$
$adjectives(L, L, Ind).$

% A modifying phrase/relative clause is a relation (verb or preposition) fol-
% lowed by a noun phrase

$mp(L_0, L_2, Subject) \leftarrow$
$\quad reln(L_0, L_1, Subject, Object) \wedge$
$\quad noun\_phrase(L_1, L_2, Object).$

% An optional modifying phrase is either a modifying phrase or nothing

$omp(L_0, L_1, Ind) \leftarrow mp(L_0, L_1, Ind).$
$omp(L, L, Ind).$

% $adj(L_0, L_1, Ind)$ is true if $L_0 - L_1$ is an adjective that is true of *Ind*

$adj(["large"|L], L, Ind) \leftarrow large(Ind).$
$adj([LangName, "speaking"|L], L, Ind) \leftarrow$
$\quad name(Lang, LangName) \wedge language(Ind, Lang).$
$adj([a \mid L], L, Ind).$

% $noun(L_0, L_1, Ind)$ is true if $L_0 - L_1$ is a noun that is true of *Ind*

$noun(["country"|L], L, Ind) \leftarrow country(Ind).$
$noun([N|L], L, E) : -name(E, N).$

% $reln(L_0, L_1, Sub, Obj)$ is true if $L_0 - L_1$ is a relation on individuals *Sub* and *Obj*

$reln(["borders"|L], L, Sub, Obj) \leftarrow borders(Sub, Obj).$
$reln(["bordering"|L], L, Sub, Obj) \leftarrow borders(Sub, Obj).$
$reln(["the", "capital", "of"|L], L, Sub, Obj) \leftarrow capital(Obj, Sub).$
$reln(["the", "name", "of"|L], L, Sub, Obj) \leftarrow name(Obj, Sub).$

Figure 15.10: Simple grammar that directly answers a question

$noun\_phrase(L, [\,], Ind).$

The following rule allows it to answer questions, such as "What large country bordering Paraguay borders Chile?"

$$question(["What" \mid L_0], L_2, Ind) \leftarrow$$
$$noun\_phrase(L_0, L_1, Ind) \wedge$$
$$mp(L_1, L_2, Ind).$$

The preceding grammar directly found an answer to the natural language question. Two problems with this way of answering questions are:

- It is difficult to separate the cases where the program could not parse the language from the case where there were no answers; in both cases the answer is "no".

- When there is ambiguity, meaning multiple legal parses, and there are possibly multiple answers for each parse, it gives all of the answers for all of the parses, without distinguishing them.

These properties make it difficult to debug the programs that use this style.

An alternative is, instead of directly querying the knowledge base while parsing, to build a **logical form** of the natural language – a logical proposition that conveys the meaning of the utterance – before asking it of the knowledge base. The semantic form can be used for other tasks, such as telling the system knowledge, paraphrasing natural language, or even translating it into a different language.

You can construct a query by allowing noun phrases to return an individual and a list of constraints imposed by the noun phrase on the individual. Appropriate grammar rules are specified in Figure 15.11 (page 685), and they are used with the dictionary of Figure 15.12 (page 686).

$$noun\_phrase(L_0, L_1, Ind, C_0, C_1)$$

means that list $L_1$ is an ending of list $L_0$, and the words in $L_0$ before $L_1$ form a noun phrase. This noun phrase refers to the individual *Ind*. $C_1$ is an ending of $C_0$, and the formulas in $C_0$ before $C_1$ are the constraints on the individual *Ind* imposed by the noun phrase.

Procedurally, $L_0$ is the list of words to be parsed, and $L_1$ is the list of remaining words after the noun phrase. $C_1$ is the list of conditions coming into the noun phrase, and $C_0$ is $C_1$ with the extra conditions imposed by the noun-phrase added.

**Example 15.37** The query

ask $noun\_phrase(["a", "Spanish", "speaking", "country",$
$"bordering", "Argentina"], [\,], E_1, C_0, [\,]).$

returns

$$C_0 = [language(E_1, A), name(A, "Spanish"), country(E_1), borders(E_1, argentina)].$$

The query

ask $mp(["the", "name", "of", "the", "capital", "of", "a", "country", "bordering", "Argentina"], [\,], Ind, C_0, [\,])$.

returns

$$C_0 = [name(A, Ind), capital(B, A), country(B), borders(B, argentina)].$$

If the elements of list $C_0$ are queried against a database that uses these relations and constants, as in Figure 15.2 (page 658), they can return a Spanish-speaking country that borders Argentina or the name of the capital of a country bordering Argentina. In Prolog, the built-in predicate *call* queries an atom.

% A noun phrase is a determiner followed by adjectives followed by a noun
% followed by an optional modifying phrase

$$noun\_phrase(L_0, L_4, Ind, C_0, C_4) \leftarrow$$
$$det(L_0, L_1, Ind, C_0, C_1) \wedge$$
$$adjectives(L_1, L_2, Ind, C_1, C_2) \wedge$$
$$noun(L_2, L_3, Ind, C_2, C_3) \wedge$$
$$omp(L_3, L_4, Ind, C_3, C_4).$$

% Adjectives consist of a sequence of adjectives.

$$adjectives(L, L, Ind, C, C).$$
$$adjectives(L_0, L_2, Ind, C_0, C_2) \leftarrow$$
$$adj(L_0, L_1, Ind, C_0, C_1) \wedge$$
$$adjectives(L_1, L_2, Ind, C_1, C_2).$$

% A modifying phrase is a relation followed by a noun phrase

$$mp(L_0, L_2, Sub, C_0, C_2) \leftarrow$$
$$relation(L_0, L_1, Sub, Obj, C_0, C_1) \wedge$$
$$noun\_phrase(L_1, L_2, Obj, C_1, C_2).$$

% An optional modifying phrase is either nothing or a modifying phrase

$$omp(L, L, Ind, C, C).$$
$$omp(L_0, L_1, Ind, C_0, C_1) \leftarrow mp(L_0, L_1, Ind, C_0, C_1).$$

Figure 15.11: Part of a grammar that constructs a query

### 15.7.4 Comparison with Large Language Models

The preceding grammars provide a different way to answer natural language queries than the **large language models** discussed in Section 8.5.5 (page 364). The differences in aims were discussed in the box on page 675.

The large language models, such as the **GPT** family (page 365), can be used to answer the questions about the geography of South America, for example. The main differences are:

- GPT models give a probabilistic prediction of the next word. The next word can be sampled, and the prediction can be repeated to give a natural language answer. The grammar of the previous section directly answers the question, giving a symbolic answer, designed for subsequent reasoning.

- The preceding grammar can be used to give all the answers and then stop when there are no more answers, whereas GPT models predict answers with a probability or sample from the distribution of answers.

- GPT models provide each answer for each parse without distinguishing the parses, similar to the grammar that directly answers questions, shown in Figure 15.10 (page 683). The grammar of Figure 15.11 can be

```
det(L, L, O, C, C).
det(["a" | T], T, O, C, C).
det(["the" | T], T, O, C, C).
noun(["country"|L], L, Ind, [country(Ind)|C], C).
noun(["city"|L], L, Ind, [city(Ind)|C], C).
noun([N|L], L, Ind, C, C) :- name(Ind, N).
adj(["large"|L], L, Ind, [large(Ind)|C], C).
adj([LangName, "speaking"|L], L, Ind,
    [language(Ind, Lang), name(Lang, LangName)|C], C).
reln(["borders"|L], L, Sub, Obj, [borders(Sub, Obj)|C], C).
reln(["bordering"|L], L, Sub, Obj, [borders(Sub, Obj)|C], C).
reln(["next", "to"|L], L, Sub, Obj, [borders(Sub, Obj)|C], C).
reln(["the", "capital", "of"|L], L, Sub, Obj, [capital(Obj, Sub)|C], C).
reln(["the", "name", "of"|L], L, Sub, Obj, [name(Obj, Sub)|C], C).
```

Figure 15.12: A dictionary for constructing a query

used to separately provide the parses and the answers for each parse, which might be useful for some applications.

- Modern large language models can output realistic-looking queries in, for example, SQL or Datalog. To actually use a generated query to interface to a database requires the language model to access the database schema to find out the predicates, their arity and meaning, etc., as well as to the database itself, to disambiguate constants such as "Chile" (which can mean the country, the football team, or is a spelling of the chili pepper).

- The preceding grammars can fail if the user does not use the appropriate grammar and vocabulary, whereas GPT models are very forgiving in the use of language.

- GPT models have a much broader coverage and can converse on arbitrary topics, whereas the preceding grammars need to be engineered for each domain.

Depending on your needs, on whether you are prepared to engineer a system for each domain, and whether the users can be trained to use the assumed grammar, either one of these techniques might be more useful.

## 15.8 Equality

Sometimes it is useful to use more than one term to name a single individual. For example, the terms $4 * 4$, $2^4$, $273 - 257$, and 16 may denote the same number. Sometimes, you want to have each name refer to a different individual. For example, you may want unique names for different courses in a university. Sometimes you do not know whether or not two names denote the same individual – for example, whether the 8 a.m. delivery person is the same as the 1 p.m. delivery person.

This section considers the role of **equality**, which allows us to represent whether or not two terms denote the same individual in the world. Note that, in the definite-clause language presented earlier in the chapter, all of the answers were valid whether or not terms denoted the same individuals.

Equality is a special predicate symbol with a standard domain-independent intended interpretation.

Term $t_1$ **equals** term $t_2$, written $t_1 = t_2$, is true in interpretation $I$ if $t_1$ and $t_2$ denote the same individual in $I$.

Equality does *not* mean similarity. If $a$ and $b$ are constants and $a = b$, it is not the case that there are two things that are similar or even identical. Rather, it means there is one thing with two names.

**Example 15.38** Consider the world consisting of two chairs given in Figure 15.13 (page 688). In this world it is *not* true that $chair1 = chair2$, even though the two chairs may be identical in all respects; without representing the exact position of the chairs, they cannot be distinguished. It may be the case that *chairOnRight* = *chair*2. It is not the case that the chair on the right is *similar* to chair2. It *is* chair2.

### 15.8.1 Allowing Equality Assertions

Without allowing equality in the head of clauses, the only thing that is equal to a term in all interpretations is itself.

It is often useful to be able to assert or infer that two terms denote the same individual, such as *chairOnRight* = *chair*2. To allow this, the representation and reasoning system must be able to derive what follows from a knowledge base that includes clauses with equality in the head of clauses. There are two ways of doing this. The first is to axiomatize equality like any other predicate. The other is to build special-purpose inference machinery for equality.

If $t_1 = t_2$, any occurrence of $t_1$ can be replaced by $t_2$. Equality can thus be treated as a **rewrite rule**, substituting equals for equals. This approach works best if you can select a **canonical representation** for each individual, which is a term that other representations for that individual can be mapped into.

One classic example is the representation of numbers. There are many terms that represent the same number (e.g., $4 * 4$, $13 + 3$, $273 - 257$, $2^4$, $4^2$, 16), but typically the sequence of digits (in base 10) is used as the canonical representation of the number.

Universities invented student numbers to provide a canonical representation for each student. Different students with the same name are distinguishable and different names for the same person can be mapped to the person's student number.

Each rewrite rule should make the description closer to the canonical representation. In theorem proving, using equality as rewriting rules is called **paramodulation**. Determining the canonical representation is sometimes referred to as determining the **identity** of the description (e.g., determining the identity of a student who submitted as assignment without a name).

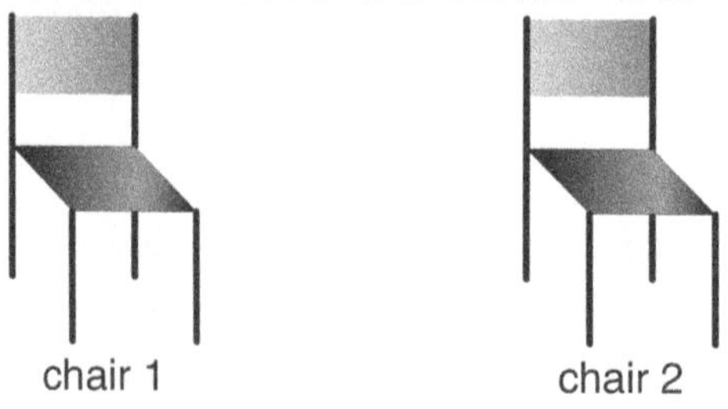


Figure 15.13: Two chairs

### 15.8.2 Unique Names Assumption

Instead of being agnostic about the equality of each term and expecting the user to axiomatize which names denote the same individual and which denote different individuals, it is often easier to have the convention that different ground terms denote different individuals.

**Example 15.39** Consider a student database example where a student must have two courses as science electives. Suppose a student has passed $math302$ and $psyc303$; then you only know whether they have passed two courses if you know $math302 \neq psyc303$. That is, the constants $math302$ and $psyc303$ denote different courses. Thus, you must know which course numbers denote different courses. Rather than writing $n * (n-1)/2$ inequality axioms for $n$ individuals, it may be better to have the convention that every course number denotes a different course and thus the use of inequality axioms is avoided.

Under the **unique names assumption (UNA)**, distinct ground terms denote different individuals. That is, for every pair of distinct ground terms $t_1$ and $t_2$, it assumes $t_1 \neq t_2$, where "$\neq$" means "not equal to."

The unique names assumption is very useful for database applications. You may not want to have to state that, for example, $kim \neq sam$ and $kim \neq chris$ and $chris \neq sam$, and similarly for each pair of entities.

The unique names assumption does *not* follow from the semantics for the definite clause language (page 650). As far as that semantics was concerned, distinct ground terms $t_1$ and $t_2$ could denote the same individual or could denote different individuals.

With the unique names assumption, inequality ($\neq$) can be in the bodies of clauses.

Ground terms are different if and only if they do not unify. This is not the case for non-ground terms. For example, $a \neq X$ has some instances that are true – for example, when $X$ has value $b$ – and an instance which is false, namely, when $X$ has value $a$.

Sometimes the unique names assumption is inappropriate – for example, $2+2 \neq 4$ is wrong, and it may not be the case that $clark\_kent \neq superman$.

#### Top-Down Proof Procedure for the Unique Names Assumption

A top-down proof procedure (page 665) incorporating the unique names assumption should not treat inequality as just another predicate, mainly because too many different individuals exist for any given individual.

If there is a subgoal (page 191) of the form $t_1 \neq t_2$, for terms $t_1$ and $t_2$ there are three cases:

1. $t_1$ and $t_2$ do not unify. In this case, $t_1 \neq t_2$ succeeds.

   For example, the inequality $f(X, a, g(X)) \neq f(t(X), X, b)$ succeeds because the two terms do not unify.

2. $t_1$ and $t_2$ are identical, including having the same variables in the same positions. In this case, $t_1 \neq t_2$ fails.

   For example, $f(X, a, g(X)) \neq f(X, a, g(X))$ fails.

   Note that, for any pair of *ground* terms, one of these first two cases must occur.

3. Otherwise, there are instances of $t_1 \neq t_2$ that succeed and instances of $t_1 \neq t_2$ that fail.

   For example, consider the subgoal $f(W, a, g(Z)) \neq f(t(X), X, Y)$. The most general unifier of $f(W, a, g(Z))$ and $f(t(X), X, Y)$ is $\{X/a,\ W/t(a),\ Y/g(Z)\}$. Some instances of the inequality, such as the ground instances consistent with the unifier, should fail. Any instance that is not consistent with the unifier should succeed. Unlike other goals, you do not want to enumerate every instance that succeeds because that would mean unifying $X$ with every function and constant different than $a$, as well as enumerating every pair of values for $Y$ and $Z$ where $Y$ is different than $g(Z)$.

The top-down proof procedure can be extended to incorporate the unique names assumption. Inequalities of the first type can succeed and those of the second type can fail. Inequalities of the third type can be **delayed**, waiting for subsequent goals to unify variables so that one of the first two cases occur. To delay a goal in the proof procedure of Figure 15.5 (page 666), when selecting an atom in the body of the answer clause $G$, the algorithm should select one of the atoms that is not being delayed. If there are no other atoms to select, and neither of the first two cases is applicable, the query should succeed. There is always an instance of the inequality that succeeds, namely, the instance where every variable gets a different constant that does not appear anywhere else. When this occurs, the user has to be careful when interpreting the free variables in the answer. The answer does not mean that it is true for every instance of the free variables, but rather that it is true for some instance.

**Example 15.40** Consider the rules that specify whether a student has passed at least two courses:

$$
\begin{aligned}
& \mathit{passed\_two\_courses}(S) \leftarrow \\
& \quad C_1 \neq C_2 \wedge \\
& \quad \mathit{passed}(S, C_1) \wedge \\
& \quad \mathit{passed}(S, C_2). \\
& \mathit{passed}(S, C) \leftarrow \\
& \quad \mathit{grade}(S, C, M) \wedge \\
& \quad M \geq 50. \\
& \mathit{grade}(\mathit{sam}, \mathit{engl}101, 87). \\
& \mathit{grade}(\mathit{sam}, \mathit{phys}101, 89).
\end{aligned}
$$

For the query

ask *passed_two_courses*(*sam*)

the subgoal $C_1 \neq C_2$ cannot be determined and so must be delayed. The top-down proof procedure can, instead, select *passed*(*sam*, $C_1$), which binds *engl*101 to $C_1$. It can then call *passed*(*sam*, $C_2$), which in turn calls *grade*(*sam*, $C_2$, $M$), which can succeed with substitution $\{C_2/engl101, M/87\}$. At this stage, the variables for the delayed inequality are bound enough to determine that the inequality should fail.

Another clause can be chosen for *grade*(*sam*, $C_2$, $M$), returning substitution $\{C_2/phys101, M/89\}$. The variables in the delayed inequality are bound enough to test the inequality and, this time, the inequality succeeds. It can then go on to prove that $89 > 50$, and the goal succeeds.

One question that may arise from this example is "why not simply make the inequality the last call, because then it does not need to be delayed?" There are two reasons. First, it may be more efficient to delay. In this example, the delayed inequality can be tested before checking whether $87 > 50$. Although this particular inequality test may be fast, in many cases substantial computation can be avoided by noticing violated inequalities as soon as possible. Second, if a subproof were to return one of the values before it is bound, the proof procedure should still remember the inequality constraint, so that any future unification that violates the constraint can fail.

## 15.9 Complete Knowledge Assumption

The complete knowledge assumption, as discussed in Section 5.7 (page 207), is the assumption that any statement that does not follow from a knowledge base is false. It also allows for proof by **negation as failure**.

The complete knowledge assumption for logic programs with variables and functions symbols requires axioms for equality, and the domain closure, and a more sophisticated notion of the completion.

**Example 15.41** Suppose a *student* relation is defined by

*student*(*huan*).
*student*(*manpreet*).
*student*(*karan*).

The complete knowledge assumption would say that these three are the only students:

$$student(X) \leftrightarrow X = huan \vee X = manpreet \vee X = karan.$$

That is, if $X$ is *huan*, *manpreet*, or *karan*, then $X$ is a student, and if $X$ is a student, $X$ must be one of these three. In particular, *kim* is not a student.

Concluding $\neg student(kim)$ requires proving $kim \neq huan \wedge kim \neq manpreet \wedge kim \neq karan$. To derive the inequalities, the unique names assumption (page 689) is required.

The complete knowledge assumption includes the unique names assumption.

The **Clark normal form** of the clause

$$p(t_1, \ldots, t_k) \leftarrow B.$$

is the clause

$$p(V_1, \ldots, V_k) \leftarrow \exists W_1 \ldots \exists W_m \; V_1 = t_1 \land \ldots \land V_k = t_k \land B.$$

where $V_1, \ldots, V_k$ are $k$ variables that did not appear in the original clause, and $W_1, \ldots, W_m$ are the original variables in the clause. "$\exists$" means "there exists" (page 649). When the clause is an **atomic clause** (page 185), $B$ is *true*.

Suppose all of the clauses for $p$ are put into Clark normal form, with the same set of introduced variables, giving

$$p(V_1, \ldots, V_k) \leftarrow B_1.$$

$$\vdots$$

$$p(V_1, \ldots, V_k) \leftarrow B_n.$$

which is equivalent to

$$p(V_1, \ldots, V_k) \leftarrow B_1 \lor \ldots \lor B_n.$$

This implication is logically equivalent to the set of original clauses.

**Clark's completion** of predicate $p$ is the equivalence

$$\forall V_1 \ldots \forall V_k \; p(V_1, \ldots, V_k) \leftrightarrow B_1 \lor \ldots \lor B_n$$

where **negation as failure** ($\sim$) in bodies is replaced by standard logical negation ($\neg$). The completion means that $p(V_1, \ldots, V_k)$ is true if and only if at least one body $B_i$ is true.

**Clark's completion** of a knowledge base consists of the completion of every predicate symbol.

**Example 15.42** For the clauses

$$student(huan).$$
$$student(manpreet).$$
$$student(karan).$$

the Clark normal form is

$$student(V) \leftarrow V = huan.$$
$$student(V) \leftarrow V = manpreet.$$
$$student(V) \leftarrow V = karan.$$

which is equivalent to

$$student(V) \leftarrow V = huan \lor V = manpreet \lor V = karan.$$

The completion of the *student* predicate is

$$\forall V \; student(V) \leftrightarrow V = huan \lor V = manpreet \lor V = karan.$$

**Example 15.43** Consider the following recursive definition:

$$\begin{aligned}&passed\_each([\,], St, MinPass).\\&passed\_each([C \mid R], St, MinPass) \leftarrow\\&\quad passed(St, C, MinPass) \land\\&\quad passed\_each(R, St, MinPass).\end{aligned}$$

In Clark normal form, with variable renaming, this can be written as

$$\begin{aligned}&passed\_each(L, S, M) \leftarrow L = [\,].\\&passed\_each(L, S, M) \leftarrow\\&\quad \exists C\, \exists R\, L = [C \mid R] \land\\&\quad passed(S, C, M) \land\\&\quad passed\_each(R, S, M).\end{aligned}$$

Clark's completion of *passed_each* is

$$\begin{aligned}&\forall L\, \forall S\, \forall M\, passed\_each(L, S, M) \leftrightarrow L = [\,] \lor\\&\quad \exists C\, \exists R\, (L = [C \mid R] \land\\&\quad passed(S, C, M) \land\\&\quad passed\_each(R, S, M)).\end{aligned}$$

Under the complete knowledge assumption, relations that cannot be defined using only definite clauses can now be defined.

**Example 15.44** Suppose you are given a database of $course(C)$ that is true if $C$ is a course, and $enrolled(S, C)$, which means that student $S$ is enrolled in course $C$. Without the complete knowledge assumption, you cannot define $empty\_course(C)$, which is true if there are no students enrolled in course $C$. This is because there is always a model of the knowledge base where every course has someone enrolled.

Using negation as failure, $empty\_course(C)$ can be defined by

$$\begin{aligned}&empty\_course(C) \leftarrow course(C) \land \sim has\_enrollment(C).\\&has\_enrollment(C) \leftarrow enrolled(S, C).\end{aligned}$$

The completion of this is

$$\begin{aligned}&\forall C\, empty\_course(C) \leftrightarrow course(C) \land \neg has\_enrollment(C).\\&\forall C\, has\_enrollment(C) \leftrightarrow \exists S\, enrolled(S, C).\end{aligned}$$

As a word of caution, you should be very careful when you include free variables within negation as failure. They usually do not mean what you think they might. The predicate *has_enrollment* was introduced in the previous example to avoid having a free variable within a negation as failure. See Exercise 15.15 (page 700).

### 15.9.1 Complete Knowledge Assumption Proof Procedures

The top-down proof procedure for negation as failure with the variables and functions is much like the top-down procedure for propositional negation as failure (page 213). As with the unique names assumption (page 689), a problem arises when there are free variables in negated goals.

**Example 15.45** Consider the clauses

$$p(X) \leftarrow \sim q(X) \wedge r(X).$$
$$q(a).$$
$$q(b).$$
$$r(d).$$

According to the semantics, there is only one answer to the query ask $p(X)$, which is $X = d$. As $r(d)$ follows, so does $\sim q(d)$ and so $p(d)$ logically follows from the knowledge base.

When the top-down proof procedure encounters $\sim q(X)$, it should not try to prove $q(X)$, which succeeds (with substitution $\{X/a\}$). This would make the goal $p(X)$ fail, when it should succeed with $X = d$. Thus, the proof procedure would be incomplete. Note that, if the knowledge base contained $s(X) \leftarrow \sim q(X)$, the failure of $q(X)$ would mean $s(X)$ succeeding. Thus, with negation as failure, incompleteness leads to unsoundness.

As with the unique names assumption (Section 15.8.2 (page 689)), a sound proof procedure should delay the negated subgoal until the free variable is bound.

A more complicated top-down procedure is required when there are calls to negation as failure with free variables:

- Negation-as-failure goals that contain free variables must not be selected in the negation-as-failure procedure of Figure 5.12 (page 213) until the variables become bound.
- If the variables never become bound, the goal **flounders**. In this case, you cannot conclude anything about the goal. The following example shows that you should do something more sophisticated for the case of floundering goals.

**Example 15.46** Consider the clauses

$$p(X) \leftarrow \sim q(X)$$
$$q(X) \leftarrow \sim r(X)$$
$$r(a)$$

and the query

ask $p(X)$.

The completion of the knowledge base is

$$p(X) \leftrightarrow \neg q(X)$$

$$q(X) \leftrightarrow \neg r(X)$$
$$r(X) \leftrightarrow X = a.$$

Substituting $X = a$ for $r$ gives $q(X) \leftrightarrow \neg X = a$, and so $p(X) \leftrightarrow X = a$. Thus, there is one answer, namely $X = a$, but delaying the goal will not help find it. A proof procedure should analyze the cases for which the goal failed to derive this answer. However, such a procedure is beyond the scope of this book.

## 15.10 Social Impact

There are numerous applications of logic programming. It is used in the Java virtual machine type checker: "The type checker enforces type rules that are specified by means of Prolog clauses. English language text is used to describe the type rules in an informal way, while the Prolog clauses provide a formal specification" [Lindholm et al., 2022]. Prolog was used for the parser for the clues in the IBM **Watson** system which beat the human world champion in the TV quiz show "Jeopardy!" [Lally et al., 2012].

The idea of a **robot scientist** [King et al., 2004, 2009a; Sparkes et al., 2010] is that a computer creates and tests hypotheses. The robot scientist **Adam** [King et al., 2009b] automatically generates functional genomics hypotheses about yeast and tests the hypotheses using a physical robot that automates a laboratory. It represents the hypotheses using a logic program. A hypothesis in the form of a logic program allows it to be interpreted and also the consequences can be tested. The robot created a hypothesis, physically runs an experiment to test the hypothesis, interprets the results, and repeats.

## 15.11 Review

The following are the main points you should have learned from this chapter:

- In domains characterized by individuals and relations, constants denoting individuals and predicate symbols denoting relations can be reasoned with to determine what is true in the domain.
- Datalog is a logical language with constants, universally quantified variables, relations, and rules.
- Substitutions are used to make instances of atoms and rules. Unification makes atoms identical for use in proofs.
- Function symbols are used to denote a possibly infinite set of individuals described in terms of other individuals. Function symbols can be used to build data structures.
- Definite-clause grammars can be used for flexible language natural language processing in cases where the language used can be controlled, such as natural language interfaces to databases.
- Equality between terms means that the terms denote the same individual.

- Clark's completion can be used to define the semantics of negation as failure under the complete knowledge assumption.
- Logic programming is useful for creating specifications, parsers, and formal scientific hypotheses.

## 15.12 References and Further Reading

Datalog and logic programs are described by Kowalski [2014], Sterling and Shapiro [1994], and Garcia-Molina et al. [2009]. The history of logic programming is described by Kowalski [1988] and Colmerauer and Roussel [1996].

The work on negation as failure (page 207), as well as the unique names assumption (page 689), is based on the work of Clark [1978]. See the book by Lloyd [1987] for a formal treatment of logic programming in general and negation as failure in particular. Apt and Bol [1994] provide a survey of different techniques for handling negation as failure.

Jurafsky and Martin [2023] provide an excellent introduction to computational linguistics. The use of definite clauses for describing natural language is described by Dahl [1994] and Pereira and Shieber [2002].

## 15.13 Exercises

**Exercise 15.1** Consider a domain with two individuals (✂ and ☎), two predicate symbols ($p$ and $q$), and three constants ($a$, $b$, and $c$). The knowledge base $KB$ is defined by

$$p(X) \leftarrow q(X).$$
$$q(a).$$

(a) Give one interpretation that is a model of $KB$.

(b) Give one interpretation that is not a model of $KB$.

(c) How many interpretations are there? Give a brief justification for your answer.

(d) How many of these interpretations are models of $KB$? Give a brief justification for your answer.

**Exercise 15.2** Suppose a language has constant symbols $a$, $b$, and $c$; predicate symbols $p$ and $q$; and no function symbols. The following knowledge bases are built from this language:

| $KB_1$ | $KB_2$ | $KB_3$ |
|---|---|---|
| $p(a).$ | $p(X) \leftarrow q(X).$ | $p(X) \leftarrow q(X).$<br>$p(a).\quad q(b).$ |

Consider possible interpretations for this language of the form $I = \langle D, \pi, \phi \rangle$, where $D = \{$✂, ☎, ✈, ✎$\}$.

(a) How many interpretations with the four domain elements exist for our simple language? Give a brief justification for your answer. [Hint: Determine the number of possible assignments $\phi$ for the constant symbols. Consider how many extensions predicates $p$ and $q$ can have to determine how many assignments $\pi$ exist.] Do not try to enumerate all possible interpretations.
(b) Of the interpretations outlined above, how many are models of $KB_1$? Give a brief justification for your answer.
(c) Of the interpretations outlined above, how many are models of $KB_2$? Give a brief justification for your answer.
(d) Of the interpretations outlined above, how many are models of $KB_3$? Give a brief justification for your answer.

**Exercise 15.3** Consider the following knowledge base:

$$
\begin{array}{lll}
r(a). & r(e). & p(c). \\
q(b). & s(a,b). & s(d,b). \\
s(e,d). & p(X) \leftarrow q(X) \wedge r(X). & q(X) \leftarrow s(X,Y) \wedge q(Y).
\end{array}
$$

Show the set of ground atomic consequences derivable from this knowledge base. Use the bottom-up proof procedure (page 662) assuming, at each iteration, the first applicable clause is selected in the order shown. Furthermore, applicable constant substitutions are chosen in "alphabetic order" if more than one applies to a given clause; for example, if $X/a$ and $X/b$ are both applicable for a clause at some iteration, derive $q(a)$ first. In what order are consequences derived?

**Exercise 15.4** Consider the following knowledge base:

*has_access(X, library)* ← *student(X).*
*has_access(X, library)* ← *faculty(X).*
*has_access(X, library)* ← *has_access(Y, library)* ∧ *parent(Y, X).*
*has_access(X, office)* ← *has_keys(X).*
*faculty(diane).* *faculty(ming).* *student(william).*
*student(mary).* *parent(diane, karen).* *parent(diane, robyn).*
*parent(susan, sarah).* *parent(sarah, ariel).* *parent(karen, chelsey).*
*parent(karen, todd).*

(a) Provide an SLD derivation of the query *has_access(todd, library)*, similar to Figure 15.6 (page 668).
(b) The query *has_access(mary, library)* has two SLD derivations. Give both, but do not show the clauses chosen or the substitutions.
(c) Is there a derivation for *has_access(ariel, library)*? Explain why, or why not.
(d) Explain why the set of answers to the query *has_access(X, office)* is empty.
(e) Suppose the following clause is added to the knowledge base:

*has_keys(X)* ← *faculty(X).*

What are the answers to the query *has_access(X, office)*?

**Exercise 15.5** What is the result of the following applications of substitutions?

(a) $f(A, X, Y, X, Y)\{A/X, Z/b, Y/c\}$.

(b) $yes(F,L) \leftarrow append(F,c(L,nil),c(l,c(i,c(s,c(t,nil)))))$
$\{F/c(l,X_1),Y_1/c(L,nil),A_1/l,Z_1/c(i,c(s,c(t,nil)))\}$.
(c) $append(c(A_1,X_1),Y_1,c(A_1,Z_1)) \leftarrow append(X_1,Y_1,Z_1)$
$\{F/c(l,X_1),Y_1/c(L,nil),A_1/l,Z_1/c(i,c(s,c(t,nil)))\}$.

**Exercise 15.6** Give a most general unifier of the following pairs of expressions:

(a) $p(f(X),g(g(b)))$ and $p(Z,g(Y))$
(b) $g(f(X),r(X),t)$ and $g(W,r(Q),Q)$
(c) $bar(val(X,bb),Z)$ and $bar(P,P)$

**Exercise 15.7** For each of the following pairs of atoms, either give a most general unifier or explain why one does not exist:

(a) $p(X,Y,a,b,W)$ and $p(E,c,F,G,F)$
(b) $p(Y,a,b,Y)$ and $p(c,F,G,F)$
(c) $foo(Z,[a,z|X],X)$ and $foo([a,m|W],W,[i,n,g])$
(d) $ap(F0,c(b,c(B0,L0)),c(a,c(b,c(a,emp))))$ and $ap(c(H1,T1),L1,c(H1,R1))$.

**Exercise 15.8** List all of the ground atomic logical consequences of the following knowledge base:

$q(Y) \leftarrow s(Y,Z) \wedge r(Z)$. $\quad p(X) \leftarrow q(f(X))$. $\quad s(f(a),b)$.
$s(f(b),b)$. $\quad s(c,b)$. $\quad r(b)$.

**Exercise 15.9** Consider the following logic program:

$rd(cons(H,cons(H,T)),T)$.
$rd(cons(H,T),cons(H,R)) \leftarrow rd(T,R)$.

Give a top-down derivation, showing all substitutions for the query

ask $rd(cons(a,cons(cons(a,X),cons(B,cons(c,Z)))),W)$.

What is the answer corresponding to this derivation?

Is there a second answer? If yes, show the derivation; if not, explain why.

**Exercise 15.10** Consider the following logic program:

$ap(emp,L,L)$.
$ap(c(H,T),L,c(H,R)) \leftarrow ap(T,L,R)$.
$adj(A,B,L) \leftarrow ap(F,c(A,c(B,E)),L)$.

(a) Give a top-down derivation (including all substitutions) for one answer to the query

ask $adj(b,Y,c(a,c(b,c(b,c(a,emp)))))$.

(b) Are there any other answers? If so, explain where a different choice could be made in the derivation in the previous answer, and continue the derivation, showing another answer. If there are no other answers, explain why not.

[You are meant to do this exercise as if you were a computer, without knowing what the symbols mean. If you want to give a meaning to this program, you could read *ap* as *append*, *c* as *cons*, *emp* as *empty*, and *adj* as *adjacent*.]

**Exercise 15.11** The aim of this question is to get practice writing simple logic programs.

(a) Write a relation $remove(E, L, R)$ that is true if $R$ is the list resulting from removing one instance of $E$ from list $L$. The relation is false if $E$ is not a member of $L$.

(b) Give all of the answers to the following queries:

$$\text{ask } remove(a, [b, a, d, a], R).$$
$$\text{ask } remove(E, [b, a, d, a], R).$$
$$\text{ask } remove(E, L, [b, a, d]).$$
$$\text{ask } remove(p(X), [a, p(a), p(p(a)), p(p(p(a)))], R).$$

(c) Write a relation $subsequence(L1, L2)$ that is true if list $L1$ contains a subset of the elements of $L2$ in the same order.

(d) How many different proofs are there for each of the following queries:

$$\text{ask } subsequence([a, d], [b, a, d, a]).$$
$$\text{ask } subsequence([b, a], [b, a, d, a]).$$
$$\text{ask } subsequence([X, Y], [b, a, d, a]).$$
$$\text{ask } subsequence(S, [b, a, d, a]).$$

Explain why there are that many.

**Exercise 15.12** In this question, you are to write a definite-clause knowledge base for the design of custom video presentations.

Assume that the video is annotated using the relation

$$segment(SegId, Duration, Covers)$$

where *SegId* is an identifier for the segment. (In a real application this will be enough information to extract the video segment.) *Duration* is the running time of the segment (in seconds). *Covers* is a list of topics covered by the video segment. An example of a video annotation is the database

$$segment(seg0, 10, [welcome]).$$
$$segment(seg1, 30, [skiing, views]).$$
$$segment(seg2, 50, [welcome, artificial\_intelligence, robots]).$$
$$segment(seg3, 40, [graphics, dragons]).$$
$$segment(seg4, 50, [skiing, robots]).$$

A presentation is a sequence of segments. Represent a presentation by a list of segment identifiers.

(a) Axiomatize a predicate

$$presentation(MustCover, Maxtime, Segments)$$

that is true if *Segments* is a presentation whose total running time is less than or equal to *Maxtime* seconds, such that all of the topics in the list *MustCover* are covered by a segment in the presentation. The aim of this predicate is to design presentations that cover a certain number of topics within a time limit.

For example, the query

ask *presentation*([*welcome*, *skiing*, *robots*], 90, *Segs*)

should return at least the following two answers (perhaps with the segments in some other order):

*presentation*([*welcome*, *skiing*, *robots*], 90, [*seg*0, *seg*4])
*presentation*([*welcome*, *skiing*, *robots*], 90, [*seg*2, *seg*1]).

Give the intended interpretation of all symbols used and demonstrate that you have tested your axiomatization (including finding all answers to your query) in AIPython (aipython.org) or Prolog. Explain briefly why each answer is an answer.

(b) Assuming you have a good user interface and a way to actually view the presentations, list *three* things that the preceding program does not do that you may want in such a presentation system. (There is no correct answer for this part. You must be creative to get full marks.)

**Exercise 15.13** The extra arguments in a definite-clause grammar makes it strictly more powerful than a context-free grammar. The language $\{a^n b^n c^n \mid n \geq 0\}$, which consists of sentences that are made up of a number of *a*s, followed by the same number of *b*s followed by the same number of *c*s cannot be defined with a context-free grammar. Define this language using a definite clause grammar. [Hint: Define a predicate *copies* for a non-terminal that creates *n* copies of one of its arguments, and represent numbers using 0 for zero and $s(N)$ for the numbers after *n*.]

**Exercise 15.14** Construct a knowledge base and a dictionary based on Figure 15.12 (page 686) to answer geographical questions such as that given in Figure 1.3 (page 13). For each query, either show how it can be answered or explain why it is difficult to answer given the tools presented in this chapter.

**Exercise 15.15** Consider what would happen in Example 15.44 (page 693) if *empty_course* had been defined as

$$empty\_course(C) \leftarrow course(C) \wedge \sim enrolled(S, C).$$

Suppose the rest of the knowledge base is

| | | |
|---|---|---|
| *course*(*cs*422). | *course*(*cs*486). | *course*(*cs*987). |
| *enrolled*(*huan*, *cs*422). | *enrolled*(*sally*, *cs*486). | |

(a) What is Clark's completion of the clause for *empty_course*?

(b) What is a counter example to the soundness of the completion? Give an instance of the clause for which the body is true and the head is false.

(c) What does an implementation with negation as failure (e.g., Prolog) give? Compare with $empty\_course(C) \leftarrow \sim enrolled(S, C) \wedge course(C)$.

# Chapter 16

# Knowledge Graphs and Ontologies

*The most serious problems standing in the way of developing an adequate theory of computation are as much ontological as they are semantical. It is not that the semantic problems go away; they remain as challenging as ever. It is just that they are joined – on center stage, as it were – by even more demanding problems of ontology.*

– Brian Cantwell Smith [1996, p. 14]

How do you represent knowledge about a world to make it easy to acquire, debug, maintain, communicate, share, and reason with that knowledge? This chapter explores flexible methods for storing and reasoning with facts, and knowledge and data sharing using ontologies. As Smith points out, the problems of ontology are central for building intelligent computational agents.

## 16.1 Knowledge Graphs

### 16.1.1 Triples

Given a logical representation language, such as the one developed in the previous chapter, and a world to reason about, people designing databases and knowledge bases have to choose which individuals and relations to represent. It may seem that a modeler can just refer to the individuals and relations that exist in the world. However, the world does not determine which individuals there are. How the world is divided into individuals is invented by whomever is modeling the world. The modeler divides the world up into things so that the agent can refer to parts of the world that make sense for the task at hand.

**Example 16.1** It may seem as though *"red"* is a reasonable property to ascribe to things in the world. You may do this because you want to tell the delivery robot to go and get the red parcel. In the world, there are surfaces absorbing some frequencies and reflecting other frequencies of light. Some user may have decided that, for some application, some particular set of reflectance properties should be called *red*. Some other modeler might decide on another mapping of the spectrum and use the terms *pink*, *scarlet*, *ruby*, and *crimson*, and yet another modeler may divide the spectrum into regions that do not correspond to words in any language but are those regions most useful to distinguish different categories of individuals.

Just as modelers choose which individuals to represent, they also choose which relations to use. There are, however, some guiding principles that are useful for choosing relations and individuals. These will be demonstrated through a sequence of examples.

**Example 16.2** Suppose you decide that "red" is an appropriate category for classifying individuals. You could treat the name *red* as a unary relation and write that parcel *a* is red:

$$red(a).$$

If you represent the color information in this way, then you can easily ask what is red:

$$\text{ask } red(X).$$

The $X$ returned are the red individuals.

With this representation, it is hard to ask the question "What color is parcel *a*?" In the syntax of definite clauses, you cannot ask

$$\text{ask } X(a).$$

because, in languages based on first-order logic (page 672), predicate names cannot be variables. In second-order or higher-order logic, this may return any property of *a*, not just its color.

There are alternative representations that allow you to ask about the color of parcel *a*. There is nothing in the world that forces you to make *red* a predicate. You could just as easily say that colors are individuals too, and you could use the constant *red* to denote the color red. Given that *red* is a constant, you can use the predicate *color* where $color(Ind, Val)$ means that physical individual *Ind* has color *Val*. "Parcel *a* is red" can now be written as

$$color(a, red).$$

What you have done is reconceive the world: the world now consists of colors as individuals that you can name. There is now a new binary relation *color* between physical individuals and colors. Under this new representation you can ask "What has color red?" with the query

$$\text{ask } color(X, red).$$

and ask "What color is block $a$?" with the query

ask $color(a, C)$.

To make an abstract concept into an entity is to **reify** it. In the preceding example, the color *red* is reified.

**Example 16.3** It seems as though there is no disadvantage to the new representation of colors in the previous example. Everything that could be done before can be done now. It is not much more difficult to write $color(X, red)$ than $red(X)$, but you can now ask about the color of things. So the question arises of whether you can do this to every relation, and what do you end up with?

You can do a similar analysis for the *color* predicate as for the *red* predicate in Example 16.2 (page 702). The representation with *color* as a predicate does not allow you to ask the question "Which property of parcel *a* has value *red*?" where the appropriate answer is "color." Carrying out a similar transformation to that of Example 16.2, you can reify properties such as *color* as individuals, and invent a relation *prop* and write "individual *a* has the *color red*" as

$prop(a, color, red)$.

This representation allows for all of the queries of this and the previous example. You do not have to do this again, because you can write all relations in terms of the *prop* relation.

The **individual–property–value** representation is in terms of a single relation *prop* where

$prop(Ind, Prop, Val)$

means that individual *Ind* has value *Val* for property *Prop*. This is also called the **triple representation** because all of the relations are represented as **triples**. The first element of the triple is called the **subject**, the second is the **verb**, and the third is the **object**, using the analogy that a triple is a simple three-word sentence.

A triple is sometimes written as a three-word sentence:

*subject verb object.*

meaning the atom

$prop(subject,\ verb,\ object)$.

or written in functional notation as

$verb(subject,\ object)$.

The verb of a triple is a **property**. The **domain** of property $p$ is the set of individuals that can appear as the subject of a triple when $p$ is the verb. The

**range** of a property $p$ is the set of values that can appear as the object of a triple that has $p$ as the verb.

An **attribute** is a property–value pair. For example, an attribute of a parcel may be that its color is red.

There are some predicates that may seem to be too simple for the triple representation:

**Example 16.4** Consider $parcel(a)$, which means that $a$ is a parcel; there are two ways to represent it using triples.

The first is to reify the concept parcel to say that $a$ is a parcel:

$$prop(a, type, parcel).$$

where *type* is a property that relates an individual to a class. The constant *parcel* denotes the class of all, real or potential, things that are parcels. This triple specifies that the individual $a$ is in the class *parcel*. The property *type* is sometimes written as **is_a**, in which case the triple represents "a is_a parcel".

The second is to make parcel a property and write "$a$ is a parcel" as

$$prop(a, parcel, true).$$

In this representation, *parcel* is a Boolean property which is true of things that are parcels. The property corresponds to an indicator variable used in CSPs (page 182) and in machine learning (page 286).

A **Boolean property** is a property whose range is $\{true, false\}$, where *true* and *false* are constant symbols in the language.

Some predicates may seem to be too complicated for the triple representation:

**Example 16.5** The verb "give" requires three participants: an agent giving, a recipient, and a patient (the item being given). The sentence "Alex gave Chris a book" loses information if only two of the entities involved are specified in a relation. It could be represented by $gave(alex, chris, book)$. It can be represented using triples by inventing a giving act, say *ga*3545, with the triples:

$$prop(ga3545, type, giving\_act).$$
$$prop(ga3545, agent, alex).$$
$$prop(ga3545, patient, b342).$$
$$prop(ga3545, recipient, chris).$$
$$prop(b342, type, book).$$

Here, *ga*3545 is a reified entity denoting the action, and *b*342 is the book given. The *agent* is the one carrying out the action, the *patient* is the object the action is carried out on, and the *recipient* is the one receiving the patient. The properties *agent*, *patient*, and *recipient* are **thematic relations** or **semantic roles** used for giving meaning to sentences. The reification allows for other properties of the giving act, such as the date or perhaps the price paid.

Words and numbers that represent reified relations are very common. For example, a booking, a reservation, a marriage, a flight number, a purchase order all denote a relation and have properties such as the participants and a start time.

### 16.1.2 Individuals and Identifiers

Individuals are denoted by unique **identifiers**. For example, in a university, a student number is an identifier used to denote a student. The name is not adequate as there might be multiple students with the same name, and some students change their name.

A **uniform resource identifier** (**URI**), or its unicode extension, an **internationalized resource identifier** (**IRI**), is a unique name that can be used to identify anything. A **resource** is anything that can be named. An IRI typically has the form of a uniform resource locator (URL), a web address, typically staring with `http://` or `https://`, because URLs are unique. The IRI denotes the entity, not the website. The idea is that if someone uses the IRI, they mean the individual denoted by the IRI. A IRI has meaning because people use it with that meaning. There need not be a formal definition; it just has to be used consistently.

**Wikidata** (https://www.wikidata.org) is a free, collaborative knowledge graph with around 1.25 billion triples describing 100 million entities (as of 2022).

**Example 16.6** Christine Sinclair is a Canadian association football (soccer) player, who has scored more goals than any other player in international play. In Wikidata [2021], Christine Sinclair is represented using the identifier "http://www.wikidata.org/entity/Q262802", which we shorten to "Q262802". Wikidata uses this to disambiguate the footballer from any other person called Christine Sinclair. The identifier "http://www.wikidata.org/entity/Q262802" denotes the footballer, not the web page (which doesn't play football).

Wikidata uses unique identifiers for properties. For example, it uses the identifier "http://schema.org/name" for the property that gives the name of the subject. We use "name", but remember that it is an abbreviation for the property defined by schema.org. If you don't want that meaning, you should use another identifier. The value of a triple with "name" as the property is the pair of a string and a language, such as ("Christine Sinclair",en).

Wikidata uses "http://www.wikidata.org/prop/direct/P27" for the property "country of citizenship", where the subject is a person and the object is a country they are a citizen of. Canada is "http://www.wikidata.org/entity/Q16", so "Christine Sinclair is a citizen of Canada" is represented using the triple

/entity/Q262802  /prop/direct/P27  /entity/Q16

but using the full IRIs (including "http://www.wikidata.org").

### 16.1.3 Graphical Representations

You can interpret the *prop* relation in terms of a **knowledge graph**, a directed labelled graph, where nodes are entities (and other values such as strings and numbers). The relation

*prop*(*Ind*, *Prop*, *Val*)

defines an arc with **tail** *Ind* and **head** *Val*, labelled with *Prop*. Such a graph is also called a **semantic network**.

**Example 16.7** Figure 16.1 shows part of the **Wikidata** knowledge graph about Christine Sinclair (Q262802). Wikidata provides over 3400 triples about her, including her name in 47 languages (as of August 2022); her name in English and Korean is shown.

Christine Sinclair is a citizen of Canada. Instead of the Wikidata name, "http://www.wikidata.org/prop/direct/P27", *country_of_citizenship* is shown.

She has played 319 games since 2000 for the Canada women's national soccer team (identifier Q499946), scoring 190 goals. The relationship between her and the team is reified using the identifier Q262802-9c5c267f (the actual identifier is longer than this), connected to her with the property "http://www.wikidata.org/prop/P54" (member of sports team). The property between the reified entity and Q499946 is "http://www.wikidata.org/prop/statement/P54", also shown as *member_of_sports_team*.

She has played 161 games for Portland Thorns (identifier Q1446672) since 2013, scoring 65 goals.

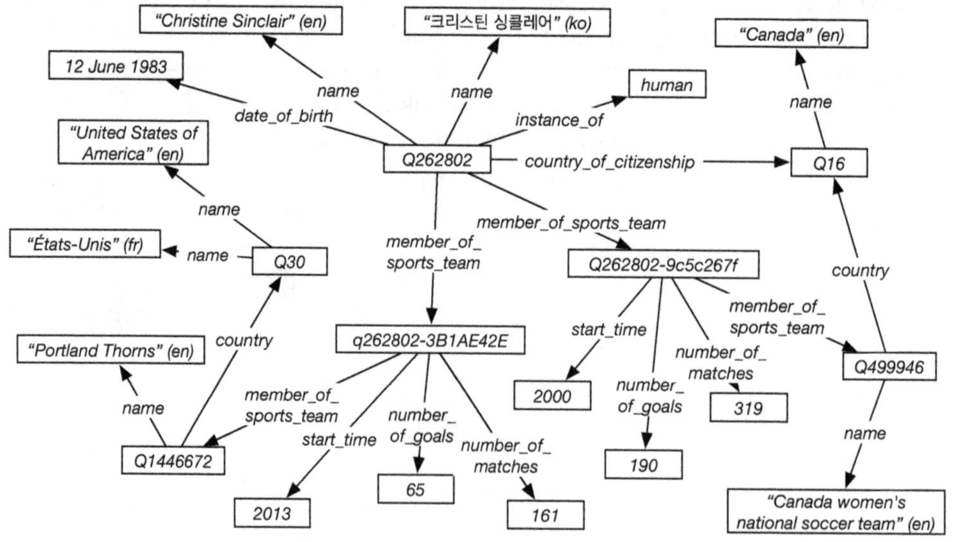


Figure 16.1: Part of the Wikidata knowledge graph about Christine Sinclair. The English names, not the IRIs, of the properties are shown

Apart from the flexibility outlined earlier, the graphical notation has a number of advantages:

- It is easy for a human to see the relationships without being required to learn the syntax of a particular logic. The graphical notation helps the builders of knowledge bases to organize their knowledge. There are many tools for creating knowledge graphs where users just draw nodes and arcs (sometimes called **knowledge maps** or **mind maps**).
- A person browsing the knowledge graph can ignore the labels of nodes that just have meaningless names – for example, the name *ga*3545 in Example 16.5 (page 704), or Q262802-9c5c267f in Figure 16.1 (page 706). A representation and visualization can just leave these nodes blank and make up an arbitrary name if they must be mapped to explicit triples.
- Triples can be stored efficiently in a **triple store**. In a relational database, the designer needs to specify the keys used to index into the database; given a key, the associated tuples can be found efficiently. A triple store needs eight indexes to be able to find the tuples associated with any combination of given positions. One extreme is where the subject, verb, and object are given and the query is to determine if a particular triple is in the store. At the other extreme, no positions are specified, and the aim is to enumerate the triples. In between these, for example, just the subject and object could be given and the aim is to enumerate the verbs that link them, or just the subject and verb are given and the aim is to enumerate the objects. Eight indexes are required because each of the subject, verb, and object could be given or not. With these indexes, the designer does not need to define keys to access the triples efficiently.

## 16.2 Classes and Properties

Typically, you know more about a domain than a database of facts; you may know general rules from which other facts can be derived. Which facts are explicitly given and which are derived is a choice to be made when designing and building a knowledge base.

**Primitive knowledge** is knowledge that is specified explicitly. **Derived knowledge** is knowledge that can be inferred from primitive knowledge and other derived knowledge.

The use of rules allows for a more compact representation of knowledge. Derived relations allow for **generalizations** to be drawn from knowing something is in a class. This is important because you do not directly observe everything about a domain. Much of what is known about a domain is inferred from the observations and more general knowledge, including learned knowledge.

A standard way to use derived knowledge is to specify attributes (property–value pairs) that hold for all members of a class. Individuals inherit the attributes associated with the classes they are in. Grouping individuals into classes enables a more concise representation than representing the attributes for each individual separately. This issue was discussed in the context of probabilistic classifiers (page 467) and unsupervised learning (page 473).

A **class** is the set of those actual and potential individuals that would be members of the class. This is typically an **intensional set** (page 131), defined by a **characteristic function** that is true of members of the set and false of other individuals. The alternative to an intensional set is an **extensional set**, which is defined by listing its elements.

For example, the class *chair* is the set of all things that would be chairs. The definition is not the set of things that *are* chairs, because chairs that have not yet been built also fall into the class of chairs. Without this definition, an agent could not design a chair, because the chair doesn't exist during the designing (and may never exist).

Two classes are not equivalent just because they have the same members. For example, the class of green unicorns and the class of chairs that are exactly 124 meters high are different classes, even though they may contain the same elements; they are both empty. A green unicorn is not a 124 meter high chair.

The definition of class allows any set that can be described to be a class. For example, the set consisting of the number 17, the Taj Mahal in Agra, and the first goal scored in the 2022 FIFA world cup final can be considered a class, but it is not very useful. A **natural kind** is a class such that describing individuals using the class is more succinct than describing individuals without the class. For example, "mammal" is a natural kind, because describing the common attributes of mammals makes a knowledge base that uses "mammal" more succinct than one that does not use "mammal" and instead repeats the attributes for every individual.

### 16.2.1 Class and Property Hierarchies

Class $S$ is a **subclass** of class $C$ means $S$ is a subset of $C$. That is, every individual of type $S$ is of type $C$.

**Example 16.8** Figure 16.2 (page 709) shows the class structure for the Brazil national football team and the Canada women's national soccer team, up to the level of organization. Shown is the English name of the entity or class with the Wikidata identifier in parentheses.

At the lowest level, the Brazil national football team is an instance of the class Q6979593, which has the name in English "national association football team". This is a subclass of the classes called "national football team" and "association football team".

The relationship between types and subclasses can be written as a definite clause:

$$\begin{aligned}&prop(E, type, C) \leftarrow\\&\quad prop(S, subClassOf, C) \wedge\\&\quad prop(E, type, S).\end{aligned}$$

or using functional notation, if $subClassOf(S, C)$ and $type(E, S)$, then $type(E, C)$.

You can treat *type* and *subClassOf* as special properties that allow **property inheritance**. Property inheritance occurs when a value for a property is specified at the class level and inherited by the members of the class. If all members of class $c$ have value $v$ for property $p$, this can be written as the definite clause

$$prop(Ind, p, v) \leftarrow$$
$$\quad prop(Ind, type, c).$$

which, together with the above rule that relates types and subclasses, can be used for property inheritance.

Property $p_1$ is a **sub-property** of property $C$ if every pair related by $p_1$ is also related by $p_2$. In functional notation this means $p_1(x, y)$ implies $p_2(x, y)$, or in triple notation $(x, p_1, y)$ implies $(x, p_2, y)$.

**Example 16.9** Some sub-properties in Wikidata are

- "member of sports team" (P54) is a sub-property of "member of" (P463)

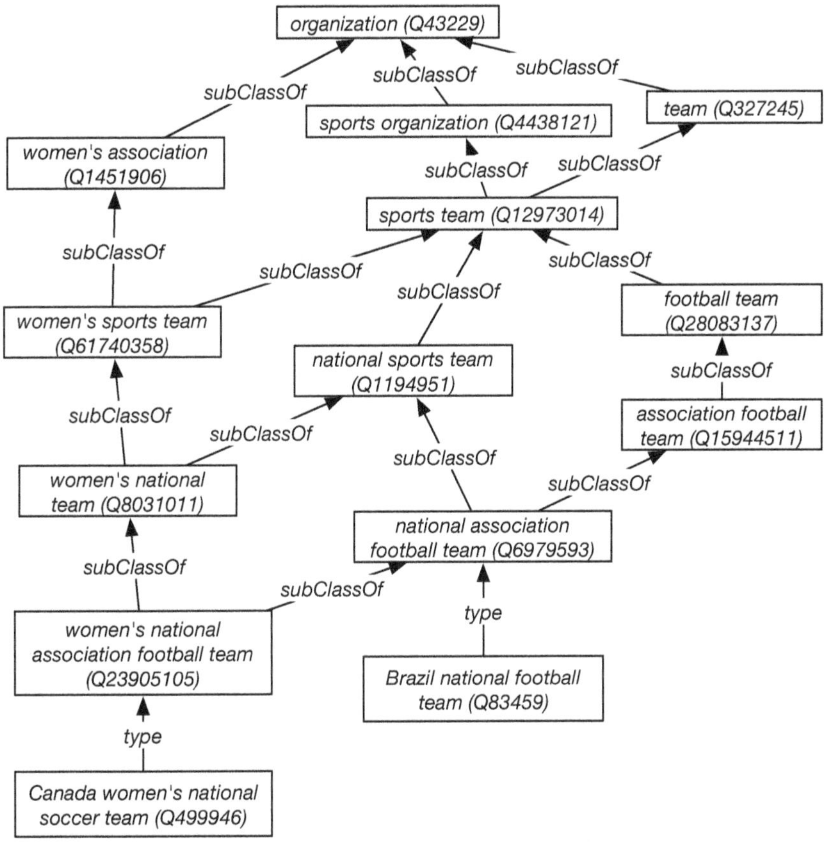


Figure 16.2: Part of the Wikidata class structure for the Brazil national football team and the Canada women's national soccer team

- "member of" (P463) is a sub-property of "affiliation" (P1416)
- "affiliation" (P1416) is a sub-property of "part of" (P361)
- "part of" (P361) is a sub-property of "partially coincident with" (P1382)
- "partially coincident with" (P1382) is a sub-property of "different from" (P1889).

The **domain** of a property is a class such that the subject (first argument) of a triple with the property has to be in the class. That is, "the domain of property $p$ is class $C$" means if $p(x, y)$ then $x \in C$. If a property $p$ has domain $C_1$ and has domain $C_2$, then every individual in the subject of $p$ must be in both $C_1$ and $C_2$.

The **range** of a property is a class such that the object (last argument) of a triple with the property has to be in the class. That is, the range of property $p$ is class $C$ means if $p(x, y)$ then $y \in C$.

A property $p$ is **functional** means that there is at most one object associated with any subject; i.e., if $p(x, y_1)$ and $p(x, y_2)$ then $y_1 = y_2$. This corresponds to the mathematical definition of a partial function.

Functional properties play a special role in relational learning and relational probabilistic models in Chapter 17, because features (page 127), as used in constraint satisfaction problems and in machine learning, and random variables (page 377) are assumed to be functional (having only one value). What is special here is that non-functional properties such as "has-friend" are allowed.

**Example 16.10** The following are not (currently) part of Wikidata, but could be:

- the domain of "member of sports team" (P54) is "human" (Q5)
- the range of "member of sports team" (P54) is "sports team" (Q12973014)
- "member of sports team" (P54) is not functional, because someone could be in multiple sports teams at the same time; as shown in Figure 16.1, Christine Sinclair was in two sports teams
- "date of birth" (P569) is functional as each person has only one date of birth.

Some general guidelines are useful for deciding what should be primitive and what should be derived:

- When associating an attribute with an individual, select the most general class $C$ that the individual is in, where all members of $C$ have that attribute, and associate the attribute with class $C$. Inheritance can be used to derive the attribute for the individual and all other members of class $C$. This representation methodology tends to make knowledge bases more concise, and it means that it is easier to incorporate new individuals because members of $C$ automatically inherit the attribute. For example, people have backbones; this is represented by having a class of vertebrates which humans are a subclass of.

- Do not associate a contingent attribute of a class with the class. A **contingent attribute** is one whose value changes when circumstances change. For example, do not define a football team in terms of having a coach; a team does not stop being a team because the coach resigns or dies.

### 16.2.2 Designing Classes

Categorizing objects, the basis for modern ontologies, has a long history. Aristotle [350 BCE] suggested the definition of a class C in terms of

- **Genus**: a superclass of C. The plural of genus is genera.
- **Differentia**: the attributes that make members of the class C different from other members of the superclass of C.

He anticipated many of the issues that arise in definitions:

> *If genera are different and co-ordinate, their differentiae are themselves different in kind. Take as an instance the genus "animal" and the genus "knowledge". "With feet", "two-footed", "winged", "aquatic", are differentiae of "animal"; the species of knowledge are not distinguished by the same differentiae. One species of knowledge does not differ from another in being "two-footed".*
>
> – Aristotle [350 BCE]

Note that "co-ordinate" here means neither is subordinate to the other.

In the style of modern ontologies, we would say that "animal" is a class and "knowledge" is a class. The property "two-footed" has domain "animal". If something is an instance of knowledge, it does not have a value for the property "two-footed".

> *The art of ranking things in genera and species is quite important, and greatly helps our judgment as well as our memory. ...This helps one not merely to retain things in one's memory, but also to find them there. Writers who have laid out all sorts of notions under certain headings or categories have done something very useful.*
>
> – Leibniz [1705]

To build an ontology based on **Aristotelian definitions**:

- For each class you may want to define, determine a relevant superclass and then select those attributes that distinguish the class from other subclasses. Each attribute gives a property and a value.

### Classes in Knowledge Bases and Object-Oriented Programming

The use of "individuals" and "classes" in knowledge-based systems is very similar to the use of "objects" and "classes" in **object-oriented programming (OOP) languages** such as **Smalltalk**, **Python**, or **Java**. This should not be too surprising because they have an interrelated history. But there are important differences that tend to make the direct analogy often more confusing than helpful:

- Objects in OOP are computational objects; they are data structures and associated programs. A "person" object in Java is not a person. However, individuals in a knowledge base (KB) are (typically) things in the real world. A "person" individual in a KB can be a real person. A "chair" individual can be a real chair you can actually sit in; it can hurt you if you bump into it. You can send a message to, and get answers from, a "chair" object in Java, whereas a chair in the real world tends to ignore what you tell it. A KB is not typically used to interact with a chair, but to reason *about* a chair. A real chair stays where it is unless it is moved by a physical agent.
- In a KB, a representation of an object is only an approximation at one (or a few) levels of abstraction. Real objects tend to be much more complicated than what is represented. You typically do not represent the individual fibers in the fabric of a chair. In an OOP system, there are only the represented properties of an object. The system can know everything about a Java object, but not about a real individual.
- The class structure of Java is intended to represent designed objects. A systems analyst or a programmer gets to create a design. For example, in Java, an object is only a member of one lowest-level class. There is no multiple inheritance. Real objects are not so rigidly constrained. The same person could be a football coach, a mathematician, and a mother.
- A computer program cannot be uncertain about its data structures; it has to select particular data structures to use. However, you can be uncertain about the types of things in the world.
- The representations in a KB do not actually do anything. In an OOP system, objects do computational work. In a KB, they just represent – that is, they just refer to objects in the world.
- While an object-oriented modeling language, like **UML**, may be used for representing KBs, it may not be the best choice. A good OO modeling tool has facilities to help build good designs. However, the world being modeled may not have a good design at all. Trying to force a good design paradigm on a messy world may not be productive.

Knublauch et al. [2006] present a more detailed comparison between object-orientated software design and the use of ontologies.

- For each property, define the most general class for which it makes sense, and define the domain (page 703) of the property to be this class. Make the range (page 704) of the property another class that makes sense (perhaps requiring this range class to be defined, either by enumerating its values or by defining it using an Aristotelian definition).

**Example 16.11** In Example 16.8 (page 708), a national sports team is a "team that represents a nation in a sport", where "team" is the genus and "represents a nation in a sport" is the differentia. An association football team is a sports team that plays association football (soccer). So a national association football team is a team that represents a nation in association football, and so is a subclass of both. A team is "a group linked in a common purpose".

In Figure 16.2 (page 709), the differentia that distinguishes the classes on the left is that the members have to be women. There can also be a women's association football team, a women's football team, and a women's team, not all of which are given identifiers in Wikidata. Note that, while "men's football team" defines a class, it does not exist in Wikidata because most teams allow women, even if none actually play.

The class hierarchy is a directed graph with arcs from subclasses to their immediate superclasses. Cyclic definitions are not useful; for example, defining $x$ is above $y$ as $y$ is below $x$ and defining $y$ is below $x$ as $x$ is above $y$ does not define either; it just creates an equivalence. Thus, it is reasonable to assume that the graph is a directed acyclic graph (DAG), forming a lattice. This methodology does not, in general, give a tree hierarchy of classes. Objects can be in many classes. Each class does not have a single most-specific superclass.

**Example 16.12** Consider the definitions of rectangle, rhombus, and square:

- A rectangle is a quadrilateral where all inside angles are right angles (90°).
- A rhombus is a quadrilateral where all four sides have the same length.
- A square is a quadrilateral where all four sides have the same length and all inside angles are right angles.

A square is both a rectangle and a rhombus; both are most specific superclasses. A square could be defined as a rectangle where all sides have the same length. It could equally well be defined as a rhombus where the inside angles are right angles.

A quadrilateral is a planar figure made up of four straight sides. The definition of square can be expanded so that a square is a planar figure made up of four straight sides of equal length and the inside angles are right angles.

In rare cases, the natural class hierarchy forms a tree, most famously in the **Linnaean taxonomy** of living things. The reason this is a tree is because of evolution. Trying to force a tree structure in other domains has been much less successful.

If the class structure is acyclic and each class – except for a top class, which we call *thing* – is defined in terms of a superclass and the attributes that form the differentia, then each class has a normal form as *thing* conjoined with attributes, by replacing each superclass by its definition. If the attributes are property–value pairs then one class is a subclass of the other if its normal form is a superset of the other; Section 16.3.1 (page 718) describes more expressive class constructs. In Example 16.12 (page 713), square is a subclass of rectangle and is a subclass of rhombus as all of the attributes are the same, with an extra one for the differentia of the square.

## 16.3 Ontologies and Knowledge Sharing

Building large knowledge-based systems is complex:

- Knowledge often comes from multiple sources, including people, sensors, and the web, which must be integrated. Moreover, these sources may not have the same division of the world. Often knowledge comes from different fields that have their own distinctive terminology and divide the world according to their own needs.
- Systems evolve over time and it is difficult to anticipate all future distinctions that should be made.
- The people involved in designing a knowledge base must choose what individuals and relationships to represent. The world is not divided into individuals; that is something done by intelligent agents to understand the world. Different people involved in a knowledge-based system should agree on this division of the world.
- It is often difficult to remember what your own notation means, let alone to discover what someone else's notation means. This has two aspects:
  - given a symbol used in the computer, determining what it means
  - given a concept in someone's mind, determining what symbol to use. This has three aspects:
    * determining whether the concept has already been defined
    * if it has been defined, discovering what symbol has been used for it
    * if it is not already defined, finding related concepts that it can be defined in terms of.

To share and communicate knowledge, it is important to be able to develop a common vocabulary and an agreed-on meaning for that vocabulary.

A **conceptualization** or **intended interpretation** (page 647) is a mapping between symbols used in the computer, the vocabulary, and the individuals and relations in the world. It provides a particular abstraction of the world and notation for that abstraction. A conceptualization for small knowledge

### The Semantic Web

The **semantic web** is a way to allow machine-interpretable knowledge to be distributed on the World Wide Web. Instead of just serving HTML pages that are meant to be read by humans, websites can also provide information that can be used by computers.

At the most basic level, **XML** (the Extensible Markup Language) provides a syntax designed to be machine readable, but which is also possible for humans to read. It is a text–based language, where items are tagged in a hierarchical manner. The syntax for XML can be quite complicated, but at the simplest level, the scope of a tag is either in the form $\langle tag \ldots / \rangle$, or in the form $\langle tag \ldots \rangle \ldots \langle / tag \rangle$.

An **IRI (internationalized resource identifier)** is used to uniquely identify a resource. A **resource** is anything that can be uniquely identified, including individuals, classes, and properties. Typically, IRIs use the syntax of web addresses (URLs).

**RDF** (the **resource description framework**) is a language built on XML, for individual–property–value triples.

**RDFS (RDF schema)** lets you define resources (classes and properties) in terms of other resources (e.g., using *subClassOf* and *subPropertyOf*). RDFS also lets you restrict the domain and range of properties and provides containers: sets, sequences, and alternatives.

RDF allows sentences in its own language to be reified. This means that it can represent arbitrary logical formulas and so is not decidable in general. Undecidability is not necessarily a bad thing; it just means that you cannot put a bound on the time a computation may take. Logic programs with function symbols and programs in virtually all programming languages are undecidable.

**OWL** (the **web ontology language**) is an ontology language for the World Wide Web. It defines some classes and properties with a fixed interpretation that can be used for describing classes, properties, and individuals. It has built-in mechanisms for equality of individuals, classes, and properties, in addition to restricting domains and ranges of properties and other restrictions on properties (e.g., transitivity, cardinality).

There have been some efforts to build large universal ontologies, such as **Cyc** (www.cyc.com), but the idea of the semantic web is to allow communities to converge on ontologies. Anyone can build an ontology. People who want to develop a knowledge base can use an existing ontology or develop their own ontology, usually building on existing ontologies. Because it is in their interest to have semantic interoperability, companies and individuals should tend to converge on standard ontologies for their domain or to develop mappings from their ontologies to others' ontologies.

bases can be in the head of the designer or specified in natural language in the documentation. This informal specification of a conceptualization does not scale to larger systems where the conceptualization must be shared.

In philosophy, **ontology** is the study of what exists. In AI, an **ontology** is a specification of the meanings of the symbols in an information system. That is, it is a specification of a conceptualization. It is a specification of what individuals and relationships are assumed to exist and what terminology is used for them. Typically, it specifies what types of individuals will be modeled, specifies what properties will be used, and gives some axioms that restrict the use of that vocabulary.

**Example 16.13** An ontology of individuals that could appear on a map could specify that the symbol "ApartmentBuilding" will represent apartment buildings. The ontology will not define an apartment building, but it will describe it well enough so that others can understand the definition. We want other people, who may call such buildings "Condos", "Flats", or "Apartment Complex" to be able to find the appropriate symbol in the ontology (see Figure 16.3). That is, given a concept, people want to be able to find the symbol, and, given the symbol, they want to be able to determine what it means.

An ontology may give axioms to restrict the use of some symbols. For example, it may specify that apartment buildings are buildings, which are human-constructed artifacts. It may give some restriction on the size of buildings so that shoeboxes cannot be buildings or that cities cannot be buildings. It may state that a building cannot be at two geographically dispersed locations at the

Figure 16.3: Mapping from a conceptualization to a symbol

same time (so if you take off some part of the building and move it to a different location, it is no longer a single building). Because apartment buildings are buildings, these restrictions also apply to apartment buildings.

Ontologies are usually written independently of a particular application and often involve a community agreeing on the meanings of symbols. An ontology consists of:

- a vocabulary of the categories of the things (both classes and properties) that a knowledge base may want to represent
- an organization of the categories, for example into an inheritance hierarchy using *subClassOf* (page 708) or *subPropertyOf* (where property $S$ is a sub-property of property $P$ if $S(x, y)$ implies $R(x, y)$ for all $x$ and $y$), or using Aristotelian definitions (page 711), and
- a set of axioms restricting the definition of some of the symbols to better reflect their intended meaning – for example, that some property is transitive, or the domain and range of a property, or restrictions on the number of values a property can take for each individual. Sometimes relationships are defined in terms of other relationships but, ultimately, the relationships are grounded out into **primitive relationships** that are not actually defined.

An ontology does not specify the individuals not known at design time. For example, an ontology of buildings would typically not include actual buildings. An ontology would specify those individuals that are fixed and should be shared, such as the days of the week, or colors.

**Example 16.14** Consider a trading agent that is designed to find accommodations. Users could use such an agent to describe what accommodation they want. The trading agent could search multiple knowledge bases to find suitable accommodations or to notify users when some appropriate accommodation becomes available. An ontology is required to specify the meaning of the symbols for the user and to allow the knowledge bases to interoperate. It provides the semantic glue to tie together the users' needs with the knowledge bases.

In such a domain, houses and apartment buildings may both be residential buildings. Although it may be sensible to suggest renting a house or an apartment in an apartment building, it may not be sensible to suggest renting an apartment building to someone who does not actually specify that they want to rent the whole building. A "living unit" could be defined to be the collection of rooms that some people, who are living together, live in. A living unit may be what a rental agency offers to rent. At some stage, the designer may have to decide whether a room for rent in a house is a living unit, or even whether part of a shared room that is rented separately is a living unit. Often the boundary cases – cases that may not be initially anticipated – are not clearly delineated but become better defined as the ontology evolves.

The ontology would not contain descriptions of actual houses or apartments because, at the time the ontology is defined, the designers will not know which houses will be described by the ontology. The ontology will change much slower than the actual available accommodation.

The primary purpose of an ontology is to document what the symbols mean – the mapping between symbols (in a computer) and concepts (in someone's head). Given a symbol, a person is able to use the ontology to determine what it means. When someone has a concept to be represented, the ontology is used to find the appropriate symbol or to determine that the concept does not exist in the ontology. The secondary purpose, achieved by the use of axioms, is to allow inference or to determine that some combination of values is inconsistent. The main challenge in building an ontology is the organization of the concepts to allow a human to map concepts into symbols in the computer, and to allow a computer to infer useful new knowledge from stated facts.

### 16.3.1 Description Logic

Modern ontology languages such as **OWL** (page 715) are based on **description logics**. A description logic is used to describe classes, properties, and individuals. One of the main ideas behind a description logic is to separate

- a **terminological knowledge base** (or **TBox**), describes the terminology; it defines what the symbols mean
- an **assertional knowledge base** (or **ABox**), specifies what is true at some point in time.

Usually, the terminological knowledge base is defined at the design time of the system and defines the ontology, and it only changes as the meaning of the vocabulary changes, which should be relatively rarely. The assertional knowledge base usually contains the knowledge that is situation specific and is only known at run time.

It is typical to use triples (page 703) to define the assertional knowledge base and a language such as OWL to define the terminological knowledge base.

The **web ontology language** (**OWL**) describes domains in terms of

- **Individuals** – things in the world that is being described (e.g., a particular house or a particular booking may be individuals).
- **Classes** – sets of individuals. A class is the set of all real or potential things that would be in that class. For example, the class "House" may be the set of all things that would be classified as a house, not just those houses that exist in the domain of interest.
- **Properties** – used to describe binary relationships between individuals and other individuals or values. A **datatype property** has values that are primitive data types, such as integers, strings, or dates. For example, "streetName" may be a datatype property between a street and a string. An **object property** has values that are other individuals. For example, "nextTo" may be a property between two houses, and "onStreet" may be a property between a house and a street.

OWL comes in a few variants that differ in restrictions imposed on the classes and properties, and how efficiently they can be implemented. For example, in OWL-DL a class cannot be an individual or a property, and a property is not an individual. In OWL-Full, the categories of individuals, properties, and classes are not necessarily disjoint. OWL-DL comes in three profiles that are targeted towards particular applications, and do not allow constructs they do not need that would make inference slower. OWL 2 EL is designed for large biohealth ontologies, allowing rich structural descriptions. OWL 2 QL is designed to be the front end of database query languages. OWL 2 RL is a language that is designed for cases where rules are important.

OWL does not make the unique names assumption (page 689); two names do not necessarily denote different individuals or different classes. It also does not make the complete knowledge assumption (page 207); it does not assume that all the relevant facts have been stated.

$C_k$ are classes, $p$ is a property, $I_k$ are individuals, and $n$ is an integer. $\#S$ is the number of elements in set $S$.

| Class | Class Contains |
|---|---|
| owl:Thing | all individuals |
| owl:Nothing | no individuals (empty set) |
| owl:ObjectIntersectionOf$(C_1, \dots, C_k)$ | individuals in $C_1 \cap \cdots \cap C_k$ |
| owl:ObjectUnionOf$(C_1, \dots, C_k)$ | individuals in $C_1 \cup \cdots \cup C_k$ |
| owl:ObjectComplementOf$(C)$ | the individuals not in $C$ |
| owl:ObjectOneOf$(I_1, \dots, I_k)$ | $I_1, \dots, I_k$ |
| owl:ObjectHasValue$(p, v)$ | individuals with value $v$ on property $p$; i.e., $\{x : p(x, v)\}$ |
| owl:ObjectAllValuesFrom$(p, C)$ | individuals with all values in $C$ on property $p$; i.e., $\{x : \forall y\, p(x, y) \to y \in C\}$ |
| owl:ObjectSomeValuesFrom$(p, C)$ | individuals with some values in $C$ on property $p$; i.e., $\{x : \exists y \in C \text{ such that } p(x, y)\}$ |
| owl:ObjectMinCardinality$(n, p, C)$ | individuals $x$ with at least $n$ individuals of class $C$ related to $x$ by $p$; i.e., $\{x : \#\{y : p(x, y) \text{ and } y \in C\} \geq n\}$ |
| owl:ObjectMaxCardinality$(n, p, C)$ | individuals $x$ with at most $n$ individuals of class $C$ related to $x$ by $p$; i.e., $\{x : \#\{y : p(x, y) \text{ and } y \in C\} \leq n\}$ |
| owl:ObjectHasSelf$(p)$ | individuals $x$ such that $p(x, x)$; i.e., $\{x : p(x, x)\}$ |

Figure 16.4: Some OWL built-in classes and class constructors

Figure 16.4 (page 719) gives some primitive classes and some class constructors. This figure uses set notation to define the set of individuals in a class. Figure 16.5 gives some primitive predicates of OWL. The owl: prefix is an abbreviation for the standard IRI for OWL.

In these figures, $p(x,y)$ is a triple. OWL defines some terminology that is used to define the meaning of the predicates, rather than any syntax. The predicates can be used with different syntaxes, such as XML, triples, or functional notation.

**Example 16.15** As an example of a class constructor in functional notation:

ObjectHasValue(country_of_citizenship, Q16)

is the class containing the citizens of Canada (Q16).

OWL has the following predicates with a fixed interpretation, where $C_k$ are classes, $p_k$ are properties, and $I_k$ are individuals; $x$ and $y$ are universally quantified variables.

| Statement | Meaning |
|---|---|
| rdf:type$(I, C)$ | $I \in C$ |
| owl:ClassAssertion$(C, I)$ | $I \in C$ |
| rdfs:subClassOf$(C_1, C_2)$ | $C_1 \subseteq C_2$ |
| owl:SubClassOf$(C_1, C_2)$ | $C_1 \subseteq C_2$ |
| rdfs:domain$(p, C)$ | if $p(x,y)$ then $x \in C$ |
| owl:ObjectPropertyDomain$(p, C)$ | if $p(x,y)$ then $x \in C$ |
| rdfs:range$(p, C)$ | if $p(x,y)$ then $y \in C$ |
| owl:ObjectPropertyRange$(p, C)$ | if $p(x,y)$ then $y \in C$ |
| owl:EquivalentClasses$(C_1, C_2, \ldots, C_k)$ | $C_i \equiv C_j$ for all $i, j$ |
| owl:DisjointClasses$(C_1, C_2, \ldots, C_k)$ | $C_i \cap C_j = \{\}$ for all $i \neq j$ |
| rdfs:subPropertyOf$(p_1, p_2)$ | $p_1(x,y)$ implies $p_2(x,y)$ |
| owl:EquivalentObjectProperties$(p_1, p_2)$ | $p_1(x,y)$ if and only if $p_2(x,y)$ |
| owl:DisjointObjectProperties$(p_1, p_2)$ | $p_1(x,y)$ implies not $p_2(x,y)$ |
| owl:InverseObjectProperties$(p_1, p_2)$ | $p_1(x,y)$ if and only if $p_2(y,x)$ |
| owl:SameIndividual$(I_1, \ldots, I_n)$ | $\forall j \forall k\ I_j = I_k$ |
| owl:DifferentIndividuals$(I_1, \ldots, I_n)$ | $\forall j \forall k\ j \neq k$ implies $I_j \neq I_k$ |
| owl:FunctionalObjectProperty$(p)$ | if $p(x,y_1)$ and $p(x,y_2)$ then $y_1 = y_2$ |
| owl:InverseFunctionalObjectProperty$(p)$ | if $p(x_1,y)$ and $p(x_2,y)$ then $x_1 = x_2$ |
| owl:TransitiveObjectProperty$(p)$ | if $p(x,y)$ and $p(y,z)$ then $p(x,z)$ |
| owl:SymmetricObjectProperty | if $p(x,y)$ then $yPx$ |
| owl:AsymmetricObjectProperty$(p)$ | $p(x,y)$ implies not $p(y,x)$ |
| owl:ReflectiveObjectProperty$(p)$ | $p(x,x)$ for all $x$ |
| owl:IrreflectiveObjectProperty$(p)$ | not $p(x,x)$ for all $x$ |

Figure 16.5: Some RDF, RDFS, and OWL built-in predicates

Q113489728 is the class of countries that are members of the Organization for Economic Co-operation and Development (OECD), so

ObjectSomeValuesFrom(country_of_citizenship, Q113489728)

is the class of people that are citizens of a country that is a member of the OECD. For people with multiple citizenships, at least one of the countries they are a citizen of has to be an OECD country.

MinCardinality(2, country_of_citizenship, Q113489728)

is the class of individuals who are citizens of two or more countries that are members of the OECD.

The class constructors must be used in a statement, for example, to say that some individual is a member of this class or to say that one class is equivalent to some other class.

OWL does not have definite clauses. To say that all of the elements of a set $S$ have value $v$ for a predicate $p$, we say that $S$ is a subset of the set of all things with value $v$ for predicate $p$.

Some of OWL and RDF or RDFS statements have the same meaning. For example, rdf:type$(I, C)$ means the same as owl:ClassAssertion$(C, I)$ and rdfs:domain means the same as owl:ObjectPropertyDomain for object properties. Some ontologies use both definitions, because the ontologies were developed over long periods of time, with contributors who adopted different conventions.

**Example 16.16** Consider an Aristotelian definition (page 711) of an apartment building. We can say that an apartment building is a residential building with multiple units and the units are rented. (This is in contrast to a condominium building, where the units are individually sold, or a house, where there is only one unit.) Suppose we have the class *ResidentialBuilding* that is a subclass of *Building*.

The following defines the functional object property *numberOfUnits*, with domain *ResidentialBuilding* and range $\{one, two, moreThanTwo\}$:

```
FunctionalObjectProperty(numberOfunits)
ObjectPropertyDomain(numberOfunits, ResidentialBuilding)
ObjectPropertyRange(numberOfunits,
                    ObjectOneOf(two, one, moreThanTwo)).
```

The functional object property *ownership* with domain *ResidentialBuilding* and range $\{rental, ownerOccupied, coop\}$ can be defined similarly.

An apartment building is a *ResidentialBuilding* where the *numberOfUnits* property has the value *moreThanTwo* and the *ownership* property has the value *rental*. To specify this in OWL, we define the class of things that have value *moreThanTwo* for the property *numberOfUnits*, the class of things that have value *rental* for the property *ownership*, and say that *ApartmentBuilding* is equivalent to the intersection of these classes. In OWL functional syntax, this is

```
EquivalentClasses(ApartmentBuilding,
    ObjectIntersectionOf(
        ResidentialBuilding,
        ObjectHasValue(numberOfunits, moreThanTwo),
        ObjectHasValue(ownership, rental))).
```

This definition can be used to answer questions about apartment buildings, such as the ownership and the number of units. Apartment buildings inherit all of the properties of residential buildings.

The previous example did not really define *ownership*. The system has no idea what ownership actually means. Hopefully, a user will know what it means. Everyone who wants to adopt an ontology should ensure that their use of a property and a class is consistent with other users of the ontology.

There is one property constructor in OWL, owl:ObjectInverseOf$(p)$, which is the inverse property of $p$; that is, it is the property $p^{-1}$ such that $p^{-1}(x,y)$ if and only if $p(x,y)$. Note that it is only applicable to object properties; datatype properties do not have inverses, because data types cannot be the subject of a triple.

The list of classes and statements in these figures is not complete. There are corresponding datatype classes for datatype properties, where appropriate. For example, owl:DataSomeValuesFrom and owl:EquivalentDataProperties have the same definitions as the corresponding object symbols, but are for datatype properties. There are also other constructs in OWL to define properties, comments, annotations, versioning, and importing other ontologies.

A **domain ontology** is an ontology about a particular domain of interest. Most existing ontologies are in a narrow domain that people write for specific applications. There are some guidelines that have evolved for writing domain ontologies to enable knowledge sharing:

- If possible, use an existing well-established ontology. This means that your knowledge base will be able to interact with others who use the same ontology.
- If an existing ontology does not exactly match your needs, import it and add to it. Do not start from scratch, because people who have used the existing ontology will have a difficult time also using yours, and others who want to select an ontology will have to choose one or the other. If your ontology includes and improves the other, others who want to adopt an ontology will choose yours, because their application will be able to interact with adopters of either ontology.
- Make sure that your ontology integrates with neighboring ontologies. For example, an ontology about resorts may have to interact with ontologies about food, beaches, recreation activities, and so on. When first designing the ontology, you may not know the full extent of what it needs to interoperate with. Try to make sure that it uses the same terminology as possibly related ontologies for the same things.

- Try to fit in with higher-level ontologies (see below). This will make it much easier for others to integrate their knowledge with yours.
- If you must design a new ontology, consult widely with other potential users. This will make it most useful and most likely to be adopted.
- Follow naming conventions. For example, call a class by the singular name of its members. For example, call a class "Resort" not "Resorts". Resist the temptation to call it "ResortConcept" (thinking it is only the concept of a resort, not a resort; see the box on page 724). When naming classes and properties, think about how they will be used. It sounds better to say that "$r1$ is a Resort" than "$r1$ is a Resorts", which is better than "$r1$ is a ResortConcept".
- As a last option, specify the matching between ontologies. Sometimes ontology matching has to be done when ontologies are developed independently. It is best if matching can be avoided; it makes knowledge using the ontologies much more complicated because there are multiple ways to say the same thing.

OWL is at a lower level than most people will want to specify or read. It is designed to be a machine-readable specification. There are many editors that let you edit OWL representation. One example is **Protégé** (http://protege.stanford.edu/). An ontology editor should support the following:

- It should provide a way for people to input ontologies at the level of abstraction that makes the most sense.
- Given a concept a user wants to use, an ontology editor should facilitate finding the terminology for that concept or determining that there is no corresponding term.
- It should be straightforward for someone to determine the meaning of a term.
- It should be as easy as possible to check that the ontology is correct (i.e., matches the user's intended interpretation for the terms).
- It should create an ontology that others can use. This means that it should use a standardized language as much as possible.

### 16.3.2 Top-Level Ontologies

Example 16.16 (page 721) defines a domain ontology for apartment building that could be used by people who want to write a knowledge base that refers to things that can appear on maps. Each domain ontology implicitly or explicitly assumes a higher-level ontology that it can fit into. The apartment building ontology assumes buildings are defined.

A **top-level ontology** provides a definition of *everything* at a very abstract level. The goal of a top-level ontology is to provide a useful categorization on which to base other ontologies. Making it explicit how domain ontologies fit into an upper-level ontology promises to facilitate the integration of these ontologies. The integration of ontologies is necessary to allow applications to refer to multiple knowledge bases, each of which may use different ontologies.

At the top is **entity**. OWL calls the top of the hierarchy **thing**. Essentially, everything is an entity.

Some of the high-level properties used to define domain ontologies include

- Concrete or abstract: physical objects and events are concrete, but mathematic objects and times are abstract.

- Continuant or occurrent: A **continuant** is something that exists at an instant in time and continues to exist through time. Examples include a person, a finger, a country, a smile, the smell of a flower, and an email. When a continuant exists at any time, so do its parts. Continuants maintain their identity through time. An **occurrent** is something that has temporal parts, for example, a life, infancy, smiling, the opening of a flower,

### Classes and Concepts

When defining an ontology, it is tempting to name the classes **concepts**, because symbols represent concepts: mappings from the internal representation into the object or relations that the symbols represent.

For example, it may be tempting to call the class of unicorns "unicornConcept" because there are no unicorns, only the concept of a unicorn. However, unicorns and the concept of unicorns are very different; one is an animal and one is a subclass of knowledge. A unicorn has four legs and a horn coming out of its head. The concept of a unicorn does not have legs or horns. You would be very surprised if a unicorn appeared in a university lecture about ontologies, but you should not be surprised if the concept of a unicorn appeared. There are no instances of unicorns, but there are many instances of the concept of a unicorn. If you mean a unicorn, you should use the term "unicorn". If you mean the concept of a unicorn, you should use "concept of a unicorn". You should not say that a unicorn concept has four legs, because instances of knowledge do not have legs; animals, furniture, and some robots have legs.

As another example, consider a tectonic plate, which is part of the Earth's crust. The plates are millions of years old. The concept of a plate is less than a hundred years old. Someone can have the concept of a tectonic plate in their head, but they cannot have a tectonic plate in their head. It should be clear that a tectonic plate and the concept of a tectonic plate are very different things, with very different properties. You should not use "concept of a tectonic plate" when you mean "tectonic plate" and vice versa.

Calling objects concepts is a common error in building ontologies. Although you are free to call things by whatever name you want, it is only useful for knowledge sharing if other people adopt your ontology. They will not adopt it if it does not make sense to them.

and sending an email. One way to think about the difference is to consider the entity's parts: a finger is part of a person, but is not part of a life; infancy is part of a life, but is not part of a person. Continuants participate in occurrents. Processes that last through time and events that occur at an instant in time are both occurrents.

An alternative to the continent/occurrent dichotomy is a four-dimensional or **perdurant** view where objects exist in the space-time, so a person is a trajectory though space and time, and there is no distinction between the person and the life. At any time, a person is a snapshot of the four-dimensional trajectory.

- Dependent or independent: An **independent continuant** is something that can exist by itself or is part of another entity. For example, a person, a face, a pen, a flower, a country, and the atmosphere are independent continuants. A dependent continuant only exists by virtue of another entity and is not a part of that entity. For example, a smile, the ability to laugh, or the inside of your mouth, or the ownership relation between a person and a phone, can only exist in relation to another object or objects. Note that something that is a part of another object is an independent continuant; for example, while a heart cannot exist without a body, it can be detached from the body and still exist. This is different from a smile; you cannot detach a smile from a cat.

  An occurrent that is dependent on an entity is a process or an event. A **process** is something that happens over time, has temporal parts, and depends on a continuant. For example, Joe's life has parts such as infancy, childhood, adolescence, and adulthood and involves a continuant, Joe. A holiday, writing an email, and a robot cleaning the lab are all processes. An **event** is something that happens at an instant, and is often a process boundary. For example, the first goal in the 2022 FIFA World Cup final is an event that happens at the instant the ball crosses the goal line; it could be seen as the end of a process that involves a team.

- Connected or scattered: A living bird is a single connected whole, but a flock of birds is a scattered entity made up of multiple birds. March 2024 is a connected single but Tuesdays from 3:00 to 4:00 GMT is a scattered temporal region.

- Material or immaterial. An independent continuant is either a **material entity** or an **immaterial entity**. A material entity has some matter as a part. Material entities are localized in space and can move in space. Examples of material entities are a person, a football team, Mount Everest, and Hurricane Katrina. Immaterial entities are abstract. Examples of immaterial entities are the first email you sent last Monday, a plan, and an experimental protocol. Note that you need a physical embodiment of an email to receive it (e.g., as text on your smartphone or spoken by a speech synthesizer), but the email is not that physical embodiment; a different physical embodiment could still be the same email.

Different categories can be formed by choosing among these dichotomies. A material entity that is a single coherent whole is an **object**. An object maintains its identity through time even if it gains or loses parts (e.g., a person who loses some hair, a belief, or even a leg, is still the same person). A person, a chair, a cake, or a computer are all objects. The left leg of a person (if it is still attached to the person), a football team, or the equator are not objects. If a robot were asked to find three objects, it would not be reasonable to bring a chair and claim the back, the seat, and the left-front leg are three objects.

Designing a top-level ontology is difficult. It probably will not satisfy everyone. There always seem to be some problematic cases. In particular, boundary cases are often not well specified. However, using a standard top-level ontology should help in connecting ontologies together.

## 16.4 Social Impact

To make predictions on data, the **provenance** of the data or **data lineage** – where the data came from and how it was manipulated – can make a difference between a good prediction and nonsense. Provenance is typically recorded as **metadata** – data about the data – including:

- Who collected each piece of data? What are their credentials?
- Who transcribed the information?
- What was the protocol used to collect the data? Was the data chosen at random or chosen because it was interesting or some other reason?
- What were the controls? What was manipulated, when?
- What sensors were used? What is their reliability and operating range?
- What processing has been done to the data?

Such metadata is needed for environmental, geospatial, and social data – data about the Earth – that is collected by people and used for environmental decision making [Gil et al., 2019].

This is particularly important if the data should be FAIR [Wilkinson et al., 2016]:

- *Findable* – the (meta)data uses unique persistent identifiers, such as IRIs.
- *Accessible* – the data is available using free and open protocols, and the metadata is accessible even when the data is not.

- *Interoperable* – the vocabulary is defined using formal knowledge representation languages (ontologies).

- *Reusable* – the data uses rich metadata, including provenance, and an appropriate open license, so that the community can use the data.

Data repositories based on these principles are available for many areas including Earth observations [NASA, 2022], social sciences [King, 2007], computational workflows [Goble et al., 2020], and all research domains [Springer Nature, 2022]. FAIR data is an important part of modern data-driven science, however, some researchers that have commercial or military reasons to think of themselves as being in competition with one another may have an incentive to not follow FAIR guidelines.

Stodden et al. [2016], Gil et al. [2017], and Sikos et al. [2021] overview ways to enhance reproducibility in data science. Gebru et al. [2021] propose 57 questions about the content of a dataset and the workflow used to produce it.

## 16.5 Review

The following are the main points you should have learned from this chapter:

- Individual–property–value triples form a flexible, universal representation for relations.
- Ontologies allow for semantic interoperability and knowledge sharing.
- OWL ontologies are built from individuals, classes, and properties. A class is a set of real and potential individuals.
- A top-level ontology allows for a framework where domain ontologies can be designed to interoperate.
- Data repositories with provenance, based on ontologies, are widely used in modern data-driven science.

## 16.6 References and Further Reading

Sowa [2000] and Brachman and Levesque [2004] give an overview of knowledge representation. Davis [1990] is an accessible introduction to a wealth of knowledge representation issues in commonsense reasoning. Brachman and Levesque [1985] present many classic knowledge representation papers. See Woods [2007] for an overview of semantic networks.

Hogan et al. [2021] and Chaudhri et al. [2022] provide a comprehensive introduction to knowledge graphs.

For an overview of the philosophical and computational aspects of ontologies, see Smith [2003] and Sowa [2011].

The semantic web and its technologies are described by Berners-Lee et al. [2001], Hendler et al. [2002], Antoniou and van Harmelen [2008], and Allemang et al. [2020]. Janowicz et al. [2015] explain the role of semantics in big data. Kendall and McGuinness [2019] overview modern ontology engineering.

The description of OWL is based on OWL-2; see W3C OWL Working Group [2012], Hitzler et al. [2012], and Motik et al. [2012]. Krötzsch [2012] describes the OWL 2 profiles. Baader et al. [2007] overview description logic.

Heath and Bizer [2011] overview the vision of **linked data**. DBpedia [Auer et al., 2007], **YAGO** [Suchanek et al., 2007; Hoffart et al., 2013; Mahdisoltani et al., 2015], **Wikidata** [Vrandečić and Krötzsch, 2014] (http://www.wikidata.org/), and Knowledge Vault [Gabrilovich et al., 2014] are large knowledge bases that use triples and ontologies to represent facts about millions of entities.

The top-level ontology is based on **BFO**, the **Basic Formal Ontology** 2.0, described by Smith [2015] and Arp et al. [2015] and the ontology of Sowa [2000]. Other top-level ontologies include DOLCE [Gangemi et al., 2003], Cyc [Panton et al., 2006], and SUMO [Niles and Pease, 2001; Pease, 2011]. A more lightweight and widely used ontology is at http://schema.org.

SNOMED Clinical Terms (SNOMED CT) [IHTSDO, 2016] is a large medical ontology that is used in clinical practice. You can explore it at http://browser.ihtsdotools.org/.

## 16.7 Exercises

**Exercise 16.1** There are many possible kinship relationships you could imagine, like mother, father, great-aunt, second-cousin-twice-removed, and natural-paternal-uncle. Some of these can be defined in terms of the others, for example:

$$\begin{aligned}&\mathit{brother}(X,Y) \leftarrow \mathit{father}(X,Z) \wedge \mathit{natural\_paternal\_uncle}(Y,Z).\\&\mathit{sister}(X,Y) \leftarrow \mathit{parent}(Z,X) \wedge \mathit{parent}(Z,Y) \wedge\\&\qquad \mathit{female}(X) \wedge \mathit{different}(X,Y).\end{aligned}$$

Give two quite different representations for kinship relationships based on different relations being primitive.

Consider representing the primitive kinship relationship using relation

$$\mathit{children}(\mathit{Mother}, \mathit{Father}, \mathit{List\_of\_children}).$$

What advantages or disadvantages may this representation have compared to the two you designed above?

**Exercise 16.2** A travel site has a database that represents information about hotels and feedback from users that uses the relations

$$\begin{aligned}&\mathit{hotel}(\mathit{Hotel\_Id}, \mathit{Name}, \mathit{City}, \mathit{Province\_or\_state}, \mathit{Country}, \mathit{Address})\\&\mathit{reported\_clean}(\mathit{Hotel\_Id}, \mathit{RoomNumber}, \mathit{Cleanliness}, \mathit{day}(\mathit{Year}, \mathit{Month}, \mathit{Day})).\end{aligned}$$

Show how the following facts can be represented using triple notation, using vocabularies that make sense:

```
hotel(h345, "The Beach Hotel", victoria, bc,
      canada, "300 Beach St").
reported_clean(h345, 127, clean, day(2023,01,25)).
```

Is it reasonable to represent the hotel name and address as strings? Explain.

**Exercise 16.3** Christine Sinclair (Q262802) was born in Burnaby (Q244025), British Columbia. Give the triples in Wikidata that relate her place of birth to the name of the province she was born in. The result should be a sequence of triples starting with one with Q262802 as the subject, and ending with "British Columbia"(en), where the object of each tuple is the subject of the next tuple. Give both the Wikidata tuples as well as the English translation. The information can be found starting from https://www.wikidata.org/wiki/Q262802. The first triple is

$$Q262802\ \ P19\ \ Q244025.\ \ \text{"Christine Sinclair's place of birth was Burnaby".}$$

The next tuple then has Q244025 as the subject.

**Exercise 16.4** Give 10 tuples that are related to the first goal scored in the 2010 FIFA World Cup Final (Q208401 in Wikidata), scored by Andrés Iniesta (Q43729) at 116 minutes. Either draw the relationships as in Figure 16.1 (page 706) or write the triples using the Wikidata names, as well as a translation into English. The triples should be connected (as they are in Figure 16.1). The information can be found at https://www.wikidata.org/wiki/Q208401.

**Exercise 16.5** Sam has proposed that any $n$-ary relation $P(X_1, X_2, X_3, \ldots, X_n)$ can be re-expressed as $n-1$ binary relations, namely

$$P_1(X_1, X_2), P_2(X_2, X_3), P_3(X_3, X_4), \ldots, P_{n-1}(X_{n-1}, X_n).$$

Explain to Sam why this may not be such a good idea. What problems would arise if Sam tried to do this? Use an example to demonstrate where the problem arises.

**Exercise 16.6** Write an ontology for the objects that often appear on your desk that may be useful for a robot that is meant to tidy your desk. Think of the categories that (a) the robot can perceive and (b) should be distinguished for the task.

**Exercise 16.7** Suppose a "beach resort" is a resort near a beach that the resort guests can use. The beach has to be near the sea or a lake, where swimming is permitted. A resort must have places to sleep and places to eat. Write a definition of beach resort in OWL.

**Exercise 16.8** A luxury hotel has multiple rooms to rent, each of which is comfortable and has a view. The hotel must also have more than one restaurant. There must be menu items for vegetarians and for meat eaters to eat in the restaurants.

(a) Define a luxury hotel in OWL, based on this description. Make reasonable assumptions where the specification is ambiguous.
(b) Suggest three other properties you would expect of a luxury hotel. For each, give the natural language definition and the OWL specification.

**Exercise 16.9** For the following, explain how each is categorized by the top-level ontology of Section 16.3.2 (page 723):

(a) your skin

(b) the period at the end of the first sentence of this chapter
(c) the excitement a child has before a vacation
(d) the trip home from a vacation
(e) a computer program
(f) summer holidays
(g) the ring of a telephone
(h) the dust on your desk
(i) the task of cleaning your office
(j) the diagnosis of flu in a person
(k) France.

Based on this experience, suggest and justify a modification of the top-level ontology. Think about categories that are not exclusive or other distinctions that seem to be fundamental.

# Chapter 17

# Relational Learning and Probabilistic Reasoning

*The mind is a neural computer, fitted by natural selection with combinatorial algorithms for causal and probabilistic reasoning about plants, animals, objects, and people.*

*In a universe with any regularities at all, decisions informed about the past are better than decisions made at random. That has always been true, and we would expect organisms, especially informavores such as humans, to have evolved acute intuitions about probability. The founders of probability, like the founders of logic, assumed they were just formalizing common sense.*

– Steven Pinker [1997, pp. 524, 343]

In the machine learning and probabilistic models presented in earlier chapters, the world is made up of features and random variables. As Pinker points out, we generally reason about things. Things are not features or random variables; it doesn't make sense to talk about the probability of an individual animal, but you could reason about the probability that it is sick, based on its symptoms. This chapter is about how to learn and make probabilistic predictions about things or entities.

The representation dimension (page 24) has, as its top level, reasoning in terms of individuals (**entities**) and **relations**. Reasoning in terms of relations allows for compact representations that can be built independently of the particular entities, but can also be used to learn and reason about each entity. This chapter outlines how feature-based representations as used in learning and probabilistic reasoning can be expanded to deal also with entities and relations. A relational model can benefit from being able to be built before the entities are known and, therefore, before the features are known.

**Statistical relational AI** or **neuro-symbolic AI** involves making predictions about relations based on **relational data** consisting of a relational database, and perhaps metadata (page 726). Statistical relational AI is a general term for relational predictions based on data, whereas neuro-symbolic AI involves using neural networks and other embedding-based techniques for predictions. This encompasses:

- Predicting attributes of entities based on their other attributes and attributes of entities they are related to.

- Predicting relations based on properties and relations of the entities involved. The simplest case is learning a single binary relation (Section 17.2.1), which is useful for domains like movie recommendations. This is extended to learning triples in Section 17.2.2, and learning more general relations in Section 17.3.

- Predicting **identity**, whether descriptions denote the same entity – the descriptions are equal (page 687) – for example, which citations refer to the same papers, or whether two descriptions refer to the same person (Section 17.4).

- Predicting **existence**, whether an entity exists that fits a description, for example whether there is a person in a particular room (Section 17.4).

The set of all entities of a type is called the **population**. In this chapter, a property where the range is an entity (e.g., a person or a movie) is called a **relation** and the term **property** is used when the range is a fixed set, such as Boolean or the reals.

## 17.1 From Relations to Features and Random Variables

The learning of Chapters 7 and 8 and the probabilistic reasoning of Chapter 9 were in terms of features (page 127) and random variables (page 377). Neither entities, properties, nor relations are features or random variables, but they can be used to construct random variables.

Unfortunately, the name "variable" is used for random variables (page 377) and logical variables (page 649), but these are not related; a logical variable denotes an entity and a random variable is a function on worlds or states. This chapter always distinguishes the two; for other sources you need to determine which is meant from the context.

The random variables from a knowledge graph (Section 16.1) are defined as follows:

- There is a random variable for each entity–property pair for functional properties and a random variable for each entity–relation pair for functional relations. Recall (page 710) that $p$ is **functional** if there is a unique object for each subject; i.e., if $(x,p,y_1)$ and $(x,p,y_2)$ then $y_1 = y_2$. The range of the property is the domain of the random variable. For example, height in centimeters (at age 20) of Christine Sinclair (Q262802 in Wikidata) is a real-valued random variable if property *height* is functional. *Month-of-birth* is a categorical random variable for each person. *Birth-mother* of a particular person is a random variable with people as the domain.

  For a functional relation (the object of each triple is an entity), such as *birth-mother*, a prediction is a probability distribution over entities. Such a probability distribution cannot be defined independently of the population; instead, the probability over entities needs to be learned for the particular population or a function of the embeddings of the entity and relationships needs to be defined.

- For non-functional properties, there is a Boolean random variable for each subject–property–value or subject–relation–object triple. For example, *participated-in* is a non-functional relation, and there is a Boolean random variable for triples such as *Q262802 participated-in Q181278* (whether Christine Sinclair participated in the 2020 Summer Olympics).

For more general relationships $r(X_1, \ldots, X_k)$:

- If one argument, say $X_k$, is a function of the other arguments, there is a random variable for each tuple $r(e_1, \ldots, e_{k-1})$ where the domain of the random variable is the set of values that $X_k$ can take. For example, the relation $rated(U, M, R)$, which means that $R$ was the rating (from 1 to 5) given by user $U$ to movie $M$, gives a random variable for each user–movie pair with domain the set of possible ratings, namely $\{1, 2, 3, 4, 5\}$. Predicting the rating for a particular user and movie can be seen as a regression task, where the prediction is a real number, or a classification task, where the prediction is a probability distribution over the numbers from 1 to 5.

- Otherwise, there is a Boolean random variable for each tuple $r(e_1, \ldots, e_k)$.

In the description below, the functional case is treated as a relation of $k-1$ arguments, with a non-Boolean prediction.

A relation of $k$ arguments gives $n^k$ random variables, where $n$ is the number of entities. This might be fewer depending on the domains of the arguments; for example, if the first argument is users and the second argument is movies, the number of random variables is the number of users times the number of movies. If arbitrary interdependence among the random variables is allowed, there are $2^{n^k} - 1$ probabilities to be assigned, just for a single Boolean relation with $k$ arguments. How to avoid this combinatorial explosion of the number of random variables is the subject of **lifted inference**.

## 17.2 Embedding-Based models

### 17.2.1 Learning a Binary Relation

Suppose you are given a database of a binary relation where both arguments are entities, and the aim is to predict whether other tuples are true. The machine learning methods of Chapters 7 and 8 are not directly applicable as the entities are represented using meaningless names (identifiers). An algorithm that does this is defined below, for the case where there are no other relations defined, but where there can also be a numeric prediction for the pair. This is explained using a particular example of predicting a user's ratings for an item such as a movie.

In a **recommender system**, users are given **personalized recommendations** of items they may like. One technique for recommender systems is to predict the rating of a user on an item from the ratings of similar users or similar items, by what is called **collaborative filtering**.

**Example 17.1** MovieLens (https://movielens.org/) is a movie recommendation system that acquires movie ratings from users. The rating is from 1 to 5 stars, where 5 stars is better. The first few tuples of one dataset are shown in Table 17.1, where each user is given a unique number, each item (movie) is given a unique number, and the timestamp is the Unix standard of seconds since 1970-01-01 UTC. Such data can be used in a recommendation system to make predictions of other movies a user might like.

One way for a recommender system to **personalize recommendations** is to present the user with the **top-*n*** items, where $n$ is a positive integer, say 10. This can be done by first estimating the rating of each item for a user and then presenting the $n$ items with the highest predicted rating. This is not a good solution in general, as all of the top items might be very similar. The system should also take diversity into account when choosing the set of items.

In the example above, the items were movies, but they could also be consumer goods, restaurants, holidays, or other items.

Suppose *Es* is a dataset of $\langle u, i, r\rangle$ triples, where $\langle u, i, r\rangle$ means user $u$ gave item $i$ a rating of $r$ (ignoring the timestamp). Let $\widehat{r}(u, i)$ be the predicted rating

| User | Item | Rating | Timestamp |
|---|---|---|---|
| 196 | 242 | 3 | 881250949 |
| 186 | 302 | 3 | 891717742 |
| 22 | 377 | 1 | 878887116 |
| 244 | 51 | 2 | 880606923 |
| 253 | 465 | 5 | 891628467 |
| ... | ... | ... | ... |

Table 17.1: Part of the MovieLens dataset

of user $u$ on item $i$. The aim is to optimize the sum-of-squares error

$$\sum_{\langle u,i,r\rangle \in Es} (\widehat{r}(u,i) - r)^2.$$

As with most machine learning, the aim is to optimize for the test examples (page 263), not for the training examples.

Following is a sequence of increasingly sophisticated models for $\widehat{r}(u,i)$, the prediction of the rating of a user for an item. Each model adds more terms to the model, in a similar way to how features are added in boosting (page 309) and residuals in deep learning (page 349).

**Make a single prediction** The simplest case is to predict the same rating for all users and items: $\widehat{r}(u,i) = \mu$, where $\mu$ is the mean rating. Recall (page 277) that when predicting the same value for every instance, predicting the mean minimizes the sum-of-squares error.

**Add user and item biases** Some users might give higher ratings than other users, and some movies may have higher ratings than other movies. You can take this into account using

$$\widehat{r}(u,i) = \mu + b_1[u] + b_2[i]$$

where user $u$ has bias $b_1[u]$ and item $i$ has bias $b_2[i]$. The parameters $b_1[u]$ and $b_2[i]$ are chosen to minimize the sum-of-squares error. If there are

Netflix Prize

There was a considerable amount of research on collaborative filtering with the **Netflix Prize** to award \$1,000,000 to the team that could improve the prediction accuracy of Netflix's proprietary system, measured in terms of sum-of-squares, by 10%. Each rating gives a user, a movie, a rating from 1 to 5 stars, and a date and time the rating was made. The dataset consisted of approximately 100 million ratings from 480,189 anonymized users on 17,770 movies that was collected over a 7-year period. The prize was won in 2009 by a team that averaged over a collection of hundreds of predictors, some of which were quite sophisticated. After 3 years of research, the winning team beat another team by just 20 minutes to win the prize. They both had solutions which had essentially the same error, which was just under the threshold to win. Interestingly, an average of the two solutions was better than either alone.

The algorithm presented here is the basic algorithm that gave the most improvement.

The Netflix dataset is no longer available because of **privacy** concerns. Although users were only identified by a number, there was enough information, if combined with other information, to potentially identify some of the users.

$n$ users and $m$ items, there are $n + m$ parameters to tune (assuming $\mu$ is fixed). Finding the best parameters is an optimization problem that can be done with a method like gradient descent (page 169), as was used for the linear learner (page 288).

One might think that $b_1[u]$ should be directly related to the average rating for user $u$ and $b_2[i]$ should be directly related to the average rating for item $i$. However, it is possible that $b_1[u] < 0$ even if all of the ratings for user $u$ were above the mean $\mu$. This can occur if user $u$ only rated popular items and rated them lower than other people.

Optimizing the $b_1[u]$ and $b_2[i]$ parameters can help get better estimates of the ratings, but it does not help in personalizing the recommendations, because the movies are still ordered the same for every user.

**Add a latent property** You could hypothesize that there is an underlying property of each user and each movie that enables more accurate predictions, such as the age of each user, and the age-appeal of each movie. A real-valued **latent property** or **hidden property** for each entity can be tuned to fit the data.

Suppose the latent property for user $u$ has a value $f_1[u]$, and the latent property for item $i$ has value $f_2[i]$. The product of these is used to offset the rating of that item for that user:

$$\widehat{r}(u,i) = \mu + b_1[u] + b_2[i] + f_1[u] * f_2[i].$$

If $f_1[u]$ and $f_2[i]$ are both positive or both negative, the property will increase the prediction. If one of $f_1[u]$ or $f_2[i]$ is negative and the other is positive, the property will decrease the prediction.

**Example 17.2** Figure 17.1 (page 737) shows a plot of the ratings as a function of a single latent property. This uses the subset of the MovieLens 100k dataset, containing the 20 movies that had the most ratings, and the 20 users who had the most ratings for these movies. It was trained for 1000 iterations of gradient descent, with a single latent property.

On the $x$-axis are the users, ordered by their value, $f_1[u]$, on the property. On the $y$-axis are the movies, ordered by their value, $f_2[i]$ on the property. Each rating is then plotted against the user and the movie, so that triple $\langle u,i,r\rangle$ is depicted by plotting $r$ at the $(x,y)$ position $(f_1[u], f_2[i])$. Thus each vertical column of numbers corresponds to a user, and each horizontal row of numbers is a movie. The columns overlap if two users have very similar values on the property. The rows overlap for movies that have very similar values on the property. The users and the movies where the property values are close to zero are not affected by this property, as the prediction uses the product of values of the properties.

In general, high ratings are in the top-right and the bottom-left, as these are the ratings that are positive in the product, and low ratings in the top-left and bottom-right, as their product is negative. Note that what is high and low is relative to the user and movie biases; what is high for one movie may be different from what is high for another movie.

**Add $k$ latent properties** Instead of using just one property, consider using $k$ latent properties for each user and item. There is a value $E_1[u][f]$ (using Python notation for matrices (page 352)) for each user $u$ and property $f \in \{0, \ldots, k-1\}$. The vector $E_1[u]$ of length $k$ is called the **user embedding** for user $u$, analogous to the **word embeddings** used in deep learning (page 350). Similarly, there is a value $E_2[i][f]$ for every item $i$ and property $f$, where $E_2[i]$ is the **item embedding** for item $i$. The contributions of the separate properties are added. This gives the prediction

$$\widehat{r}(u,i) = \mu + b_1[u] + b_2[i] + \sum_f E_1[u][f] * E_2[i][f].$$

This is often called a **matrix factorization** method as the summation corresponds to **matrix multiplication** (page 352) of $E_1$ and the transpose –

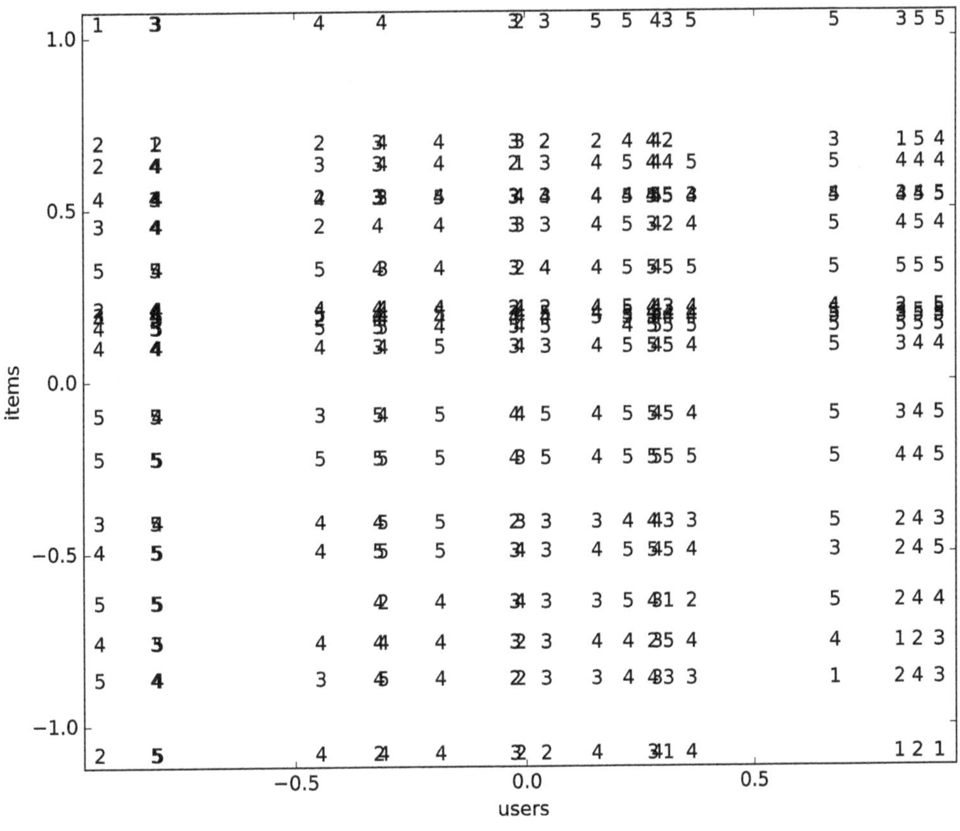


Figure 17.1: Movie ratings as a function of a single latent property; see Example 17.2 (page 736)

flipping the arguments – of $E_2$.

**Regularize** To avoid overfitting, a **regularization** (page 302) term can be added to prevent the parameters from growing too much and overfitting the given data. Here an $L_2$ regularizer (page 303) for each of the parameters is added to the optimization. The goal is to choose the parameters to

$$minimize \left( \sum_{\langle u,i,r\rangle \in Es} (\widehat{r}(u,i) - r)^2 \right)$$
$$+ \lambda \left( \sum_u (b_1[u]^2 + \sum_f E_1[u][f]^2) + \sum_i (b_2[i]^2 + \sum_f E_2[i][f]^2) \right) \quad (17.1)$$

where $\lambda$ is a regularization parameter, which can be tuned by cross validation (page 304).

The parameters $b_1$, $b_2$, $E_1$, and $E_2$ can be optimized using stochastic gradient descent (page 293), as shown in Figure 17.2 (page 739). The parameters there are adjusted in each iteration, but regularized after going through the dataset, which might not be the best choice; see Exercise 17.3 (page 761). Note that the elements of $E_1[i][f]$ and $E_2[u][f]$ need to be initialized randomly (and not to the same value) to force each property to be different.

To understand what is being learned, consider the following thought experiment:

**Example 17.3** In the rating running example, suppose there is a genre of movies that some people really like and others hate. Suppose property $f$ has 1 for movies of that genre, and 0 for other movies. Users who like that genre more than would be expected from other properties have a high value for property $f$, those that dislike it more have a negative value, and others have values close to zero. This can be seen as a soft clustering – as in expectation maximization (EM) (page 478) – for users into the categories of *likes*, *dislikes*, and *indifferent*. Suppose now that the user property $f$ is fixed to these values, but the corresponding property for the movie is learned, so it might not exactly correspond to the genre. The movies that have a high value for the property are the movies that are liked by the people who like the genre and disliked by those who hate the genre. Thus it learns which movies those people like or dislike. Again it is providing a soft clustering of movies. With multiple latent properties, it can find multiple soft clusterings, with the values added together in a similar way to boosting (page 309) and residuals in deep learning (page 349).

The **alternating least squares** algorithm acts like the above description, alternating fixing user or item properties and optimizing the other, but starting with random assignments. Optimizing Equation (17.1) with user or item parameters fixed gives a linear regression on the other parameters. The adjustments in Figure 17.2 (page 739) are more fine grained, but the results are similar.

This algorithm can be evaluated by how well it predicts future ratings by training it with the data up to a certain time, and testing it on future data.

The algorithm can be modified to take into account observed attributes of items and users by fixing some of the properties. For example, the Movielens dataset includes 19 genres, which can be represented using 19 of the embedding positions, one position for each genre (forming a one-hot encoding (page 331) for part of the embedding space). If position $g$ represents a particular genre, a movie has 1 at position $g$ if the movie has the corresponding

```
procedure Collaborative_filter_learner(Es, η, λ)
    Inputs
        Es: set of ⟨user, item, rating⟩ triples
        η: gradient descent step size
        λ: regularization parameter
    Output
        function to predict rating for a ⟨user, item⟩ pair
    μ := average rating
    assign E1[u][f], E2[i][f] randomly
    assign b1[u], b2[i] arbitrarily
    define r̂(u,i) = μ + b1[u] + b2[i] + Σ_f E1[u][f] * E2[i][f]
    repeat
                # Update parameters from training data:
        for each ⟨u,i,r⟩ ∈ Es do
            error := r̂(u,i) − r
            b1[u] := b1[u] − η * error
            b2[i] := b2[i] − η * error
            for each property f do
                E1[u][f] := E1[u][f] − η * error * E2[i][f]
                E2[i][f] := E2[i][f] − η * error * E1[u][f]
                # Regularize the parameters:
        for each item i do
            b1[u] := b1[u] − η * λ * b1[u]
            for each property f do
                E1[u][f] := E1[u][f] − η * λ * E1[u][f]
        for each user u do
            b2[i] := b2[i] − η * λ * b2[i]
            for each property f do
                E2[i][f] := E2[i][f] − η * λ * E2[i][f]
    until termination
    return r̂
```

Figure 17.2: Gradient descent for collaborative filtering

genre and 0 otherwise. Each user has a learnable parameter at position $g$ to indicate whether the genre is positive or negative for that user, as in Example 17.3 (page 738). Different positions are used for user properties. Using explicit properties is useful when users or items have few ratings from which to learn, or for the **cold-start problem**, which is how to make recommendations about new items or for new users; predictions can be made just on the observed properties, without any ratings needed.

This algorithm ignores the timestamp, but using the timestamp may help as users' preferences may change and items may come in and out of fashion. The dynamics of preferences becomes important when predicting future ratings – which is usually what is wanted – but there is usually very little data to learn the dynamics for each user.

The above was for regression, predicting the numerical rating of an item for a user. For Boolean classification, for example, whether the rating is greater than 3, the sigmoid (page 290) of a linear function provides a probabilistic prediction. When trained to optimize binary log loss (page 276), the algorithm can remain unchanged, except for an added sigmoid in the definition of $\widehat{r}$ on line 11 of Figure 17.2.

The Boolean function of whether a rating is greater than 3 is atypical because both positive and negative examples are provided. Most relations do not contain negative examples. For some, the closed-world assumption (page 207) – everything not stated is false – may be appropriate, but then there is nothing to learn. For relations where only positive examples are provided, for example predicting *rated*, which is true when a rating is provided, the above algorithm will conclude that everything is true, as that prediction minimizes Equation (17.1). The mean value ($\mu$ in Figure 17.2 (page 739)) is not defined. To handle this case, either $\mu$ can be treated as a parameter which must be regularized, or negative examples need to be provided. The ratio of positive to negative examples and the regularization parameter both provide a prior assumption of the probability, which is not something that can be estimated from the data. Because the algorithm can handle noise, it is reasonable to just choose random cases as negative examples, even though they could be positive. The absence of negative examples also makes evaluation challenging and is one reason why relational prediction methods are often judged using **ranking**, such as predicting the **top-*n*** (page 734) items for each user.

When used for recommendations, it might be better to take the diversity of the recommendations into account and recommend very different items than to recommend similar items. Thus, while predicting the ratings is useful, it does not lead directly to useful recommendations.

### 17.2.2 Learning Knowledge Graphs

Suppose the aim is to learn the triples of a knowledge graph (page 701). Consider predicting the truth of the triple $(s, r, o)$, where $s$ is the subject, $r$ is the relation (verb), and $o$ the object of the triple. A straightforward extension to matrix factorization (page 737) to predict triples is the **polyadic decomposition**, which decomposes a tensor (page 352) into matrices. It can be used to predict the probability of a triple – an element of a three-dimensional tensor – as

$$\widehat{p}((s,r,o)) = sigmoid(\mu + b_1[s] + b_2[r] + b_3[o] + \sum_f E_1[s][f] * E_2[r][f] * E_3[o][f])$$

using the tunable parameters

- a global bias $\mu$
- two biases for each entity $e$, namely $b_1[e]$, used when $e$ is in the first position, and $b_3[e]$, used when $e$ is in the third position
- a bias for each relation $r$, given by $b_2[r]$
- a matrix $E_1$, indexed by entities and properties, so that $E_1[e]$ is the vector of length $k$, called the **subject embedding** for $e$, used when $e$ appears as the first item of a triple, and a matrix $E_3$, providing the **object embedding** for each entity when it appears as the third item of a triple
- a matrix $E_2$, indexed by relations and properties, where $E_2[r]$ is the **relation embedding** for relation $r$.

All of the embeddings $E_1[e]$, $E_2[r]$, and $E_3[e]$ are the same length.

Training this model on a dataset of triples, minimizing categorical log loss (page 273) with L2 regularization (page 303), is like the algorithm of Figure 17.2 (page 739), but with a different predictor and more parameters to tune and regularize. With only a knowledge graph of triples with no negative examples, as with the binary case above, without regularizing $\mu$, all triples being true minimizes the error. Either negative examples need to be added or regularization of $\mu$ is required. The ratio of positive to negative examples, and the regularization of $\mu$, convey prior information about the proportion of tuples expected to be true, which cannot be obtained from a dataset of only positive triples.

The polyadic decomposition, however, does not work well because the subject and object embeddings are independent of each other.

**Example 17.4** Suppose user $u$ likes movies directed by a particular person $d$, and the knowledge is represented as $(u, likes, m)$ and $(m, directed\_by, d)$. Whether someone likes a movie only depends on the object embedding of the movie, but the directorship depends only on the subject embedding of the movie. As these embeddings do not interact, there is no way for the above embedding model to represent the interdependence. A solution to this is to also represent the inverse of the relations where $(m, likes^{-1}, u) \leftrightarrow (u, likes, m)$ and $(d, directed\_by^{-1}, m) \leftrightarrow (m, directed\_by, d)$.

The **polyadic decomposition with inverses** has embeddings for each relation $r$ and its inverse $r^{-1}$, where $(s,r,o) = (o,r^{-1},s)$, to make the prediction that is the average of the prediction from the two ways of representing the same tuple:

$$\widehat{p}(s,r,o) = \frac{1}{2}(\widehat{pd}(s,r,o) + \widehat{pd}(o,r^{-1},s))$$

where $\widehat{pd}$ is the prediction from the polyadic decomposition. This allows the interdependence of the subject and object embeddings, which can solve the problem of Example 17.4 (page 741).

The polyadic decomposition with inverses is **fully expressive**, meaning it can approximate any relation with a log loss less than and $\epsilon > 0$, even if all embeddings are restricted to be non-negative, and the value of all embedding values is bounded by a constant (which may depend on $\epsilon$). This means that it can memorize any relation, which is the best it can do in general; see the no-free-lunch theorem (page 315). It also means that there are no inherent restrictions on what can be represented. If the same embedding is used for the subject and the object, only symmetric relations can be represented or approximated.

Example 17.3 (page 738) explains how the user and items embedding used in prediction can be used to understand what is being learned. That explanation holds for a relation, for each embedding position where the relation has a non-zero value. In particular, for the case where all embeddings are non-negative:

- For the subject embedding, each embedding position is a soft clustering (page 478) of entities. Those entities in the cluster have a large value for that position, where large is relative to the other values. Similarly, for the object embedding.

- For each position, the product of the subject, relation, and object embeddings is only large if all three are large. When the relation embedding is large at a position, the entities in the subject clustering for that position are related to the entities in the corresponding object clustering.

- The addition ($\sum_f$) provides for multiple clusterings to be added together.

In the general case, when an even number of the values being multiplied are negative, the result is positive and it acts like the above. When an odd number of the values is negative (one or three of the subject, relation, and object is negative), the product is negative and this position can act like exceptions.

This method – and related methods – is clustering entities in various ways to provide the best predictions. What is learned is not general knowledge that can be applied to other populations. If the goal is to model a single population, for example in a social network, that might be adequate. However, if the aim is to learn knowledge that can be applied to new populations, this method does not work.

Decomposing a relation into matrices does not work well for relations with multiple arguments. If the relation is converted to triples using reification (page 703), the introduced entity has very few instances – the number of arguments to the relation – which makes learning challenging. If the polyadic deposition is used directly, the problem of independent positions – which motivated the inverses above – occurs for every pair of positions. Modeling the interaction between every pair of argument predictions leads to overfitting.

Embedding-based models that decompose a relation do not work for predicting properties with a fixed range, such as the age of users, because they rely on a lower-dimensional representation and there isn't one for properties. The vector for a user can be used to memorize the age in one or more of the embedding positions, which means it does not generalize.

# 17.3 Learning Interdependence of Relations

## 17.3.1 Relational Probabilistic Models

An alternative to the previous models that learn embedding of entities and relations is to learn the interdependencies of relations, building models that predict some relations in terms of others, similar to how graphical models of Chapter 9 represented the interdependencies of random variables.

The belief networks of Chapter 9 were defined in terms of random variables. Many domains are best modeled in terms of entities and relations. Agents must often build models before they know what entities are in the domain and, therefore, before they know what random variables exist. When the probabilities are being learned, the probabilities often do not depend on the identity of the entities. Probability models with entities and relations are studied in the area of **statistical relational AI**, and the models are referred to as **relational probabilistic models**, **probabilistic relational models**, or **probabilistic logic models**.

**Example 17.5** Consider the problem of predicting how well students will do in courses they have not taken. Figure 17.3 (page 744) shows some fictional data designed to show what can be done. Students $s_3$ and $s_4$ have a B average, on courses both of which have B averages. However, you should be able to distinguish them as you know something about the courses they have taken.

A **relational probabilistic model** (**RPM**) is a model in which the probabilities are specified on the relations, independently of the actual entities. The entities share the probability parameters. The sharing of the parameters is known as **parameter sharing** or **weight tying**, as in **convolutional neural networks** (page 347).

A **parameterized random variable** is of the form $R(t_1, \ldots, t_k)$, where each $t_i$ is a term (a logical variable or a constant). The parameterized random variable is said to be parameterized by the logical variables that appear in it. A **ground instance** of a parameterized random variable is obtained by substituting constants for the logical variables in the parameterized random variable. The ground instances of a parameterized random variable correspond to random variables, as in Section 17.1 (page 732). The domain of the random variable is the range of $R$. A Boolean parameterized random variable $R$ corresponds to a predicate symbol. For example, $Grade(S, C)$ is a parameterized random variable, and $Grade(s_3, c_4)$ is a random variable with domain the set of all possible grades.

We use the Datalog convention (page 655) that logical variables start with an upper-case letter and constants start with a lower-case letter. Parameterized random variables are written starting with an upper-case letter, with the corresponding proposition in lower case (e.g., $Diff(c_1) = true$ is written as $diff(c_1)$, and $Diff(c_1) = false$ is written as $\neg diff(c_1)$), similar to the convention for random variables (page 377).

A **plate model** consists of

- a directed graph in which the nodes are parameterized random variables
- a population of entities for each logical variable, and
- a conditional probability of each node given its parents.

A rectangle – a **plate** – is drawn around the parameterized random variables that share a logical variable. There is a plate for each logical variable. This notation is redundant, as the logical variables are specified in both the plates and the arguments. Sometimes one of these is omitted; often the arguments are omitted when they can be inferred from the plates.

**Example 17.6** Figure 17.4 (page 745) gives a plate model for predicting student grades. There is a plate $C$ for the courses and a plate $S$ for the students. The parameterized random variables are

- $Int(S)$, which represents whether student $S$ is intelligent

| *Student* | *Course* | *Grade* |
|---|---|---|
| $s_1$ | $c_1$ | A |
| $s_2$ | $c_1$ | C |
| $s_1$ | $c_2$ | B |
| $s_2$ | $c_3$ | B |
| $s_3$ | $c_2$ | B |
| $s_4$ | $c_3$ | B |
| $s_3$ | $c_4$ | ? |
| $s_4$ | $c_4$ | ? |

Figure 17.3: Predict which student is likely to do better in course $c_4$

- *Diff*(*C*), which represents whether course *C* is difficult,
- *Grade*(*S*, *C*), which represents the grade of student *S* in course *C*.

The probabilities for $P(Int(S))$, $P(DiffC))$, and $P(Grade(S,C) \mid Int(S), DiffC))$ need to be specified. If *I* and *D* are Boolean (with range *true* and *false*) and *Gr* has range $\{A, B, C\}$, then there are 10 parameters that define the probability distribution. Suppose $P(Int(S)) = 0.5$ and $P(DiffC)) = 0.5$ and $P(Grade(S,C) \mid Int(S), DiffC))$ is defined by the following table:

| *Int*(*S*) | *DiffC*) | *Grade*(*S*, *C*) | | |
|---|---|---|---|---|
| | | *A* | *B* | *C* |
| *true* | *true* | 0.5 | 0.4 | 0.1 |
| *true* | *false* | 0.9 | 0.09 | 0.01 |
| *false* | *true* | 0.01 | 0.1 | 0.9 |
| *false* | *false* | 0.1 | 0.4 | 0.5 |

Eight parameters are required to define $P(Grade(S,C) \mid Int(S), Diff(C))$ because there are four cases, and each case requires two numbers to be specified; the third can be inferred to ensure the probabilities sum to one.

If there were $n$ students and $m$ courses, in the grounding there would be $n$ instances of *Int*(*S*), $m$ instances of *DiffC*), and $n * m$ instances of *Grade*(*S*, *C*). So there would be $n + m + n * m$ random variables in the grounding.

A model that contains parametrized random variables is called a **lifted model**. A plate model means its **grounding** – the belief network in which nodes are all ground instances of the parameterized random variables (each logical variable replaced by an entity in its population) and the arcs are preserved. That is, the parametrized random variables in each plate are replicated for each entity. The conditional probabilities of the grounded belief network are the same as the corresponding instances of the plate model.

**Example 17.7** Consider conditioning the plate model of Figure 17.4 on the data given in Figure 17.3 (page 744), and querying the random variables corresponding to the last two rows. There are 4 courses and 4 students, and so there would be 24 random variables in the grounding. All of the instances

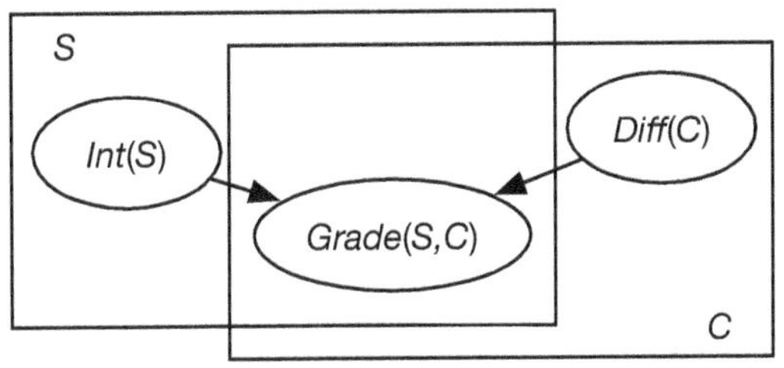


Figure 17.4: A plate model to predict the grades of students

of *Grade*$(S, C)$ that are not observed or queried can be pruned (page 417) or never constructed in the first place, resulting in the belief network of Figure 17.5. From this network, conditioned on the *obs*, the observed grades of Figure 17.3, and using the probabilities of Example 17.6, the following posterior probabilities can be derived:

| | $A$ | $B$ | $C$ |
|---|---|---|---|
| $P(Grade(s_3, c_4) \mid obs)$ | 0.491 | 0.245 | 0.264 |
| $P(Grade(s_4, c_4) \mid obs)$ | 0.264 | 0.245 | 0.491 |

Thus, this model predicts that $s_3$ is likely to do better than $s_4$ in course $c_4$.

Figure 17.6 (page 747) shows the three cases of how a directed arc interacts with a plate. The population of logical variable $X$ is $\{x_1, \ldots, x_n\}$. The random variable $A(x_i)$ is written as $A_i$, and similarly for $B$. The parametrization can be inferred from the plates.

In Figure 17.6(a), $A$ and $B$ are both within the plate, and so represent the parametrized random variables $A(X)$ and $B(X)$. In the grounding, the arc is replicated for every value of $X$. The conditional probability $P(B_i \mid A_i)$ is the same for every $i$, and is the one modeled by $P(B \mid A)$ in the lifted model. $A_i$ and $B_i$ are independent of $A_j$ and $B_j$ for $i \neq j$, unless there is another arc to make them dependent.

In Figure 17.6(b), the parent is outside of the plate, and so it is not replicated for each element of the population. $P(B_i \mid A)$ is the same for all $i$. This

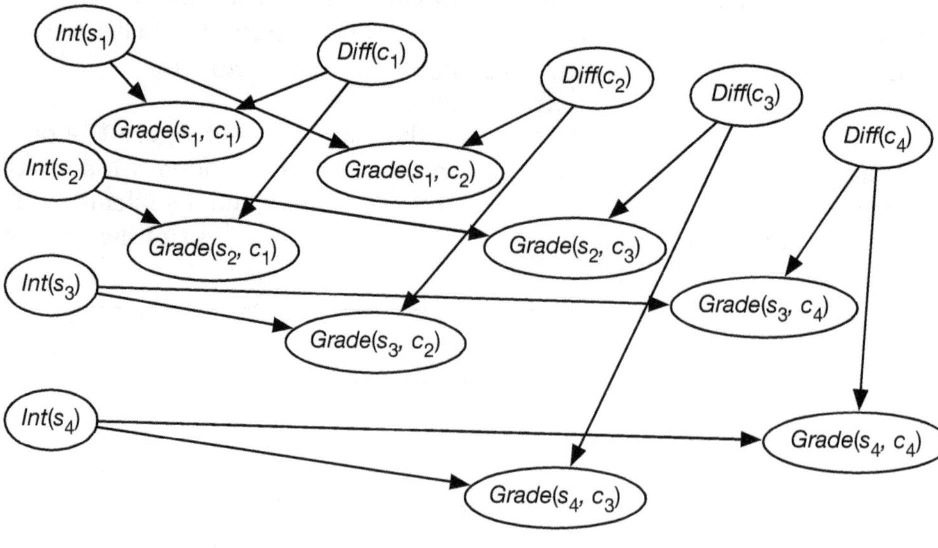


Figure 17.5: A grounding that is sufficient to predict from the data in Figure 17.3. Instances of *Grade*$(S, C)$ that are not observed or queried do not need to be created.

makes the $B_i$ dependent on each other when $A$ is not observed. The number of parameters in the lifted models of Figure 17.6(a) and (b) is the same as the network without the plates, and so is independent of the population size $n$.

In Figure 17.6(c), the child is outside of the plate, with a variable number of parents. In this case $B$ has $n$ parents and so cannot use the conditional probability $P(B \mid A)$. It needs an **aggregator** to compute the probability from arbitrary many parents. The aggregator is symmetric, as the index is of no significance; exchanging the names has no effect. This symmetry is called **exchangeability**. Some aggregators are the following:

- If the model is specified as a **probabilistic logic program** (page 397) with Boolean logical variables, the existential quantification of the logical variables in the body of a clause (page 649) results in a **noisy-or** (page 398) aggregation. In the aggregator of Figure 17.6(c), the noisy-or is equivalent to $b \leftarrow (\exists X\; a(X) \wedge n(X)) \vee n_0$, where $n_0$ and $n(x)$ are independent random variables for all instances $x$ of $X$.

- The model can be specified using weighted logical formulas (page 401), extended to first-order logic. A **first-order weighted logical formula** is a pair of a first-order logic formula and a weight. The conditional probability is proportional to the exponential of the sum of weights of the

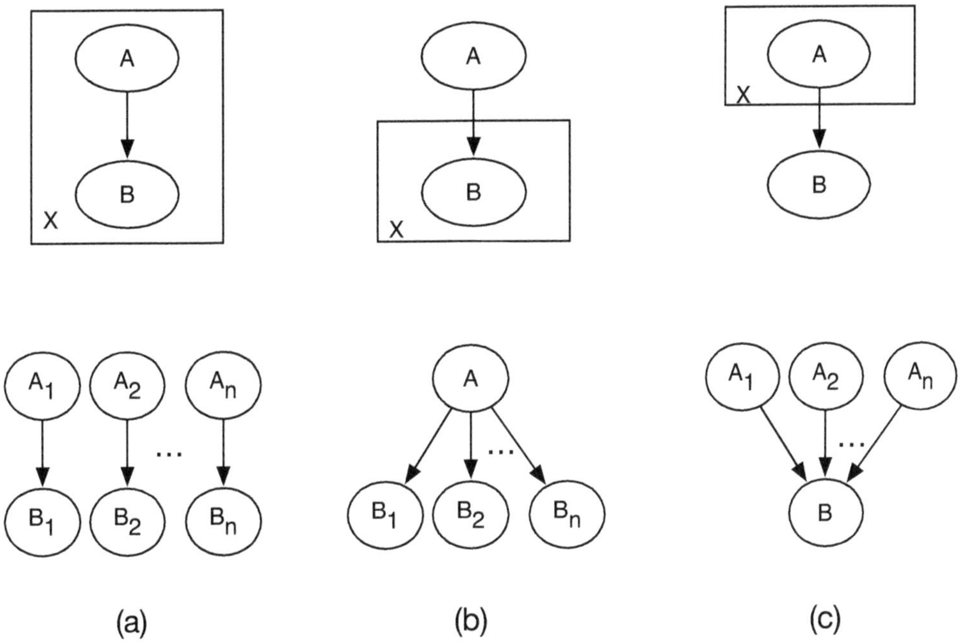


Figure 17.6: Three cases of arcs with plates: (a) an arc inside a plate; (b) an arc going into a plate; (c) an arc going out of a plate. On the top is a plate model and underneath is its grounding

groundings of formulas that are true. In this case, the aggregation becomes a case of **logistic regression** (page 400), called **relational logistic regression**.

For example, the first-order weighted formulas $(b : w_0)$, $(b \wedge a(X), w_1)$ and $(b \wedge \neg a(X), w_2)$ result in $P(b \mid as) = sigmoid(w_0 + c_1 * w_1 + c_2 * w_2)$, where *as* is an assignment of values to the parents consisting of $c_1$ entities with $A(e) = true$ and $c_2$ entities with $A(e) = false$.

- Standard database aggregators such as average, sum, or max of some values of the parents can be used.

- A more sophisticated aggregation, **latent Dirichlet allocation (LDA)**, is when the population of the plate corresponds to the domain of the child. The value of $A(v)$ can be used to compute $P(B = v)$. For example, using a softmax

$$P(B = v) = \frac{\exp(A(v))}{\sum_{v'} exp(A(v'))}$$

(or perhaps without the exponentiation, if $A(v) \geq 0$). The aggregation is thus implementing an **attention** mechanism, similar to that used in transformers (page 360).

For overlapping plates, the values are duplicated for each plate separately, as in the following example.

**Example 17.8** Suppose someone was shot and the problem is to determine who did it. Assume the shooting depends on having motive, opportunity, and

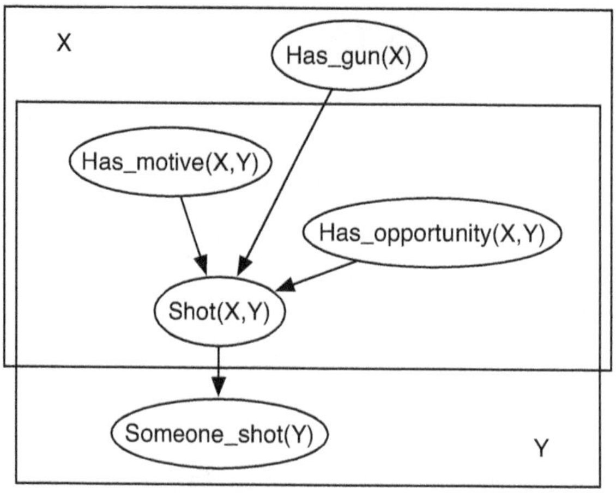


Figure 17.7: A plate model for determining who shot someone

a gun. A plate model for this is shown in Figure 17.7 (page 748), where $Y$ is the person shot and $X$ is the shooter.

When a particular person $y$ is observed to be shot, the aim is to determine which person $x$ could have shot them. The motive and the opportunity depend on both $x$ and $y$, but whether the shooter, $x$, has a gun does not depend on $y$. Noisy-or is an appropriate aggregator here; $y$ is shot if there exists someone who shot them, but there is some chance they were shot even if no one shot them (e.g., a gun went off randomly). There are probably different probabilities for the cases where $X = Y$ (they shot themself) and for $X \neq Y$ (the shooter and victim were different people). If there are 1000 people, there are 3,002,000 random variables in the grounding, including a million instances of $Has\_motive(X, Y)$ and a thousand instances of $Has\_gun(X)$. If all of the variables are Boolean, there are 13 parameters to be assigned: eight for *Shot*, two for *Someone_shot*, and one each for the other (parameterized) random variables. Each of these other variables could have parents; see Exercise 17.5 (page 761).

### 17.3.2 Collective Classification and Crowd Sourcing

Suppose there are many true/false questions that you would like the answer to. One way to find the answer might be to ask many people using **crowd sourcing**, where the users might be paid for reliable answers. Each person answers some subset of the questions; the aim is to determine which questions are true, and who to pay. Some people and bots may give random answers, in the hope of being paid for very little work. The problem of determining truth from crowd sourcing is called **truth discovery**.

One application for truth discovery is to evaluate predictions of an AI algorithm on a knowledge graph. You cannot just use a held-out test set for evaluation as there are only positive examples in a knowledge graph. Negative examples are required to evaluate probabilistic predictions, for example, using log loss. Negative examples can be acquired by crowd sourcing.

One way to represent this problem is the plate model of Figure 17.8, where $Answer(U, Q)$, the provided answer by user $U$ to question $Q$, depends on the reliability of $U$ and the truth of $Q$.

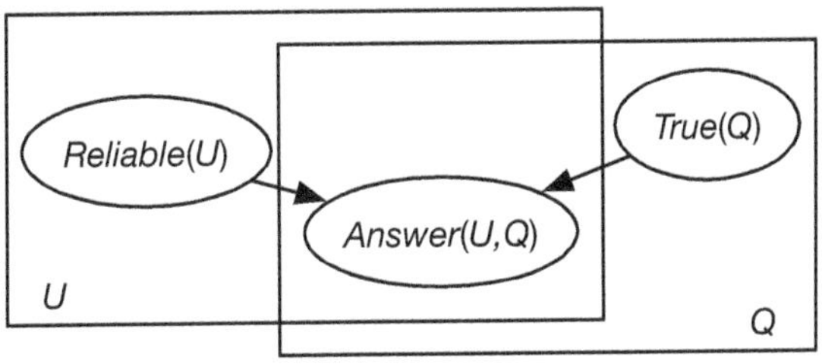


Figure 17.8: A plate model for truth discovery

The conditional probabilities can specify that the answer provided by reliable users is highly likely to be the truth, and the answer provided by an unreliable person is likely to be random. When conditioned on the answers provided, the users are classified as reliable or not and the questions are classified as true or false. It may not take many reliable users answering a particular question to make us quite sure of the truth of the question, but users who answer randomly provide no information about the answer. Simultaneously classifying multiple entities, as in this case, is called **collective classification**.

Exact inference in this model is intractable because the treewidth (page 417) of the grounding containing the *Reliable*, *True*, and observed *Answer* random variables grows quickly; see Exercise 17.6 (page 761). One way to carry out inference is to use **Markov-chain Monte Carlo (MCMC)** (page 447), alternating between the truth random variables and reliability random variables.

Once there is a rough division into reliable and unreliable users and the truth of questions, **expectation maximization (EM)** (page 478) can be used to learn the probability that a reliable user will give the correct answer and the prior probability that a user is reliable.

Such methods, however, can be manipulated by **collusion** among the users to give **misinformation**, which for this case means wrong answers. When some users are colluding to give misinformation, other methods can be used to help determine which users are reliable. You could start with some questions for which you know the truth; probabilistic inference can be used to determine reliability. Alternatively, some users can be deemed to be reliable; users that agree with them will be more likely to be reliable. It is also possible to have more than two classes as the domain of *Reliable*; how many classes to use is beyond the scope of the book, but the *Chinese restaurant process* provides one answer to that question. It is very difficult to counter the case where a group of people collude to give correct answers to all of the questions except for one; you can just hope that non-colluding reliable users will out number the colluding ones. Sometimes the best one can do is to check answers and find that collusion probably has occurred. Be warned, however, that just because people agree that something is true does not mean that it is true.

### 17.3.3 Language and Topic Models

The **probabilistic language models** of Section 9.6.6 (page 430), including the **topic models** (page 435) of Figure 9.38, are simpler when viewed as relational models. Inferring the topic(s) of a document can help disambiguate the words in a document, as well as classify the documents.

Figure 17.9 (page 751) shows a plate representation of a model where a document, represented as a **set of words** (page 430), has a single topic. In this model:

- $D$ is the set of all documents
- $W$ is the set of all words

- $A(W, D)$ is a parametrized random variable such that Boolean $A(w, d)$ is true if word $w$ appears in document $d$
- $T(D)$ is a parametrized random variable such that $T(d)$, with domain the set of all topics, is the topic of document $d$.

In this model, the topic for a document is connected to all words. There is no aggregation, as there are no arcs out of a plate. The documents are independent of each other.

Figure 17.10 shows a plate representation of a model where a document, represented as a set of words, can have multiple topics. Instead of having a random variable with domain the set of all topics – implying a document can only have a single topic – there is a Boolean random variable for each topic and document:

- $D$ is the set of all documents
- $W$ is the set of all words
- $T$ is the set of all topics (with a slight abuse of notation from the previous model)
- Boolean $A(w, d)$ is true if word $w$ appears in document $d$
- Boolean $S(t, d)$ is true if topic $t$ is a subject of document $d$.

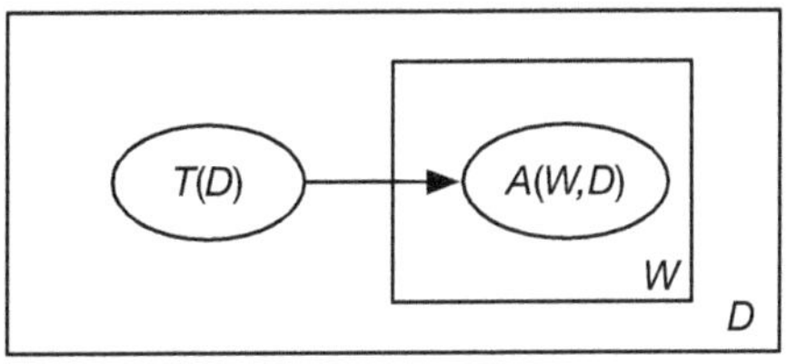


Figure 17.9: Topic model: single topic and a set of words

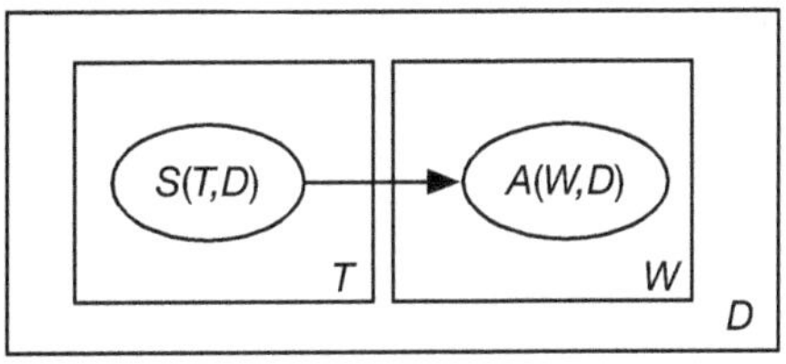


Figure 17.10: Topic model using plates: multiple topics and a set of words

In this model, all topics for a document are connected to all words. The documents are independent of each other. The grounding for a single document is show in Figure 9.29 (page 435). Because there is an arc out of a plate, this model requires a form of aggregation. Noisy-or (page 398) was used in **Google**'s **Rephil**; see Example 9.38 (page 435).

Figure 17.11 is like the previous case, but with a **bag-of-words** (page 432) (**unigram**) model of each document. In this model

- $D$ is the set of all documents
- $I$ is the set of indexes of words in the document; $I$ ranges from 1 to the number of words in the document
- $T$ is the set of all topics
- $W(d,i)$ is the $i$'th word in document $d$; the domain of $W$ is the set of all words.
- $S(t,d)$ is true if topic $t$ is a subject of document $d$; $S$ is Boolean.

**Example 17.9** Consider a document, $d_1$, that just consists of the words "the cat sat on the mat", and suppose there are three topics, *animals*, *football*, and *AI*.

In a set-of-words model, there is a Boolean random variable for each word. To condition on this document, $A(\text{"the"}, d_1)$ and $A(\text{"cat"}, d_1)$ are observed to be true. $A(\text{"neural"}, d_1)$ is observed to be false, because the word "neural" does not appear in the document. Similarly for the other words.

In a bag-of-words model, there is a random variable for each position in the document, with domain the set of all words. In this model, the observation about document $d_1$ is $w(1, d_1) = \text{"the"}$, $w(2, d_1) = \text{"cat"}$, etc., and $w(7, d_1) = \bot$ where $\bot$ is a value representing the end of the document.

In Figure 17.9 (page 751) there is a single topic for each document. This is represented by the random variable $T(d_1)$ with domain $\{animals, football, AI\}$.

In the other two models, with document possibly containing multiple topics, there is a Boolean random variable for each topic. In this case there are three random variables, including $S(animals, d_1)$ that is true when animals is a topic of document $d_1$, and $S(football, d_1)$ that is true when football is a topic of document $d_1$.

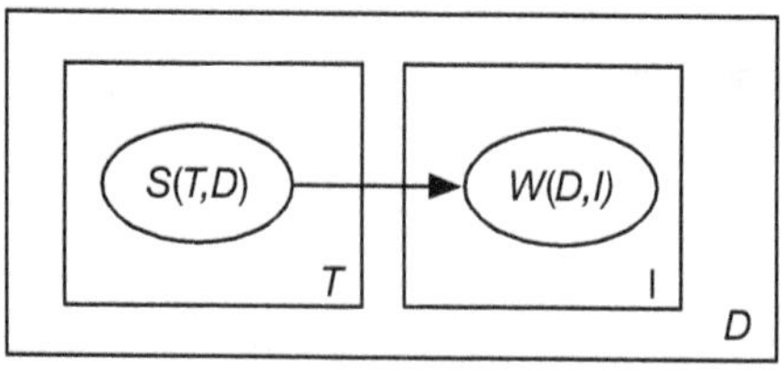


Figure 17.11: Topic model using plates: multiple topics and a bag of words

Figure 17.12 shows a model called **latent Dirichlet allocation (LDA)**, with the following meaning:

- $D$ is the document and $I$ is the index of a word in the document.
- $T$ is the topic.
- $w(d,i)$ is the $i$th word in document $d$. The domain of $w$ is the set of all words; thus, this is a bag-of-words model.
- $to(d,i)$ is the topic of the $i$th word of document $d$. The domain of $to$ is the set of all topics. $P(w(d,i) \mid to(d,i)$ gives the word distribution over each topic.
- $pr(d,t)$ represents the proportion of document $d$ that is about topic $t$. The domain of $pr$ is the reals. If $pr(d,t)$ is positive (pseudo)counts, this is a **Dirichlet distribution** (page 465), with

$$P(to(D,I)=t \mid pr(D,T)) = \frac{pr(D,T=t)}{\sum_{t'} pr(D,T=t)}.$$

Alternatively, $pr(d,t)$ could be represented as a softmax, with

$$P(to(D,I)=t \mid pr(D,T)) = \frac{\exp(pr(D,T=t))}{\sum_{t'} \exp(pr(D,T=t'))}$$

which is similar to an **attention** mechanism (page 360), where each word pays attention to the topics.

To go beyond set-of-words and bag-of-words, for example, to model the sequence of words an $n$-gram (page 433), more structure is needed than is specified by a plate model. In particular, these require the ability to refer to the sequence previous words, which can be represented using structure in the logical variables (plates), such as can be provided by function symbols in logic (page 667).

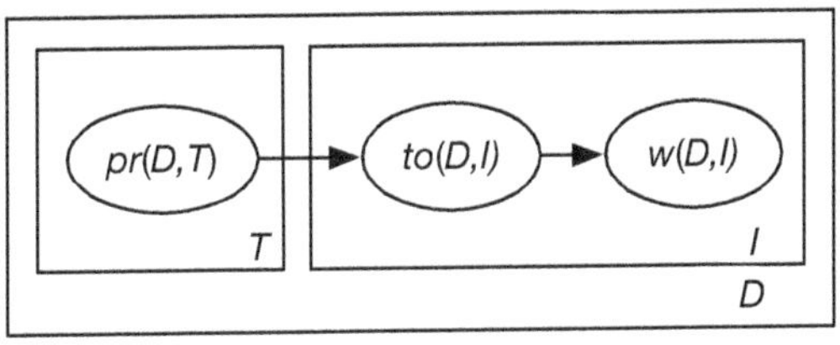


Figure 17.12: Topic model using plates: latent Dirichlet allocation

### 17.3.4 Some Specific Representations

Any of the representations of belief networks can be used for representing relational probabilistic models. However, because plates correspond to logical variables, representations defined in terms of first-order logic most naturally represent these models. The models can also provide structure in the logical variables. In the neural network literature, plate models are referred to as **convolutional models**, due to the parameter sharing, which also corresponds to universal quantification in logic (page 652).

The representations mainly differ in the way they handle aggregation, and whether latent features are random variables or tunable weighted formulas (as in neural networks).

Some notable representations include the following.

#### Probabilistic Logic Programs

In a **probabilistic logic program**, the model is described in terms of a logic program with parametrized noise variables (page 397). Plates correspond to logical variables.

**Example 17.10** To represent the domain of Figure 17.7 (page 748), as described in Example 17.8:

$$is\_shot(Y) \leftarrow shot\_by\_no\_one(Y)$$
$$is\_shot(Y) \leftarrow shot(X, Y) \land shot\_succeeds(X, Y).$$

Each instance of *shot_by_no_one* and *shot_succeeds* are parameterized **noise variables** (page 397). $P(shot\_by\_no\_one(Y))$ is the probability that $Y$ was shot even if no one shot them. $P(shot\_succeeds(X, Y))$ is the probability that $Y$ would be shot if $X$ shot $Y$. These two rules implement a **noisy-or** (page 398) over the instances of $X$ for each $Y$. The parametrized random variable *shot* can be represented using rules such as:

$$shot(X, Y) \leftarrow has\_motive(X, Y) \land has\_gun(X)$$
$$\land\, has\_opportunity(X, Y) \land actually\_shot(X, Y).$$

$P(actually\_shot(X, Y))$ is the probability that $X$ would shoot $Y$ if they had a motive, gun, and opportunity. Other rules could cover cases such as where $X$ doesn't have motive.

Probabilistic logic programs go beyond the plate model, as they can handle recursion, which gives loops in the lifted model.

#### Weighted First-Order Logic Formulas

An alternative is to use weighted formulas (page 401), where the formulas contain logical variables, corresponding to the plates. The formulas can either define a directed model, called **relational logistic regression** (page 748), or an undirected (page 403), called a **Markov logic network (MLN)**.

**Example 17.11** The domain of Figure 17.7 (page 748) can be represented using the weighted formulas

$$(is\_shot(Y), w_0)$$
$$(is\_shot(Y) \vee \neg shot(X,Y), w_1)$$
$$(shot(X,Y) \vee \neg has\_motive(X,Y) \vee \neg has\_gun(X)$$
$$\vee \neg has\_opportunity(X,Y) \vee \neg actually\_shot(X,Y), w_2)$$

where $w_0$, $w_2$, and $w_3$ are weights that are shared by all ground instances of the corresponding formula. Note that the last weighted formula has the same form as an implication with conjunctions in the body; it is true for all cases except for exceptions to the rule.

Inference in Markov logic networks and in models with relational logistic regression require marginalizing (page 405) unobserved variables in the grounding. **Probabilistic soft logic** has weighted logical formulas like Markov logic networks, but the latent variables are represented like latent features in neural networks. This means that inference is much faster, as marginalization is avoided, and learning can use standard gradient descent methods. It means that the latent variables cannot be interpreted as random variables, which may make interpretation more difficult.

Directed models, such as probabilistic logic programs, have the advantages of being able to prune irrelevant variables in the grounding – in cases such as truth discovery, most are pruned – and being able to be learned modularly. One problem with the grounding being a belief network is the need for it to be acyclic, for example *friends*$(X,Y)$ might depend on *friends*$(Y,Z)$, and making the grounding acyclic entails arbitrary orderings. **Relational dependency networks** are directed models that allow cycles. The probabilities in the model define the transitions in a Markov chain (page 418). The distribution defined by the model is the stationary distribution (page 419) of the induced Markov chain.

## Graph Neural Networks

**Graph neural networks** are neural networks that act on graph data. Each node has an embedding that is inferred from parametrized linear functions and activation functions of the node's neighbors, and their neighbors, to some depth.

A **relational graph convolutional network (R-GCN)** is used to learn embeddings for **knowledge graphs** (page 701), where nodes are entities and arcs are labelled with relations. The properties for entity $e$ in the knowledge graph are used to give an embedding $h_e^{(0)}$, similar to the encoder used for word embeddings (page 350). These embeddings provide inputs to the neural network. There are multiple layers, with shared parameters, that follow the graph structure to give an output embedding for each entity.

The output embedding for an entity can be used to predict properties of the entity, or can be used in models such as polyadic decomposition (page 740) to predict arcs. It is called *convolutional* because, like other relational models, the same learnable parameters for the layers are used for each entity. These layers provide separate embeddings for each entity based on the properties of the entity and its local neighborhood.

The layers are defined as follows. The embedding of layer $l+1$ for entity $e$ is the vector $h_e^{(l+1)}$ defined in terms of the embeddings of $e$ and its neighbors in the knowledge graph in the previous layer:

$$h_e^{(l+1)} = \phi\left(W_0^{(l)} h_e^{(l)} + \sum_{r \in R} \sum_{\{n:(e,r,n) \in KG\}} \frac{1}{C_{e,r}} W_r^{(l)} h_n^{(l)}\right)$$

where $\phi$ is an activation function (page 289), such as ReLU, defined by $\phi(x) = max(x, 0)$. $R$ is the set of all relations and $KG$ is the set of triples in the knowledge graph. $h_e^{(l)}$ is the embedding for entity $e$ from layer $l$. $W_r^{(l)}$ is a matrix (page 352) for relation $r$ for layer $l$, which is multiplied by the vector $h_n^{(l)}$ for each neighbor $n$. $W_0^{(l)}$ is a matrix defining how the embedding for entity $e$ in layer $l$ affects the same entity in the next layer. $C_{e,r}$ is a normalization constant, such as $|\{n : (e, r, n) \in KG\}|$, which gives an average for each relation. The base case is $h_e^{(0)}$, which doesn't use any neighborhood information.

This model uses separate parameters for each relation, which can result in overfitting for relations with few instances. To help solve this, the relation matrices, $W_r^{(l)}$, can be represented as a linear combination of learned basis matrices which are shared among the relation; the weights in the linear combination depend on the relation.

Whereas the embedding-based models of Section 17.2.2 (page 740) did not work well for reified entities, because reified entities had very few instances, the use of two or more layers in relational graph convolutional network allows a node to depend on the neighbors of neighbors.

The depth of the network is directly related to the size of the neighborhood of a node used. A network of size $k$ uses paths of length $k$ from each node.

The methods based on lifted graphical models work the same whether the intermediate variables are observed or not. For example, in the shooting example, $Has\_motive(X, Y)$ can depend on other parametrized random variables, such as whether someone hired $X$ to shoot $Y$ (see Example 17.5), in which case $Has\_motive(X, Y)$ needs to be marginalized out. However, graph neural networks treat relations specified in the knowledge graph differently from inferred relations, and thus need to learn the model as a function of the specified relations. This lack of modularity makes them less flexible.

## 17.4 Existence and Identity Uncertainty

The models of Section 17.3 are concerned with **relational uncertainty**; uncertainty about whether a relation is true of some entities. For example, a probabilistic model of $likes(X, Y)$ for $X \neq Y$, whether different people like each other, could depend on properties of $X$ and $Y$ and other relations they are involved in. A probabilistic model for $likes(X, X)$ is about whether people like themselves. Models about who likes whom may be useful, for example, for a tutoring agent to determine whether two people should work together.

The problem of **identity uncertainty** concerns uncertainty of whether two symbols (terms or descriptions) are equal (page 687) (denote the same entity).

**Example 17.12** Figure 17.13 shows the denotation for some symbols; each arrow indicates what entity a symbol denotes. *Huan* = *Jing's twin*, because they denote the same entity. *Huan's glasses* ≠ *Kiran's glasses*, because they denote different pairs of glasses, even though the glasses might be identical; they would only be equal if they shared the same pair of glasses. *Milo's glasses* might not exist because Milo doesn't have a pair of glasses.

Identity partitions the symbols. *Huan*, *Jing's twin*, and *Kiran's teacher* are in the same partition as they denote the same entity. They are in a different partition from *Jing*. The symbols with no entity, *Milo's glasses* and *cat in the yard*, can be in a special partition.

Identity uncertainty is a problem for medical systems, where it is important to determine whether the person who is interacting with the system now is the same person as one who visited yesterday. This problem is particularly difficult if the patient is non-communicative or wants to deceive the system, for example, to get drugs. This problem is also referred to as **record linkage**, as the problem is to determine which (medical) records are for the same person. This

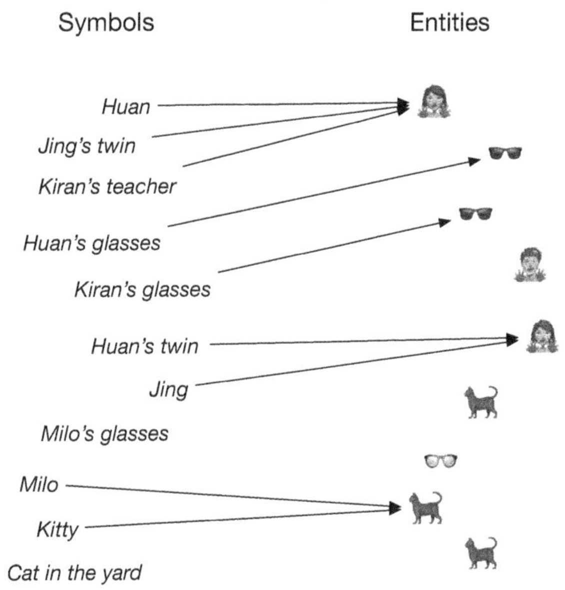


Figure 17.13: Existence and identity

problem also arises in **citation matching**, determining if authors on different papers are the same person, or if two citations denote the same paper.

Identity uncertainty is computationally intractable because it is equivalent to partitioning the symbols. For citation matching, the partition is over the citations; the citations denoting the same paper are in the same partition. The number of partitions of $n$ items is called the **Bell number**, which grows faster than any exponential in $n$. The most common way to find the distribution over partitions is to use **Markov-chain Monte Carlo (MCMC)** (page 447). Given a partition, entities can be moved to different partitions or to new partitions.

The techniques of the previous sections assumed the entities are known to exist. Given a description, the problem of determining whether there exists an entity that fits the description is the problem of **existence uncertainty**. Existence uncertainty is problematic because there may be no entities who fit a description or there may be multiple entities. For example, for the description "the cat in the yard", there may be no cats in the yard or there might be multiple cats. You cannot give properties to non-existent entities, because entities that do not exist do not have properties. If you want to give a name to an entity that exists, we need to be concerned about which entity you are referring to if there are multiple entities that exist.

One particular case of existence uncertainty is **number uncertainty**, about the number of entities that exist. For example, a purchasing agent may be uncertain about the number of people who would be interested in a package tour, and whether to offer the tour depends on the number of people who may be interested.

Reasoning about existence uncertainty can be tricky if there are complex roles involved, and the problem is to determine whether there are entities to fill the roles. Consider a purchasing agent who must find an apartment for Sam and Sam's child Chris. Whether Sam wants an apartment probabilistically depends, in part, on the size of Sam's room and the color of Chris's room. However, entity apartments do not come labeled with Sam's room and Chris's room, and there may not exist a room for each of them. Given a model of an apartment Sam would want, it is not obvious how to condition on the observations.

## 17.5 Social Impact

Recommender systems are the most commercial offshoot of AI. Many of the largest companies, including Meta (Facebook) and Alphabet (Google), make their money from advertising. When the companies get paid by clicks, the profitability is directly related to how well they target advertisements to individual users, and how well they keep people **engaged** on their platform. Streaming services, such as Netflix, have competitive advantages if good recommendations help to keep people going back to their sites.

These systems use a diverse collection of AI tools for their recommendations. Steck et al. [2021] describe challenges that arise in the Netflix recommendation system, in particular, integrating deep learning into their recommender systems. "Through experimentation with various kinds of recommendation algorithms, we found that there is no 'silver bullet'; the best-performing method (whether deep learning or other) depends on the specific recommendation task to be solved as well as on the available data. For this reason, different kinds of machine learning models are used to generate personalized recommendations for the different parts (e.g., rows) of the Netflix homepage" [Steck et al., 2021].

The recommendations of social media companies trying to maximize **engagement**, and so their profits, leads to increased polarization [Sunstein, 2018; Levy, 2021]. People engage more with extreme views than with moderate, considered content, forming **filter bubbles** and **echo chambers** where users only communicate with like-minded people [Acemoglu et al., 2021]. Because the content is targeted, public people, including politicians, can tell different people different, even inconsistent, messages. With technologies where the messages are public, many people moderate their messages to not turn off other people. This mix of relative privacy and optimization for engagement makes for toxic online forums.

## 17.6 Review

The following are the main points you should have learned from this chapter:

- Relational representations are used when an agent requires models to be given or learned before it knows which entities it will encounter, or when the data includes identifiers (page 705), such as part numbers and booking numbers.
- Collaborative filtering and other embedding-based methods can be used to make predictions about instances of relations from other instances by inventing latent properties.
- Plate models allow for the specification of probabilistic models before the entities are known.
- Many of the probabilistic representations in earlier chapters can be made relational by including universally quantified logical variables and parameter sharing.
- The recommendation systems at the heart of many large corporations are optimizing engagement, which leads to increased polarization.

## 17.7 References and Further Reading

Jannach et al. [2021] overview recommender systems. The Netflix prize and the best algorithms are described by Bell and Koren [2007] and Jahrer et al. [2010].

The collaborative filtering algorithm is based on Koren et al. [2009]; see also Koren and Bell [2011]. The MovieLens datasets are described by Harper and Konstan [2015] and available from http://grouplens.org/datasets/movielens/. Jannach and Bauer [2020] explain why recommendations require more than optimizing an easy-to-optimize criteria.

The polyadic decomposition by Hitchcock [1927] was used in knowledge graph completion by Trouillon et al. [2016]. Its use with inverses for knowledge graph prediction was independently proposed by Kazemi and Poole [2018] and Lacroix et al. [2018]. Fatemi et al. [2020] extend this method for relations with multiple arguments.

Statistical relational AI is overviewed by De Raedt et al. [2016]. Plate models are due to Buntine [1994], who used them to characterize learning. Latent Dirichlet allocation and the plate models of language are by Blei et al. [2003].

Li et al. [2016] discuss truth discovery from crowdsourcing, which can be more general than the Boolean case presented here. Van den Broeck et al. [2021] provide an introduction to lifted inference, which allows inference without grounding.

Probabilistic logic programming was proposed by Poole [1993] and implemented in Problog [De Raedt et al., 2007]. De Raedt et al. [2008] and Getoor and Taskar [2007] provide collections of papers that overview probabilistic relational models and how they can be learned. Domingos and Lowd [2009] discuss Markov logic networks and how (undirected) relational models can provide a common target representation for AI. Pujara et al. [2015] discuss how statistical relational AI techniques and ontological constraints are used for making predictions on knowledge graphs. Probabilistic soft logic is described by Bach et al. [2017]. Relational dependency networks are by Neville and Jensen [2007].

Graph neural networks are described by Xu et al. [2019], Hamilton [2020], and Chaudhri et al. [2022]. Schlichtkrull et al. [2018] define relational graph convolutional networks (R-GCNs).

The classic method existence and identity uncertainty, called *record linkage*, is by Fellegi and Sunter [1969]. The integration of existence and identity uncertainty into relational graphical models are discussed by Pasula et al. [2003], Milch et al. [2005], and Poole [2007].

## 17.8 Exercises

**Exercise 17.1** A variant of the gradient descent algorithm for collaborative filtering (Figure 17.2) can be used to predict $P(rating > threshold)$ for various values of threshold in $\{1,2,3,4\}$. Modify the code so that it learns such a probability. [Hint: Make the prediction the sigmoid of the linear function as in logistic regression.] Does this modification work better for the task of recommending the top-$n$ movies, for, say $n = 10$, where the aim is to have the maximum number of movies rated 5 in the top-$n$ list? Which threshold works best? What if the top-$n$ is judged by the number of movies rated 4 or 5?

**Exercise 17.2** An alternative regularization for collaborative filtering is to minimize

$$\sum_{\langle u,i,r\rangle \in D} \left( (\hat{r}(u,i) - r)^2 + \lambda(ib[i]^2 + ub[u]^2 + \sum_{p}(ip[i,p]^2 + up[u,p]^2)) \right).$$

(a) How doe this differ from the regularization of formula (17.1) (page 738)? [Hint: Compare the regularization for the items or users with few ratings with those with many ratings.]

(b) How does the code of Figure 17.2 (page 739) need to be modified to implement this regularization?

(c) Which works better on test data? [Hint: You will need to set $\lambda$ to be different for each method; for each method, choose the value of $\lambda$ by cross validation.]

**Exercise 17.3** Change the stochastic gradient descent algorithm of Figure 17.2 (page 739) that minimizes formula (17.1) so it adjusts the parameters, including regularization, after a batch of examples. How does the complexity of this algorithm differ from the algorithm of Figure 17.2? Which one works better in practice? [Hint: Think about whether you need to regularize all of the parameters or just those used in the batch.]

**Exercise 17.4** Suppose Boolean parameterized random variables $young(Person)$ and $cool(Item)$ are parents of Boolean $buys(Person, Item)$. Suppose there are 3000 people and 200 items.

(a) Draw this in plate notation.

(b) How many random variables are in the grounding of this model?

(c) How many numbers need to be specified for a tabular representation of this model. (Do not include any numbers that are functions of other specified numbers.)

(d) Draw the grounding belief network assuming the population of $Person$ is $\{sam, chris\}$ and the population of $Item$ is $\{iwatch, mortgage, spinach\}$.

(e) What could be observed to make $cool(iwatch)$ and $cool(mortgage)$ probabilistically dependent on each other given the observations?

**Exercise 17.5** Consider Example 17.8 (page 748). Suppose that the motive for $X$ to shoot $Y$ is that they are being paid by someone else, $Z$, who needs to have motive to kill $Y$. Draw the corresponding plate model. (If the plates become complicated to draw, just use the arguments of the parametrized random variables). It must be clear what logical variables the parametrized random variables depend on.

**Exercise 17.6** Suppose you have a relational probabilistic model for movie prediction, which represents

$$P(likes(P,M) \mid age(P), genre(M))$$

where $age(P)$ and $genre(M)$ are a priori independent.

(a) What is the treewidth (page 417) of the ground belief network (after pruning irrelevant variables) for querying *age*(*Sam*) given *age* and *genre* are not observed and given the observations for *likes* in Figure 17.14.
(b) For the same probabilistic model, for $m$ movies, $n$ people, and $r$ ratings, what is the worst-case treewidth of the corresponding graph (after pruning irrelevant variables), where only ratings are observed? [Hint: The treewidth depends on the structure of the observations; think about how the observations can be structured to maximize the treewidth.]
(c) For the same probabilistic model, for $m$ movies, $n$ people, and $r$ ratings, what is the worst-case treewidth of the corresponding graph, where only some of the ratings but all of the genres are observed?

**Exercise 17.7** Consider diagnosing the errors school students make when adding multi-digit numbers. Consider adding two multi-digit numbers to form a third multi-digit number, as in

$$\begin{array}{rrr} & A_1 & A_0 \\ + & B_1 & B_0 \\ \hline C_2 & C_1 & C_0 \end{array}$$

where $A_i$, $B_i$, and $C_i$ are all digits.

(a) Suppose you want to model whether students know the skills of single-digit addition and carrying. If students know how, they usually get the correct answer, but sometimes make mistakes. Students who do not know simply guess. Draw a belief network for a single student and problem involving adding two 2-digit numbers to get a 3-digit number. [Hint: Each of the $A_i$, $B_i$, and $C_i$, and the carries, are variables, and there is a variable for each skill of the student.]
(b) Suppose there are multiple students and multiple problems. Give a plate representation, either drawing plates or specifying the parametrized random variables. There should be plates for students and problems. Think about what variables depend on the student, the problem, or both.

| Person | Movie | Likes |
|---|---|---|
| Sam | Hugo | yes |
| Chris | Hugo | no |
| Sam | Avatar | no |
| Sam | Harry Potter 6 | yes |
| Chris | Harry Potter 6 | yes |
| Chris | AI | no |
| Chris | Avatar | no |
| David | AI | yes |
| David | Avatar | yes |

Figure 17.14: Data for Example 17.6 (page 761)

(c) Suppose now you want to also represent multiple digits and multiple times. Assume that the students' knowledge can change through time. Draw the plate model. What challenge arises in plate models for times and digits that did not arise for students and problems?

**Exercise 17.8** Represent the electrical domain of previous chapters as a probabilistic logic program, so that it will run in AIPython (aipython.org) or Problog. The representation should include the probabilistic dependencies of Example 9.15 (page 391) and the relations of Example 15.11 (page 656).

# Part VI

# The Big Picture

What are the social impacts of AI, and what are the likely future scenarios for AI science and technology?

# Chapter 18

# The Social Impact of Artificial Intelligence

*Never in the history of humanity have we allowed a machine to autonomously decide who should live and who should die, in a fraction of a second, without real-time supervision. We are going to cross that bridge any time now, and it will not happen in a distant theatre of military operations; it will happen in that most mundane aspect of our lives, everyday transportation. Before we allow our cars to make ethical decisions, we need to have a global conversation to express our preferences to the companies that will design moral algorithms, and to the policymakers that will regulate them.*

– Awad et al. [2018, p. 63]

Artificial intelligence is a transformational set of ideas, algorithms, and tools. AI systems are now increasingly deployed at scale in the real world [Littman et al., 2021; Zhang et al., 2022a]. They have significant impact across almost all forms of human activity, including the economic, social, psychological, healthcare, legal, political, government, scientific, technological, manufacturing, military, media, educational, artistic, transportation, agricultural, environmental, and philosophical spheres. Those impacts can be beneficial but they may also be harmful. Ethical and, possibly, regulatory concerns, as raised by Awad et al. [2018], apply to all the spheres of AI application, not just to self-driving cars.

**Autonomous agents** (page 14) perceive, decide, and act on their own. They, along with **semi-autonomous agents** (page 14), represent a radical, qualitative change in technology and in our image of technology. Such agents can take unanticipated actions beyond human control. As with any disruptive technology, there may be substantial beneficial and harmful consequences – many that are difficult to evaluate and many that humans simply cannot, or will not, foresee.

Consider social media platforms, which rely on AI algorithms, such as deep learning and probabilistic models, trained on huge datasets generated by users. These platforms allow people to connect, communicate, and form social groups across the planet in healthy ways. However, the platforms typically optimize a user's feed to maximize engagement, thereby increasing advertising revenue. Maximizing engagement often leads to adversarial behavior and polarization (page 758). The platforms can also be manipulated to drive divisive political debates adversely affecting democratic elections, and produce other harmful outcomes such as **deep fakes** (page 366). They can also be very invasive of users' privacy. Automated decision systems, possibly biased, are used to qualify people for loans, mortgages, and insurance policies, and even to screen potential employees.

People expect to have the right to receive fair and equitable treatment, to appeal decisions, to ask for accountability and trustworthiness, and to expect privacy. Is it possible to ensure that those rights are indeed available?

## 18.1 The Digital Economy

The science, the technology and the applications of AI have developed rapidly in the era of ubiquitous digital communication and the Internet. The world economy has been transformed by these developments. Most of the ten largest global corporations, measured by market capitalization, rely heavily upon AI applications. Those companies are centred more on the use of information than on the production of material goods. The shift from matter to information is characterized as **dematerialization**.

Physical mail has been disrupted by email, texting, and social media. Incidentally, email was overwhelmed by spam until AI methods were used to filter it out (page 486). Printed books are now supplemented by e-books. Analog photography, film, and video are supplanted by digital media. Some travel in planes and cars has been replaced by digital communication. CDs have been replaced by streaming audio and newspapers by news websites. This process, the **atoms-to-bits** transformation, allows transactions with less friction and more speed. It is easier, quicker, cheaper, and more material and energy efficient to stream music than to go to a store to buy a CD.

Digitalization, in turn, leads to a general temporal speedup of society and the economy. It also shrinks distances through telecommunication. We all live now in a global village, as characterized by Marshall McLuhan [1962]. Furthermore, the digital revolution reduces or eliminates the need for intermediaries, such as retail clerks, bank tellers, and travel agents, between the producers and consumers of goods and services – a process known as **disintermediation**.

The digital revolution and AI are transforming the world economy. These effects are beneficial for some but harmful for others. The benefits, and the harms, are far from evenly distributed in the new economy. There is a **winner-take-all** dynamic as the most powerful corporations use their power to increase their dominance until a monopoly, or oligopoly, market position is established. AI and machine learning algorithms, relying on tracking and modeling users, are central to this dynamic. Zuboff [2019] characterized the new economy as **surveillance capitalism**, epitomized by the large-scale harvesting of personal data online to facilitate targeted monitoring and advertising for commercial and political purposes. Human values such as privacy, dignity, equity, diversity, and inclusion are compromised.

**Human attention**, selective concentration on available information, is a critical and limited resource. Attention is a psychological issue but it is also an economic issue, as pointed out long ago by Simon [1971] when he created the key concept of the **attention economy**. He observed:

> *In an information-rich world, the wealth of information means a dearth of something else: a scarcity of whatever it is that information consumes. What information consumes is rather obvious: it consumes the attention of its recipients. Hence a wealth of information creates a poverty of attention and a need to allocate that attention efficiently among the overabundance of information sources that might consume it.*

In English, a person is said to be "paying attention" to a salient event. In other words, attention is a currency to be spent, like money, in this economy. The central role of human attention in our screen-filled digital age is described by Richtel [2014]. Turning attention into a commodity requires monitoring users, which, in turn, triggers privacy concerns. Corporations, and other actors, not only want to know a lot about us but they also use that knowledge to manipulate our attention, our thoughts, and our actions.

## 18.2 Values and Bias

Learning systems, trained on large datasets, produce outputs that reflect any bias present in the training sets. Since the datasets were acquired in the past, using them to predict outcomes in the future propagates any bias from the past to the future. What if the future will not, or should not, resemble the past?

In machine learning, **bias** has a neutral technical meaning (page 262), "the tendency to prefer one hypothesis over another". The **no-free-lunch theorem** (page 315) implies that any effective learning algorithm *must* have a bias in that sense. But in ordinary language use, human **bias** has a negative connotation, meaning "prejudice in favor of or against one thing, person, or group compared with another, usually in a way considered to be unfair" [Stevenson and Lindberg, 2010].

Training sets for **facial recognition**, often acquired without informed consent, typically do not represent people equitably, thereby causing misclassification, often with harmful effect as discussed in Section 7.7 (page 317). **Large language models** (page 364), pre-trained on vast text corpora, when prompted often produce new text that is racist, sexist, or otherwise demeaning of human dignity.

Any AI-based decision system inherently reflects certain implicit values, or preferences. The key question to ask is: whose values are they? Typically, the values embedded in an AI system are the values of the designer or owner of the system, or the values implicit in a deep learning training set. Further questions arise. Can those values be made explicit? Can they be specified? Is it possible to ensure those are democratic values, avoiding discrimination and prejudice? Can they be transparent to the users, or targets, of the system? Do they reflect the values of everyone who may be affected, directly or indirectly? Can systems be designed that respect privacy, dignity, equity, diversity, and inclusion?

The role of social bias in training data is described in Section 7.7 (page 317). Bias and other social impact concerns in modern deep learning systems trained on large corpora are discussed in Section 8.7 (page 367). These questions, ongoing challenges to AI system designers, are examined critically by O'Neil [2016], Eubanks [2018], Noble [2018], Broussard [2018], Benjamin [2019], and Bender et al. [2021].

## 18.3 Human-Centred Artificial Intelligence

Mary Wollstonecraft Shelley's *Frankenstein; or, The Modern Prometheus* [Shelley, 1818], is the first true science fiction novel. It can be read as a morality tale, as signaled by Shelley's alternate title, *The Modern Prometheus*. According to ancient Greek mythology, Prometheus stole fire from the gods and gave it to humanity. Zeus punished that theft, of technology and knowledge, by sentencing Prometheus to eternal torment. Dr. Frankenstein's creature attempted to assimilate into human society by learning human customs and language, but humankind rejected him and misinterpreted his genuine acts of kindness. That rejection and his loneliness, given his lack of a companion, led to his choice to exact revenge. Frankenstein's monster has now come to symbolize unbridled, uncontrolled technology turning against humans.

Concerns about the control of technology are now increasingly urgent as AI transforms our world. Discussions of so-called **artificial general intelligence (AGI)** envisage systems that outperform humans on a wide range of tasks, unlike so-called "narrow" AI that develops and trains systems for specific tasks. Some believe that AGI may lead to a **singularity** when AGI bootstraps to a **superintelligence**, that could dominate humans [Good, 1965]. Or, as Bostrom [2014] hypothesized, an imagined AGI system, given a goal that includes maximizing the number of paperclips in the universe, could consume every resource available to it, including those required by humans. This seemingly absurd thought experiment purports to show that an apparently innocuous AGI, without **common sense**, could pose an existential threat to humanity if its goals are misspecified or otherwise not aligned with the long-term survival of humans and the natural environment. This **safety** concern has come to be known as the **alignment problem** [Christian, 2020].

A more immediate threat is that AI systems, such as self-driving cars and lethal autonomous weapons, may make life-or-death decisions without meaningful human oversight. Less dramatically, AI systems may make harmful, even if not life-threatening, value-laden decisions impinging on human welfare, such as deciding who should get a mortgage or a job offer. This has given rise to a focus on autonomy and human control. How can designers create **human-centred AI** or **human-compatible AI**? Can human values be instilled in AI systems? These questions are examined by Russell [2019], Marcus and Davis [2019], and Shneiderman [2022]. One proposed technique for incorporating human values is **Reinforcement Learning from Human Feedback (RLHF)** [Knox and Stone, 2009]. RLHF is the framework for a key module of **ChatGPT** (page 6) [OpenAI, 2022].

Increasingly, especially in high-stakes applications, human decision-makers are assisted by **semi-autonomous agents**; this combination is known as **human-in-the-loop**. As shown in Chapter 2, intelligent systems are often structured as a hierarchy of controllers (page 58), with the lower levels operating very quickly, on short time horizons, while the higher levels have longer time horizons, operating slowly on more symbolic data. Human interaction with hierarchically structured systems typically occurs at the higher levels. Human drivers cannot meaningfully modify the anti-lock braking systems on a car in real time, but they can provide high-level navigation preferences or directions. Humans can steer or brake to avoid accidents but only if they are paying attention; however, as vehicles become more automated the driver may well be distracted, or asleep, and unable to redirect their attention in time.

The concept of **attention** in neural networks (page 360) is inspired by the concept of **human attention** (page 769). Concepts directly related to human attention include **vigilance**, the state of keeping careful watch for possible danger, and **salience**, the quality of being particularly noticeable or important. Designing AI systems so that humans can meaningfully interact with them requires designers who understand the economic, social, psychological, and ethical roles of vigilance, salience, and attention. Early research on human attention and vigilance is reported by N. H. Mackworth [1948] and J. F. Mackworth [1970]. Mole [2010] presents a philosophical theory of attention. The papers collected in Archer [2022] show how issues concerning salience, attention, and ethics intersect.

Designers of interactive AI systems must be well versed in the principles and practices of both **human–computer interaction (HCI)** [Rogers et al., 2023] and AI. Good designs for AI can go a long way in creating trustworthy systems. For example, the "Guidelines for Human–AI Interaction" by Amershi et al. [2019] give strategies for doing less when the system is uncertain to reduce the costs and consequences of incorrect predictions.

**Assistive technology** for disabled and aging populations is being pioneered by many researchers and companies. **Assisted cognition**, including memory prompts, is one application. **Assisted perception** and **assisted action**, in the form of smart wheelchairs, companions for older people, and nurses' assistants in long-term care facilities, are beneficial technologies. Assistive technology systems are described by Pollack [2005], Liu et al. [2006], and Yang and Mackworth [2007]. **Semi-autonomous** smart wheelchairs are discussed by Mihailidis et al. [2007] and Viswanathan et al. [2011]. However, Sharkey [2008] and Shneiderman [2022] warn of some dangers of relying upon robotic assistants as companions for the elderly and the very young. As with autonomous vehicles, researchers must ask cogent questions about the development and use of their creations. Researchers and developers of assistive technology, and other AI applications, should be aware of the dictum of the disability rights movement presented by Charlton [1998], "Nothing about us without us."

A plethora of concepts are used to evaluate AI systems from a human perspective, including **transparency**, **interpretability**, **explainability**, **fairness**, **safety**, **accountability**, and **trustworthiness**. They are useful concepts but they have multiple, overlapping, shifting, and contested meanings. **Transparency** typically refers to the complete ecosystem surrounding an AI application, including the description of the training data, the testing and certification of the application, and user privacy concerns. But transparency is also used to describe an AI system whose outcomes can be interpreted or explained, where humans can understand the models used and the reasons behind a particular decision. Black-box AI systems, based, say, on deep learning, are not transparent in that sense. Systems that have some understanding of how the world works, using causal models, may be better able to provide explanations. See, for example, this presentation on explainable human–AI interaction from a planning perspective by Sreedharan et al. [2022]. Enhancements in explainability may make an application more trustworthy, as Russell [2019] suggests.

Enhanced transparency, interpretability, and fairness may also improve trustworthiness. Interpretability is useful for developers to evaluate, debug and mitigate issues. However, the evidence that it is always useful for end-users is less convincing. Understanding the reasons behind predictions and actions is the subject of **explainable AI**. It might seem obvious that it is better if a system can explain its conclusion. However, having a system that can explain an incorrect conclusion, particularly if the explanation is approximate, might do more harm than good. Bansal et al. [2021] show that "Explanations increased the chance that humans will accept the AI's recommendation, regardless of its correctness."

As discussed in Section 7.7 (page 317), models built by computational systems are open to probing in ways that humans are not. Probing and testing cannot cover all rare events, or **corner cases**, for real-world domains. Verification of systems, proving that their behaviors must always satisfy a formal specification that includes explicit **safety** and **goal constraints** (page 244) could make them more trusted [Mackworth and Zhang, 2003]. **Semi-autonomous** systems that interact and collaborate with humans on an ongoing basis can become more trusted, if they prove to be reliable; however, that trust may prove to be misplaced for corner cases. The role of explicit utilities in open and accountable group decision making is described in Section 12.6 (page 571). In Section 13.10 (page 604), concerns about real-world deployment of reinforcement learning are outlined. Trust has to be earned.

## 18.4 Work and Automation

The impact of automation, in general, and AI, in particular, on the nature of work and employment has been widely studied by economists and sociologists; however, there is no consensus yet on the impact of automation or AI. Some claim that AI, including robotics, will lead to large-scale unemployment; others claim that many new job categories will develop based on AI-enabled developments. A better way to look at the phenomenon is to understand that any particular job requires a suite of skills. Some of those skills may indeed be rendered redundant. Other skills may become more necessary and may also require upgrading. As discussed above, **disintermediation** eliminates many job categories but also requires "upskilling" other job categories. These issues are explored by Brynjolfsson and McAfee [2014], Agrawal et al. [2019], and Ford [2021]. One theme, developed by Agrawal et al. [2022], is that business decisions require prediction and judgment. Machine learning is now enabling automated prediction so human judgment and decision analysis skills become relatively more valuable. Danaher [2021] considers the ethics of automation and the future of work.

AI and related technologies are creating many new job categories; however, the new post-industrial high-tech corporations typically employ many fewer people than corporations based in the older industrial economy, with similar market size. AI is now permeating the entire economy, with AI-related jobs being created in the older industrial corporations, such as the auto industry and other manufacturing sectors as well as in the health, legal, education, entertainment, and financial sectors. One aspect of the role of AI in the video game industry is described in Section 6.6 (page 252). Perhaps fewer people will be required to produce society's goods and services. Moreover, AI could generate so many significant new wealth opportunities that a **universal basic income** (UBI) guaranteed to everyone, without qualification, is possible, and necessary, to redistribute some of that wealth equitably [Ford, 2021]. The argument for UBI is that AI will reduce the need for much manual and mental labour, so the human rights to housing and sustenance should not be tied entirely to employment income. This could allow more creative leisure time and informal caregiving.

It is already the case that the employment picture is changing significantly, disrupted by AI. Many workers now have a portfolio of employment gigs, working on short-term ad hoc contracts. The so-called **gig economy** allows AI-enabled scheduling and organizing of the resources needed for just-in-time ordering and delivery of consumer goods and services, including ride-hailing and food delivery. This has produced radical changes in the nature of retail shopping and employment. A permanent full-time job with a single employer for life is no longer the standard model. The gig economy has the benefit of flexibility, for both the employee and the employer. On the downside, workers are losing the advantages and protections of organizing in unions, including security of employment, bargaining for wages and salaries, and benefits such as vacations, paid sick leave, pensions and health care coverage (if it is not universal). Enhancements to government legislation, regulation, and enforcement are being proposed to cope with these emerging challenges.

## 18.5 Transportation

Transportation, of people and cargo, is a key sector of the economy, satisfying a variety of social needs. It serves as a useful case study to examine the social and economic impact of AI. **Autonomous vehicles** are being developed and deployed. The technologies used for accurate positioning in self-driving vehicles are covered in Section 9.8 (page 449). Some of the ethical choices surrounding self-driving cars are considered in Section 2.4 (page 71). The role of preferences in automated route planning is discussed in Section 3.9 (page 120). Using constraints to schedule deliveries by a fleet of vehicles is described in Section 4.9 (page 170). The positive impact of having intelligent cars and trucks could be large [Thrun, 2006]. There is the **safety** aspect of reducing the annual carnage on the roads; it is estimated that 1.2 million people are killed, and more than 50 million are injured, in traffic accidents each year worldwide [Peden et al., 2004]. Vehicles could communicate and negotiate at intersections. Besides the consequent reduction in accidents, there could be up to three times the traffic throughput [Dresner and Stone, 2008].

The improvements in road usage efficiency come both from smarter intersection management and from platooning effects, whereby automated, communicating vehicles can safely follow each other closely because they can communicate their intentions before acting and they react much quicker than human drivers. This increase in road utilization has potential positive side-effects. It not only decreases the capital and maintenance cost of highways, but has potential ecological savings of using highways so much more efficiently instead of paving over farmland, forests, or wilderness.

With full autonomy, elderly and disabled people would be able to get around on their own, without a driver. People could dispatch vehicles to the parking warehouse autonomously and then recall them later. Individual car ownership could become mostly obsolete, when an autonomous taxi ride becomes cheaper and more convenient than a private vehicle. Most private vehicles are used only about 5% of the time. Better utilization of the vehicle fleet would significantly reduce the demand for vehicle production and storage. Supported by AI systems, people could simply order up the most suitable available vehicle for their trips. Automated robotic warehouses could store vehicles more efficiently than using surface land for parking. In very dense cities, private car ownership is already becoming obsolete. This trend would accelerate with autonomous vehicles. Much of the current paved space in urban areas could be used for housing, or for environmentally enhancing uses such as parks, playgrounds, or urban farms. The rigid distinction between private vehicles and public transit could dissolve.

These speculations are, at the moment, mostly science fiction. Many early promises of full autonomy have not materialized. The transition to a mixed transportation system of human drivers, autonomous vehicles, transit, pedestrians, cyclists, and so on is challenging.

Short of full vehicle autonomy, many smart driving features such as self-parking, lane keeping, lane changing, adaptive cruise control, emergency braking, and automated avoidance of pedestrians and cyclists are now routine driver aides and safety enhancements. A variety of vehicles, other than cars and trucks, including microcars, e-bikes, e-scooters, and e-unicycles, are now available under the rubric **micromobility**, often with AI enhancements for semi-autonomy, routing, and vehicle sharing. Public transit, with intelligent crew and vehicle scheduling, and some autonomy is also improving.

Experimental autonomous vehicles are seen by many as precursors to robot tanks, military cargo movers, and automated warfare. Although there may be, in some sense, significant benefits to robotic warfare, there are also very real dangers. In the past, these were only the nightmares of science fiction. Now, as automated warfare becomes a reality, those dangers have to be confronted. Sharkey [2008], Singer [2009a,b], Russell [2019], and Robillard [2021] discuss the dangers and ethics of autonomous weapon systems and robotic warfare.

## 18.6 Sustainability

The sustainability crisis now facing humanity has many facets, including the climate emergency, global inequity, biodiversity loss, and scarcity of water and food resources. **Sustainability** is the ability to maintain the balance of a process in a system over the long term. **Ecological sustainability** is the ability of an ecosystem to maintain ecological processes, functions, biodiversity, and productivity into the future. Ecosystem **resilience** is the capacity of an ecosystem to tolerate disturbance without collapsing into a qualitatively different state. In social systems, resilience is enhanced by the capacity of humans to anticipate and plan for the future [Holling, 1973].

**Sustainable development** is the ability to recognize and meet the needs of the present without compromising the ability of future generations to meet their own needs. In the United Nations Brundtland Report, "Our Common Future" [Brundtland et al., 1987], sustainable development was emphasized. Sustainable development requires satisfying environmental, societal, and economic **constraints** [Rockström et al., 2009; United Nations, 2015b]. Environmental, social, and economic issues are intertwined.

In *An Essay on the Principle of Population*, Malthus [1798] was concerned primarily with the imbalance between population growth, which has grown exponentially, and the supply of food, which is limited. He wrote:

> *This natural inequality of the two powers, of population, and of production of the earth, and that great law of our nature which must constantly keep their effects equal, form the great difficulty.*

In other words, the global planetary system must satisfy the constraint that the consumption by the growing population is limited by the food production of the Earth. It is just one of many constraints that must be satisfied for our planetary system to be sustainable and resilient.

What is the relationship between sustainability and computation, in general, and AI, in particular? Computation is a double-edged sword with respect to sustainability. The amazing increase in the power of our computational and communication networks has been significantly beneficial to sustainability as the digital age unfolds. Computation is transforming society and the economy. As discussed in Section 18.1 (page 768), computation has, at its core, an inherent sustainable dynamic, **dematerialization**, replacing atoms by bits. Dematerialization, inherently, saves many resources.

On the other hand, many resources are consumed and wasted in the digital revolution. Mining to produce the materials needed to manufacture computers, devices, and batteries can have serious environmental effects. At the end of the short product lifecycles, many million tonnes of electronic waste are produced each year, with devastating environmental consequences, especially in the Global South. The power used by massive cloud servers is another major resource consumed. In particular, the training of large models, discussed in Section 8.5.5 (page 364), requires huge computational resources. AI is characterized as a "technology of extraction" by Crawford [2021]. Similarly, the mining of some **cryptocurrency** coins, such as Bitcoin, and the verification of cryptocurrency transactions are also major resource sinks.

Countering these trends is the so-called **green information technology** movement, which aims to design, manufacture, use, repair, and dispose of computers, servers, and other devices with minimal energy use and impact on the environment.

A new discipline, **computational sustainability**, is emerging [Gomes et al., 2019]. It applies techniques from AI, computer science, information science, operations research, applied mathematics, and statistics for balancing environmental, societal, and economic needs for sustainable development. Computational sustainability has two main themes:

- Developing computational models and methods for **offline** decision making for the management and allocation of ecosystem resources.

- Developing computational modules embedded directly in **online** real-time ecosystem monitoring, management, and control.

AI plays a key role in both themes.

In *Planetary Boundaries: Exploring the Safe Operating Space for Humanity*, Rockström et al. [2009] identified nine critical boundaries on the Earth's biophysical processes to ensure the sustainability of the planet. The boundaries are **goal constraints** (page 244) on:

- climate change
- rate of biodiversity loss (terrestrial and marine)
- interference with the nitrogen and phosphorus cycles
- stratospheric ozone depletion
- ocean acidification
- global freshwater use
- change in land use
- chemical pollution
- atmospheric aerosol loading.

For example, a constraint on anthropogenic **climate change** requires atmospheric carbon dioxide concentration to be less than 350 ppmv (parts per million by volume). The pre-industrial value was 280 ppmv; in 2009 it was 387 ppmv and 412 ppmv in 2023. The rate of biodiversity loss is determined by the extinction rate (number of species lost per million per year). Its boundary value is set at 10, whereas it is greater than 100 in 2023. **Constraint satisfaction**, as covered in Chapter 4 and Section 6.4 (page 244), is at the core of computational sustainability.

In 2015, the United Nations adopted the "2030 Agenda for Sustainable Development" [United Nations, 2015a] which specifies 17 **Sustainable Development Goals (SDGs)** [United Nations, 2015b]. The SDGs cover the nine biophysical planetary boundary constraints and extend them to cover human social and economic goals such as reducing poverty, hunger, and inequality, while improving health, education, and access to justice. Many systems, using the full spectrum of AI methods, including deep learning, reinforcement learning, constraint satisfaction, planning, vision, robotics, and language understanding, are being developed to help achieve the SDGs. For example, as described earlier (page 638), Perrault et al. [2020] show how multiagent techniques based on **Stackelberg security games** can enhance public health, security, and social justice. Multiagent methods also address the so-called **tragedy of the commons** (page 637), which is at the heart of sustainability concerns [Hardin, 1968]. Ostrom [1990] showed that institutions for collective action can evolve to govern the commons.

AI researchers and development engineers have some of the skills required to address aspects of concerns about global warming, poverty, food production, arms control, health, education, the aging population, and demographic issues. They will have to work with domain experts, and be able to convince domain experts that the AI solutions are not just new snake oil. As a simple example, open access to tools for learning about AI, such as this book and **AIspace** [Knoll et al., 2008], empowers people to understand and try AI techniques on their own problems, rather than relying upon opaque black-box commercial systems. Games and competitions based upon AI systems can be very effective learning, teaching, and research environments, as shown by the success of **RoboCup** for robot soccer [Visser and Burkhard, 2007]. Some of the positive environmental impacts of intelligent vehicles and smart traffic control were discussed in Section 18.5 (page 774). Bakker et al. [2020] present an overview of digital technology applications for dynamic environmental management.

Environmental decision making often requires choosing a set of components that work together as parts of a complex system. A **combinatorial auction** is an auction in which agents bid on packages, consisting of combinations of discrete items [Shoham and Leyton-Brown, 2008]. Determining the winner is difficult because preferences are usually not additive (page 526), but items are typically complements or substitutes (page 526). Work on combinatorial auctions, already applied to spectrum allocation (allocation of radio frequencies to companies for television or cell phones) [Leyton-Brown et al., 2017], logistics (planning for transporting goods), and supply chain configuration [Sandholm, 2007], could further be applied to support carbon markets, to optimize energy supply and demand, and to mitigate climate change. There is much work on smart energy controllers using distributed sensors and actuators which improve energy use in buildings.

## 18.7 Ethics

**Moral** and **ethical** issues abound in considering the impacts of AI. Morals are guidelines that apply to an individual's sense of right and wrong. Ethical principles apply at the level of a community, an organization, or a profession. Morals and ethics are, of course, intimately connected: an individual may have personal morals that derive from various sources, including the ethical principles of groups they belong to. Normative ethical codes are categorized, by philosophers, as either virtue-based, consequentialist, or deontological [Hursthouse and Pettigrove, 2018]:

- **Virtue** ethics emphasize the values and character traits that a virtuous agent possesses [Vallor, 2021].

- **Consequentialist** (or **utilitarian**) ethics focus on the outcomes of possible actions that the agent can take, measuring the global **utility** (page 518) of each outcome.

- **Deontological** (or **Kantian**) ethical codes are based on a set of rules the agent should follow.

A focus on **AI ethics** has arisen, motivated, in part, by worries about whether AI systems can be expected to behave properly. Reliance on autonomous intelligent agents raises the question: can we **trust** AI systems? They are not fully trustworthy and reliable, given the way they are built now. So, can they do the right thing? Will they do the right thing? But trust is not just about the system doing the right thing. A human will only see a system as trustworthy if they are confident that it will *reliably* do the right thing. As evidenced by popular movies and books, in our collective unconscious, the fear exists that robots, and other AI systems, are untrustworthy. They may become completely autonomous, with free will, intelligence, and consciousness. They may rebel against us as Frankenstein-like monsters.

Issues of trust raise questions about ethics. If the designers, implementers, deployers, and users of AI systems are following explicit ethical codes, those systems are more likely to be trusted. Moreover, if those systems actually embody explicit ethical codes, they are also more likely to be trusted. The discipline of AI ethics is concerned with answering questions such as:

- Should AI scientists be guided by ethical principles in developing theories, algorithms, and tools?
- What are ethical activities for designers and developers of AI systems?
- For deployers of AI systems, are there applications that should not be considered?
- Should humans be guided by ethical principles when interacting with AI systems?
- Should AI systems be guided by ethical principles, in their interactions with humans, other agents, or the rest of the world?
- What data should be used to train AI systems?
- For each of these concerns, who determines the ethical codes that apply?

AI ethics, as an emerging and evolving discipline, addresses two, distinct but related, issues:

A. **AI ethics for humans**: researchers, designers, developers, deployers, and users.

B. **AI ethics for systems**: software agents and embodied robots.

Each is concerned with developing and examining ethical codes, of one of the three code types, either for humans or for systems.

With regard to AI ethics for humans, many perceive a need for strong professional codes of ethics for AI designers and engineers, just as there are for engineers in all other disciplines. Others disagree. The legal, medical, and computing professions all have explicit **deontological** ethics codes that practitioners are expected or required to follow. For computing, the ACM Committee on Professional Ethics [2018], AAAI [2019], and IEEE [2020] have established ethics codes that apply to their members.

There are several issues around what should be done ethically in designing, building, and deploying AI systems. What ethical issues arise for us, as humans, as we interact with them? Should we give them any rights? There are human rights codes; will there be AI systems rights codes, as well?

Philosophers distinguish among **moral agents**, **moral patients**, and other agents. Moral agents can tell right from wrong and can be held responsible for their actions. A moral patient is an agent who should be treated with moral principles by a moral agent. So, for example, a typical adult human is a moral agent, and a moral patient; a baby is a moral patient but not a moral agent, whereas a (traditional) car is neither. There is an ongoing debate as to whether an AI agent could ever be (or should ever be) a moral agent. Moreover, should current AI systems be considered as moral patients, warranting careful ethical treatment by humans? Presumably not, but is it conceivable that future AI systems, including robots, could be, or should be, ever treated as moral patients? Some of the underlying issues are covered by Bryson [2011], Mackworth [2011], Bryson [2018], Gunkel [2018], and Nyholm [2021]. These issues are partially addressed by the multitude of proposed codes of AI ethics such as those developed by the IEEE Global Initiative on Ethics of Autonomous and Intelligent Systems [2019], OECD [2019], and UNESCO [2022].

With regard to AI ethics for systems, how should AI systems make decisions as they develop more autonomy? Consider some interesting, if perhaps naive, proposals put forward by the science fiction novelist Isaac Asimov [1950], one of the earliest thinkers about these issues. Asimov's **Laws of Robotics** are a good basis to start from because, at first glance, they seem logical and succinct.

Asimov's original three laws are:

I. A robot may not harm a human being, or, through inaction, allow a human being to come to harm.

II. A robot must obey the orders given to it by human beings except where such orders would conflict with the First Law.

III. A robot must protect its own existence, as long as such protection does not conflict with the First or Second Laws.

Asimov proposed those prioritized laws should be followed by all robots and, by statute, manufacturers would have to guarantee that. The laws constitute a deontological code of ethics for robots, imposing constraints on acceptable robotic behavior. Asimov's plots arise mainly from the conflict between what the humans intend the robot to do and what it actually does, or between literal and sensible interpretations of the laws, because they are not codified in any formal language. Asimov's fiction explored many hidden implicit contradictions in the laws and their consequences.

There are ongoing discussions of AI ethics for systems, but the discussions often presuppose technical abilities to impose and verify AI system safety requirements that just do not exist yet. Some progress on formal hardware and

**Facial Recognition**

Selinger and Leong [2021], studying the ethics of facial recognition technology, define four forms of **facial recognition**, each with their own risks and benefits:

- **facial detection** finds the location of faces in images, it is common in phones, putting square overlays on faces
- **facial characterization** finds features of individual faces, such as approximate age, emotions (e.g., smiling or sad), and what the person is looking at
- **facial verification** determines whether the person matches a single template; it is used to verify the user of a phone and in airport security
- **facial identification** is used to identify each person in an image from a database of faces; it is used in common photo library software to identify friends and family members.

Facial identification, usually considered the most problematic, has problems that arise both when it is perfect and when it makes mistakes.

If facial identification is perfect and pervasive, people will know they are constantly under surveillance. This means they will be very careful to not do anything that is illegal or anything out of narrow social norms. People's behavior is self-censored, even if they have no intention to commit any wrongdoing. Preventing illegal activity becomes problematic when any criticism of the ruling order or anything that deviates from a narrow definition of normal behavior becomes illegal. Surveillance has a chilling effect that limits self-expression, creativity, and growth, and deprives the marketplace of ideas.

When facial identification makes mistakes, they usually do not affect all groups equally. The error rate is usually much worse for socially disadvantaged people, which can result in those people becoming more targeted.

Given a database of faces, facial identification becomes a combination of facial detection and facial verification. The facial verification on an iPhone uses multiple sensors to build a three-dimensional model of a face based on 30,000 points. It has **privacy-by-design**; the information is stored locally on the phone and not in a server. It has a false-positive rate of 1 in 10 million, which means it is unlikely to have a false positive in normal use. If the same error rate was used on a database of everyone, on average there are about 800 people on Earth who match a particular face. Vision-only techniques have much higher error rates, which would mean that mis-identification would be very common.

People have argued that making facial recognition, in any of its forms, part of normal life provides a slippery slope where it is easy to slip into problematic cases. For example, if a community already has surveillance cameras to detect and prevent crime, it can be very cheap to get extra value out of the cameras by adding on facial recognition.

software verification is described in Section 5.10 (page 219). Joy [2000] was so concerned about our inability to control the dangers of new technologies that he called, unsuccessfully, for a moratorium on the development of robotics (and AI), nanotechnology, and genetic engineering.

Perhaps the intelligent agent design space and the agent design principles developed in this book could provide a more technically informed framework for the development of social, ethical, and legal codes for intelligent agents.

However, in skeptical opposition, Munn [2022] argues that "AI ethical principles are useless, failing to mitigate the racial, social, and environmental damages of AI technologies in any meaningful sense." But see also "In defense of ethical guidelines" by Lundgren [2023].

## 18.8 Governance and Regulation

It is increasingly apparent that ethical codes are necessary but not sufficient to address some of the actual and potential harms induced by the widespread use of AI technologies. There are already AI liability and insurance issues. Legislation targeting AI issues is coming into force worldwide. Many countries are now developing AI regulations and laws. A survey of the national AI policies and practices in 50 countries is presented by the Center for AI and Digital Policy [2023]. Issues in robot regulation and robot law are covered in Calo [2014] and Calo et al. [2016].

Zuboff [2019] used the term **surveillance capitalism** (page 769) to characterize the nexus among AI-based user tracking, social media, and modern commerce. This issue is hard to address solely at the national level since it is a global concern. In 2016, the European Union (EU) adopted the **General Data Protection Regulation** (**GDPR**) [European Commission, 2021] as a regulation in EU law on data protection and privacy, as a part of the human right to privacy regime in the EU. The GDPR has influenced similar legislation in many nations outside the EU. Given the size of the European market, many corporations welcomed the GDPR as giving uniformity to data protection; however, GDPR has not put an end to surveillance capitalism. The EU also adopted the **Digital Services Act** (**DSA**) in 2022 [European Commission, 2022c]. The DSA defines a digital service as any intermediary that connects consumers with content, goods, or other services, including social media. It is designed to protect the rights of children and other users, and to prevent consumer fraud, disinformation, misogyny, and electoral manipulation. There are substantial penalties for infringement.

The OECD AI Principles [OECD, 2019] presented the first global framework for AI policy and governance. In 2022, the EU was debating a draft of the **Artificial Intelligence Act** (**AI Act**) [European Commission, 2022b], the first legislation globally aiming to regulate AI across all sectors. It is designed primarily to address harms caused by the use of AI systems, as explained by Algorithm Watch [2022]. The underlying principle of the AI Act is that the more serious the harms, the more restrictions are placed on the systems. Systems with unacceptable risks are prohibited. High-risk systems must satisfy certain constraints. Low-risk systems are not regulated. For example, social scoring, evaluating individual trustworthiness, would be banned if government-led but not if done by the private sector. Predictive policing would be banned. **Facial recognition** (page 781) in public places by law enforcement would be restricted. Subsequently, the EU followed up with the AI Liability Directive [European Commission, 2022d,a] which would, if enacted, make it more feasible for people and companies to sue for damages if they have been harmed by an AI system. The US Office of Science and Technology Policy [2022] has developed a "Blueprint for an AI Bill of Rights", a set of five principles and associated practices to help guide the design, use, and deployment of automated systems.

**Governance** covers government legislation and regulation, **external governance**, but it also refers to **internal governance**, within corporations, government agencies, and other actors who are developing and deploying AI products and services. Many of those actors are putting in place internal governance measures, including ethics codes, to ensure responsible AI guidelines are followed [Amershi et al., 2019; World Economic Forum, 2021]. The cultural and organizational challenges that need to be addressed to create responsible AI systems are described by Rakova et al. [2021]. As a note of caution, Green [2022] suggests, "Rather than protect against the potential harms of algorithmic decision making in government, human oversight policies provide a false sense of security in adopting algorithms and enable vendors and agencies to shirk accountability for algorithmic harms." Professional standards, product certification, and independent oversight are other means, beyond external and internal governance, to ensure AI **safety**, as discussed by Falco et al. [2021].

The scope of government regulation is hotly debated and subject to intense lobbying efforts. Multinational corporations are alleged to use **ethics washing** to fend off further regulation, arguing that the introduction of internal ethical codes is sufficient to prevent harms. Moreover, the extent of **regulatory capture**, whereby legislators and regulators are influenced by, and aligned with, the corporations they are supposed to regulate, is pervasive. It is a real and significant concern for AI governance.

## 18.9 Review

The following are the main points you should have learned from this chapter:

- The digital economy puts the emphasis on information rather than matter.

- The **atoms-to-bits** transformation, **dematerialization**, and AI reduce friction in economic transactions, speeding them up.

- The process of **disintermediation**, the elimination of intermediary roles, is enabled by AI. It is disruptive to employment patterns in the digital economy.
- Machine learning systems, trained on massive datasets, may embody racist, sexist, and other attitudes demeaning of human dignity.
- There are concerns about the alignment between human values and AI systems, in both the short term and the long term.
- AI applications are permeating the economy, eliminating the need for many skills and increasing the demand for other skills.
- Transportation and sustainability are two areas of potentially beneficial applications of AI.
- Ethical codes, legislation, regulation, and certification are being developed to restrict harmful applications of AI.

## 18.10 Exercises

**Exercise 18.1** There have been proposals made for a global ban on the use of **lethal autonomous weapon systems** (LAWS). Investigate and describe the current status of action on a ban on the use of LAWS. Present a brief argument in favor or against such a ban.

**Exercise 18.2** Consider the use of robots and companions for the elderly, the disabled, or infants. Investigate and describe briefly the current state of the art for these companions for one of those populations. Present three reasons in favor of their use and three reasons against.

**Exercise 18.3** Human rights and animal rights are well recognized. Outline a case for or against robot rights. Be specific about the robot rights you are discussing.

**Exercise 18.4** Estimate and compare the energy use of deep learning systems and Bitcoin miners, globally. Compare your results to the energy use of a typical city.

**Exercise 18.5** Discuss how one of the normative ethical systems discussed (virtue, consequentialism, and deontological) could be used in design guidelines for an autonomous car.

**Exercise 18.6** Consider the proposal to require strong professional codes of ethics for AI designers and engineers. Give three reasons in favor of requiring such codes and three reasons against. Which, on balance, do you support?

**Exercise 18.7** Consider the need for government legislation, regulation, and enforcement of restrictions on the use of AI. Give three reasons in favor of restrictions and three reasons against. Which, on balance, do you support?

# Chapter 19

# Retrospect and Prospect

*Computation is the fire in our modern-day caves. By 2056, the computational revolution will be recognised as a transformation as significant as the industrial revolution. The evolution and widespread diffusion of computation and its analytical fruits will have major impacts on socioeconomics, science and culture.*

– Eric Horvitz [2006]

This chapter starts with the state-of-the-art in deploying AI for applications, then looks at the big picture in terms of the agent design space (page 21), and speculates on the future of AI. By placing many of the representations covered in the agent design space, the relationships among them become more apparent. This helps us to see where the frontier of AI research lies and provides a sense of the evolution of the field. As Horvitz points out above, computation is changing the world; its beneficial and harmful effects will impact us all.

## 19.1 Deploying AI

During **deployment**, when AI is used in an application, the data comes from the world, and rather than using a test set to evaluate predictions, actions are carried out in the world. Figure 19.1 (page 786) gives a decision tree to help choose which AI technologies to use.

The conditions in this tree are:

- At the top level is the choice of whether the **stakes** are high or low. The stakes are **low** when there are not severe consequences for errors, for example, in a game, for recommending what videos to watch, or suggesting a way to fold proteins when any resulting medicine will be fully tested.

If a medical diagnostic agent is reminding doctors of possibilities they might have forgotten, it might have low stakes, even if it would have high stakes if it is relied on. In low-stakes cases, being better than the competition may be enough.

The stakes are **high** when people or the environment can be harmed or when a large amount of resources are spent for each decision. For decisions that are repeated, there are typically many possible outcomes that each have a low probability, but where the probability of one of them arising is very high. For example, in a self-driving car, there are many unusual things that could be on the road, each of which is unlikely, but with millions of cars, the probability that one of these will eventually be encountered by someone is very high. If the cost of errors is high, having a low error rate may mean an application is still high stakes.

- When there is **abundant homogenous data**, for example from online images, text, high-throughput science experiments or when there is a simulator to generate data, as in a game, data-hungry machine learning tools

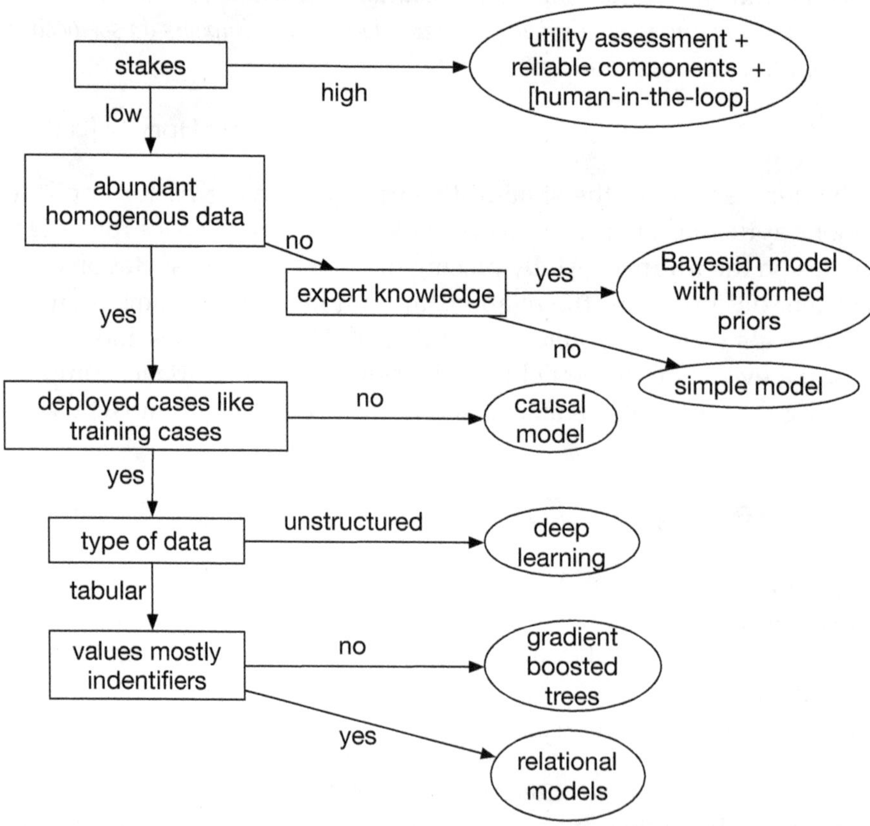


Figure 19.1: Choice of AI technology in deployment

can be used. Sometimes there is a lot of data, but it is heterogenous. For example, governments publish pollution data where there is, say, monthly or irregular testing of multiple pollutants at many locations, which become voluminous, even though there may be only tens or hundreds of data points for any particular location and pollutant. As another example, in medicine there are many rare diseases which have few (recorded) cases. Although each disease is rare, there are so many diseases that in a community it is common to find someone who has one of them. Because there are so many diseases, for most pairs of diseases, no one in the world has both, even though there are many people with multiple diseases.

- When there is not a lot of data, often there is **expert knowledge** that can be applied. Experts have the advantage that they do more than learning from examples; they can build on established theories they learned in school or from reading books, and can bring in diverse knowledge.

- Many machine learning algorithms assume that **deployed cases are like training cases**: the data used in deployment is from the same distribution as the training data. That assumption needs to be verified, and is often not appropriate. In real-world domains, as opposed to games, the future is typically not like the past, for example due to technology advances or global warming. You might not want the future to be like the past.

- There are a number of **types of data** that arise. Some methods are used for **unstructured** and perceptual data, such as text, speech, images, video, and protein sequences, where there are no readily available features. **Tabular** data sometimes has values, such as categories, Booleans, and numbers, that can be used to form features. Sometimes in tabular data the **values are mostly identifiers** (page 705), such as student numbers, product ids, or transaction numbers, which contain no information in themselves about what they refer to.

When the stakes are low, there is abundant homogenous data and the deployed cases are expected to be like the training cases, pure machine learning can be used. Deep learning (page 327) has proved to be the choice for unstructured and perceptual data where there are not pre-defined features, such as images, speech, text, and protein sequences. For tabular data where the values in the tables can be used to construct features, **gradient-boosted trees** (page 311), which use linear functions of conjunctions of propositions about these values, work well. Relational models (page 731) are designed for tabular data with identifiers.

If the assumption that deployment is like training is inappropriate, a causal model (page 491)) can be built that takes into account possible changes or missing data. Observational data alone is provably not sufficient to predict the effect of actions, such as in Simpson's paradox (page 504). The conditional probabilities of a causal model can be learned using the methods of Chapters 7 or 8, or the whole model can be learned (page 481), taking into account the causality.

If there is not much data, but there is expert knowledge, building a causal model with informed priors (e.g., using a Dirichlet distribution (page 465)) is a way to combine expertise and data in a way that smoothly interpolates between the case with no data, and when the data is overwhelming (page 466). If there is little data and no expertise, a simple model such as a decision tree (page 281) or a linear model (page 288) is typically the best that can be done, where the simplicity depends on the amount of data.

When the stakes are high, a complex cost–benefit analysis is appropriate, based on the utility (page 518) of all stakeholders who might be affected by the decision. When considerable resources are required for the actions, or when poor outcomes can arise, decisions need to be explained. The system needs to be able to be debugged when errors arise. High-stakes cases typically use a combination of techniques, where each component is well tested and reliable.

## 19.2 Agent Design Space Revisited

The agent design space (page 21) provides a way to understand the frontier of knowledge about AI. It is instructive to see how representations presented in the book can be positioned in that space.

Figure 19.2 (page 789) reviews the dimensions of complexity and classifies, in terms of the values for each dimension, some of the agent models covered in the book. These agent models were selected because they have different values in the dimensions.

### Agent Models

The following describes the agent models that form the columns of Figure 19.2.

- **Hier. Control**, hierarchical control (page 58), means reasoning at multiple levels of abstraction. As presented it was non-planning, and it did not take goals or utility into account.

- State-space **search**, as presented in Chapter 3, allows for an indefinite horizon but otherwise gives the simplest value in all the other dimensions. **Det. planning**, deterministic planning (Chapter 6), either regression planning, forward planning, or CSP planning, extends state-space search to reason in terms of features.

- **Decision Net.**, decision networks (page 537), extend belief networks to include decision and utility nodes, and can represent features, stochastic effects, partial observability, and complex preferences in terms of utilities. However, these networks only model a finite-stage planning horizon. **Markov decision processes (MDPs)** (page 552) allow for indefinite

| | Hier. Control | Search | Det. Planning | Decision Net | MDP | Dynamic DN | POMDP | Extensive game | Q-Learning | Deep RL | Stochastic PI |
|---|---|---|---|---|---|---|---|---|---|---|---|
| **Modularity** | | | | | | | | | | | |
| flat | ✔ | ✔ | ✔ | ✔ | ✔ | ✔ | ✔ | ✔ | ✔ | ✔ | ✔ |
| modular | ✔ | | | | | | | | | | |
| hierarchical | ✔ | | | | | | | | | | |
| **Planning Horizon** | | | | | | | | | | | |
| non-planning | ✔ | | | | | | | | | | |
| finite | | ✔ | ✔ | ✔ | | | | ✔ | | | ✔ |
| indefinite | | ✔ | ✔ | | ✔ | ✔ | ✔ | ✔ | ✔ | ✔ | |
| infinite | | | | | ✔ | ✔ | ✔ | | ✔ | ✔ | |
| **Representation** | | | | | | | | | | | |
| states | ✔ | ✔ | | | ✔ | | ✔ | ✔ | ✔ | | ✔ |
| features | ✔ | | ✔ | ✔ | | ✔ | | | | ✔ | |
| relational | | | | | | | | | | | |
| **Computational Limits** | | | | | | | | | | | |
| perfect | ✔ | ✔ | ✔ | ✔ | | | | ✔ | | | |
| bounded | | | | | ✔ | ✔ | ✔ | | ✔ | ✔ | ✔ |
| **Learning** | | | | | | | | | | | |
| given | ✔ | ✔ | ✔ | ✔ | ✔ | ✔ | ✔ | ✔ | | | |
| learned | | | | | | | | | ✔ | ✔ | ✔ |
| **Sensing Uncertainty** | | | | | | | | | | | |
| fully obs. | ✔ | ✔ | ✔ | | ✔ | ✔ | | | ✔ | ✔ | ✔ |
| partial obs. | | | | ✔ | | | ✔ | ✔ | | | |
| **Effect Uncertainty** | | | | | | | | | | | |
| deterministic | ✔ | ✔ | ✔ | | | | | | | | |
| stochastic | | | | ✔ | ✔ | ✔ | ✔ | ✔ | ✔ | ✔ | ✔ |
| **Preference** | | | | | | | | | | | |
| goals | | ✔ | ✔ | | | | | | | | |
| utility | | | | ✔ | ✔ | ✔ | ✔ | ✔ | ✔ | ✔ | ✔ |
| **Number of Agents** | | | | | | | | | | | |
| single | ✔ | ✔ | ✔ | ✔ | ✔ | ✔ | ✔ | | ✔ | ✔ | |
| adversary | | | | | | | | ✔ | ✔ | ✔ | ✔ |
| multiple | ✔ | | | | | | | ✔ | | | ✔ |
| **Interactivity** | | | | | | | | | | | |
| offline | | ✔ | ✔ | ✔ | ✔ | ✔ | ✔ | ✔ | | | |
| online | ✔ | | | | | | | | ✔ | ✔ | ✔ |

Figure 19.2: Some agent models rated by dimensions of complexity

and infinite-stage problems with stochastic actions and complex preferences; however, they are state-based representations that assume the state is fully observable. Dynamic decision networks (dynamic DN) (page 565) extend MDPs to allow feature-based representation of states. Partially observable MDPs (POMDPs) (page 569) allow for partially observable states but are much more difficult to solve.

- **Game tree search** for the **extensive form of a game** (page 612) extends state-space search to include multiple agents and utility. It can handle partially observable domains through the use of information sets (page 614).

- **Q-learning** (page 589) extends MDPs to allow for online learning, but only deals with states. **Deep reinforcement learning (Deep RL)** (page 600), and other methods that use function approximation in reinforcement learning (page 599), do reinforcement learning with features. These work for single agents or adversaries, but not for arbitrary multiagent domains.

- **Stochastic PI**, stochastic policy iteration (page 634), allows for learning with multiple agents but needs to play the same game repeatedly with the same agents to coordinate.

## Dimensions Revisited

None of the planning representations presented in Figure 19.2 handle **hierarchical control** (page 58). In hierarchical control, low-level controls act faster than high-level deliberation. While deep reinforcement learning (page 600) uses hierarchies in its representation of the state, it only plans at a single level of abstraction. Hierarchical planning and hierarchical reinforcement learning are not presented in this book, although much research exists. Hierarchical reasoning does not need to work as a monolith; different techniques can be used at low levels than used at high levels. There is evidence (page 58) that humans have quite different systems for high-level deliberative reasoning than for low-level perception and reactions.

Some of the representations (such as decision networks) model each decision separately and are only applicable for a finite sequence of decisions. Some allow for indefinitely many decisions, but then the policies are typically stationary (not dependent on time, unless time is part of the state space). The planning systems based on (discounted or average) rewards can handle infinite-stage planning, where the agents go on forever collecting rewards. It does not make sense for goal-oriented systems to go on forever.

All of the representations can handle states as the degenerate case of having a single feature. Reasoning in terms of features is the main design choice for many of the representations, either engineered features or learned features. Reasoning in terms of features can be much more efficient than reasoning in terms of states, as the number of states is exponentially more than the number of features. None of the representations in Figure 19.2 allow for relational models, although many of the algorithms can be made relational.

**Bounded rationality** (page 26) underlies many of the approximation methods used for applications; however, making the explicit trade-off between thinking and acting, in which the agent reasons about whether it should act immediately or think more, is still relatively rare.

Figure 19.2 only shows three learning algorithms, although it is possible to learn the models for the others, for example, learning the conditional probabilities (page 461) or the structure (page 484) of probabilistic models, as, for example, model-based reinforcement learning (page 597) learns the transition and reward probabilities for an MDP.

The dimension that adds the most difficulty to the task of building an agent is **sensing uncertainty** (page 29). With partial observability, there are many possible states the world could be in. The outcome of an action by the agent can depend on the actual state of the world. All the agent has access to is its history (page 55) of past percepts and actions. There are many ways to represent the function from the history of the agent to its actions. Ways to extend planning with sensing uncertainty and indefinite and infinite-horizon problems are discussed in the context of POMDPs (page 569). How to handle sensing in all of its forms is one of the most active areas of current AI research.

The models that can use stochastic actions can also handle deterministic actions (as deterministic is a special case of stochastic). Some of them, such as MDPs and the reinforcement learning algorithms, work well in deterministic domains.

Preferences are either specified in terms of goals or utilities; Proposition 12.3 (page 522) proved that complex preferences, under very mild assumptions, can be represented in terms of utility. The models that can handle complex cardinal preferences can also handle goals by giving a reward to goal achievement. A preference to the shortest path to a goal can be achieved by negative rewards for actions that do not lead to a goal or discounting (page 556). In general, utilities are more expressive than goals.

Dealing with multiple agents is much more difficult than planning for a single agent. The case of an agent with a single adversary agent is simpler than the more general cases. Multiple agents can be cooperative or competitive, or more often somewhere in between, where they can compete in some aspects and cooperate in others. Communication between agents is a standard way to achieve cooperation in society. Another way to achieve cooperation between self-interested agents is in the design of mechanisms (page 630) for making society work, including money and legislation. This book has hardly scratched the surface of what can be done.

**Interactivity** (page 34) is a single dimension, whereas real agents have to make quick online decisions as well as make more long-term decisions. Agents need to reason about multiple time-scales, and what can appear as offline in relation to a decision that has to be made in a second could be seen as an online decision at the scale of days. Unlimited offline computation risks the possibility of the agent never actually acting.

This book has presented the details of a small part of the design space of AI. The current frontier of research goes beyond what is covered in this textbook. There is much active research in all areas of AI. There have been and continue to be impressive advances in planning, learning, perception, natural language understanding, robotics, and other subareas of AI. Most of this work considers multiple dimensions and how they interact. There is growing interest in considering all of the dimensions and multiple tasks simultaneously (for example, under the rubric of **artificial general intelligence**), but doing everything well is difficult.

The decomposition of AI into subareas is not surprising. The design space is too big to explore all at once. Once a researcher has decided to handle, say, relational domains and reasoning about the existence of objects, it is difficult to add sensor uncertainty. If a researcher starts with learning with infinite horizons, it is difficult to add hierarchical reasoning, let alone learning with infinite horizons and relations together with hierarchies.

As AI practitioners, we still do not know how to build an agent that acts rationally in infinite-stage, partially observable domains consisting of individuals and relations in which there are multiple agents acting autonomously. Arguably humans do this, perhaps by reasoning hierarchically and approximately. Although we may not yet be able to build an intelligent artificial agent with human-level performance, we may have the building blocks to develop one. The main challenge is handling the complexity of the real world. However, so far there seem to be no intrinsic obstacles to building computational embodied agents capable of human-level performance or beyond.

## 19.3 Looking Ahead

> *The Navy revealed the embryo of an electronic computer today that it expects will be able to walk, talk, see, write, reproduce itself and be conscious of its existence. . . . The service said it would . . . build the first of its Perceptron thinking machines that will be able to read and write. It is expected to be finished in about a year at a cost of $100,000.*
>
> – New York Times [1958]

Predicting the future is always perilous. Brooks [2018] gives more recent informed predictions, and updates the progress every year.

Over the last decade there has been an explosion of applications that rely on large datasets and immense computation power, fueled by online datasets and the use of vector processing units (including GPUs), especially by large corporations that can afford huge computation centers. However, in the science of AI, integrating more of the dimensions is happening much more slowly.

For the technology, there are some predictions that seem safe, given the current state of the art in Figure 19.1 (page 786).

For low-stakes decisions where there is abundant homogeneous data, such as vision, text, video, and big-data science, it is likely that more data and more compute power, together with improved algorithms that are being developed, will lead to better predictions in these cases. **Universal function approximators**, functions that can approximate any functions on bounded domains, such as neural networks, have been shown to be very effective when provided with abundant data and computation power.

Generating images, video, text, code, and novel designs for drugs and other chemicals, in what is known as **generative AI**, will get more sophisticated. When used for high-stakes decisions, unless they are generated to be provably correct, the predictions will need to undergo critical evaluation to ensure they can be used as reliable components for the decision task.

Improvements in predictive technology are likely to have beneficial outcomes because better predictions lead to better decisions. However, they can also have harmful outcomes for people when the values embedded in decisions do not coincide with the wellbeing of those people. For example, the use of generative AI to produce text, images, video, and music is likely to explode. These techniques could be used in the workflow to create **art**, possibly enhancing human creativity, or to create deep fakes (page 367), designed to mislead. There is an arms race to build and detect these fakes, but note that adversarial networks (including GANs) (page 366) explicitly build models to counter efforts to detect them.

One medium-term development we can expect is for cases when the world in deployment is different than the world the training data is from, or in **transfer learning**, when using data from one domain in another. Observational data alone is not sufficient to predict the effect of actions; causality and expert knowledge needs to be taken into account. We expect more interactions between subareas.

There are many cases where there is no abundant data. For example, the SNOMED CT (page 728) medical ontology has about 100,000 terms for diseases and other underlying causes that humans can have. The long tail of the probability of diseases means that for most diseases there are very few people with the disease. For nearly all of the pairs of diseases, no one in the world has both. We cannot learn the interactions of these diseases from data alone, as there are not enough people to cover all of the interactions. For these cases, more sophisticated models need to be considered, and expert knowledge cannot be ignored. We expect to see more integration of data that has rich metadata (page 726) and expert knowledge to build hypotheses that match both the data and prior expectation.

For decision making in the world, an agent cannot learn from passive observation, such as text or video alone. Text only contains what someone thought was interesting, and does not contain mundane details that everyone knows. Video does not specify the actions of the agent, and if it did, it does not specify what the agent would have done in other circumstances, which is counterfactual reasoning (page 508). Except in artificial domains, an agent is never in the same state twice. An agent that is **embodied** interacts with the environment. An embodied agent in the real world needs **common sense** (page 8) [Brachman and Levesque, 2022b]. This includes being ready to react to the unexpected; something never experienced before.

For high-stakes decisions, **preference elicitation** (page 526) from affected stakeholders needs to be taken into account. In general, preferences are not obtainable by learning from data. While maybe it is possible to hypothesize someone's preferences from their actions, in what is called **inverse reinforcement learning**, it is difficult to know what they would have done in other circumstances, or they might regret their actions, or their preferences may have changed. The various stakeholders may have very different preferences, and somehow these need to be combined in a fair and transparent way for an agent that affects multiple stakeholders.

Some have suggested that computers will become more intelligent than people, reaching a **singularity** (page 770), in which case people might not be needed. There is much speculation about when computers will be more intelligent than humans. This is difficult to define, as it is not clear what "humans" or "computers" mean. Humans could refer to a random person answering questions about a random culture, an educated person answering questions about their own culture, a world expert, or a person who has access to the Internet and others who are connected. A computer could refer to a standalone phone or laptop, a phone or laptop connected to the Internet, the whole World Wide Web without the humans in the loop, or the World Wide Web with humans in the loop. At the most general level of these it isn't clear what the difference is.

Some have predicted that AI will lead to a dystopian future ruled by machines, but others see a nirvana – an ideal or idyllic place – where good decisions are made and people are looked after. Which of these arises depends on the people who build the AI and those who regulate the AI.

Turing [1950] concluded his seminal paper with "We can only see a short distance ahead, but we can see plenty there that needs to be done." This is still true today, even though there have been considerable advances since then.

## 19.4 References and Further Reading

Some of the other combinations of the dimensions include the following. Hierarchical planning is discussed by Nau [2007]. Hierarchical reinforcement learning is covered by Dietterich [2000b]. Multiagent reinforcement learning is addressed by Stone [2007]. Inverse reinforcement learning is introduced by Ng and Russell [2000] and discussed by Russell [2019]. Dzeroski et al. [2001] overview relational reinforcement learning. Khardon and Sanner [2021] discuss relational decision-theoretic planning.

Challenges for the future of AI are described by Russell [2019], Marcus and Davis [2019], Littman et al. [2021] and Brachman and Levesque [2022a].

## 19.5 Exercises

**Exercise 19.1** For each leaf in the decision tree of Figure 19.1 (page 786) (starting with "use" or "do"), give an example of an application that has the characteristics that would end at that leaf. For example, for the first leaf, give an application where the stakes are low, there is abundant homogeneous data, etc.

Suggest an application that should not follow the advice of Figure 19.1. Explain why.

**Exercise 19.2** Consider one of the following scenarios.

(i) You are working for a company and have been asked about the feasibility of building a tool for predicting the results of an upcoming election so they can plan appropriately. You will have access to data about the outcome of previous elections, demographic data from the census about the voters, information about the parties and candidates. The goal is to predict the probability of which party or parties will form government. A rival company has proposed solving it by combining hidden Markov models and gradient-boosted trees.

(ii) A large national coffee and donut shop is looking to modernize their donut production operations. Currently they have a single production machine that bakes and decorates the many kinds of donuts and pastries they make and dumps them onto a single line. The donuts on this line are then sorted by human operators into boxes for display and delivery. They need to fill two types of boxes: boxes where all the donuts are the same type, and boxes containing 12 unique types of donuts (there are more than 12 types of donuts). The company is proposing to replace these human sorters with robots. Your job is to advise them. A rival company has proposed using deep learning with deterministic planning.

(iii) A biomedical firm approaches your company to develop a drug interaction advisor for doctors to understand the interaction of different drugs on their patients. They have access to a number of large databases of leading research on the effects of different drugs. However, the databases overlap on some drugs and diseases but not others. The databases use different notation for representing drugs, diseases, and their impact. Each database makes probabilistic predictions about drugs curing specific diseases, causing negative side-effects, or having no impact. A rival company has proposed using a mix of ontologies and probabilistic relational models to solve this problem.

(a) Explain how the problem fits into the abstraction of an agent.

(b) Explain how the rival company's solution may work, and explain why they may have chosen the technologies they proposed.

(c) What is the most challenging part of solving this problem? What would you recommend as a way to solve this? Justify any recommendation made.

**Exercise 19.3** Find some current AI applications and classify the state-of-the-art for that application in terms of the dimensions. Does the application automate what Kahneman [2011] calls System 1 or System 2 (page 58) or neither or both?

**Exercise 19.4** Give an argument for and against each of these propositions, about the possibility of a singularity, when computers will be more intelligent than people.

(a) The singularity will never occur as people have common sense that can never be matched by a computer.
(b) The singularity has already occurred; I would trust an answer that Google provides more than I would trust an answer from a random person.
(c) The singularity is meaningless as humans are so tightly integrated with computers that the interaction will always be more intelligent than either one.
(d) The singularity will happen in a few decades and will make humans subservient to computers.

# Appendix A

# Mathematical Preliminaries and Notation

This appendix gives some definitions of fundamental mathematical concepts used in AI, but which are traditionally taught in other courses. It also introduces some notation and data structures that are used in various parts of the book.

## A.1 Rolling Average

It is common to get information sequentially, and require a rolling average, the mean of the values already seen, or the mean of the most recent values.

Suppose there is a sequence of numerical values, $v_1, v_2, v_3, \ldots$, and the goal is to predict the mean after the first $k$ values for each $k$. The **rolling average**, $A_k$, is the mean of the first $k$ data points $v_1, \ldots, v_k$, namely

$$A_k = \frac{v_1 + \cdots + v_k}{k} .$$

Thus

$$\begin{aligned} k * A_k &= v_1 + \cdots + v_{k-1} + v_k \\ &= (k-1)A_{k-1} + v_k. \end{aligned}$$

Dividing by $k$ gives

$$A_k = \left(1 - \frac{1}{k}\right) * A_{k-1} + \frac{v_k}{k} .$$

Let $\alpha_k = \frac{1}{k}$, then

$$A_k = (1 - \alpha_k) * A_{k-1} + \alpha_k * v_k$$

$$=A_{k-1} + \alpha_k * (v_k - A_{k-1}). \tag{A.1}$$

Predicting the mean makes sense if all of the values have an equal weight. However, suppose you are keeping an estimate of the expected price of some item in the grocery store. Prices go up and down in the short term, but tend to increase slowly; the newer prices are more useful for the estimate of the current price than older prices, and so they should be weighted more in predicting new prices.

Suppose, instead, you want to maintain the average of the previous $n$ values. The first $n$ values need to be treated specially. Each example (after the $n$th) contributes $1/n$ to the average. When a new value arrives, the oldest is dropped. If $A_{k-1}$ is the average of the previous $n$ values, the next average is

$$A_k = A_{k-1} + \frac{v_k - v_{k-n}}{n}.$$

To implement this, the $n$ most recent values need to be stored, and the average is sensitive to what happened $n$ steps ago. One way to simplify this is to use the rolling average, $A_{k-1}$, instead of $v_{k-n}$. This results in Equation (A.1), but with $\alpha_k$ a constant, namely $1/n$.

Having $\alpha_k = \frac{1}{k}$ averages out noise, but treats all data equally. Having $\alpha_k$ a constant means more recent data is used, but any noise in the data become noise in the rolling average. Using a constant, $\alpha$, gives an **exponentially-decaying rolling average** as item $v_{k-n}$, which is $n$ steps before the current value, has weight $(1 - \alpha)^n$ in the average.

You could reduce $\alpha$ more slowly and potentially have the benefits of both approaches: weighting recent observations more and still converging to the mean. You can guarantee convergence if

$$\sum_{k=1}^{\infty} \alpha_k = \infty \quad \text{and} \quad \sum_{k=1}^{\infty} \alpha_k^2 < \infty.$$

The first condition is to ensure that random fluctuations and initial conditions get averaged out, and the second condition guarantees convergence.

The rolling average is used for the simple controller of Example 2.3 (page 57), some of the optimizers for neural networks in Section 8.2 (page 336), and for reinforcement learning in Section 13.3 (page 588).

## A.2 Discrete Mathematics

The mathematical concepts we build on include:

**sets** A **set** has elements (members). $s \in S$ means $s$ is an element of set $S$. The elements in a set define the set, so that two sets are equal if they have the same elements.

**tuples** An $n$-tuple is an ordered grouping of $n$ elements, written $\langle x_1, \ldots, x_n \rangle$. A 2-tuple is a **pair**, and a 3-tuple is a **triple**. Two $n$-tuples are equal if they have the same members in the corresponding positions. If $S$ is a set, $S^n$ is the set of $n$-tuples $\langle x_1, \ldots, x_n \rangle$, where $x_i$ is a member of $S$. $S_1 \times S_2 \times \cdots \times S_n$ is the set of $n$-tuples $\langle x_1, \ldots, x_n \rangle$, where each $x_i$ is in $S_i$.

**relations** A **relation** is a set of n-tuples. The tuples in the relation are said to be *true* of the relation. An alternative definition is in terms of the relation's **characteristic function**, a function on tuples that is true for a tuple when the tuple is in the relation and false when it is not.

**functions** A **function**, or **mapping**, $f$ from set $D$, the **domain**, into set $R$, the **range**, written $f : D \to R$, is a subset of $D \times R$ such that for every $d \in D$ there is a unique $r \in R$ such that $\langle d, r \rangle \in f$. We write $f(d) = r$ if $\langle d, r \rangle \in f$.

While these may seem like obscure definitions for commonsense concepts, you can now use these concepts comfortable in the knowledge that you can check the definitions.

## A.3 Functions, Factors, and Arrays

Many of the algorithms in this book manipulate representations of functions. We extend the standard definition of functions on sets to include functions on variables. A **factor** is a representation of a function. An **array** is an explicit representation of a function that can have its individual components modified.

If $S$ is a set, we write $f(S)$ to be a function, with domain $S$. Thus, if $c \in S$, then $f(c)$ is a value in the range of $f$. $f[S]$ is like $f(S)$, but individual components can be updated. This notation is based on that of Python, C, and Java (but C and Java only allow $S$ to be the set of integers $\{0, \ldots, n-1\}$ for arrays of size $n$). Thus $f[c]$ is a value in the range of $f$. If $f[c]$ is assigned a new value, it will return that new value.

This notation can be extended to (algebraic) variables. If $X$ is an algebraic variable with domain $D$, then $f(X)$ is a function that given a value $x \in D$, returns a value in the range of $f$. This value is often written as $f(X = x)$ or simply as $f(x)$. Similarly, $f[X]$ is an array indexed by $X$, that is, it is a function of $X$ whose components can be modified.

This notation can also be extended to set of variables. $f(X_1, X_2, \ldots, X_n)$ is a function such that given a value $v_1$ for $X_1$, a value $v_2$ for $X_2, \ldots,$ and a value $v_n$ for $X_n$, returns a value in the range of $f$. Note that it is the name of the variable that is important, not the position. This factor applied to the specific values is written as $f(X_1 = v_1, X_2 = v_2, \ldots, X_n = v_n)$. The set of variables, $X_1, X_2, \ldots, X_n$ is called the **scope** of $f$. The array $f[X_1, X_2, \ldots, X_n]$ is a function on $X_1, X_2, \ldots, X_n$ where the values can be updated.

Assigning just some of the variables gives a function on the remaining variables. Thus, for example, if $f$ is a function with scope $X_1, X_2, \ldots, X_n$, then

$f(X_1 = v_1)$ is a function of $X_2, \ldots, X_n$, such that

$$(f(X_1 = v_1))(X_2 = v_2, \ldots, X_n = v_n) = f(X_1 = v_1, X_2 = v_2, \ldots, X_n = v_n).$$

Factors can be added, multiplied, or composed with any other operation level on the elements. If $f_1$ and $f_2$ are factors, then $f_1 + f_2$ is a factor with scope the union of the scopes of $f_1$ and $f_2$, defined point-wise:

$$\begin{aligned}(f_1 + f_2)&(X_1 = v_1, X_2 = v_2, \ldots, X_n = v_n) \\ &= f_1(X_1 = v_1, X_2 = v_2, \ldots, X_n = v_n) + f_2(X_1 = v_1, X_2 = v_2, \ldots, X_n = v_n)\end{aligned}$$

where we assume that $f_1$ and $f_2$ ignore variables not in their scope. Multiplication and other binary operators work similarly.

**Example 1.1** Suppose $f_1(X, Y) = X + Y$ and $f_2(Y, Z) = Y + Z$. Then $f_1 + f_2$ is $X + 2Y + Z$, which is a function of $X$, $Y$, and $Z$. Similarly, $f_1 \times f_2 = (X + Y) \times (Y + Z)$.

$f_1(X = 2)$ is a function of $Y$, defined by $2 + Y$.

Suppose that variable $W$ has domain $\{0, 1\}$ and $X$ has domain $\{1, 2\}$, the factor $f_3(W, X)$ can be defined by a table such as

| $W$ | $X$ | Value |
|---|---|---|
| 0 | 1 | 2 |
| 0 | 2 | 1 |
| 1 | 1 | 0 |
| 1 | 2 | 3 |

$f_3 + f_1$ is a function on $W$, $X$, and $Y$ such that, for example

$$(f_3 + f_1)(W = 1, X = 2, Y = 3) = 3 + 5 = 8.$$

Similarly, $(f_3 \times f_1)(W = 1, X = 2, Y = 3) = 3 \times 5 = 15$.

Other operations on factors are defined in the book.

## A.4 Relations and the Relational Algebra

Relations are common in AI and database systems. The **relational algebra** defines operations on relations and is the basis of relational databases.

A **scope** $S$ is a set of variables. A **tuple** $t$ on scope $S$ has a value on each variable in its scope. A variable can be seen as a function on tuples; one that returns the value for that variable for that tuple. We write $X(t)$ to be the value of tuple $t$ on variable $X$. The value of $X(t)$ must be in $dom(X)$. This is like the mathematical notion of tuple, except the index is given by a variable, not by an integer.

A **relation** is a set of tuples, all with the same scope. A relation is often given a name. The scope of the tuples is often called the **relation scheme**. A

**relational database** is a set of relations. A scheme of a relational database is the set of pairs of relation names and relation schemes.

A relation with scope $X_1, \ldots, X_n$ can be seen as a Boolean factor on $X_1, \ldots, X_n$, where the true elements are represented as tuples.

Often a relation is written as a table.

**Example 1.2** The following is a tabular depiction of a relation, *enrolled*:

| *Course* | *Year* | *Student* | *Grade* |
|---|---|---|---|
| cs322 | 2008 | *fran* | 77 |
| cs111 | 2009 | *billie* | 88 |
| cs111 | 2009 | *jess* | 78 |
| cs444 | 2008 | *fran* | 83 |
| cs322 | 2009 | *jordan* | 92 |

The heading gives the scheme, namely $\{Course, Year, Student, Grade\}$, and every other row is a tuple. The first tuple, call it $t_1$, is defined by $Course(t_1) = cs322$, $Year(t_1) = 2008$, $Student(t_1) = fran$, $Grade(t_1) = 77$.

The order of the columns and the order of the rows is not significant.

If $r$ is a relation with scheme $S$, and $c$ is a condition on the variables in $S$, the **selection** of $c$ in $r$, written $\sigma_c(r)$, is the set of tuples in $r$ for which $c$ holds. The selection has the same scheme as $r$.

If $r$ is a relation with scheme $S$, and $S_0 \subseteq S$, the **projection** of $r$ onto $S_0$, written $\pi_{S_0}(r)$, is the set of tuples of $r$ where the scope is restricted to $S_0$.

**Example 1.3** Suppose *enrolled* is the relation given in Example A.2.

The relation $\sigma_{Grade>79}(enrolled)$ selects those tuples in *enrolled* where the grade is over 79. This is the relation:

| *Course* | *Year* | *Student* | *Grade* |
|---|---|---|---|
| cs111 | 2009 | *billie* | 88 |
| cs444 | 2008 | *fran* | 83 |
| cs322 | 2009 | *jordan* | 92 |

The relation $\pi_{\{Student,Year\}}(enrolled)$ specifies what years students were enrolled:

| *Student* | *Year* |
|---|---|
| *fran* | 2008 |
| *billie* | 2009 |
| *jess* | 2009 |
| *jordan* | 2009 |

Notice how the first and the fourth tuple of *enrolled* become the same tuple in the projection; they represent the same function on $\{Student, Year\}$.

If two relations are on the same scheme, the **union**, **intersection**, and **set difference** of these are defined as the corresponding operations on the set of tuples.

If $r_1$ and $r_2$ are two relations, the natural **join** of $r_1$ and $r_2$, written $r_1 \bowtie r_2$, is a relation where

- the scheme of the join is the union of the scheme of $r_1$ and the scheme of $r_2$
- a tuple is in the join if the tuple restricted to the scope of $r_1$ is in the relation $r_1$ and the tuple restricted to the scope of $r_2$ is in the relation $r_2$.

**Example 1.4** Consider the relation *assisted*:

| *Course* | *Year* | *TA* |
|---|---|---|
| cs322 | 2008 | *yuki* |
| cs111 | 2009 | *sam* |
| cs111 | 2009 | *chris* |
| cs322 | 2009 | *yuki* |

The join of *enrolled* and *assisted*, written *enrolled* ⋈ *assisted*, is the relation

| *Course* | *Year* | *Student* | *Grade* | *TA* |
|---|---|---|---|---|
| cs322 | 2008 | *fran* | 77 | *yuki* |
| cs111 | 2009 | *billie* | 88 | *sam* |
| cs111 | 2009 | *jess* | 78 | *sam* |
| cs111 | 2009 | *billie* | 88 | *chris* |
| cs111 | 2009 | *jess* | 78 | *chris* |
| cs322 | 2009 | *jordan* | 92 | *yuki* |

Note how in the join, the information about *cs*444 was lost, as there was no TA in that course.

# Appendix B

# Mapping to Open-Source Packages

## B.1 Gradient-Boosted Trees

The open-source tools for gradient tree boosting **XGBoost** [Chen and Guestrin, 2016] and **LightGBM** [Ke et al., 2017] have been used for many winning entries in machine learning competitions; see https://xgboost.readthedocs.io/ and https://lightgbm.readthedocs.io/.

Table B.1 provides the mapping from the code of Table 7.21 into both XGBoost and LightGBM. They each have many parameters not shown here.

| Figure 7.21 | XGBoost | | LightGBM | |
|---|---|---|---|---|
| Parameter | Parameter | Default | Parameter | Default |
| $K$ | `num_boost_round` | 10 | `num_iterations` | 100 |
| $\lambda$ | `lambda_reg` | 1 | `lambda_l2` | 0 |
| $\eta$ | `eta` | 0.3 | `learning_rate` | 0.1 |
| $\gamma$ | `gamma` | 0 | `min_gain_to_split` | 0 |
| $css$ | `colsample_bytree` | 1 | `feature_fraction` | 1 |
| $ss$ | `subsample` | 1 | `bagging_fraction` | 1 |

Table B.1: Hyperparameters for two open-source gradient-boosted trees learning packages

## B.2 Deep Learning

Table B.2 (page 805) gives the defaults for two common Python-based deep learning frameworks, **Keras** [Chollet, 2021], a high-level interface to **tensorflow**, and **PyTorch**. For documentation on Keras, see https://keras.io. For documentation on PyTorch, see https://pytorch.org.

In Keras and PyTorch, the optimizers are specified separately. The one corresponding to the update of Figure 8.9 (page 347) is SGD (stochastic gradient descent). In both, momentum is a parameter of SGD.

In Keras, the number of input features is implicit, matching the output of the lower layer that the layer is connected to.

Our definition of RMS-Prop follows the original and Keras. In PyTorch, the RMS-Prop update has $\epsilon$ outside of the square root (Line 5 of the method *update* for RMP-Prop on page 340), similar to Adam.

| This Book | | | Keras | | PyTorch | |
|---|---|---|---|---|---|---|
| Algorithm | Page | Name | Name | Default | Name | Default |
| Dense | 334 | *Dense* | Dense | | Linear | |
| | | $n_o$ | units | – | out_features | – |
| | | $n_i$ | (implicit) | | in_features | – |
| update | 334 | *update* | SGD | | SGD | |
| | | $\eta$ | learning_rate | 0.01 | lr | – |
| **momentum** | 339 | $\alpha$ | momentum | 0 | momentum | 0 |
| **RMS-Prop** | 339 | | RMSprop | | RMSprop | |
| | | $\eta$ | learning_rate | 0.001 | lr | 0.01 |
| | | $\rho$ | rho | 0.9 | alpha | 0.99 |
| | | $\epsilon$ | epsilon | $10^{-7}$ | eps | $10^{-8}$ |
| **Adam** | 340 | | Adam | | Adam | |
| | | $\eta$ | learning_rate | 0.001 | lr | 0.01 |
| | | $\beta_1$ | beta_1 | 0.9 | betas[0] | 0.9 |
| | | $\beta_2$ | beta_2 | 0.999 | betas[1] | 0.999 |
| | | $\epsilon$ | epsilon | $10^{-7}$ | eps | $10^{-8}$ |
| Dropout | 343 | *Dropout* | Dropout | | Dropout | |
| | | rate | rate | – | p | 0.5 |
| 2D Conv | 347 | *Conv2D* | Conv2D | | Conv2D | |
| | | $k$ | kernel_size | | kernel_size | |
| | | # output channels | filters | – | out_channels | – |
| | | # input channels | (implicit) | | in_channels | – |

Table B.2: Hyperparameters for two deep learning packages

# References


AAAI [2019]. AAAI code of professional ethics and conduct. https://www.aaai.org/Conferences/code-of-ethics-and-conduct.php.

Abelson, H. and DiSessa, A. [1981]. *Turtle Geometry: The Computer as a Medium for Exploring Mathematics*. MIT Press.

Acemoglu, D., Ozdaglar, A., and Siderius, J. [2021]. A model of online misinformation. Working Paper 28884, National Bureau of Economic Research. http://dx.doi.org/10.3386/w28884.

ACM Committee on Professional Ethics [2018]. ACM code of ethics and professional conduct. https://ethics.acm.org.

Agrawal, A., Gans, J., and Goldfarb, A. [2019]. *The Economics of Artificial Intelligence: An Agenda*. National Bureau of Economic Research Conference Report. University of Chicago Press.

Agrawal, A., Gans, J., and Goldfarb, A. [2022]. *Prediction Machines, Updated and Expanded: The Simple Economics of Artificial Intelligence*. Harvard Business Review Press.

Agre, P. E. [1995]. Computational research on interaction and agency. *Artificial Intelligence*, 72:1–52.

Ajunwa, I. [2020]. The paradox of automation as anti-bias intervention. *Cardozo, L. Rev.*, 167.

Alammar, J. [2018]. The illustrated transformer. https://jalammar.github.io/illustrated-transformer/.

Albus, J. S. [1981]. *Brains, Behavior and Robotics*. BYTE Publications.

Algorithm Watch [2022]. A guide to the AI act. https://algorithmwatch.org/en/ai-act-explained/.

Allais, M. and Hagen, O. (eds.) [1979]. *Expected Utility Hypothesis and the Allais Paradox*. Reidel.

Allemang, D., Hendler, J., and Gandon, F. [2020]. *Semantic Web for the Working Ontologist: Effective Modeling for Linked Data, RDFS and OWL.* ACM Books, 3rd edition.

Amershi, S., et al. [2019]. Guidelines for human–AI interaction. In *CHI 2019.* ACM. https://www.microsoft.com/en-us/research/publication/guidelines-for-human-ai-interaction/. CHI 2019 Honorable Mention Award.

Amodei, D., et al. [2016]. Concrete Problems in AI Safety. *ArXiv e-prints,* arXiv:1606.06565.

Andreae, J. H. [1963]. STELLA: A scheme for a learning machine. In *2nd IFAC Congress,* pp. 497–502.

Andrieu, C., de Freitas, N., Doucet, A., and Jordan, M. I. [2003]. An introduction to MCMC for machine learning. *Machine Learning,* 50(1–2):5–43.

Antoniou, G. and van Harmelen, F. [2008]. *A Semantic Web Primer.* MIT Press, 2nd edition.

Apt, K. and Bol, R. [1994]. Logic programming and negation: A survey. *Journal of Logic Programming,* 19/20:9–71.

Archer, S. [2022]. *Salience: A Philosophical Inquiry.* Routledge.

Aristotle [350 BCE]. *Categories.* Translated by E. M. Edghill. http://classics.mit.edu/Aristotle/categories.html.

Arp, R., Smith, B., and Spear, A. [2015]. *Building Ontologies with Basic Formal Ontology.* MIT Press.

Arrow, K. [1963]. *Social Choice and Individual Values.* Wiley, 2nd edition.

Asimov, I. [1950]. *I, Robot.* Doubleday.

Auer, P., Cesa-Bianchi, N., and Fischer, P. [2002]. Finite-time analysis of the multiarmed bandit problem. *Machine Learning,* 47(2):235–256. http://dx.doi.org/10.1023/A:1013689704352.

Auer, S., et al. [2007]. DBpedia: A nucleus for a web of open data. In *6th International Semantic Web Conference (ISWC).*

Awad, E., et al. [2018]. The moral machine experiment. *Nature,* 563(7729):59–64. http://dx.doi.org/10.1038/s41586-018-0637-6.

Awad, E., et al. [2020]. Crowdsourcing moral machines. *Communications of the ACM,* 63(3):Pages 48–55.

Baader, F., et al. (eds.) [2007]. *The Description Logic Handbook: Theory, Implementation and Applications.* Cambridge University Press, 2nd edition. http://dx.doi.org/10.1017/CBO9780511711787.

Bacchus, F. and Grove, A. [1995]. Graphical models for preference and utility. In *Uncertainty in Artificial Intelligence (UAI-95),* pp. 3–10.

Bacchus, F. and Kabanza, F. [1996]. Using temporal logic to control search in a forward chaining planner. In Ghallab, M. and Milani, A. (eds.), *New Directions in AI Planning,* pp. 141–153. ISO Press.

Bach, S. H., Broecheler, M., Huang, B., and Getoor, L. [2017]. Hinge-loss Markov random fields and probabilistic soft logic. *Journal of Machine Learning Research (JMLR),* 18:1–67.

Bäck, T. [1996]. *Evolutionary Algorithms in Theory and Practice.* Oxford University Press.

Baek, M., et al. [2021]. Accurate prediction of protein structures and interactions using a three-track neural network. *Science*, 373(6557):871–876. http://dx.doi.org/10.1126/science.abj8754.

Bahdanau, D., Cho, K., and Bengio, Y. [2015]. Neural machine translation by jointly learning to align and translate. In *International Conference on Learning Represenations (ICLR).* http://dx.doi.org/10.48550/arXiv.1409.0473.

Bakhtin, A., et al. [2022]. Human-level play in the game of Diplomacy by combining language models with strategic reasoning. *Science*, 378(6624):1067–1074. http://dx.doi.org/10.1126/science.ade9097.

Bakker, K., et al. [2020]. Digital technologies and dynamic resource management. *2020 IEEE International Conference on Smart Computing (SMARTCOMP)*, pp. 368–373.

Ballard, B. W. [1983]. The ∗-minimax search procedure for trees containing chance nodes. *Artificial Intelligence*, 21(3):327–350.

Bansal, G., et al. [2021]. Does the whole exceed its parts? The effect of AI explanations on complementary team performance. In *2021 CHI Conference on Human Factors in Computing Systems.* http://dx.doi.org/10.1145/3411764.3445717.

Bartlett, F. C. [1932]. *Remembering: A Study in Experimental and Social Psychology.* Cambridge University Press. http://dx.doi.org/10.1017/CBO9780511759185.

Baum, E. B. [2004]. *What is Thought?* MIT Press.

Bayes, T. [1763]. An essay towards solving a problem in the doctrine of chances. *Philosophical Transactions of the Royal Society of London*, 53:370–418. https://doi.org/10.1098/rstl.1763.0053.

Bell, R. M. and Koren, Y. [2007]. Lessons from the netflix prize challenge. *SIGKDD Explor. Newsl.*, 9(2):75–79. http://dx.doi.org/10.1145/1345448.1345465.

Bellman, R. [1957]. *Dynamic Programming.* Princeton University Press.

Bender, E. M., Gebru, T., McMillan-Major, A., and Shmitchell, S. [2021]. On the dangers of stochastic parrots: Can language models be too big? In *2021 ACM Conference on Fairness, Accountability, and Transparency*, pp. 610–623. http://dx.doi.org/10.1145/3442188.3445922.

Bender, E. M. and Koller, A. [2020]. Climbing towards NLU: On meaning, form, and understanding in the age of data. In *58th Annual Meeting of the Association for Computational Linguistics*, pp. 5185–5198. http://dx.doi.org/10.18653/v1/2020.acl-main.463.

Bengio, Y., Ducharme, R., Vincent, P., and Janvin, C. [2003]. A neural probabilistic language model. *J. Mach. Learn. Res. (JMLR)*, 3:1137–1155.

Benjamin, R. [2019]. *Race After Technology : Abolitionist Tools for the New Jim Code.* Polity.

Bent, R. and Van Hentenryck, P. [2004]. A two-stage hybrid local search for the vehicle routing problem with time windows. *Transportation Science*, 38(4):515–530.

Berners-Lee, T., Hendler, J., and Lassila, O. [2001]. The semantic web: A new form of web content that is meaningful to computers will unleash a revolution of new possibilities. *Scientific American*, May:28–37.

Bertelè, U. and Brioschi, F. [1972]. *Nonserial Dynamic Programming*. Academic Press.

Bertsekas, D. P. [2017]. *Dynamic Programming and Optimal Control*. Athena Scientific, 4th edition.

Besnard, P. and Hunter, A. [2008]. *Elements of Argumentation*. MIT Press.

Bickel, P. J., Hammel, E. A., and O'Connell, J. W. [1975]. Sex bias in graduate admissions: Data from Berkeley. *Science*, 187(4175):398–404.

Biere, A., Heule, M., van Maaren, H., and Walsh, T. (eds.) [2021]. *Handbook of Satisfiability*. IOS Press, 2nd edition.

Bishop, C. M. [2008]. *Pattern Recognition and Machine Learning*. Springer-Verlag.

Bisk, Y., et al. [2020]. Experience grounds language. *CoRR*, abs/2004.10151. https://arxiv.org/abs/2004.10151.

Blei, D. M., Ng, A. Y., and Jordan, M. I. [2003]. Latent Dirichlet allocation. *Journal of Machine Learning Research (JMLR)*, 3:993–1022.

Bleichrodt, H., Rohde, K. I., and Wakker, P. P. [2008]. Koopmans' constant discounting for intertemporal choice: A simplification and a generalization. *Journal of Mathematical Psychology*, 52(6):341–347. http://dx.doi.org/https://doi.org/10.1016/j.jmp.2008.05.003.

Blodgett, S. L., Barocas, S., Daumé III, H., and Wallach, H. [2020]. Language (technology) is power: A critical survey of "bias" in NLP. In *58th Annual Meeting of the Association for Computational Linguistics*. http://dx.doi.org/10.18653/v1/2020.acl-main.485.

Blum, A. and Furst, M. [1997]. Fast planning through planning graph analysis. *Artificial Intelligence*, 90:281–300.

Bobrow, D. G. [1967]. Natural language input for a computer problem solving system. In Minsky, M. (ed.), *Semantic Information Processing*, pp. 133–215. MIT Press.

Bobrow, D. G. [1993]. Artificial intelligence in perspective: a retrospective on fifty volumes of *Artificial Intelligence*. *Artificial Intelligence*, 59:5–20.

Boddy, M. and Dean, T. L. [1994]. Deliberation scheduling for problem solving in time-constrained environments. *Artificial Intelligence*, 67(2):245–285.

Bodlaender, H. L. [1993]. A tourist guide through treewidth. *Acta Cybernetica*, 11(1–2):1–21.

Bommasani, R. et al. [2021]. On the opportunities and risks of foundation models. *CoRR*, abs/2108.07258. https://arxiv.org/abs/2108.07258.

Bonnefon, J.-F. [2021]. *The Car That Knew Too Much Can a Machine Be Moral?* MIT Press.

Bostrom, N. [2014]. *Superintelligence: Paths, Dangers, Strategies.* Oxford University Press.

Boutilier, C., Dean, T., and Hanks, S. [1999]. Decision-theoretic planning: Structual assumptions and computational leverage. *Journal of Artificial Intelligence Research*, 11:1–94.

Boutilier, C., et al. [2004]. CP-nets: A tool for representing and reasoning with conditional ceteris paribus preference statements. *Journal of Artificial Intelligence Research*, 21:135–191.

Brachman, R. J. and Levesque, H. J. (eds.) [1985]. *Readings in Knowledge Representation.* Morgan Kaufmann.

Brachman, R. J. and Levesque, H. J. [2004]. *Knowledge Representation and Reasoning.* Morgan Kaufmann.

Brachman, R. J. and Levesque, H. J. [2022a]. *Machines like Us: Toward AI with Common Sense.* MIT Press.

Brachman, R. J. and Levesque, H. J. [2022b]. Toward a new science of common sense. In *Thirty-Sixth AAAI Conference on Artificial Intelligence (AAAI-22).*

Breiman, L. [2001]. Random forests. *Machine Learning*, 45(1):5–32.

Breiman, L., Friedman, J. H., Olshen, R. A., and Stone, C. J. [1984]. *Classification and Regression Trees.* Wadsworth & Brooks.

Brémaud, P. [1999]. *Markov Chains: Gibbs Fields, Monte Carlo Simulation and Queues.* Springer.

Brin, S. and Page, L. [1998]. The anatomy of a large-scale hypertextual web search engine. *Computer Networks and ISDN Systems*, 30(1–7):107–117. http://www.sciencedirect.com/science/article/pii/S016975529800110X.

Brooks, R. A. [1986]. A robust layered control system for a mobile robot. *IEEE Journal of Robotics and Automation*, 2(1):14–23.

Brooks, R. A. [1990]. Elephants don't play chess. *Robotics and Autonomous Systems*, 6:3–15.

Brooks, R. A. [1991]. Intelligence without representation. *Artificial Intelligence*, 47:139–159.

Brooks, R. A. [2018]. My dated predictions. https://rodneybrooks.com/my-dated-predictions/.

Broussard, M. [2018]. *Artificial Unintelligence: How Computers Misunderstand the World.* MIT Press. http://dx.doi.org/10.7551/mitpress/11022.001.0001.

Brown, N. and Sandholm, T. [2019]. Superhuman AI for multiplayer poker. *Science*, 365(6456):885–890. http://dx.doi.org/10.1126/science.aay2400.

Brown, T., et al. [2020]. Language models are few-shot learners. In *Advances in Neural Information Processing Systems*, volume 33, pp. 1877–1901. https://arxiv.org/abs/2005.14165.

Brundtland, G. H. et al. [1987]. *Our Common Future.* United Nations, Report of the World Commission on Environment and Development. https://sustainabledevelopment.un.org/content/documents/5987our-common-future.pdf.

Bryce, D. and Kambhampati, S. [2007]. A tutorial on planning graph-based reachability heuristics. *AI Magazine*, 28(1):47–83.

Brynjolfsson, E. and McAfee, A. [2014]. *The Second Machine Age: Work, Progress, and Prosperity in a Time of Brilliant Technologies*. W. W. Norton & Co.

Bryson, J. J. [2011]. AI robots should not be considered moral agents. In Berlatsky, N. (ed.), *Artificial Intelligence, Opposing Viewpoints*, pp. 155–168. Greenhaven Press.

Bryson, J. J. [2018]. Patiency is not a virtue: the design of intelligent systems and systems of ethics. *Ethics and Information Technology*, 20(1):15–26. http://dx.doi.org/10.1007/s10676-018-9448-6.

Buchanan, B. G. [2005]. A (very) brief history of artificial intelligence. *AI Magazine*, 26(4):53–60.

Buchanan, B. G. and Feigenbaum, E. A. [1978]. Dendral and Meta-Dendral: Their applications dimension. *Artificial Intelligence*, 11:5–24.

Buchanan, B. G. and Shortliffe, E. (eds.) [1984]. *Rule-Based Expert Systems: The MYCIN Experiments of the Stanford Heuristic Programming Project*. Addison-Wesley.

Buntine, W. [1992]. Learning classification trees. *Statistics and Computing*, 2:63–73.

Buntine, W. L. [1994]. Operations for learning with graphical models. *Journal of Artificial Intelligence Research*, 2:159–225.

Buolamwini, J. and Gebru, T. [2018]. Gender shades: Intersectional accuracy disparities in commercial gender classification. In *1st Conference on Fairness, Accountability and Transparency*. https://proceedings.mlr.press/v81/buolamwini18a.html.

Burch, R. [2022]. Charles Sanders Peirce. *The Stanford Encyclopedia of Philosophy*. http://plato.stanford.edu/archives/sum2022/entries/peirce/.

Busoniu, L., Babuska, R., and Schutter, B. D. [2008]. A comprehensive survey of multiagent reinforcement learning. *IEEE Transactions on Systems, Man, and Cybernetics, Part C: Applications and Reviews*, 38(2):156–172.

Calo, R. [2014]. The case for a federal robotics commission. *Brookings Institution Center for Technology Innovation*.

Calo, R., Froomkin, A. M., and Kerr, I. [2016]. *Robot Law*. Edward Elgar.

Campbell, M., Hoane Jr., A. J., and Hse, F.-h. [2002]. Deep Blue. *Artificial Intelligence*, 134(1–2):57–83.

Caswell, I. and Liang, B. [2020]. Recent advances in Google translate. https://ai.googleblog.com/2020/06/recent-advances-in-google-translate.html.

Cauchy, A. [1847]. Méthode générale pour la résolution des systèmes d'équations simultanées. *C. R. Acad. Sci. Paris*, 25:536–538.

Center for AI and Digital Policy [2023]. Artificial intelligence and democratic values. https://www.caidp.org/reports/aidv-2021/.

Chapman, D. [1987]. Planning for conjunctive goals. *Artificial Intelligence*, 32(3):333–377.

Charlton, J. I. [1998]. *Nothing About Us Without Us: Disability Oppression and Empowerment*. University of California Press, 1st edition. http://www.jstor.org/stable/10.1525/j.ctt1pnqn9.

Chaudhri, V. K., et al. [2022]. Knowledge graphs: Introduction, history and, perspectives. *AI Magazine*, 43(1):17–29.

Cheeseman, P., et al. [1988]. Autoclass: A Bayesian classification system. In *Fifth International Conference on Machine Learning*, pp. 54–64. Reprinted in Shavlik and Dietterich [1990].

Chen, J., Holte, R. C., Zilles, S., and Sturtevant, N. R. [2017]. Front-to-end bidirectional heuristic search with near-optimal node expansions. In *IJCAI-2017*.

Chen, T. and Guestrin, C. [2016]. Xgboost: A scalable tree boosting system. In *KDD '16: 22nd ACM SIGKDD International Conference on Knowledge Discovery and Data Mining*, pp. 785–794. https://doi.org/10.1145/2939672.2939785.

Cheng, J. and Druzdzel, M. [2000]. AIS-BN: An adaptive importance sampling algorithm for evidential reasoning in large Bayesian networks. *Journal of Artificial Intelligence Research*, 13:155–188. http://www.jair.org/papers/paper764.html.

Chesnevar, C., Maguitman, A., and Loui, R. [2000]. Logical models of argument. *ACM Computer Surveys*, 32(4):337–383.

Choi, Y., Vergari, A., and Van den Broeck, G. [2020]. Probabilistic circuits: A unifying framework for tractable probabilistic models. Technical report, UCLA StarAI Lab. http://starai.cs.ucla.edu/papers/ProbCirc20.pdf.

Chollet, F. [2021]. *Deeep Learning with Python*. Manning.

Chomsky, N. [1957]. *Syntactic Structures*. Mouton & Co.

Chowdhery, A., et al. [2022]. PaLM: Scaling language modeling with pathways. http://dx.doi.org/10.48550/arXiv.2204.02311.

Chrisley, R. and Begeer, S. [2000]. *Artificial intelligence: Critical Concepts in Cognitive Science*. Routledge.

Christian, B. [2020]. *The Alignment Problem: Machine Learning and Human Values*. W. W. Norton & Co.

Clark, K. L. [1978]. Negation as failure. In Gallaire, H. and Minker, J. (eds.), *Logic and Databases*, pp. 293–322. Plenum Press.

Cohen, P. R. [2005]. If not Turing's test, then what? *AI Magazine*, 26(4):61–67.

Colledanchise, M. and Ögren, P. [2018]. *Behavior Trees in Robotics and AI: An Introduction*. CRC Press.

Colmerauer, A., Kanoui, H., Roussel, P., and Pasero, R. [1973]. Un système de communication homme-machine en français. Technical report, Groupe de Researche en Intelligence Artificielle, Université d'Aix-Marseille.

Colmerauer, A. and Roussel, P. [1996]. The birth of Prolog. In Bergin, T. J. and Gibson, R. G. (eds.), *History of Programming Languages–II*, pp. 331–367. ACM Press/Addison-Wesley.

Conati, C., Gertner, A. S., and VanLehn, K. [2002]. Using Bayesian networks to manage uncertainty in student modeling. *User Modeling and User-Adapted Interaction*, 12(4):371–417. http://dx.doi.org/10.1023/A:1021258506583.

Confucius [500 BCE]. *Confucian Analects*. translated by James Legge [1893]. https://www.sacred-texts.com/cfu/conf1.htm.

Cormen, T. H., Leiserson, C. E., Rivest, R. L., and Stein, C. [2022]. *Introduction to Algorithms*. MIT Press, 4th edition.

Cover, T. M. and Thomas, J. A. [2006]. *Elements of Information Theory*. Wiley, 2nd edition.

Cramer, J. [2002]. The origins of logistic regression. Working Paper 2002-119/4, Tinbergen Institute. http://dx.doi.org/10.2139/ssrn.360300.

Crawford, K. [2021]. *The Atlas of AI: Power, Politics, and the Planetary Costs of Artificial Intelligence*. Yale University Press.

Culberson, J. and Schaeffer, J. [1998]. Pattern databases. *Computational Intelligence*, 14(3):318–334.

Dadich, S. [2016]. Barack Obama, neural nets, self-driving cars, and the future of the world. *Wired*.

Dahl, V. [1994]. Natural language processing and logic programming. *Journal of Logic Programming*, 19/20:681–714.

Danaher, J. [2021]. Automation and the future of work. In *The Oxford Handbook of Digital Ethics*. Oxford University Press. http://dx.doi.org/10.1093/oxfordhb/9780198857815.013.37.

Darwiche, A. [2001]. Recursive conditioning. *Artificial Intelligence*, 126(1-2):5–41.

Darwiche, A. [2009]. *Modeling and Reasoning with Bayesian Networks*. Cambridge University Press.

Darwiche, A. [2018]. Human-level intelligence or animal-like abilities? *Communication of the ACM*, 61(10):56–67. http://dx.doi.org/10.1145/3271625.

Davis, E. [1990]. *Representations of Commonsense Knowledge*. Morgan Kaufmann.

Davis, E. [2015]. A collection of Winograd schemas. http://www.cs.nyu.edu/faculty/davise/papers/WinogradSchemas/WSCollection.html.

Davis, J. and Goadrich, M. [2006]. The relationship between precision-recall and ROC curves. In *23rd International Conference on Machine Learning (ICML)*, pp. 233–240.

Davis, M., Logemann, G., and Loveland, D. [1962]. A machine program for theorem proving. *Communications of the ACM*, 5(7):394–397.

Davis, M. and Putnam, H. [1960]. A computing procedure for quantification theory. *Journal of the ACM*, 7(3):201–215.

De Jong, K. A. [2006]. *Evolutionary Computation: A Unified Approach*. MIT Press.

de Kleer, J. [1986]. An assumption-based TMS. *Artificial Intelligence*, 28(2):127–162.

de Kleer, J., Mackworth, A. K., and Reiter, R. [1992]. Characterizing diagnoses and systems. *Artificial Intelligence*, 56:197–222.

De Raedt, L., Frasconi, P., Kersting, K., and Muggleton, S. H. (eds.) [2008]. *Probabilistic Inductive Logic Programming*. Springer.

De Raedt, L., Kersting, K., Natarajan, S., and Poole, D. [2016]. *Statistical Relational Artificial Intelligence: Logic, Probability, and Computation*. Morgan & Claypool. http://dx.doi.org/10.2200/S00692ED1V01Y201601AIM032.

De Raedt, L., Kimmig, A., and Toivonen, H. [2007]. ProbLog: A probabilistic Prolog and its application in link discovery. In *20th International Joint Conference on Artificial Intelligence (IJCAI)*, pp. 2462–2467.

Dean, T. and Kanazawa, K. [1989]. A model for reasoning about persistence and causation. *Computational Intelligence*, 5(3):142–150.

Dean, T. L. and Wellman, M. P. [1991]. *Planning and Control*. Morgan Kaufmann.

Dechter, R. [1996]. Bucket elimination: A unifying framework for probabilistic inference. In *Twelfth Conference on Uncertainty in Artificial Intelligence (UAI-96)*, pp. 211–219.

Dechter, R. [2003]. *Constraint Processing*. Morgan Kaufmann.

Dechter, R. [2019]. *Reasoning with Probabilistic and Deterministic Graphical Models*. Morgan & Claypool, 2nd edition.

Dechter, R. and Pearl, J. [1985]. Generalized best-first search strategies and the optimality of A*. *Journal of the Association for Computing Machinery*, 32(3):505–536.

Dellaert, F., Fox, D., Burgard, W., and Thrun, S. [1999]. Monte Carlo localization for mobile robots. In *IEEE International Conference on Robotics and Automation (ICRA)*.

Delling, D., Goldberg, A. V., Pajor, T., and Werneck, R. F. [2015]. Customizable route planning in road networks. *Transportation Science*, 51(2):566–591. https://doi.org/10.1287/trsc.2014.0579.

Dempster, A., Laird, N., and Rubin, D. [1977]. Maximum liklihood from incomplete data via the EM algorithm. *Journal of the Royal Statistical Society, Series B*, 39:1–38. With discussion.

Deng, J., et al. [2009]. ImageNet: A large-scale hierarchical image database. In *Computer Vision and Pattern Recognition Conference (CVPR)*.

Denil, M., Matheson, D., and de Freitas, N. [2014]. Narrowing the gap: Random forests in theory and in practice. In *International Conference on Machine Learning (ICML)*.

Devlin, J., Chang, M.-W., Lee, K., and Toutanova, K. [2019]. BERT: Pre-training of deep bidirectional transformers for language understanding. In *2019 Conference of the North American Chapter of the Association for Computational Linguistics: Human Language Technologies*, pp. 4171–4186. http://dx.doi.org/10.18653/v1/N19-1423.

Dietterich, T. G. [2000a]. An experimental comparison of three methods for constructing ensembles of decision trees: Bagging, boosting, and randomization. *Machine Learning*, 40(2):139–158.

Dietterich, T. G. [2000b]. Hierarchical reinforcement learning with the MAXQ value function decomposition. *Journal of Artificial Intelligence Research*, 13:227–303.

Dietterich, T. G. [2002]. Ensemble learning. In Arbib, M. (ed.), *The Handbook of Brain Theory and Neural Networks*, pp. 405–408. MIT Press, 2nd edition.

Dijkstra, E. W. [1959]. A note on two problems in connexion with graphs. *Numerische Mathematik*, 1:269–271. https://doi.org/10.1007/BF01386390.

Dijkstra, E. W. [1976]. *A Discipline of Programming*. Prentice-Hall.

Dolgov, D., Thrun, S., Montemerlo, M., and Diebel, J. [2010]. Path planning for autonomous vehicles in unknown semi-structured environments. *The International Journal of Robotics Research*, 29(5):485–501. http://dx.doi.org/10.1177/0278364909359210.

Domingos, P. and Lowd, D. [2009]. *Markov Logic: An Interface Layer for Artificial Intelligence*. Synthesis Lectures on Artificial Intelligence and Machine Learning. Morgan & Claypool. http://dx.doi.org/doi:10.2200/S00206ED1V01Y200907AIM007.

Doucet, A., de Freitas, N., and Gordon, N. (eds.) [2001]. *Sequential Monte Carlo in Practice*. Springer-Verlag.

Doyle, J. [1979]. A truth maintenance system. AI Memo 521, MIT AI Laboratory.

Dresner, K. and Stone, P. [2008]. A multiagent approach to autonomous intersection management. *Journal of Artificial Intelligence Research*, 31:591–656.

du Boulay, B., Mitrovic, T., and Yacef, K. (eds.) [2023]. *Handbook of Artificial Intelligence in Education*. Edward Elgar.

Dua, D. and Graff, C. [2017]. UCI machine learning repository. http://archive.ics.uci.edu/ml.

Duda, R. O., Hart, P. E., and Stork, D. G. [2001]. *Pattern Classification*. Wiley-Interscience, 2nd edition.

Dung, P. [1995]. On the acceptability of arguments and its fundamental role in nonmonotonic reasoning, logic programming and *n*-person games. *Artificial Intelligence*, 77(2):321–357.

Dzeroski, S., De Raedt, L., and Driessens, K. [2001]. Relational reinforcement learning. *Machine Learning,*, 43:7–52.

Einstein, A. [1934]. On the method of theoretical physics. *Philosophy of Science*, 1(2):163–169.

Eubanks, V. [2018]. *Automating Inequality: How High-Tech Tools Profile, Police, and Punish the Poor*. St. Martin's Publishing Group.

European Commission [2021]. The general data protection regulation. https://commission.europa.eu/law/law-topic/data-protection/data-protection-eu_en.

European Commission [2022a]. AI liability directive. https://www.europarl.europa.eu/RegData/etudes/BRIE/2023/739342/EPRS_BRI(2023)739342_EN.pdf.

European Commission [2022b]. The artificial intelligence act. https://eur-lex.europa.eu/legal-content/EN/TXT/?uri=CELEX:52021PC0206.

European Commission [2022c]. The digital services act package. https://digital-strategy.ec.europa.eu/en/policies/digital-services-act-package.

European Commission [2022d]. New liability rules on products and AI to protect consumers. https://ec.europa.eu/commission/presscorner/detail/en/ip_22_5807.

Falco, G., et al. [2021]. Governing AI safety through independent audits. *Nature Machine Intelligence*, 3(7):566–571. http://dx.doi.org/10.1038/s42256-021-00370-7.

Fanshel, S. and Bush, J. [1970]. Health-status index and its application to health-services outcomes. *Operations Research*, 18.

Fatemi, B., Taslakian, P., Vazquez, D., and Poole, D. [2020]. Knowledge hypergraphs: Prediction beyond binary relations. In *29th International Joint Conference on Artificial Intelligence (IJCAI)*.

Fedus, W., Zoph, B., and Shazeer, N. [2021]. Switch transformers: Scaling to trillion parameter models with simple and efficient sparsity. http://dx.doi.org/10.48550/arXiv.2101.03961.

Fellegi, I. and Sunter, A. [1969]. A theory for record linkage. *Journal of the American Statistical Association*, 64(328):1183–1280.

Felner, A., Korf, R. E., and Hanan, S. [2004]. Additive pattern database heuristics. *Journal of Artificial Intelligence Research*, 22:279–318.

Feurer, M. and Hutter, F. [2019]. Hyperparameter optimization. In *Automated Machine Learning*. Springer. http://dx.doi.org/https://doi.org/10.1007/978-3-030-05318-5_1.

Fikes, R. E. and Nilsson, N. J. [1971]. STRIPS: A new approach to the application of theorem proving to problem solving. *Artificial Intelligence*, 2(3–4):189–208.

Foot, P. [1967]. The problem of abortion and the doctrine of the double effect. *Oxford Review*, 5:5–15. https://philpapers.org/archive/FOOTPO-2.pdf.

Forbus, K. [2019]. *Qualitative Representations: How People Reason and Learn about the Continuous World*. MIT Press.

Forbus, K. D. and Hinrich, T. [2017]. Analogy and relational representations in the companion cognitive architecture. *AI Magazine*, 38(4):34–42. http://dx.doi.org/10.1609/aimag.v38i4.2743.

Ford, M. [2021]. *Rule of the Robots: How Artificial Intelligence Will Transform Everything*. John Murray Press.

François-Lavet, V., et al. [2018]. An introduction to deep reinforcement learning. *CoRR*, abs/1811.12560. http://arxiv.org/abs/1811.12560.

Freuder, E. C. and Mackworth, A. K. [2006]. Constraint satisfaction: An emerging paradigm. In Rossi, F., Van Beek, P., and Walsh, T. (eds.), *Handbook of Constraint Programming*, pp. 13–28. Elsevier.

Friedman, J. H. [2001]. Greedy function approximation: A gradient boosting machine. *The Annals of Statistics*, 29(5):1189–1232. http://www.jstor.org/stable/2699986.

Friedman, N., Greiger, D., and Goldszmidt, M. [1997]. Bayesian network classifiers. *Machine Learning*, 29:103–130.

Gabrilovich, E., et al. [2014]. Knowledge vault: A web-scale approach to probabilistic knowledge fusion. In *20th ACM SIGKDD Conference on Knowledge Discovery and Data Mining*.

Gal, K. and Grosz, B. J. [2022]. Multi-agent systems: Technical & ethical challenges of functioning in a mixed group. *Daedalus*.

Galton, F. [1886]. Regression towards mediocrity in hereditary stature. *Journal of the Anthropological Institute*, 15:246–263. http://galton.org/essays/1880-1889/galton-1886-jaigi-regression-stature.pdf.

Gangemi, A., Guarino, N., Masolo, C., and Oltramari, A. [2003]. Sweetening WordNet with DOLCE. *AI Magazine*, 24(3):13–24.

Garcia-Molina, H., Ullman, J. D., and Widom, J. [2009]. *Database Systems: The Complete Book*. Prentice Hall, 2nd edition.

Gardner, H. [1985]. *The Mind's New Science*. Basic Books.

Gebru, T., et al. [2021]. Datasheets for datasets. *Communication of the ACM*, 64(12):86–92. http://dx.doi.org/10.1145/3458723.

Geffner, H. and Bonet, B. [2013]. *A Concise Introduction to Models and Methods for Automated Planning*. Springer. http://dx.doi.org/doi:10.2200/S00513ED1V01Y201306AIM022.

Geffner, H., Dechter, R., and Halpern, J. Y. (eds.) [2022]. *Probabilistic and Causal Inference: The Works of Judea Pearl*. ACM Books.

Gelman, A., Carlin, J. B., Stern, H. S., and Rubin, D. B. [2013]. *Bayesian Data Analysis*. Chapman & Hall/CRC, 3rd edition. http://www.stat.columbia.edu/~gelman/book/.

Gelman, A., Hill, J., and Vehtari, A. [2020]. *Regression and Other Stories*. Cambridge University Press.

Genesereth, M. and Thielscher, M. [2014]. *General Game Playing*. Morgan & Claypool. http://dx.doi.org/doi:10.2200/S00564ED1V01Y201311AIM024.

Gers, F. A., Schmidhuber, J., and Cummins, F. [2000]. Learning to forget: Continual prediction with LSTM. *Neural Computation*, 12(10):2451–2471. http://dx.doi.org/https://doi.org/10.1162/089976600300015015.

Getoor, L. and Taskar, B. (eds.) [2007]. *Introduction to Statistical Relational Learning*. MIT Press.

Ghahramani, Z. [2015]. Probabilistic machine learning and artificial intelligence. *Nature*, 521(7553):452–459. http://dx.doi.org/10.1038/nature14541.

Ghallab, M., Nau, D., and Traverso, P. [2004]. *Automated Planning: Theory and Practice*. Elsevier.

Gibbard, A. [1973]. Manipulation of voting schemes: A general result. *Econometrica*, 41:587–601.

Gil, Y., et al. [2017]. Towards continuous scientific data analysis and hypothesis evolution. In *Thirty-First AAAI Conference on Artificial Intelligence (AAAI-17)*. http://www.isi.edu/~gil/papers/gil-etal-aaai17.pdf.

Gil, Y., et al. [2019]. Intelligent systems for geosciences: An essential research agenda. *Communications of the ACM*, 62. http://dx.doi.org/10.1145/3192335.

Glorot, X. and Bengio, Y. [2010]. Understanding the difficulty of training deep feedforward neural networks. In *Thirteenth International Conference on Artificial Intelligence and Statistics*, pp. 249–256. https://proceedings.mlr.press/v9/glorot10a.html.

Glorot, X., Bordes, A., and Bengio, Y. [2011]. Deep sparse rectifier neural networks. In *14th International Conference on Artificial Intelligence and Statistics*, pp. 315–323.

Goble, C., et al. [2020]. FAIR Computational Workflows. *Data Intelligence*, 2(1-2):108–121. http://dx.doi.org/10.1162/dint_a_00033.

Goldberg, D. E. [2002]. *The Design of Innovation: Lessons from and for Competent Genetic Algorithms*. Addison-Wesley.

Goldberg, Y. [2016]. A primer on neural network models for natural language processing. *Journal of Artificial Intelligence Research*, 57:345–420. http://dx.doi.org/doi:10.1613/jair.4992.

Gomes, C., et al. [2019]. Computational sustainability: Computing for a better world and a sustainable future. *Communication of the ACM*, 62(9):56–65. http://dx.doi.org/10.1145/3339399.

Good, I. J. [1965]. Speculations concerning the first ultraintelligent machine. In Alt, F. and Ruminoff, M. (eds.), *Advances in Computers*, volume 6. Academic Press.

Goodfellow, I., Bengio, Y., and Courville, A. [2016]. *Deep Learning*. MIT Press. http://www.deeplearningbook.org.

Goodfellow, I. J., et al. [2014]. Generative adversarial networks. In *Advances in Neural Information Processing Systems 27 (NIPS 2014)*. http://dx.doi.org/10.48550/arXiv.1406.2661.

Gordon, M. L., et al. [2021]. The disagreement deconvolution: Bringing machine learning performance metrics in line with reality. In *2021 CHI Conference on Human Factors in Computing Systems*. http://dx.doi.org/10.1145/3411764.3445423.

Green, B. [2022]. The flaws of policies requiring human oversight of government algorithms. *Computer Law and Security Review*, 45:105681. http://dx.doi.org/https://doi.org/10.1016/j.clsr.2022.105681.

Green, C. [1969]. Application of theorem proving to problem solving. In *1st International Joint Conference on Artificial Intelligence*, pp. 219–237.

Grosz, B. [2012]. What question would Turing pose today? *AI Magazine*, 33(4):73. http://dx.doi.org/10.1609/aimag.v33i4.2441.

Grosz, B. J. [2018]. Smart enough to talk with us? Foundations and challenges for dialogue capable AI systems. *Computational Linguistics*, 44(1):1–15. http://dx.doi.org/10.1162/COLI_a_00313.

Grünwald, P. D. [2007]. *The Minimum Description Length Principle*. MIT Press.

Gunkel, D. [2018]. *Robot Rights*. MIT Press.

Halevy, A., Norvig, P., and Pereira, F. [2009]. The unreasonable effectiveness of data. *IEEE Intelligent Systems*, 24(2):8–12.

Halpern, J. Y. [2003]. *Reasoning about Uncertainty*. MIT Press.

Hamilton, W. L. [2020]. *Graph Representation Learning*. Morgan & Claypool.

Hardin, G. [1968]. The tragedy of the commons: The population problem has no technical solution; it requires a fundamental extension in morality. *Science*, 162(3859):1243–1248.

Harper, F. M. and Konstan, J. A. [2015]. The MovieLens datasets: History and context. *ACM Transactions on Interactive Intelligent Systems*, 5(4). http://dx.doi.org/10.1145/2827872.

Hart, P. E., Nilsson, N. J., and Raphael, B. [1968]. A formal basis for the heuristic determination of minimum cost paths. *IEEE Transactions on Systems Science and Cybernetics*, 4(2):100–107.

Hart, T. P. and Edwards, D. J. [1961]. The tree prune (TP) algorithm. Memo 30, MIT Artificial Intelligence Project.

Haslum, P., Lipovetzky, N., Magazzeni, D., and Muise, C. [2019]. *An Introduction to the Planning Domain Definition Language*. Morgan & Claypool. https://doi.org/10.2200/S00900ED2V01Y201902AIM042.

Hastie, T., Tibshirani, R., and Friedman, J. [2009]. *The Elements of Statistical Learning: Data Mining, Inference, and Prediction*. Springer, 2nd edition.

Haugeland, J. [1985]. *Artificial Intelligence: The Very Idea*. MIT Press.

Haugeland, J. (ed.) [1997]. *Mind Design II: Philosophy, Psychology, Artificial Intelligence*. MIT Press, revised and enlarged edition.

Hayes, P. J. [1973]. Computation and deduction. In *2nd Symposium on Mathematical Foundations of Computer Science*, pp. 105–118. Czechoslovak Academy of Sciences.

He, K., Zhang, X., Ren, S., and Sun, J. [2015]. Deep residual learning for image recognition. *CoRR*, abs/1512.03385. http://arxiv.org/abs/1512.03385.

Heath, T. and Bizer, C. [2011]. *Linked Data: Evolving the Web into a Global Data Space*. Springer.

Heckerman, D. [1999]. A tutorial on learning with Bayesian networks. In Jordan, M. (ed.), *Learning in Graphical Models*. MIT Press.

Hendler, J., Berners-Lee, T., and Miller, E. [2002]. Integrating applications on the semantic web. *Journal of the Institute of Electrical Engineers of Japan*, 122(10):676–680. http://www.w3.org/2002/07/swint.

Henrion, M. [1988]. Propagating uncertainty in Bayesian networks by probabilistic logic sampling. In Lemmer, J. F. and Kanal, L. N. (eds.), *Uncertainty in Artificial Intelligence 2*, pp. 149–163. Elsevier Science.

Hewitt, C. [1969]. Planner: A language for proving theorems in robots. In *1st International Joint Conference on Artificial Intelligence*, pp. 295–301.

Hinton, G., et al. [2012a]. Deep neural networks for acoustic modeling in speech recognition: The shared views of four research groups. *Signal Processing Magazine, IEEE*, 29(6):82–97. http://dx.doi.org/10.1109/MSP.2012.2205597.

Hinton, G. E., et al. [2012b]. Improving neural networks by preventing co-adaptation of feature detectors. *CoRR*, abs/1207.0580. http://arxiv.org/abs/1207.0580.

Hitchcock, F. L. [1927]. The expression of a tensor or a polyadic as a sum of products. *Studies in Applied Mathematics*, 6(1–4):164–189.

Hitzler, P., et al. (eds.) [2012]. *OWL 2 Web Ontology Language Primer (Second Edition)*. W3C Recommendation 11 December 2012. http://www.w3.org/TR/owl2-primer/.

Ho, J., Jain, A., and Abbeel, P. [2020]. Denoising diffusion probabilistic models. In *Advances in Neural Information Processing Systems*, volume 33, pp. 6840–6851. https://proceedings.neurips.cc/paper_files/paper/2020/file/4c5bcfec8584af0d967f1ab10179ca4b-Paper.pdf.

Hochreiter, S. and Schmidhuber, J. [1997]. Long short-term memory. *Neural Computation*, 9:1735–1780.

Hoffart, J., Suchanek, F., Berberich, K., and Weikum, G. [2013]. YAGO2: A spatially and temporally enhanced knowledge base from Wikipedia. *Artificial Intelligence*, 194:28–61.

Hofstadter, D. [2022]. Artificial neural networks today are not conscious, according to Douglas Hofstadter. *The Economist*, June 11th 2022.

Hogan, A. et al. [2021]. Knowledge graphs. *ACM Computing Surveys*, 54(4). https://doi.org/10.1145/3447772.

Holland, J. H. [1975]. *Adaption in Natural and Artificial Systems: An Introductory Analysis with Applications to Biology, Control, and Artificial Intelligence*. University of Michigan Press.

Holling, C. S. [1973]. Resilience and stability of ecological systems. *Annual Review of Ecology and Systematics*, 4(1):1–23. http://dx.doi.org/10.1146/annurev.es.04.110173.000245.

Hoos, H. H. and Stützle, T. [2004]. *Stochastic Local Search: Foundations and Applications*. Morgan Kaufmann.

Horvitz, E. J. [1989]. Reasoning about beliefs and actions under computational resource constraints. In Kanal, L., Levitt, T., and Lemmer, J. (eds.), *Uncertainty in Artificial Intelligence 3*, pp. 301–324. Elsevier.

Horvitz, E. J. [2006]. Eric Horvitz forecasts the future. *New Scientist*, 2578:72.

Howard, R. A. and Matheson, J. E. [1984]. Influence diagrams. In Howard, R. A. and Matheson, J. E. (eds.), *The Principles and Applications of Decision Analysis*. Strategic Decisions Group.

Howson, C. and Urbach, P. [2006]. *Scientific Reasoning: The Bayesian Approach*. Open Court, 3rd edition.

Huang, Y. and Valtorta, M. [2006]. Pearl's calculus of intervention is complete. In *Conference on Uncertainty in Artificial Intelligence*, pp. 217–224.

Hume, D. [1739–40]. *A Treatise of Human Nature: Being an Attempt to Introduce the Experimental Method of Reasoning into Moral Subjects*. https://gutenberg.org/files/4705/4705-h/4705-h.htm.

Hursthouse, R. and Pettigrove, G. [2018]. Virtue ethics. In Zalta, E. N. (ed.), *The Stanford Encyclopedia of Philosophy*. Winter 2018 edition. https://plato.stanford.edu/archives/win2018/entries/ethics-virtue/.

Hutter, F., Kotthoff, L., and Vanschoren, J. (eds.) [2019]. *Automated Machine Learning Methods, Systems, Challenges*. Springer.

IEEE [2020]. IEEE code of ethics. https://www.ieee.org/about/corporate/governance/p7-8.html.

IEEE Global Initiative on Ethics of Autonomous and Intelligent Systems [2019]. Ethically aligned design: A vision for prioritizing human well-being with autonomous and intelligent systems. https://standards.ieee.org/content/ieee-standards/en/industry-connections/ec/autonomous-systems.html.

IHTSDO [2016]. *SNOMED CT Starter Guide*. International Health Terminology Standards Development Organisation. http://snomed.org.

Jackson, M. O. [2011]. *A Brief Introduction to the Basics of Game Theory*. SSRN. http://dx.doi.org/10.2139/ssrn.1968579.

Jacobs, A. Z. and Wallach, H. [2021]. Measurement and fairness. In *2021 ACM Conference on Fairness, Accountability, and Transparency*, FAccT '21, pp. 375–385. http://dx.doi.org/10.1145/3442188.3445901.

Jahrer, M., Töscher, A., and Legenstein, R. [2010]. Combining predictions for accurate recommender systems. In *16th ACM SIGKDD International Conference on Knowledge Discovery and Data Mining*, pp. 693–702. http://dx.doi.org/10.1145/1835804.1835893.

Jannach, D. and Bauer, C. [2020]. Escaping the McNamara fallacy: Towards more impactful recommender systems research. *AI Magazine*, 41(4):79–95. http://dx.doi.org/10.1609/aimag.v41i4.5312.

Jannach, D., Pu, P., Ricci, F., and Zanker, M. [2021]. Recommender systems: Past, present, future. *AI Magazine*, 42(3):3–6. http://dx.doi.org/10.1609/aimag.v42i3.18139.

Janowicz, K., van Harmelen, F., Hendler, J. A., and Hitzler, P. [2015]. Why the data train needs semantic rails. *AI Magazine*, 36(1):5–14.

Jarrett, K., Kavukcuoglu, K., Ranzato, M., and LeCun, Y. [2009]. What is the best multi-stage architecture for object recognition? In *2009 IEEE 12th International Conference on Computer Vision*. http://dx.doi.org/10.1109/ICCV.2009.5459469.

Jaynes, E. T. [2003]. *Probability Theory: The Logic of Science*. Cambridge University Press. https://bayes.wustl.edu/etj/prob/book.pdf.

Jordan, M. I. [2019]. Artificial intelligence – the revolution hasn't happened yet. *Harvard Data Science Review*, 1(1). https://hdsr.mitpress.mit.edu/pub/wot7mkc1.

Joy, B. [2000]. Why the future doesn't need us. *Wired*. http://www.wired.com/wired/archive/8.04/joy.html.

Jozefowicz, R., Zaremba, W., and Sutskever, I. [2015]. An empirical exploration of recurrent network architectures. In *32nd International Conference on Machine Learning*, ICML'15, pp. 2342–2350.

Jumper, J., et al. [2021]. Highly accurate protein structure prediction with AlphaFold. *Nature*, 596(7873):583–589. http://dx.doi.org/10.1038/s41586-021-03819-2.

Jurafsky, D. and Martin, J. H. [2023]. *Speech and Language Processing*. Unpublished, 3rd edition. https://web.stanford.edu/~jurafsky/slp3/.

Kahneman, D. [2011]. *Thinking, Fast and Slow*. Allen Lane.

Kakas, A. and Denecker, M. [2002]. Abduction in logic programming. In Kakas, A. and Sadri, F. (eds.), *Computational Logic: Logic Programming and Beyond*, pp. 402–436. Springer-Verlag.

Kambhampati, S., Knoblock, C. A., and Yang, Q. [1995]. Planning as refinement search: A unified framework for evaluating design tradeoffs in partial order planning. *Artificial Intelligence*, 76:167–238.

Kant, I. [1787]. *The Critique of Pure Reason*. https://gutenberg.org/ebooks/4280.

Karimi, H., Nutini, J., and Schmidt, M. [2016]. Linear convergence of gradient and proximal-gradient methods under the Polyak–Łojasiewicz condition. In *European Conference on Machine Learning (ECML)*.

Karpathy, A. [2015]. The unreasonable effectiveness of recurrent neural networks. http://karpathy.github.io/2015/05/21/rnn-effectiveness/.

Katoch, S., Chauhan, S. S., and Kumar, V. [2021]. A review on genetic algorithm: past, present, and future. *Multimedia Tools and Applications*, 80(5):8091–8126. http://dx.doi.org/10.1007/s11042-020-10139-6.

Kautz, H. and Selman, B. [1996]. Pushing the envelope: Planning, propositional logic and stochastic search. In *13th National Conference on Artificial Intelligence*, pp. 1194–1201.

Kazemi, S. M. and Poole, D. [2018]. SimplE embedding for link prediction in knowledge graphs. In *32nd Conference on Neural Information Processing Systems*.

Ke, G., et al. [2017]. LightGBM: A highly efficient gradient boosting decision tree. In *Advances in Neural Information Processing Systems 30*.

Kearns, M., Mansour, Y., and Ng, A. [2002]. A sparse sampling algorithm for near-optimal planning in large Markovian decision processes. *Machine Learning*, 49:193–208.

Keeney, R. L. and Raiffa, H. [1976]. *Decisions with Multiple Objectives*. Wiley.

Kendall, E. F. and McGuinness, D. L. [2019]. *Ontology Engineering*. Springer. http://dx.doi.org/10.1007/978-3-031-79486-5.

Khardon, R. and Sanner, S. [2021]. Stochastic planning and lifted inference. In Van den Broeck, G., Kersting, K., Natarajan, S., and Poole, D. (eds.), *Introduction to Lifted Inference*. MIT Press.

King, G. [2007]. An introduction to the dataverse network as an infrastructure for data sharing. *Sociological Methods and Research*, 36(2):173–199.

King, R., et al. [2004]. Functional genomic hypothesis generation and experimentation by a robot scientist. *Nature*, 427:247–252. http://www.doc.ic.ac.uk/~shm/Papers/Oliver_Jan15_hi.pdf.

King, R. D., et al. [2009a]. The automation of science. *Science*, 324(5923):85–89. http://dx.doi.org/10.1126/science.1165620.

King, R. D., et al. [2009b]. The robot scientist Adam. *Computer*, 42(8):46–54. http://dx.doi.org/10.1109/MC.2009.270.

Kirkpatrick, S., Gelatt, C. D., and Vecchi, M. P. [1983]. Optimization by simulated annealing. *Science*, 220:671–680.

Kirsh, D. [1991a]. Foundations of AI: The big issues. *Artificial Intelligence*, 47:3–30.

Kirsh, D. [1991b]. Today the earwig, tomorrow man? *Artificial Intelligence*, 47:161–184.

Kleinberg, J., Ludwig, J., Mullainathan, S., and Sunstein, C. R. [2020]. Algorithms as discrimination detectors. In *National Academy of Sciences*.

Knoll, B., et al. [2008]. AIspace: Interactive tools for learning artificial intelligence. In *AAAI 2008 AI Education Workshop*, p. 3.

Knox, W. B. and Stone, P. [2009]. Interactively shaping agents via human reinforcement: The TAMER framework. In *Fifth International Conference on Knowledge Capture*, pp. 9–16. http://dx.doi.org/10.1145/1597735.1597738.

Knublauch, H., Oberle, D., Tetlow, P., and Wallace, E. [2006]. A semantic web primer for object-oriented software developers. Working Group Note 9 March 2006, W3C. http://www.w3.org/TR/sw-oosd-primer/.

Knuth, D. E. and Moore, R. W. [1975]. An analysis of alpha-beta pruning. *Artificial Intelligence*, 6(4):293–326.

Kochenderfer, M. J. [2015]. *Decision Making Under Uncertainty*. MIT Press.

Kochenderfer, M. J., Wheeler, T. A., and Wray, K. H. [2022]. *Algorithms for Decision Making*. MIT Press. https://algorithmsbook.com.

Kocsis, L. and Szepesvári, C. [2006]. Bandit based Monte-Carlo planning. In *17th European Conference on Machine Learning (ECML)*, pp. 282–293.

Koller, D. and Friedman, N. [2009]. *Probabilisitic Graphical Models: Principles and Techniques*. MIT Press.

Koller, D. and Milch, B. [2003]. Multi-agent influence diagrams for representing and solving games. *Games and Economic Behavior*, 45(1):181–221. http://people.csail.mit.edu/milch/papers/geb-maid.pdf.

Koopmans, T. [1972]. Representations of preference orderings over time. In McGuire, C. and Radner, R. (eds.), *Decisions and Organization*. North-Holland.

Koren, Y. and Bell, R. [2011]. Advances in collaborative filtering. In Ricci, F., Rokach, L., Shapira, B., and Kantor, P. B. (eds.), *Recommender Systems Handbook*, pp. 145–186. Springer. http://dx.doi.org/10.1007/978-0-387-85820-3_5.

Koren, Y., Bell, R., and Volinsky, C. [2009]. Matrix factorization techniques for recommender systems. *IEEE Computer*, 42(8):30–37.

Korf, K. E. [1985]. Depth-first iterative deepening: An optimal admissible tree search. *Artificial Intelligence*, 27(1):97–109.

Kowalski, R. [1979]. Algorithm = logic + control. *Communications of the ACM*, 22:424–431.

Kowalski, R. A. [1974]. Predicate logic as a programming language. In *Information Processing 74*, pp. 569–574. North-Holland.

Kowalski, R. A. [1988]. The early history of logic programming. *Communications of the ACM*, 31(1):38–43.

Kowalski, R. A. [2014]. *Logic for Problem Solving, Revisited*. Books on Demand.

Kramár, J., et al. [2022]. Negotiation and honesty in artificial intelligence methods for the board game of diplomacy. *Nature Communications*, 13(1):7214. http://dx.doi.org/10.1038/s41467-022-34473-5.

Krizhevsky, A., Sutskever, I., and Hinton, G. [2012]. Imagenet classification with deep convolutional neural networks. In *Advances in Neural Information Processing Systems 25*, pp. 1090–1098.

Krötzsch, M. [2012]. OWL 2 Profiles: An introduction to lightweight ontology languages. In Eiter, T. and Krennwallner, T. (eds.), *8th Reasoning Web Summer School, Vienna, Austria*, pp. 112–183. Springer. http://korrekt.org/page/OWL_2_Profiles.

Kuppe, M. A., Lamport, L., and Ricketts, D. [2019]. The TLA+ toolbox. *Electronic Proceedings in Theoretical Computer Science*, 310:50–62. http://dx.doi.org/10.4204/eptcs.310.6.

Lacroix, T., Usunier, N., and Obozinski, G. [2018]. Canonical tensor decomposition for knowledge base completion. In *35th International Conference on Machine Learning (ICML)*.

Lakshmanan, V., Görner, M., and Gillard, R. [2021]. *Practical Machine Learning for Computer Vision: End-to-End Machine Learning for Images*. O'Reilly.

Lally, A., et al. [2012]. Question analysis: How Watson reads a clue. *IBM Journal of Research and Development*, 56(3/4).

Lamport, L. [2002]. *Specifying Systems: The TLA+ Language and Tools for Hardware and Software Engineers*. Addison-Wesley Longman.

Langley, P., Iba, W., and Thompson, K. [1992]. An analysis of Bayesian classifiers. In *10th National Conference on Artificial Intelligence*, pp. 223–228.

Langton, C. G. [1997]. *Artificial Life: An Overview*. MIT Press.

Laplace, P. [1812]. *Théorie Analytique de Probabilités*. Courcier.

Latombe, J.-C. [1991]. *Robot Motion Planning*. Kluwer Academic.

Lawler, E. L. and Wood, D. E. [1966]. Branch-and-bound methods: A survey. *Operations Research*, 14(4):699–719.

LeCun, Y., Bengio, Y., and Hinton, G. [2015]. Deep learning. *Nature*, 521(7553):436–444.

LeCun, Y., Bottou, L., Bengio, Y., and Haffner, P. [1998a]. Gradient-based learning applied to document recognition. *IEEE*, 86(11):2278–2324. http://dx.doi.org/10.1109/5.726791.

LeCun, Y., Bottou, L., Orr, G., and Muller, K. [1998b]. Efficient backprop. In Orr, G. and Muller, K.-R. (eds.), *Neural Networks: Tricks of the Trade*. Springer. http://yann.lecun.com/exdb/publis/pdf/lecun-98b.pdf.

Lehman, J., Clune, J., Misevic, D., et al. [2018]. The surprising creativity of digital evolution: A collection of anecdotes from the evolutionary computation and artificial life research communities. *CoRR*. http://arxiv.org/abs/1803.03453.

Leibniz, G. W. [1677]. *The Method of Mathematics: Preface to the General Science*. Selections reprinted by Chrisley and Begeer [2000].

Leibniz, G. W. [1705]. *New Essays on Human Understanding*. Book 3. www.earlymoderntexts.com.

Lenat, D. B. and Feigenbaum, E. A. [1991]. On the thresholds of knowledge. *Artificial Intelligence*, 47:185–250.

Lepikhin, D., et al. [2021]. GShard: Scaling giant models with conditional computation and automatic sharding. In *International Conference on Learning Representations*. https://openreview.net/pdf?id=qrwe7XHTmYb.

Lertvittayakumjorn, P. and Toni, F. [2021]. Explanation-based human debugging of NLP models: A survey. *Transactions of the Association for Computational Linguistics*, 9:1508–1528. http://dx.doi.org/10.1162/tacl_a_00440.

Levesque, H. J. [1984]. Foundations of a functional approach to knowledge representation. *Artificial Intelligence*, 23(2):155–212.

Levesque, H. J. [2012]. *Thinking as Computation*. MIT Press.

Levesque, H. J. [2014]. On our best behaviour. *Artificial Intelligence*, 212:27–35.

Levy, R. [2021]. Social media, news consumption, and polarization: Evidence from a field experiment. *American Economic Review*, 111(3):831–70. http://dx.doi.org/10.1257/aer.20191777.

Leyton-Brown, K., Milgrom, P. R., and Segal, I. [2017]. Economics and computer science of a radio spectrum reallocation. *National Academy of Sciences*, 114:7202 – 7209.

Leyton-Brown, K. and Shoham, Y. [2008]. *Essentials of Game Theory*. Morgan & Claypool.

Li, Y. [2018]. Deep reinforcement learning. *CoRR*, abs/1810.06339. http://arxiv.org/abs/1810.06339.

Li, Y., et al. [2016]. A survey on truth discovery. *SIGKDD Explorations Newsletter*, 17(2):1–16. http://dx.doi.org/10.1145/2897350.2897352.

Liao, T., Taori, R., Raji, D., and Schmidt, L. [2021]. Are we learning yet? A meta review of evaluation failures across machine learning. In *Neural Information Processing Systems (NeurIPS) Track on Datasets and Benchmarks*. https://datasets-benchmarks-proceedings.neurips.cc/paper/2021/hash/757b505cfd34c64c85ca5b5690ee5293-Abstract-round2.html.

Lin, A. Y., Kuehl, K., Schöning, J., and Hecht, B. [2017]. Understanding "death by GPS": A systematic study of catastrophic incidents associated with personal navigation technologies. In *CHI Conference on Human Factors in Computing Systems*. http://dx.doi.org/10.1145/3025453.3025737.

Lindholm, T., et al. [2022]. *The Java Virtual Machine Specification: Java SE 19 Edition*. Oracle America, Inc. https://docs.oracle.com/javase/specs/jvms/se19/jvms19.pdf.

Little, R. J. A. and Rubin, D. B. [1987]. *Statistical Analysis with Missing Data*. Wiley.

Littman, M. L., et al. [2021]. *Gathering Strength, Gathering Storms: The One Hundred Year Study on Artificial Intelligence (AI100) 2021 Study Panel Report*. Stanford University. http://ai100.stanford.edu/2021-report.

Liu, A. L., et al. [2006]. Indoor wayfinding: Developing a functional interface for individuals with cognitive impairments. In *8th International ACM SIGACCESS Conference on Computers and Accessibility*.

Lloyd, J. W. [1987]. *Foundations of Logic Programming*. Symbolic Computation Series. Springer-Verlag, 2nd edition.

Lloyd, S. [1982]. Least squares quantization in PCM. *IEEE Transactions on Information Theory*, 28(2):129–137. http://dx.doi.org/10.1109/TIT.1982.1056489.

Lopez, A. and Bacchus, F. [2003]. Generalizing GraphPlan by formulating planning as a CSP. In *18th International Joint Conference Artificial Intelligence (IJCAI)*, pp. 954–960.

Luenberger, D. G. [1979]. *Introduction to Dynamic Systems: Theory, Models and Applications*. Wiley.

Lum, K. and Isaac, W. [2016]. To predict and serve? *Significance*, 13(5).

Lundgren, B. [2023]. In defense of ethical guidelines. *AI and Ethics*. http://dx.doi.org/10.1007/s43681-022-00244-7.

Ma, Y., et al. [2022]. Identification of antimicrobial peptides from the human gut microbiome using deep learning. *Nature Biotechnology*, 40(6):921–931. http://dx.doi.org/10.1038/s41587-022-01226-0.

MacKay, D. [2003]. *Information Theory, Inference, and Learning Algorithms*. Cambridge University Press.

Mackworth, A. K. [1977a]. Consistency in networks of relations. *Artificial Intelligence*, 8:99–118.

Mackworth, A. K. [1977b]. On reading sketch maps. In *Fifth International Joint Conference on Artificial Intelligence*, pp. 598–606.

Mackworth, A. K. [1993]. On seeing robots. In Basu, A. and Li, X. (eds.), *Computer Vision: Systems, Theory, and Applications*, pp. 1–13. World Scientific Press.

Mackworth, A. K. [2009]. Agents, bodies, constraints, dynamics and evolution. *AI Magazine*.

Mackworth, A. K. [2011]. Architectures and ethics for robots: Constraint satisfaction as a unitary design framework. In Anderson, M. and Anderson, S. L. (eds.), *Machine Ethics*, pp. 335–360. Cambridge University Press. http://dx.doi.org/10.1017/CBO9780511978036.024.

Mackworth, A. K. and Zhang, Y. [2003]. A formal approach to agent design: An overview of constraint-based agents. *Constraints*, 8(3):229–242.

Mackworth, J. F. [1970]. *Vigilance and Attention: A Signal Detection Approach*. Penguin.

Mackworth, N. H. [1948]. The breakdown of vigilance during prolonged visual search. *Quarterly Journal of Experimental Psychology*, 1(1):6–21. http://dx.doi.org/10.1080/17470214808416738.

Mahdisoltani, F., Biega, J., and Suchanek, F. M. [2015]. YAGO3: A knowledge base from multilingual wikipedias. In *Conference on Innovative Data Systems Research (CIDR 2015)*. http://suchanek.name/work/publications/cidr2015.pdf.

Malthus, T. R. [1798]. *An Essay on the Principle of Population: As it Affects the Future Improvement of Society*. J. Johnson.

Manning, C. and Schütze, H. [1999]. *Foundations of Statistical Natural Language Processing*. MIT Press.

Marcus, G. and Davis, E. [2019]. *Rebooting AI: Building Artificial Intelligence We Can Trust*. Pantheon.

Marlin, B. M., Zemel, R. S., Roweis, S. T., and Slaney, M. [2011]. Recommender systems, missing data and statistical model estimation. In *22nd International Joint Conference on Artificial Intelligence (IJCAI)*, pp. 2686–2691.

Matheson, J. E. [1990]. Using influence diagrams to value information and control. In Oliver, R. M. and Smith, J. Q. (eds.), *Influence Diagrams, Belief Nets and Decision Analysis*, chapter 1, pp. 25–48. Wiley.

Mausam and Kolobov, A. [2012]. *Planning with Markov Decision Processes: An AI Perspective*. Morgan & Claypool. http://dx.doi.org/doi:10.2200/S00426ED1V01Y201206AIM017.

McAllester, D. and Rosenblitt, D. [1991]. Systematic nonlinear planning. In *9th National Conference on Artificial Intelligence*, pp. 634–639.

McCarthy, J. [1958]. Programs with common sense. In *Teddington Conference on the Mechanization of Thought Processes*. http://jmc.stanford.edu/articles/mcc59/mcc59.pdf.

McCarthy, J. [1986]. Applications of circumscription to formalizing commonsense knowledge. *Artificial Intelligence*, 28(1):89–116.

McCarthy, J. and Hayes, P. J. [1969]. Some philosophical problems from the standpoint of artificial intelligence. In Meltzer, M. and Michie, D. (eds.), *Machine Intelligence 4*, pp. 463–502. Edinburgh University Press.

McCulloch, W. and Pitts, W. [1943]. A logical calculus of ideas immanent in nervous activity. *Bulletin of Mathematical Biophysics*, 5:115–133.

McDermott, D. and Hendler, J. [1995]. Planning: What it is, what it could be, an introduction to the special issue on planning and scheduling. *Artificial Intelligence*, 76:1–16.

McElreath, R. [2020]. *Statistical Rethinking: A Bayesian Course with Examples in R and STAN*. Chapman & Hall. https://xcelab.net/rm/statistical-rethinking/.

McFadden, D. L. [2000]. Prize lecture. *The Sveriges Riksbank Prize in Economic Sciences in Memory of Alfred Nobel 2000*. https://www.nobelprize.org/prizes/economic-sciences/2000/mcfadden/lecture/.

McGuffie, K. and Newhouse, A. [2020]. The radicalization risks of GPT-3 and advanced neural language model. Technical report, Center on Terrorism, Extremism, and Counterterrorism, Middlebury Institute of International Studies at Monterrey. https://www.middlebury.edu/institute/sites/www.middlebury.edu.institute/files/2020-09/gpt3-article.pdf.

McLuhan, M. [1962]. *The Gutenberg Galaxy: The Making of Typographic Man*. University of Toronto Press.

Meir, R. and Rätsch, G. [2003]. An introduction to boosting and leveraging. In *Advanced Lectures on Machine Learning*, pp. 119–184. Springer.

Michie, D. [1963]. Experiments on the mechanisation of game learning. 1. Characterization of the model and its parameters. *Computer Journal*, 1:232–263.

Michie, D., Spiegelhalter, D. J., and Taylor, C. C. (eds.) [1994]. *Machine Learning, Neural and Statistical Classification*. Series in Artificial Intelligence. Ellis Horwood.

Mihailidis, A., Boger, J., Candido, M., and Hoey, J. [2007]. The use of an intelligent prompting system for people with dementia. *ACM Interactions*, 14(4):34–37.

Mikolov, T., Chen, K., Corrado, G., and Dean, J. [2013]. Efficient estimation of word representations in vector space. http://dx.doi.org/10.48550/arXiv.1301.3781.

Milch, B., et al. [2005]. BLOG: Probabilistic models with unknown objects. In *19th International Joint Conference Artificial Intelligence (IJCAI-05)*.

Minaee, S., et al. [2021]. Deep learning–based text classification: A comprehensive review. *ACM Computing Surveys*, 54(3). http://dx.doi.org/10.1145/3439726.

Minsky, M. L. [1952]. A neural-analogue calculator based upon a probability model of reinforcement. Technical report, Harvard University Psychological Laboratories.

Minsky, M. L. [1961]. Steps towards artificial intelligence. *IEEE*, 49:8–30. http://web.media.mit.edu/~minsky/papers/steps.html.

Minsky, M. L. [1975]. A framework for representing knowledge. In Winston, P. (ed.), *The Psychology of Computer Vision*, pp. 211–277. McGraw-Hill. Alternative version is in Haugeland [1997].

Minsky, M. L. [1986]. *The Society of Mind*. Simon & Schuster.

Minsky, M. L. and Papert, S. [1988]. *Perceptrons: An Introduction to Computational Geometry*. MIT Press, expanded edition.

Minton, S., Johnston, M. D., Philips, A. B., and Laird, P. [1992]. Minimizing conflicts: A heuristic repair method for constraint satisfaction and scheduling problems. *Artificial Intelligence*, 58(1–3):161–205.

Mitchell, M. [1996]. *An Introduction to Genetic Algorithms*. MIT Press.

Mitchell, T. [1997]. *Machine Learning*. McGraw-Hill. http://www.cs.cmu.edu/afs/cs.cmu.edu/user/mitchell/ftp/mlbook.html.

Mnih, V. et al. [2015]. Human-level control through deep reinforcement learning. *Nature*, 518:529–533. http://www.nature.com/nature/journal/v518/n7540/abs/nature14236.html.

Mohan, K. [2022]. Causal graphs for missing data: A gentle introduction. In *Probabilistic and Causal Inference: The Works of Judea Pearl*. ACM Books.

Mohan, K., Pearl, J., and Tian, J. [2013]. Graphical models for inference with missing data. In *Advances in Neural Information Processing Systems*, volume 26, pp. 1277–1285.

Mole, C. [2010]. *Attention Is Cognitive Unison: An Essay in Philosophical Psychology*. Oxford University Press. http://dx.doi.org/10.1093/acprof:oso/9780195384529.001.0001.

Moore, E. F. [1959]. The shortest path through a maze. In *International Symposium on the Theory of Switching*, pp. 285–292. Harvard University Press.

Moore, T. J., Heyward, J., Anderson, G., and Alexander, G. C. [2020]. Variation in the estimated costs of pivotal clinical benefit trials supporting the US approval of new therapeutic agents, 2015–2017: A cross-sectional study. *BMJ Open*, 10(6). http://dx.doi.org/10.1136/bmjopen-2020-038863.

Morin, F. and Bengio, Y. [2005]. Hierarchical probabilistic neural network language model. In *international Workshop on Artificial Intelligence and Statistics*, pp. 246–252,.

Motik, B., Patel-Schneider, P. F., and Grau, B. C. (eds.) [2012]. *OWL 2 Web Ontology Language: Direct Semantics*. W3C Recommendation 11 December 2012, 2nd edition. http://www.w3.org/TR/owl2-direct-semantics/.

Munn, L. [2022]. The uselessness of AI ethics. *AI and Ethics*. https://doi.org/10.1007/s43681-022-00209-w.

Murphy, K. P. [2022]. *Probabilistic Machine Learning: An Introduction*. MIT Press. https://probml.github.io/pml-book/book1.html.

Murphy, K. P. [2023]. *Probabilistic Machine Learning: Advanced Topics*. MIT Press. http://probml.github.io/book2.

Muscettola, N., Nayak, P., Pell, B., and Williams, B. [1998]. Remote agent: To boldly go where no AI system has gone before. *Artificial Intelligence*, 103:5–47.

NASA [2022]. EarthData: Open access for open science. https://www.earthdata.nasa.gov.

Nash, J. F. [1950]. Equilibrium points in N-person games. *National Academy of Sciences of the United States of America*, 36:48–49.

Nau, D. S. [2007]. Current trends in automated planning. *AI Magazine*, 28(4):43–58.

Neufeld, X., Mostaghim, S., Sancho-Pradel, D. L., and Brand, S. [2019]. Building a planner: A survey of planning systems used in commercial video games. *IEEE Transactions on Games*, 11(2):91–108. http://dx.doi.org/10.1109/TG.2017.2782846.

Neumann, J. V. and Morgenstern, O. [1953]. *Theory of Games and Economic Behavior*. Princeton University Press, 3rd edition.

Neville, J. and Jensen, D. [2007]. Relational dependency networks. *Journal of Machine Learning Research (JMLR)*, 8:653–692.

New York Times [1958]. New Navy device learns by doing: Psychologist shows embryo of computer designed to read and grow wiser. https://timesmachine.nytimes.com/timesmachine/1958/07/08/83417341.html?pageNumber=25.

Newell, A. and Simon, H. A. [1956]. The logic theory machine: A complex information processing system. Technical Report P-868, The Rand Corporation. http://shelf1.library.cmu.edu/IMLS/MindModels/logictheorymachine.pdf.

Newell, A. and Simon, H. A. [1976]. Computer science as empirical enquiry: Symbols and search. *Communications of the ACM*, 19:113–126.

Ng, A. [2018]. *Machine Learning Yearning*. deeplearning.ai. https://www.deeplearning.ai/resources/.

Ng, A. Y. [2004]. Feature selection, L1 vs. L2 regularization, and rotational invariance. In *Twenty-First International Conference on Machine Learning*.

Ng, A. Y. and Russell, S. J. [2000]. Algorithms for inverse reinforcement learning. In *International Conference on Machine Learning (ICML)*, pp. 663–670.

Niles, I. and Pease, A. [2001]. Towards a standard upper ontology. In Welty, C. and Smith, B. (eds.), *2nd International Conference on Formal Ontology in Information Systems (FOIS-2001)*.

Nilsson, N. J. [2007]. The physical symbol system hypothesis: Status and prospects. In Lungarella, M. et al. (eds.), *50 Years of AI, Festschrift*, pp. 9–17. Springer. http://ai.stanford.edu/~nilsson/OnlinePubs-Nils/PublishedPapers/pssh.pdf.

Nilsson, N. J. [2010]. *The Quest for Artificial Intelligence: A History of Ideas and Achievements*. Cambridge University Press.

Nisan, N. [2007]. Introduction to mechanisn design (for computer scientists). In Nisan, N. et al. (eds.), *Algorithmic Game Theory*, chapter 9, pp. 209–242. Cambridge University Press.

Noble, S. U. [2018]. *Algorithms of Oppression: How Search Engines Reinforce Racism*. NYU Press.

Nocedal, J. and Wright, S. [2006]. *Numerical Optimization*. Springer-Verlag.

Nyholm, S. [2021]. The ethics of human-robot interaction and traditional moral theories. In *The Oxford Handbook of Digital Ethics*. Oxford University Press. http://dx.doi.org/10.1093/oxfordhb/9780198857815.013.3.

Obermeyer, Z., Powers, B., Vogeli, C., and Mullainathan, S. [2019]. Dissecting racial bias in an algorithm used to manage the health of populations. *Science*, 366(6464):447–453.

OECD [2019]. OECD AI principles. https://oecd.ai/en/ai-principles.

Office of Science and Technology Policy [2022]. The blueprint for an AI bill of rights. https://www.whitehouse.gov/ostp/ai-bill-of-rights/.

Olah, C. [2015]. Understanding LSTM networks. https://colah.github.io/posts/2015-08-Understanding-LSTMs/.

O'Neil, C. [2016]. *Weapons of Math Destruction: How Big Data Increases Inequality and Threatens Democracy*. Crown.

OpenAI [2022]. ChatGPT: Optimizing language models for dialogue. https://openai.com/blog/chatgpt/.

OpenAI [2023]. GPT-4 technical report. *ArXiv e-prints*, arXiv:2303.08774.

Ordeshook, P. C. [1986]. *Game Theory and Political Theory: An Introduction*. Cambridge University Press.

Orkin, J. [2006]. Three states and a plan: The AI of F.E.A.R. In *Game Developers Conference*.

Ostrom, E. [1990]. *Governing the Commons: The Evolution of Institutions for Collective Action*. Cambridge University Press.

Page, L., Brin, S., Motwani, R., and Winograd, T. [1999]. The PageRank citation ranking: Bringing order to the Web. Technical Report SIDL-WP-1999-0120, Stanford InfoLab.

Panton, K., et al. [2006]. Common sense reasoning – from Cyc to intelligent assistant. In Cai, Y. and Abascal, J. (eds.), *Ambient Intelligence in Everyday Life*, pp. 1–31. Springer.

Pasula, H., et al. [2003]. Identity uncertainty and citation matching. In *Advances in Neural Information Processing Systems*, volume 15.

Pearl, J. [1984]. *Heuristics*. Addison-Wesley.

Pearl, J. [1988]. *Probabilistic Reasoning in Intelligent Systems: Networks of Plausible Inference*. Morgan Kaufmann.

Pearl, J. [2009]. *Causality: Models, Reasoning and Inference*. Cambridge University Press, 2nd edition.

Pearl, J. and Mackenzie, D. [2018]. *The Book of Why: The New Science of Cause and Effect*. Basic Books.

Pease, A. [2011]. *Ontology: A Practical Guide*. Articulate Software Press.

Peden, M. et al. (eds.) [2004]. *World Report on Road Traffic Injury Prevention*. World Health Organization.

Pereira, F. C. N. and Shieber, S. M. [2002]. *Prolog and Natural-Language Analysis*. Microtome Publishing.

Perrault, A., Fang, F., Sinha, A., and Tambe, M. [2020]. Artificial intelligence for social impact: Learning and planning in the data-to-deployment pipeline. *AI Magazine*, 41(4):3–16. http://dx.doi.org/10.1609/aimag.v41i4.5296.

Peters, M. E., et al. [2018]. Deep contextualized word representations. In *2018 Conference of the North American Chapter of the Association for Computational Linguistics: Human Language Technologies*. http://dx.doi.org/10.18653/v1/N18-1202.

Phuong, M. and Hutter, M. [2022]. Formal algorithms for transformers. http://dx.doi.org/10.48550/arXiv.2207.09238.

Piaget, J. [1953]. *The Origin of Intelligence in the Child*. Routledge & Kegan Paul.

Pinker, S. [1997]. *How the Mind Works*. Norton.

Pohl, I. [1971]. Bi-directional search. *Machine Intelligence*, 6(127–140).

Pollack, M. E. [2005]. Intelligent technology for an aging population: The use of AI to assist elders with cognitive impairment. *AI Magazine*, 26(2):9–24.

Poole, D. [1993]. Probabilistic Horn abduction and Bayesian networks. *Artificial Intelligence*, 64(1):81–129.

Poole, D. [2007]. Logical generative models for probabilistic reasoning about existence, roles and identity. In *22nd AAAI Conference on AI (AAAI-07)*. http://cs.ubc.ca/~poole/papers/AAAI07-Poole.pdf.

Poole, D., Goebel, R., and Aleliunas, R. [1987]. Theorist: A logical reasoning system for defaults and diagnosis. In Cercone, N. and McCalla, G. (eds.), *The Knowledge Frontier: Essays in the Representation of Knowledge*, pp. 331–352. Springer-Verlag.

Posner, M. I. (ed.) [1989]. *Foundations of Cognitive Science*. MIT Press.

Powell, W. B. [2022]. *Reinforcement Learning and Stochastic Optimization: A Unified Framework for Sequential Decisions*. Wiley. https://castlelab.princeton.edu/RLSO/.

Prabhu, V. U. and Birhane, A. [2020]. Large image datasets: A pyrrhic win for computer vision? http://dx.doi.org/10.48550/arXiv.2006.16923.

Pujara, J., Miao, H., Getoor, L., and Cohen, W. W. [2015]. Using semantics and statistics to turn data into knowledge. *AI Magazine*, 36(1):65–74. http://dx.doi.org/10.1609/aimag.v36i1.2568.

Puterman, M. [1994]. *Markov Decision Processes: Discrete Stochastic Dynamic Programming*. Wiley.

Qian, K., et al. [2021]. XNLP: A living survey for XAI research in natural language processing. In *26th International Conference on Intelligent User Interfaces*, pp. 78–80. http://dx.doi.org/10.1145/3397482.3450728.

Qiu, X., et al. [2020]. Pre-trained models for natural language processing: A survey. *CoRR*, abs/2003.08271. https://arxiv.org/abs/2003.08271.

Quinlan, J. R. [1993]. *C4.5 Programs for Machine Learning*. Morgan Kaufmann.

Rabiner, L. [1989]. A tutorial on hidden Markov models and selected applications in speech recognition. *IEEE*, 77(2):257–286.

Rae, J. W., et al. [2021]. Scaling language models: Methods, analysis & insights from training gopher. *CoRR*, abs/2112.11446. https://arxiv.org/abs/2112.11446.

Rakova, B., Yang, J., Cramer, H., and Chowdhury, R. [2021]. Where responsible AI meets reality: Practitioner perspectives on enablers for shifting organizational practices. *Proceedings of the ACM on Human-Computer Interaction*, 5. http://dx.doi.org/10.1145/3449081.

Randell, B. [1982]. From analytical engine to electronic digital computer: The contributions of ludgate, torres, and bush. *Annals of the History of Computing*, 4(4).

Real, E., Liang, C., So, D. R., and Le, Q. V. [2020]. AutoML-Zero: Evolving machine learning algorithms from scratch. In *37th International Conference on Machine Learning*. http://dx.doi.org/10.48550/arXiv.2003.03384.

Richtel, M. [2014]. *A Deadly Wandering: A Mystery, a Landmark Investigation, and the Astonishing Science of Attention in the Digital Age*. HarperCollins.

Roberts, L. [1965]. *Machine Perception of 3-D Solids*. MIT Press.

Robillard, M. [2021]. The ethics of weaponized AI. In *The Oxford Handbook of Digital Ethics*. Oxford University Press. http://dx.doi.org/10.1093/oxfordhb/9780198857815.013.29.

Robinson, J. A. [1965]. A machine-oriented logic based on the resolution principle. *Journal ACM*, 12(1):23–41.

Rockström, J., et al. [2009]. A safe operating space for humanity. *Nature*, 461(7263):472–475.

Rogers, Y., Sharp, H., and Preece, J. [2023]. *Interaction Design: Beyond Human-Computer Interaction*. Wiley, 6th edition.

Rosenblatt, F. [1958]. The perceptron: A probabilistic model for information storage and organization in the brain. *Psychological Review*, 65(6):386–408.

Rosenschein, S. J. and Kaelbling, L. P. [1995]. A situated view of representation and control. *Artificial Intelligence*, 73:149–173.

Rossi, F., Venable, K. B., and Walsh, T. [2011]. *A Short Introduction to Preferences: Between Artificial Intelligence and Social Choice*. Morgan & Claypool. http://dx.doi.org/doi:10.2200/S00372ED1V01Y201107AIM014.

Rubin, D. B. [1976]. Inference and missing data. *Biometrika*, 63(3):581–592.

Rubinstein, R. Y. [1981]. *Simulation and the Monte Carlo Method*. Wiley.

Ruder, S. [2016]. An overview of gradient descent optimization algorithms. *CoRR*, abs/1609.04747. http://arxiv.org/abs/1609.04747.

Rudin, C., et al. [2022]. Interpretable machine learning: Fundamental principles and 10 grand challenges. *Statistics Surveys*, 16:1–85. http://dx.doi.org/10.1214/21-SS133.

Rumelhart, D. E., Hinton, G. E., and Williams, R. J. [1986]. Learning internal representations by error propagation. In Rumelhart, D. E. and McClelland, J. L. (eds.), *Parallel Distributed Processing*, chapter 8, pp. 318–362. MIT Press.

Russakovsky, O., et al. [2014]. Imagenet large scale visual recognition challenge. *CoRR*, abs/1409.0575. http://arxiv.org/abs/1409.0575.

Russell, S. [1997]. Rationality and intelligence. *Artificial Intelligence*, 94:57–77.

Russell, S. [2019]. *Human Compatible: AI and the Problem of Control*. Penguin Books Limited.

Russell, S. and Norvig, P. [2020]. *Artificial Intelligence: A Modern Approach (4th Edition)*. Pearson. http://aima.cs.berkeley.edu/.

Russo, D., et al. [2018]. A tutorial on Thompson sampling. *Foundations and Trends in Machine Learning,*, 11(1):1–96. http://dx.doi.org/10.48550/arXiv.1707.02038.

Sacerdoti, E. D. [1975]. The nonlinear nature of plans. In *4th International Joint Conference on Artificial Intelligence*, pp. 206–214.

Salimans, T., et al. [2017]. Evolution strategies as a scalable alternative to reinforcement learning. http://dx.doi.org/10.48550/arXiv.1703.03864.

Samuel, A. L. [1959]. Some studies in machine learning using the game of checkers. *IBM Journal on Research and Development*, 3(3):210–229.

Sandholm, T. [2007]. Expressive commerce and its application to sourcing: How we conducted $35 billion of generalized combinatorial auctions. *AI Magazine*, 28(3):45–58.

Satterthwaite, M. [1975]. Strategy-proofness and Arrow's conditions: Existence and correspondence theorems for voting procedures and social welfare functions. *Journal of Economic Theory*, 10:187–217.

Savage, L. J. [1972]. *The Foundation of Statistics*. Dover, 2nd edition.

Schank, R. C. [1990]. What is AI, anyway? In Partridge, D. and Wilks, Y. (eds.), *The Foundations of Artificial Intelligence*, pp. 3–13. Cambridge University Press.

Schapire, R. E. [2002]. The boosting approach to machine learning: An overview. In *MSRI Workshop on Nonlinear Estimation and Classification*. Springer-Verlag.

Schlichtkrull, M., et al. [2018]. Modeling relational data with graph convolutional networks. In *European Semantic Web Conference (ESWC 2018)*, pp. 593–607. Springer. https://arxiv.org/abs/1703.06103.

Schmidhuber, J. [1990]. Making the world differentiable: On using fully recurrent self-supervised neural networks for dynamic reinforcement learning and planning in non-stationary environments. Technical Report FKI-126-90, T.U. Munich.

Schmidhuber, J. [2015]. Deep learning in neural networks: An overview. *Neural Networks*, 61:85–117. http://dx.doi.org/10.1016/j.neunet.2014.09.003.

Schubert, E. [2022]. Stop using the elbow criterion for k-means and how to choose the number of clusters instead. http://dx.doi.org/10.48550/arXiv.2212.12189.

Schwarz, G. [1978]. Estimating the dimension of a model. *Annals of Statistics*, 6(2):461–464. https://projecteuclid.org/euclid.aos/1176344136.

Seger, C.-J. H. [2021]. Formal verification of complex data paths: An industrial experience. In *FM*.

Selinger, E. and Leong, B. [2021]. The ethics of facial recognition technology. In *The Oxford Handbook of Digital Ethics*. Oxford University Press. http://dx.doi.org/10.1093/oxfordhb/9780198857815.013.32.

Senior, A. W., et al. [2020]. Improved protein structure prediction using potentials from deep learning. *Nature*, 577(7792):706–710. http://dx.doi.org/10.1038/s41586-019-1923-7.

Settles, B. [2012]. *Active Learning*. Synthesis Lectures on Artificial Intelligence and Machine Learning. Morgan & Claypool. http://dx.doi.org/doi:10.2200/S00429ED1V01Y201207AIM018.

Shachter, R. and Peot, M. A. [1992]. Decision making using probabilistic inference methods. In *Eighth Conference on Uncertainty in Artificial Intelligence (UAI-92)*, pp. 276–283.

Shahriari, B., et al. [2016]. Taking the human out of the loop: A review of Bayesian optimization. *IEEE*, 104(1):148–175. http://dx.doi.org/10.1109/JPROC.2015.2494218.

Shanahan, M. [2022]. Talking about large language models. http://dx.doi.org/10.48550/arXiv.2212.03551.

Shannon, C. E. and Weaver, W. [1949]. *The Mathematical Theory of Communication*.

Sharkey, N. [2008]. The ethical frontiers of robotics. *Science*, 322(5909):1800–1801. DOI:10.1126/science.1164582.

Shavlik, J. W. and Dietterich, T. G. (eds.) [1990]. *Readings in Machine Learning*. Morgan Kaufmann.

Shelley, M. W. [1818]. *Frankenstein; or, The Modern Prometheus*. Lackington, Hughes, Harding, Mavor & Jones.

Shneiderman, B. [2022]. *Human-Centered AI*. Oxford University Press.

Shoeybi, M., et al. [2019]. Megatron-LM: Training multi-billion parameter language models using model parallelism. *CoRR*, abs/1909.08053. http://arxiv.org/abs/1909.08053.

Shoham, Y. [2016]. Why knowledge representation matters. *Communications of the ACM*, 59(1):47–49.

Shoham, Y. and Leyton-Brown, K. [2008]. *Multiagent Systems: Algorithmic, Game Theoretic, and Logical Foundations*. Cambridge University Press.

Shpitser, I. and Pearl, J. [2008]. Complete identification methods for the causal hierarchy. *Journal of Machine Learning Research*, 9:1941–1979.

Sikos, L., Seneviratne, O., and McGuinness, D. L. [2021]. *Provenance in Data Science: From Data Models to Context-Aware Knowledge Graphs*. Springer. https://www.springer.com/gp/book/9783030676803.

Silver, D., Singh, S., Precup, D., and Sutton, R. S. [2021]. Reward is enough. *Artificial Intelligence*, 299. http://dx.doi.org/https://doi.org/10.1016/j.artint.2021.103535.

Silver, D., et al. [2016]. Mastering the game of Go with deep neural networks and tree search. *Nature*, 529(7587):484–489.

Silver, D., et al. [2017]. Mastering chess and shogi by self-play with a general reinforcement learning algorithm. *CoRR*, abs/1712.01815. http://arxiv.org/abs/1712.01815.

Simon, H. A. [1971]. Designing organizations for an information rich world. In Greenberger, M. (ed.), *Computers, Communications, and the Public Interest*, pp. 37–72. Johns Hopkins Press.

Simon, H. A. [1995]. Artificial intelligence: An empirical science. *Artificial Intelligence*, 77(1):95–127.

Simon, H. A. [1996]. *The Sciences of the Artificial*. MIT Press, 3rd edition.

Singer, P. W. [2009a]. Robots at war: The new battlefield. *The Wilson Quarterly*.

Singer, P. W. [2009b]. *Wired for War: The Robotics Revolution and Conflict in the 21st Century*. Penguin.

Sinz, C., Kaiser, A., and Küchlin, W. [2003]. Formal methods for the validation of automotive product configuration data. *Artificial Intelligence for Engineering Design, Analysis and Manufacturing*, 17:75 – 97.

Siu, H. C., et al. [2021]. Evaluation of human-AI teams for learned and rule-based agents in Hanabi. In *Neural Information Processing Systems (NeurIPS)*. http://dx.doi.org/10.48550/arXiv.2107.07630.

Smith, B. [2003]. Ontology. In Floridi, L. (ed.), *Blackwell Guide to the Philosophy of Computing and Information*, pp. 155–166. Blackwell. http://ontology.buffalo.edu/smith/articles/ontologies.htm.

Smith, B. [2015]. Basic formal ontology 2.0: Specification and user's guide. Technical report, Institute for Formal Ontology and Medical Information Science (IFOMIS). https://github.com/bfo-ontology/BFO/wiki.

Smith, B. C. [1996]. *On the Origin of Objects*. MIT Press.

Sohl-Dickstein, J., Weiss, E., Maheswaranathan, N., and Ganguli, S. [2015]. Deep unsupervised learning using nonequilibrium thermodynamics. In *32nd International Conference on Machine Learning*, pp. 2256–2265. https://proceedings.mlr.press/v37/sohl-dickstein15.html.

Sowa, J. F. [2000]. *Knowledge Representation: Logical, Philosophical, and Computational Foundations*. Brooks Cole.

Sowa, J. F. [2011]. Future directions for semantic systems. In Tolk, A. and Jain, L. C. (eds.), *Intelligence-Based Software Engineering*, pp. 23–47. Springer-Verlag. http://www.jfsowa.com/pubs/futures.pdf.

Spall, J. C. [2003]. *Introduction to Stochastic Search and Optimization: Estimation, Simulation*. Wiley.

Sparkes, A., et al. [2010]. Towards robot scientists for autonomous scientific discovery. *Automated Experimentation*, 2(1):1. http://dx.doi.org/10.1186/1759-4499-2-1.

Spencer, A., et al. [2022]. The QALY at 50: One story many voices. *Social Science and Medicine*, 296:114653. http://dx.doi.org/https://doi.org/10.1016/j.socscimed.2021.114653.

Spiegelhalter, D. J., Franklin, R. C. G., and Bull, K. [1990]. Assessment, criticism and improvement of imprecise subjective probabilities for a medical expert system. In Henrion, M., Shachter, R. D., Kanal, L., and Lemmer, J. (eds.), *Uncertainty in Artificial Intelligence 5*, pp. 285–294. North-Holland.

Spirtes, P., Glymour, C., and Scheines, R. [2001]. *Causation, Prediction, and Search*. MIT Press, 2nd edition.

Springer Nature [2022]. SN SciGraph: A linked open data platform for the scholarly domain. https://www.springernature.com/gp/researchers/scigraph.

Sreedharan, S., Kulkarni, A., and Kambhampati, S. [2022]. *Explainable Human–AI Interaction: A Planning Perspective*. Morgan & Claypool. https://doi.org/10.2200/S01152ED1V01Y202111AIM050.

Srivastava, A. et al. [2022]. Beyond the imitation game: Quantifying and extrapolating the capabilities of language models. http://dx.doi.org/10.48550/arXiv.2206.04615.

Stanley, K. O., Clune, J., Lehman, J., and Miikkulainen, R. [2019]. Designing neural networks through neuroevolution. *Nature Machine Intelligence*, 1(1):24–35. http://dx.doi.org/10.1038/s42256-018-0006-z.

Steck, H., et al. [2021]. Deep learning for recommender systems: A netflix case study. *AI Magazine*, 42(3):7–18. http://dx.doi.org/10.1609/aimag.v42i3.18140.

Sterling, L. S. and Shapiro, E. Y. [1994]. *The Art of Prolog: Advanced Programming Techniques*. MIT Press, 2nd edition.

Stevenson, A. and Lindberg, C. A. (eds.) [2010]. *The New Oxford American Dictionary*. Oxford University Press.

Stillings, N. A., et al. [1987]. *Cognitive Science: An Introduction*. MIT Press.

Stodden, V., et al. [2016]. Enhancing reproducibility for computational methods. *Science*, 354. http://dx.doi.org/10.1126/science.aah6168.

Stone, P. [2007]. Learning and multiagent reasoning for autonomous agents. In *The 20th International Joint Conference on Artificial Intelligence (IJCAI-07)*, pp. 13–30. http://www.cs.utexas.edu/~pstone/Papers/bib2html-links/IJCAI07-award.pdf.

Stone, P. and Veloso, M. [2000]. Multiagent systems: A survey from a machine learning perspective. *Autonomous Robots*, 8:345–383.

Such, F. P., et al. [2017]. Deep neuroevolution: Genetic algorithms are a competitive alternative for training deep neural networks for reinforcement learning. *CoRR*, abs/1712.06567. http://arxiv.org/abs/1712.06567.

Suchanek, F. M., Kasneci, G., and Weikum, G. [2007]. YAGO: A core of semantic knowledge – unifying WordNet and Wikipedia. In *16th International World Wide Web Conference (WWW 2007)*.

Sundermann, C., et al. [2021]. Applications of #SAT solvers on feature models. *15th International Working Conference on Variability Modelling of Software-Intensive Systems*.

Sunstein, C. R. [2018]. *#Republic: Divided Democracy in the Age of Social Media*. Princeton University Press. http://www.jstor.org/stable/j.ctv8xnhtd.

Sutton, R. S. [1988]. Learning to predict by the methods of temporal differences. *Machine Learning*, 3(1):9–44. http://dx.doi.org/10.1007/BF00115009.

Sutton, R. S. and Barto, A. G. [2018]. *Reinforcement Learning: An Introduction*. MIT Press, 2nd edition.

Szepesvári, C. [2010]. *Algorithms for Reinforcement Learning*. Morgan & Claypool. http://dx.doi.org/doi:10.2200/S00268ED1V01Y201005AIM009.

Tarski, A. [1956]. *Logic, Semantics, Metamathematics*. Clarendon Press. Papers from 1923 to 1938 collected and translated by J. H. Woodger.

Tate, A. [1977]. Generating project networks. In *5th International Joint Conference on Artificial Intelligence*, pp. 888–893.

Tay, Y., Dehghani, M., Bahri, D., and Metzler, D. [2022]. Efficient transformers: A survey. *ACM Computing Surveys*. http://dx.doi.org/10.1145/3530811.

Thompson, W. [1933]. On the likelihood that one unknown probability exceeds another in view of the evidence of two samples". *Biometrika*, 25(3/4):285–294.

Thrun, S. [2006]. Winning the DARPA grand challenge. In *Innovative Applications of Artificial Intelligence Conference (IAAI-06)*, pp. 16–20.

Thrun, S., Burgard, W., and Fox, D. [2005]. *Probabilistic Robotics*. MIT Press.

Torrance, G. [1970]. A generalized cost-effectiveness model for the evaluation of health programs. Technical report, Faculty of Business, McMaster University. http://hdl.handle.net/11375/5559.

Trouillon, T., et al. [2016]. Complex embeddings for simple link prediction. In *ICML*, volume abs/1606.06357. http://arxiv.org/abs/1606.06357.

Turing, A. [1950]. Computing machinery and intelligence. *Mind*, 59:433–460. https://doi.org/10.1093/mind/LIX.236.433.

Tversky, A. and Kahneman, D. [1974]. Judgment under uncertainty: Heuristics and biases. *Science*, 185:1124–1131.

UNESCO [2022]. Recommendation on the ethics of artificial intelligence. https://unesdoc.unesco.org/ark:/48223/pf0000381137.

United Nations [2015a]. Transforming our world: The UN 2030 agenda for sustainable development. https://sdgs.un.org/2030agenda.

United Nations [2015b]. The UN sustainable development goals. https://sdgs.un.org/goals.

U.S. Government [2022]. GPS accuracy. https://www.gps.gov/systems/gps/performance/accuracy/.

Vallor, S. [2021]. Virtues in the digital age. In *The Oxford Handbook of Digital Ethics*. Oxford University Press. http://dx.doi.org/10.1093/oxfordhb/9780198857815.013.2.

van Beek, P. and Chen, X. [1999]. Cplan: A constraint programming approach to planning. In *AAAI-99*, pp. 585–590.

van de Meent, J.-W., Paige, B., Yang, H., and Wood, F. [2018]. An introduction to probabilistic programming. https://arxiv.org/abs/1809.10756.

Van den Broeck, G., Kersting, K., Natarajan, S., and Poole, D. (eds.) [2021]. *Introduction to Lifted Inference*. MIT Press.

van Diggelen, F. and Enge, P. [2015]. The world's first GPS MOOC and worldwide laboratory using smartphones. In *28th International Technical Meeting of the Satellite Division of The Institute of Navigation*.

van Emden, M. H. and Kowalski, R. A. [1976]. The semantics of predicate logic as a programming language. *Journal ACM*, 23(4):733–742.

Vaswani, A., et al. [2017]. Attention is all you need. In *31st Conference on Neural Information Processing Systems*. https://arxiv.org/abs/1706.03762.

Veitch, V. and D'Amour, A. [2023]. Causality. In *Murphy [2023]*, chapter 36. MIT Press.

Visser, U. and Burkhard, H.-D. [2007]. Robocup: 10 years of achievements and challenges. *AI Magazine*, 28(2):115–130.

Viswanathan, P., Little, J., Mackworth, A. K., and Mihailidis, A. [2011]. Navigation and obstacle avoidance help (NOAH) for older adults with cognitive impairment: A pilot study. In *International ACM SIGACCESS Conference on Computers and Accessibility*.

Vlassis, N. [2007]. *A Concise Introduction to Multiagent Systems and Distributed Artificial Intelligence*. Morgan & Claypool. http://dx.doi.org/doi:10.2200/S00091ED1V01Y200705AIM002.

Vrandečić, D. and Krötzsch, M. [2014]. Wikidata: A free collaborative knowledgebase. *Communications of the ACM*, 57(10):78–85.

W3C OWL Working Group (ed.) [2012]. *OWL 2 Web Ontology Language Document Overview*. W3C Recommendation 11 December 2012, 2nd edition. http://www.w3.org/TR/owl2-overview/.

Wakker, P. P. [2010]. *Prospect Theory: For Risk and Ambiguity*. Cambridge University Press.

Waldinger, R. [1977]. Achieving several goals simultaneously. In Elcock, E. and Michie, D. (eds.), *Machine Intelligence 8: Machine Representations of Knowledge*, pp. 94–136. Ellis Horwood.

Walsh, T. [2007]. Representing and reasoning with preferences. *AI Magazine*, 28(4):59–69.

Walter, W. G. [1950]. An imitation of life. *Scientific American*, 182(5):42–45.

Walter, W. G. [1951]. A machine that learns. *Scientific American*, 185(2):60–63.

Wang, H. [1960]. Toward mechanical mathematics. *IBM Journal of Research and Development*, 4(1):2–22. http://dx.doi.org/doi:10.1147/rd.41.0002.

Warren, D. H. D. and Pereira, F. C. N. [1982]. An efficient easily adaptable system for interpreting natural language queries. *Computational Linguistics*, 8(3–4):110–122. http://portal.acm.org/citation.cfm?id=972944.

Watkins, C. J. C. H. and Dayan, P. [1992]. Q-learning. *Machine Learning*, 8(3):279–292. http://dx.doi.org/10.1007/BF00992698.

Weidinger, L., et al. [2021]. Ethical and social risks of harm from language models. http://dx.doi.org/10.48550/arXiv.2112.04359.

Weizenbaum, J. [1976]. *Computer Power and Human Reason: From Judgment to Calculation*. Freeman.

Weld, D. S. [1994]. An introduction to least commitment planning. *AI Magazine*, 15(4):27–61.

Weld, D. S. [1999]. Recent advances in AI planning. *AI Magazine*, 20(2).

Wellman, M. P. [2011]. *Trading Agents*. Morgan & Claypool. http://dx.doi.org/doi:10.2200/S00370ED1V01Y201107AIM012.

Whitehead, A. N. and Russell, B. [1925, 1927]. *Principia Mathematica*. Cambridge University Press, 2nd edition.

Wikidata [2021]. Q262802 – wikidata. https://www.wikidata.org/wiki/Q262802.

Wilkins, D. E. [1988]. *Practical Planning: Extending the Classical AI Planning Paradigm*. Morgan Kaufmann.

Wilkinson, M. D., et al. [2016]. The fair guiding principles for scientific data management and stewardship. *Scientific Data*, 3(1):160018. http://dx.doi.org/10.1038/sdata.2016.18.

Winograd, T. [1972]. *Understanding Natural Language*. Academic Press.

Winograd, T. [1990]. Thinking machines: Can there be? Are we? In Partridge, D. and Wilks, Y. (eds.), *The Foundations of Artificial Intelligence: A Sourcebook*, pp. 167–189. Cambridge University Press.

Wolpert, D. H. [1996]. The lack of a priori distinctions between learning algorithms. *Neural Computation*, 8(7):1341–1390. http://dx.doi.org/10.1162/neco.1996.8.7.1341.

Woods, W. A. [2007]. Meaning and links. *AI Magazine*, 28(4):71–92.

Wooldridge, M. [2009]. *An Introduction to MultiAgent Systems*. Wiley.

World Economic Forum [2021]. Responsible use of technology: The IBM case study. https://www.weforum.org/whitepapers/responsible-use-of-technology-the-ibm-case-study/.

Xu, K., Hu, W., Leskovec, J., and Jegelka, S. [2019]. How powerful are graph neural networks? In *ICLR*.

Xu, L., Hutter, F., Hoos, H. H., and Leyton-Brown, K. [2008]. SATzilla: Portfolio-based algorithm selection for SAT. *Journal of Artificial Intelligence Research*, 32:565–606. https://www.aaai.org/Papers/JAIR/Vol32/JAIR-3214.pdf.

Yang, Q. [1997]. *Intelligent Planning: A Decomposition and Abstraction-Based Approach*. Springer-Verlag.

Yang, S. and Mackworth, A. K. [2007]. Hierarchical shortest pathfinding applied to route-planning for wheelchair users. In *Canadian Conference on Artificial Intelligence, AI-2007*.

Yannakakis, G. N. and Togelius, J. [2018]. *Artificial Intelligence and Games*. Springer. http://gameaibook.org.

Zador, A., et al. [2023]. Catalyzing next-generation artificial intelligence through NeuroAI. *Nature Communications*, 14(1):1597. http://dx.doi.org/10.1038/s41467-023-37180-x.

Zhang, B. H., Lemoine, B., and Mitchell, M. [2018]. Mitigating unwanted biases with adversarial learning. In *2018 AAAI/ACM Conference on AI, Ethics, and Society*, pp. 335–340. http://dx.doi.org/10.1145/3278721.3278779.

Zhang, D., et al. [2022a]. *The AI Index 2022 Annual Report*. AI Index Steering Committee, Stanford Institute for Human-Centered AI, Stanford University. https://aiindex.stanford.edu/wp-content/uploads/2022/03/2022-AI-Index-Report_Master.pdf.

Zhang, H., et al. [2022b]. On the paradox of learning to reason from data. http://starai.cs.ucla.edu/papers/ZhangArxiv22.pdf.

Zhang, N. L. [2004]. Hierarchical latent class models for cluster analysis. *Journal of Machine Learning Research*, 5(6):697–723.

Zhang, N. L. and Poole, D. [1994]. A simple approach to Bayesian network computations. In *10th Canadian Conference on Artificial Intelligence*, pp. 171–178.

Zhang, Y. and Mackworth, A. K. [1995]. Constraint nets: A semantic model for hybrid dynamic systems. *Theoretical Computer Science*, 138:211–239.

Zilberstein, S. [1996]. Using anytime algorithms in intelligent systems. *AI Magazine*, 17(3):73–83.

Zimmer, M. [2022]. A celebrated AI has learned a new trick: How to do chemistry. *The Conversation.* https://theconversation.com/a-celebrated-ai-has-learned-a-new-trick-how-to-do-chemistry-182031.

Zuboff, S. [2019]. *The Age of Surveillance Capitalism : The Fight for a Human Future at the New Frontier of Power.* Profile Books.

# Index of Algorithms

# Index

www.ingramcontent.com/pod-product-compliance
Lightning Source LLC
Chambersburg PA
CBHW082153270125
20954CB00005B/109
* 9 7 8 1 0 0 9 2 5 8 1 9 7 *